THE
MACMILLAN
VISUAL
DICTIONARY

THE
MACMILLAN
VISUAL
DICTIONARY

MACMILLAN PUBLISHING COMPANY
NEW YORK

MAXWELL MACMILLAN INTERNATIONAL
NEW YORK   OXFORD   SINGAPORE   SYDNEY

Library of Congress Cataloging-in-Publication Data

Corbeil, Jean-Claude

The Macmillan visual dictionary / Jean-Claude Corbeil, Ariane Archambault.

p.   cm.

ISBN 0-02-528160-7

1. Picture dictionaries, English. 2. Handbooks, vade-mecums, etc.
I. Archambault, Ariane. II. Title.

PE1629. C64 1992

423'. 1—dc20   91-34460

                                                                                      CIP

Created and produced
by Québec/Amérique International
a division of
Éditions Québec/Amérique Inc.
425, rue Saint-Jean-Baptiste, Montréal, Québec H2Y 2Z7
Tel. : (514) 393-1450 Fax : (514) 866-2430

Copyright © 1992, by Éditions Québec/Amérique Inc.

Macmillan Publishing Company, 866 Third Avenue, New York, NY 10022

Macmillan Publishing Company is part of the Maxwell Communication Group of Companies.

Macmillan books are available at special discounts for bulk purchases for sales promotions, premiums, fund-raising, or educational use. For details, contact:

Special Sales Director, Macmillan Publishing Company, 866 Third Avenue, New York, NY 10022

First American Edition, 10 9 8 7 6 5 4 3 2 1

Printed in Canada

ENGLISH LANGUAGE EDITION

William Rosen - *Publisher*
Natalie Chapman - *Senior Editor*
Camillo LoGiudice - *Production Director*
Brian Holmes - *Production Editor*

EDITORIAL STAFF FOR THE ORIGINAL EDITION

Jacques Fortin - *Publisher*
Jean-Claude Corbeil - *Editor-in-chief*
Ariane Archambault - *Assistant Editor*
François Fortin - *Illustrations Editor*
Jean-Louis Martin - *Art Director*

COMPUTER GRAPHIC ARTISTS

Jacques Perrault
Anne Tremblay
Jocelyn Gardner
Christiane Beauregard
Michel Blais
Rielle Lévesque
Marc Lalumière
Stéphane Roy
Alice Comtois
Jean-Yves Ahern
Benoît Bourdeau

COMPUTER COPYEDITING

Yves Ferland

RESEARCH EDITOR

Serge D'Amico

PAGE SETUP

Pascal Goyette
Lucie Mc Brearty
Martin Langlois

PRODUCTION

François Fortin
Jean-Louis Martin
Tony O'Riley

GRAPHIC DESIGN

Emmanuel Blanc

ACKNOWLEDGMENTS

In preparing *The Macmillan Visual Dictionary*, we have benefited from the help of numerous groups, organizations and companies, which have provided us with up-to-date technical documents. We have also received judicious advice from various specialists, colleagues, terminologists and translators. We extend a special thank-you to our initial contributors, Édith Girard, René St-Pierre, Marielle Hébert, Christiane Vachon and Anik Lapointe. In addition, we wish to express our sincere gratitude to the following individuals and organizations:

A.C. Delco
Aérospatiale (France)
Aérospatiale Canada (ACI) Inc.
Air Canada (Linguistic Policy and Services)
Amity-Leather Products Company
Animat Inc.
Archambault Musique
International Association of Lighthouse Authorities (Marie-Hélène Grillet)
Association des groupes d'astronomes amateurs (Jean-Marc Richard)
Atlas Copco
Atomic Energy of Canada Ltd. (Pierre Giguère)
Bell Canada
Bell Helicopter Textron
Bellefontaine
Benoît, Richard
Beretta
Black & Decker
Bombardier Inc.
Boutique de harnais Pépin
British Hovercraft Corporation Ltd. (Division of Westland Aerospace)
C. Plath North American Division
Caloritech Inc.
Cambridge Instruments (Canada) Inc.
CAMIF (Direction relations extérieures)
Canada Billard & Bowling Inc. (Bernard Monsec)
Canadian National (Information and Linguistic Services)
Canadian Kenworth Company
Canadian Coleman Supply Inc.
Canadian Liquid Air Ltd.
Canadian Curling Association
Canadian Coast Guard
Canadian Broadcasting Corporation (Gilles Amyot, Pierre Beaucage, Claude L'Hérault, Pierre Laroche)
Carpentier, Jean-Marc
Casavant Frères Limitée (Gilbert Lemieux)
Centre de Tissage Leclerc Inc.
Chromalox Inc.
Clerc, Redjean
Club de tir à l'arc de Montréal
Club de planeur Champlain
Collège Jean de Brébeuf (Paul-Émile Tremblay)
Collège militaire royal de Saint-Jean
Communauté urbaine de Montréal (Bureau de transport métropolitain)
Complexe sportif Claude-Robillard
Control Data Canada Ltd.
Cycles Performance
David M. Stewart Museum (Philippe Butler)
Department of National Defence of Canada (Public Relations)
Detson
Direction des constructions navales (Programmes internationaux) (France)
Distributions TTI Inc.
Energy, Mines and Resources Canada (Canada Centre for Remote Sensing)
Environment Canada (Atmospheric Environment Service, Gilles Sanscartier)
FACOM
Fédération québécoise des échecs
Fédération québécoise de tennis
Fédération québécoise de luge et bobsleigh
Fédération québécoise de canot-camping
Fédération québécoise de boxe olympique
Fédération québécoise de badminton
Fédération québécoise d'haltérophilie

Fédération québécoise d'escrime
Fédération de patinage de vitesse du Québec
Festival des Montolfières du Haut-Richelieu
Fincantieri Naval Shipbuilding Division
Fisher Scientific Ltd.
Ford New-Holland Inc.
Gadbois, Alain
GAM Pro Plongée
G.E. Astro-Space Division
G.T.E. Sylvania Canada Ltd.
General Electric Canada Inc. (Dominion Engineering Works, Mony Schinasi)
General Motors of Canada Ltd.
GIAT Industries
Government of Canada Terminology Bank
Gym Plus
Harrison (1985) Inc.
Hewitt Equipment Ltd.
Hippodrome Blue Bonnets (Robert Perez)
Honeywell Ltd.
Hortipro
Hughes Aircraft Company
Hydro-Québec (Centre de documentation, Anne Crépeau)
IBM Canada Ltd.
Imperial Oil Ltd.
Institut de recherche d'Hydro-Québec (IREQ)
International Telecommunications Satellite Organization (Intelsat)
International Civil Aviation Organization (IATA)
Jardin Botanique de Montréal
John Deere Ltd.
Johnson & Johnson Inc.
La Maison Olympique (Sylvia Doucette)
La Cordée
Le Beau Voyage
Le Coz, Jean-Pierre
Lee Valley Tools Ltd.
Leica Camera
Les Manufacturiers Draco ltée
Les Instruments de Musique Twigg Inc.
Les Équipements Chalin ltée
Les Appareils orthopédiques BBG Inc.
Leviton Manufacturing of Canada Ltd.
Liebherr-Québec
Manac Inc.
Manutan
Marcoux, Jean-Marie
Marrazza Musique
MATRA S.A.
Matra Défense (Direction de la communication)
Mazda Canada
Médiatel
Mendes Inc. (François Caron)
Michelin
MIL Tracy (Henri Vacher)
Ministère des transports du Québec (Sécurité routière, Signalisation routière)
Monette Sport Inc.
Moto Internationale
National Oceanic and Atmospheric Administration (NOAA) — National Environmental Satellite and Information Service (Frank Lepore)
National Aeronautics and Space Administration (NASA)
Nikon Canada Inc.
Northern Telecom Canada Ltd.
Office de la langue française du Québec (Chantal Robinson)
Ogilvie Mills Ltd. (Michel Ladouceur)

Olivetti Systems and Networks Canada Ltd.
Ontario Hydro
Paterson Darkroom Necessities
Petro-Canada (Calgary)
Philips Electronics Ltd. (Philips Lighting)
Philips Electronics Ltd. (Scientific and Analytical Equipment)
Pierre-Olivier Decor
Planétarium Dow (Pierre Lacombe)
Plastimo
Port of Montreal (Public Affairs)
Pratt & Whitney Canada Inc.
Quincaillerie A.C.L. Inc.
Radio-Québec
Remington Products (Canada) Inc.
Russell Rinfret
Rodriguez Cantieri navali S.p.A.
S.A. Redoute Catalogue (Relations extérieures)
Samsonite
Secretary of State of Canada (Translation Bureau)
Shell Canada
SIAL Poterie
Smith-Corona (Canada) Ltd.
SNC Defence Products Ltd.
Société Nationale des Chemins de Fer français (S.N.C.F.) (Direction de la communication)
Société de transport de la Communauté urbaine de Montréal
Spalding Canada
Spar Aerospace Ltd. (Hélène Lapierre)
St. Lawrence Seaway Authority (Normand Dodier)
Sunbeam Corporation (Canada) Ltd.
Swimming Canada
Teleglobe Canada Inc. (Roger Leblanc)
Telesat Canada (Yves Comtois)
The Coal Association of Canada
The British Petroleum Company p.l.c. (Photographic Services)
Thibault
Tideland Signal Canada Ltd.
Transport Canada (Montreal Airports, Gilbert L'Espérance, Koos R. Van der Peijl)
Ultramar Canada Inc.
United States Department of Defense (Department of the Navy, Office of Information)
Université du Québec à Montréal (Module des arts, Michel Fournier)
Université du Québec (Institut national de la recherche scientifique, Benoît Jean)
Varin, Claude
Via Rail Canada Inc.
Viala L.R. Inc. (Jean Beaudin)
Ville de Montréal (Bureau du cinéma; Service de l'habitation et du développement urbain; Service de la prévention des incendies, Robert Gilbert, Réal Audet; Service des travaux publics)
Volcano Inc.
Volkswagen Canada Inc.
Volvo Canada Ltd.
Water Ski Canada
Weider
Wild Leitz Canada ltée
Xerox Canada Inc.
Yamaha Canada Music Ltd.

The Macmillan Visual Dictionary is quite unlike other dictionaries with respect to both contents and presentation. Given its uniqueness, a few words of explanation will help you appreciate its usefulness and the quality of the information it contains. The following introduction explains how and why The Macmillan Visual Dictionary differs from language dictionaries and encyclopedias. For dictionary "fans" and professional lexicographers, we have included a brief description of the principles and methods that guided us in producing the dictionary.

A PICTURE/WORD DICTIONARY

The Macmillan Visual Dictionary closely links pictures and words.

The pictures describe and analyze today's world: the objects of everyday life, our physical environment, the animal and vegetable life that surrounds us, the communication and work techniques that are changing our lifestyles, the weapons that preoccupy us, the means of transportation that are breaking down geographical barriers, the sources of energy on which we depend, etc.

Illustrations play a specific role in our dictionary: they serve to define words, enabling dictionary users to "see" immediately the meaning of each term. Users can thus recognize the objects they are looking for and, at a single glance, find the corresponding vocabulary.

The Macmillan Visual Dictionary provides users with the words they need to accurately name the objects that make up the world around them.

The terms in the dictionary have been carefully selected from current documents written by experts in each area. In case of doubt, the vocabulary has been studied by specialists in the corresponding field and cross-checked in encyclopedias and language dictionaries. We have taken these precautions to ensure the accuracy of each word and a high level of standardization.

A DICTIONARY FOR ONE AND ALL

The Macmillan Visual Dictionary is aimed at all persons who participate in one way or another in contemporary civilization and, as a consequence, need to know and use a great number of technical terms from a wide range of fields.

It thus addresses the needs and curiosity of each and every one of us. It is not designed only for specialists.

The depth of analysis varies according to the subject. Rather than arbitrarily providing a uniform breakdown of each subject, the authors have acknowledged that people's degrees of knowledge differ from one field to another, and that the complexity of the topics dealt with varies widely. For example, more people are familiar with clothing and automobiles than with atomic energy or telecommunications satellites, and find the former subjects simpler than the latter. Another aspect of the same problem is that, in describing human anatomy, we are obliged to use medical terminology, even though the terms seem more complicated than those for fruits and vegetables. In addition, our world is changing: photographic vocabulary, for example, has become much more complicated due to camera automation. Similarly, although microcomputer fans are

familiar with computer terminology, the field remains a mystery for much of the rest of the population.

The Macmillan Visual Dictionary allows for these phenomena, and thus reflects the specialized vocabulary commonly used in each field.

AN EASY-TO-CONSULT DICTIONARY

People may use The Macmillan Visual Dictionary in several different ways, thanks to the List of Chapters (page xxxi), the detailed table of contents (page xv), and the index (page 833).

Users may consult the dictionary:

By going from an idea to a word, if they are familiar with an object and can clearly visualize it, but cannot find or do not know the name for it. The table of contents breaks down each subject according to an easy-to-consult, stratified classification system. The Macmillan Visual Dictionary is the only dictionary that allows users to find a word from its meaning.

By going from a word to an idea, if they want to check the meaning of a term. The index refers users to the illustrations, which provide the names for the individual features.

At a glance, by using the List of Chapters. The colored page edges help users find the chapters they are looking for.

For sheer pleasure, by flipping from one illustration to another, or from one word to another, for the sole purpose of enjoying the illustrations and enriching their knowledge.

A DICTIONARY WITH A DIFFERENCE

We are all familiar with several types of dictionaries and encyclopedias. It is not always easy, however, to grasp their distinguishing features. The following overview highlights the main differences between The Macmillan Visual Dictionary and other reference works.

a) Language dictionaries

These dictionaries describe the meanings given by speakers to the general vocabulary of their language.

They provide two major types of information: headwords (vocabulary), and a list of the meanings of each term (dictionary entries).

The vocabulary, which comprises all of the words covered by lexicographical descriptions, constitutes the framework of the dictionary. For consultation purposes, the headwords are arranged in alphabetical order. Generally speaking, the vocabulary includes common, contemporary language, archaic words useful for understanding the texts or history of a civilization, and a certain number of widely used technical terms.

Each dictionary entry provides an itemized, semantic description of the corresponding headword. Generally, the entry indicates the part of speech for the headword, its etymology and its various meanings, as well as the word's social usage (familiar, colloquial, vulgar, etc.) according to criteria that, even today, remain somewhat "impressionistic."

In general, language dictionaries are classified according to their target users and the number of terms in the vocabulary, which, in addition to nouns, includes all other parts of speech (verbs, pronouns, adjectives, adverbs, prepositions, conjunctions, etc.). A 5,000-word dictionary is intended for children, one with 15,000 words is suitable for elementary schools and a 50,000-word dictionary covers the needs of the general public.

b) Encyclopedic dictionaries

In addition to the information included in language dictionaries, encyclopedic dictionaries provide details about the nature, functioning, and history of things, thus enabling laymen with solid general knowledge and specialists to understand the scope of a word. They devote much more space to technical terms, and reflect current scientific and technological developments. Generally speaking, pictures play an important role in illustrating the text. The size of encyclopedic dictionaries varies according to the breadth of the vocabulary, the length of the entries, the emphasis placed on proper nouns and the number of fields of specialization covered.

c) Encyclopedias

Unlike the preceding category of reference works, encyclopedias do not deal with language. They are devoted to providing scientific, technical, occasionally economic, historical and geographic descriptions. The arrangement of the entries varies, as all classification systems are valid: alphabetic, conceptual, chronological, by field of specialization, etc. The number of different encyclopedias is virtually unlimited, given the fragmentation of civilization into multiple categories. There is, however, a distinction between universal encyclopedias and specialized encyclopedias.

d) Specialized lexicons and vocabularies

These works usually address specific needs created by scientific and technological progress. They focus on ensuring efficient communication through precise, standardized terminology. They vary in all respects: the method of compilation, the authors' approach to the subject matter, the scope of the vocabulary, the number of languages, and the means of establishing equivalents in the various languages (i.e., by simple translation or by a comparison of unilingual terminologies). Specialized lexicography has become an area of intense activity. The number of works is multiplying in all sectors and in all language combinations.

e) *The Macmillan Visual Dictionary*

The Macmillan Visual Dictionary is a terminology-oriented dictionary. It is aimed at providing members of the general public with the specific terms they need to name the objects of daily life, and helping them grasp the meaning of words through illustrations. Grouped together in interlocking categories, the various elements are interde-

fined. The dictionary is thus organized according to chapters, subjects, specific objects, and features of these objects. Depending on a person's degree of familiarity with a given chapter, the terminology may seem simple or technical. The fundamental goal, however, is to provide non-specialists with a coherent analysis of useful, necessary vocabulary for each subject.

The Macmillan Visual Dictionary is not an encyclopedia, for at least two reasons: rather than describing objects, it names them; in addition, it avoids listing all the objects in a given category. For example, rather than enumerating the various types of trees, it focuses on a typical representative of the category, and examines its structure and individual parts.

It may even less be considered a language dictionary: like other terminological works, it contains no written definitions and covers only nouns and, in particular, noun phrases.

Nor may it be seen as a compendium of specialized vocabularies, as it avoids terminology used only by specialists, focusing instead on more widespread terms—at the risk of being considered simplistic by experts in specific fields.

The Macmillan Visual Dictionary is the first terminology-oriented dictionary to group together in a single volume the thousands of technical and not-so-technical terms most commonly used in our society, where science, technology, and their end products are part of everyday life.

This is the editorial policy that has guided us in creating this dictionary. Consequently, the number of words it contains does not have the same significance as for a language dictionary, for several reasons: in keeping with our editorial policy, we have deliberately chosen to limit the number of words; unlike conventional dictionaries, this work focuses exclusively on nouns, the most significant words in the language, to the exclusion of adjectives, verbs, prepositions, etc.; and finally no one is sure exactly how to count compound terms!

COMPUTER-PRODUCED ILLUSTRATIONS

The illustrations in *The Macmillan Visual Dictionary* have been created by computer from recent documents and original photographs.

The use of computers has given the illustrations a highly realistic, almost photographic look, while allowing us to highlight the essential features corresponding to the vocabulary. The graphic precision of *The Macmillan Visual Dictionary* is one of the main sources of its excellence as an encyclopedic and lexicographical reference tool.

In addition, thanks to computers, we have been able to improve the accuracy of the lines joining objects to their names, thus enhancing the clarity of the link between words and the things they describe.

CAREFULLY ESTABLISHED VOCABULARY

In creating *The Macmillan Visual Dictionary*, we have used the method of systematic and comparative terminological research, which is standard practice among professionals who prepare works of this type.

This method comprises several steps, which follow one another in a logical order. The following paragraphs provide a brief description of each of these steps.

Field delimitation

First of all, on the basis of our objectives, we defined the scope and contents of the proposed work.

We began by choosing the chapters we felt it necessary to cover. We then divided each chapter into fields and sub-fields, taking care to abide by our editorial policy and avoiding overspecialization and the temptation to cover all subjects in detail. This step resulted in a working table of contents, the dictionary framework, which guided our subsequent steps and was refined as the work progressed. The detailed table of contents is the end result of this process.

Documentary research

In keeping with our production plan, we assembled pertinent documents likely to provide us with the required information about words and concepts in each subject matter.

In order of reliability, our documentary sources were as follows:

• Articles and books by experts in the various fields, written in their native language, with an acceptable degree of specialization. Translations of such texts provide revealing information about vocabulary usage, but must be used with due caution;

• Technical documents, such as national standards or the guidelines of the International Standard Organization (ISO), product instructions, technical documents provided by manufacturers, official government publications, etc.;

• Catalogs, commercial texts, advertisements from specialized magazines and major newspapers;

• Encyclopedias, encyclopedic dictionaries, and unilingual language dictionaries;

• Unilingual, bilingual, and multilingual specialized vocabularies and dictionaries. The quality and reliability of these works, however, must be carefully assessed;

• Bilingual and multilingual language dictionaries.

In all, we consulted four to five thousand references. The selected bibliography included in the dictionary indicates only the general documentary sources consulted, and does not include specialized sources.

Sifting through the documents

A terminologist went through the documents for each subject, in search of specific concepts and the words used to express them by different authors and works. Gradually, a framework was established, as the terminologist noted the use of the same term for a given concept from one source to another, or, on the contrary, the use of several terms for the same idea. In the latter case, the terminologist continued his research until he was able to form a well-documented opinion of each competing term. All of this research was recorded, with reference notes.

Creation of terminological files

The preceding step enabled us to assemble all of the elements for our terminological files.

Each concept identified and defined by an illustration has been paired with the term most frequently used to describe it by the leading authors or in the most reliable sources. Where several competing terms were found in the reference material, following discussion and consensus between the terminologist and the scientific director, a single term was chosen.

Terminological variants

Frequently, several words may be used to designate virtually the same concept.

We dealt with such situations as follows:

• In some cases, a term was used by a single author or appeared only once in our documentary sources. We retained the most frequently used competing term.

• Technical terms are often compound words with or without a hyphen, or several-word expressions. This results in at least two types of terminological variants:

a) The compound technical term may be shortened by the deletion of one or more of its elements, especially where the meaning is clear in the context. The shortened expression may even become the normal term for the concept. In such cases, we retained the compound form, leaving users the freedom to abbreviate it according to the context.

b) An element of the compound term may itself have equivalents (most often synonyms from the commonly spoken language). We retained the most frequently used form.

Variants may stem from the evolution of the language, without terminological consequences. We therefore retained the most contemporary or well-known form.

TERMINOLOGICAL APPROACH

A few comments about the terminological approach, as compared to the lexicographical approach, are in order.

Language dictionaries have a long history. They are familiar reference works, used by most people since early school age, with a well-established, widely known and accepted tradition. We all know how to consult a dictionary and interpret the information it provides—or fails to provide.

Terminological dictionaries are either very recent or intended for a specialized public. There is no solid tradition to guide those who design and produce such works. Although specialists know how to interpret dictionaries pertaining to their own fields, given that they are familiar with the terminology, the same cannot be said for the layperson, who is confused by variants. Finally, whereas language dictionaries have to a certain extent established standard word usage among their users, specialized vocabularies are characterized by competing terms in new fields of specialization.

Users of a reference work such as *The Macmillan Visual Dictionary* should take into account these elements in assessing this new type of reference tool.

JEAN-CLAUDE CORBEIL
ARIANE ARCHAMBAULT

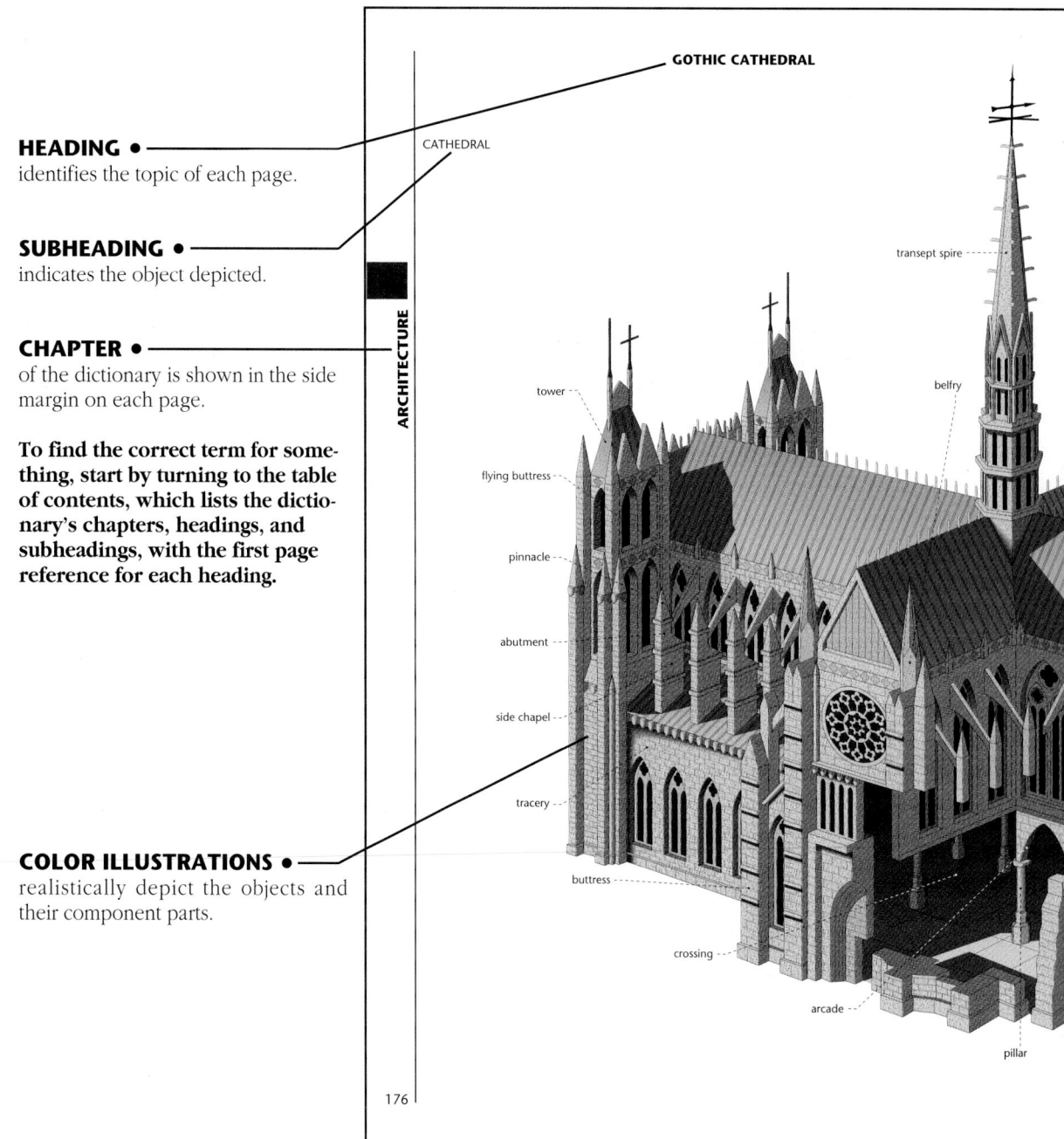

HEADING ●
identifies the topic of each page.

SUBHEADING ●
indicates the object depicted.

CHAPTER ●
of the dictionary is shown in the side margin on each page.

To find the correct term for something, start by turning to the table of contents, which lists the dictionary's chapters, headings, and subheadings, with the first page reference for each heading.

COLOR ILLUSTRATIONS ●
realistically depict the objects and their component parts.

GOTHIC CATHEDRAL

CATHEDRAL

ARCHITECTURE

transept spire

tower

belfry

flying buttress

pinnacle

abutment

side chapel

tracery

buttress

crossing

arcade

pillar

176

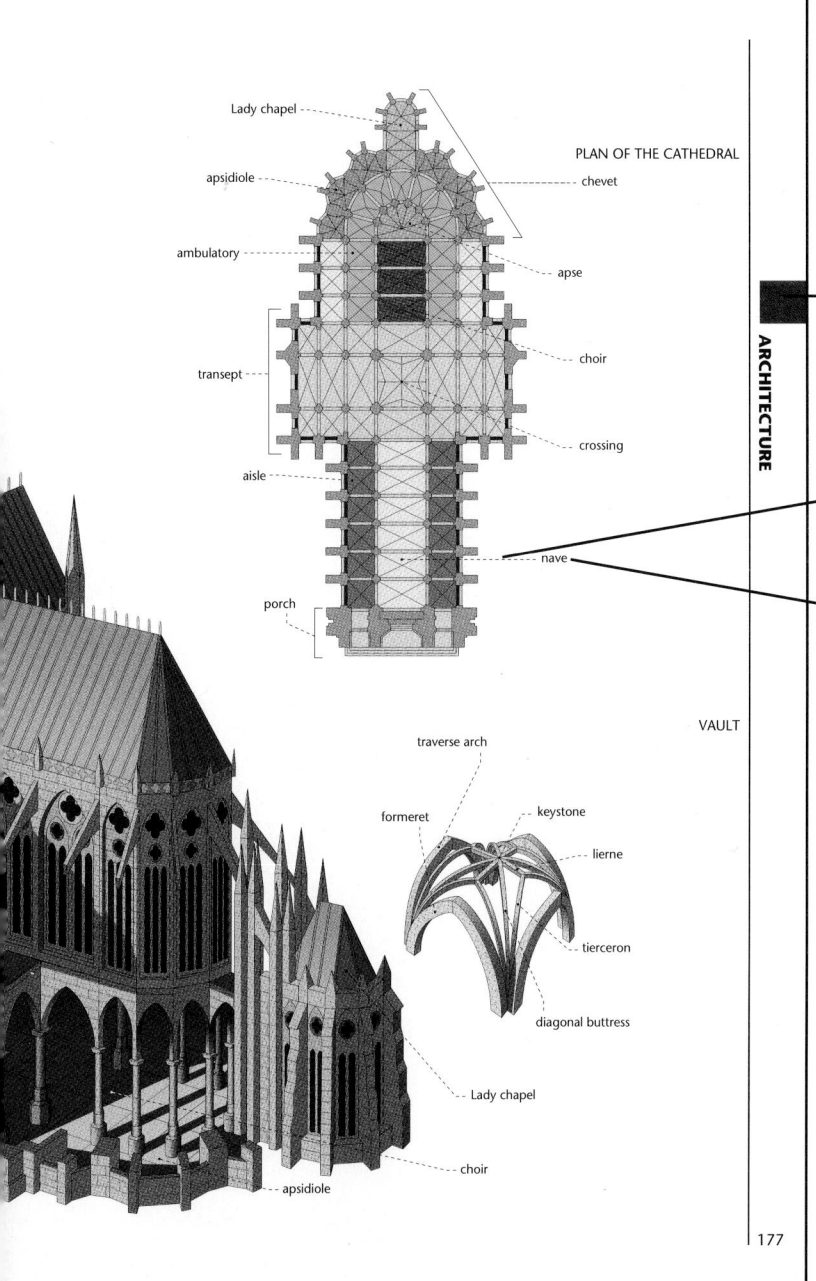

PLAN OF THE CATHEDRAL

Lady chapel

apsidiole — chevet

ambulatory

apse

transept

choir

crossing

aisle

nave

porch

ARCHITECTURE

VAULT

traverse arch

formeret

keystone

lierne

tierceron

diagonal buttress

Lady chapel

choir

apsidiole

177

● **COLORED TAB**
on the edge of the page corresponds
to the chapter as shown in the List of
Chapters. This color-coding allows
you to find, at a glance, the subject
you are looking for.

● **DOTTED LINES**
link the terms with the objects they
describe.

● **TERMS**
are included in the index, with references to all pages on
which they appear.

**To see an illustration depicting
a term that you know,
consult the index.**

SELECTED BIBLIOGRAPHY

DICTIONARIES

- *Gage Canadian Dictionary.* Toronto: Gage Publishing Limited, 1983, 1313 p.
- *The New Britannica/Webster Dictionary and Reference Guide.* Chicago, Toronto: Encyclopedia Britannica, 1981, 1505 p.
- *The Oxford English Dictionary.* Second edition. Oxford: Clarendon Press, 1989, 20 vol.
- *The Oxford Illustrated Dictionary.* Oxford: Clarendon Press, 1967, 974 p.
- *Oxford American Dictionary.* Eugene Ehrlich, et al. New York, Oxford: Oxford University Press, 1980, 816 p.
- *The Random House Dictionary of the English Language.* Second edition. New York: Random House 1983, 2059 p.
- *Webster's Encyclopedic Unabridged Dictionary of the English Language.* New York: Portland House, 1989, 2078 p.
- *Webster's Third New International Dictionary.* Springfield: Merriam-Webster, 1986, 2662 p.
- *Webster's Ninth New Collegiate Dictionary.* Springfield: Merriam-Webster, 1984, 1563 p.
- *Webster's New World Dictionary of American Language.* New York: The World Pub., 1953.

ENCYCLOPEDIAS

- *Academic American Encyclopedia.* Princeton: Arete Publishing Company, 1980, 21 vol.
- *Architectural Graphic Standards.* Eighth edition. New York: John Wiley & Sons, 1988, 854 p.
- *Chamber's Encyclopedia.* New rev. edition. London: International Learning System, 1989.
- *Collier's Encyclopedia.* New York: Macmillan Educational Company, 1984, 24 vol.
- *Compton's Encyclopedia.* Chicago: F.E. Compton Company, Division of Encyclopedia Britannica Inc., 1982, 26 vol.
- *Encyclopedia Americana.* International Edition, Danbury: Grolier, 1981, 30 vol.
- *How It Works, The Illustrated Science and Invention Encyclopedia.* New York: H.S. Stuttman, 1977, 21 vol.
- *McGraw-Hill Encyclopedia of Science & Technology.* New York: McGraw-Hill Book Company, 1982, 15 vol.
- *Merit Students Encyclopedia.* New York: Macmillan Educational Company, 1984, 20 vol.
- *New Encyclopedia Britannica.* Chicago, Toronto: Encyclopedia Britannica, 1985, 32 vol.
- *The Joy of Knowledge Encyclopedia.* London: Mitchell Beazley Encyclopedias, 1976, 7 vol.
- *The Random House Encyclopedia.* New York: Random House, 1977, 2 vol.
- *The World Book Encyclopedia.* Chicago: Field Enterprises Educational Corporation, 1973.

FRENCH AND ENGLISH DICTIONARIES

- Collins-Robert, *French-English, English-French Dictionary,* London, Glasgow, Cleveland, Toronto: Collins-Robert, 1978, 781 p.
- Dubois, Marguerite, *Dictionnaire moderne français-anglais.* Paris: Larousse, 1980, 752 p.
- Harrap's *New Standard French and English Dictionary.* Part one, French-English. London: Harrap's 1977, 2 vol. Part two, English-French. London: Harrap's 1983, 2 vol.
- Harrap's *Shorter French and English Dictionary,* London, Toronto, Willington, Sydney: Harrap's 1953, 940 p.

CONTENTS

ASTRONOMY

Earth coordinate system.. 3
celestial coordinate system... 3
solar system.. 4
    planets and moons, orbits of the planets
Sun... 6
    structure of the Sun
Moon.. 7
    phases of the Moon, lunar features
solar eclipse.. 8
lunar eclipse.. 8
seasons of the year.. 8
comet... 9
galaxy... 9
    Hubble's classification
constellations of the northern hemisphere.. 10
constellations of the southern hemisphere 12
astronomical observatory.. 14
    observatory, telescope
radio telescope 15
    altazimuth mounting
Hubble space telescope... 16
planetarium 16

GEOGRAPHY

profile of the Earth's atmosphere... 19
configuration of the continents.. 20
structure of the Earth 22
section of the Earth's crust... 22
earthquake 23
cave 24
volcano... 25
glacier... 26
mountain.. 27
ocean floor... 28
    mid-ocean ridge, topographic features, abyssal plain, continental margin
wave 30
common coastal features... 30
ecology... 31
    structure of the biosphere, food chain, pollution of food on ground, pollution of
    food in water, atmospheric pollution, hydrologic cycle
precipitations... 36
    stormy sky, classification of snow crystals
meteorology... 38
    weather map, station model, wind
international weather symbols... 39
    fronts, sky coverage, present weather
meteorological measuring instruments 40
    measure of sunshine, measure of rainfall, measure of temperature, measure of
    air pressure, measure of wind direction, measure of wind strength, measure of
    humidity, measure of snowfall, measure of cloud ceiling, instrument shelter
weather satellite 42
    geostationary satellite, polar-orbiting satellite, orbit of the satellites
clouds and meteorological symbols.. 44
    high clouds, middle clouds, low clouds, clouds of vertical development

CONTENTS

climates of the world...45
    tropical climates, continental climates, temperate climates, subtropical climates, polar climates, highland climates, subarctic climates
desert..46
cartography...47
    grid system, hemispheres, map projections, political map, physical map, urban map, road map
remote detection satellite..48
    Radarsat satellite

VEGETABLE KINGDOM
mushroom...55
    structure of a mushroom, edible mushrooms, deadly poisonous mushroom, poisonous mushroom
leaf...56
    leaf margin, types of leaves, compound leaves, simple leaves
structure of a plant...57
conifer..58
    branch, types of leaves
structure of a tree..59
    tree, cross section of a trunk, stump
structure of a flower...60
    types of inflorescences
grape..61
    maturing steps, vine stock, grape leaf, bunch of grapes
fleshy fruits: berry fruits...62
    section of a berry, section of a raspberry, section of a strawberry, major types of berries
stone fleshy fruits..63
    section of a stone fruit, major types of stone fruits
pome fleshy fruits..64
    section of a pome fruit, major types of pome fruits
fleshy fruits: citrus fruits..65
    section of a citrus fruit, major types of citrus fruits
dry fruits: nuts...66
    section of a hazelnut, section of a walnut, major types of nuts, husk
various dry fruits...67
    section of a follicle, section of a legume, section of a silique, section of a capsule
tropical fruits...68
    major types of tropical fruits
vegetables..69
    fruit vegetables, inflorescent vegetables, bulb vegetables, tuber vegetables, root vegetables, stalk vegetables, seed vegetables, leaf vegetables
herbs..74

ANIMAL KINGDOM
insects and spider..77
butterfly...78
    caterpillar, chrysalis, hind leg
honeybee..80
    foreleg (outer surface), middle leg (outer surface), hind leg (inner surface), mouthparts, worker, queen, drone, honeycomb section, hive
gastropod...83
    snail, major edible gastropods

CONTENTS

amphibians 84
    frog, life cycle of the frog, eggs, tadpole, major amphibians
fish 86
    morphology, gills, anatomy
crustacean 90
    lobster, major edible crustaceans
mollusk 92
    oyster, major edible mollusks
univalve shell 94
bivalve shell 95
    dorsal view, left valve
reptile 96
    rattlesnake, venomous snake's head, turtle
types of jaws 98
    rodent's jaw, carnivore's jaw, herbivore's jaw
major types of horns 99
major types of tusks 99
types of hoofs 99
horse 100
    morphology, skeleton, gaits, horseshoe, hoof
deer family 105
    deer antlers, kinds of deer
dog 106
    morphology, dog's forepaw
cat 107
    cat's head, retracted claw, extended claw
bird 108
    morphology, head, egg, wing, contour feather, principal types of bills, principal types of feet
bat 112

HUMAN BEING
plant cell 115
animal cell 115
human body 116
muscles 120
    anterior view, posterior view
skeleton 122
    anterior view, posterior view
blood circulation 124
    schema of circulation, heart, principal veins and arteries
male genital organs 127
    spermatozoon
female genital organs 128
    egg
breast 129
respiratory system 130
digestive system 131
    large intestine, small intestine
urinary system 132
nervous system 133
    peripheral nervous system, central nervous system, lumbar vertebra, chain of neurons, sensory impulse
sense organs: touch 136
    skin, finger, hand

CONTENTS

sense organs: hearing 138
   parts of the ear, auditory ossicles, auricle
sense organs: sight 140
   eye, eyeball
sense organs: smell 141
   external nose, nasal fossae
senses of smell and taste 142
   mouth, dorsum of tongue, taste sensations
teeth 144
   human denture, cross section of a molar

FARMING
tractor 147
farmstead 148
farm animals 150
major types of cereals 152
bread 153
steps for cultivating soil 154
   ribbing plow, manure spreader, tandem disk harrow, cultivator, seed drill, flail
   mower, rake, hay baler, combine harvester, forage harvester, forage blower

ARCHITECTURE
traditional houses 165
architectural styles 166
   ionic order, doric order, corinthian order
Greek temple 168
Roman house 170
mosque 172
arch 174
   semicircular arch, types of arches
gothic cathedral 175
Vauban fortification 178
castle 180
roofs 182
downtown 184
cross section of a street 186
city houses 187
theater 188
   stage
office building 190

HOUSE
blueprint reading 193
   elevation, site plan, mezzanine floor, second floor, first floor
exterior of a house 196
structure of a house 198
   frame, roof truss, foundations
wood flooring 200
   wood flooring on cement screed, wood flooring on wooden structure, wood
   flooring arrangements
stairs 201
door 202
   types of doors
window 203
   structure, types of windows

CONTENTS

heating 204
    fireplace, slow-burning stove, chimney, fire irons, forced warm-air system,
    electric furnace, types of registers, forced hot-water system, column radiator,
    boiler, oil burner, humidifier, hygrometer, electric baseboard radiator,
    convector, auxiliary heating, heat pump, room thermostat
air conditioning 214
    ceiling fan, room air conditioner
plumbing system 215
pedestal-type sump pump 216
septic tank 216

HOUSE FURNITURE
table 219
    major types of tables
armchair 220
    principal types of armchairs
seats 222
side chair 223
    types of chairs
bed 224
    linen
storage furniture 225
    armoire
window accessories 228
    types of curtains, types of pleats, types of headings, curtain pole, curtain track,
    traverse rod, roller shade, Venetian blind
lights 232
    incandescent lamp, fluorescent tube, tungsten-halogen lamp, energy saving
    bulb, adjustable lamp, track lighting, chandelier
glassware 237
dinnerware 238
silverware 239
    major types of knives, major types of forks, major types of spoons
kitchen utensils 242
    types of kitchen knives, for straining and draining, for grinding and grating, set
    of utensils, for opening, for measuring, baking utensils
coffee makers 247
    automatic drip coffee maker, vacuum coffee maker, percolator, plunger,
    Neapolitan coffee maker, espresso coffee maker
cooking utensils 248
    wok set, fish poacher, fondue set, pressure cooker
domestic appliances 250
    hand blender, beaters, blender, hand mixer, table mixer, food processor, citrus
    juicer, juicer, ice cream freezer, kettle, toaster, deep fryer, waffle iron,
    microwave oven, griddle, refrigerator, range hood, electric range, steam iron,
    coffee mill, can opener, dishwasher, washer, electric dryer, hand vacuum
    cleaner, canister vacuum cleaner

GARDENING
pleasure garden 263
tools and equipment 264
    impulse sprinkler, hose trolley, watering can, hedge trimmer, wheelbarrow,
    motorized earth auger, hand mower, edger, power mower, chainsaw, tiller

CONTENTS

DO-IT-YOURSELF

carpentry: tools 275
    nail, mallet, claw hammer, ball-peen hammer, screwdriver, spiral screwdriver,
    crescent wrench, hacksaw, plane, handsaw, slip joint pliers, rib joint pliers,
    locking pliers, washers, screw, bolt, nut, electric drill, hand drill, twist drill,
    brace, auger bit, C-clamp, vise, router, drill press, circular saw, table saw

building materials 286
    basic building materials, covering materials, insulating materials, wood, board,
    wood-based materials

lock 290
    mortise lock, tubular lock

masonry 291
    caulking gun, mason's trowel

plumbing: bathroom 292
    toilet

plumbing 294
    stem faucet, ball-type faucet, disc faucet, cartridge faucet, garbage disposal
    sink, gas water-heater tank

plumbing: examples of branching 298
    washer, dishwasher

plumbing 299
    plumbing tools, fittings, transition fittings

ladders and stepladders 302
    extension ladder, stepladder, platform ladder

painting upkeep 304
    spray paint gun, brush, scraper, paint roller

soldering and welding 305
    arc welding, soldering gun, cutting torch, welding torch, oxyacetylene welding,
    pressure regulator, butt welding, soldering torch, striker

soldering and welding: protective clothing 308

electricity 309
    American plug, lamp socket, European plug, electrician's tools, multimeter,
    voltage tester, drop light, multipurpose tool, lineman's pliers, fuse box, fuses

CLOTHING

elements of ancient costume 315

men's clothing 319
    raincoat, trench coat, duffle coat, overcoat, windbreaker, jacket, parka, dou-
    ble-breasted jacket, vest, single-breasted jacket, belt, pants, suspenders, shirt,
    necktie, athletic shirt, underwear, socks, briefs

sweaters 326
    V-neck cardigan

gloves 327

headgear 328
    felt hat

women's clothing 330
    types of coats, pea jacket, raglan, pelerine, suit, types of dresses, types of skirts,
    types of pleats, types of pants, types of blouses, jackets, vest and sweaters,
    types of pockets, types of sleeves, types of collars, necklines and necks, hose,
    underwear, bra, nightwear

children's clothing 349
    bathing wrap, plastic pants, blanket sleepers, high-back overalls, sleepers,
    grow sleepers, training set, crossover back straps overalls, snowsuit

sportswear 352
    running shoe, training suit, exercise wear

CONTENTS

shoes 354
    parts of a shoe, major types of shoes, accessories, shoeshine kit

PERSONAL ADORNMENT
jewelry 361
    earrings, necklaces, precious stones, semiprecious stones, cut for gemstones,
    brilliant cut facets, rings, bracelets, pins, charms
manicure 365
    manicure set, manicuring implements, nail clippers
makeup 366
    lip makeup, eye makeup, sponges
hairdressing 368
    lighted mirror, hairbrushes, styling brush, combs, haircutting scissors, notched
    single-edged thinning scissors, notched double-edged thinning scissors, hair
    roller, curling iron, hair dryer

PERSONAL ARTICLES
dental care 373
    toothbrush, oral hygiene center
razors 374
    straight razor, double-edge razor, electric razor, shaving brush
umbrella and stick 375
    umbrella, stick umbrella, telescopic umbrella
eyeglasses 376
    eyeglasses parts, bifocal lens, frames, major types of eyeglasses
leather goods 378
    attaché case, bottom-fold portfolio, briefcase, checkbook/secretary clutch, card
    case
handbags 380
    satchel bag, shoulder bag, accordion bag, drawstring bag
luggage 382
    garment bag, carry-on bag, vanity case, luggage carrier, weekender, pullman
    case, trunk
smoking accessories 384
    cigar, cigarette, cigarette pack, pipe, pipe tools, matchbook, gas lighter,
    matchbox, ashtray

COMMUNICATIONS
writing instruments 389
    fountain pen, ballpoint pen
photography 390
    cross section of a reflex camera, camera back, single-lens reflex (SLR) camera,
    lenses, electronic flash, tripod, still cameras, films, exposure meter, spotmeter,
    slide projector, projection screen, transparency slide, developing tank, enlarger,
    negative carrier, developing baths, print washer
sound reproducing system 400
    system components, loudspeaker, tuner, amplifier, cassette, cassette tape deck,
    record, turntable, compact disk, compact disk player
dynamic microphone 406
headphone 406
radio: studio and control room 407
portable sound systems 408
    personal AM-FM cassette player, portable AM-FM cassette recorder
video camera 409

CONTENTS

television 410
    television set, picture tube, remote control, videocassette recorder, studio and
    control rooms, production control room, studio floor, camera
mobile unit 415
broadcast satellite communication 416
telecommunications by satellite 417
telecommunication satellites 418
    examples of satellites, Eutelsat II, launching into orbit
communication by telephone 420
    telephone answering machine, telephone set, telex, facsimile machine, types of
    telephones, telecommunication terminal, pay phone

ROAD TRANSPORT
automobile 425
    types of bodies, body, bucket seat, rear seat, lights, door, dashboard,
    instrument panel, windshield wiper, disk brake, drum brake, wheel, tire, gasoline
    engine, turbo-compressor engine, radiator, exhaust system, battery, spark plug
types of engines 436
    four-stroke-cycle engine, two-stroke-cycle engine, diesel engine, rotary engine
trucking 440
    truck tractor, tandem tractor trailer, semitrailer, flatbed
motorcycle 442
    protective helmet, motorcycle dashboard
snowmobile 445
bicycle 446
    power train, accessories
caravan 449
    trailer, motor home
road system 450
    cross section of a road, major types of interchanges, cloverleaf
service station 453
    gasoline pump, service station
fixed bridges 454
    types of beam bridges, types of arch bridges, types of arches, suspension
    bridge, cable-stayed bridges
movable bridges 457
    swing bridge, single-leaf bascule bridge, floating bridge, lift bridge, transporter
    bridge

RAIL TRANSPORT
high-speed train 458
types of passenger cars 460
    coach car, sleeping car, dining car
passenger station 462
railroad station 464
yard 465
railroad track 466
    rail joint, rail section, remote-controlled switch, manually-operated switch
diesel-electric locomotive 468
car 470
    box car, container, coupler head
highway crossing 471
types of freight cars 472
subway 474
    subway station, subway train, truck and track, passenger car

CONTENTS

MARITIME TRANSPORT

four-masted bark 478
   masting and rigging, sails
types of sails.. 482
types of rigs 482
anchor... 483
   ship's anchor, types of anchors
navigation devices.. 484
   sextant, liquid compass, echo sounder
maritime signals 486
   lighthouse lantern, cylindrical buoy, lighthouse, high focal plane buoy
maritime buoyage system 488
   cardinal marks, buoyage regions, rhythm of marks by night, daymarks
harbor 490
canal lock... 492
hovercraft 492
ferry 494
container ship 494
hydrofoil boat 495
passenger liner... 496

AIR TRANSPORT

long-range jet 498
types of tail shapes.. 498
types of wing shapes... 499
flight deck... 500
turbofan engine 501
airport... 502
   passenger terminal, runway, ground airport equipment
helicopter.. 508
rocket 509
space shuttle... 510
   space shuttle at takeoff, space shuttle in orbit
spacesuit 512

OFFICE SUPPLIES

stationery.. 515
office furniture 520
calculator 523
   pocket calculator, printing calculator
electronic typewriter.. 524

OFFICE AUTOMATION

configuration of an office automation system 526
   input devices, communication devices, data storage devices, output devices
basic components 528
   personal computer, video monitor, floppy disk, mini-floppy disk, hard disk drive,
   keyboard, mouse, dot matrix printer
photocopier 532
   control panel

MUSIC

traditional musical instruments 535
   zither, balalaika, mandolin, lyre, banjo, accordion, bagpipes, Jew's harp

CONTENTS

musical notation 537
  staff, clefs, time signatures, scale, intervals, note symbols, rest symbols,
  accidentals, ornaments, chord, other signs
musical accessories 539
  tuning fork, quartz metronome, metronome, music stand
keyboard instruments 540
  upright piano, upright piano action
organ 542
  organ console, flue pipe, reed pipe, mechanism of the organ, production of
  sound
stringed instruments 544
  violin, bow, violin family, harp, acoustic guitar, electric guitar
wind instruments 548
  saxophone, woodwind family, reeds, trumpet, brass family
percussion instruments 552
  drums, snare drum, kettledrum, xylophone, triangle, tambourine
electronic instruments 555
  synthesizer, electronic piano
symphony orchestra 556
examples of instrumental groups 558

CREATIVE LEISURE ACTIVITIES

sewing 561
  sewing machine, foot control, presser foot, needle, tension block, bobbin case,
  pin cushion, tracing wheel, scissors, underlying fabrics, pattern, fasteners, hook
  and eyes, fabric structure, zipper, snap, buckle
knitting 567
  knitting needles, stitch patterns, crochet hook
knitting machine 568
  needle bed and carriages, latch needle, tension block
bobbin lace 570
  pillow, bobbin
embroidery 571
  frame, hoop, cross stitches, flat stitches, couched stitches, knot stitches, loop
  stitches
weaving 572
  low warp loom, shuttle, heddles, high warp loom, warping frame, bobbin
  winder, ball winder, diagram of weaving principle, basic weaves, other
  techniques
fine bookbinding 577
  bound book, gathering, trimming, sawing-in, sewing, board cutter, sewing
  frame, backing, backing press, backing hammer, covering, bookbinding
  leather, pressing, standing press
printing 580
  relief printing, intaglio printing, lithographic printing
relief printing process 581
  inking slab, equipment, etching press
intaglio printing process 582
  equipment
lithography 583
  equipment, lithographic press, levigator
pottery 584
  turning, coiling, tools, slab building, turning wheel, electric kiln, firing
wood carving 586
  steps, accessories, types of tools, major types of blades

CONTENTS

painting and drawing 588
    major techniques, equipment, supports, airbrush, drafting table, utility liquids

TEAM GAMES
baseball 595
    catcher, batter, bat, fielder's glove, baseball, field
cricket 598
    cricket player, cricket ball, bat, wicket, field, pitch
soccer 600
    soccer player, soccer ball, playing field
football 602
    football player, protective equipment, football, offense, scrimmage, defense,
    playing field for American football, playing field for Canadian football,
    scrimmage in Canadian football
rugby 606
    field, rugby ball
field hockey 607
    playing field, stick, hockey ball
ice hockey 608
    puck, rink, player's stick, goalkeeper, ice hockey player
basketball 610
    court, basket, basketball
netball 611
    netball, court
handball 612
    handball, court
volleyball 613
    court, net, volleyball
tennis 614
    court, net, tennis ball, tennis player, tennis racket
squash 616
    squash racket, international singles court, squash ball
racquetball 617
    racquetball racket, court, racquetball
badminton 618
    badminton racket, shuttlecock, court, net
table tennis 619
    table tennis paddle, table, types of grips
curling 620
    curling brooms, curling stone, rink

WATER SPORTS
swimming 621
    competitive course, starting block, front crawl stroke, breaststroke, butterfly
    stroke, backstroke, backstroke start
diving 624
    diving installations, starting positions, flights, entries, forward dive, twist dive,
    armstand dive, inward dive, backward dive, reverse dive
water polo 626
    playing area, goal, water polo ball
scuba diving 627
    scuba diver
sailing 628
    points of sailing, sailboat, upperworks, traveler
sailboard 631

CONTENTS

rowing and sculling 632
   rowing (one oar), sculling boats, rowing boats, sculling (two oars), types of oars
water skiing 633
   types of skis, twin skis, slalom ski, figure ski, types of handles

AERIAL SPORTS
ballooning 634
   balloon, basket
sky diving 635
   sky diver
paragliding 636
   canopy
hang gliding 637
   hang glider
gliding 638
   glider, cockpit

WINTER SPORTS
alpine skiing 640
   alpine skier, safety binding, ski boot
cross-country skiing 642
   cross-country skier, cross-country ski
luge 643
bobsled 643
skating 644
   figure skate, hockey skate, skate guard, speed skate
roller skate 645
snowshoe 645
   Michigan snowshoe

EQUESTRIAN SPORTS
riding 646
   competition ring, obstacles, rider, saddle, bridle
types of bits 650
   snaffle bit, curb bit
horse racing 651
   jockey, stand and track
harness racing 652
   standardbred pacer

ATHLETICS
track and field athletics 654
   arena, starting block, high jump, pole vault, throwings, hammer, discus,
   javelins, shot
gymnastics 659
   asymmetrical bars, balance beam, trampoline, vaulting horse, springboard,
   rings, horizontal bar, pommel horse, parallel bars
weightlifting 662
   weightlifter, two-hand snatch, two-hand clean and jerk
fitness equipment 663
   weight stack exercise unit, barbell, stationary bicycle, rower, climber,
   handgrips, ankle/wrist weight, chest expander, jump rope, dumbbell, twist bar

COMBAT SPORTS
fencing 666
   piste, fencing weapons, parts of the weapon, fencer, positions, target areas

CONTENTS

judo 668
    judo suit, mat, examples of holds
boxing 669
    ring, boxing gloves, bandage, mouthpiece

LEISURE SPORTS
fishing 670
    fly rod, artificial fly, fly reel, spinning rod, open-face spinning reel, fishhook,
    spinner, fishing garment, accessories, terminal tackles
billiards 673
    carom billiards, English billiards, pool, snooker, table, bridge, billiards cue
golf 676
    course, golf ball, golf clubs, wood, iron, golf bag, electric golf cart, golf cart,
    head cover, golf glove, golf shoe
mountaineering 680
    mountaineer, descender, hammer ax, piton, carabiner, ice ax, tubular ice
    screw, chock
bowls and petanque 682
    green, delivery
bowling 683
    types of pins, setup, lane, bowling ball
archery 684
    target, arrow, archer, compound bow
camping 685
    two-persons tent, family tent, pup tent, major types of tents, bed and mattress,
    sleeping bags, Swiss army knife, cooking set, cutlery set, two-burner camp stove,
    propane or butane accessories, single-burner camp stove, heater, lantern, tools
knots 691
cable 692
    shot splice, twisted rope, braided rope

INDOOR GAMES
card games 695
    symbols, standard poker hands
dominoes 695
chess 696
    chessboard, types of movements, men
backgammon 697
go 697
    board, major motions
game of darts 698
    dartboard, dart, playing area
video entertainment system 699
dice 699
roulette table 700
    American roulette wheel, American betting layout, French roulette wheel,
    French betting layout
slot machine 702

MEASURING DEVICES
measure of temperature 705
    thermometer, bimetallic thermometer, clinical thermometer, room thermostat
measure of time 706
    stopwatch, mechanical watch, digital watch, analog watch, sundial,
    grandfather clock, weight-driven clock mechanism

CONTENTS

measure of weight..708
  beam balance, steelyard, Roberval's balance, spring balance, bathroom scale,
  electronic scales, analytical balance
measure of pressure..710
  barometer/thermometer, tensiometer
measure of length 711
  tape measure
measure of distance 711
  pedometer
measure of thickness 711
  micrometer caliper
watt-hour meter..712
  exterior view, mechanism
measure of angles..713
  bevel square, theodolite, protractor
measure of seismic waves..714
  detection of seismic waves, amplification of seismic waves, transcription of
  seismic waves, visualization of seismic waves

OPTICAL INSTRUMENTS
electron microscope..717
  cross section of an electron microscope, electron microscope elements
binocular microscope..718
telescopic sight..718
prism binoculars..719
magnetic compass 719
reflecting telescope..720
refracting telescope 721
lenses..722
  converging lenses, diverging lenses
radar..722

HEALTH AND SAFETY
first aid kit..725
first aid equipment..726
  stethoscope, cot, stretcher, syringe
wheelchair..727
walking aids..728
  forearm crutch, canes, underarm crutch
ear protection 729
  safety earmuff, ear plugs
eye protection..729
  safety goggles, safety glasses
head protection..729
  safety cap
respiratory system protection..730
  respirator, half-mask respirator
safety vest..730
feet protection 730

ENERGY
coal mine..733
  open-pit mine, strip mine, pithead, underground mine, jackleg drill, pneumatic
  hammer

CONTENTS

oil 737
    *drilling rig, rotary system, production platform, offshore drilling, Christmas tree,
    crude-oil pipeline, fixed-roof tank, floating-roof tank, tank trailer, tanker, tank
    car, refinery products*
electricity 746
    *hydroelectric complex, cross section of hydroelectric power station,
    embankment dam, gravity dam, arch dam, buttress dam, tidal power plant,
    generator unit, Francis turbine, Kaplan turbine, Pelton turbine, steps in
    production of electricity, tower, electricity transmission, overhead connection*
nuclear energy 758
    *nuclear generating station, carbon dioxide reactor, heavy-water reactor,
    pressurized-water reactor, boiling-water reactor, fuel handling sequence, fuel
    bundle, nuclear reactor, production of electricity from nuclear energy*
solar energy 768
    *solar cell, flat-plate solar collector, solar-cell system, solar furnace, production
    of electricity from solar energy, solar house, Trombe wall*
wind energy 773
    windmill, post mill, horizontal-axis wind turbine, vertical-axis wind turbine

HEAVY MACHINERY
fire prevention 777
    fireman, helmet, hand lamp, ladder and hose strap
fire engine 778
    *pumper, nozzle, fire hose, dividing breeching, fire hydrant wrench, aerial
    ladder truck, portable fire extinguisher, pike pole, percussion bar, hook ladder,
    fireman's hatchet*
heavy vehicles 782
    wheel loader, bulldozer, scraper, grader, dump truck, hydraulic shovel
material handling 786
    *tower crane, truck crane, gantry crane, forklift truck, hydraulic pallet truck,
    wing pallet, box pallet*

WEAPONS
Stone Age arms 791
weapons in the age of the Romans 791
    Gallic warrior, Roman legionary
armor 792
    armet
bows and crossbow 793
    modern bow, bow, arrow, crossbow
thrusting and cutting weapons 794
harquebus 795
    flintlock
submachine gun 795
automatic rifle 796
light machine gun 796
revolver 797
pistol 797
hunting weapons 798
    rifle (rifled bore), cartridge (rifle), shotgun (smooth-bore), cartridge (shotgun)
seventeenth century cannon 800
    muzzle loading, cross section of a muzzle loading, firing accessories, projectiles
modern howitzer 802
mortar 803
    seventeenth century mortar, modern mortar

CONTENTS

hand grenade 804

bazooka 804

recoilless rifle 804

tank 805

submarine 806

frigate 808

aircraft carrier 810

combat aircraft 812
   in-flight refueling

missiles 814
   structure of a missile, major types of missiles

SYMBOLS

heraldry 817
   *parts of a flag, flag shapes, shield divisions, examples of partitions, examples of
   ordinaries, examples of charges, examples of colors, examples of metals,
   examples of furs*

signs of the zodiac 820
   fire signs, earth signs, air signs, water signs

safety symbols 821
   dangerous materials, protection

common symbols 822

road signs 824
   major North American road signs, major international road signs

fabric care 829
   washing, drying, ironing

common scientific symbols 830
   mathematics, geometry, biology, chemistry, miscellaneous symbols

diacritic symbols 832

punctuation marks 832

examples of currency abbreviations 832

GENERAL INDEX 833

1 **ASTRONOMY**

17 **GEOGRAPHY**

53 **VEGETABLE KINGDOM**

75 **ANIMAL KINGDOM**

113 **HUMAN BEING**

145 **FARMING**

163 **ARCHITECTURE**

191 **HOUSE**

217 **HOUSE FURNITURE**

261 **GARDENING**

273 **DO-IT-YOURSELF**

313 **CLOTHING**

359 **PERSONAL ADORNMENT**

371 **PERSONAL ARTICLES**

387 **COMMUNICATIONS**

423 **TRANSPORT**

513 **OFFICE SUPPLIES**

533 **MUSIC**

559 **CREATIVE LEISURE ACTIVITIES**

593 **SPORTS**

693 **INDOOR GAMES**

703 **MEASURING DEVICES**

715 **OPTICAL INSTRUMENTS**

723 **HEALTH AND SAFETY**

731 **ENERGY**

775 **HEAVY MACHINERY**

789 **WEAPONS**

815 **SYMBOLS**

833 **INDEX**

LIST OF CHAPTERS

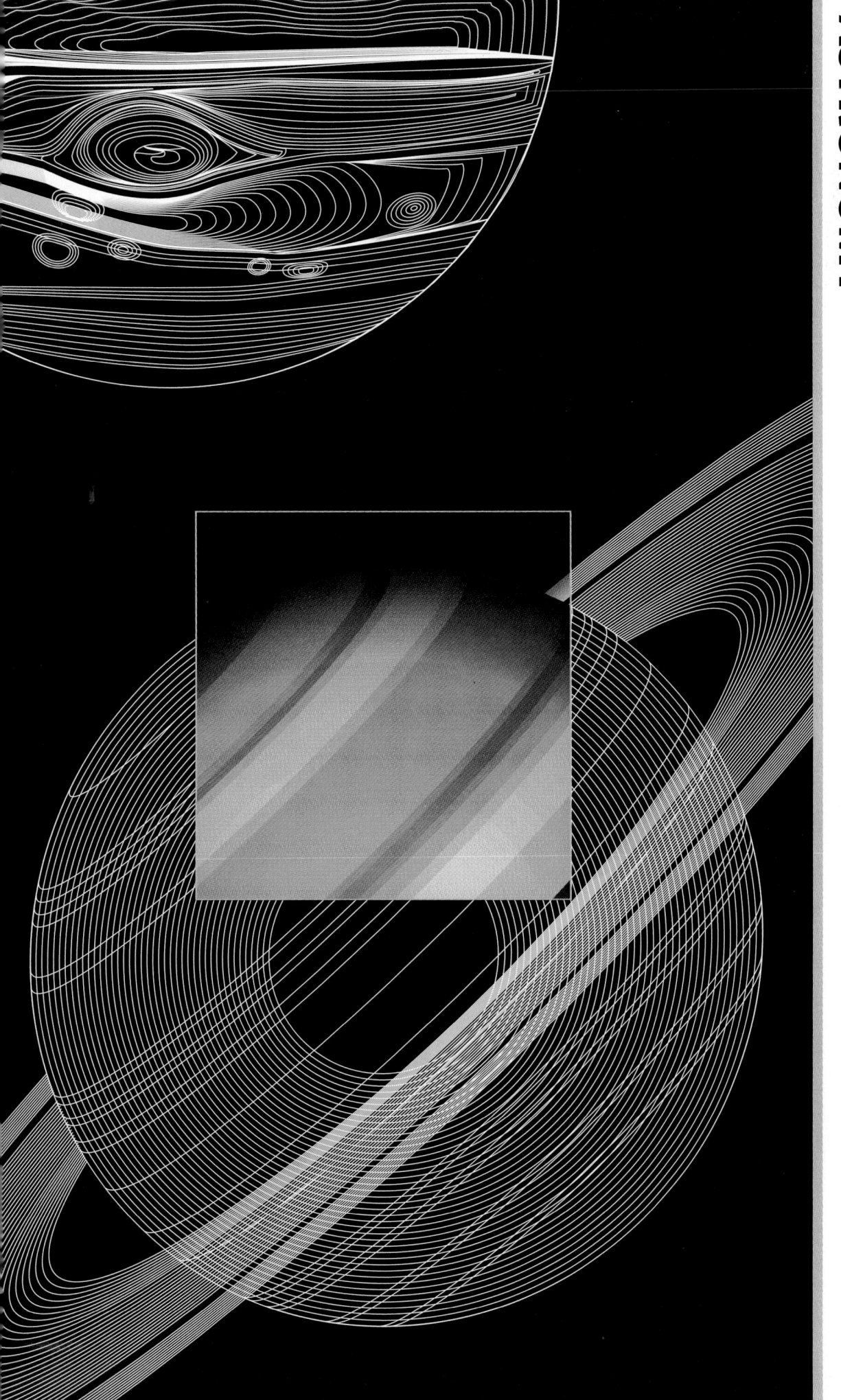

CONTENTS

EARTH COORDINATE SYSTEM..3

CELESTIAL COORDINATE SYSTEM...3

SOLAR SYSTEM 4

SUN 6

PHASES OF THE MOON 6

MOON..7

SEASONS OF THE YEAR 8

SOLAR ECLIPSE..8

LUNAR ECLIPSE 8

GALAXY 9

COMET 9

CONSTELLATIONS OF THE NORTHERN HEMISPHERE 10

CONSTELLATIONS OF THE SOUTHERN HEMISPHERE........................12

ASTRONOMICAL OBSERVATORY..14

RADIO TELESCOPE 15

PLANETARIUM 16

HUBBLE SPACE TELESCOPE 16

CELESTIAL COORDINATE SYSTEM

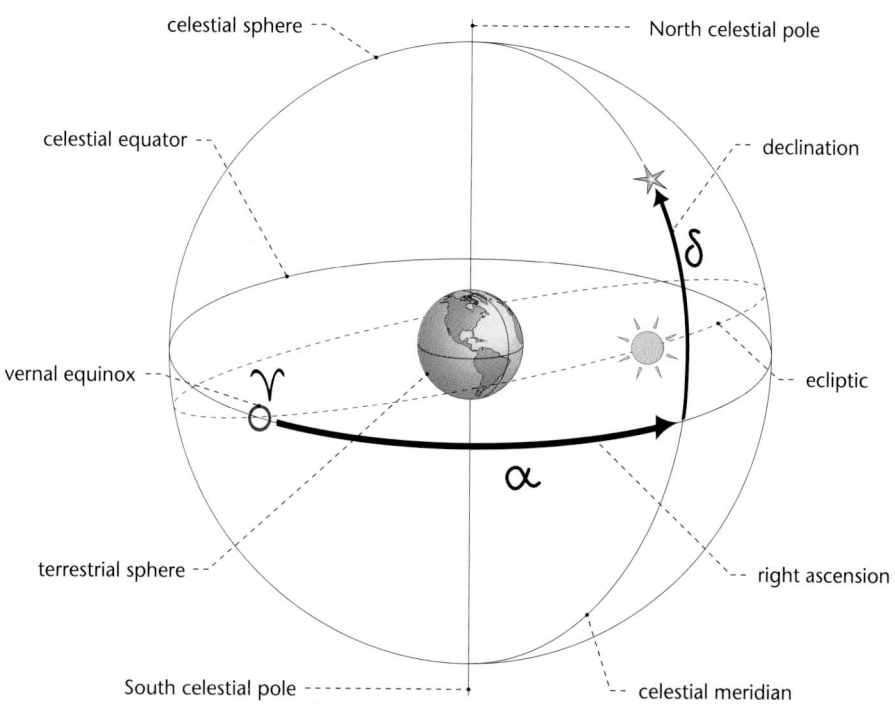

celestial sphere

North celestial pole

celestial equator

declination

δ

vernal equinox

γ

ecliptic

α

terrestrial sphere

right ascension

South celestial pole

celestial meridian

EARTH COORDINATE SYSTEM

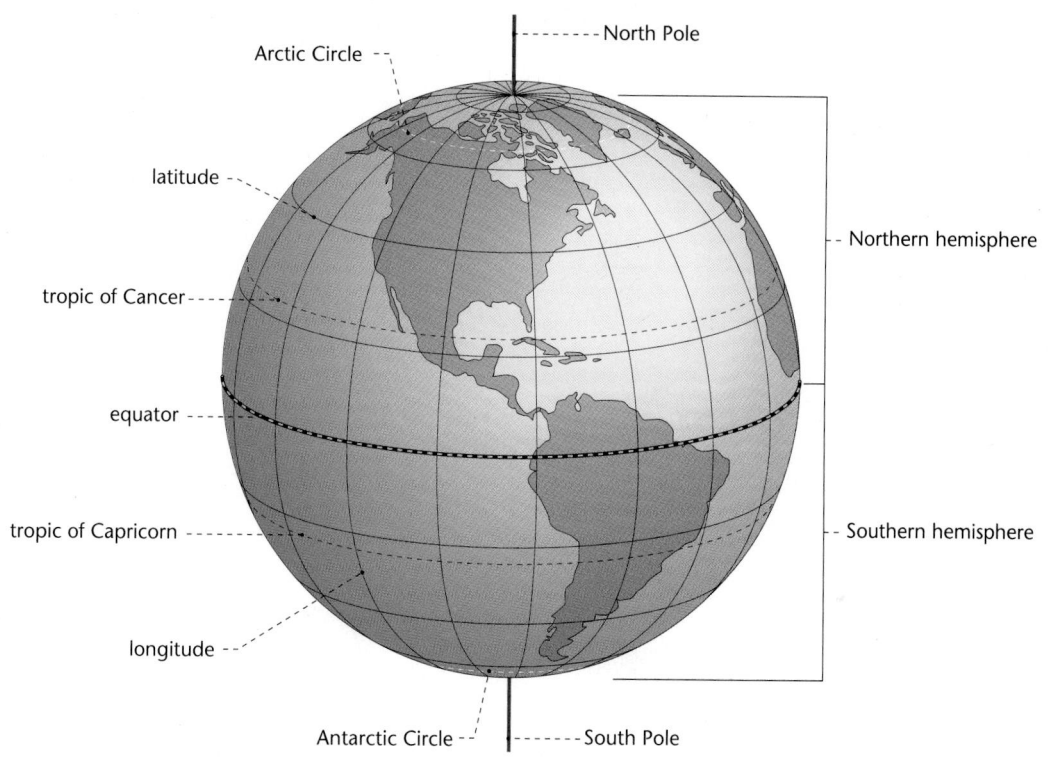

North Pole

Arctic Circle

latitude

Northern hemisphere

tropic of Cancer

equator

tropic of Capricorn

Southern hemisphere

longitude

Antarctic Circle

South Pole

SOLAR SYSTEM

PLANETS AND MOONS

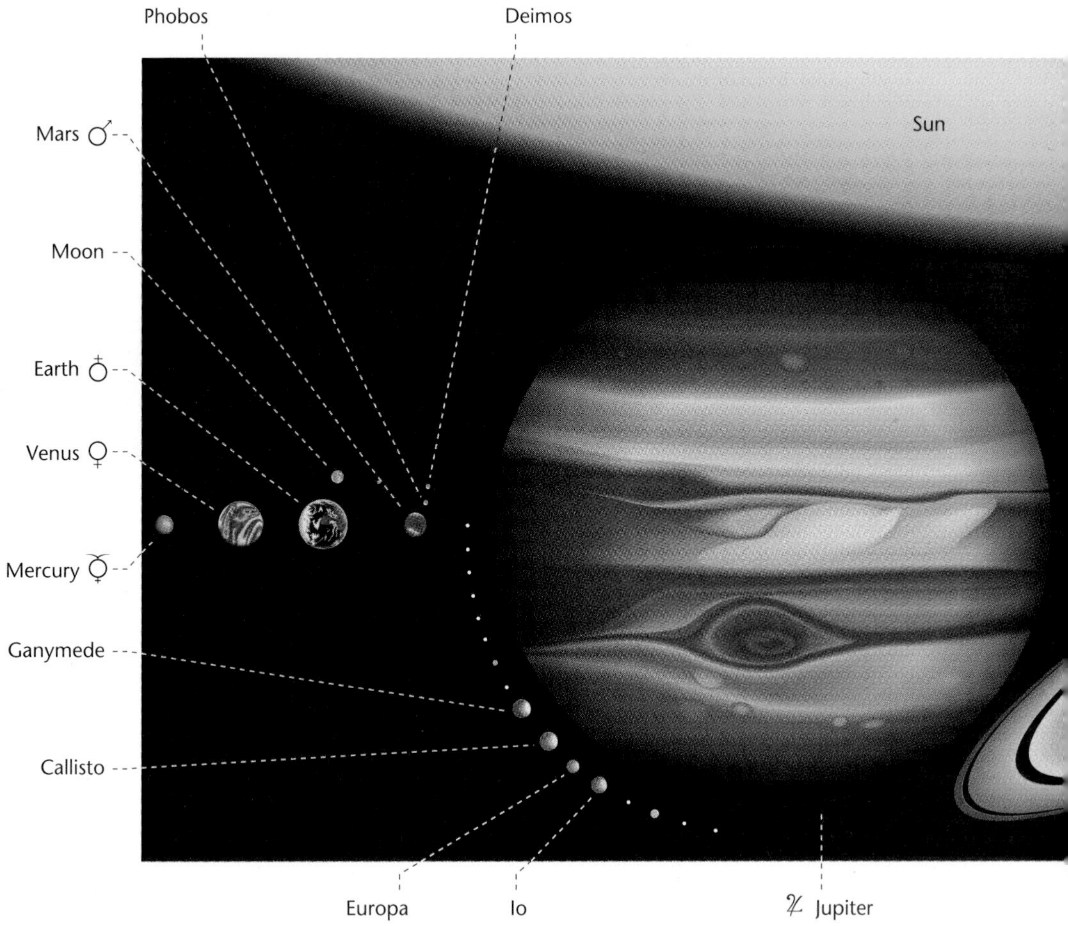

Phobos

Deimos

Mars ♂

Sun

Moon

Earth ♁

Venus ♀

Mercury ☿

Ganymede

Callisto

Europa

Io

♃ Jupiter

ORBITS OF THE PLANETS

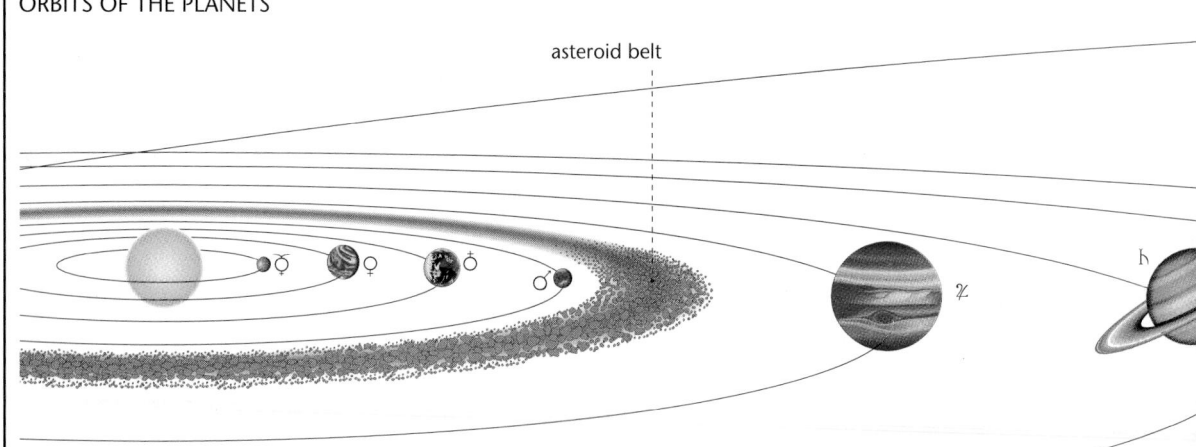

asteroid belt

♃

♄

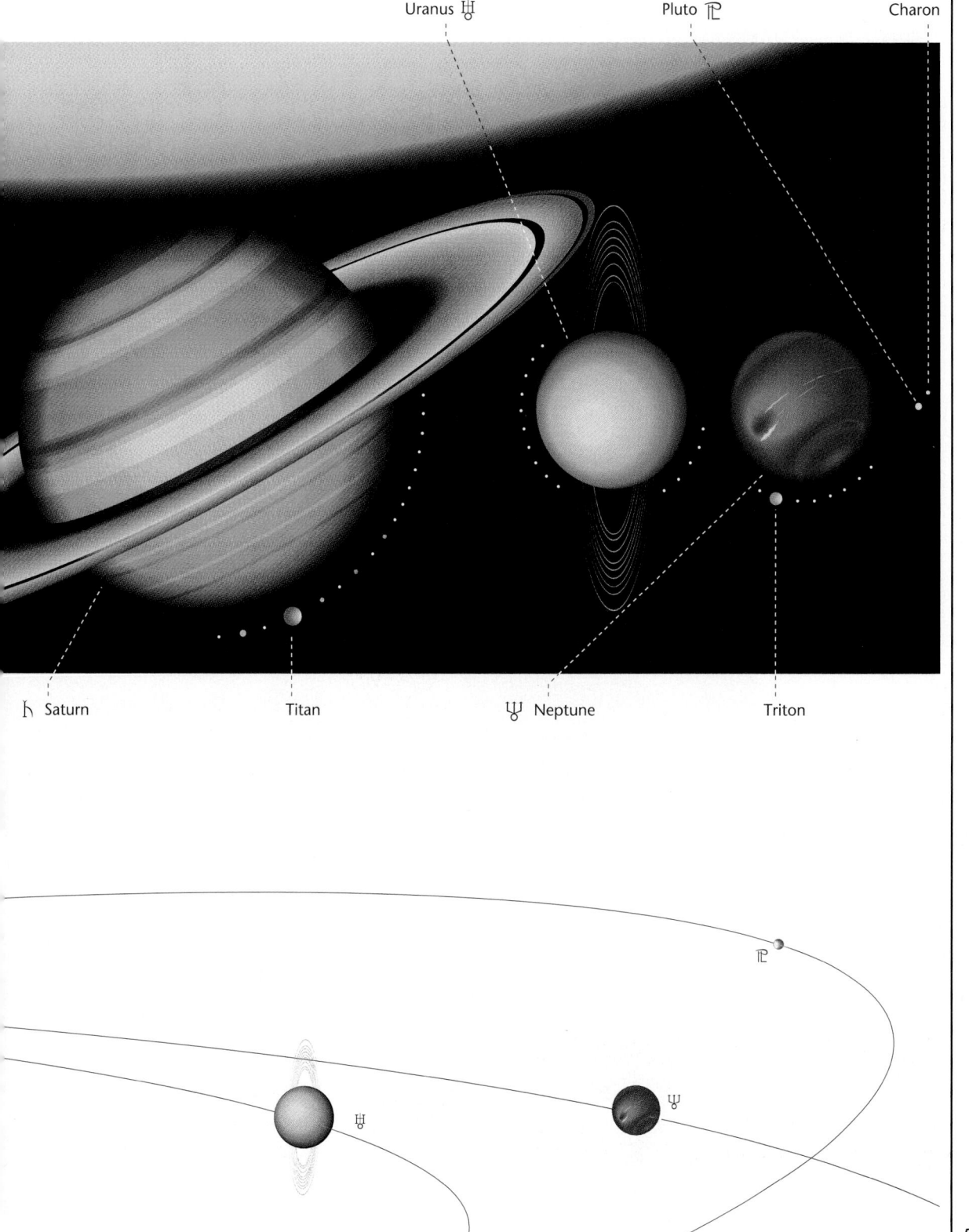

Uranus ♅

Pluto ♇

Charon

♄ Saturn

Titan

♆ Neptune

Triton

SUN

STRUCTURE OF THE SUN

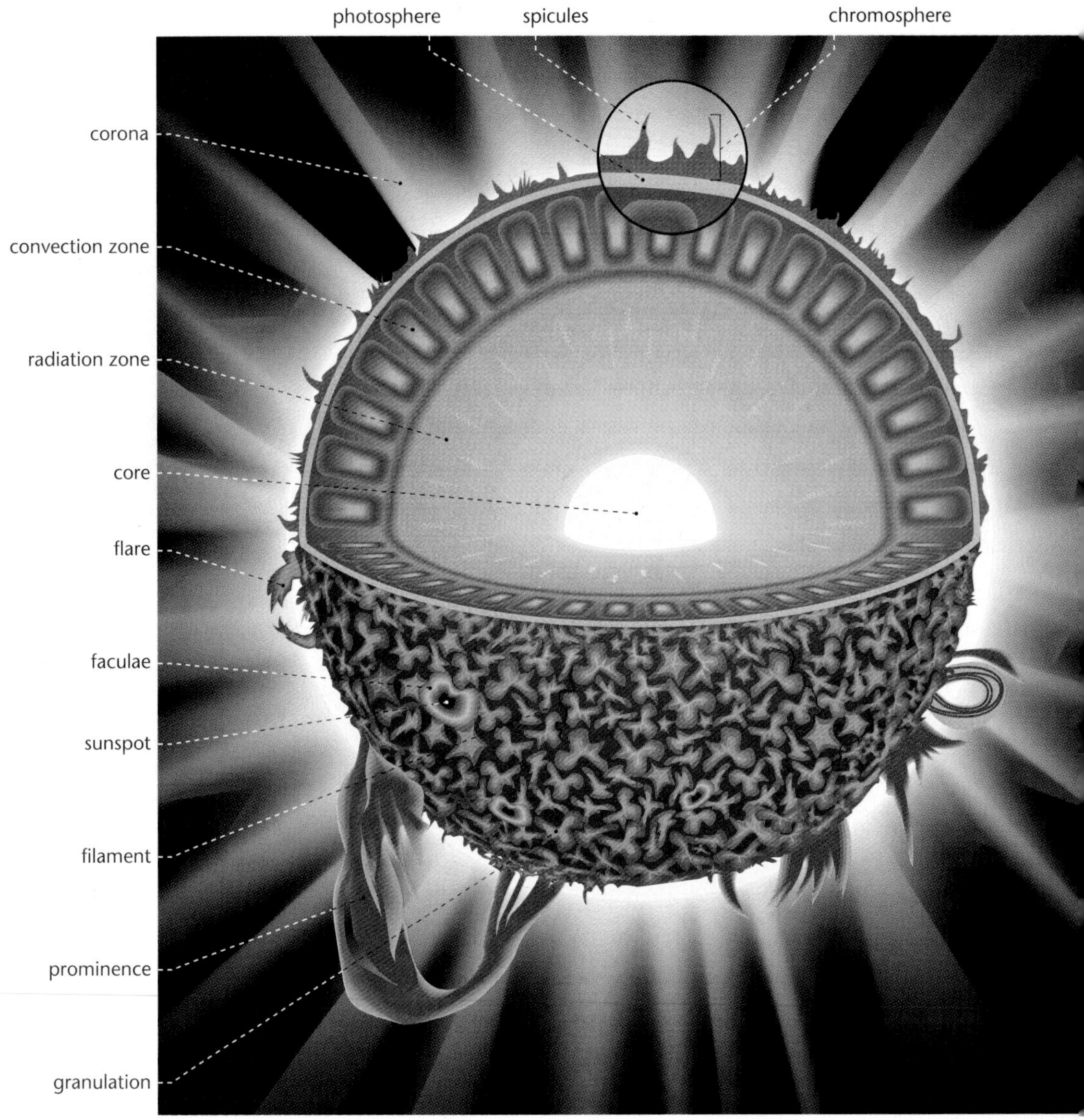

photosphere   spicules   chromosphere

corona

convection zone

radiation zone

core

flare

faculae

sunspot

filament

prominence

granulation

PHASES OF THE MOON

new moon   new crescent   first quarter   waxing gibbous

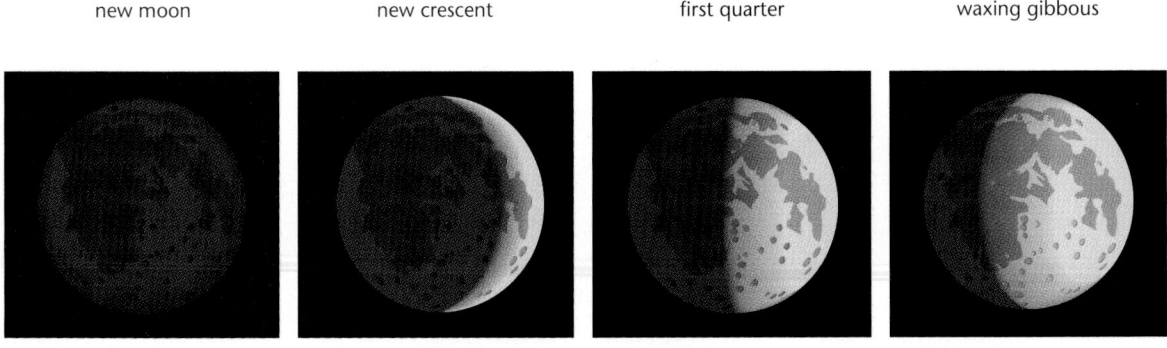

MOON

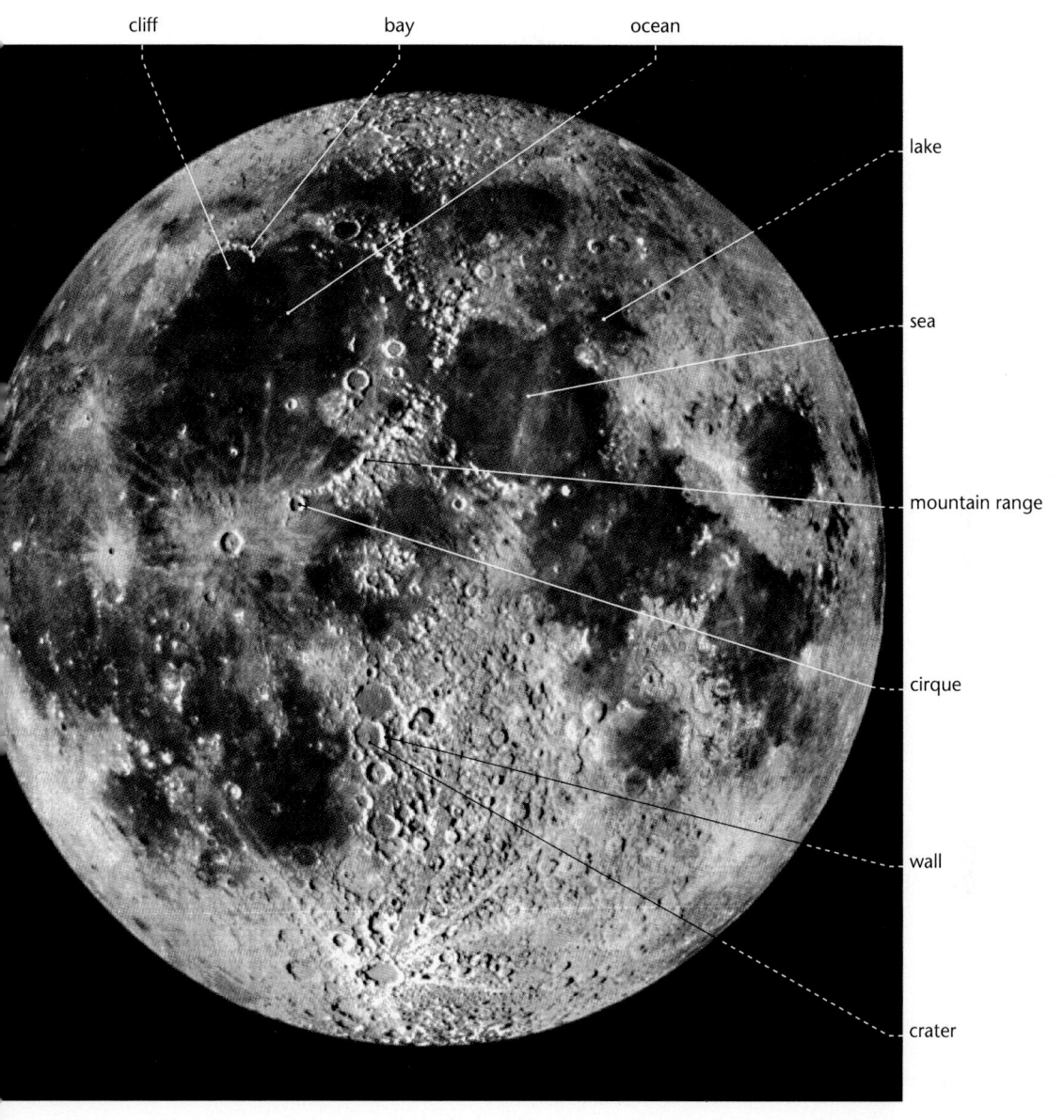

cliff

bay

ocean

lake

sea

mountain range

cirque

wall

crater

full moon

waning gibbous

last quarter

old crescent

SOLAR ECLIPSE

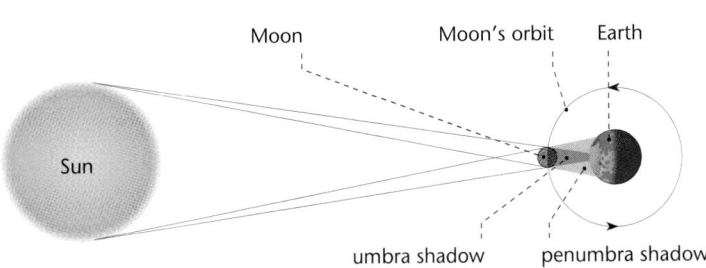

Moon   Moon's orbit   Earth

Sun

umbra shadow   penumbra shadow

TYPES OF ECLIPSES

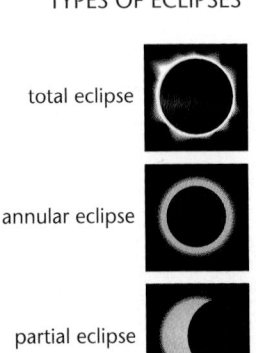

total eclipse

annular eclipse

partial eclipse

LUNAR ECLIPSE

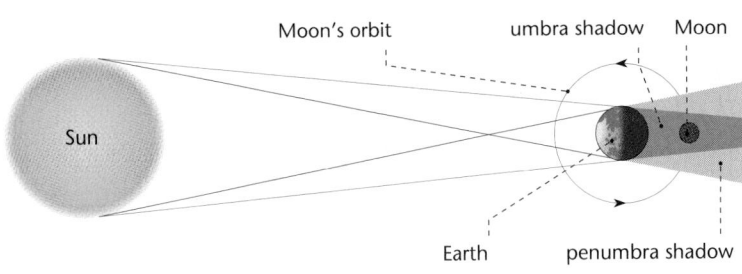

Moon's orbit   umbra shadow   Moon

Sun

Earth   penumbra shadow

TYPES OF ECLIPSES

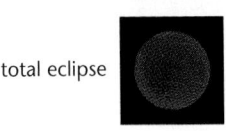

partial eclipse

total eclipse

SEASONS OF THE YEAR

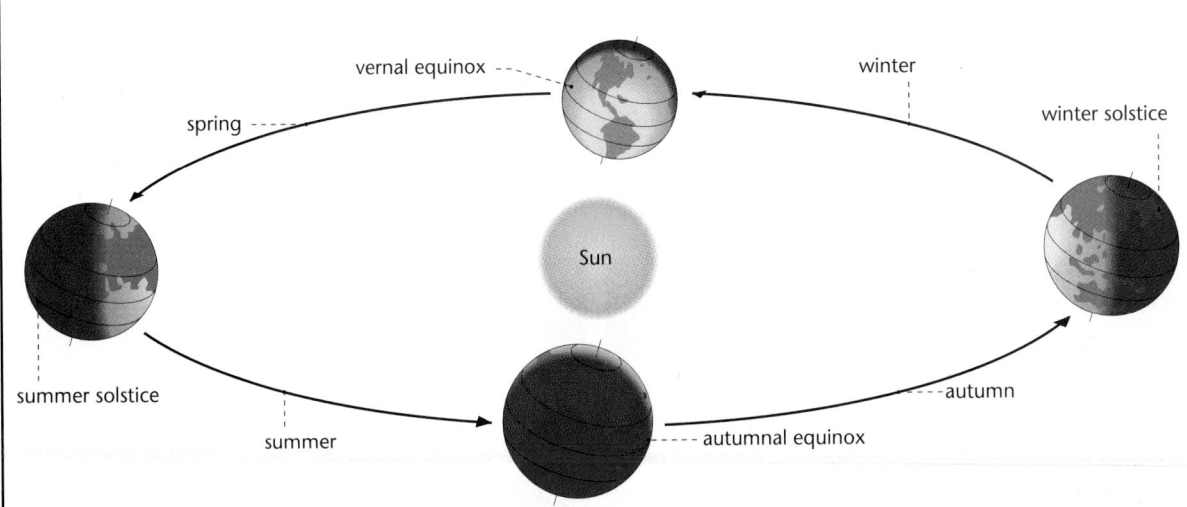

vernal equinox   winter

spring   winter solstice

Sun

summer solstice   autumn

summer   autumnal equinox

COMET

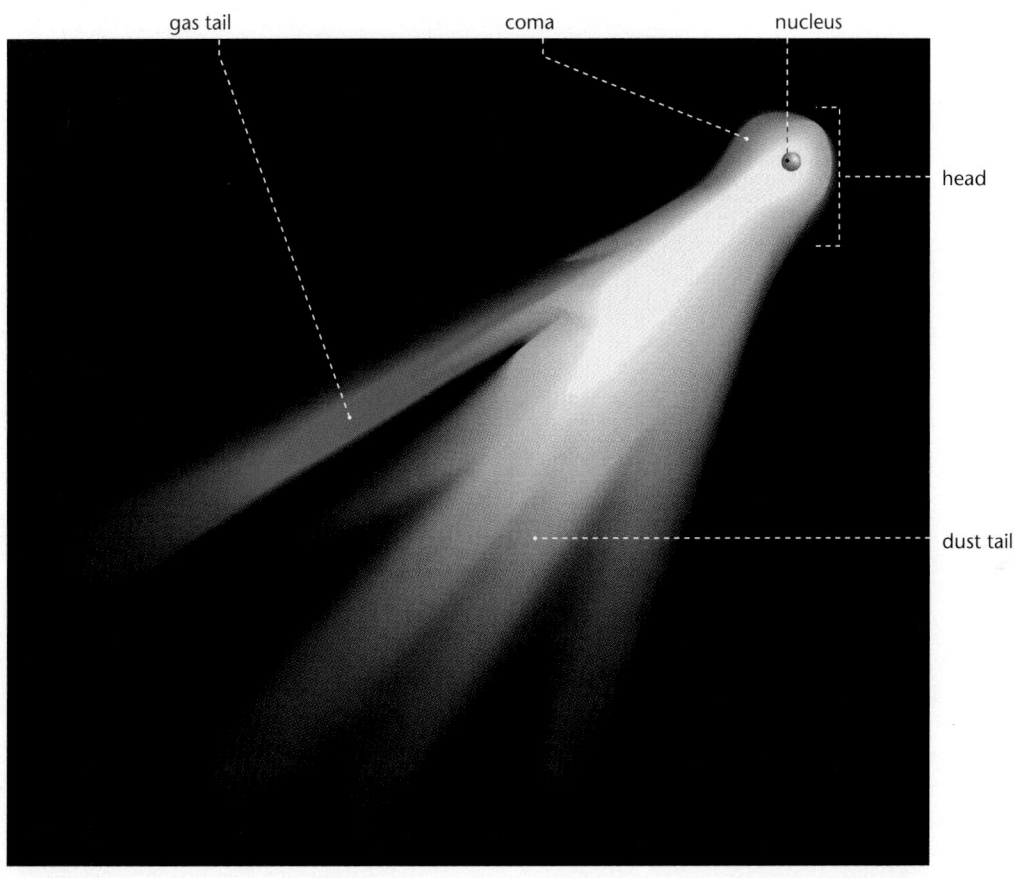

gas tail coma nucleus

head

dust tail

GALAXY

HUBBLE'S CLASSIFICATION

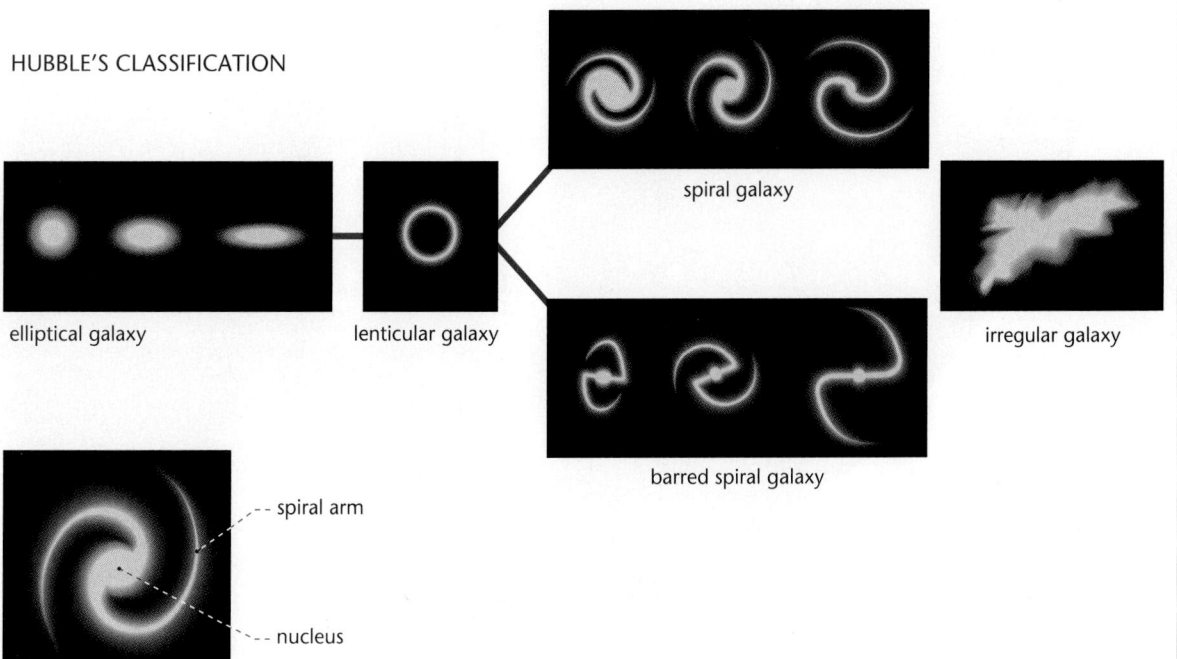

elliptical galaxy

lenticular galaxy

spiral galaxy

barred spiral galaxy

irregular galaxy

spiral arm

nucleus

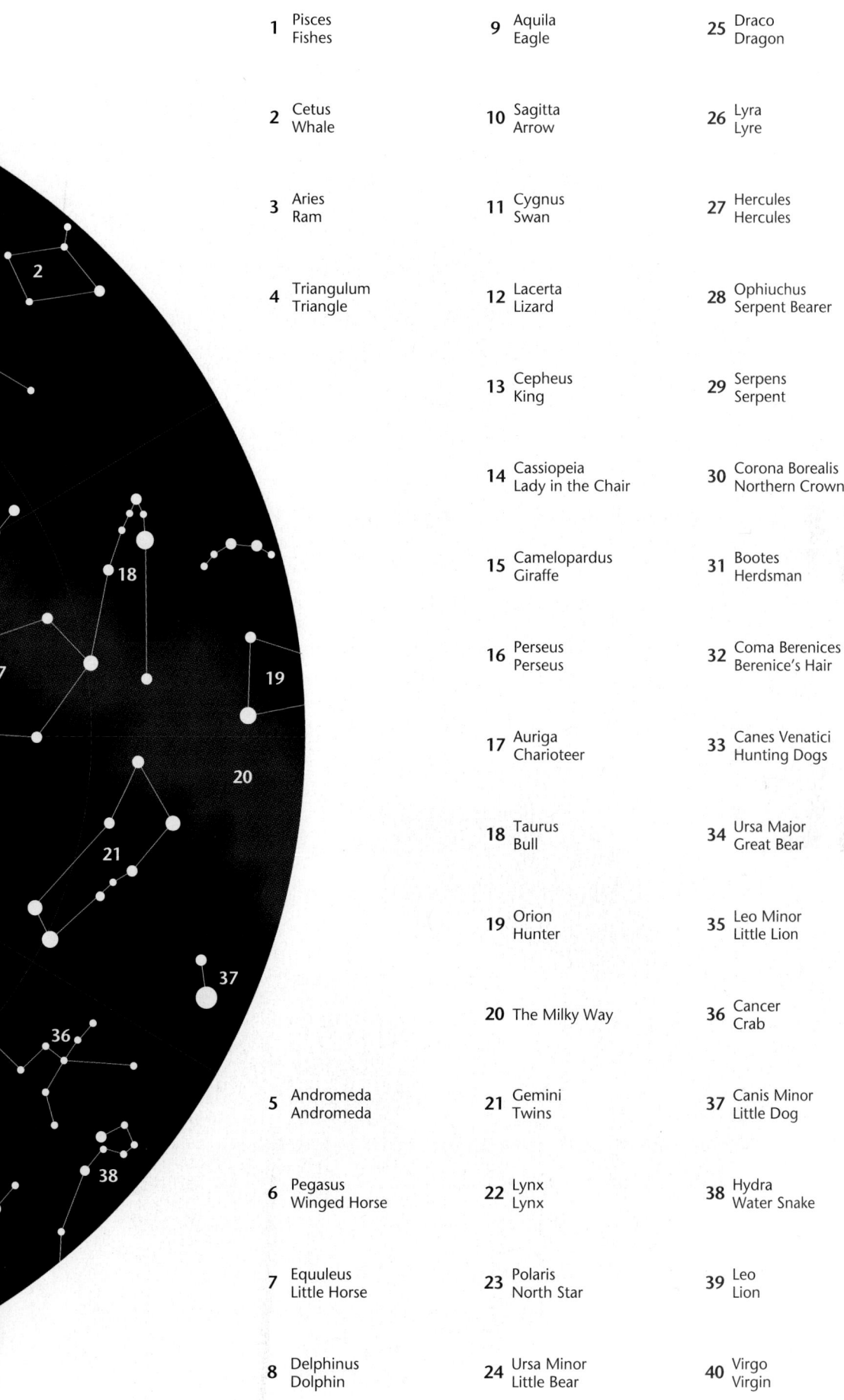

1 Pisces
Fishes

2 Cetus
Whale

3 Aries
Ram

4 Triangulum
Triangle

5 Andromeda
Andromeda

6 Pegasus
Winged Horse

7 Equuleus
Little Horse

8 Delphinus
Dolphin

9 Aquila
Eagle

10 Sagitta
Arrow

11 Cygnus
Swan

12 Lacerta
Lizard

13 Cepheus
King

14 Cassiopeia
Lady in the Chair

15 Camelopardus
Giraffe

16 Perseus
Perseus

17 Auriga
Charioteer

18 Taurus
Bull

19 Orion
Hunter

20 The Milky Way

21 Gemini
Twins

22 Lynx
Lynx

23 Polaris
North Star

24 Ursa Minor
Little Bear

25 Draco
Dragon

26 Lyra
Lyre

27 Hercules
Hercules

28 Ophiuchus
Serpent Bearer

29 Serpens
Serpent

30 Corona Borealis
Northern Crown

31 Bootes
Herdsman

32 Coma Berenices
Berenice's Hair

33 Canes Venatici
Hunting Dogs

34 Ursa Major
Great Bear

35 Leo Minor
Little Lion

36 Cancer
Crab

37 Canis Minor
Little Dog

38 Hydra
Water Snake

39 Leo
Lion

40 Virgo
Virgin

CONSTELLATIONS OF THE SOUTHERN HEMISPHERE

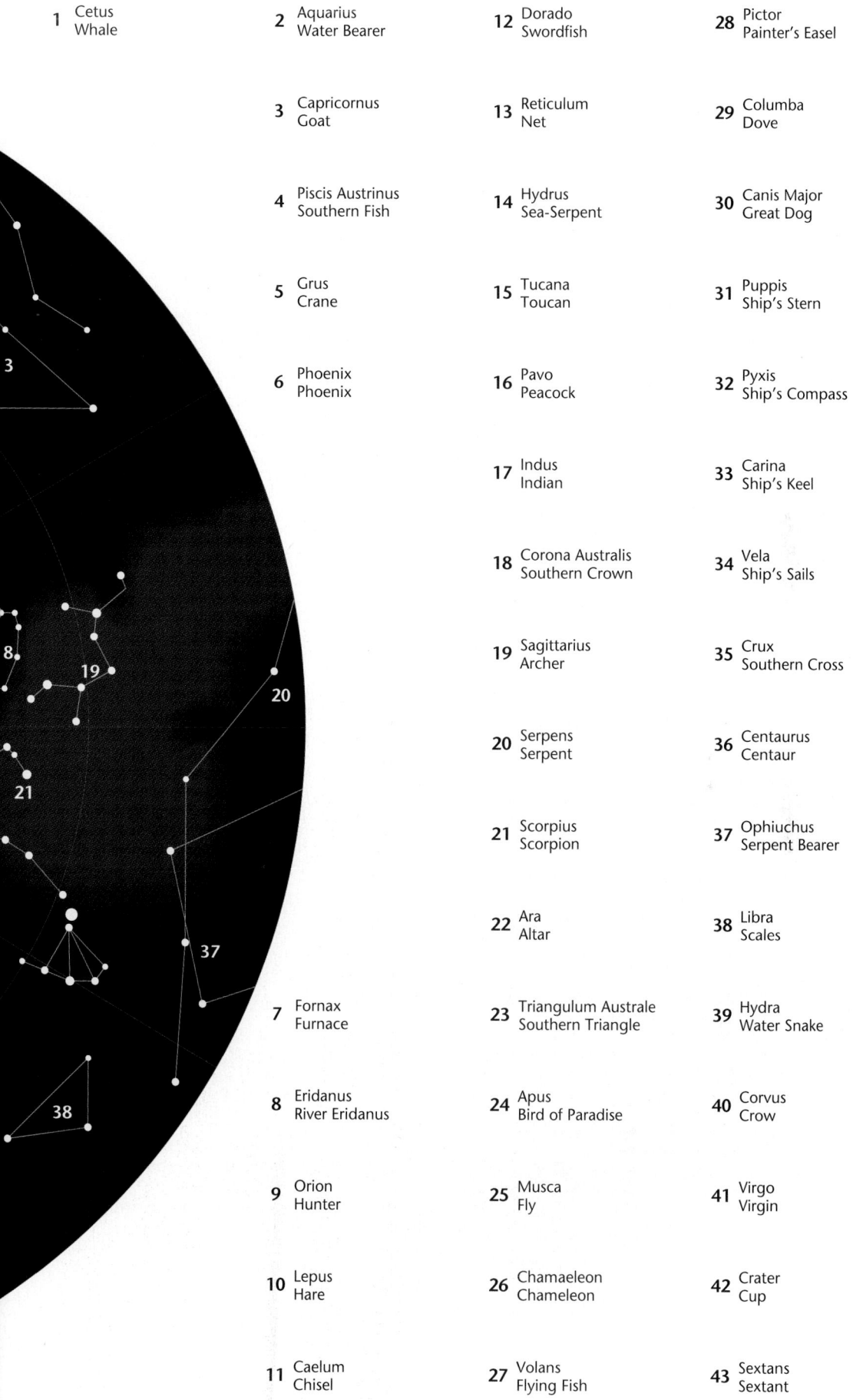

1 Cetus
Whale

2 Aquarius
Water Bearer

3 Capricornus
Goat

4 Piscis Austrinus
Southern Fish

5 Grus
Crane

6 Phoenix
Phoenix

7 Fornax
Furnace

8 Eridanus
River Eridanus

9 Orion
Hunter

10 Lepus
Hare

11 Caelum
Chisel

12 Dorado
Swordfish

13 Reticulum
Net

14 Hydrus
Sea-Serpent

15 Tucana
Toucan

16 Pavo
Peacock

17 Indus
Indian

18 Corona Australis
Southern Crown

19 Sagittarius
Archer

20 Serpens
Serpent

21 Scorpius
Scorpion

22 Ara
Altar

23 Triangulum Australe
Southern Triangle

24 Apus
Bird of Paradise

25 Musca
Fly

26 Chamaeleon
Chameleon

27 Volans
Flying Fish

28 Pictor
Painter's Easel

29 Columba
Dove

30 Canis Major
Great Dog

31 Puppis
Ship's Stern

32 Pyxis
Ship's Compass

33 Carina
Ship's Keel

34 Vela
Ship's Sails

35 Crux
Southern Cross

36 Centaurus
Centaur

37 Ophiuchus
Serpent Bearer

38 Libra
Scales

39 Hydra
Water Snake

40 Corvus
Crow

41 Virgo
Virgin

42 Crater
Cup

43 Sextans
Sextant

ASTRONOMICAL OBSERVATORY

TELESCOPE

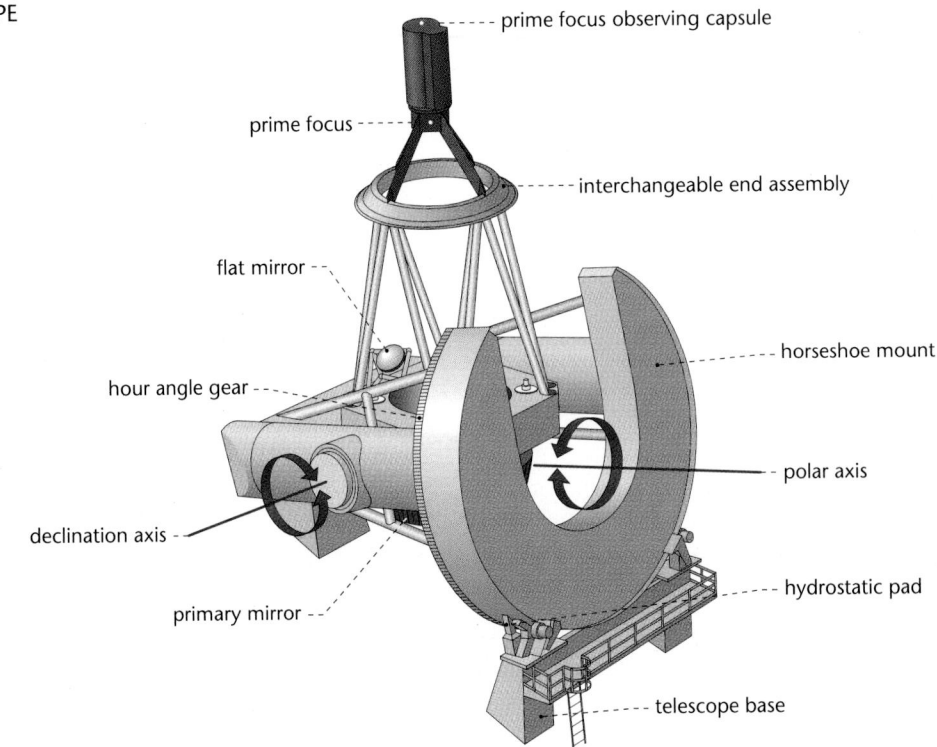

prime focus observing capsule

prime focus

interchangeable end assembly

flat mirror

hour angle gear

horseshoe mount

polar axis

declination axis

primary mirror

hydrostatic pad

telescope base

OBSERVATORY

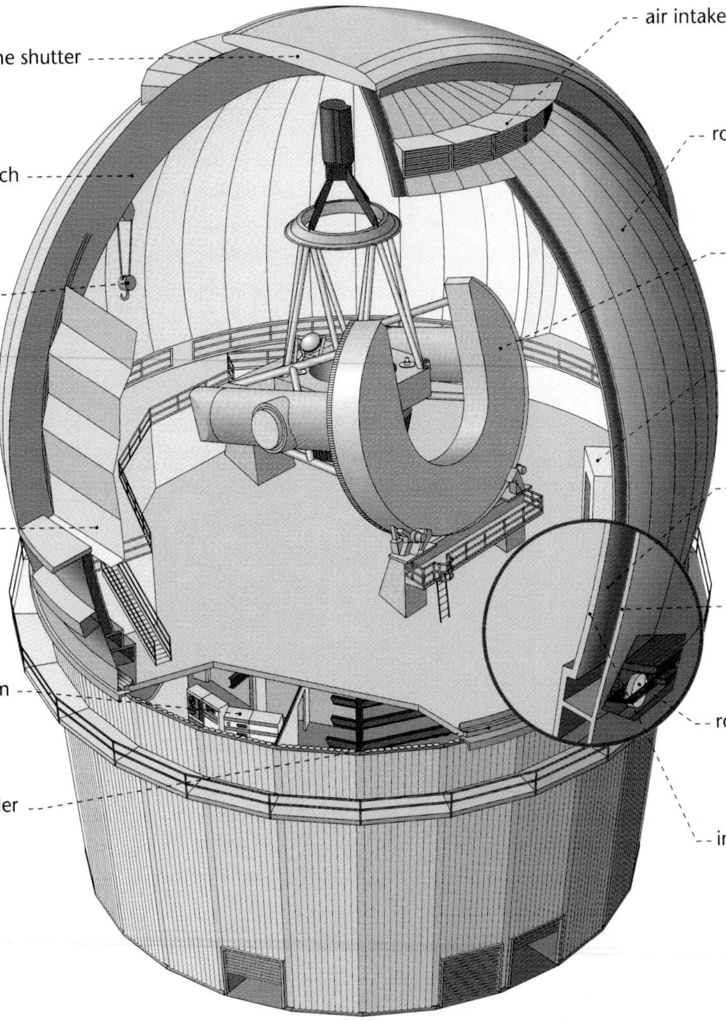

air intake

dome shutter

rotating dome

arch

telescope

crane

airlock

air space

windscreen

exterior dome shell

control room

rotating dome truck

girder

interior dome shell

RADIO TELESCOPE

ALTAZIMUTH MOUNTING

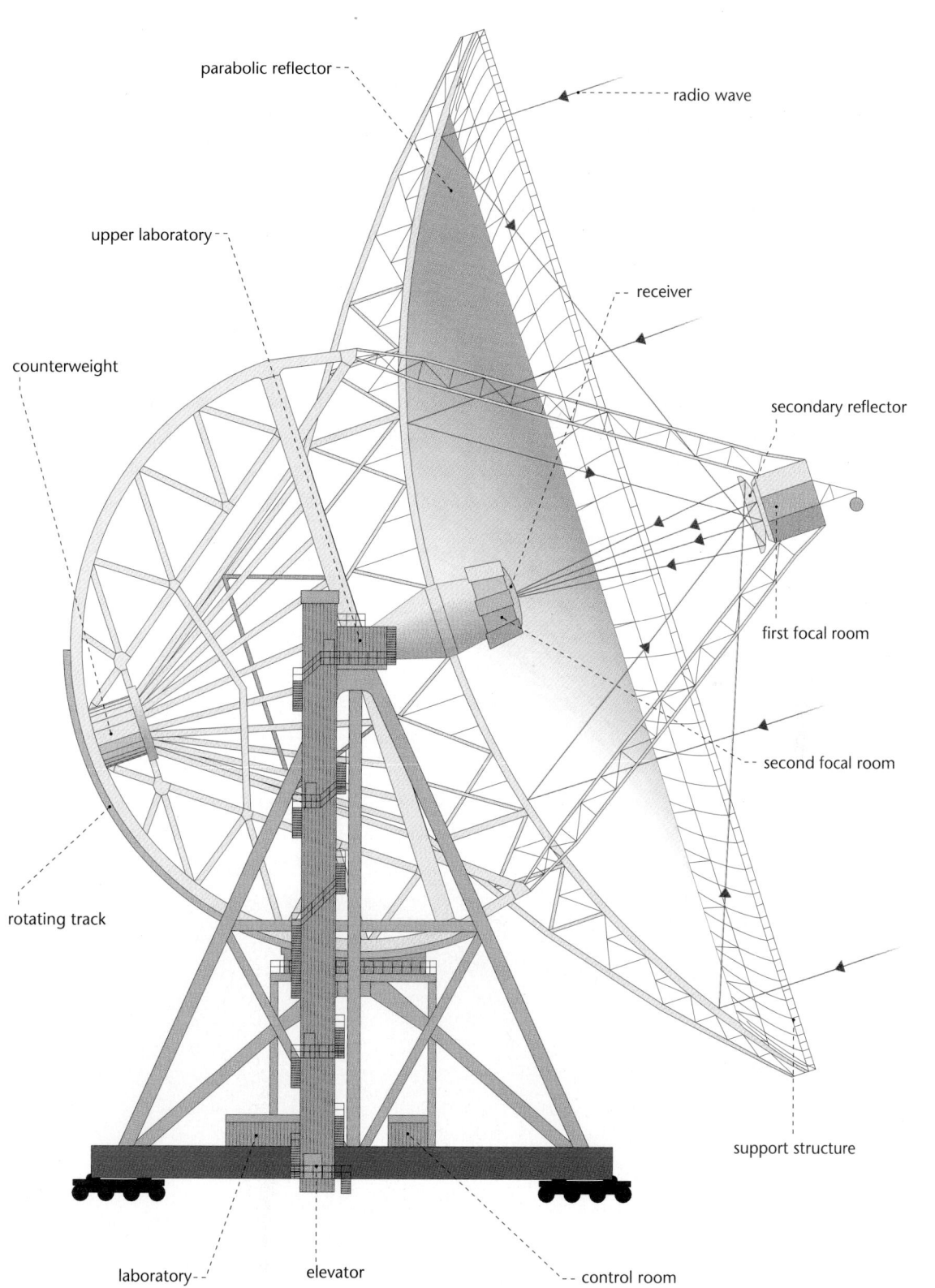

parabolic reflector

radio wave

upper laboratory

receiver

counterweight

secondary reflector

first focal room

rotating track

second focal room

support structure

laboratory

elevator

control room

HUBBLE SPACE TELESCOPE

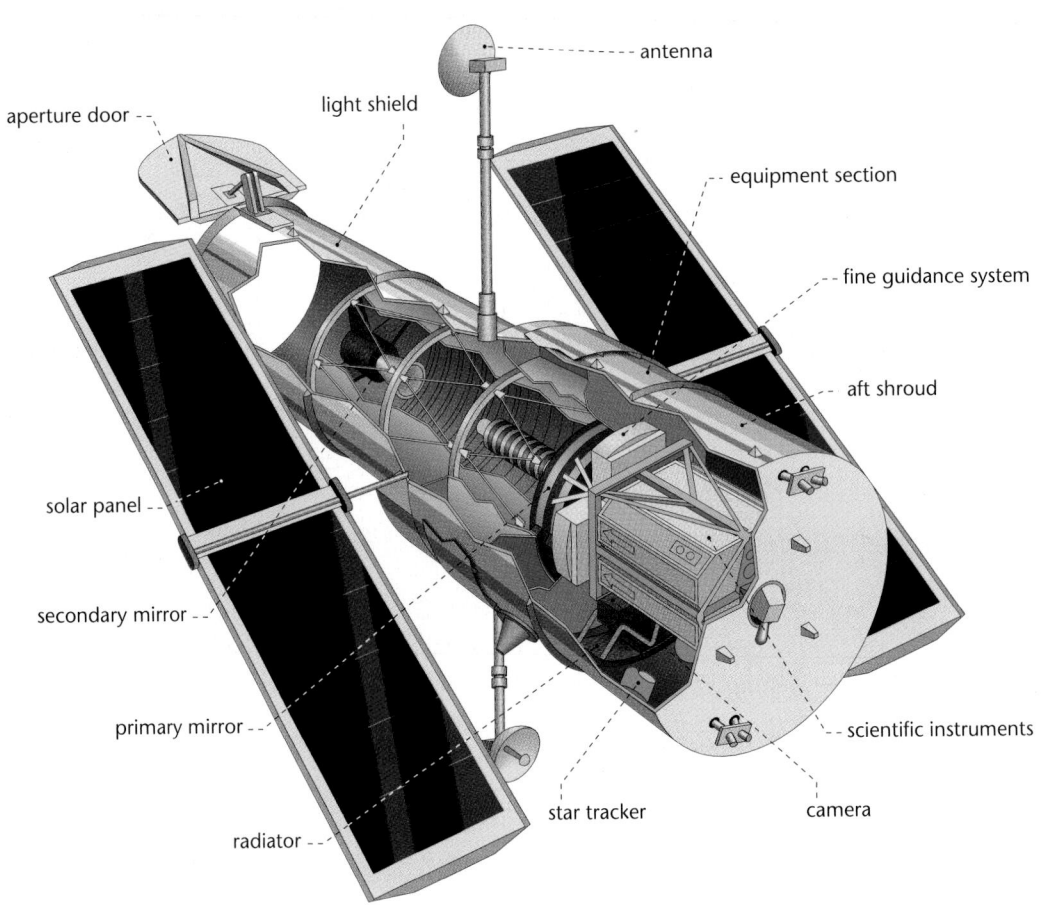

antenna

aperture door

light shield

equipment section

fine guidance system

aft shroud

solar panel

secondary mirror

primary mirror

scientific instruments

radiator

star tracker

camera

PLANETARIUM

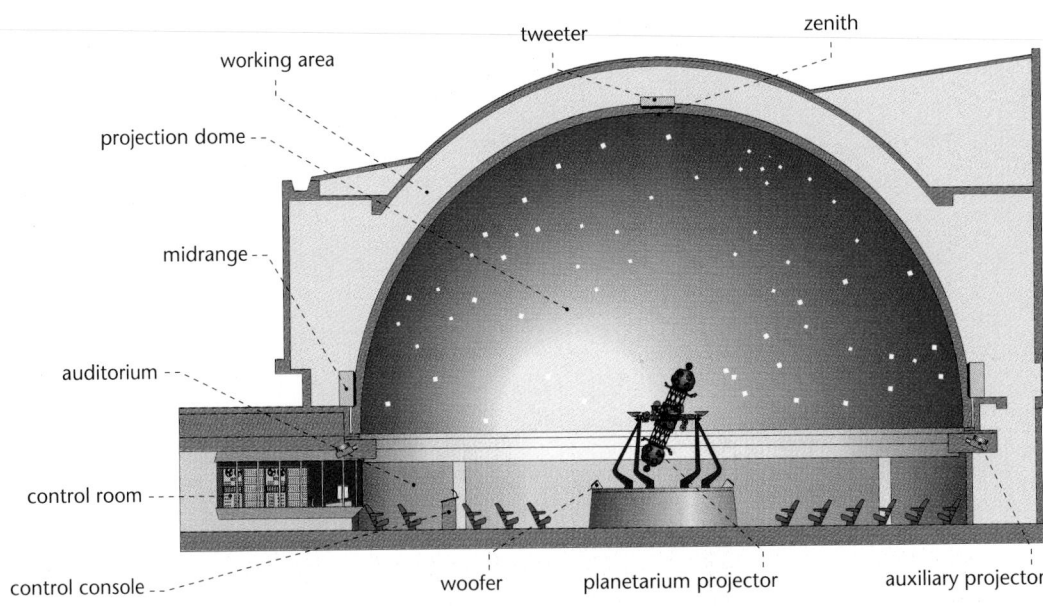

tweeter

zenith

working area

projection dome

midrange

auditorium

control room

control console

woofer

planetarium projector

auxiliary projector

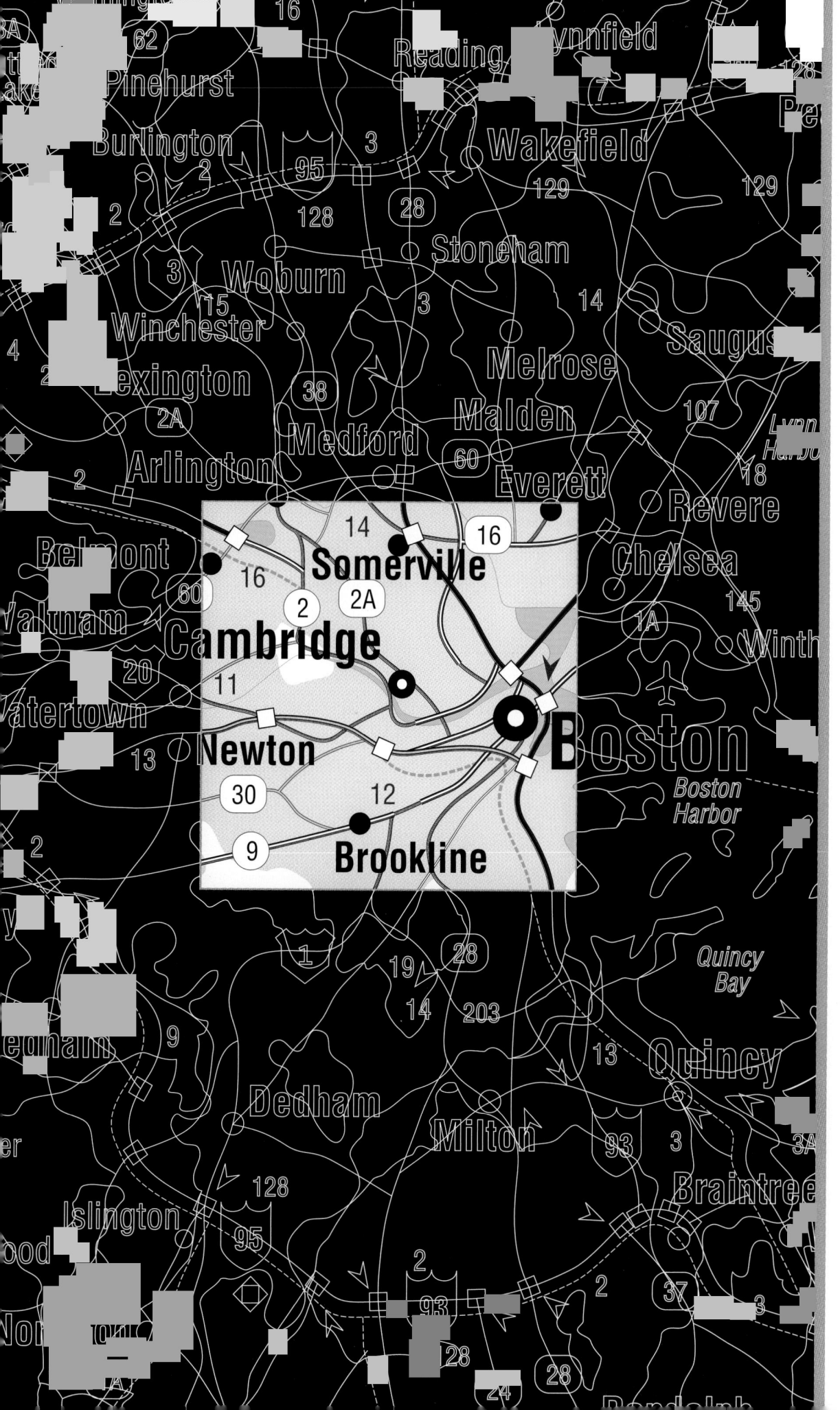

CONTENTS

PROFILE OF THE EARTH'S ATMOSPHERE 19

CONFIGURATION OF THE CONTINENTS 20

STRUCTURE OF THE EARTH 22

SECTION OF THE EARTH'S CRUST 22

EARTHQUAKE 23

CAVE 24

VOLCANO 25

GLACIER 26

MOUNTAIN 27

OCEAN FLOOR 28

WAVE 30

COMMON COASTAL FEATURES 30

ECOLOGY 31

PRECIPITATIONS 36

METEOROLOGY 38

INTERNATIONAL WEATHER SYMBOLS 39

METEOROLOGICAL MEASURING INSTRUMENTS 40

WEATHER SATELLITE 42

CLOUDS AND METEOROLOGICAL SYMBOLS 44

CLIMATES OF THE WORLD 45

DESERT 46

CARTOGRAPHY 47

REMOTE DETECTION SATELLITE 48

CARTOGRAPHY 50

GEOGRAPHY

PROFILE OF THE EARTH'S ATMOSPHERE

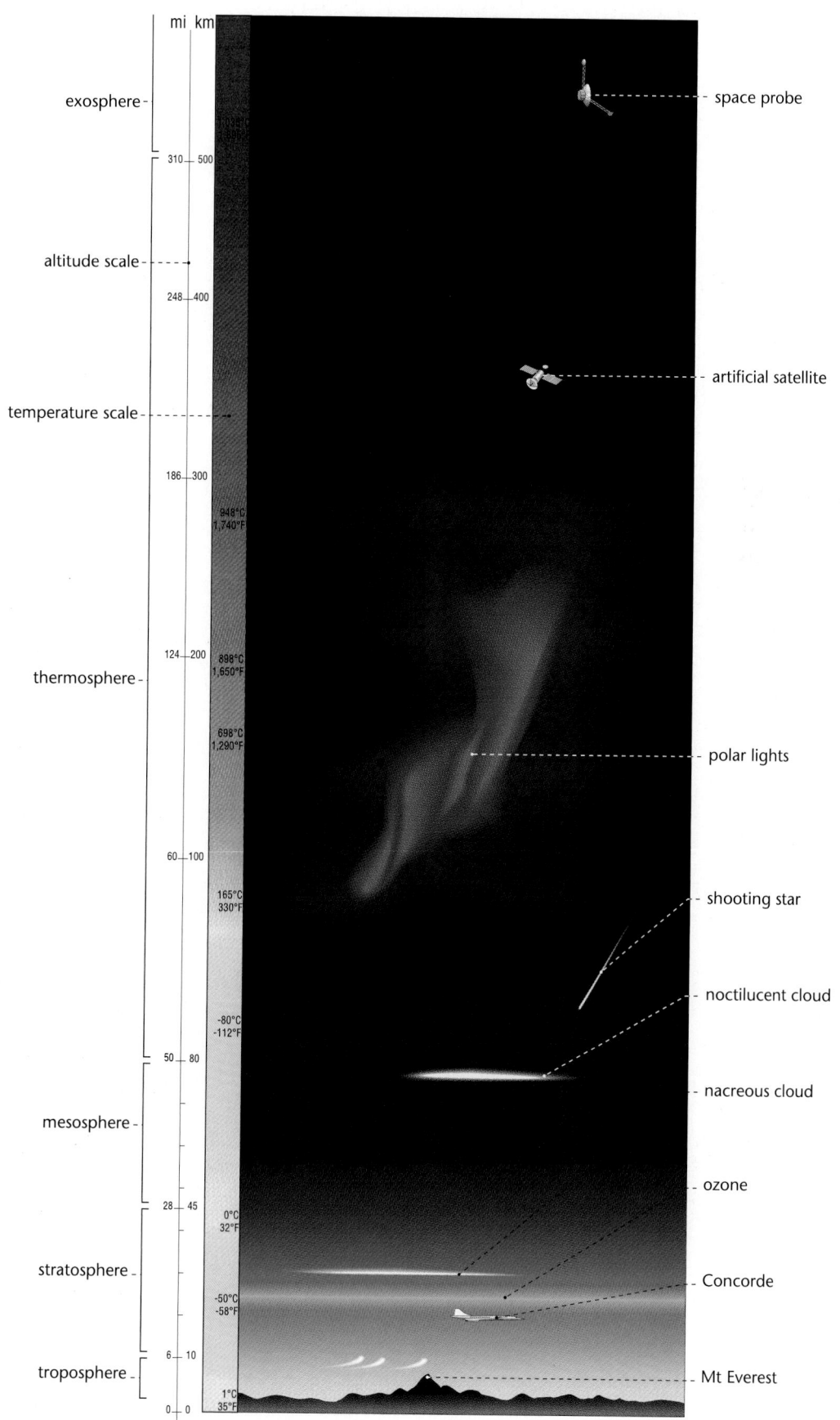

exosphere

altitude scale

temperature scale

thermosphere

mesosphere

stratosphere

troposphere

mi km

310 — 500

248 — 400

186 — 300

948°C
1,740°F

124 — 200   898°C
1,650°F

698°C
1,290°F

60 — 100

165°C
330°F

-80°C
-112°F

50 — 80

28 — 45   0°C
32°F

-50°C
-58°F

6 — 10

1°C
35°F
0 — 0

space probe

artificial satellite

polar lights

shooting star

noctilucent cloud

nacreous cloud

ozone

Concorde

Mt Everest

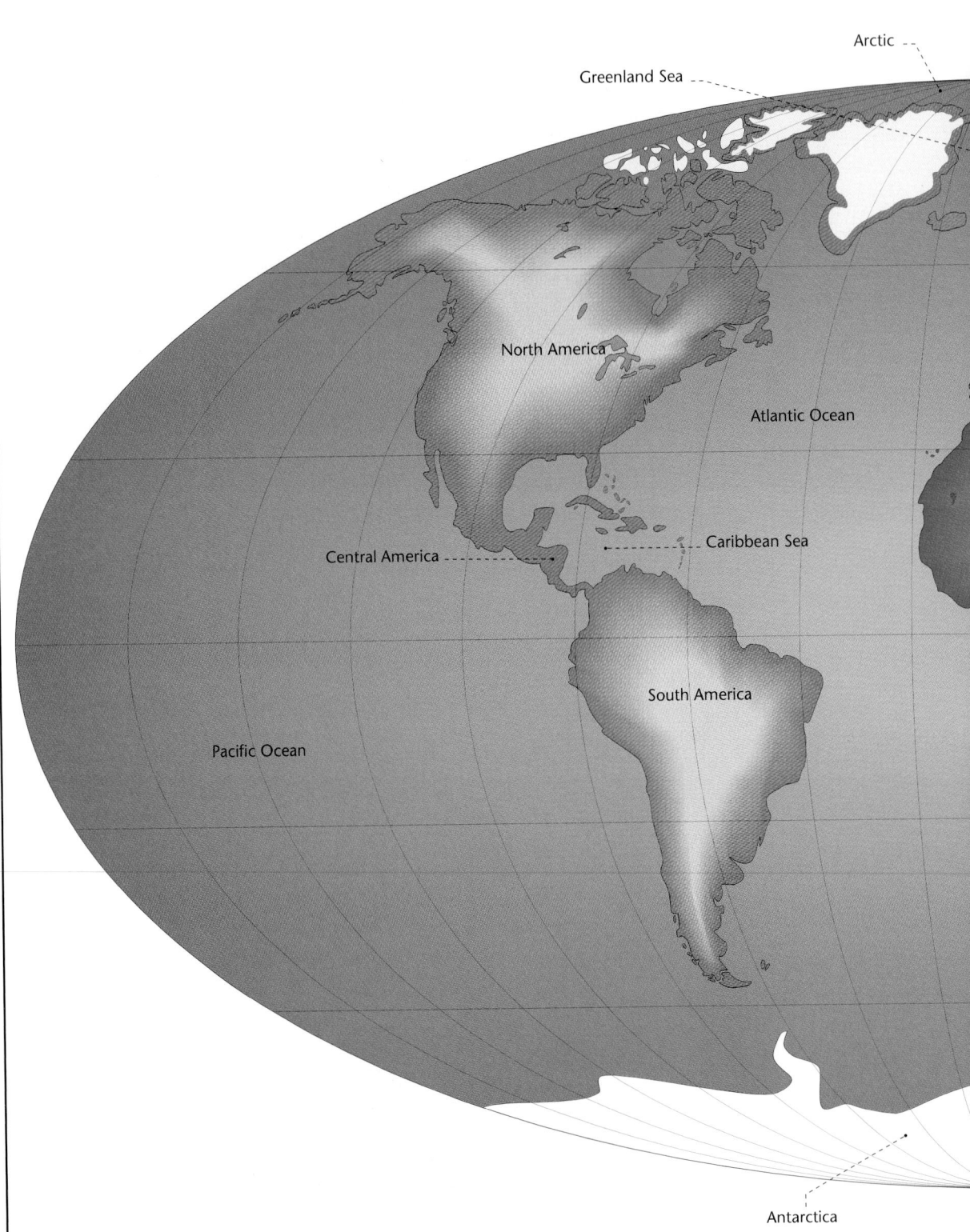

Arctic

Greenland Sea

North America

Atlantic Ocean

Caribbean Sea

Central America

South America

Pacific Ocean

Antarctica

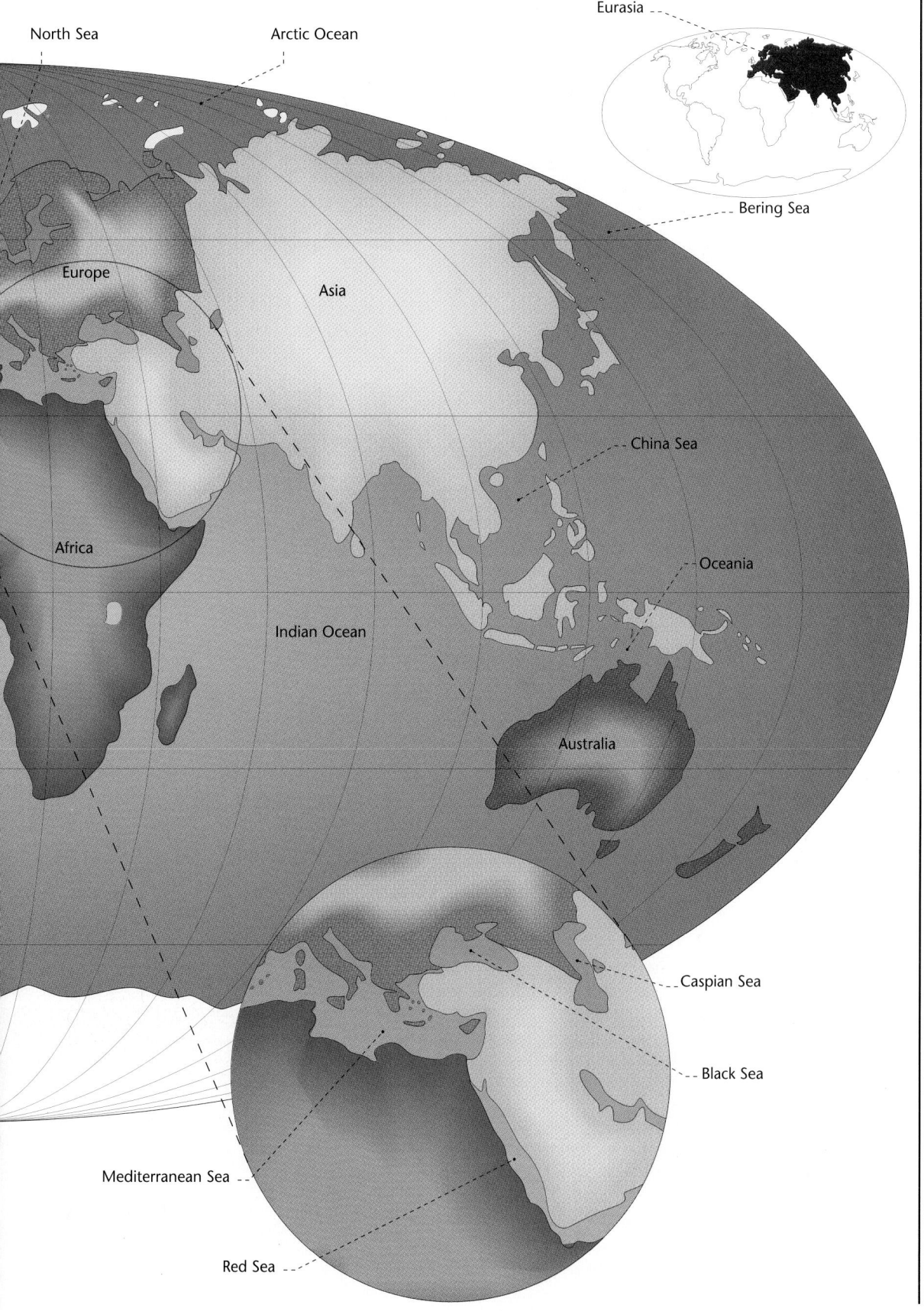

North Sea

Arctic Ocean

Eurasia

Bering Sea

Europe

Asia

China Sea

Africa

Oceania

Indian Ocean

Australia

Caspian Sea

Black Sea

Mediterranean Sea

Red Sea

STRUCTURE OF THE EARTH

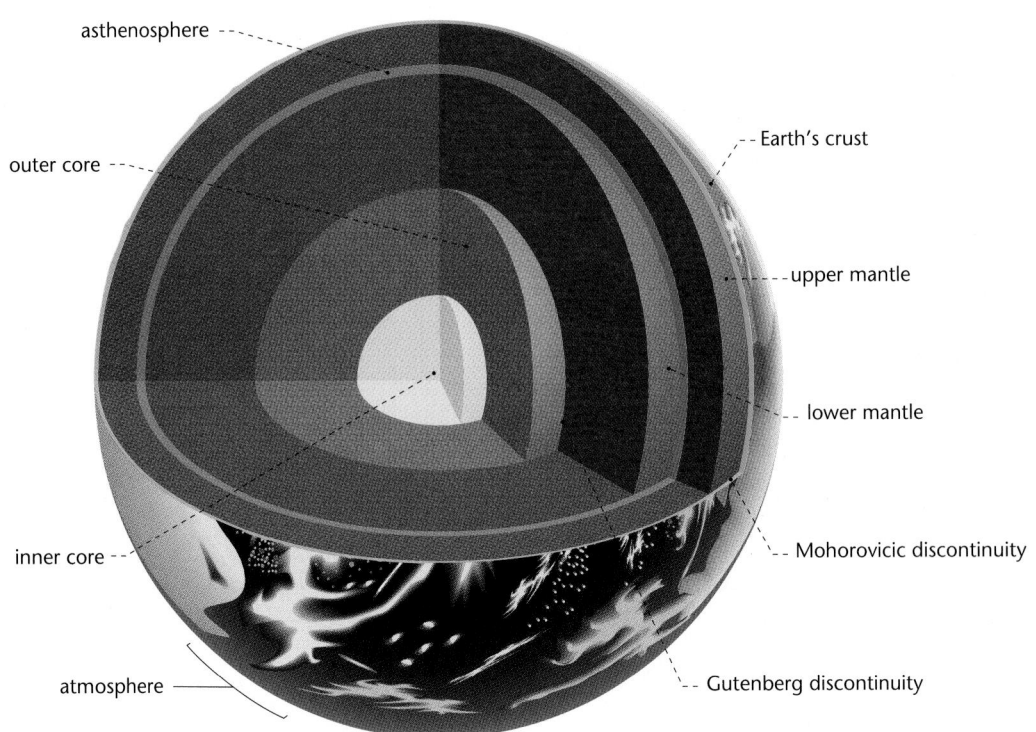

asthenosphere

outer core

inner core

atmosphere

Earth's crust

upper mantle

lower mantle

Mohorovicic discontinuity

Gutenberg discontinuity

SECTION OF THE EARTH'S CRUST

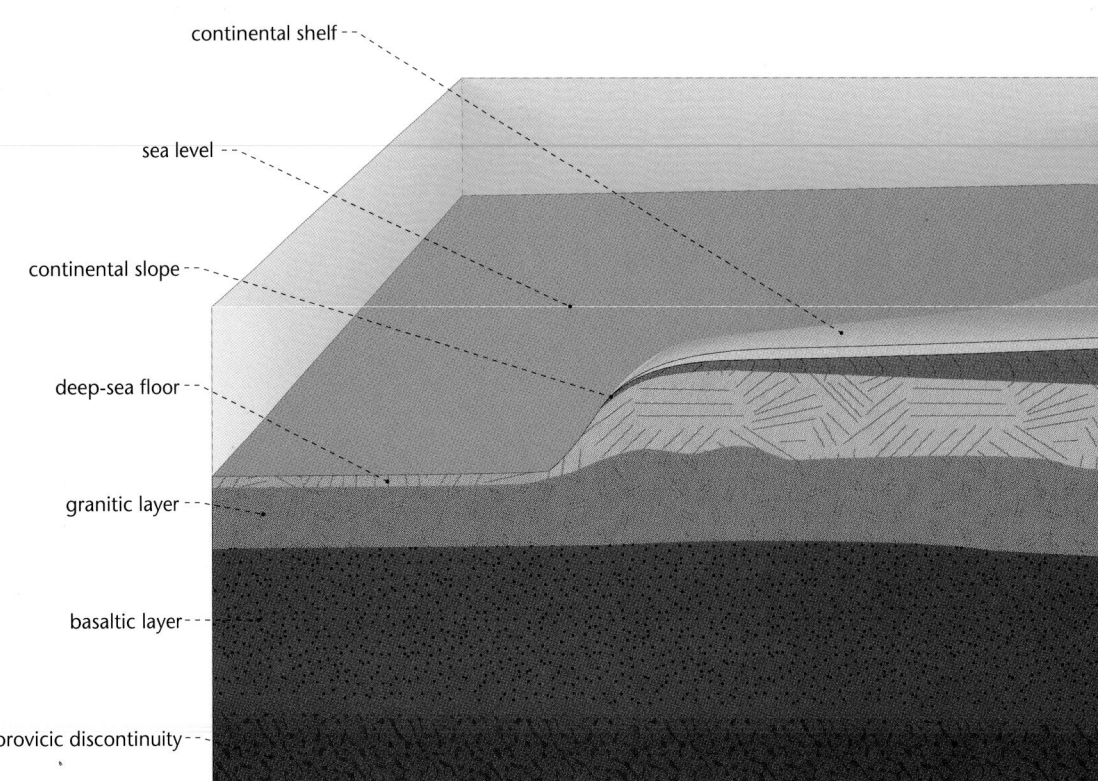

continental shelf

sea level

continental slope

deep-sea floor

granitic layer

basaltic layer

Mohorovicic discontinuity

EARTHQUAKE

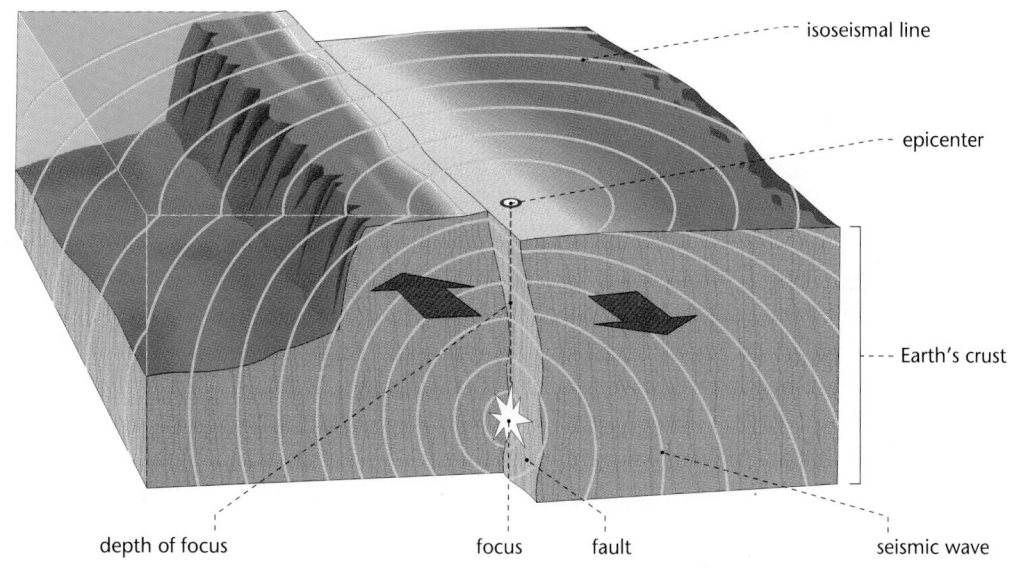

isoseismal line

epicenter

Earth's crust

depth of focus

focus

fault

seismic wave

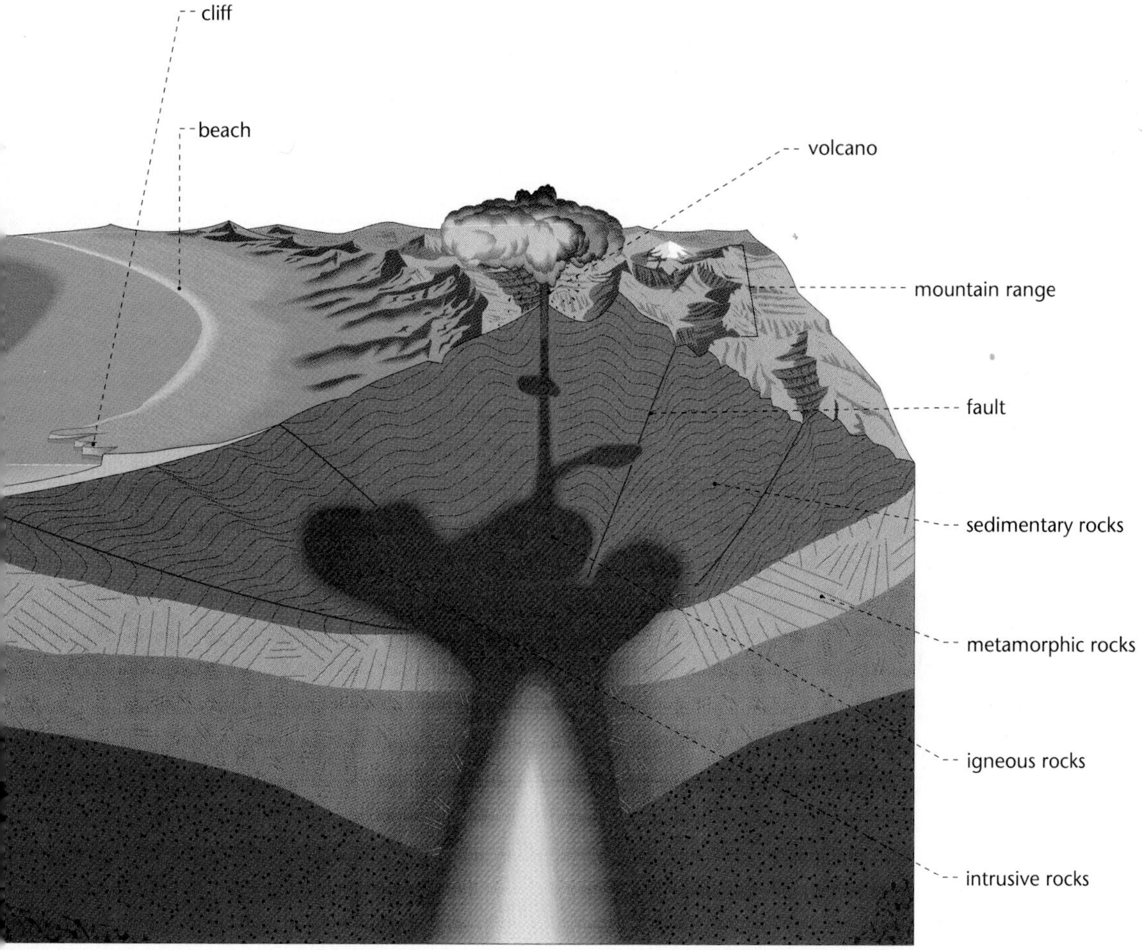

cliff

beach

volcano

mountain range

fault

sedimentary rocks

metamorphic rocks

igneous rocks

intrusive rocks

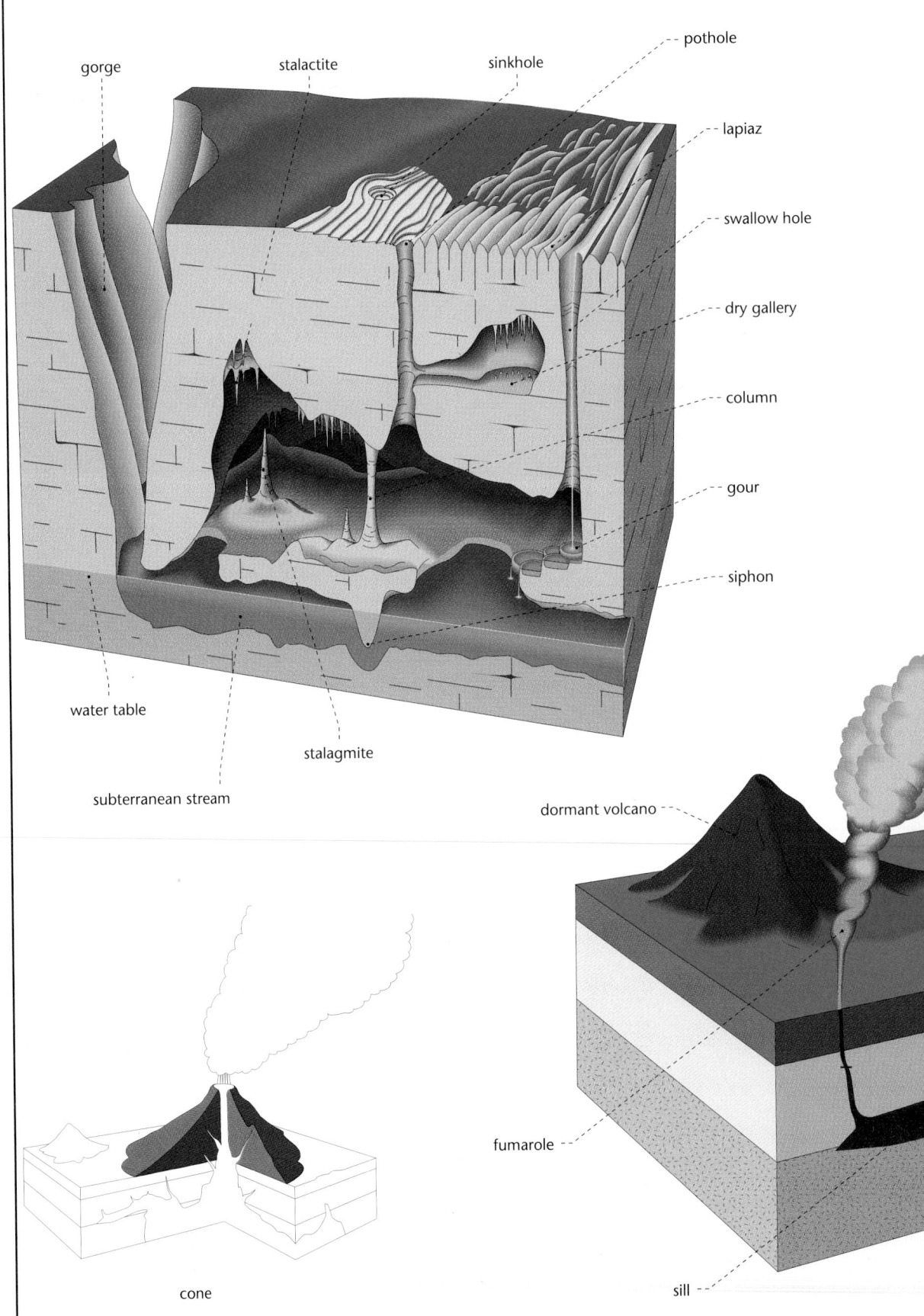

gorge

stalactite

sinkhole

pothole

lapiaz

swallow hole

dry gallery

column

gour

siphon

water table

stalagmite

subterranean stream

dormant volcano

fumarole

cone

sill

VOLCANO

VOLCANO DURING ERUPTION

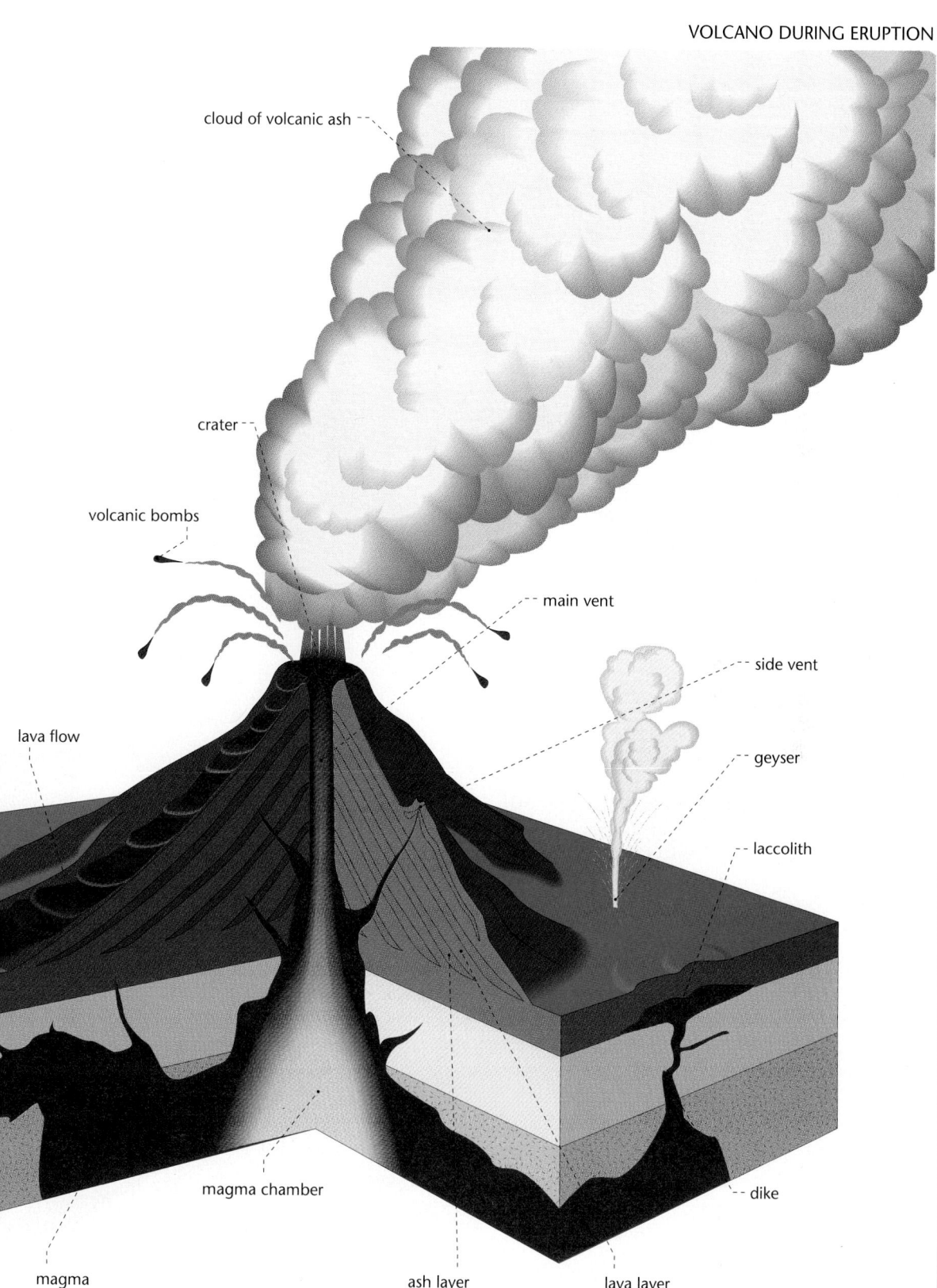

cloud of volcanic ash

crater

volcanic bombs

main vent

side vent

lava flow

geyser

laccolith

magma chamber

dike

magma

ash layer

lava layer

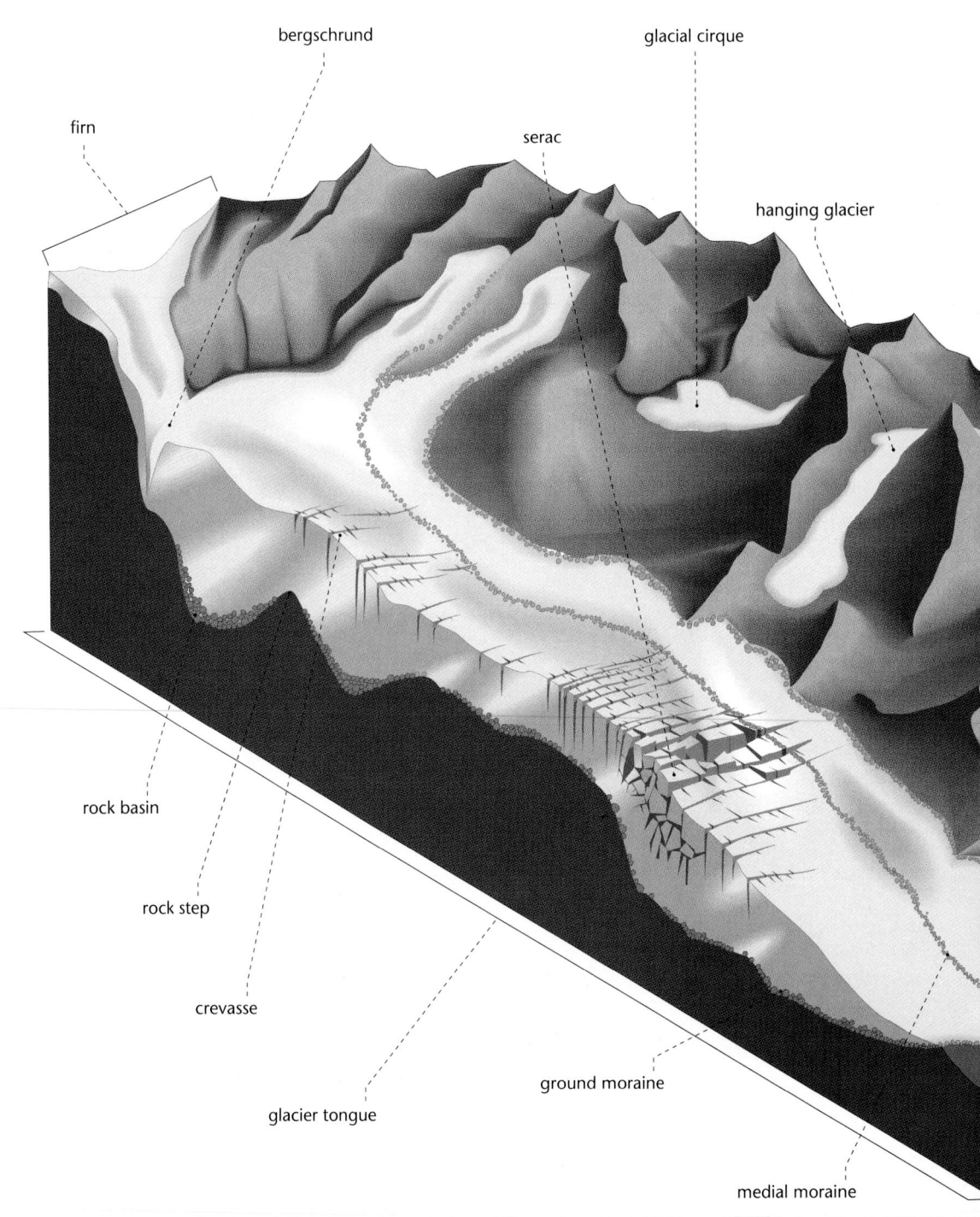

bergschrund

glacial cirque

firn

serac

hanging glacier

rock basin

rock step

crevasse

glacier tongue

ground moraine

medial moraine

MOUNTAIN

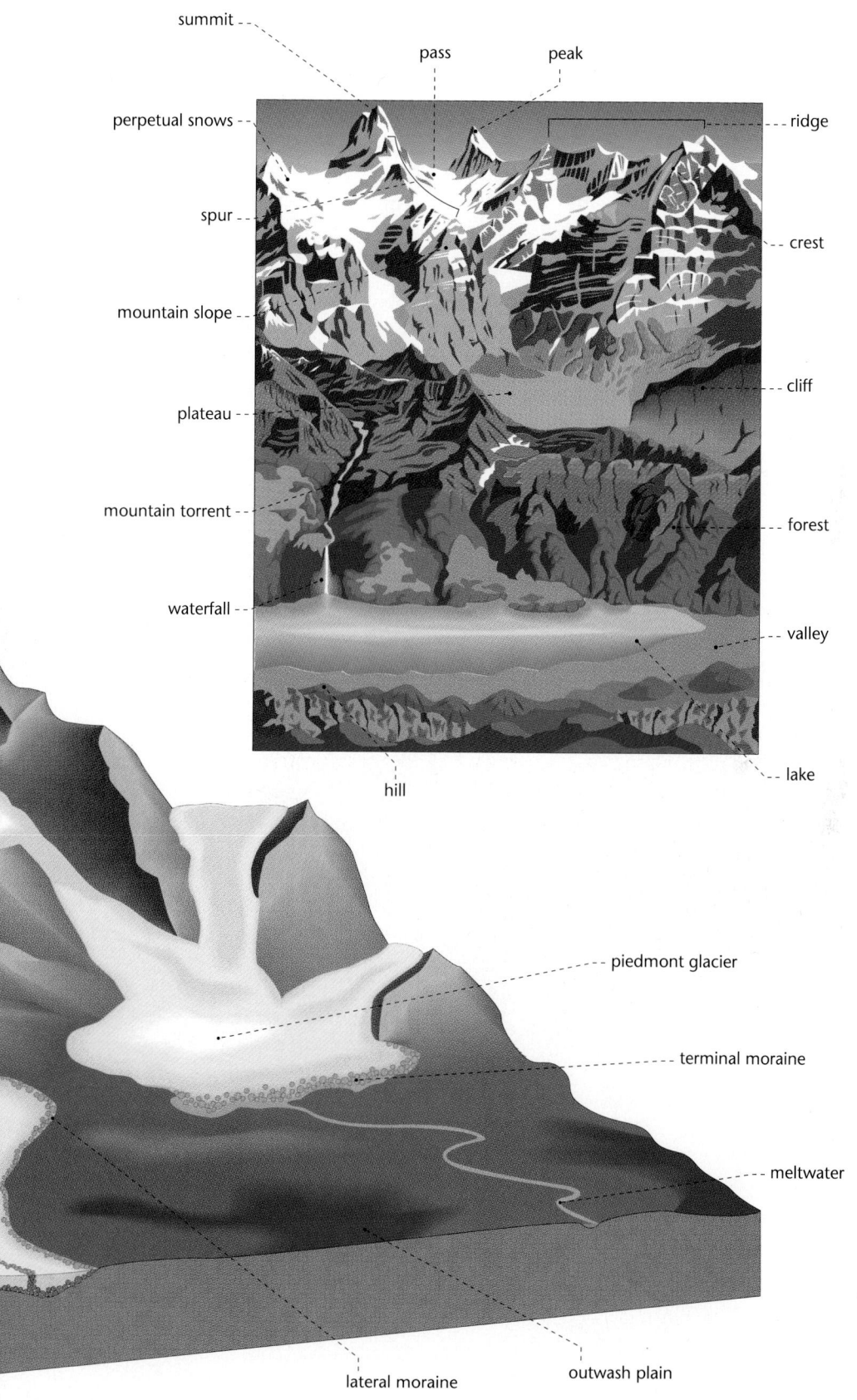

summit

pass

peak

ridge

perpetual snows

spur

crest

mountain slope

cliff

plateau

mountain torrent

forest

waterfall

valley

hill

lake

piedmont glacier

terminal moraine

meltwater

lateral moraine

outwash plain

MID-OCEAN RIDGE

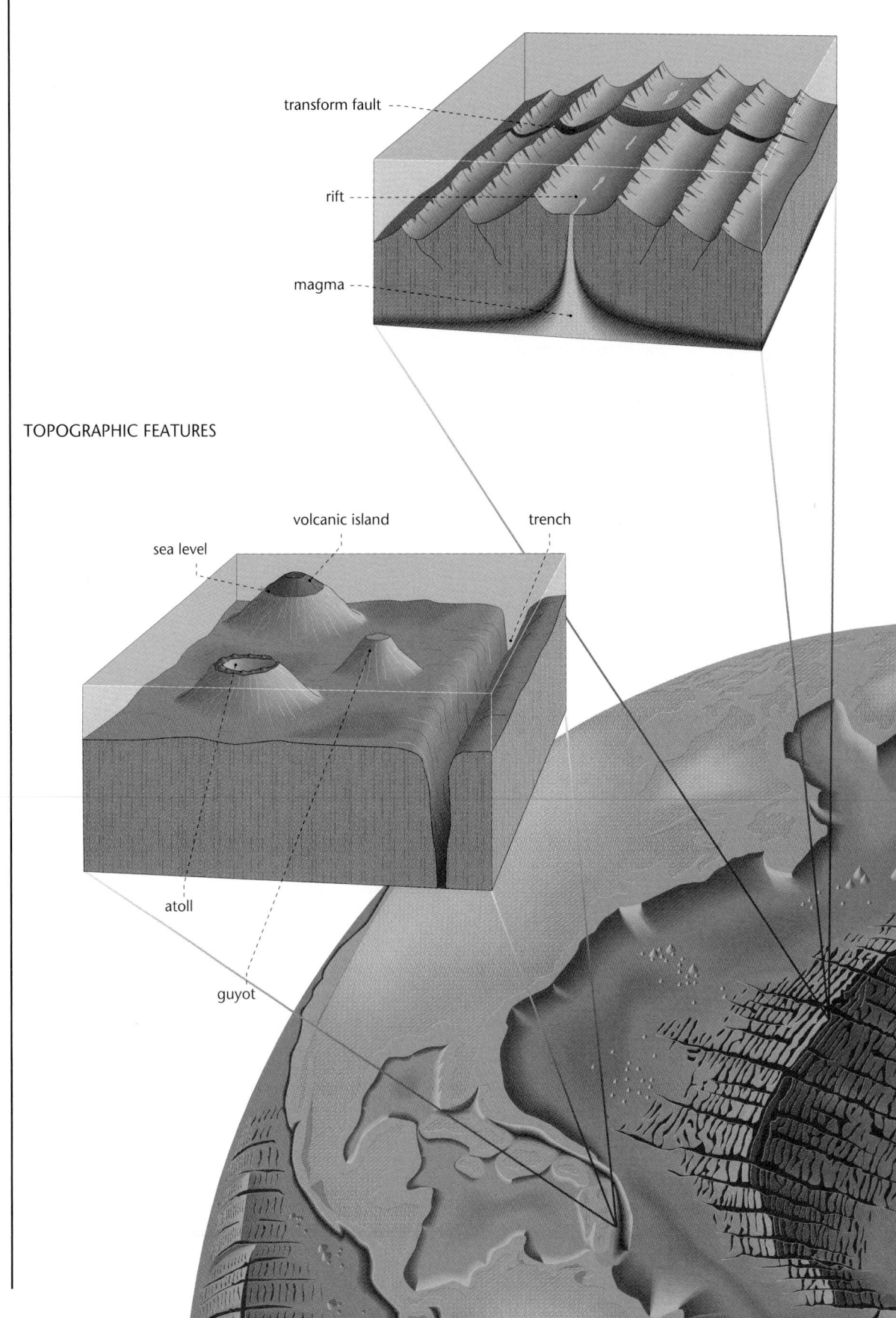

transform fault

rift

magma

TOPOGRAPHIC FEATURES

volcanic island

trench

sea level

atoll

guyot

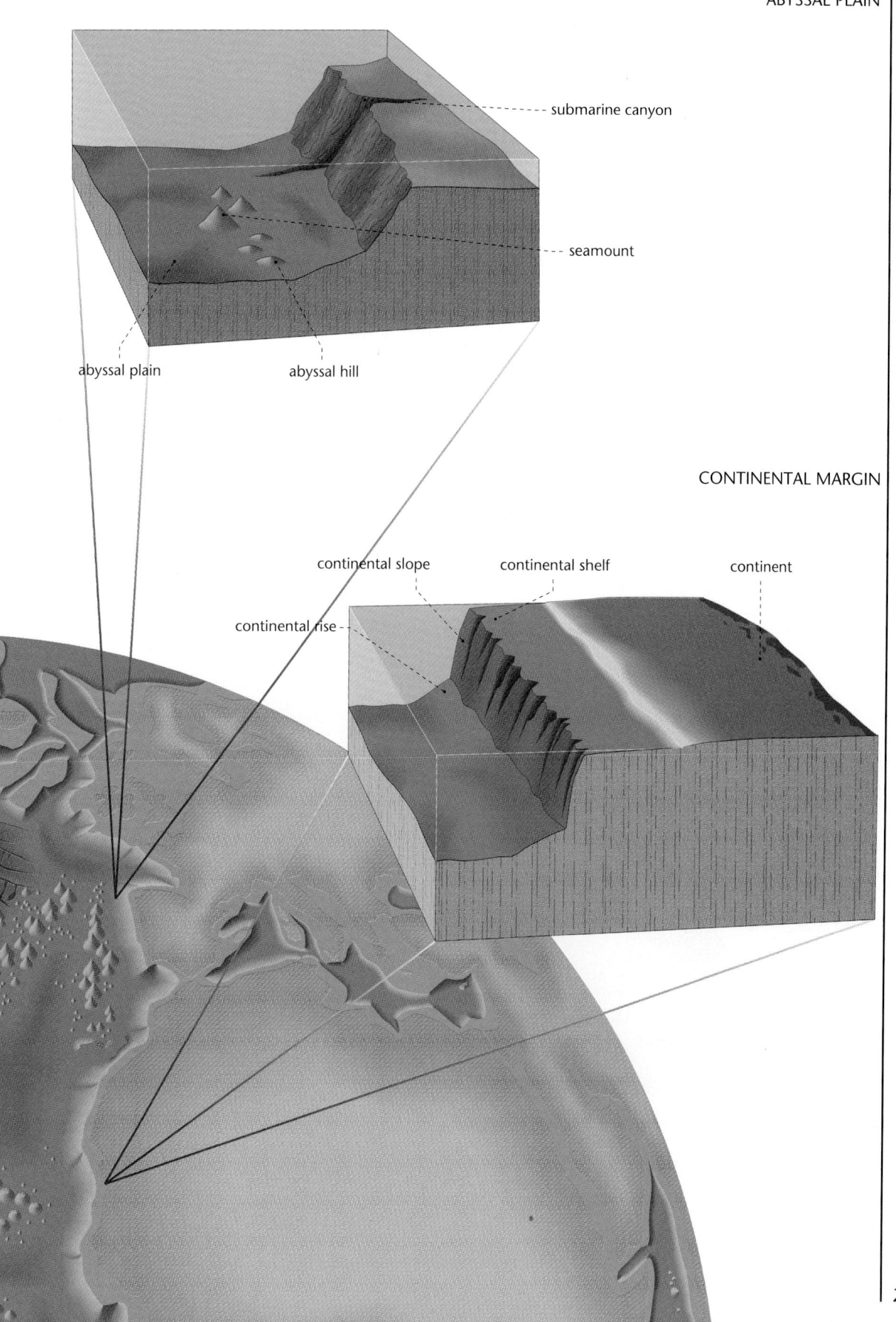

ABYSSAL PLAIN

submarine canyon

seamount

abyssal plain

abyssal hill

CONTINENTAL MARGIN

continental slope

continental shelf

continent

continental rise

WAVE

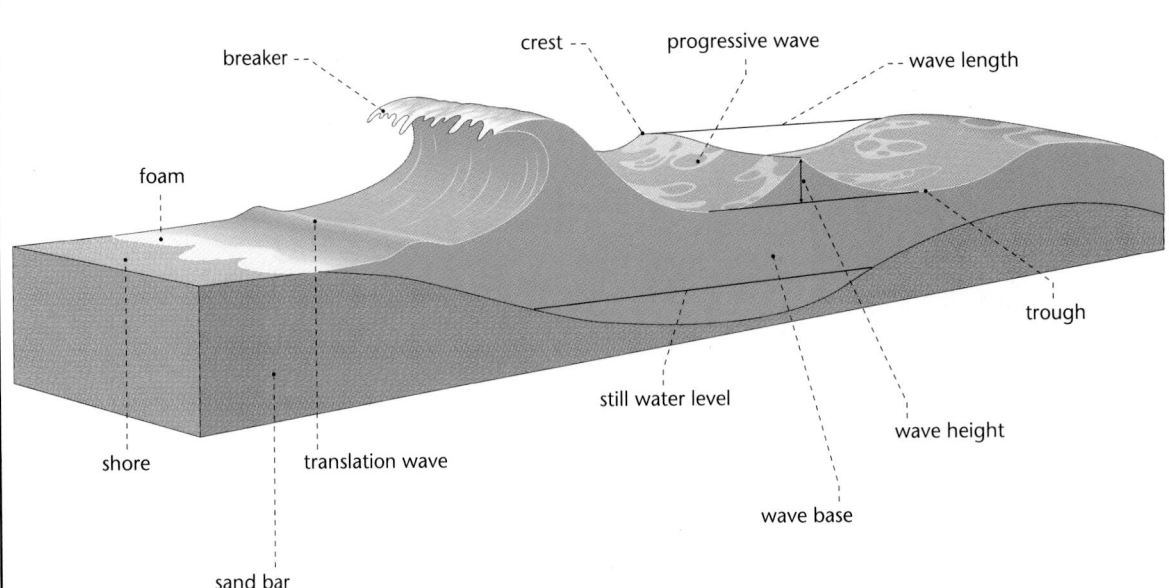

breaker

crest

progressive wave

wave length

foam

wave base

still water level

wave height

trough

shore

translation wave

sand bar

COMMON COASTAL FEATURES

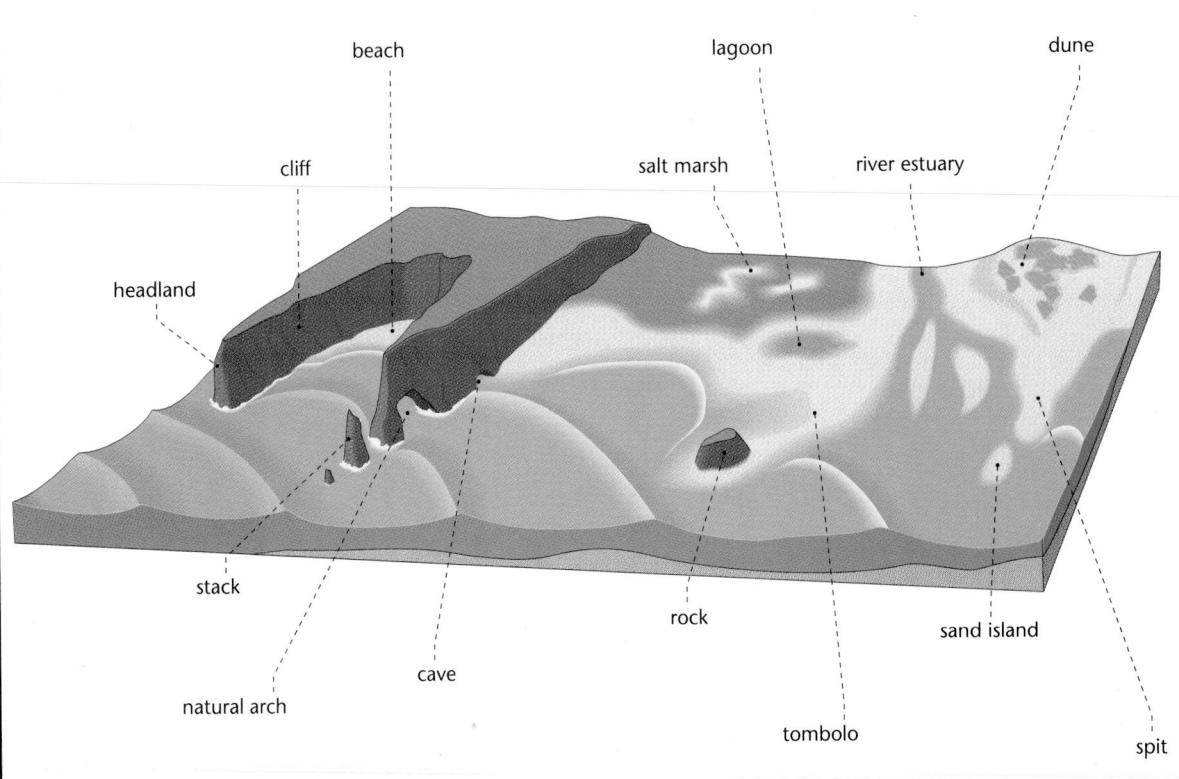

beach

lagoon

dune

cliff

salt marsh

river estuary

headland

stack

rock

sand island

natural arch

cave

tombolo

spit

ECOLOGY

STRUCTURE OF THE BIOSPHERE

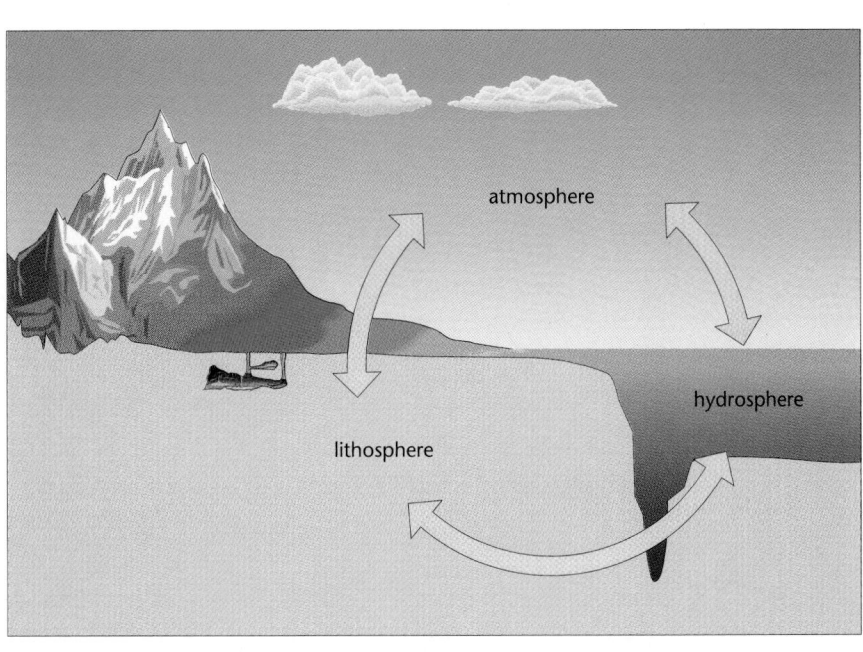

atmosphere

hydrosphere

lithosphere

FOOD CHAIN

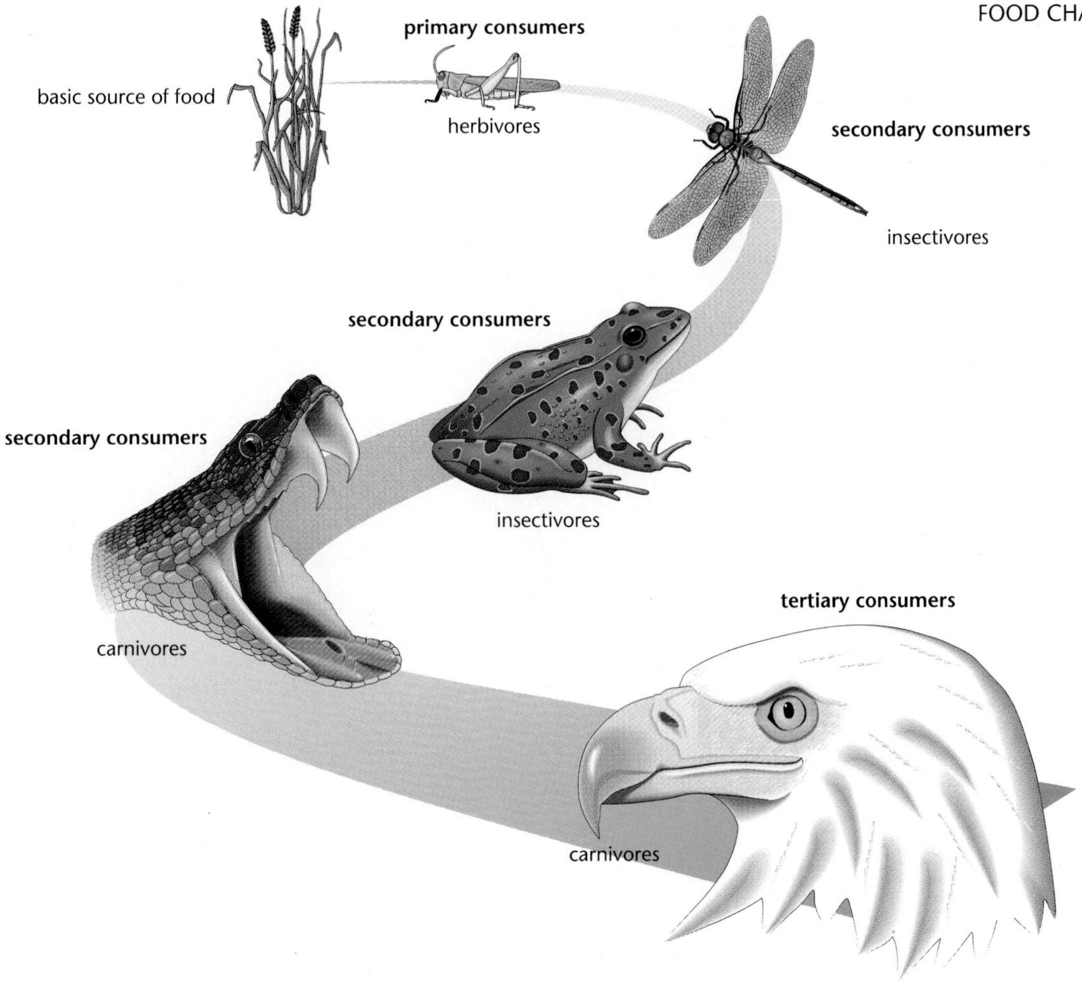

primary consumers

basic source of food

herbivores

secondary consumers

insectivores

secondary consumers

insectivores

secondary consumers

carnivores

tertiary consumers

carnivores

POLLUTION OF FOOD ON GROUND

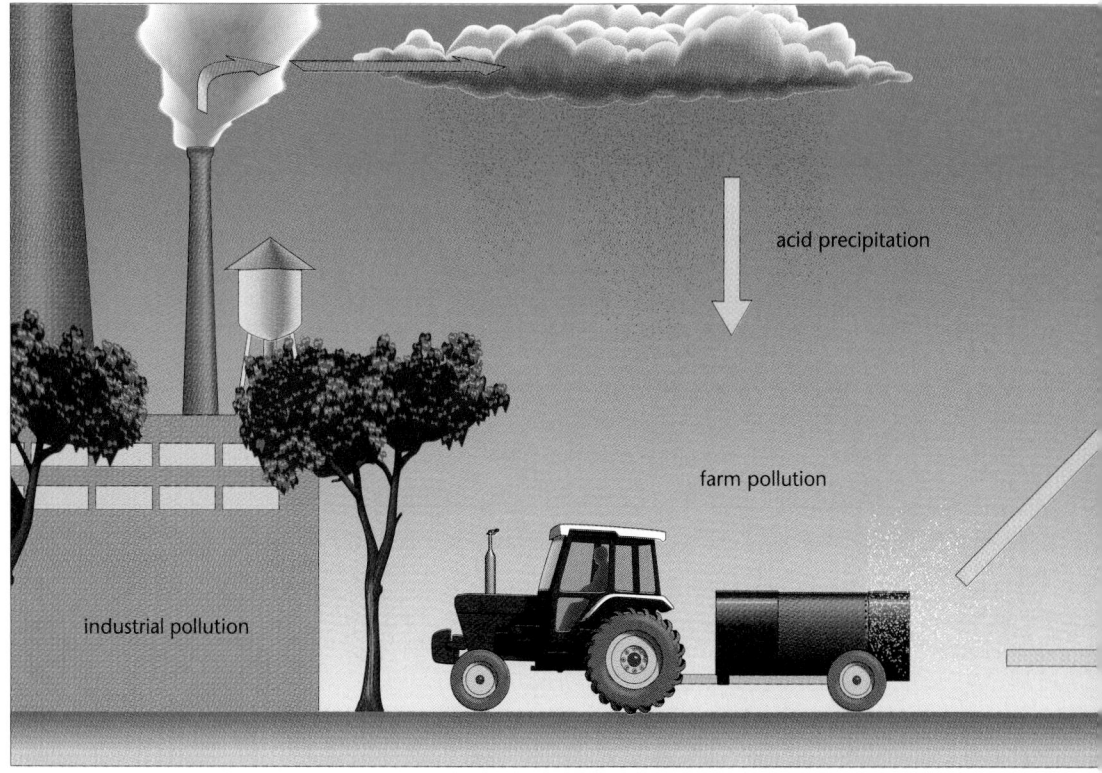

acid precipitation

farm pollution

industrial pollution

POLLUTION OF FOOD IN WATER

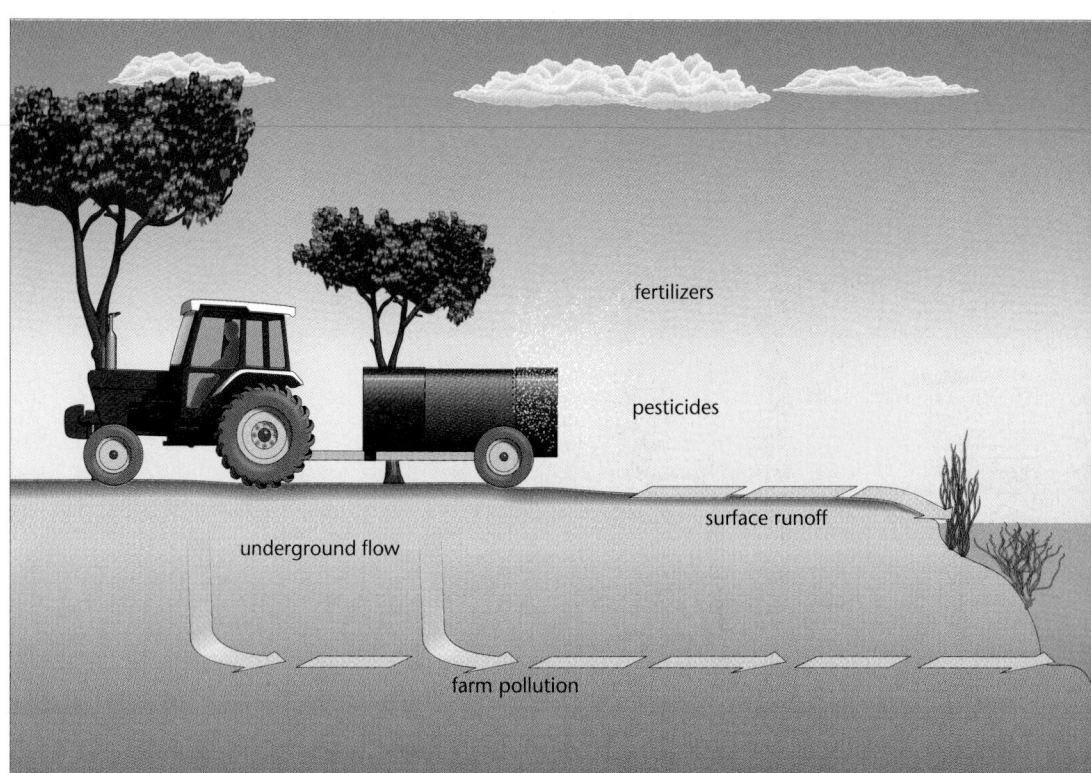

fertilizers

pesticides

surface runoff

underground flow

farm pollution

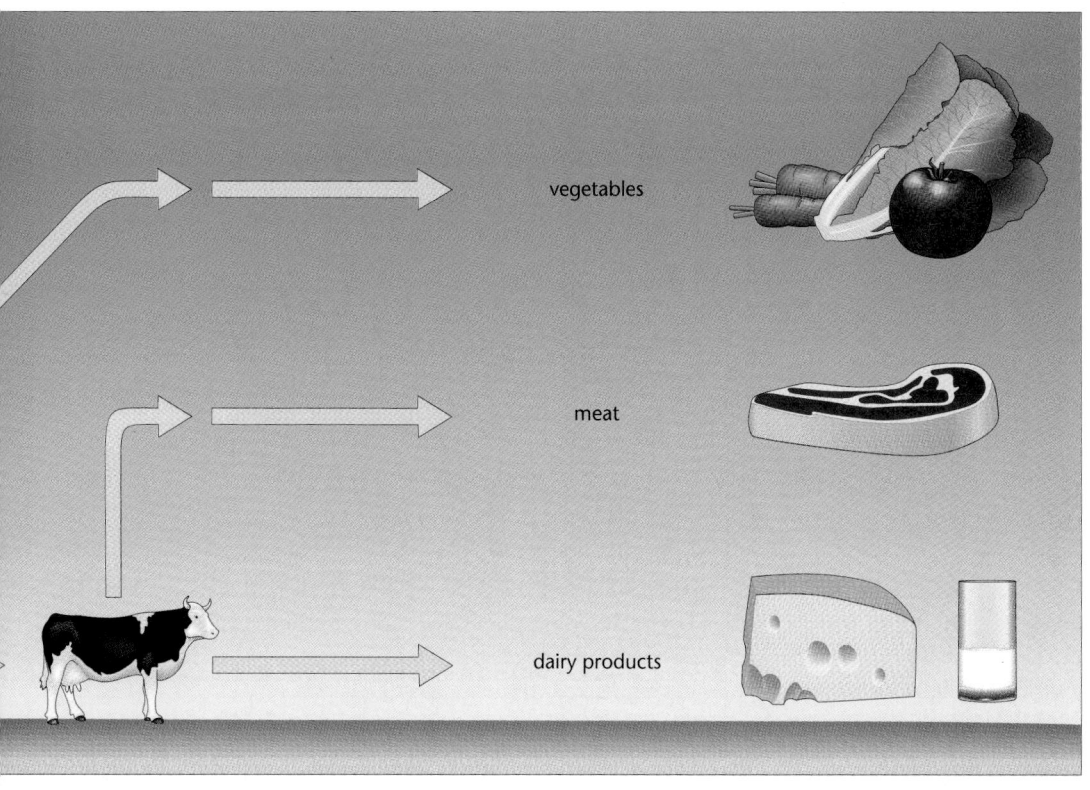

vegetables

meat

dairy products

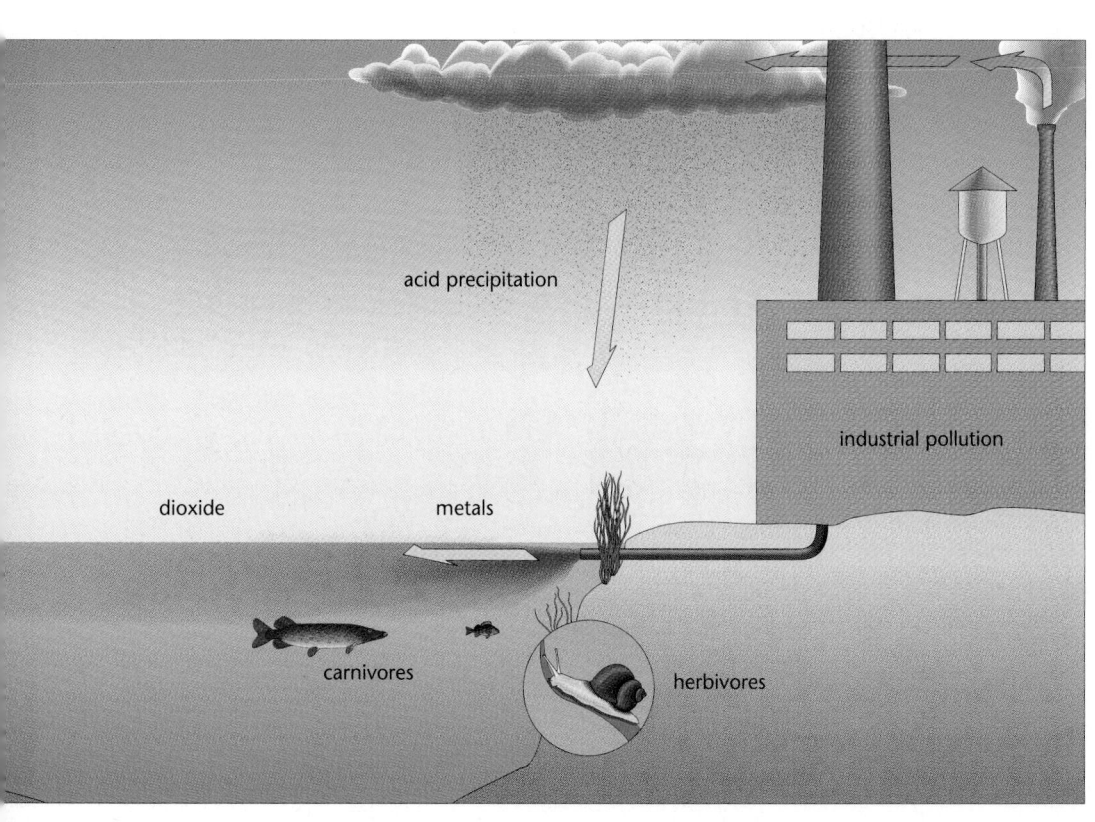

acid precipitation

industrial pollution

dioxide

metals

carnivores

herbivores

ATMOSPHERIC POLLUTION

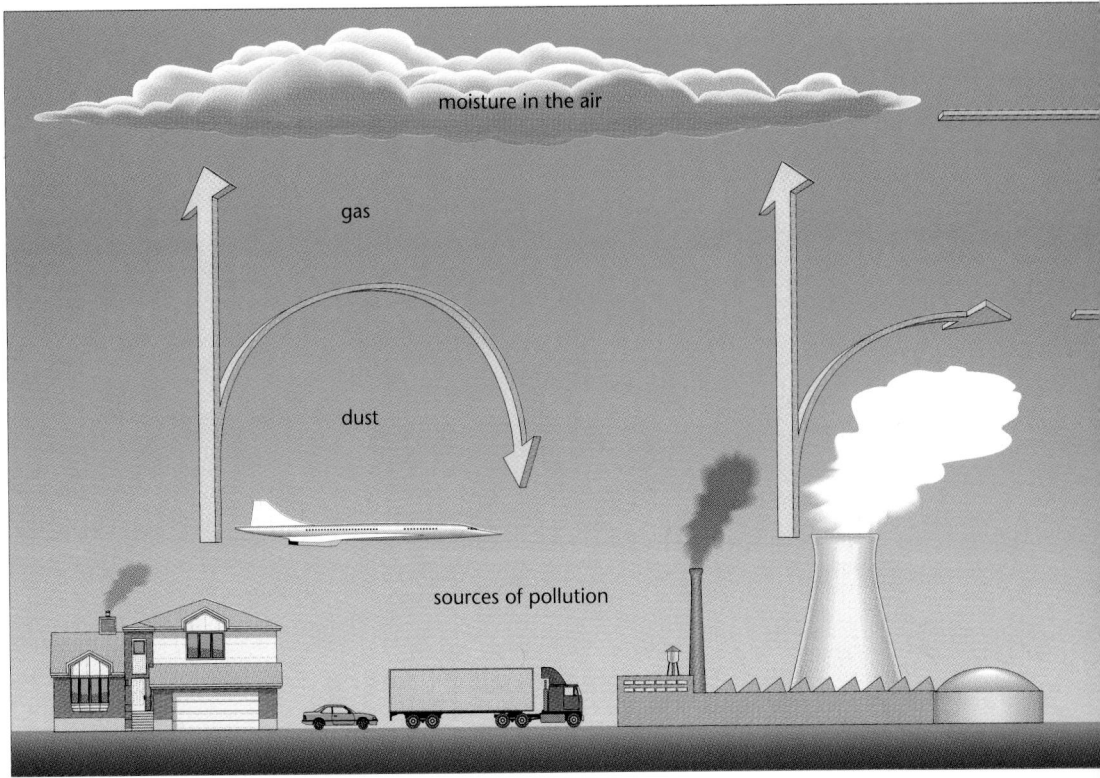

moisture in the air

gas

dust

sources of pollution

HYDROLOGIC CYCLE

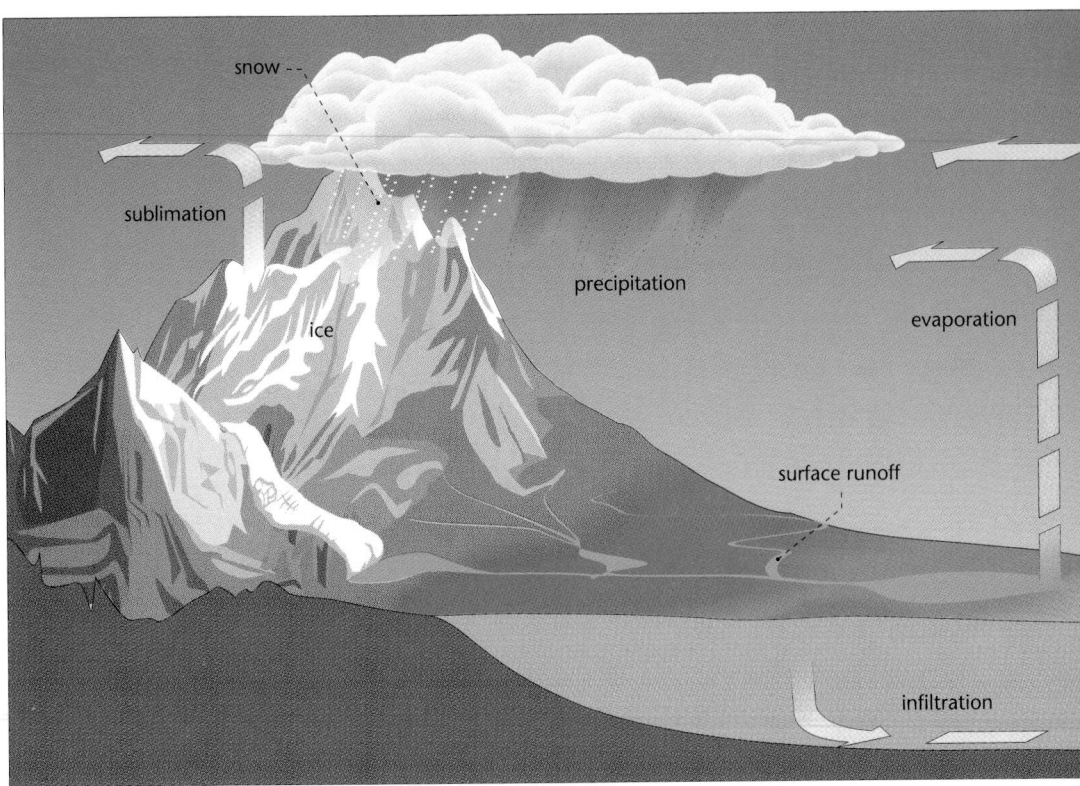

snow

sublimation

precipitation

ice

evaporation

surface runoff

infiltration

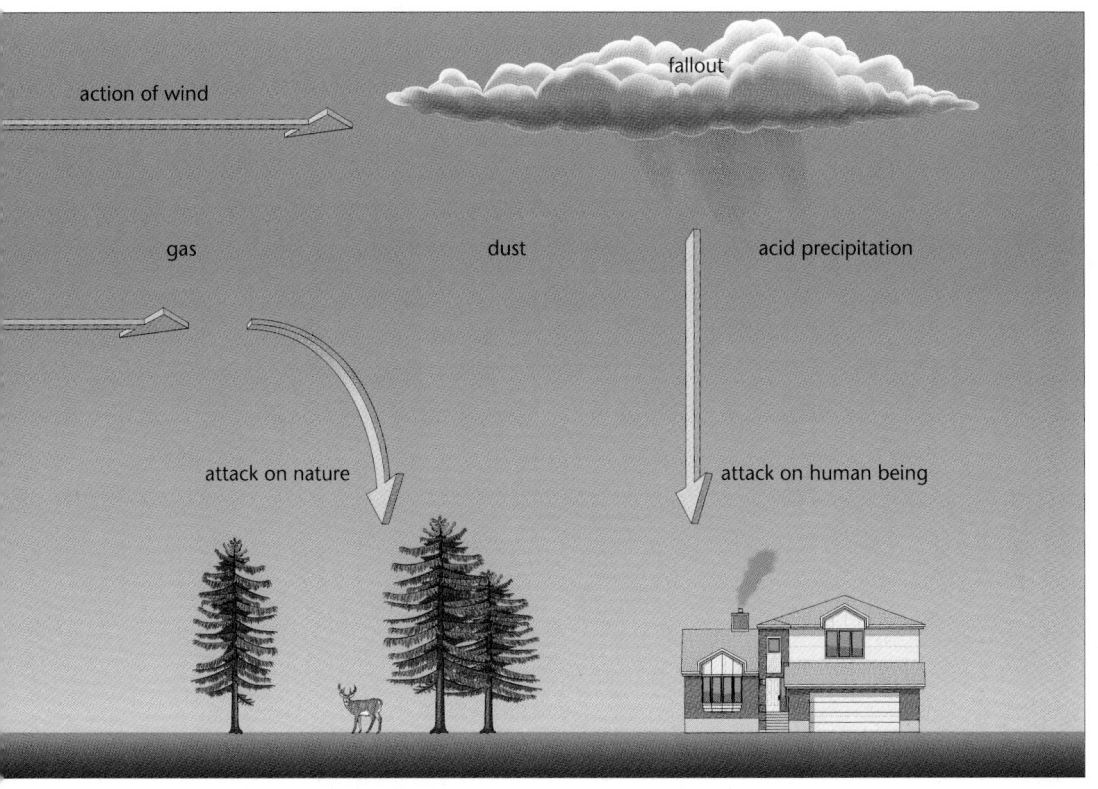

action of wind

fallout

gas

dust

acid precipitation

attack on nature

attack on human being

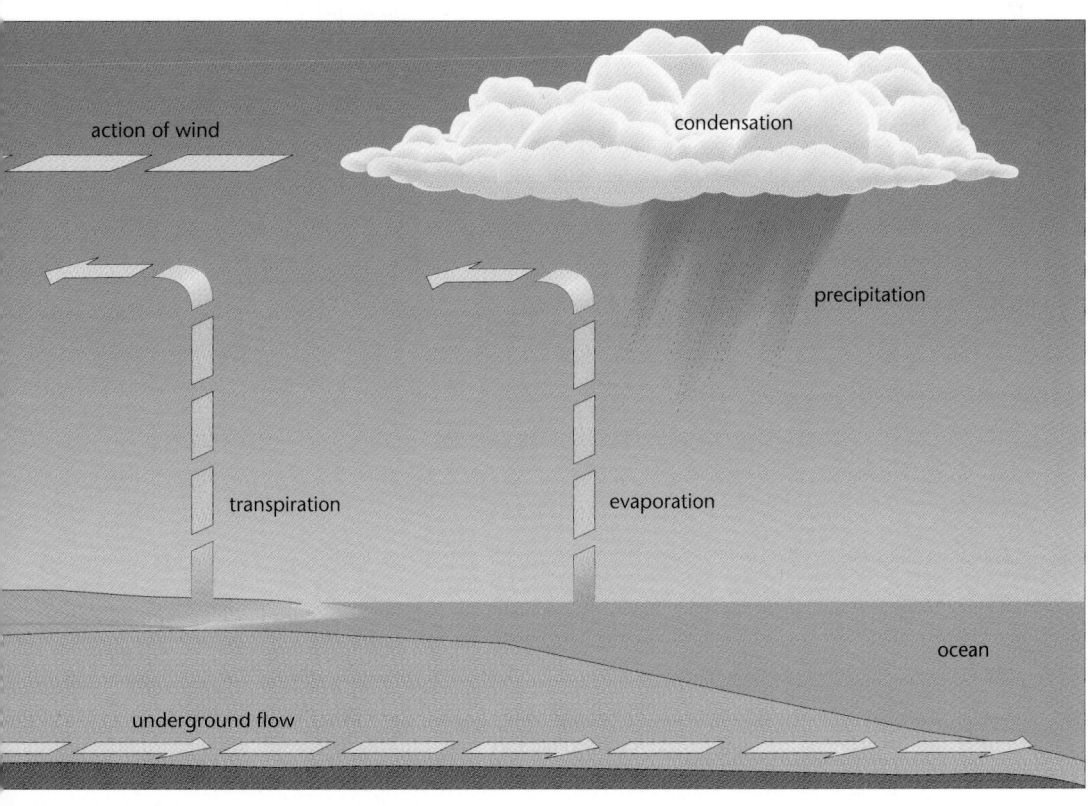

action of wind

condensation

precipitation

transpiration

evaporation

ocean

underground flow

PRECIPITATIONS

STORMY SKY

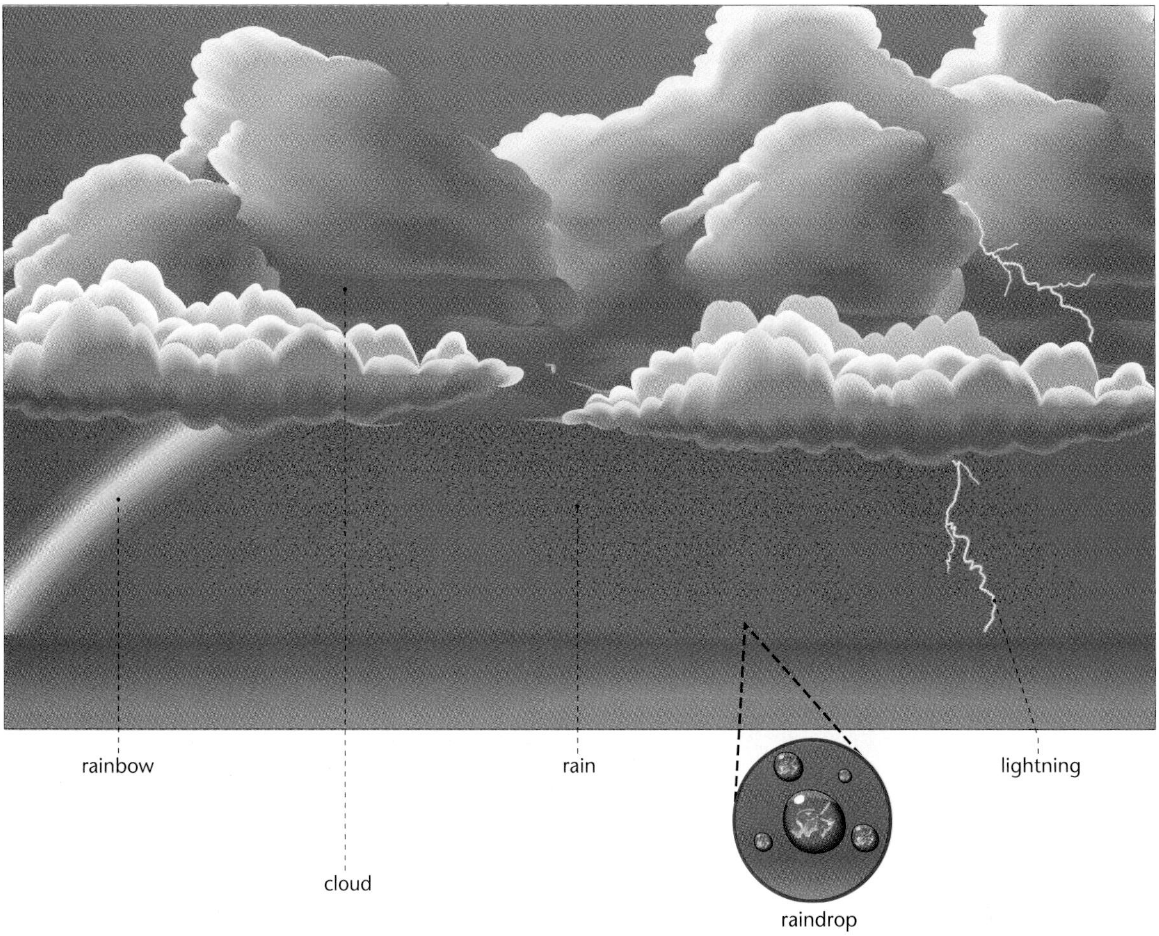

rainbow

rain

lightning

cloud

raindrop

CLASSIFICATION OF SNOW CRYSTALS

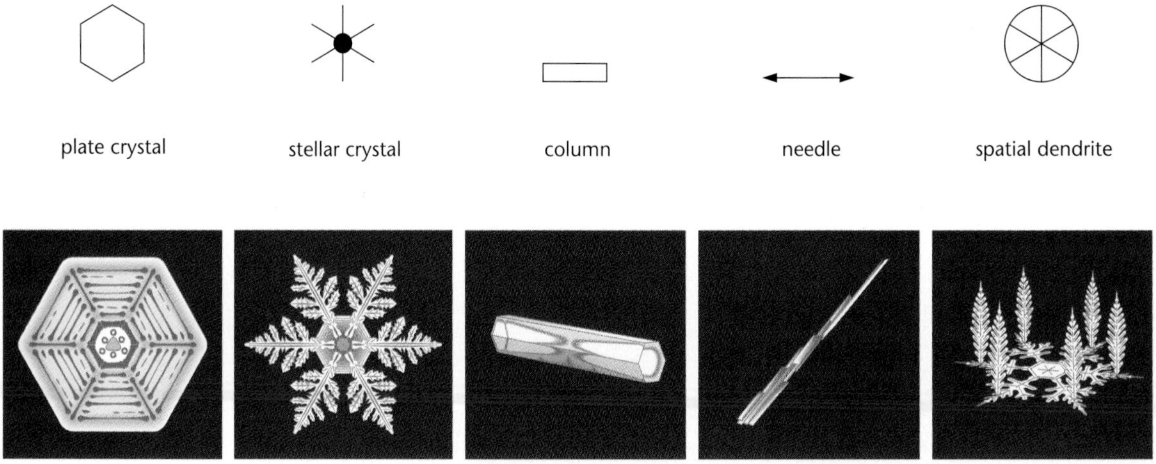

plate crystal

stellar crystal

column

needle

spatial dendrite

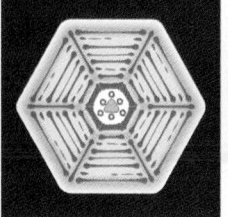

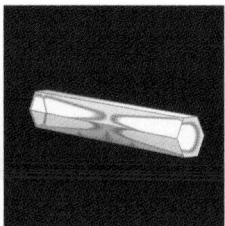

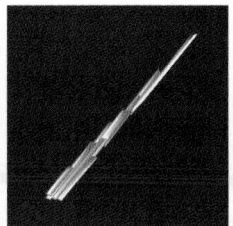

mist

fog

dew

frost

capped column

irregular crystal

snow pellet

sleet

hail

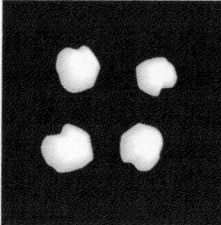

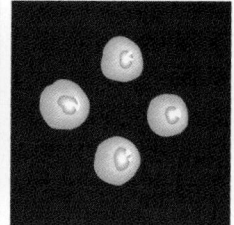

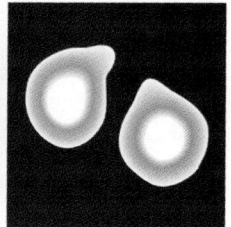

37

WEATHER MAP

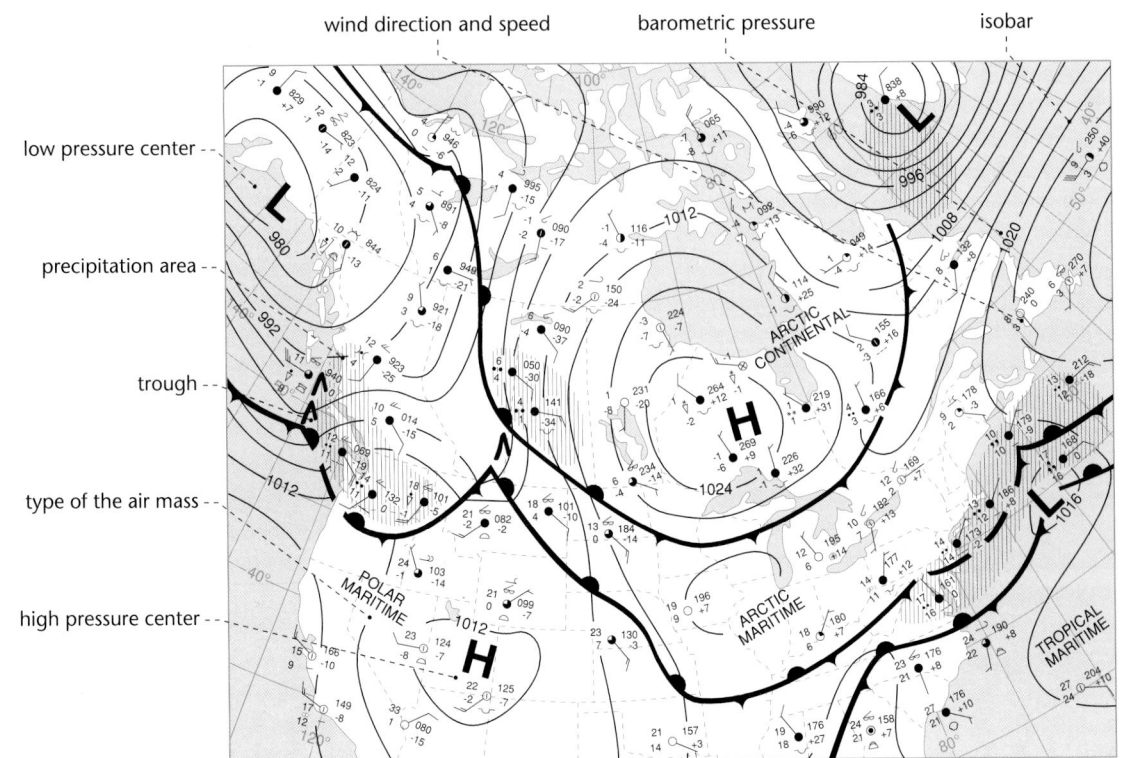

- wind direction and speed
- barometric pressure
- isobar
- low pressure center
- precipitation area
- trough
- type of the air mass
- high pressure center

STATION MODEL

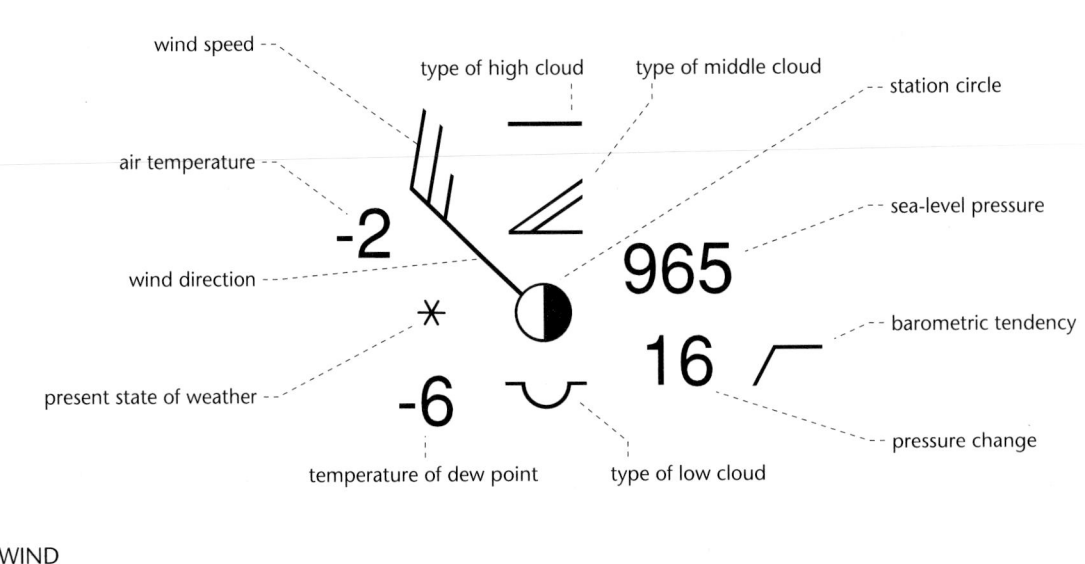

- wind speed
- type of high cloud
- type of middle cloud
- station circle
- air temperature
- sea-level pressure
- wind direction
- barometric tendency
- present state of weather
- pressure change
- temperature of dew point
- type of low cloud

-2

965

16

*

-6

WIND

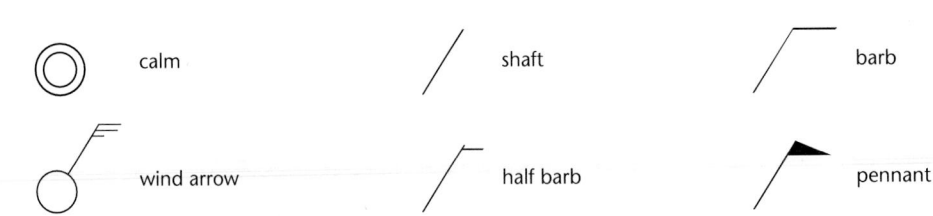

- calm
- shaft
- barb
- wind arrow
- half barb
- pennant

INTERNATIONAL WEATHER SYMBOLS

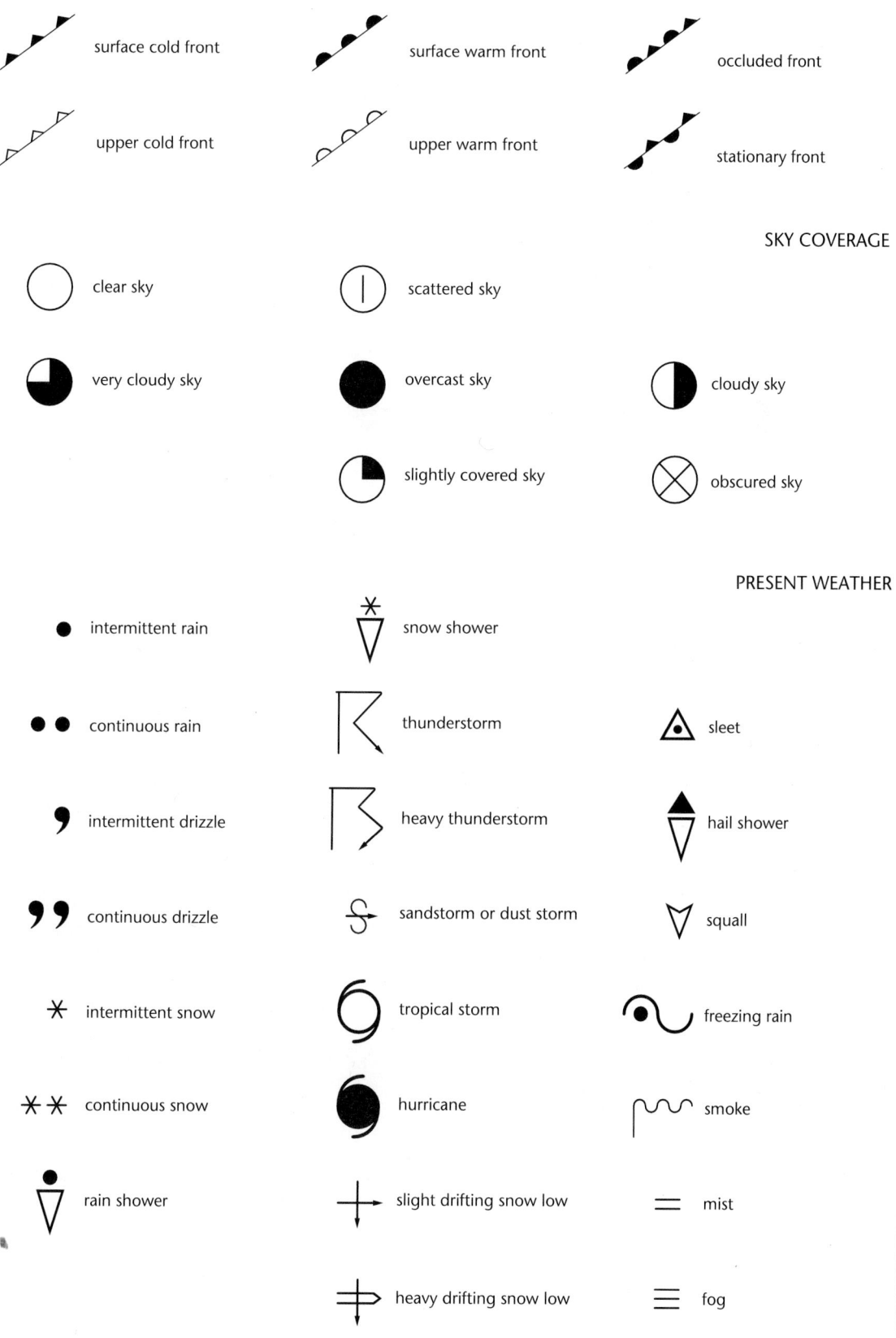

FRONTS

surface cold front

surface warm front

occluded front

upper cold front

upper warm front

stationary front

SKY COVERAGE

clear sky

scattered sky

very cloudy sky

overcast sky

cloudy sky

slightly covered sky

obscured sky

PRESENT WEATHER

intermittent rain

snow shower

continuous rain

thunderstorm

sleet

intermittent drizzle

heavy thunderstorm

hail shower

continuous drizzle

sandstorm or dust storm

squall

intermittent snow

tropical storm

freezing rain

continuous snow

hurricane

smoke

rain shower

slight drifting snow low

mist

heavy drifting snow low

fog

39

METEOROLOGICAL MEASURING INSTRUMENTS

MEASURE OF SUNSHINE

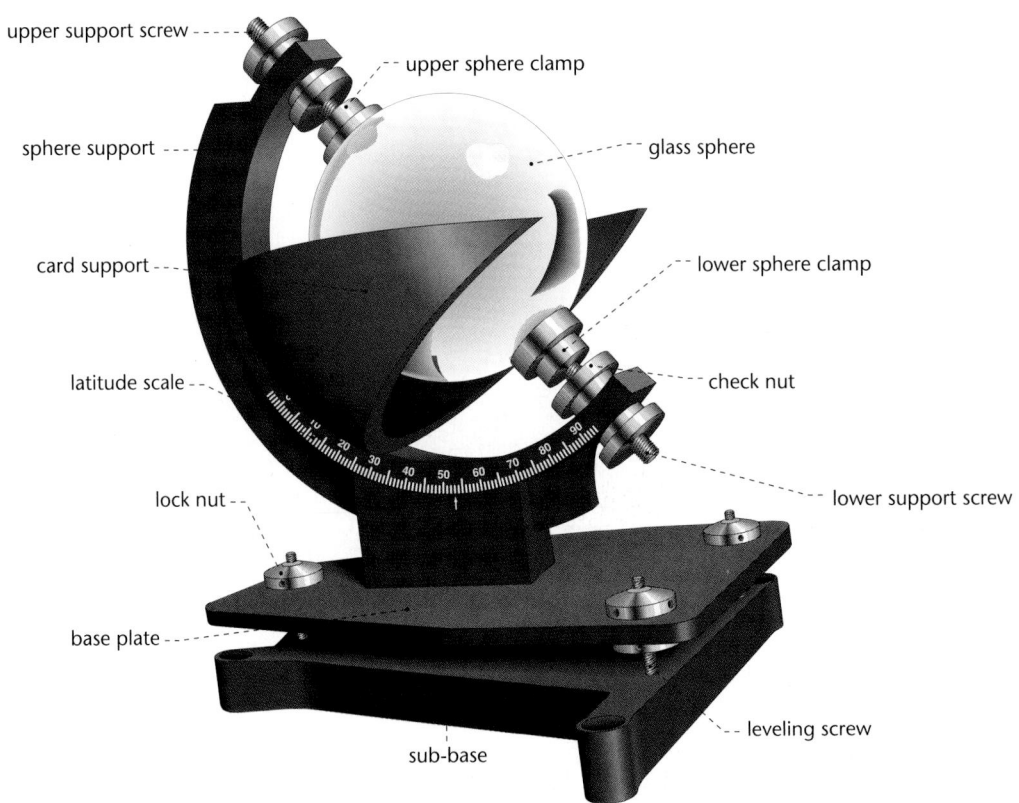

sunshine recorder

upper support screw

upper sphere clamp

sphere support

glass sphere

card support

lower sphere clamp

latitude scale

check nut

lock nut

lower support screw

base plate

sub-base

leveling screw

MEASURE OF RAINFALL

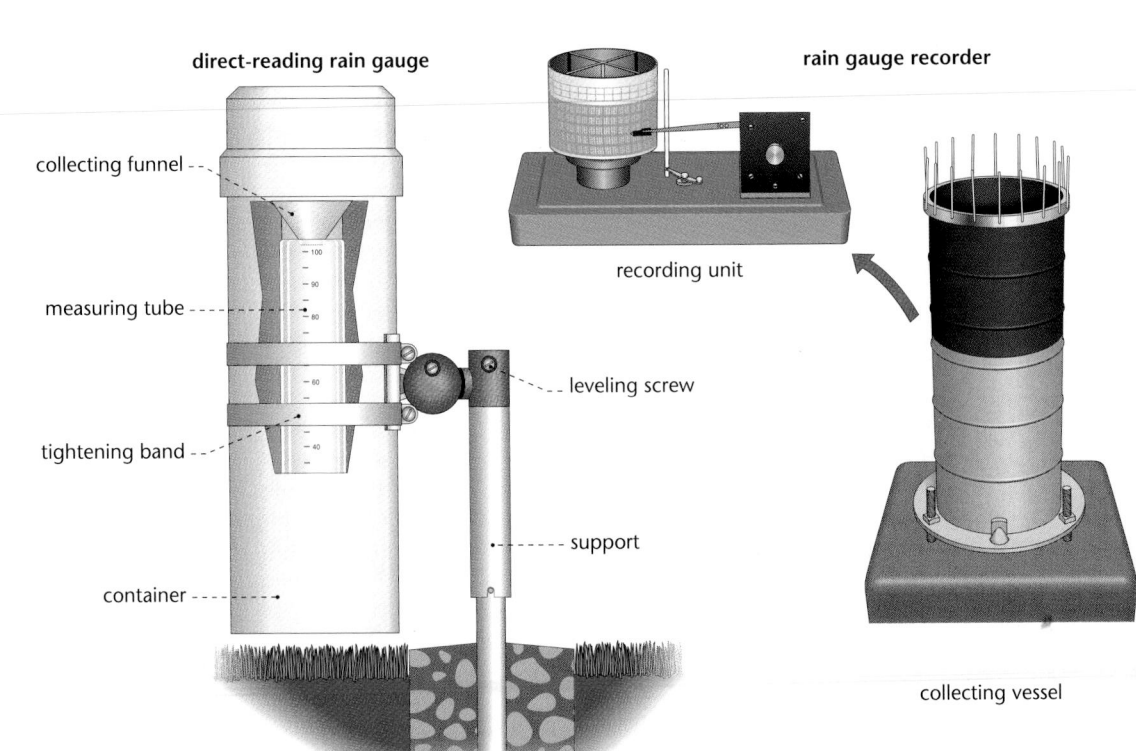

direct-reading rain gauge

rain gauge recorder

collecting funnel

measuring tube

recording unit

tightening band

leveling screw

support

container

collecting vessel

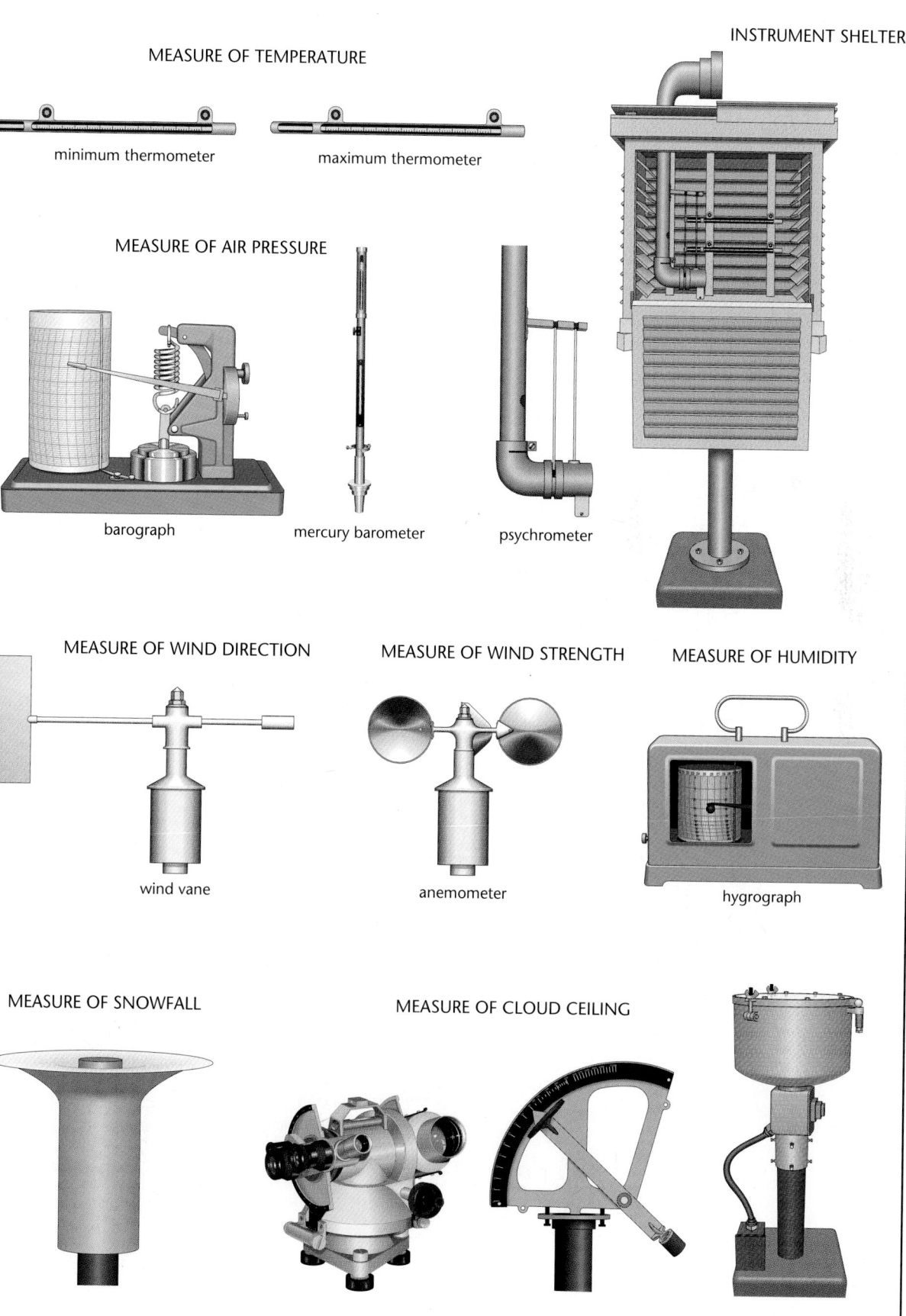

MEASURE OF TEMPERATURE

minimum thermometer

maximum thermometer

INSTRUMENT SHELTER

MEASURE OF AIR PRESSURE

barograph

mercury barometer

psychrometer

MEASURE OF WIND DIRECTION

wind vane

MEASURE OF WIND STRENGTH

anemometer

MEASURE OF HUMIDITY

hygrograph

MEASURE OF SNOWFALL

snow gauge

MEASURE OF CLOUD CEILING

theodolite

alidade

ceiling projector

WEATHER SATELLITE

GEOSTATIONARY SATELLITE

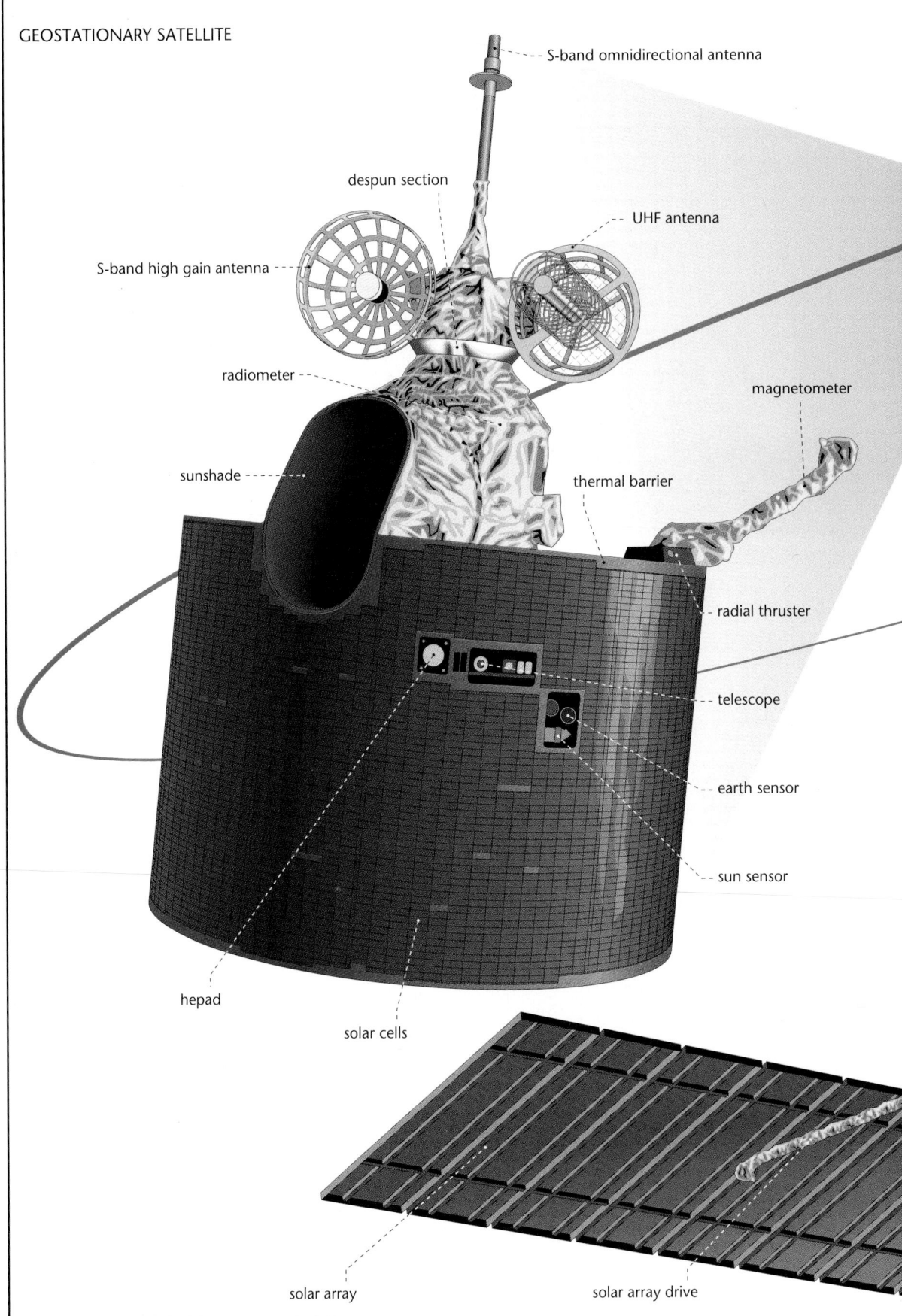

S-band omnidirectional antenna

despun section

UHF antenna

S-band high gain antenna

radiometer

magnetometer

sunshade

thermal barrier

radial thruster

telescope

earth sensor

sun sensor

hepad

solar cells

solar array

solar array drive

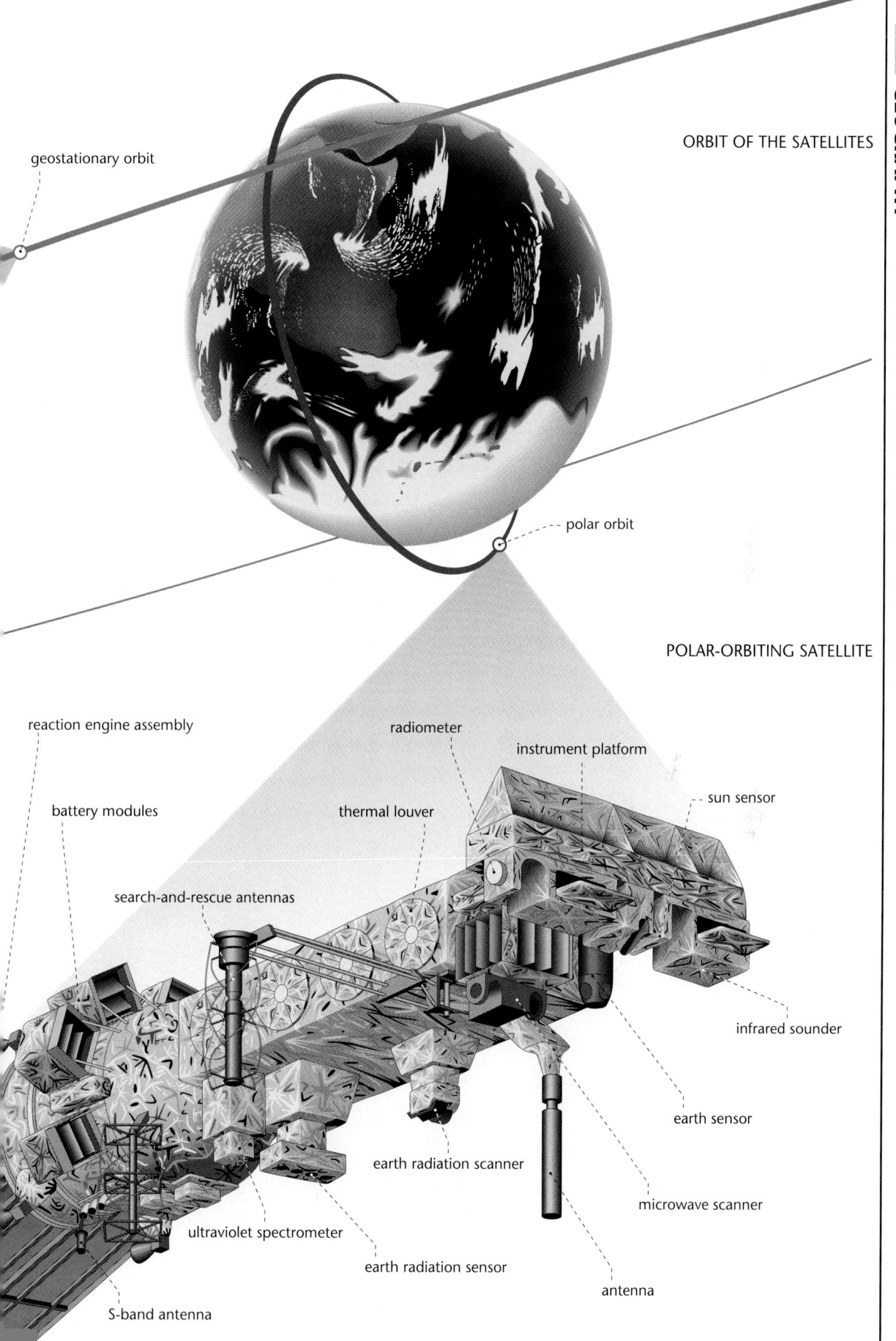

ORBIT OF THE SATELLITES

geostationary orbit

polar orbit

POLAR-ORBITING SATELLITE

reaction engine assembly

radiometer

instrument platform

sun sensor

battery modules

thermal louver

search-and-rescue antennas

infrared sounder

earth sensor

earth radiation scanner

microwave scanner

ultraviolet spectrometer

earth radiation sensor

antenna

S-band antenna

CLOUDS AND METEOROLOGICAL SYMBOLS

HIGH CLOUDS

CLOUDS OF VERTICAL DEVELOPMENT

cirrus

cumulonimbus

cirrocumulus

cirrostratus

MIDDLE CLOUDS

altostratus

altocumulus

stratocumulus

LOW CLOUDS

nimbostratus

stratus

cumulus

CLIMATES OF THE WORLD

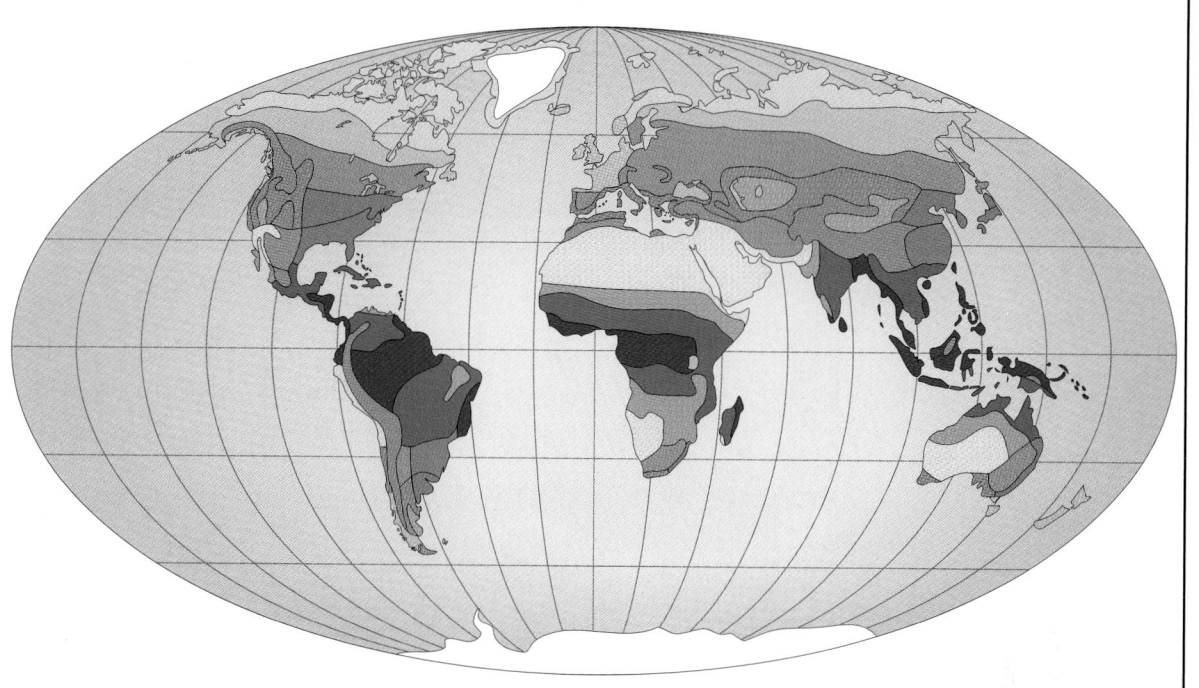

TROPICAL CLIMATES

tropical rain forest

tropical savanna

steppe

desert

TEMPERATE CLIMATES

humid - long summer

humid - short summer

marine

POLAR CLIMATES

polar tundra

polar ice cap

HIGHLAND CLIMATES

highland climates

SUBTROPICAL CLIMATES

Mediterranean subtropical

humid subtropical

dry subtropical

CONTINENTAL CLIMATES

dry continental - arid

dry continental - semiarid

SUBARCTIC CLIMATES

subarctic climates

DESERT

oasis   palm grove

mesa   butte

rocky desert

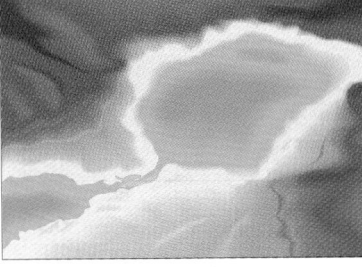

saline lake

sandy desert

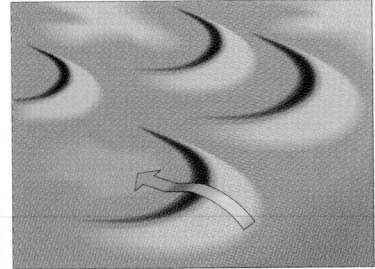

crescentic dune

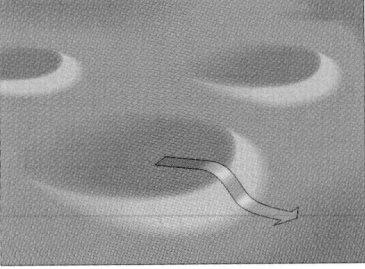

parabolic dune

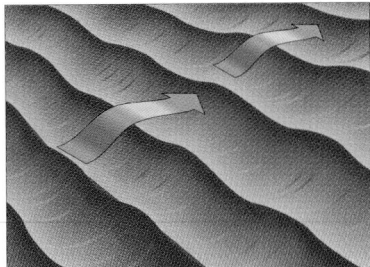

transverse dunes

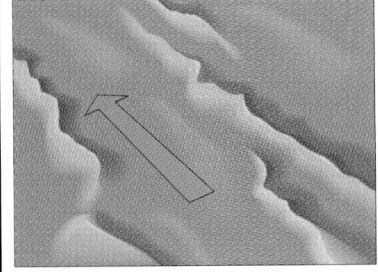

chain of dunes

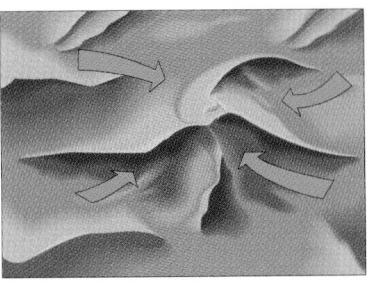

complex dune

longitudinal dunes

CARTOGRAPHY

HEMISPHERES

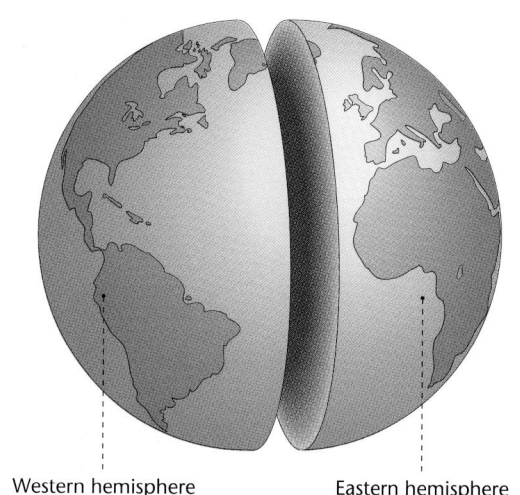

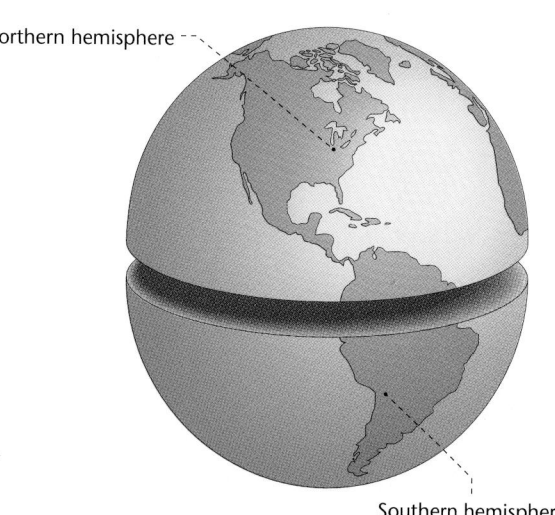

Northern hemisphere

Western hemisphere   Eastern hemisphere

Southern hemisphere

GRID SYSTEM

lines of latitude

lines of longitude

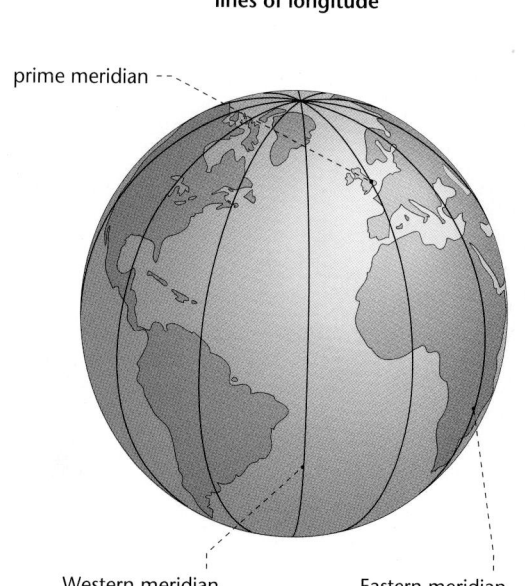

Arctic Circle

tropic of Cancer

tropic of Capricorn

equator   parallel

prime meridian

Western meridian   Eastern meridian

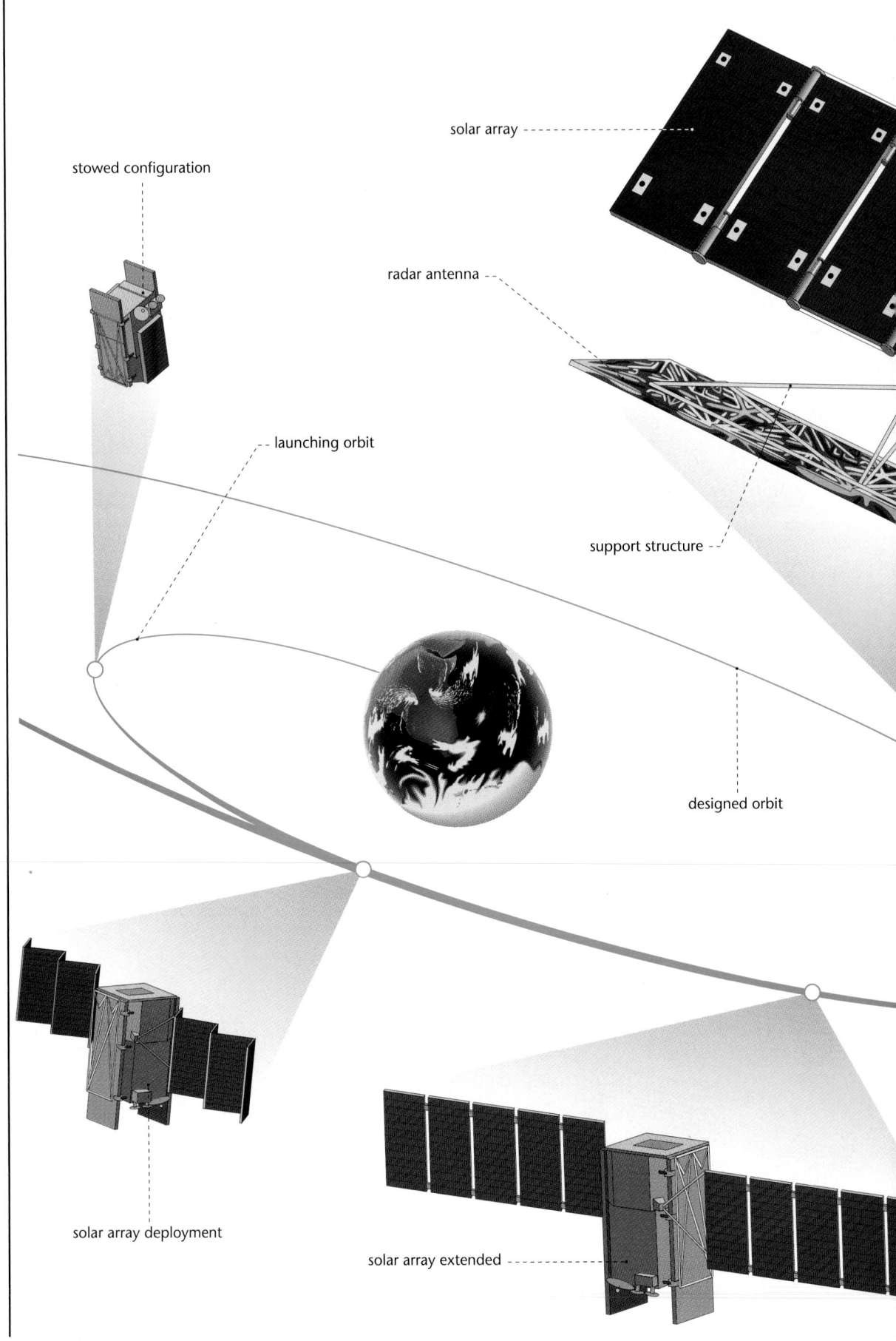

stowed configuration

solar array

radar antenna

launching orbit

support structure

designed orbit

solar array deployment

solar array extended

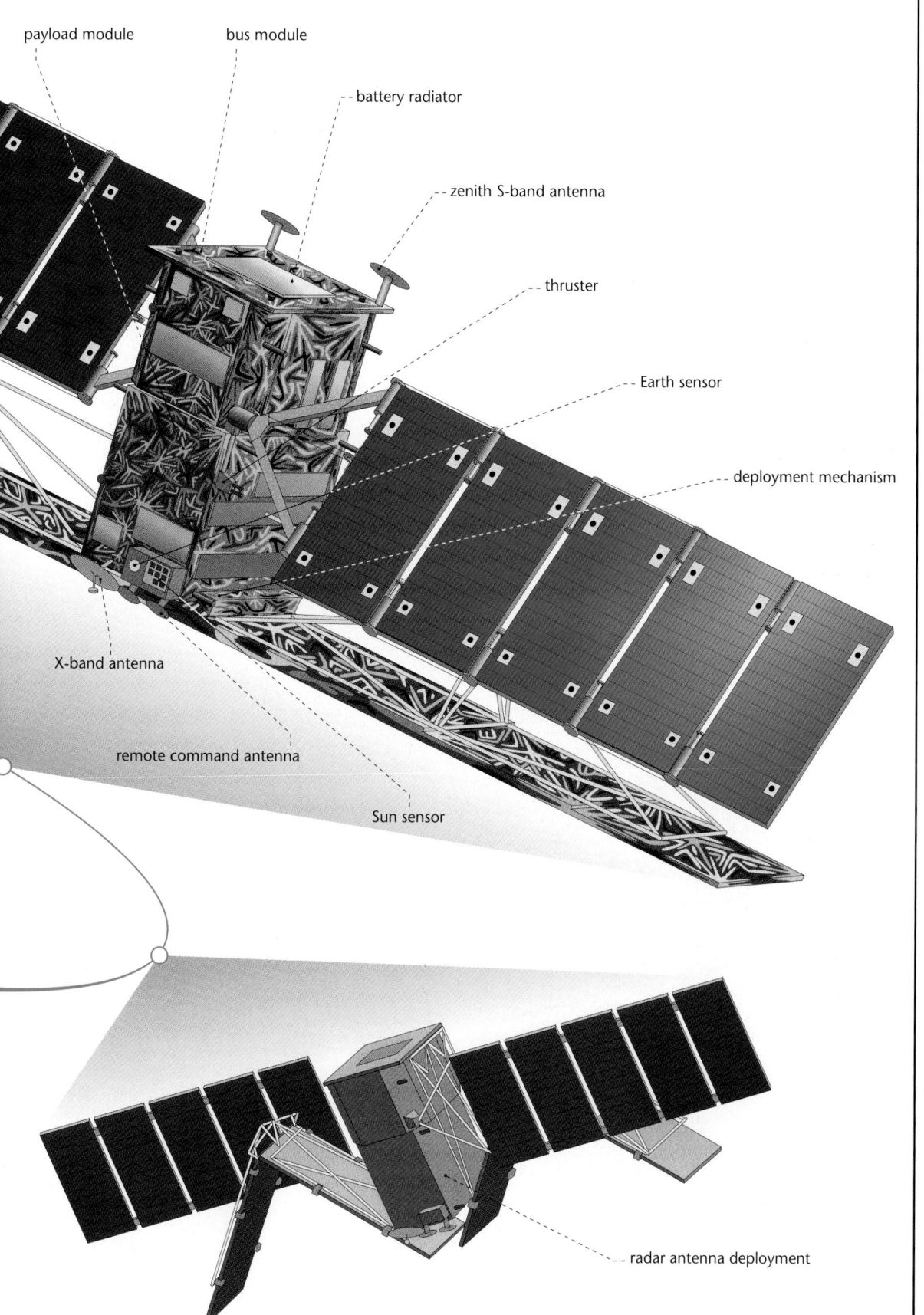

payload module

bus module

battery radiator

zenith S-band antenna

thruster

Earth sensor

deployment mechanism

X-band antenna

remote command antenna

Sun sensor

radar antenna deployment

MAP PROJECTIONS

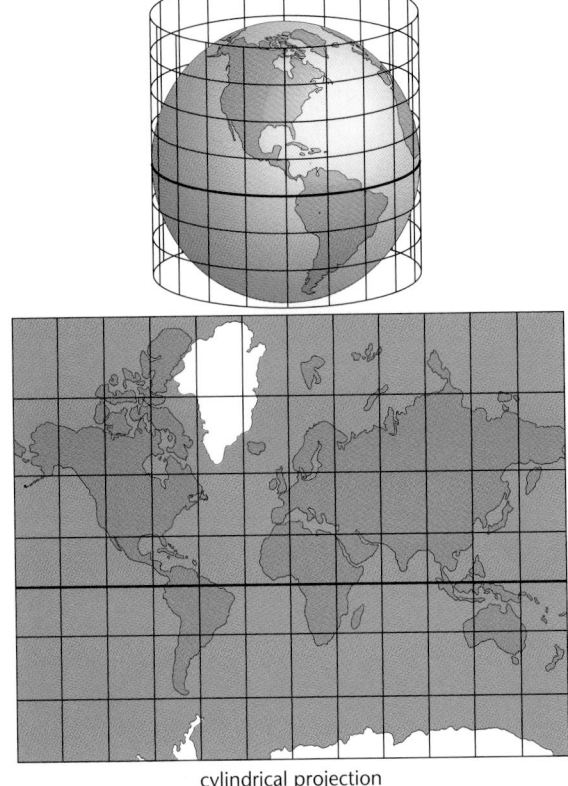

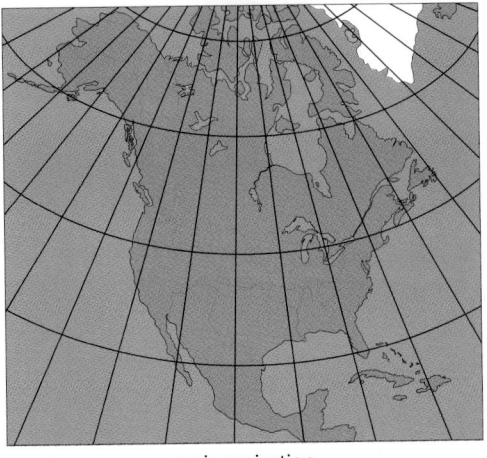

conic projection

cylindrical projection

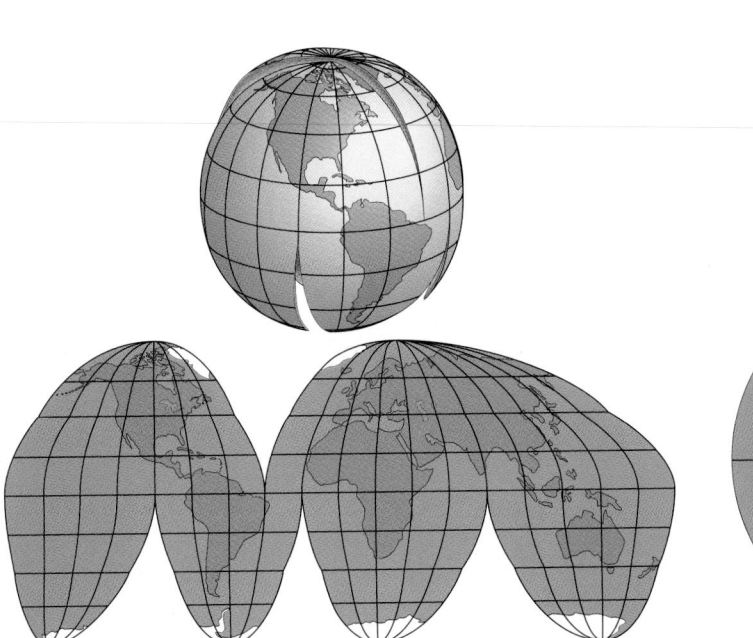

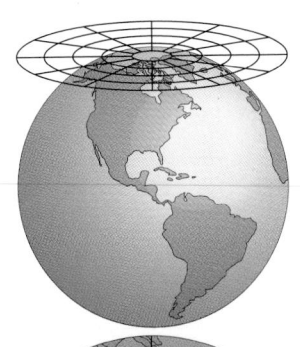

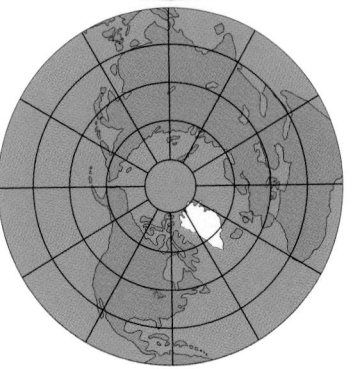

interrupted projection

plane projection

POLITICAL MAP

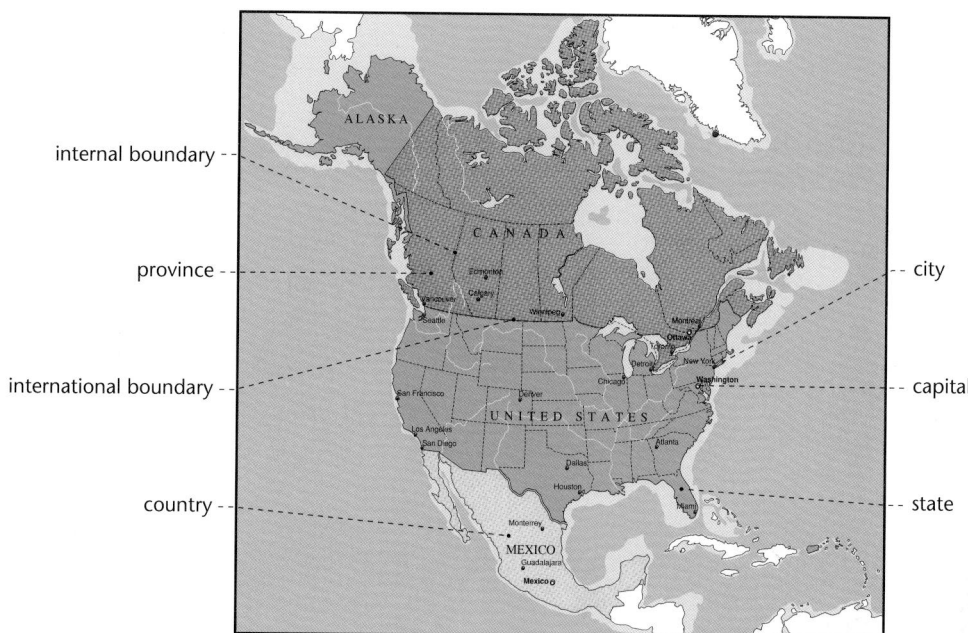

internal boundary
province
international boundary
country
city
capital
state
ALASKA
CANADA
UNITED STATES
MEXICO
Edmonton
Calgary
Vancouver
Seattle
Winnipeg
Montreal
Ottawa
Toronto
Detroit
New York
Washington
Chicago
San Francisco
Denver
Los Angeles
San Diego
Atlanta
Dallas
Houston
Miami
Monterrey
Guadalajara
Mexico

PHYSICAL MAP

mountain range
bay
prairie
mountain mass
ocean
river
river
gulf
sea
strait
island
river estuary
lake
archipelago
peninsula
cape
plateau
isthmus
plain

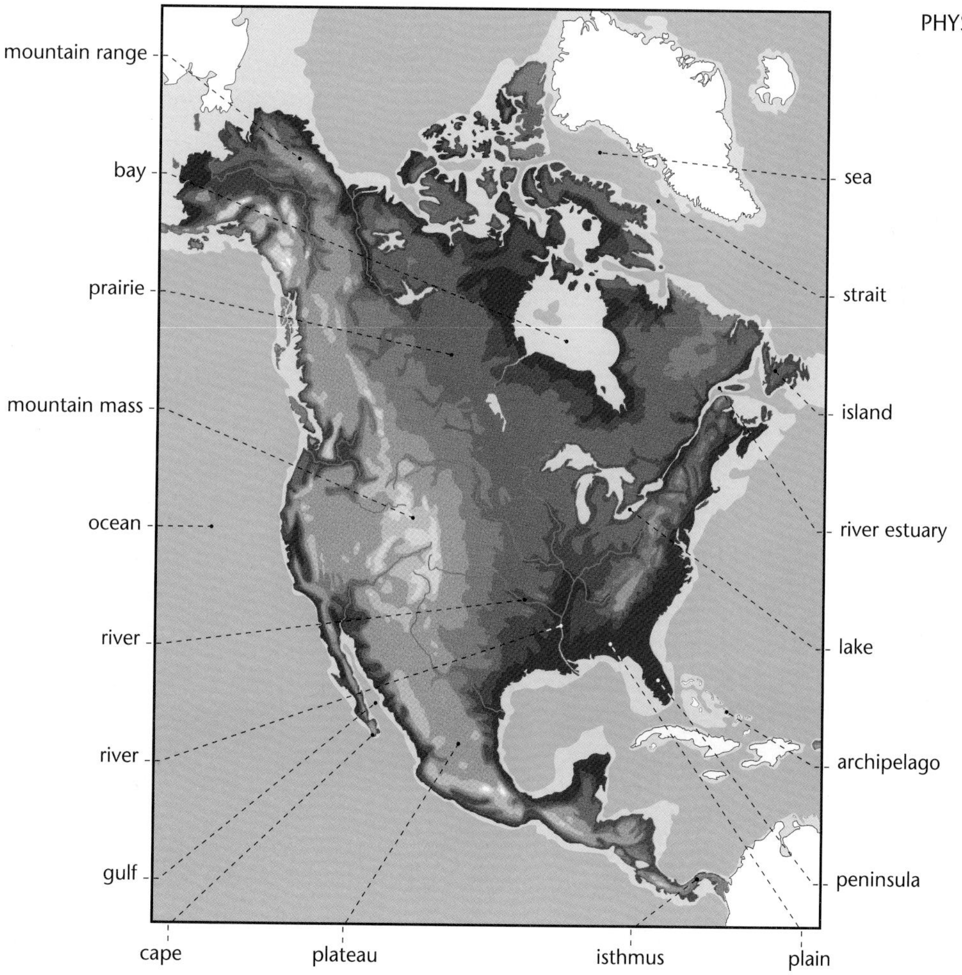

CARTOGRAPHY

URBAN MAP

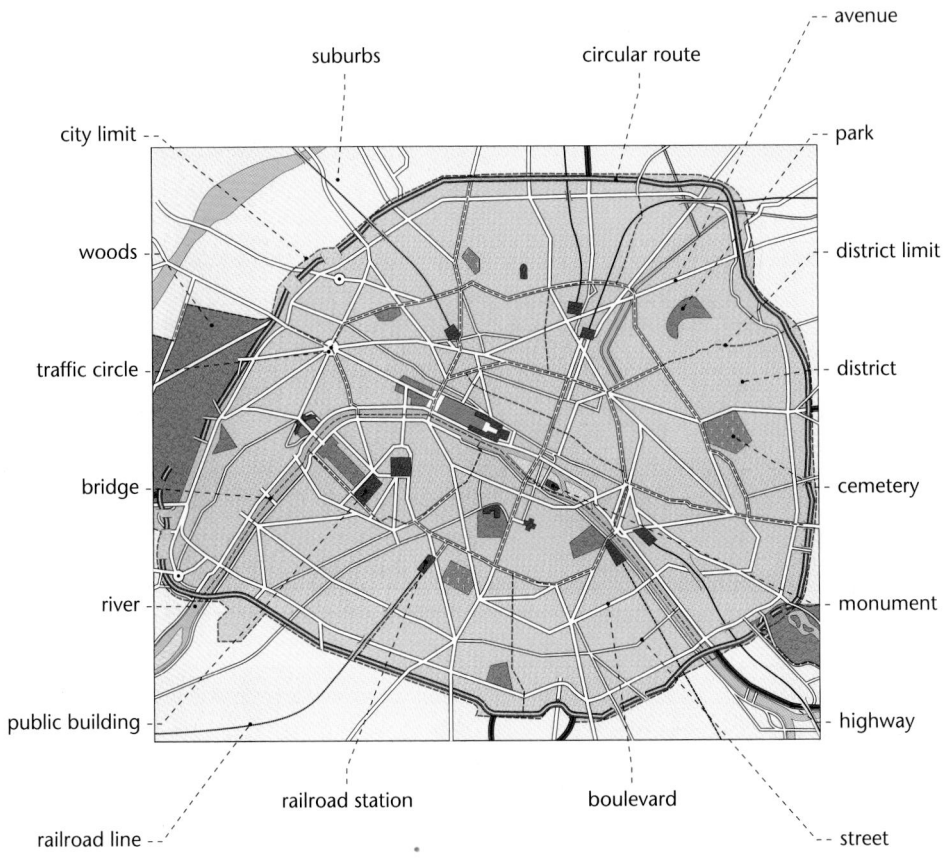

avenue

city limit

suburbs

circular route

park

woods

district limit

traffic circle

district

bridge

cemetery

river

monument

public building

highway

railroad station

boulevard

railroad line

street

ROAD MAP

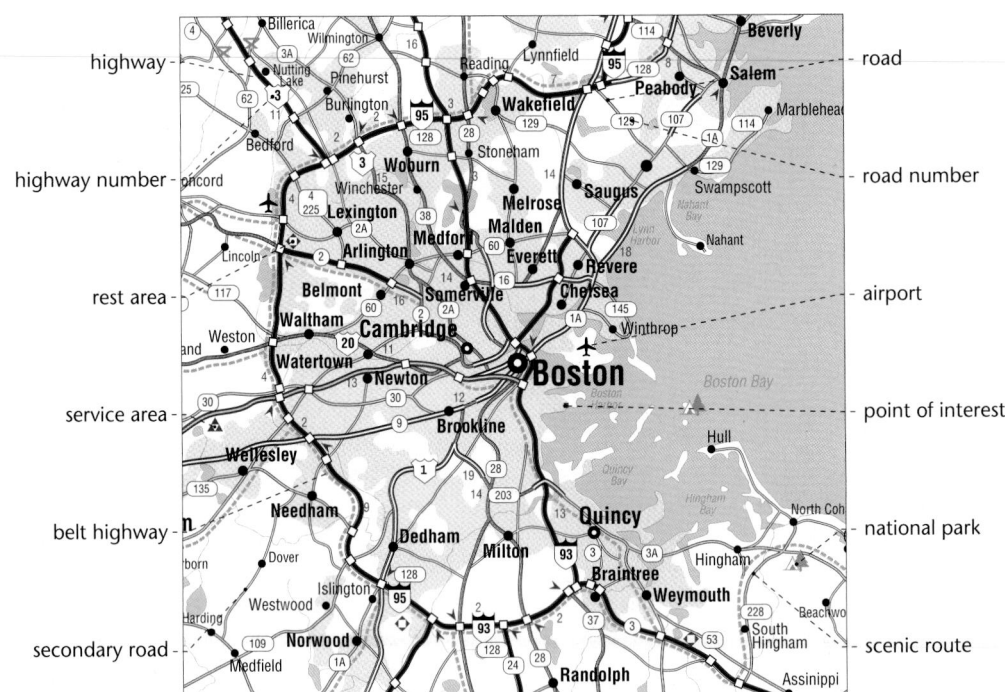

highway

road

highway number

road number

rest area

airport

service area

point of interest

belt highway

national park

secondary road

scenic route

CONTENTS

MUSHROOM 55

TYPES OF LEAVES 56

STRUCTURE OF A PLANT 57

CONIFER 58

STRUCTURE OF A TREE 59

STRUCTURE OF A FLOWER 60

GRAPE 61

FLESHY FRUITS: BERRY FRUITS 62

STONE FLESHY FRUITS 63

POME FLESHY FRUITS 64

FLESHY FRUITS: CITRUS FRUITS 65

DRY FRUITS: NUTS 66

VARIOUS DRY FRUITS 67

TROPICAL FRUITS 68

VEGETABLES 69

HERBS 74

VEGETABLE KINGDOM

54

MUSHROOM

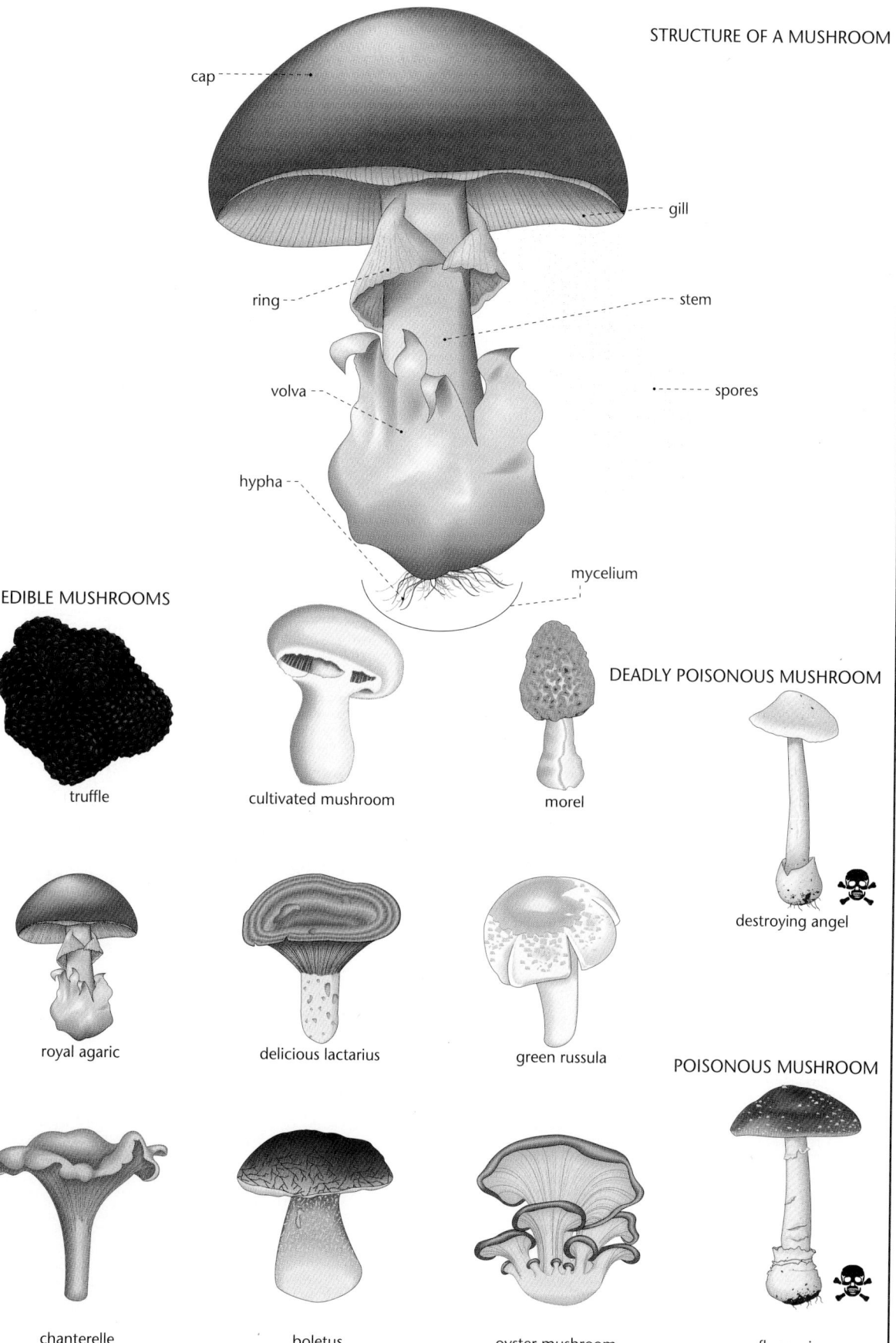

STRUCTURE OF A MUSHROOM

cap

gill

ring

stem

volva

spores

hypha

mycelium

EDIBLE MUSHROOMS

truffle

cultivated mushroom

morel

DEADLY POISONOUS MUSHROOM

destroying angel

royal agaric

delicious lactarius

green russula

POISONOUS MUSHROOM

chanterelle

boletus

oyster mushroom

fly agaric

55

TYPES OF LEAVES

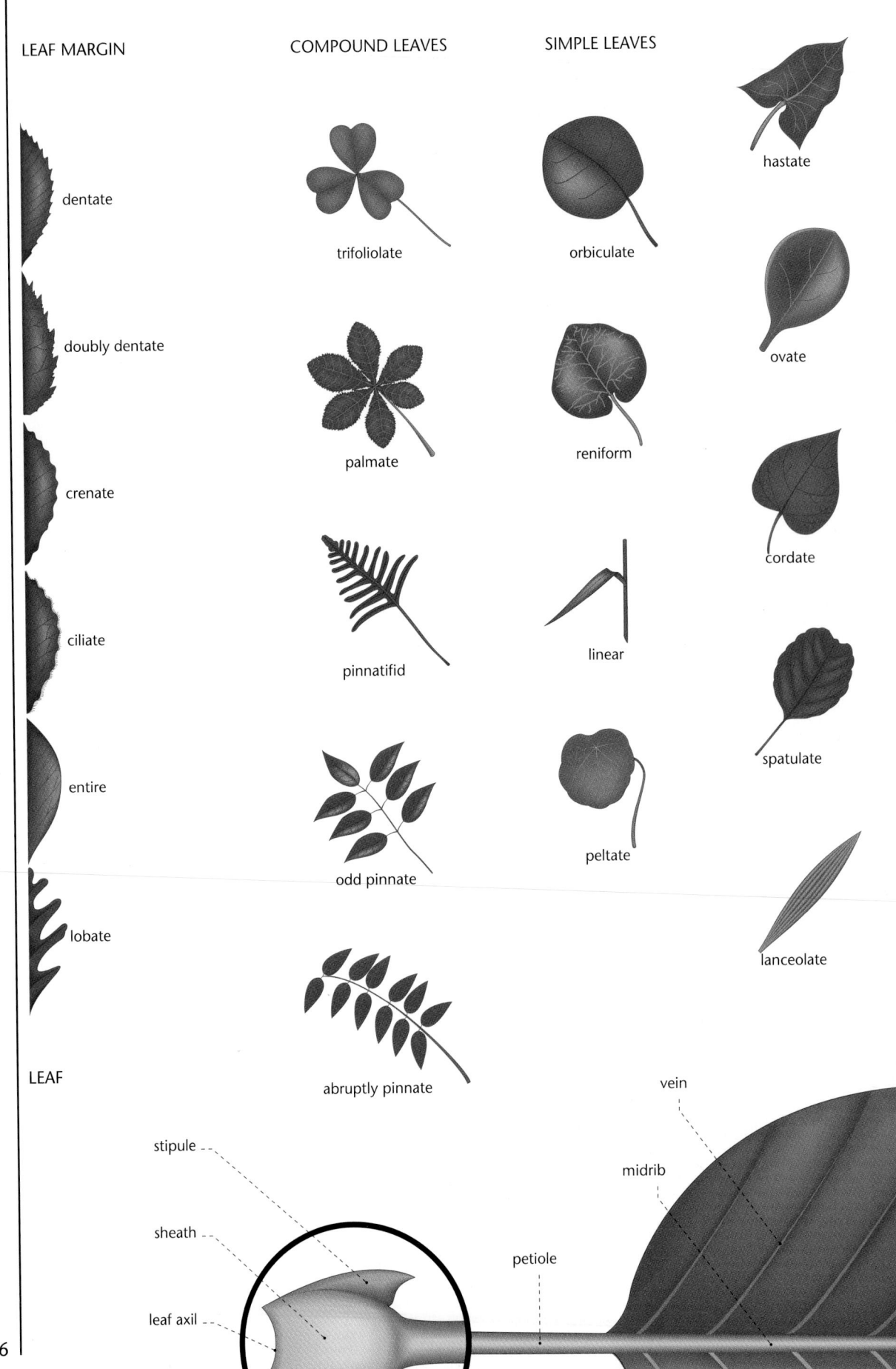

LEAF MARGIN

dentate

doubly dentate

crenate

ciliate

entire

lobate

LEAF

COMPOUND LEAVES

trifoliolate

palmate

pinnatifid

odd pinnate

abruptly pinnate

SIMPLE LEAVES

orbiculate

reniform

linear

peltate

hastate

ovate

cordate

spatulate

lanceolate

stipule

sheath

leaf axil

petiole

vein

midrib

STRUCTURE OF A PLANT

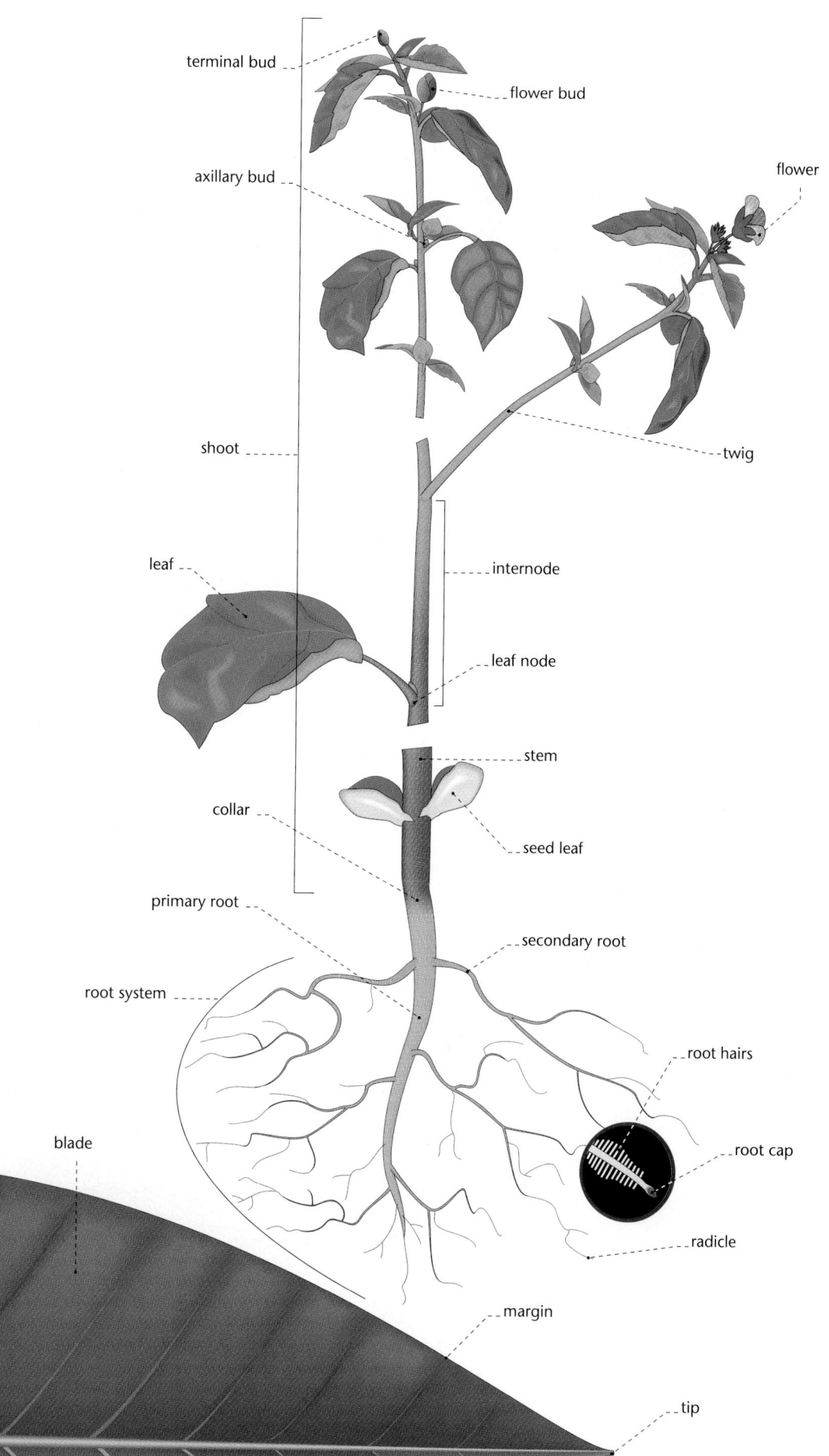

terminal bud

flower bud

axillary bud

flower

shoot

twig

internode

leaf

leaf node

stem

collar

seed leaf

primary root

secondary root

root system

root hairs

blade

root cap

radicle

margin

tip

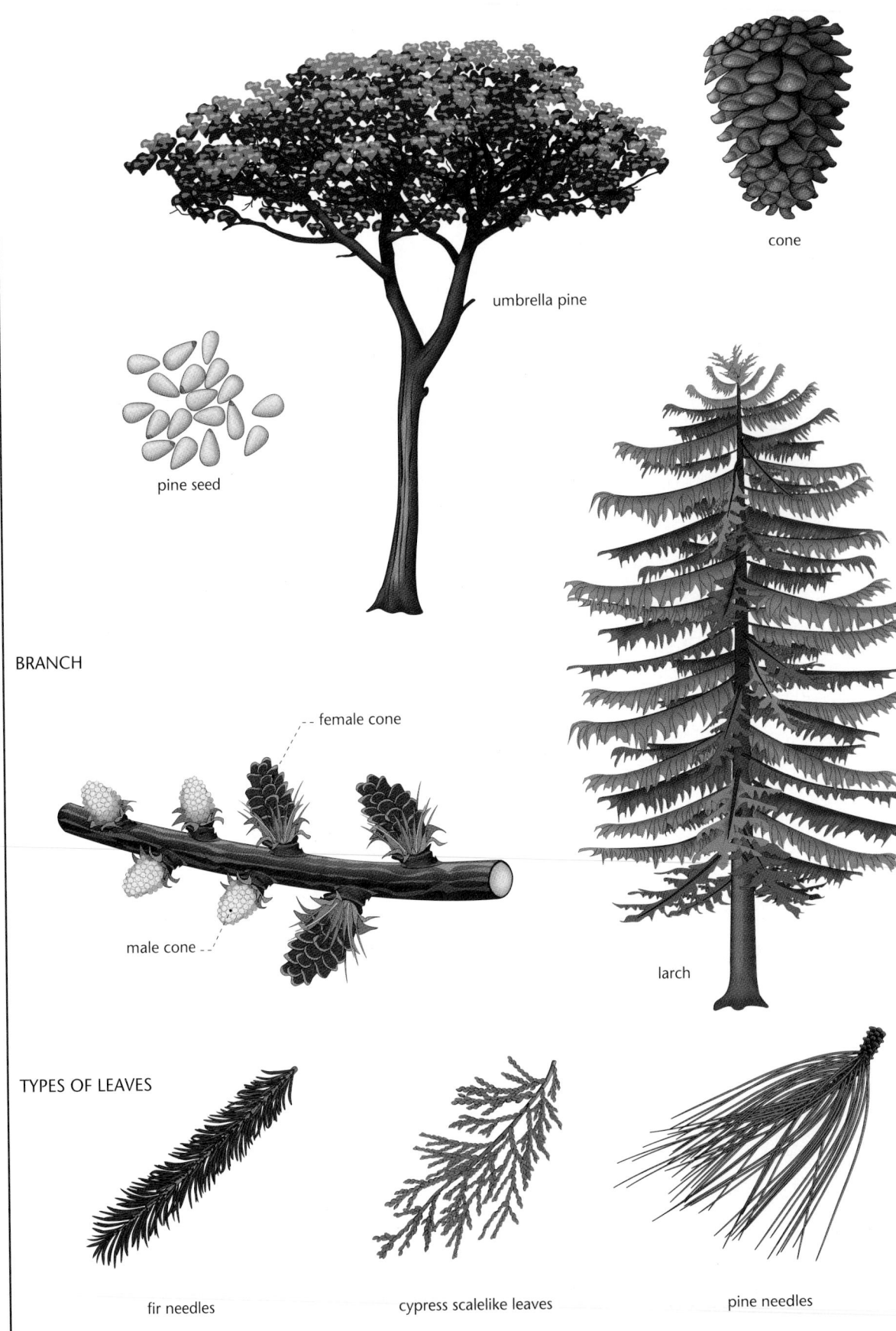

cone

umbrella pine

pine seed

BRANCH

female cone

male cone

larch

TYPES OF LEAVES

fir needles

cypress scalelike leaves

pine needles

STRUCTURE OF A TREE

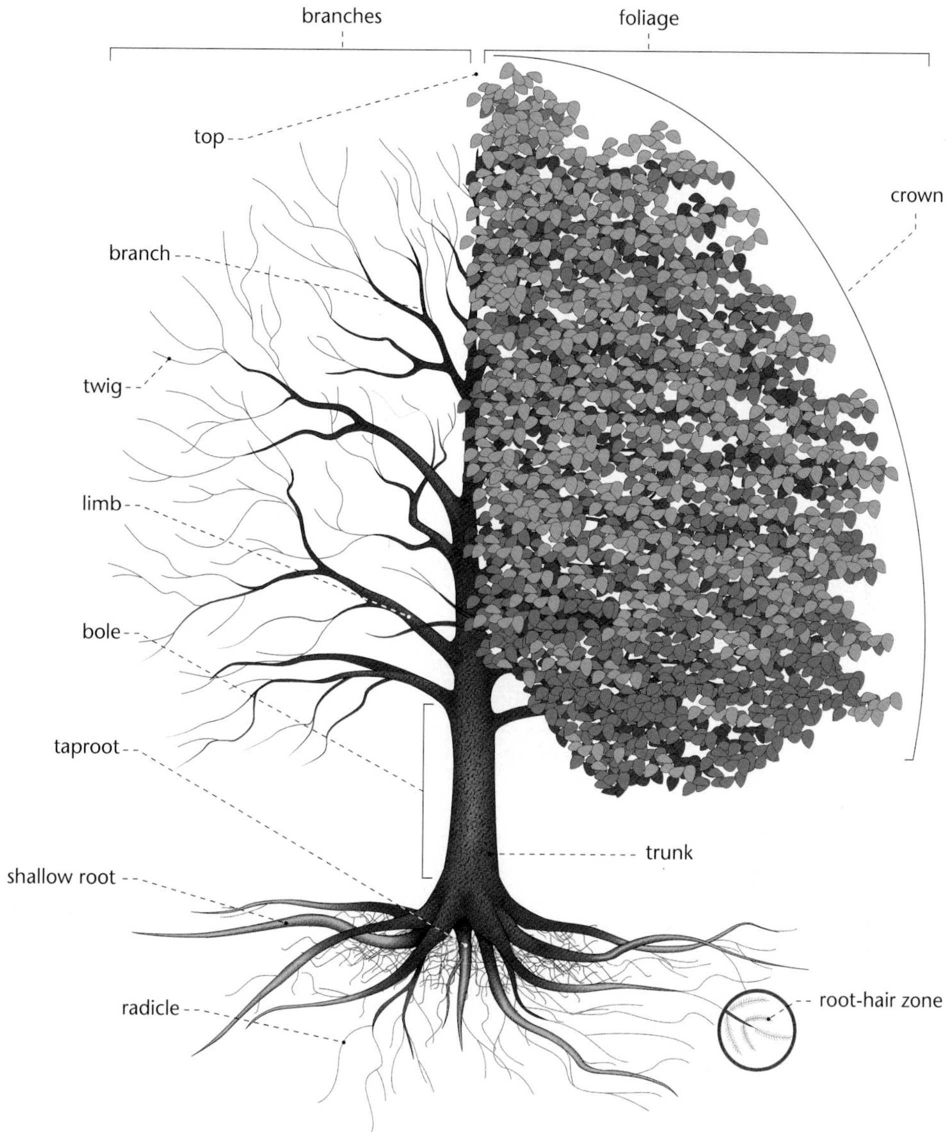

branches

foliage

top

crown

branch

twig

limb

bole

taproot

trunk

shallow root

radicle

root-hair zone

CROSS SECTION OF A TRUNK

wood ray

pith

annual ring

bark

heartwood

phloem

sapwood

cambium

STUMP

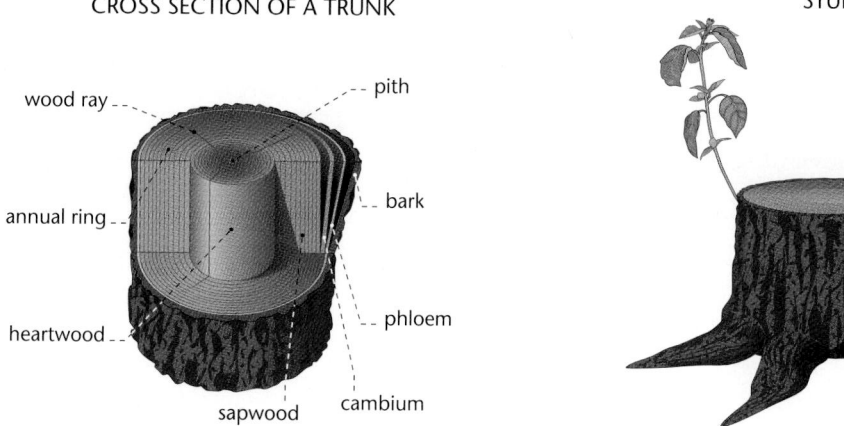

shoot

STRUCTURE OF A FLOWER

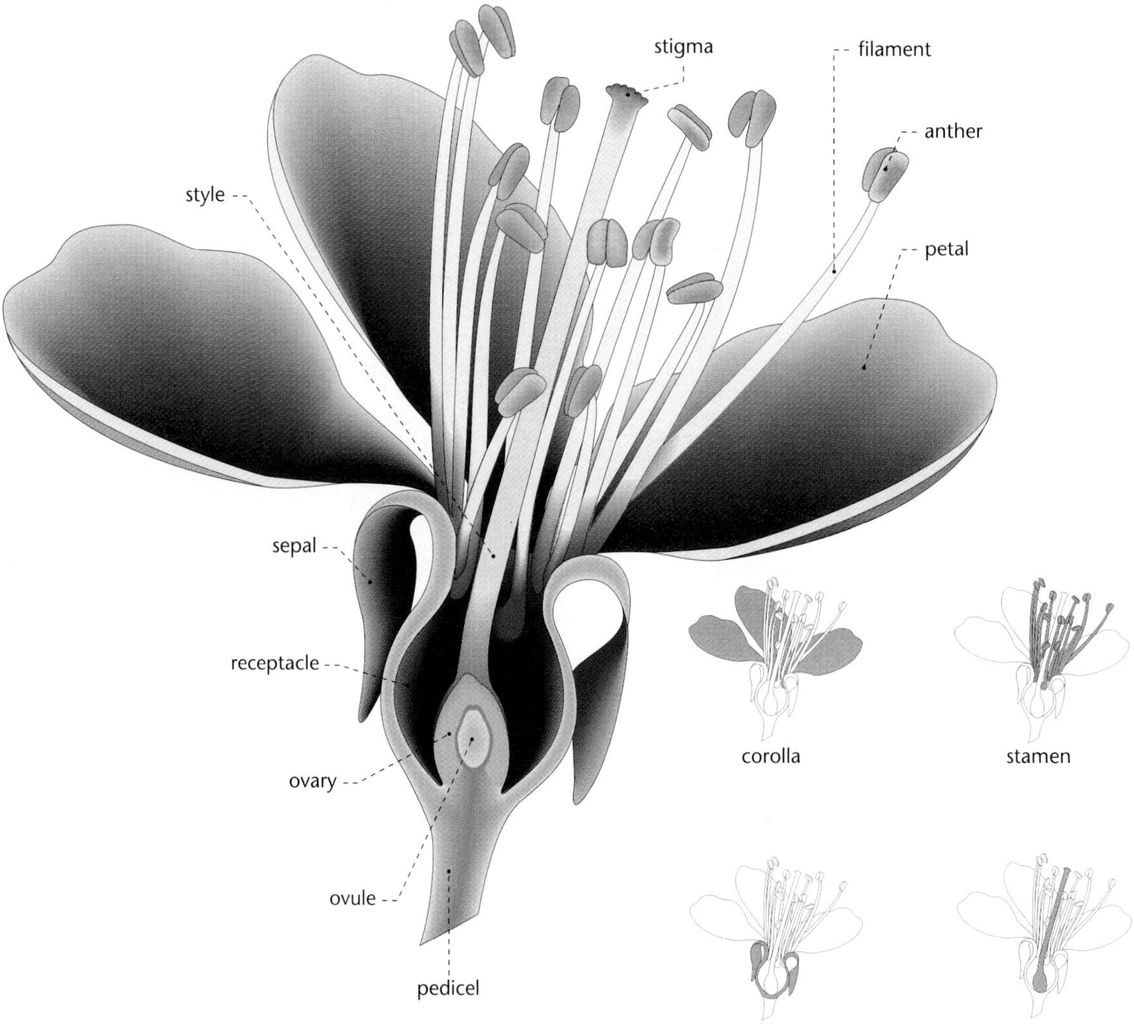

stigma

filament

anther

style

petal

sepal

receptacle

ovary

ovule

pedicel

corolla

stamen

calyx

pistil

TYPES OF INFLORESCENCES

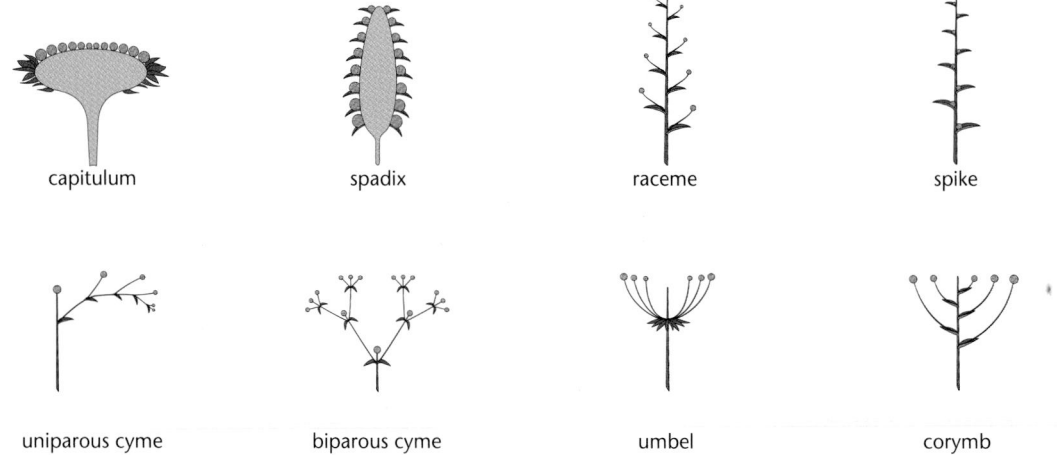

capitulum

spadix

raceme

spike

uniparous cyme

biparous cyme

umbel

corymb

GRAPE

VINE STOCK

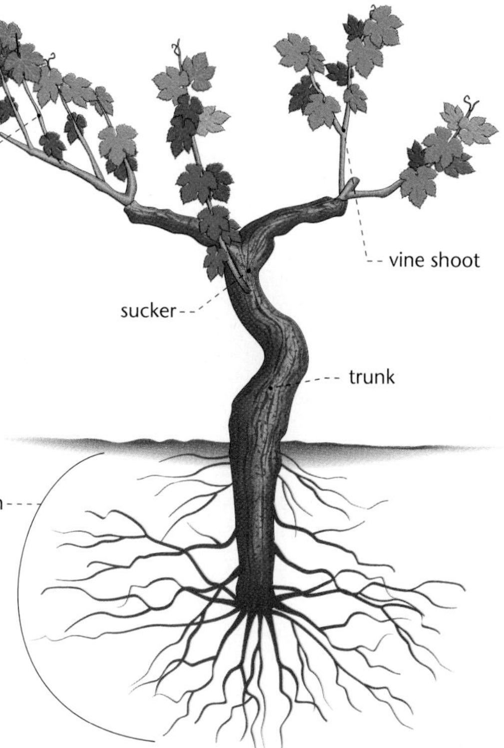

fruit branch

vine shoot

sucker

trunk

root system

MATURING STEPS

flowering

fruition

ripening

ripeness

BUNCH OF GRAPES

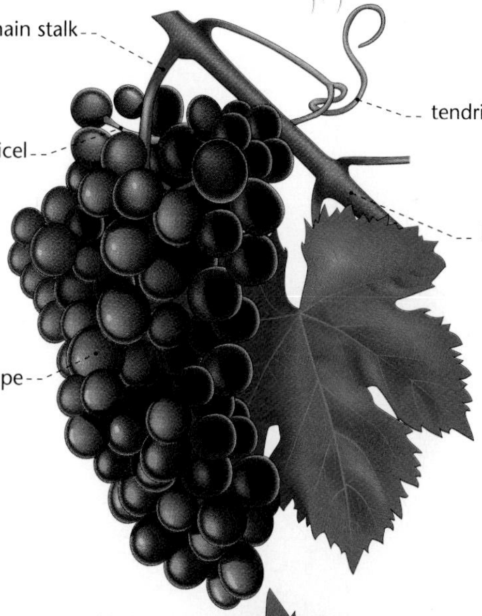

main stalk

tendril

pedicel

branch

grape

GRAPE LEAF

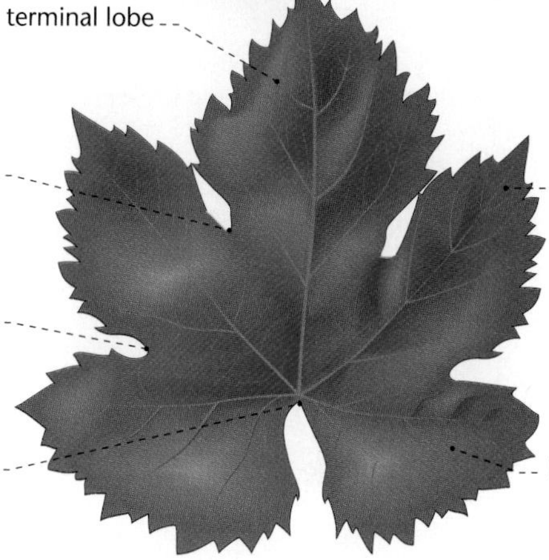

terminal lobe

upper lateral sinus

upper lateral lobe

lower lateral sinus

petiolar sinus

lower lateral lobe

FLESHY FRUITS: BERRY FRUITS

SECTION OF A BERRY

MAJOR TYPES OF BERRIES

GRAPE

usual terms   technical terms

style

skin   exocarp

pip   seed

flesh   mesocarp

funiculus

stalk

pedicel

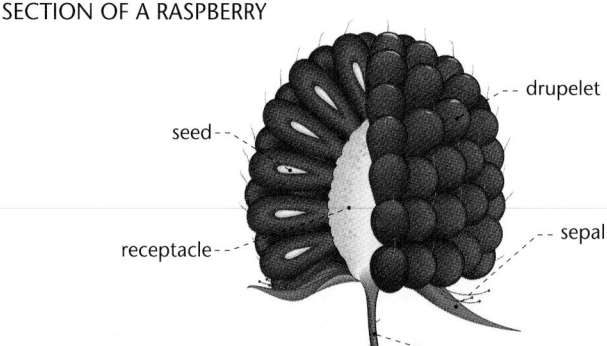

SECTION OF A RASPBERRY

drupelet

seed

receptacle   sepal

pedicel

SECTION OF A STRAWBERRY

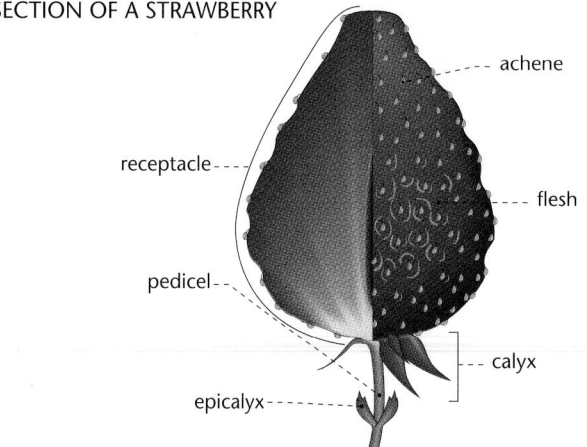

achene

receptacle

flesh

pedicel

calyx

epicalyx

black currant

currant

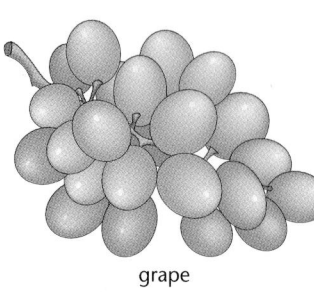

grape

gooseberry

blueberry

huckleberry

cranberry

62

STONE FLESHY FRUITS

SECTION OF A STONE FRUIT

PEACH

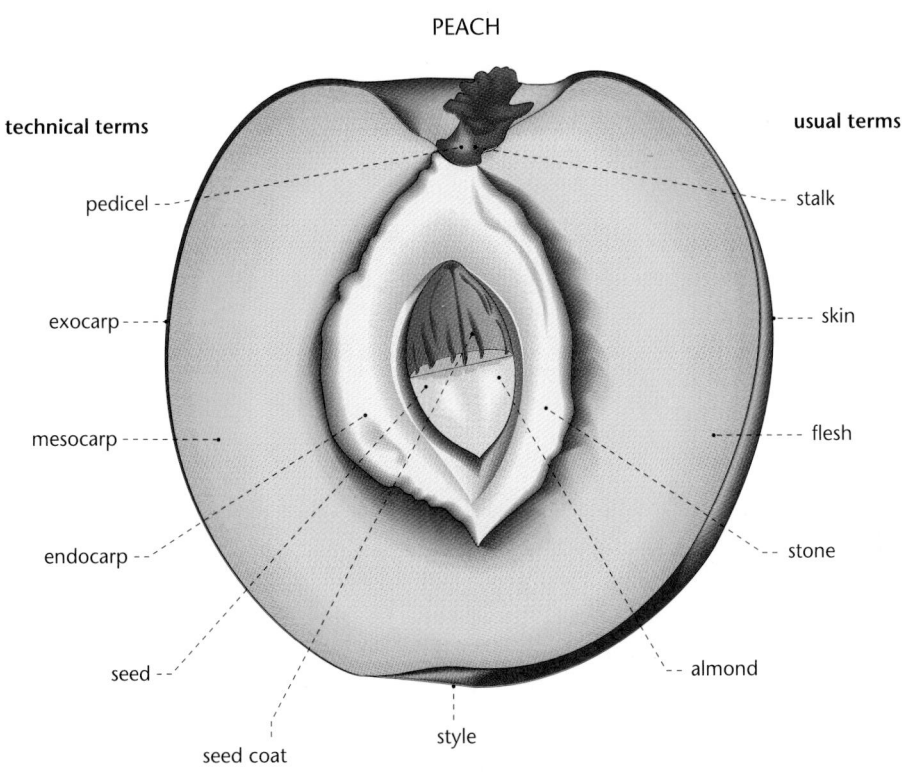

technical terms

usual terms

pedicel --- --- stalk

exocarp --- --- skin

mesocarp --- --- flesh

endocarp --- --- stone

seed ---

seed coat

style

--- almond

MAJOR TYPES OF STONE FRUITS

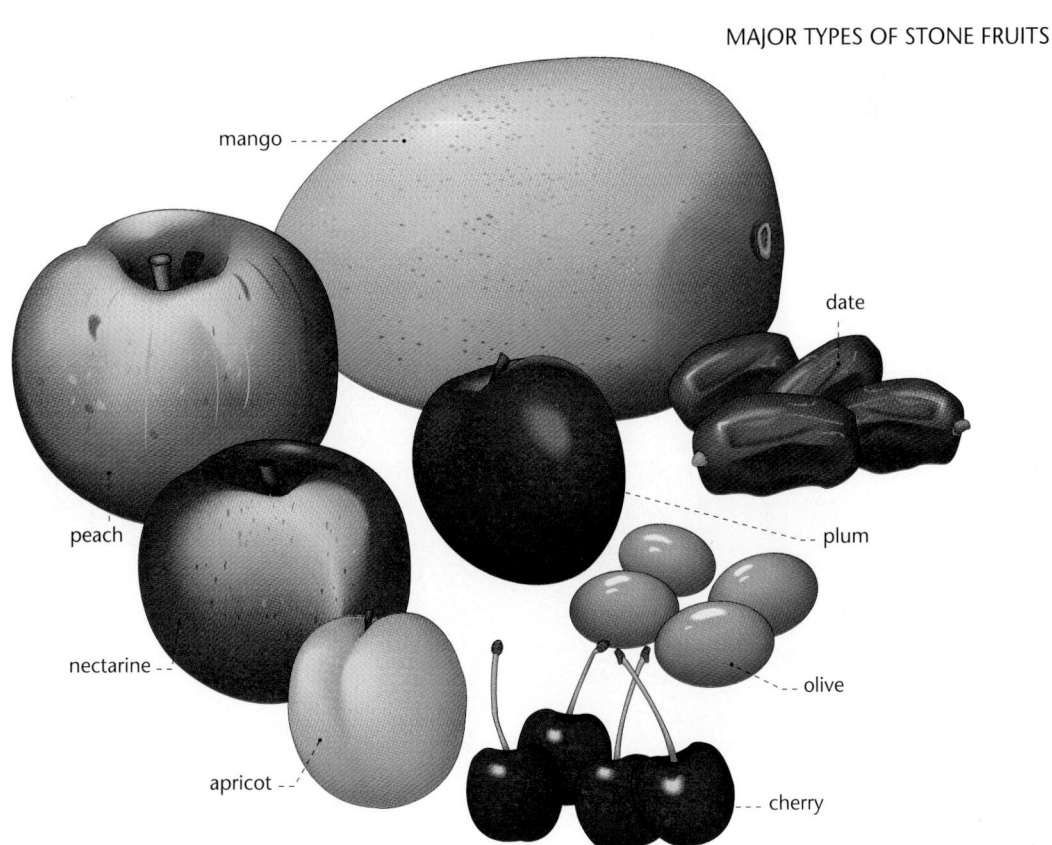

mango ---

date

peach

plum

nectarine ---

olive

apricot ---

cherry

63

VEGETABLE KINGDOM

SECTION OF A POME FRUIT

APPLE

technical terms   **usual terms**

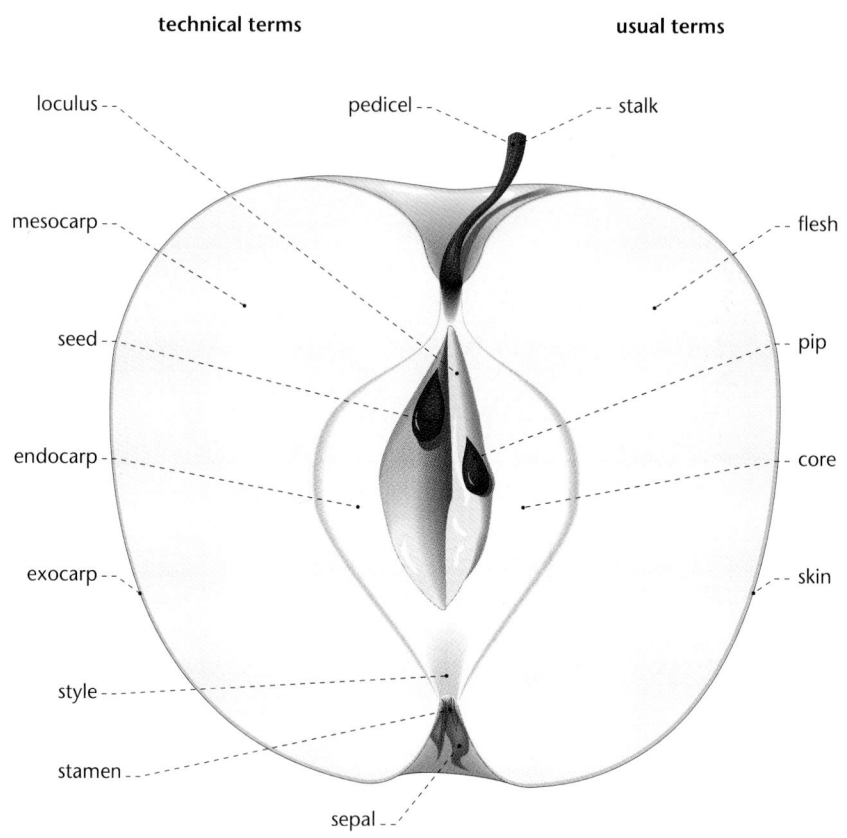

loculus

mesocarp

seed

endocarp

exocarp

style

stamen

sepal

pedicel

stalk

flesh

pip

core

skin

MAJOR TYPES OF POME FRUITS

pear

quince

apple

Japan plum

FLESHY FRUITS: CITRUS FRUITS

SECTION OF A CITRUS FRUIT

ORANGE

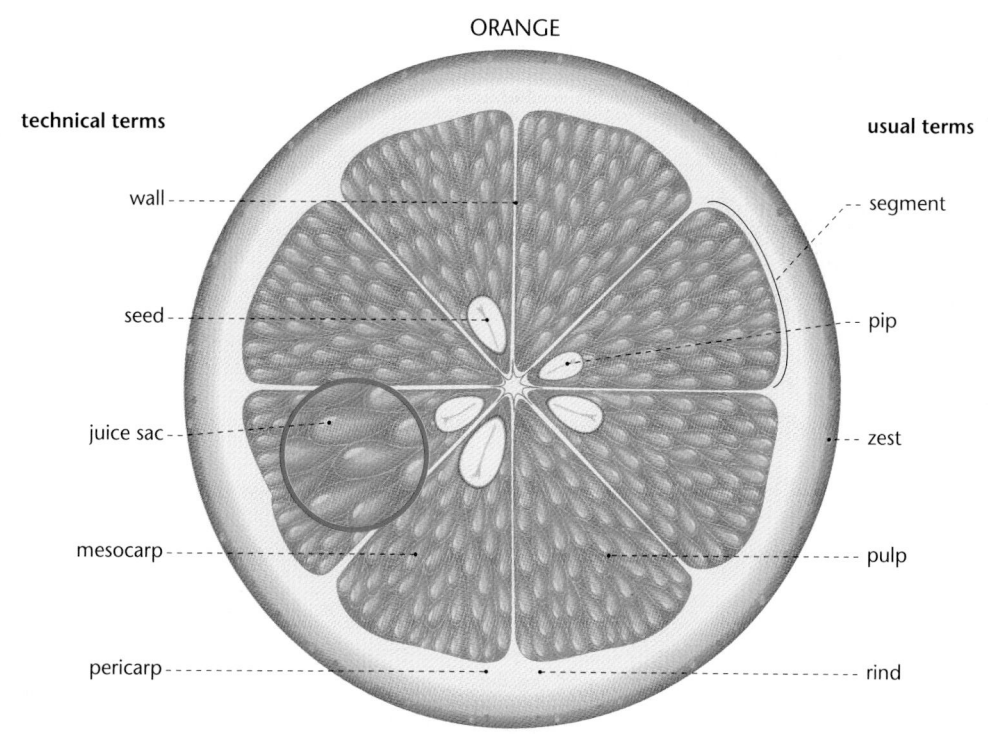

technical terms

wall

seed

juice sac

mesocarp

pericarp

usual terms

segment

pip

zest

pulp

rind

MAJOR TYPES OF CITRUS FRUITS

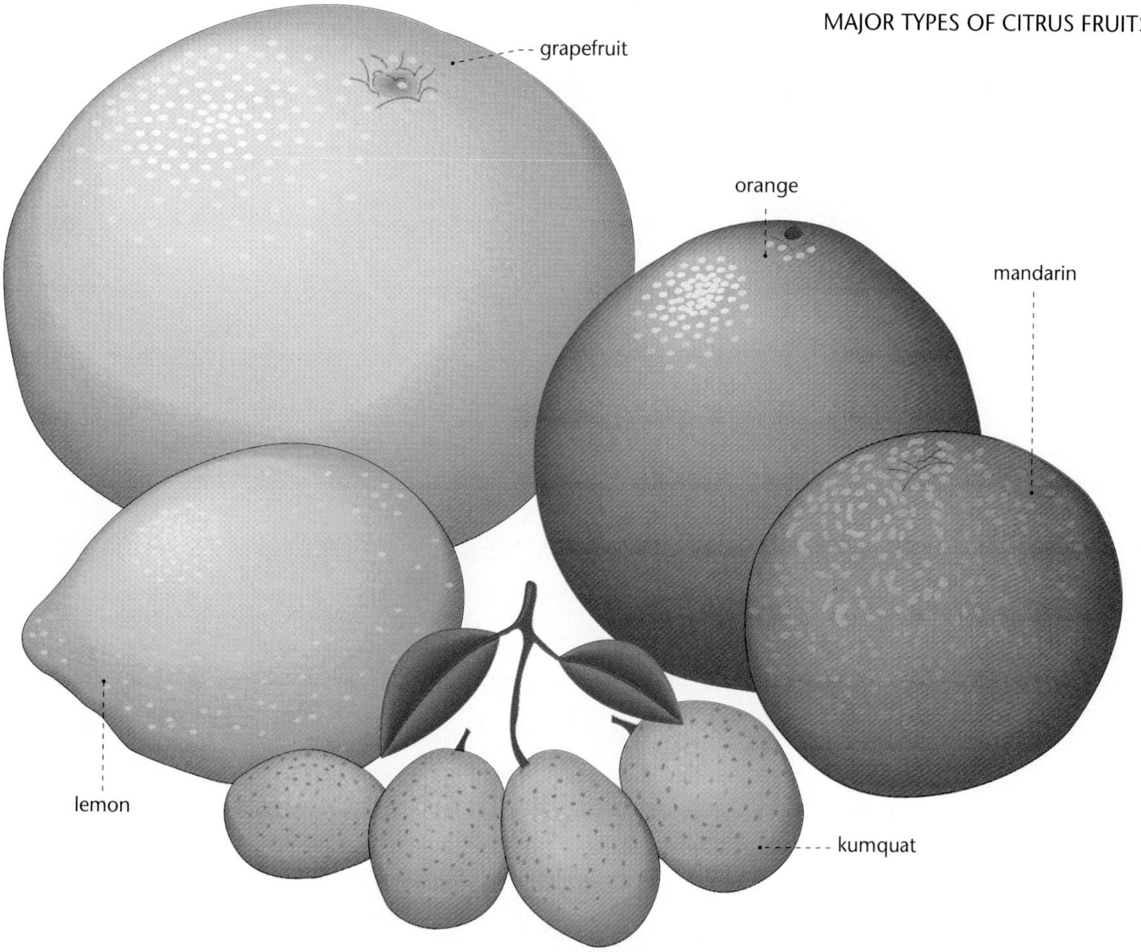

grapefruit

orange

mandarin

lemon

kumquat

VEGETABLE KINGDOM

SECTION OF A HAZELNUT

SECTION OF A WALNUT

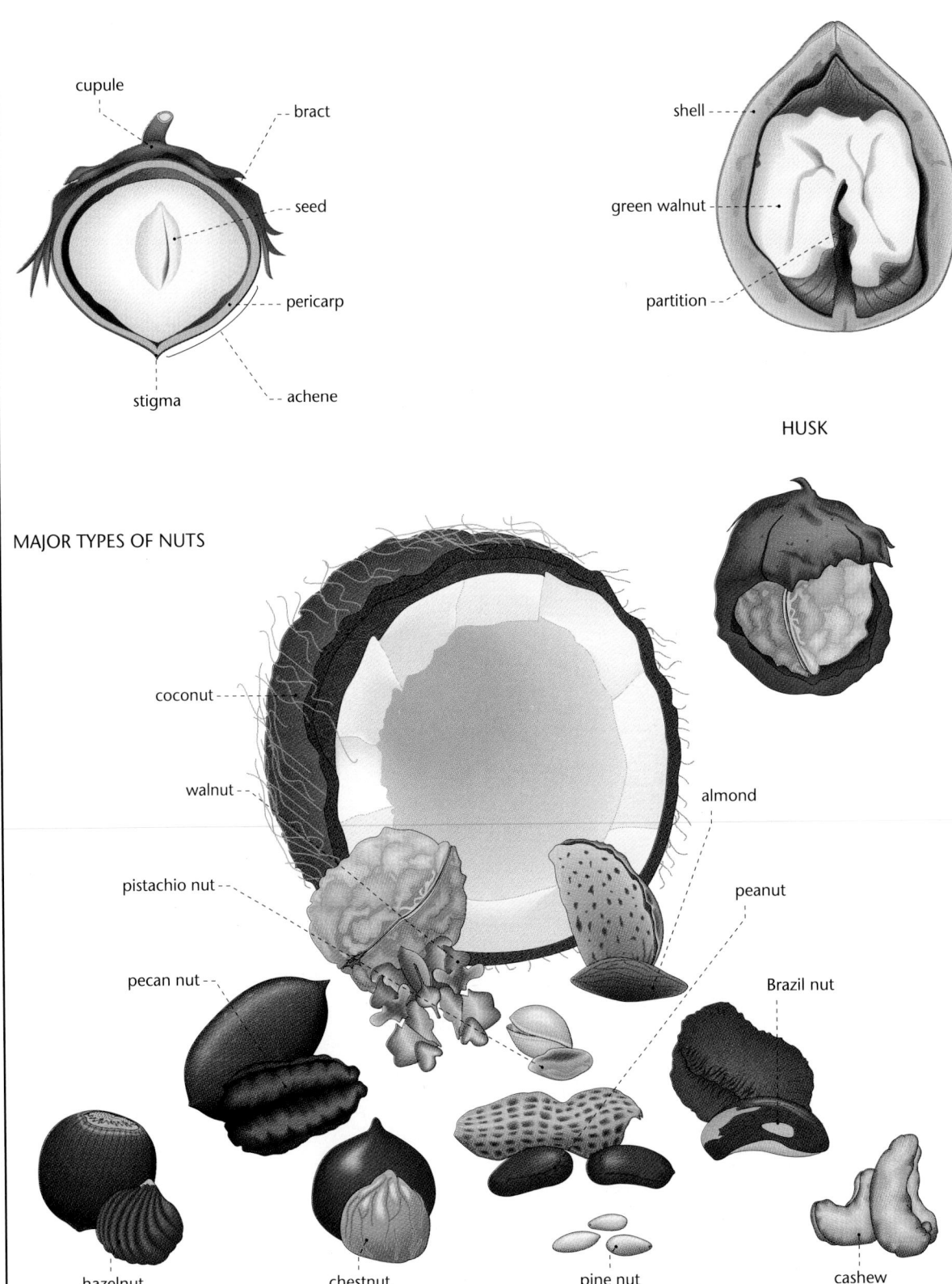

cupule

bract

seed

pericarp

achene

stigma

shell

green walnut

partition

HUSK

MAJOR TYPES OF NUTS

coconut

walnut

pistachio nut

pecan nut

hazelnut

chestnut

almond

peanut

Brazil nut

pine nut

cashew

VARIOUS DRY FRUITS

SECTION OF A FOLLICLE

star anise

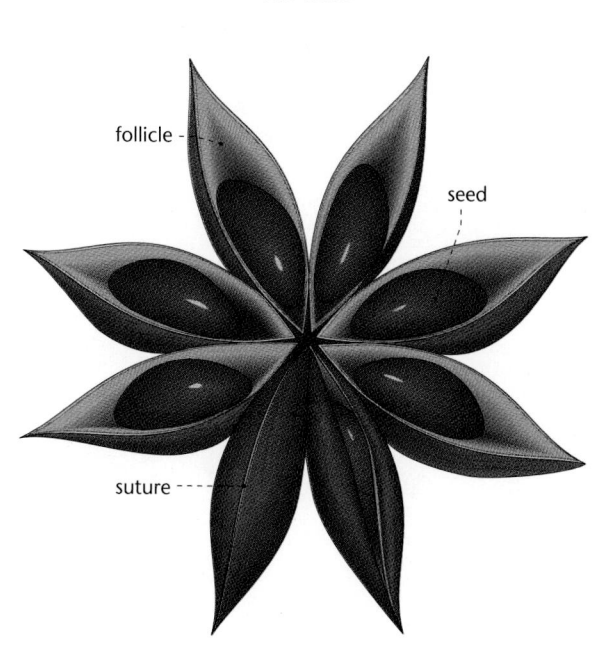

follicle

seed

suture

SECTION OF A SILIQUE

mustard

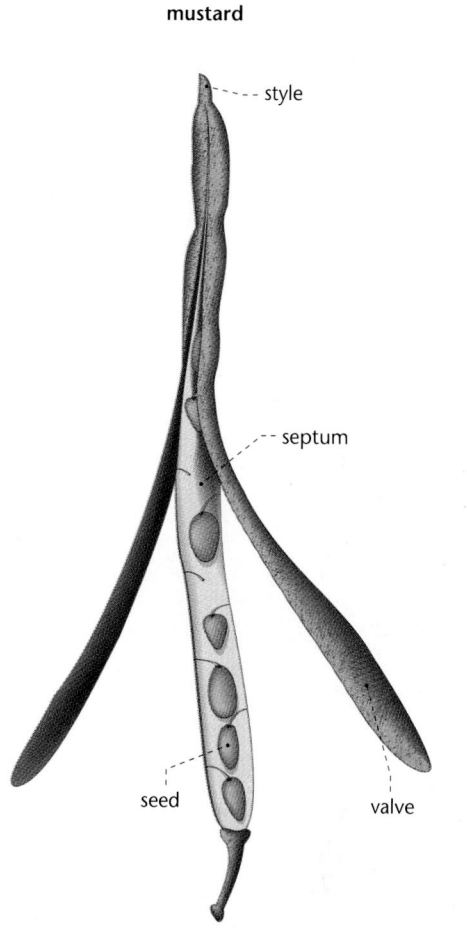

style

septum

seed

valve

SECTION OF A LEGUME

pea

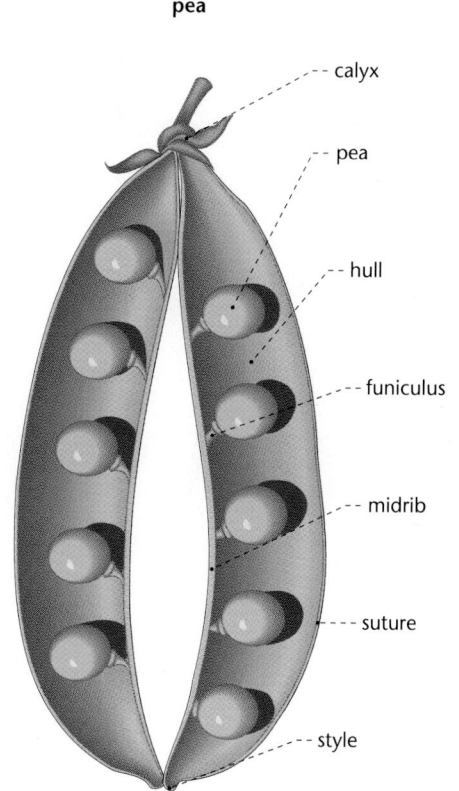

calyx

pea

hull

funiculus

midrib

suture

style

SECTION OF A CAPSULE

poppy

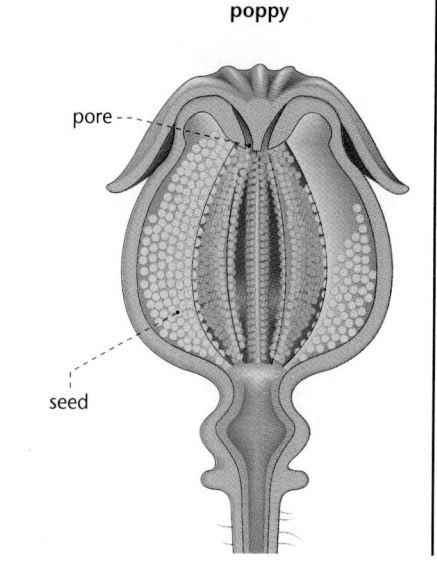

pore

seed

67

VEGETABLE KINGDOM

MAJOR TYPES OF TROPICAL FRUITS

litchi

Japanese persimmon

papaya

banana

kiwi

pomegranate

cherimoya

Indian fig

avocado

guava

pineapple

VEGETABLES

FRUIT VEGETABLES

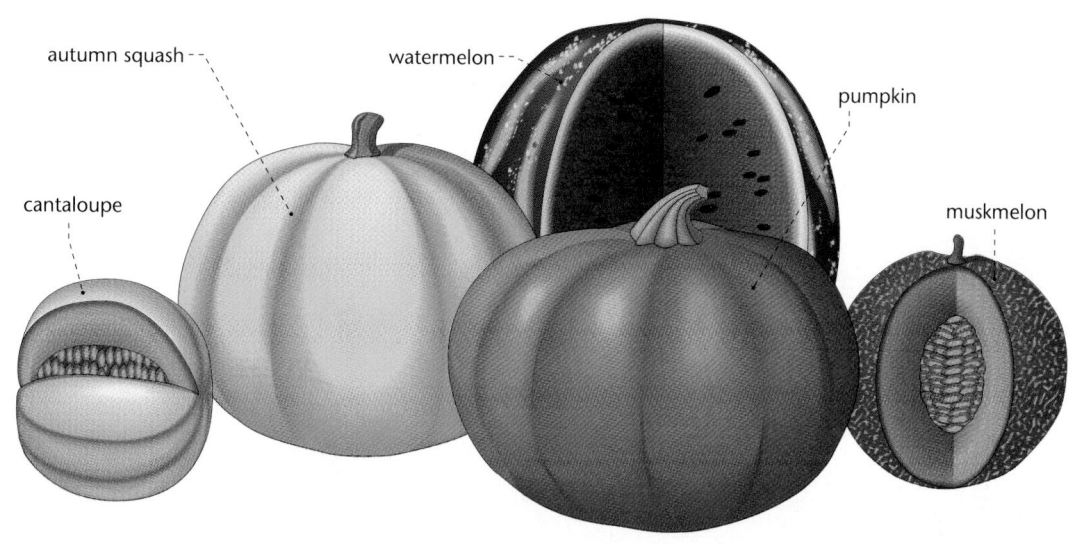

autumn squash

watermelon

pumpkin

cantaloupe

muskmelon

summer squash

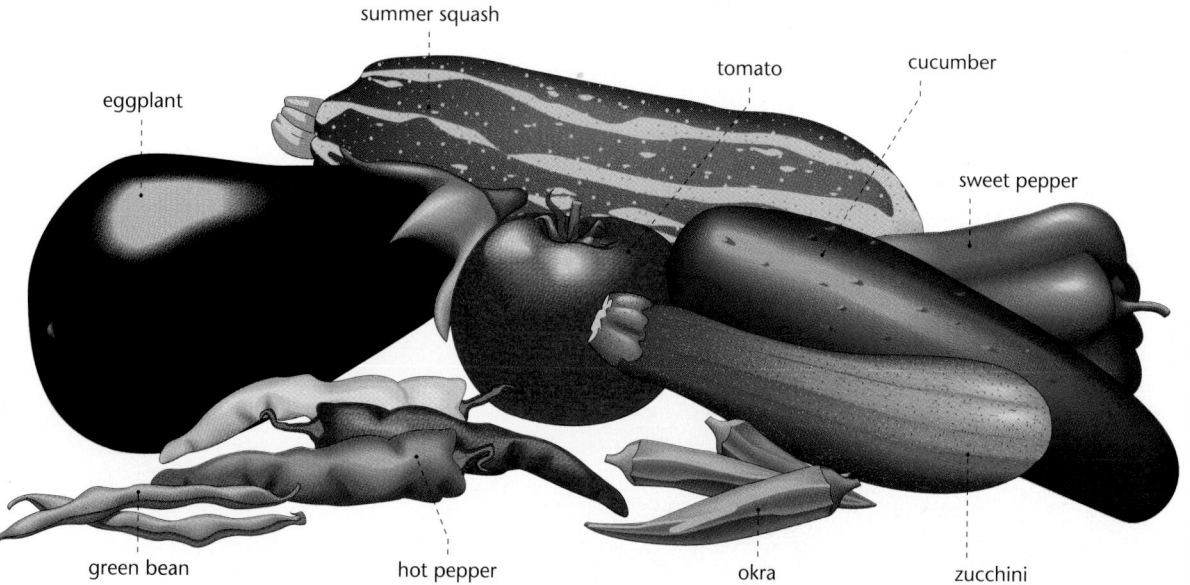

eggplant

tomato

cucumber

sweet pepper

green bean

hot pepper

okra

zucchini

INFLORESCENT VEGETABLES

broccoli

cauliflower

artichoke

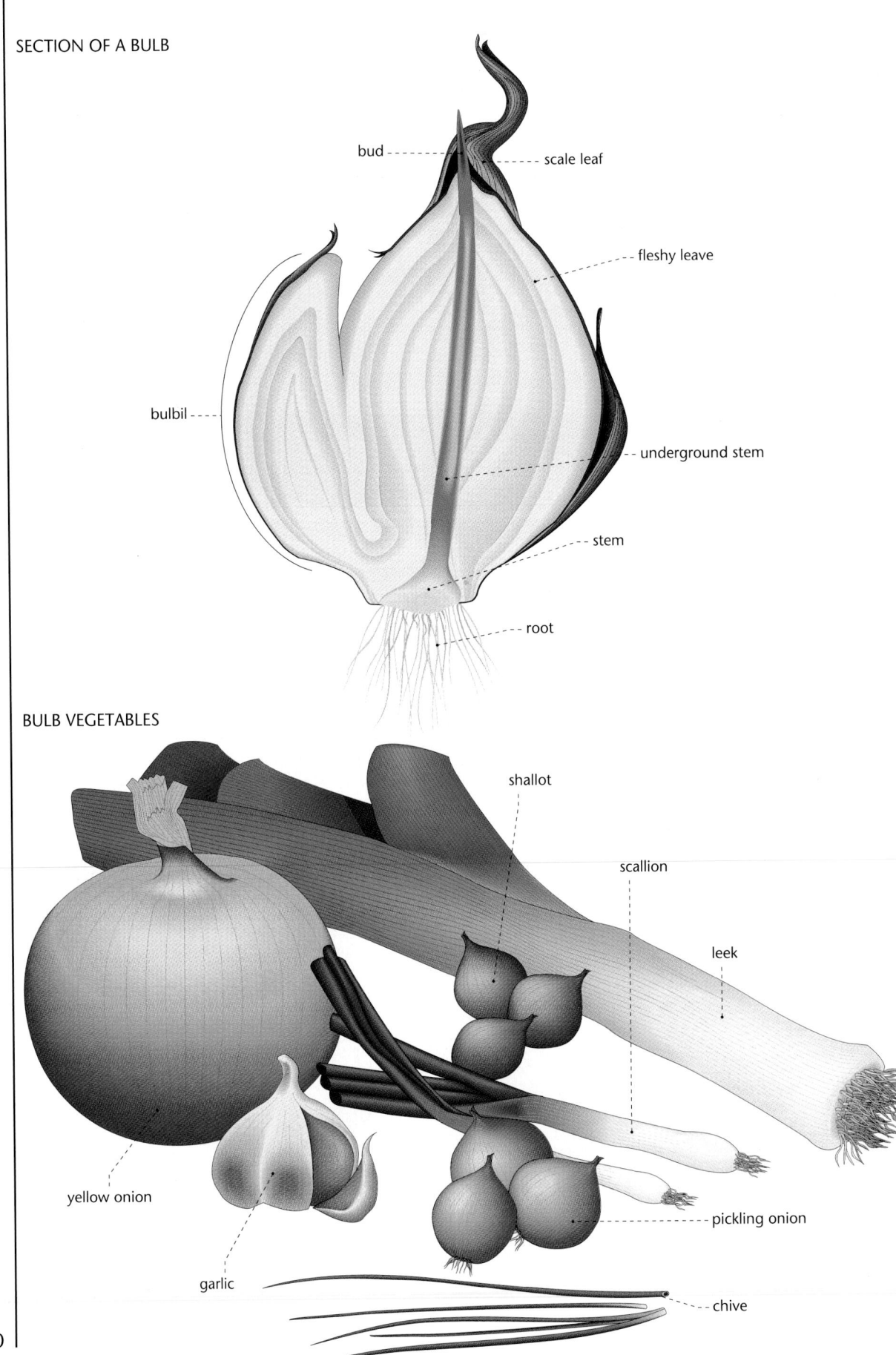

SECTION OF A BULB

bud
scale leaf
fleshy leave
bulbil
underground stem
stem
root

BULB VEGETABLES

shallot
scallion
leek
yellow onion
garlic
pickling onion
chive

VEGETABLES

TUBER VEGETABLES

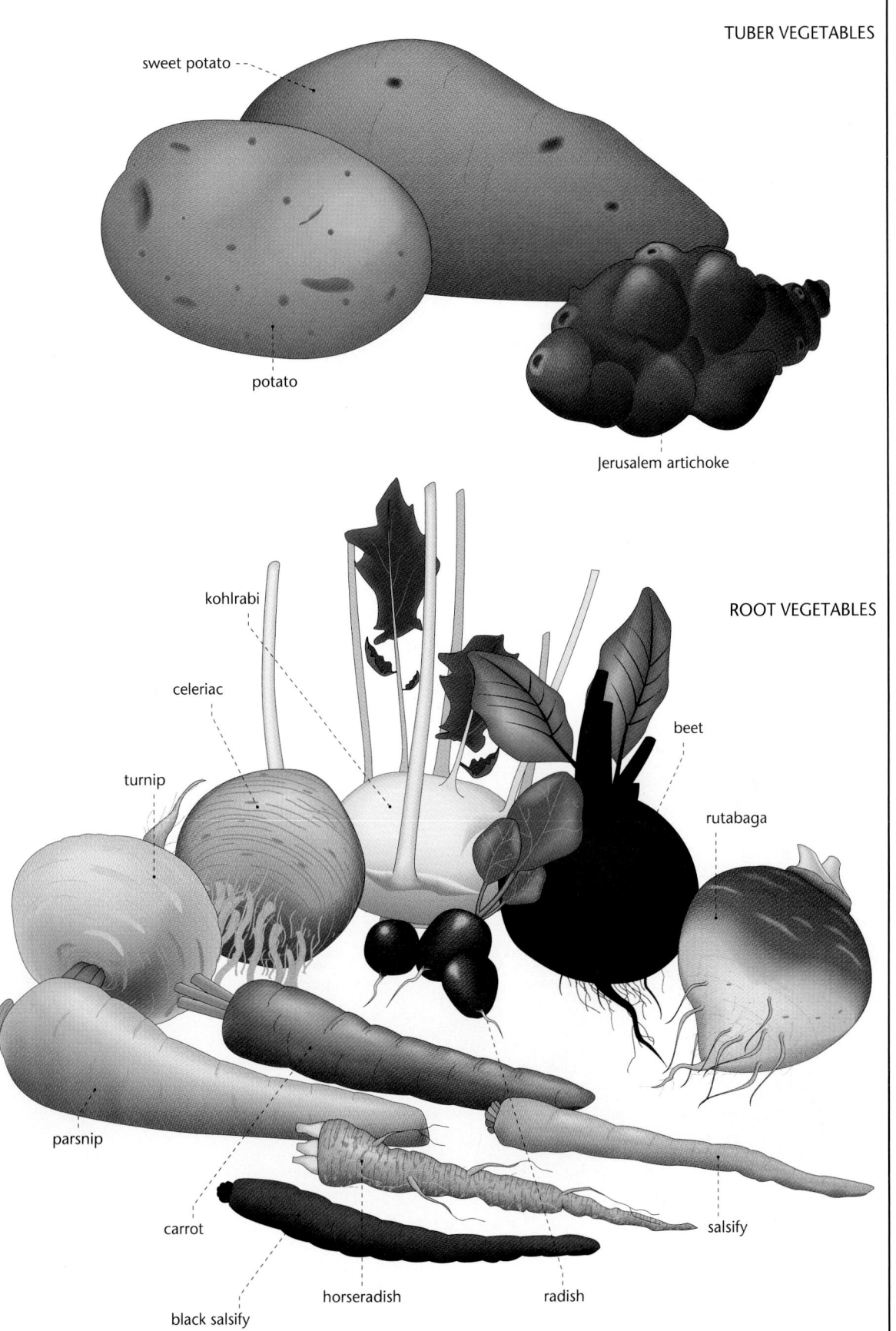

sweet potato

potato

Jerusalem artichoke

ROOT VEGETABLES

kohlrabi

celeriac

turnip

beet

rutabaga

parsnip

carrot

black salsify

horseradish

radish

salsify

VEGETABLE KINGDOM

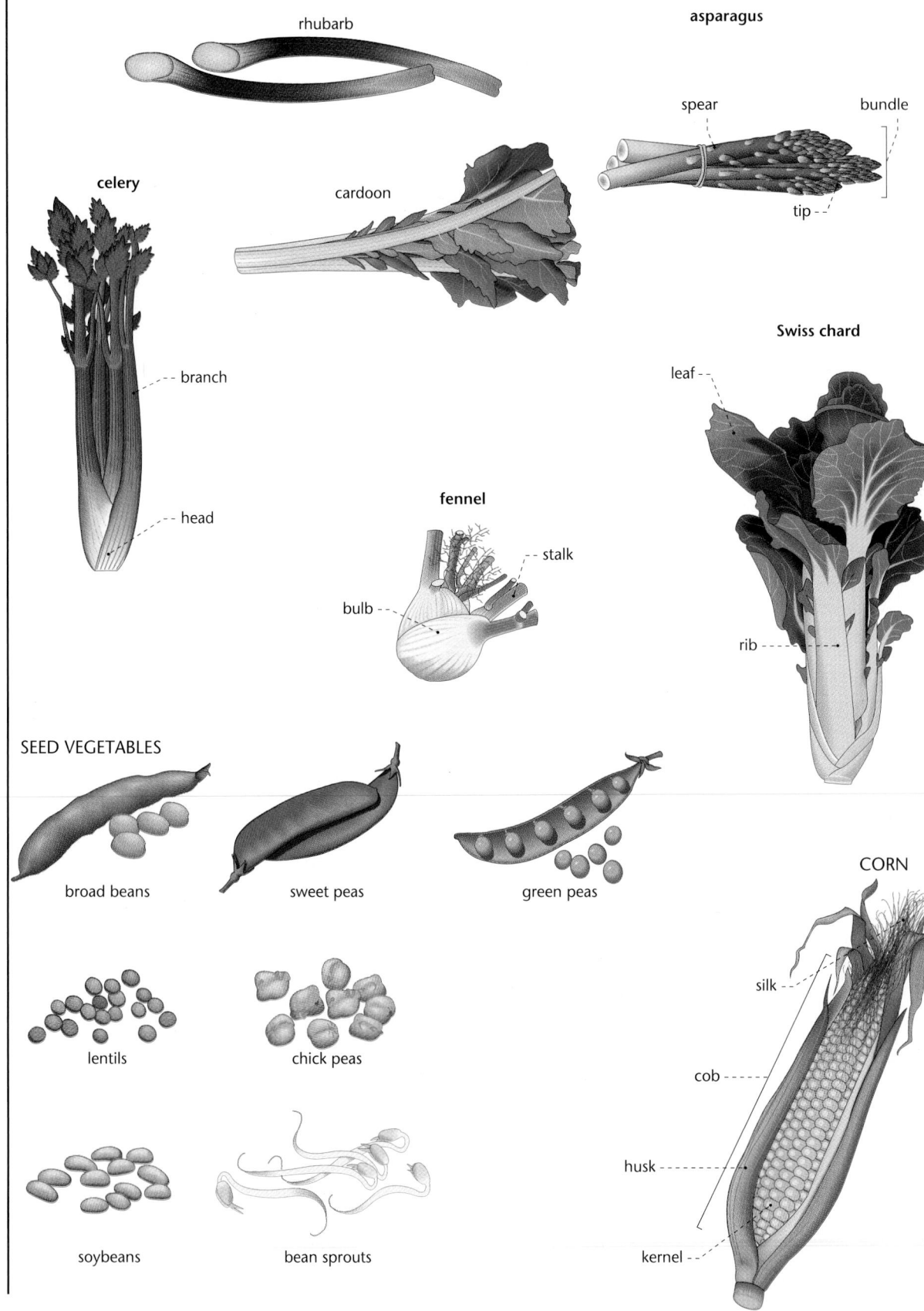

STALK VEGETABLES

rhubarb

asparagus

spear

bundle

tip

celery

cardoon

Swiss chard

leaf

branch

head

fennel

stalk

bulb

rib

SEED VEGETABLES

broad beans

sweet peas

green peas

CORN

lentils

chick peas

silk

cob

husk

soybeans

bean sprouts

kernel

LEAF VEGETABLES

corn salad

watercress

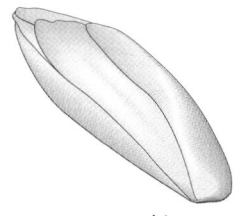

chicory

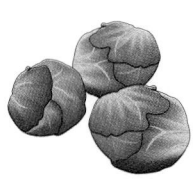

Brussels sprouts

curled kale

grape leaf

garden sorrel

spinach

curled endive

broad-leaved endive

romaine lettuce

dandelion

white cabbage

cabbage lettuce

green cabbage

Chinese cabbage

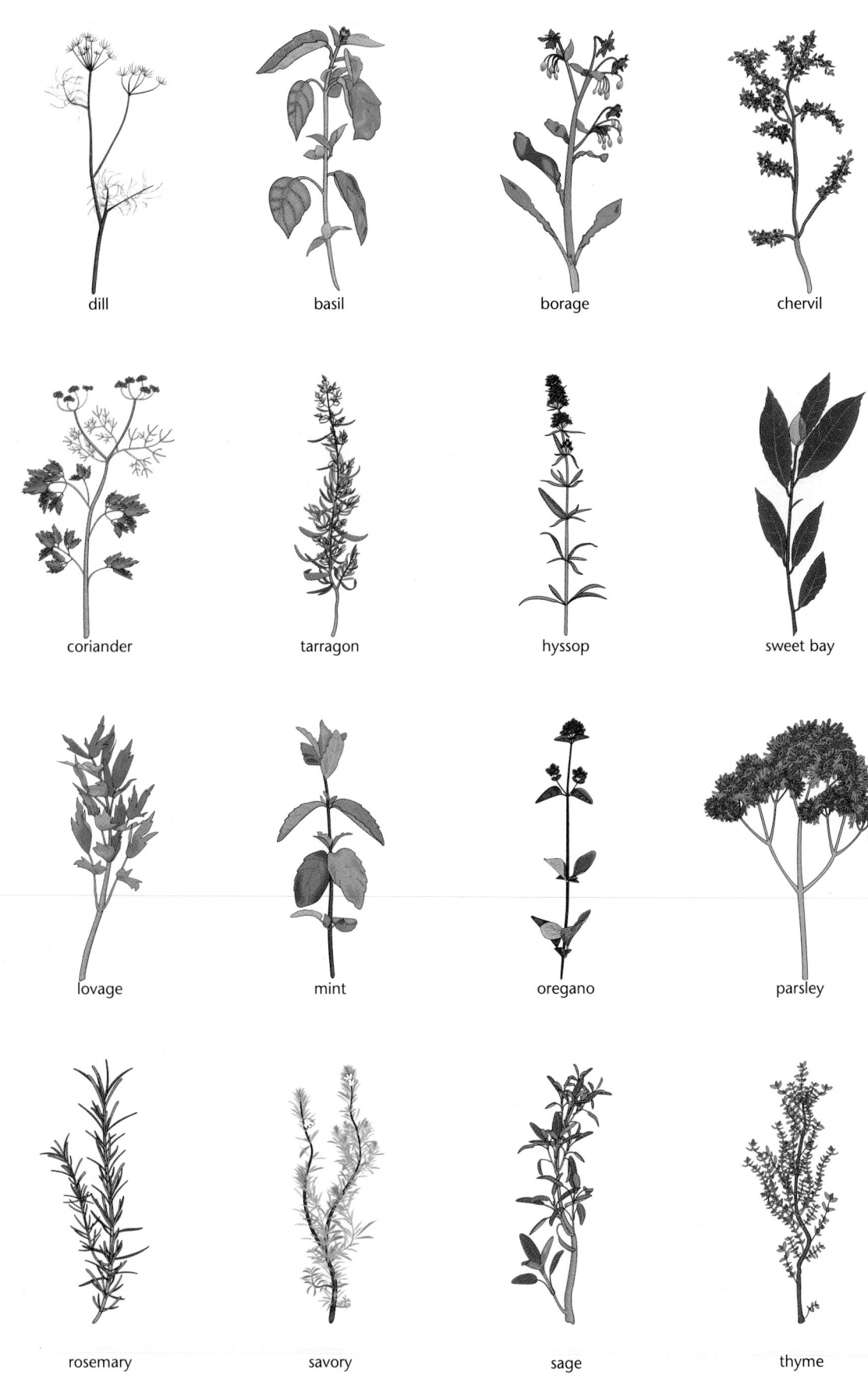

dill

basil

borage

chervil

coriander

tarragon

hyssop

sweet bay

lovage

mint

oregano

parsley

rosemary

savory

sage

thyme

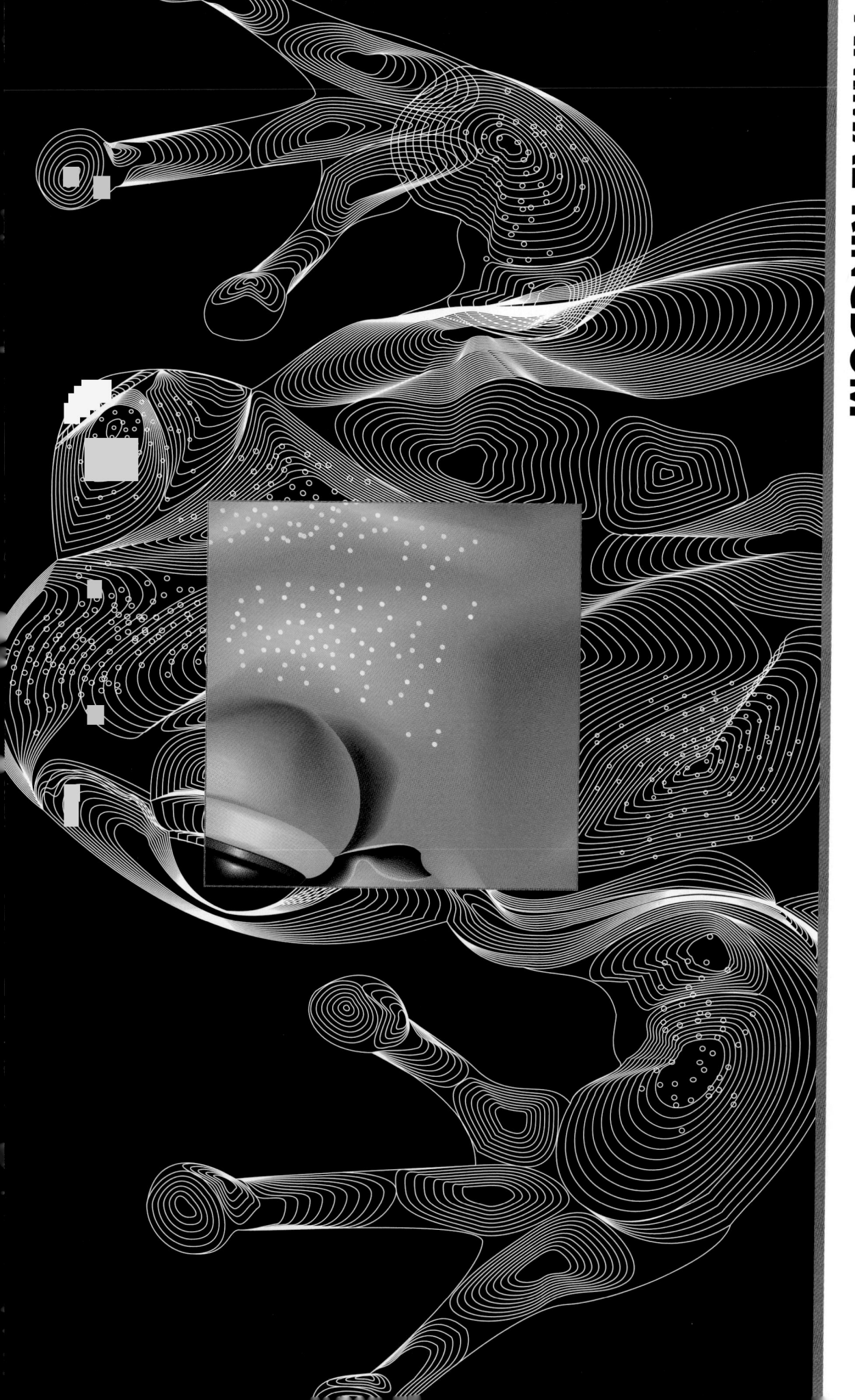

CONTENTS

INSECTS AND SPIDER 77

BUTTERFLY 78

HONEYBEE 80

GASTROPOD 83

AMPHIBIANS 84

FISH 86

CRUSTACEAN 90

MOLLUSK 92

UNIVALVE SHELL 94

BIVALVE SHELL 95

REPTILE 96

TYPES OF JAWS 98

MAJOR TYPES OF HORNS 99

MAJOR TYPES OF TUSKS 99

TYPES OF HOOFS 99

HORSE 100

DEER FAMILY 105

DOG 106

CAT 107

BIRD 108

BAT 112

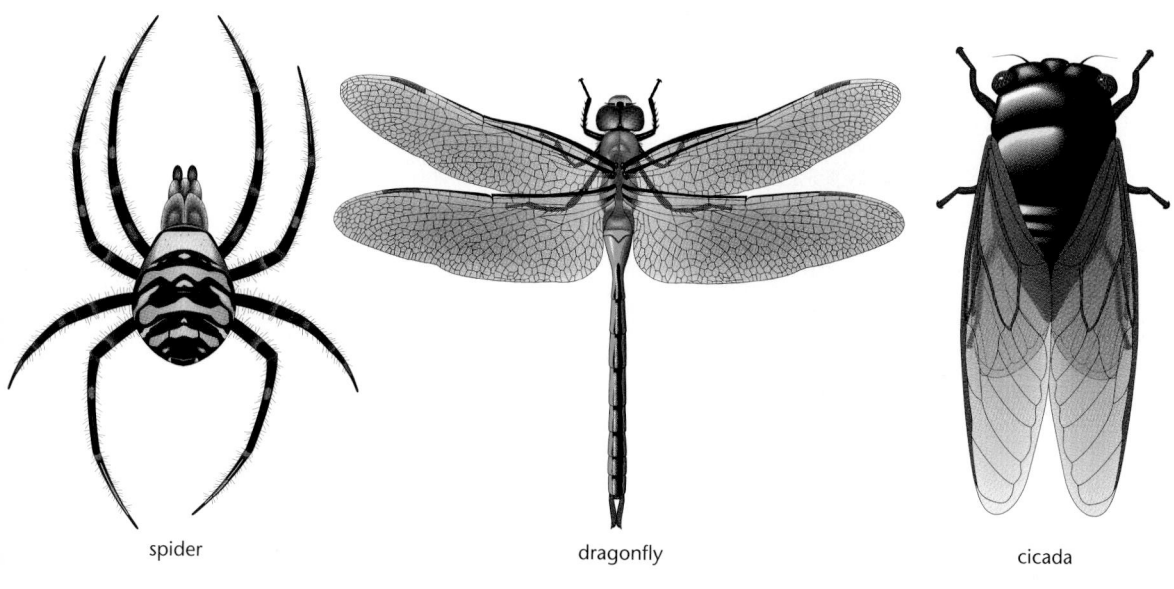

spider   dragonfly   cicada

fly   ladybug   ant

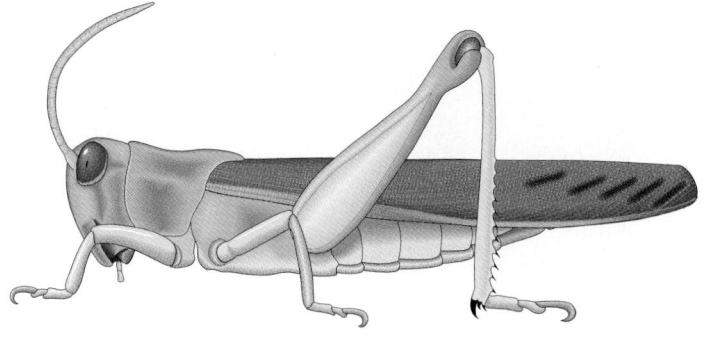

grasshopper

BUTTERFLY

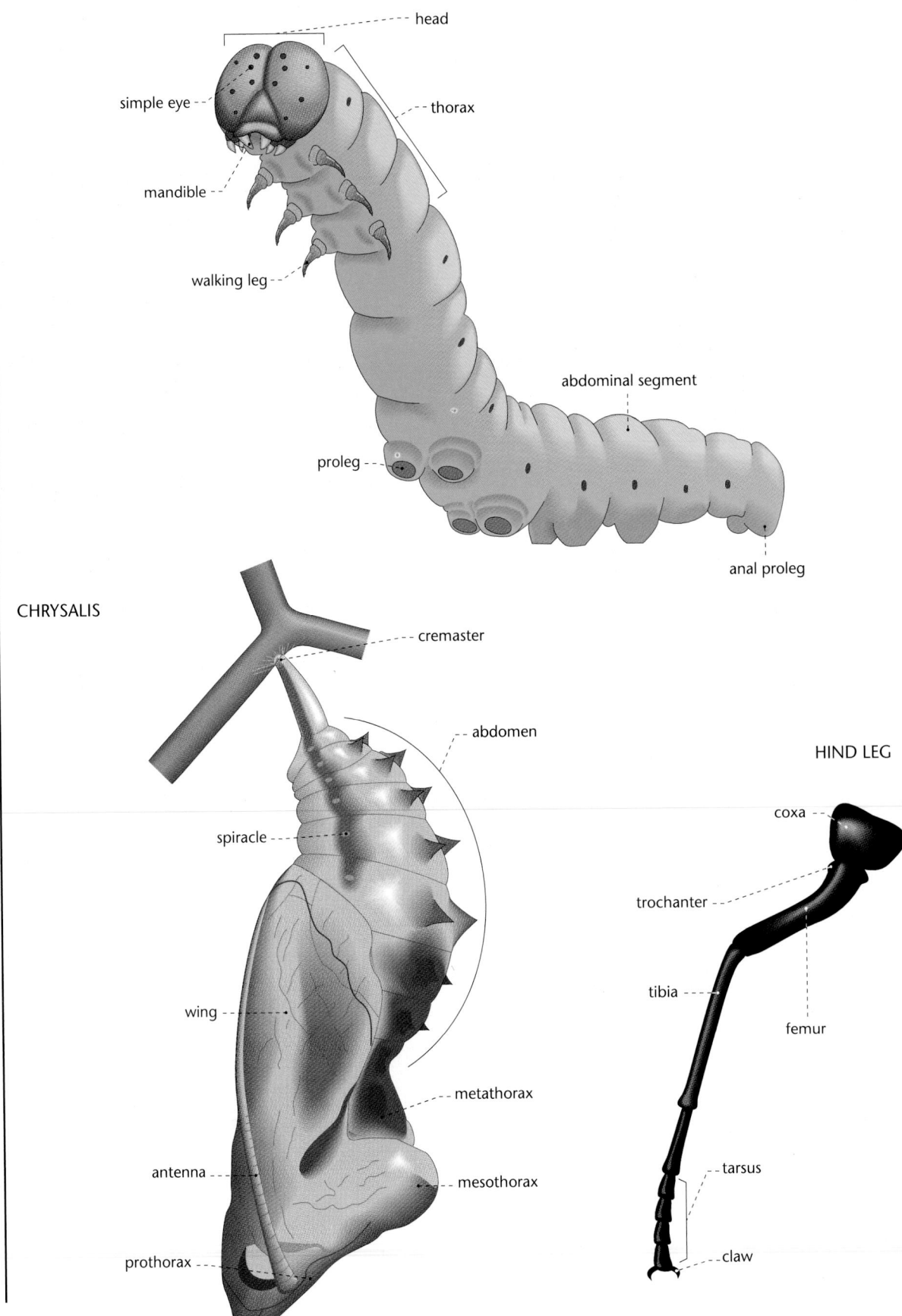

CATERPILLAR

head

simple eye

mandible

thorax

walking leg

abdominal segment

proleg

anal proleg

CHRYSALIS

cremaster

abdomen

HIND LEG

spiracle

coxa

trochanter

tibia

femur

wing

metathorax

antenna

mesothorax

tarsus

prothorax

claw

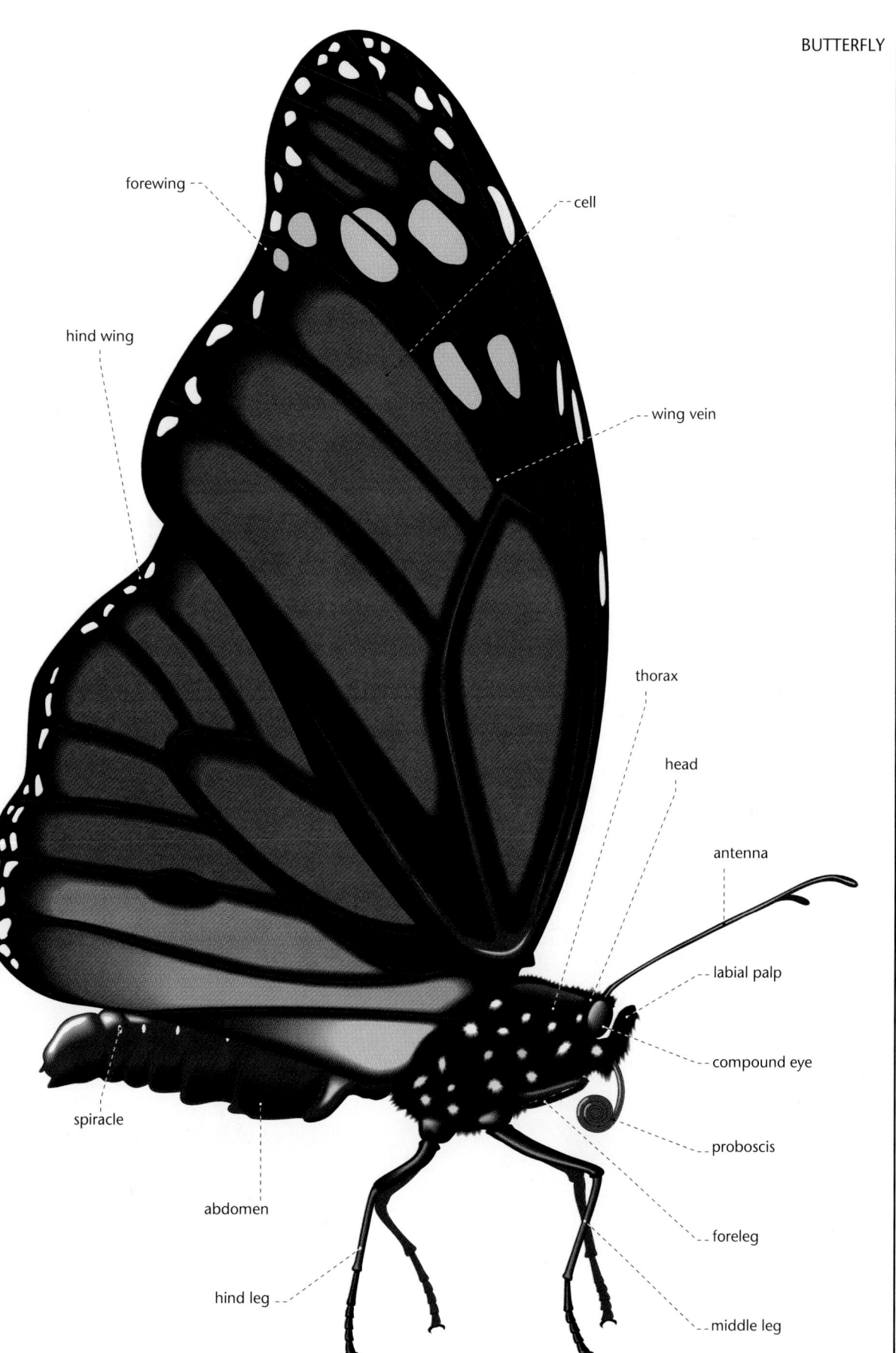

forewing

cell

hind wing

wing vein

thorax

head

antenna

labial palp

compound eye

proboscis

foreleg

spiracle

abdomen

hind leg

middle leg

HONEYBEE

WORKER

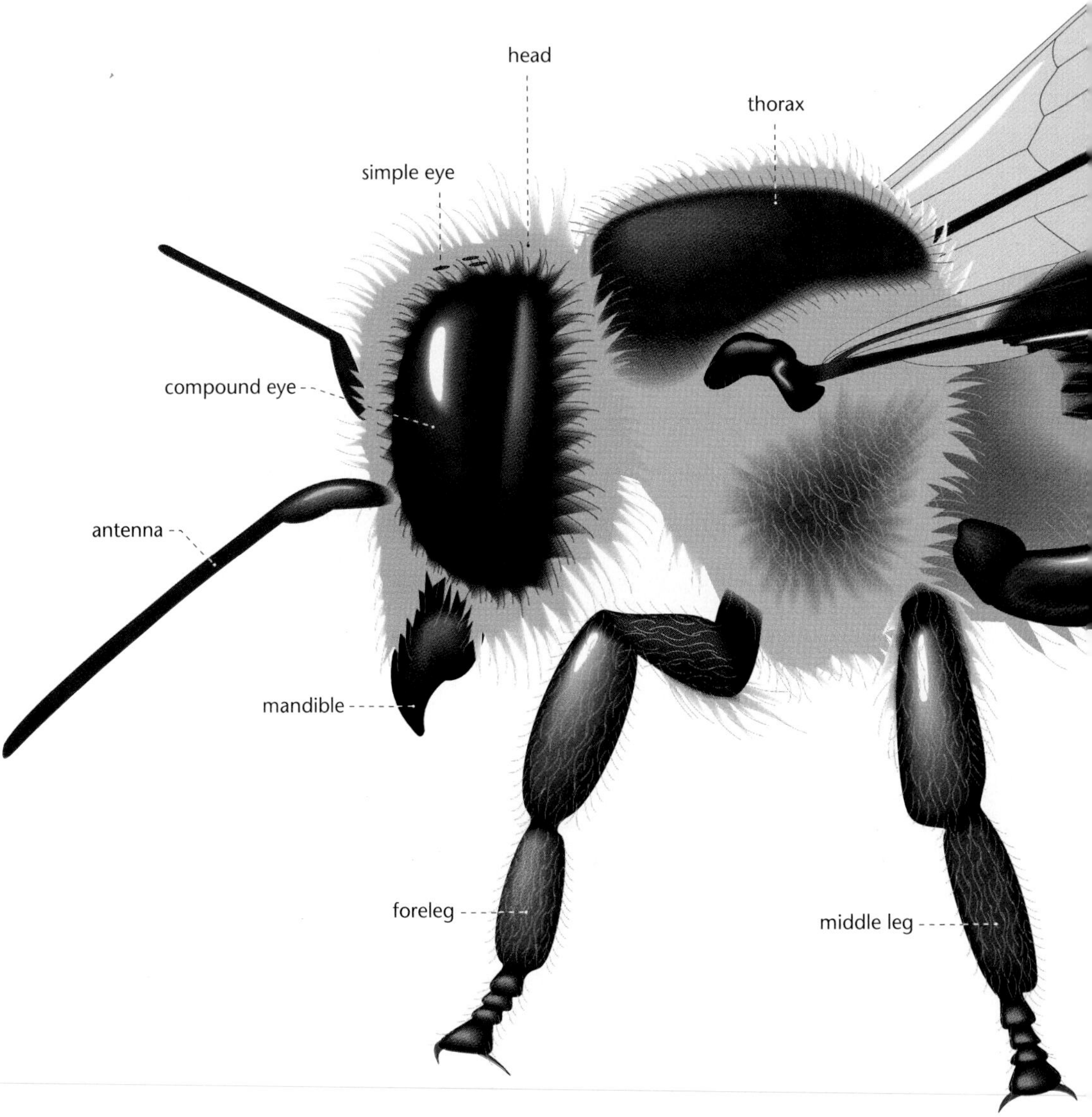

head

thorax

simple eye

compound eye

antenna

mandible

foreleg

middle leg

FORELEG (OUTER SURFACE)

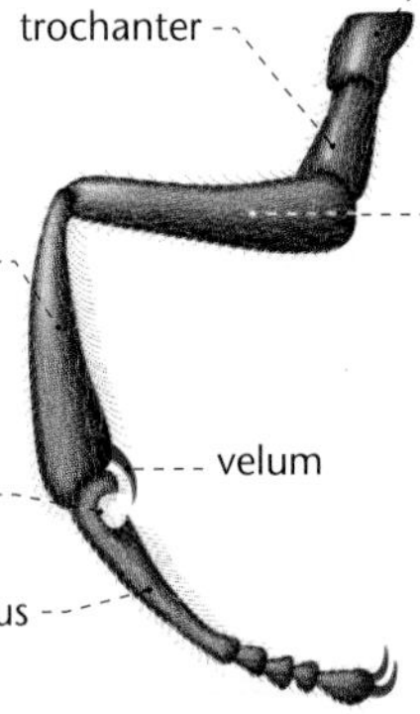

coxa

trochanter

femur

tibia

velum

antennae cleaner

metatarsus

MIDDLE LEG (OUTER SURFACE)

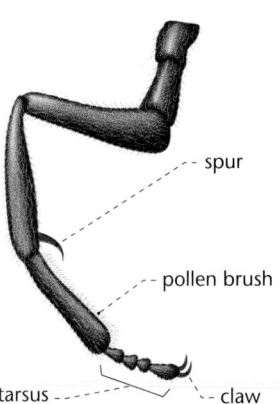

spur

pollen brush

tarsus

claw

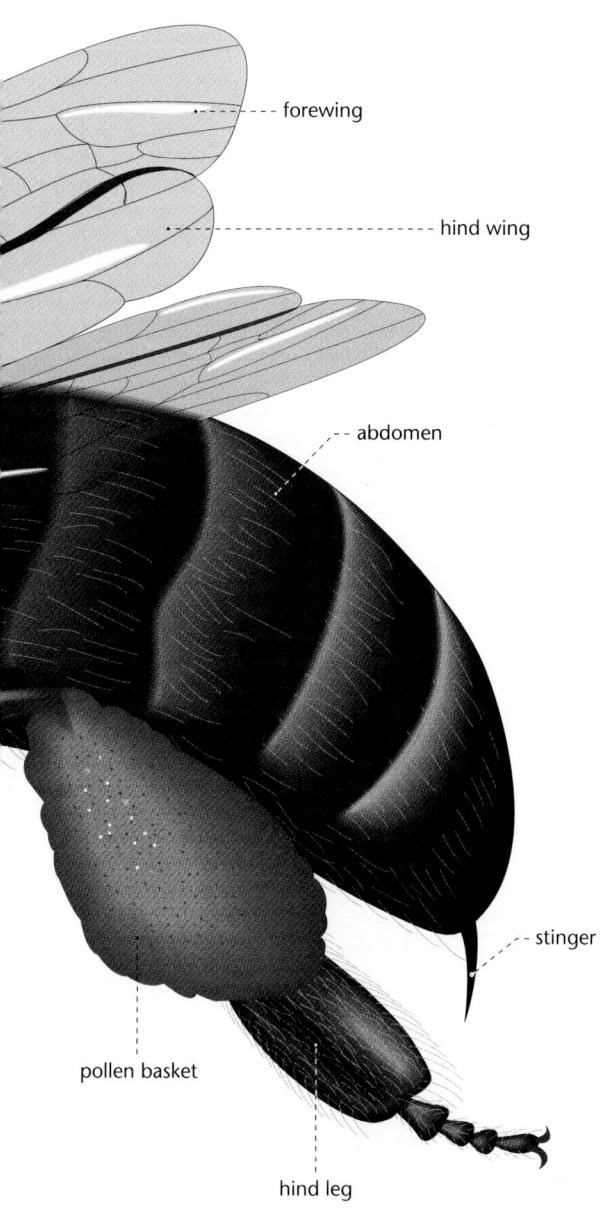

forewing

hind wing

abdomen

stinger

pollen basket

hind leg

QUEEN

DRONE

WORKER

MOUTHPARTS

HIND LEG (INNER SURFACE)

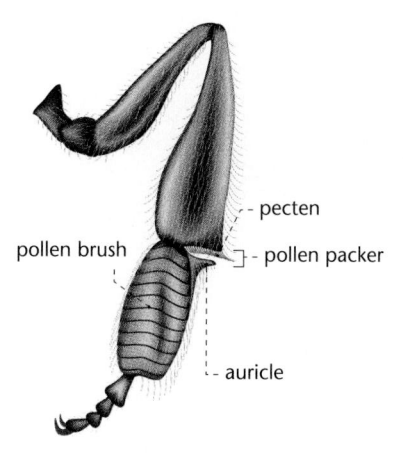

pecten

pollen brush

pollen packer

auricle

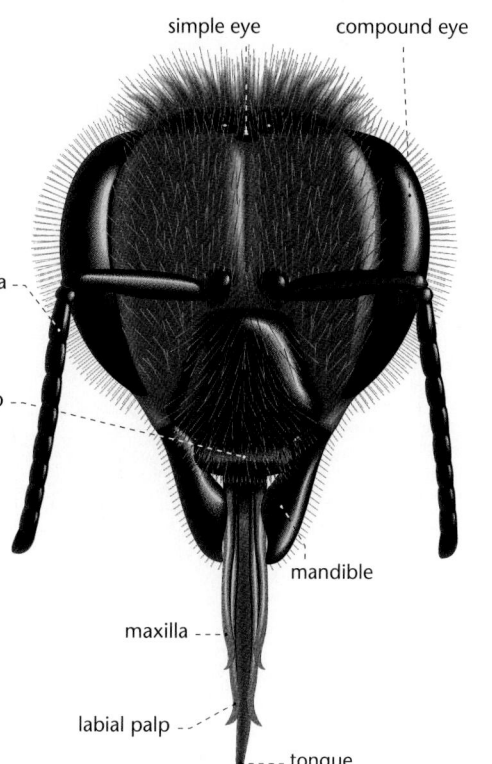

simple eye

compound eye

antenna

upper lip

mandible

maxilla

labial palp

tongue

HONEYCOMB SECTION

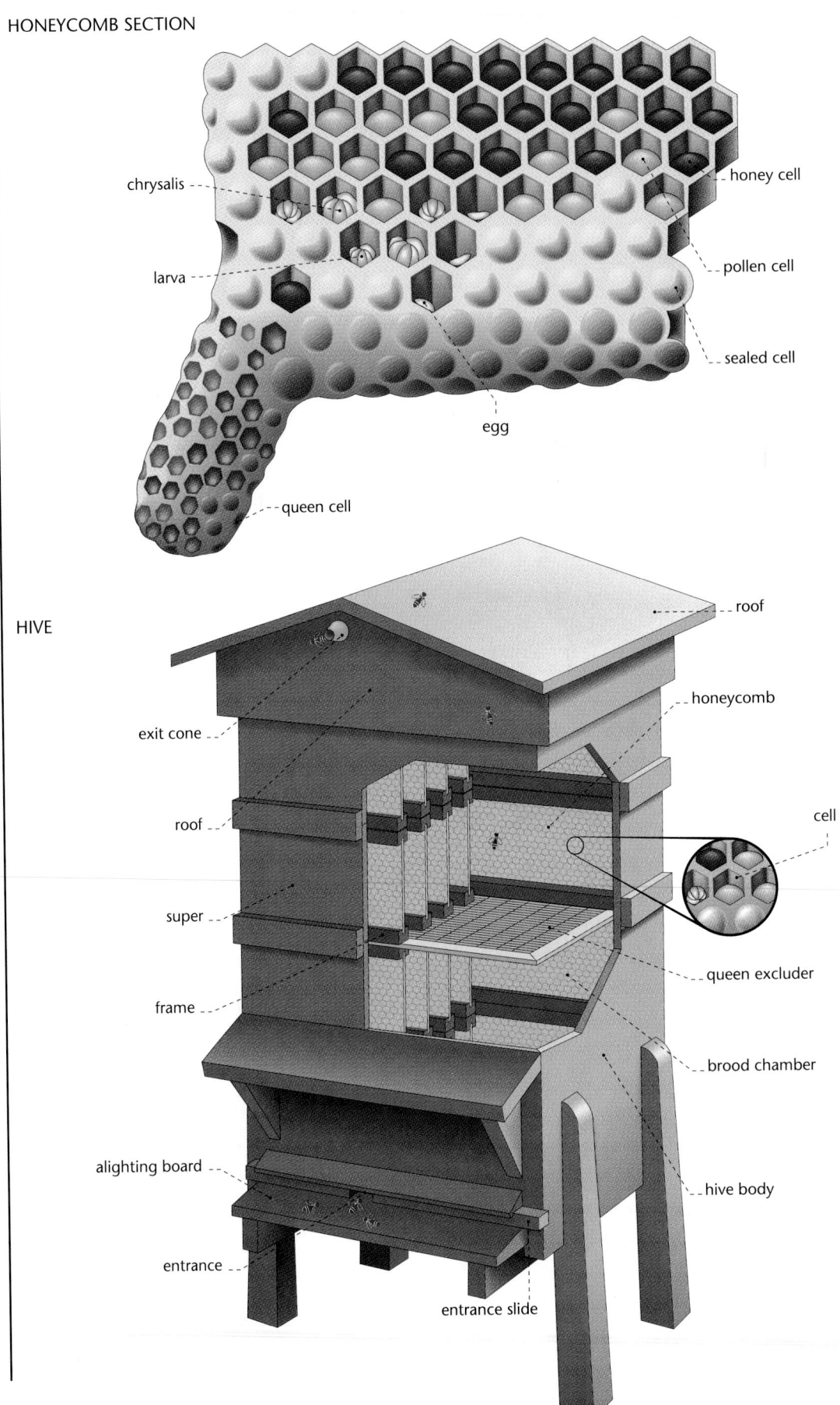

chrysalis

larva

honey cell

pollen cell

sealed cell

egg

queen cell

HIVE

roof

honeycomb

exit cone

roof

cell

super

queen excluder

frame

brood chamber

alighting board

hive body

entrance

entrance slide

GASTROPOD

apex

shell

whorl

growth line

horns

eye

pulmonary opening

eyestalk

foot

excretory opening

genital opening

head

mouth

tentacle

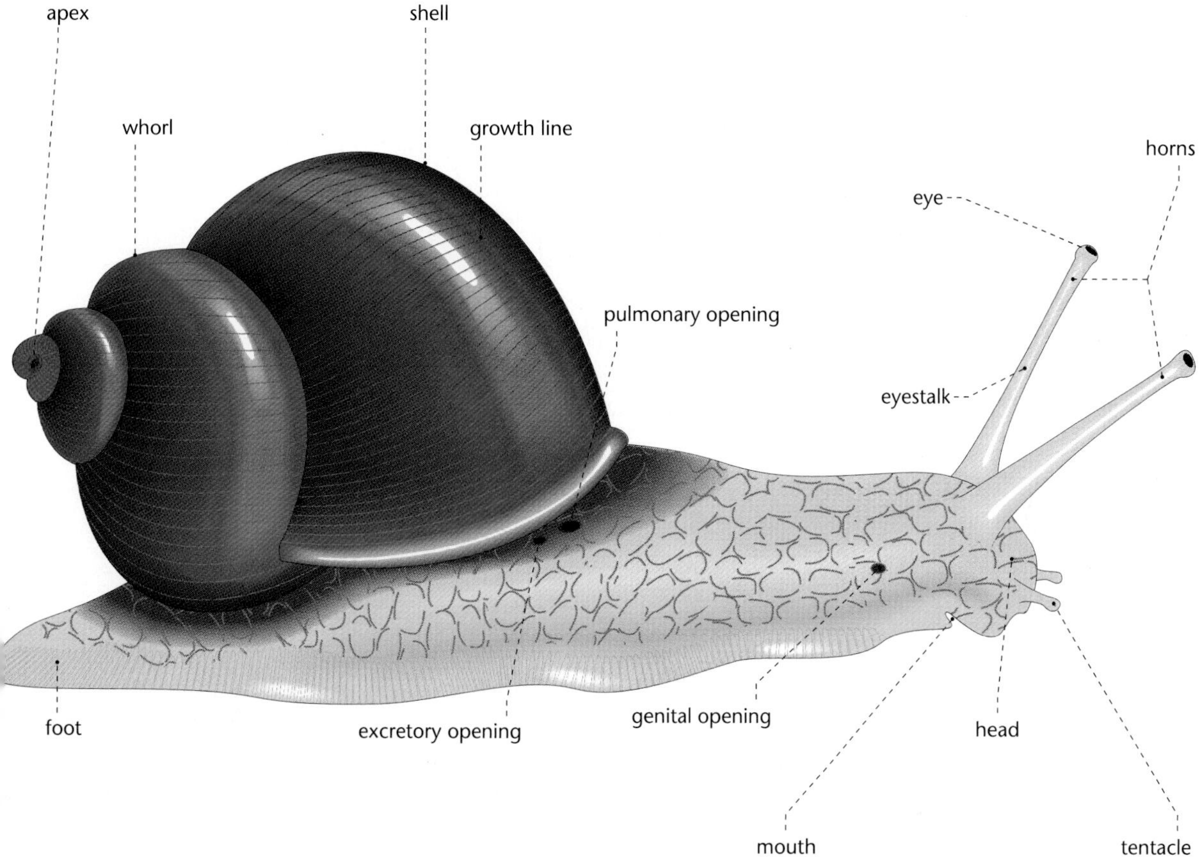

MAJOR EDIBLE GASTROPODS

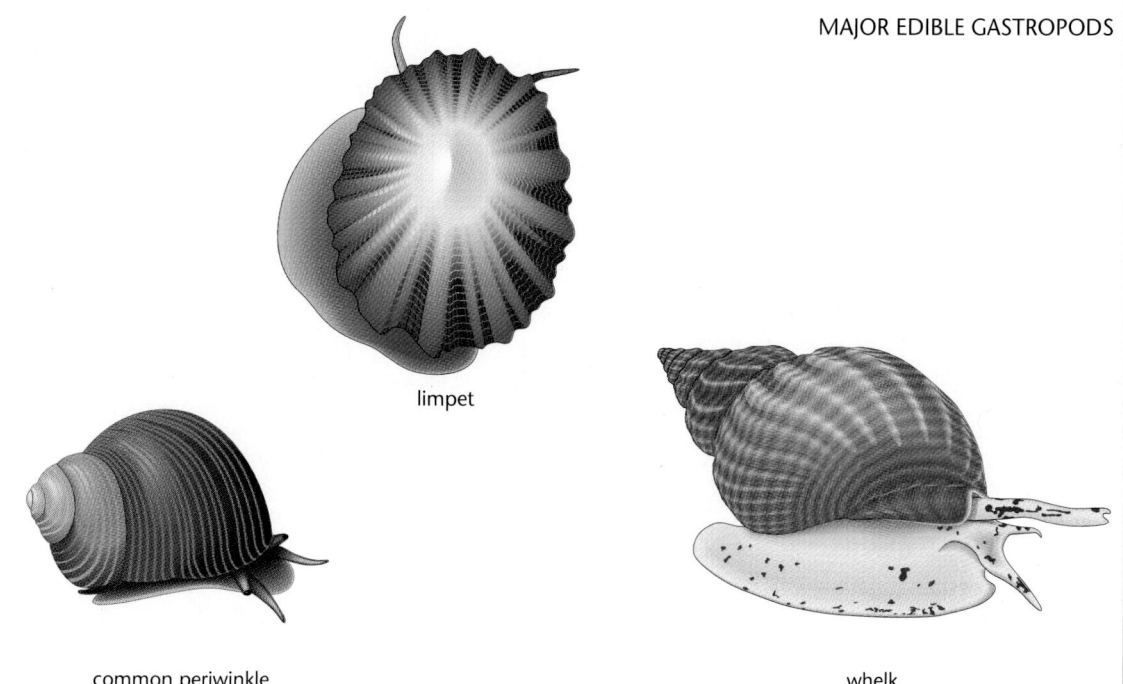

limpet

common periwinkle

whelk

83

ANIMAL KINGDOM

FROG

eyeball

upper eyelid

tympanum

snout

nostril

mouth

lower eyelid

skin

forelimb

digit

web

webbed foot

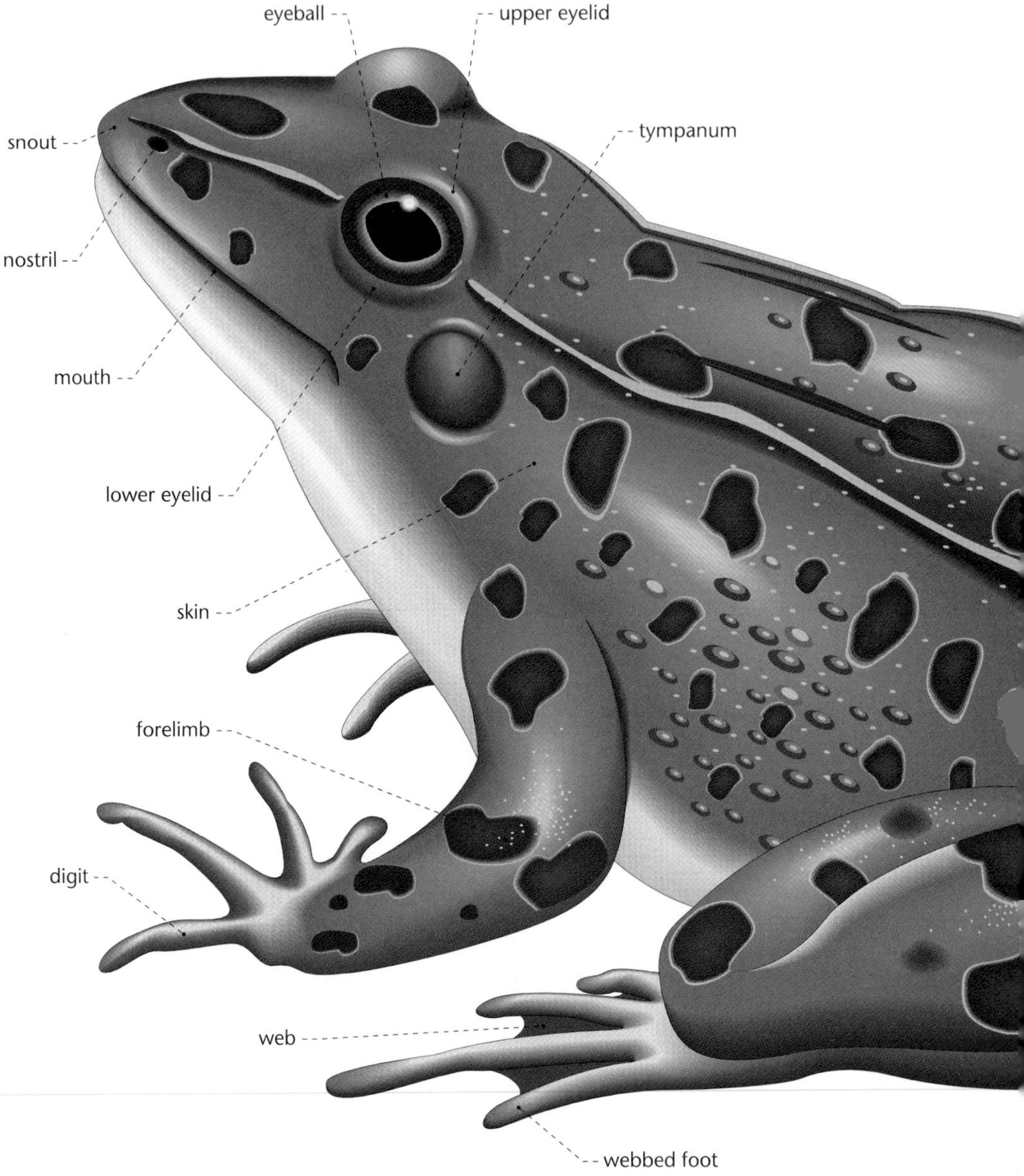

LIFE CYCLE OF THE FROG

eggs

tadpole

hind limb

forelimb

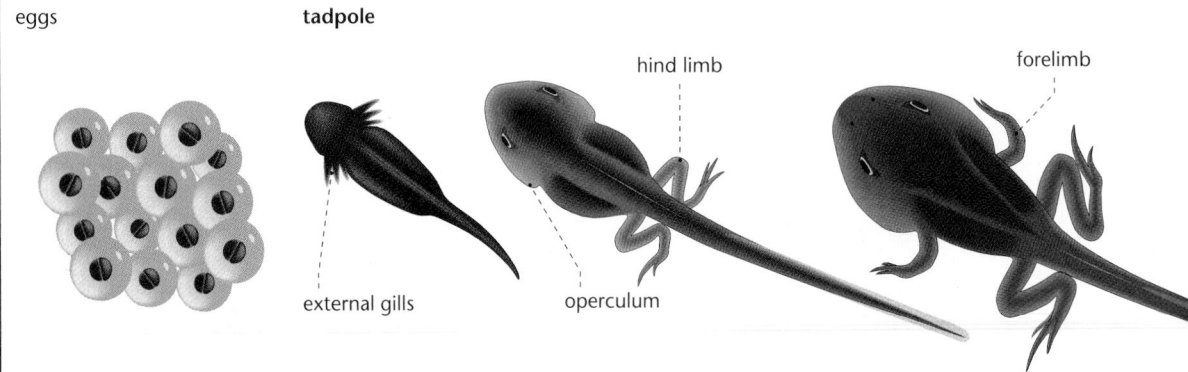

external gills

operculum

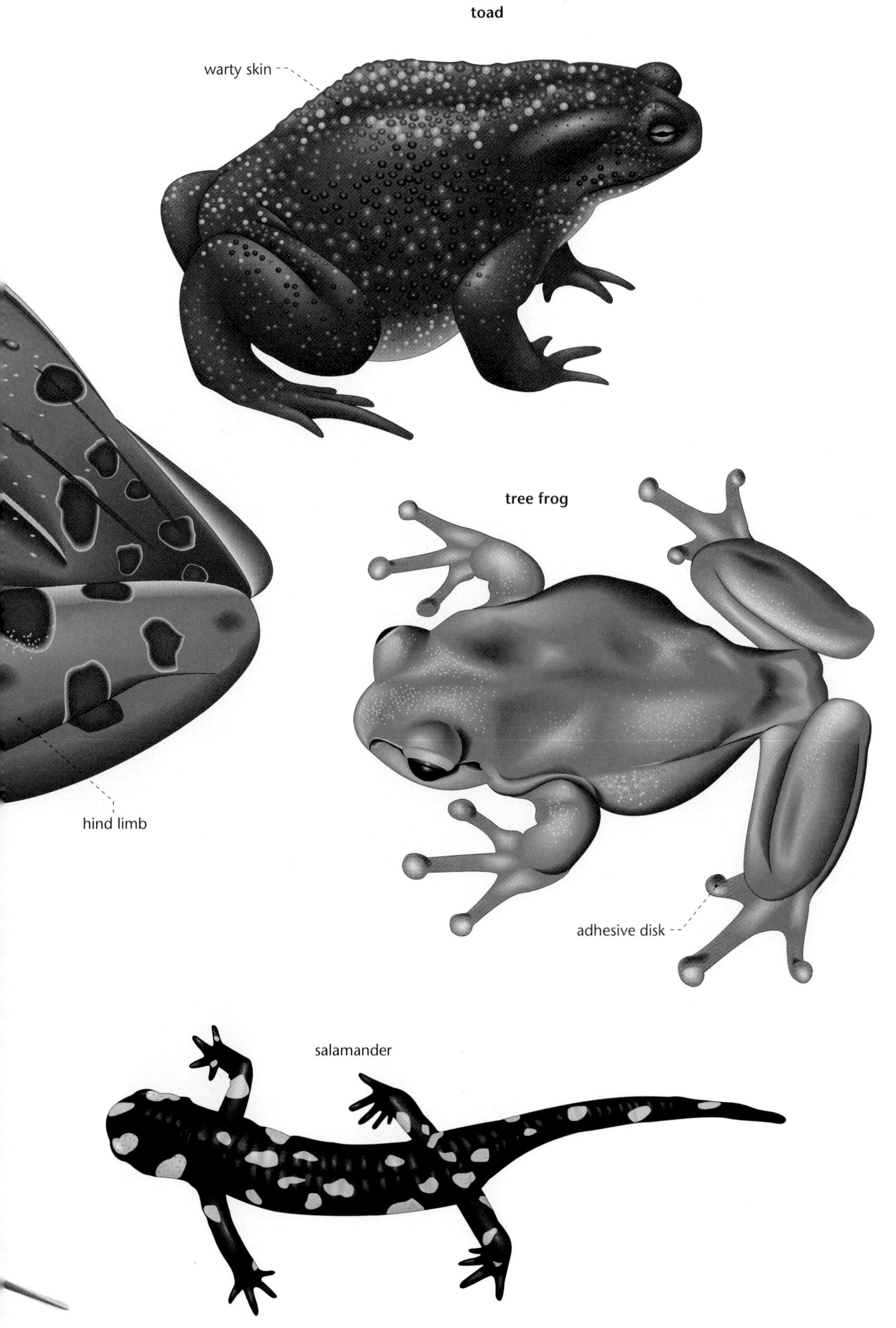

toad

warty skin ------

hind limb

tree frog

adhesive disk ---

salamander

MORPHOLOGY

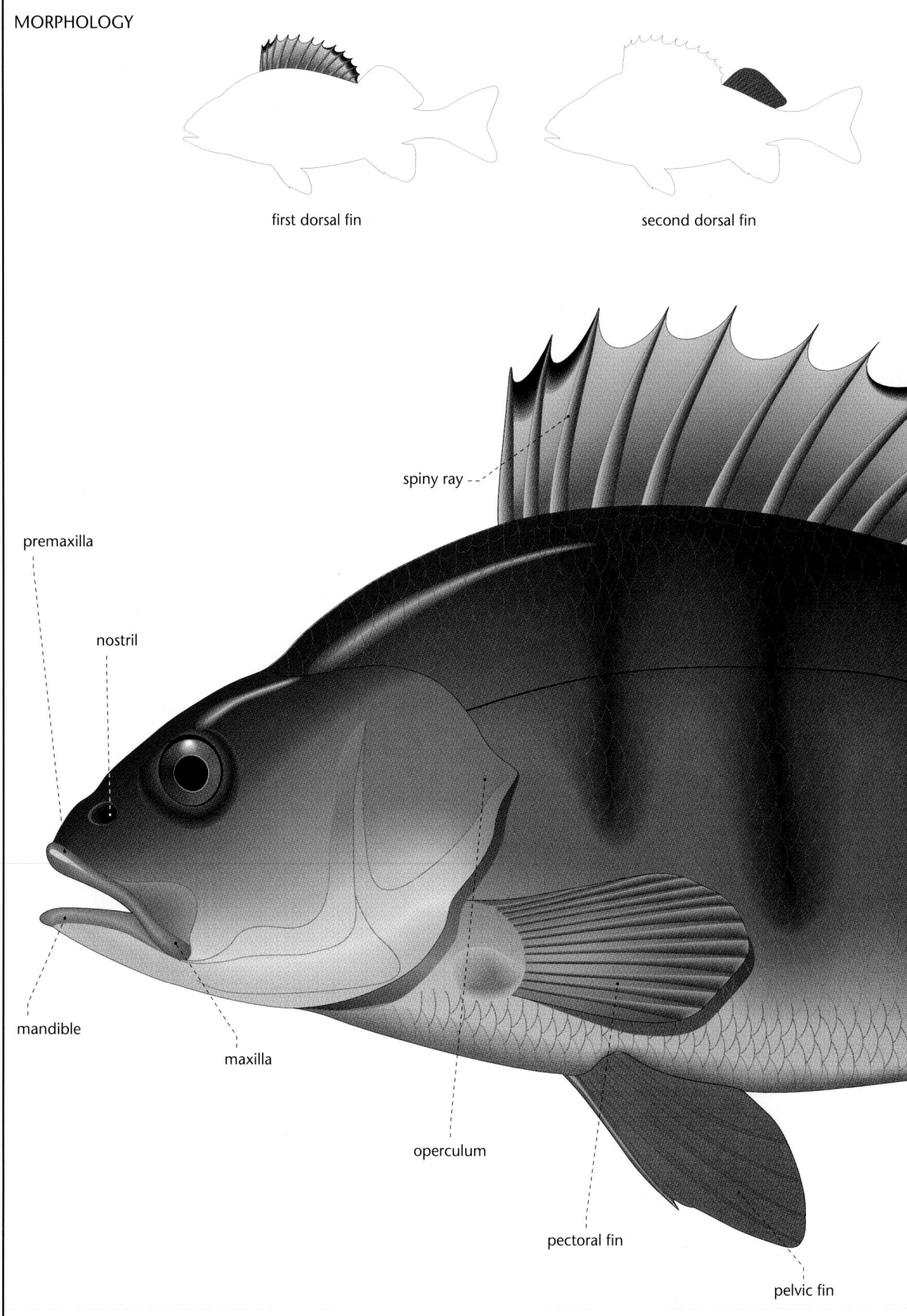

first dorsal fin

second dorsal fin

spiny ray

premaxilla

nostril

mandible

maxilla

operculum

pectoral fin

pelvic fin

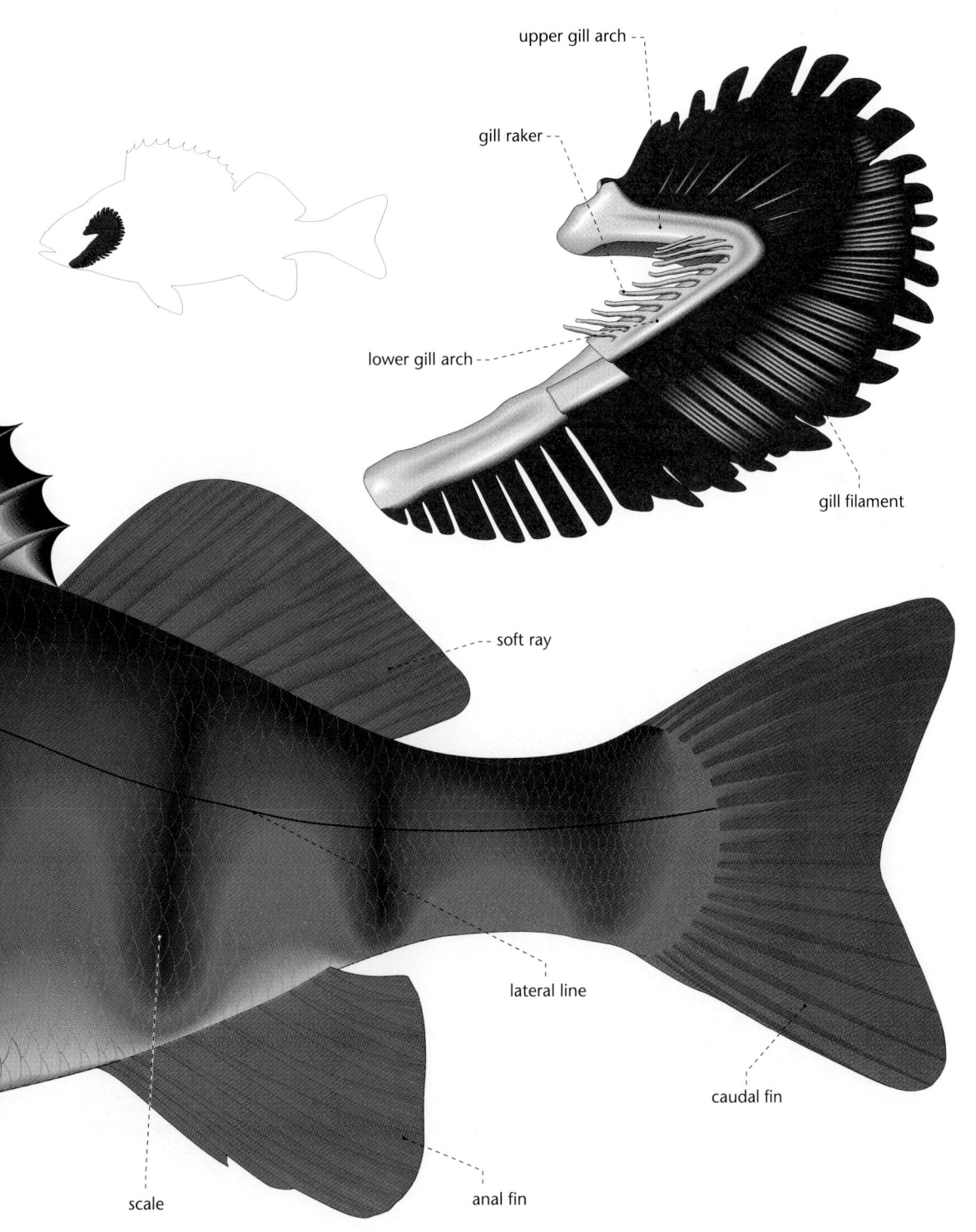

upper gill arch

gill raker

lower gill arch

gill filament

soft ray

lateral line

caudal fin

scale

anal fin

ANATOMY

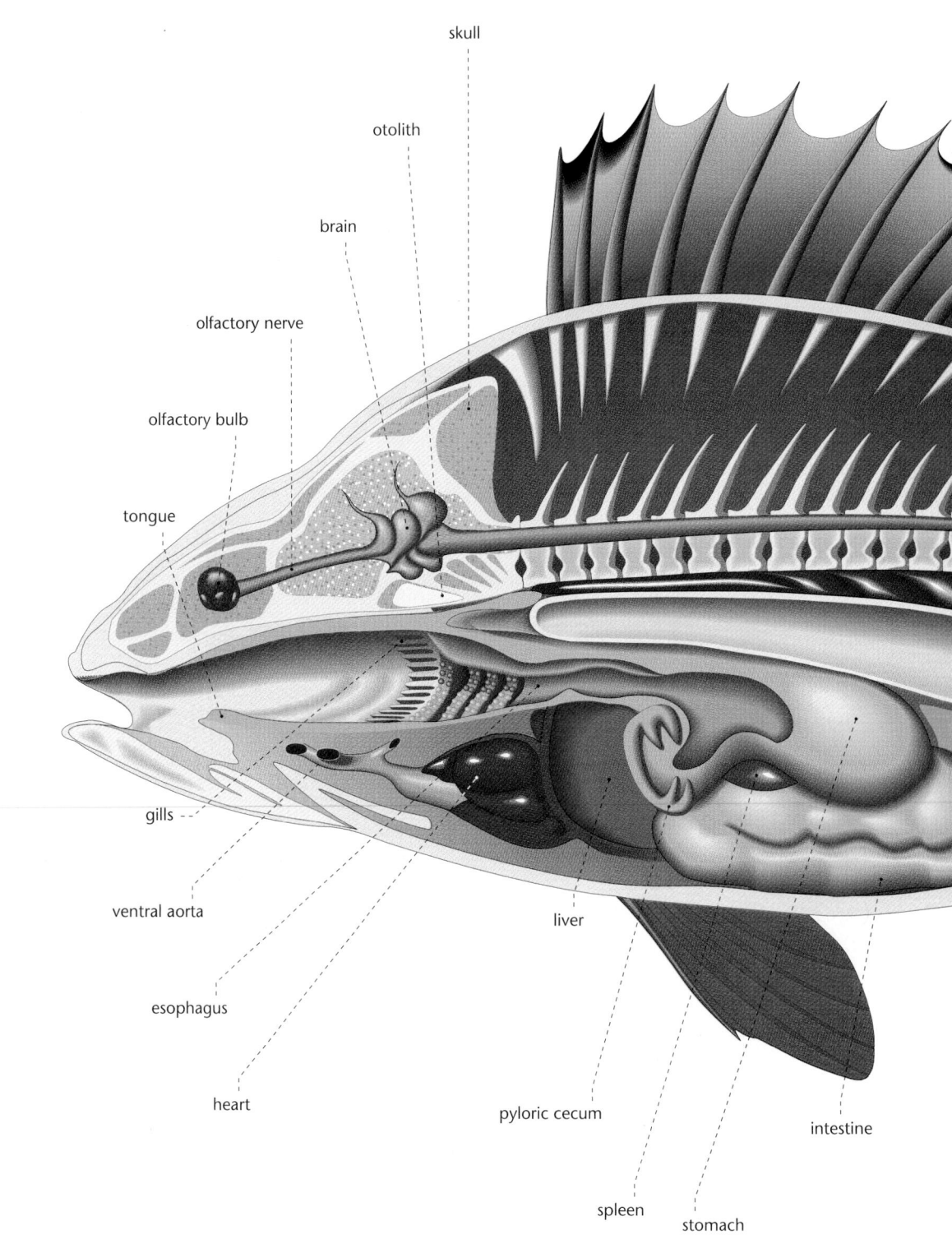

skull

otolith

brain

olfactory nerve

olfactory bulb

tongue

gills

ventral aorta

esophagus

heart

liver

pyloric cecum

spleen

stomach

intestine

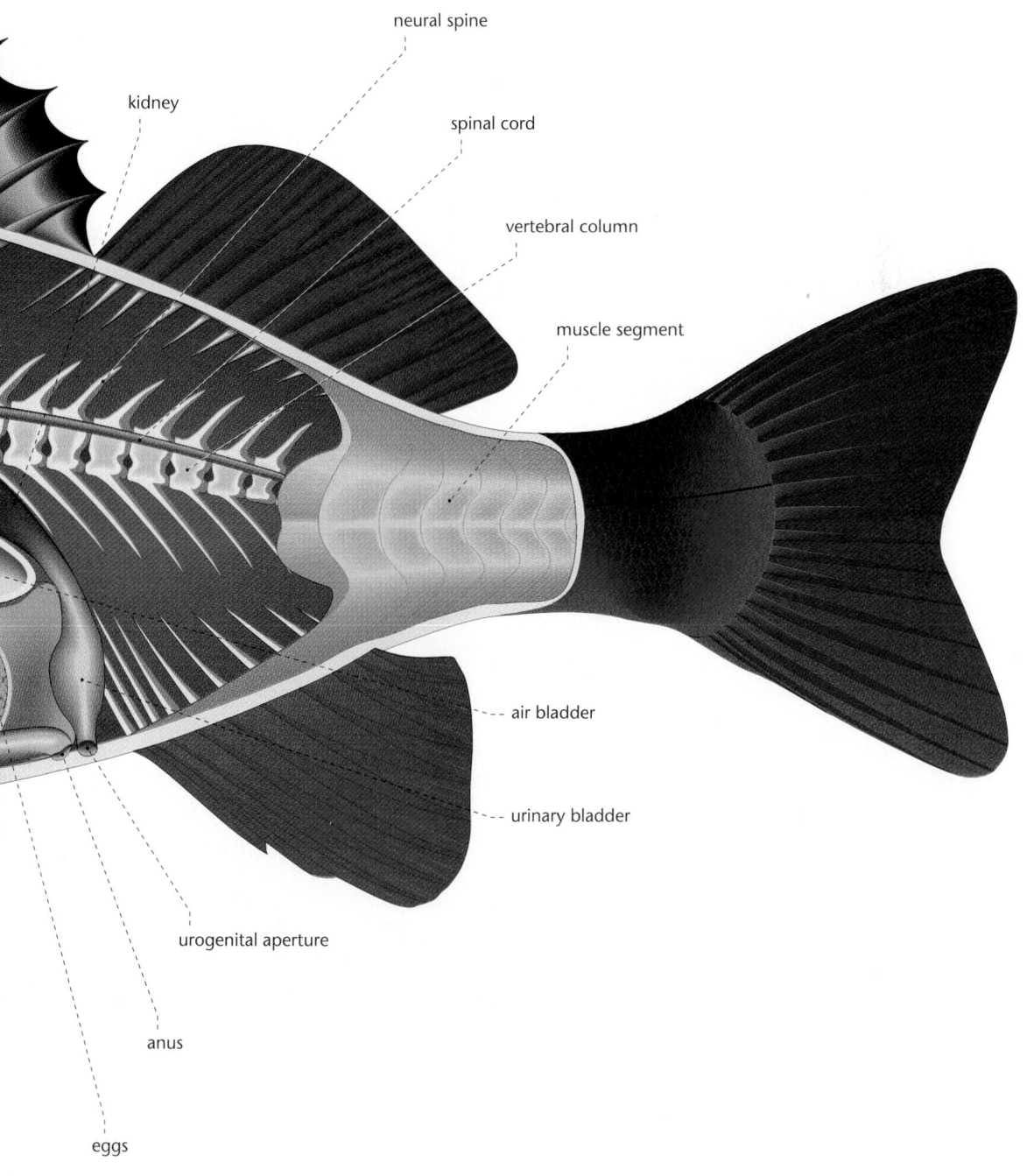

neural spine

kidney

spinal cord

vertebral column

muscle segment

air bladder

urinary bladder

urogenital aperture

anus

eggs

ANIMAL KINGDOM

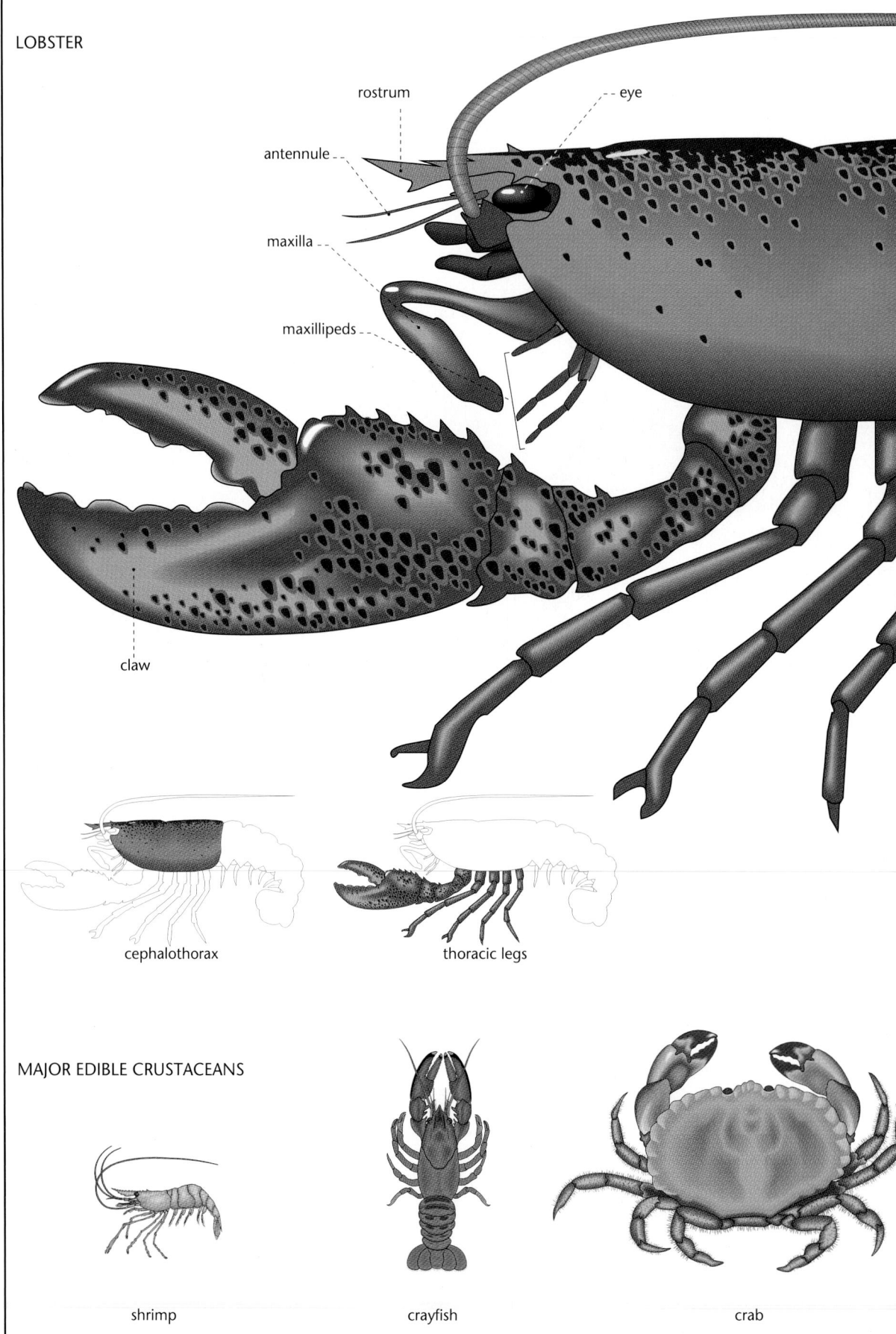

LOBSTER

rostrum

antennule

maxilla

maxillipeds

eye

claw

cephalothorax

thoracic legs

MAJOR EDIBLE CRUSTACEANS

shrimp

crayfish

crab

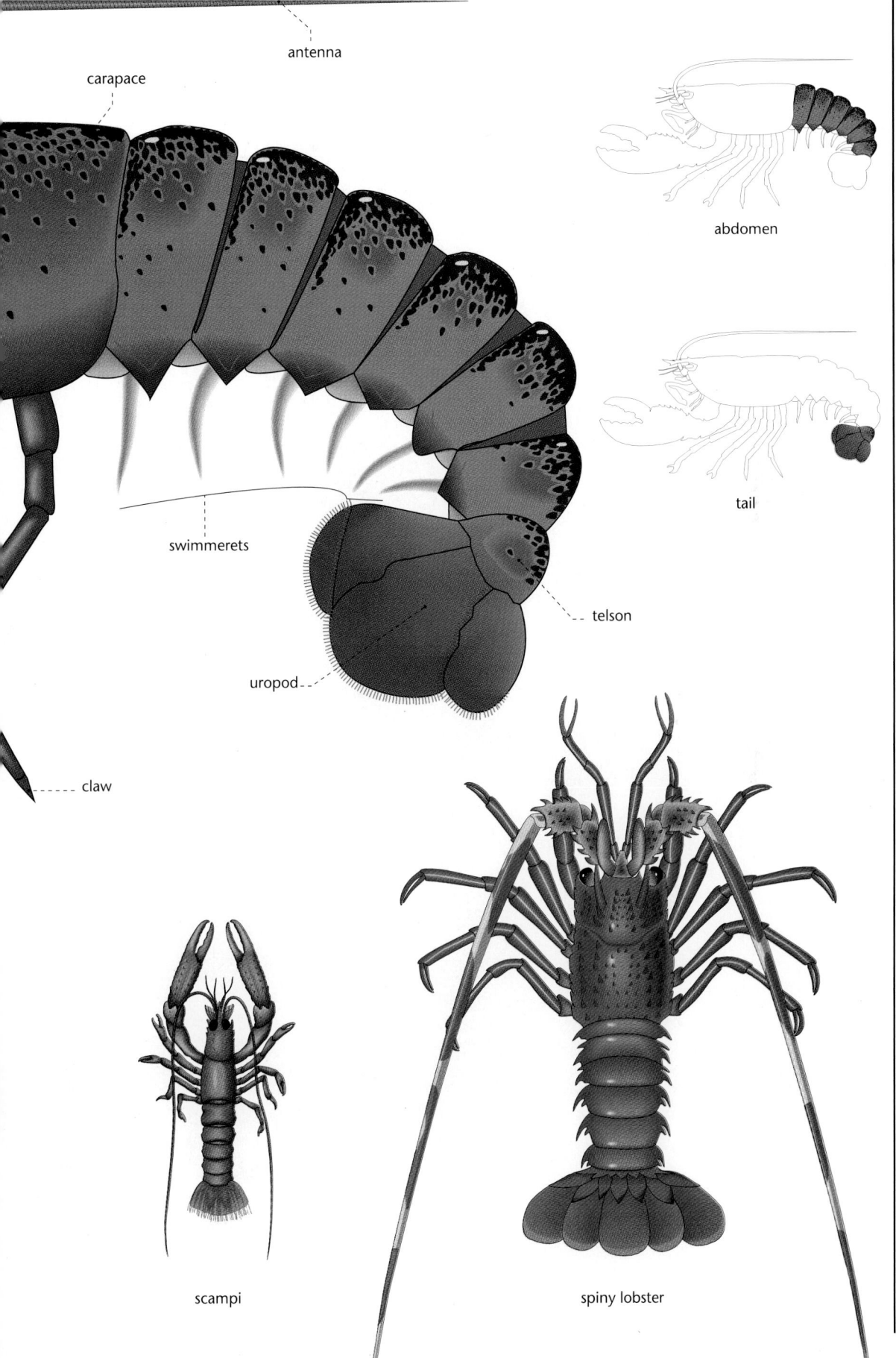

antenna

carapace

abdomen

tail

swimmerets

telson

uropod

claw

scampi

spiny lobster

ANIMAL KINGDOM

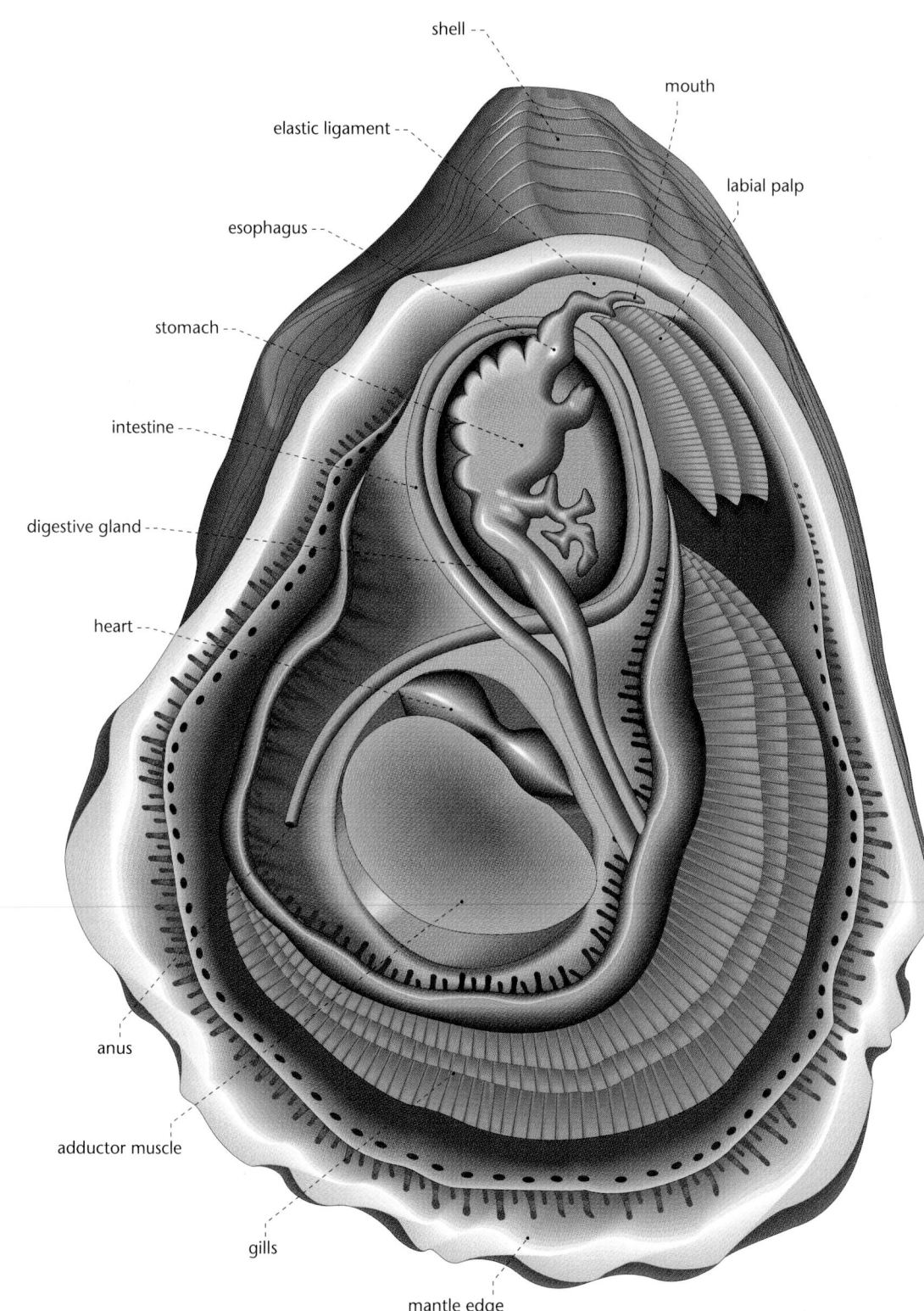

shell

mouth

elastic ligament

labial palp

esophagus

stomach

intestine

digestive gland

heart

anus

adductor muscle

gills

mantle edge

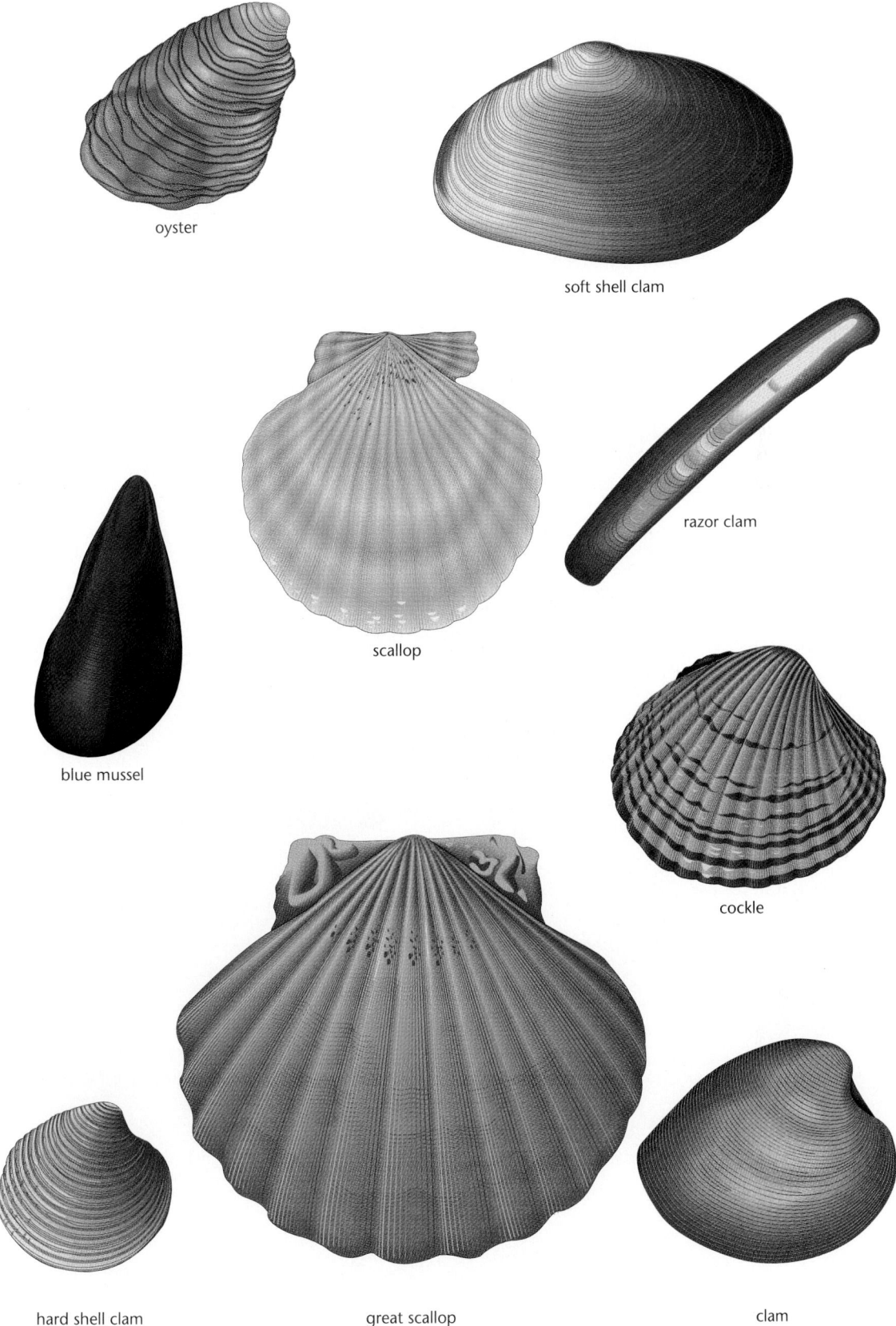

oyster

soft shell clam

razor clam

scallop

blue mussel

cockle

hard shell clam

great scallop

clam

UNIVALVE SHELL

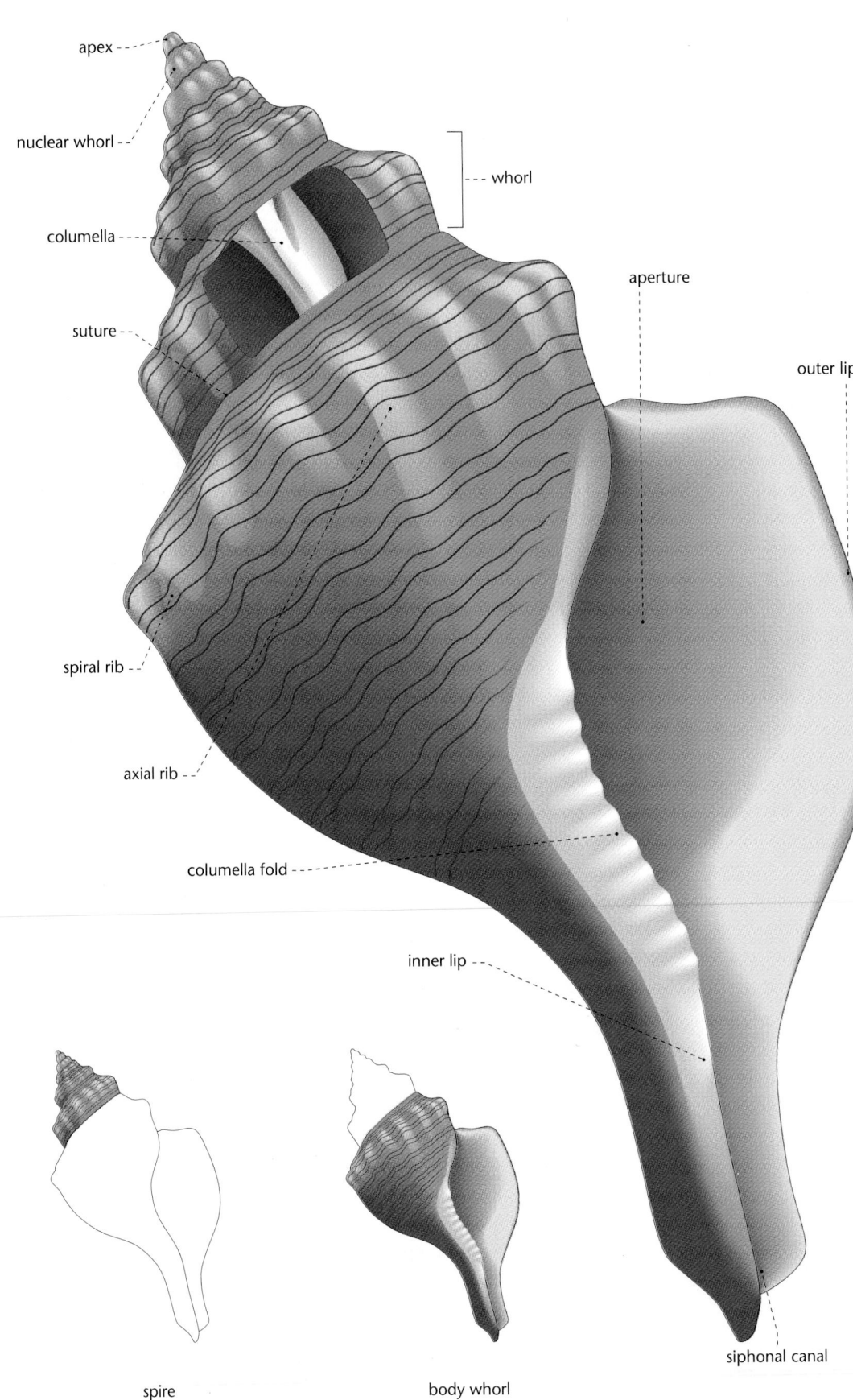

apex

nuclear whorl

columella

whorl

suture

aperture

outer lip

spiral rib

axial rib

columella fold

inner lip

siphonal canal

spire

body whorl

BIVALVE SHELL

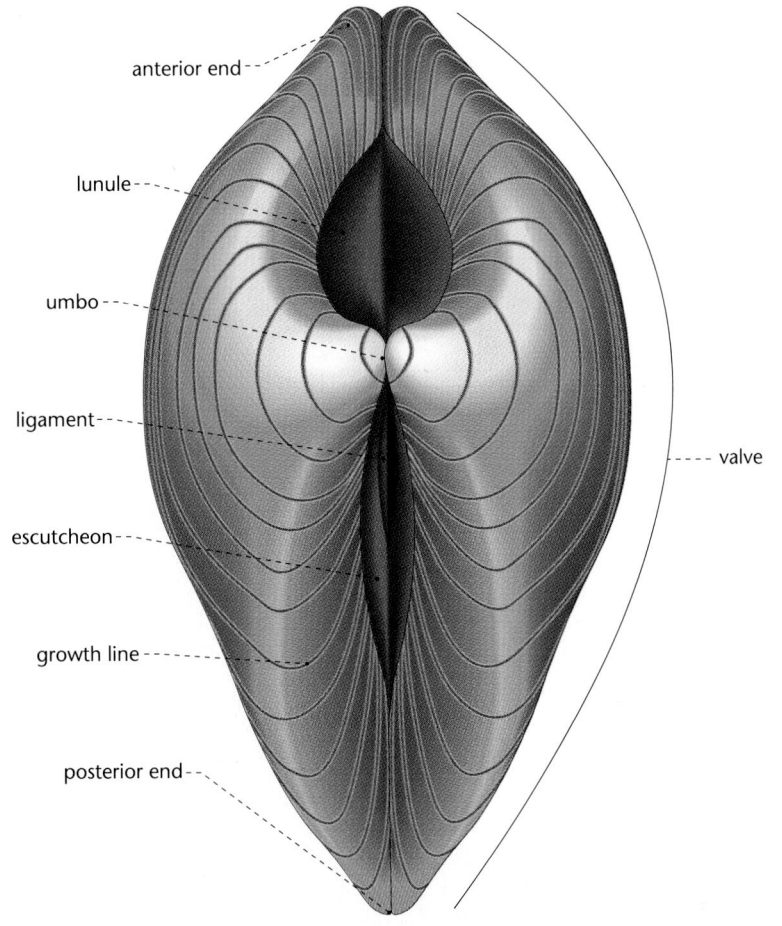

anterior end

lunule

umbo

ligament

escutcheon

growth line

posterior end

valve

LEFT VALVE

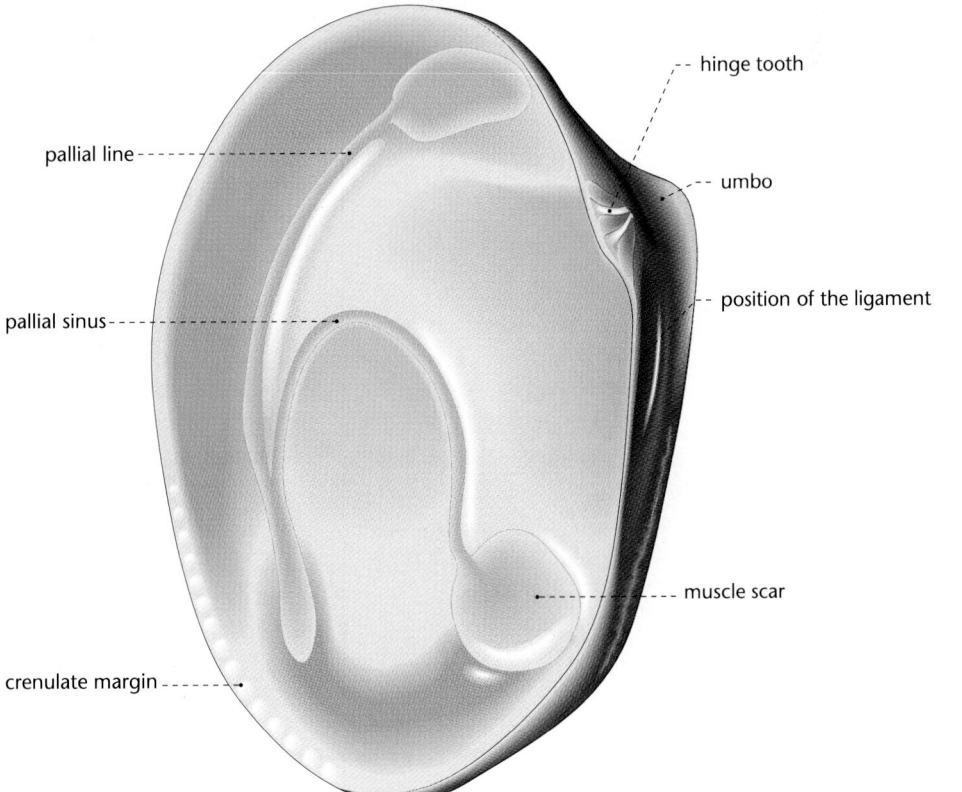

pallial line

pallial sinus

crenulate margin

hinge tooth

umbo

position of the ligament

muscle scar

ANIMAL KINGDOM

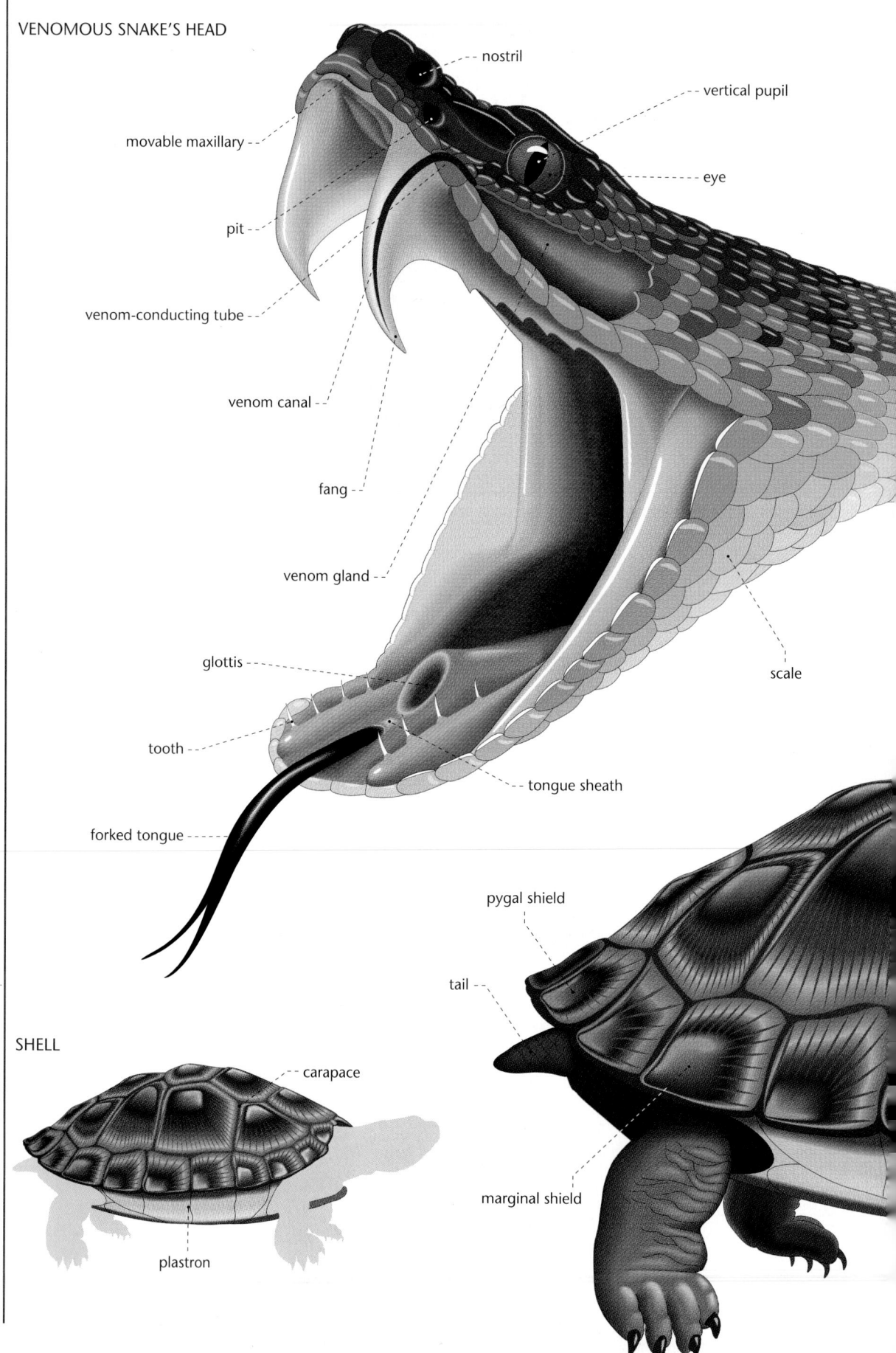

VENOMOUS SNAKE'S HEAD

nostril

vertical pupil

movable maxillary

eye

pit

venom-conducting tube

venom canal

fang

venom gland

scale

glottis

tooth

tongue sheath

forked tongue

pygal shield

tail

SHELL

carapace

plastron

marginal shield

RATTLESNAKE

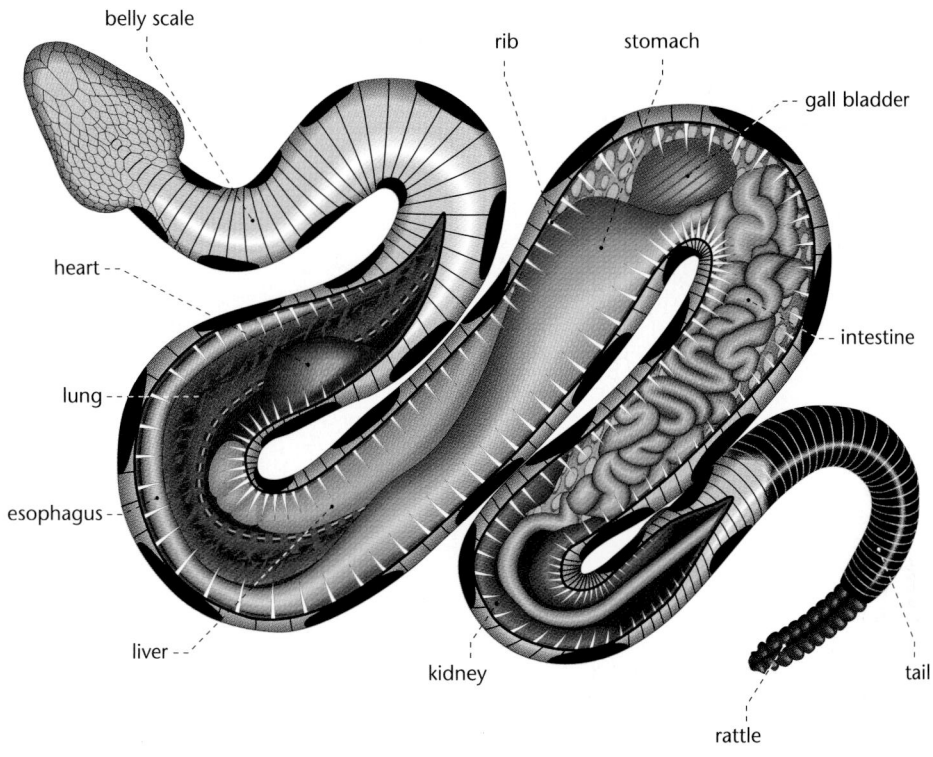

belly scale
rib
stomach
gall bladder
heart
intestine
lung
esophagus
liver
kidney
tail
rattle

TURTLE

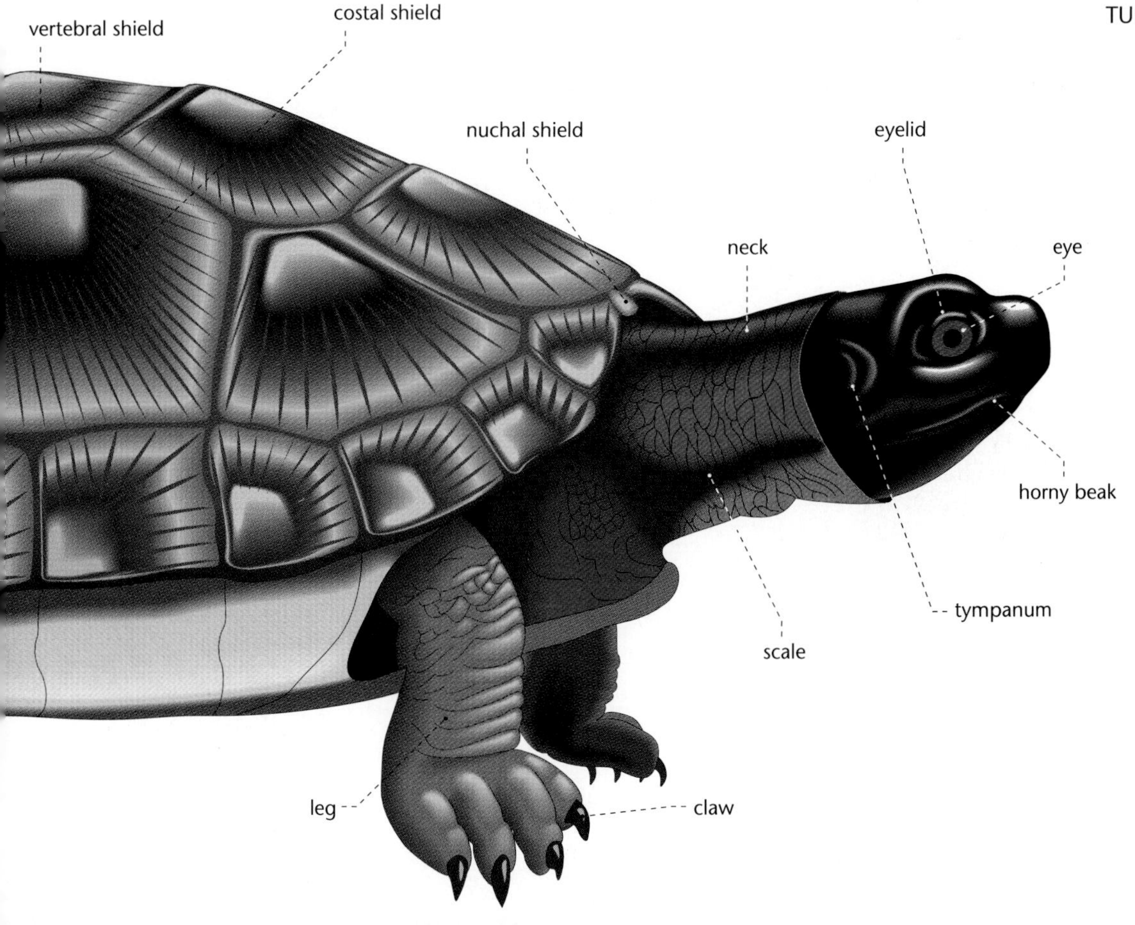

vertebral shield
costal shield
nuchal shield
eyelid
neck
eye
horny beak
tympanum
scale
leg
claw

TYPES OF JAWS

BEAVER

RODENT'S JAW

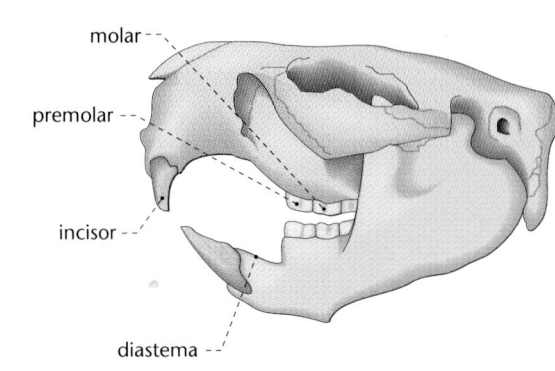

molar
premolar
incisor
diastema

LION

CARNIVORE'S JAW

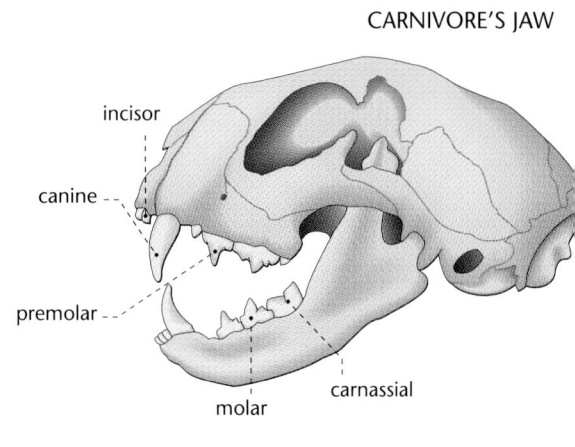

incisor
canine
premolar
molar
carnassial

HORSE

HERBIVORE'S JAW

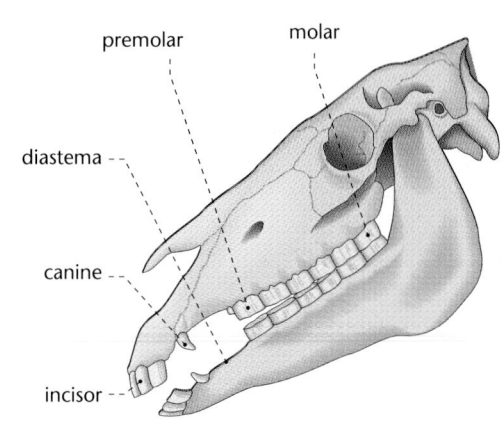

premolar
molar
diastema
canine
incisor

MAJOR TYPES OF HORNS

horns of mouflon

horns of giraffe

horns of rhinoceros

MAJOR TYPES OF TUSKS

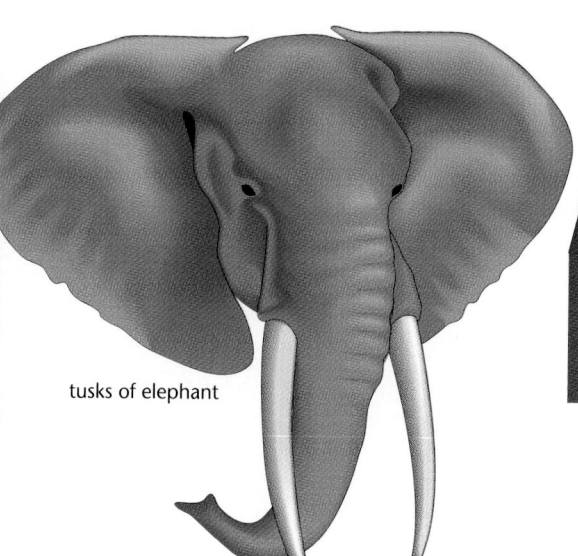

tusks of elephant

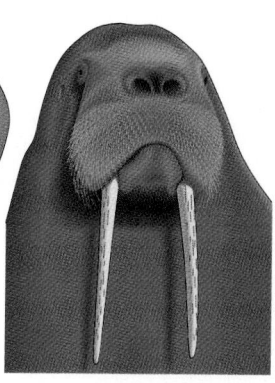

tusks of walrus

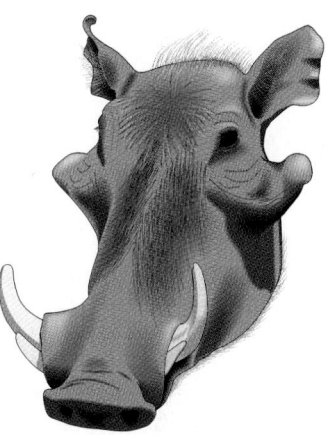

tusks of wart hog

TYPES OF HOOFS

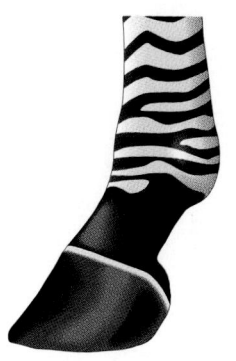

one-toe hoof

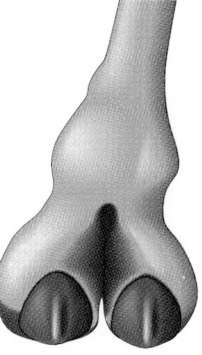

two-toed hoof

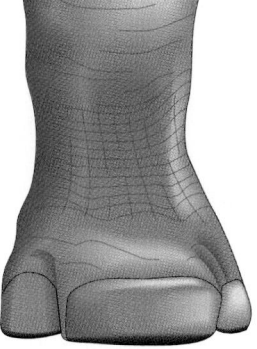

three-toed hoof

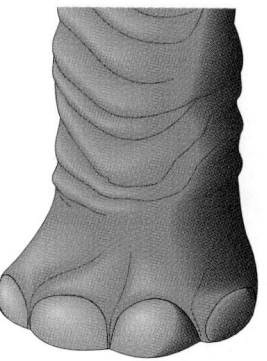

four-toed hoof

MORPHOLOGY

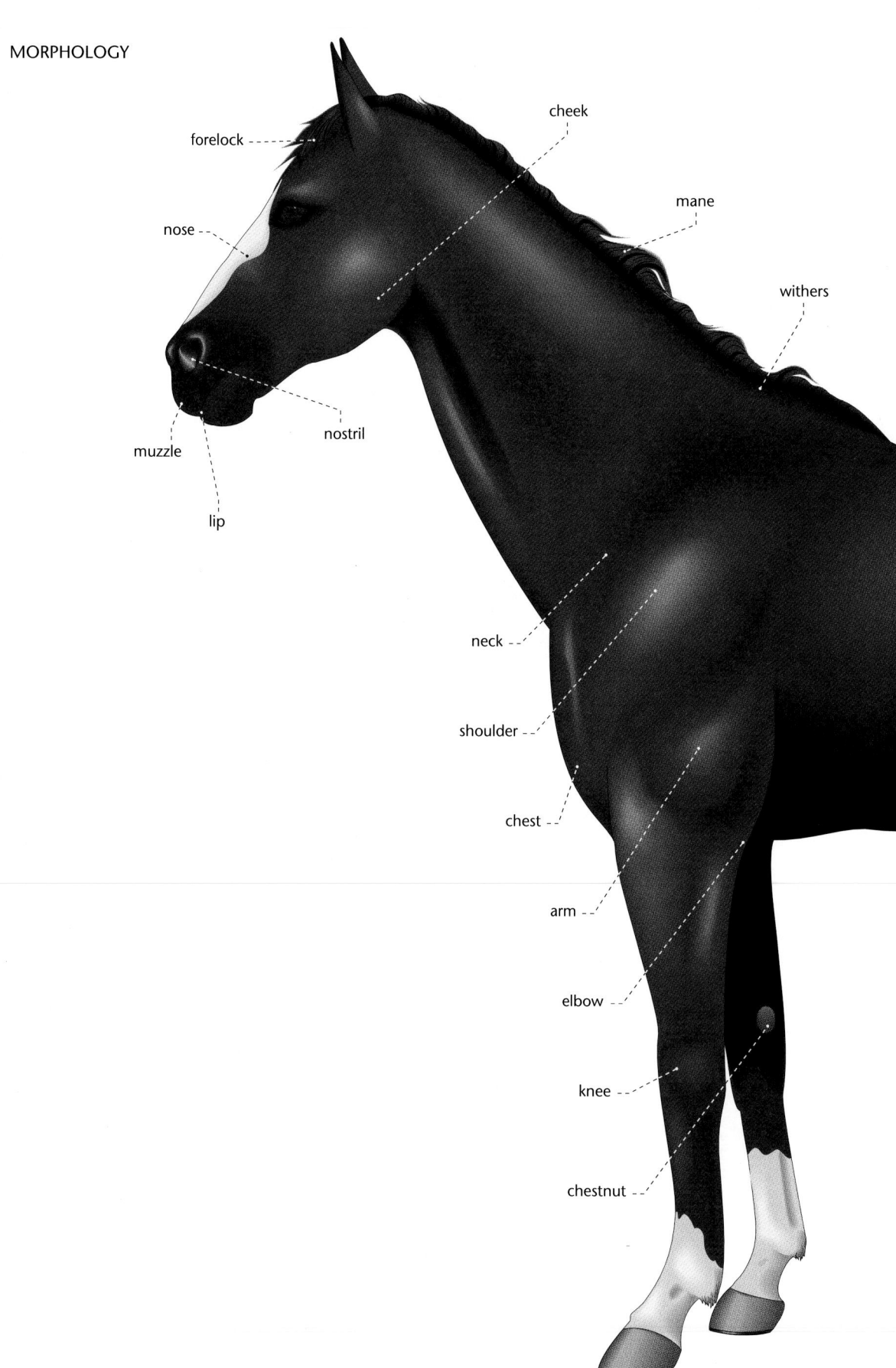

forelock

cheek

mane

withers

nose

muzzle

nostril

lip

neck

shoulder

chest

arm

elbow

knee

chestnut

ANIMAL KINGDOM

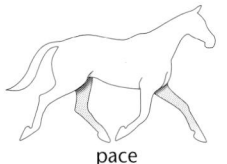
pace

walk

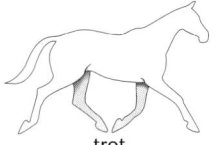
trot

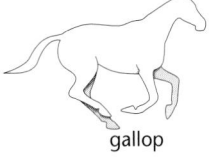
gallop

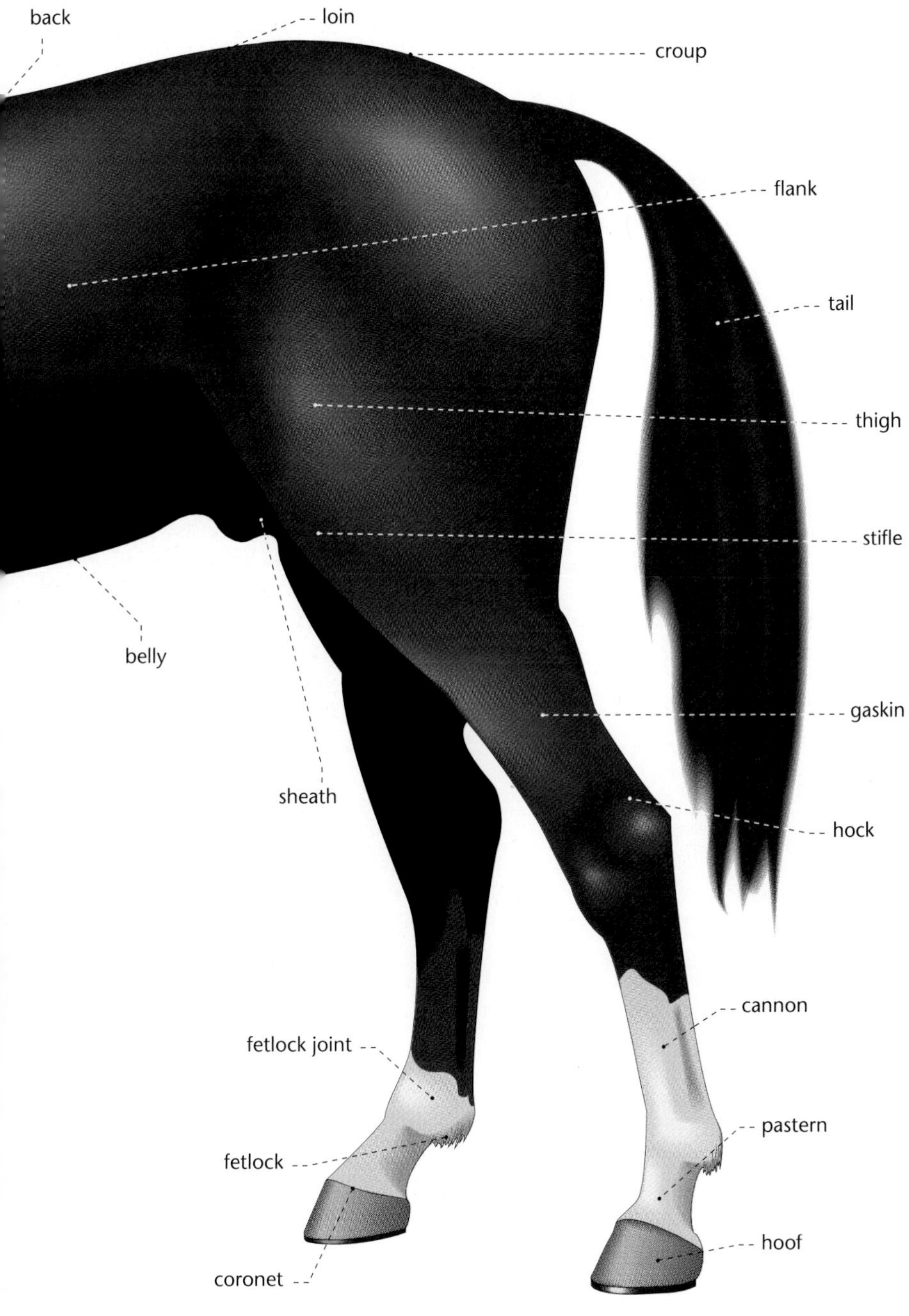

back

loin

croup

flank

tail

thigh

stifle

belly

gaskin

sheath

hock

cannon

fetlock joint

pastern

fetlock

hoof

coronet

ANIMAL KINGDOM

SKELETON

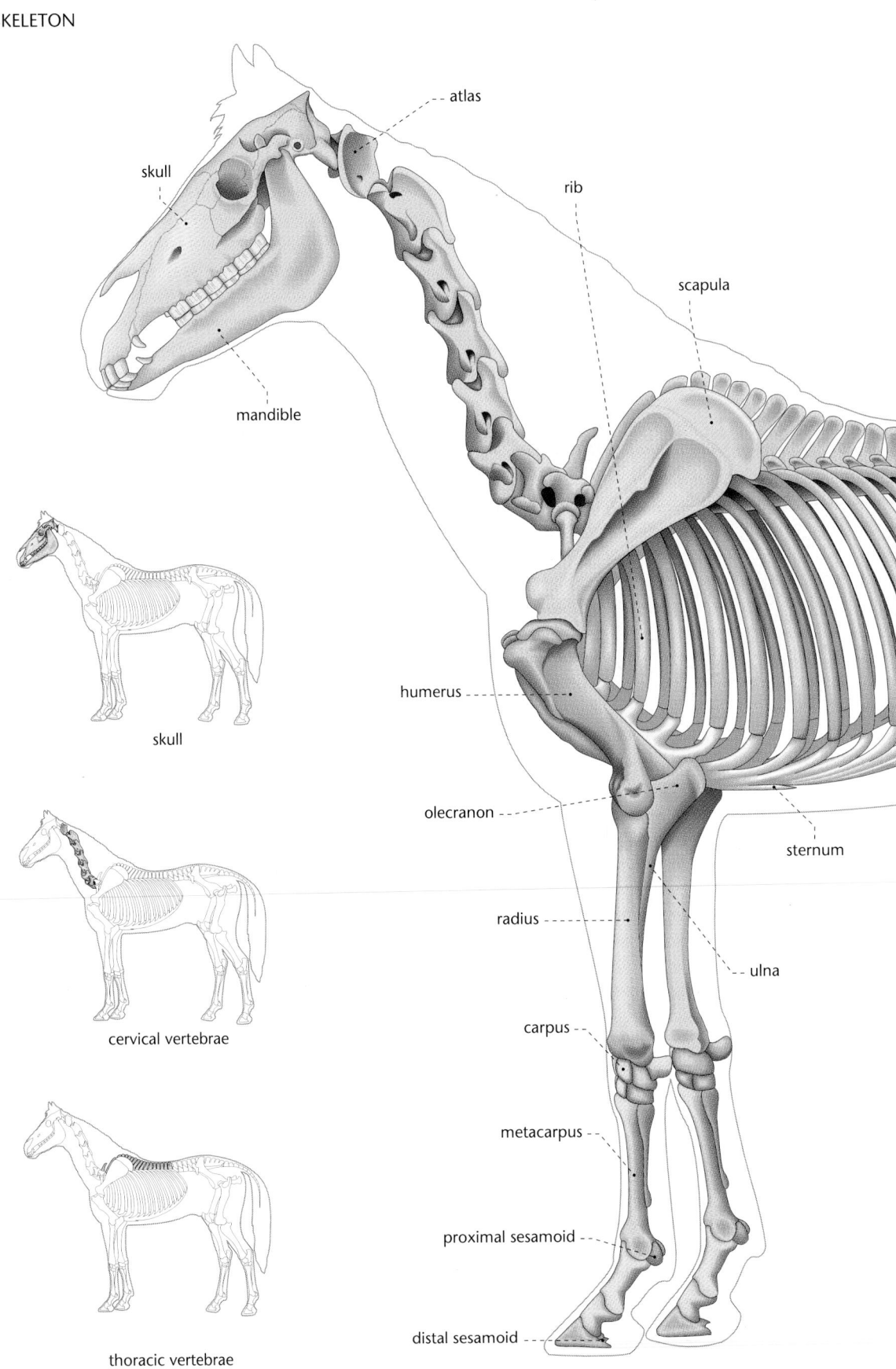

skull

atlas

rib

scapula

mandible

skull

cervical vertebrae

thoracic vertebrae

humerus

olecranon

sternum

radius

ulna

carpus

metacarpus

proximal sesamoid

distal sesamoid

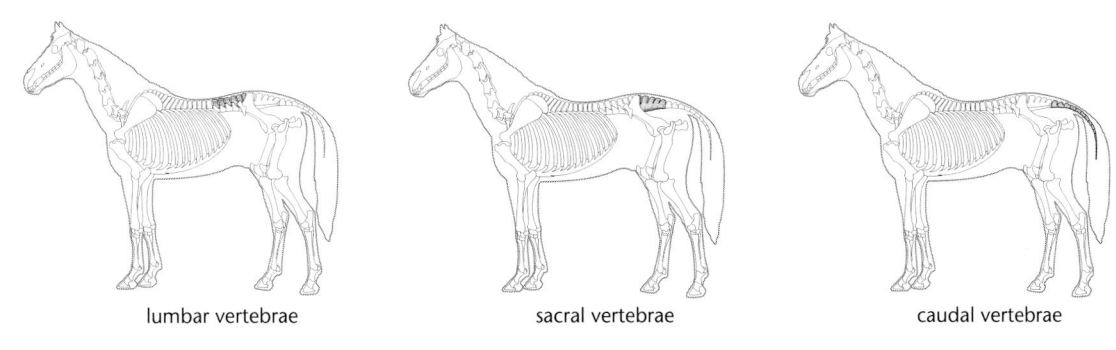

lumbar vertebrae

sacral vertebrae

caudal vertebrae

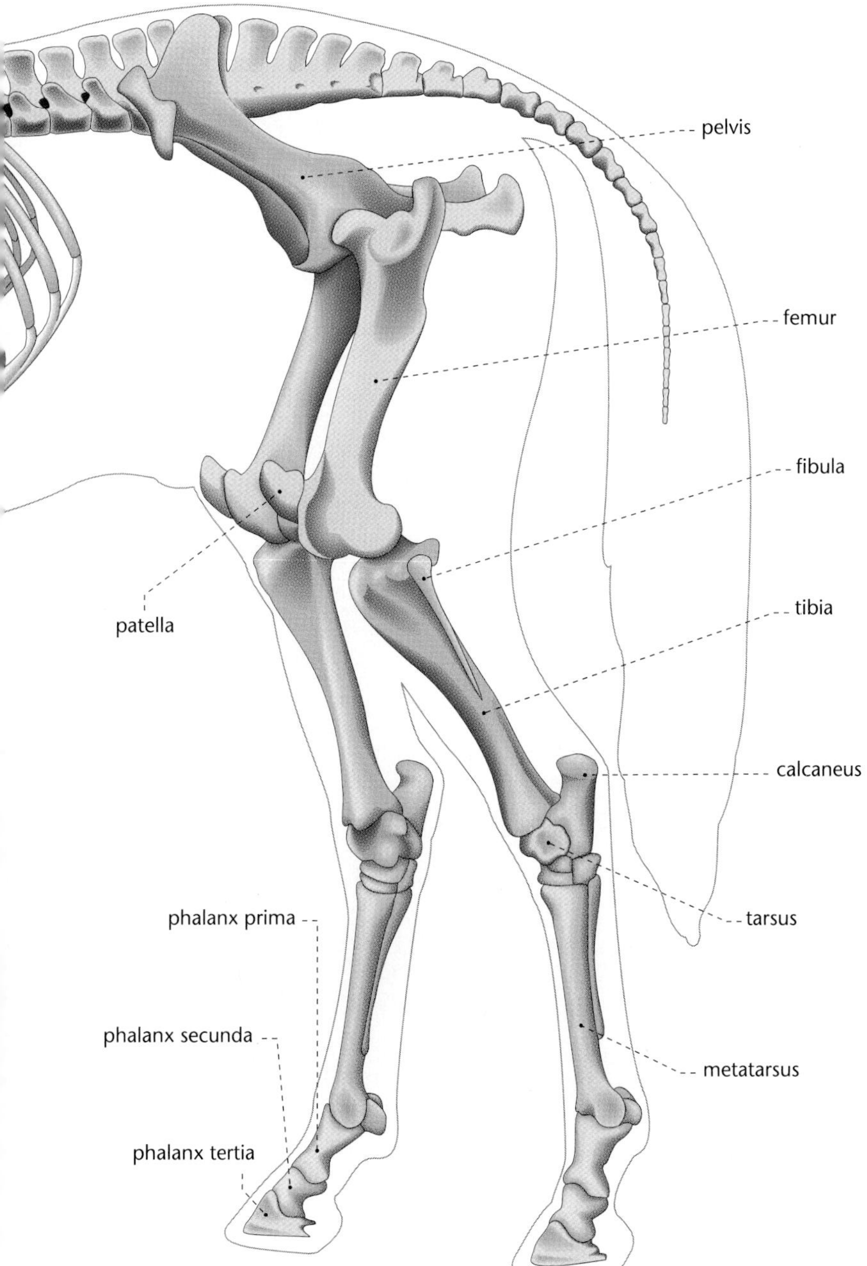

pelvis

femur

fibula

tibia

calcaneus

patella

tarsus

phalanx prima

phalanx secunda

metatarsus

phalanx tertia

PLANTAR SURFACE OF THE HOOF

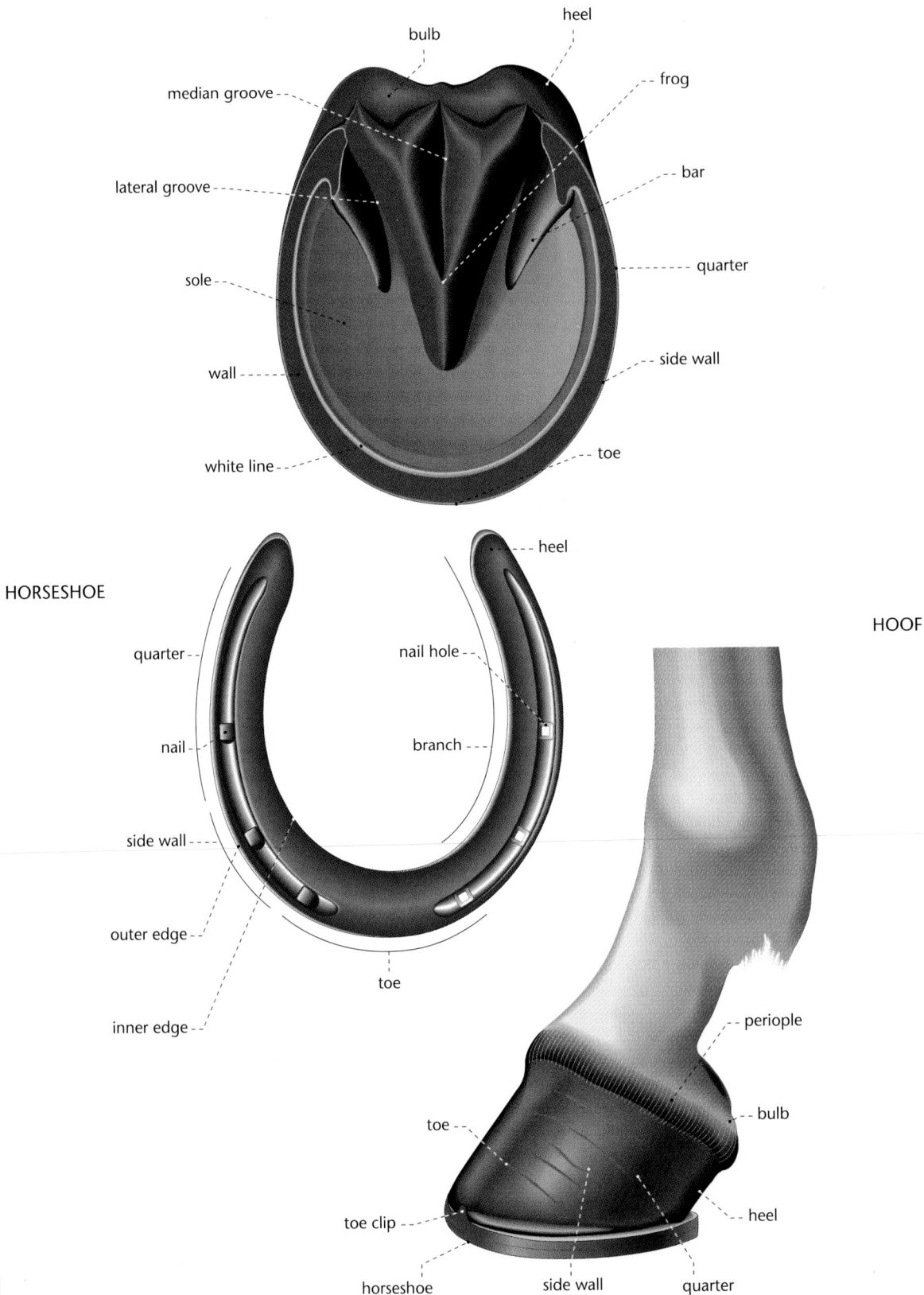

bulb

heel

median groove

frog

lateral groove

bar

sole

quarter

wall

side wall

white line

toe

HORSESHOE

heel

HOOF

quarter

nail hole

nail

branch

side wall

outer edge

toe

inner edge

periople

toe

bulb

heel

toe clip

horseshoe

side wall

quarter

DEER FAMILY

DEER ANTLERS

fork

palm

crown tine

pearl

royal antler

gutter

surroyal antler

bay antler

beam

brow tine

burr

pearls

pedicle

KINDS OF DEER

caribou

white-tailed deer

moose

wapiti

DOG

MORPHOLOGY

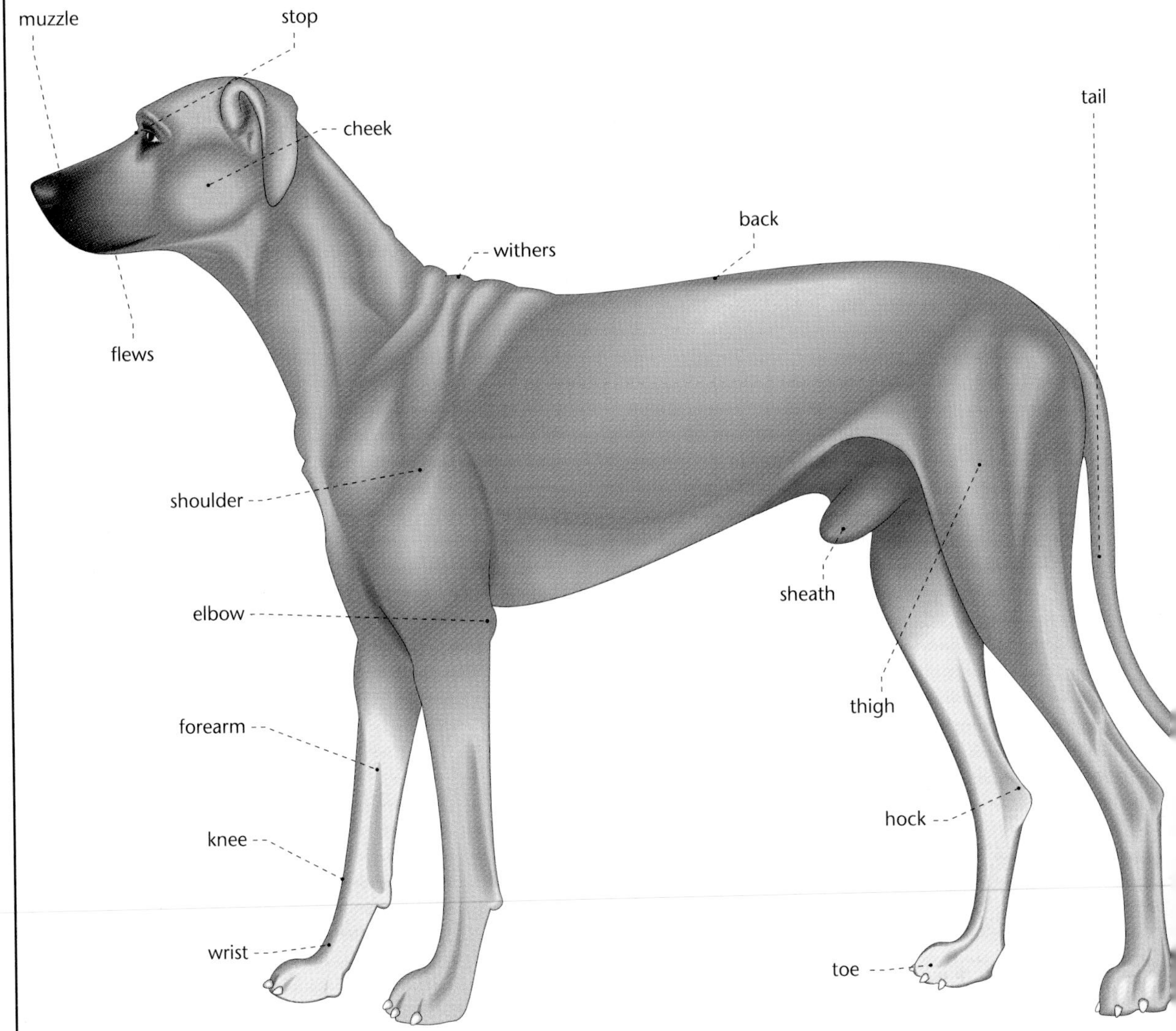

muzzle

stop

cheek

tail

back

withers

flews

shoulder

sheath

elbow

thigh

forearm

hock

knee

wrist

toe

DOG'S FOREPAW

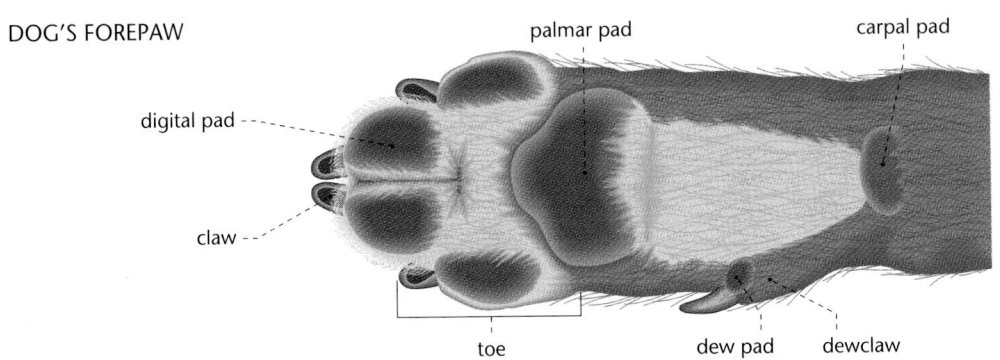

palmar pad

carpal pad

digital pad

claw

toe

dew pad

dewclaw

106

CAT

CAT'S HEAD

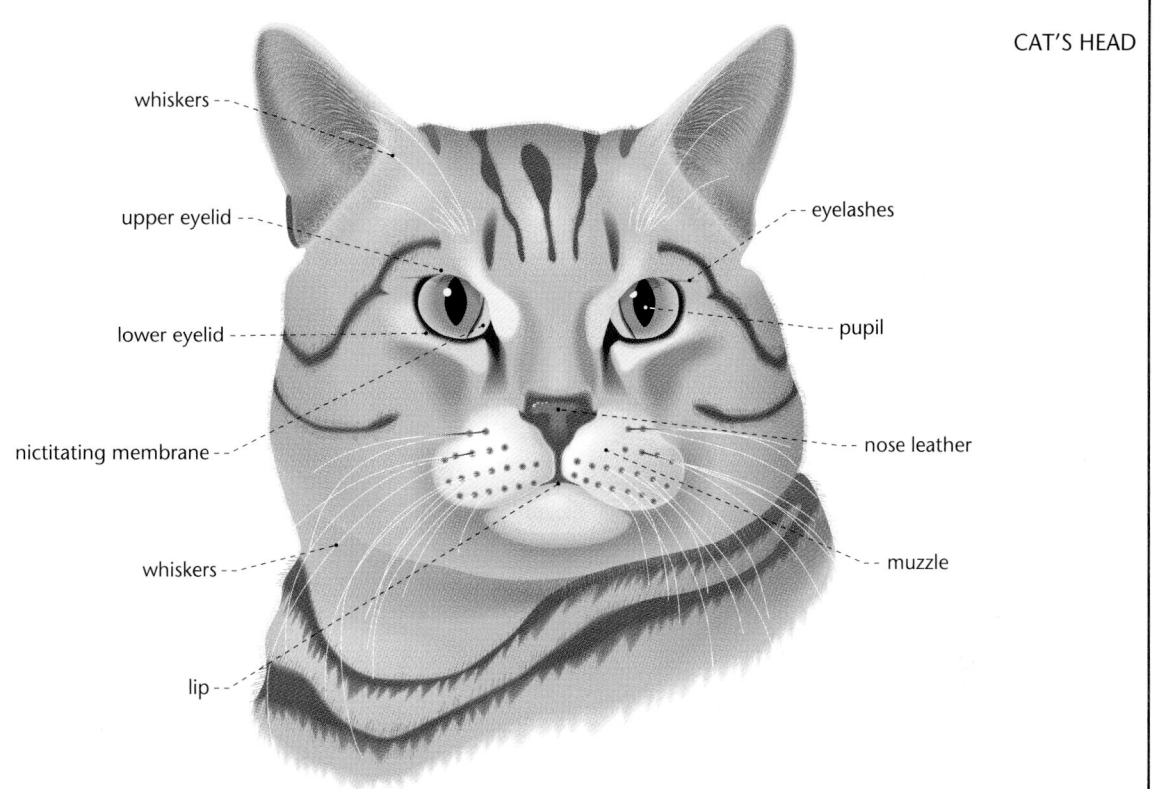

whiskers
upper eyelid
lower eyelid
nictitating membrane
whiskers
lip
eyelashes
pupil
nose leather
muzzle

EXTENDED CLAW

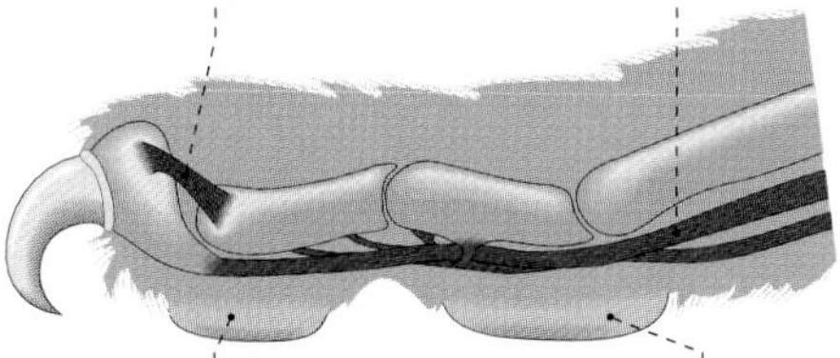

elastic ligament
tendon
digital pad
plantar pad

RETRACTED CLAW

middle phalanx
claw
metacarpus
tendon
proximal phalanx
distal phalanx

ear
eye
tail
fur

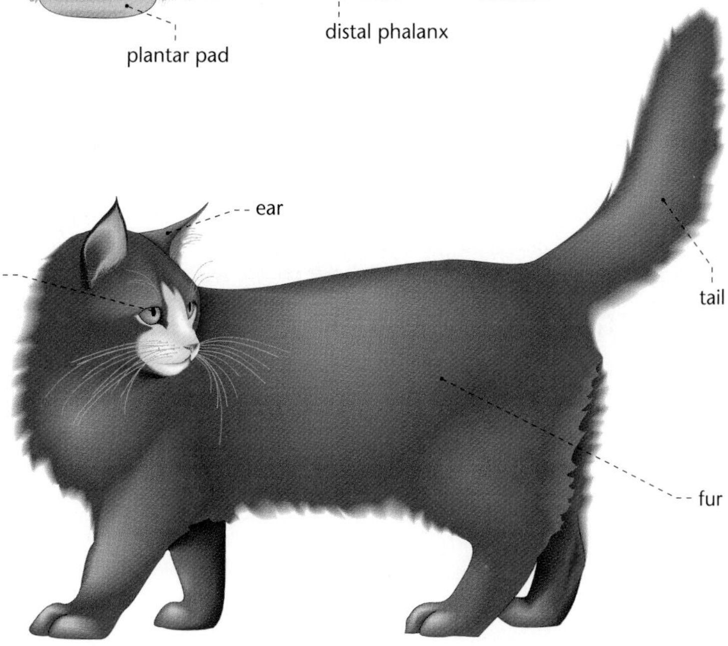

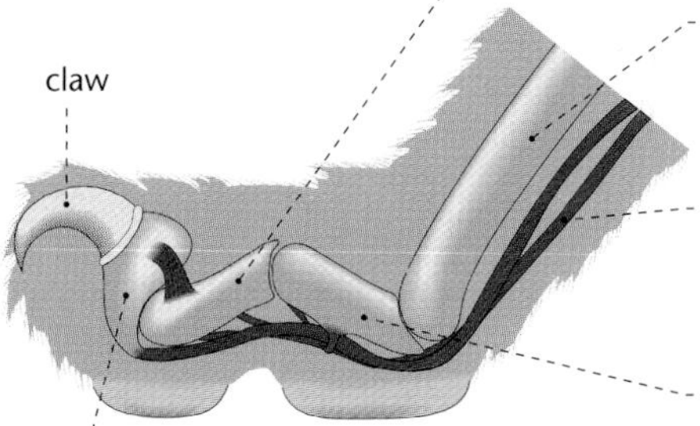

MORPHOLOGY

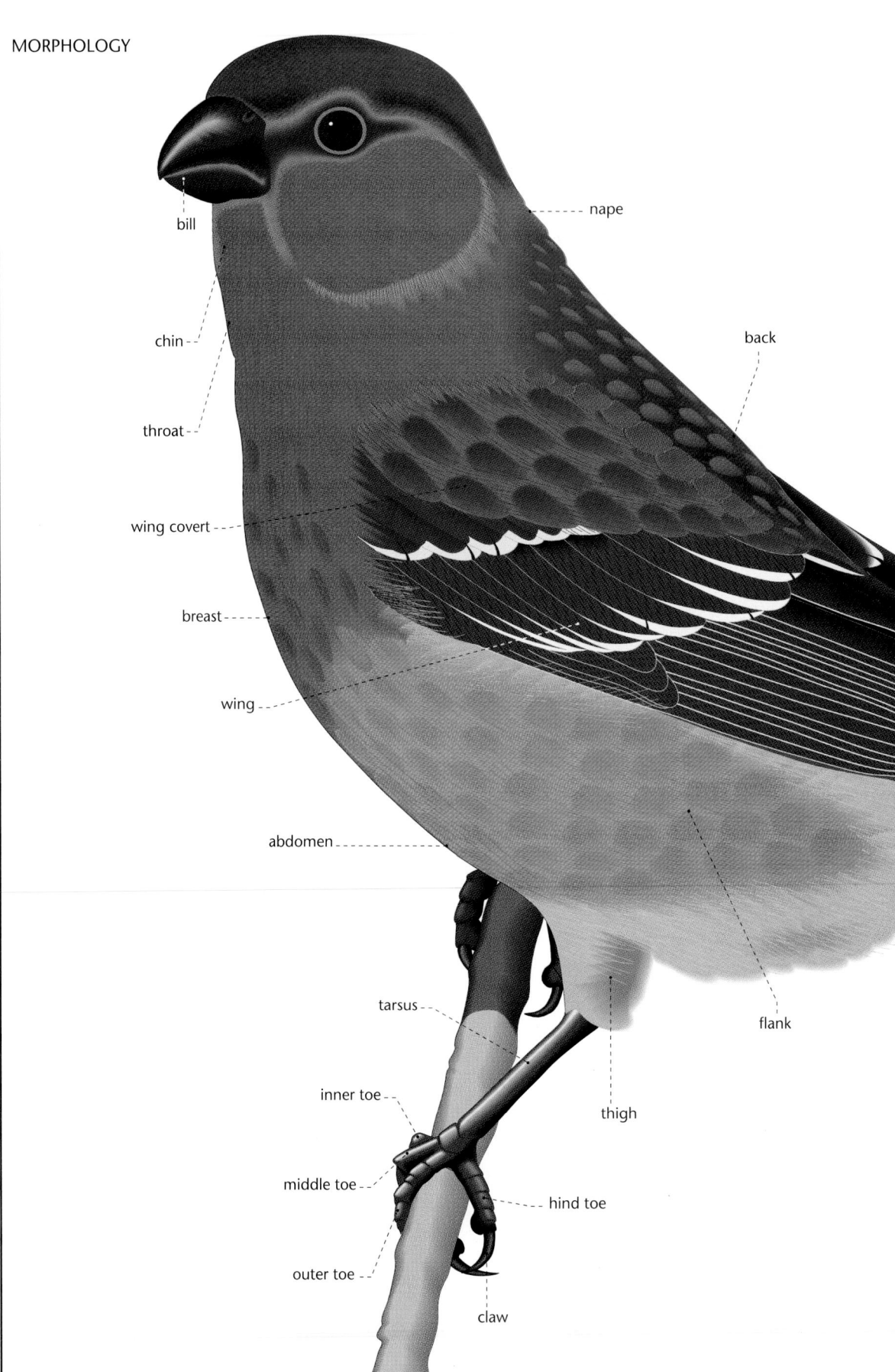

bill

nape

chin

back

throat

wing covert

breast

wing

abdomen

flank

tarsus

inner toe

thigh

middle toe

hind toe

outer toe

claw

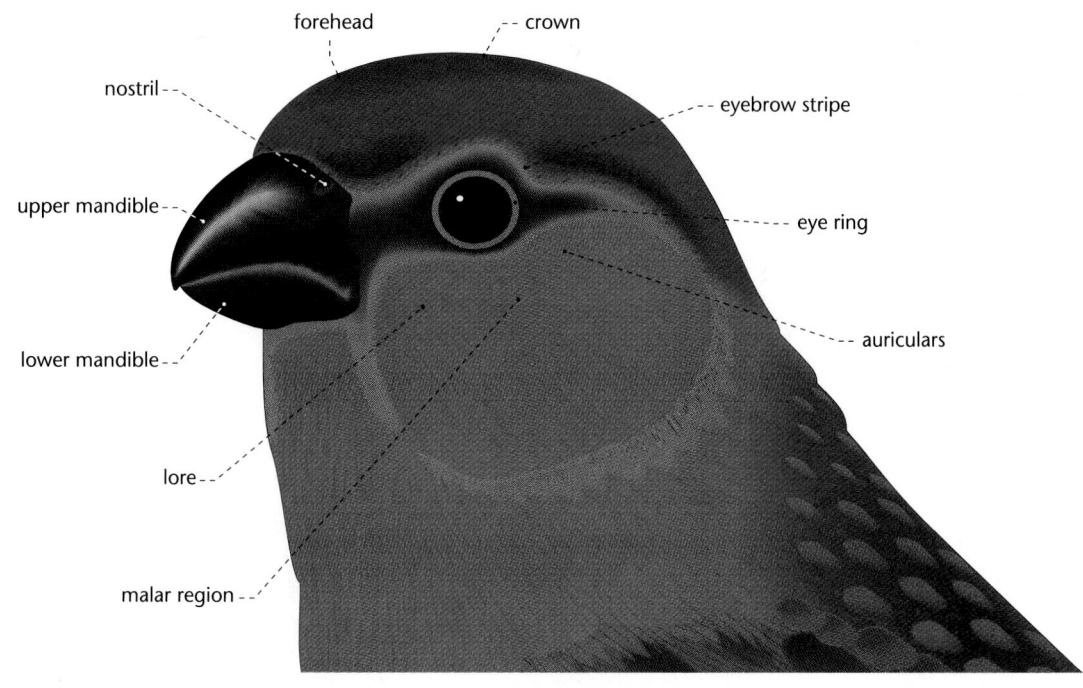

forehead

crown

nostril

eyebrow stripe

upper mandible

eye ring

lower mandible

auriculars

lore

malar region

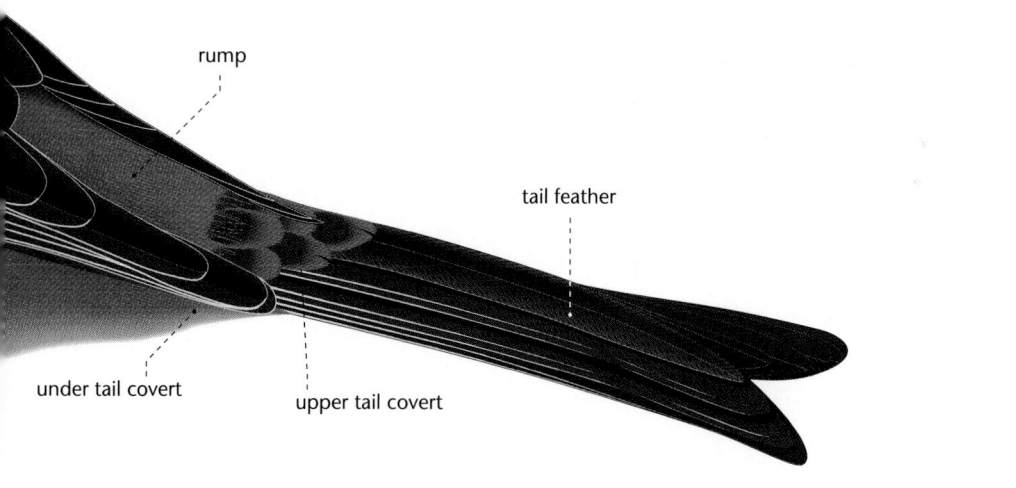

rump

tail feather

under tail covert

upper tail covert

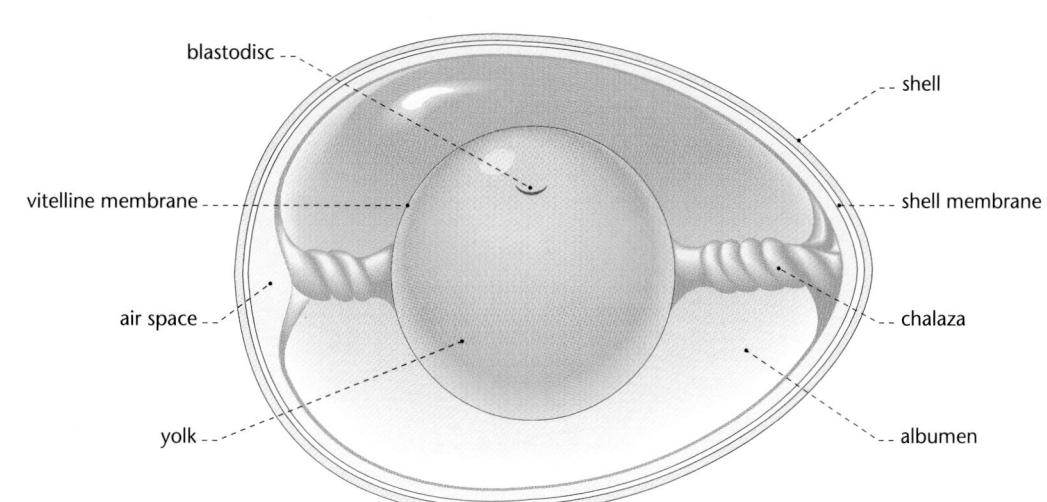

blastodisc

shell

vitelline membrane

shell membrane

air space

chalaza

yolk

albumen

WING

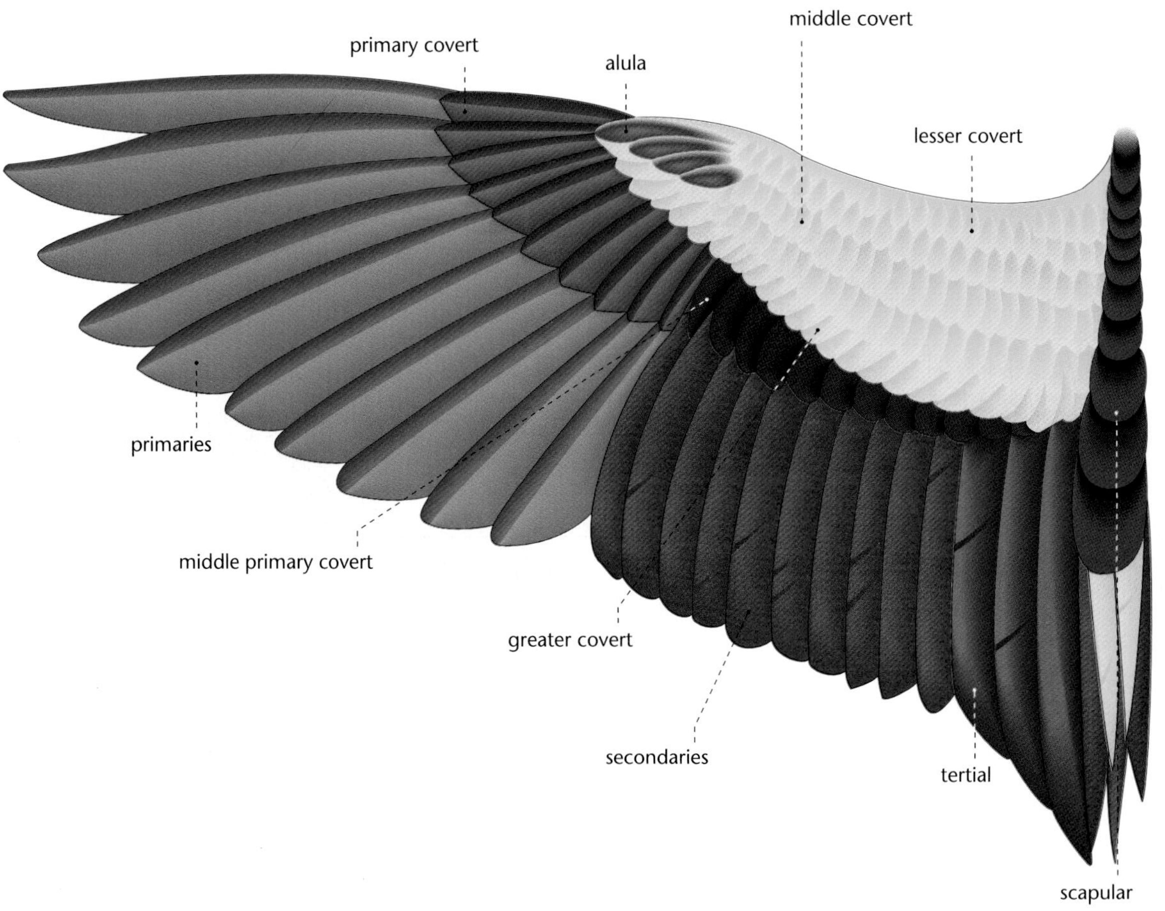

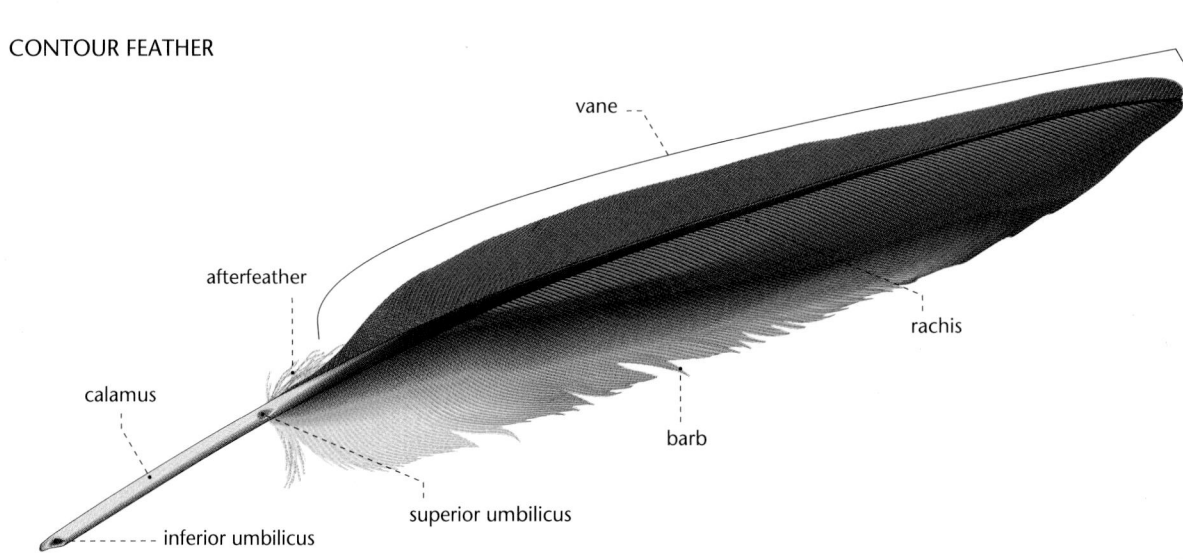

primary covert

alula

middle covert

lesser covert

primaries

middle primary covert

greater covert

secondaries

tertial

scapular

CONTOUR FEATHER

vane

afterfeather

rachis

calamus

barb

superior umbilicus

inferior umbilicus

PRINCIPAL TYPES OF BILLS

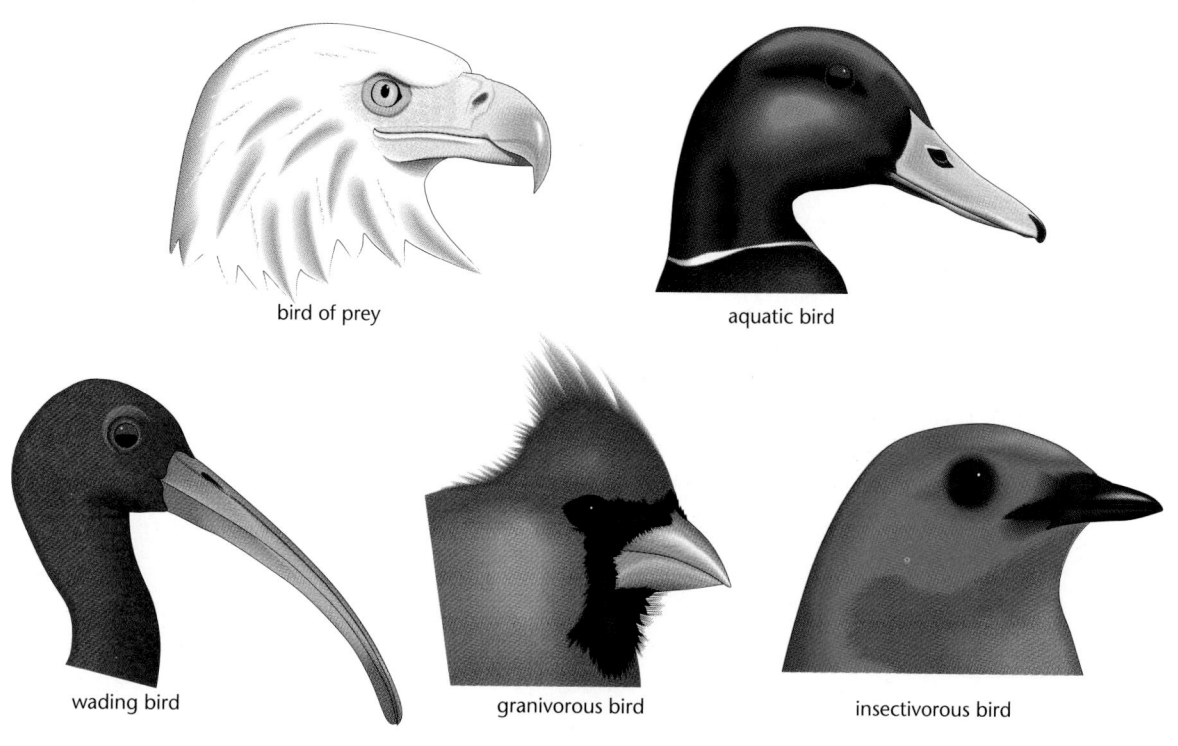

bird of prey

aquatic bird

wading bird

granivorous bird

insectivorous bird

PRINCIPAL TYPES OF FEET

perching bird

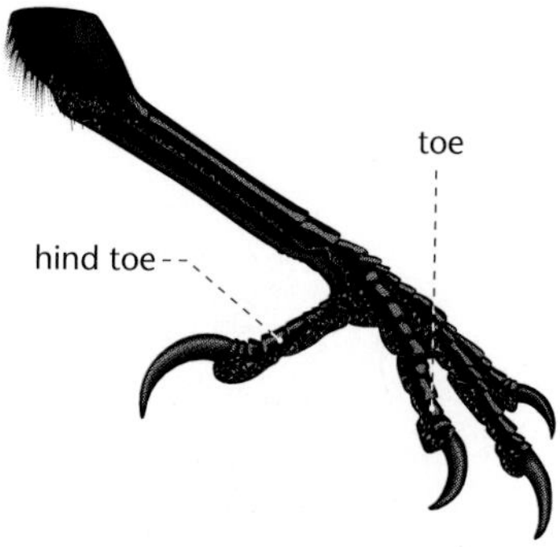
toe
hind toe

bird of prey

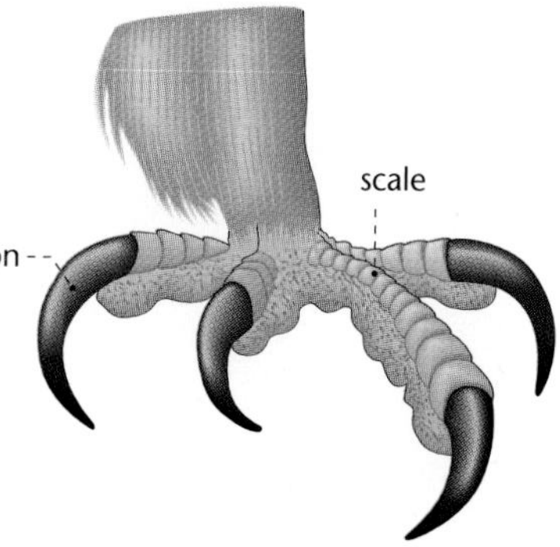
scale
talon

aquatic bird

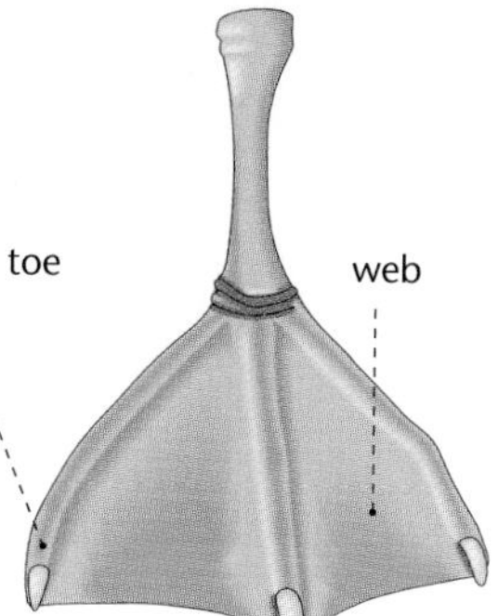
webbed toe
web

aquatic bird

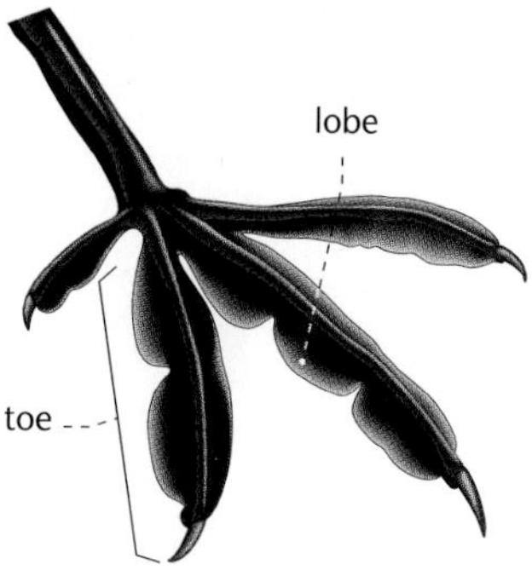
lobe
lobate toe

BAT

BAT'S HEAD

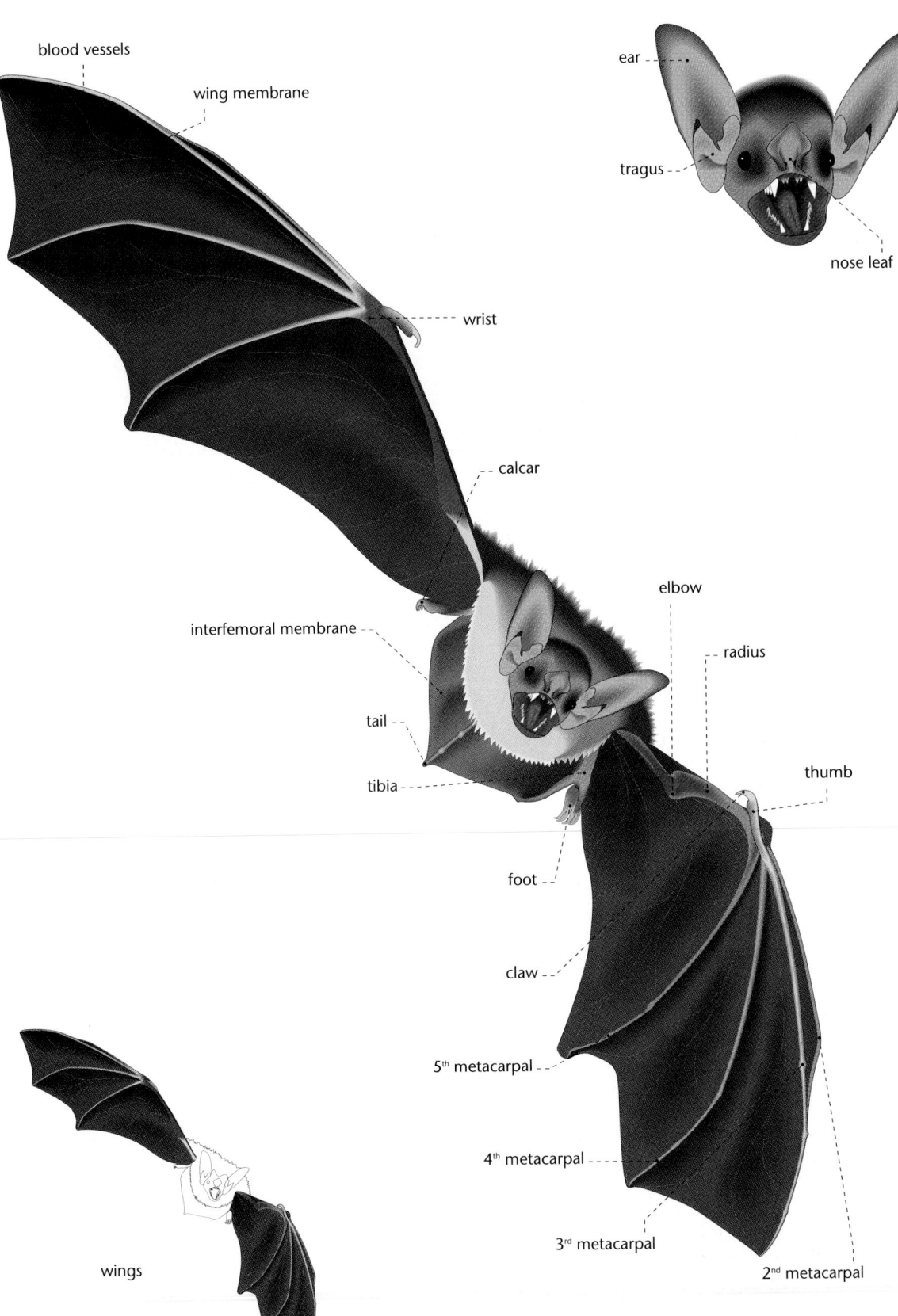

blood vessels

wing membrane

ear

tragus

nose leaf

wrist

calcar

elbow

radius

interfemoral membrane

tail

tibia

thumb

foot

claw

5th metacarpal

4th metacarpal

3rd metacarpal

2nd metacarpal

wings

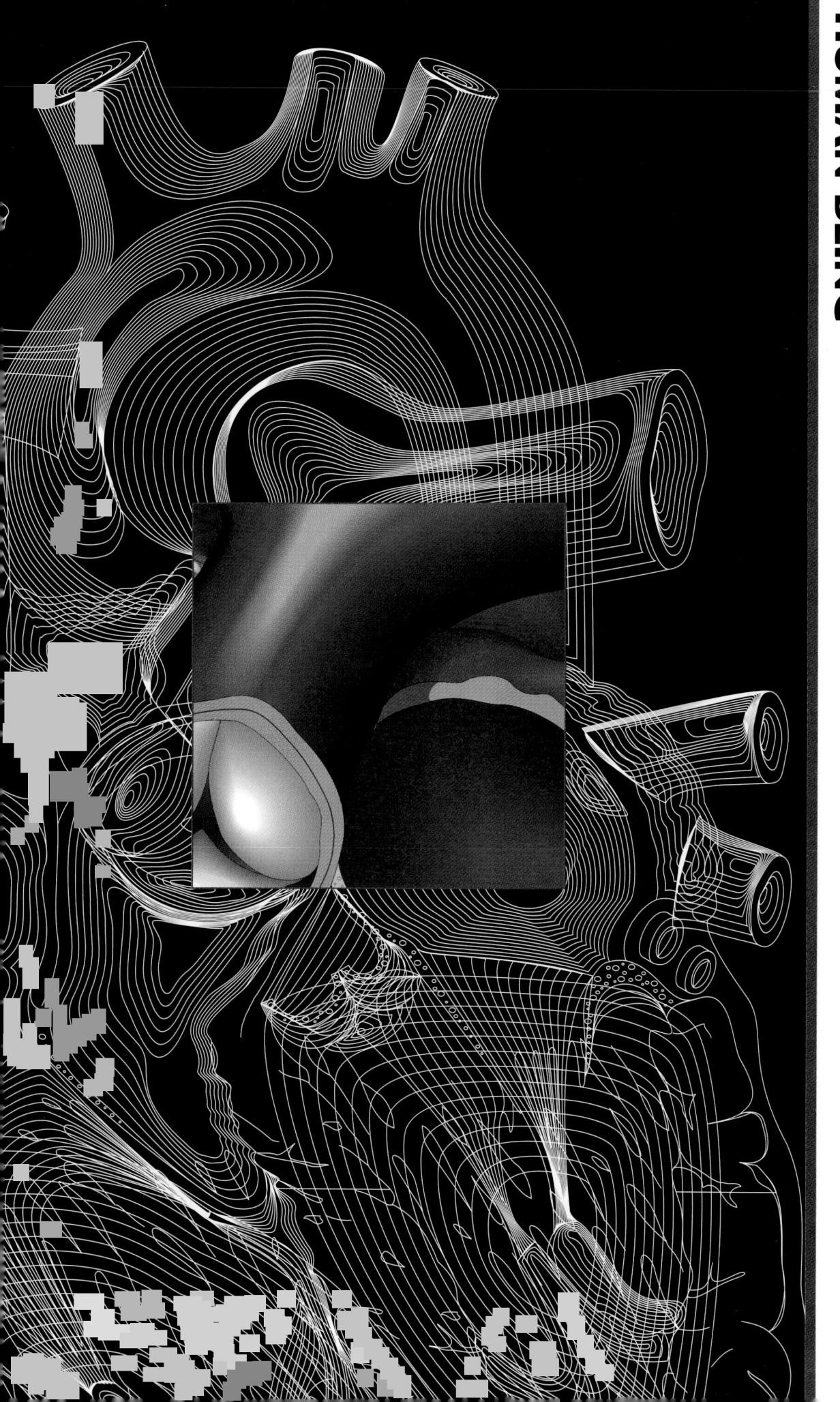

CONTENTS

PLANT CELL 115

ANIMAL CELL..115

HUMAN BODY 116

MUSCLES 120

SKELETON..122

BLOOD CIRCULATION 124

MALE GENITAL ORGANS..127

FEMALE GENITAL ORGANS 128

BREAST 129

RESPIRATORY SYSTEM 130

DIGESTIVE SYSTEM 131

URINARY SYSTEM..132

NERVOUS SYSTEM 133

SENSE ORGANS: TOUCH 136

SENSE ORGANS: HEARING 138

SENSE ORGANS: SIGHT...140

SENSE ORGANS: SMELL 141

SENSES OF SMELL AND TASTE..142

TEETH 144

PLANT CELL

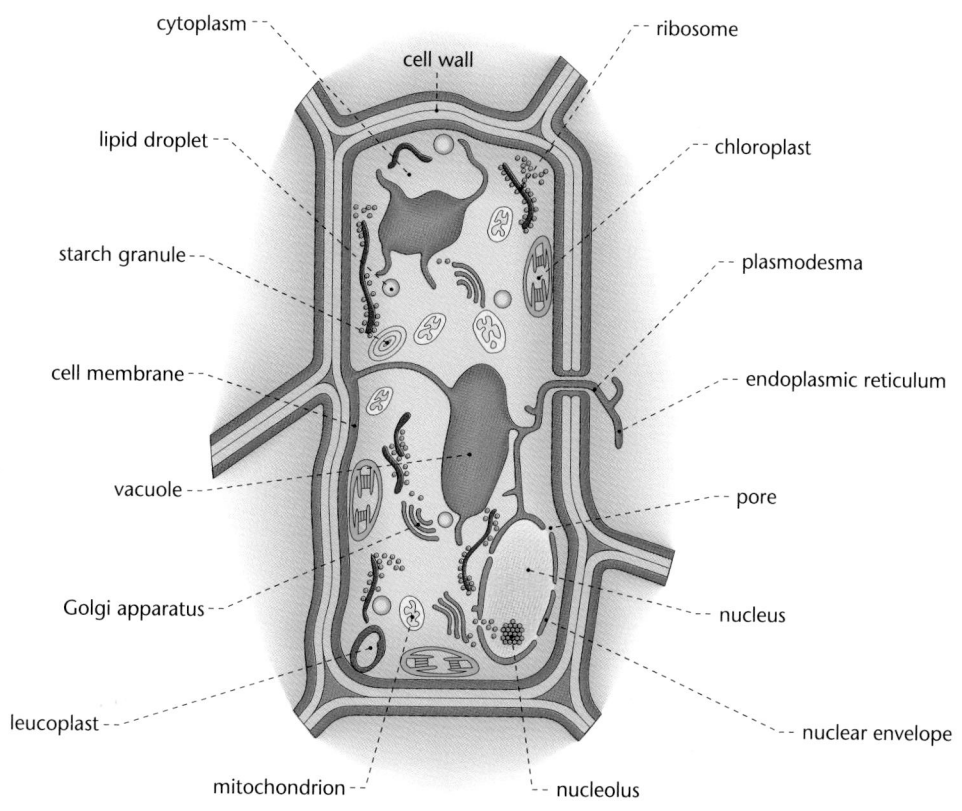

cytoplasm

cell wall

ribosome

lipid droplet

chloroplast

starch granule

plasmodesma

cell membrane

endoplasmic reticulum

vacuole

pore

Golgi apparatus

nucleus

leucoplast

nuclear envelope

mitochondrion

nucleolus

ANIMAL CELL

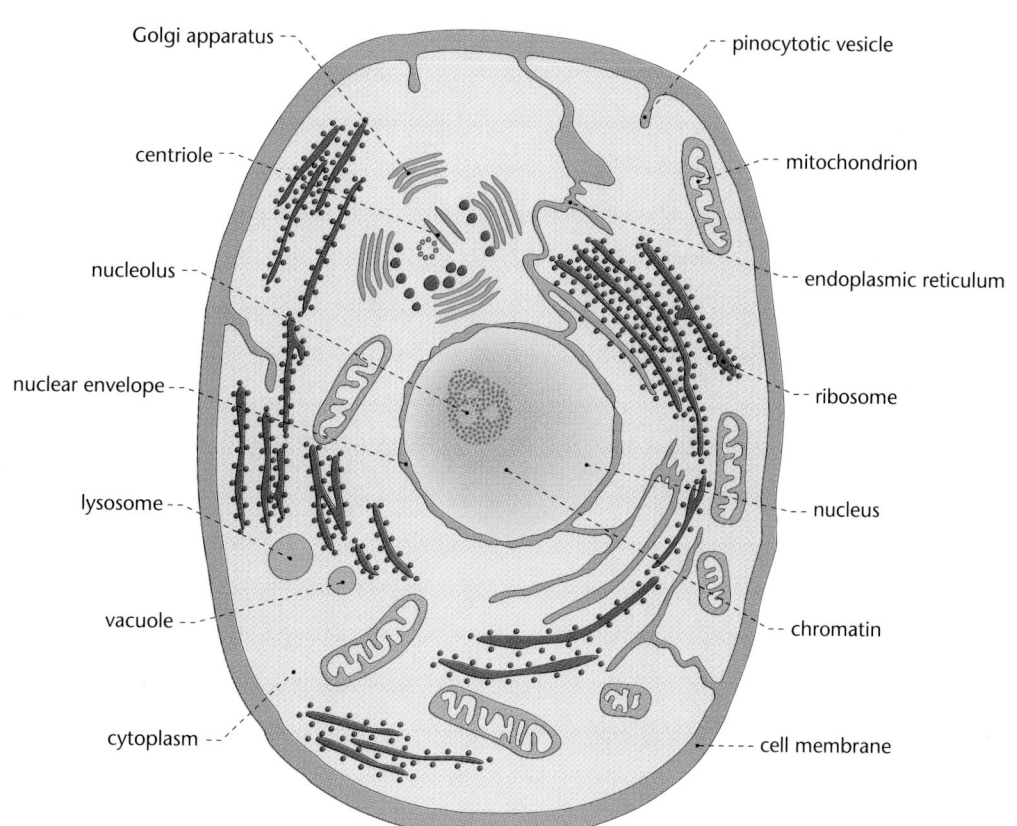

Golgi apparatus

pinocytotic vesicle

centriole

mitochondrion

nucleolus

endoplasmic reticulum

nuclear envelope

ribosome

lysosome

nucleus

vacuole

chromatin

cytoplasm

cell membrane

HUMAN BODY

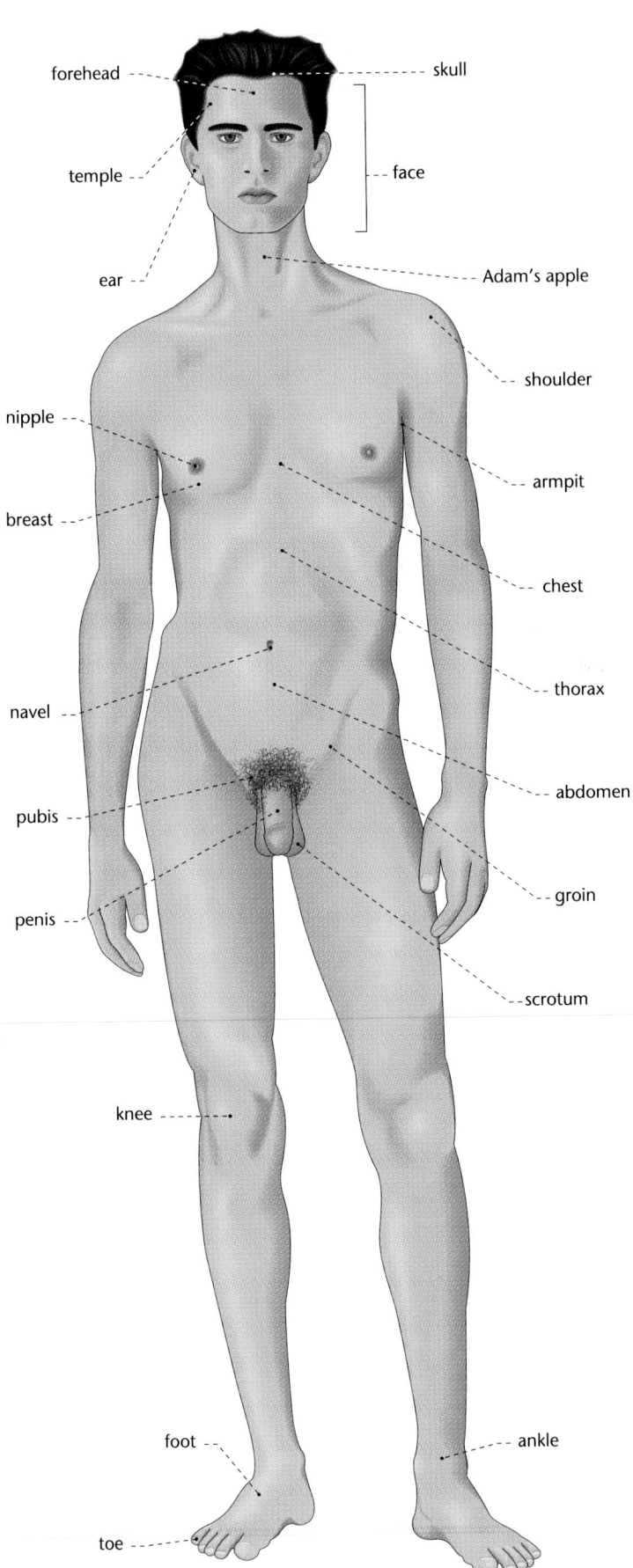

forehead —— skull

temple —— face

ear ——

—— Adam's apple

—— shoulder

nipple —— —— armpit

breast —— —— chest

—— thorax

navel —— —— abdomen

pubis —— —— groin

penis —— —— scrotum

knee ——

foot —— —— ankle

toe ——

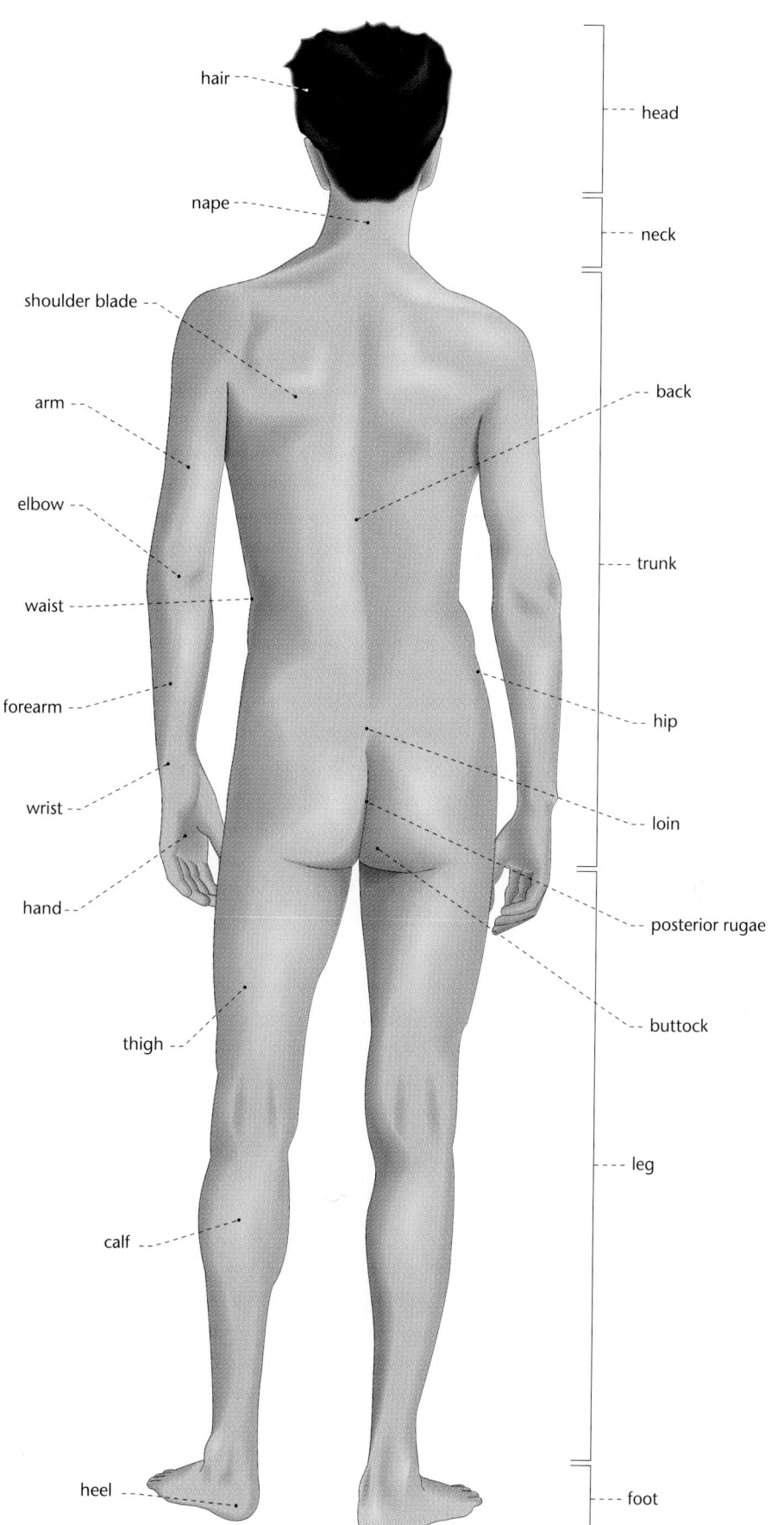

hair -----

nape -----

shoulder blade ---

arm ---

elbow ---

waist -----

forearm ---

wrist ---

hand ---

thigh ---

calf ---

heel ---

head

neck

back

trunk

hip

loin

posterior rugae

buttock

leg

foot

HUMAN BODY

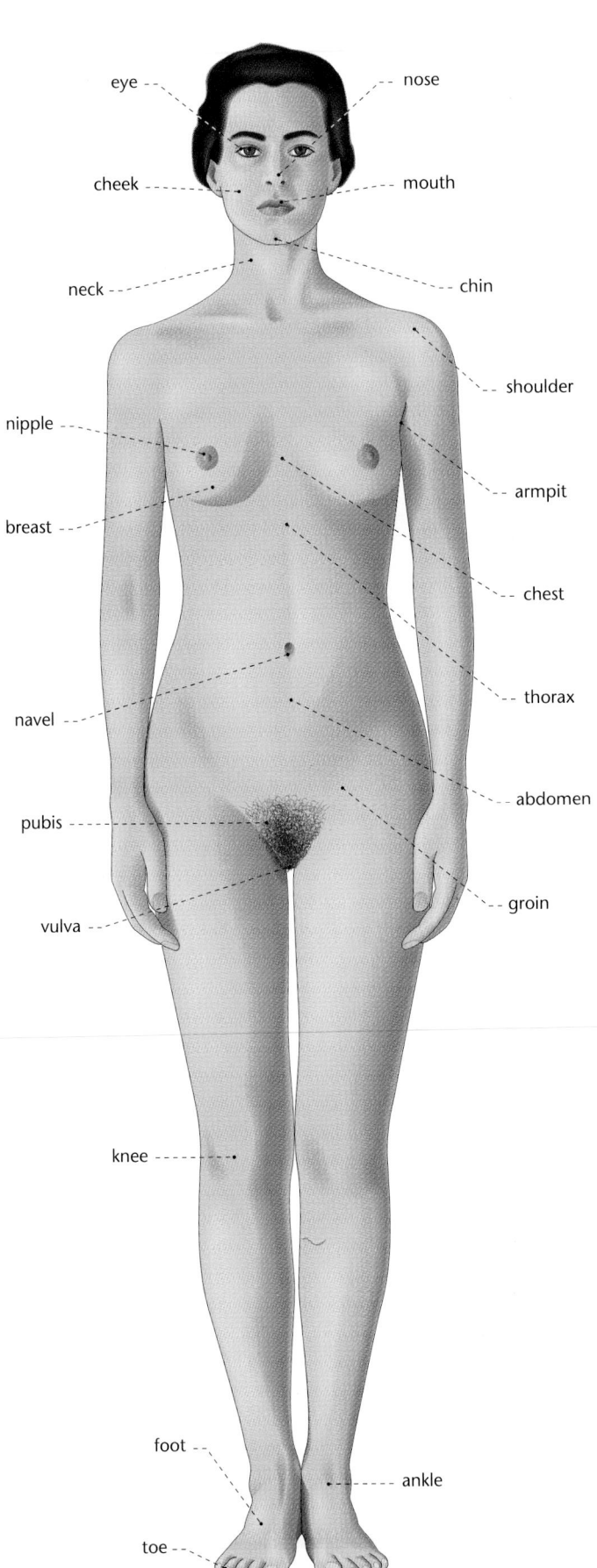

eye

nose

cheek

mouth

neck

chin

shoulder

nipple

armpit

breast

chest

navel

thorax

pubis

abdomen

vulva

groin

knee

foot

ankle

toe

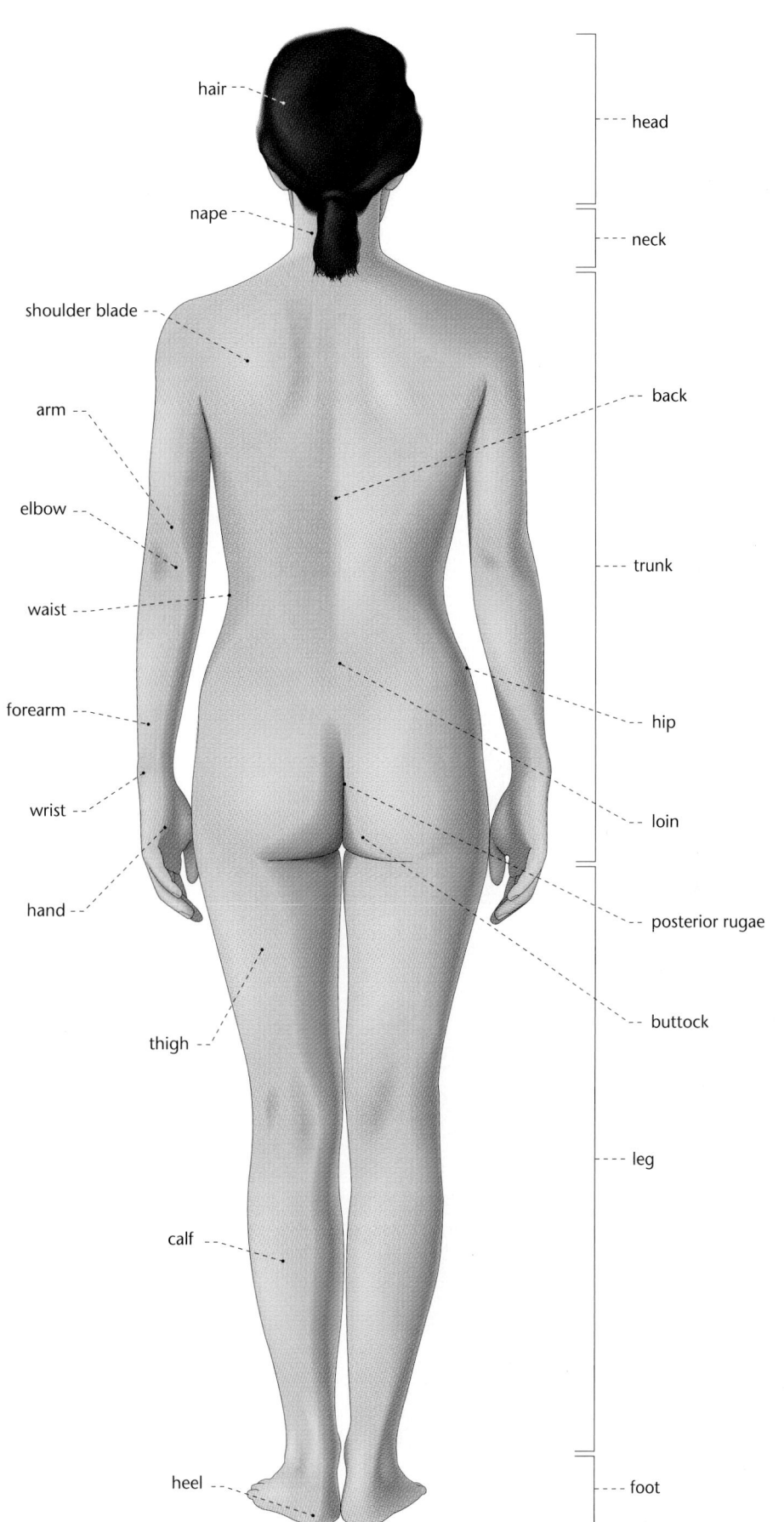

hair

nape

shoulder blade

arm

elbow

waist

forearm

wrist

hand

thigh

calf

heel

head

neck

back

trunk

hip

loin

posterior rugae

buttock

leg

foot

MUSCLES

ANTERIOR VIEW

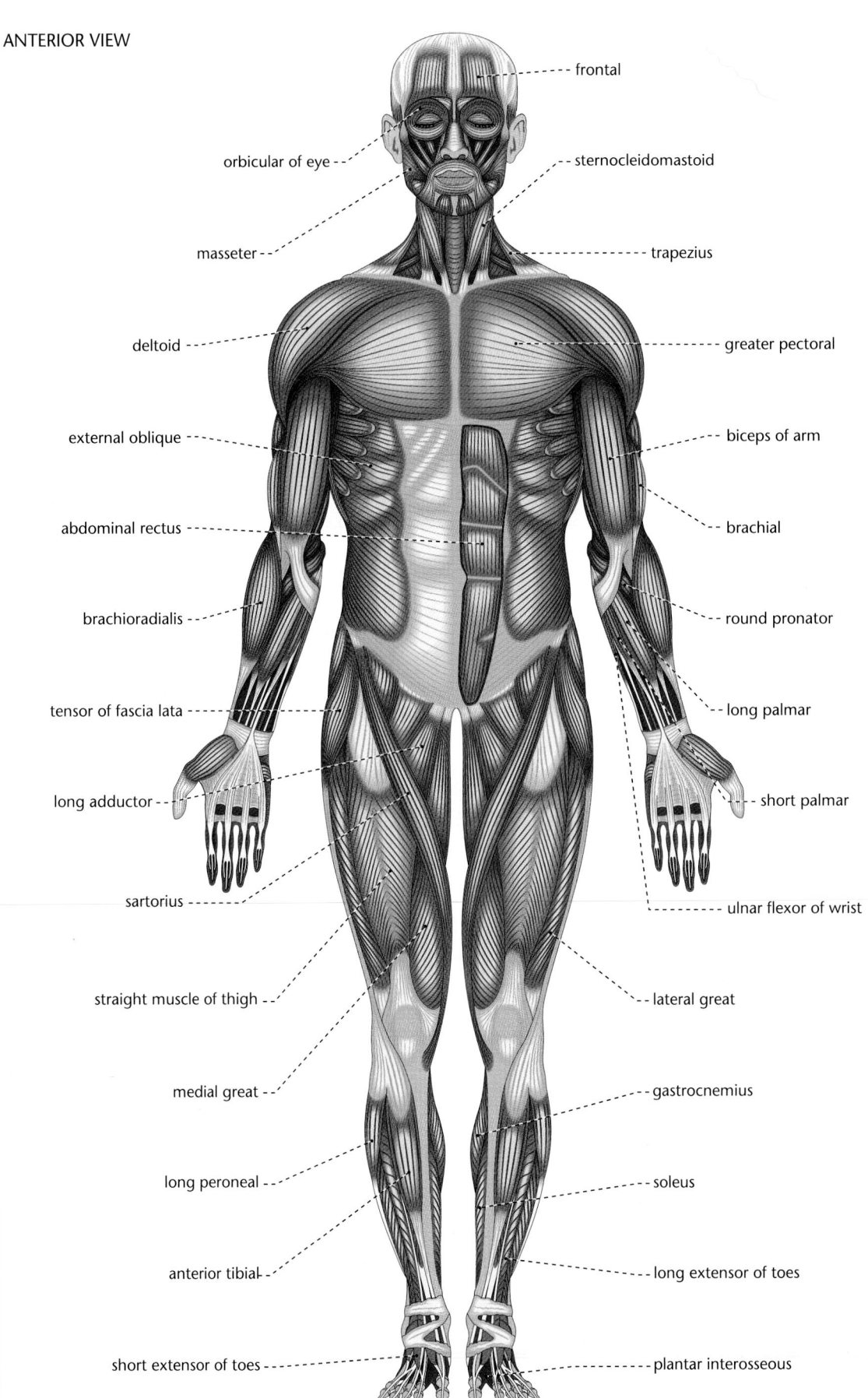

frontal

orbicular of eye

sternocleidomastoid

masseter

trapezius

deltoid

greater pectoral

external oblique

biceps of arm

abdominal rectus

brachial

brachioradialis

round pronator

tensor of fascia lata

long palmar

long adductor

short palmar

sartorius

ulnar flexor of wrist

straight muscle of thigh

lateral great

medial great

gastrocnemius

long peroneal

soleus

anterior tibial

long extensor of toes

short extensor of toes

plantar interosseous

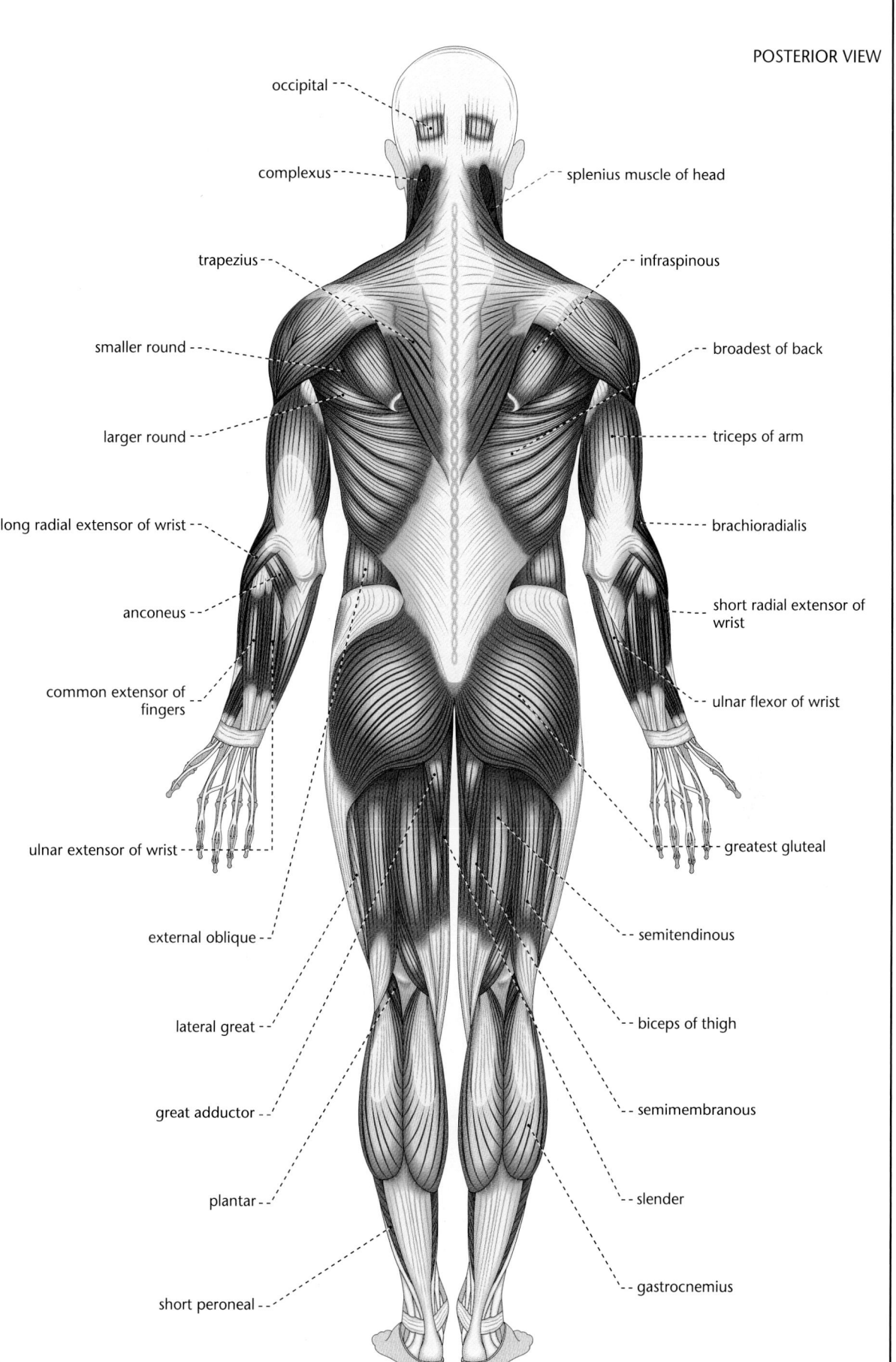

occipital

complexus

splenius muscle of head

trapezius

infraspinous

smaller round

broadest of back

larger round

triceps of arm

long radial extensor of wrist

brachioradialis

anconeus

short radial extensor of wrist

common extensor of fingers

ulnar flexor of wrist

ulnar extensor of wrist

greatest gluteal

external oblique

semitendinous

lateral great

biceps of thigh

great adductor

semimembranous

plantar

slender

short peroneal

gastrocnemius

SKELETON

ANTERIOR VIEW

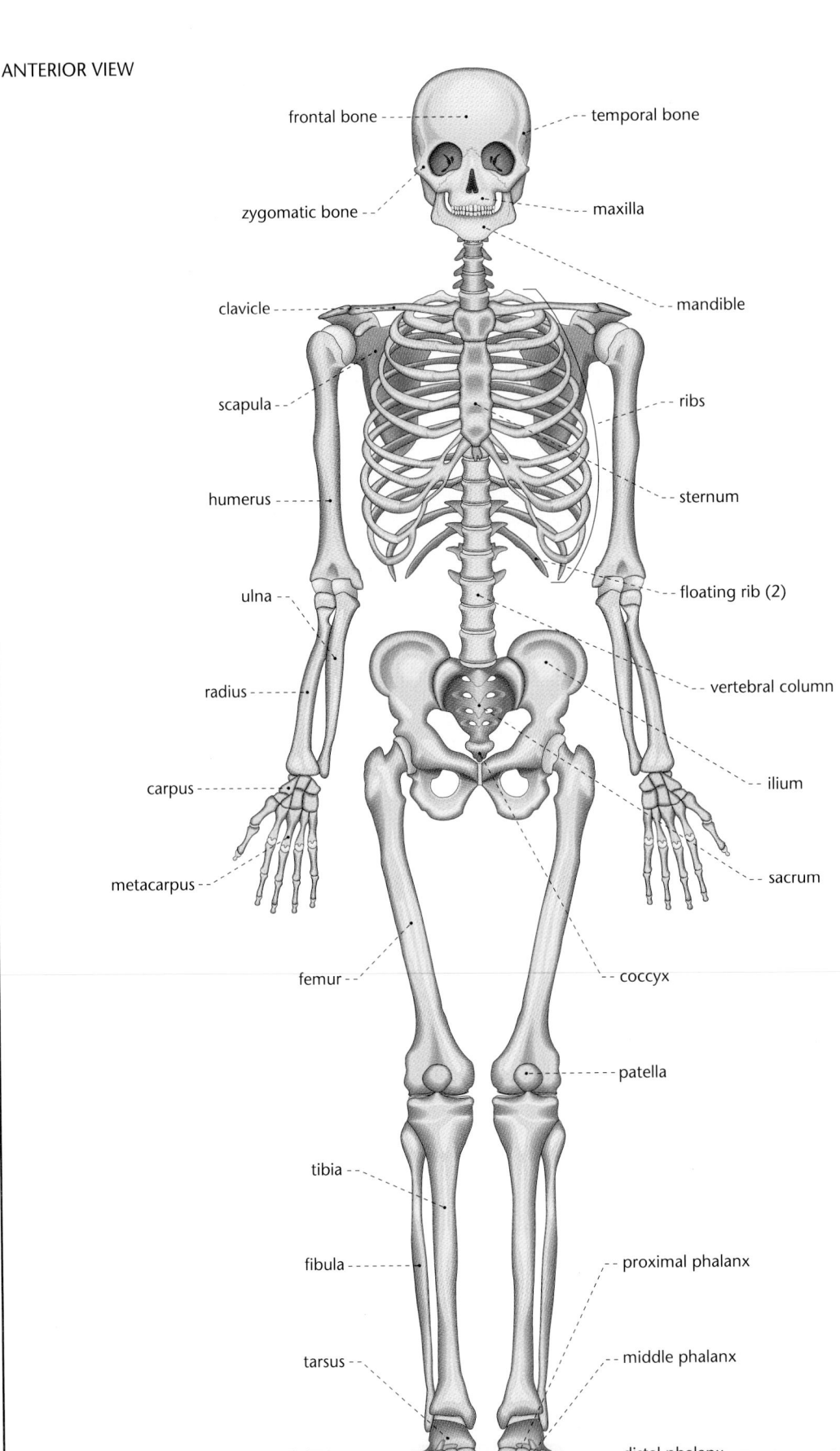

frontal bone

temporal bone

zygomatic bone

maxilla

mandible

clavicle

scapula

ribs

humerus

sternum

ulna

floating rib (2)

radius

vertebral column

carpus

ilium

metacarpus

sacrum

femur

coccyx

patella

tibia

fibula

proximal phalanx

tarsus

middle phalanx

metatarsus

distal phalanx

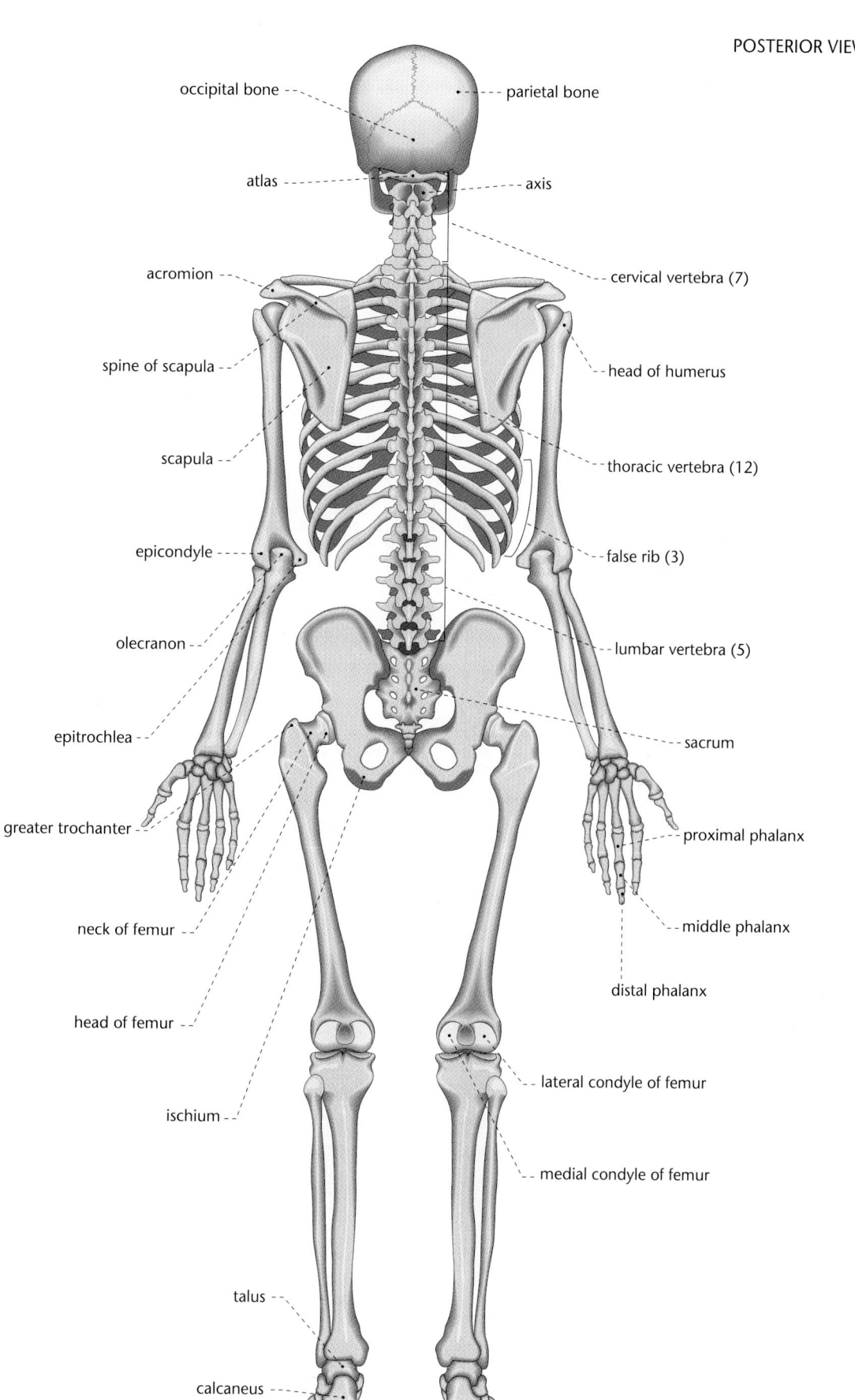

occipital bone

parietal bone

atlas

axis

cervical vertebra (7)

acromion

head of humerus

spine of scapula

scapula

thoracic vertebra (12)

false rib (3)

epicondyle

olecranon

lumbar vertebra (5)

epitrochlea

sacrum

greater trochanter

proximal phalanx

neck of femur

middle phalanx

head of femur

distal phalanx

ischium

lateral condyle of femur

medial condyle of femur

talus

calcaneus

HUMAN BEING

SCHEMA OF CIRCULATION

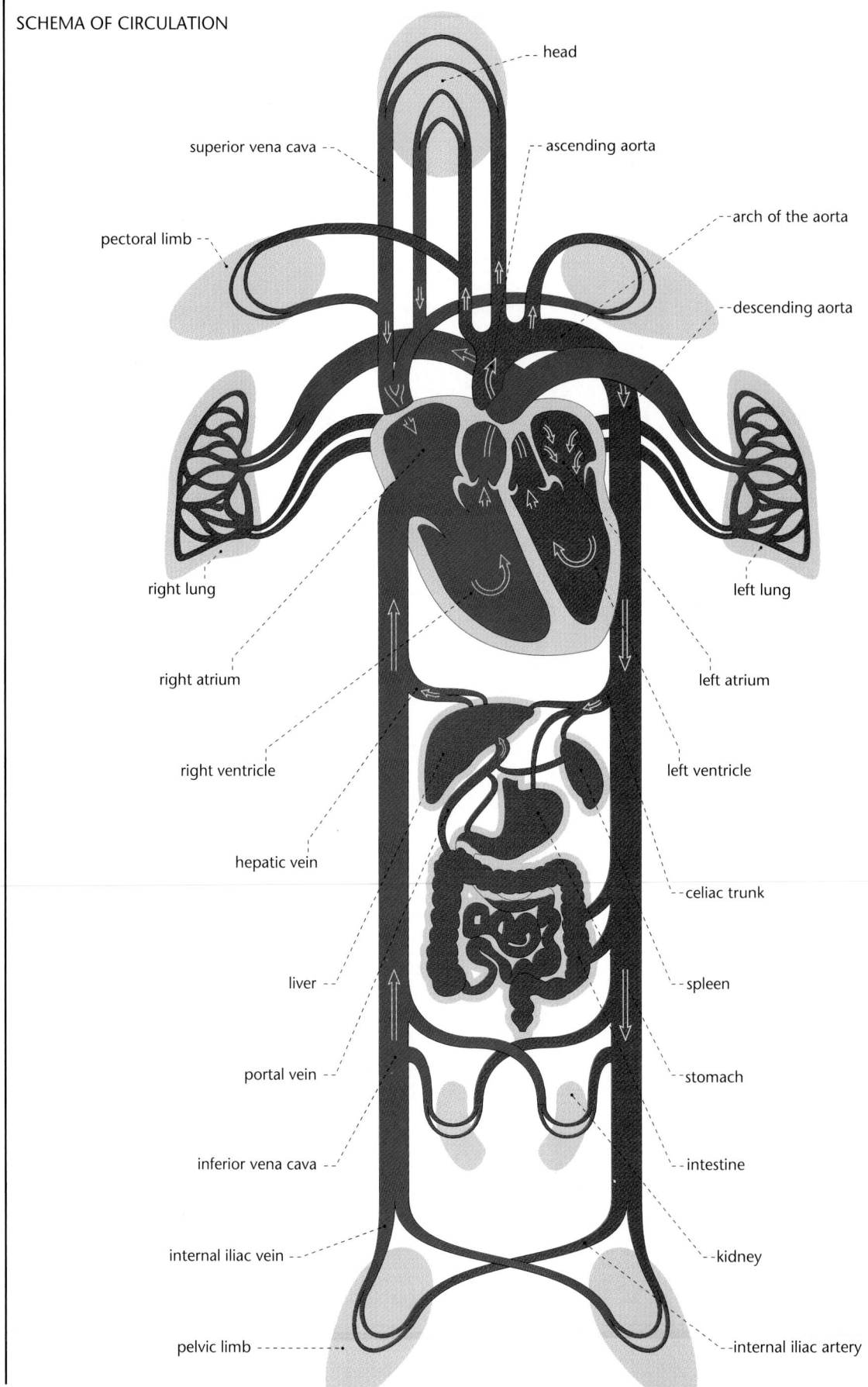

head

superior vena cava

ascending aorta

arch of the aorta

pectoral limb

descending aorta

right lung

left lung

right atrium

left atrium

right ventricle

left ventricle

hepatic vein

celiac trunk

liver

spleen

portal vein

stomach

inferior vena cava

intestine

internal iliac vein

kidney

pelvic limb

internal iliac artery

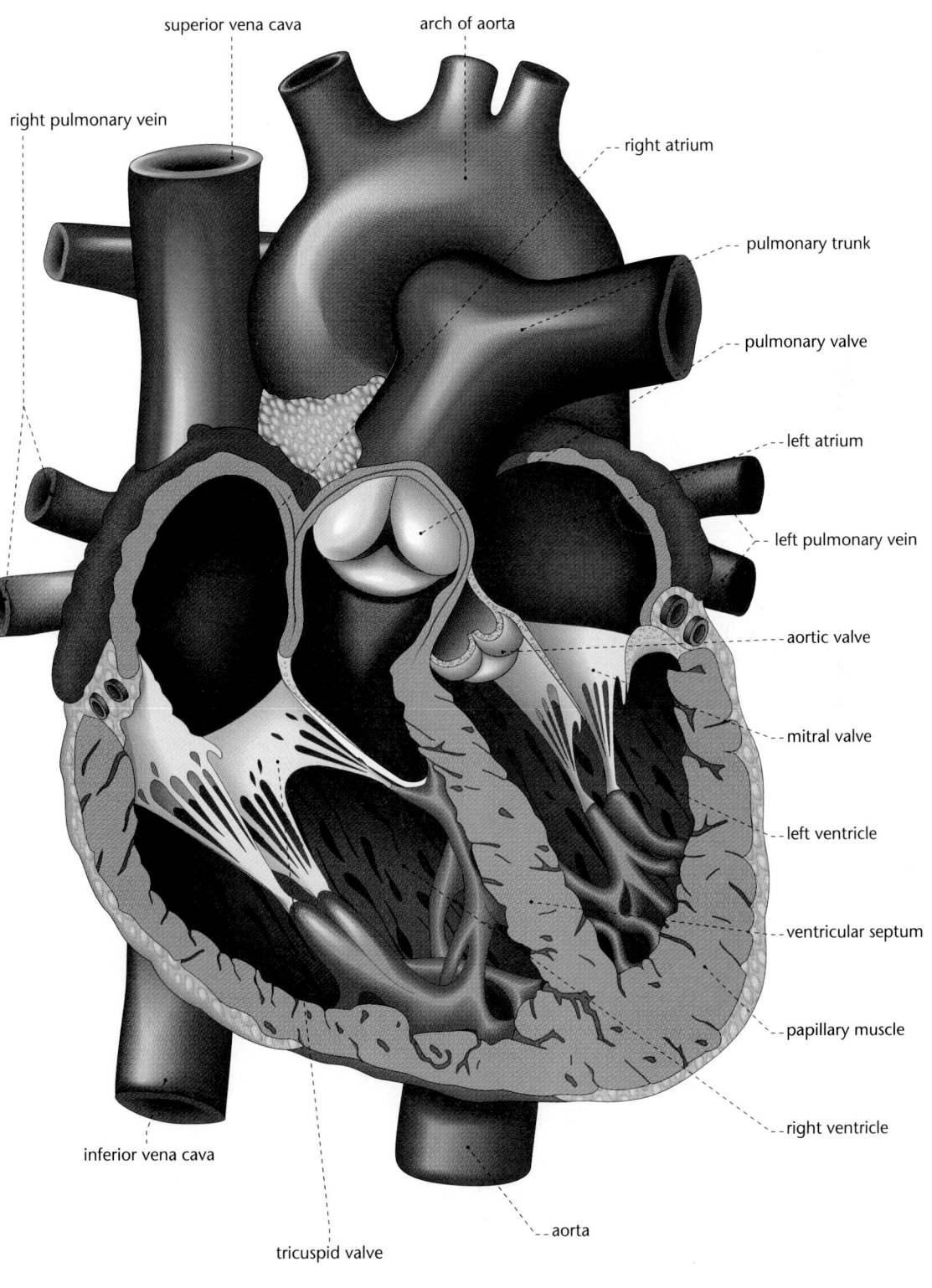

superior vena cava

arch of aorta

right pulmonary vein

right atrium

pulmonary trunk

pulmonary valve

left atrium

left pulmonary vein

aortic valve

mitral valve

left ventricle

ventricular septum

papillary muscle

right ventricle

inferior vena cava

tricuspid valve

aorta

PRINCIPAL VEINS AND ARTERIES

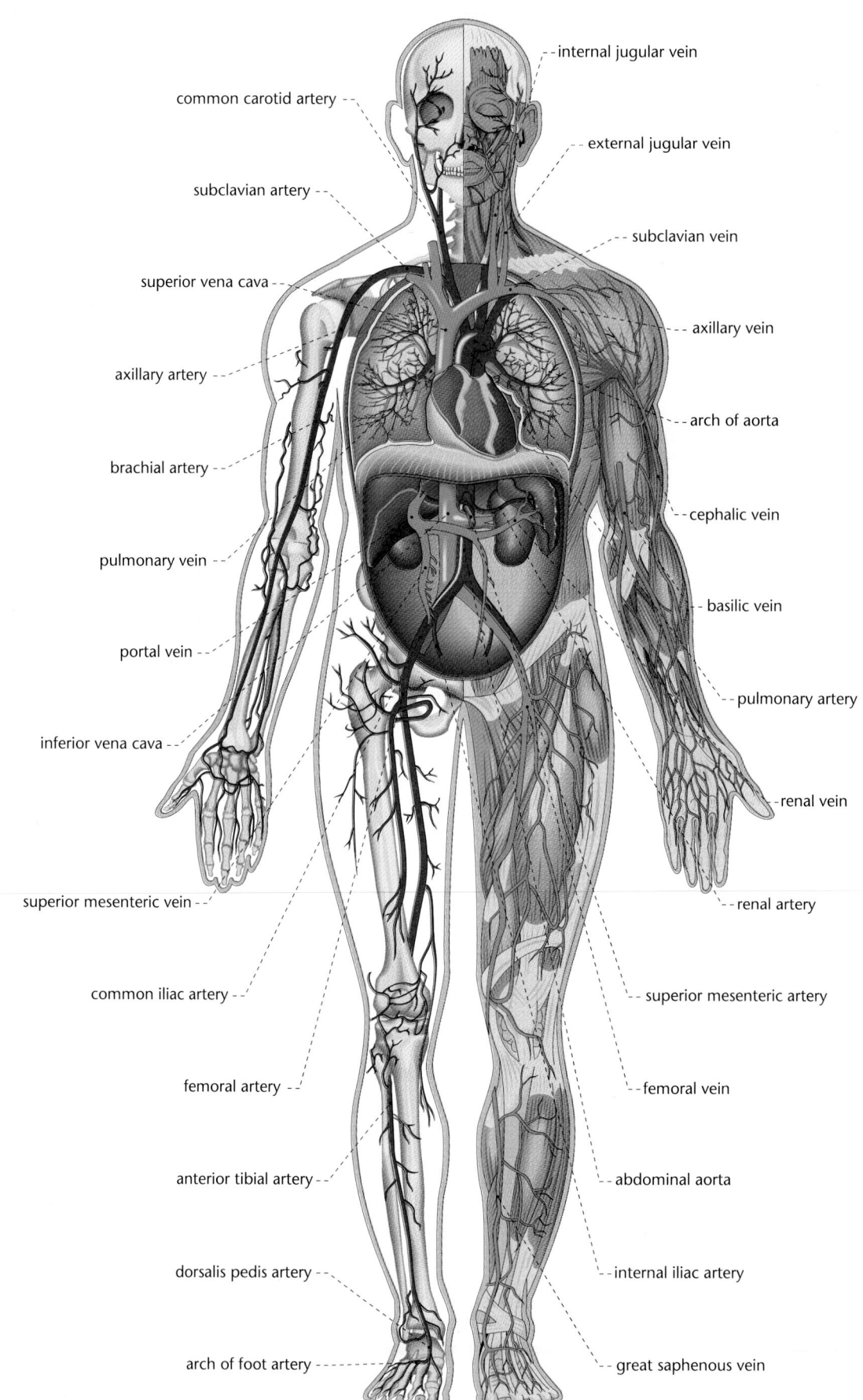

internal jugular vein

common carotid artery

external jugular vein

subclavian artery

subclavian vein

superior vena cava

axillary vein

axillary artery

arch of aorta

brachial artery

cephalic vein

pulmonary vein

basilic vein

portal vein

pulmonary artery

inferior vena cava

renal vein

superior mesenteric vein

renal artery

common iliac artery

superior mesenteric artery

femoral artery

femoral vein

anterior tibial artery

abdominal aorta

internal iliac artery

dorsalis pedis artery

arch of foot artery

great saphenous vein

MALE GENITAL ORGANS

SAGITTAL SECTION

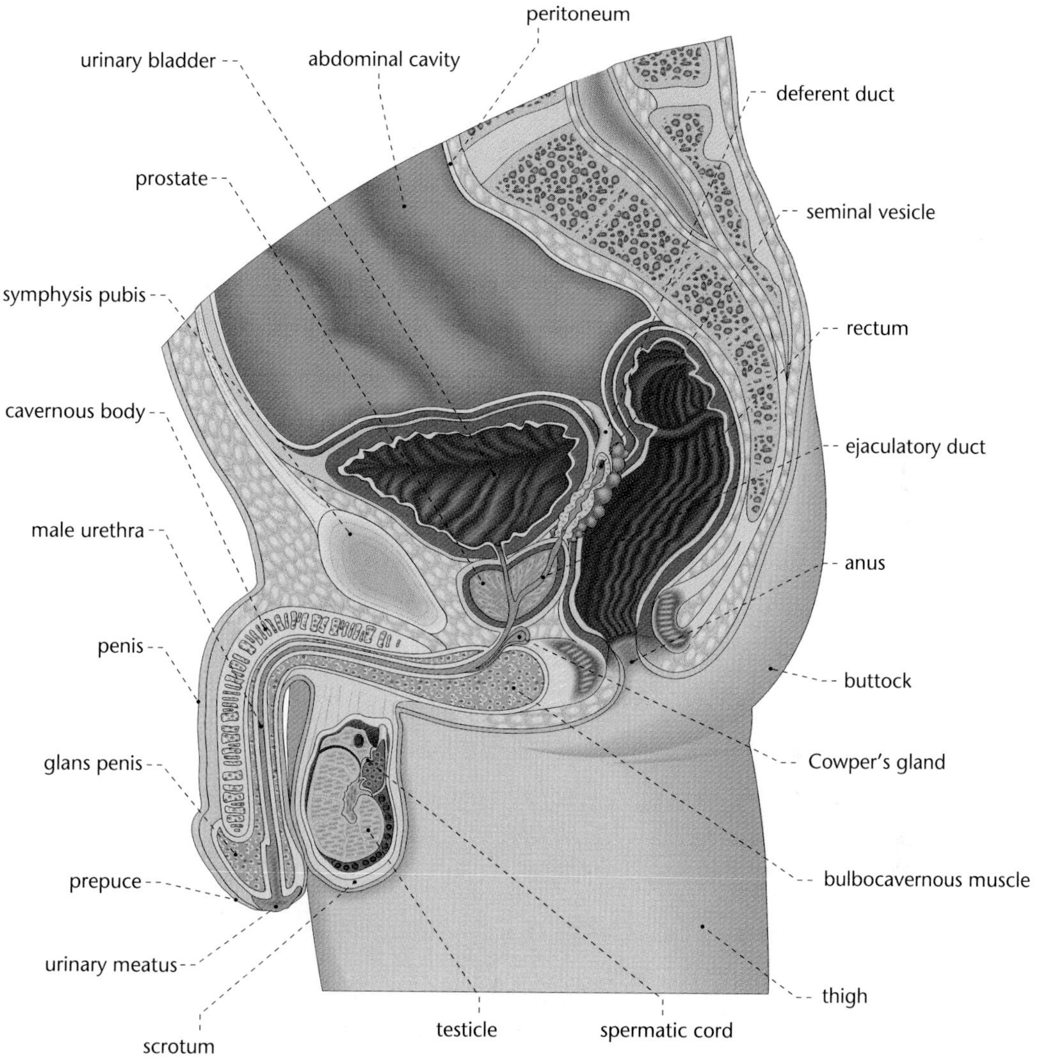

peritoneum

urinary bladder

abdominal cavity

deferent duct

prostate

seminal vesicle

symphysis pubis

rectum

cavernous body

ejaculatory duct

male urethra

anus

penis

buttock

glans penis

Cowper's gland

prepuce

bulbocavernous muscle

urinary meatus

thigh

scrotum

testicle

spermatic cord

SPERMATOZOON

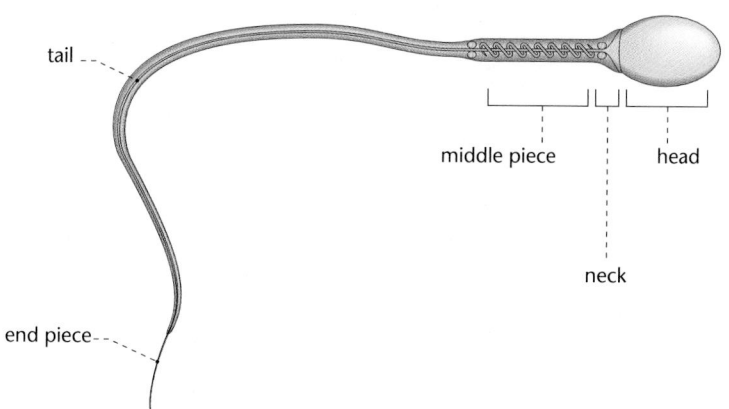

tail

middle piece

head

neck

end piece

FEMALE GENITAL ORGANS

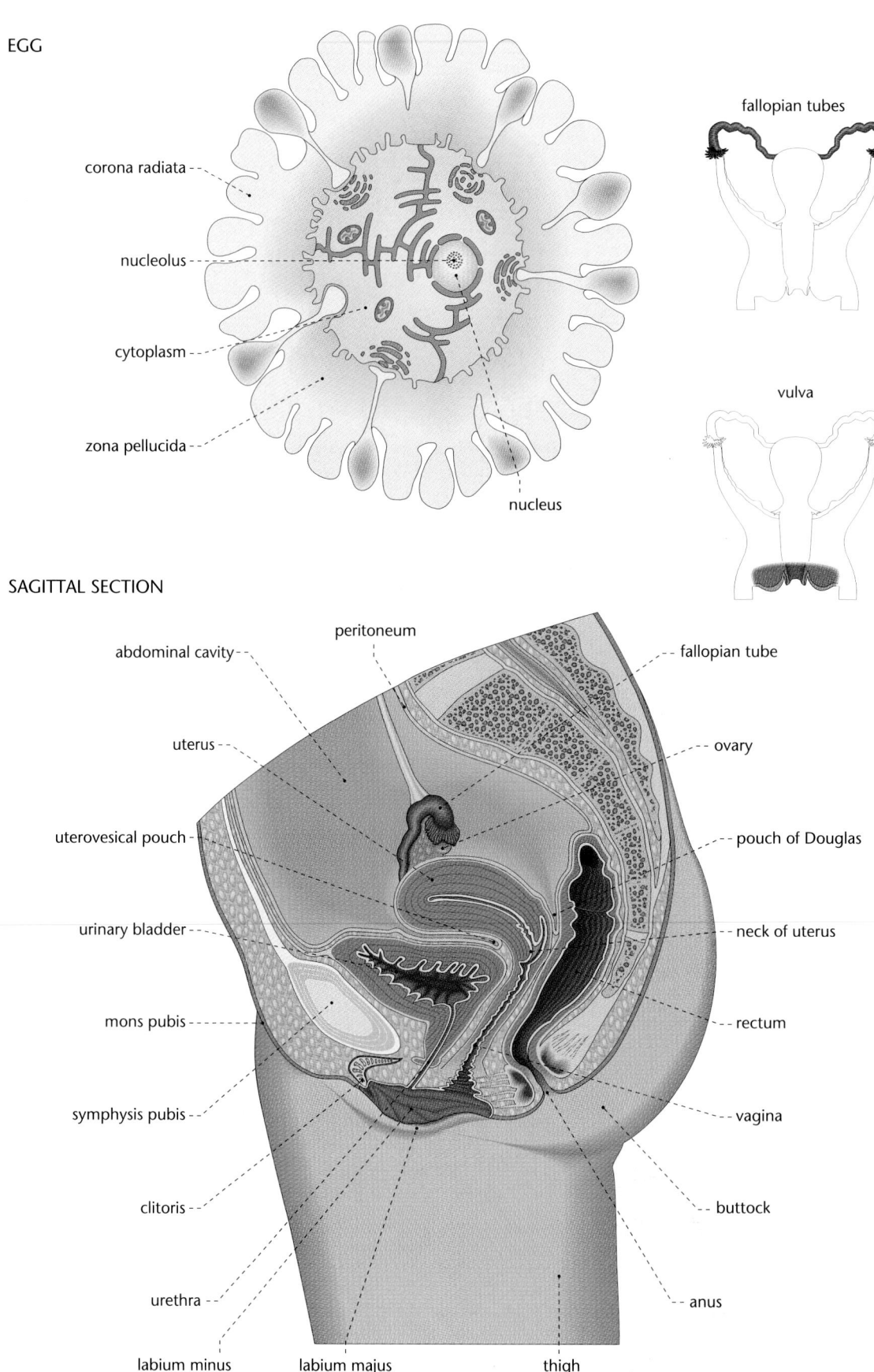

EGG

corona radiata

nucleolus

cytoplasm

zona pellucida

nucleus

fallopian tubes

vulva

SAGITTAL SECTION

peritoneum

abdominal cavity

fallopian tube

uterus

ovary

uterovesical pouch

pouch of Douglas

urinary bladder

neck of uterus

mons pubis

rectum

symphysis pubis

vagina

clitoris

buttock

urethra

anus

labium minus

labium majus

thigh

FEMALE GENITAL ORGANS

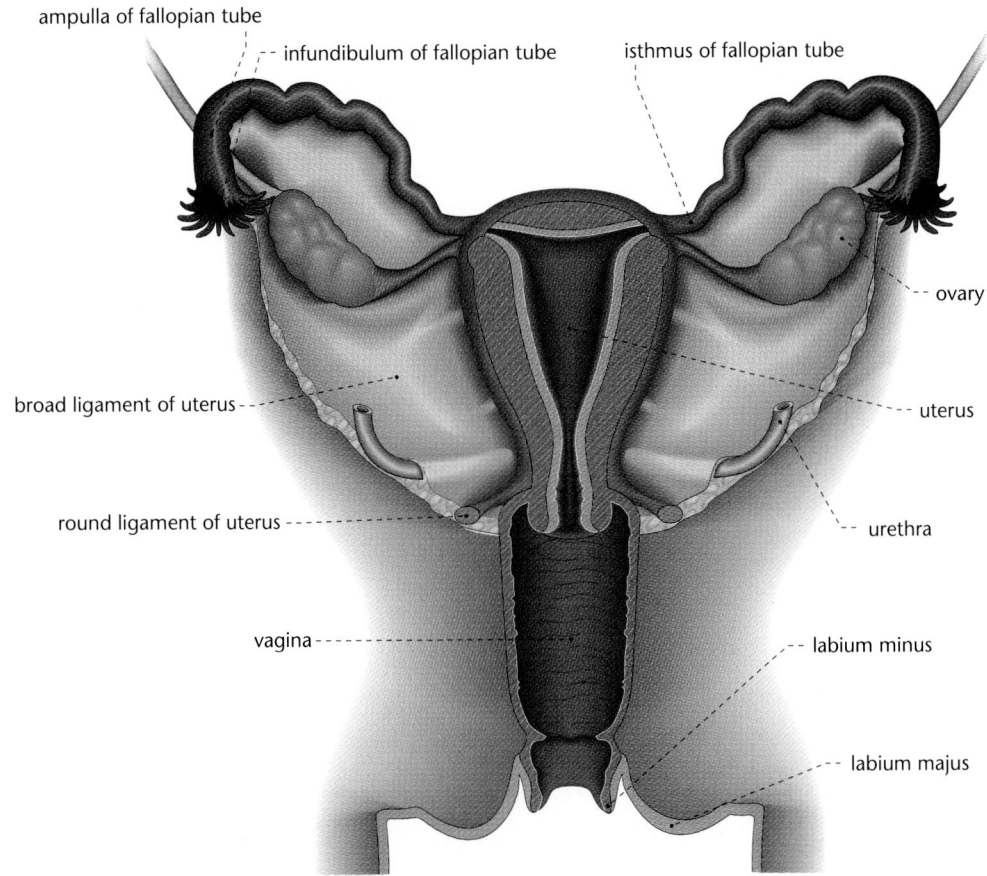

ampulla of fallopian tube

infundibulum of fallopian tube

isthmus of fallopian tube

ovary

broad ligament of uterus

uterus

round ligament of uterus

urethra

vagina

labium minus

labium majus

BREAST

SAGITTAL SECTION

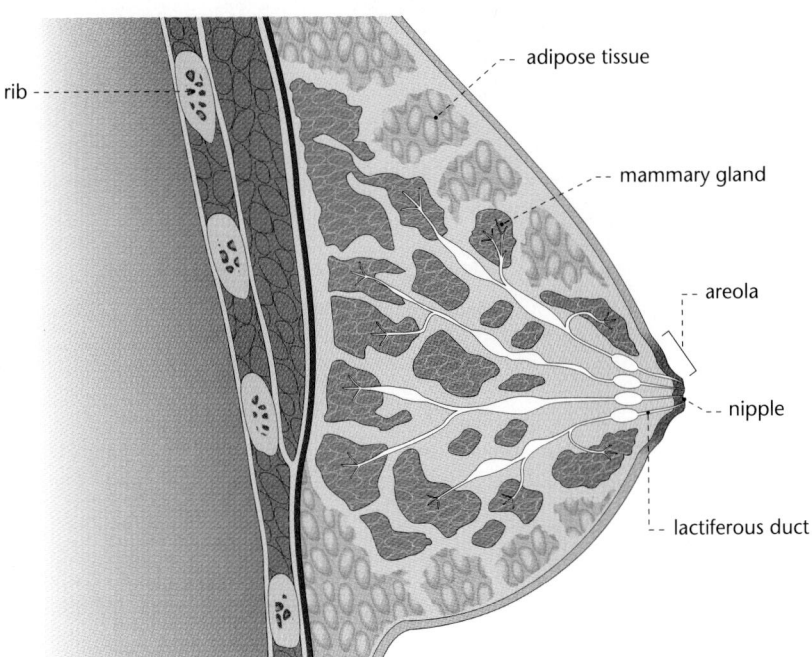

rib

adipose tissue

mammary gland

areola

nipple

lactiferous duct

129

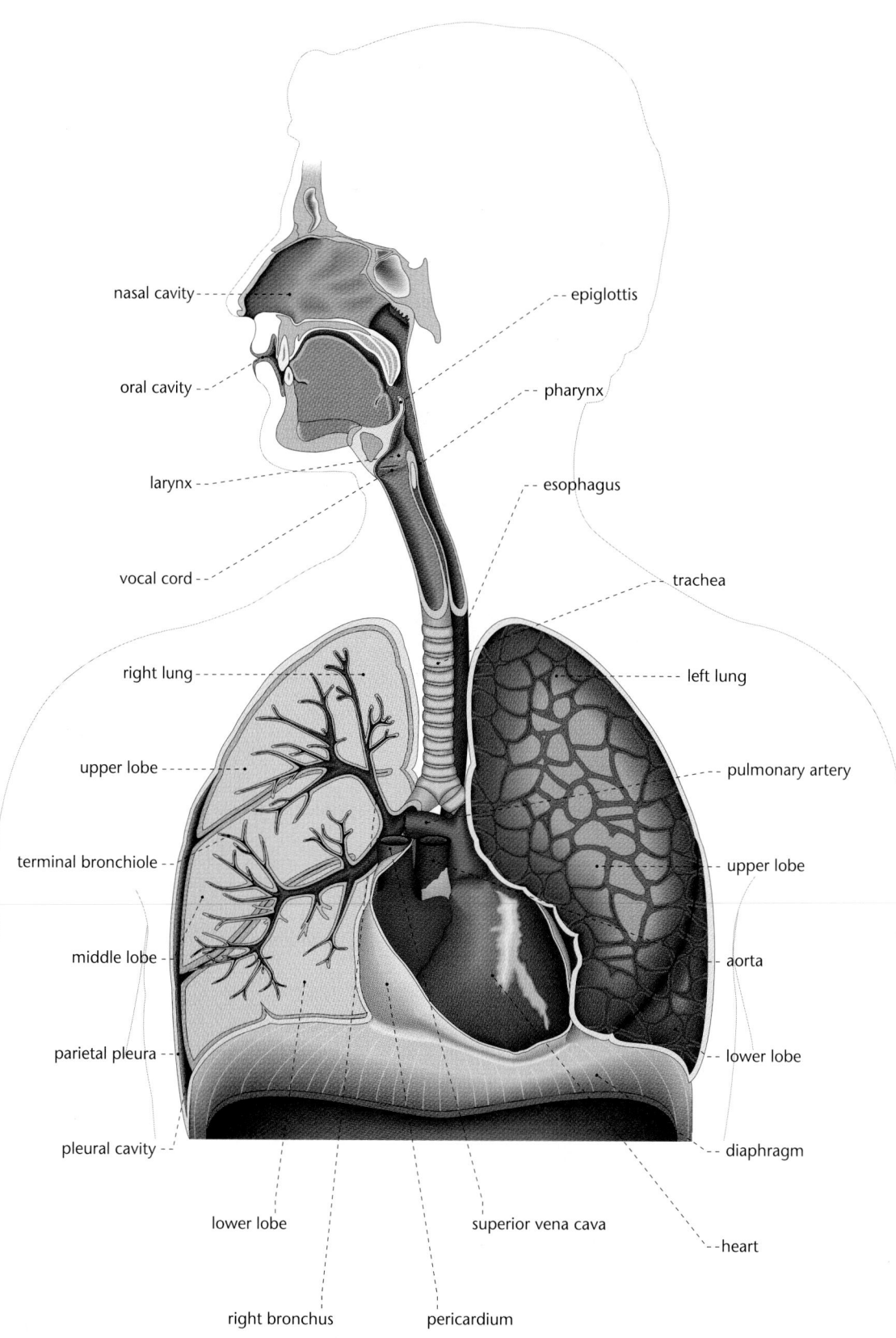

nasal cavity

oral cavity

larynx

vocal cord

right lung

upper lobe

terminal bronchiole

middle lobe

parietal pleura

pleural cavity

epiglottis

pharynx

esophagus

trachea

left lung

pulmonary artery

upper lobe

aorta

lower lobe

diaphragm

heart

lower lobe

superior vena cava

right bronchus

pericardium

DIGESTIVE SYSTEM

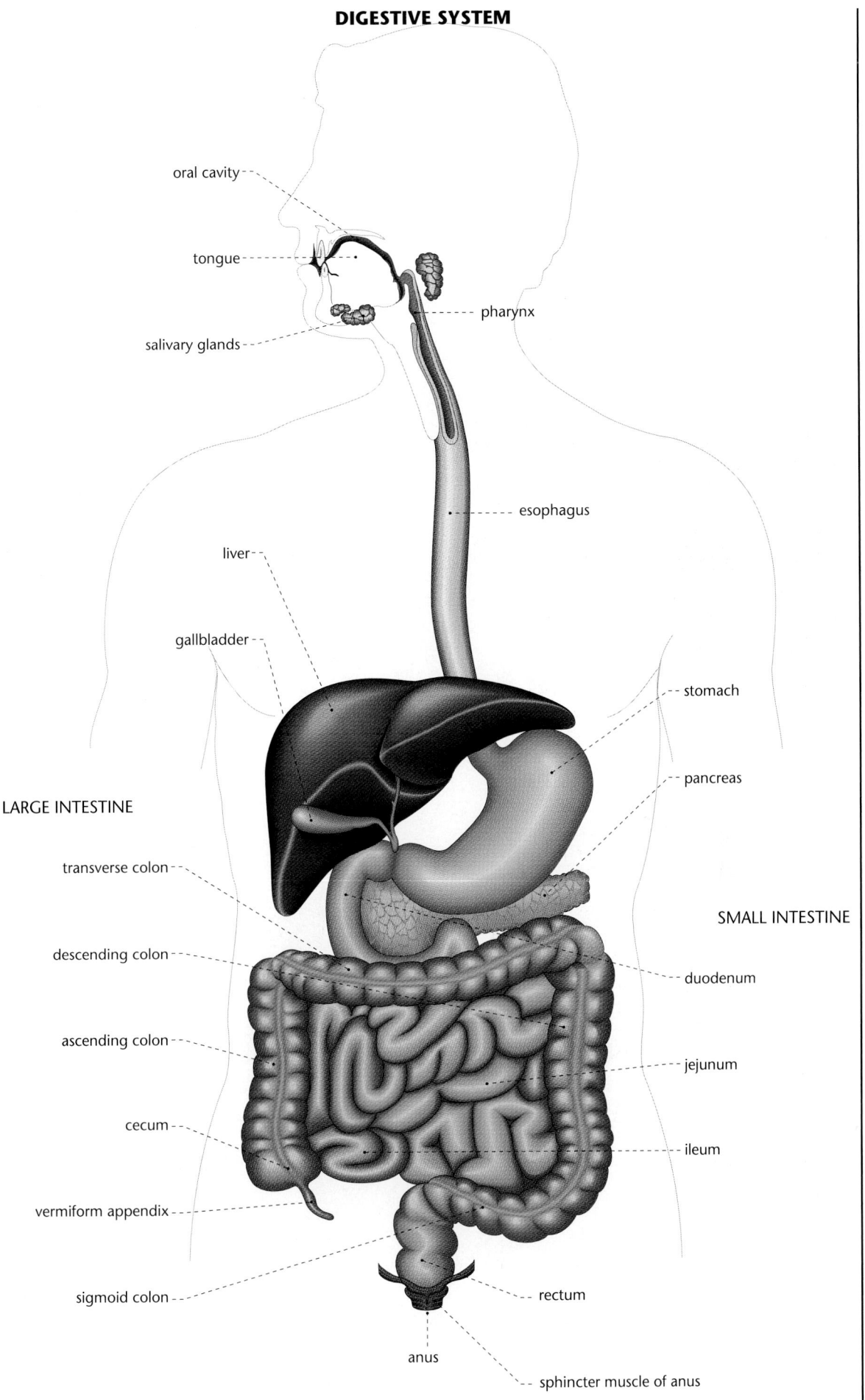

oral cavity

tongue

salivary glands

pharynx

esophagus

liver

gallbladder

stomach

pancreas

LARGE INTESTINE

transverse colon

descending colon

ascending colon

cecum

vermiform appendix

sigmoid colon

anus

SMALL INTESTINE

duodenum

jejunum

ileum

rectum

sphincter muscle of anus

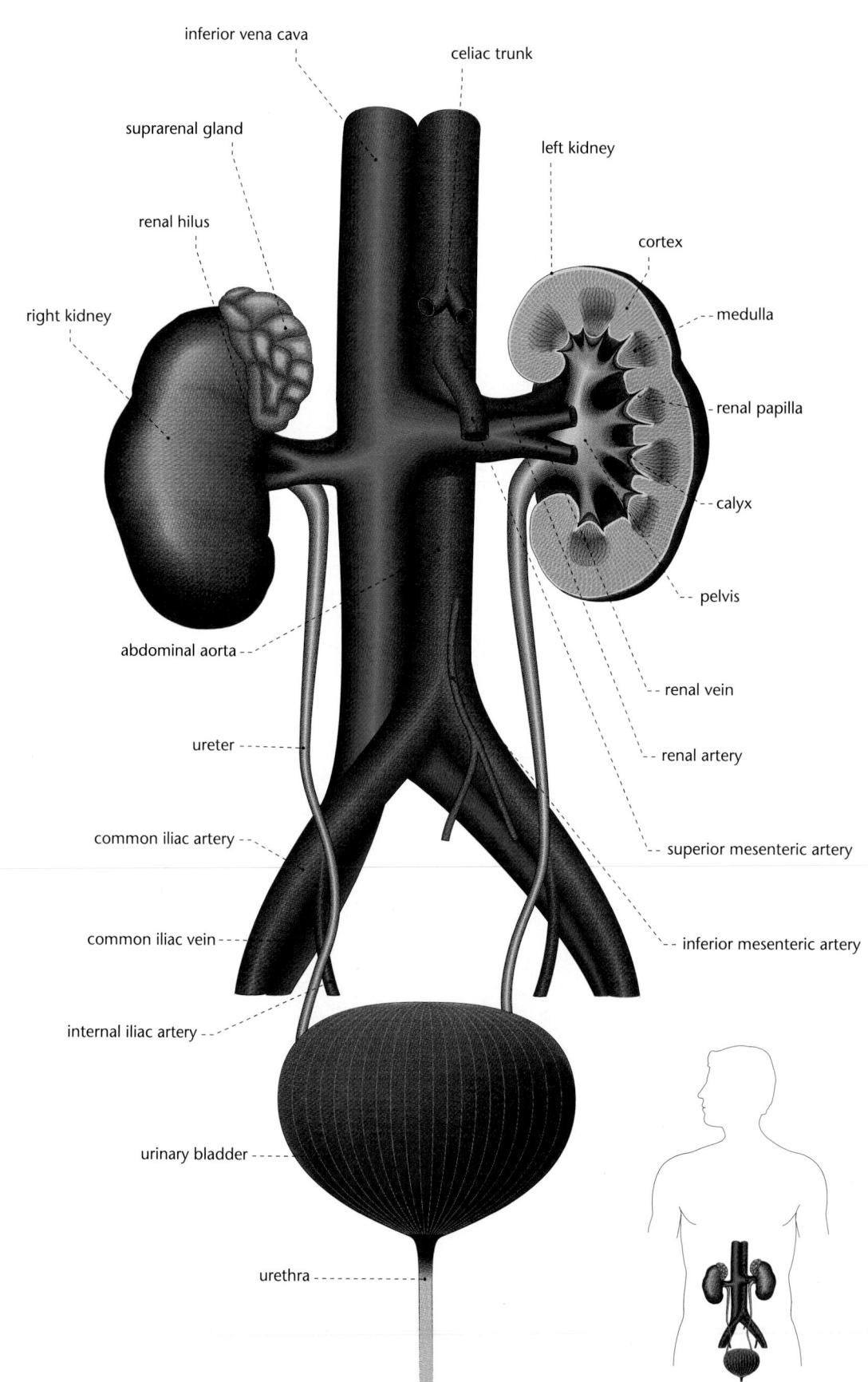

inferior vena cava

celiac trunk

suprarenal gland

left kidney

renal hilus

cortex

right kidney

medulla

renal papilla

calyx

pelvis

abdominal aorta

renal vein

renal artery

ureter

common iliac artery

superior mesenteric artery

common iliac vein

inferior mesenteric artery

internal iliac artery

urinary bladder

urethra

NERVOUS SYSTEM

PERIPHERAL NERVOUS SYSTEM

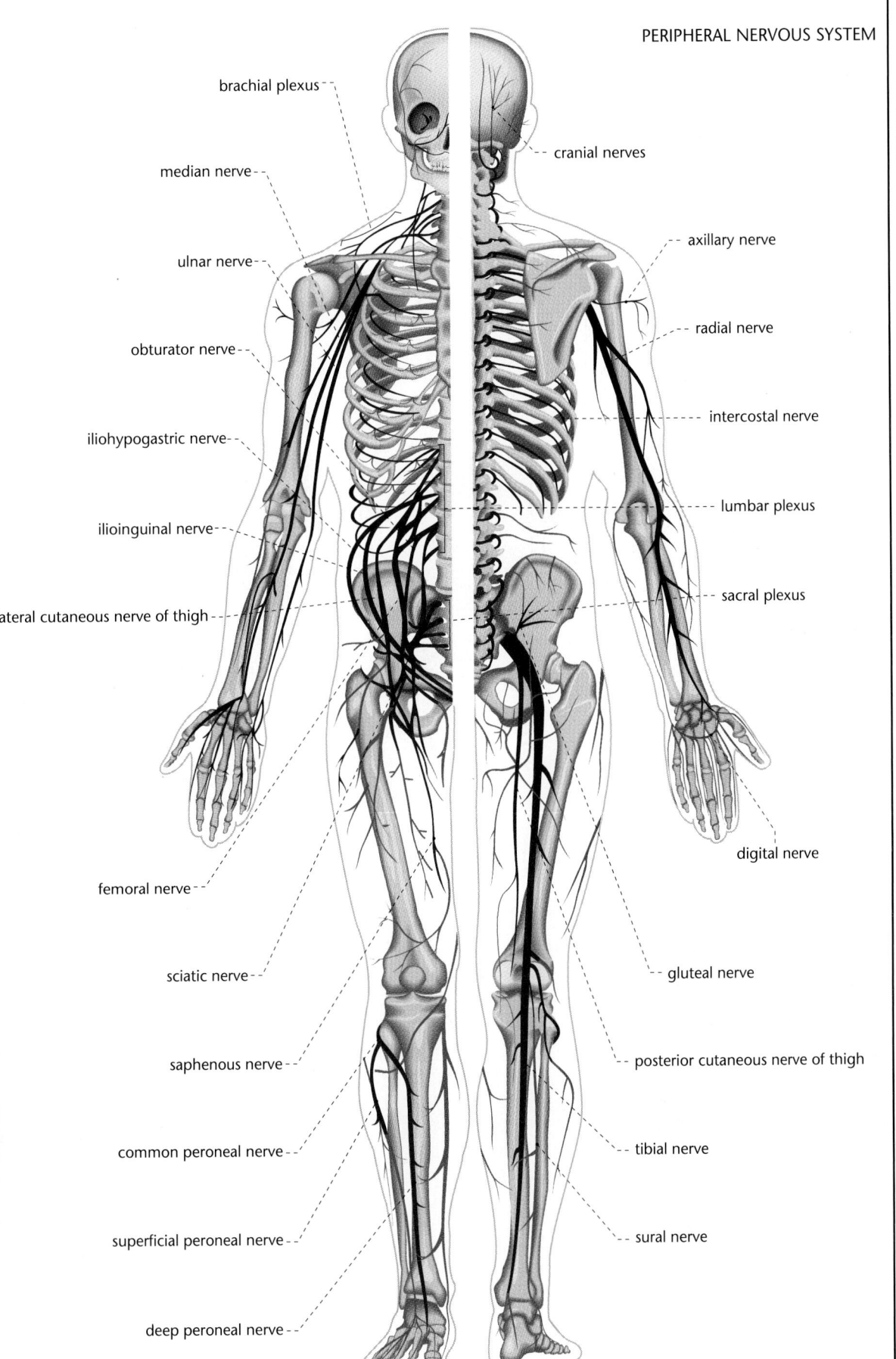

brachial plexus

cranial nerves

median nerve

axillary nerve

ulnar nerve

radial nerve

obturator nerve

intercostal nerve

iliohypogastric nerve

lumbar plexus

ilioinguinal nerve

sacral plexus

lateral cutaneous nerve of thigh

digital nerve

femoral nerve

gluteal nerve

sciatic nerve

saphenous nerve

posterior cutaneous nerve of thigh

common peroneal nerve

tibial nerve

superficial peroneal nerve

sural nerve

deep peroneal nerve

CENTRAL NERVOUS SYSTEM

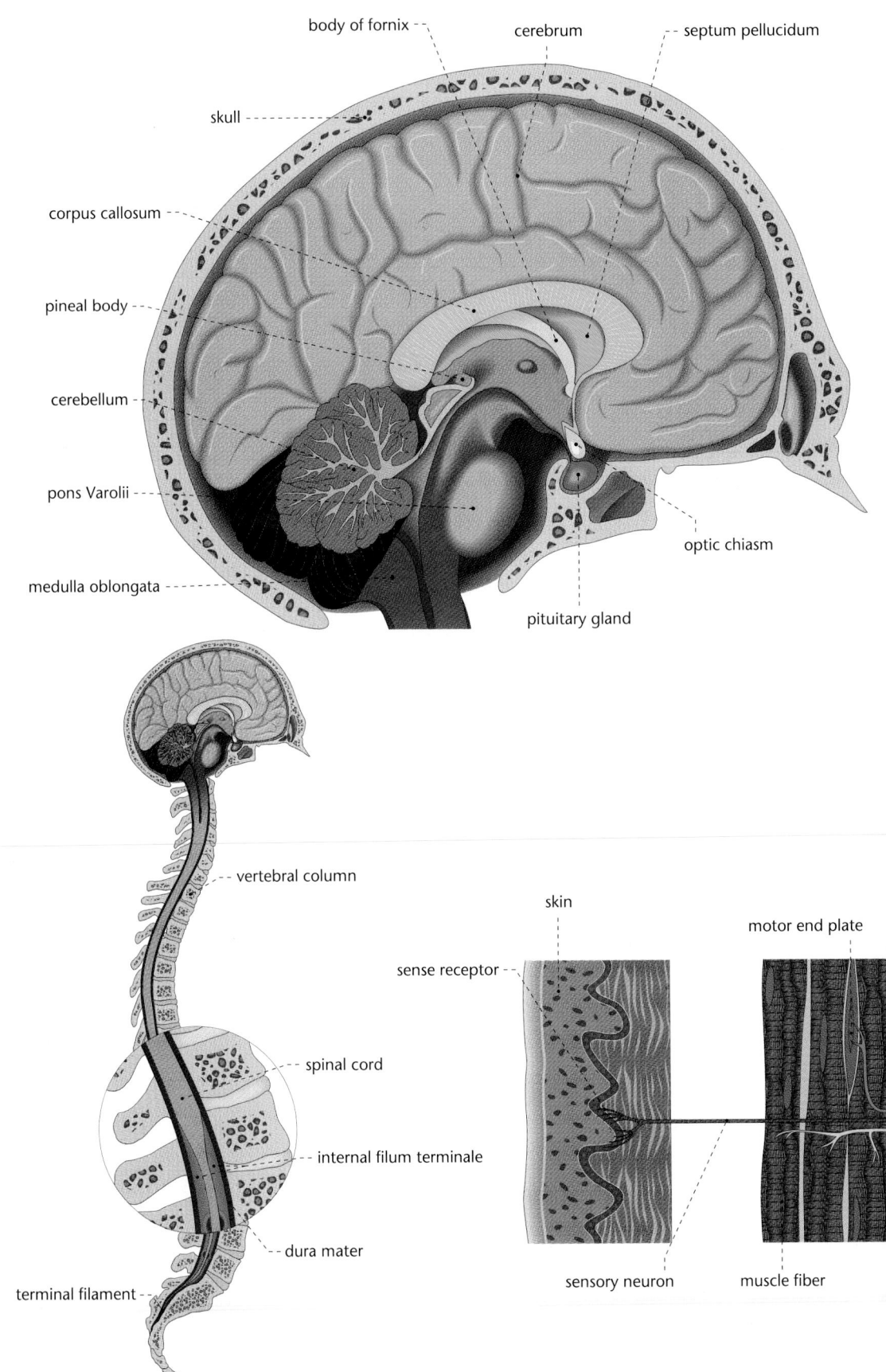

body of fornix
cerebrum
septum pellucidum
skull
corpus callosum
pineal body
cerebellum
pons Varolii
medulla oblongata
optic chiasm
pituitary gland

vertebral column
skin
sense receptor
motor end plate
spinal cord
internal filum terminale
dura mater
terminal filament
sensory neuron
muscle fiber

LUMBAR VERTEBRA

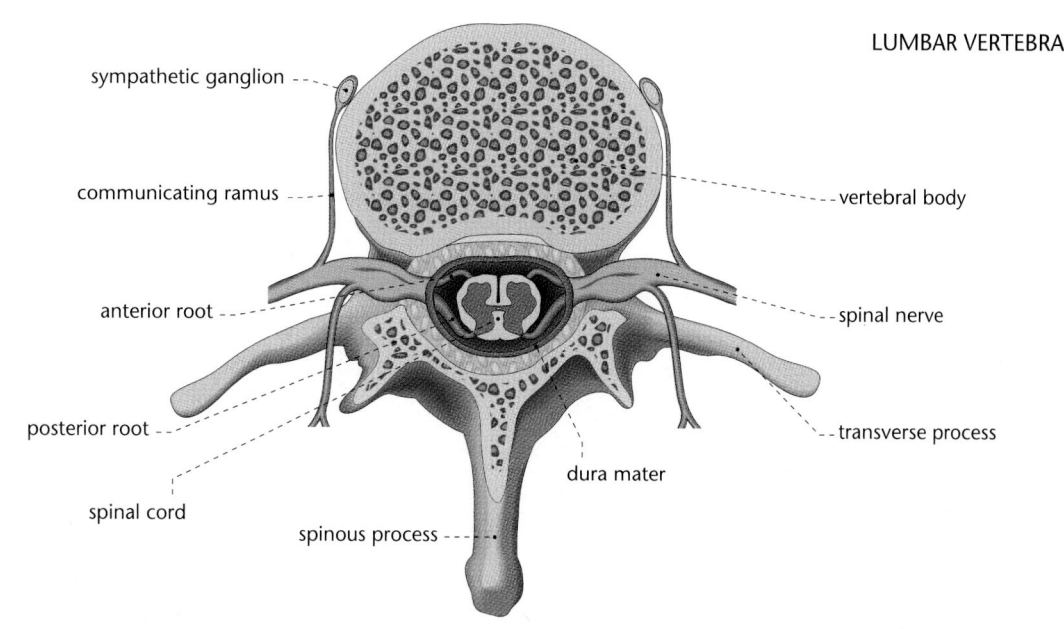

sympathetic ganglion

communicating ramus

anterior root

posterior root

spinal cord

spinous process

vertebral body

spinal nerve

transverse process

dura mater

CHAIN OF NEURONS

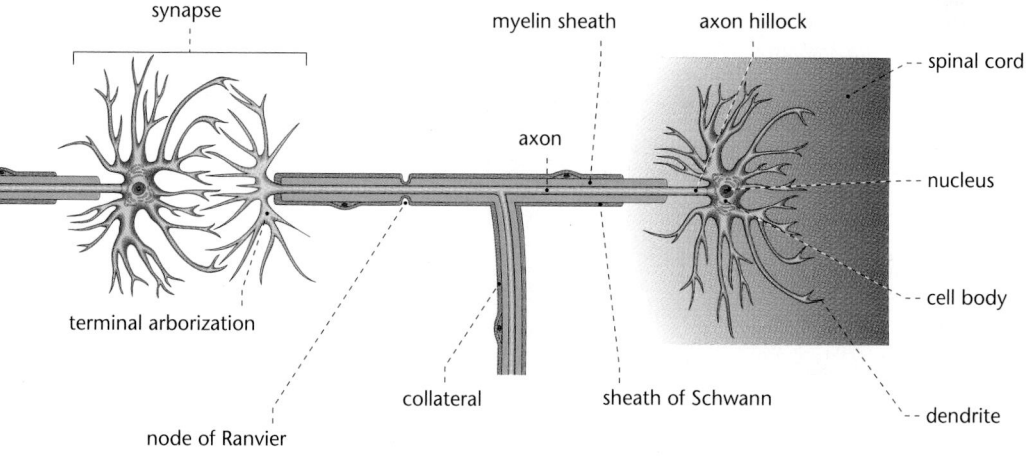

synapse

myelin sheath

axon hillock

axon

spinal cord

nucleus

terminal arborization

cell body

node of Ranvier

collateral

sheath of Schwann

dendrite

SENSORY IMPULSE

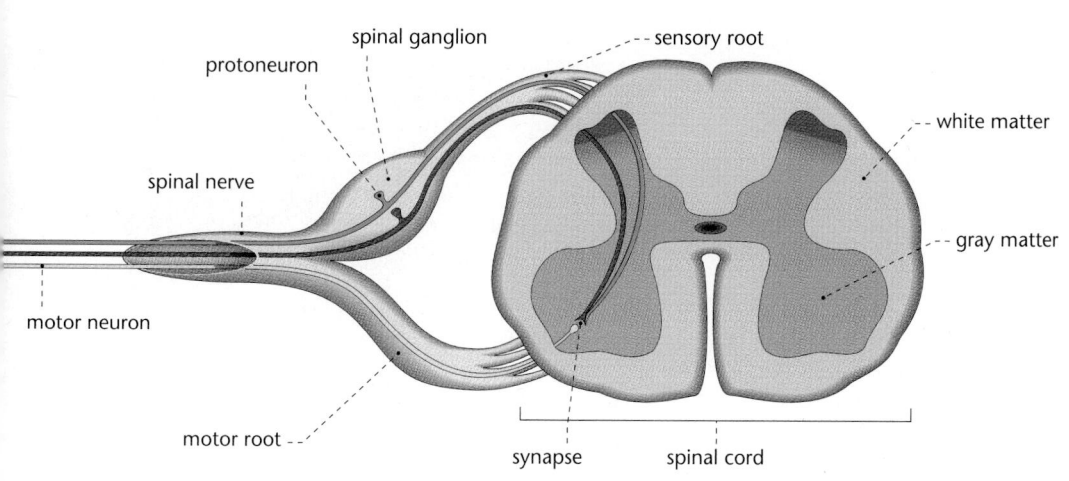

protoneuron

spinal ganglion

sensory root

spinal nerve

white matter

motor neuron

gray matter

motor root

synapse

spinal cord

SKIN

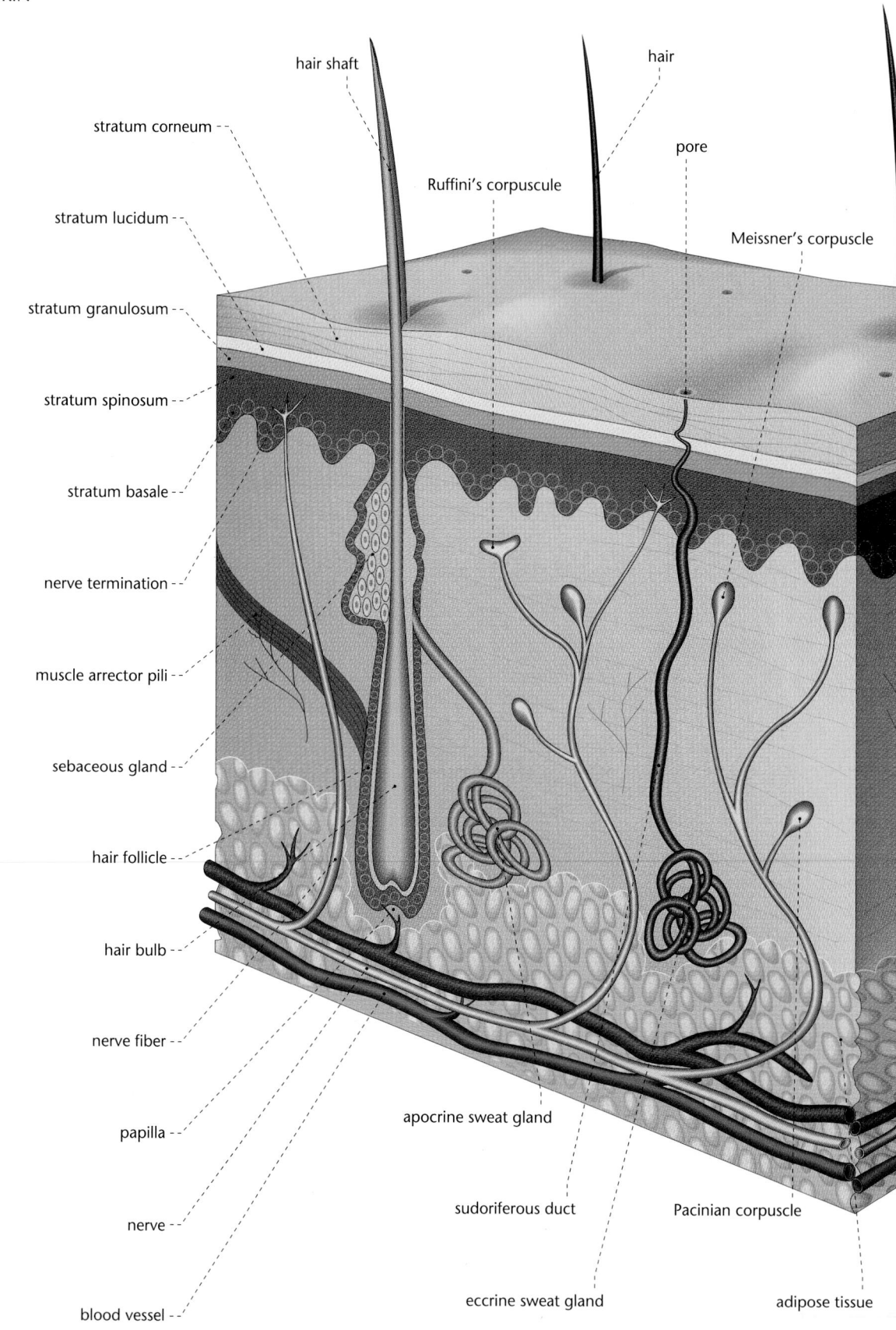

hair shaft

hair

stratum corneum

pore

Ruffini's corpuscle

stratum lucidum

Meissner's corpuscle

stratum granulosum

stratum spinosum

stratum basale

nerve termination

muscle arrector pili

sebaceous gland

hair follicle

hair bulb

nerve fiber

papilla

apocrine sweat gland

nerve

sudoriferous duct

Pacinian corpuscle

blood vessel

eccrine sweat gland

adipose tissue

136

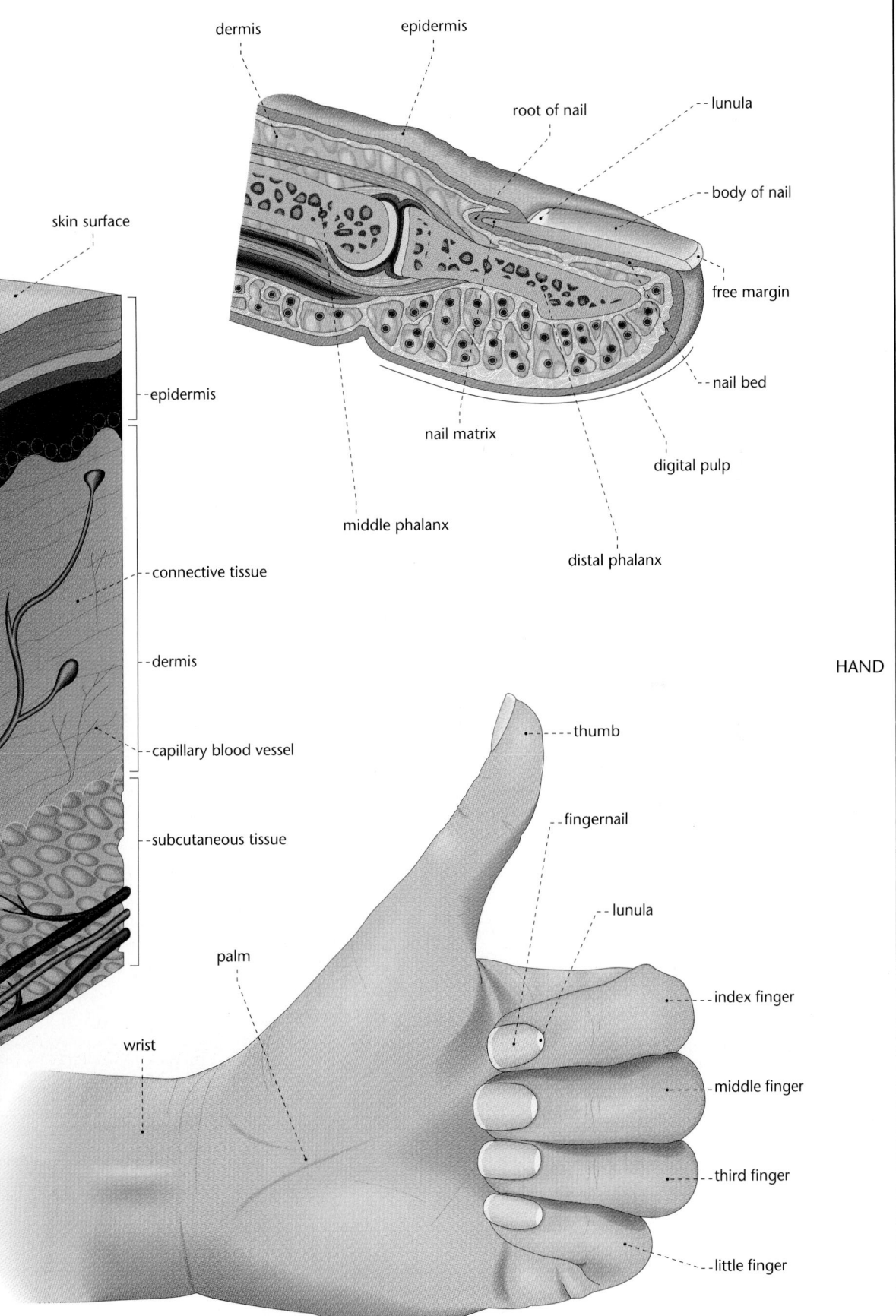

dermis

epidermis

root of nail

lunula

body of nail

skin surface

epidermis

free margin

nail bed

connective tissue

nail matrix

dermis

digital pulp

capillary blood vessel

middle phalanx

distal phalanx

subcutaneous tissue

thumb

fingernail

palm

lunula

index finger

wrist

middle finger

third finger

little finger

PARTS OF THE EAR

AUDITORY OSSICLES

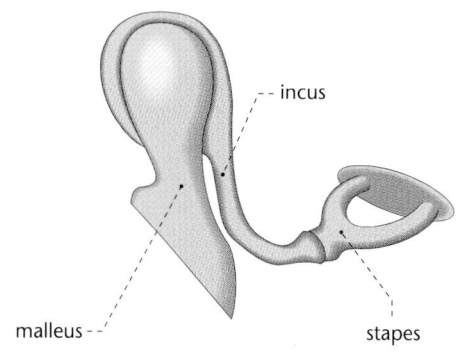

incus

malleus

stapes

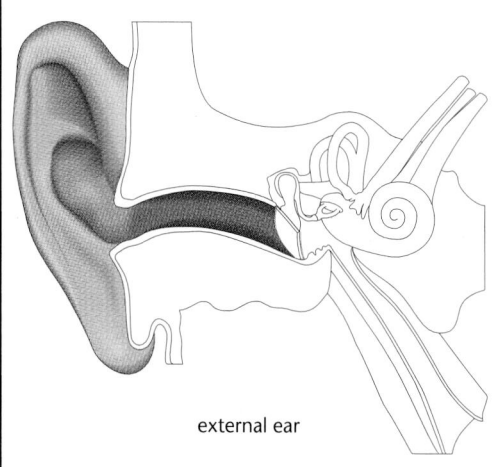

external ear

auricle

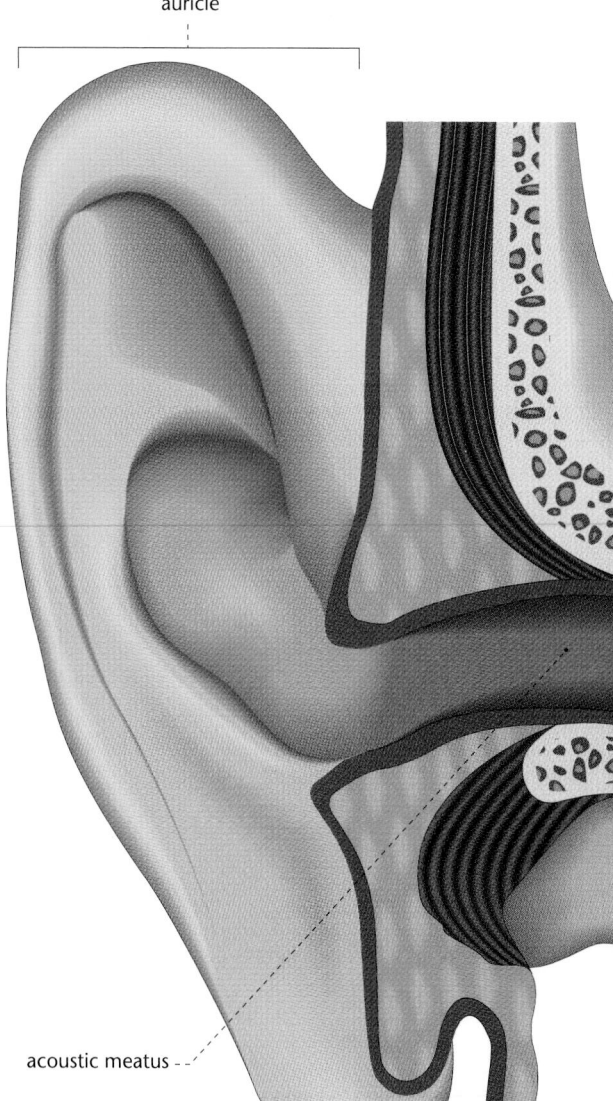

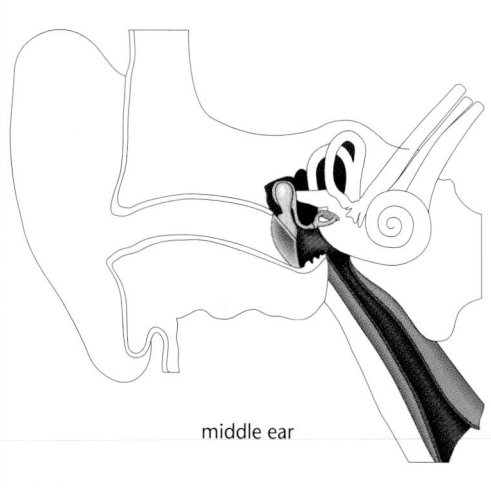

middle ear

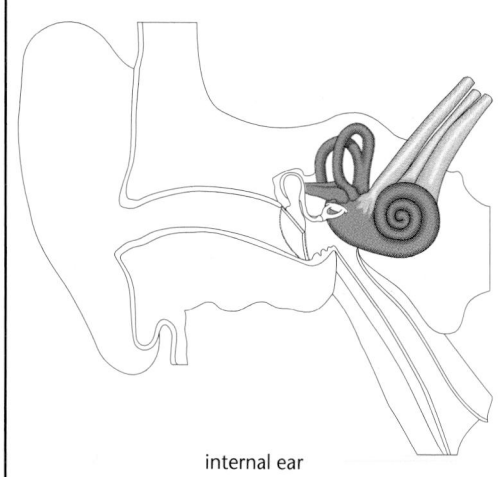

internal ear

acoustic meatus

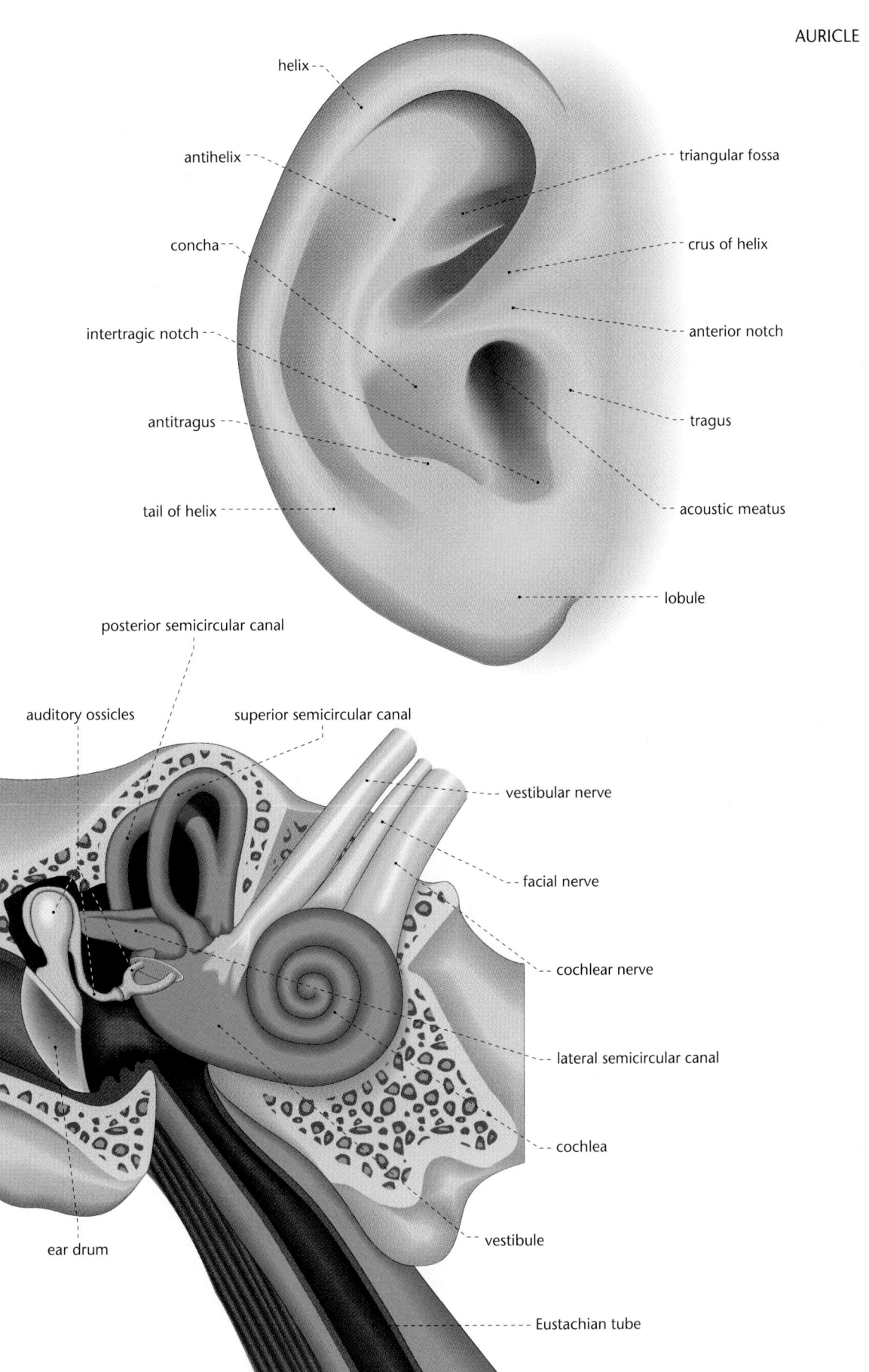

helix

antihelix

concha

intertragic notch

antitragus

tail of helix

triangular fossa

crus of helix

anterior notch

tragus

acoustic meatus

lobule

posterior semicircular canal

auditory ossicles

superior semicircular canal

vestibular nerve

facial nerve

cochlear nerve

lateral semicircular canal

cochlea

vestibule

ear drum

Eustachian tube

EYE

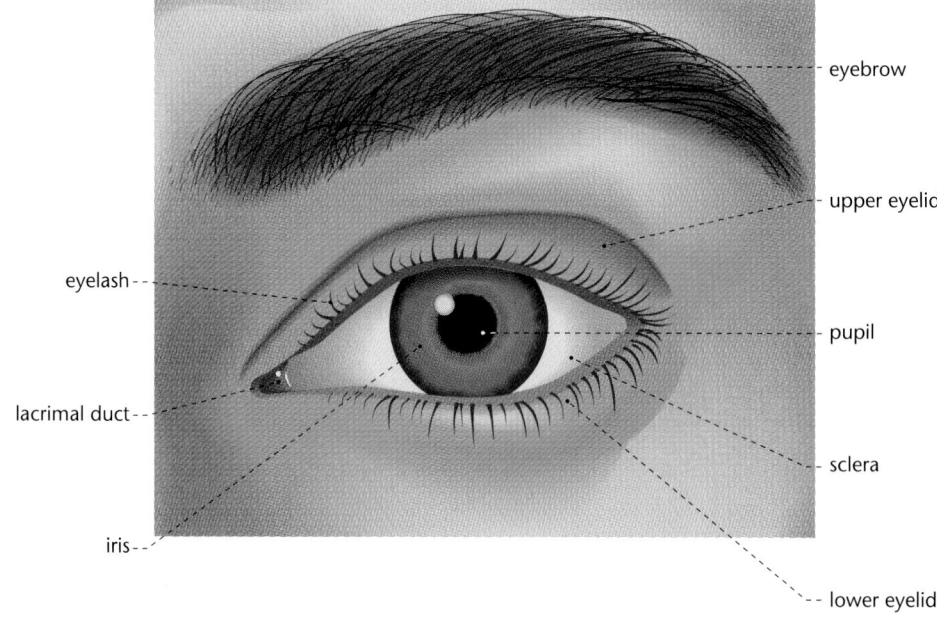

eyebrow

upper eyelid

eyelash

pupil

lacrimal duct

sclera

iris

lower eyelid

EYEBALL

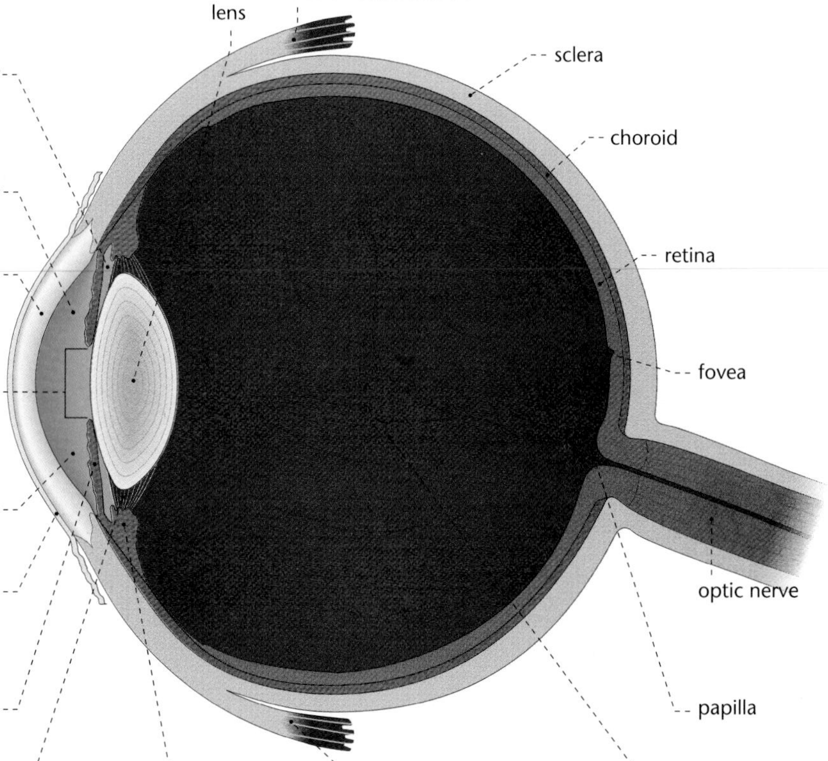

medial rectus muscle

lens

posterior chamber

sclera

anterior chamber

choroid

cornea

retina

pupil

fovea

aqueous humor

conjunctiva

optic nerve

iris

papilla

suspensory ligament

ciliary body

lateral rectus muscle

vitreous body

EXTERNAL NOSE

root of nose

dorsum of nose

septum

philtrum

ala

naris

tip of nose

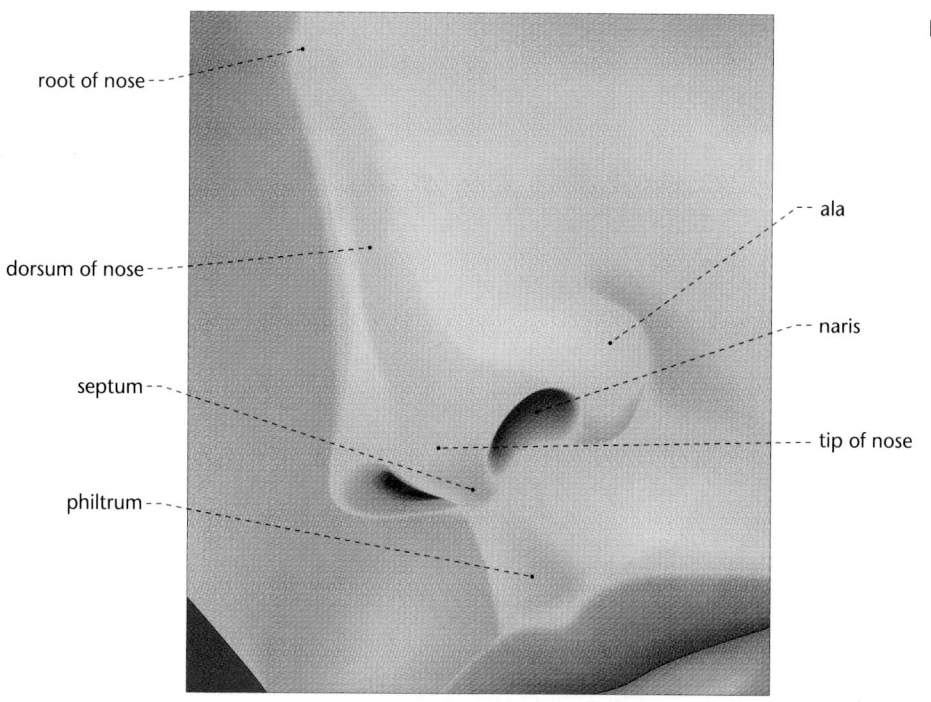

NASAL FOSSAE

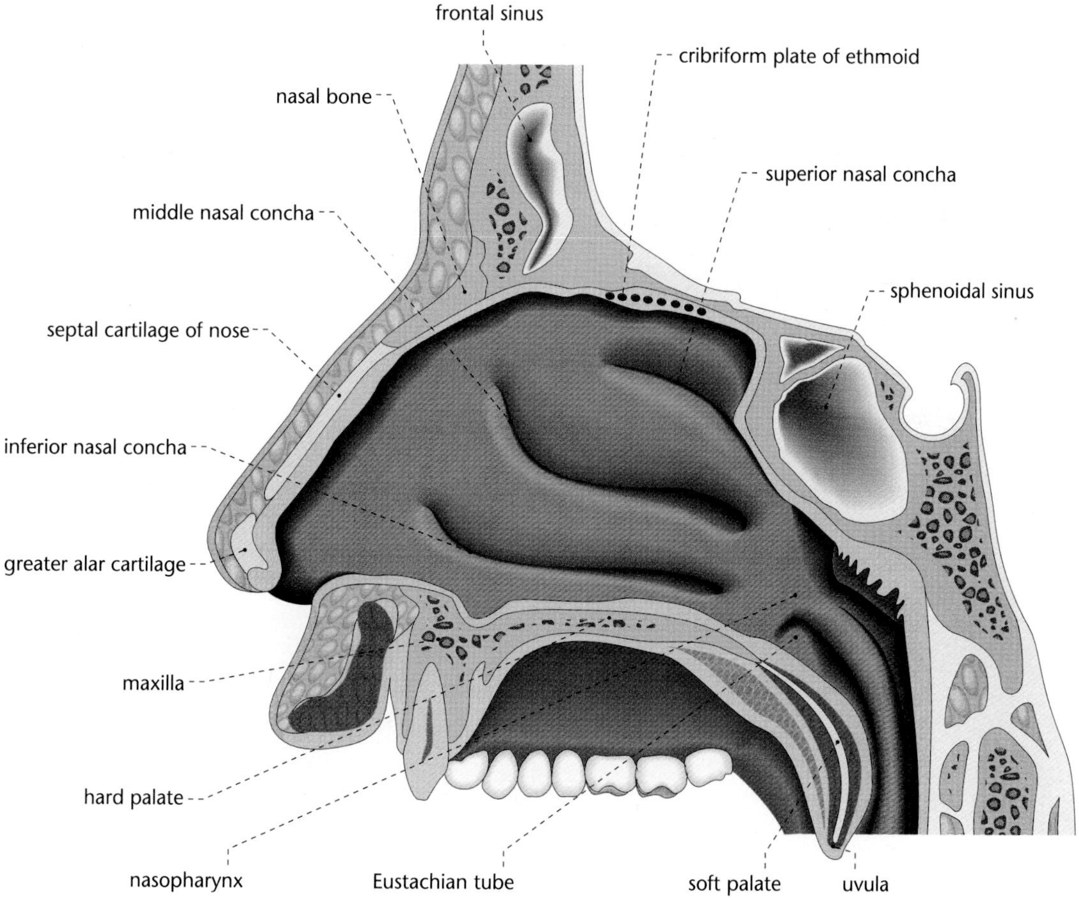

frontal sinus

cribriform plate of ethmoid

nasal bone

superior nasal concha

middle nasal concha

sphenoidal sinus

septal cartilage of nose

inferior nasal concha

greater alar cartilage

maxilla

hard palate

nasopharynx

Eustachian tube

soft palate

uvula

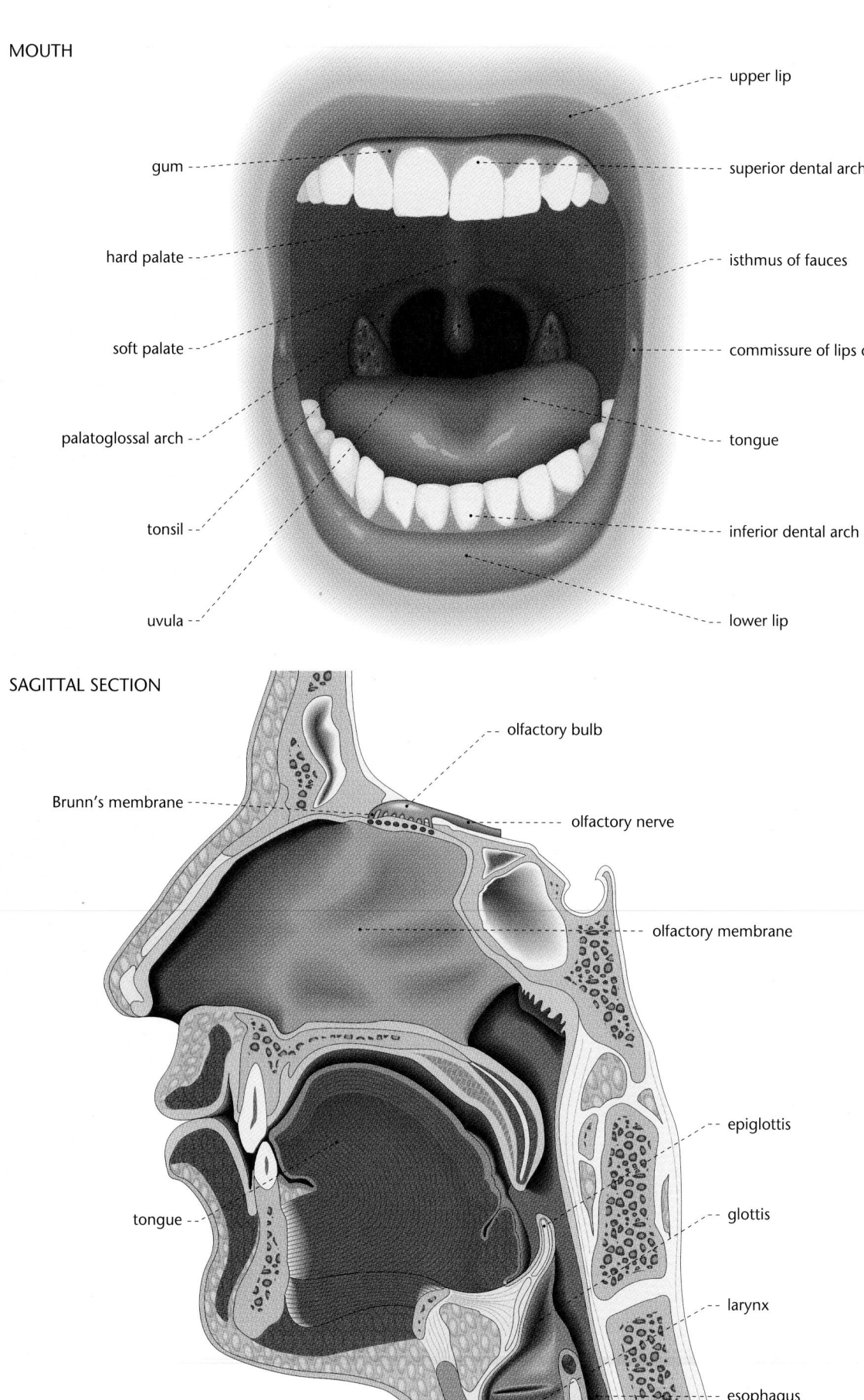

MOUTH

upper lip

gum

superior dental arch

hard palate

isthmus of fauces

soft palate

commissure of lips of mouth

palatoglossal arch

tongue

tonsil

inferior dental arch

uvula

lower lip

SAGITTAL SECTION

olfactory bulb

Brunn's membrane

olfactory nerve

olfactory membrane

epiglottis

glottis

tongue

larynx

esophagus

HUMAN BEING

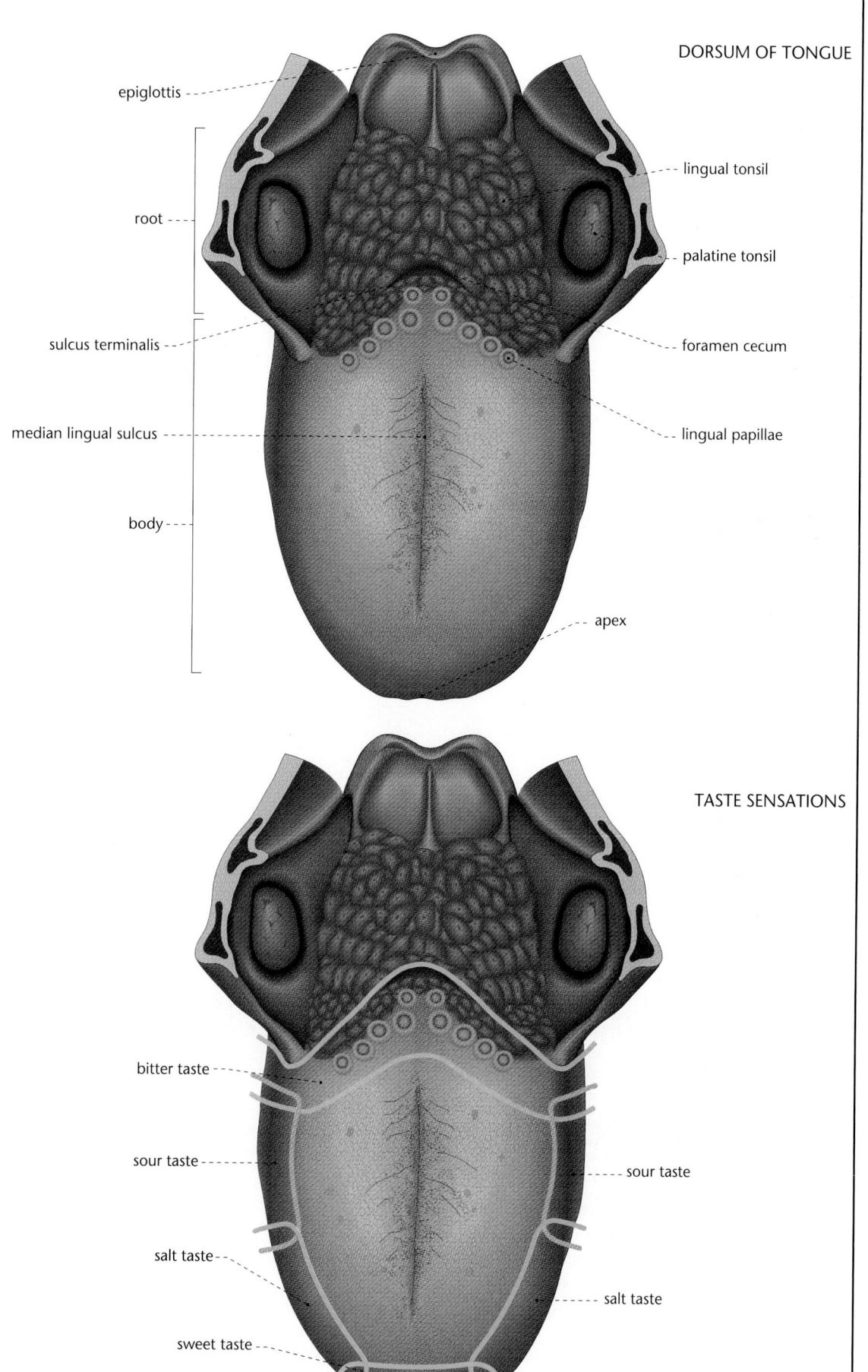

epiglottis

lingual tonsil

root

palatine tonsil

sulcus terminalis

foramen cecum

median lingual sulcus

lingual papillae

body

apex

TASTE SENSATIONS

bitter taste

sour taste

sour taste

salt taste

salt taste

sweet taste

143

TEETH

HUMAN DENTURE

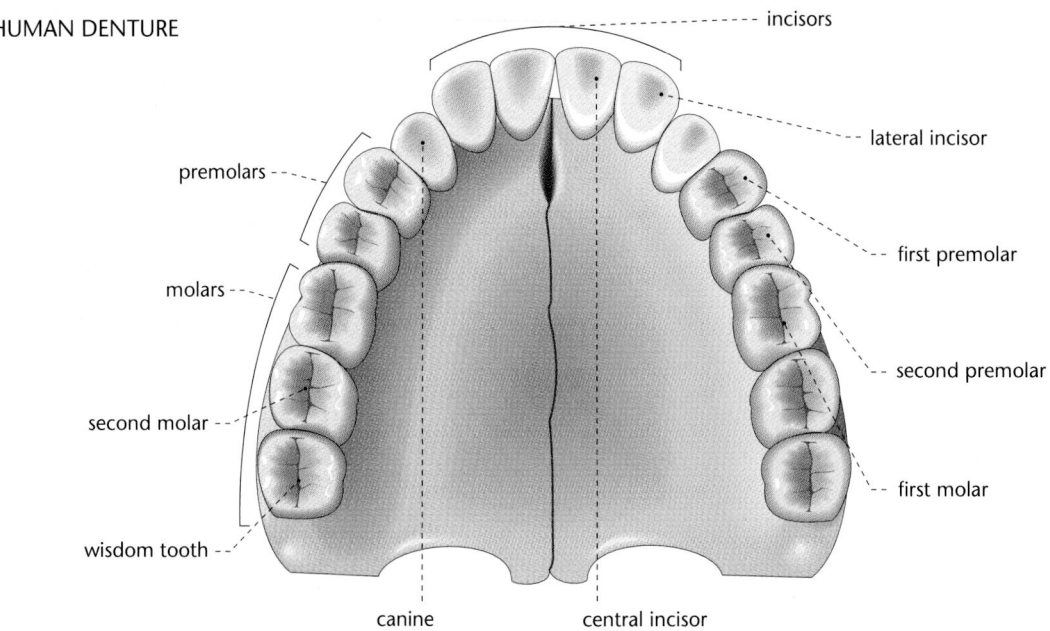

incisors

lateral incisor

first premolar

second premolar

first molar

premolars

molars

second molar

wisdom tooth

canine

central incisor

CROSS SECTION OF A MOLAR

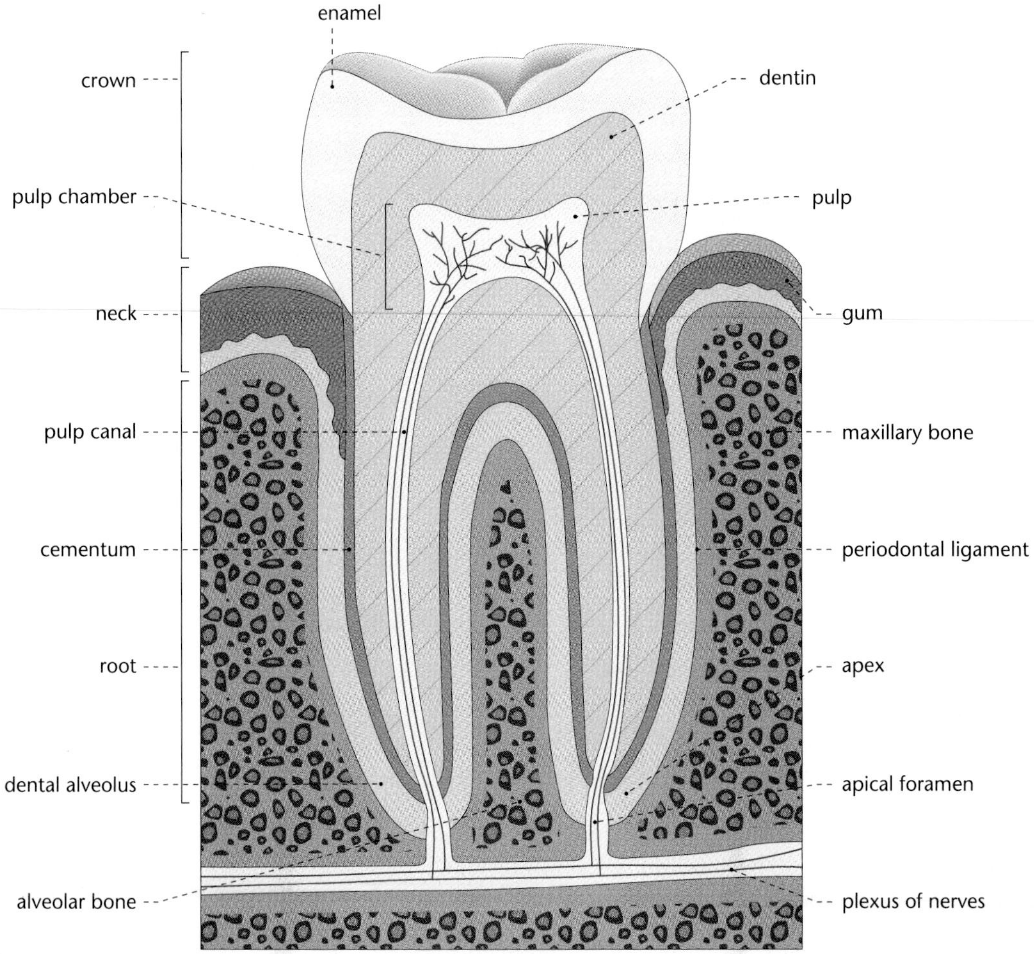

enamel

dentin

crown

pulp chamber

pulp

neck

gum

pulp canal

maxillary bone

cementum

periodontal ligament

root

apex

dental alveolus

apical foramen

alveolar bone

plexus of nerves

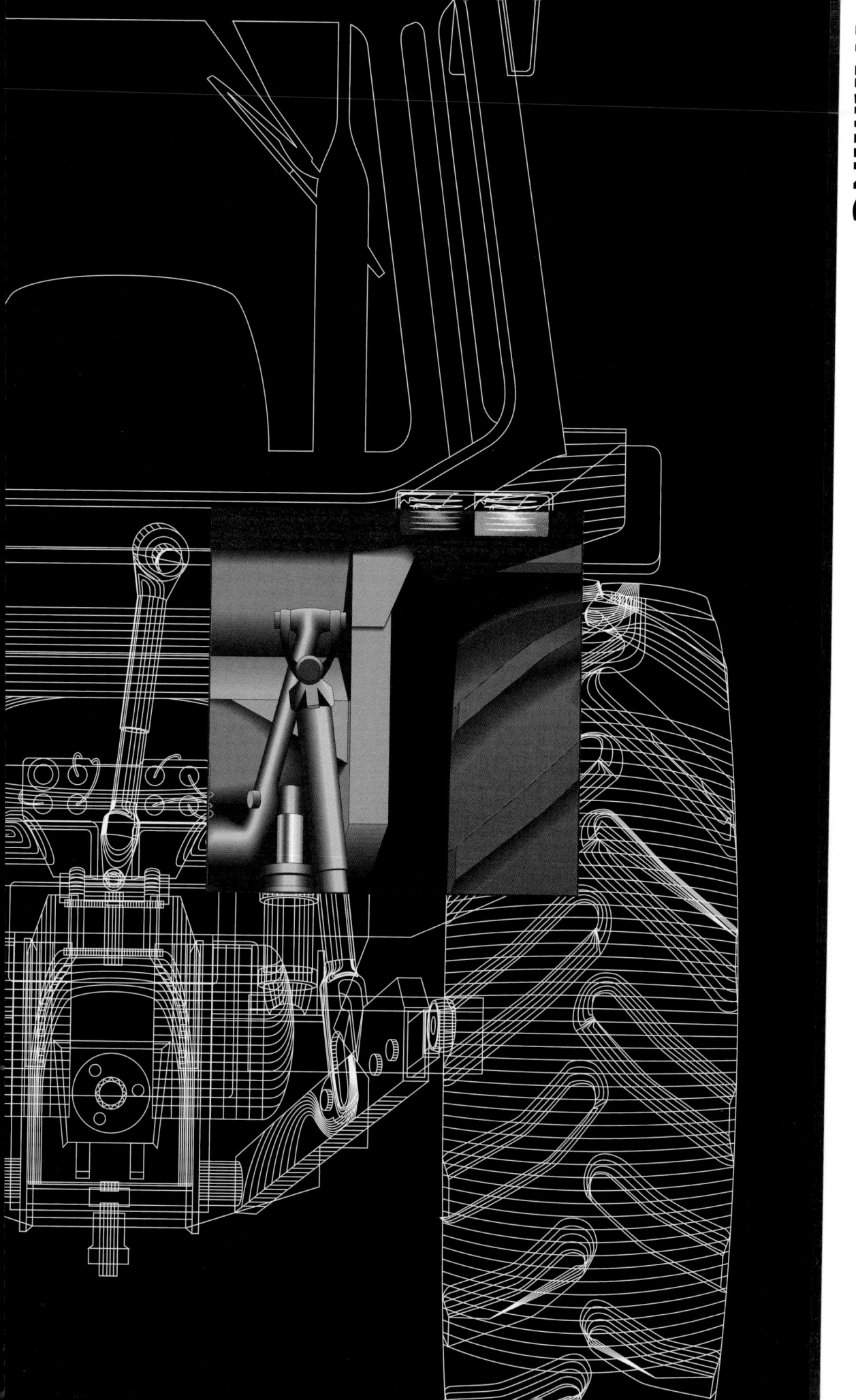

CONTENTS

TRACTOR 147

FARMSTEAD 148

FARM'S ANIMALS..150

MAJOR TYPES OF CEREALS 152

BREAD..153

STEPS FOR CULTIVATING SOIL..154

PLOWING SOIL 156

FERTILIZING SOIL..156

PULVERIZING SOIL..157

PLANTING 158

MOWING...158

TEDDING 159

HARVESTING..159

ENSILING 162

FARMING

146

TRACTOR

REAR VIEW

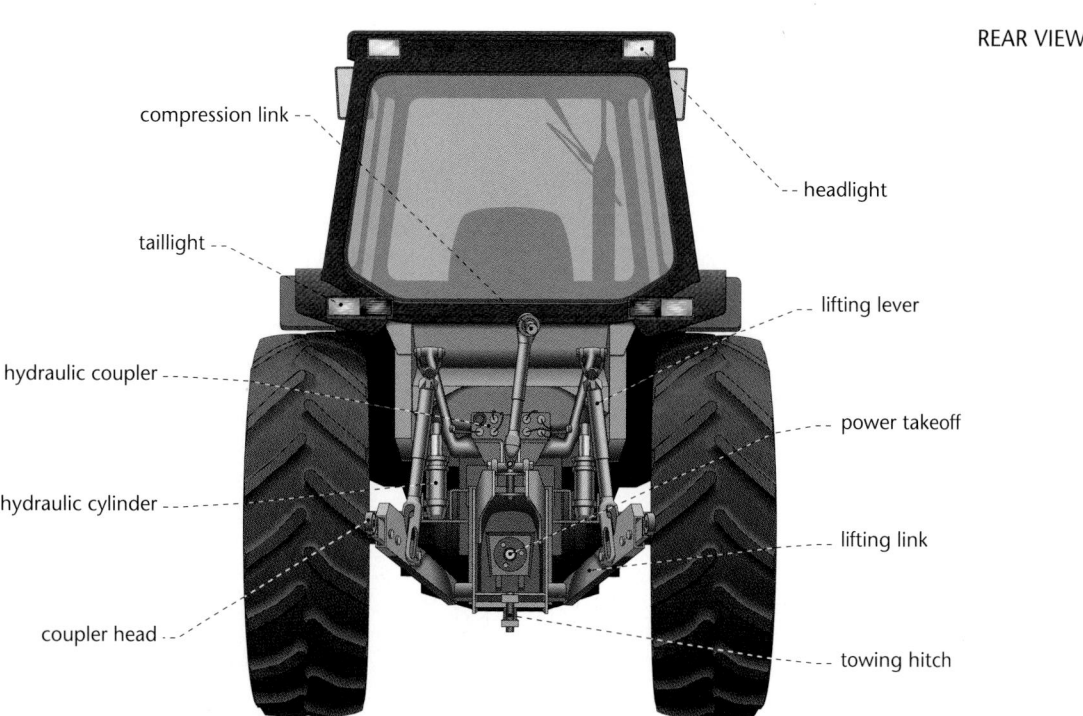

compression link

headlight

taillight

lifting lever

hydraulic coupler

power takeoff

hydraulic cylinder

lifting link

coupler head

towing hitch

FRONT VIEW

steering wheel

cab

exhaust stack

mudguard

headlight

rim

step

driving wheel

front wheel

tread bar

engine

counterweight

147

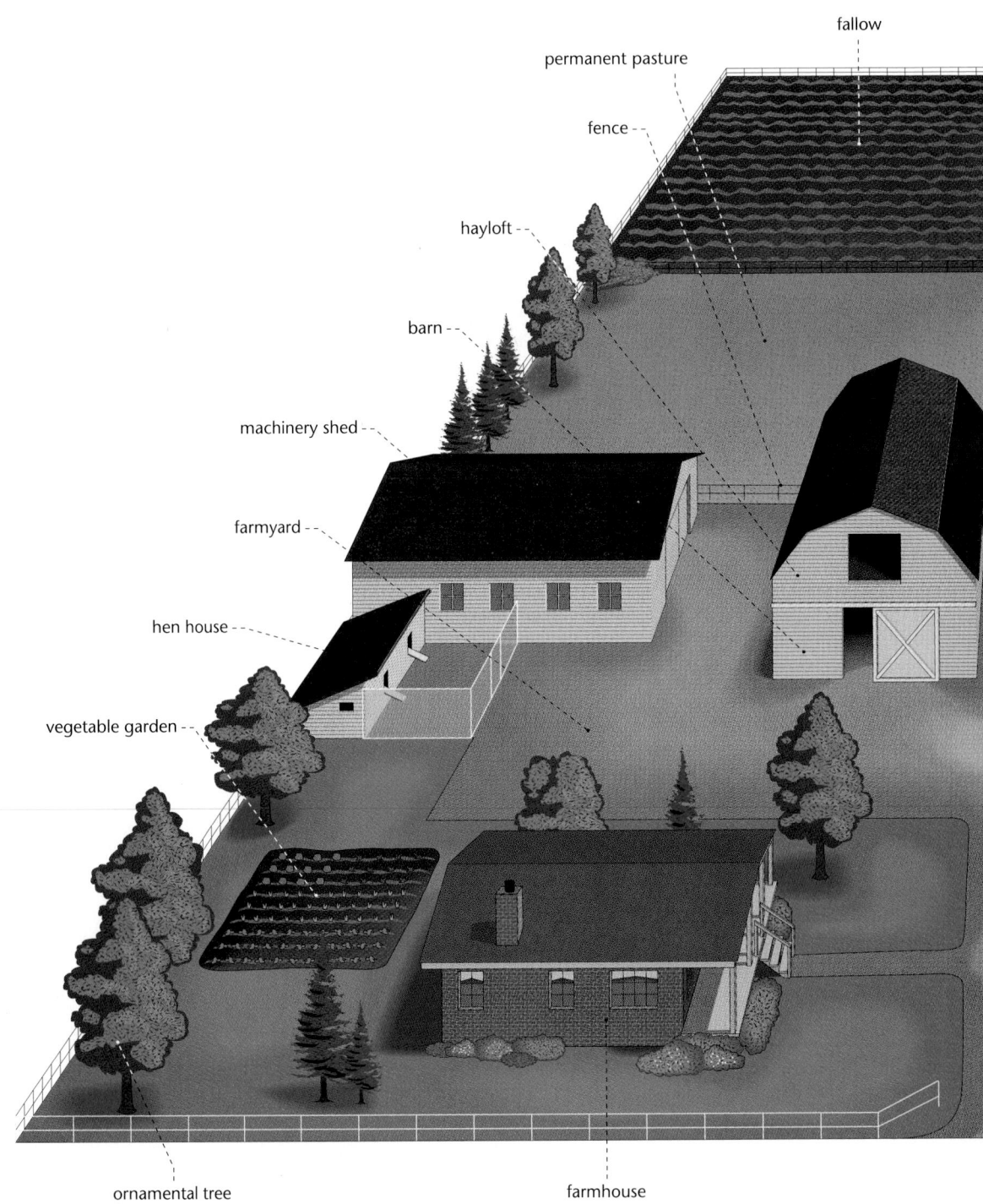

permanent pasture

fallow

fence

hayloft

barn

machinery shed

farmyard

hen house

vegetable garden

ornamental tree

farmhouse

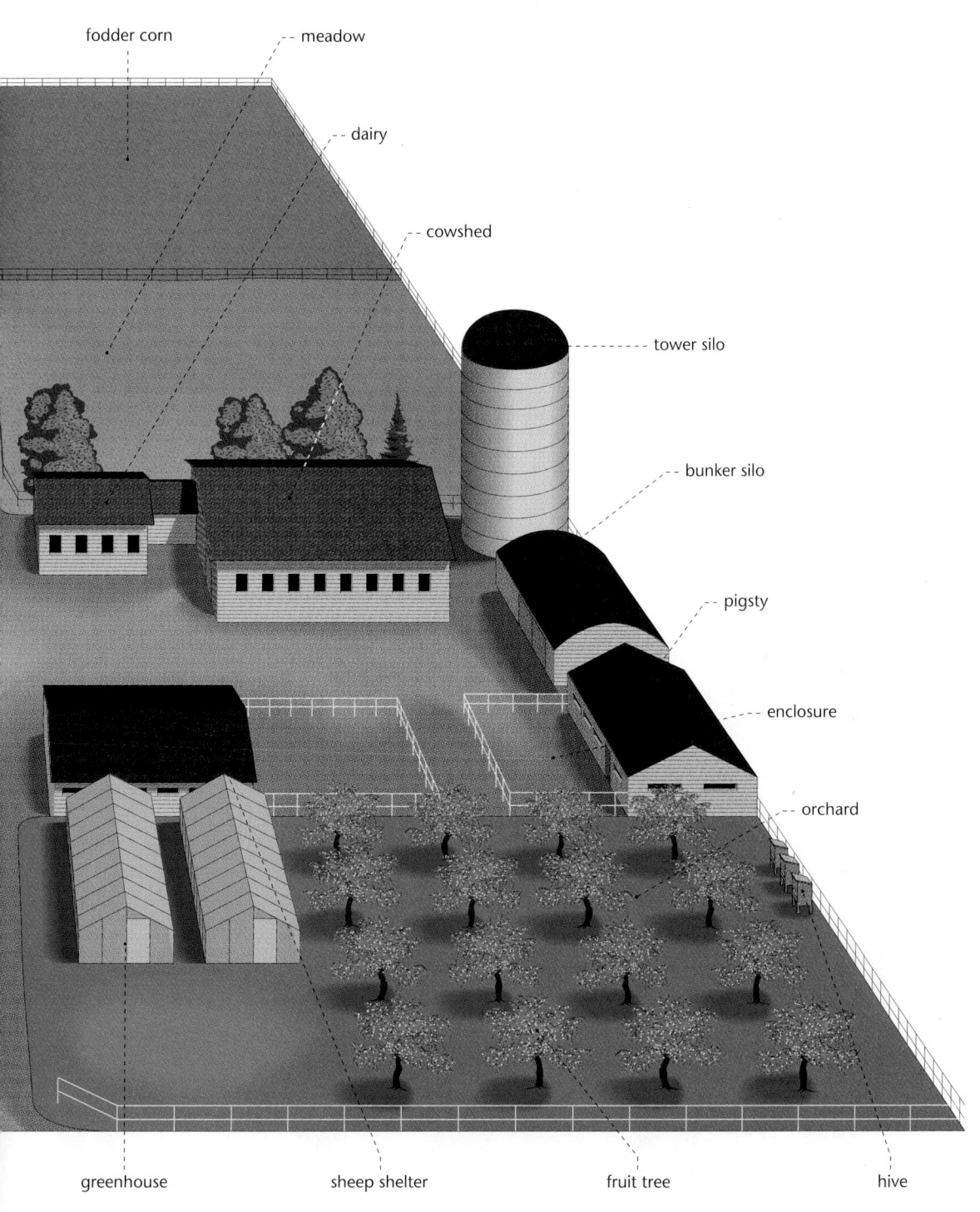

fodder corn

meadow

dairy

cowshed

tower silo

bunker silo

pigsty

enclosure

orchard

greenhouse

sheep shelter

fruit tree

hive

FARM ANIMALS

hen

chick

rooster

duck

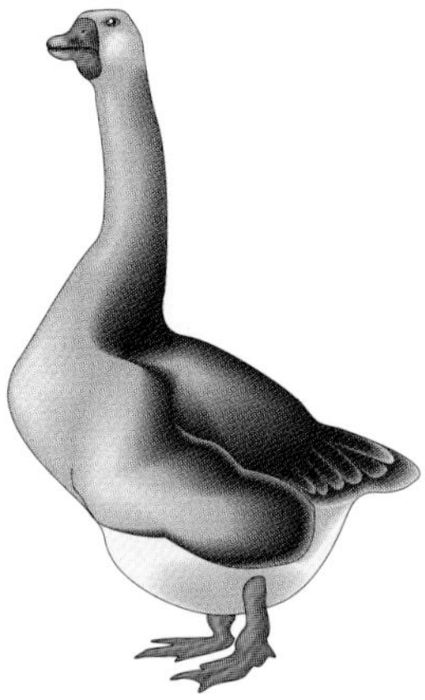

goose

turkey

goat

lamb

sheep

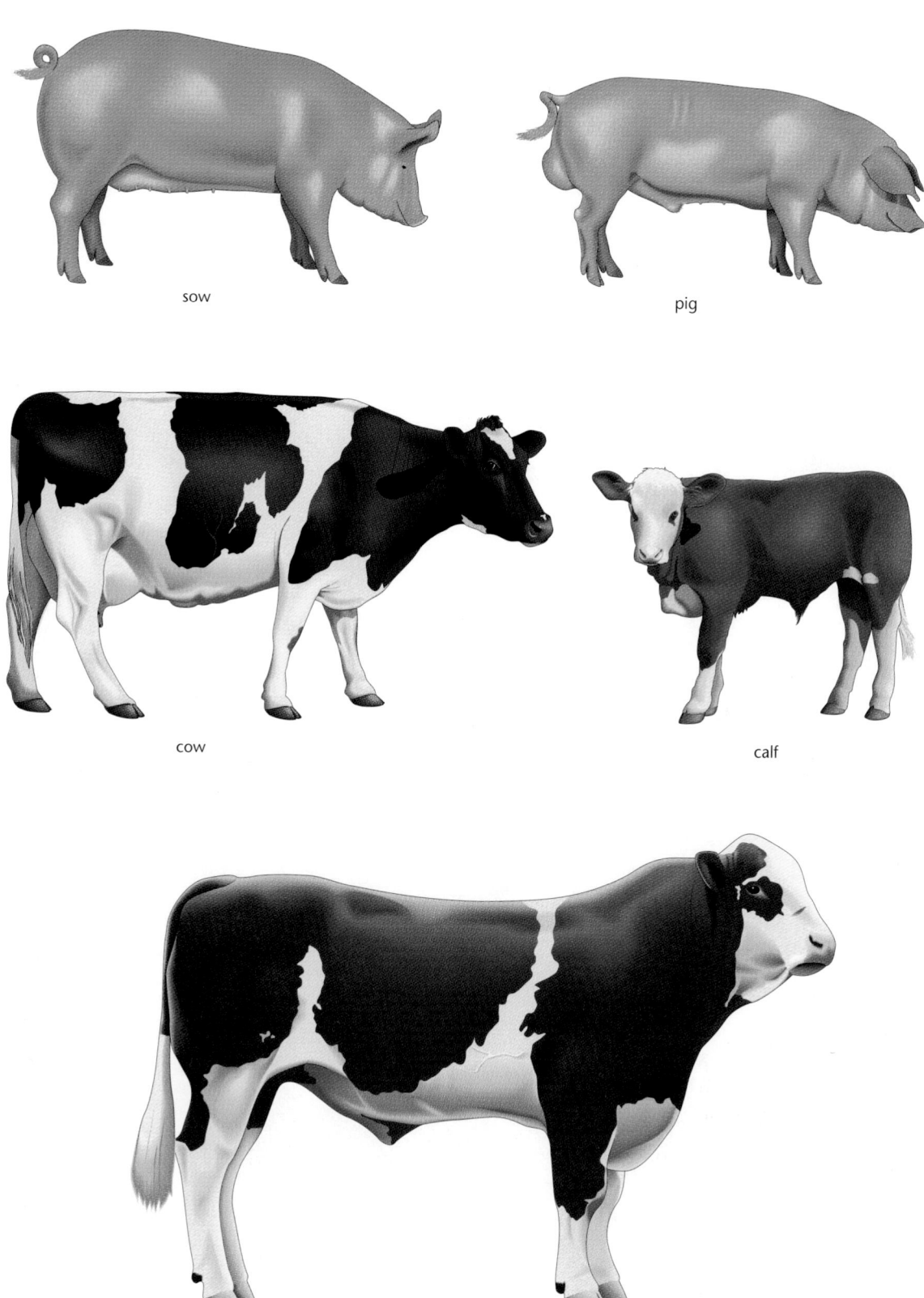

sow

pig

cow

calf

ox

MAJOR TYPES OF CEREALS

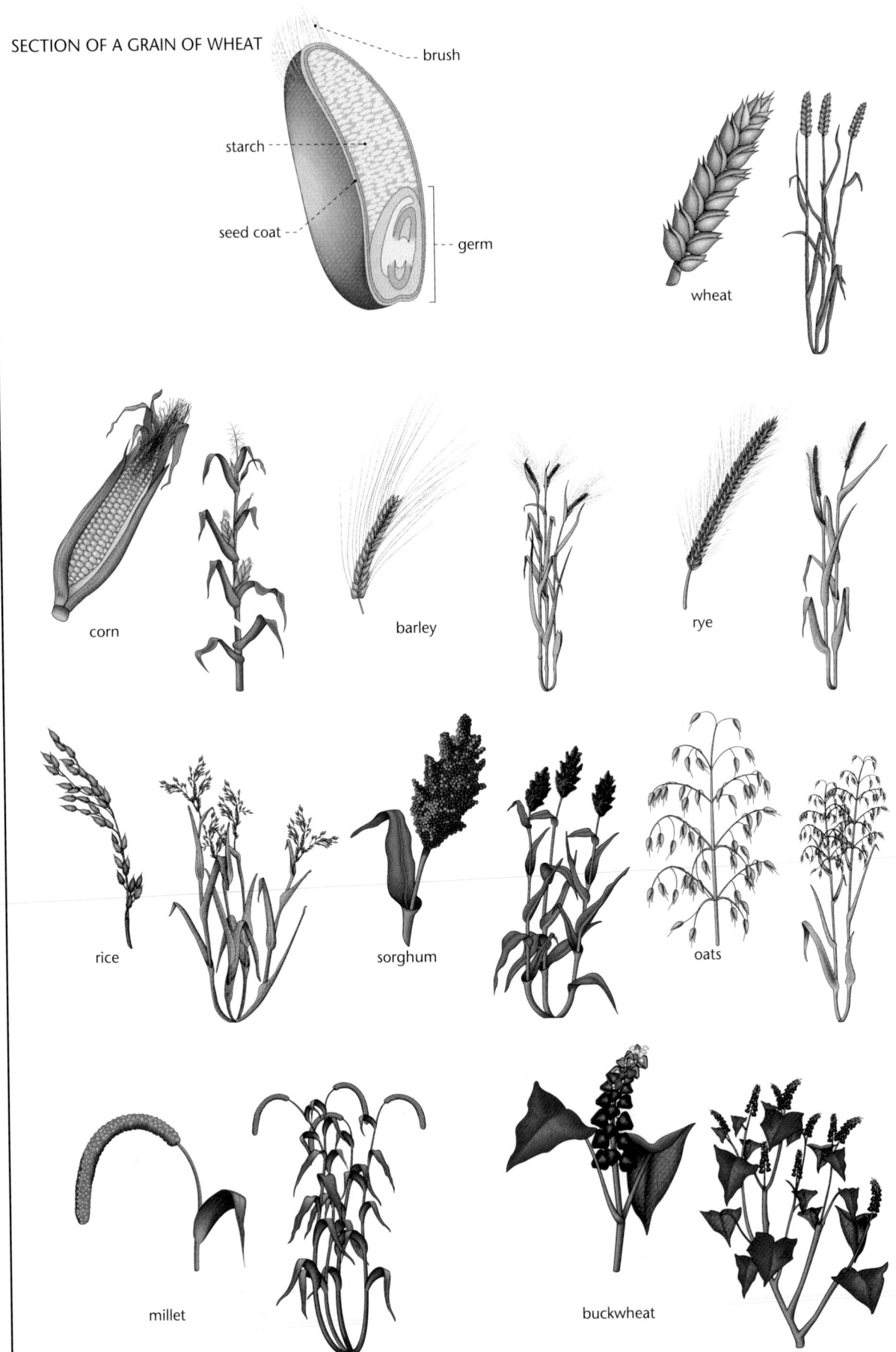

SECTION OF A GRAIN OF WHEAT

brush

starch

seed coat

germ

wheat

corn

barley

rye

rice

sorghum

oats

millet

buckwheat

BREAD

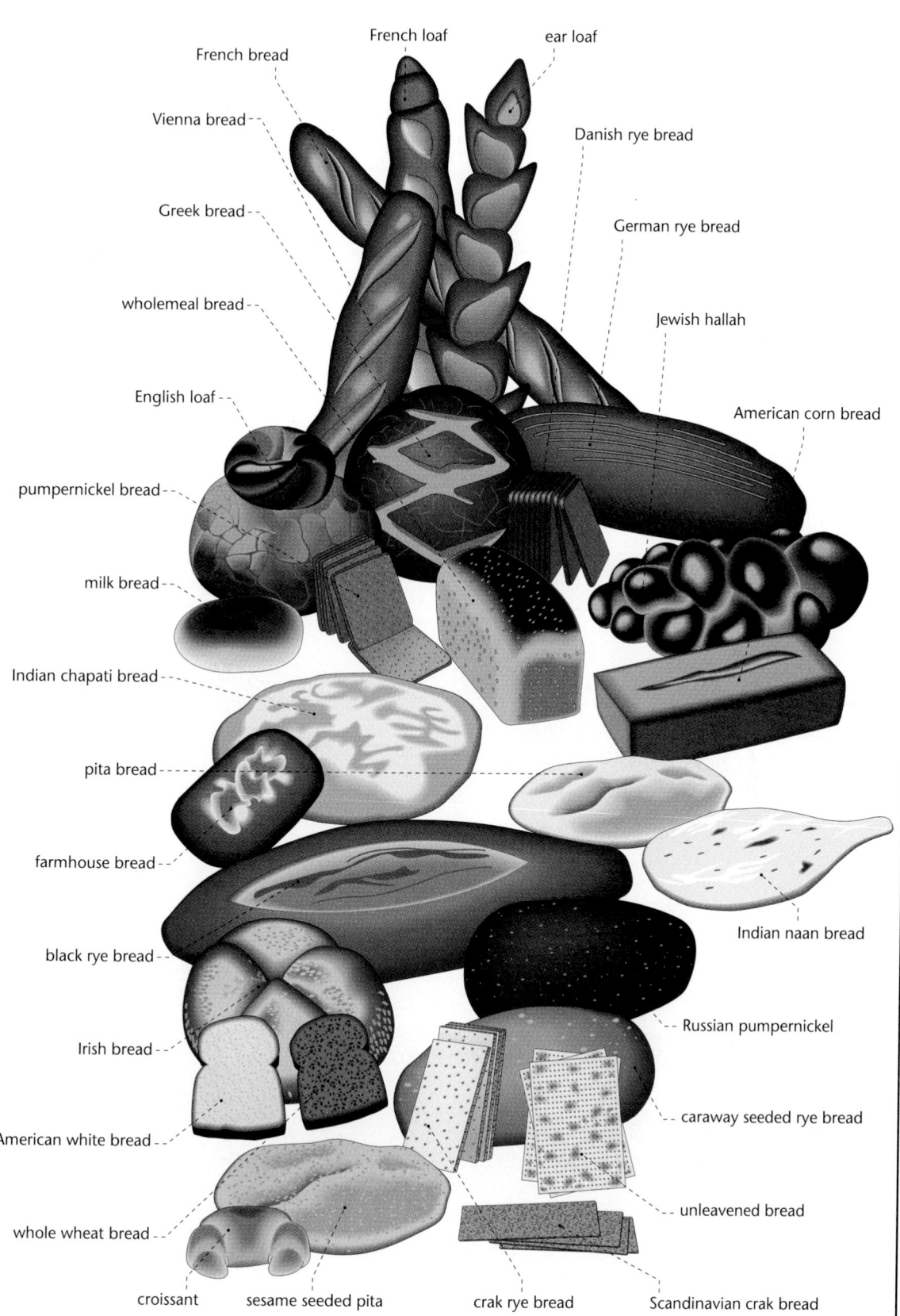

French bread

French loaf

ear loaf

Vienna bread

Danish rye bread

Greek bread

German rye bread

wholemeal bread

Jewish hallah

English loaf

American corn bread

pumpernickel bread

milk bread

Indian chapati bread

pita bread

farmhouse bread

Indian naan bread

black rye bread

Russian pumpernickel

Irish bread

caraway seeded rye bread

American white bread

unleavened bread

whole wheat bread

croissant   sesame seeded pita   crak rye bread   Scandinavian crak bread

STEPS FOR CULTIVATING SOIL

PLOWING SOIL

ribbing plow

FERTILIZING SOIL

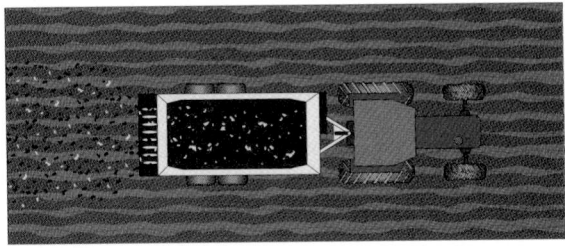

manure spreader

PULVERIZING SOIL

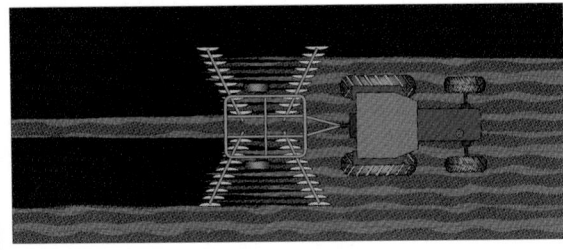

tandem disk harrow

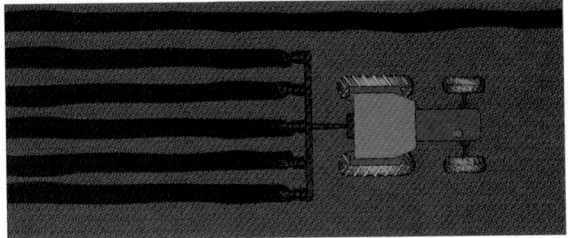

cultivator

PLANTING

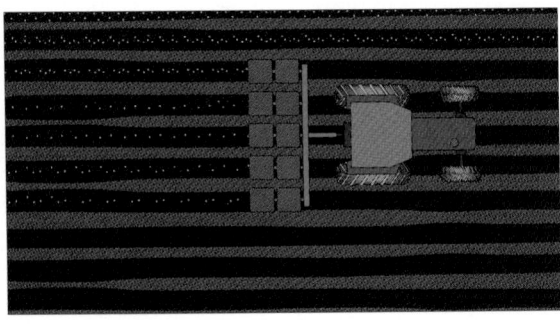

seed drill

MOWING

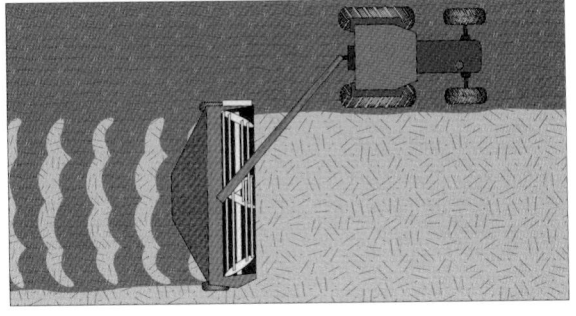

flail mower

TEDDING

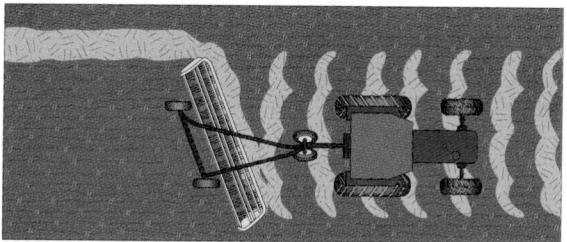

rake

HARVESTING

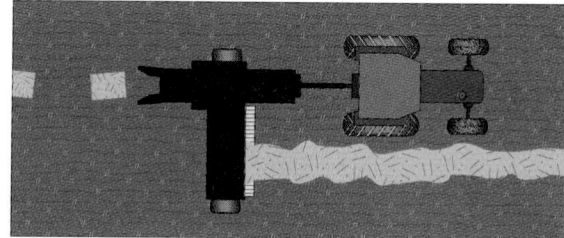

hay baler

HARVESTING

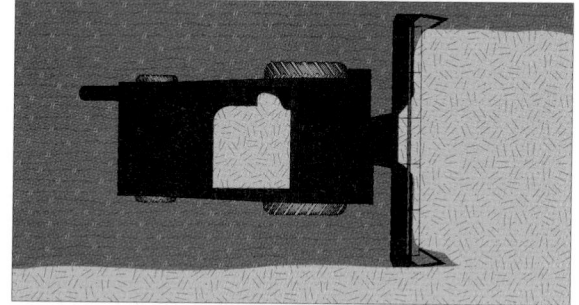

combine harvester

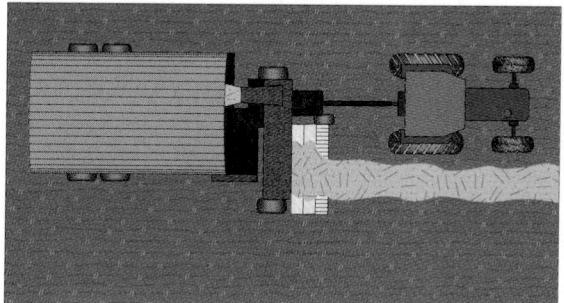

forage harvester

ENSILING

forage blower

PLOWING SOIL

RIBBING PLOW

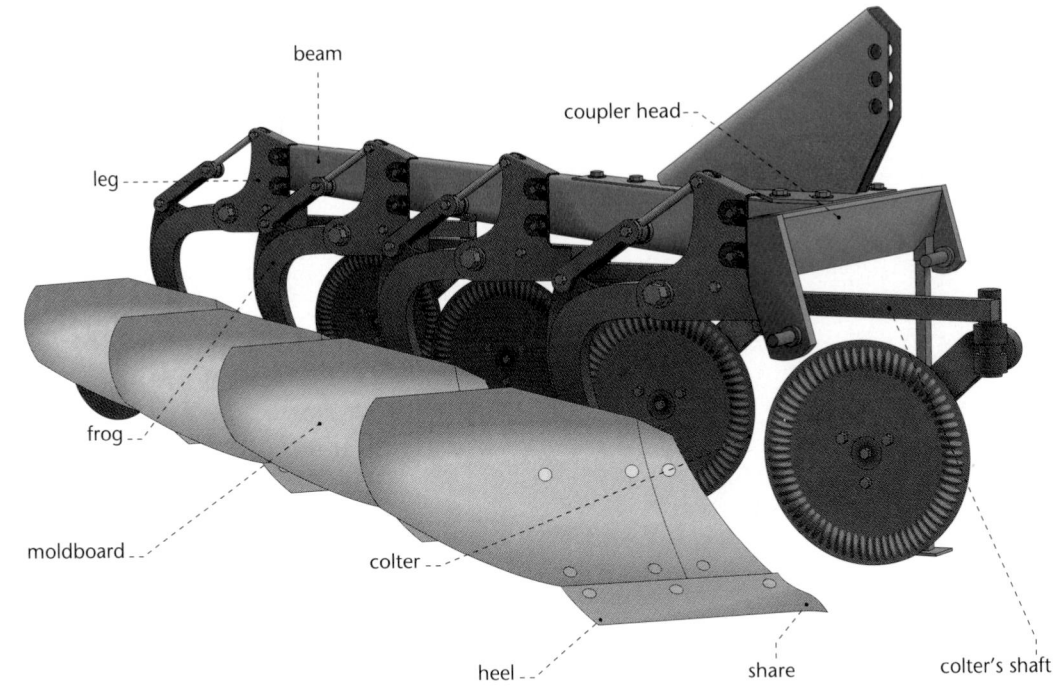

beam

coupler head

leg

frog

moldboard

colter

heel

share

colter's shaft

FERTILIZING SOIL

MANURE SPREADER

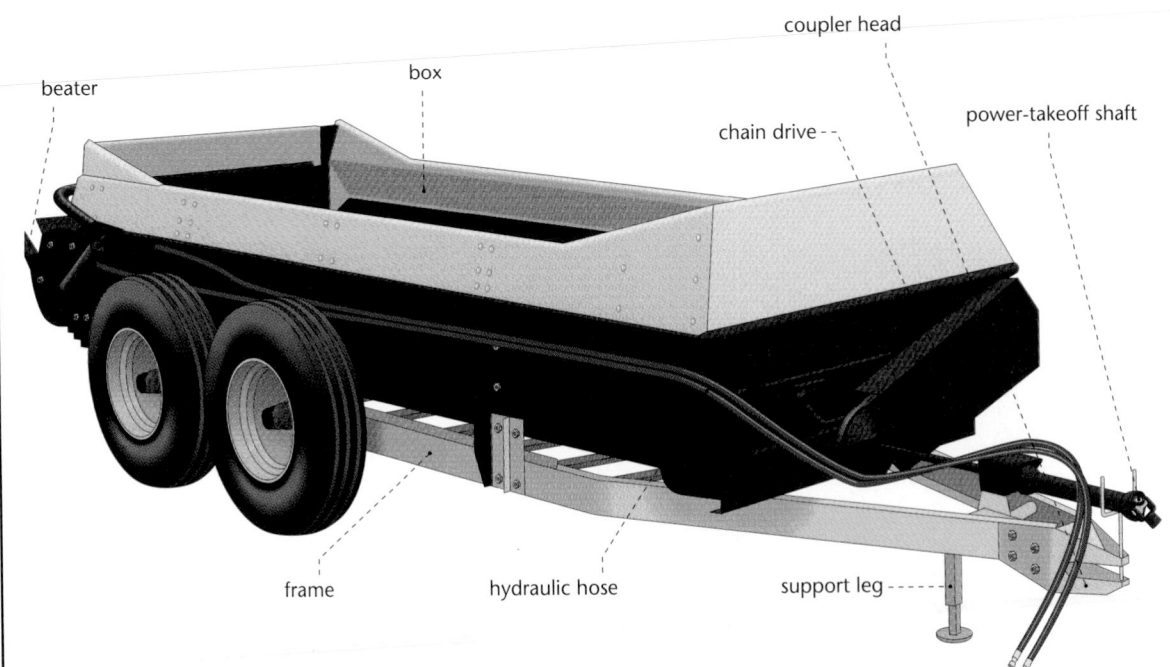

coupler head

box

beater

chain drive

power-takeoff shaft

frame

hydraulic hose

support leg

TANDEM DISK HARROW

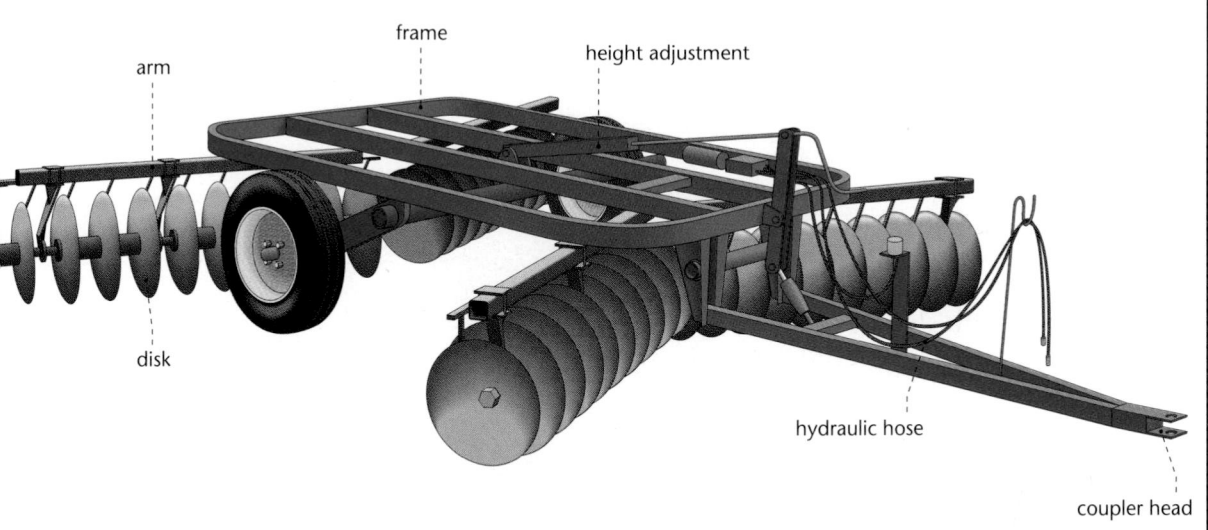

frame

height adjustment

arm

disk

hydraulic hose

coupler head

CULTIVATOR

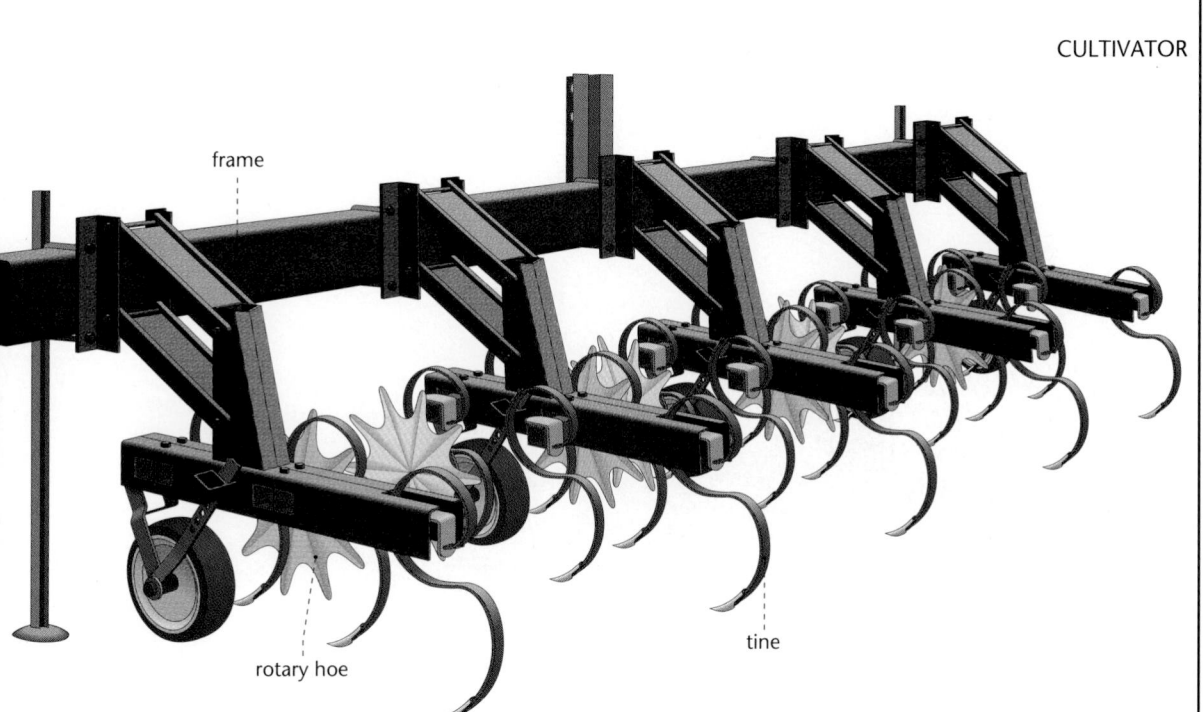

frame

rotary hoe

tine

PLANTING

SEED DRILL

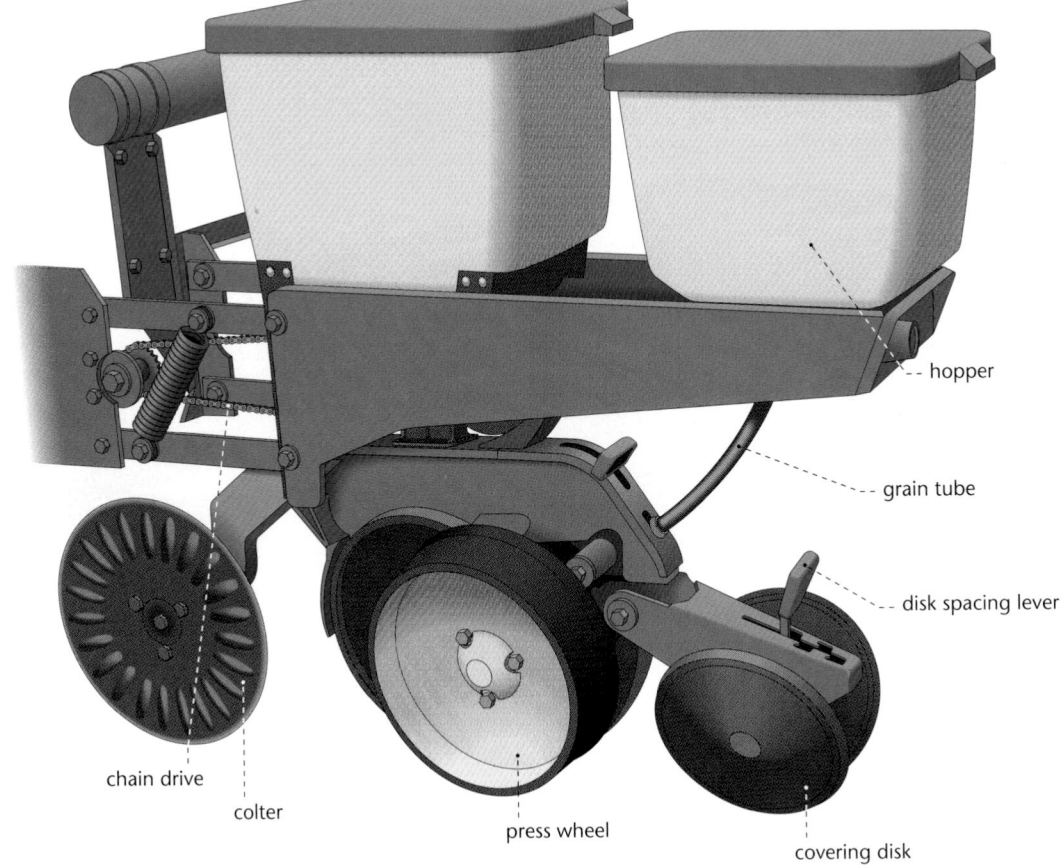

hopper

grain tube

disk spacing lever

chain drive

colter

press wheel

covering disk

MOWING

FLAIL MOWER

crushing roll

pickup reel

tow bar

tooth

hydraulic hose

cutter bar

coupler head

TEDDING

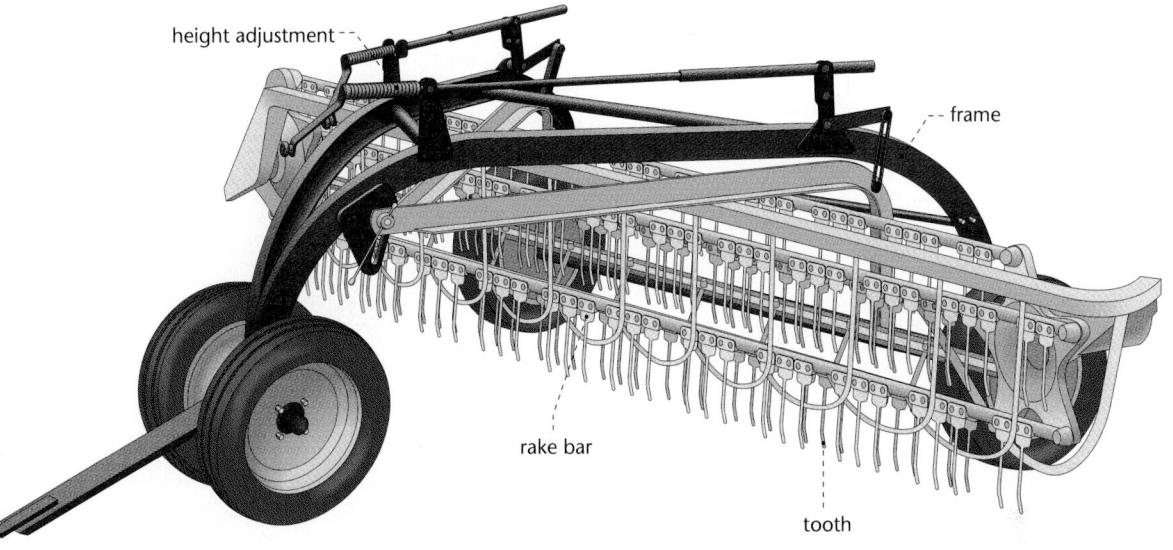

height adjustment

frame

rake bar

tooth

HARVESTING

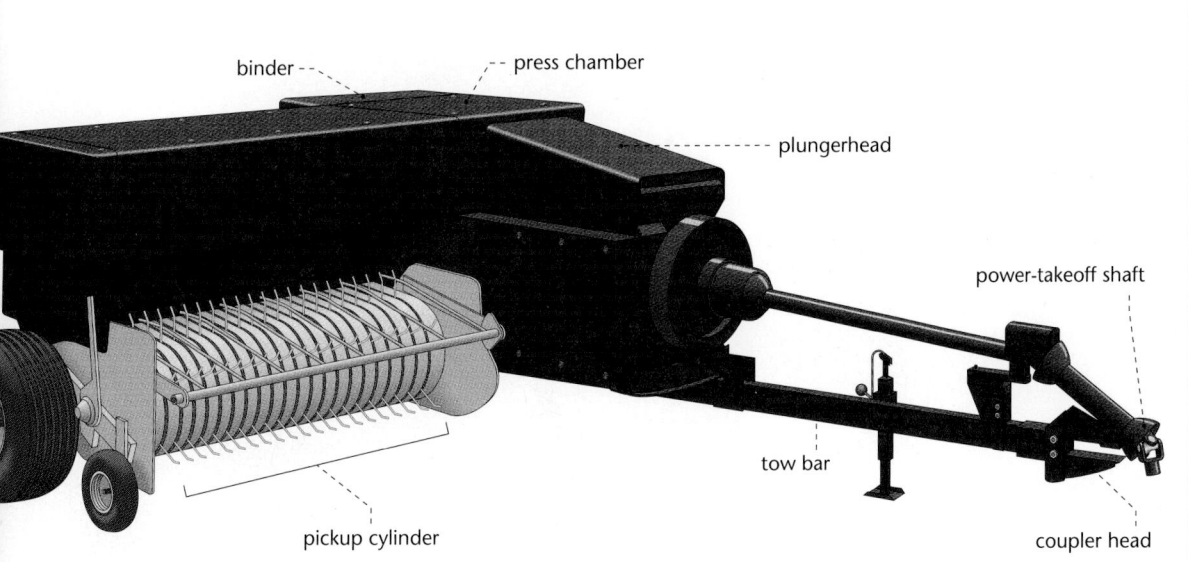

binder

press chamber

plungerhead

power-takeoff shaft

tow bar

pickup cylinder

coupler head

159

COMBINE HARVESTER

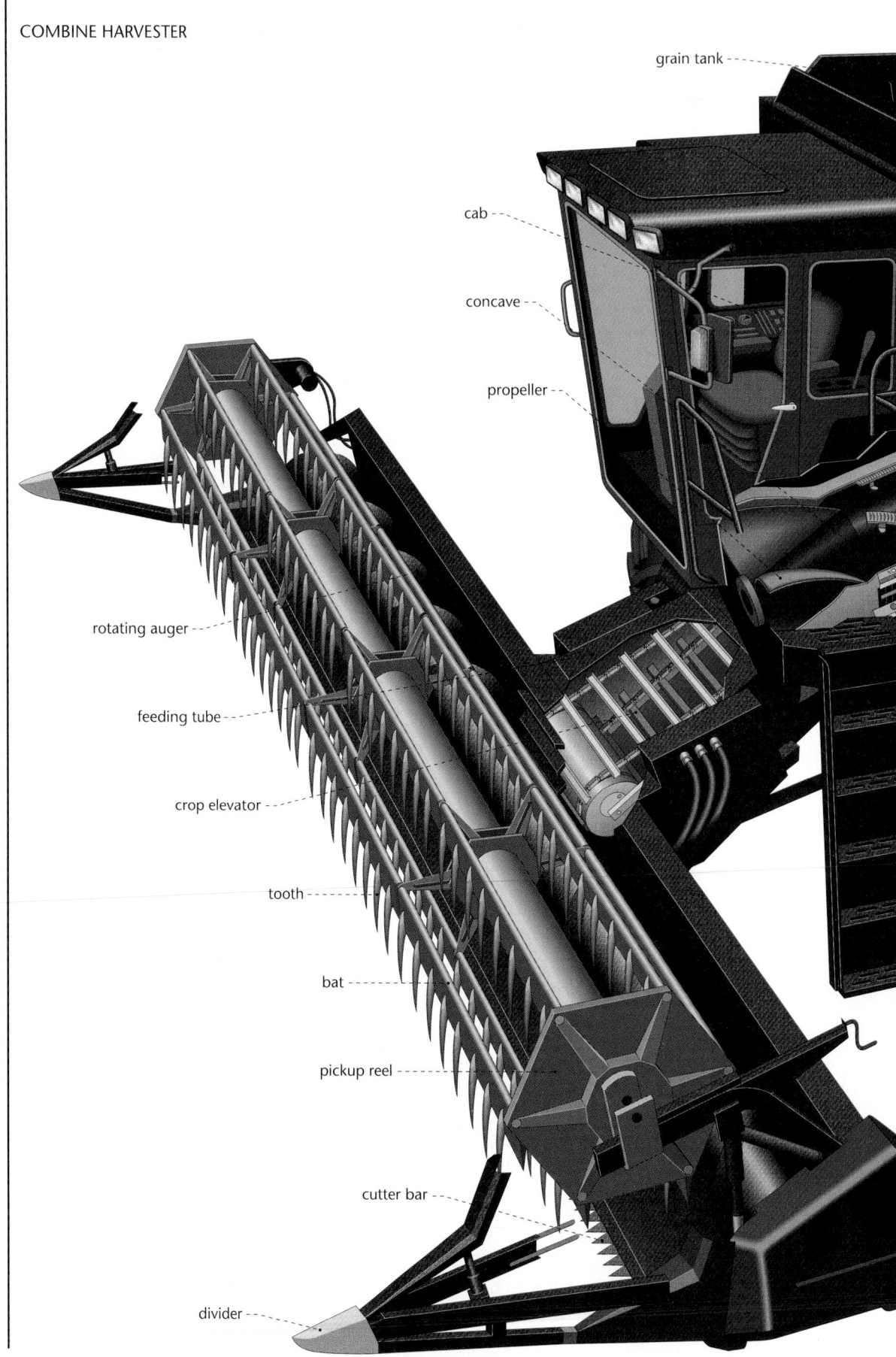

grain tank

cab

concave

propeller

rotating auger

feeding tube

crop elevator

tooth

bat

pickup reel

cutter bar

divider

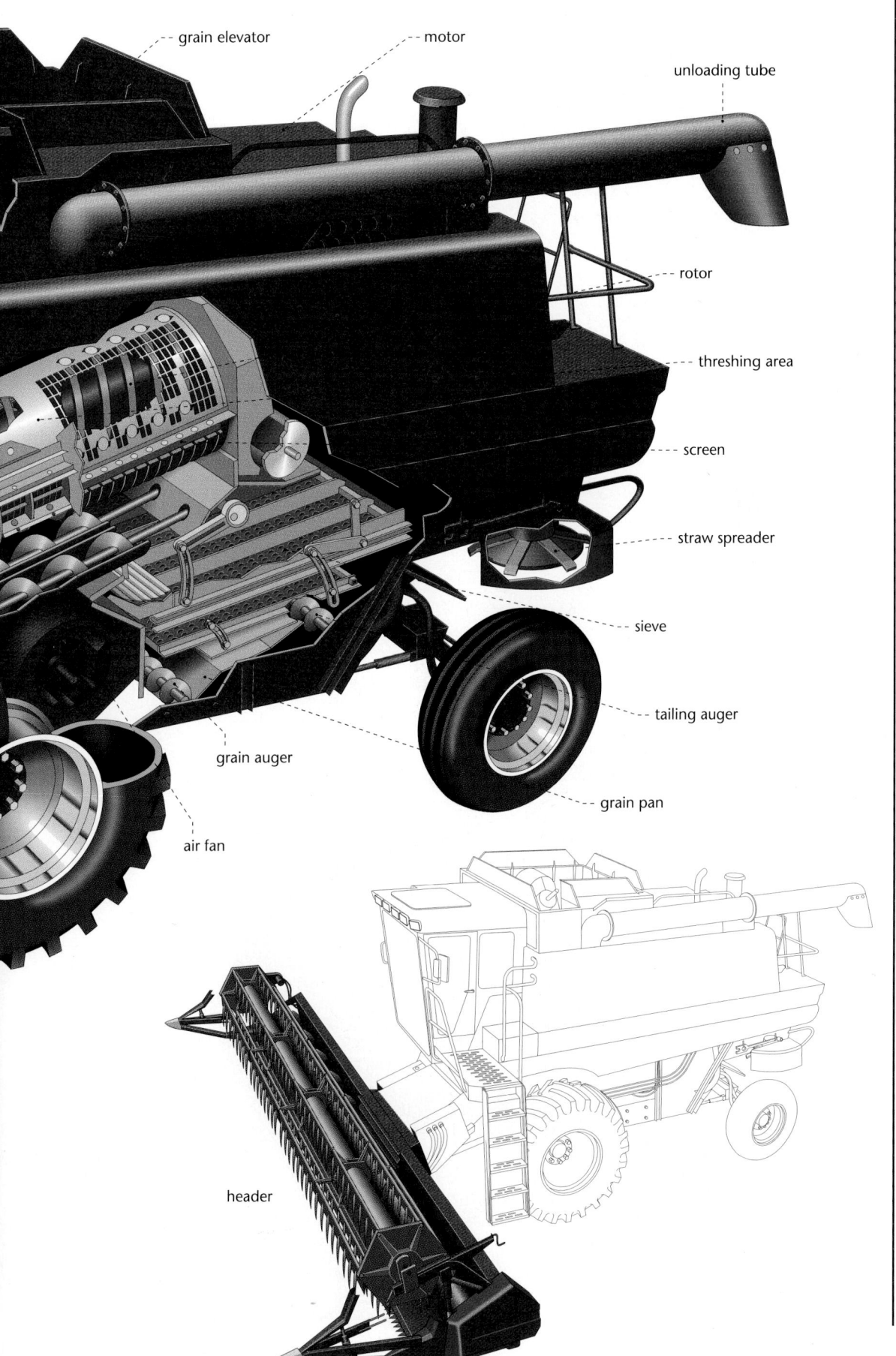

grain elevator

motor

unloading tube

rotor

threshing area

screen

straw spreader

sieve

tailing auger

grain auger

grain pan

air fan

header

FORAGE HARVESTER

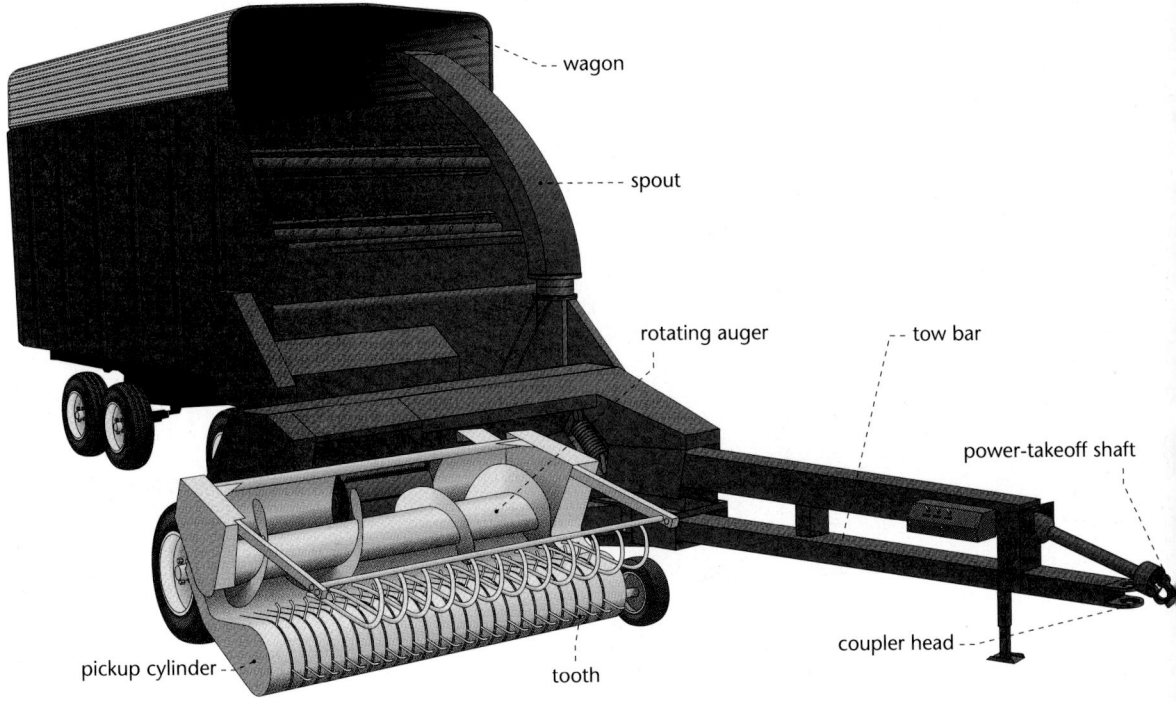

wagon

spout

rotating auger

tow bar

power-takeoff shaft

coupler head

pickup cylinder

tooth

ENSILING

FORAGE BLOWER

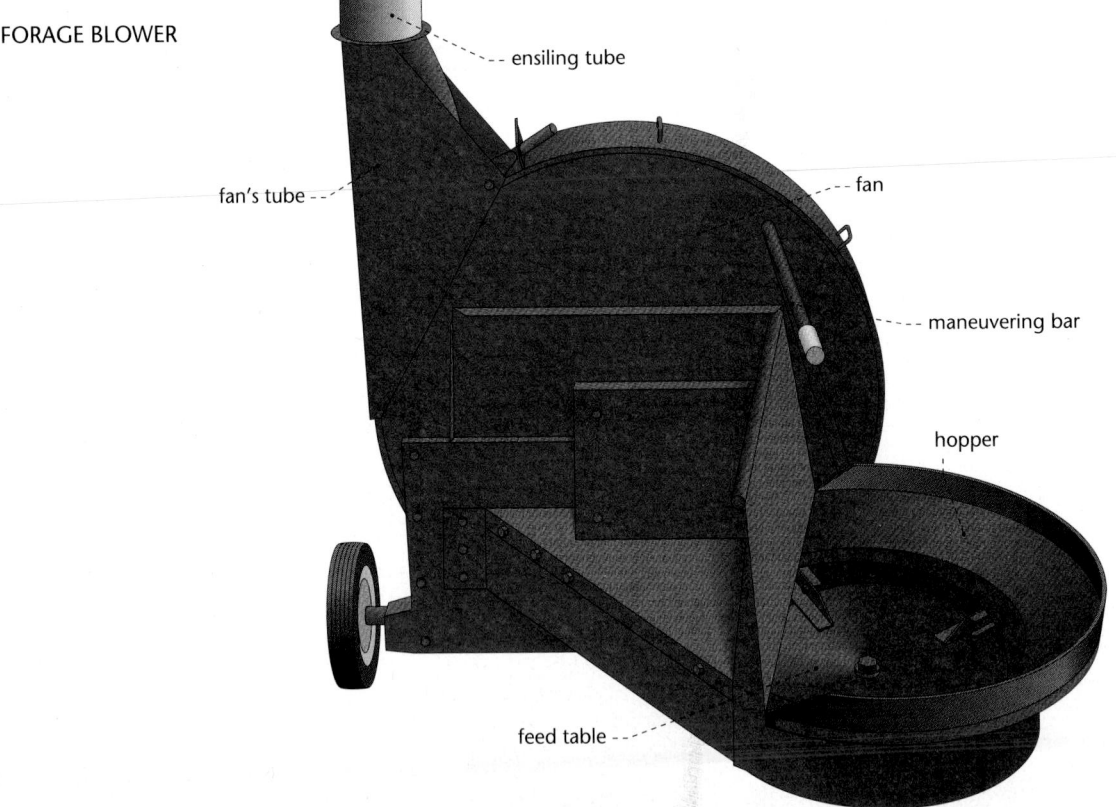

ensiling tube

fan's tube

fan

maneuvering bar

hopper

feed table

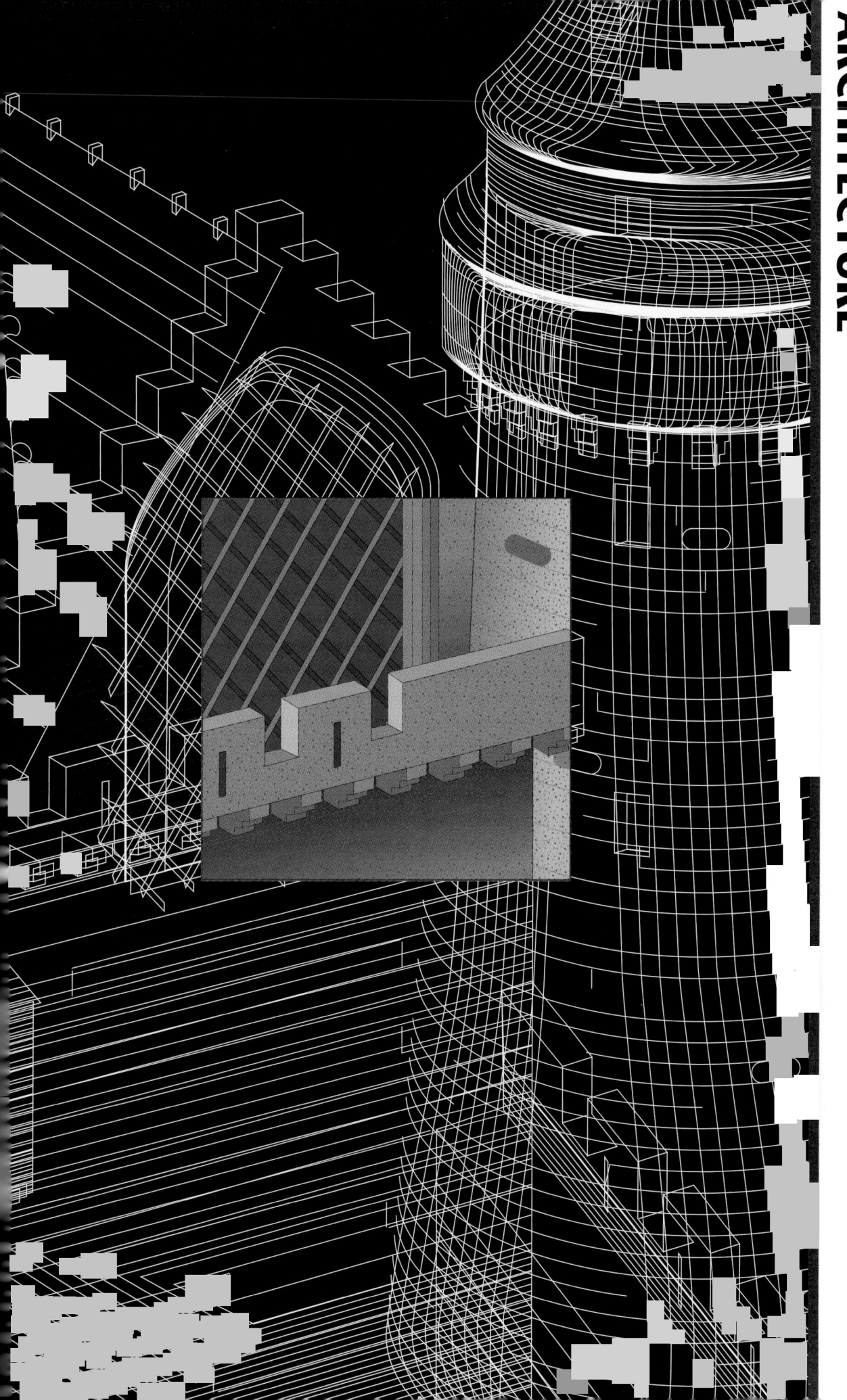

CONTENTS

TRADITIONAL HOUSES 165

ARCHITECTURAL STYLES 166

GREEK TEMPLE..168

ROMAN HOUSE 170

MOSQUE 172

ARCH 174

GOTHIC CATHEDRAL 175

VAUBAN FORTIFICATION 178

CASTLE 180

ROOFS 182

DOWNTOWN 184

CROSS SECTION OF A STREET 186

CITY HOUSES 187

THEATER 188

OFFICE BUILDING 190

ARCHITECTURE

igloo

wigwam

yurt

isba

hut

hut

tepee

pile dwelling

IONIC ORDER

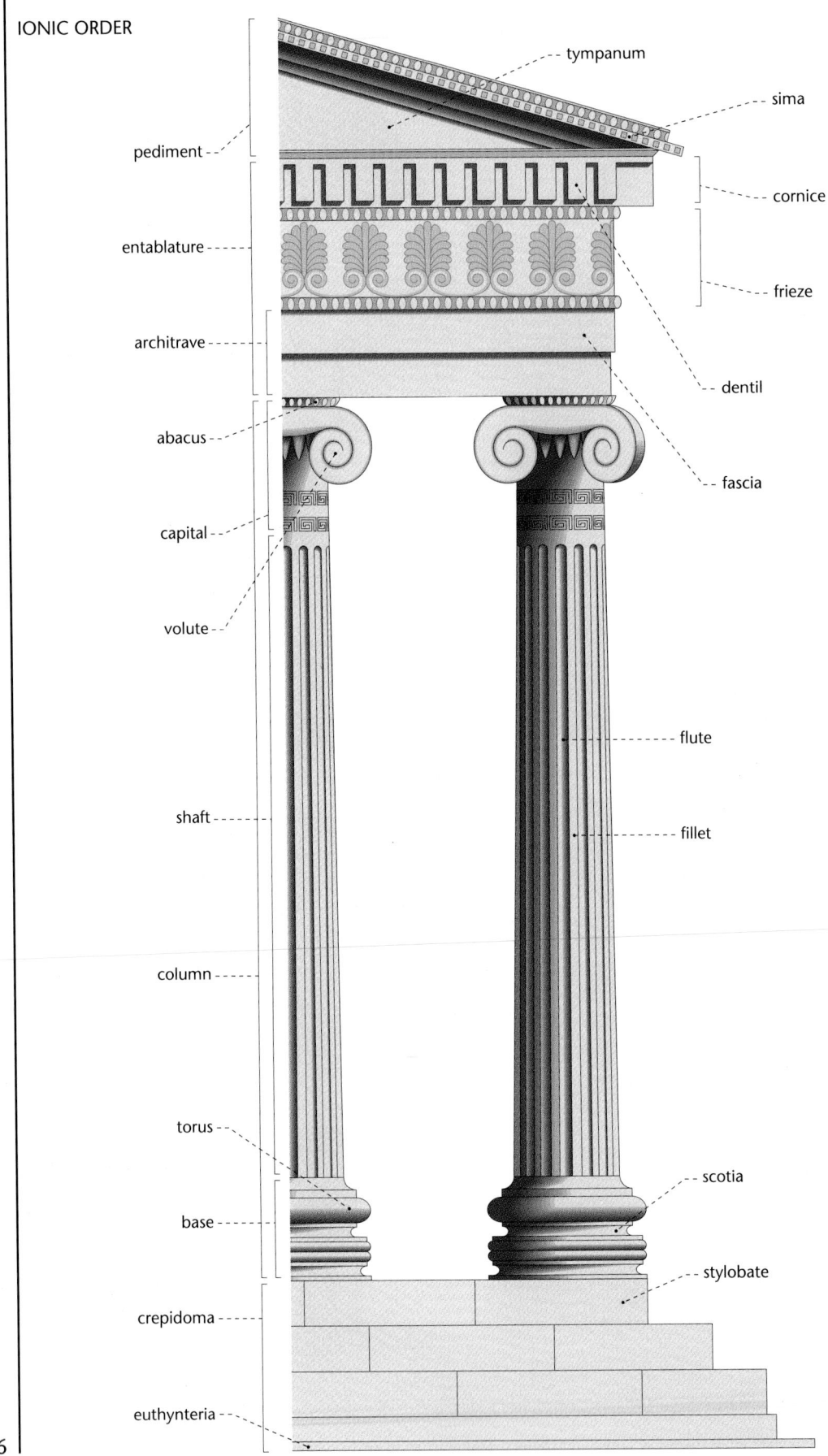

tympanum

sima

pediment

cornice

entablature

frieze

architrave

dentil

abacus

fascia

capital

volute

flute

shaft

fillet

column

torus

scotia

base

stylobate

crepidoma

euthynteria

DORIC ORDER

CORINTHIAN ORDER

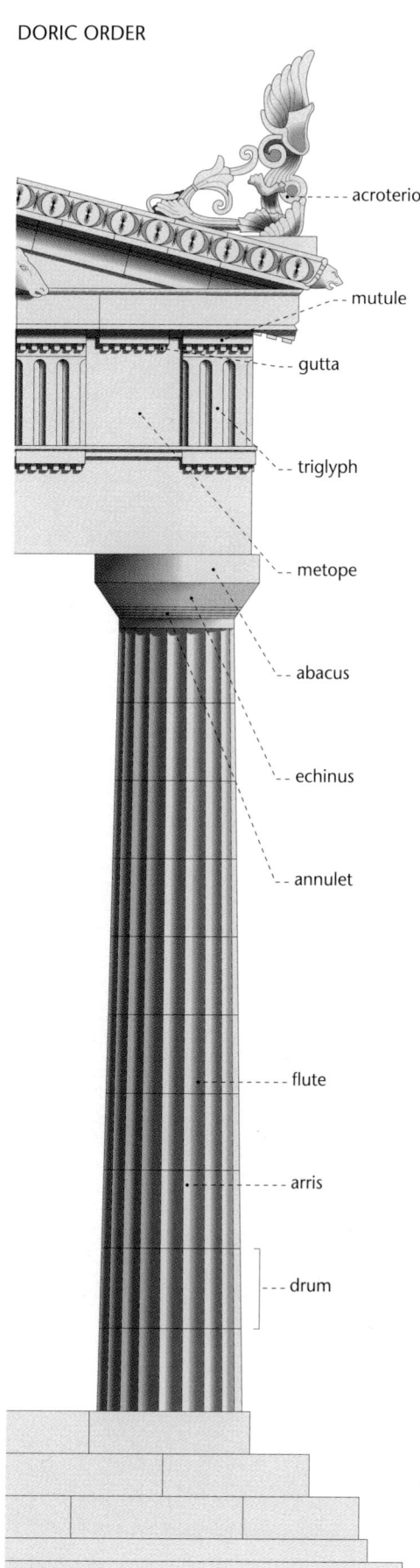

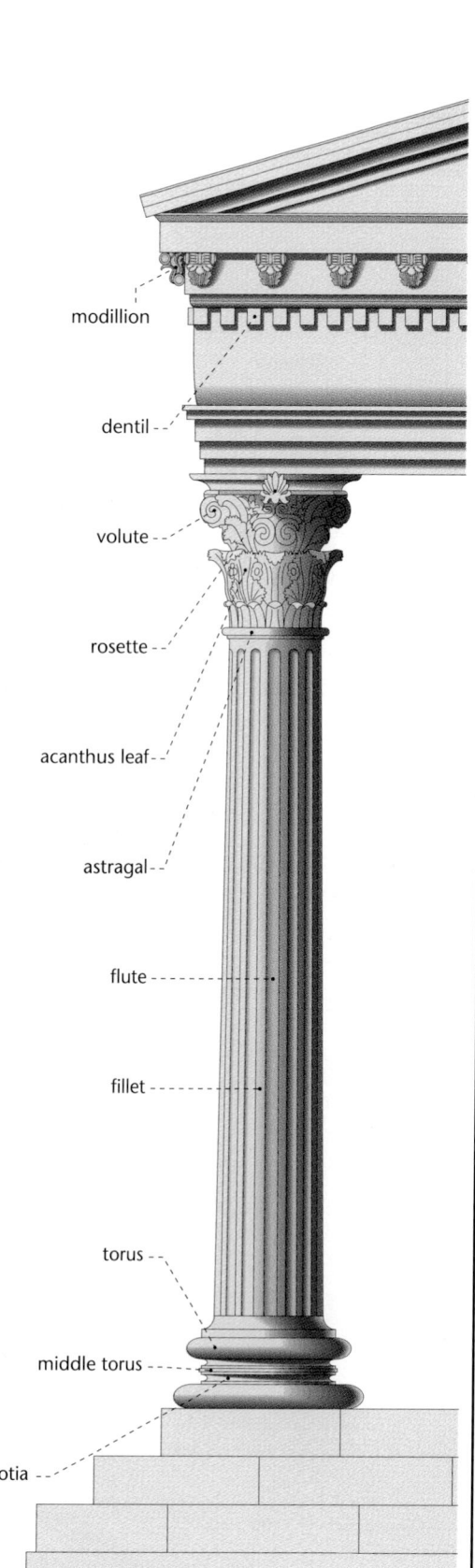

acroterion

mutule

gutta

triglyph

metope

abacus

echinus

annulet

flute

arris

drum

modillion

dentil

volute

rosette

acanthus leaf

astragal

flute

fillet

torus

middle torus

scotia

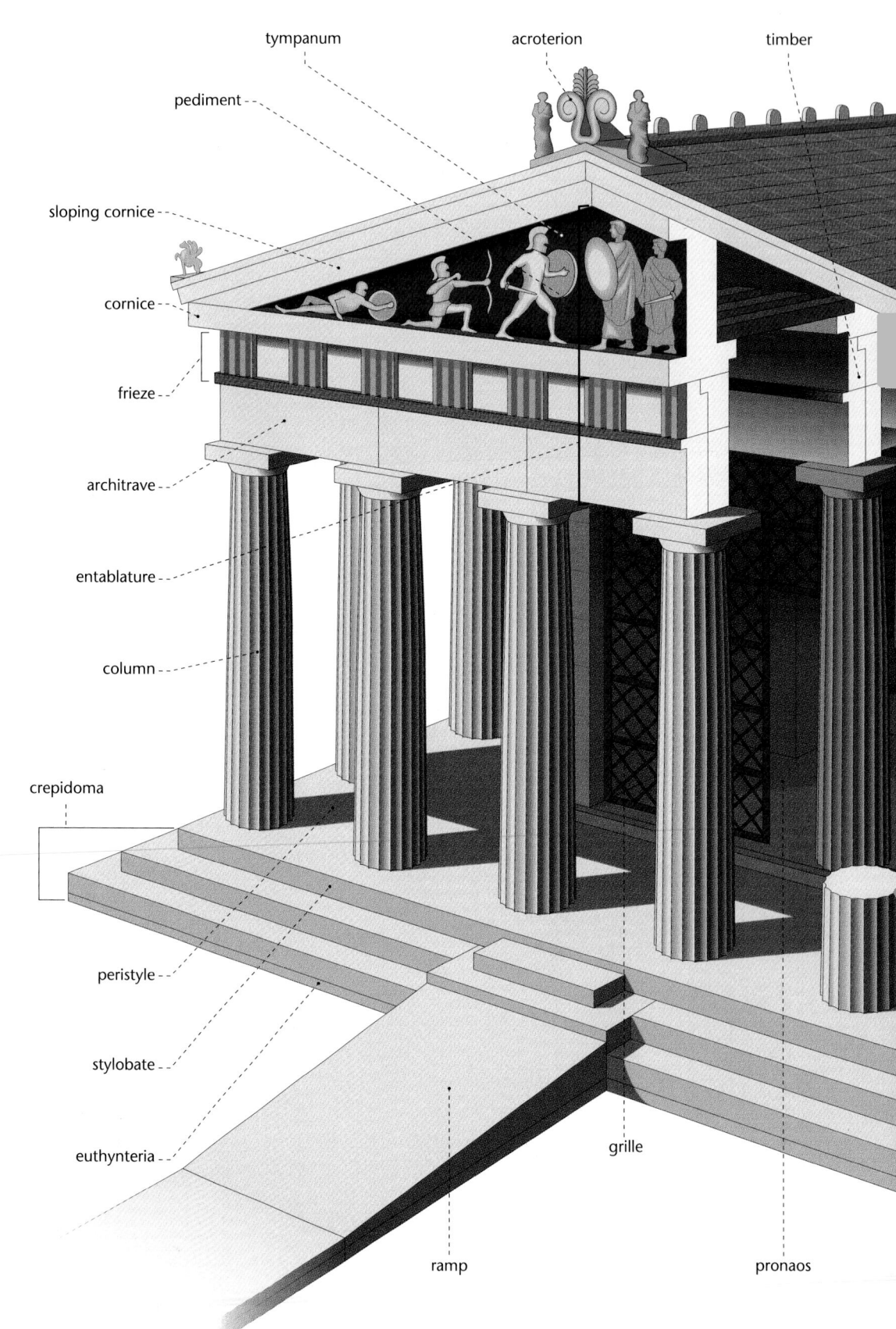

tympanum

acroterion

timber

pediment

sloping cornice

cornice

frieze

architrave

entablature

column

crepidoma

peristyle

stylobate

euthynteria

ramp

grille

pronaos

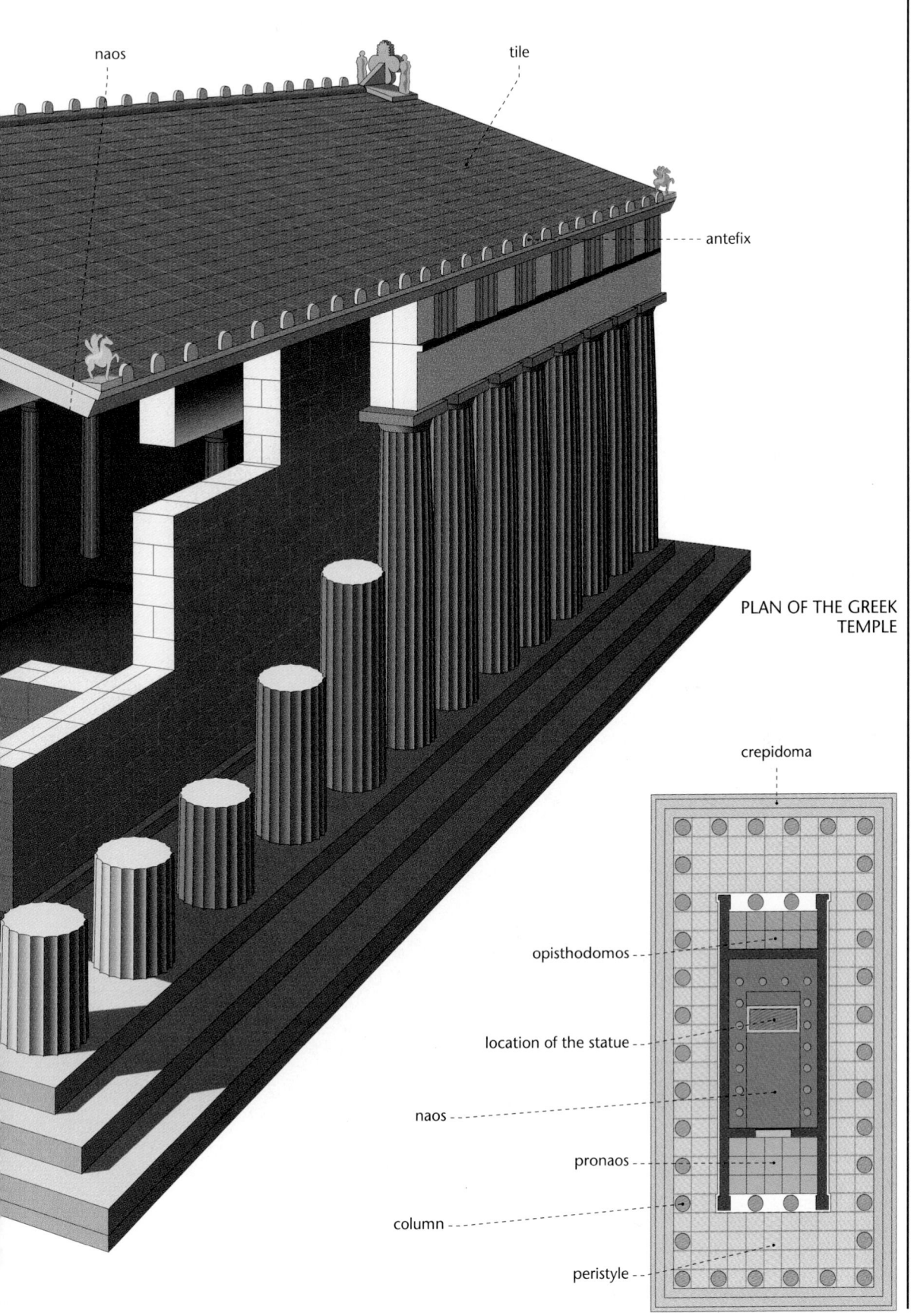

naos

tile

antefix

PLAN OF THE GREEK
TEMPLE

crepidoma

opisthodomos

location of the statue

naos

pronaos

column

peristyle

169

ROMAN HOUSE

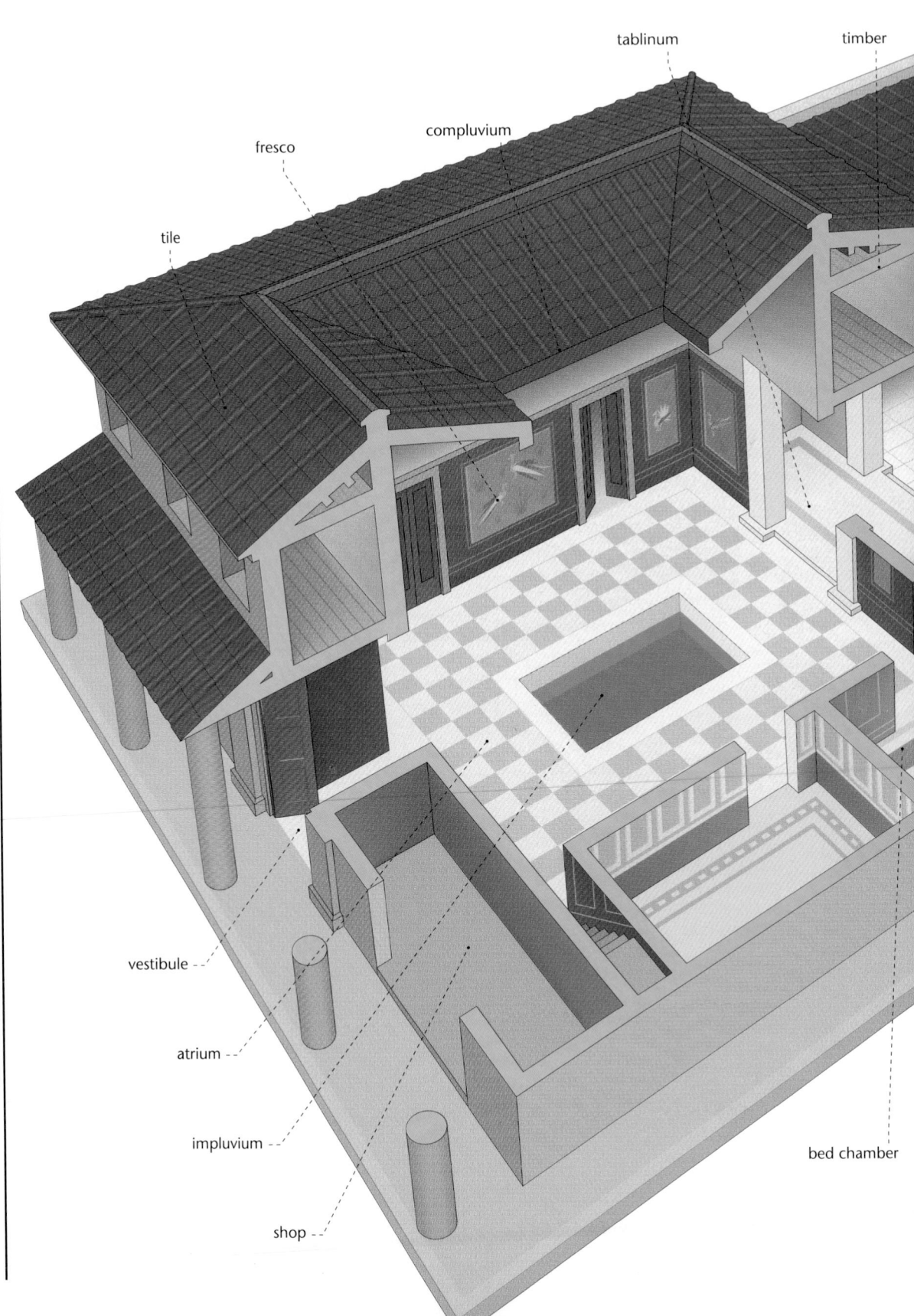

tablinum

timber

compluvium

fresco

tile

vestibule

atrium

impluvium

bed chamber

shop

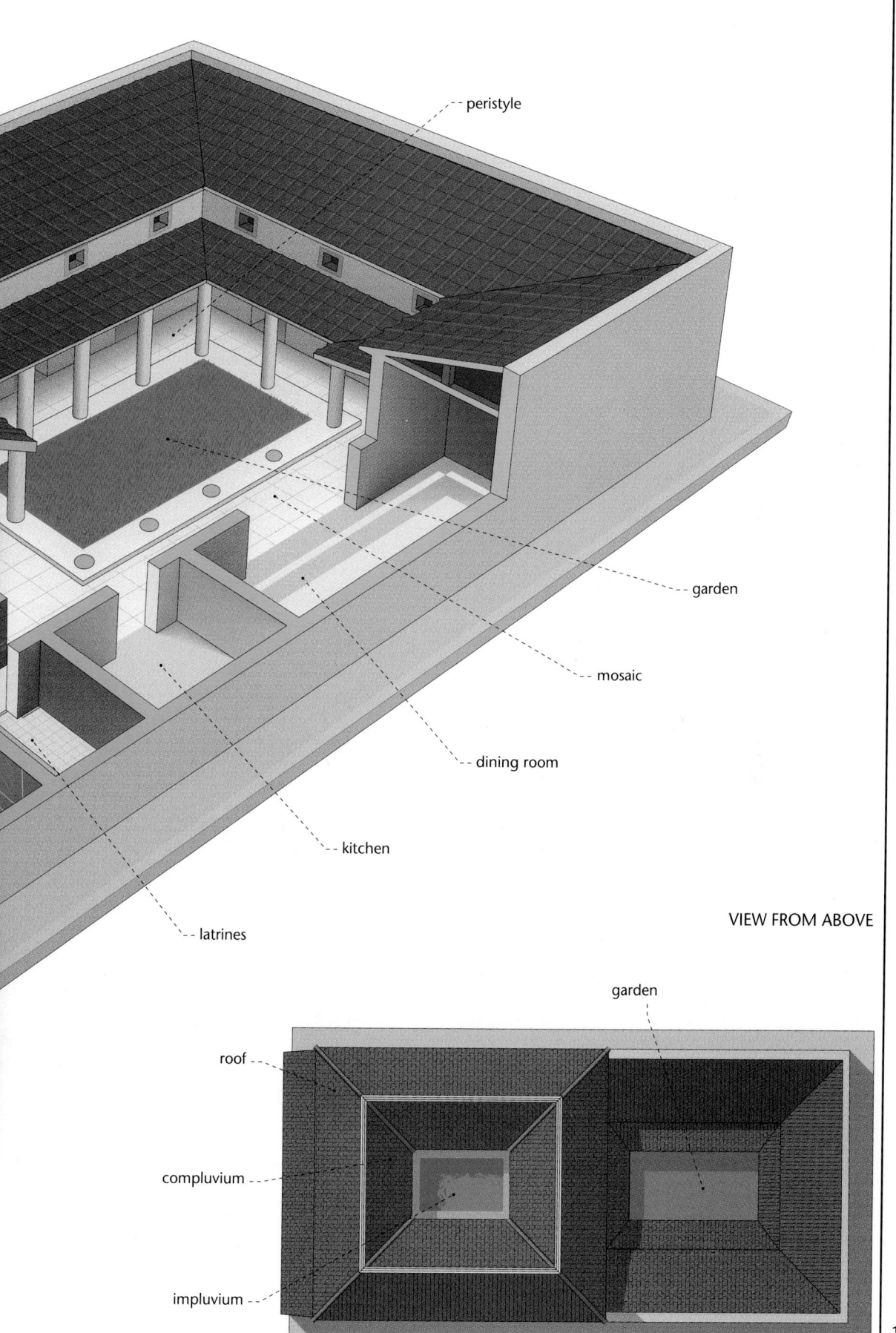

peristyle

garden

mosaic

dining room

kitchen

latrines

VIEW FROM ABOVE

garden

roof

compluvium

impluvium

MOSQUE

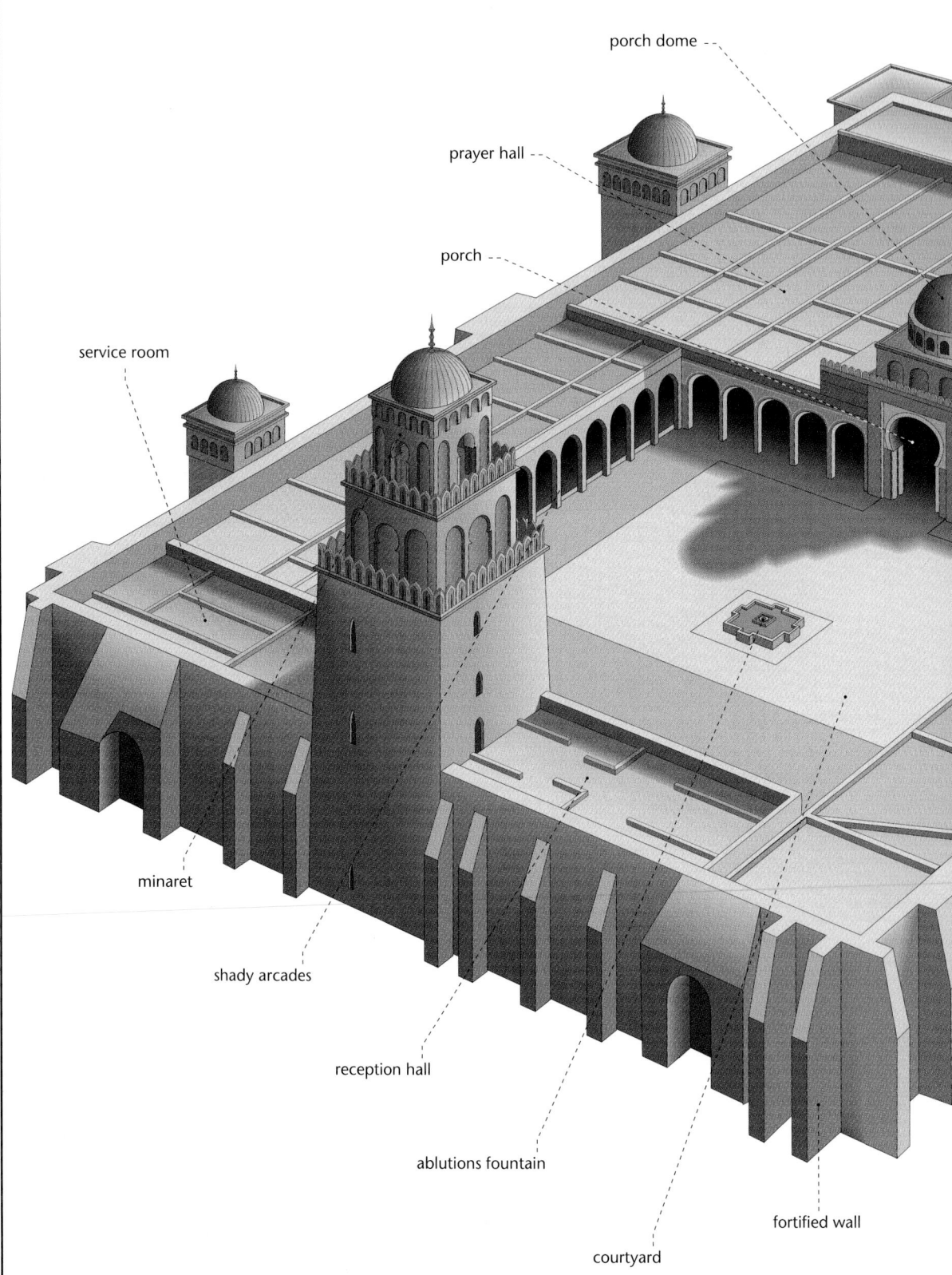

porch dome

prayer hall

porch

service room

minaret

shady arcades

reception hall

ablutions fountain

courtyard

fortified wall

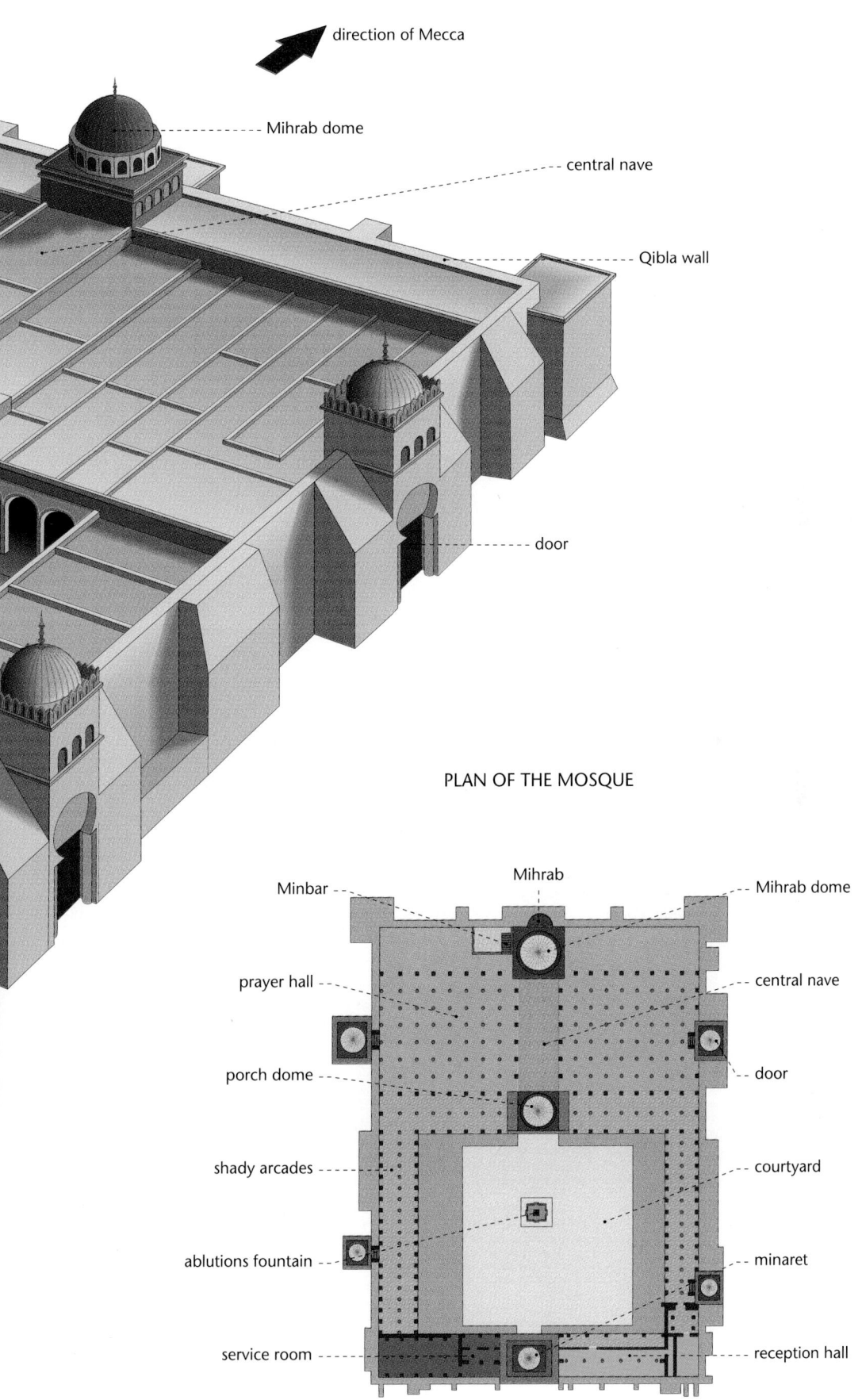

direction of Mecca

Mihrab dome

central nave

Qibla wall

door

PLAN OF THE MOSQUE

Minbar

Mihrab

Mihrab dome

prayer hall

central nave

porch dome

door

shady arcades

courtyard

ablutions fountain

minaret

service room

reception hall

ARCH

SEMICIRCULAR ARCH

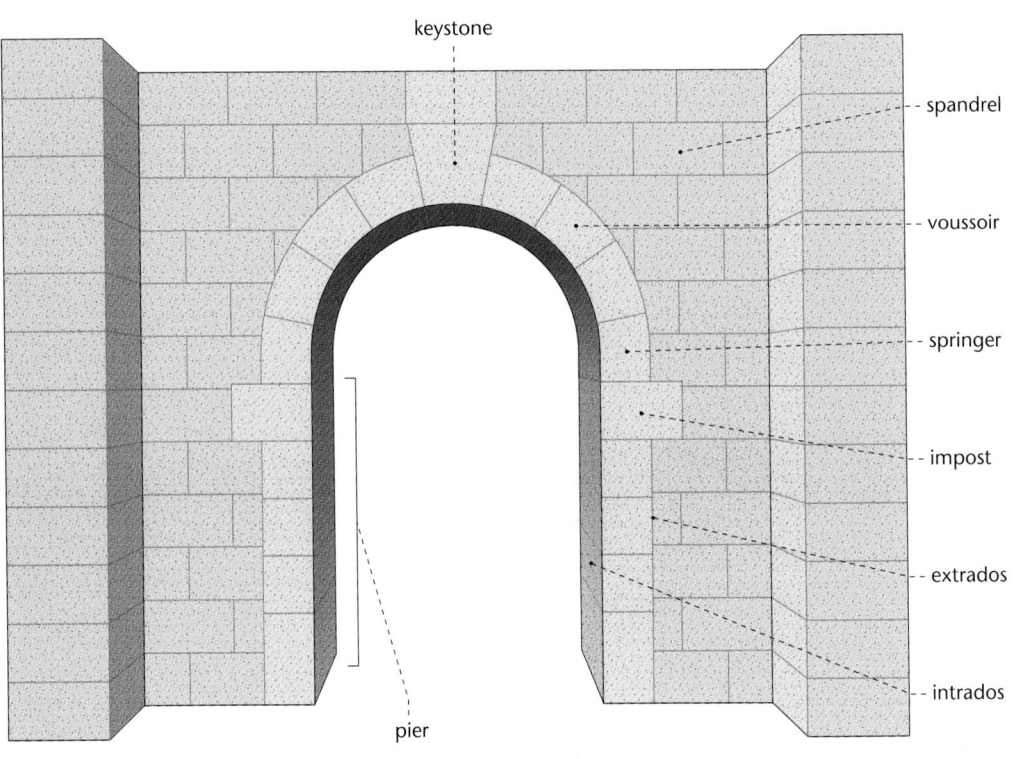

keystone

spandrel

voussoir

springer

impost

extrados

intrados

pier

TYPES OF ARCHES

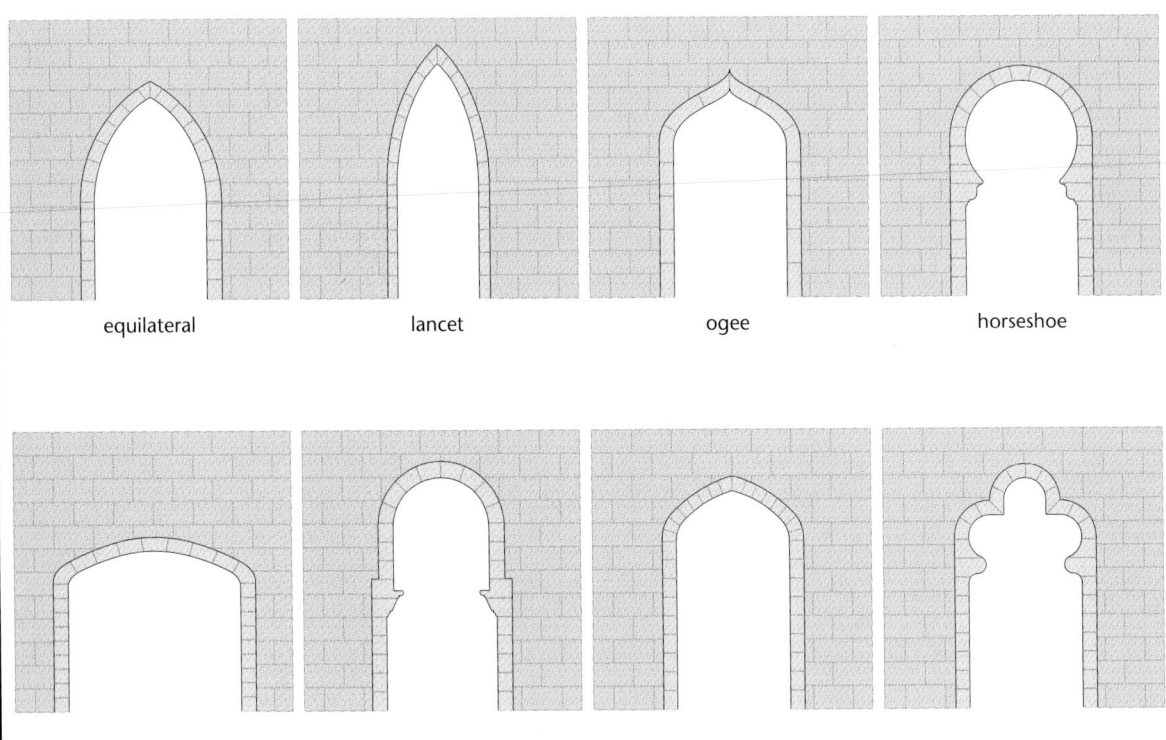

equilateral

lancet

ogee

horseshoe

basket handle

stilted

Tudor

trefoil

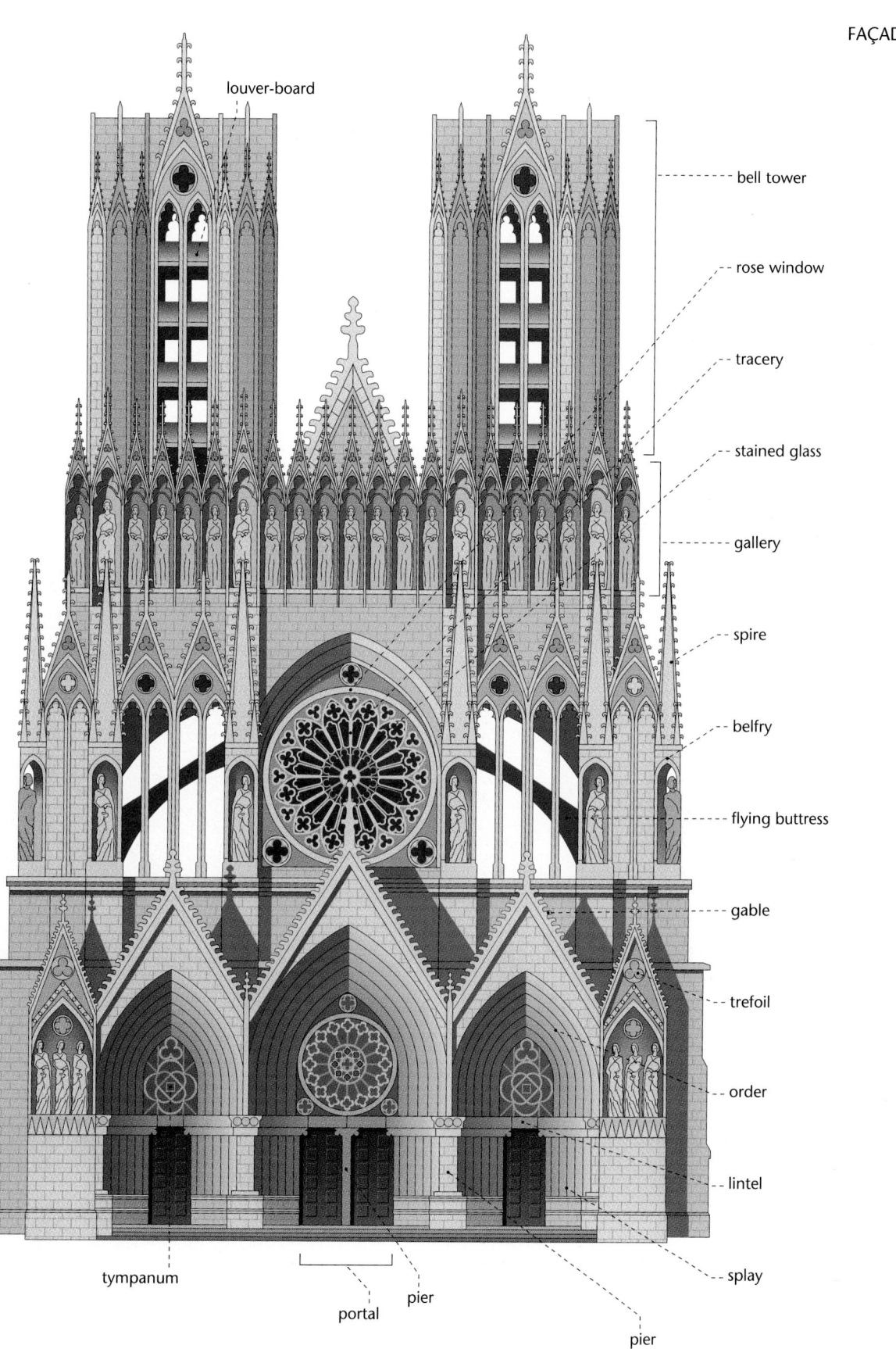

louver-board

bell tower

rose window

tracery

stained glass

gallery

spire

belfry

flying buttress

gable

trefoil

order

lintel

splay

tympanum

portal

pier

pier

GOTHIC CATHEDRAL

CATHEDRAL

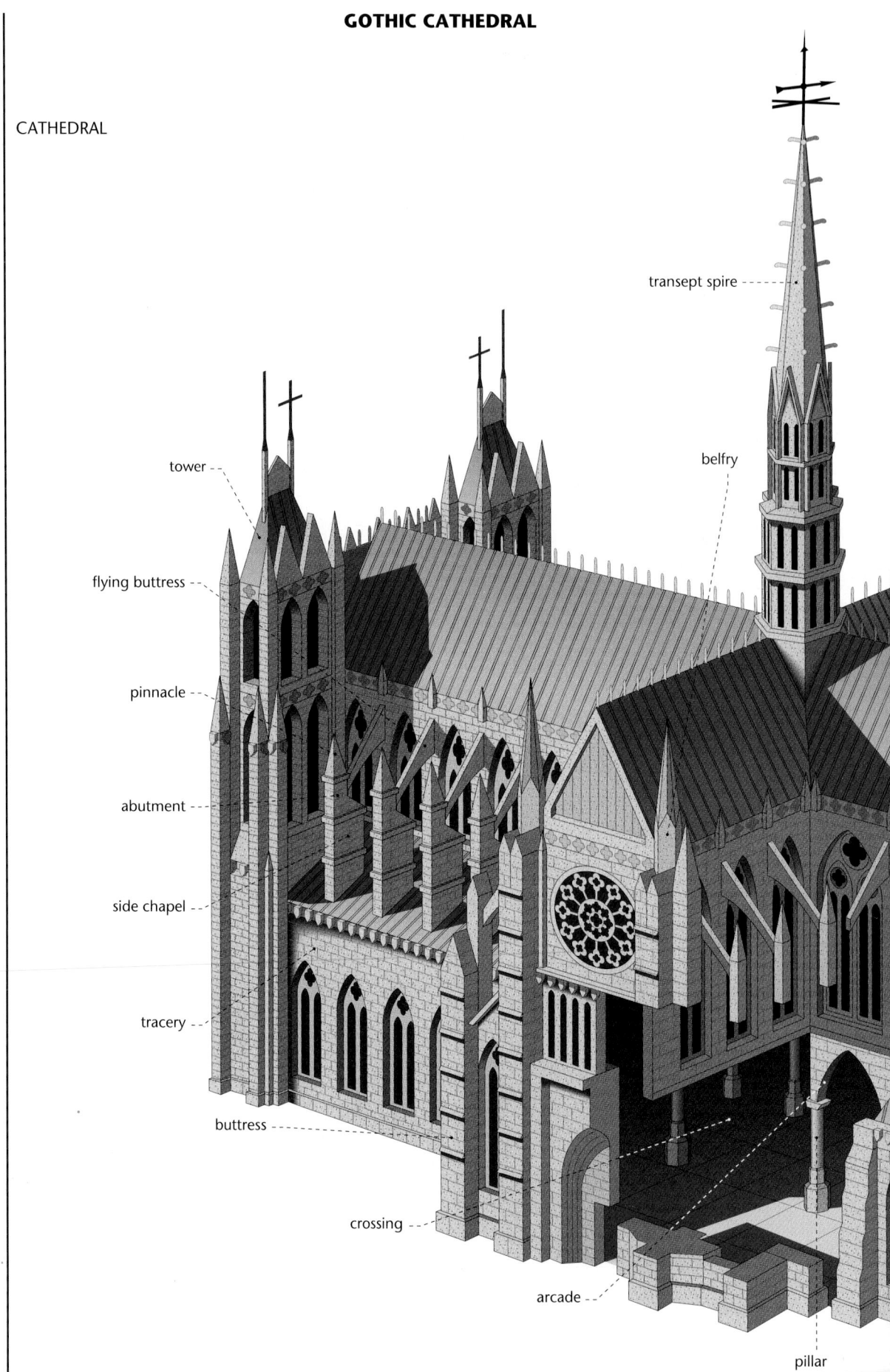

tower

flying buttress

pinnacle

abutment

side chapel

tracery

buttress

crossing

arcade

pillar

transept spire

belfry

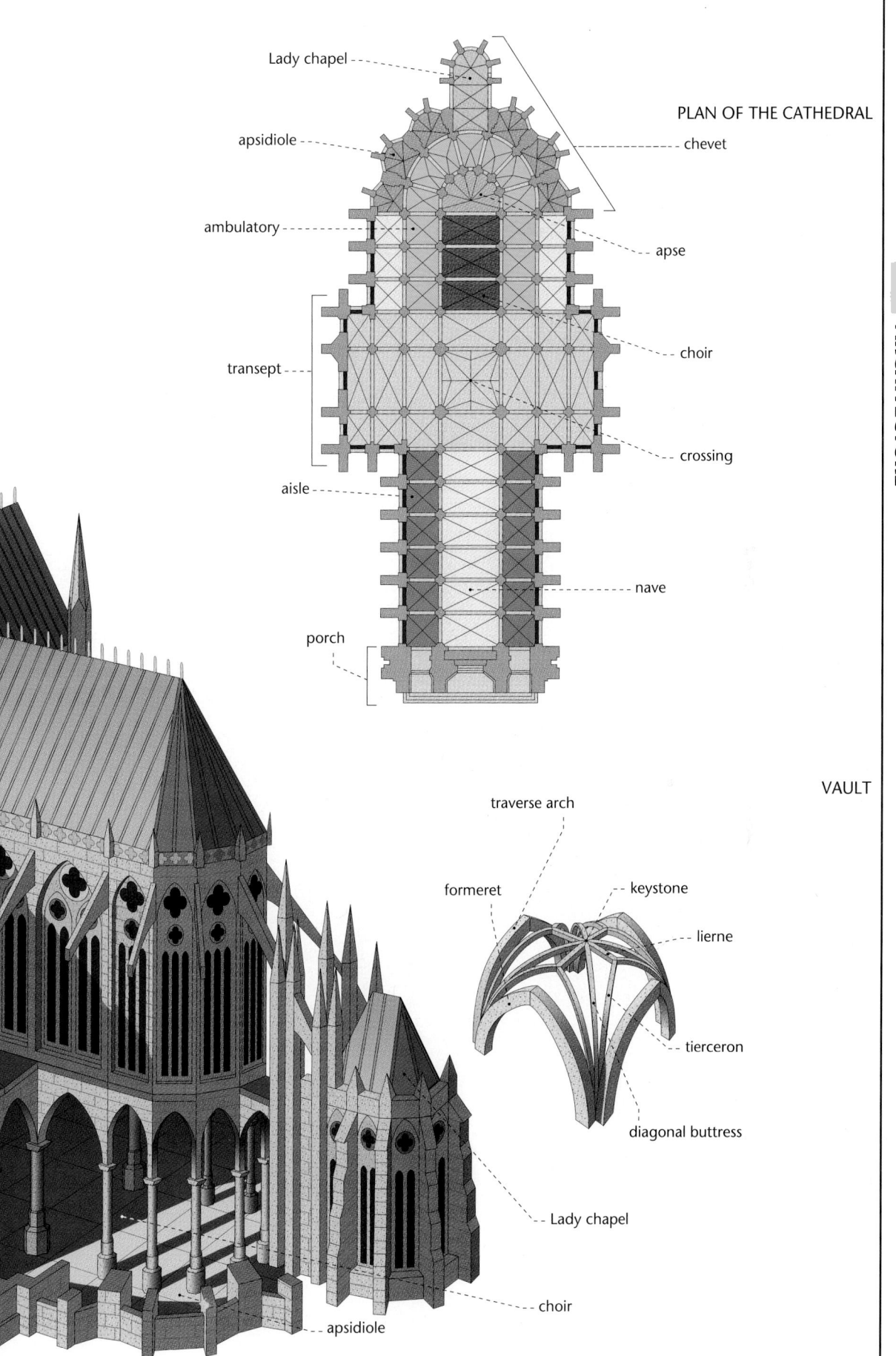

PLAN OF THE CATHEDRAL

Lady chapel

apsidiole

chevet

ambulatory

apse

transept

choir

crossing

aisle

nave

porch

VAULT

traverse arch

formeret

keystone

lierne

tierceron

diagonal buttress

Lady chapel

choir

apsidiole

VAUBAN FORTIFICATION

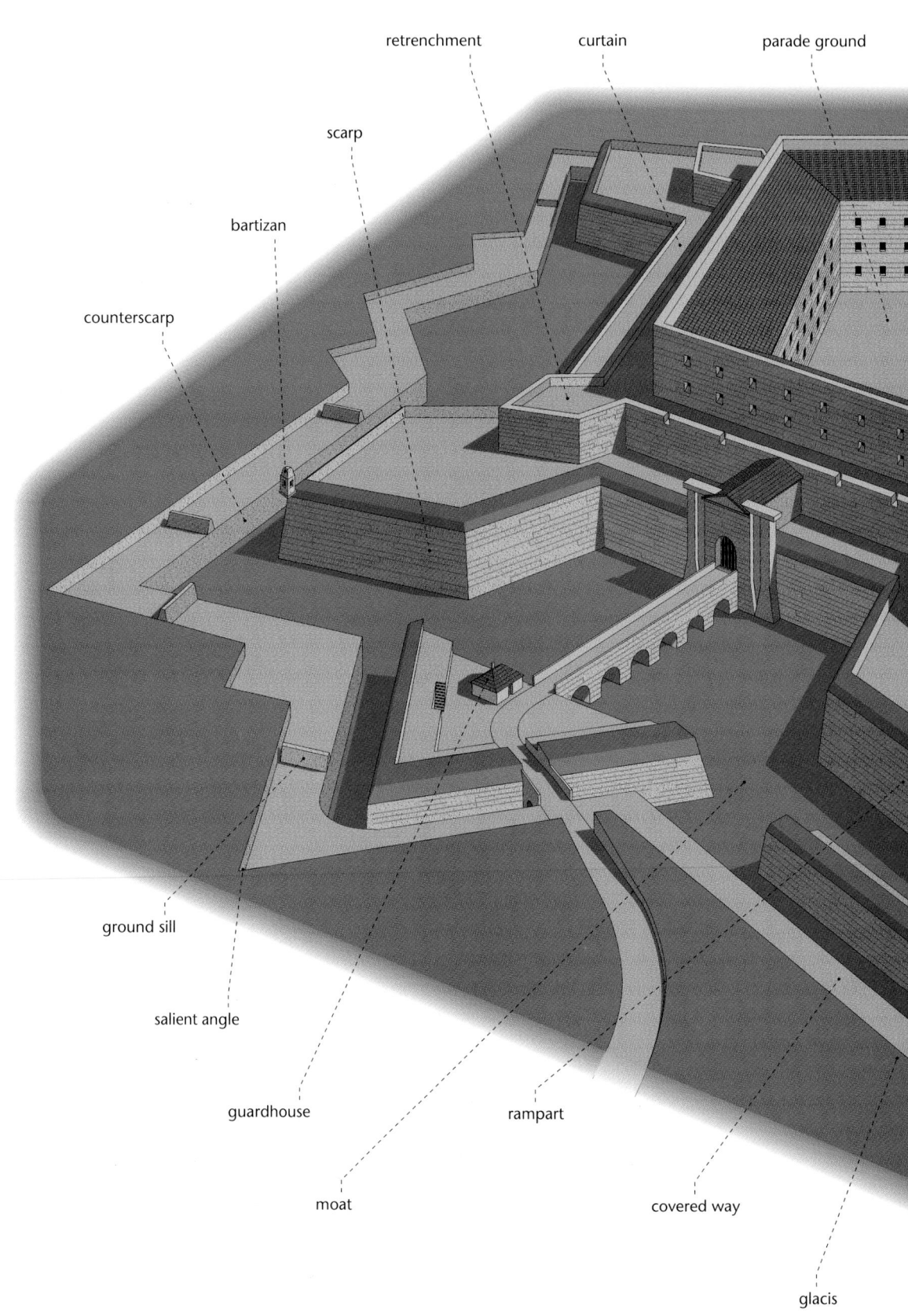

retrenchment

curtain

parade ground

scarp

bartizan

counterscarp

ground sill

salient angle

guardhouse

moat

rampart

covered way

glacis

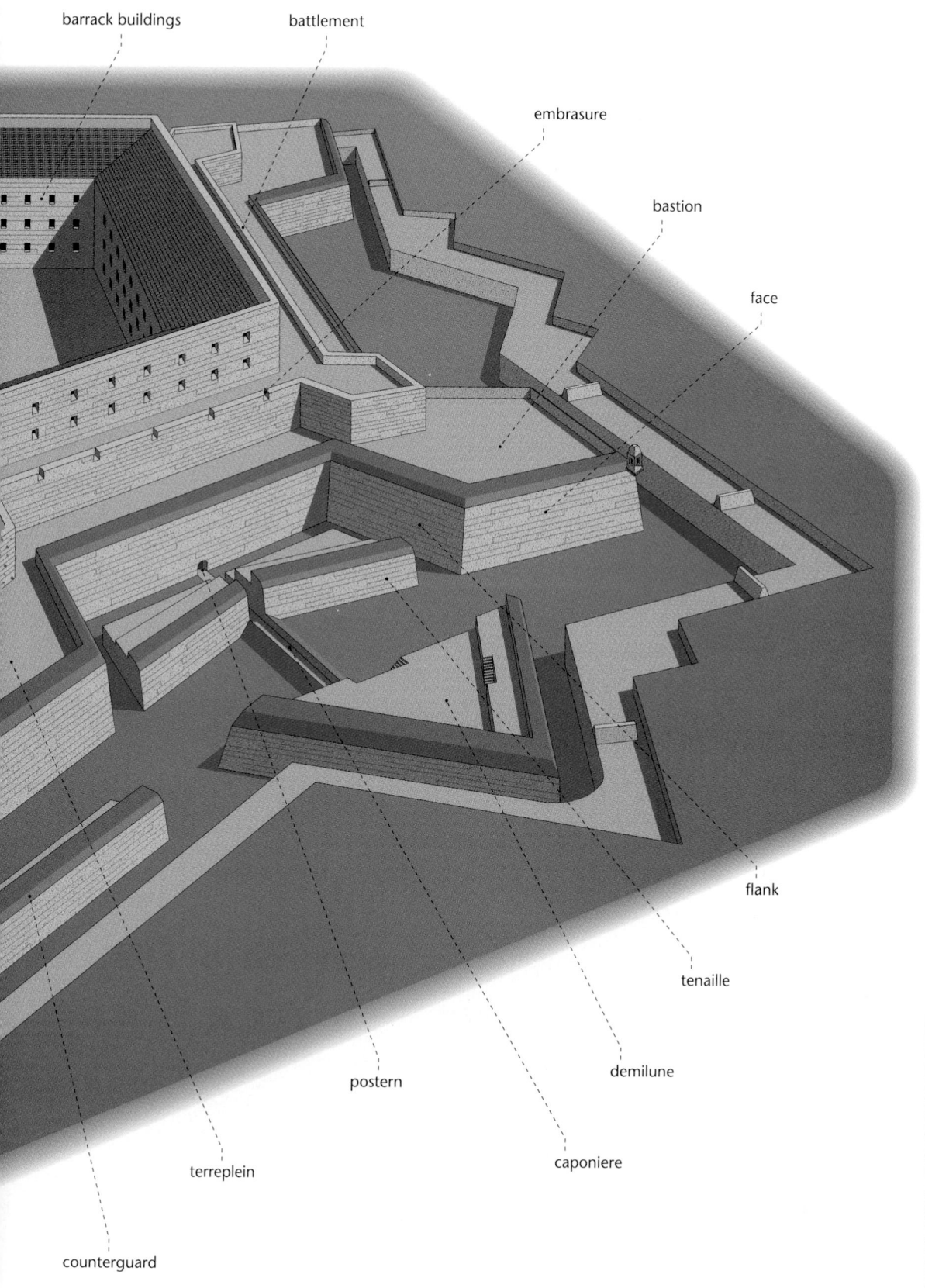

barrack buildings

battlement

embrasure

bastion

face

flank

tenaille

demilune

postern

caponiere

terreplein

counterguard

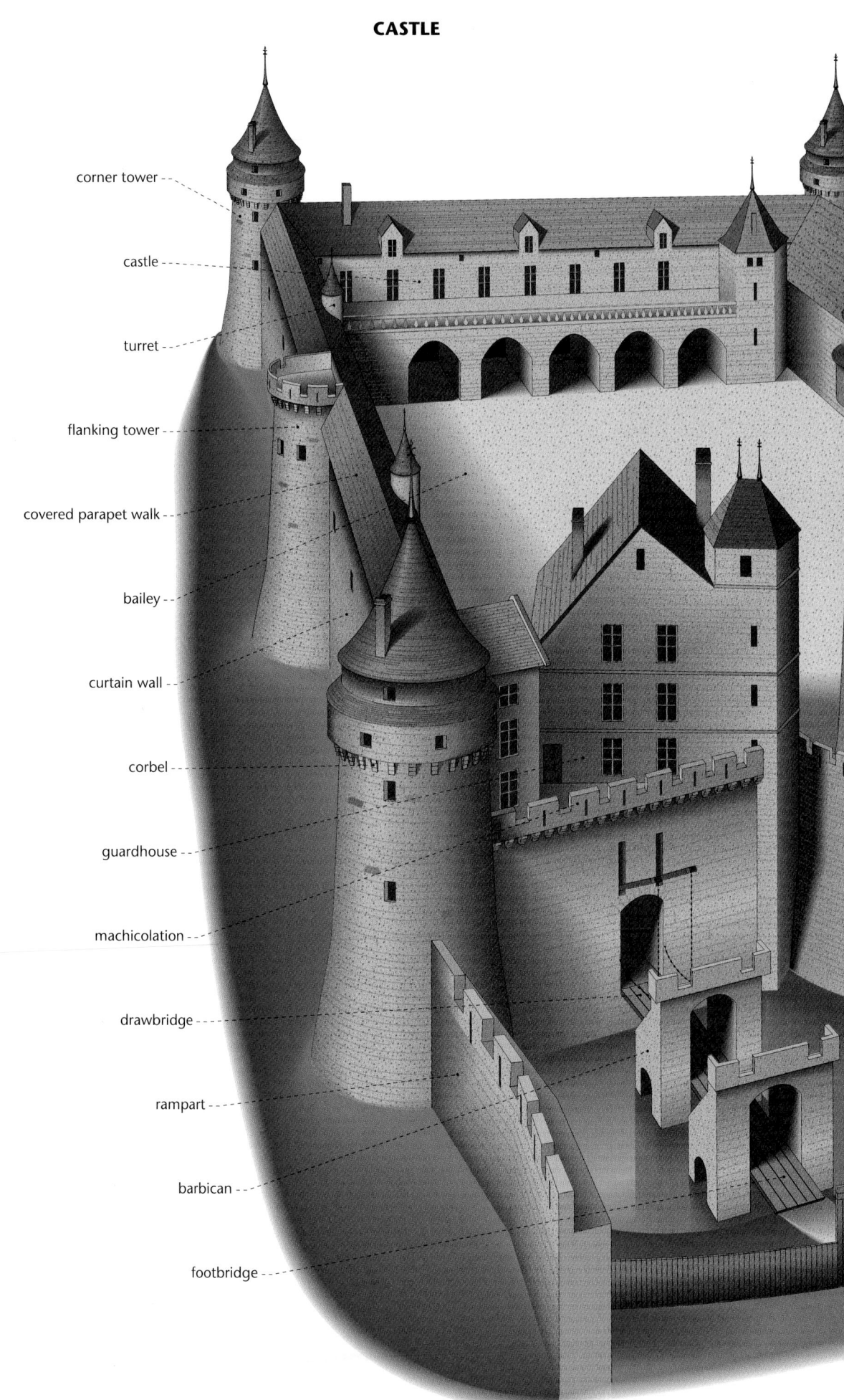

corner tower

castle

turret

flanking tower

covered parapet walk

bailey

curtain wall

corbel

guardhouse

machicolation

drawbridge

rampart

barbican

footbridge

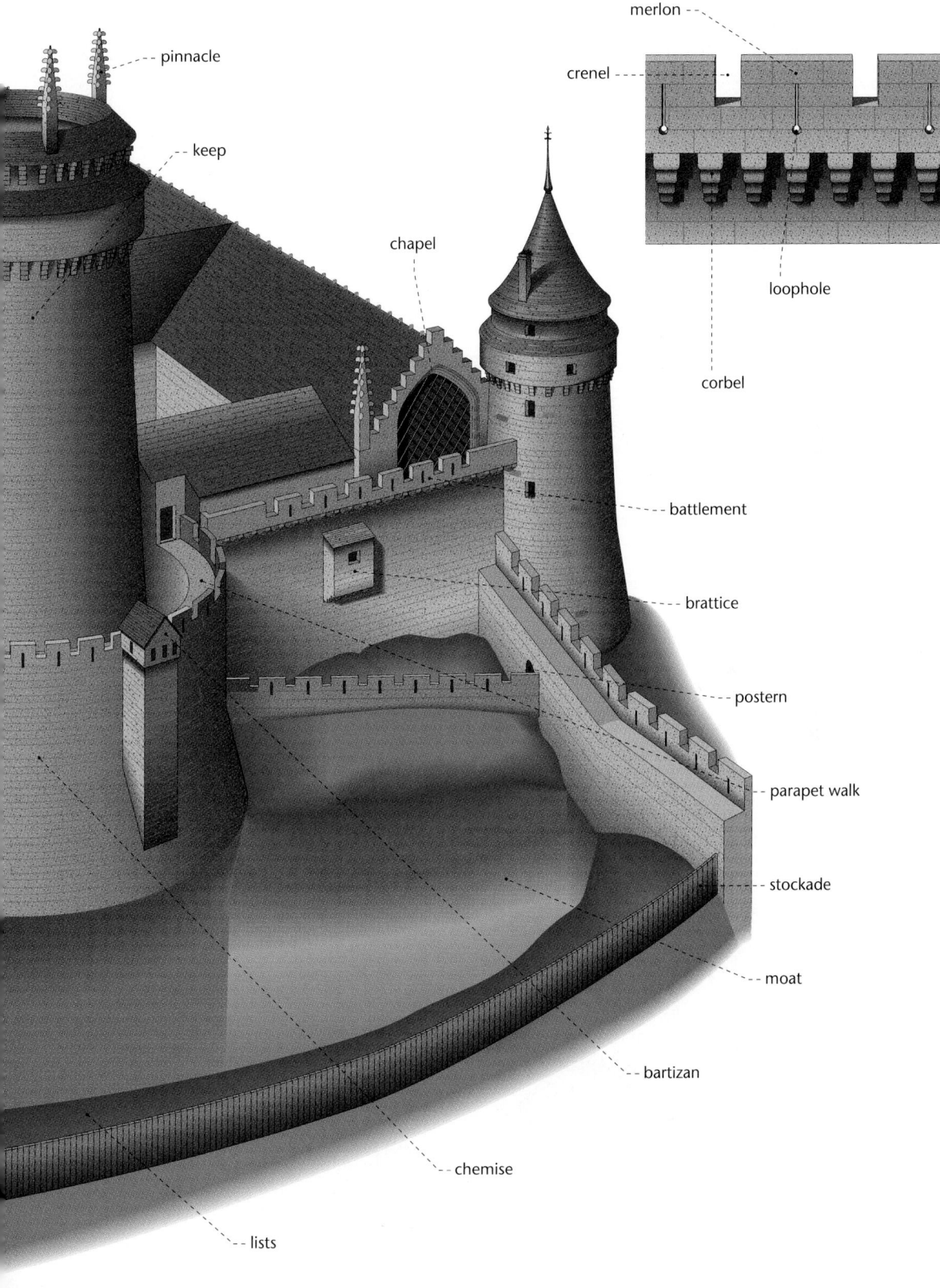

pinnacle

keep

chapel

merlon

crenel

loophole

corbel

battlement

brattice

postern

parapet walk

stockade

moat

bartizan

chemise

lists

ROOFS

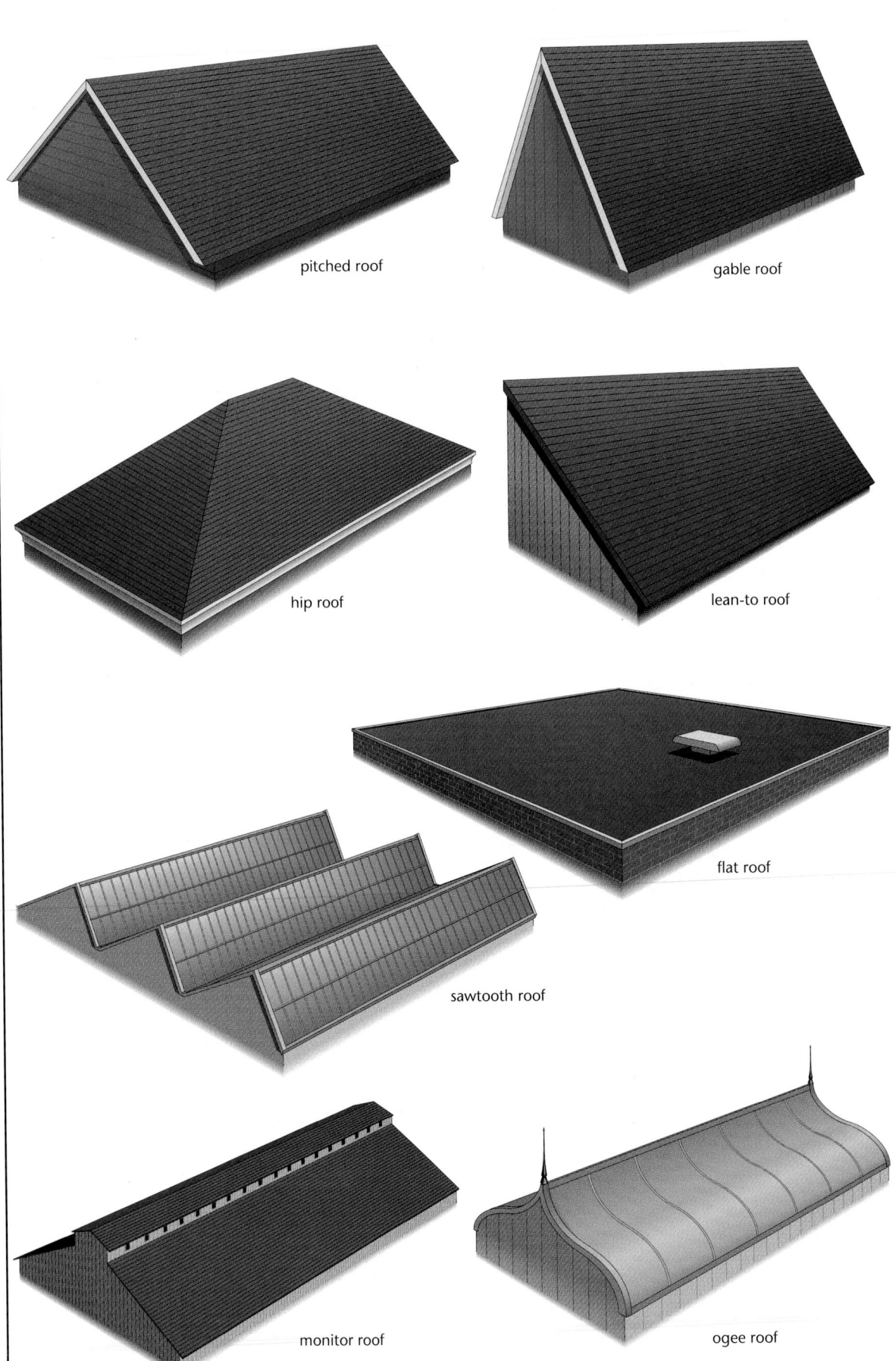

pitched roof

gable roof

hip roof

lean-to roof

flat roof

sawtooth roof

monitor roof

ogee roof

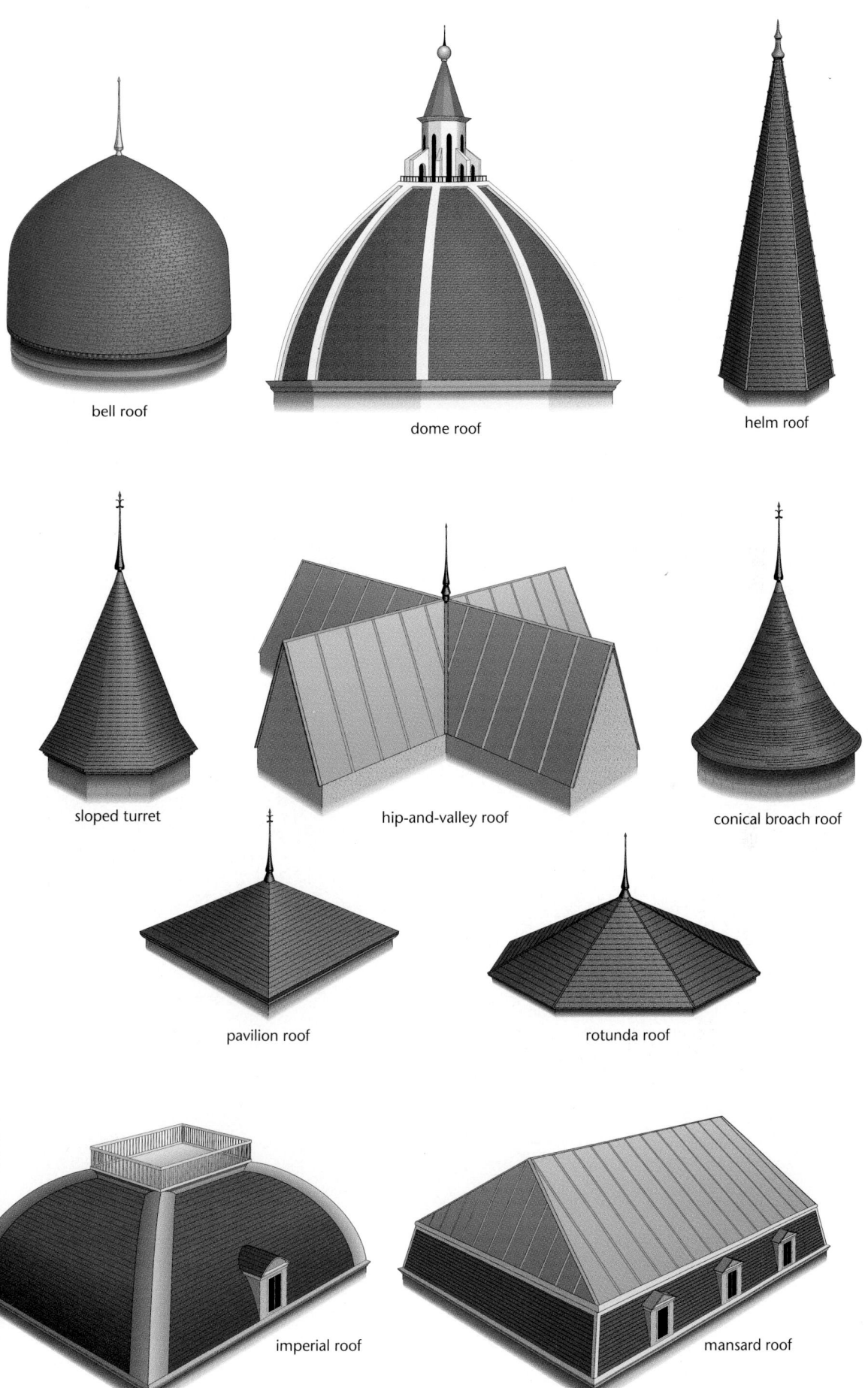

bell roof

dome roof

helm roof

sloped turret

hip-and-valley roof

conical broach roof

pavilion roof

rotunda roof

imperial roof

mansard roof

DOWNTOWN

park

convention center

office tower

square

cathedral

passenger station

median strip

planetarium

railroad

traffic island

boulevard

hotel

skyscraper

restaurant

church

high-rise apartment

street light

parking lot

trade building

office building

museum

stadium

ARCHITECTURE

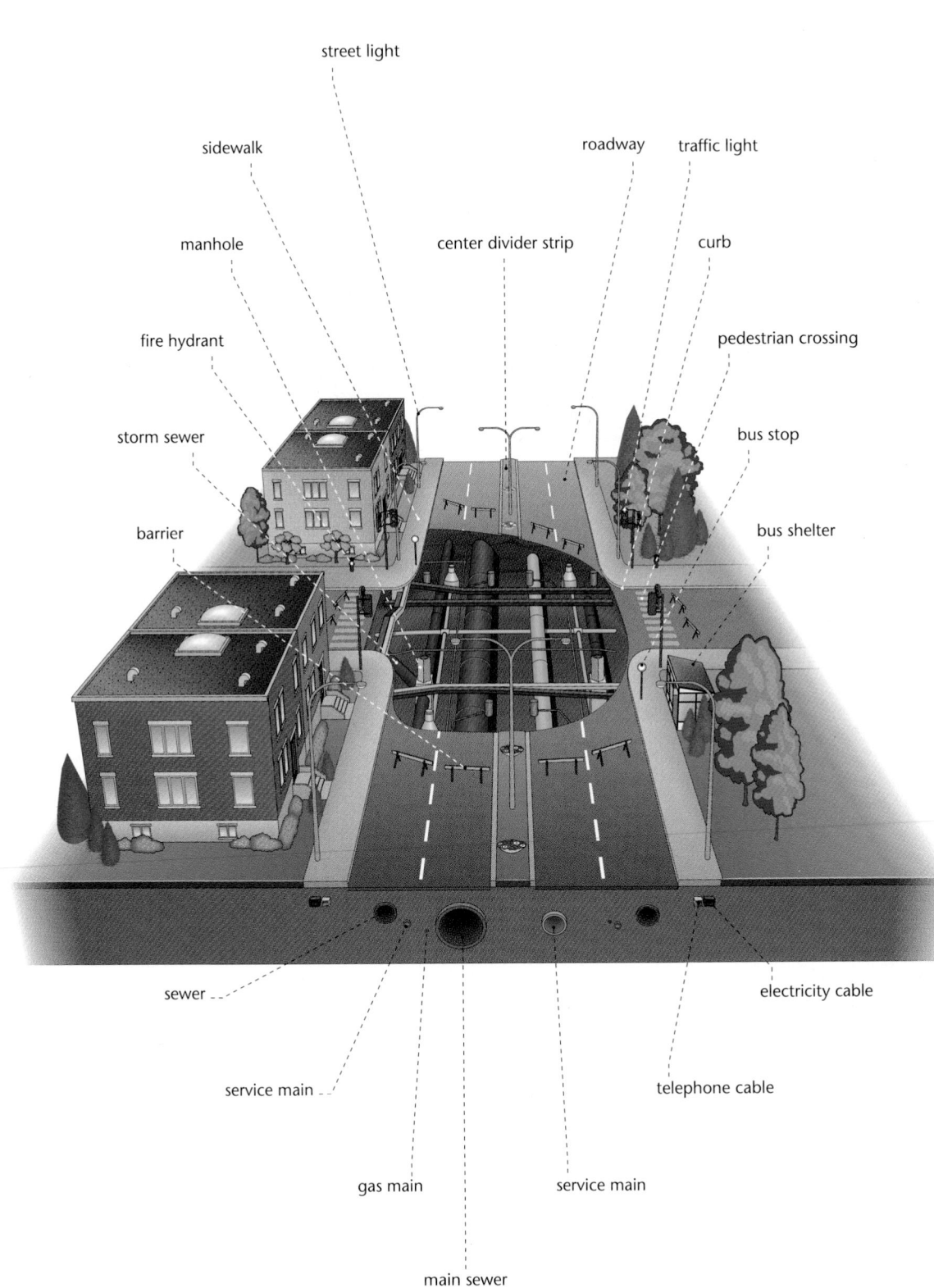

street light

sidewalk

roadway   traffic light

manhole

center divider strip

curb

fire hydrant

pedestrian crossing

storm sewer

bus stop

barrier

bus shelter

sewer

electricity cable

service main

telephone cable

gas main

service main

main sewer

CITY HOUSES

cottage

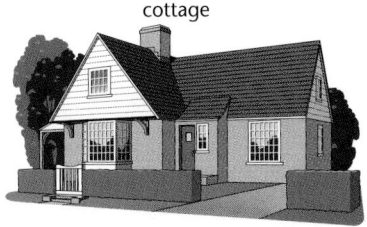

single-family home

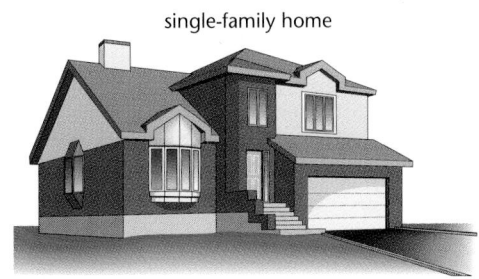

condominiums

semi-detached cottage

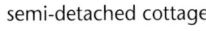

town houses

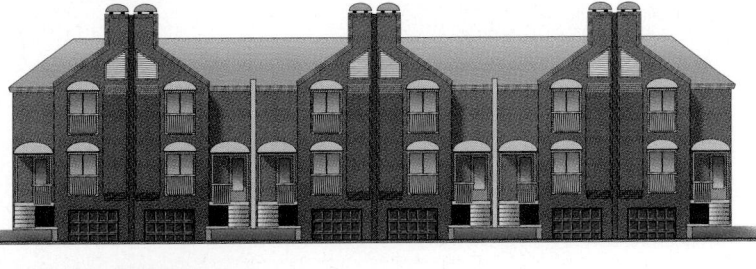

high-rise apartment

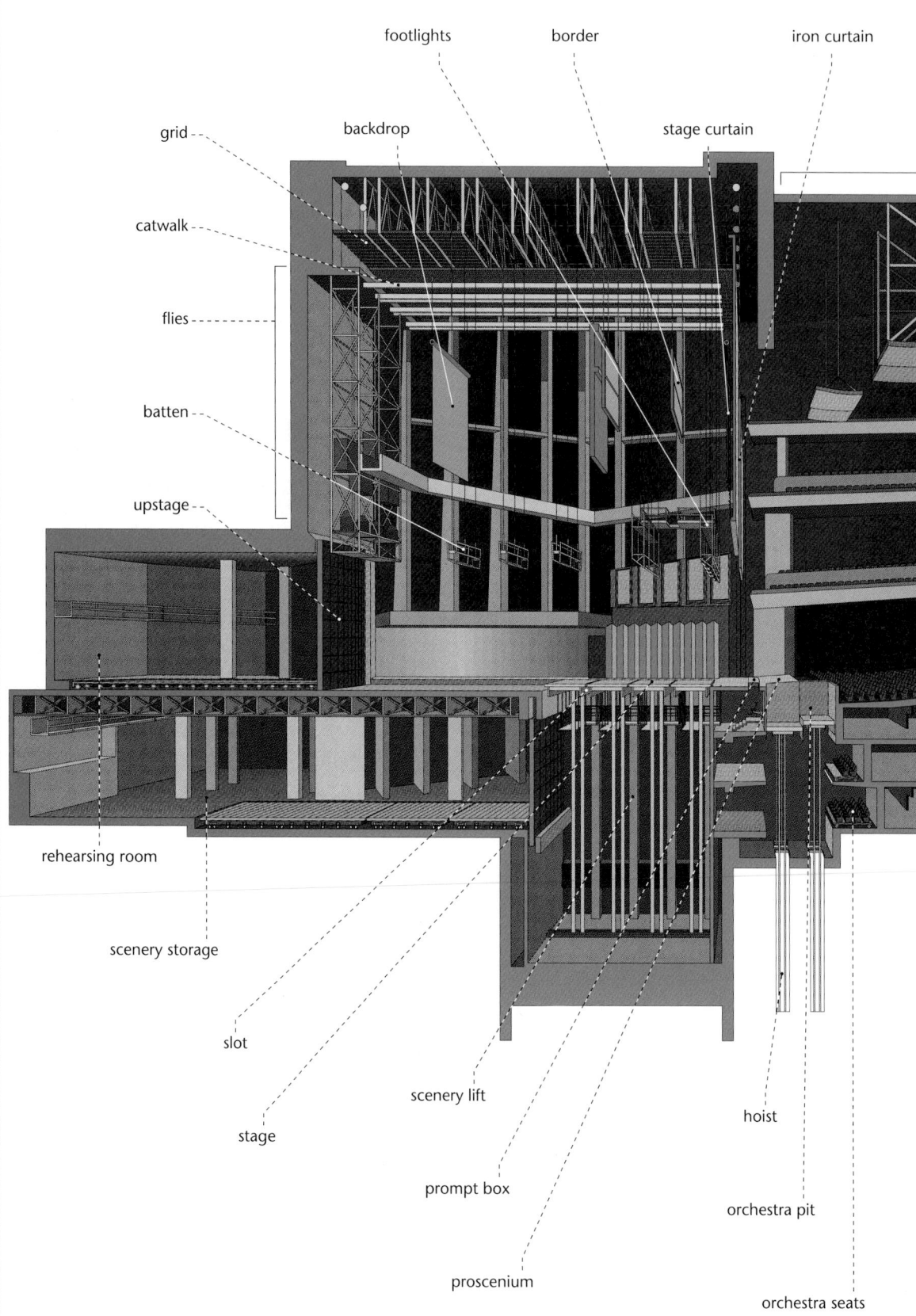

footlights

border

iron curtain

grid

backdrop

stage curtain

catwalk

flies

batten

upstage

rehearsing room

scenery storage

slot

scenery lift

stage

hoist

prompt box

orchestra pit

proscenium

orchestra seats

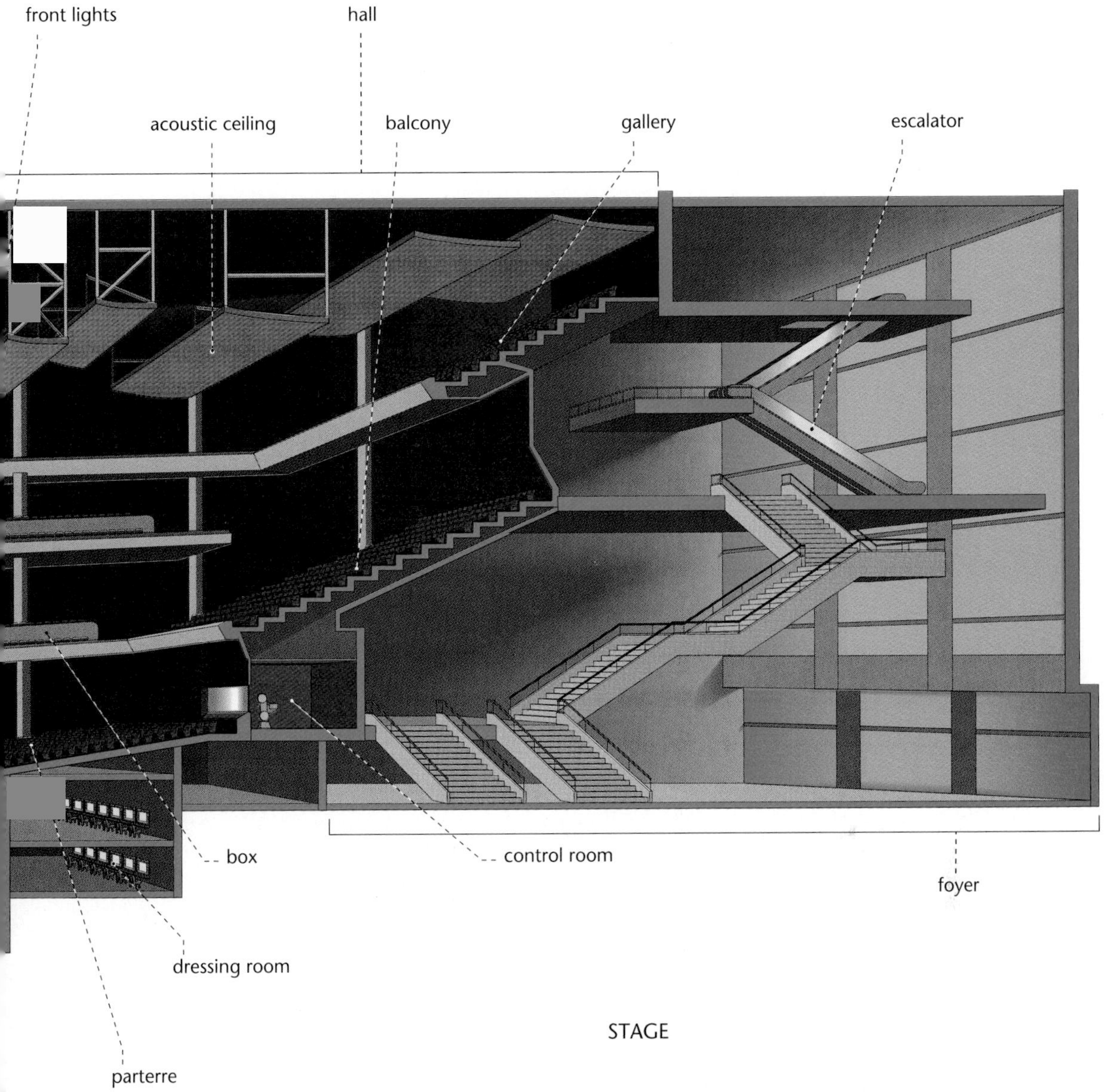

front lights

hall

acoustic ceiling

balcony

gallery

escalator

box

control room

foyer

dressing room

STAGE

parterre

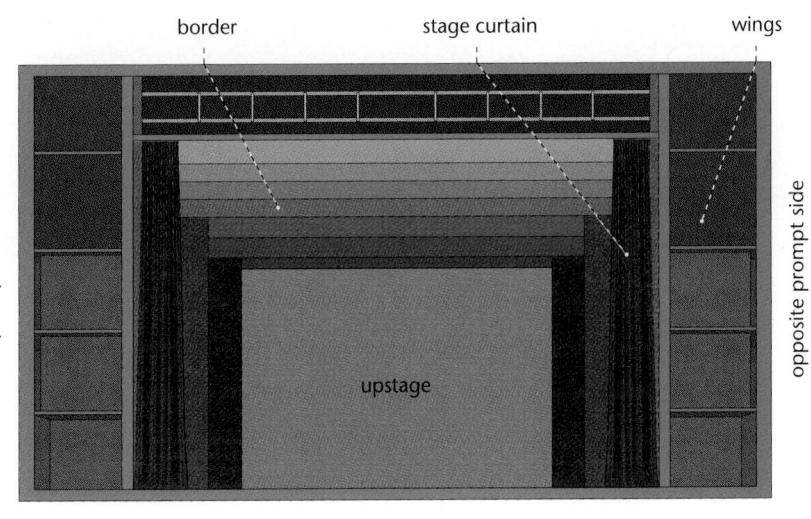

border

stage curtain

wings

prompt side

opposite prompt side

upstage

OFFICE BUILDING

ARCHITECTURE

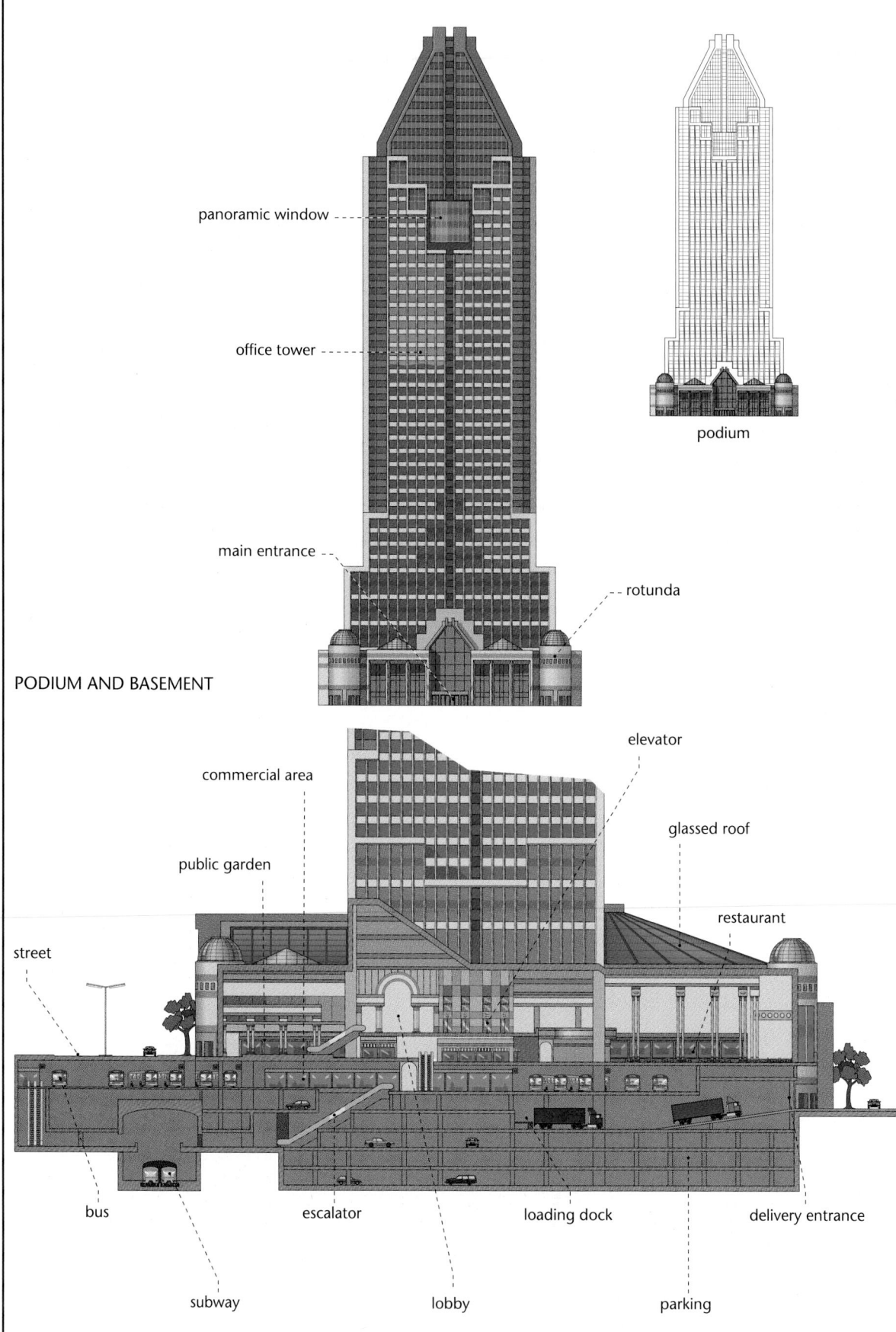

panoramic window

office tower

main entrance

rotunda

podium

PODIUM AND BASEMENT

elevator

commercial area

glassed roof

public garden

restaurant

street

bus

escalator

loading dock

delivery entrance

subway

lobby

parking

190

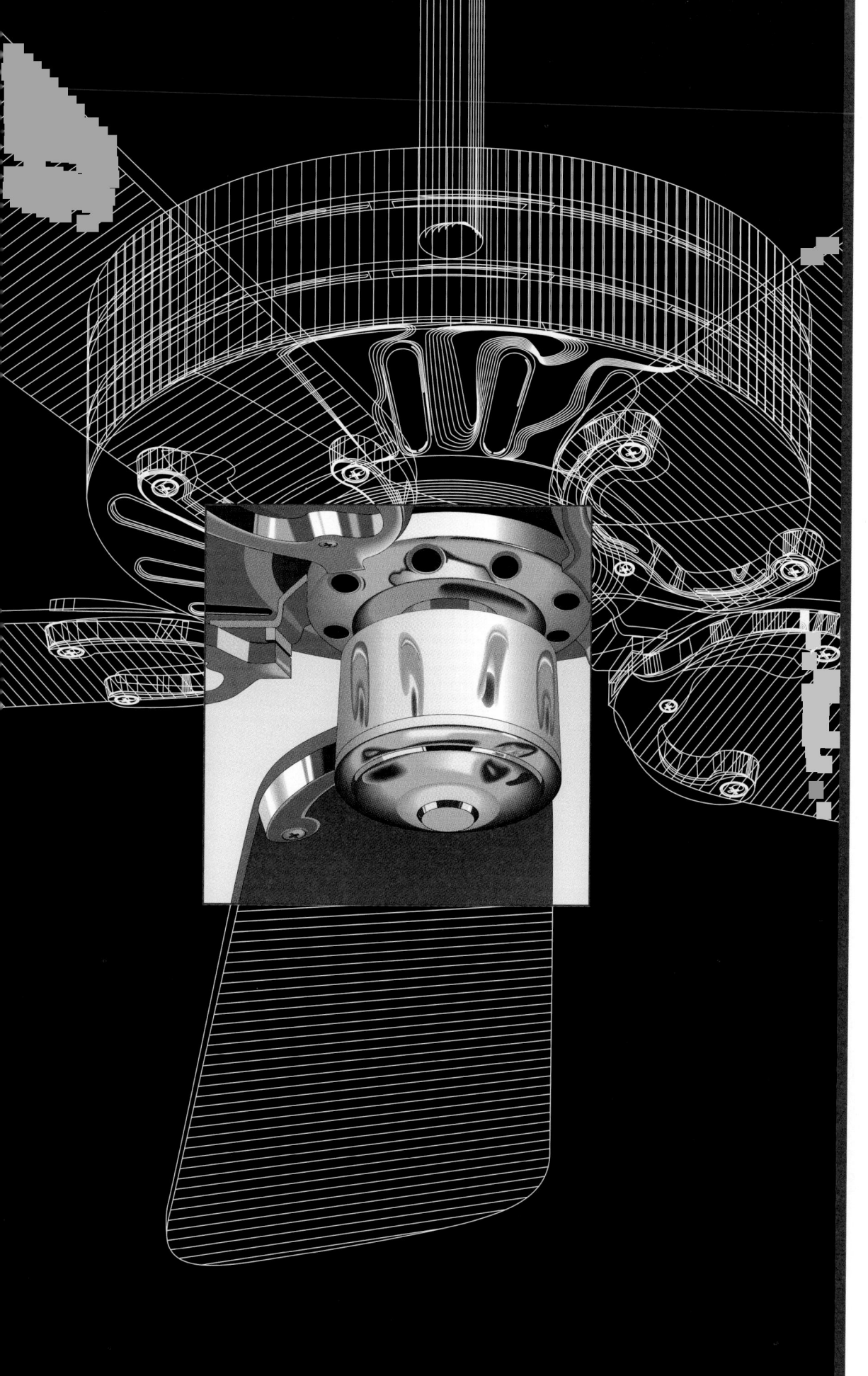

CONTENTS

BLUEPRINT READING 193

EXTERIOR OF A HOUSE 196

STRUCTURE OF A HOUSE..198

WOOD FLOORING...200

STAIRS 201

DOOR...202

WINDOW..203

HEATING...204

AIR CONDITIONING 214

PLUMBING SYSTEM 215

SEPTIC TANK..216

PEDESTAL-TYPE SUMP PUMP 216

HOUSE

BLUEPRINT READING

ELEVATION

SITE PLAN

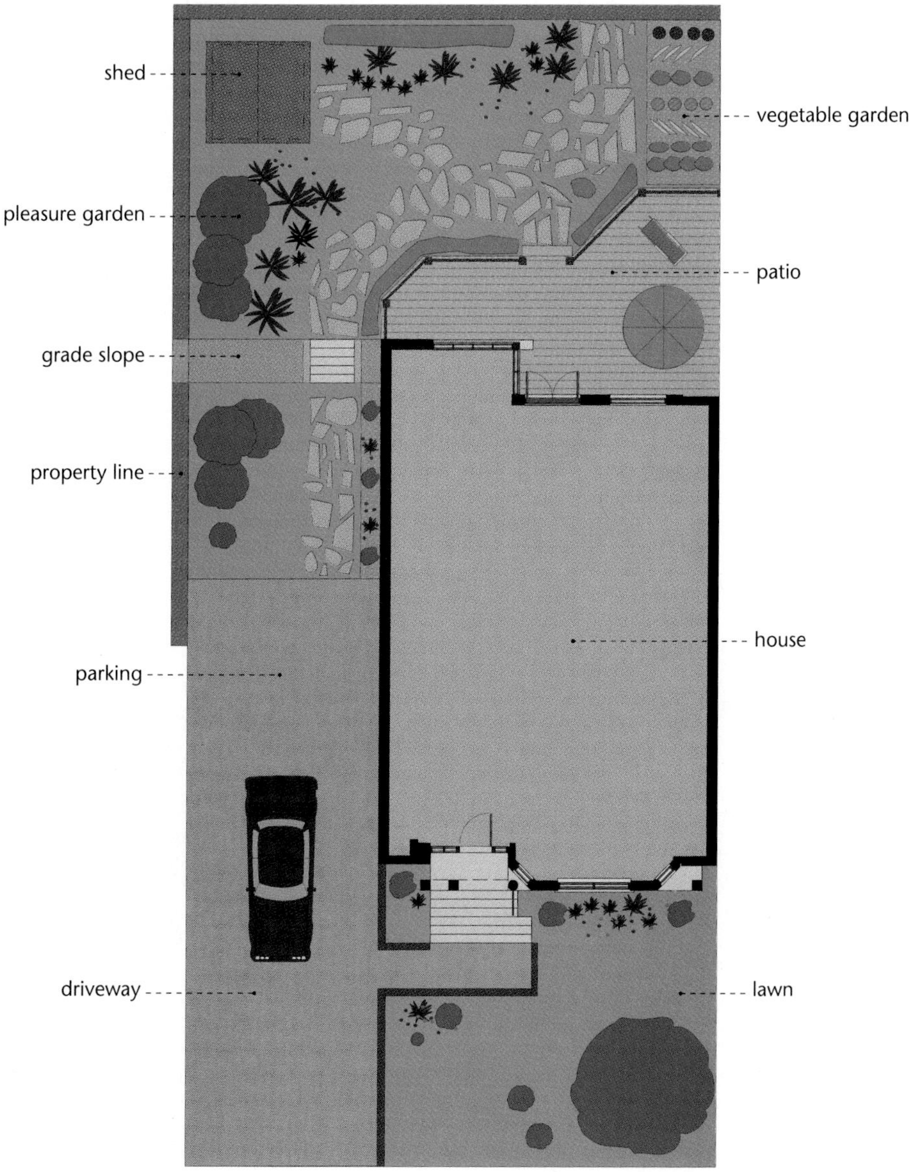

shed

pleasure garden

grade slope

property line

parking

driveway

vegetable garden

patio

house

lawn

193

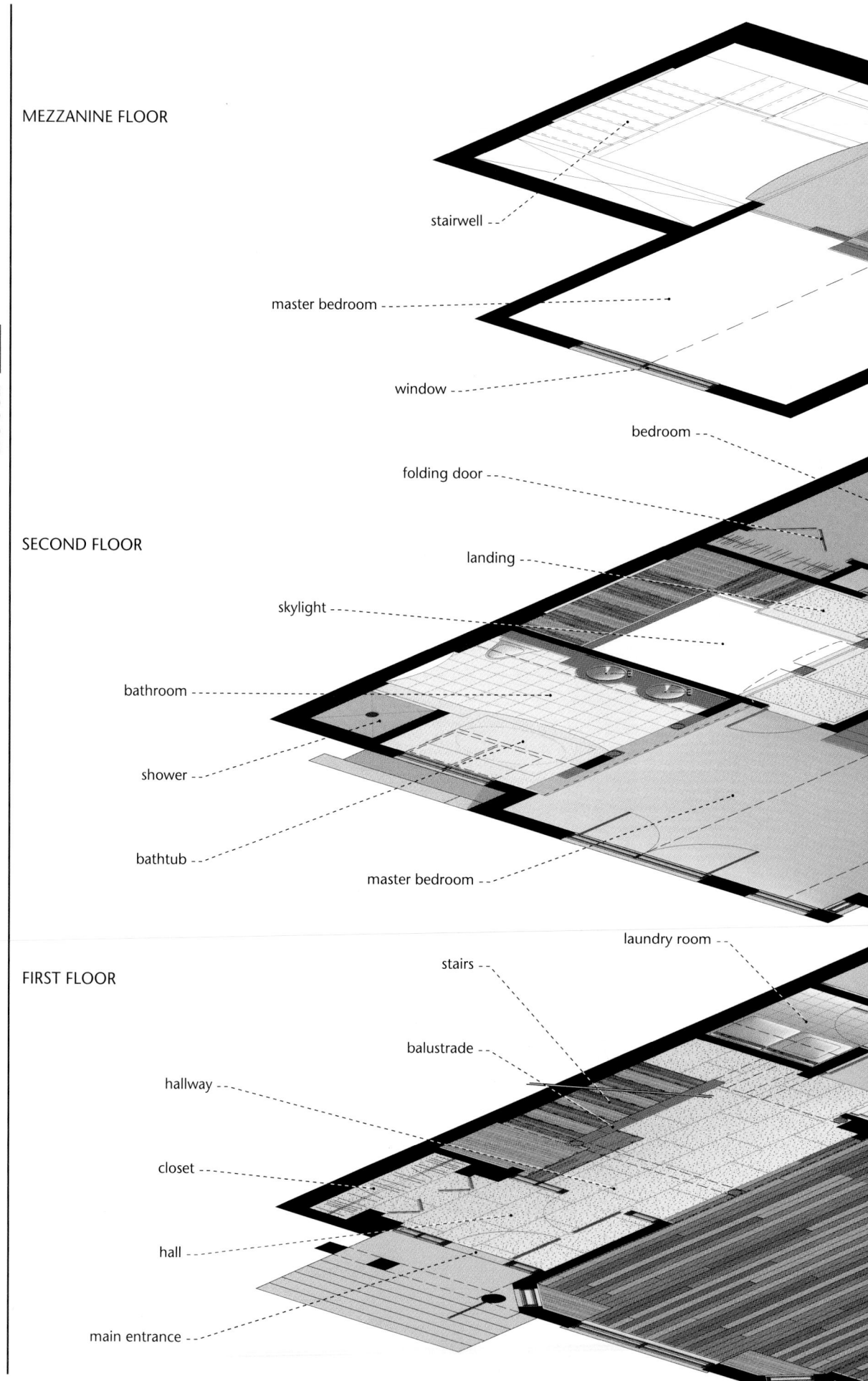

MEZZANINE FLOOR

stairwell

master bedroom

window

bedroom

folding door

SECOND FLOOR

landing

skylight

bathroom

shower

bathtub

master bedroom

laundry room

stairs

FIRST FLOOR

balustrade

hallway

closet

hall

main entrance

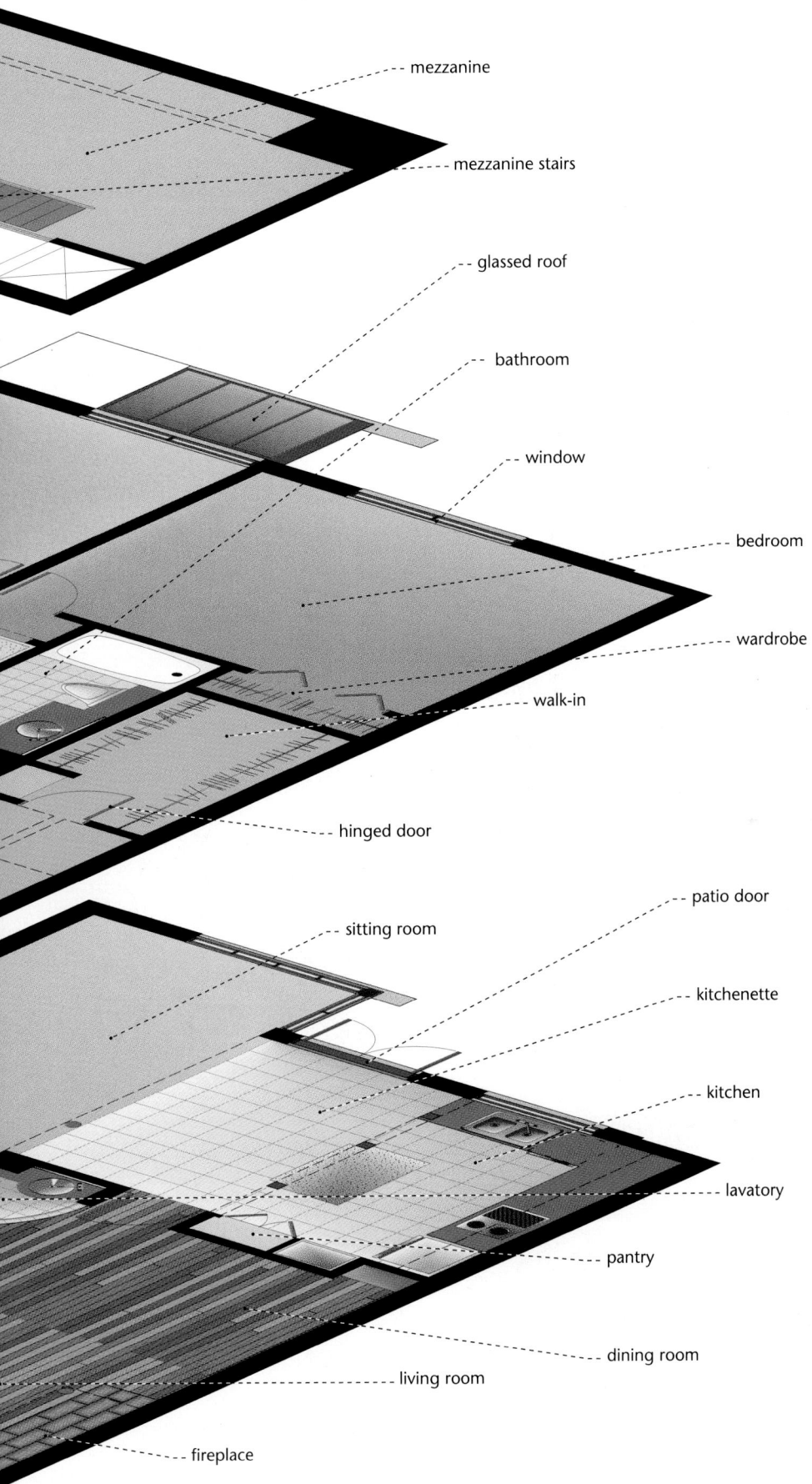

mezzanine

mezzanine stairs

glassed roof

bathroom

window

bedroom

wardrobe

walk-in

hinged door

patio door

sitting room

kitchenette

kitchen

lavatory

pantry

dining room

living room

fireplace

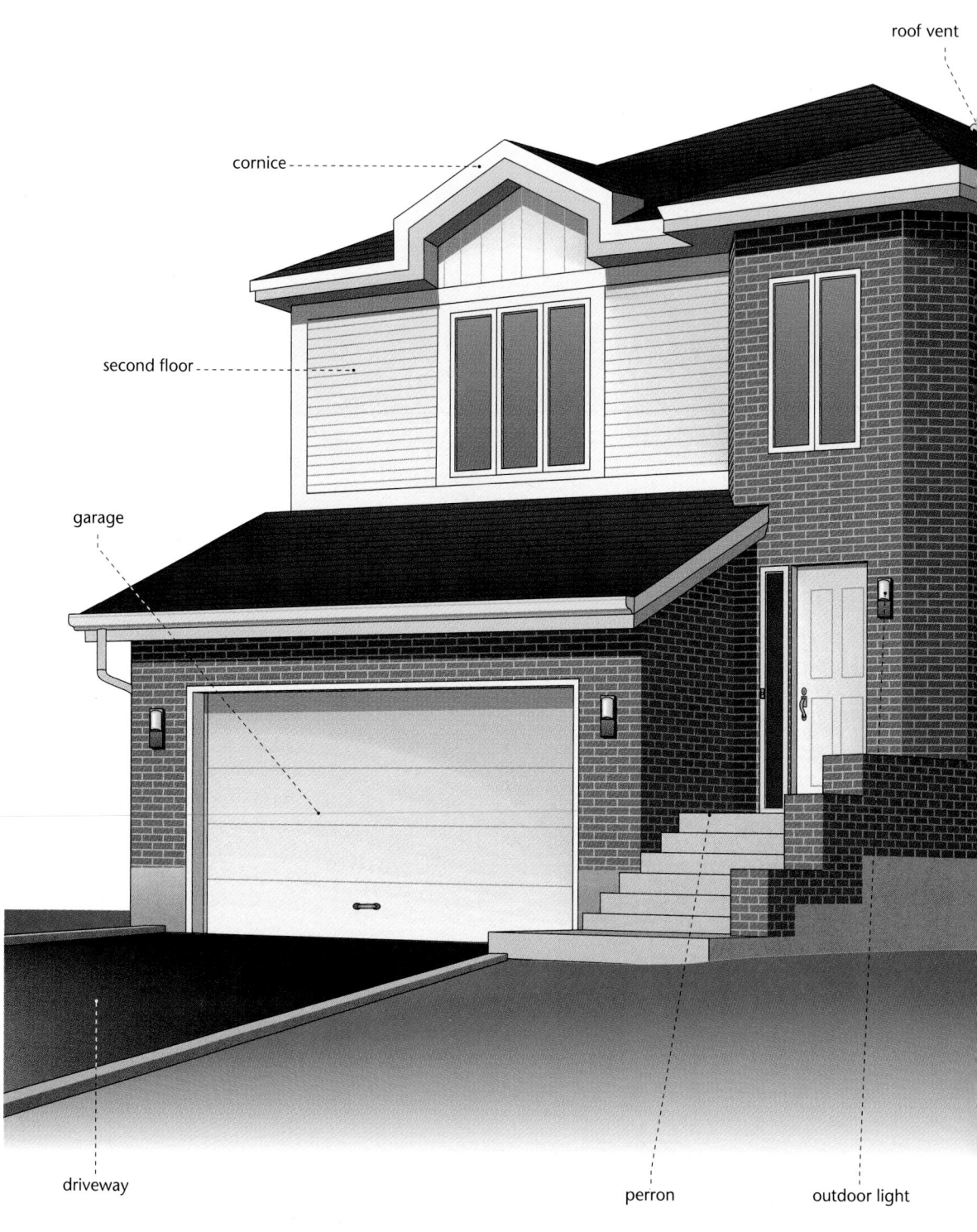

roof vent

cornice

second floor

garage

driveway

perron

outdoor light

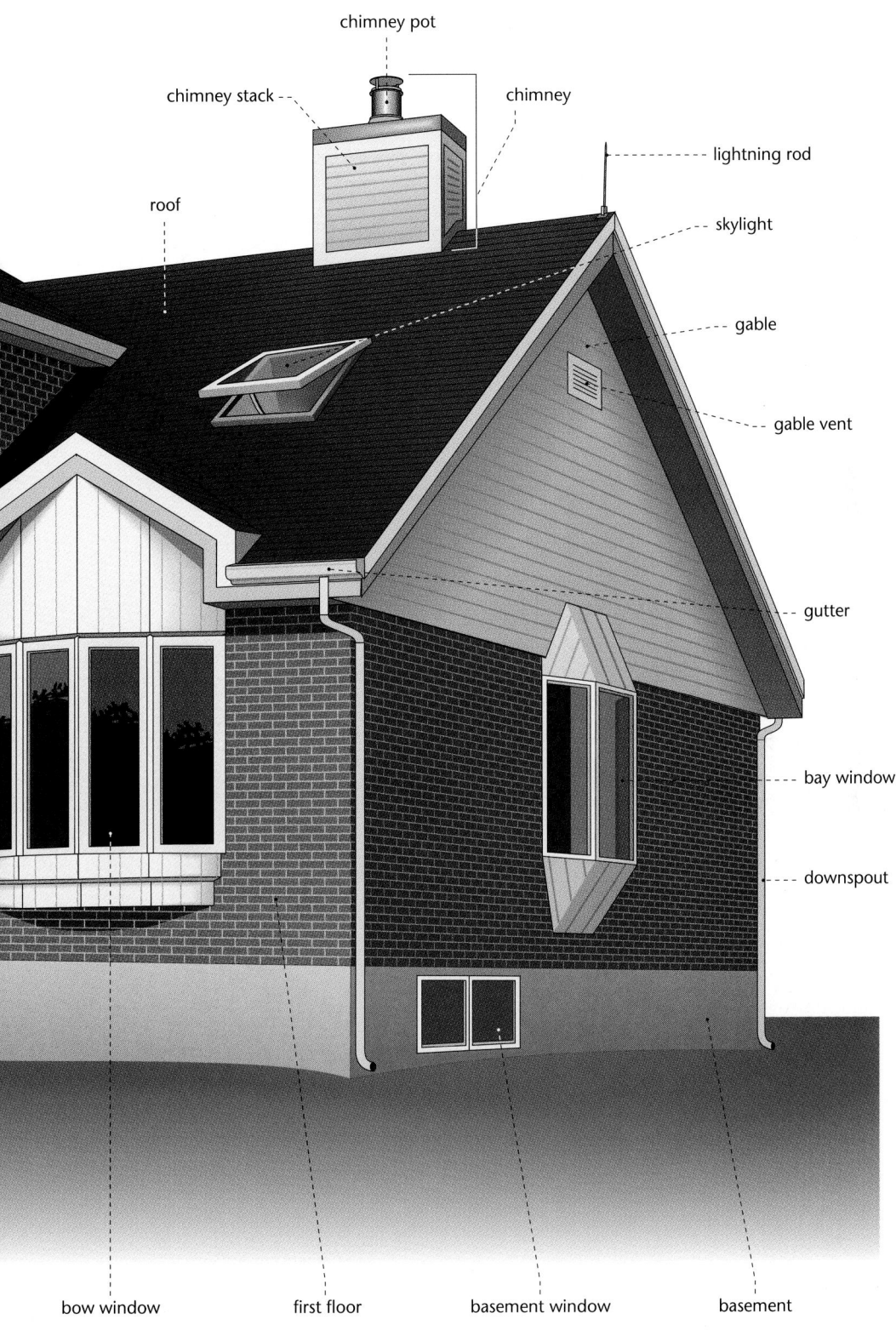

chimney pot

chimney stack

chimney

roof

lightning rod

skylight

gable

gable vent

gutter

bay window

downspout

bow window

first floor

basement window

basement

FRAME

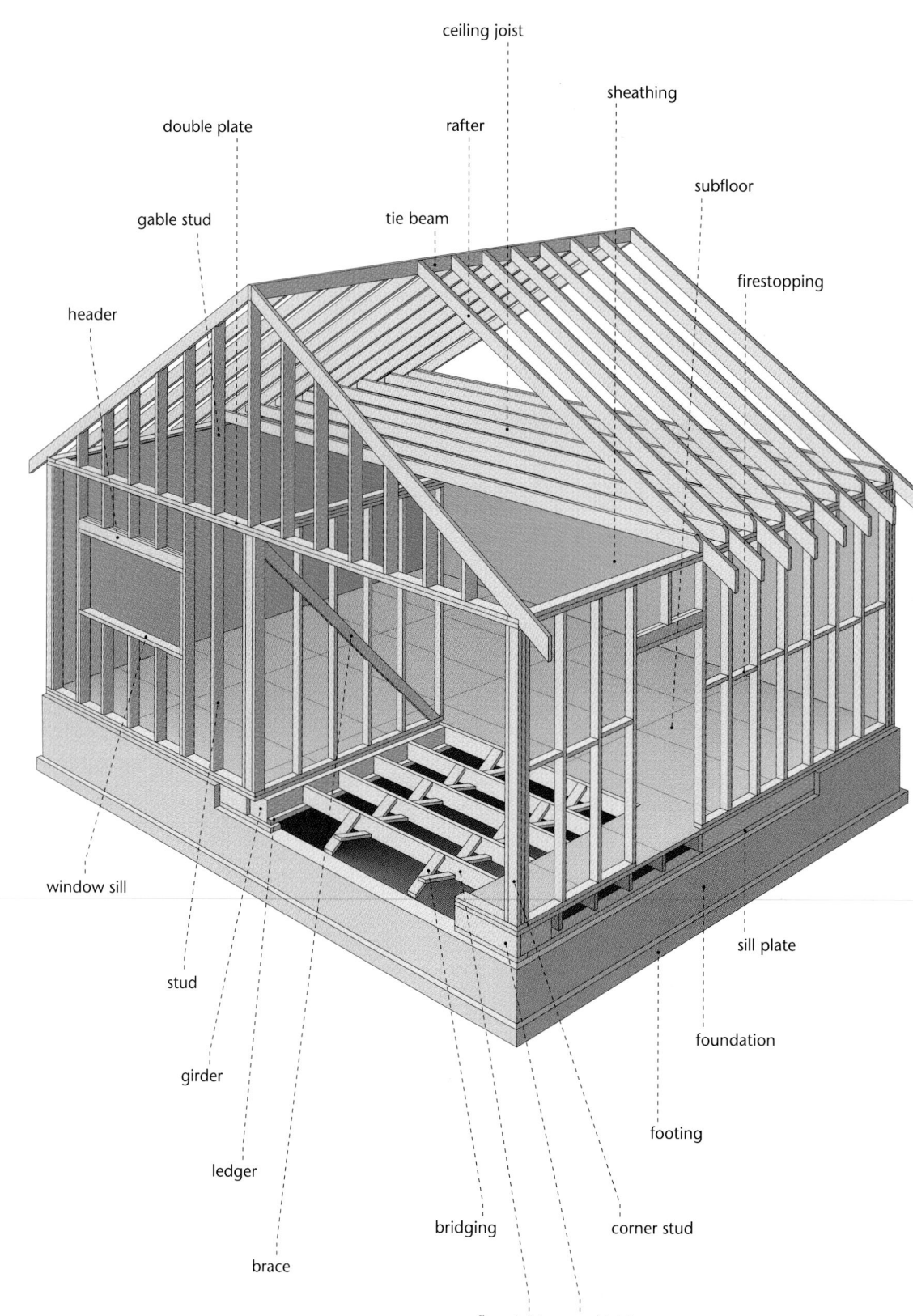

ceiling joist

sheathing

double plate

rafter

subfloor

gable stud

tie beam

firestopping

header

window sill

stud

girder

ledger

brace

floor joist

bridging

end joist

corner stud

footing

foundation

sill plate

ROOF TRUSS

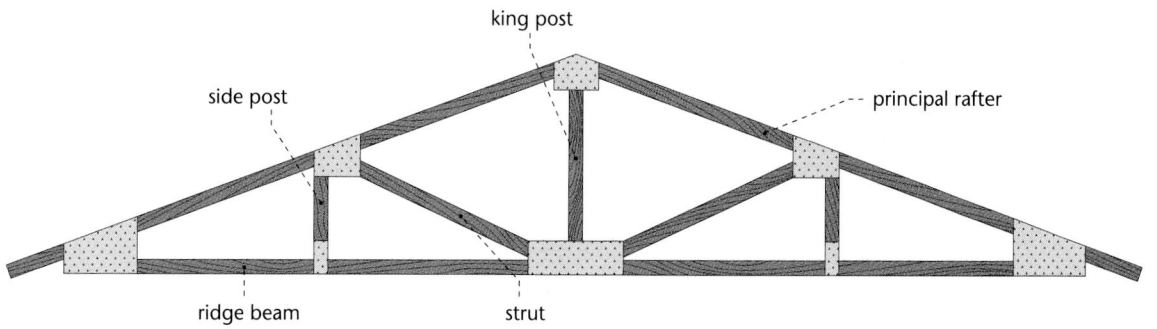

king post
side post
principal rafter
ridge beam
strut

FOUNDATIONS

sheathing
subfloor
wall stud
baseboard
brick wall
molding
insulating material
wood flooring
sill
foundation
floor joist
end joist
sill plate
footing
gravel
drain tile

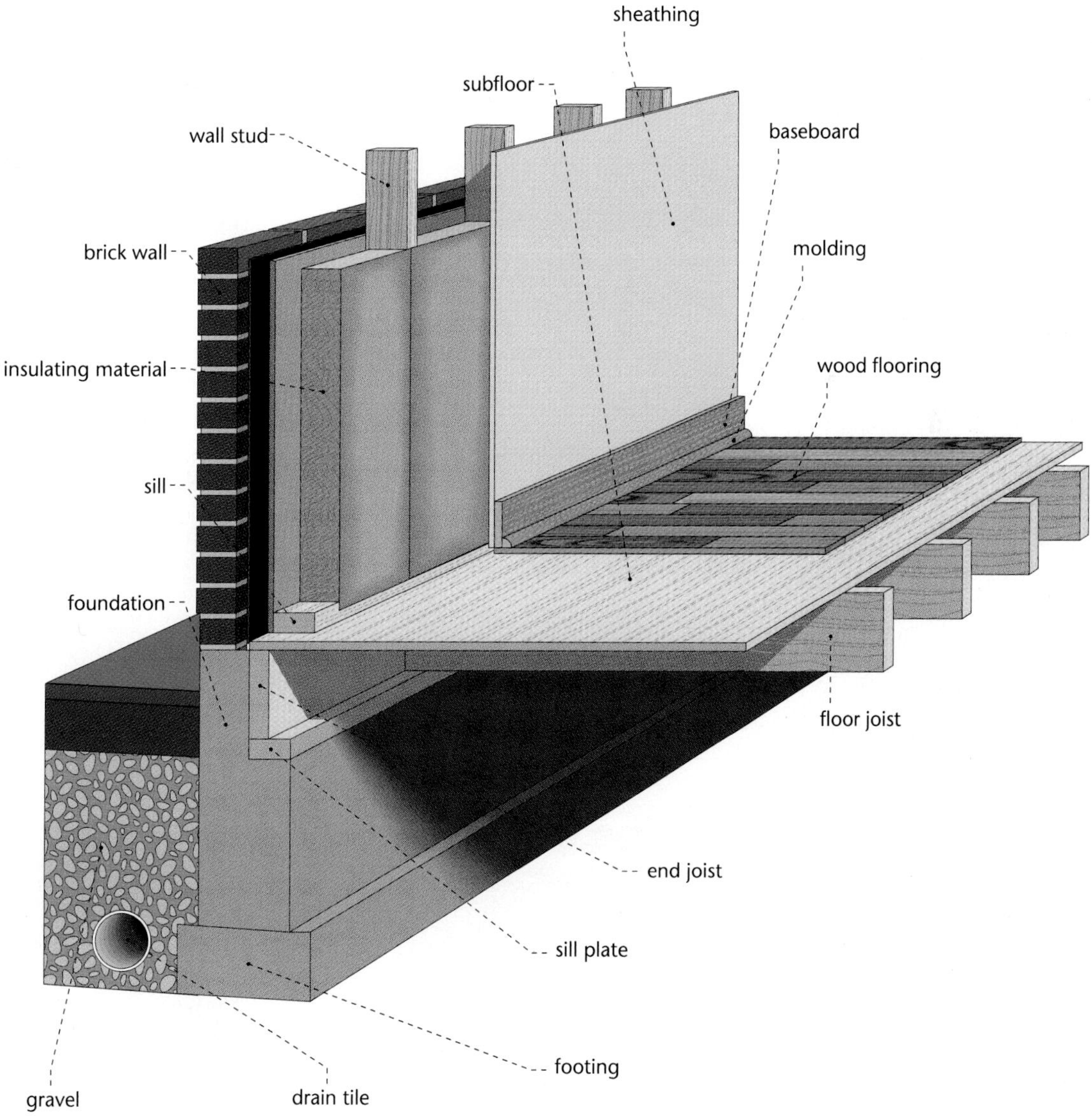

WOOD FLOORING

WOOD FLOORING ON CEMENT SCREED

WOOD FLOORING ON WOODEN STRUCTURE

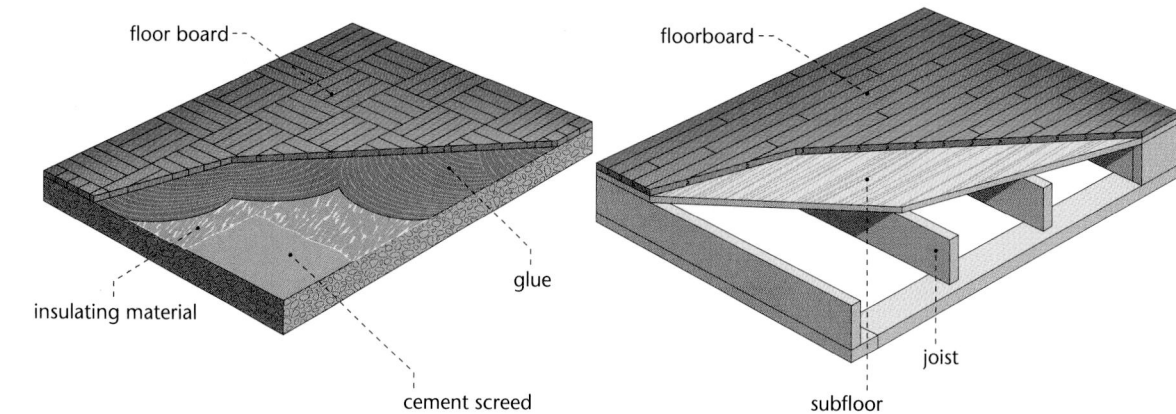

floor board

insulating material

glue

cement screed

floorboard

joist

subfloor

WOOD FLOORING ARRANGEMENTS

overlay flooring

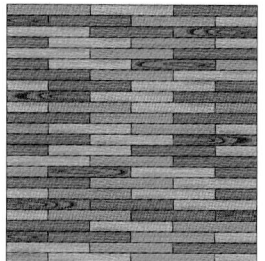

strip flooring with alternate joints

herringbone parquet

herringbone pattern

inlaid parquet

basket weave pattern

Arenberg parquet

Chantilly parquet

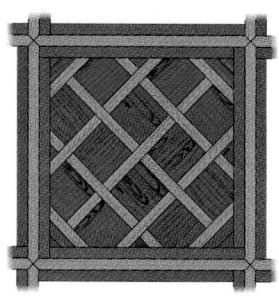

Versailles parquet

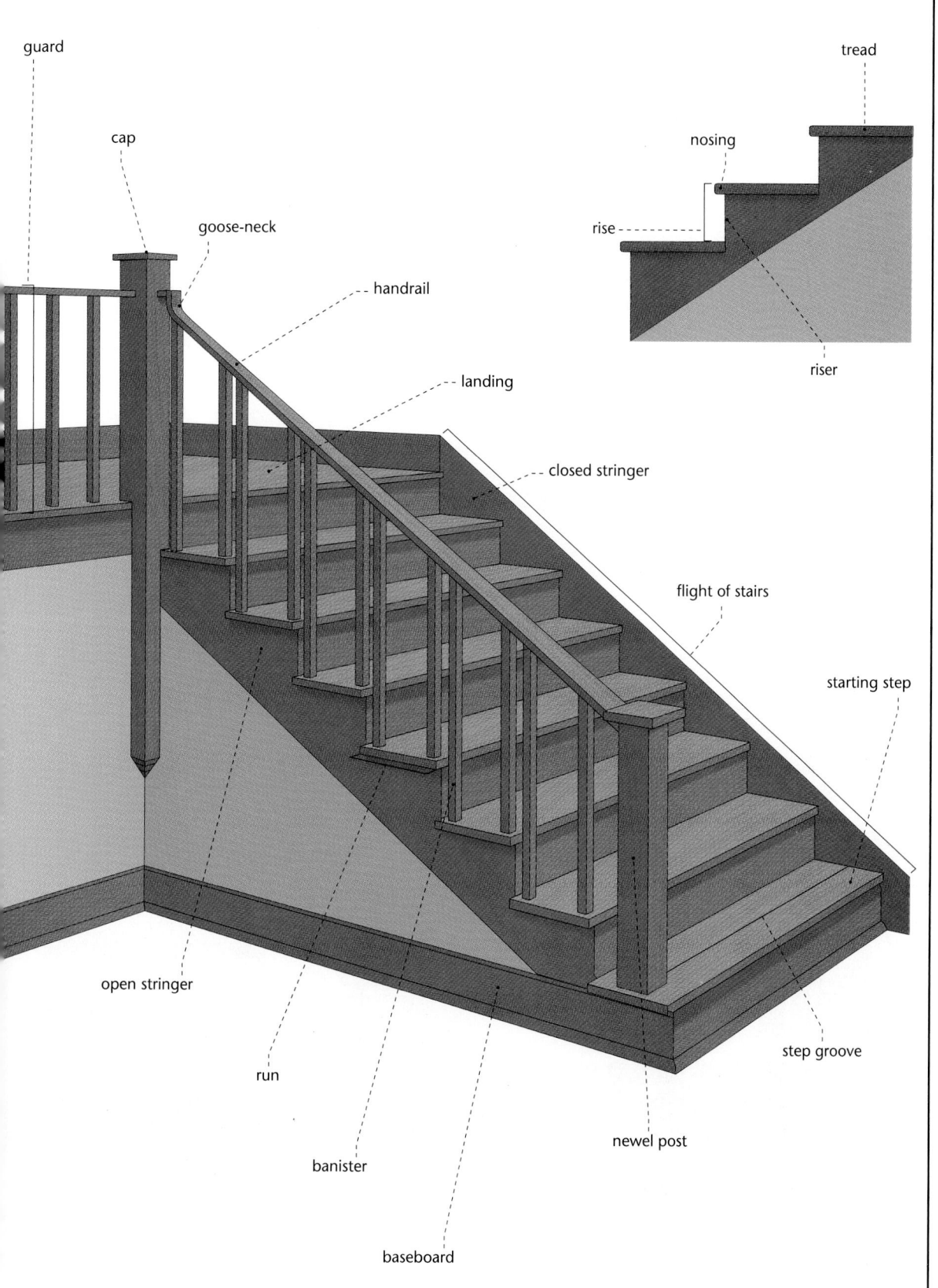

guard

cap

goose-neck

handrail

landing

closed stringer

flight of stairs

starting step

open stringer

run

banister

baseboard

newel post

step groove

tread

nosing

rise

riser

EXTERIOR DOOR

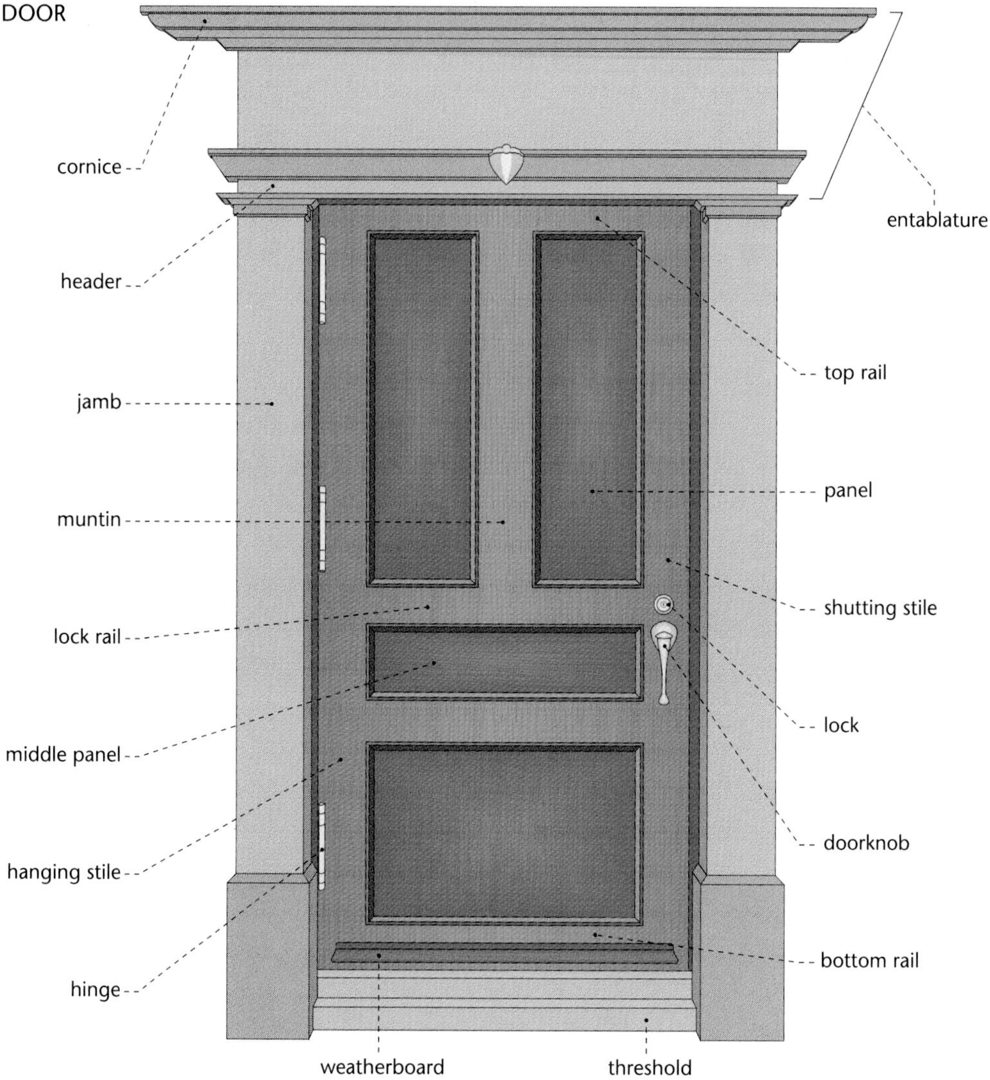

cornice

header

jamb

muntin

lock rail

middle panel

hanging stile

hinge

entablature

top rail

panel

shutting stile

lock

doorknob

bottom rail

weatherboard

threshold

TYPES OF DOORS

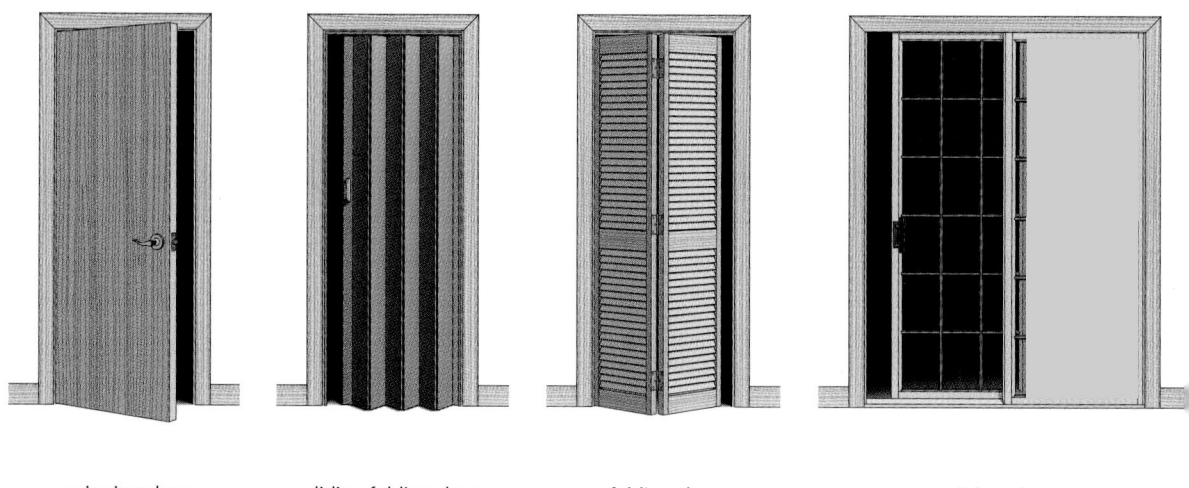

swinging door

sliding folding door

folding door

sliding door

WINDOW

STRUCTURE

muntin
head of frame
pane
top rail of sash
jamb
jalousie
casement
hanging stile
sash frame
hook
shutter
stile tongue of sash
sill of frame
hinge
weatherboard
stile groove of sash

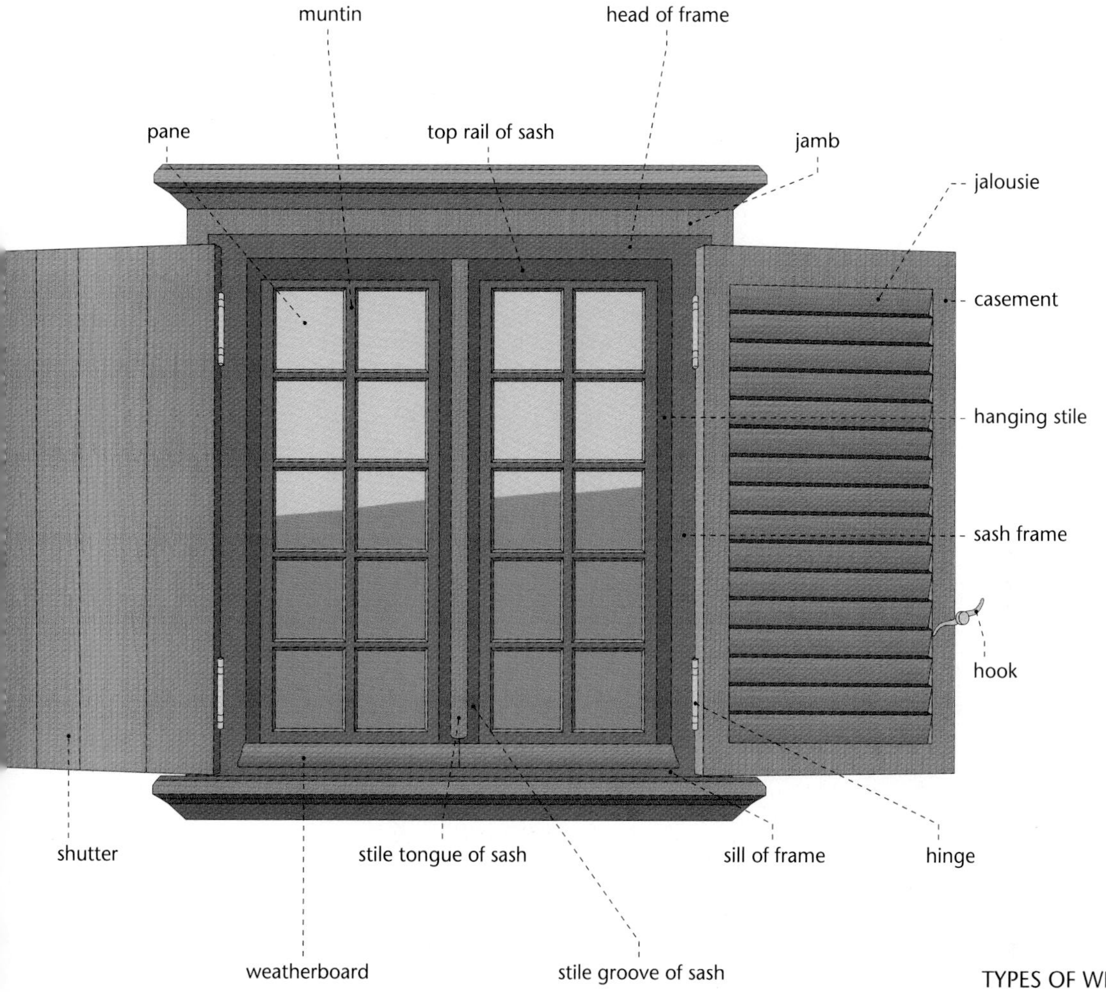

TYPES OF WINDOWS

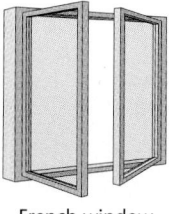

French window

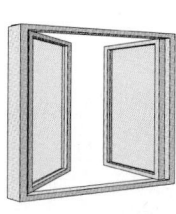

casement window

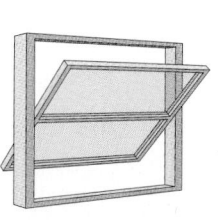

horizontal pivoting window

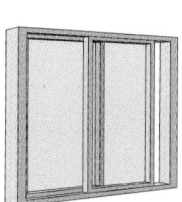

sliding window

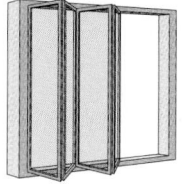

sliding folding window

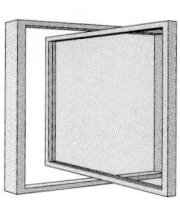

vertical pivoting window

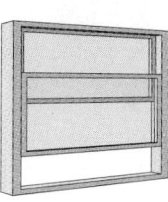

sash window

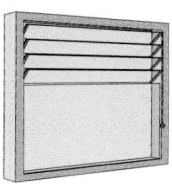

louvered window

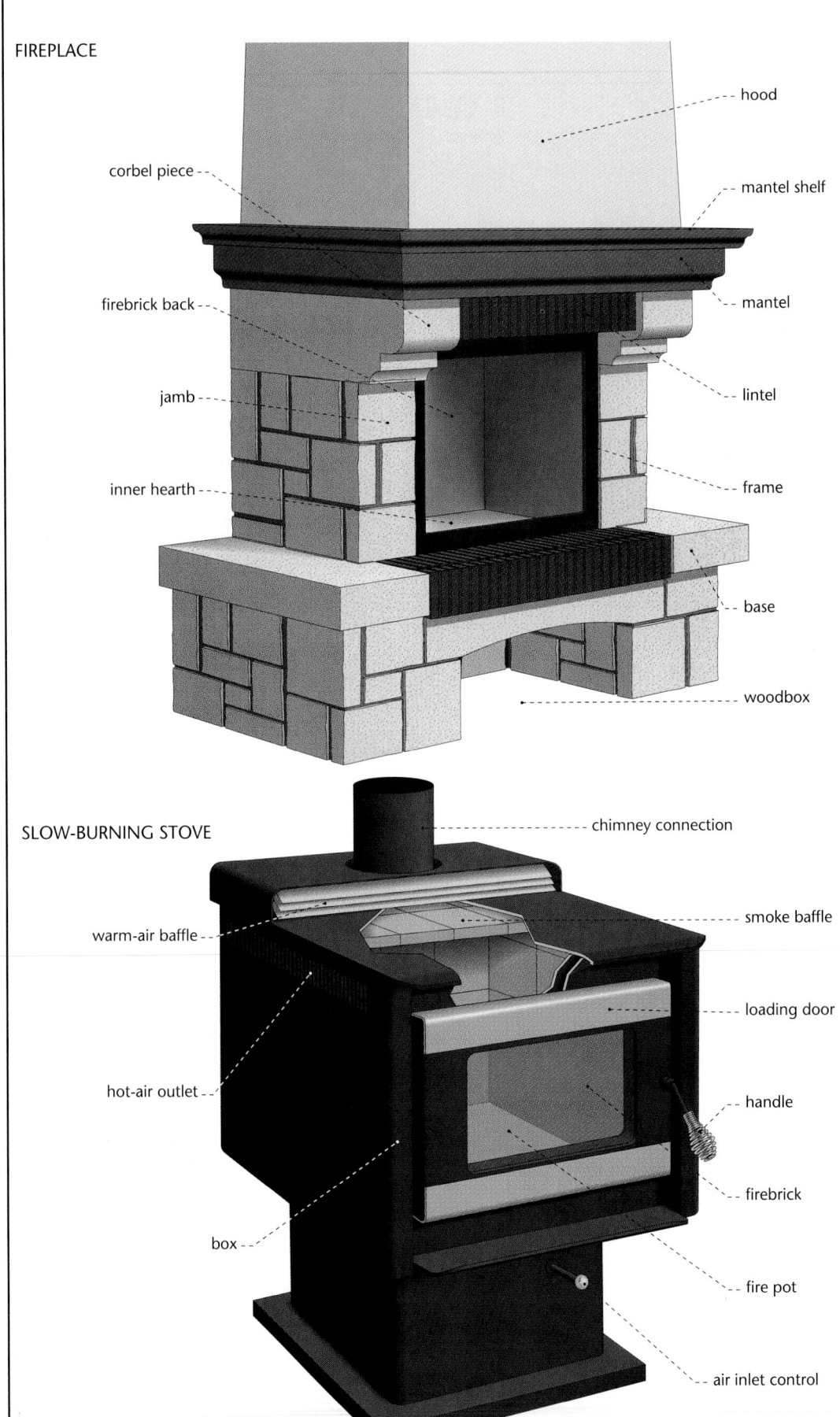

FIREPLACE

hood

corbel piece

mantel shelf

firebrick back

mantel

jamb

lintel

inner hearth

frame

base

woodbox

SLOW-BURNING STOVE

chimney connection

smoke baffle

warm-air baffle

loading door

hot-air outlet

handle

firebrick

box

fire pot

air inlet control

HOUSE

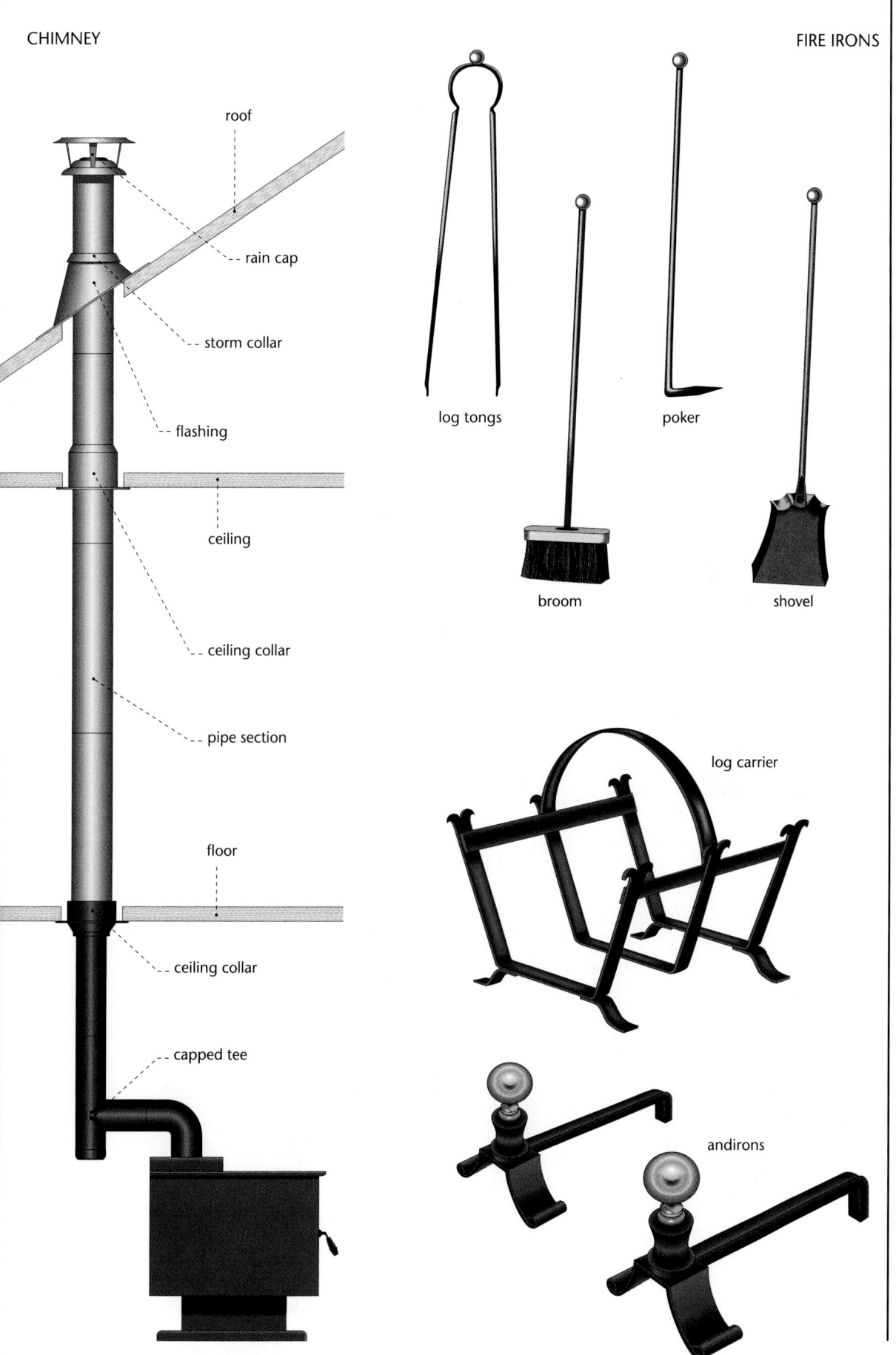

roof

rain cap

storm collar

flashing

ceiling

ceiling collar

pipe section

floor

ceiling collar

capped tee

log tongs

broom

poker

shovel

log carrier

andirons

FORCED WARM-AIR SYSTEM

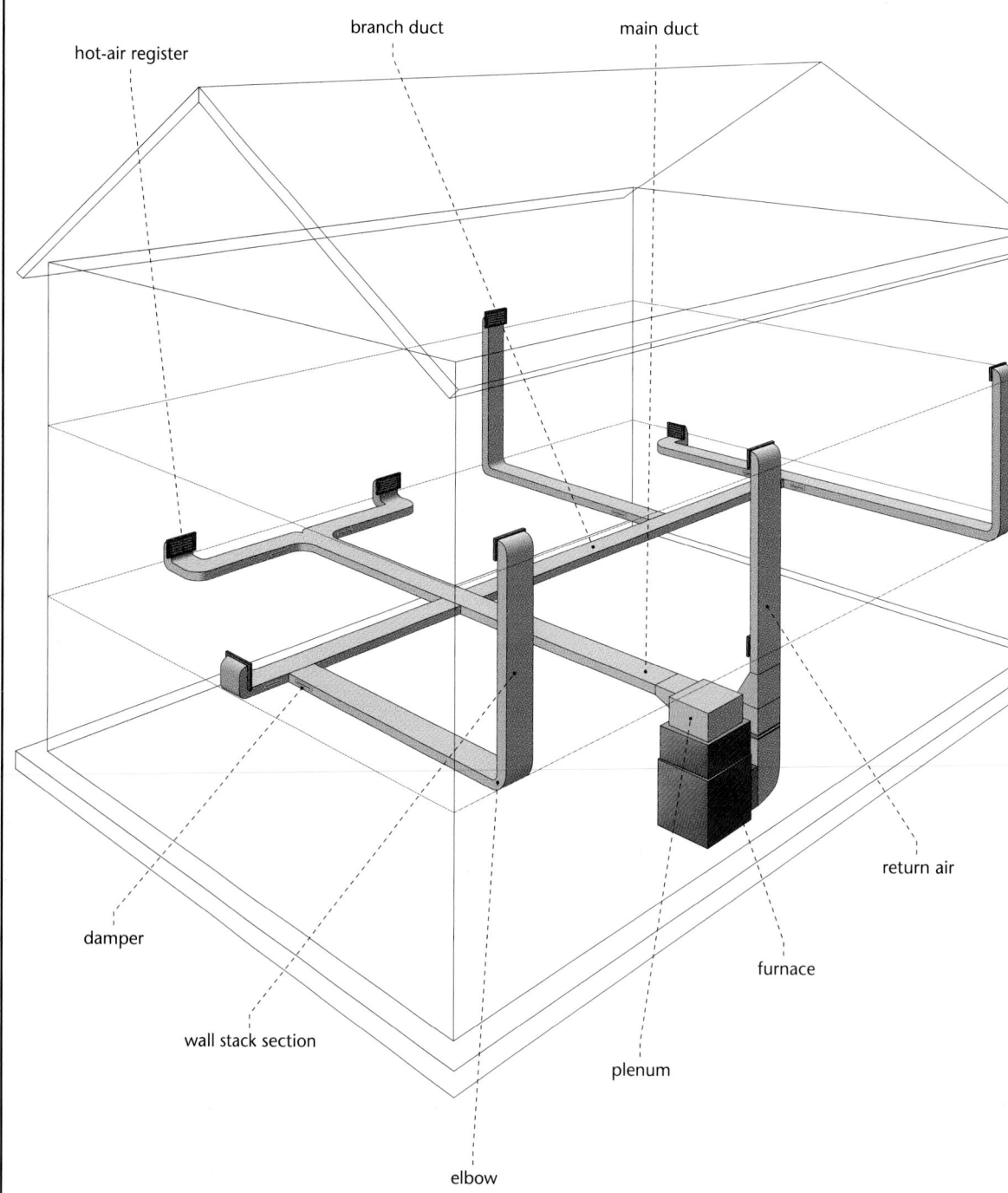

hot-air register

branch duct

main duct

damper

wall stack section

elbow

plenum

furnace

return air

ELECTRIC FURNACE

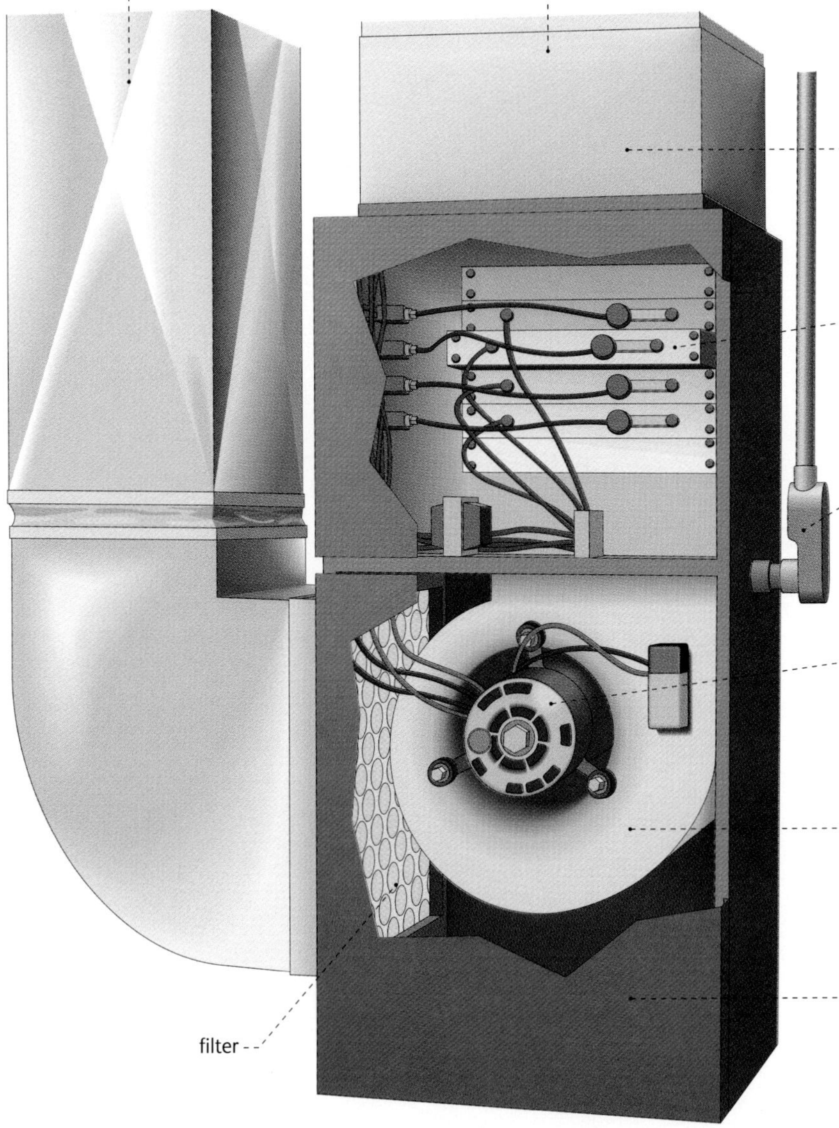

return air

hot-air outflow

plenum

heating element

electric connection

blower motor

blower

access panel

filter

TYPES OF REGISTERS

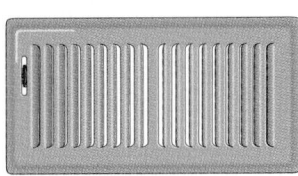

baseboard register

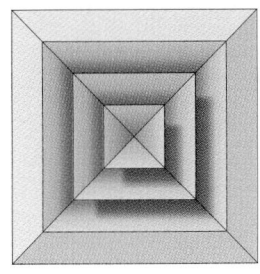

ceiling register

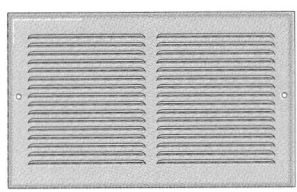

wall register

FORCED HOT-WATER SYSTEM

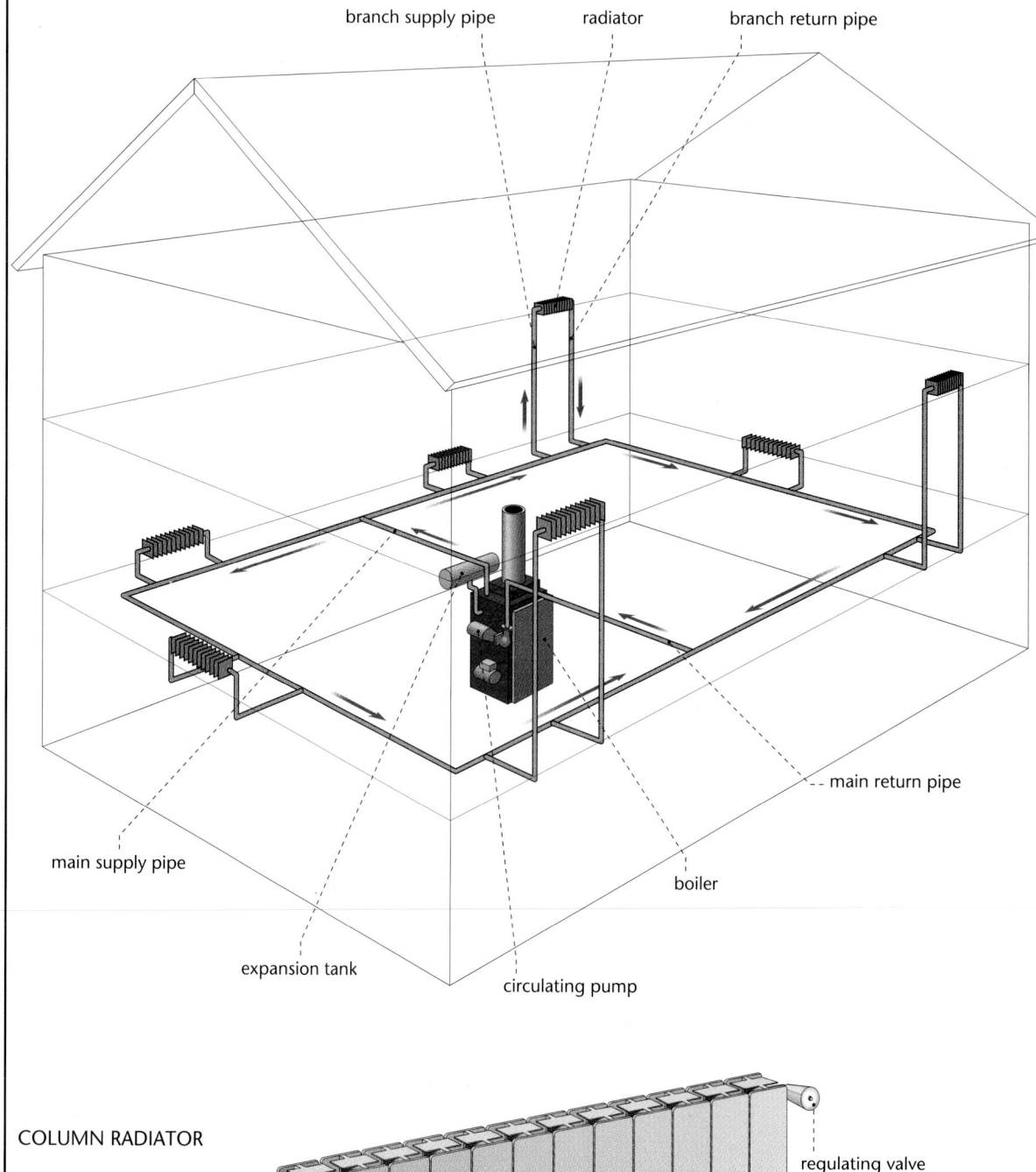

branch supply pipe   radiator   branch return pipe

main return pipe

main supply pipe

boiler

expansion tank   circulating pump

COLUMN RADIATOR

regulating valve

bleeder valve

covering grille

column

hot-water outlet

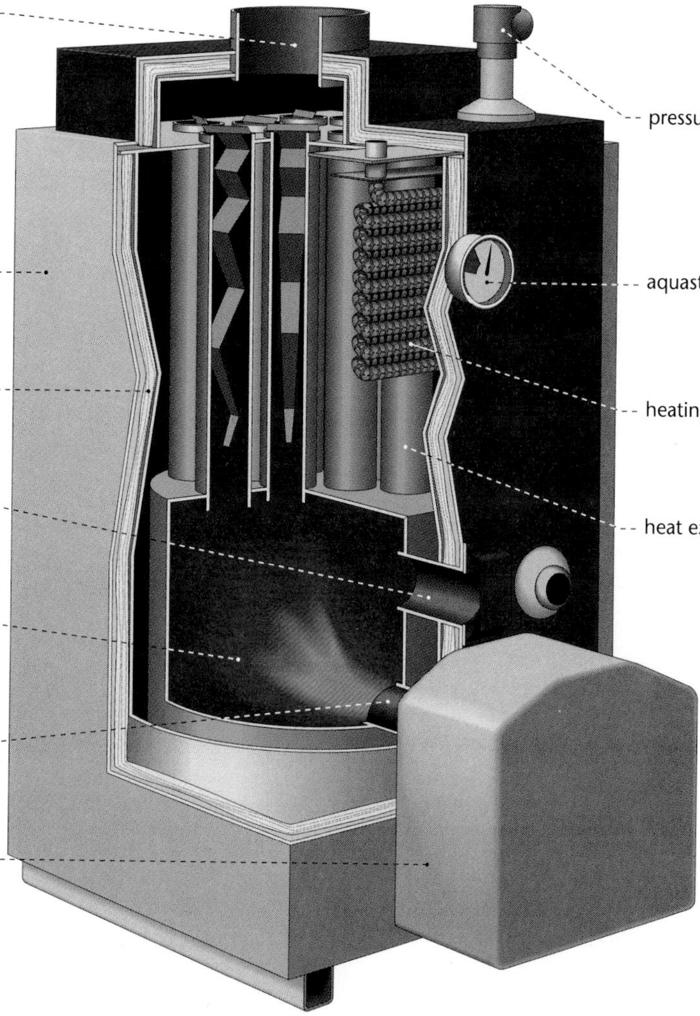

chimney ----
pressure relief valve ----
box ----
aquastat ----
insulation ----
heating element ----
draft hole ----
heat exchanger ----
fire pot ----
air tube ----
burner ----

OIL BURNER

nozzle
electrode assembly ----
ignition transformer
heat control ----
air tube ----
oil supply line ----
oil pump ----
electric motor ----
oil supply inlet ----
fan ----

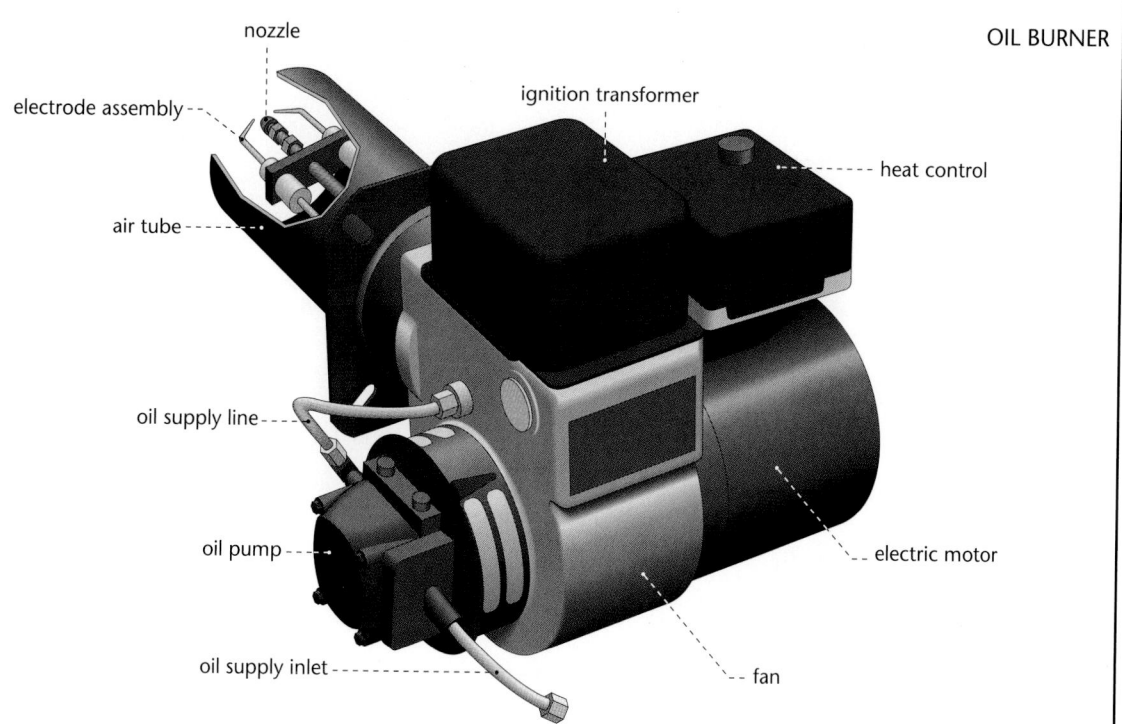

209

HEATING

HUMIDIFIER

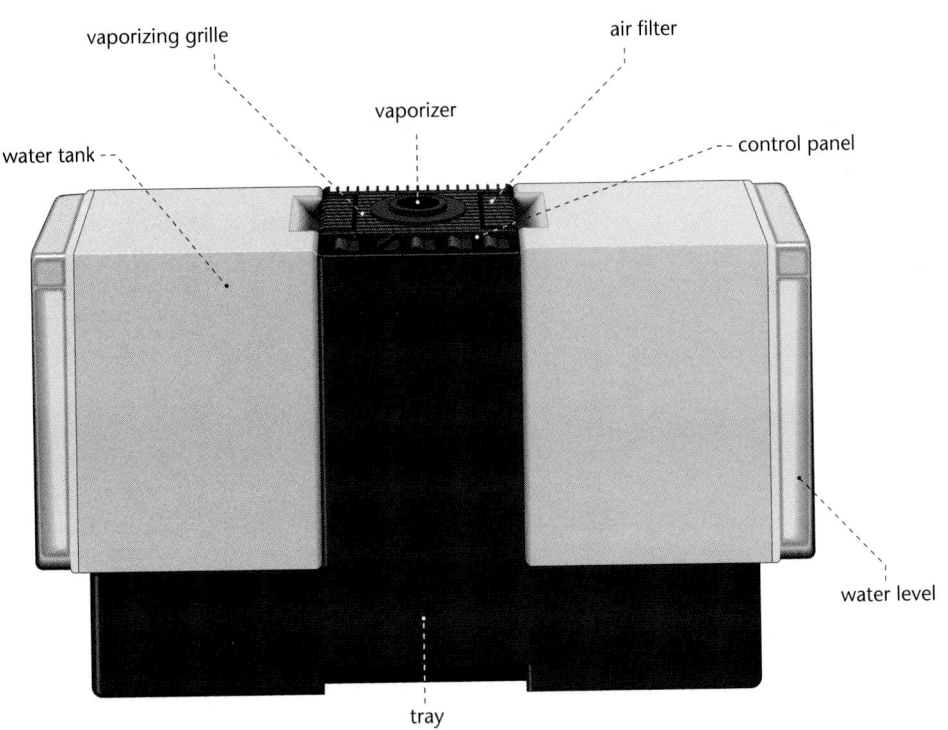

vaporizing grille

air filter

vaporizer

water tank

control panel

water level

tray

HYGROMETER

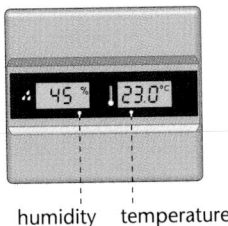

humidity temperature

air purifier

ELECTRIC BASEBOARD RADIATOR

thermostat

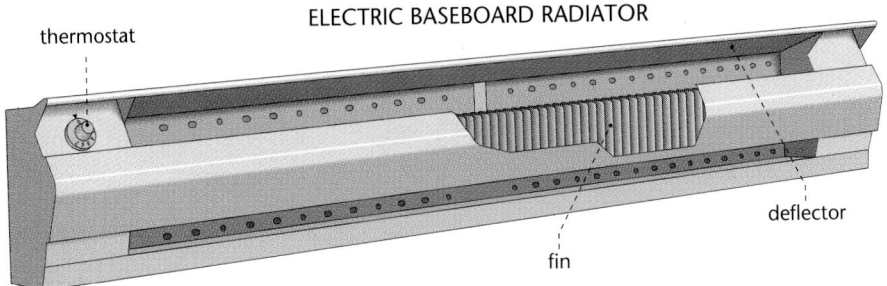

deflector

fin

CONVECTOR

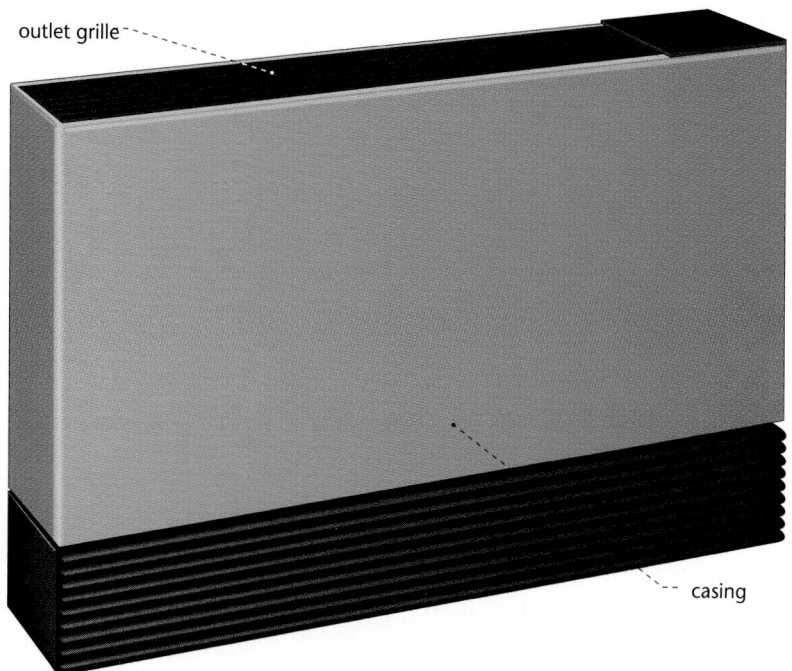

outlet grille

casing

AUXILIARY HEATING

radiant heater

oil-filled heater

fan heater

HEAT PUMP

OUTDOOR UNIT

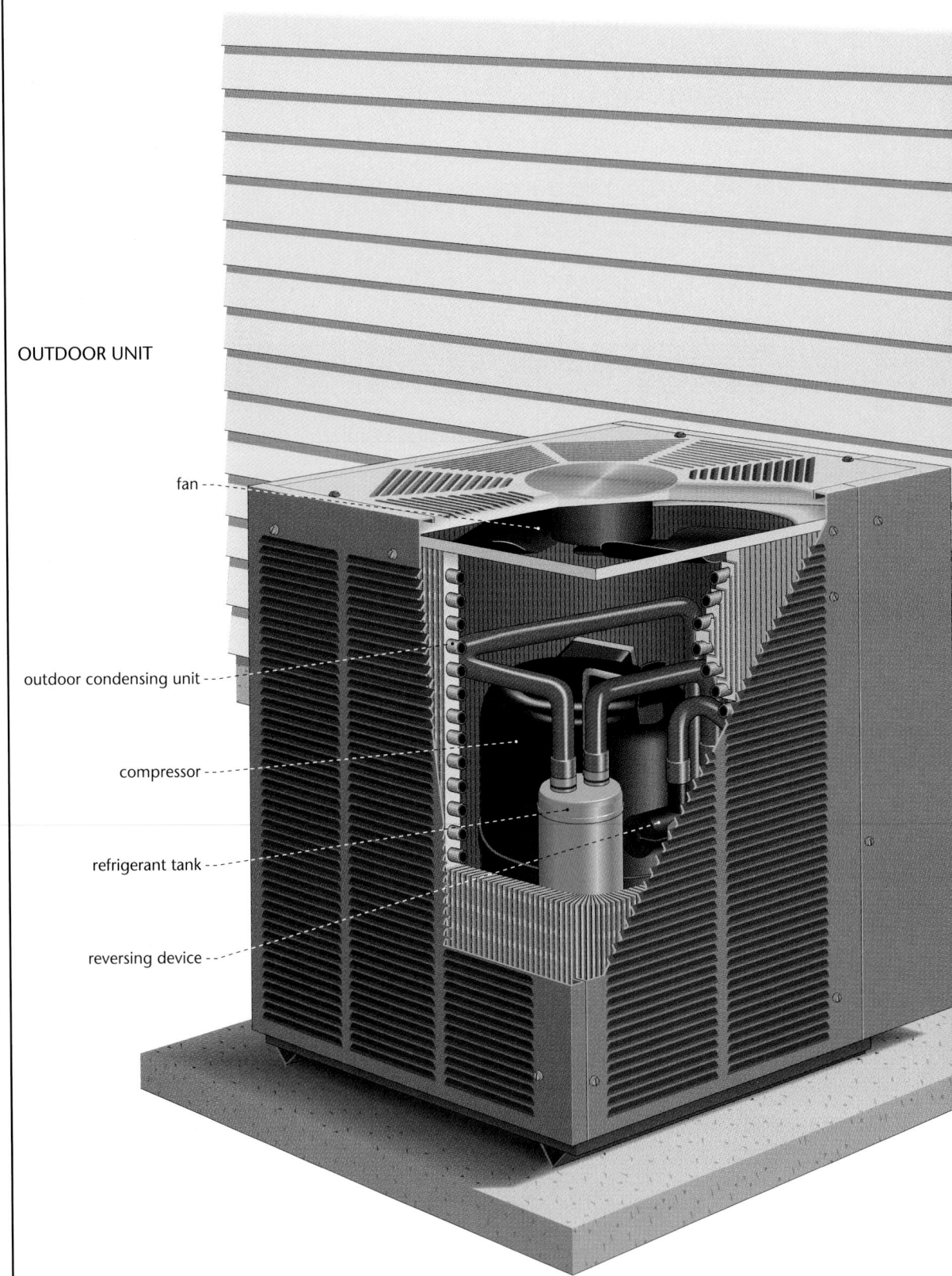

fan

outdoor condensing unit

compressor

refrigerant tank

reversing device

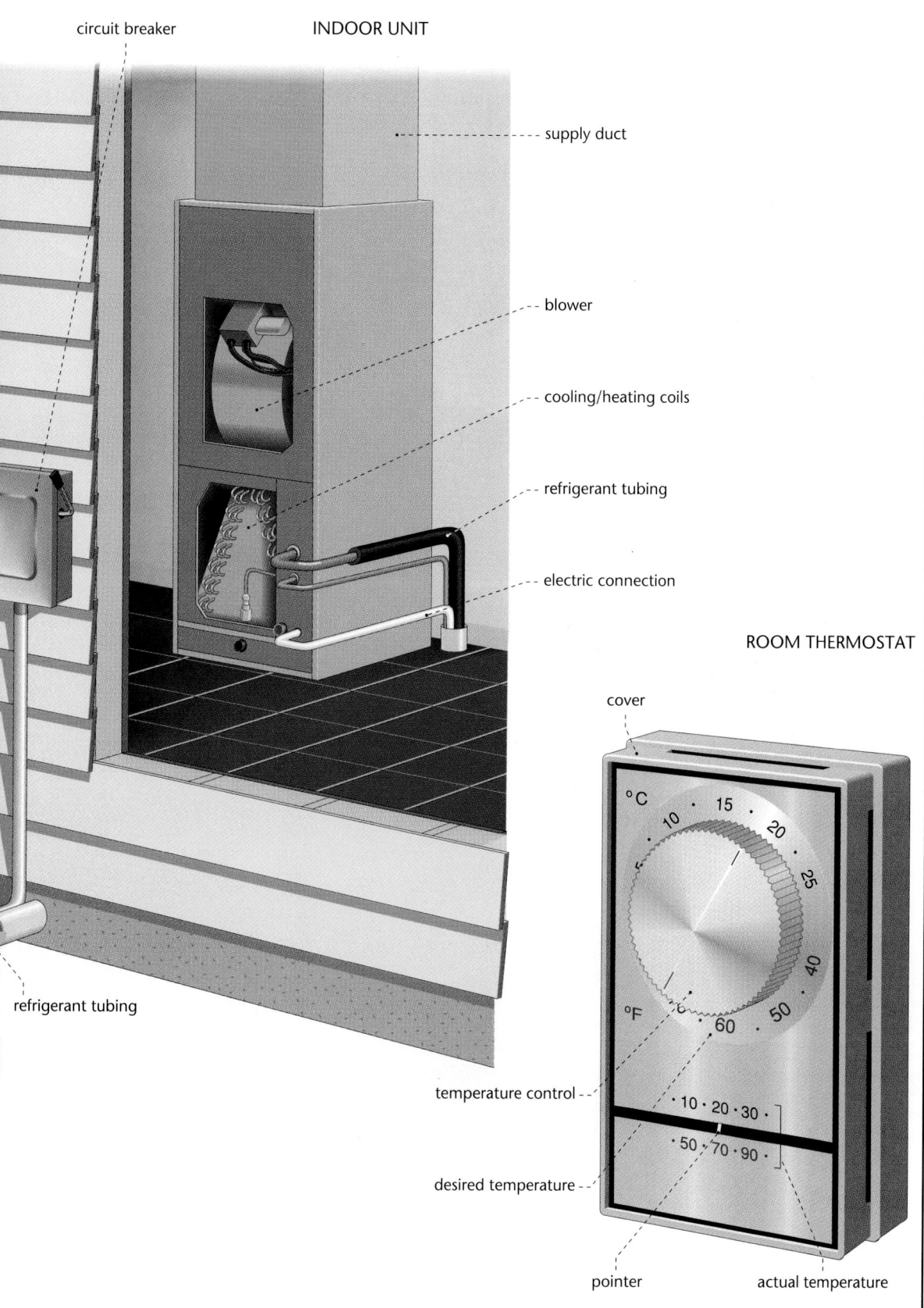

circuit breaker

INDOOR UNIT

supply duct

blower

cooling/heating coils

refrigerant tubing

electric connection

refrigerant tubing

ROOM THERMOSTAT

cover

°C

10 · 15 · 20 · 25 · 40 · 50 · 60

°F

temperature control

10 · 20 · 30

50 · 70 · 90

desired temperature

pointer

actual temperature

HOUSE

CEILING FAN

rod

motor

blade

ROOM AIR CONDITIONER

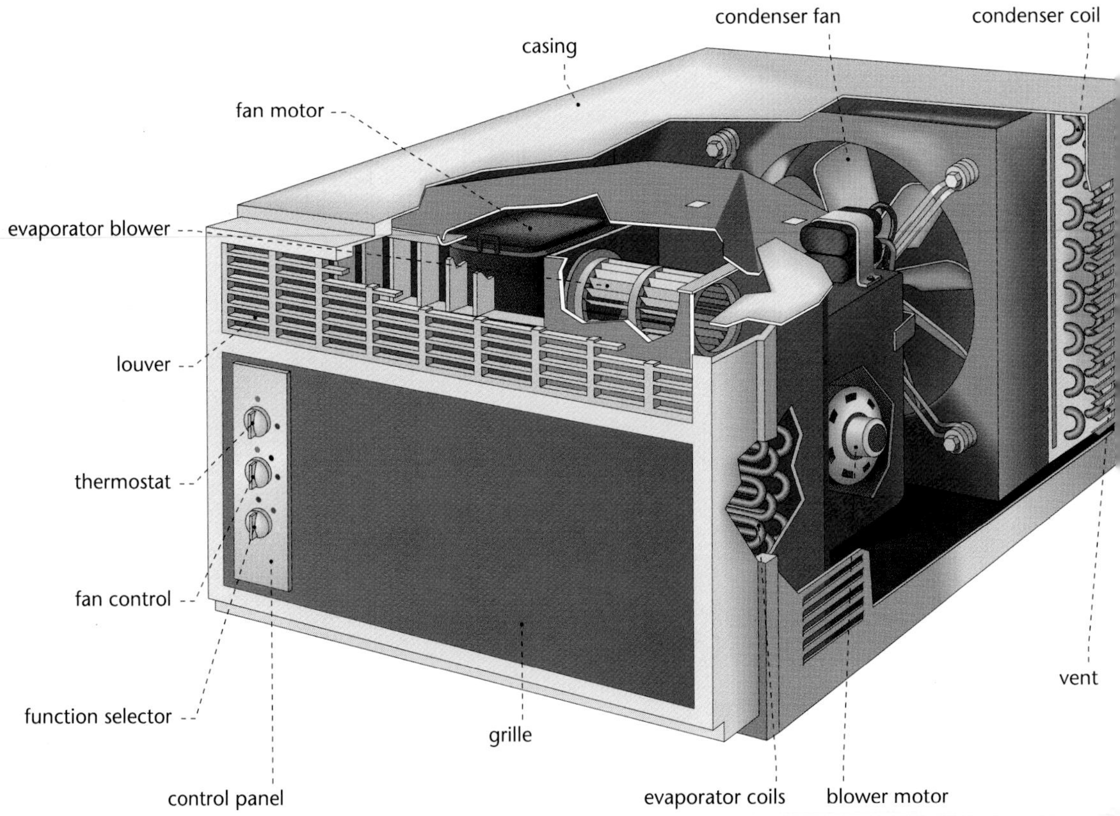

condenser fan

condenser coil

casing

fan motor

evaporator blower

louver

thermostat

fan control

function selector

control panel

grille

evaporator coils

blower motor

vent

PLUMBING SYSTEM

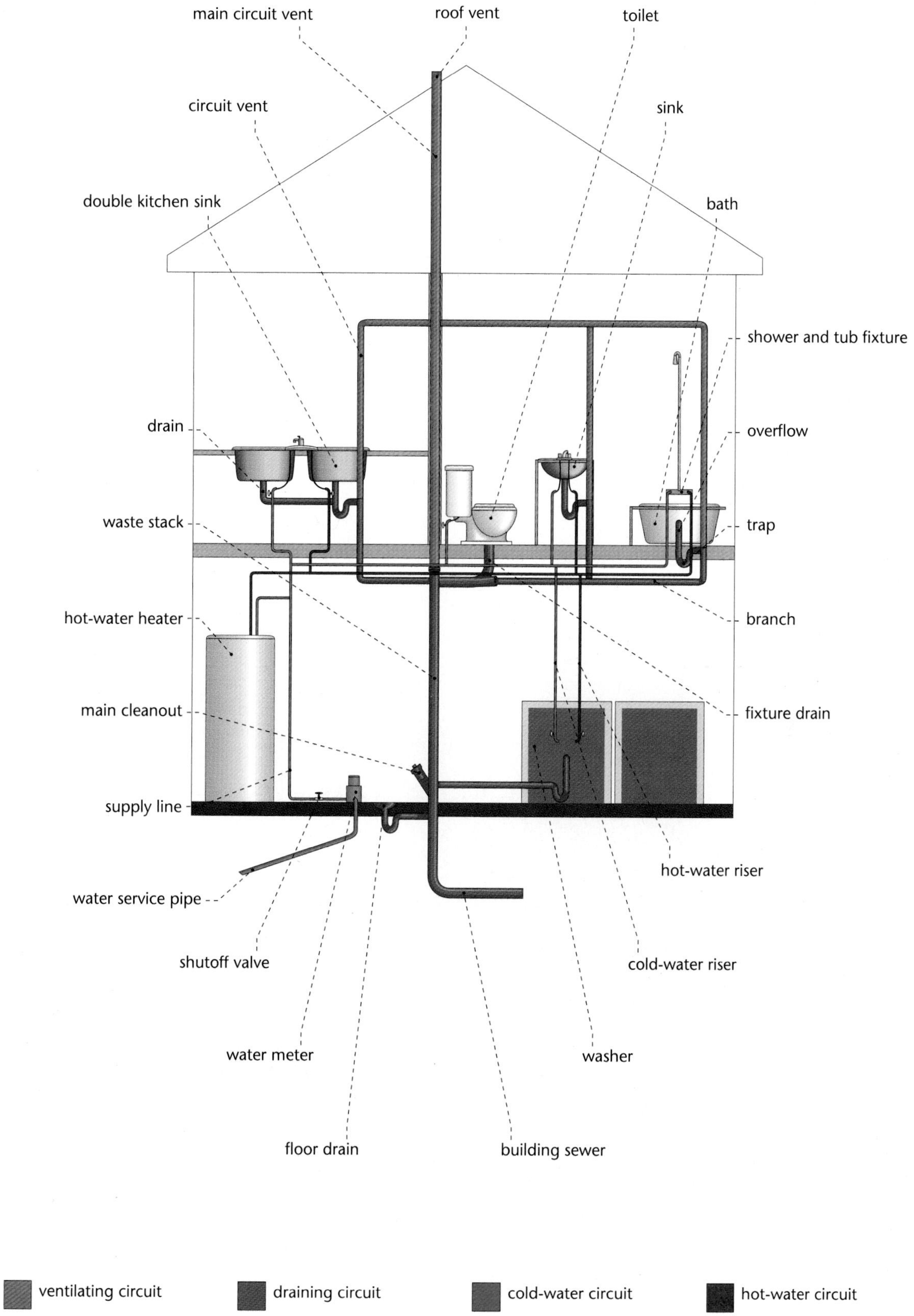

main circuit vent

roof vent

toilet

circuit vent

sink

double kitchen sink

bath

shower and tub fixture

drain

overflow

waste stack

trap

hot-water heater

branch

main cleanout

fixture drain

supply line

hot-water riser

water service pipe

cold-water riser

shutoff valve

water meter

washer

floor drain

building sewer

 ventilating circuit    draining circuit   cold-water circuit   hot-water circuit

PEDESTAL-TYPE SUMP PUMP

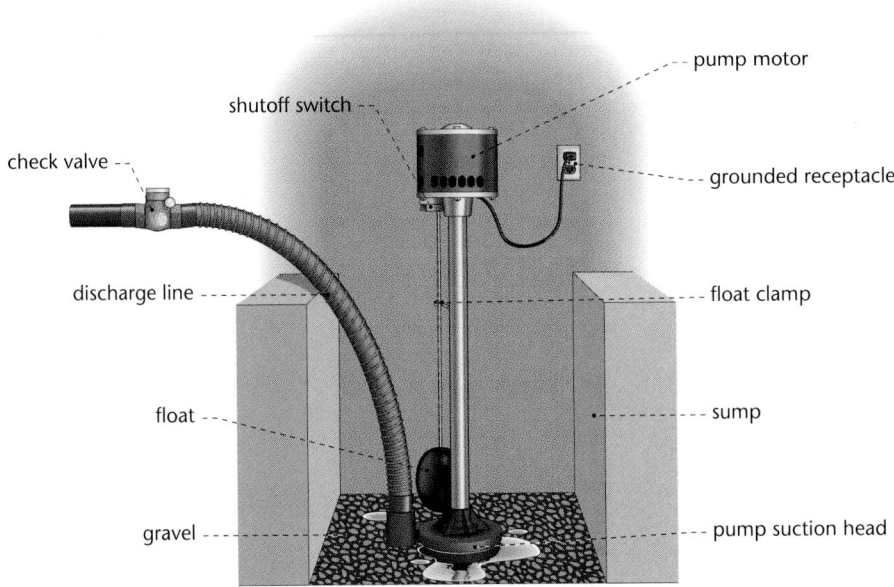

pump motor

shutoff switch

check valve

grounded receptacle

discharge line

float clamp

float

sump

gravel

pump suction head

SEPTIC TANK

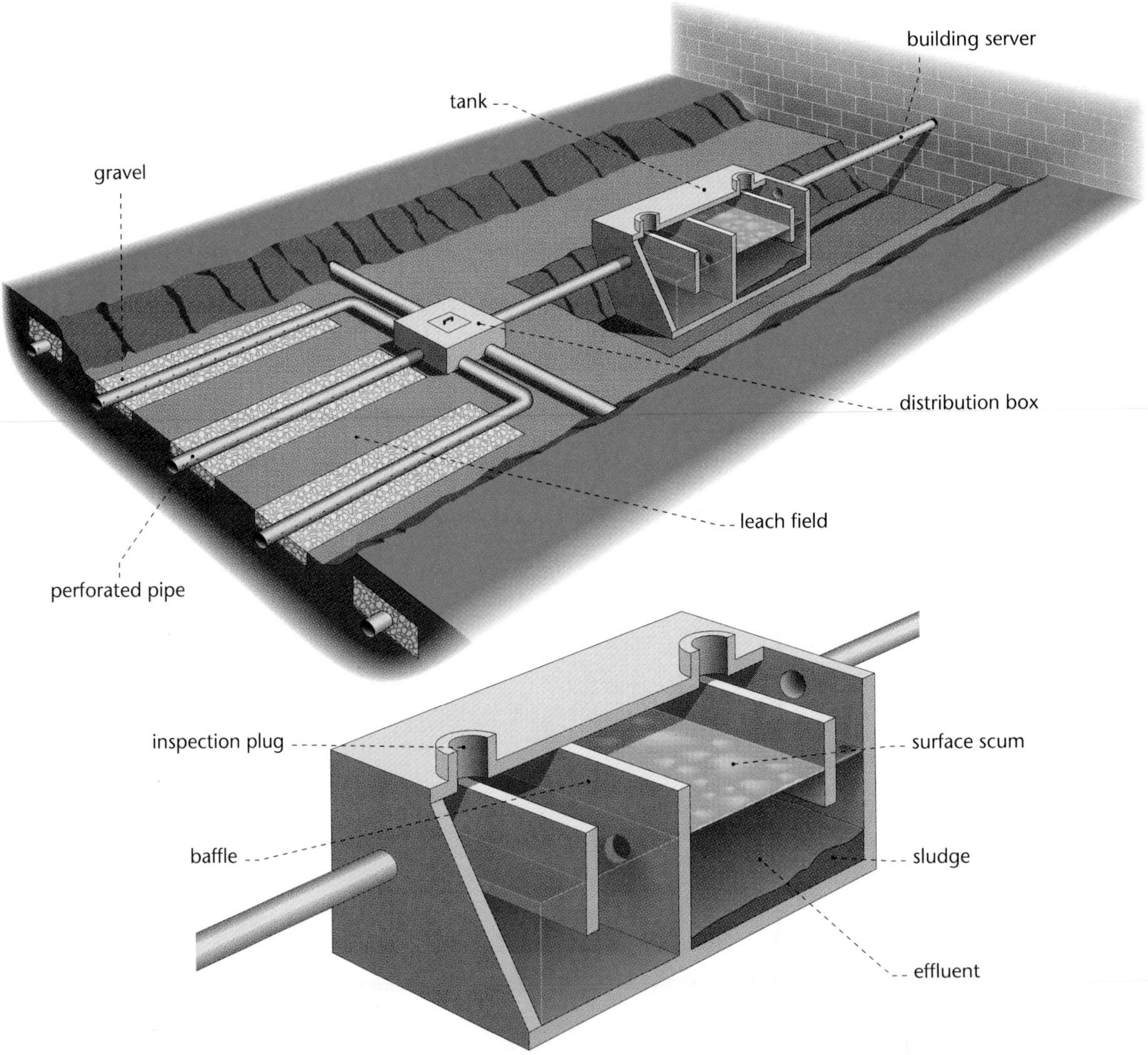

building server

tank

gravel

distribution box

leach field

perforated pipe

inspection plug

surface scum

baffle

sludge

effluent

HOUSE FURNITURE

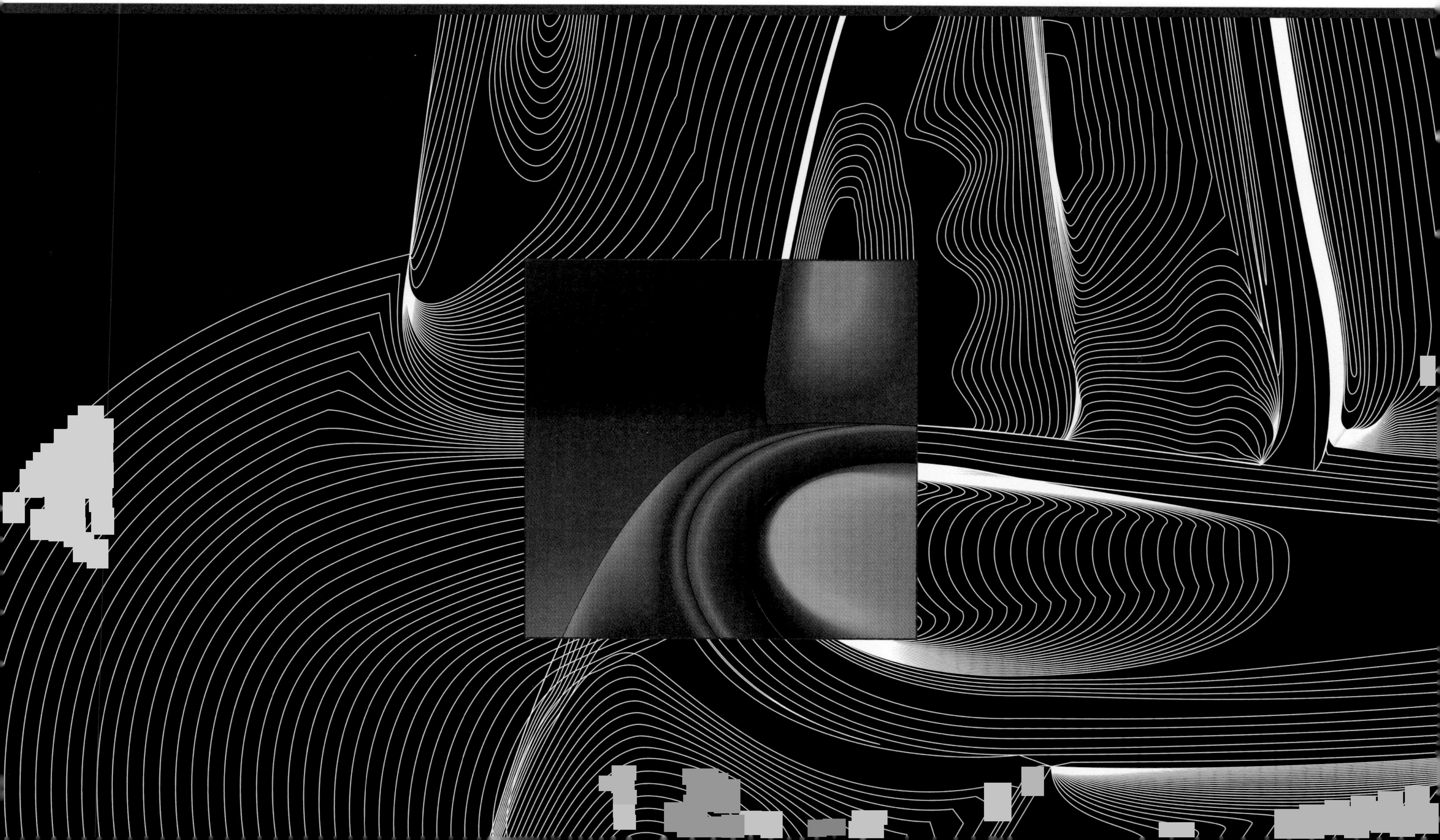

CONTENTS

TABLE...219

ARMCHAIR...220

SEATS..222

SIDE CHAIR 223

BED...224

STORAGE FURNITURE 225

WINDOW ACCESSORIES 228

LIGHTS..232

GLASSWARE..237

DINNERWARE 238

SILVERWARE..239

KITCHEN UTENSILS 242

COFFEE MAKERS 247

COOKING UTENSILS...248

DOMESTIC APPLIANCES 250

TABLE

GATE-LEG TABLE

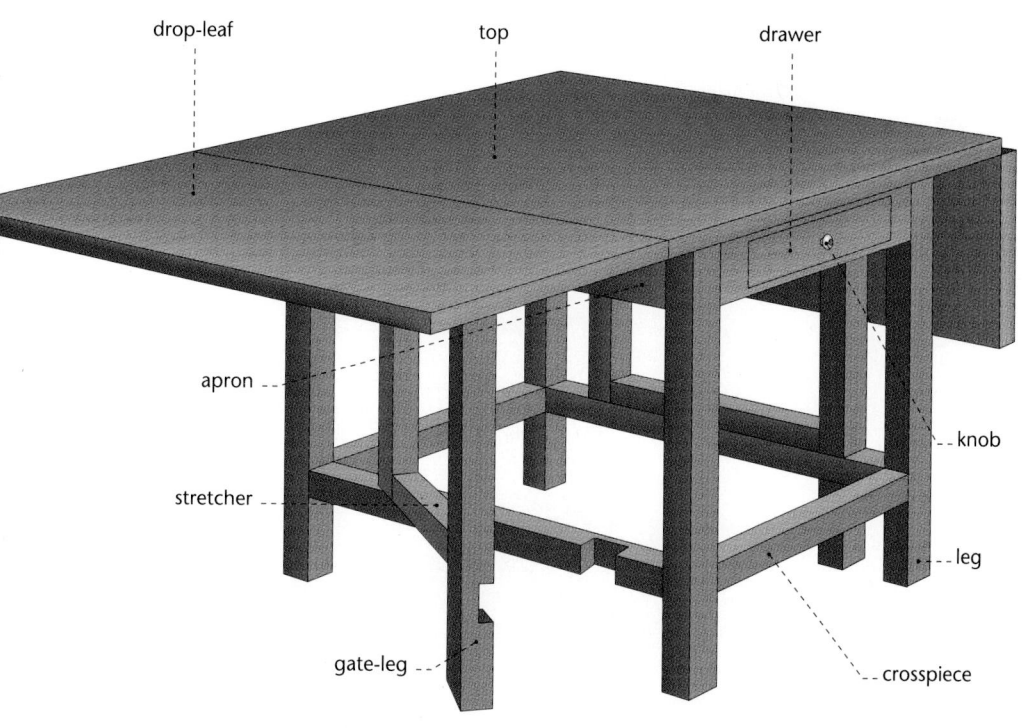

drop-leaf

top

drawer

apron

stretcher

gate-leg

knob

leg

crosspiece

MAJOR TYPES OF TABLES

extension table

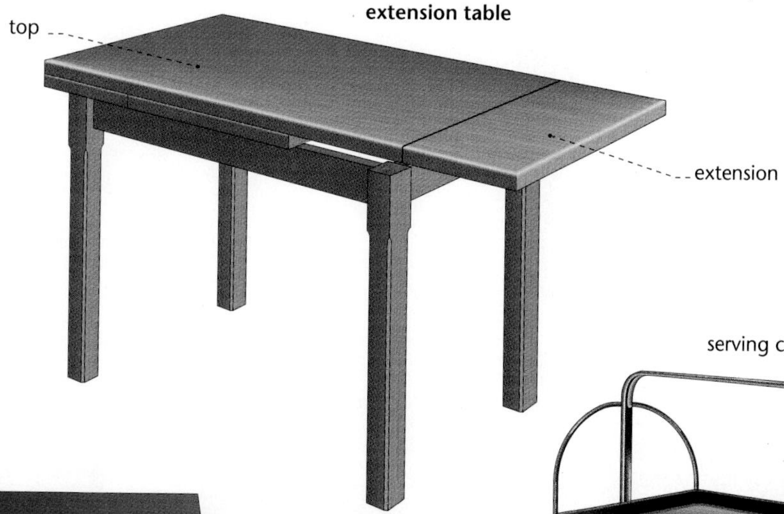

top

extension

serving cart

nest of tables

HOUSE FURNITURE

PARTS

palmette

patera

rinceau

arm

volute

arm stump

splat

seat

base of splat

apron

cockleshell

cabriole leg

scroll foot

acanthus leaf

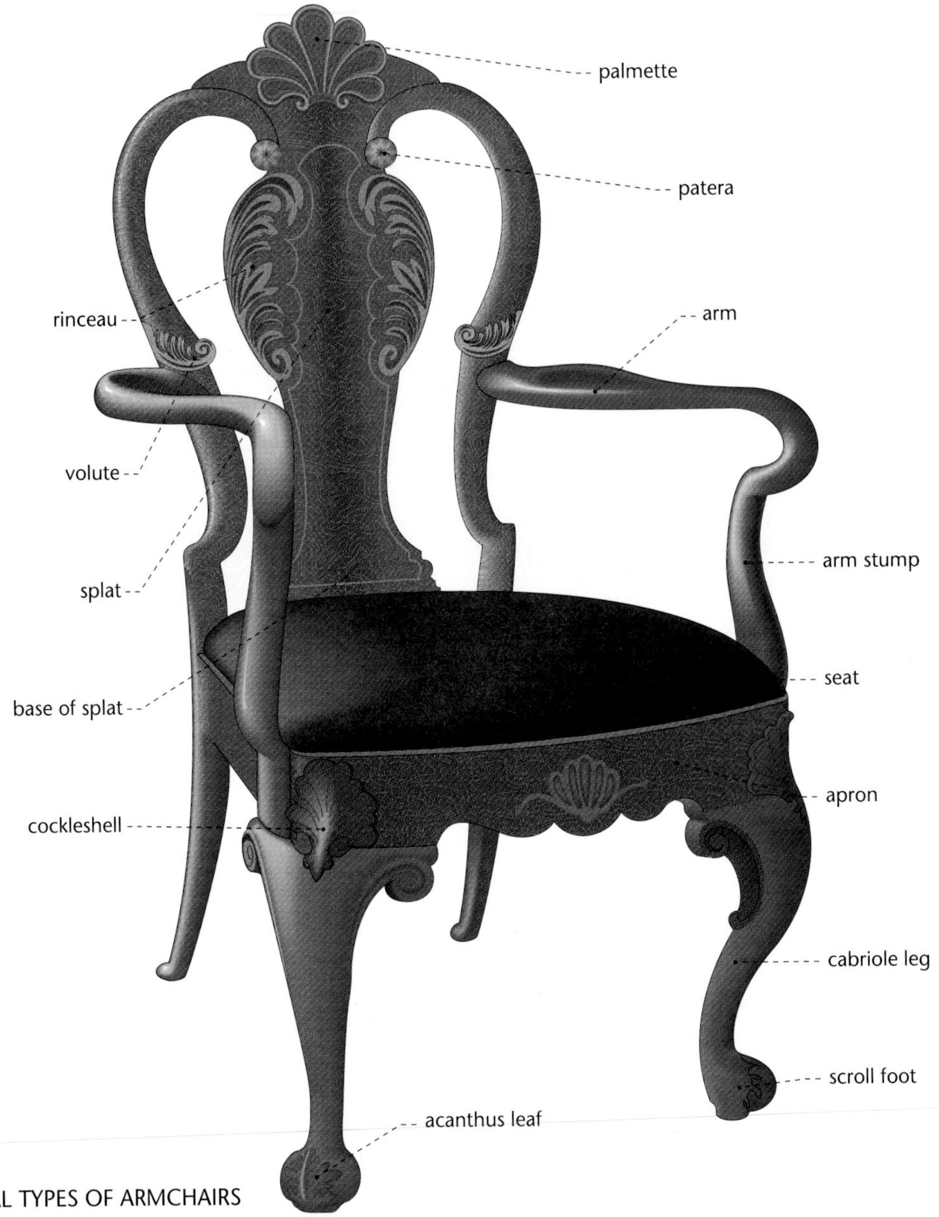

PRINCIPAL TYPES OF ARMCHAIRS

bergère

cabriolet

director's chair

sofa

love seat

récamier

chesterfield

méridienne

Wassily chair

rocking chair

club chair

HOUSE FURNITURE

banquette

ottoman

bean bag chair

bench

bar stool

footstool

step chair

SIDE CHAIR

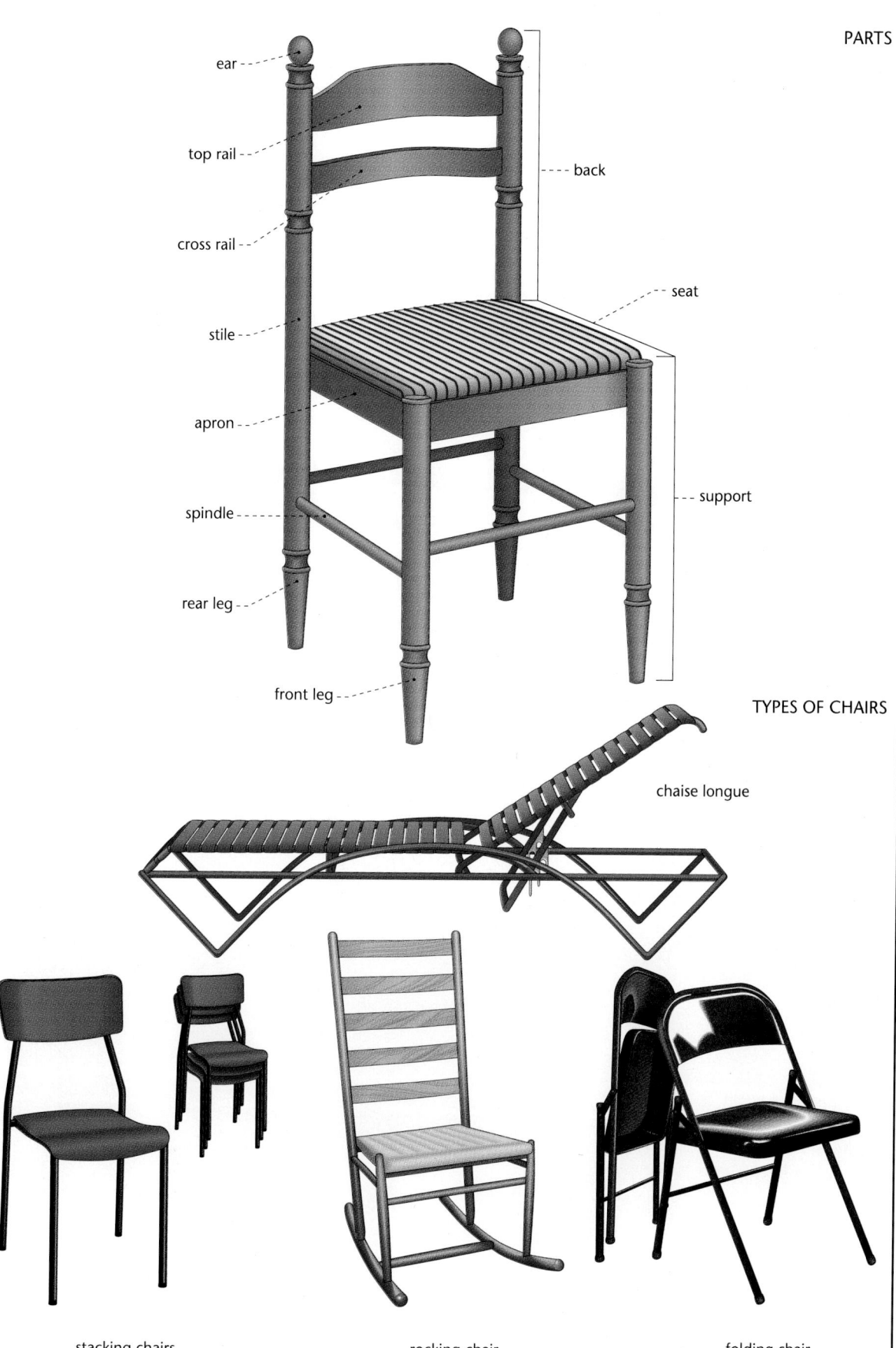

ear

top rail

cross rail

stile

apron

spindle

rear leg

front leg

back

seat

support

HOUSE FURNITURE

TYPES OF CHAIRS

chaise longue

stacking chairs

rocking chair

folding chair

223

HOUSE FURNITURE

PARTS

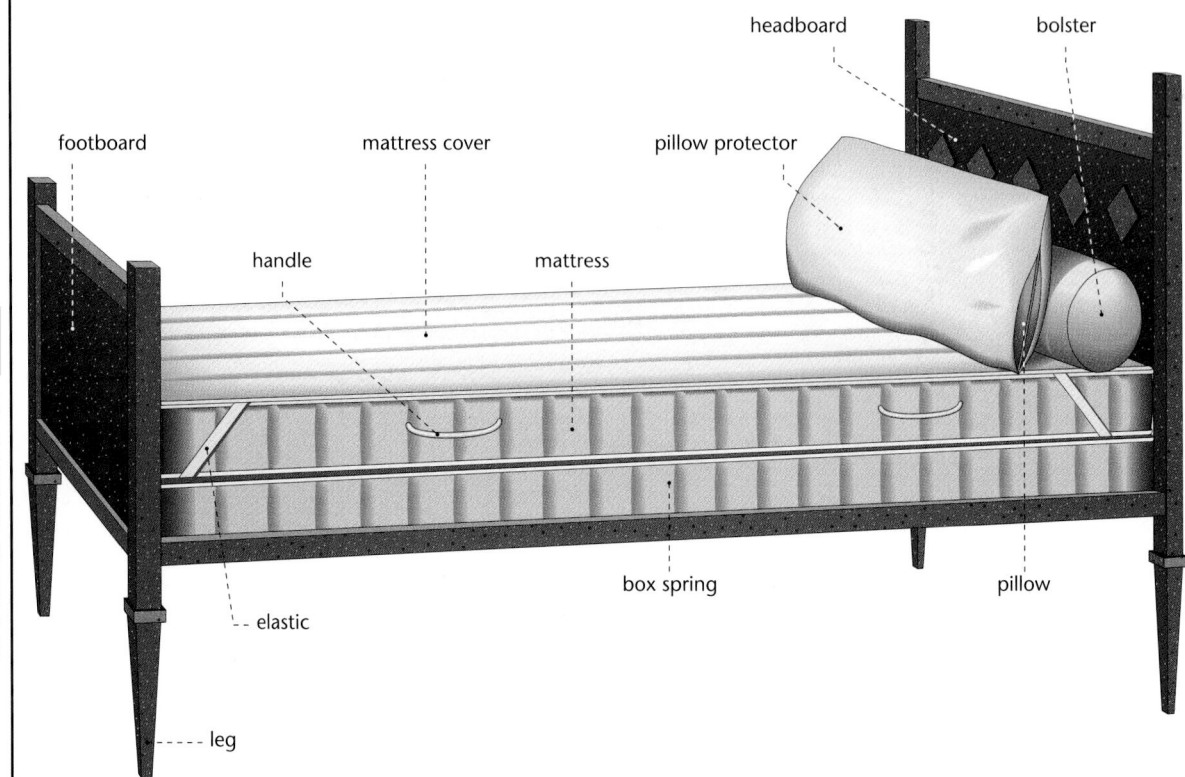

headboard

bolster

footboard

mattress cover

pillow protector

handle

mattress

box spring

pillow

elastic

leg

LINEN

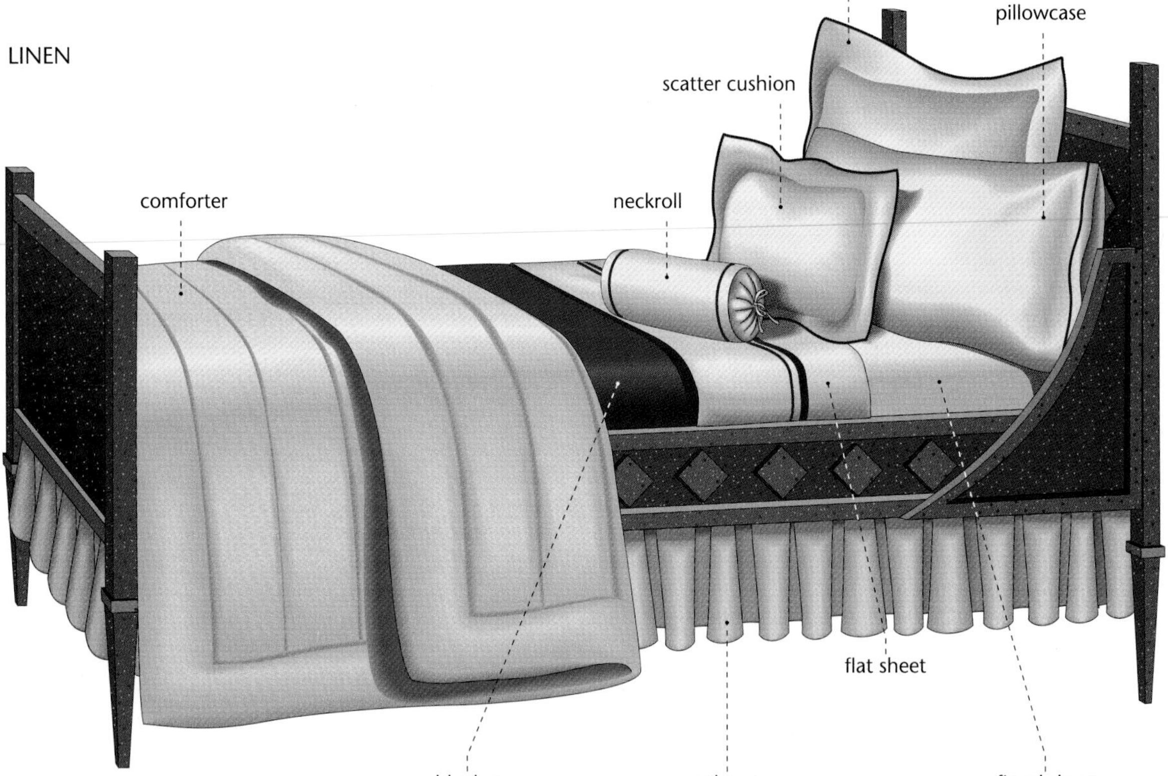

sham

pillowcase

scatter cushion

comforter

neckroll

blanket

valance

flat sheet

fitted sheet

ARMOIRE

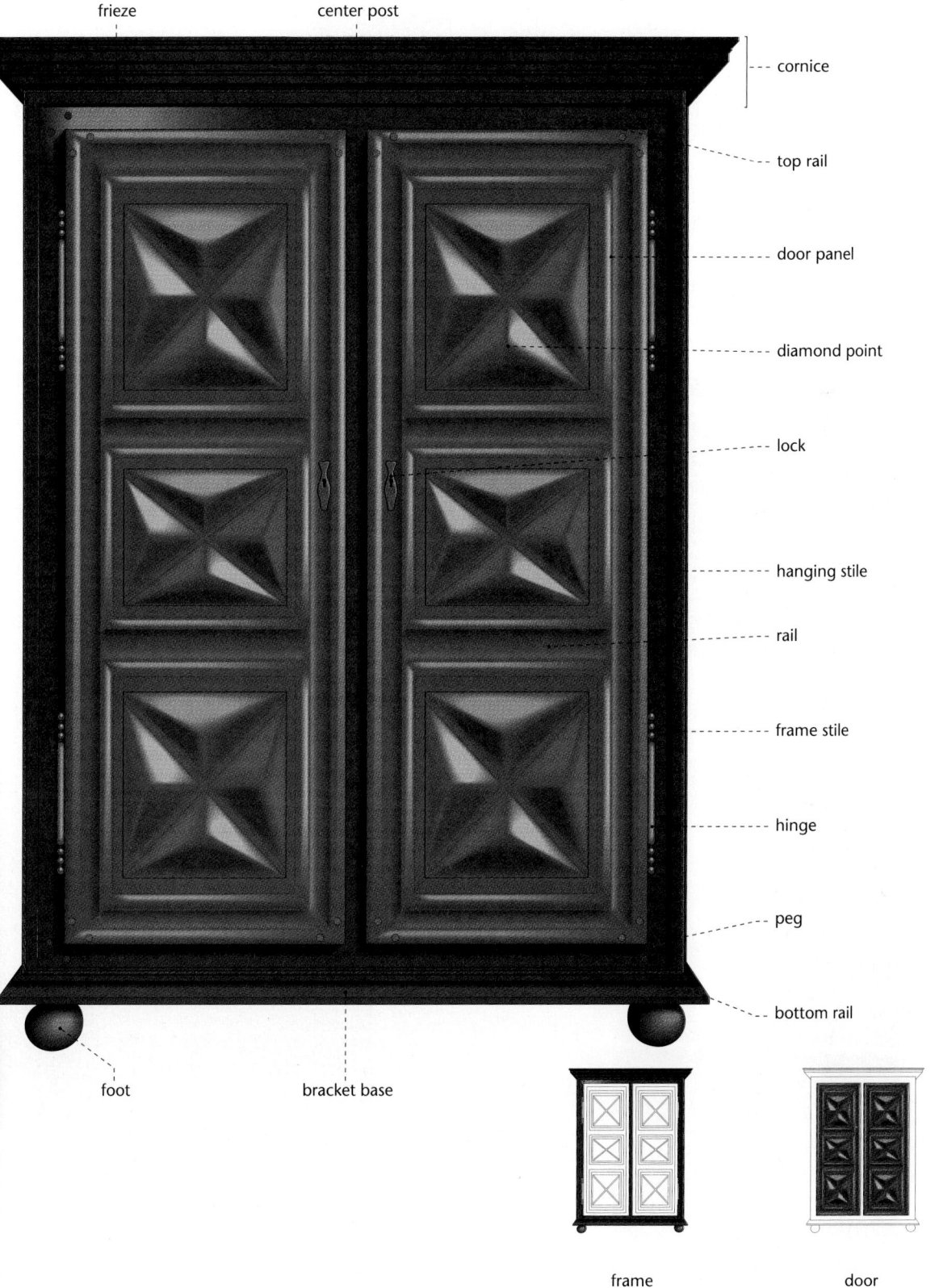

frieze

center post

cornice

top rail

door panel

diamond point

lock

hanging stile

rail

frame stile

hinge

peg

bottom rail

foot

bracket base

frame

door

linen chest

dresser

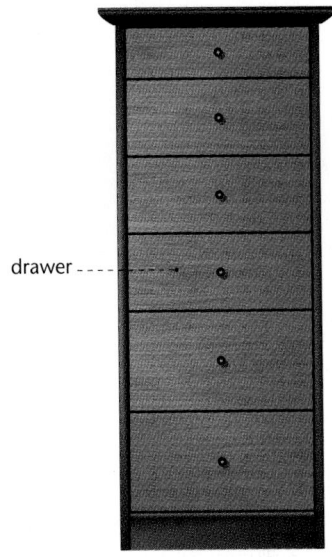

drawer

chiffonier

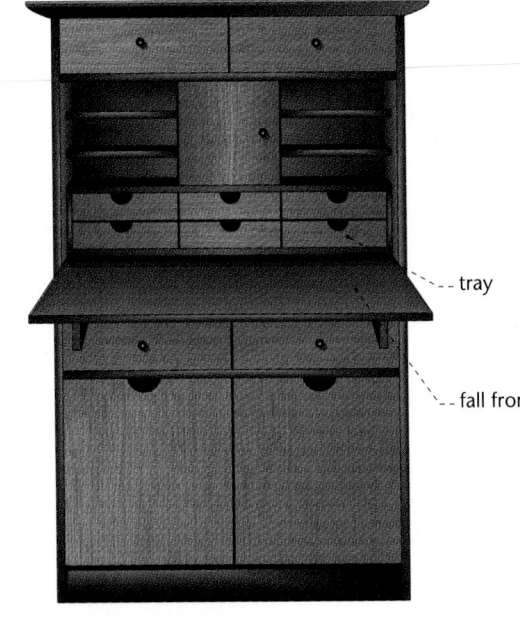

tray

fall front

secretary

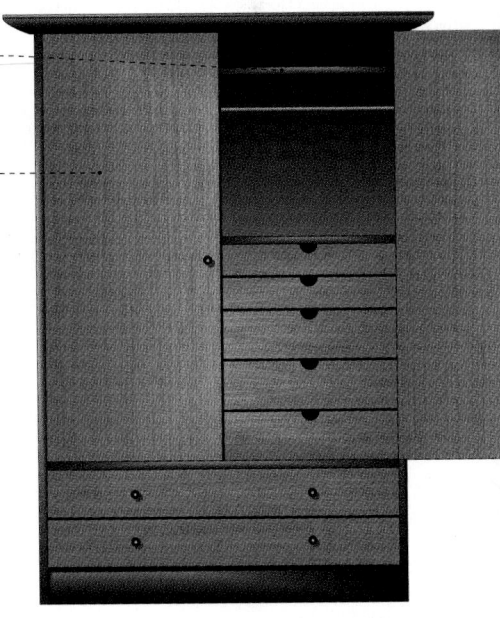

shelf

closet

wardrobe

display cabinet

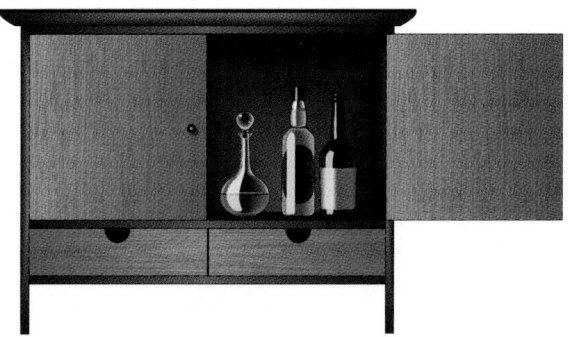

cocktail cabinet

glass-fronted display cabinet

corner cupboard

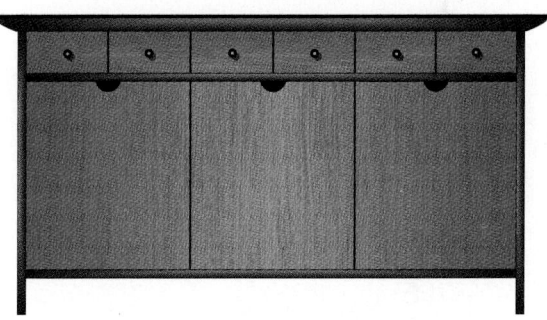

buffet

TYPES OF CURTAINS

HOUSE FURNITURE

GLASS CURTAIN

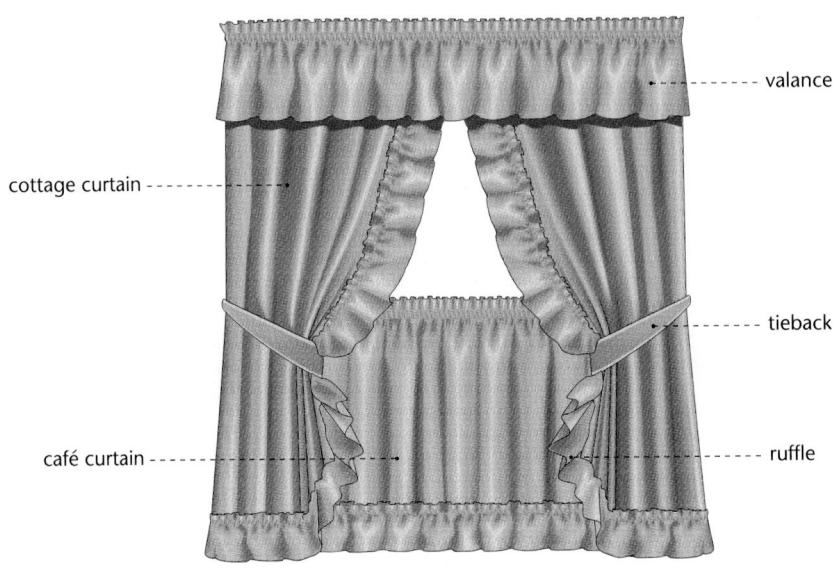

cottage curtain

café curtain

valance

tieback

ruffle

ATTACHED CURTAIN

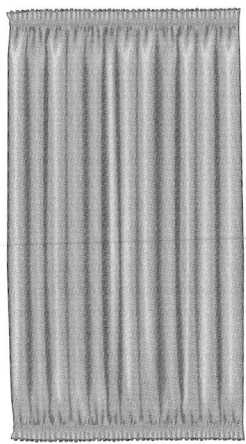

LOOSE CURTAIN

TYPES OF PLEATS

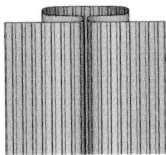

box pleat

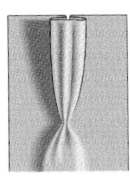

pinch pleat

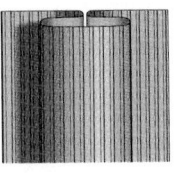

inverted pleat

CURTAIN

overdrapery

cornice

draw drapery

holdback

cord tieback

sheer curtain

tassel

BALLOON CURTAIN

CRISSCROSS CURTAINS

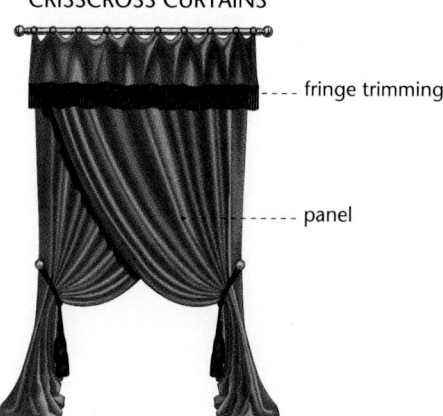

fringe trimming

panel

TYPES OF HEADINGS

draped swag

pencil pleat heading

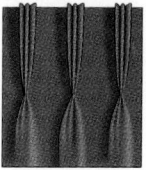

pleated heading

shirred heading

HOUSE FURNITURE

CURTAIN POLE

plain pole

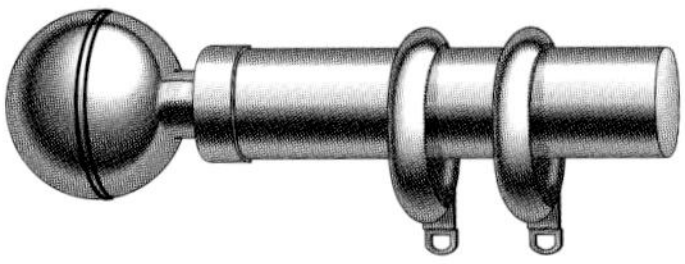

fluted pole

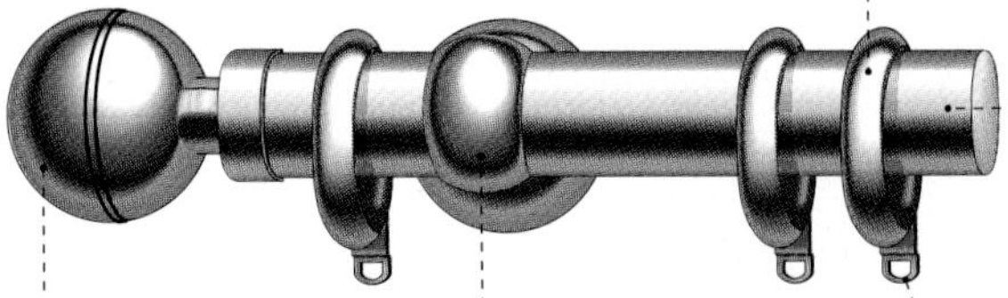

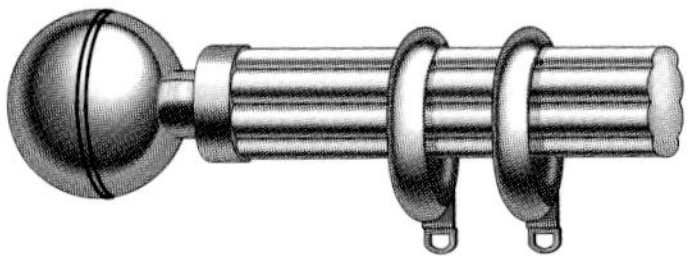

ring

pole

end cap

block bracket

eyelet

single curtain rod

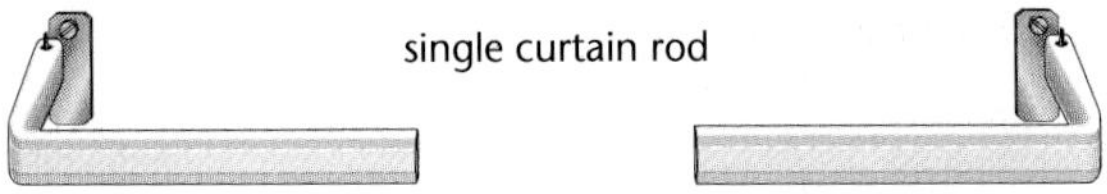

double curtain rod

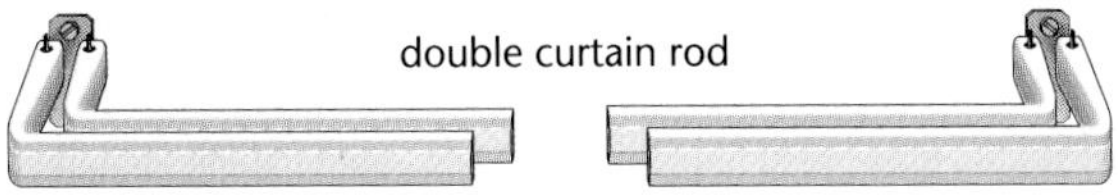

CURTAIN TRACK

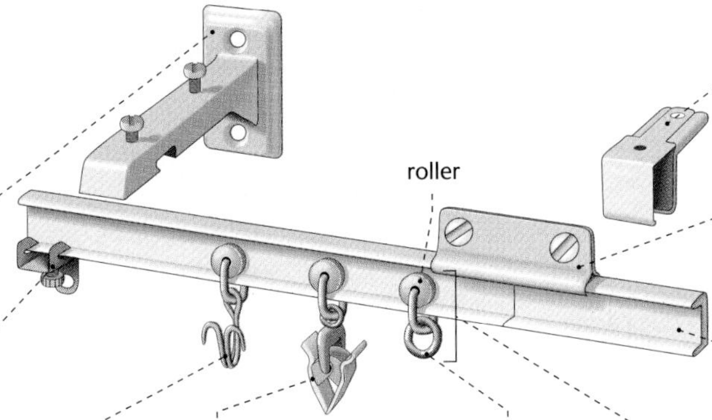

ceiling bracket

roller

bridge

wall bracket

track

end stop

ring

clip

carrier

hook

TRAVERSE ROD

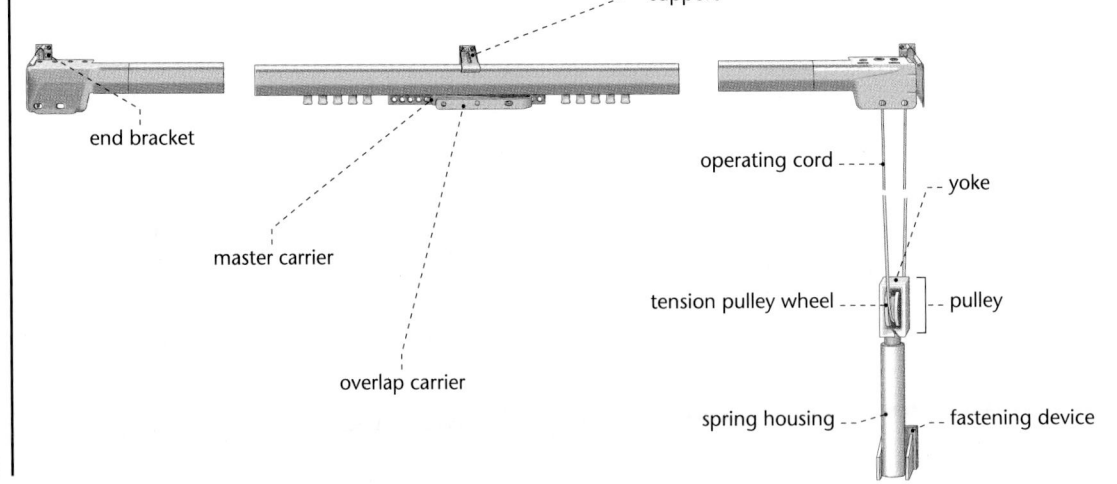

support

end bracket

operating cord

yoke

master carrier

tension pulley wheel

pulley

overlap carrier

spring housing

fastening device

ROLLER SHADE

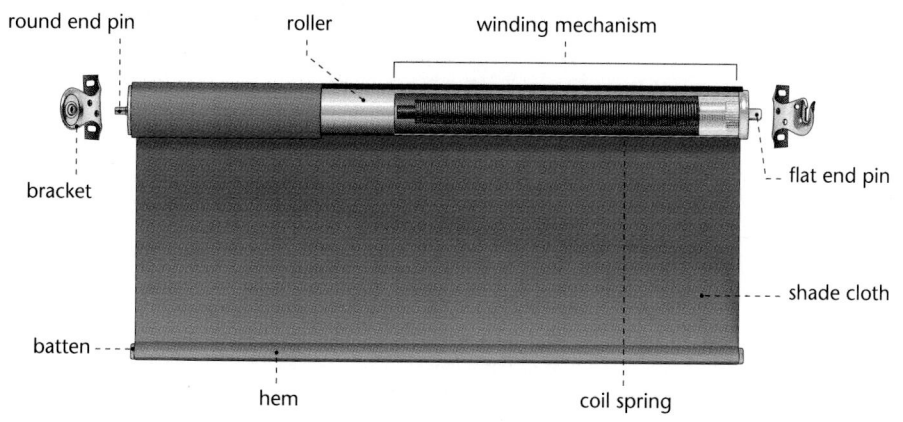

round end pin

roller

winding mechanism

bracket

flat end pin

batten

shade cloth

hem

coil spring

VENETIAN BLIND

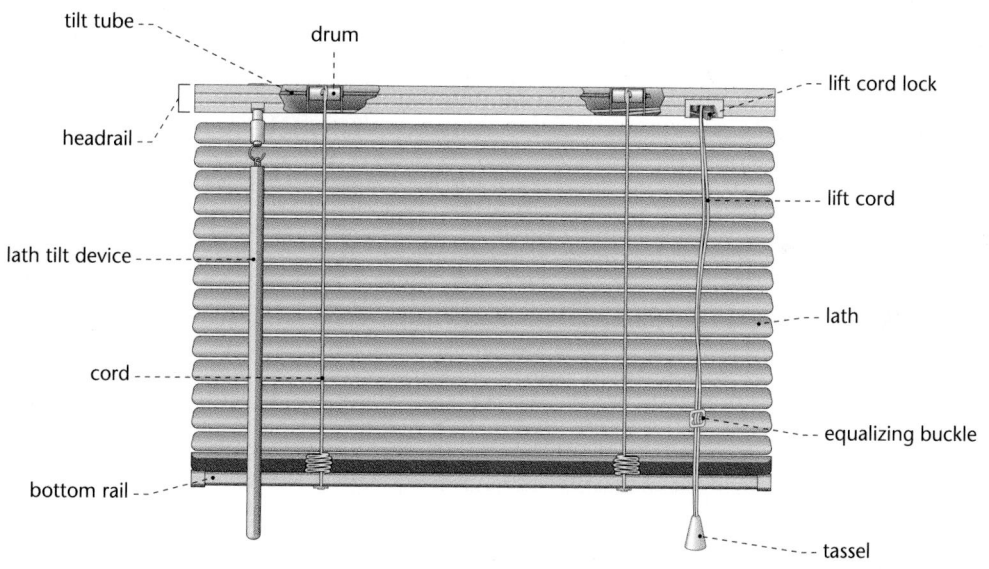

tilt tube

drum

lift cord lock

headrail

lath tilt device

lift cord

cord

lath

bottom rail

equalizing buckle

tassel

roll-up blind

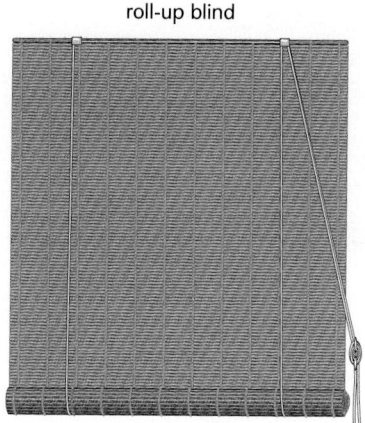

roman shade

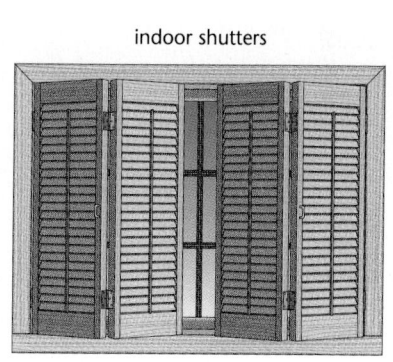

indoor shutters

231

LIGHTS

INCANDESCENT LAMP

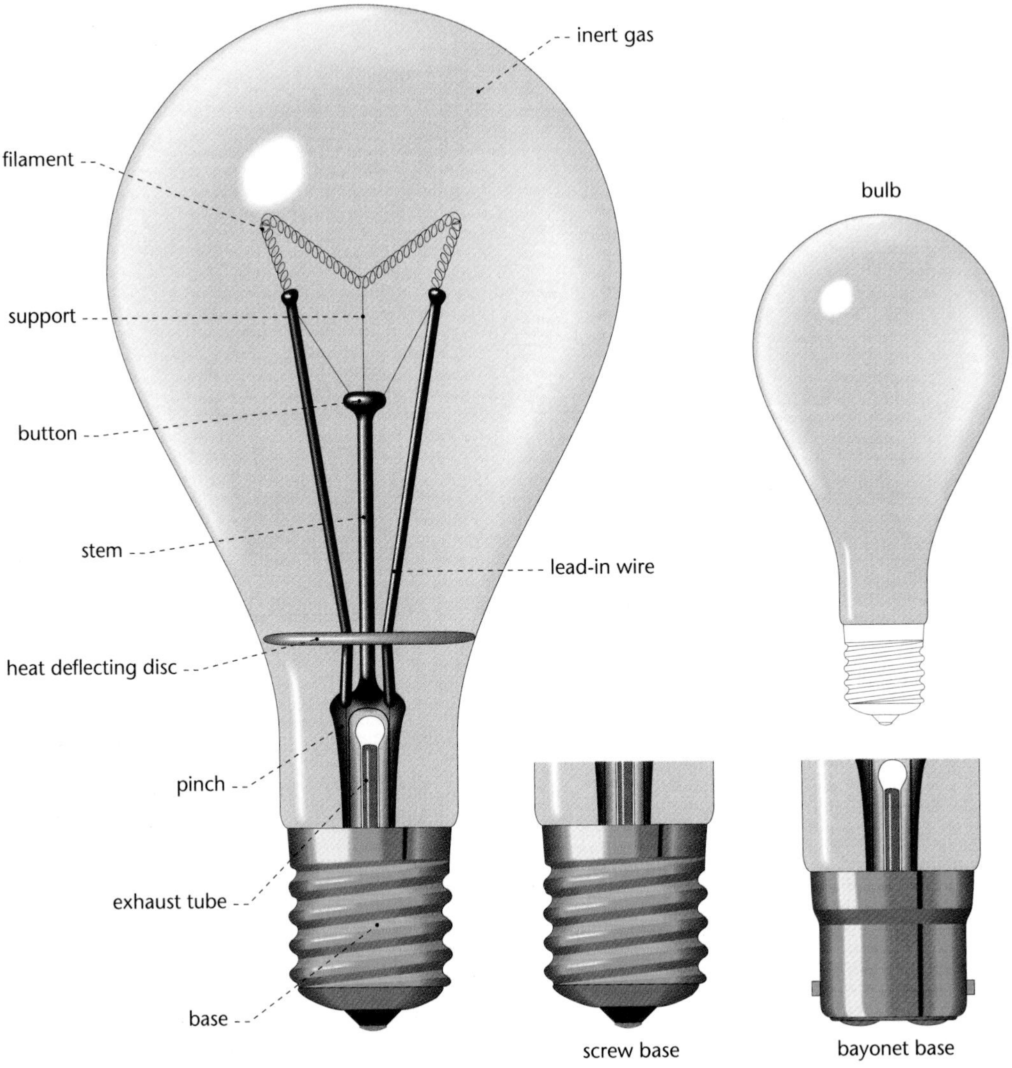

inert gas

filament

support

button

stem

lead-in wire

heat deflecting disc

pinch

exhaust tube

base

bulb

screw base

bayonet base

FLUORESCENT TUBE

pin base

phosphorescent coating

electrode

lead-in wire

exhaust tube

pinch

pin

bulb

gas

mercury

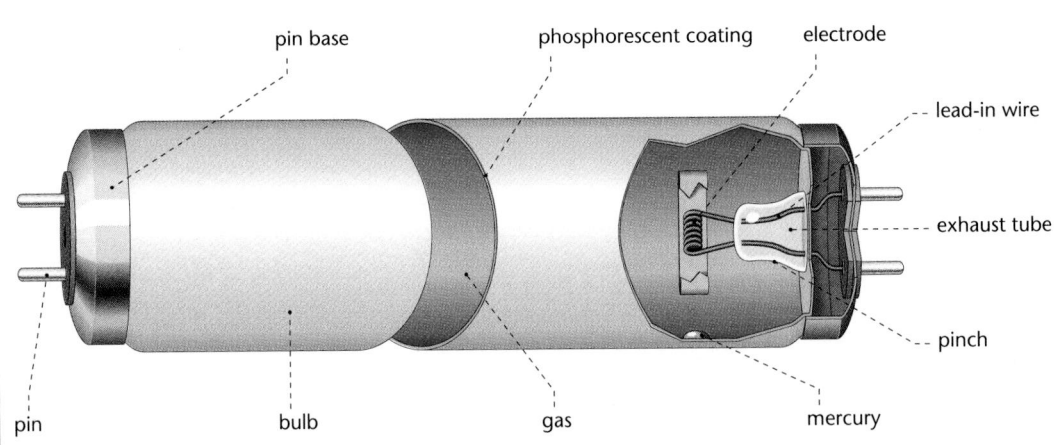

TRACK LIGHTING

bar frame

contact lever

transformer

spot

post lantern

clamp spotlight

wall lantern

strip light

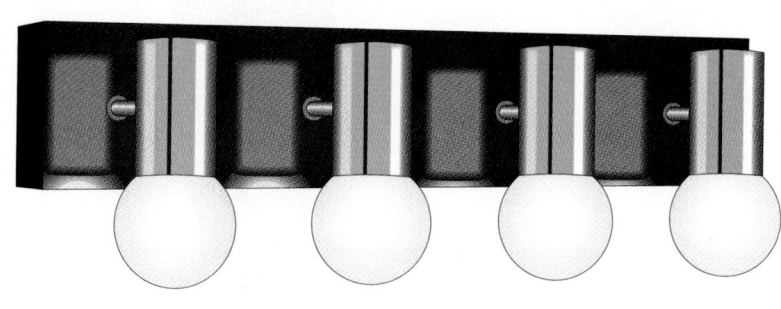

CHANDELIER

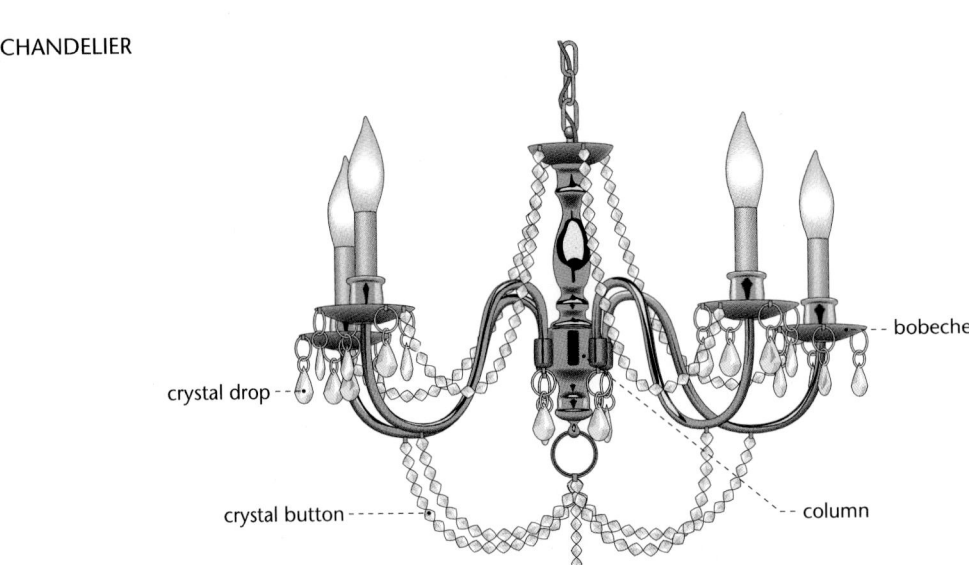

bobeche

crystal drop

crystal button

column

floor lamp

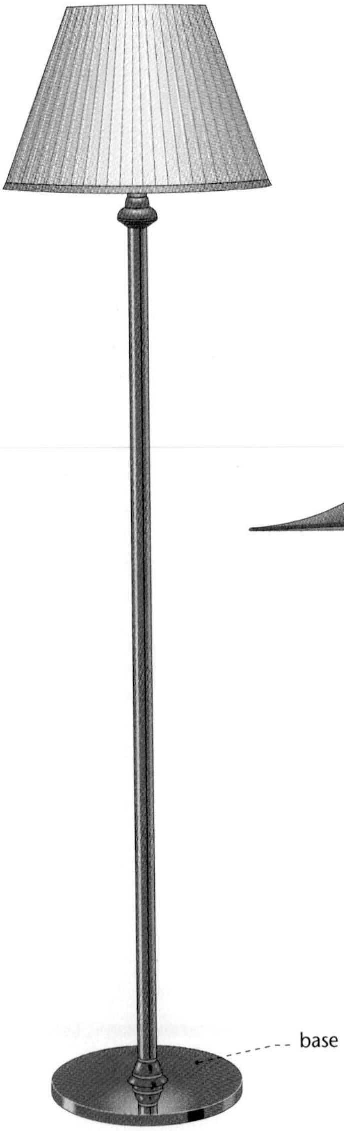

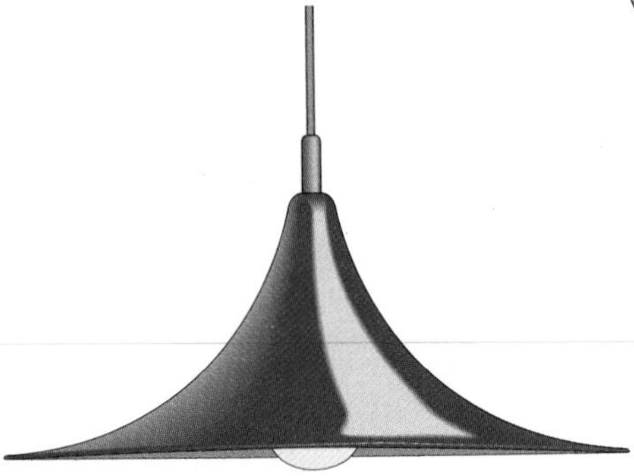

ceiling fitting

hanging pendant

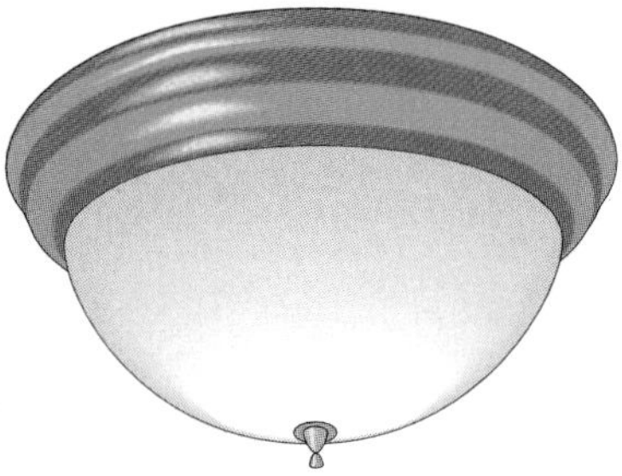

table lamp

shade

stand

base

GLASSWARE

port glass

sparkling wine glass

brandy snifter

liqueur glass

white wine glass

bordeaux glass

burgundy glass

Alsace glass

old-fashioned glass

highball glass

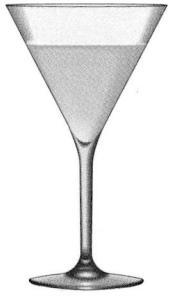

cocktail glass

water goblet

decanter

small decanter

champagne flute

beer mug

237

DINNERWARE

demitasse

cup

coffee mug

creamer

sugar bowl

pepper shaker

salt shaker

gravy boat

butter dish

ramekin

soup bowl

rim soup bowl

dinner plate

salad plate

bread and butter plate

teapot

platter

vegetable bowl

fish platter

hors d'oeuvre dish

water pitcher

salad bowl

serving bowl

soup tureen

SILVERWARE

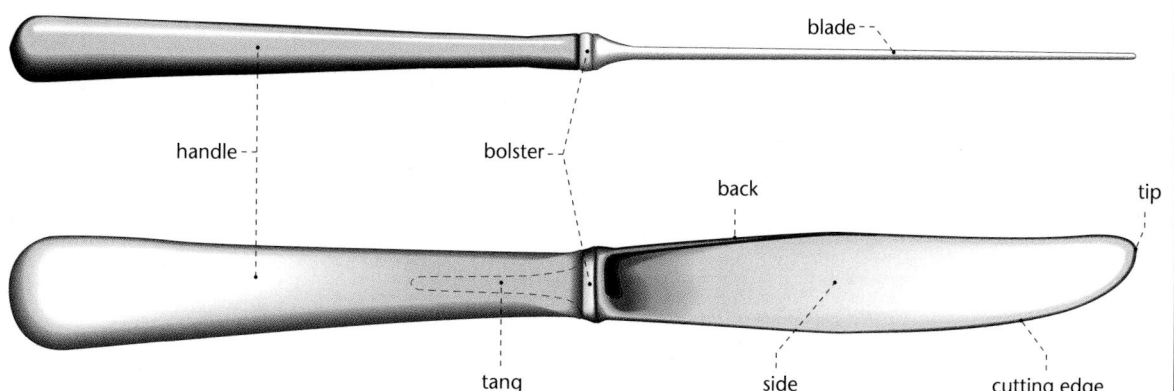

handle —   bolster —   blade - - -

back   tip

tang   side   cutting edge

HOUSE FURNITURE

MAJOR TYPES OF KNIVES

butter knife

dessert knife

fish knife

cheese knife

dinner knife

steak knife

239

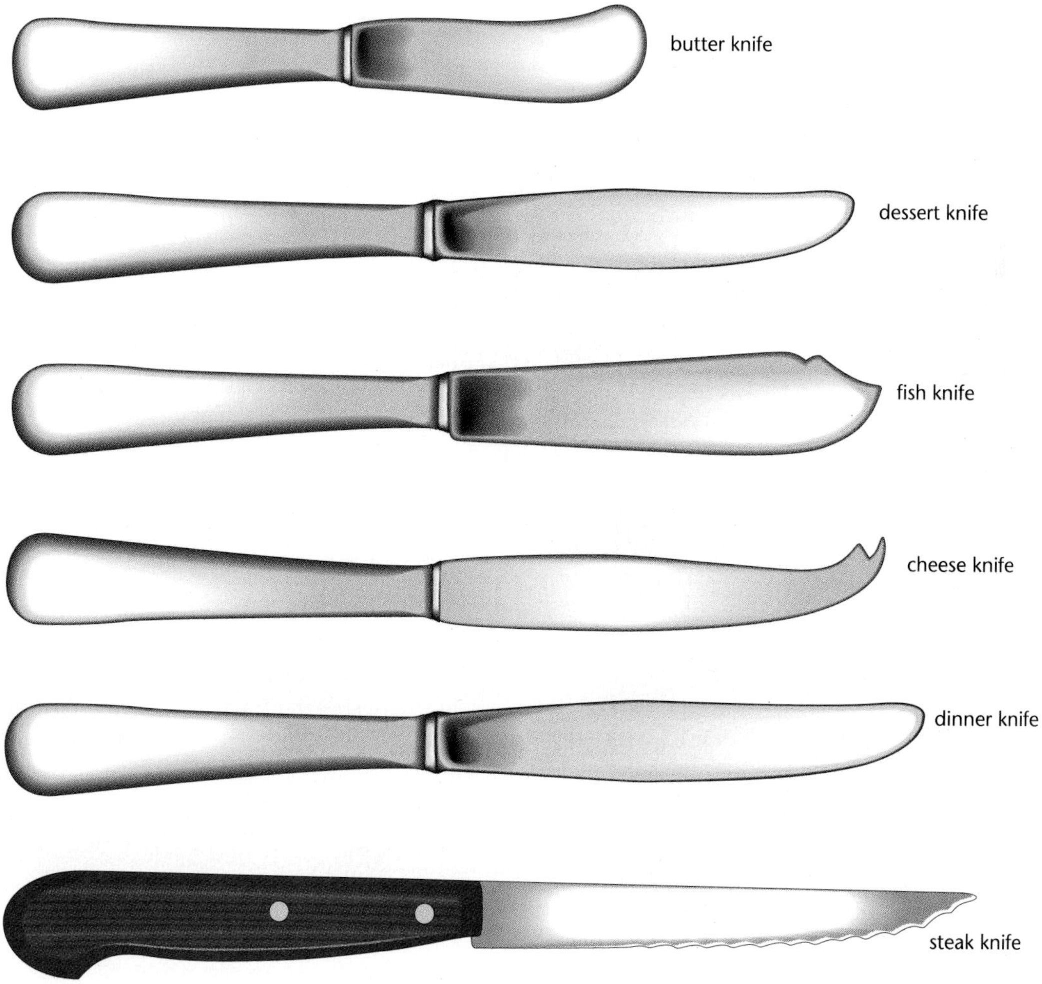

HOUSE FURNITURE

FORK

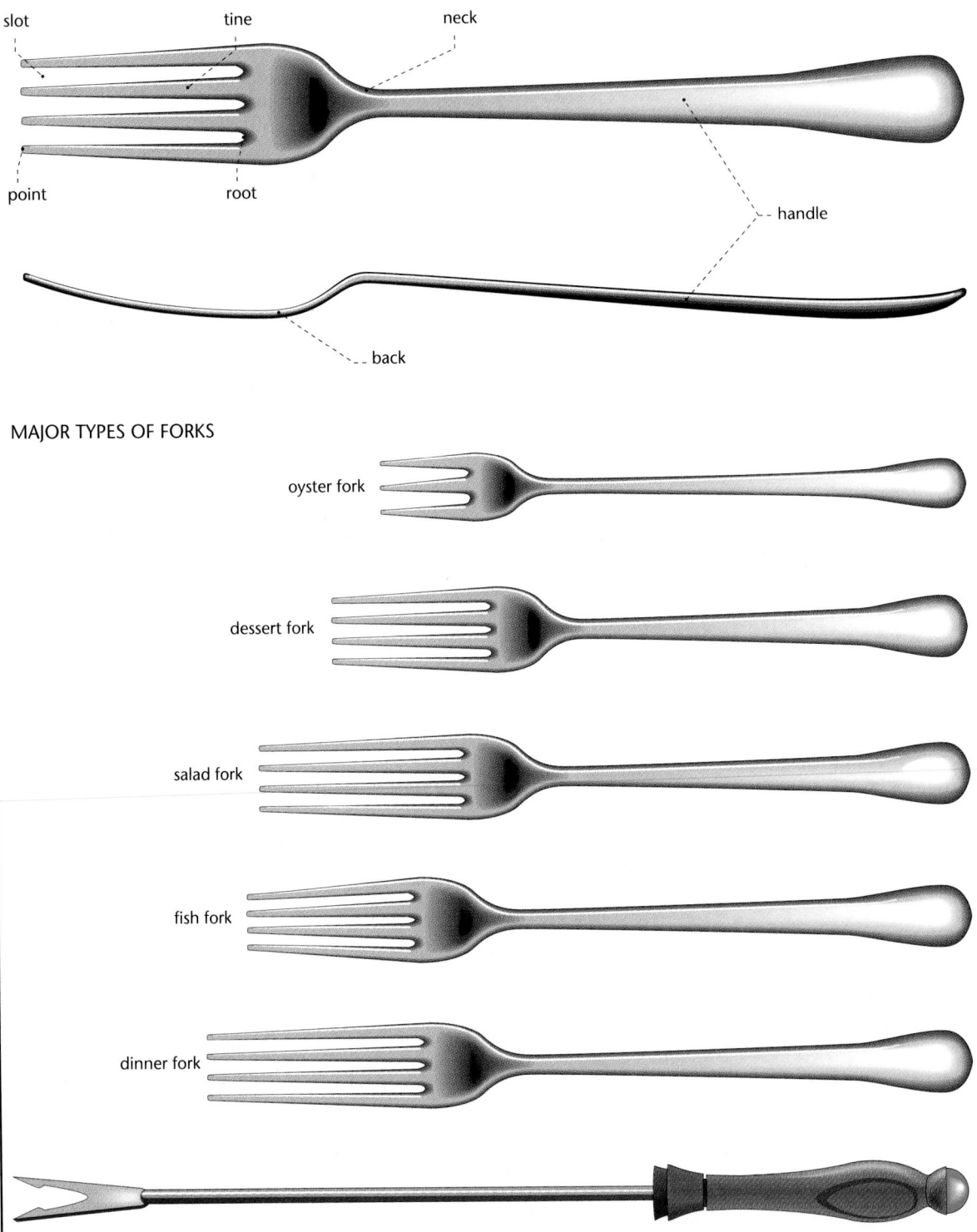

slot

tine

neck

point

root

handle

back

MAJOR TYPES OF FORKS

oyster fork

dessert fork

salad fork

fish fork

dinner fork

fondue fork

SPOON

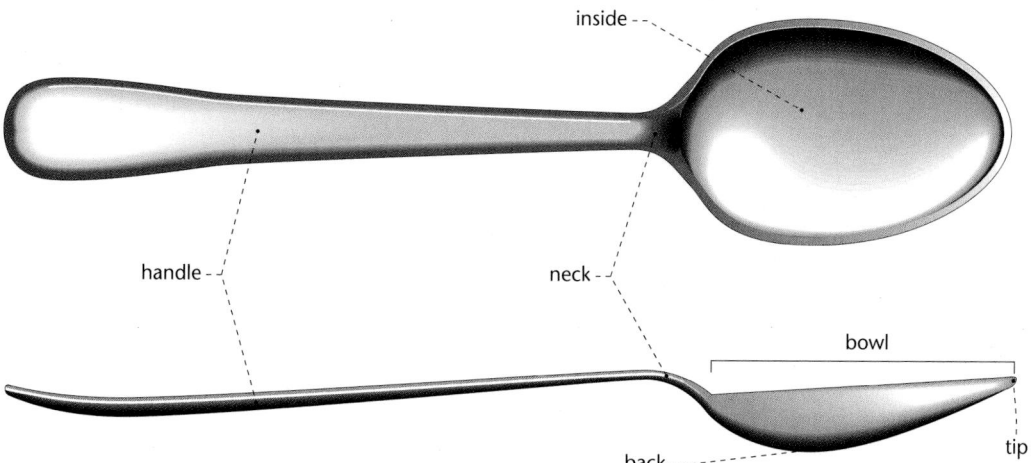

inside
handle
neck
bowl
back
tip

MAJOR TYPES OF SPOONS

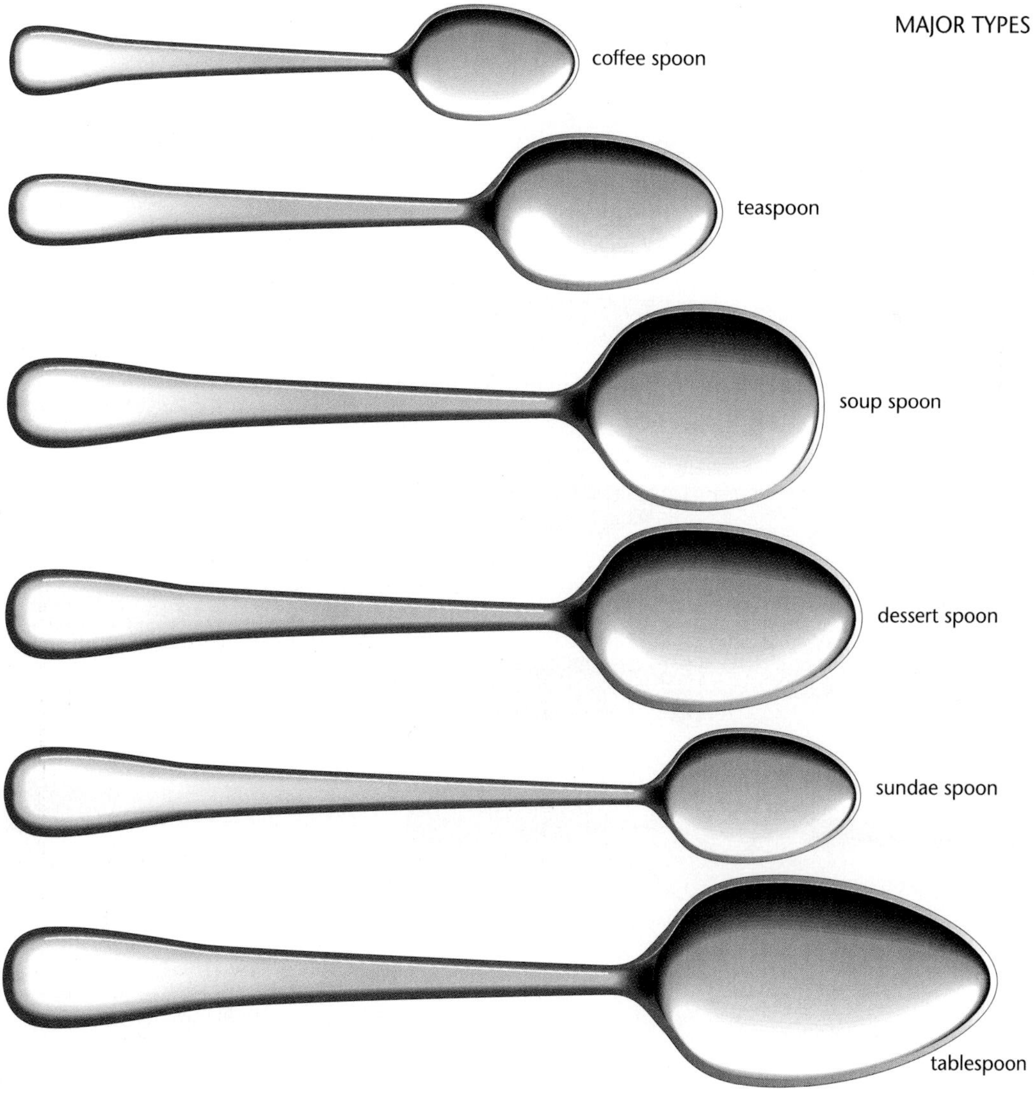

coffee spoon
teaspoon
soup spoon
dessert spoon
sundae spoon
tablespoon

KITCHEN UTENSILS

KITCHEN KNIFE

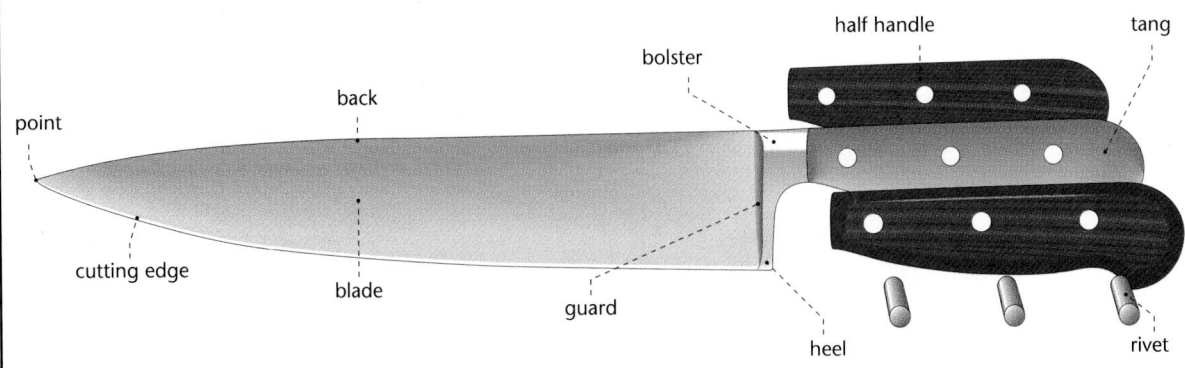

point · back · bolster · half handle · tang · cutting edge · blade · guard · heel · rivet

TYPES OF KITCHEN KNIVES

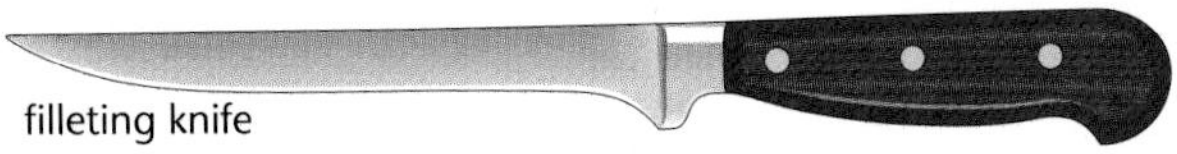

filleting knife

cleaver

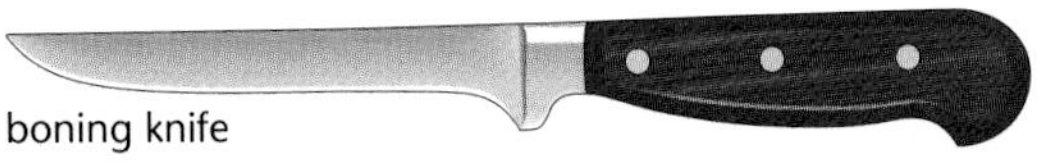

boning knife

bread knife

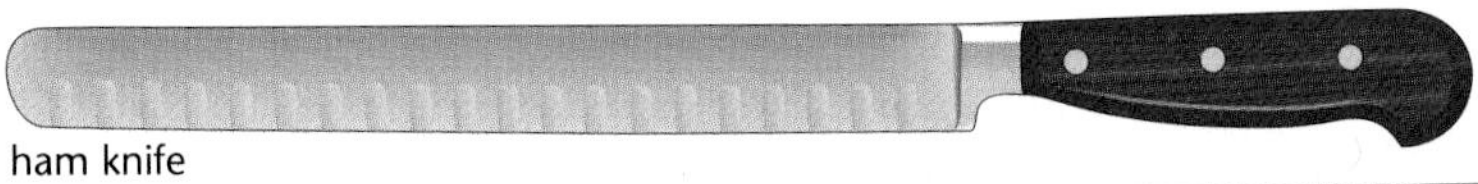

ham knife

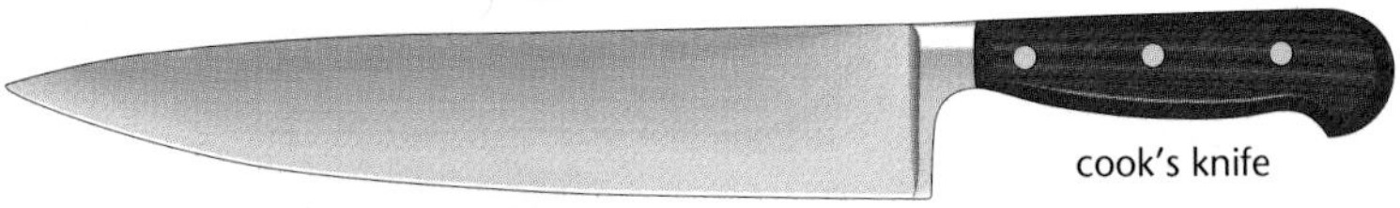

cook's knife

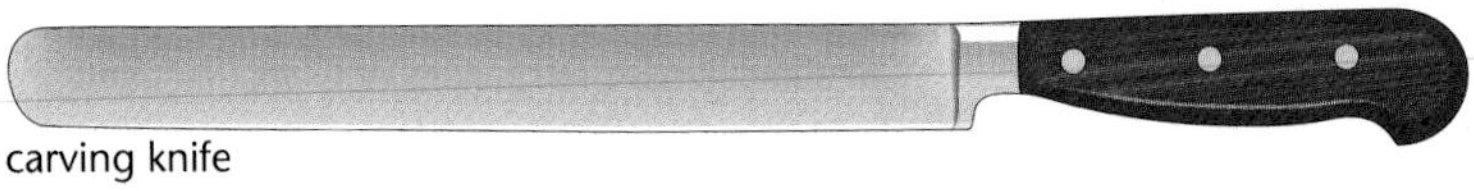

carving knife

carving fork

sharpening steel

grapefruit knife

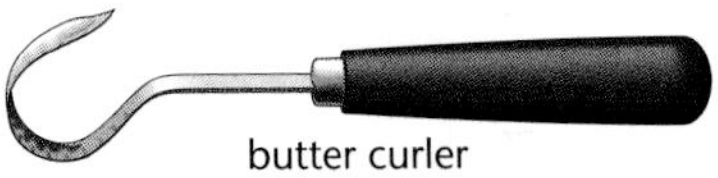

butter curler

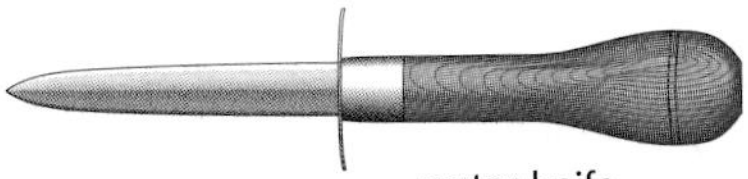

oyster knife

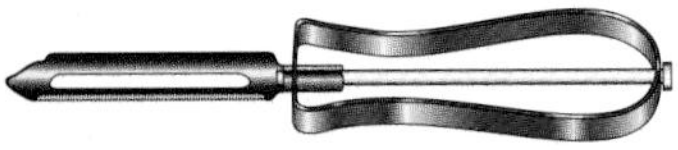

peeler

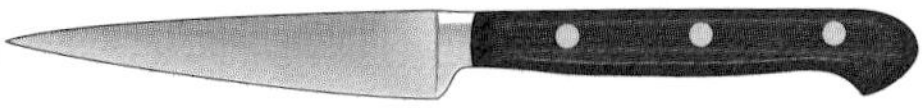

paring knife

zester

funnel

colander

strainer

salad spinner

FOR GRINDING AND GRATING

pestle

mortar

nutcracker

garlic press

citrus juicer

meat grinder

grater

pasta maker

KITCHEN UTENSILS

SET OF UTENSILS

ladle

potato masher

turner

spatula

draining spoon

skimmer

FOR OPENING

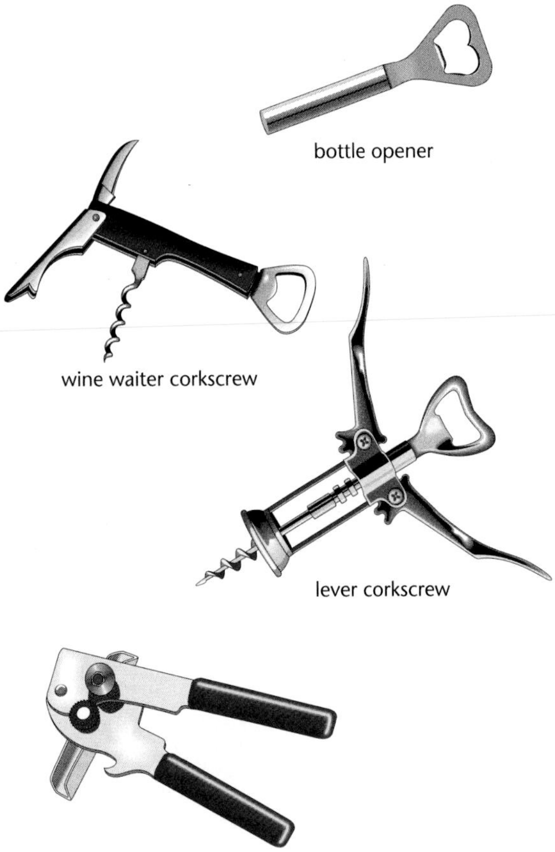

bottle opener

wine waiter corkscrew

lever corkscrew

can opener

kitchen timer

meat thermometer

kitchen scale

FOR MEASURING

egg timer

measuring spoons

measuring cups

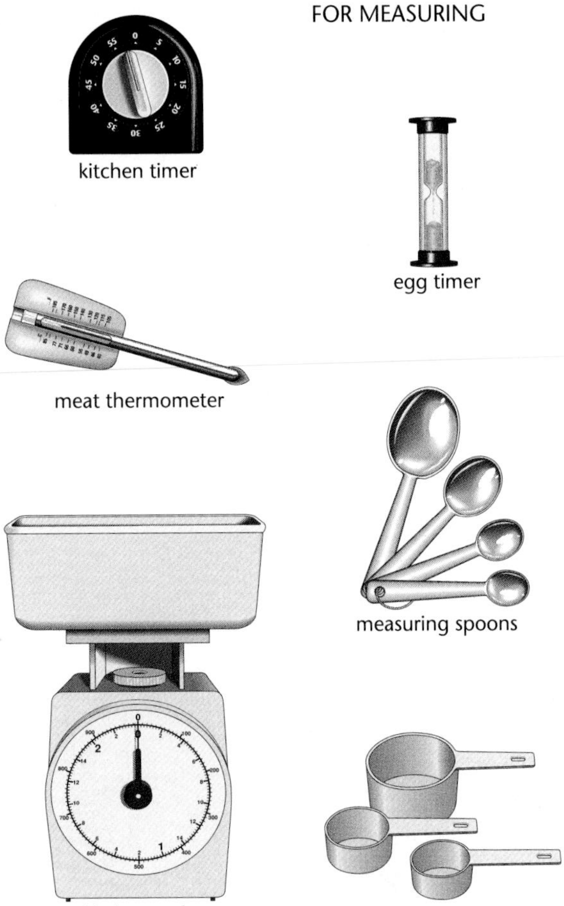

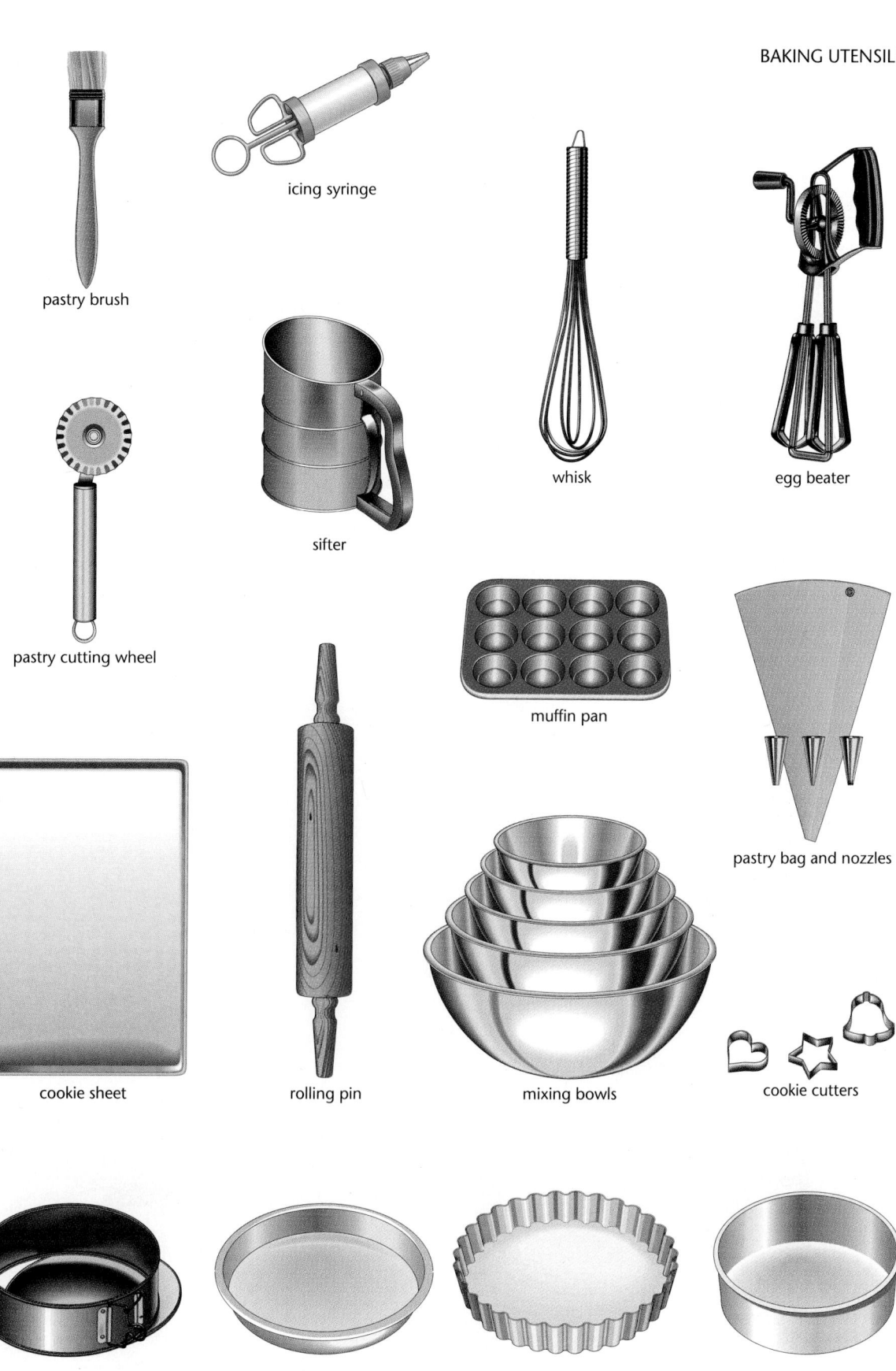

pastry brush

icing syringe

whisk

egg beater

pastry cutting wheel

sifter

muffin pan

pastry bag and nozzles

cookie sheet

rolling pin

mixing bowls

cookie cutters

removable-bottomed pan

pie pan

quiche plate

cake pan

HOUSE FURNITURE

MISCELLANEOUS UTENSILS

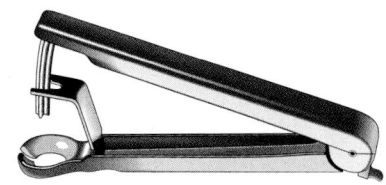

stoner

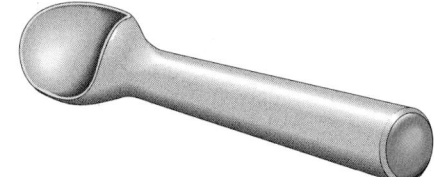

ice cream scoop

poultry shears

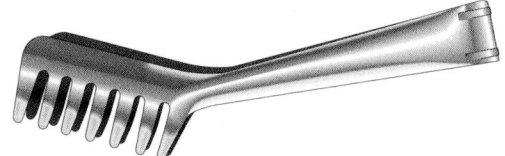

spaghetti tongs

baster

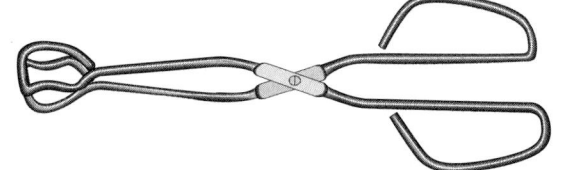

tongs

vegetable brush

tea ball

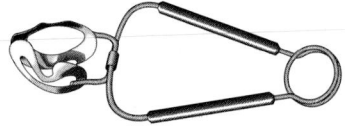

snail tongs

dredger

egg slicer

snail dish

COFFEE MAKERS

AUTOMATIC DRIP COFFEE MAKER

lid

reservoir

basket

water level

signal lamp

carafe

on-off switch

warming plate

PERCOLATOR

spout

signal lamp

VACUUM COFFEE MAKER

upper bowl

stem

lower bowl

plunger

Neapolitan coffee maker

espresso coffee maker

247

COOKING UTENSILS

WOK SET

lid

rack

wok

burner ring

FISH POACHER

rack

lid

FONDUE SET

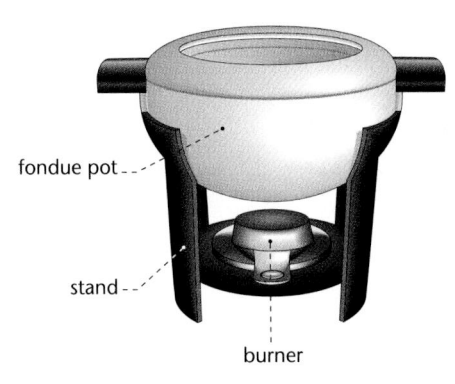

fondue pot

stand

burner

roasting pans

PRESSURE COOKER

pressure regulator

safety valve

Dutch oven

stock pot

frying pan

pancake pan

couscous kettle

egg poacher

sauté pan

vegetable steamer

double boiler

saucepan

BLENDER

cap

container

cutting blade

motor unit

push button

HAND MIXER

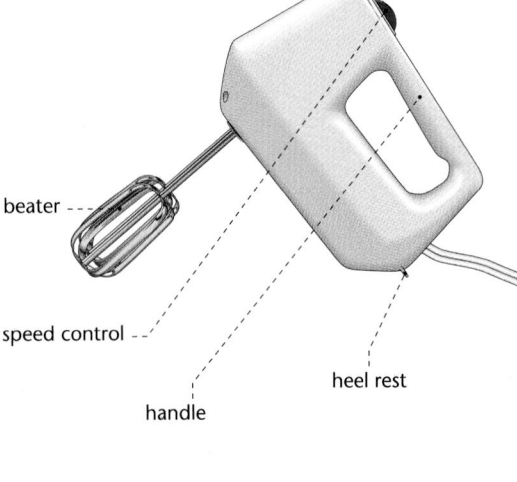

beater ejector

beater

speed control

handle

heel rest

HAND BLENDER

motor unit

blending attachment

TABLE MIXER

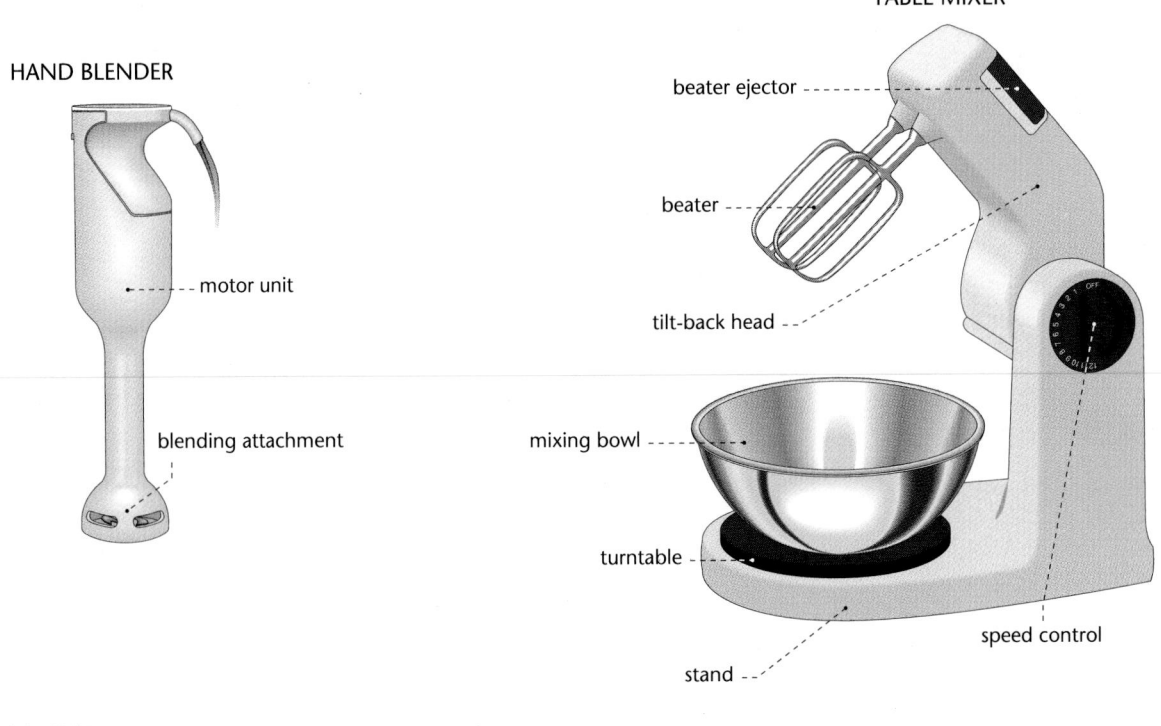

beater ejector

beater

tilt-back head

mixing bowl

turntable

stand

speed control

BEATERS

four blade beater

spiral beater

wire beater

dough hook

FOOD PROCESSOR

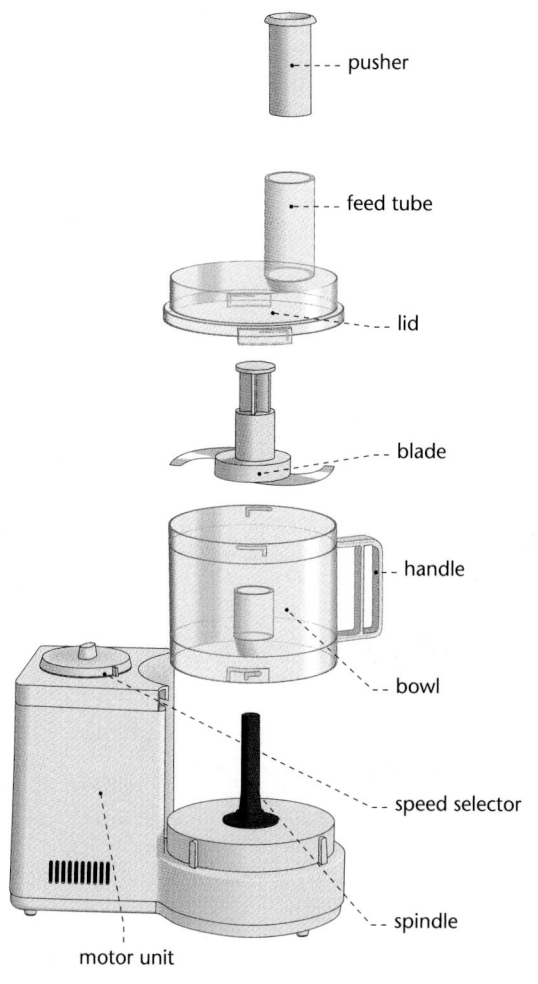

pusher

feed tube

lid

blade

handle

bowl

speed selector

spindle

motor unit

disks

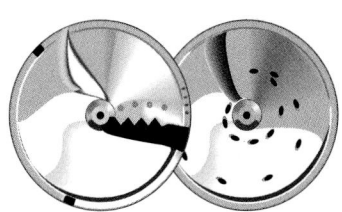

CITRUS JUICER

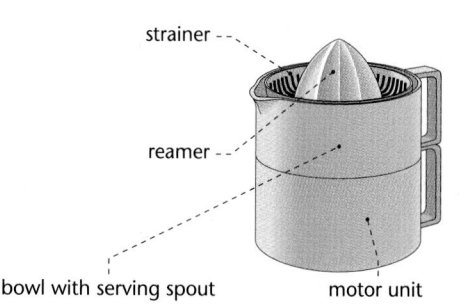

strainer

reamer

bowl with serving spout

motor unit

JUICER

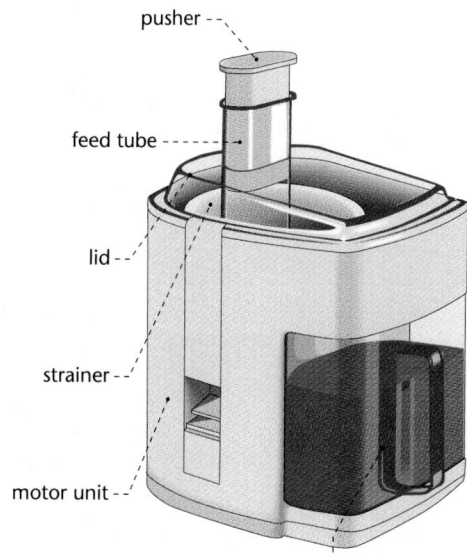

pusher

feed tube

lid

strainer

motor unit

bowl

ICE CREAM FREEZER

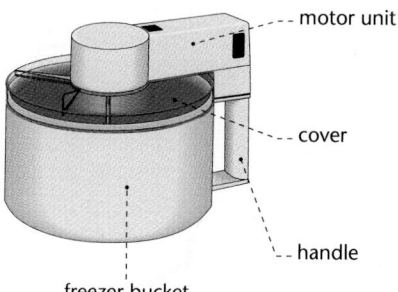

motor unit

cover

handle

freezer bucket

KETTLE

handle

whistle

signal lamp

spout

body

base

TOASTER

slot

bread guide

lever

handle

temperature control

DEEP FRYER

basket

rack

lid

timer

filter

thermostat

signal lamp

WAFFLE IRON

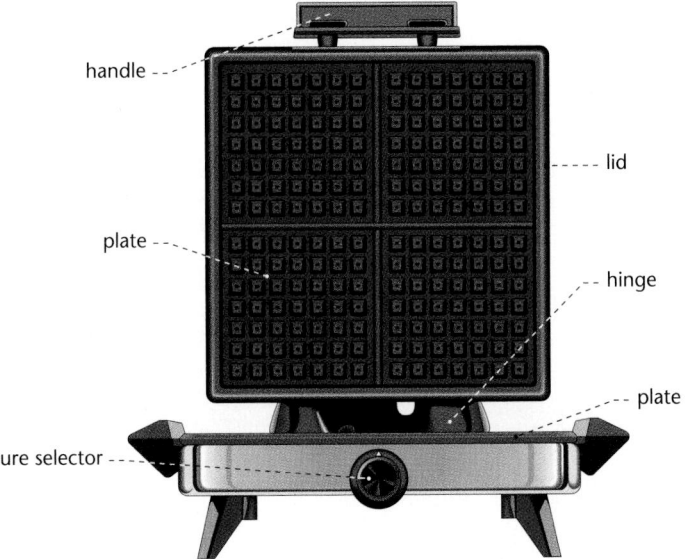

handle

lid

plate

hinge

plate

temperature selector

MICROWAVE OVEN

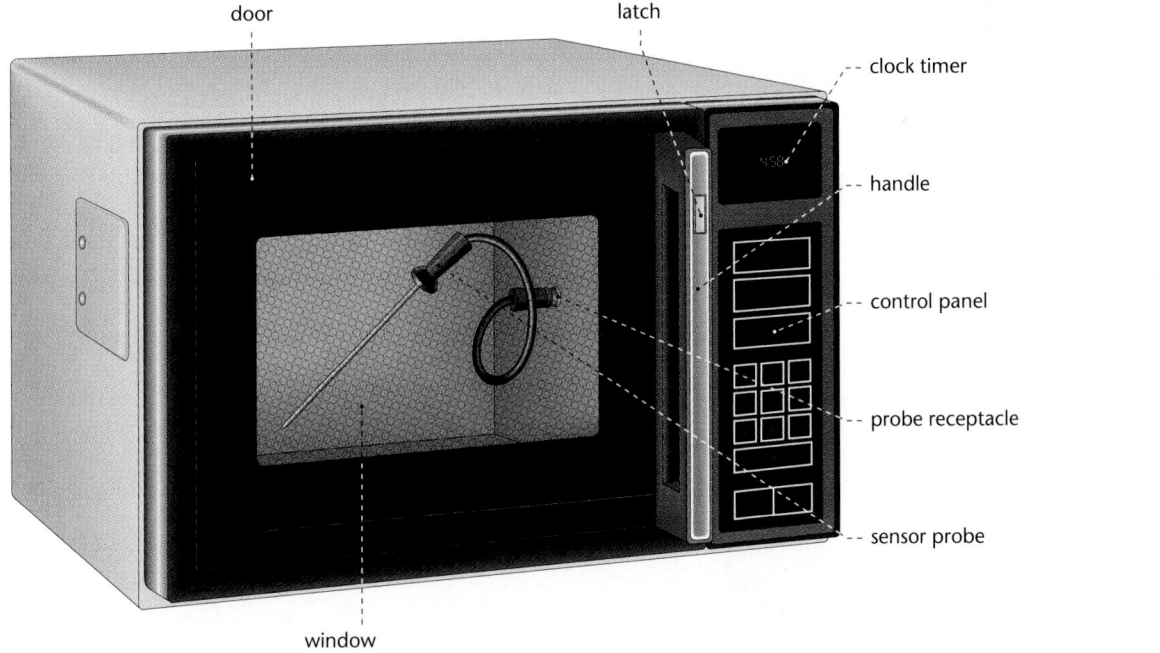

door

latch

clock timer

handle

control panel

probe receptacle

sensor probe

window

GRIDDLE

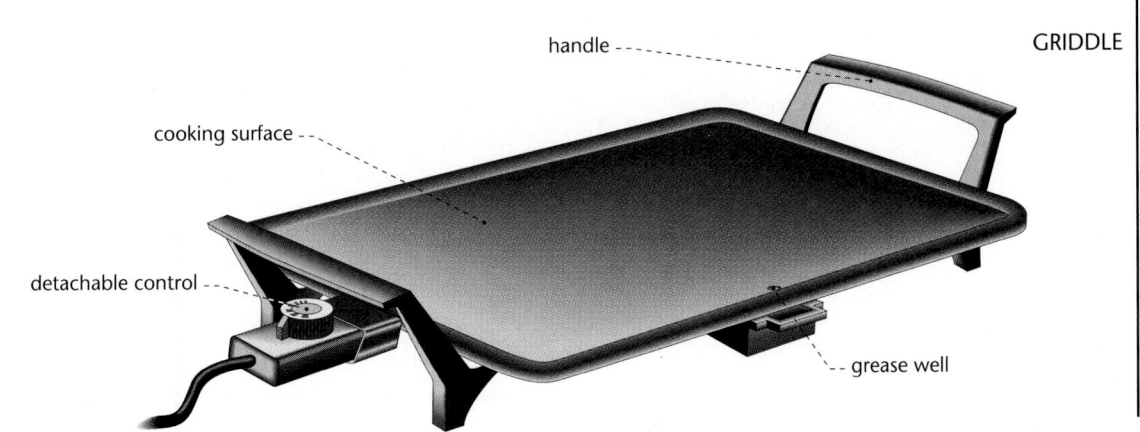

handle

cooking surface

detachable control

grease well

253

REFRIGERATOR

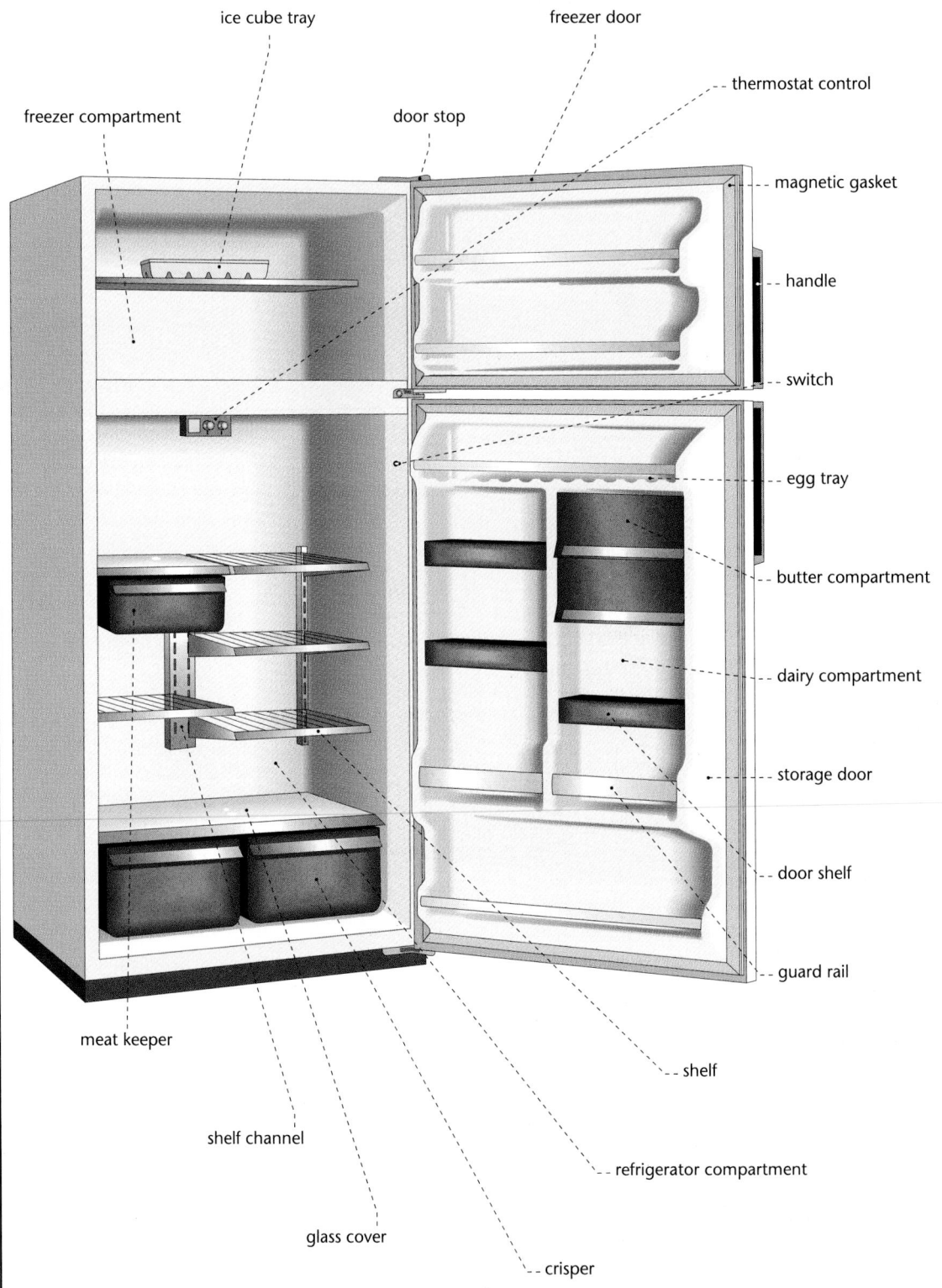

ice cube tray

freezer door

thermostat control

freezer compartment

door stop

magnetic gasket

handle

switch

egg tray

butter compartment

dairy compartment

storage door

door shelf

guard rail

meat keeper

shelf

shelf channel

refrigerator compartment

glass cover

crisper

RANGE HOOD

filter

ELECTRIC RANGE

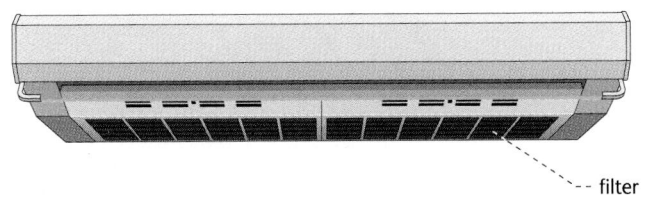

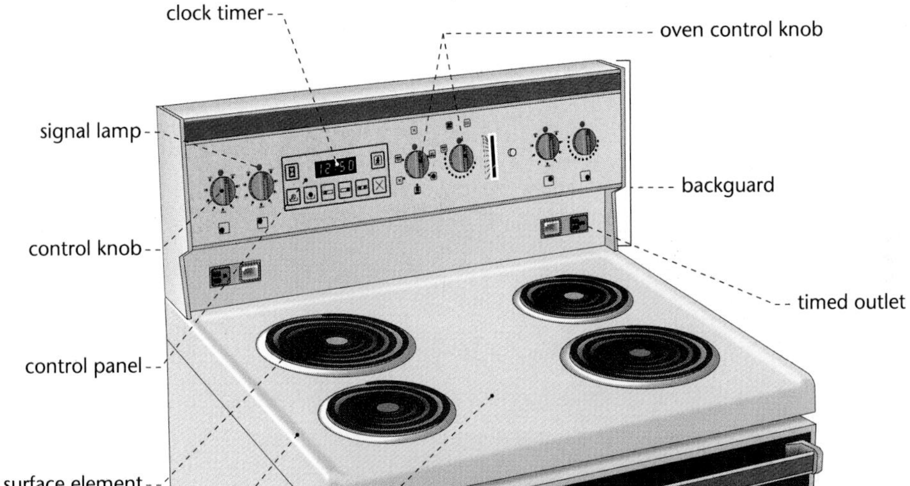

clock timer

oven control knob

signal lamp

backguard

control knob

timed outlet

control panel

surface element

oven

cooktop edge

rack

cooktop

window

handle

drawer

trim ring

drip bowl

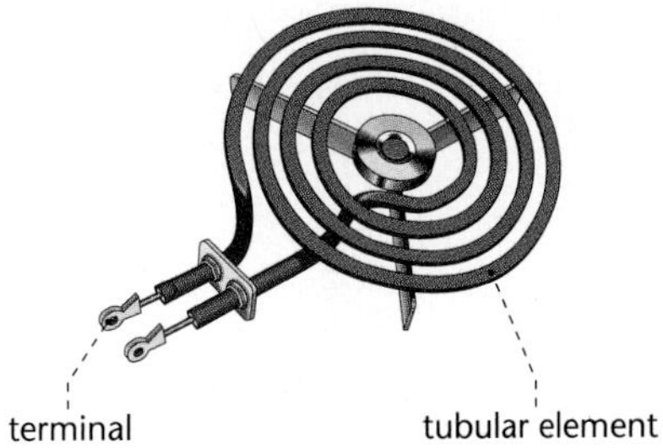

terminal

tubular element

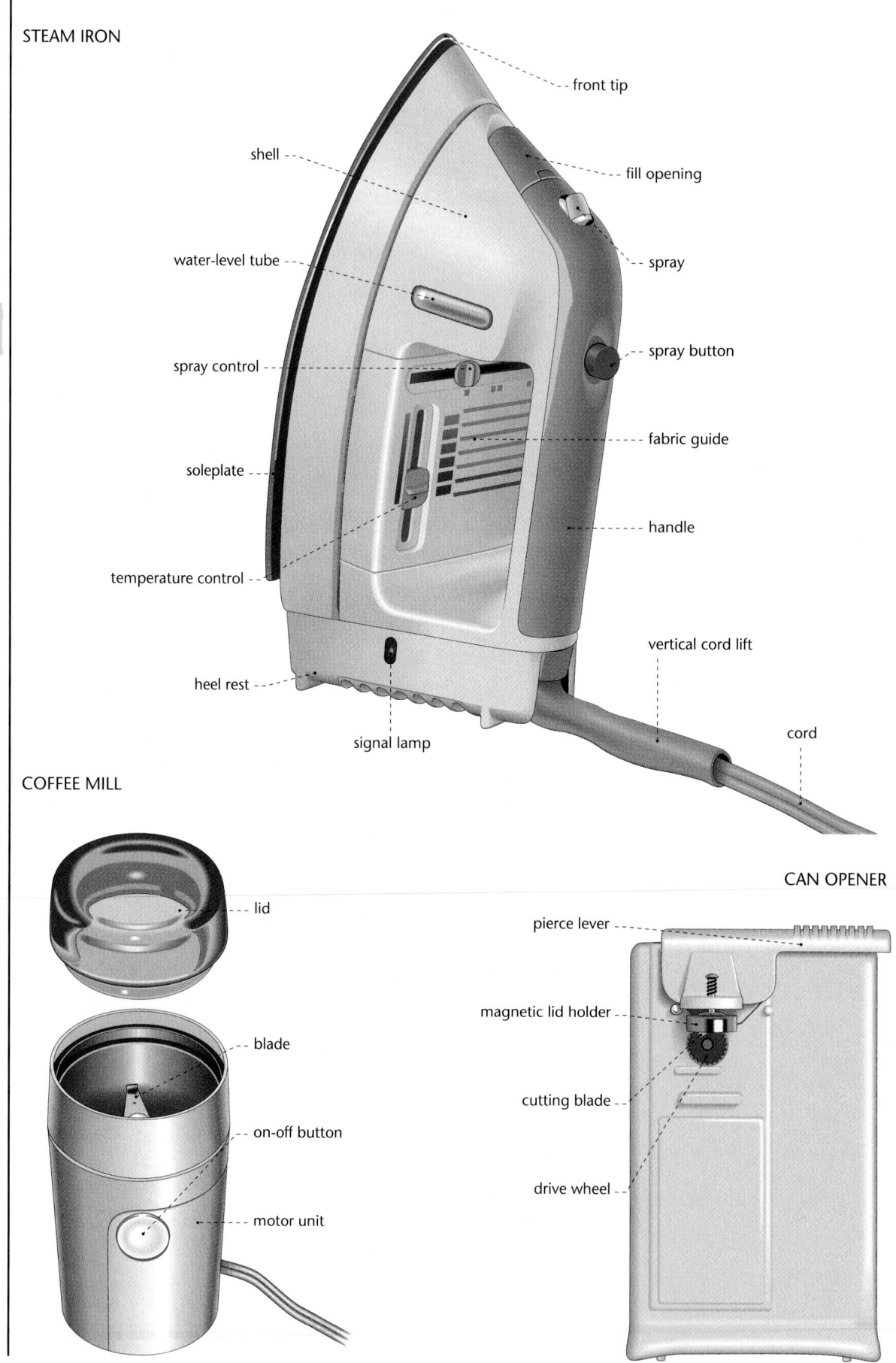

STEAM IRON

front tip

shell

fill opening

water-level tube

spray

spray button

spray control

fabric guide

soleplate

handle

temperature control

vertical cord lift

heel rest

cord

signal lamp

COFFEE MILL

lid

blade

on-off button

motor unit

CAN OPENER

pierce lever

magnetic lid holder

cutting blade

drive wheel

HOUSE FURNITURE

DOMESTIC APPLIANCES

CONTROL PANEL

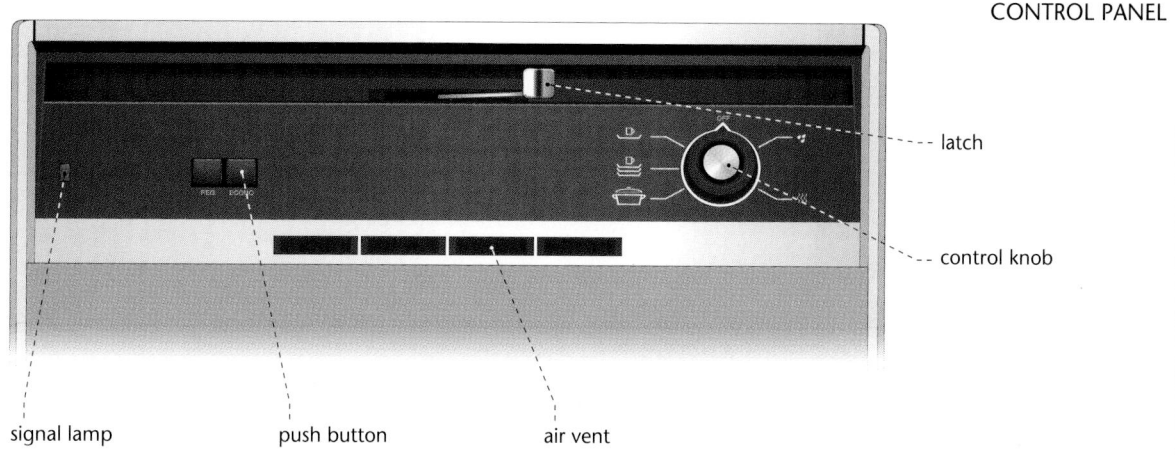

latch

control knob

signal lamp   push button   air vent

DISHWASHER

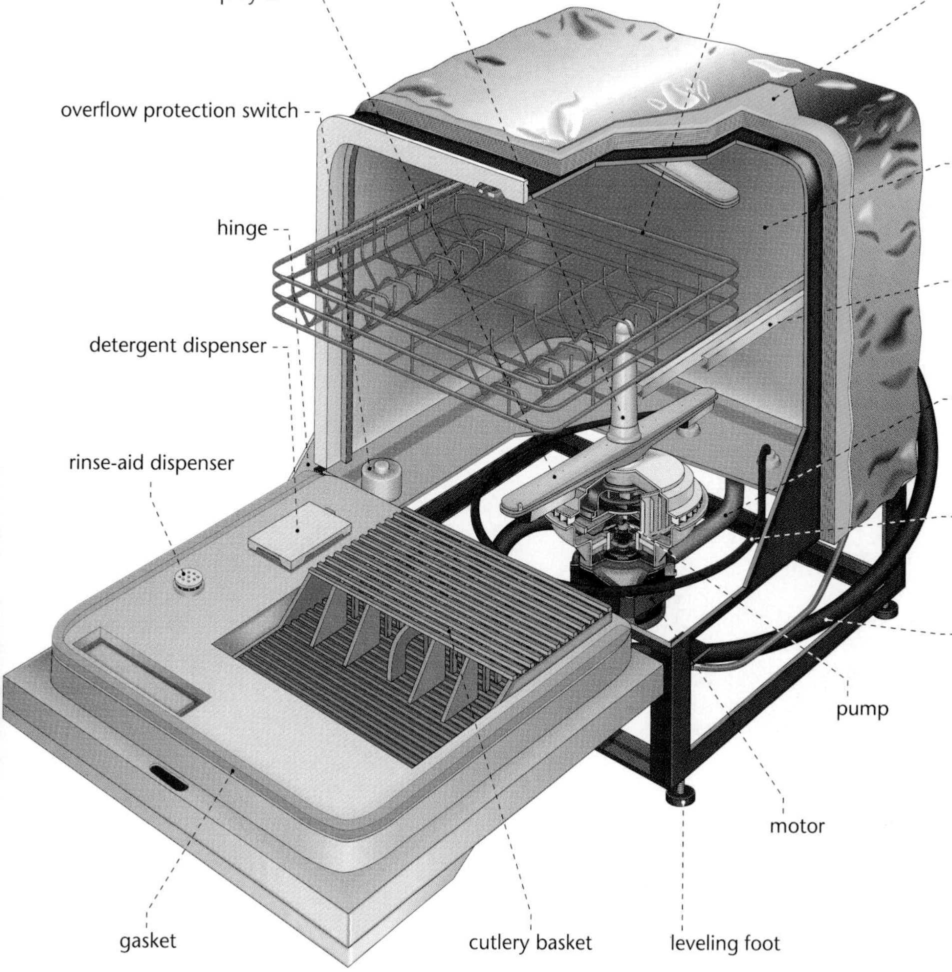

spray arm

wash tower   rack   insulating material

overflow protection switch

tub

hinge

slide

detergent dispenser

water hose

rinse-aid dispenser

heating element

drain hose

pump

motor

gasket   cutlery basket   leveling foot

WASHER

HOUSE FURNITURE

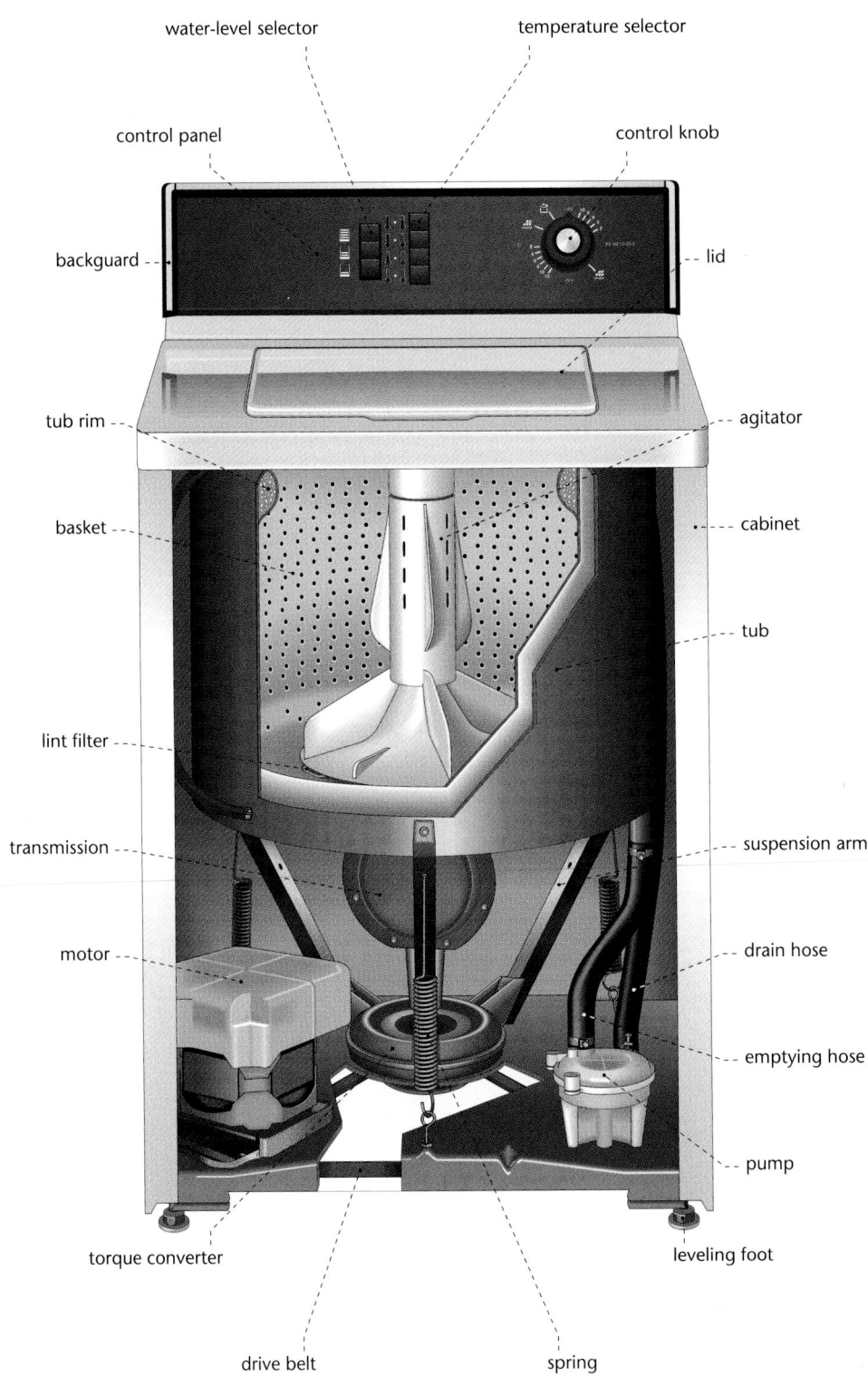

water-level selector

temperature selector

control panel

control knob

backguard

lid

tub rim

agitator

basket

cabinet

tub

lint filter

transmission

suspension arm

motor

drain hose

emptying hose

pump

torque converter

leveling foot

drive belt

spring

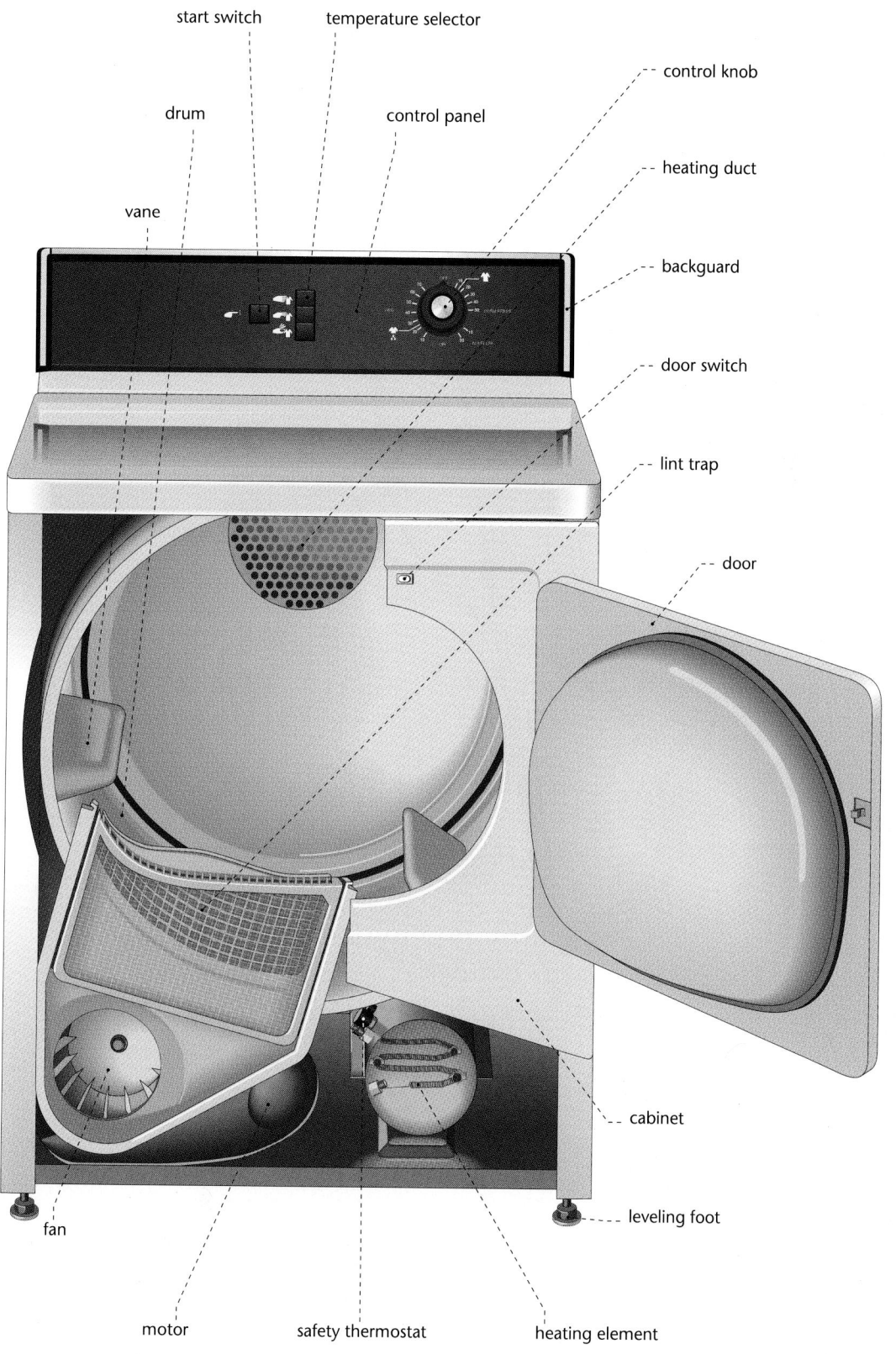

start switch

temperature selector

control knob

drum

control panel

heating duct

vane

backguard

door switch

lint trap

door

cabinet

leveling foot

fan

motor

safety thermostat

heating element

HOUSE FURNITURE

HAND VACUUM CLEANER

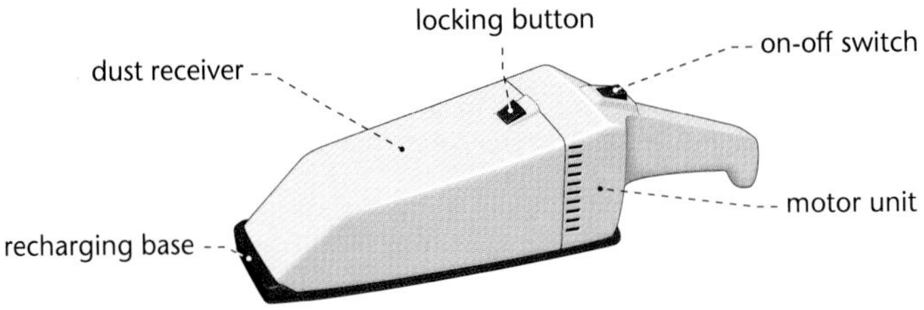

locking button

on-off switch

dust receiver

motor unit

recharging base

CANISTER VACUUM CLEANER

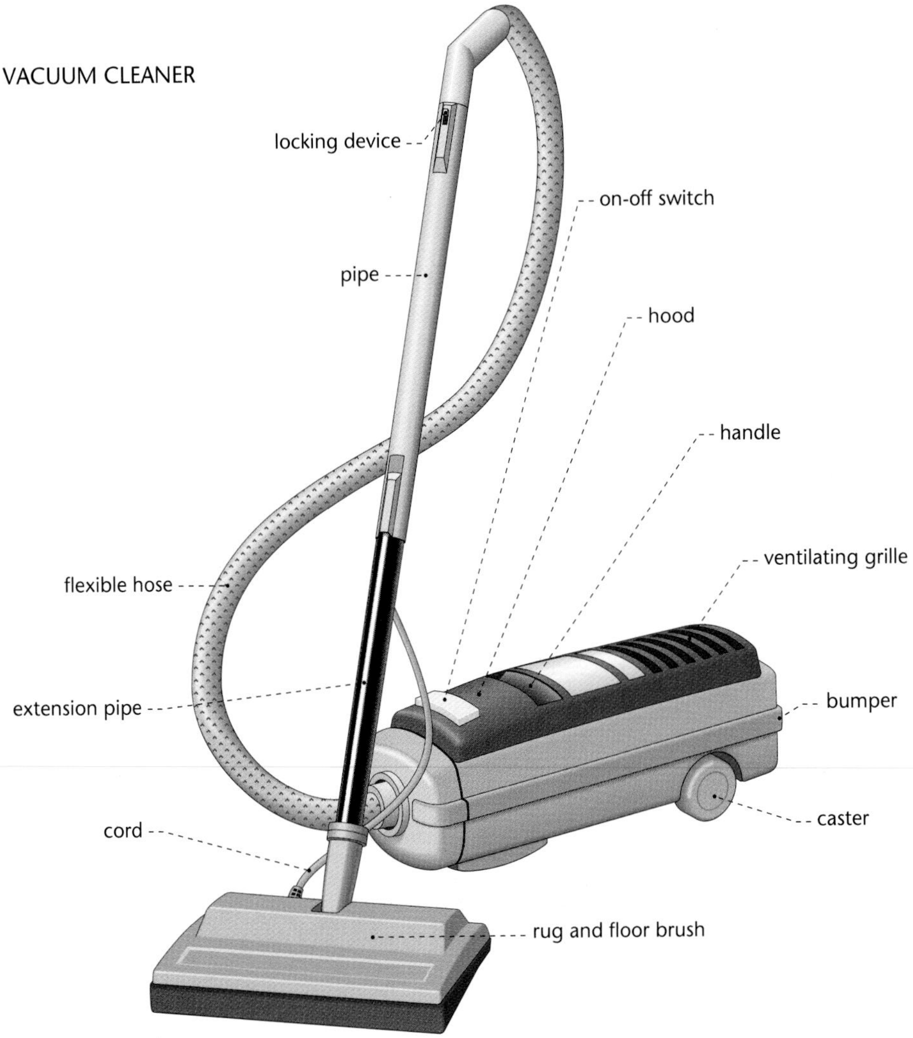

locking device

on-off switch

pipe

hood

handle

ventilating grille

flexible hose

extension pipe

bumper

cord

caster

rug and floor brush

CLEANING TOOLS

upholstery nozzle

crevice tool

floor brush

dusting brush

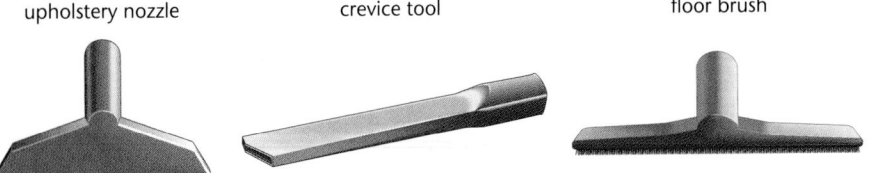

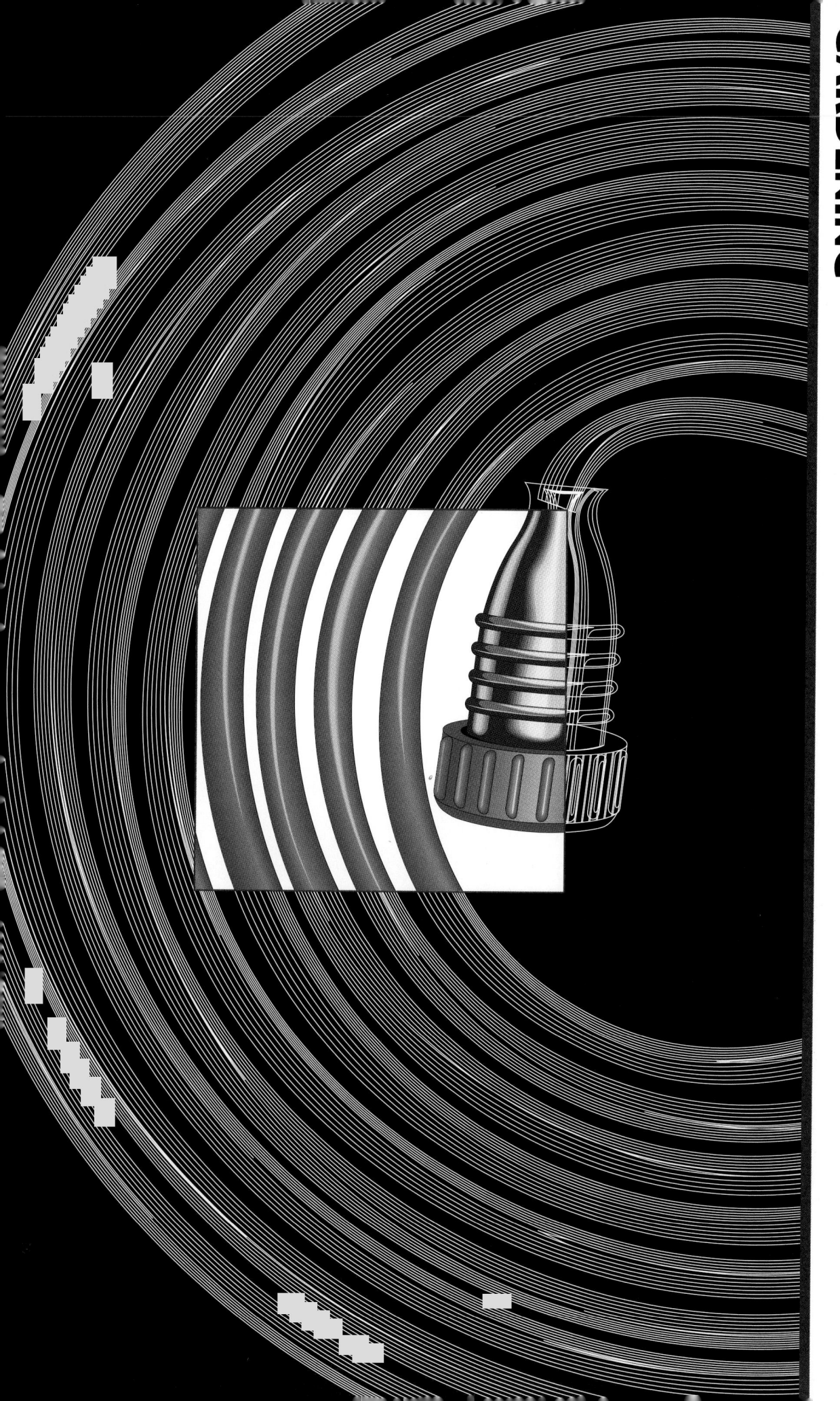

CONTENTS

PLEASURE GARDEN 263

TOOLS AND EQUIPMENT 264

GARDENING

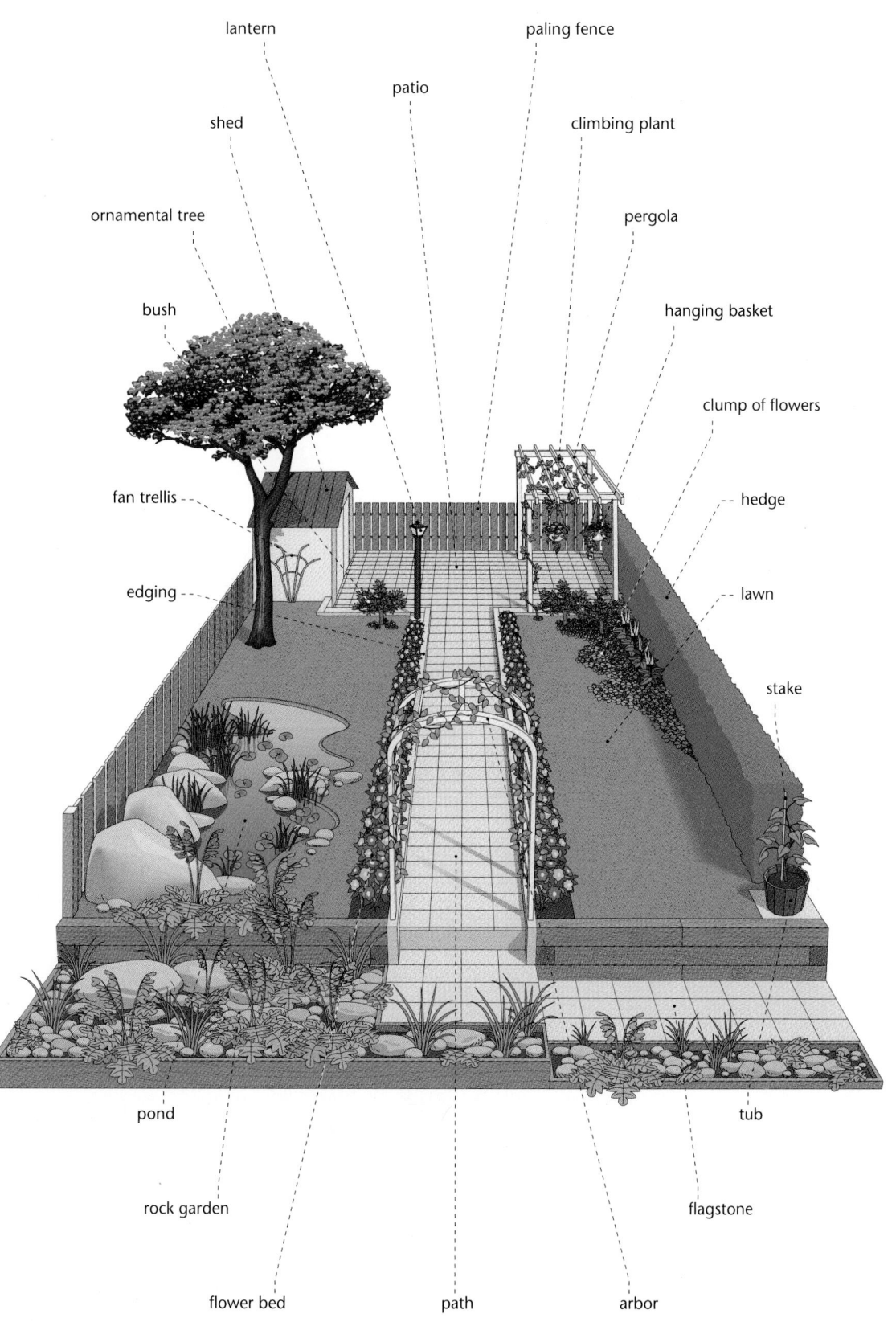

lantern

paling fence

patio

shed

climbing plant

ornamental tree

pergola

bush

hanging basket

clump of flowers

fan trellis

hedge

edging

lawn

stake

pond

tub

rock garden

flagstone

flower bed

path

arbor

TOOLS AND EQUIPMENT

pistol nozzle

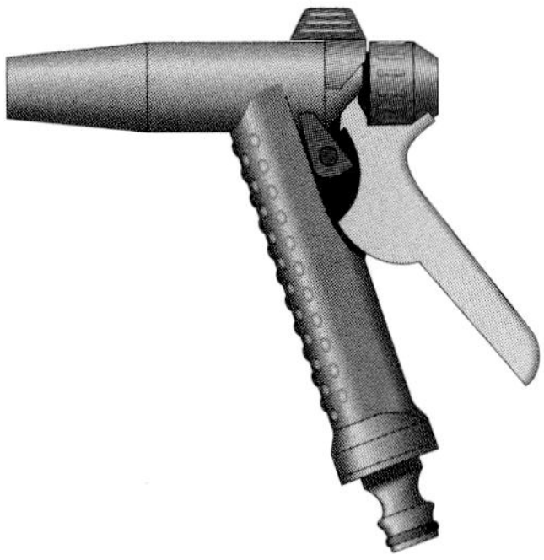

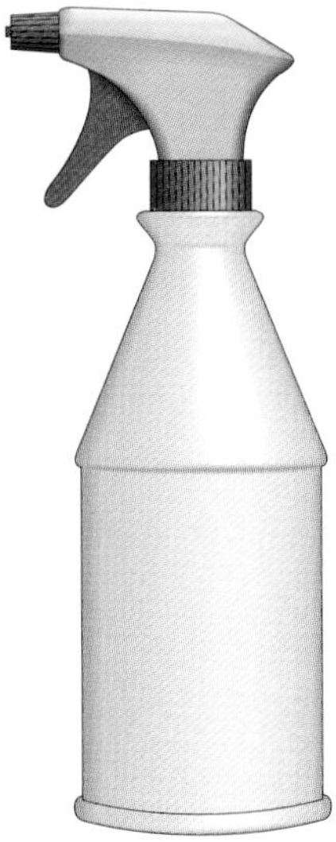

spray nozzle

sprayer

arm

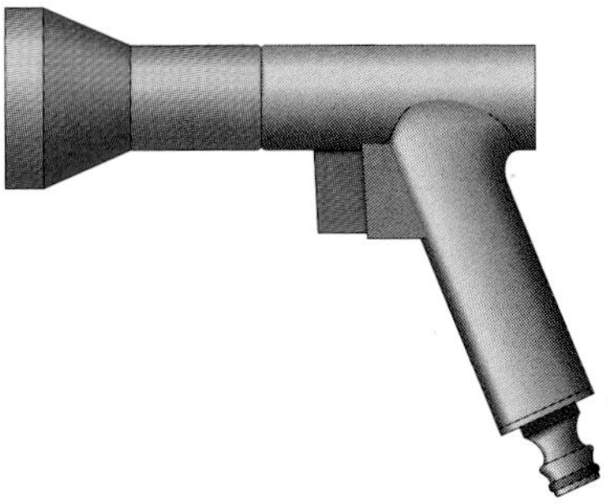

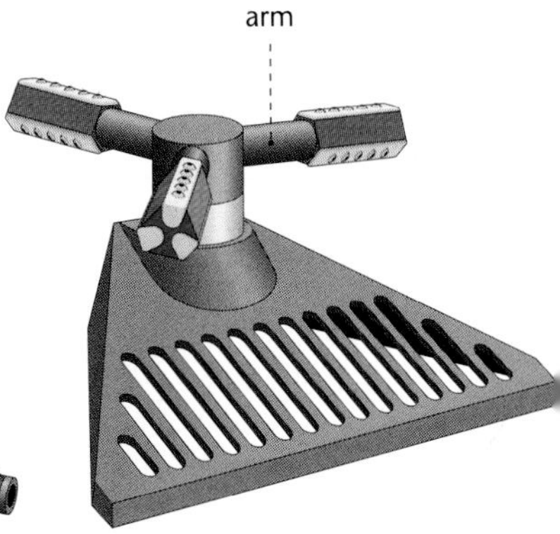

REVOLVING SPRINKLER

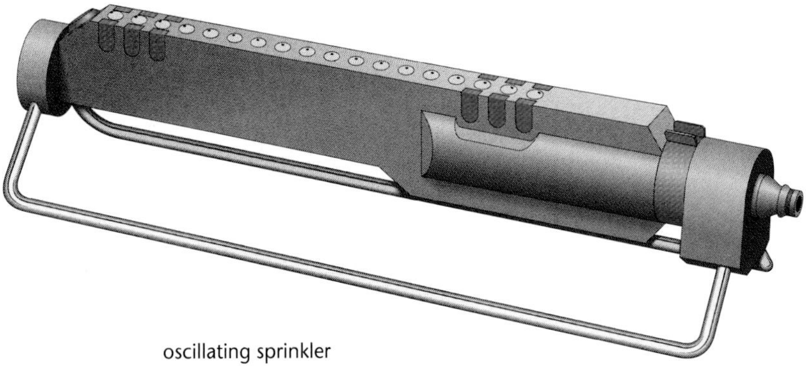

oscillating sprinkler

IMPULSE SPRINKLER

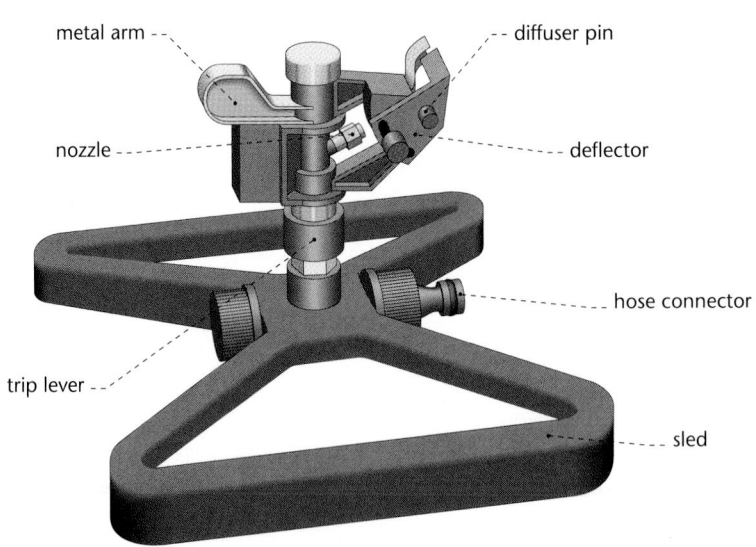

metal arm

diffuser pin

nozzle

deflector

hose connector

trip lever

sled

HOSE TROLLEY

sprinkler hose

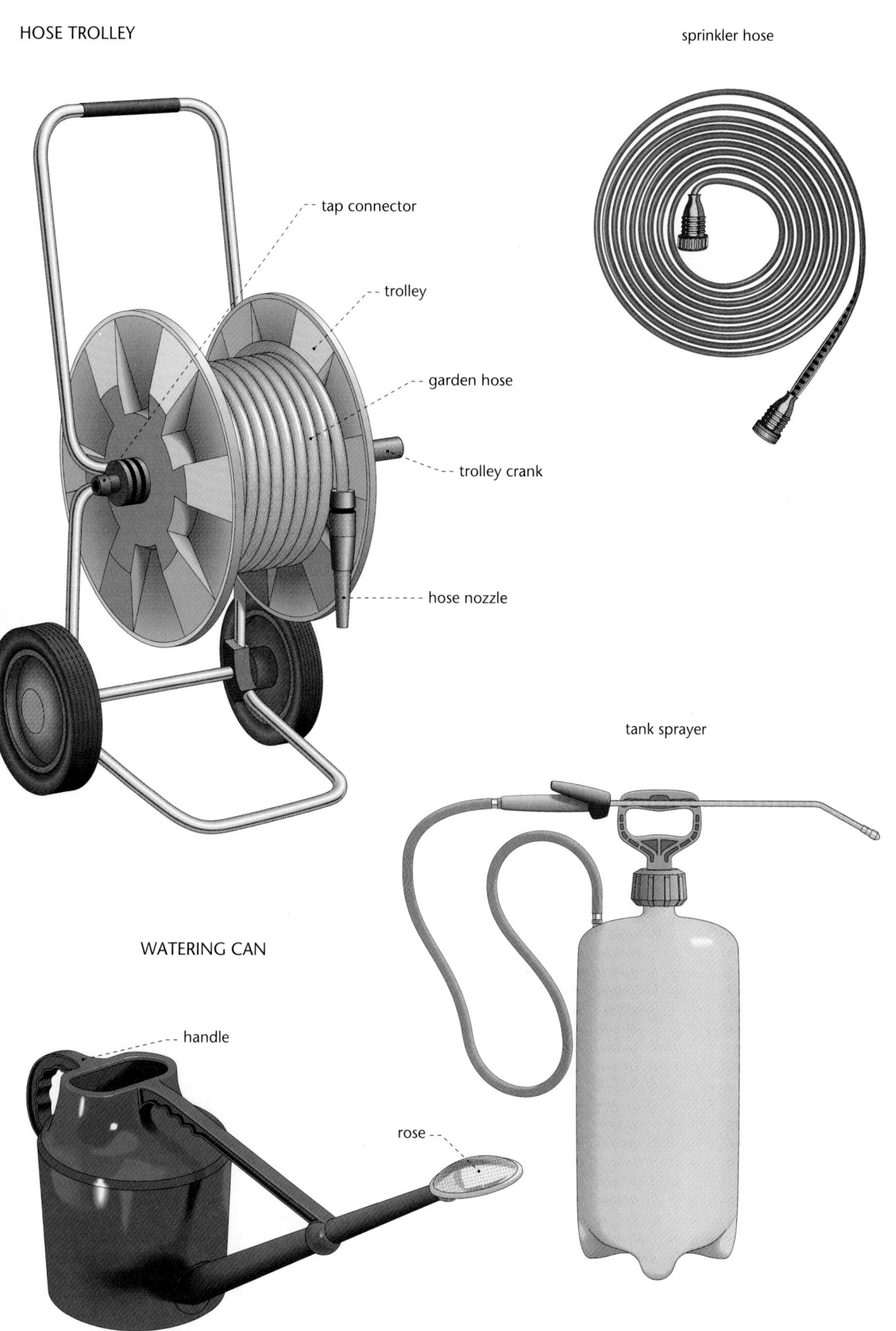

tap connector

trolley

garden hose

trolley crank

hose nozzle

tank sprayer

WATERING CAN

handle

rose

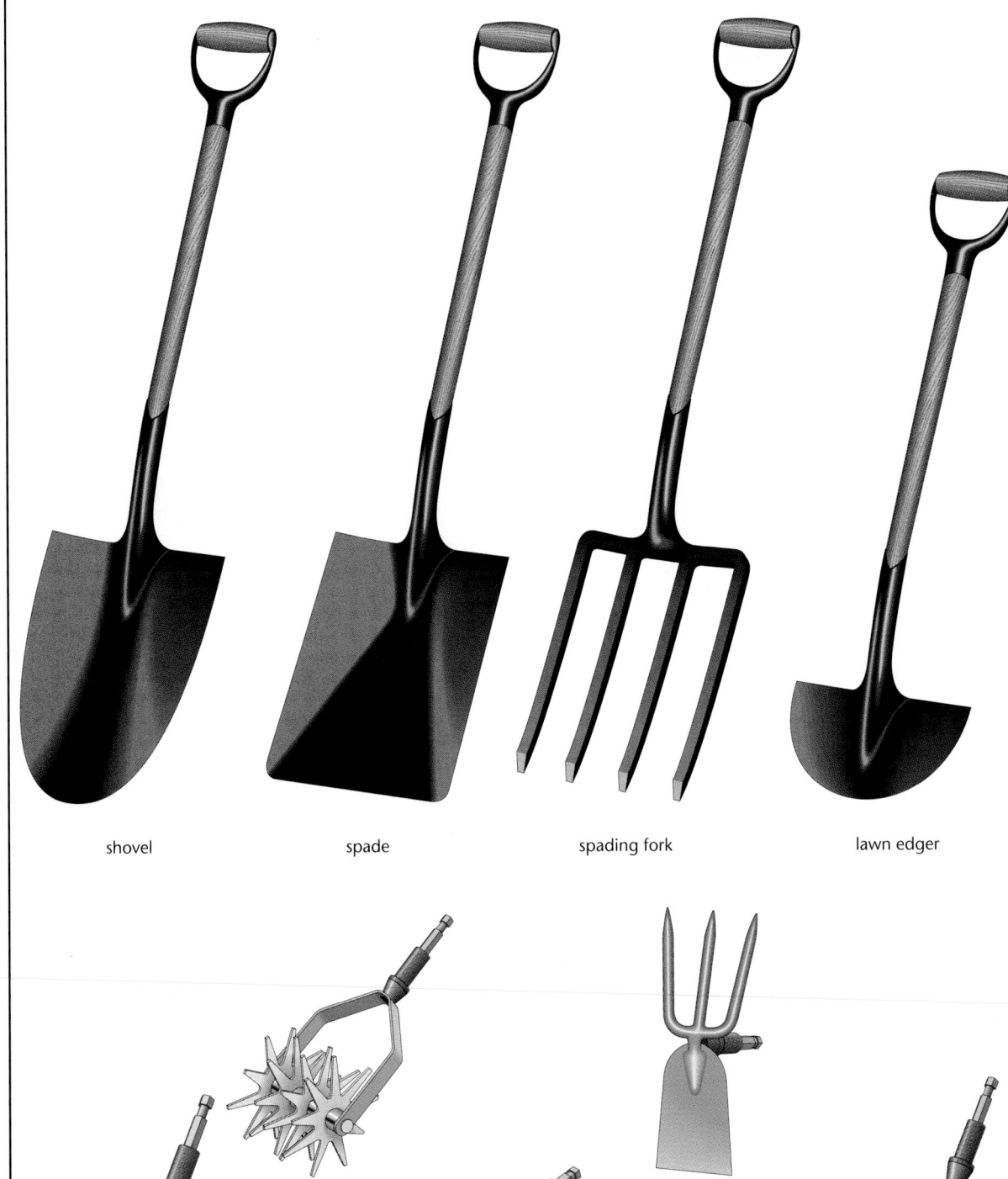

shovel

spade

spading fork

lawn edger

lawn aerator

hoe-fork

scuffle hoe

draw hoe

weeding hoe

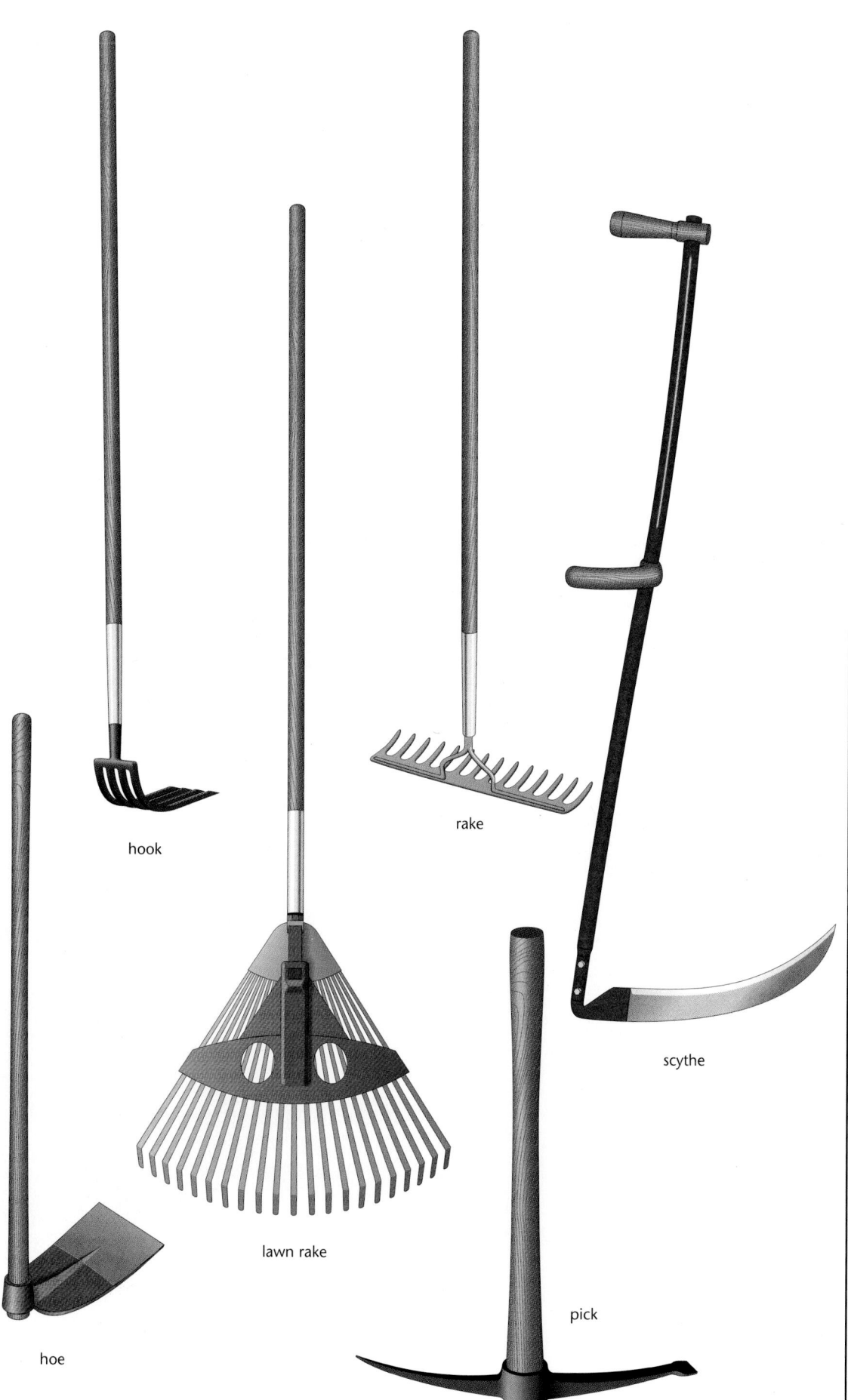

hook

rake

scythe

lawn rake

pick

hoe

GARDENING

hand fork

weeder

trowel

small hand cultivator

seeder

garden line

dibble

bulb dibble

HEDGE TRIMMER

cord

hand protector

trigger

tooth

blade

electric motor

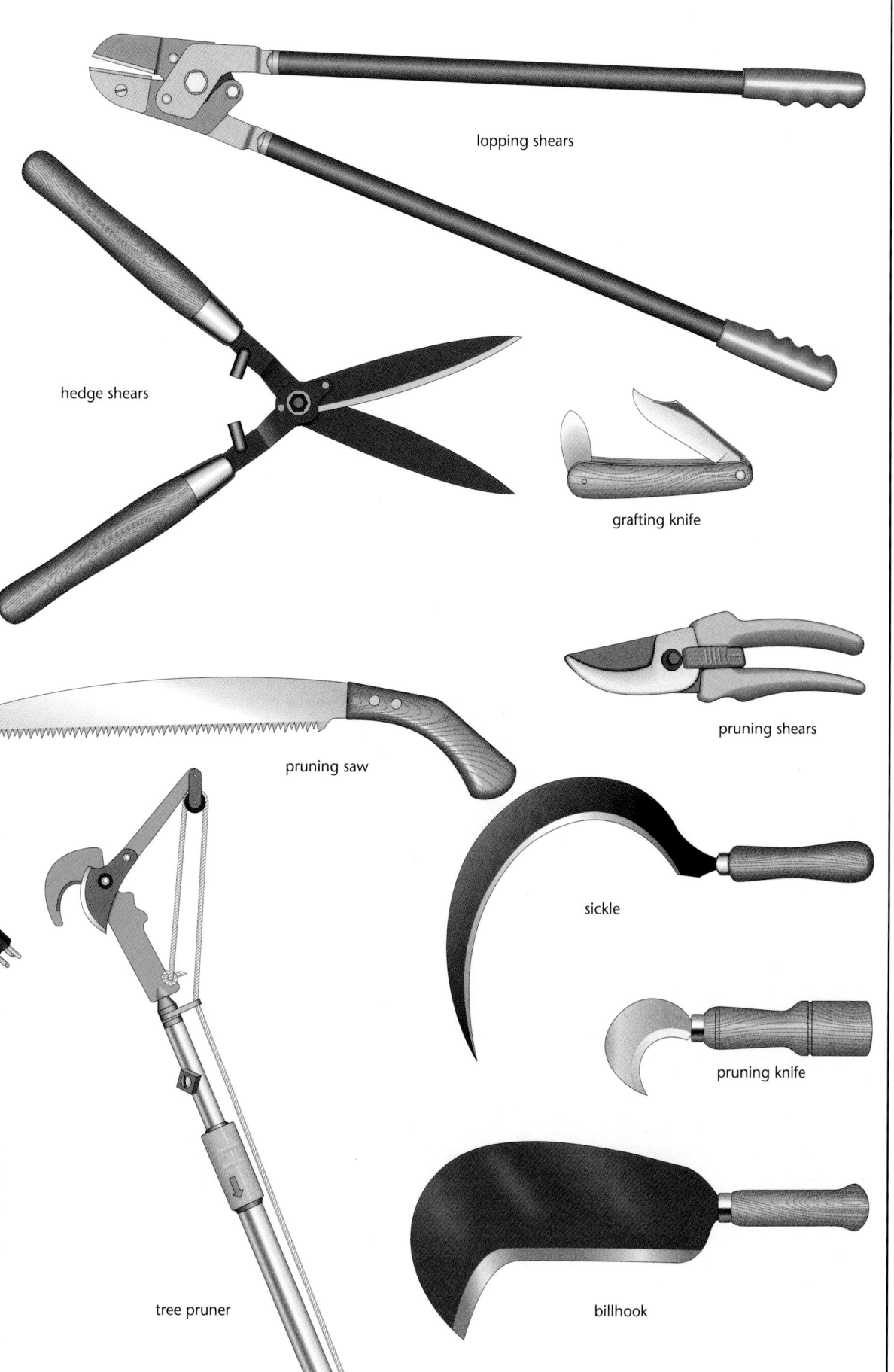

lopping shears

hedge shears

grafting knife

pruning shears

pruning saw

sickle

pruning knife

tree pruner

billhook

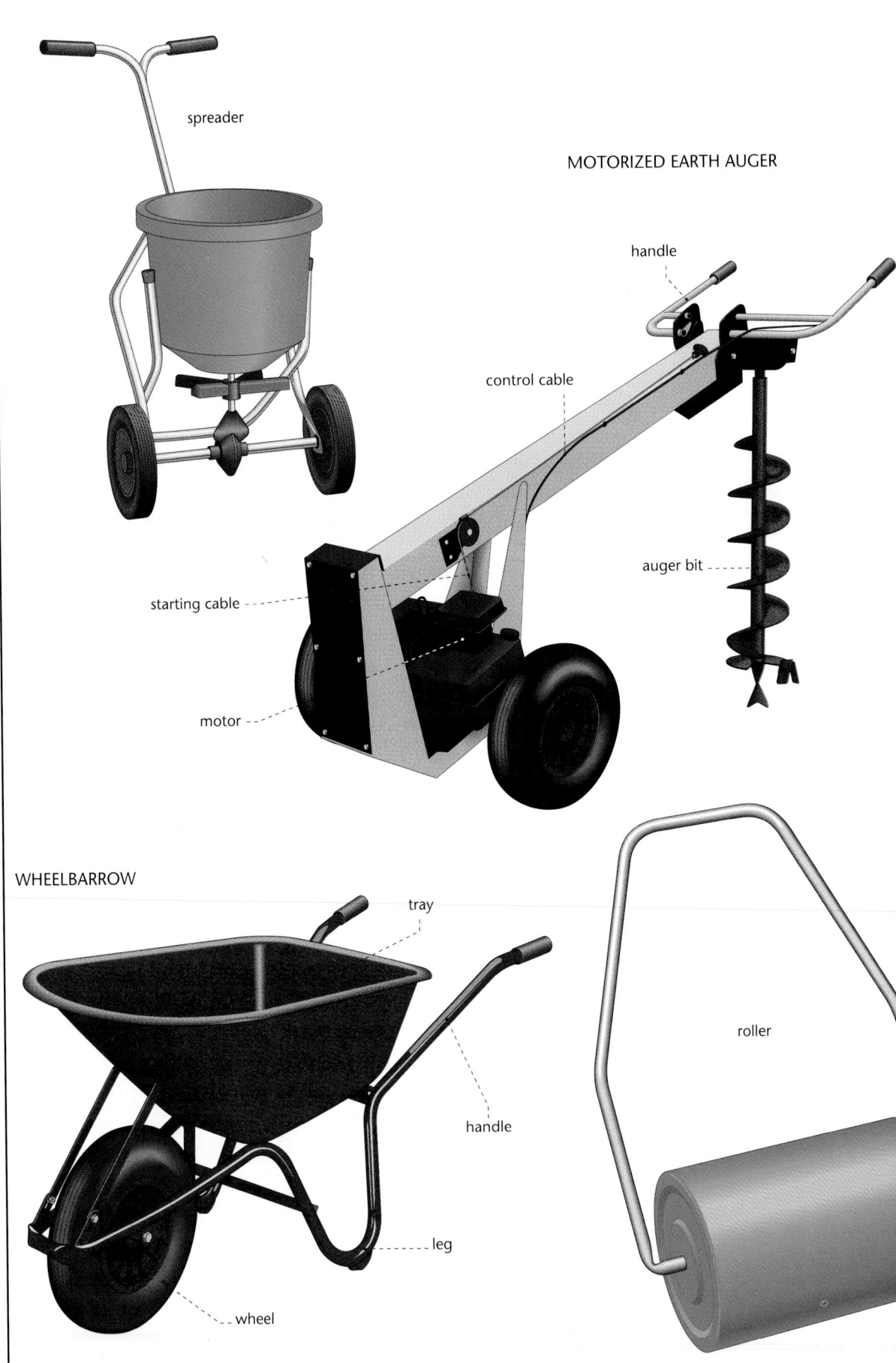

spreader

MOTORIZED EARTH AUGER

handle

control cable

auger bit

starting cable

motor

WHEELBARROW

tray

roller

handle

leg

wheel

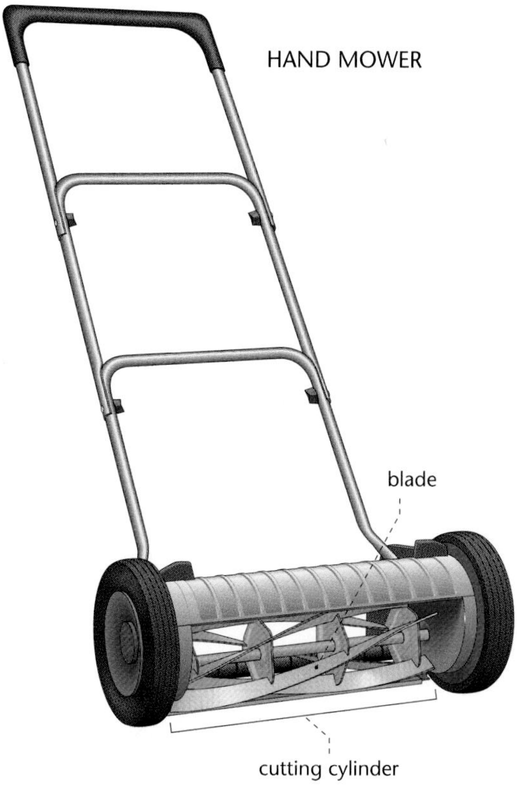

HAND MOWER

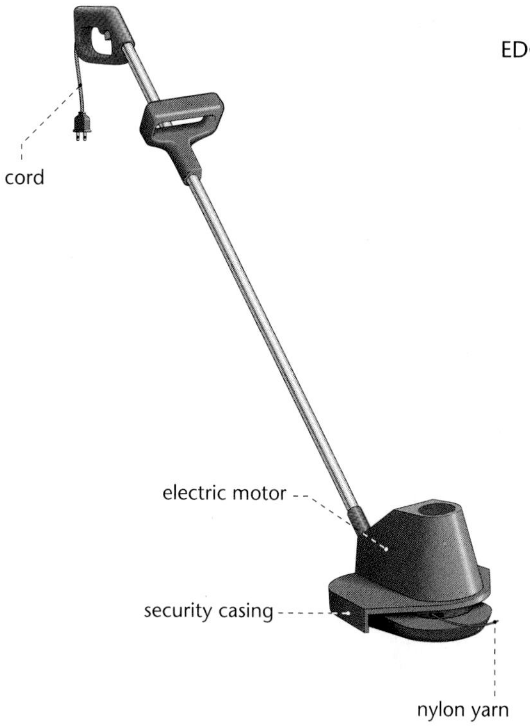

EDGER

cord

blade

electric motor

security casing

nylon yarn

cutting cylinder

POWER MOWER

handle

speed control

safety handle

ignition key

grassbox

motor

starter

accelerator cable

filler cap

spark plug

deflector

casing

CHAINSAW

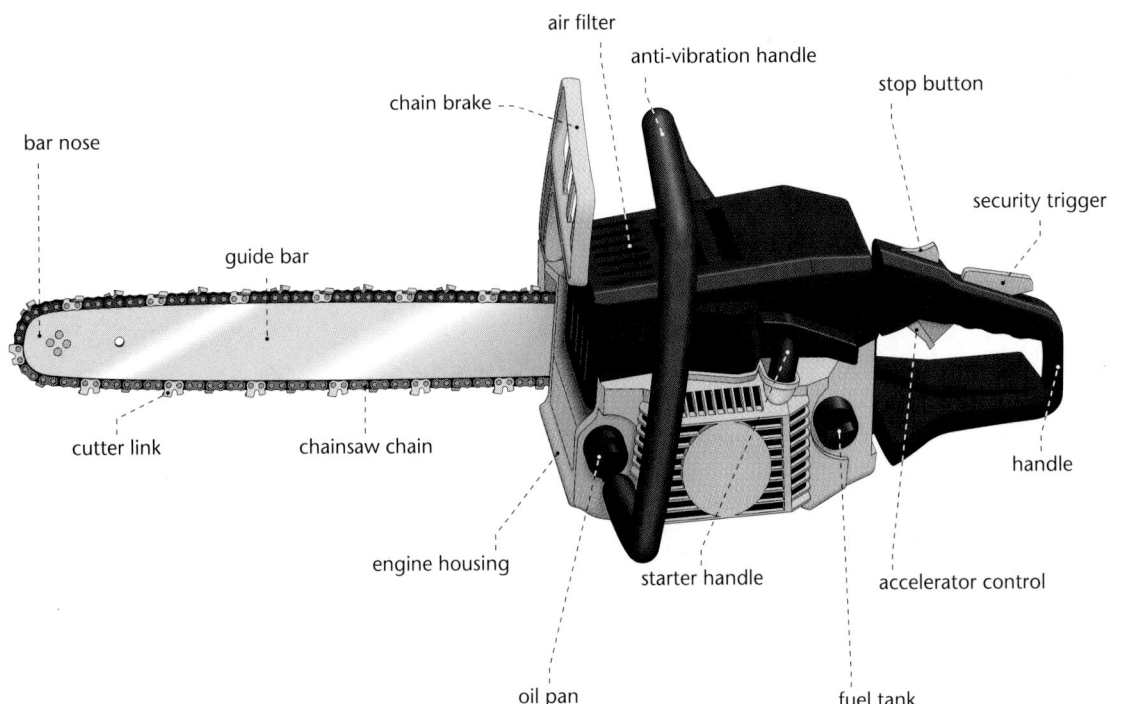

air filter

anti-vibration handle

stop button

chain brake

security trigger

bar nose

guide bar

handle

cutter link

chainsaw chain

engine housing

starter handle

accelerator control

oil pan

fuel tank

TILLER

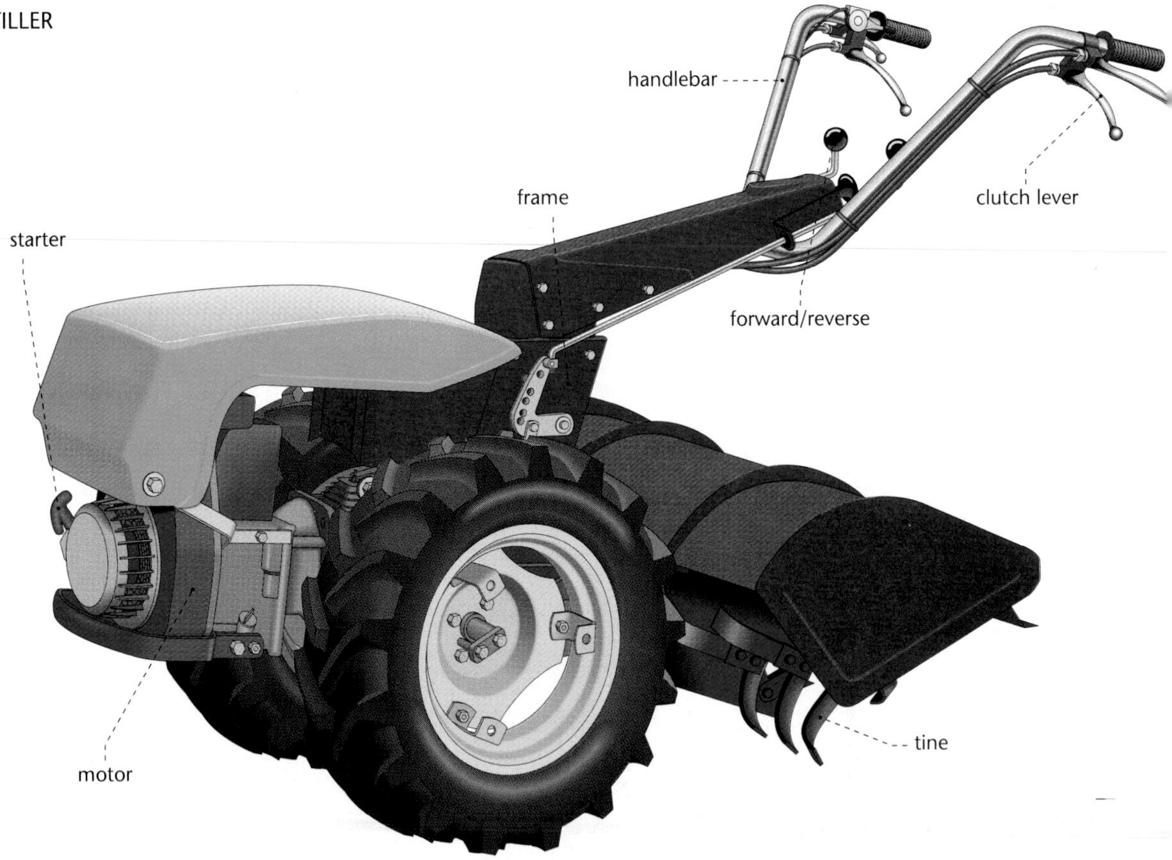

handlebar

frame

clutch lever

starter

forward/reverse

motor

tine

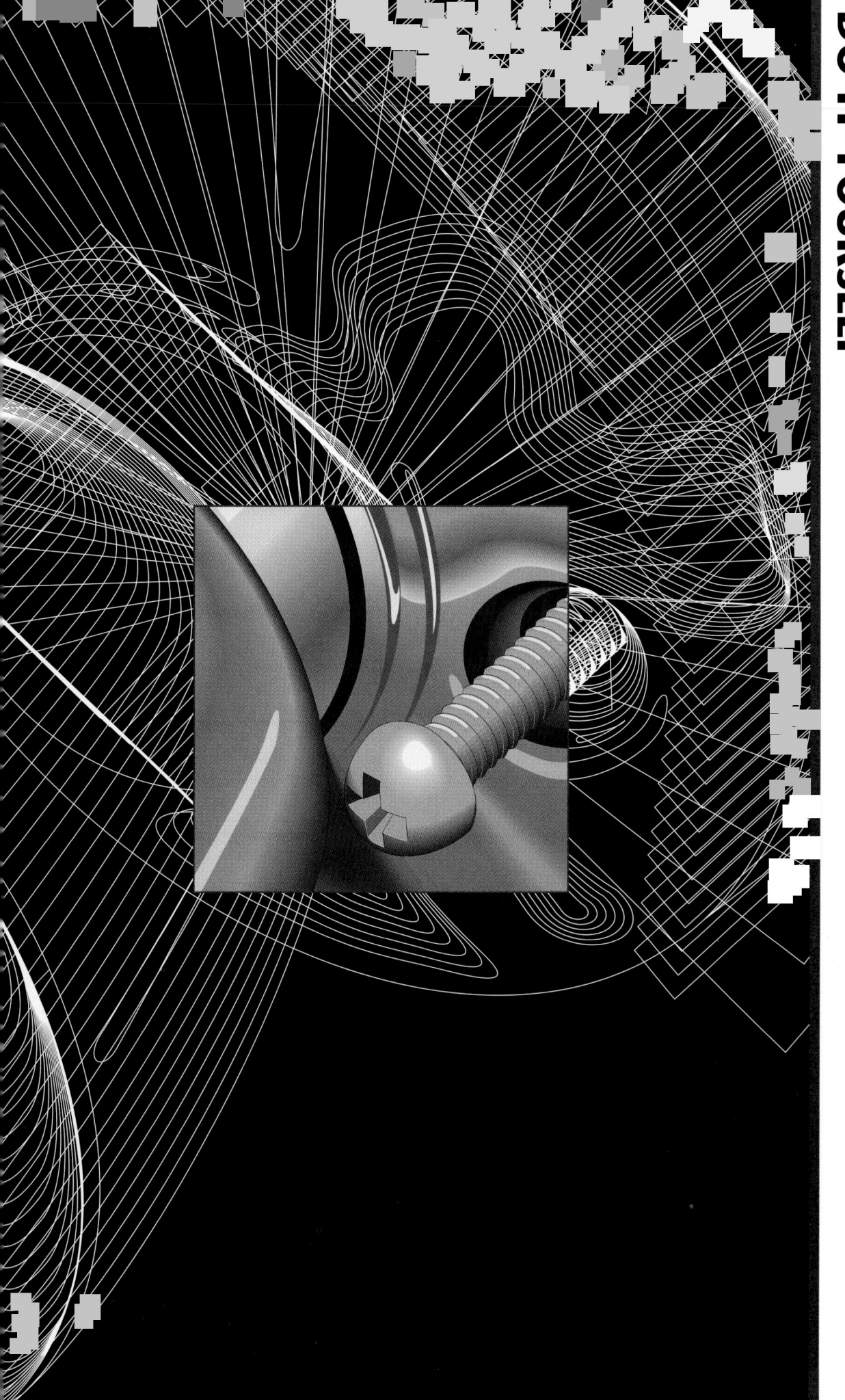

CONTENTS

CARPENTRY: TOOLS...275

BUILDING MATERIALS...286

LOCK 289

MASONRY...291

PLUMBING: BATHROOM 292

PLUMBING..294

LADDERS AND STEPLADDERS 302

PAINTING UPKEEP...304

SOLDERING AND WELDING 305

ELECTRICITY..309

DO-IT-YOURSELF

CARPENTRY: TOOLS

CLAW HAMMER

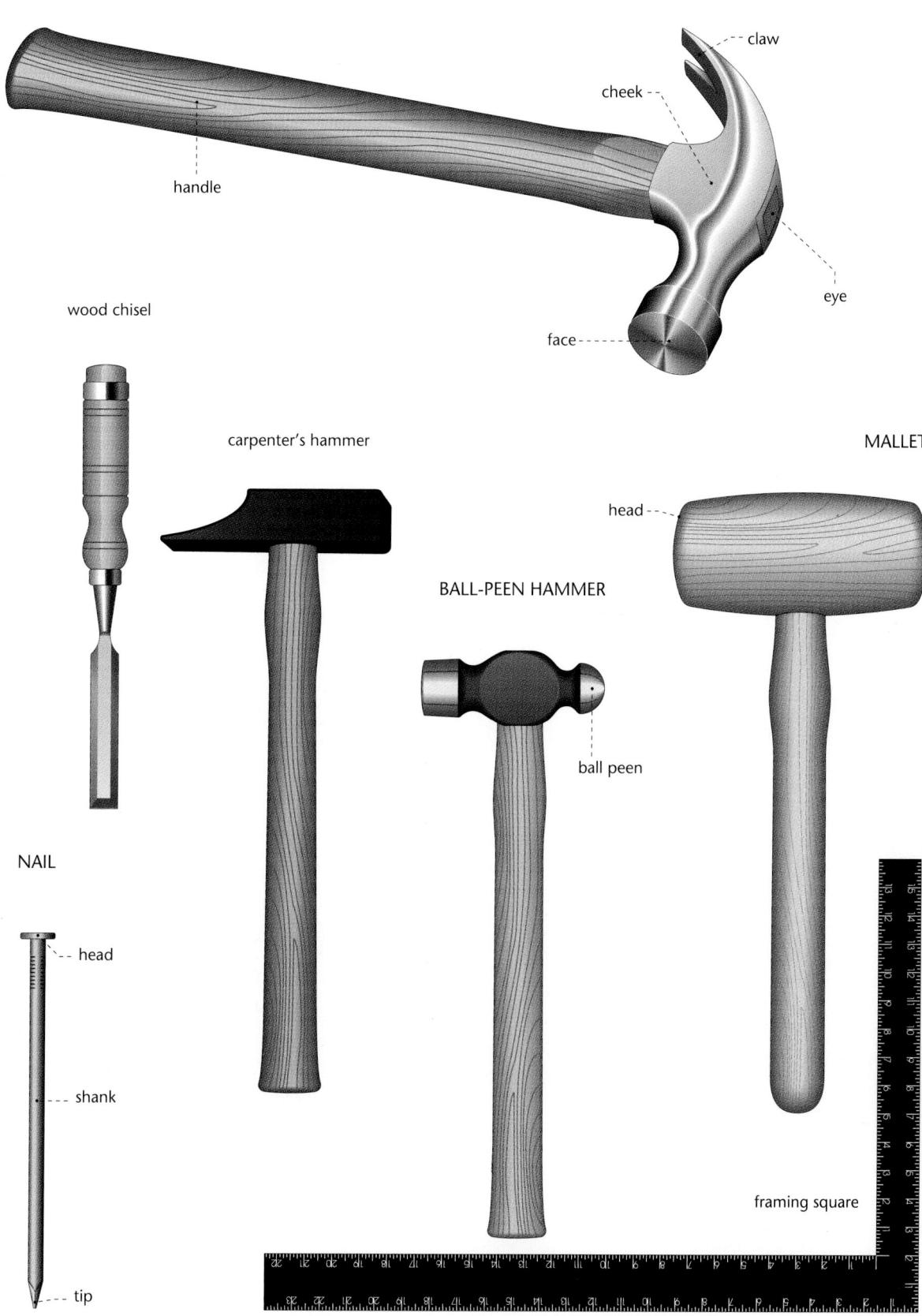

claw

cheek

handle

eye

wood chisel

face

carpenter's hammer

MALLET

head

BALL-PEEN HAMMER

ball peen

NAIL

head

shank

framing square

tip

CARPENTRY: TOOLS

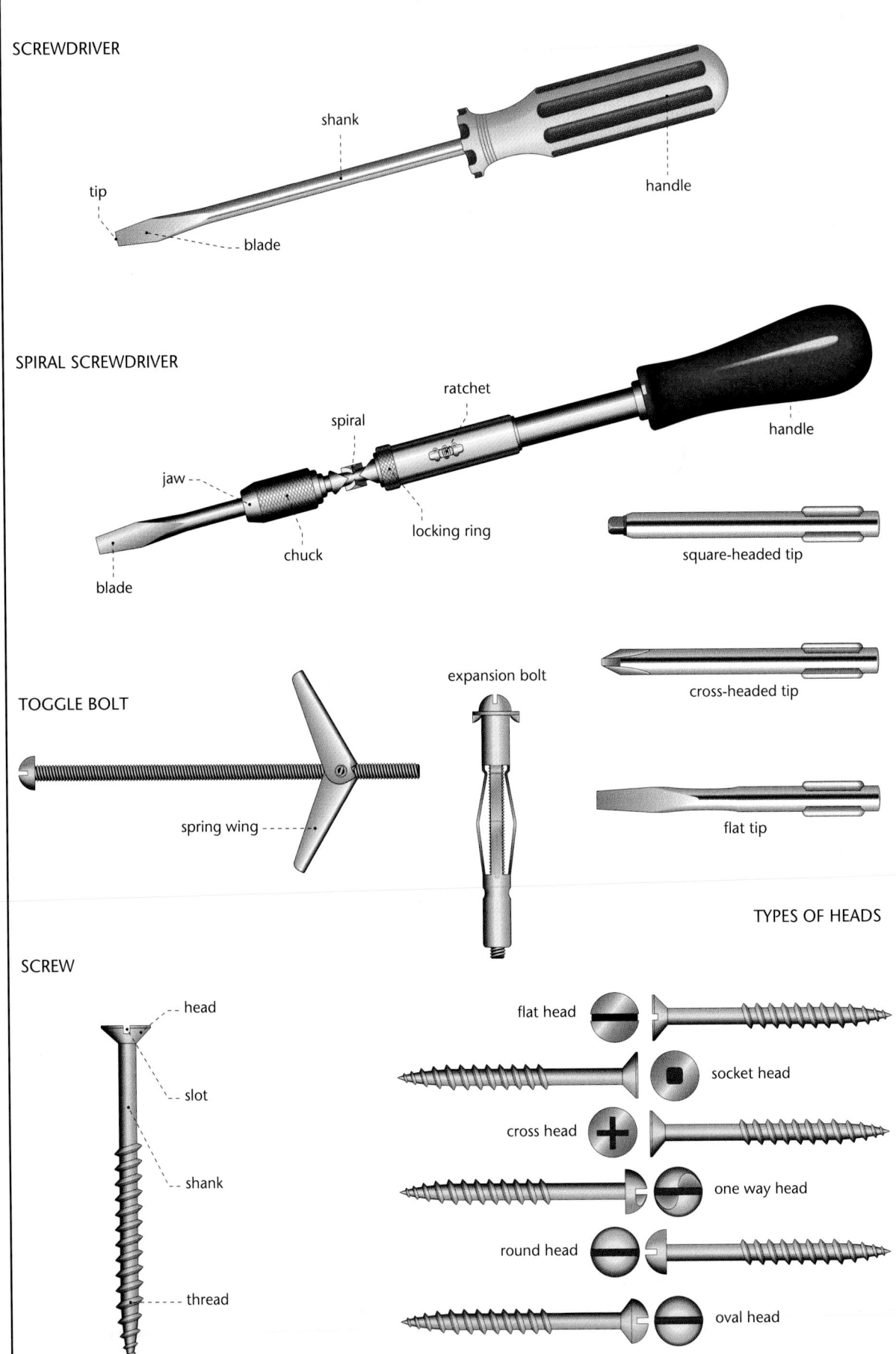

SCREWDRIVER

shank

tip

blade

handle

SPIRAL SCREWDRIVER

ratchet

spiral

jaw

locking ring

chuck

blade

handle

square-headed tip

cross-headed tip

TOGGLE BOLT

expansion bolt

spring wing

flat tip

TYPES OF HEADS

SCREW

head

slot

shank

thread

flat head

socket head

cross head

one way head

round head

oval head

276

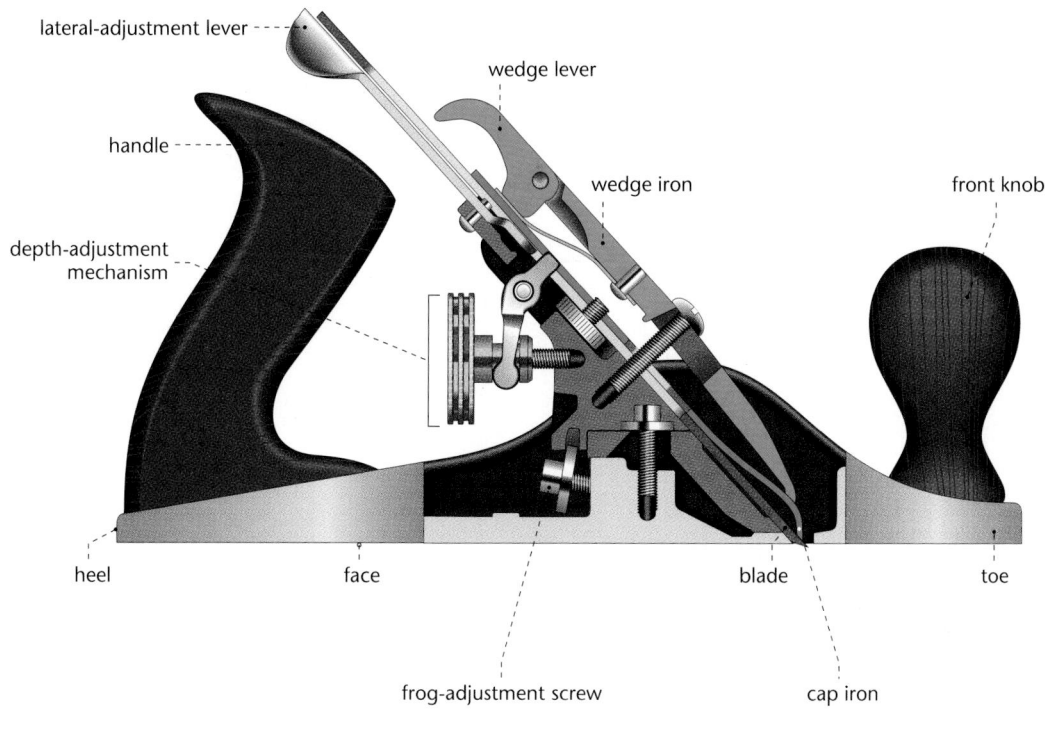

lateral-adjustment lever

handle

depth-adjustment mechanism

wedge lever

wedge iron

front knob

heel

face

blade

toe

frog-adjustment screw

cap iron

DO-IT-YOURSELF

HACKSAW

adjustable frame

grip handle

blade

file

HANDSAW

handle

blade

back

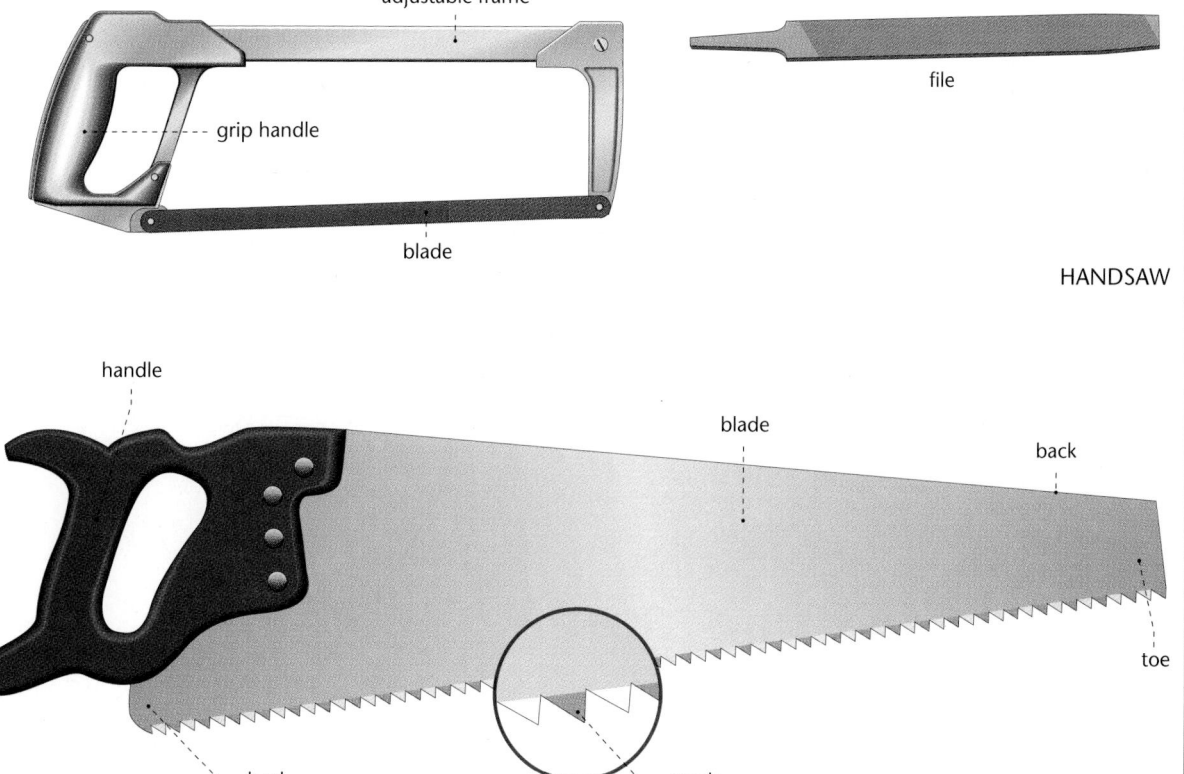

heel

tooth

toe

SLIP JOINT PLIERS

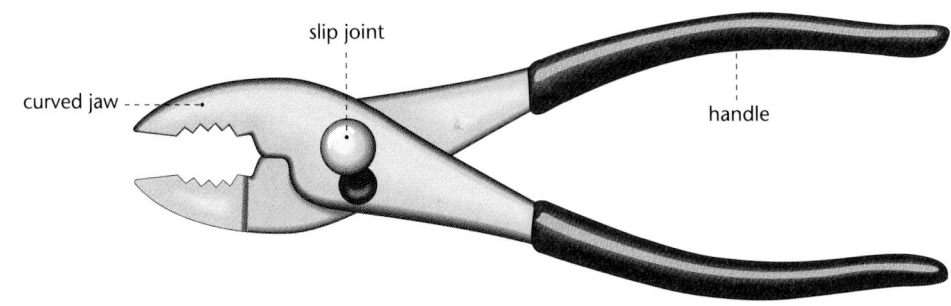

slip joint

curved jaw

handle

RIB JOINT PLIERS

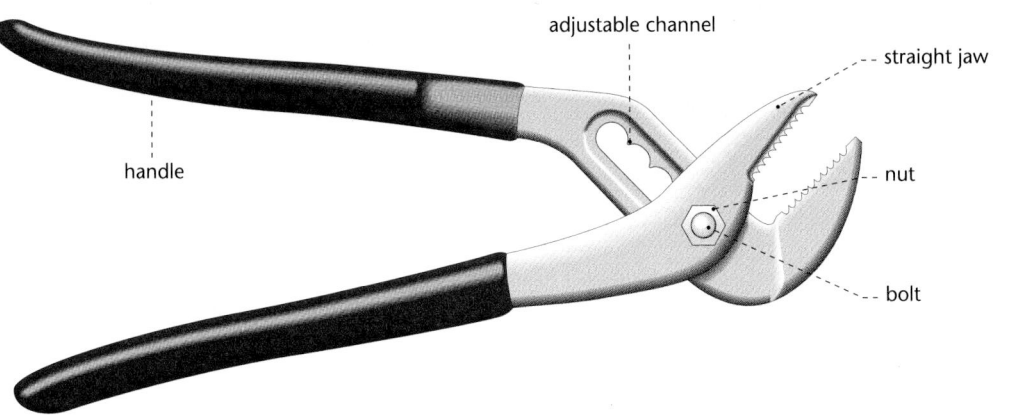

adjustable channel

straight jaw

handle

nut

bolt

LOCKING PLIERS

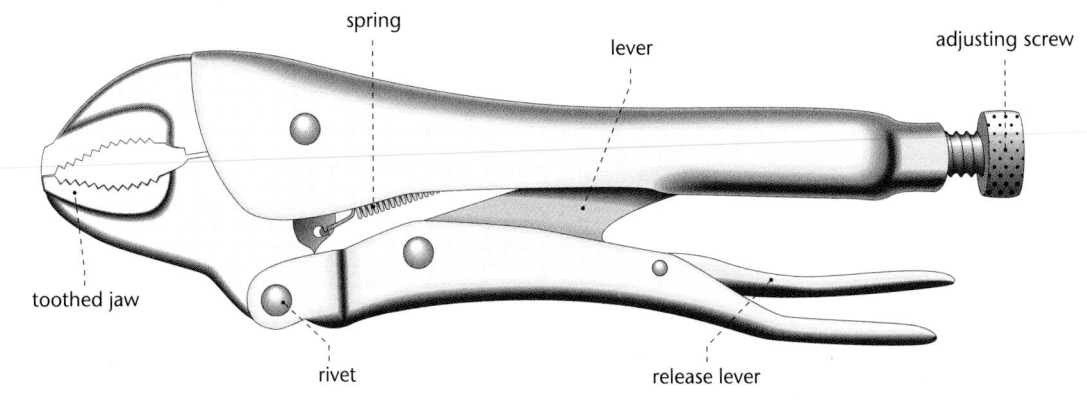

spring

lever

adjusting screw

toothed jaw

rivet

release lever

WASHERS

flat washer

lock washer

internal tooth lock washer

external tooth lock washer

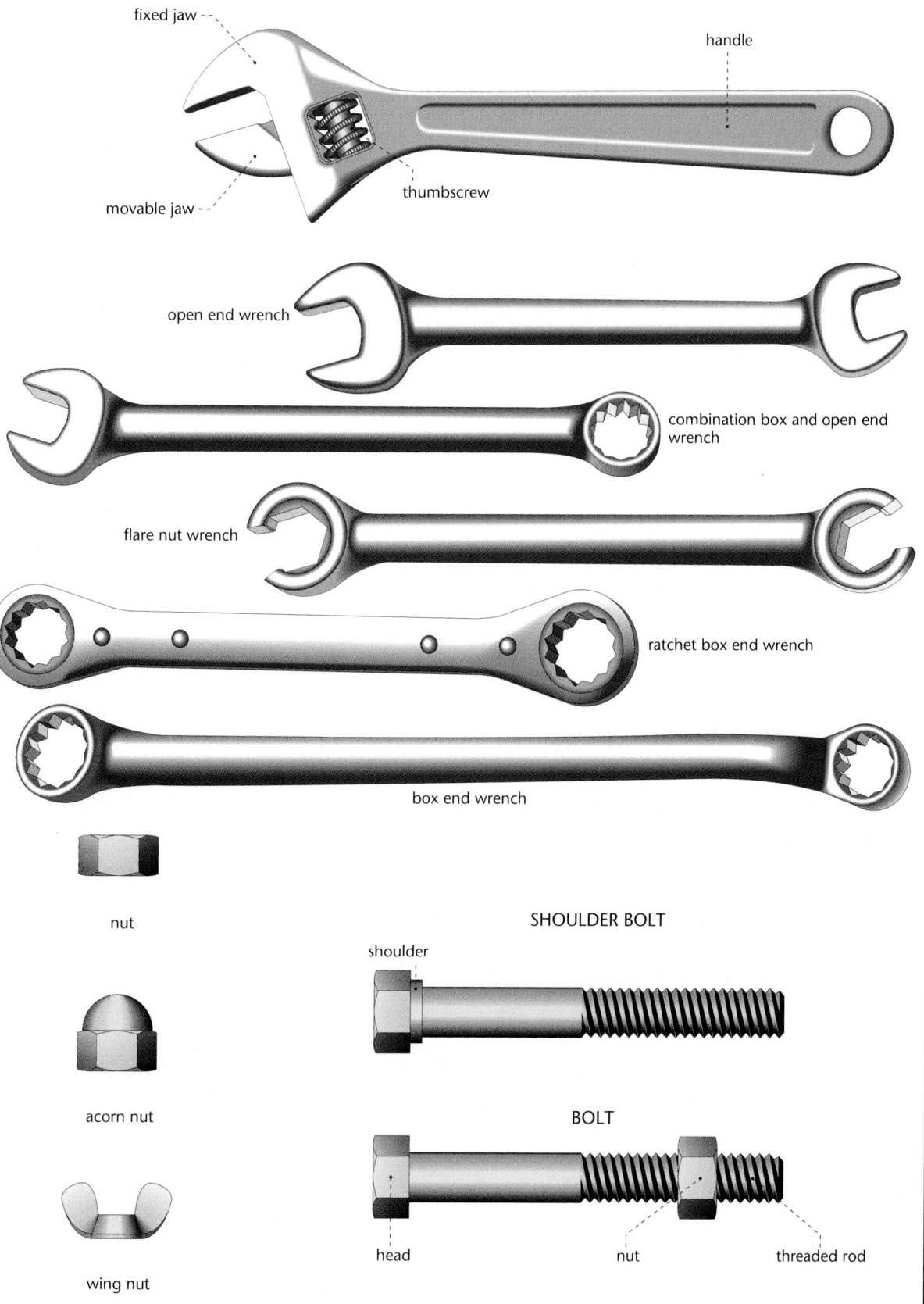

CRESCENT WRENCH

fixed jaw

handle

movable jaw

thumbscrew

open end wrench

combination box and open end wrench

flare nut wrench

ratchet box end wrench

box end wrench

nut

acorn nut

wing nut

SHOULDER BOLT

shoulder

BOLT

head

nut

threaded rod

CARPENTRY: TOOLS

ELECTRIC DRILL

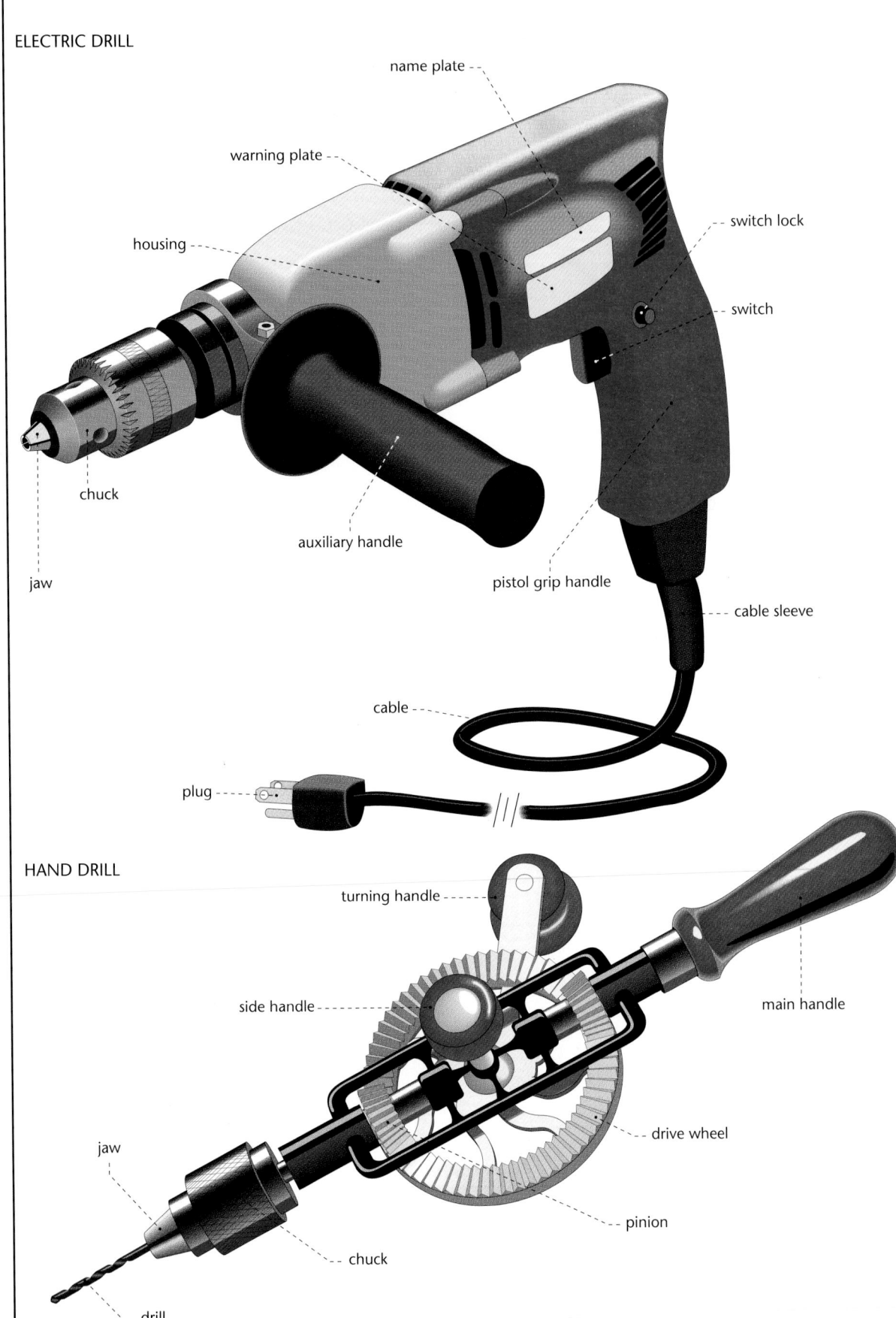

name plate

warning plate

switch lock

housing

switch

chuck

jaw

auxiliary handle

pistol grip handle

cable sleeve

cable

plug

HAND DRILL

turning handle

main handle

side handle

drive wheel

jaw

pinion

chuck

drill

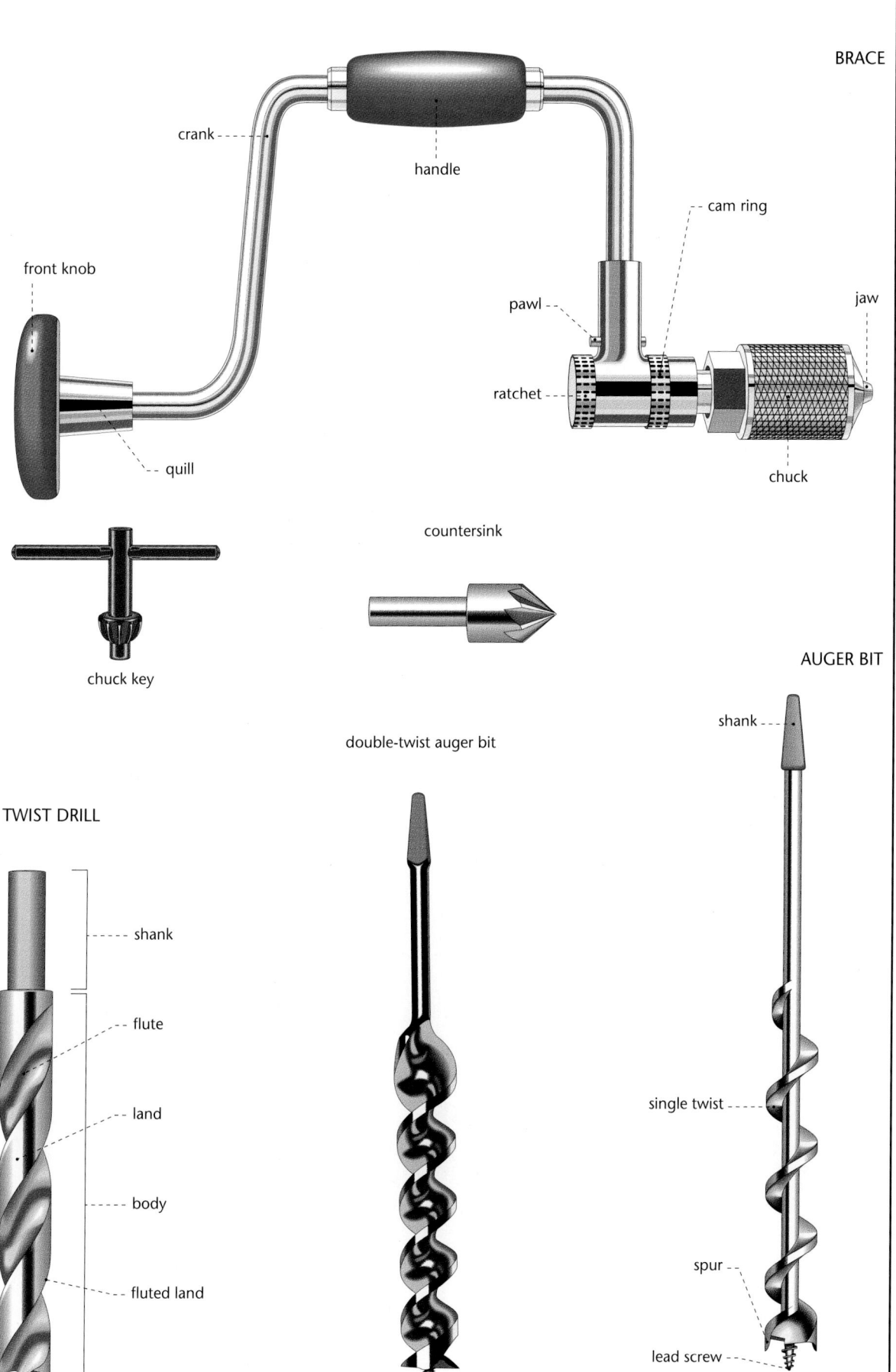

crank

handle

cam ring

front knob

pawl

jaw

ratchet

quill

chuck

chuck key

countersink

AUGER BIT

shank

double-twist auger bit

TWIST DRILL

shank

flute

single twist

land

body

fluted land

spur

lead screw

lead screw

C-CLAMP

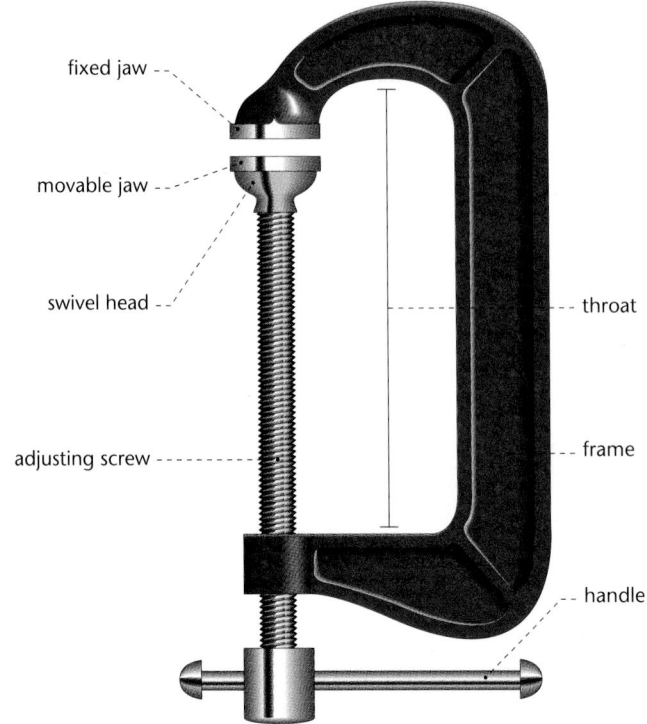

fixed jaw

movable jaw

swivel head

throat

adjusting screw

frame

handle

VISE

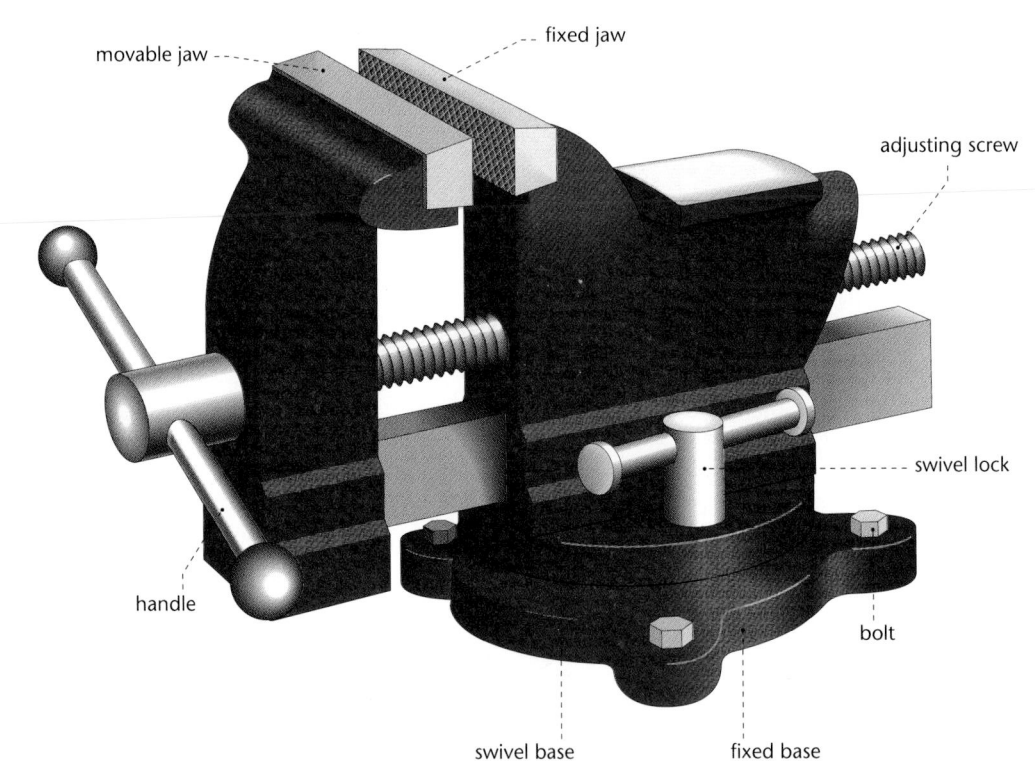

movable jaw

fixed jaw

adjusting screw

swivel lock

handle

bolt

swivel base

fixed base

head ---- ‥

cord sleeve ---- ‥

motor

switch

guide handle ---- ‥

depth adjustment

collet ---- ‥

tool holder

base ---- ‥

DO-IT-YOURSELF

pulley safety guard ---- ‥

motor

switch ---- ‥

feed lever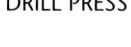

depth stop ---- ‥

quill ---- ‥

chuck ---- ‥

table-locking clamp

table ---- ‥

column

base ---- ‥

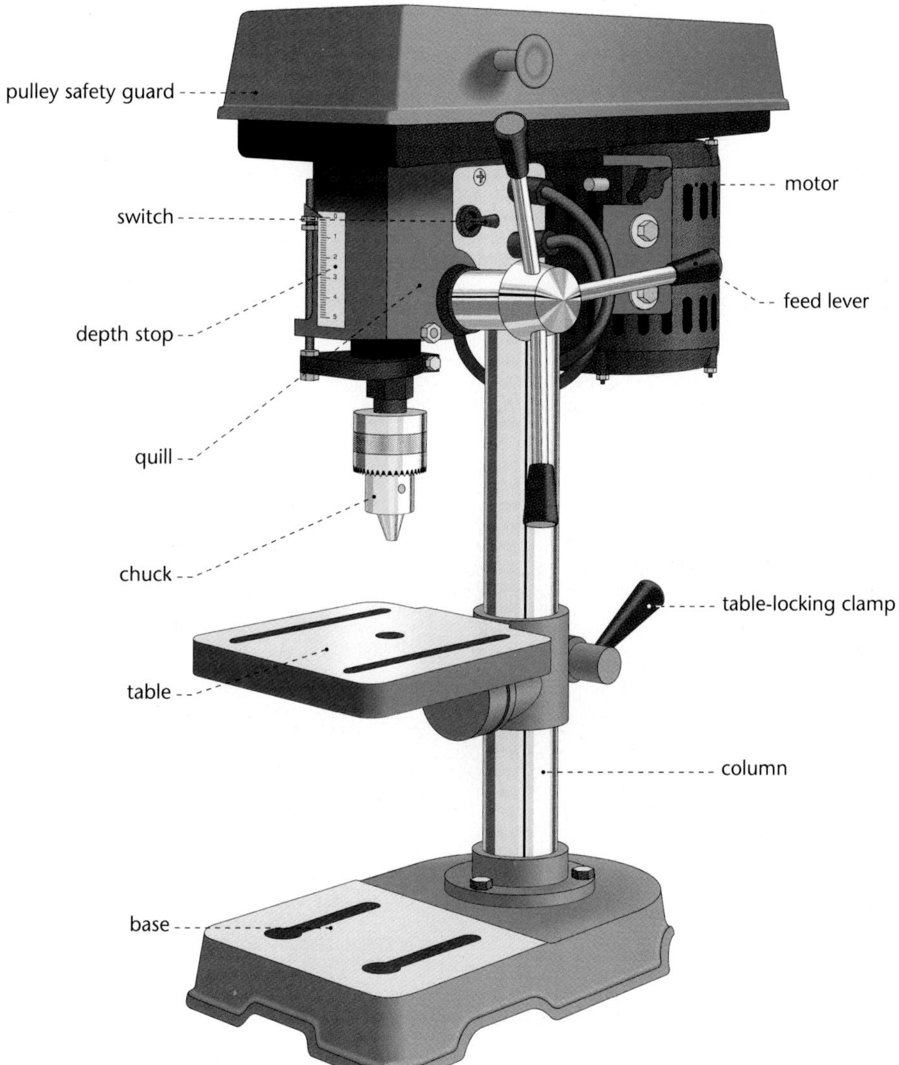

CIRCULAR SAW BLADE

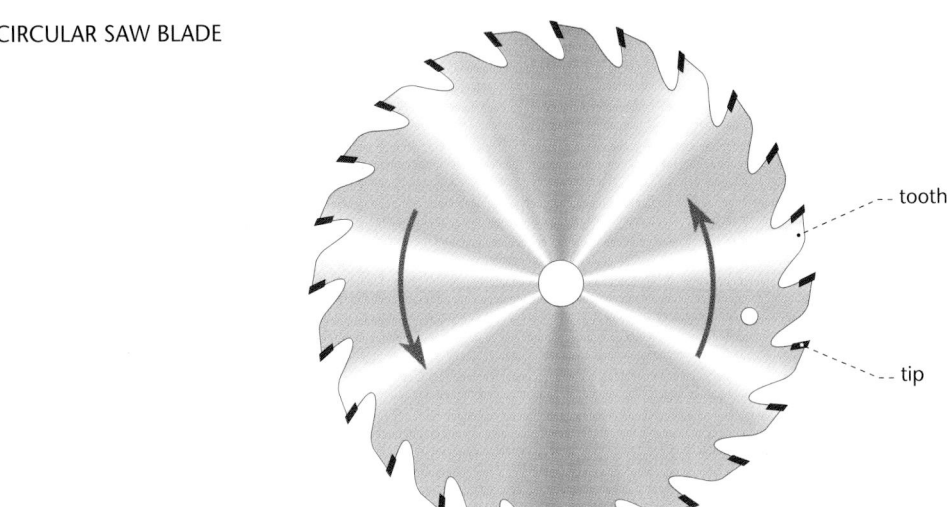

tooth

tip

CIRCULAR SAW

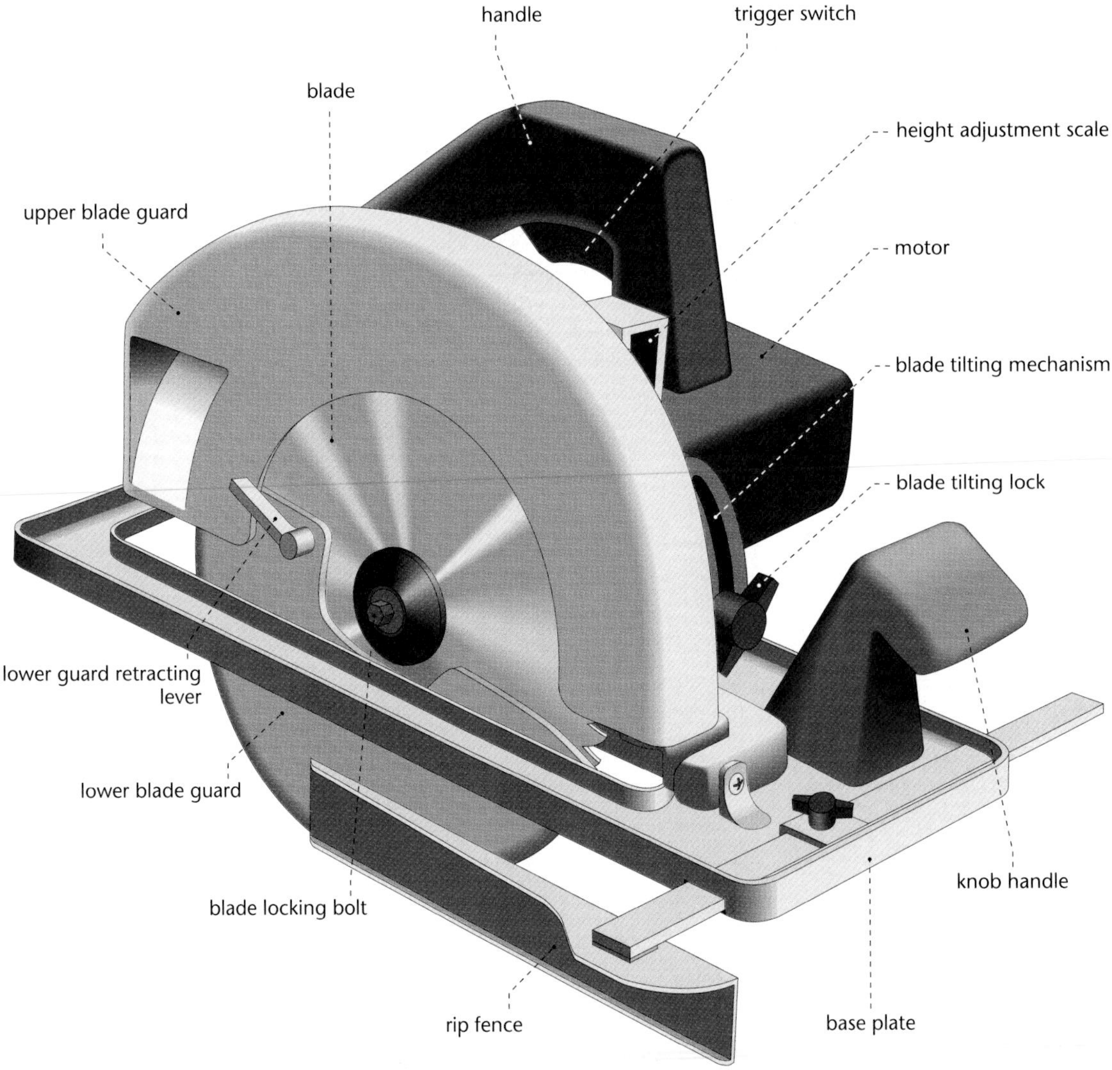

DO-IT-YOURSELF

handle

trigger switch

blade

height adjustment scale

upper blade guard

motor

blade tilting mechanism

blade tilting lock

lower guard retracting lever

lower blade guard

blade locking bolt

knob handle

rip fence

base plate

284

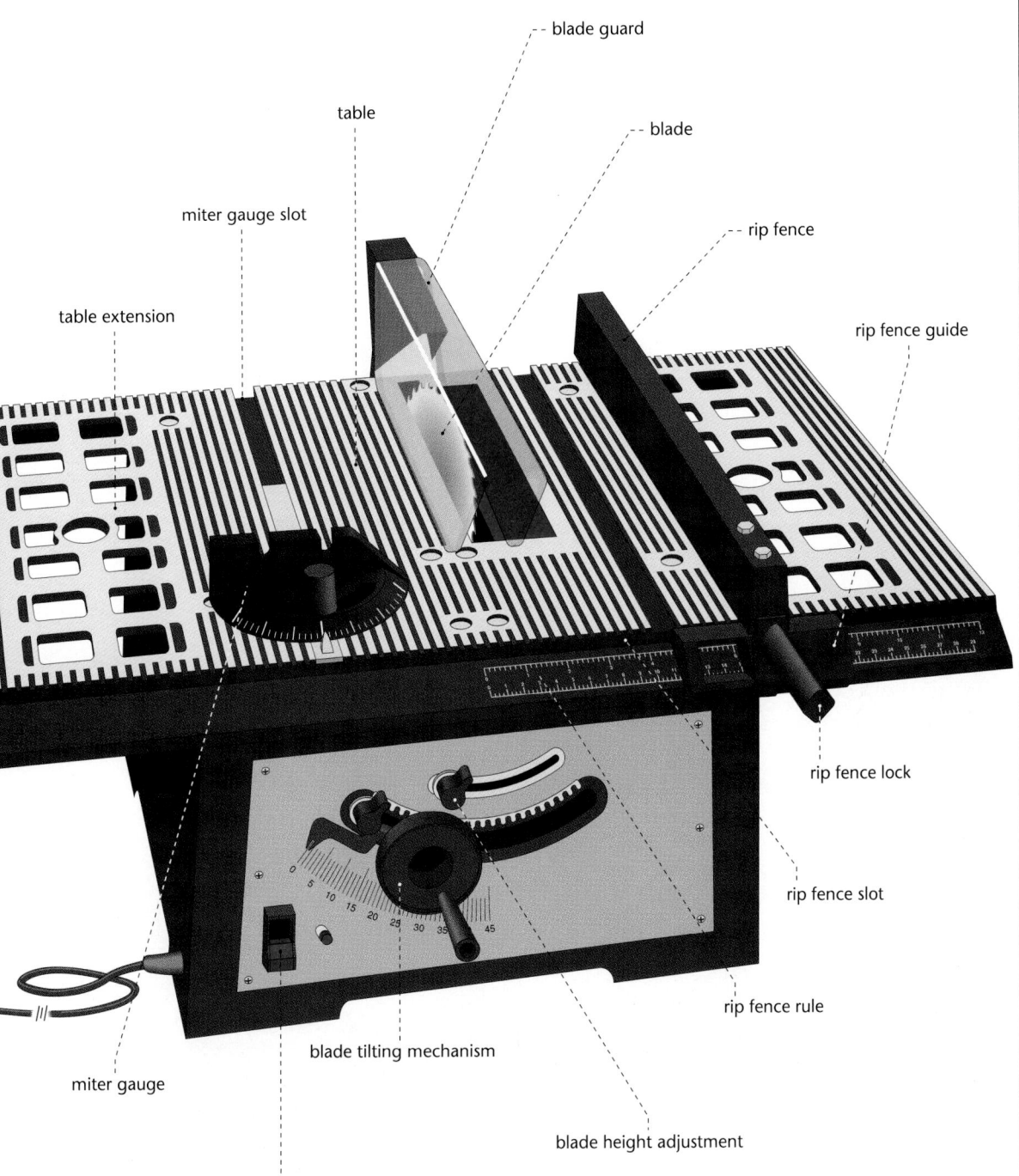

blade guard

table

blade

miter gauge slot

rip fence

table extension

rip fence guide

rip fence lock

rip fence slot

rip fence rule

miter gauge

blade tilting mechanism

blade height adjustment

switch

DO-IT-YOURSELF

BASIC BUILDING MATERIALS

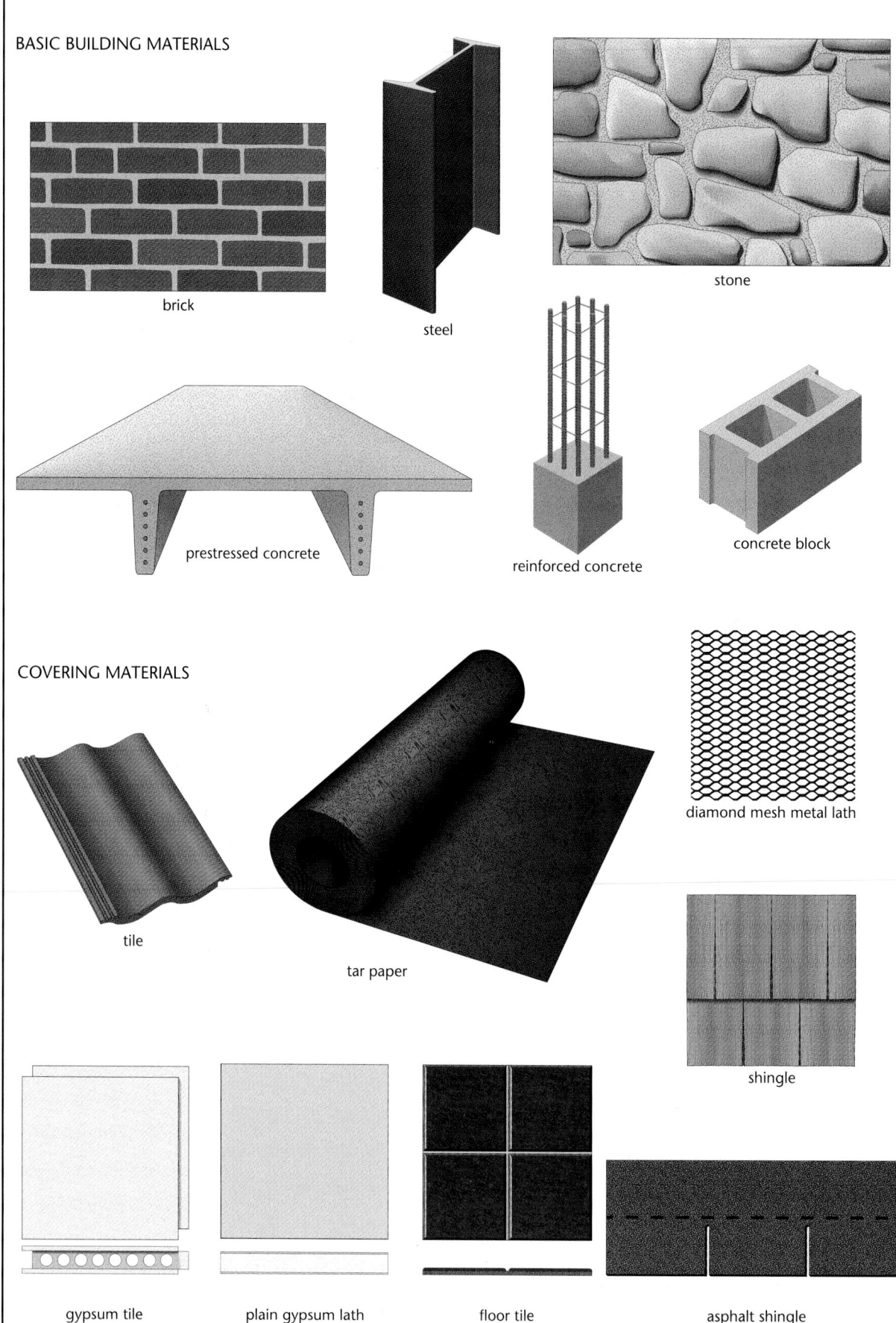

brick

steel

stone

prestressed concrete

reinforced concrete

concrete block

COVERING MATERIALS

tile

tar paper

diamond mesh metal lath

shingle

gypsum tile

plain gypsum lath

floor tile

asphalt shingle

spring-metal insulation

foam insulation

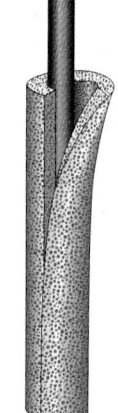
molded insulation

foam-rubber insulation

board insulation

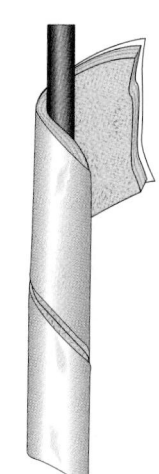
pipe-wrapping insulation

vinyl insulation

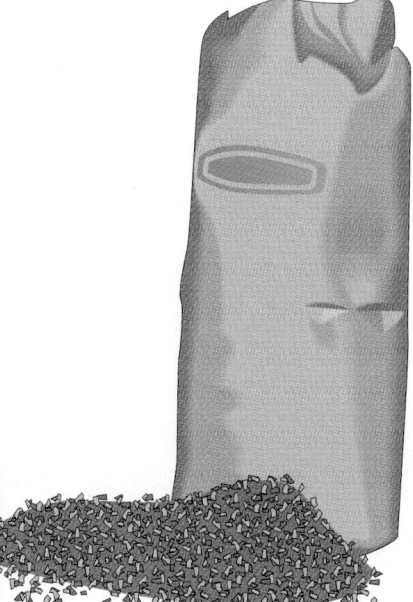
loose fill insulation

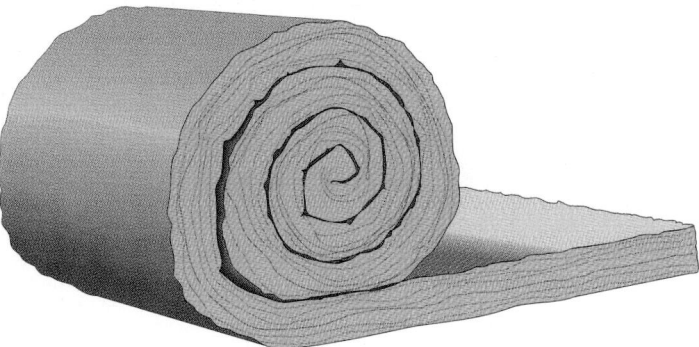
blanket insulation

DO-IT-YOURSELF

WOOD

SECTION OF A LOG

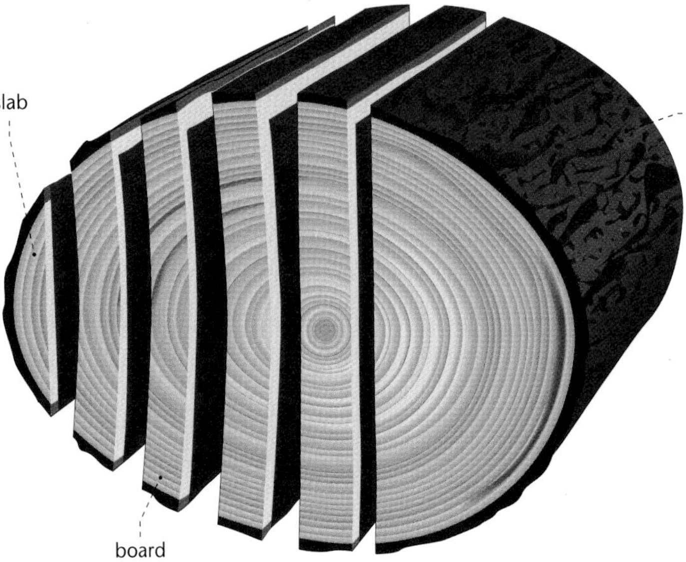

slab

log

board

BOARD

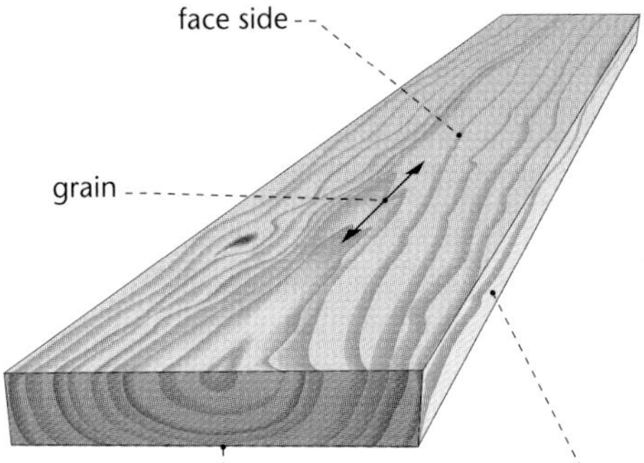

face side

grain

end grain

back

edge

WOOD-BASED MATERIALS

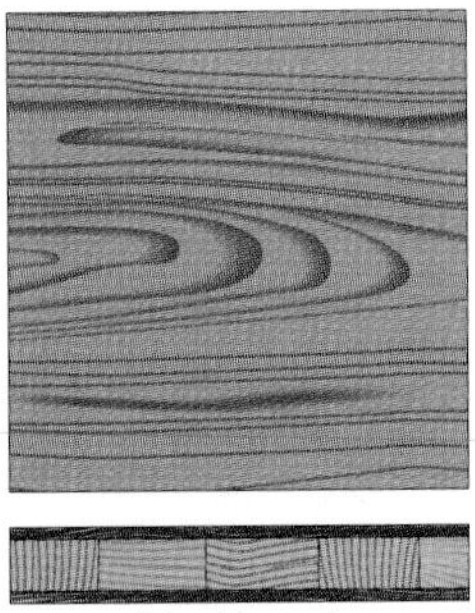

ply

blockboard

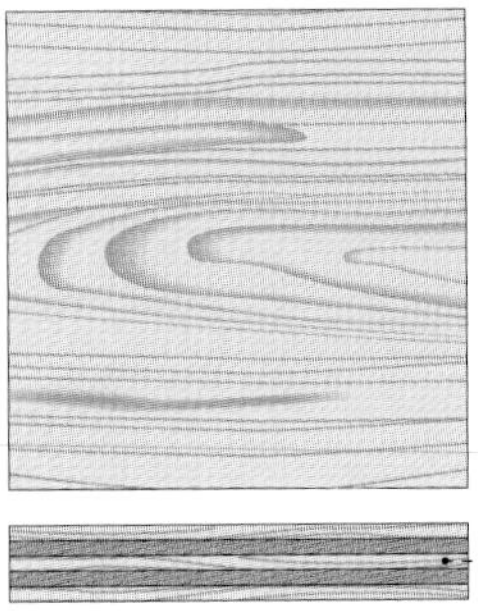

multi-ply plywood

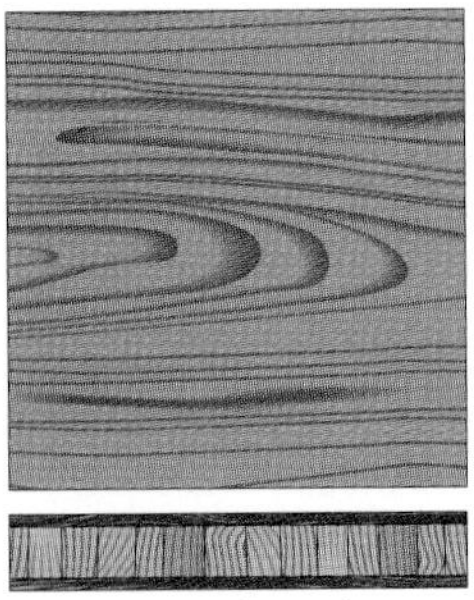

laminboard

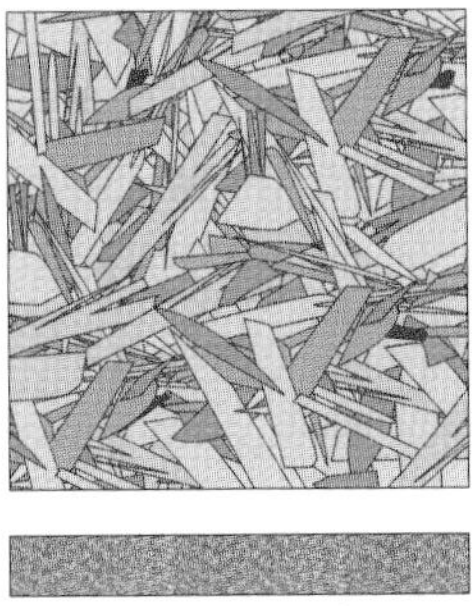

waferboard

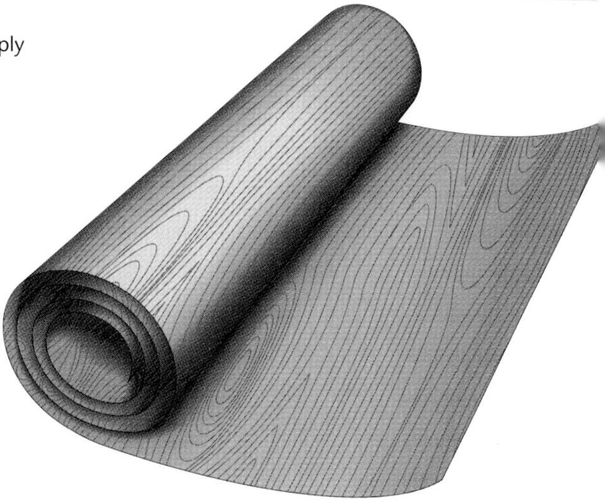

peeled veneer

hardboard

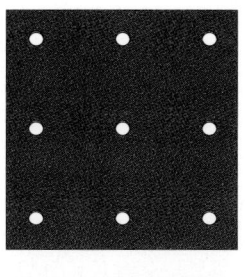

perforated hardboard

plastic-laminated particle board

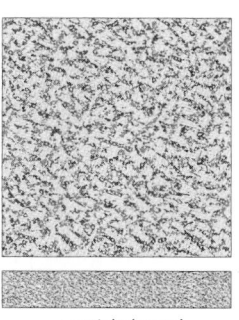

particle board

LOCK

GENERAL VIEW

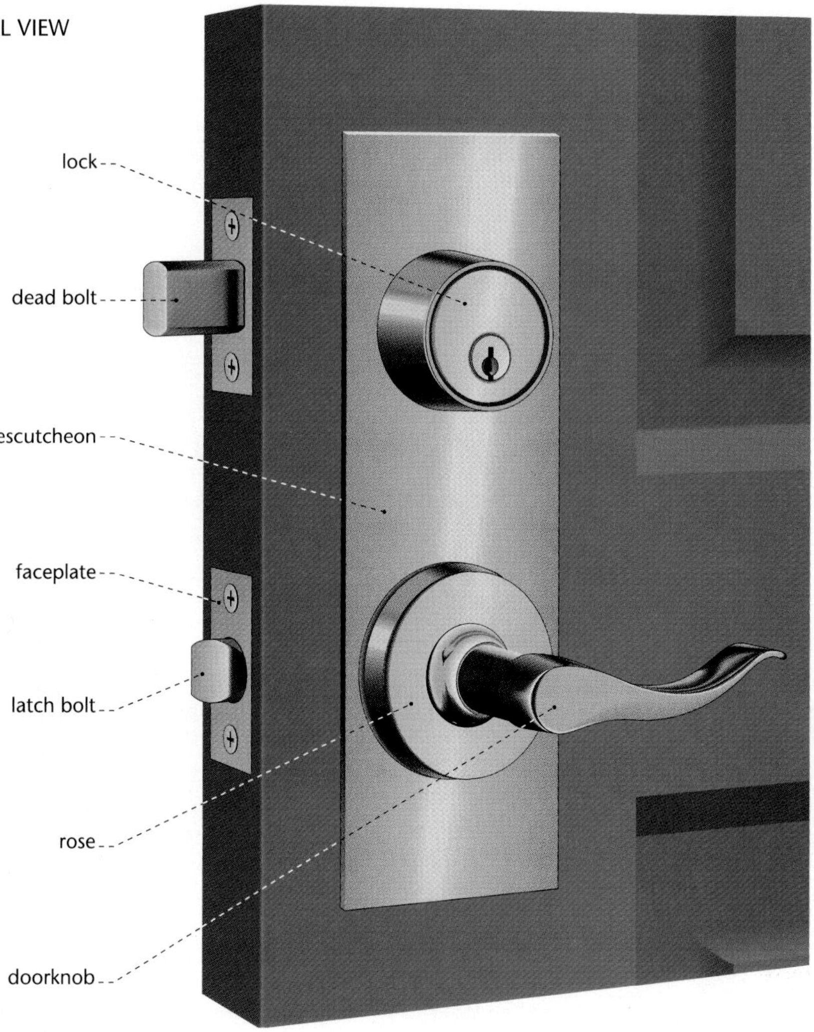

lock

dead bolt

escutcheon

faceplate

latch bolt

rose

doorknob

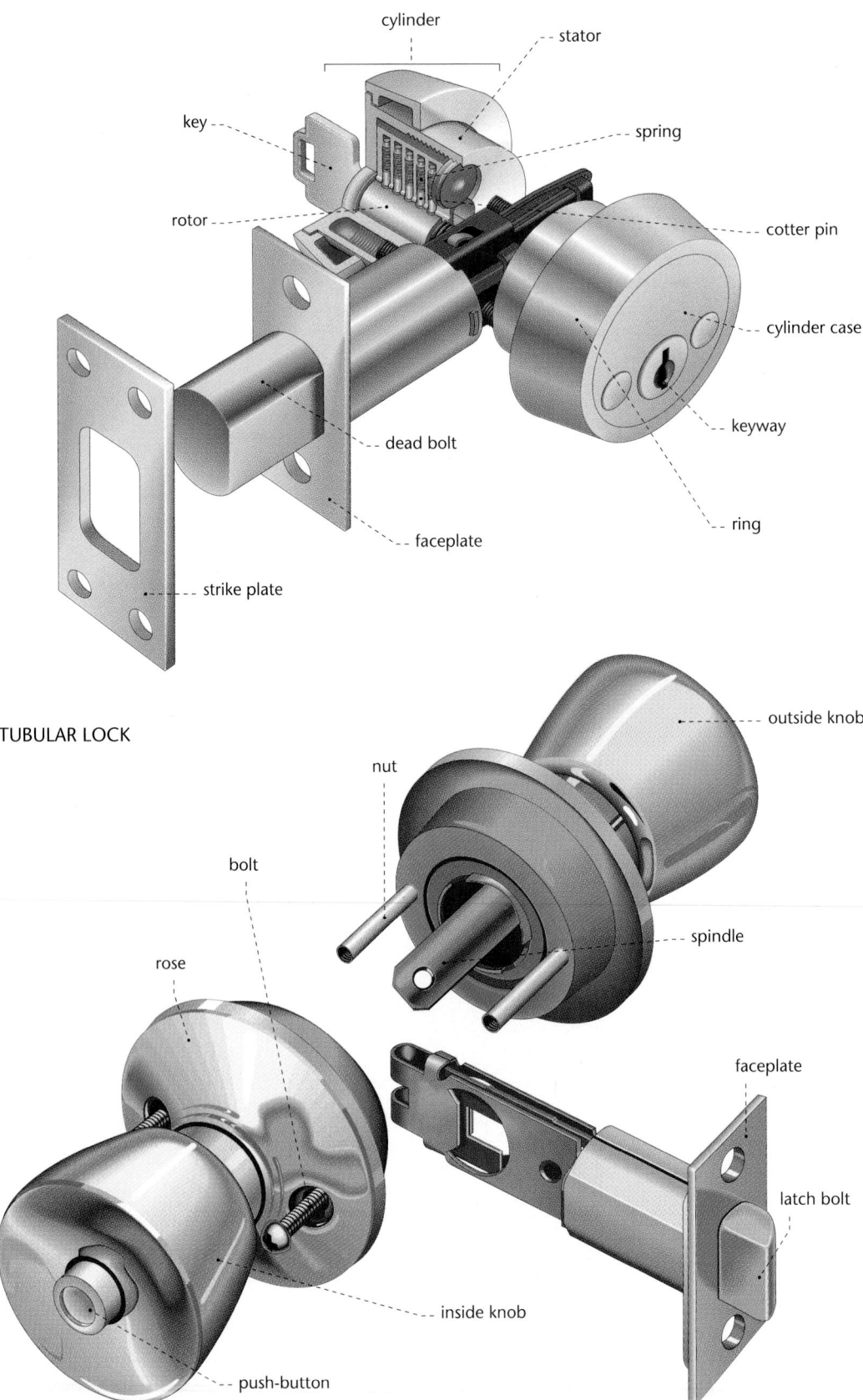

MORTISE LOCK

cylinder

stator

key

spring

rotor

cotter pin

cylinder case

dead bolt

keyway

faceplate

ring

strike plate

TUBULAR LOCK

outside knob

nut

bolt

spindle

rose

faceplate

latch bolt

inside knob

push-button

MASONRY

MASON'S TROWEL

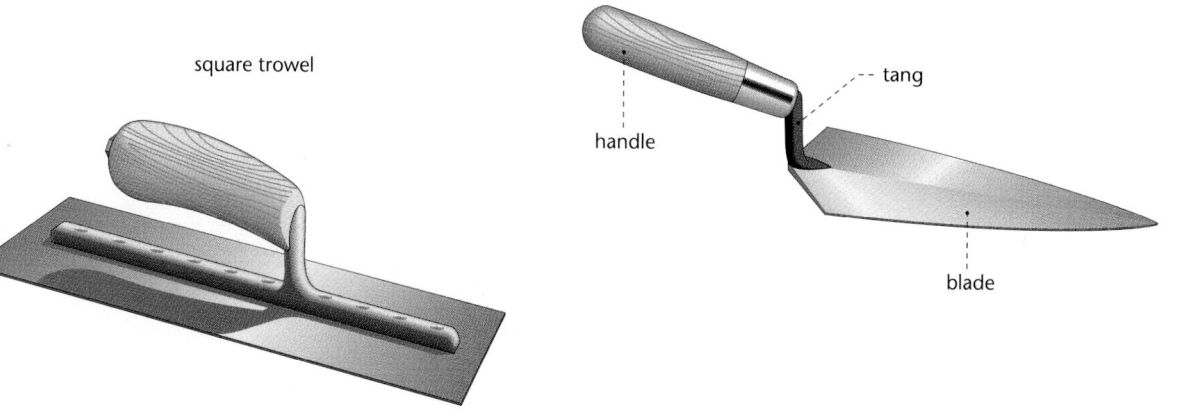

square trowel

handle

tang

blade

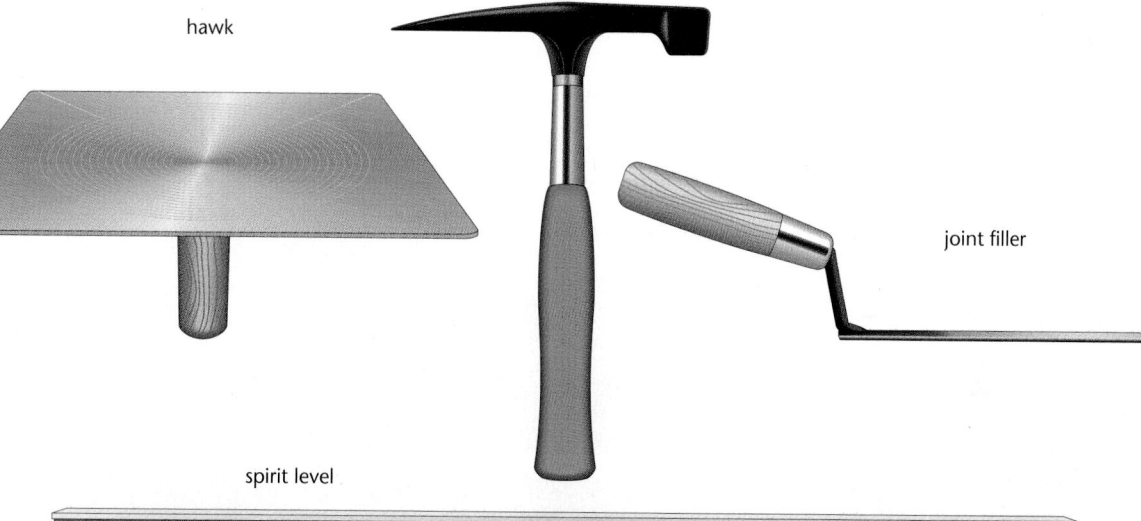

bricklayer's hammer

hawk

joint filler

spirit level

CAULKING GUN

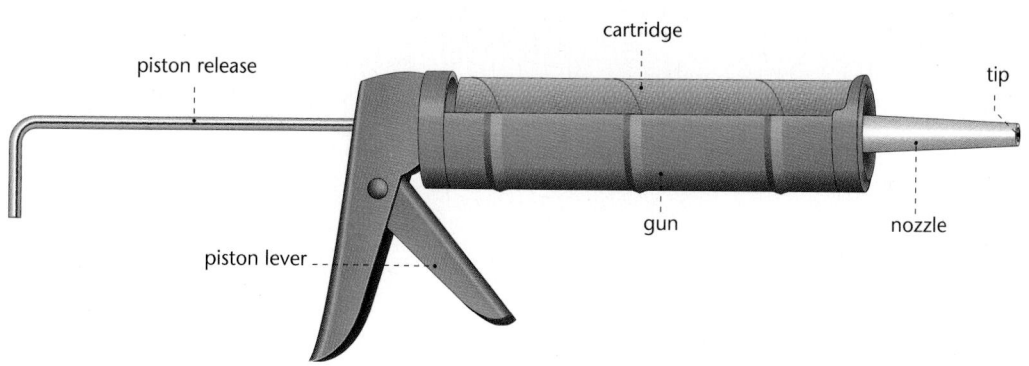

piston release

cartridge

tip

gun

nozzle

piston lever

DO-IT-YOURSELF

folding door

shower stall

spray hose

portable shower head

overflow

shower head

faucet

mirror

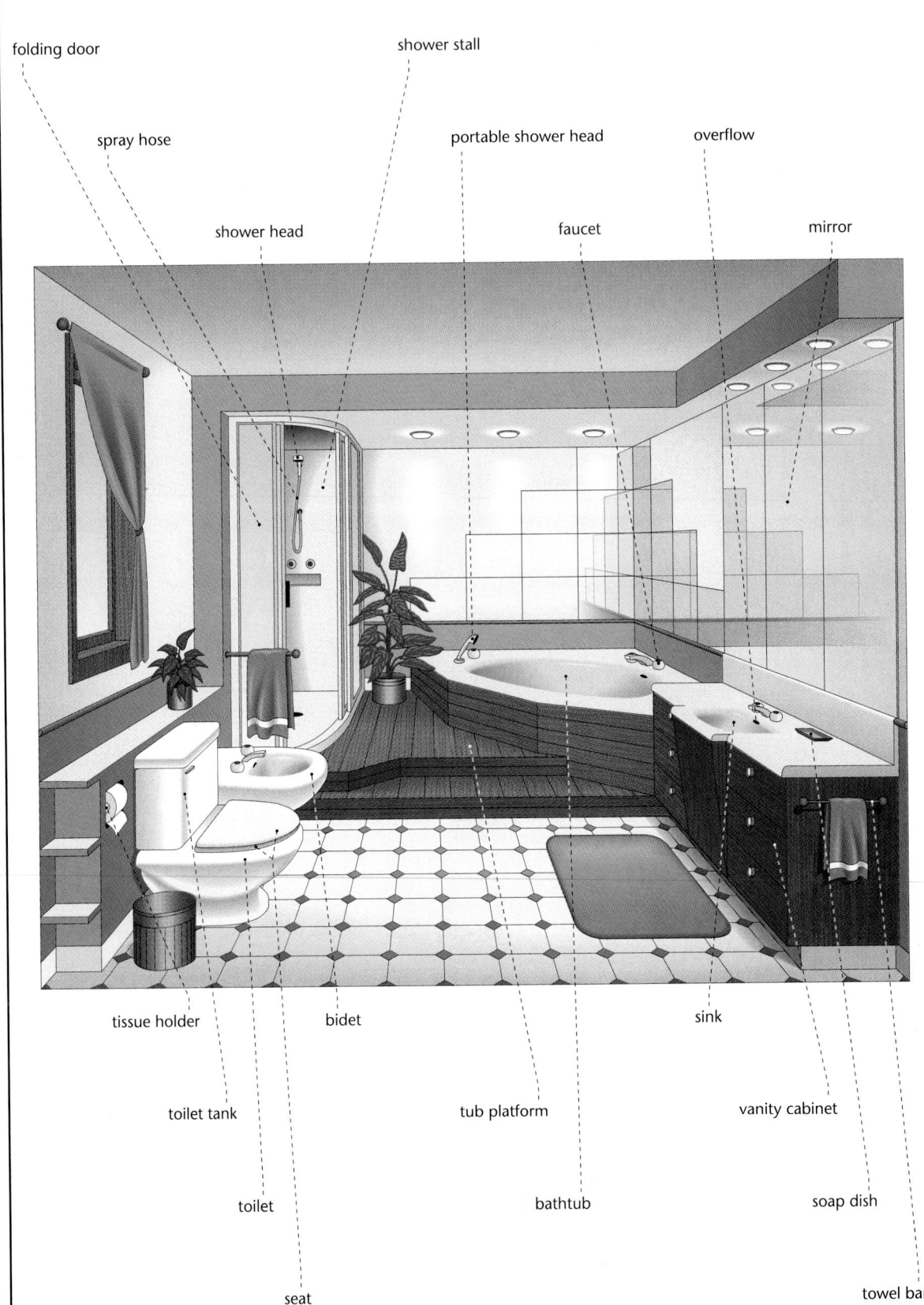

tissue holder

bidet

sink

toilet tank

tub platform

vanity cabinet

toilet

bathtub

soap dish

seat

towel bar

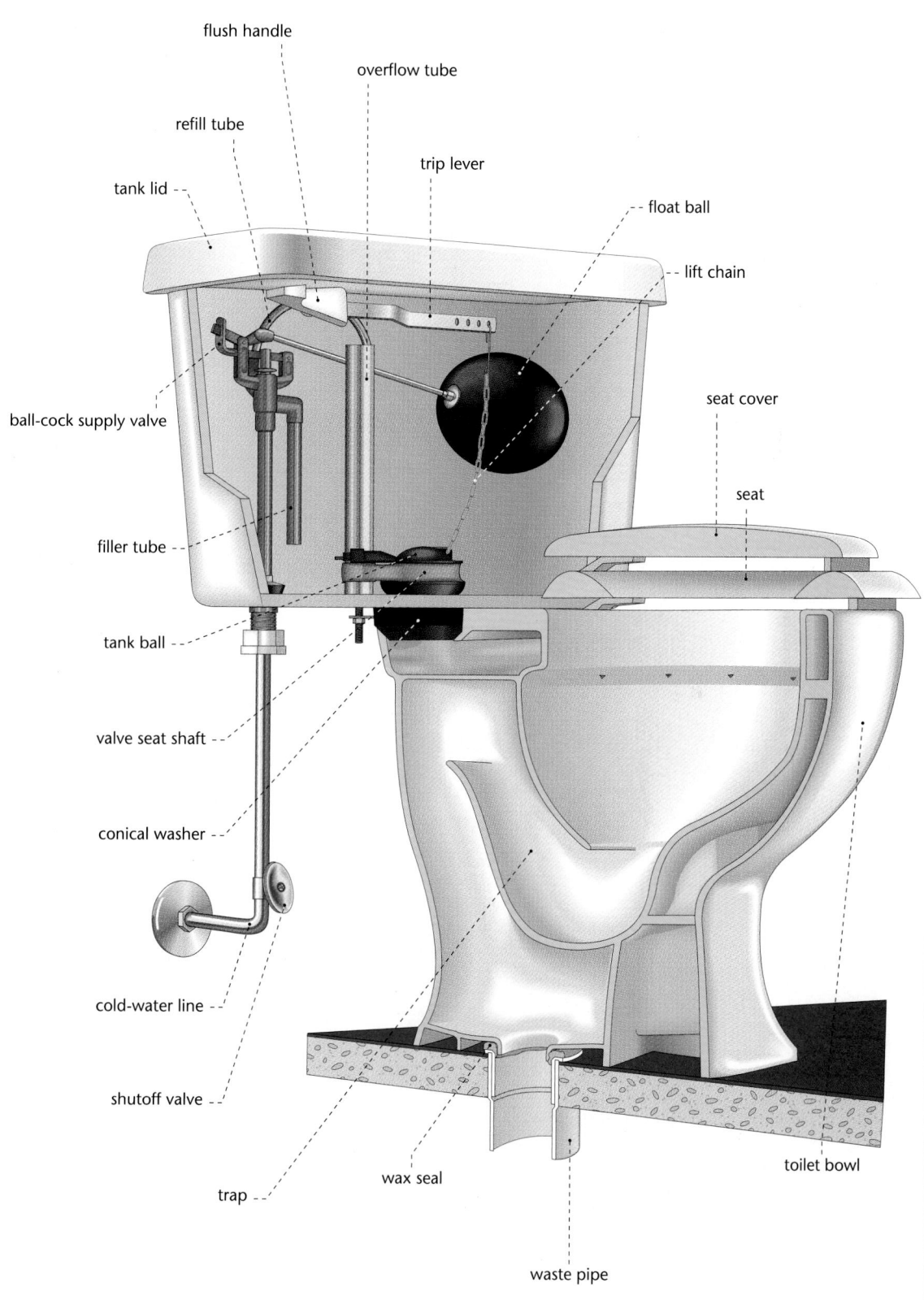

flush handle

overflow tube

refill tube

trip lever

tank lid

float ball

lift chain

ball-cock supply valve

seat cover

seat

filler tube

tank ball

valve seat shaft

conical washer

cold-water line

shutoff valve

trap

wax seal

toilet bowl

waste pipe

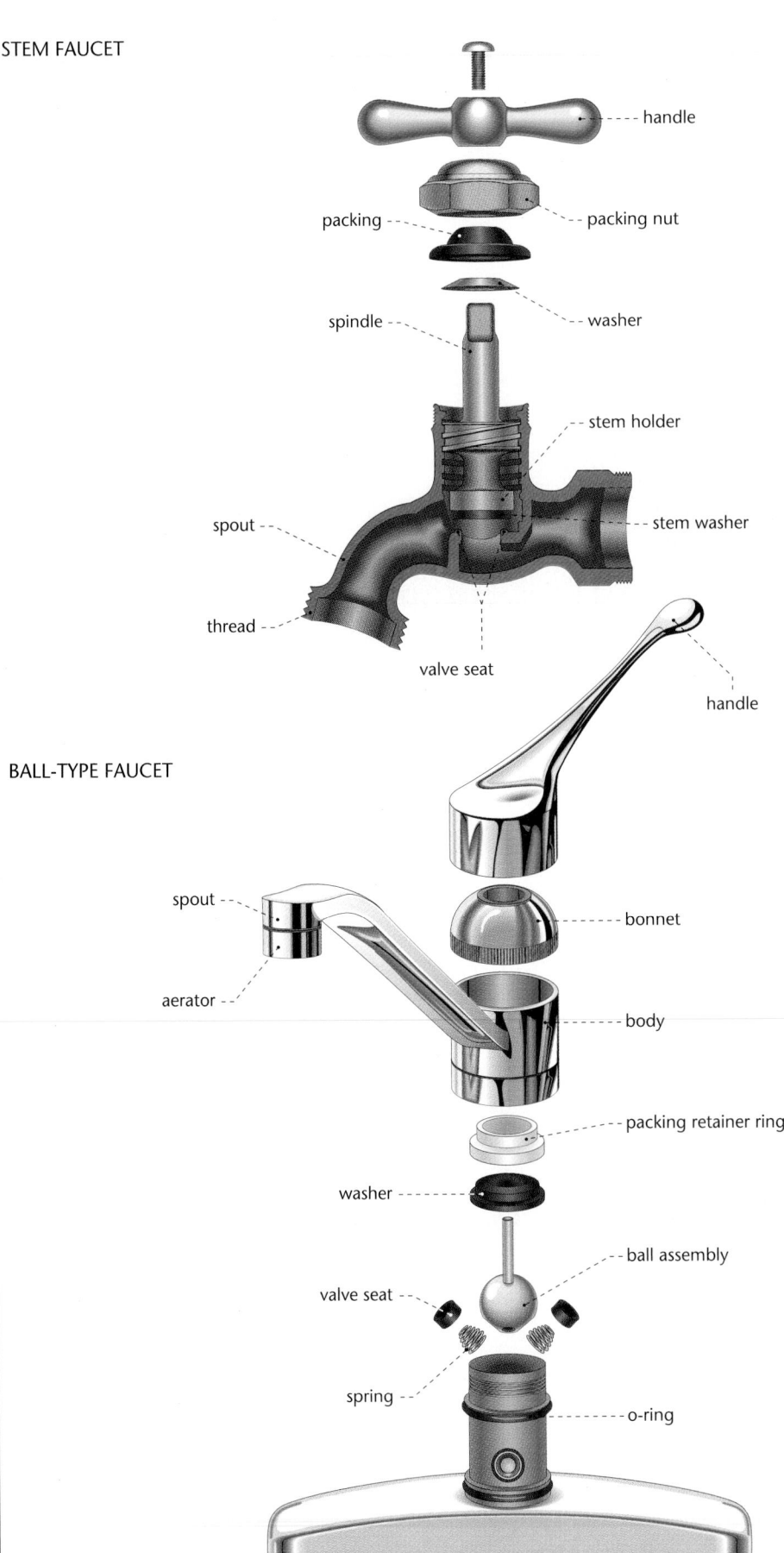

STEM FAUCET

handle

packing — packing nut

spindle — washer

stem holder

spout — stem washer

thread

valve seat

handle

BALL-TYPE FAUCET

spout — bonnet

aerator — body

packing retainer ring

washer

ball assembly

valve seat

spring — o-ring

DO-IT-YOURSELF

handle

bonnet

cylinder

seal

spout

aerator

water inlet

escutcheon

CARTRIDGE FAUCET

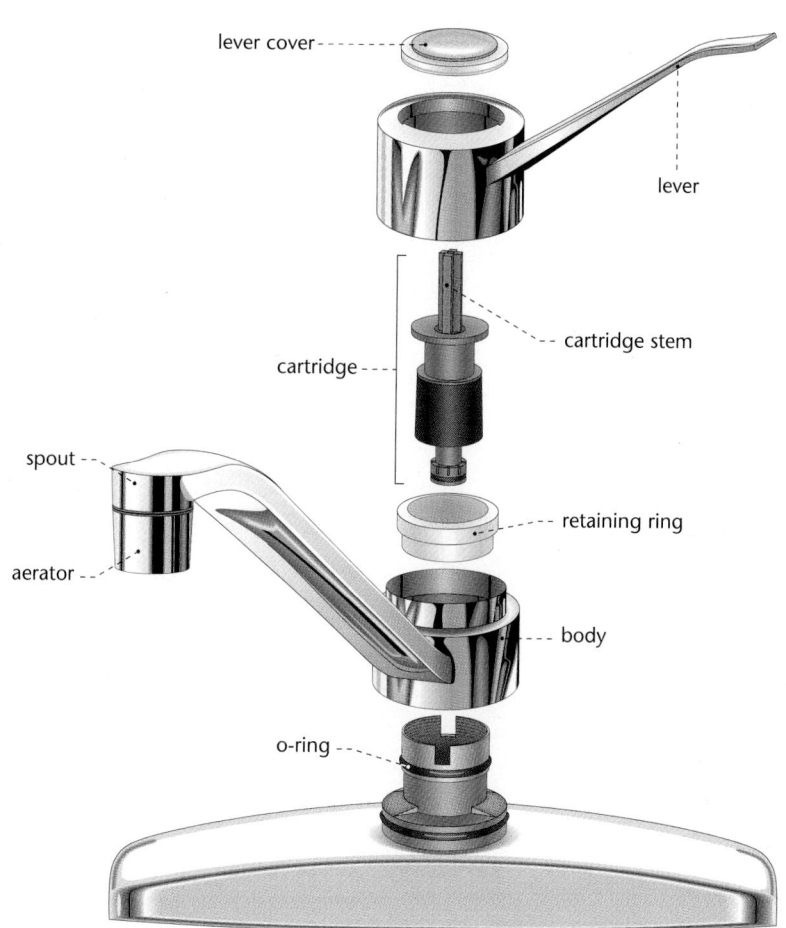

lever cover

lever

cartridge stem

cartridge

spout

retaining ring

aerator

body

o-ring

GARBAGE DISPOSAL SINK

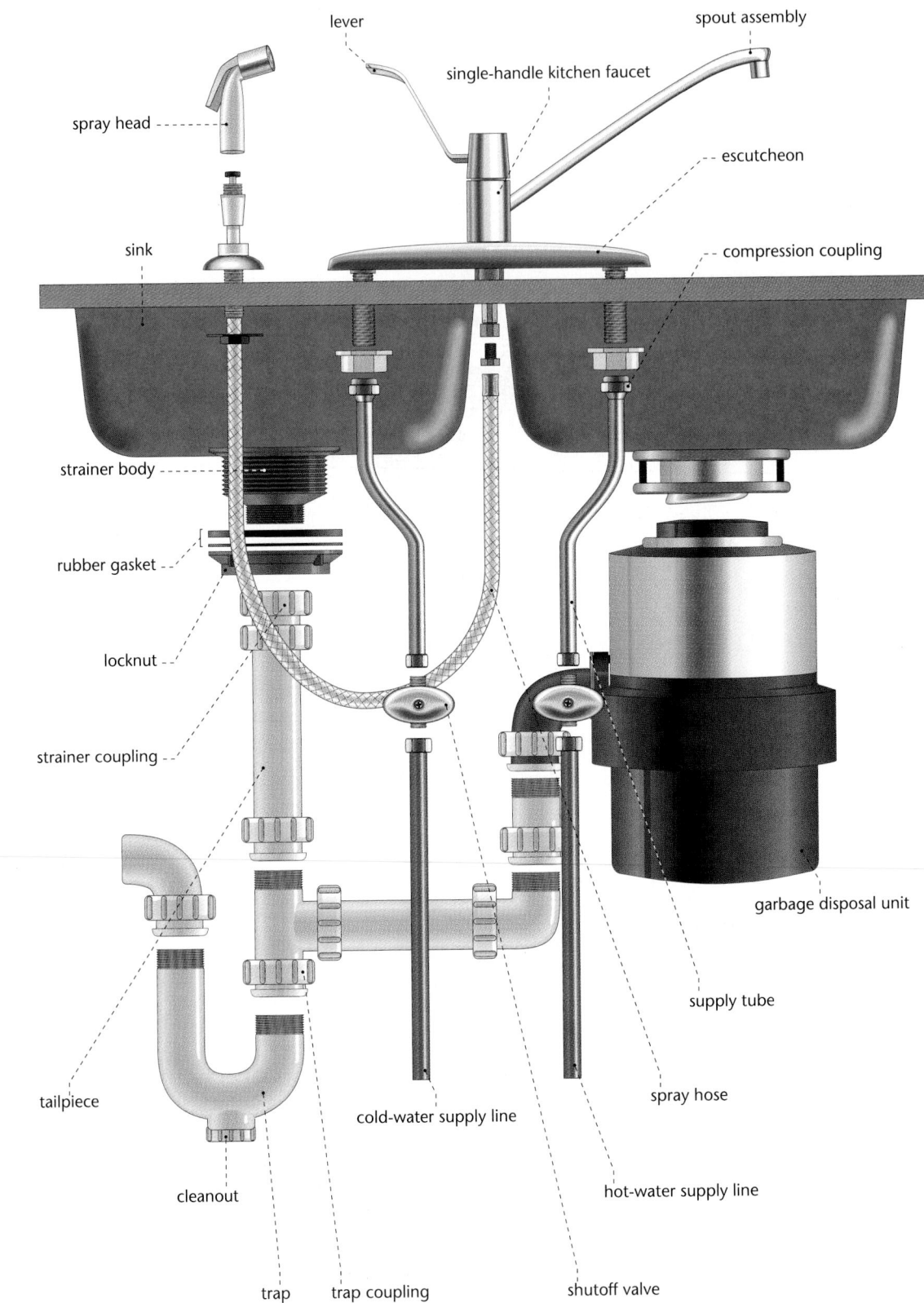

lever

spout assembly

single-handle kitchen faucet

spray head

escutcheon

sink

compression coupling

strainer body

rubber gasket

locknut

strainer coupling

garbage disposal unit

supply tube

spray hose

tailpiece

cold-water supply line

cleanout

hot-water supply line

trap

trap coupling

shutoff valve

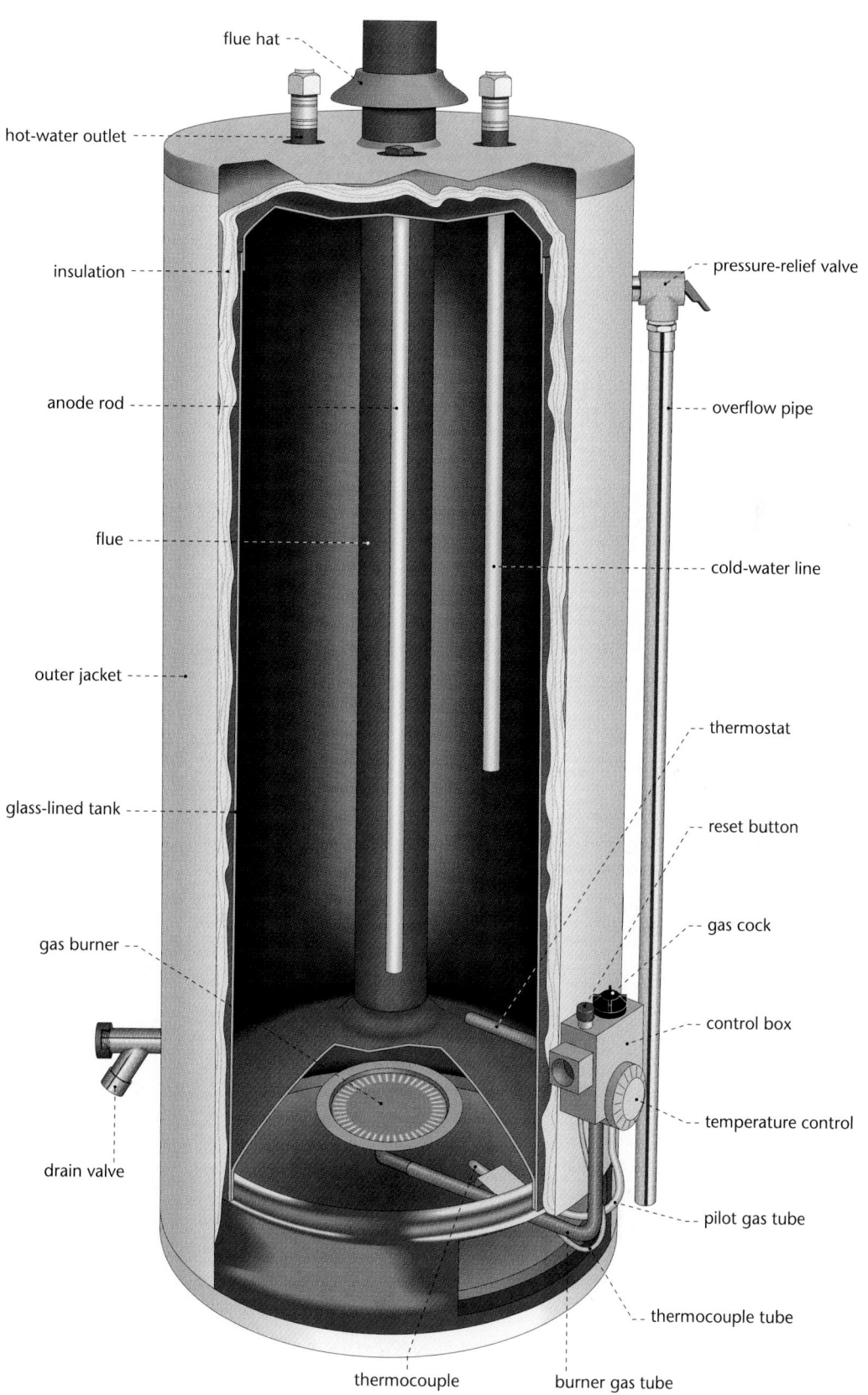

flue hat

hot-water outlet

insulation

anode rod

flue

outer jacket

glass-lined tank

gas burner

drain valve

pressure-relief valve

overflow pipe

cold-water line

thermostat

reset button

gas cock

control box

temperature control

pilot gas tube

thermocouple tube

thermocouple

burner gas tube

DO-IT-YOURSELF

PLUMBING: EXAMPLES OF BRANCHING

WASHER

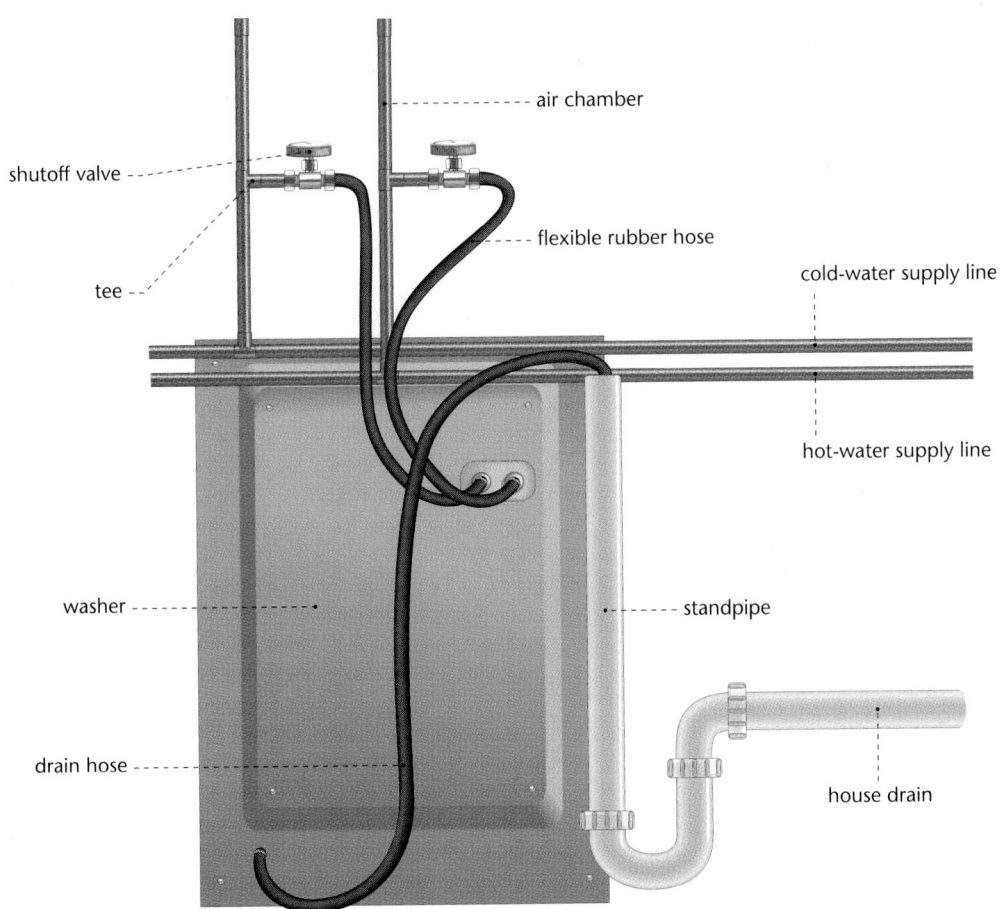

air chamber

shutoff valve

flexible rubber hose

tee

cold-water supply line

hot-water supply line

washer

standpipe

drain hose

house drain

DISHWASHER

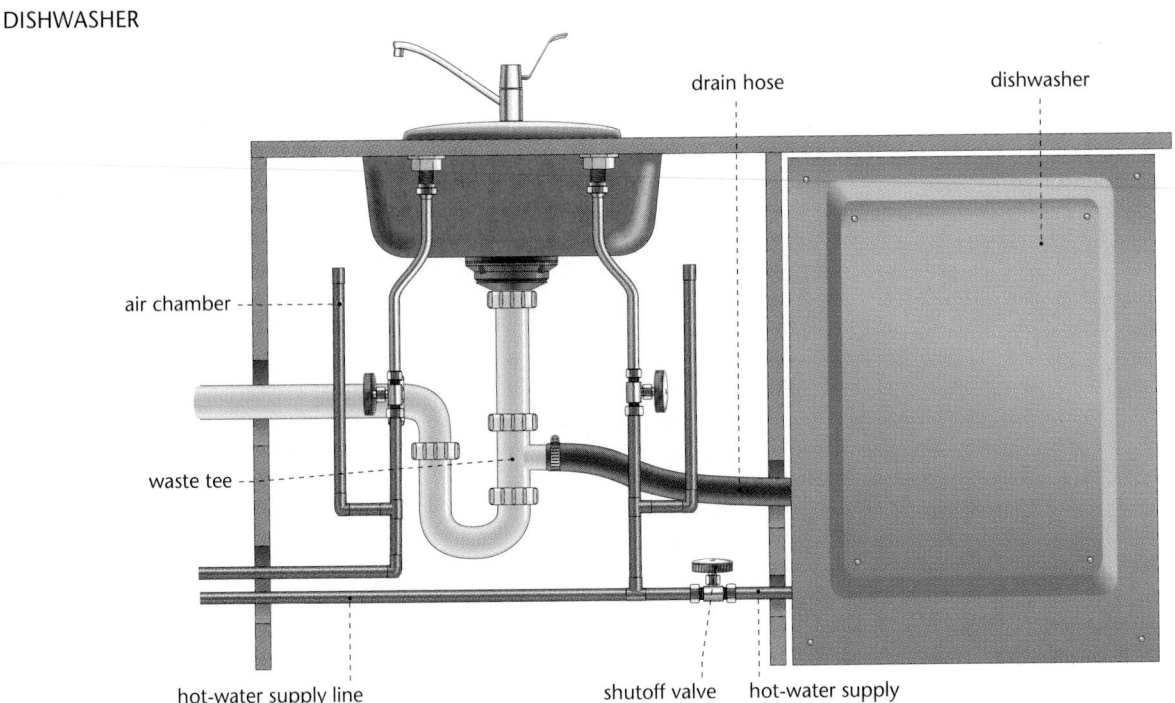

drain hose

dishwasher

air chamber

waste tee

hot-water supply line

shutoff valve

hot-water supply

PLUMBING

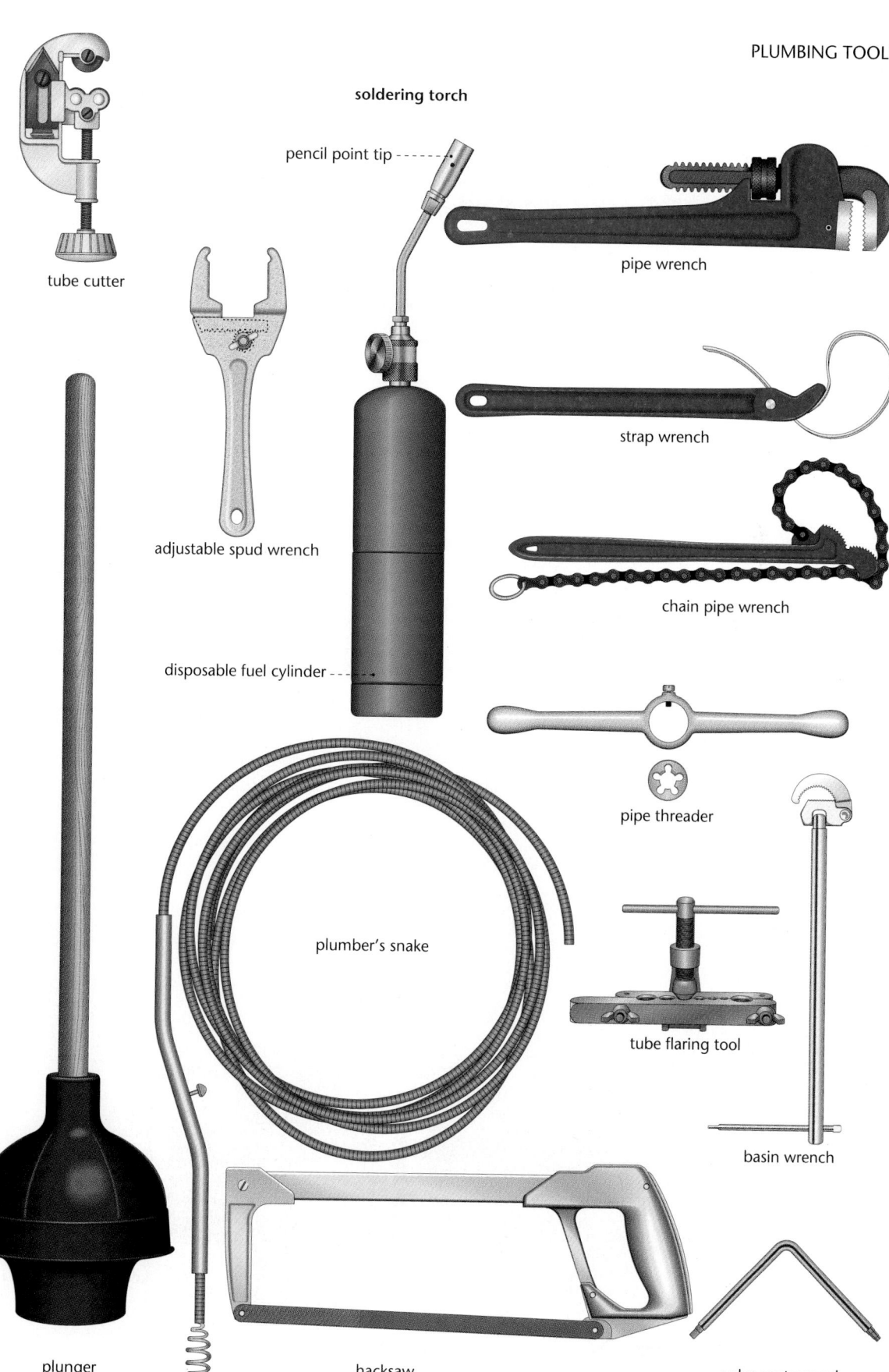

tube cutter

soldering torch

pencil point tip

pipe wrench

adjustable spud wrench

strap wrench

chain pipe wrench

disposable fuel cylinder

pipe threader

plumber's snake

tube flaring tool

basin wrench

plunger

hacksaw

valve seat wrench

MECHANICAL CONNECTORS

compression fitting

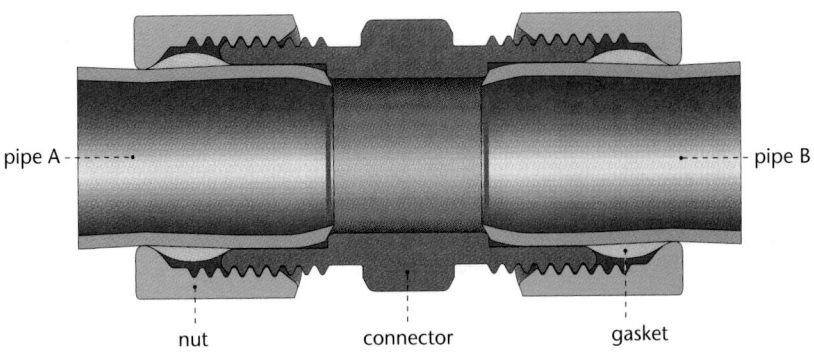

pipe A — — — — pipe B

nut — connector — gasket

flare joint

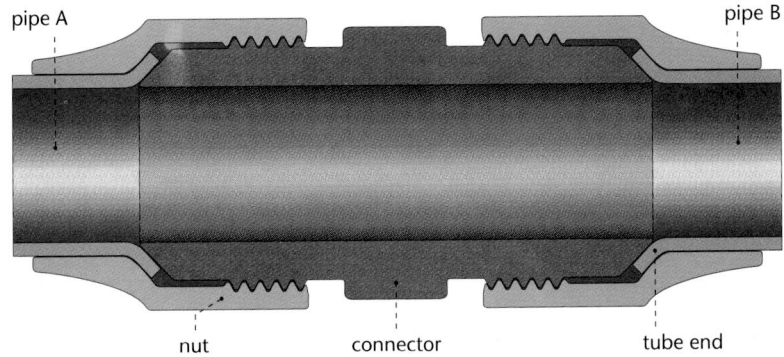

pipe A — pipe B

nut — connector — tube end

union

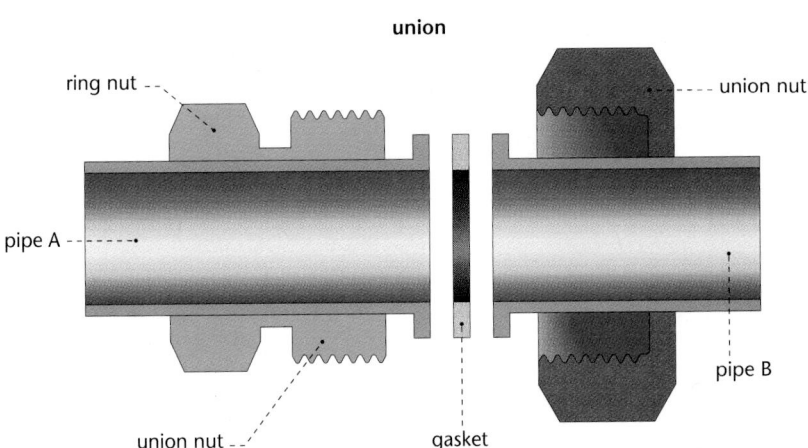

ring nut — — — union nut

pipe A — — —

union nut — — gasket — pipe B

steel to plastic

copper to plastic

copper to steel

FITTINGS

45° elbow

elbow

U-bend

tee

Y-branch

offset

trap

square head plug

cap

flush bushing

nipple

reducing coupling

threaded cap

pipe coupling

hexagon bushing

LADDERS AND STEPLADDERS

STEPLADDER

EXTENSION LADDER

tool tray

top

step

brace

step stool

rung

side rail

pulley

locking device

PLATFORM LADDER

safety rail

shelf

platform

frame

step

rubber tip

hoisting rope

anti-slip shoe

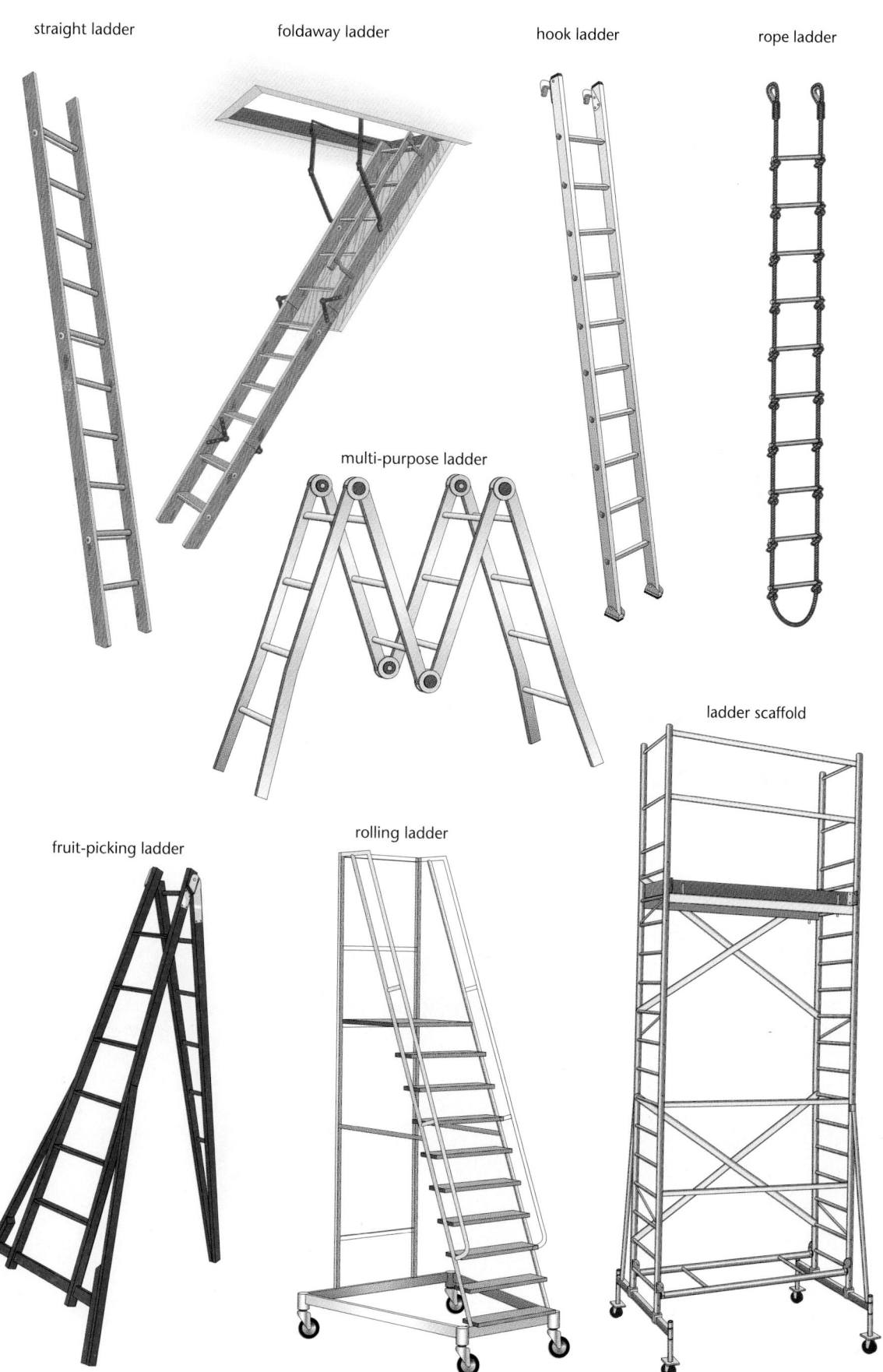

straight ladder

foldaway ladder

hook ladder

rope ladder

multi-purpose ladder

ladder scaffold

fruit-picking ladder

rolling ladder

PAINTING UPKEEP

SPRAY PAINT GUN

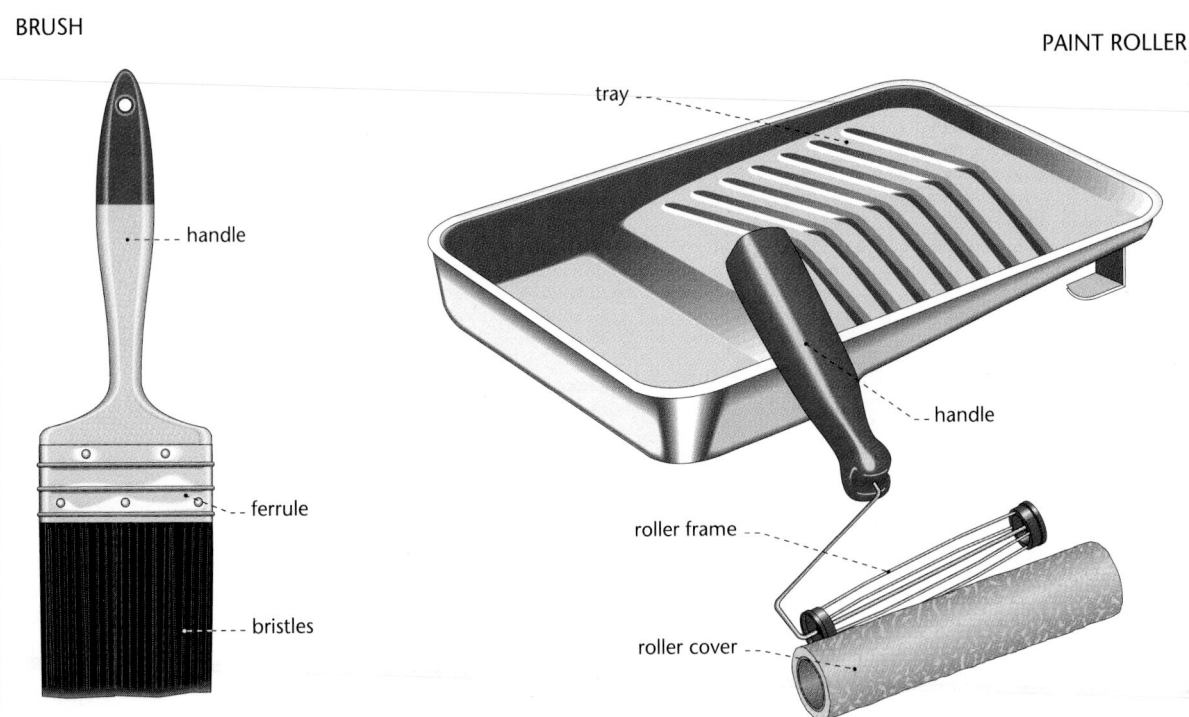

spreader adjustment valve

fluid adjustment screw

nozzle

air valve

air cap

gun body

trigger

air hose connection

vent hole

SCRAPER

blade

container

knurled bolt

handle

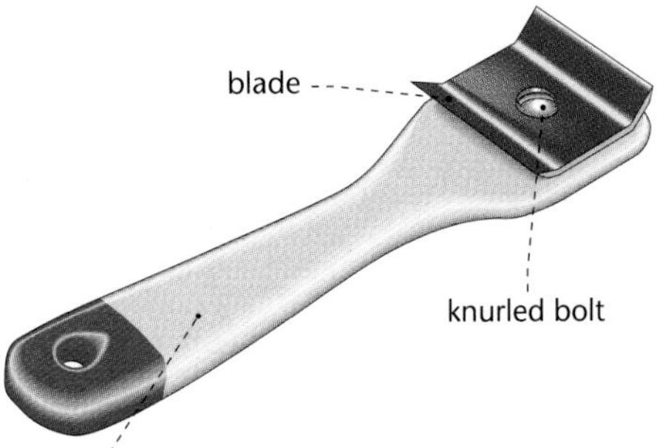

BRUSH

PAINT ROLLER

tray

handle

handle

ferrule

roller frame

bristles

roller cover

304

SOLDERING AND WELDING

soldering iron

SOLDERING GUN

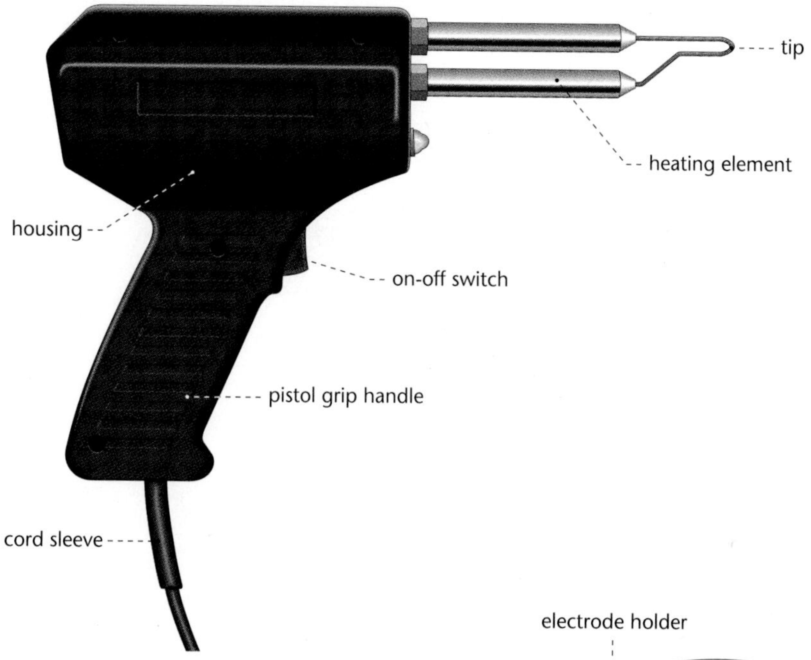

---- tip

---- heating element

housing -- ·

---- on-off switch

---- pistol grip handle

cord sleeve - - - -

ARC WELDING

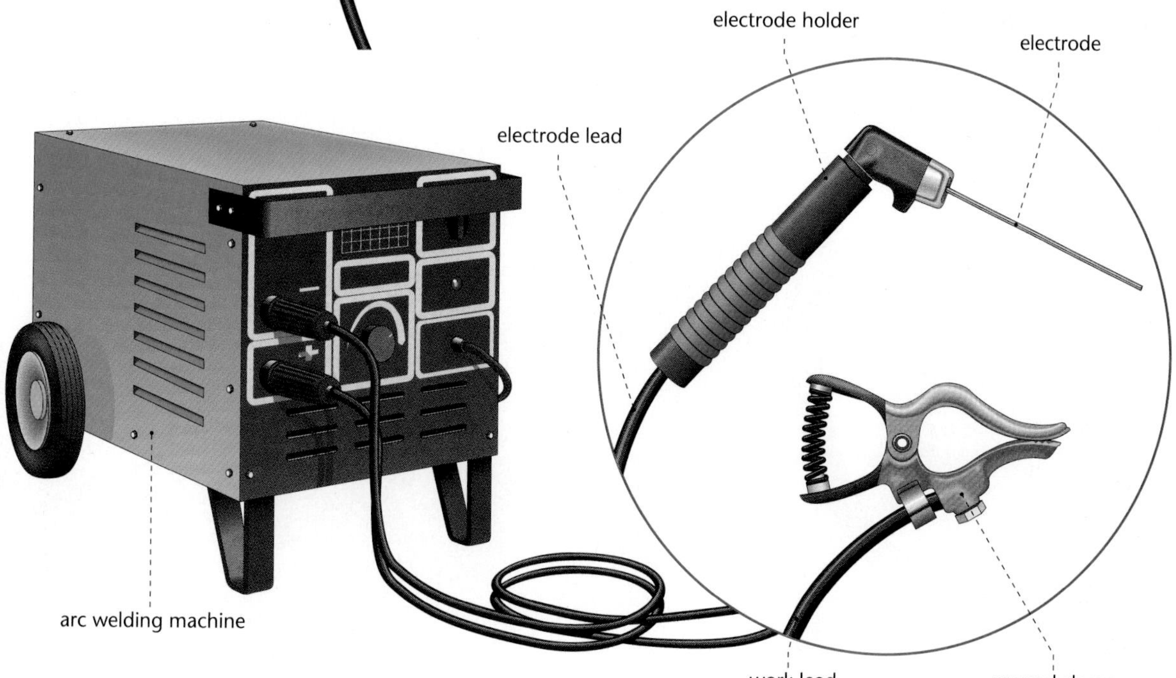

electrode holder

electrode

electrode lead

arc welding machine

work lead

ground clamp

SOLDERING AND WELDING

CUTTING TORCH

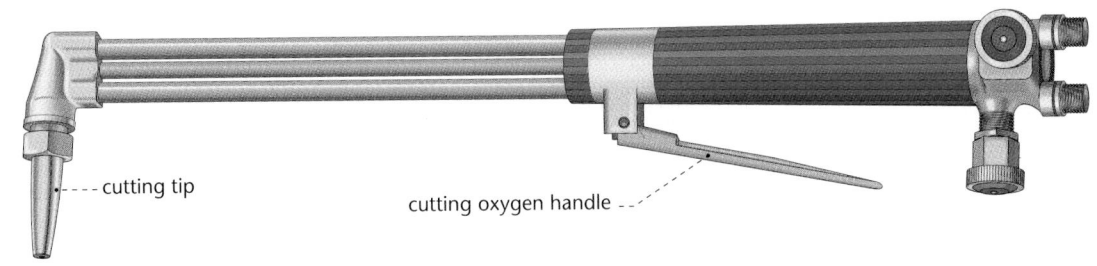

cutting tip

cutting oxygen handle

WELDING TORCH

oxygen valve

head tube

handle

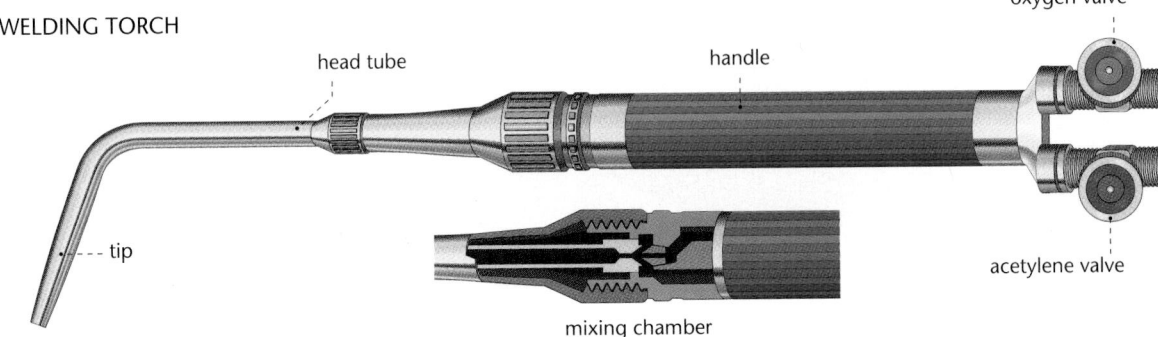

tip

acetylene valve

mixing chamber

OXYACETYLENE WELDING

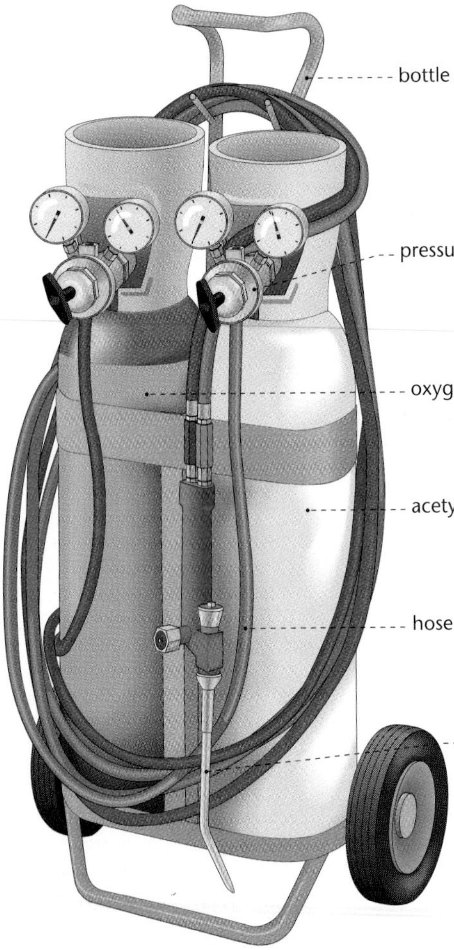

bottle cart

pressure regulator

oxygen cylinder

acetylene cylinder

hose

welding torch

PRESSURE REGULATOR

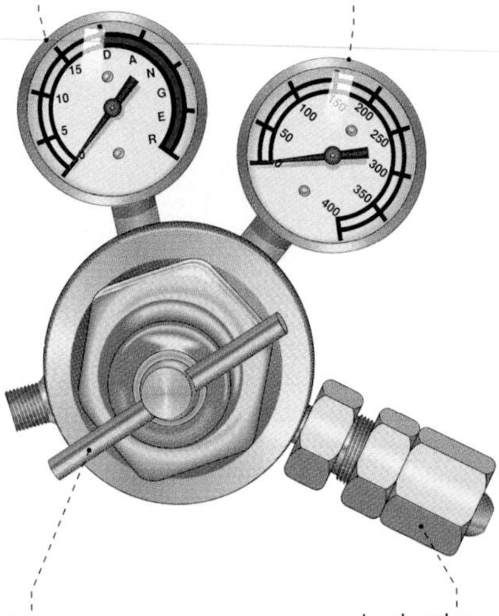

working pressure gauge

cylinder pressure gauge

adjusting screw

check valve

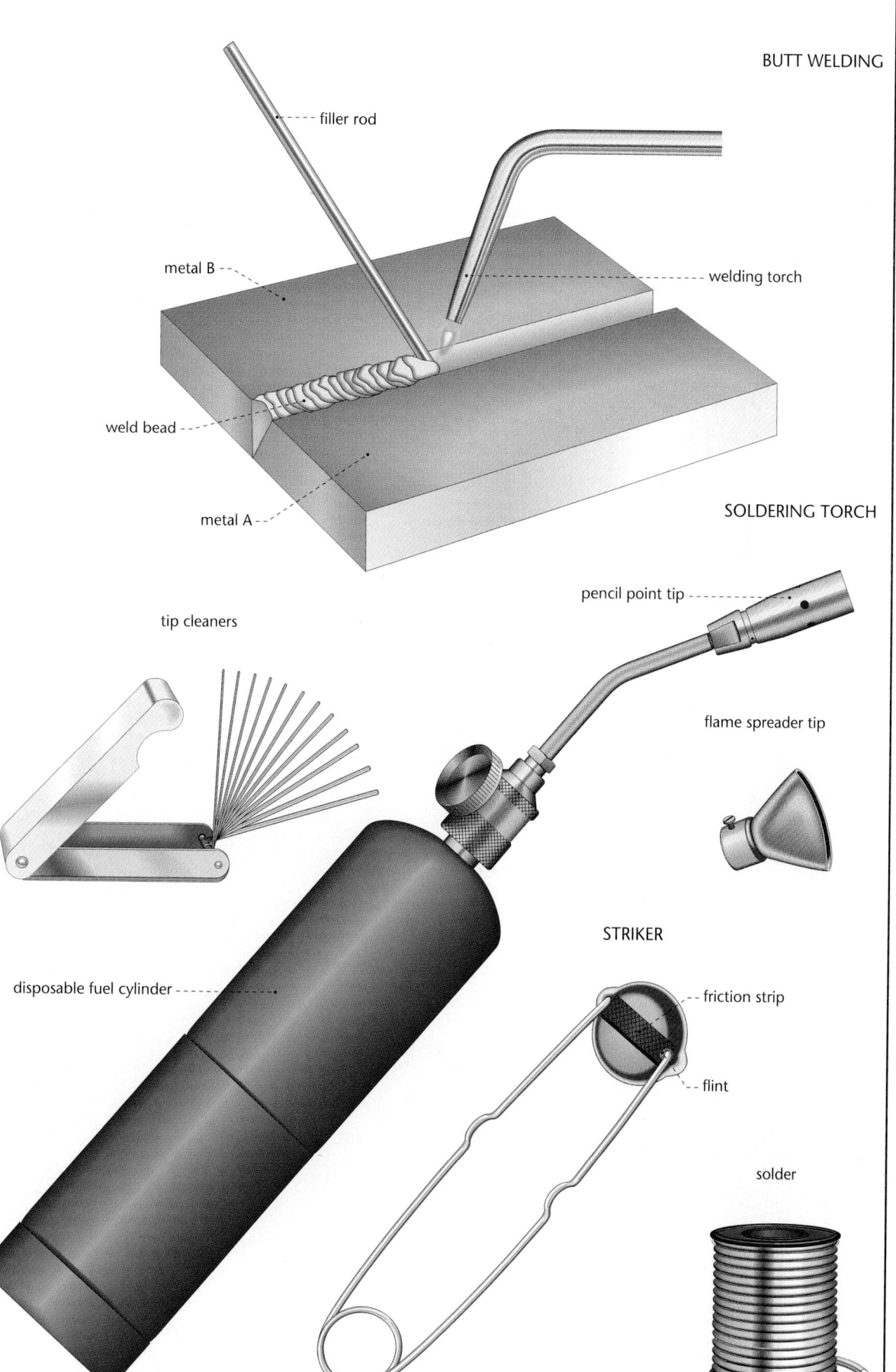

BUTT WELDING

filler rod

metal B

welding torch

weld bead

metal A

SOLDERING TORCH

pencil point tip

tip cleaners

flame spreader tip

STRIKER

disposable fuel cylinder

friction strip

flint

solder

goggles

hand shield

face shield

gauntlet

welding curtain

mitten

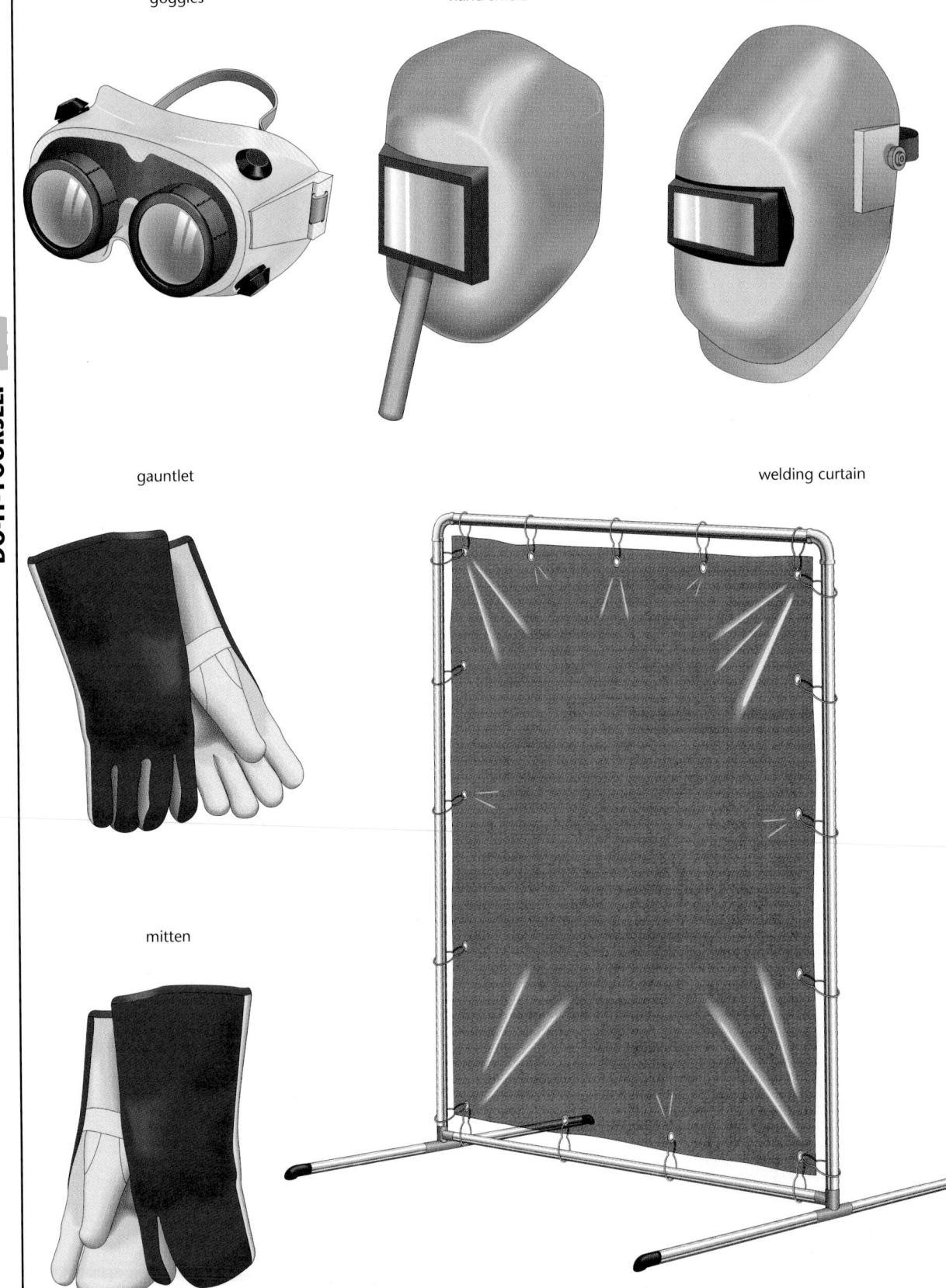

ELECTRICITY

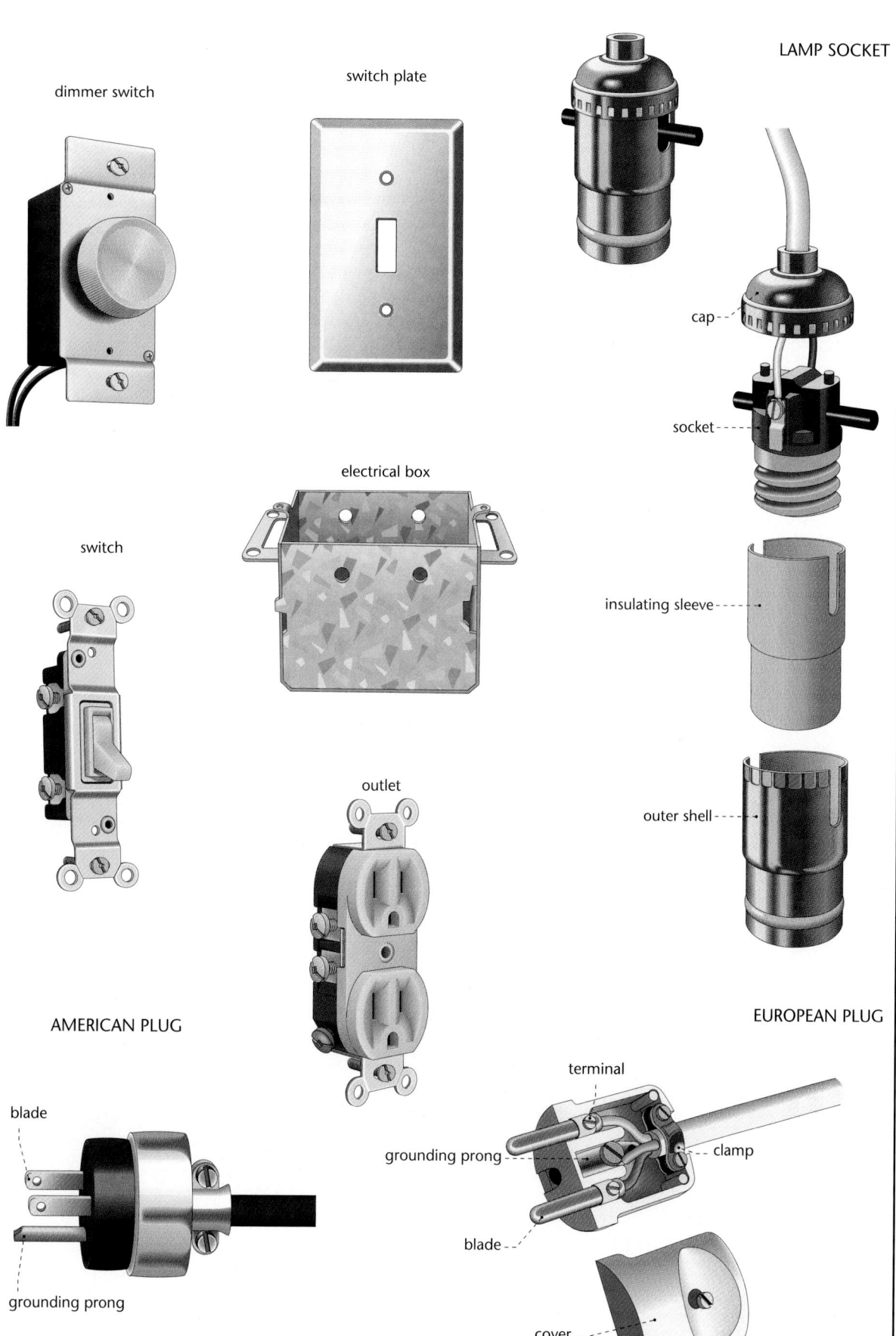

dimmer switch

switch plate

LAMP SOCKET

cap

socket

insulating sleeve

outer shell

switch

electrical box

outlet

AMERICAN PLUG

blade

grounding prong

EUROPEAN PLUG

terminal

grounding prong

clamp

blade

cover

ELECTRICIAN'S TOOLS

multimeter

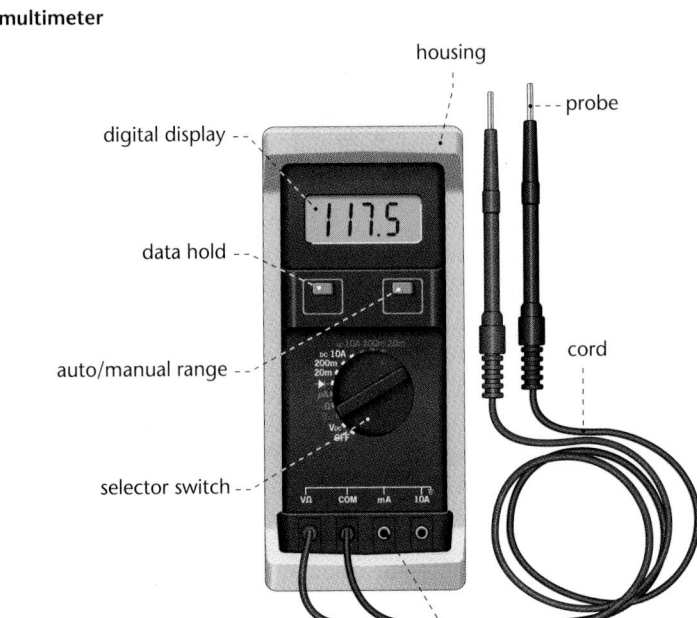

housing

probe

digital display

data hold

auto/manual range

cord

selector switch

input terminal

voltage tester

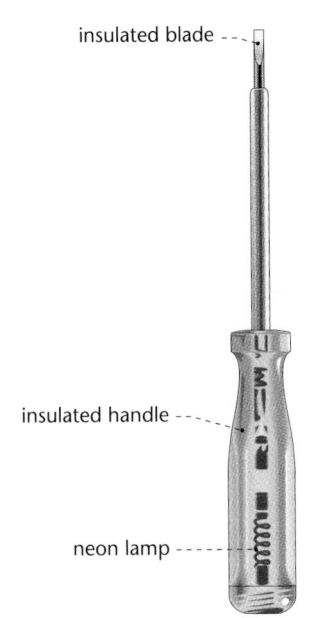

insulated blade

insulated handle

neon lamp

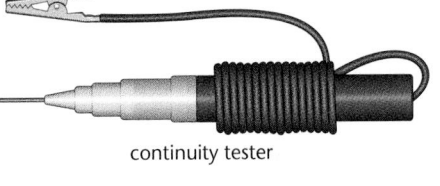

continuity tester

drop light

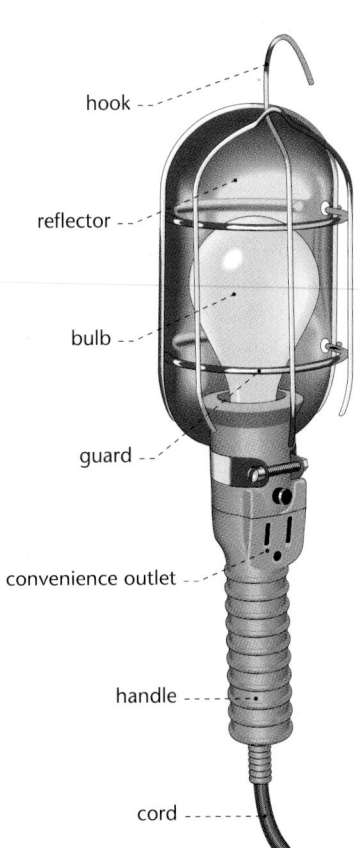

hook

reflector

bulb

guard

convenience outlet

handle

cord

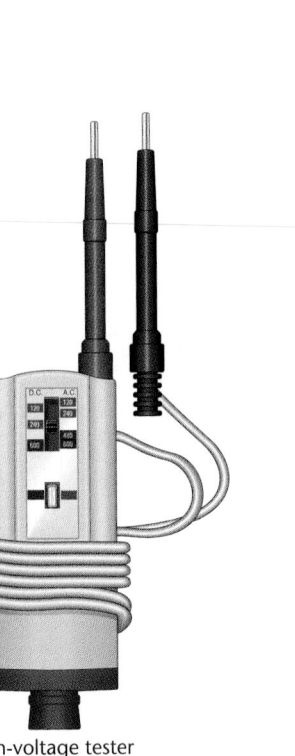

receptacle analyzer

neon tester

high-voltage tester

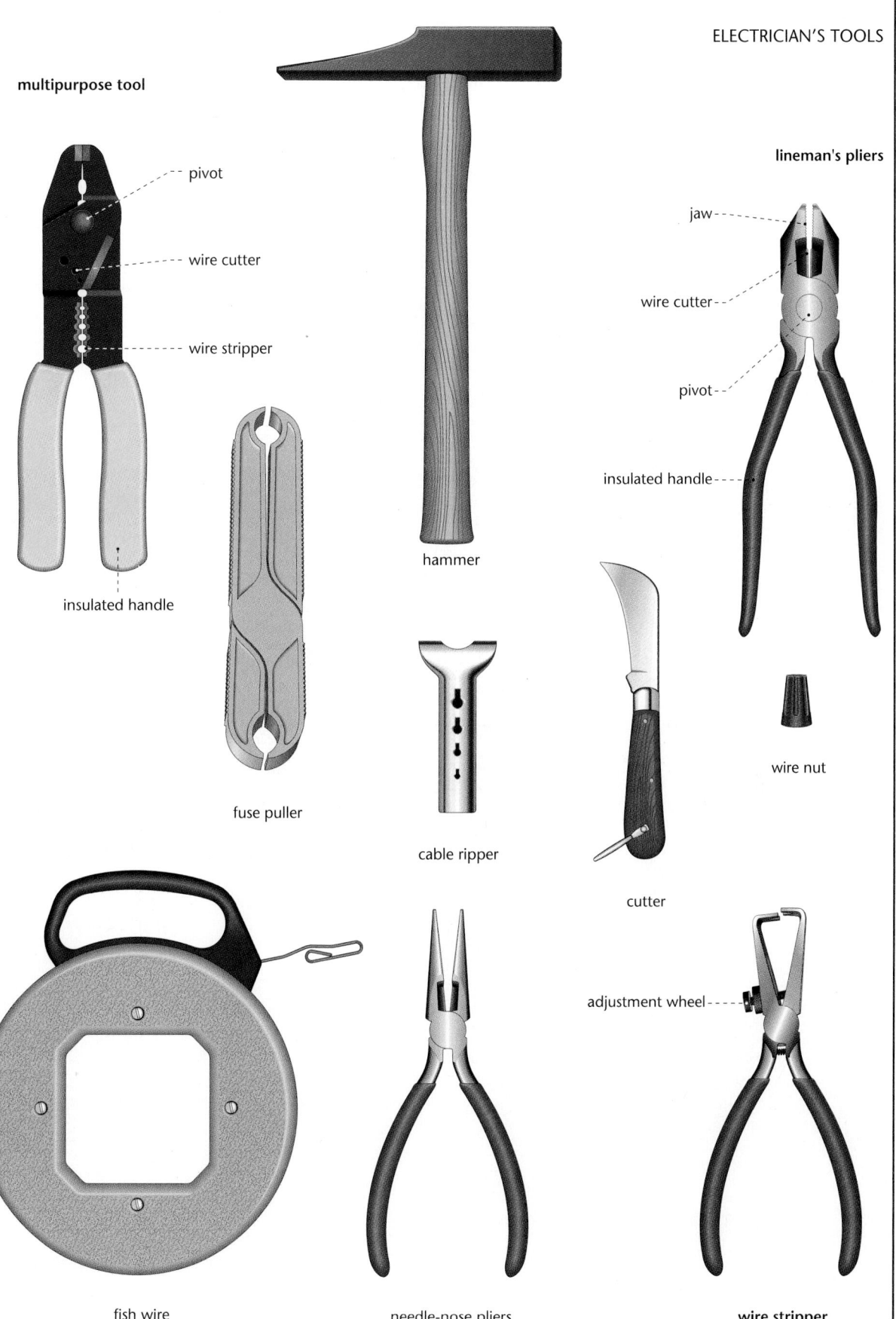

multipurpose tool

pivot

wire cutter

wire stripper

insulated handle

fuse puller

hammer

cable ripper

cutter

lineman's pliers

jaw

wire cutter

pivot

insulated handle

wire nut

fish wire

needle-nose pliers

wire stripper

adjustment wheel

DO-IT-YOURSELF

FUSE BOX

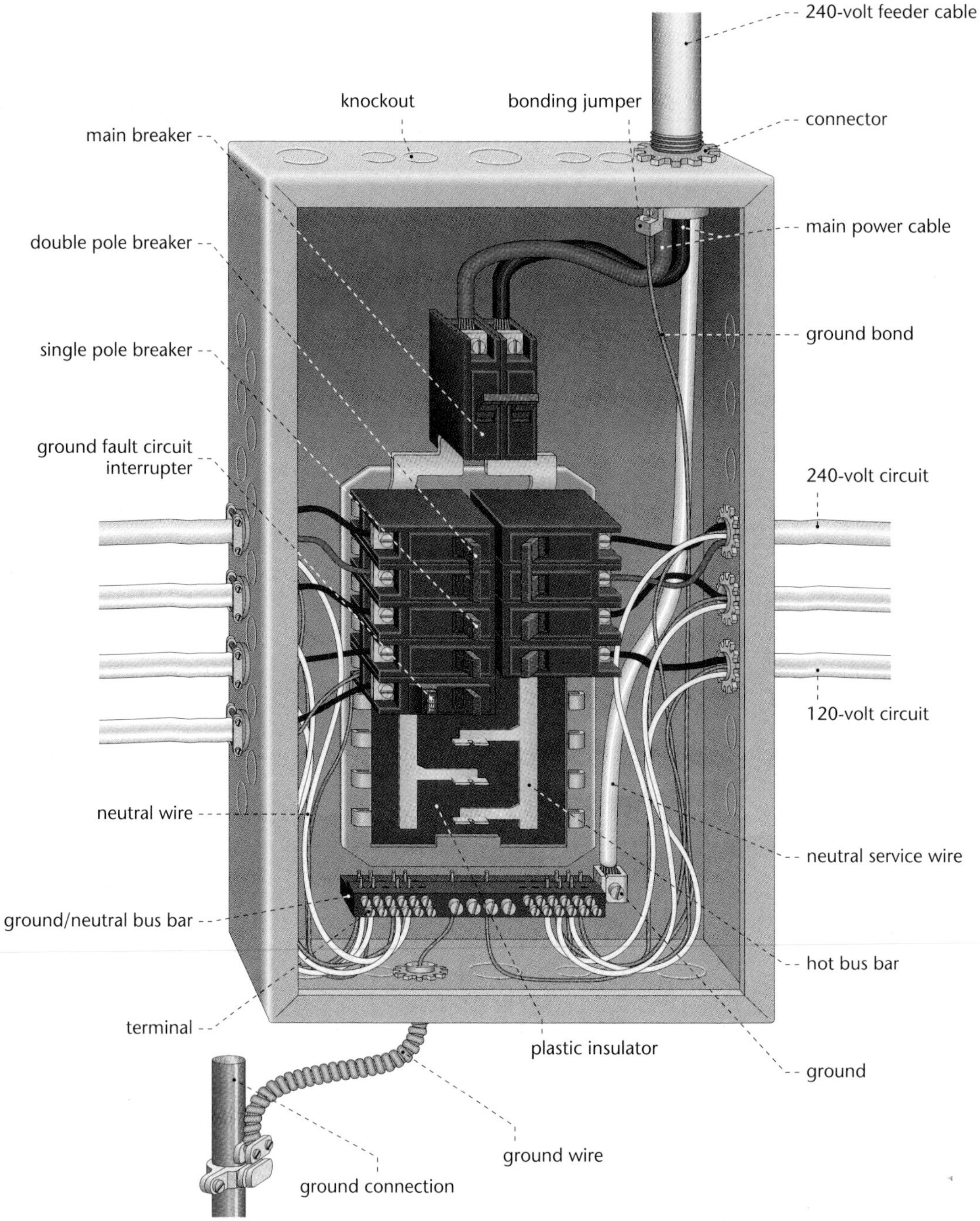

240-volt feeder cable

knockout

bonding jumper

connector

main breaker

main power cable

double pole breaker

ground bond

single pole breaker

ground fault circuit interrupter

240-volt circuit

neutral wire

120-volt circuit

ground/neutral bus bar

neutral service wire

hot bus bar

terminal

plastic insulator

ground

ground wire

ground connection

FUSES

cartridge fuse

plug fuse

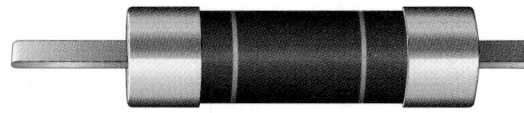

knife-blade cartridge fuse

CONTENTS

ELEMENTS OF ANCIENT COSTUME 315

MEN'S CLOTHING 319

SWEATERS...326

GLOVES 327

HEADGEAR..328

WOMEN'S CLOTHING 330

CHILDREN'S CLOTHING 349

SPORTSWEAR..352

SHOES 354

CLOTHING

ELEMENTS OF ANCIENT COSTUME

PEPLOS

TOGA

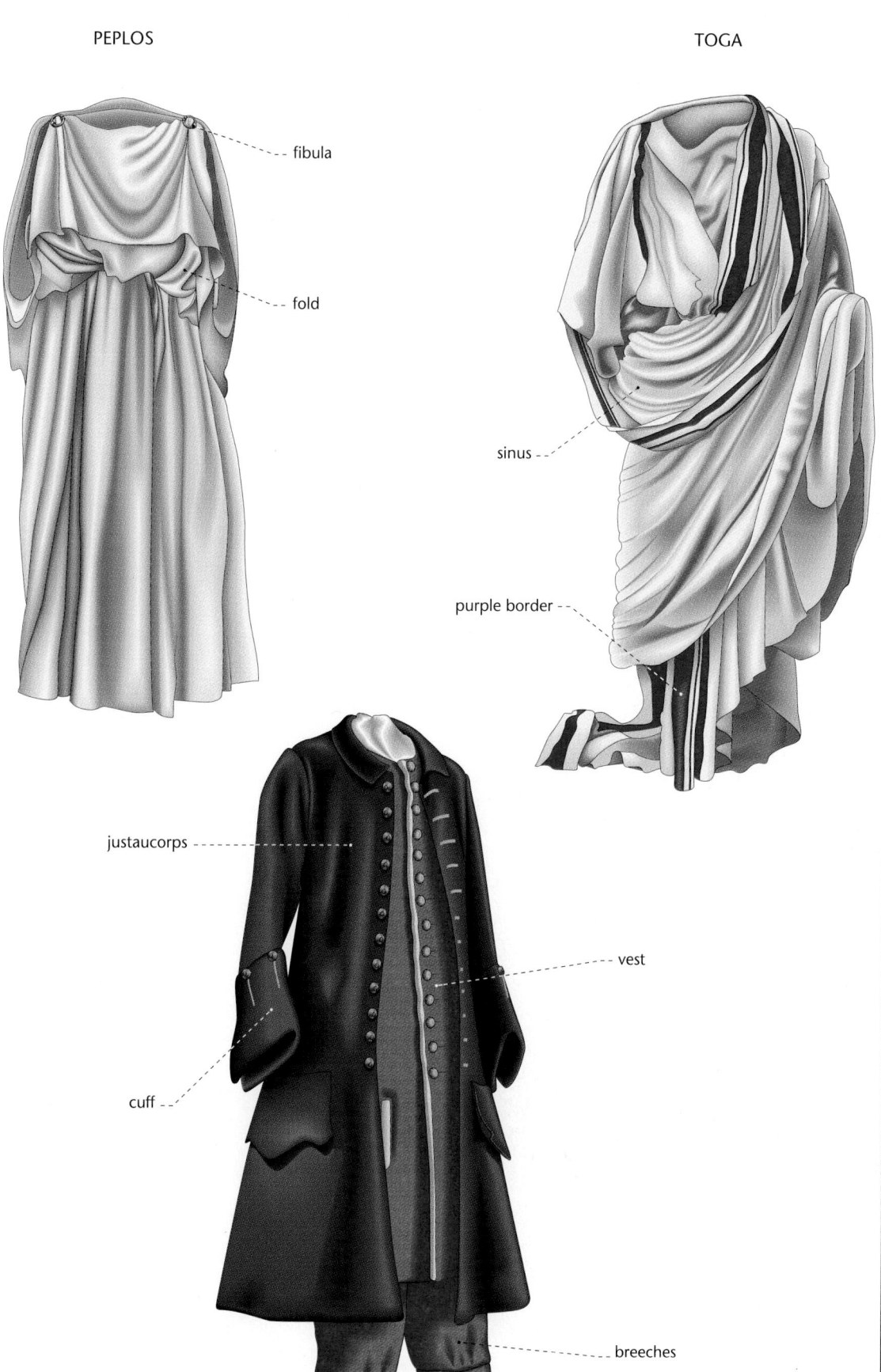

fibula

fold

sinus

purple border

justaucorps

vest

cuff

breeches

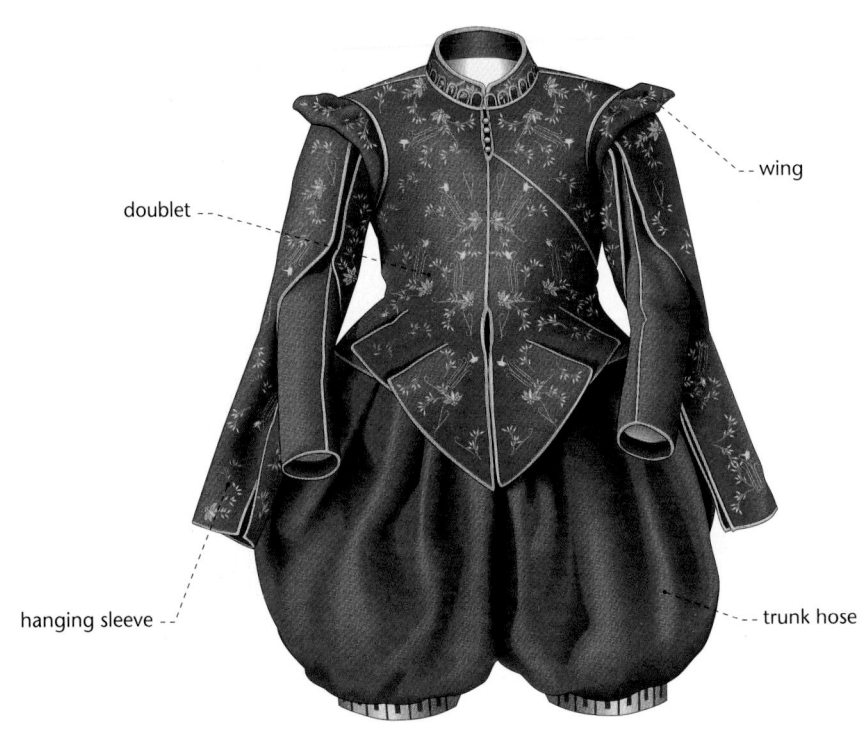

doublet

wing

hanging sleeve

trunk hose

COTEHARDIE

floating sleeve

vertical pocket

DRESS WITH BUSTLE

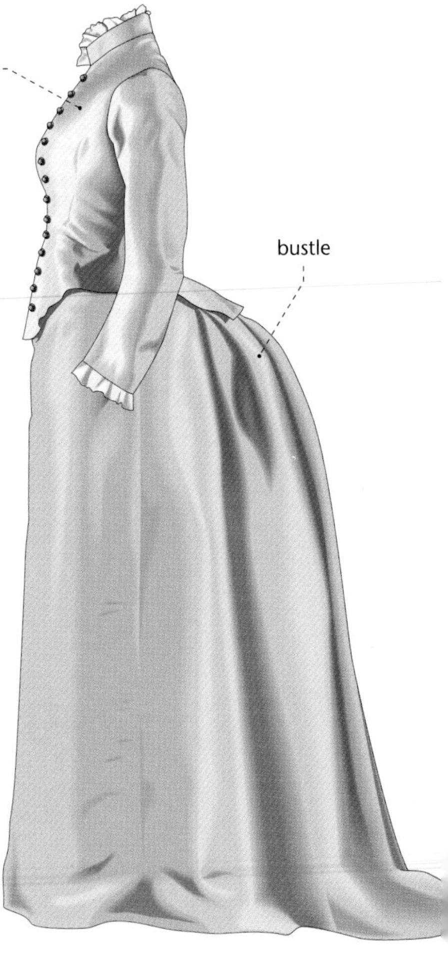

caraco jacket

bustle

CLOTHING

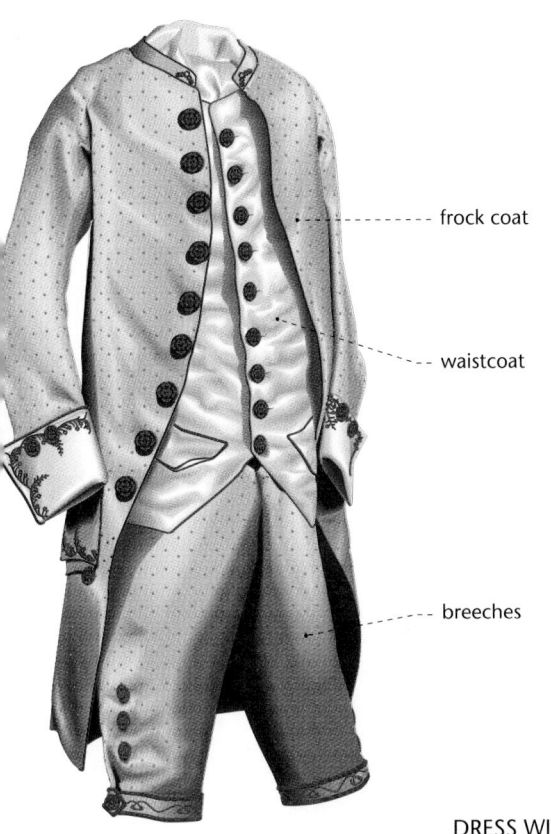

frock coat

waistcoat

breeches

houppelande

DRESS WITH PANNIERS

ruffle

stomacker

ELEMENTS OF ANCIENT COSTUME

DRESS WITH CRINOLINE

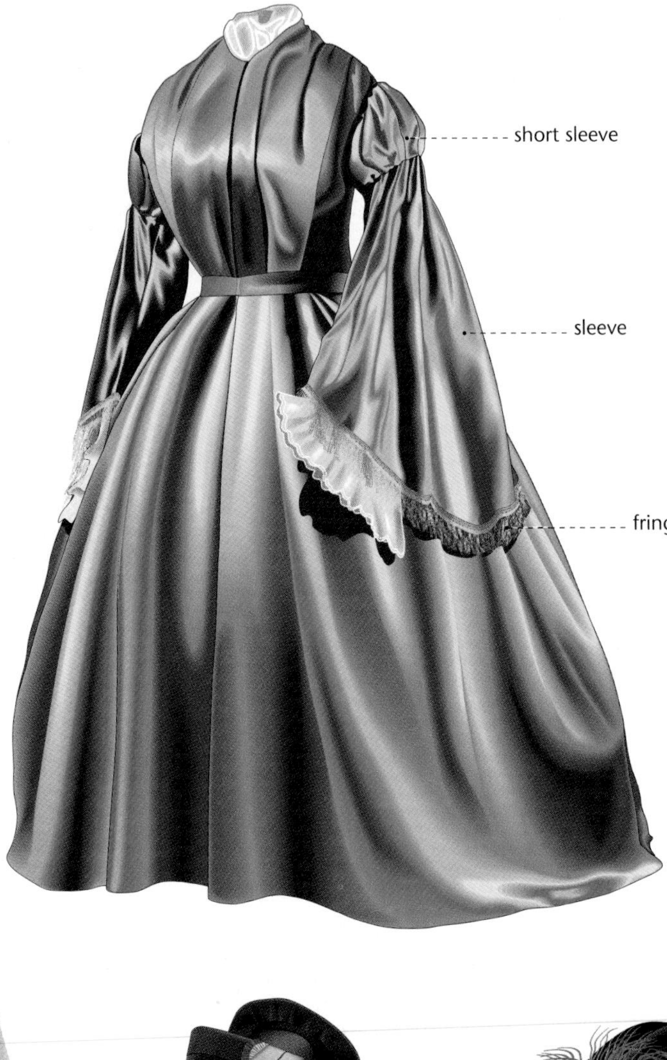
short sleeve
sleeve
fringe

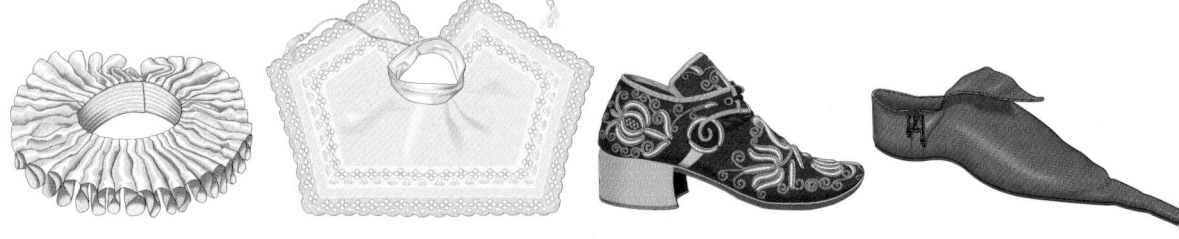

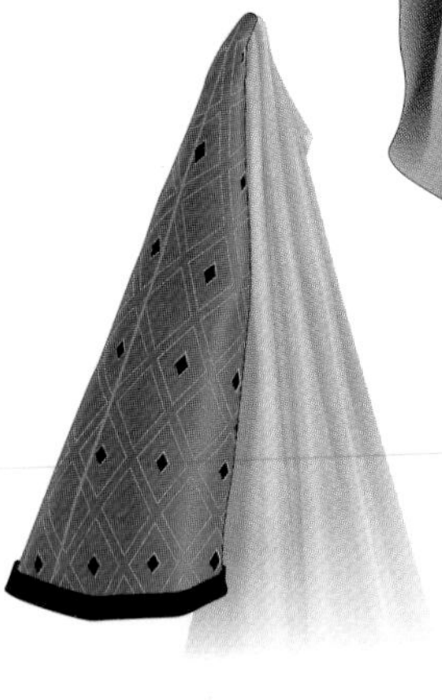
hennin

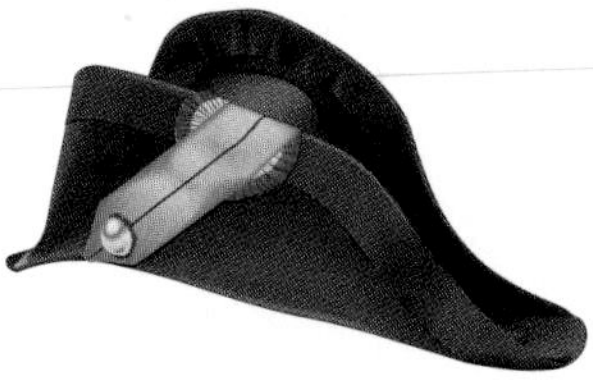
bicorne

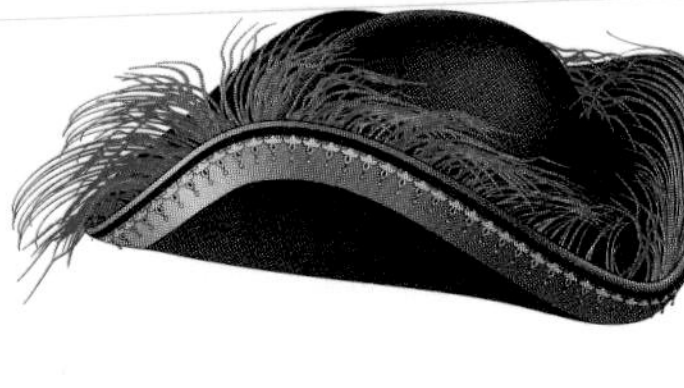
tricorne

fraise

collaret

heeled shoe

crakow

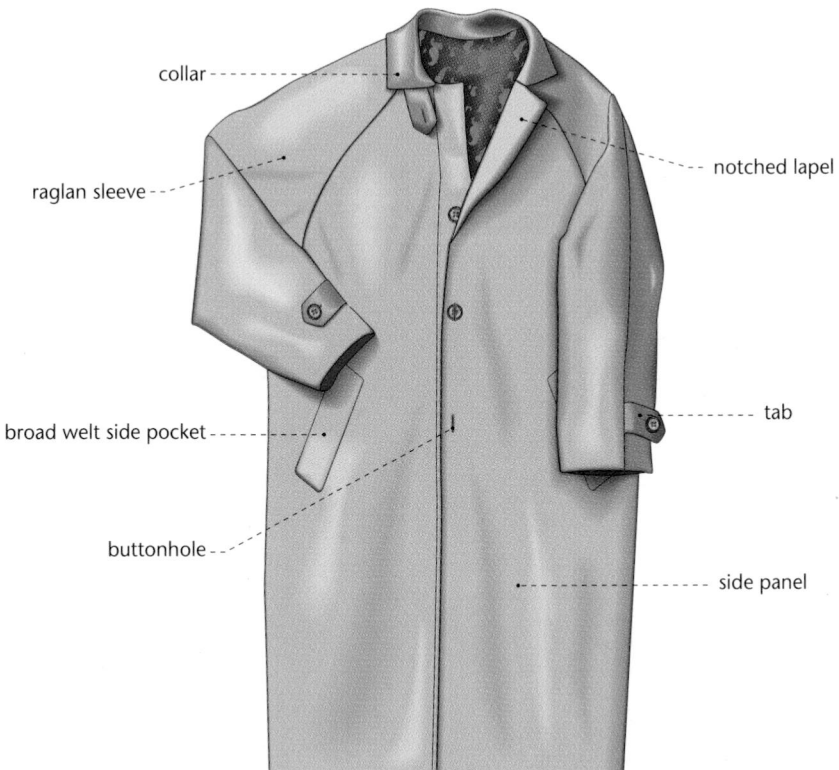

RAINCOAT

collar - - - -

raglan sleeve - - -

- - - notched lapel

- - - tab

broad welt side pocket - - - -

buttonhole - - -

- - - side panel

TRENCH COAT

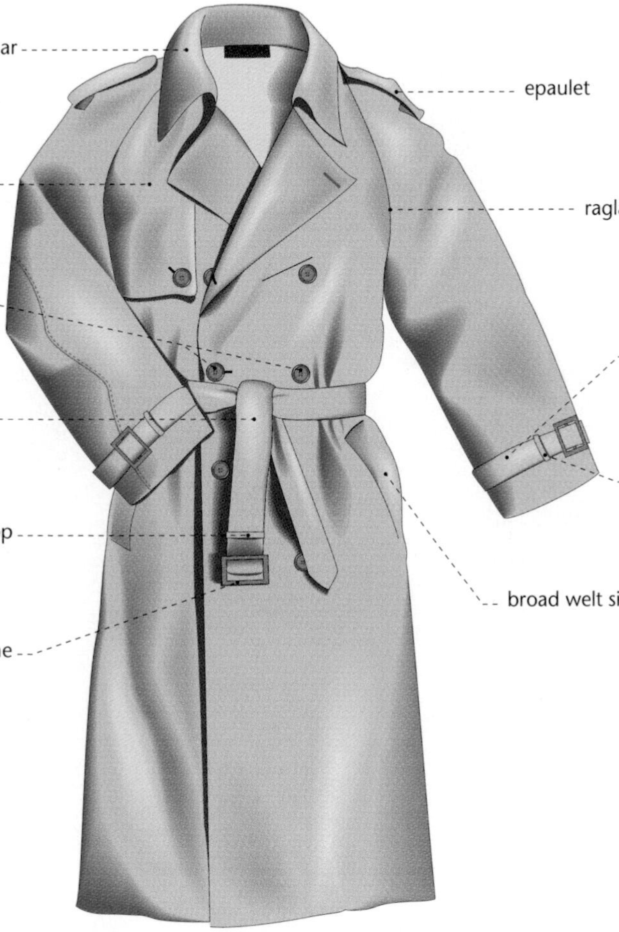

two-way collar - - - - - - - -

gun flap - - - -

- - - epaulet

- - - raglan sleeve

double-breasted buttoning - - -

belt - - - -

- - sleeve strap

- - - sleeve strap loop

belt loop - - - - -

- - - broad welt side pocket

frame - - -

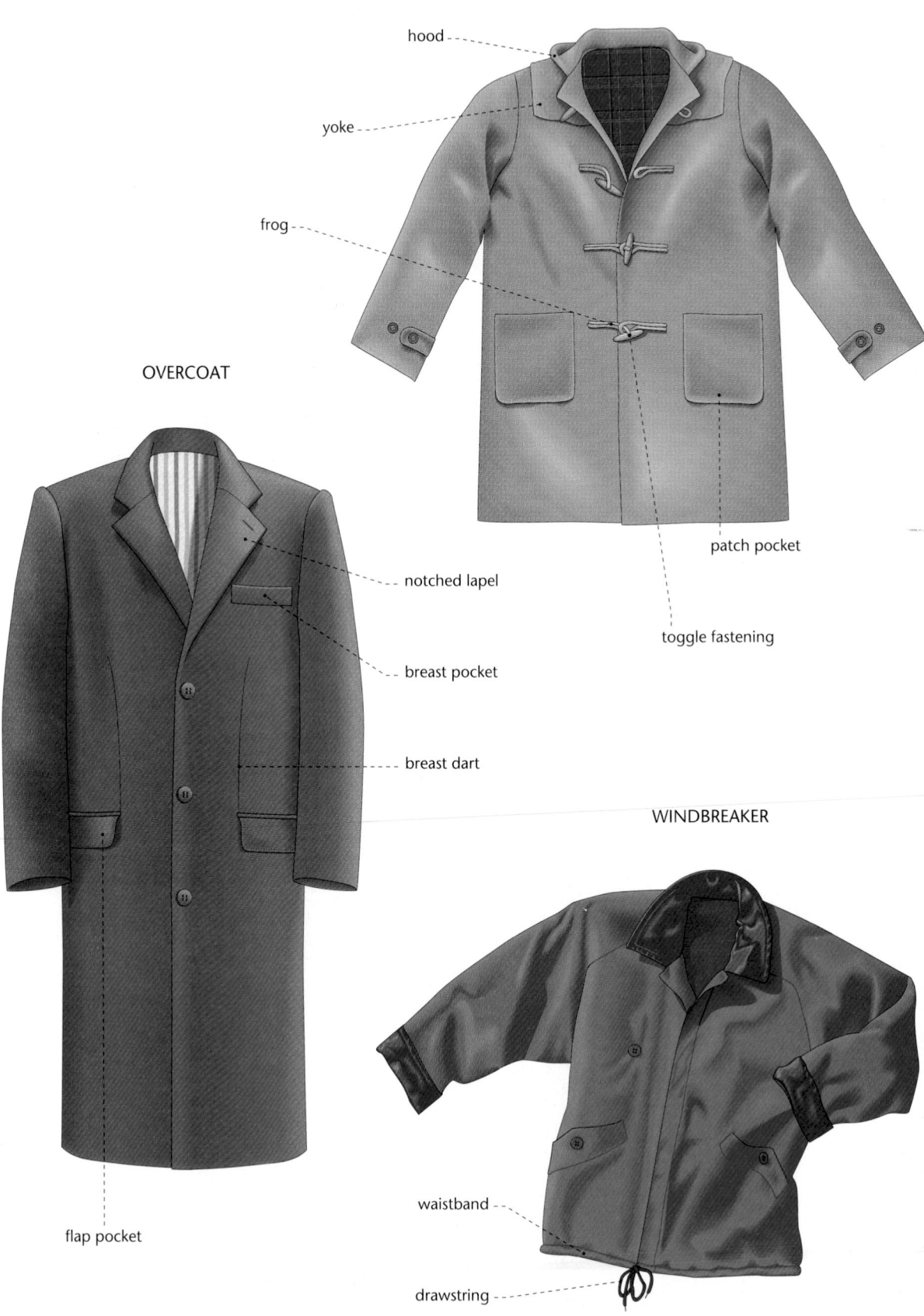

DUFFLE COAT

hood

yoke

frog

patch pocket

toggle fastening

OVERCOAT

notched lapel

breast pocket

breast dart

WINDBREAKER

flap pocket

waistband

drawstring

three-quarter coat

PARKA

zipper

snap-fastening tab

JACKET

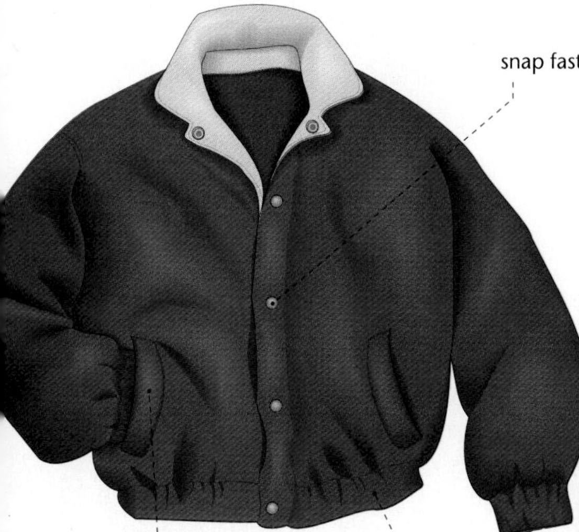

snap fastener

sheepskin jacket

hand-warmer pocket

elastic waistband

DOUBLE-BREASTED JACKET

lining

peaked lapel

collar

breast welt pocket

sleeve

flap

outside ticket pocket

patch pocket

side back vent

VEST

V-neck

lining

welt

front

seaming

welt pocket

adjustable waist tab

SINGLE-BREASTED JACKET

notch

lining

pocket handkerchief

lapel

sleeve

front

back

flap pocket

center back vent

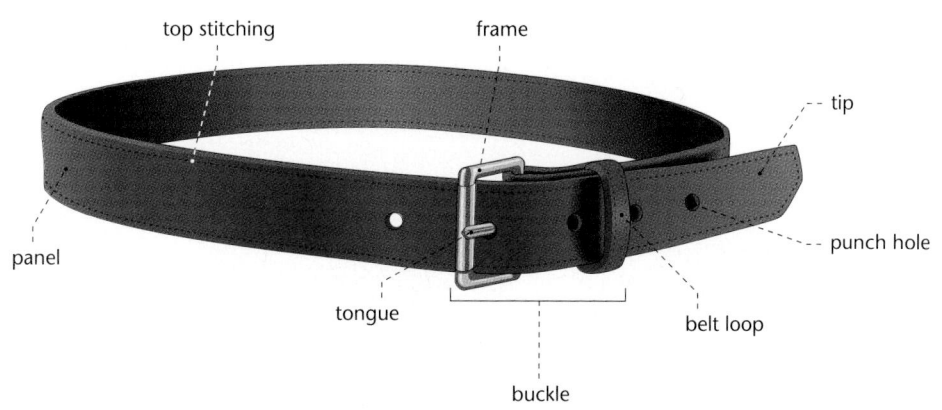

top stitching

frame

tip

panel

tongue

buckle

belt loop

punch hole

SUSPENDERS

PANTS

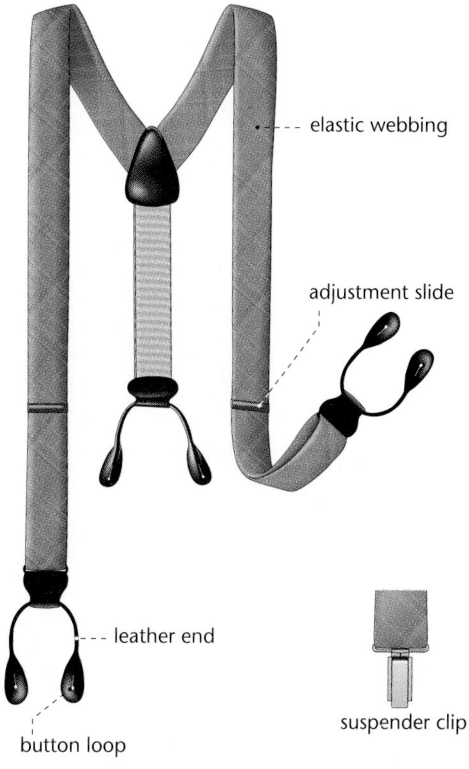

elastic webbing

adjustment slide

leather end

button loop

suspender clip

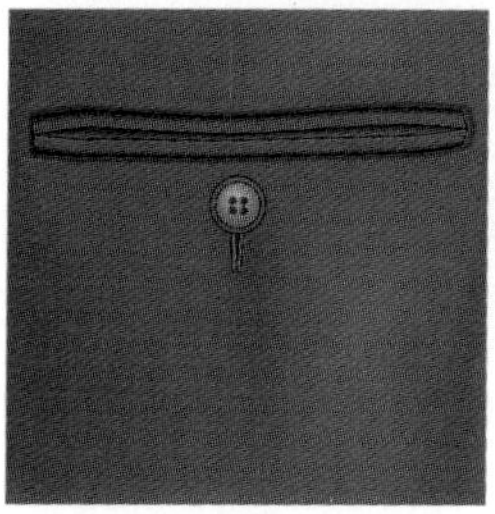

waistband

belt loop

front top pocket

waistband extension

fly

knife pleat

crease

back pocket

cuff

323

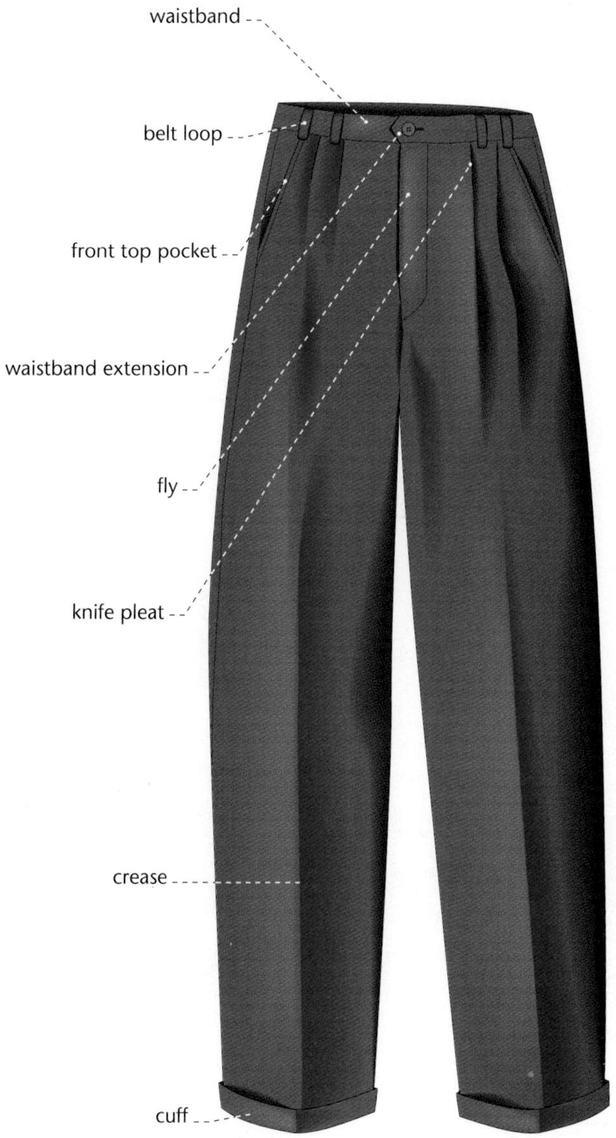

CLOTHING

SHIRT

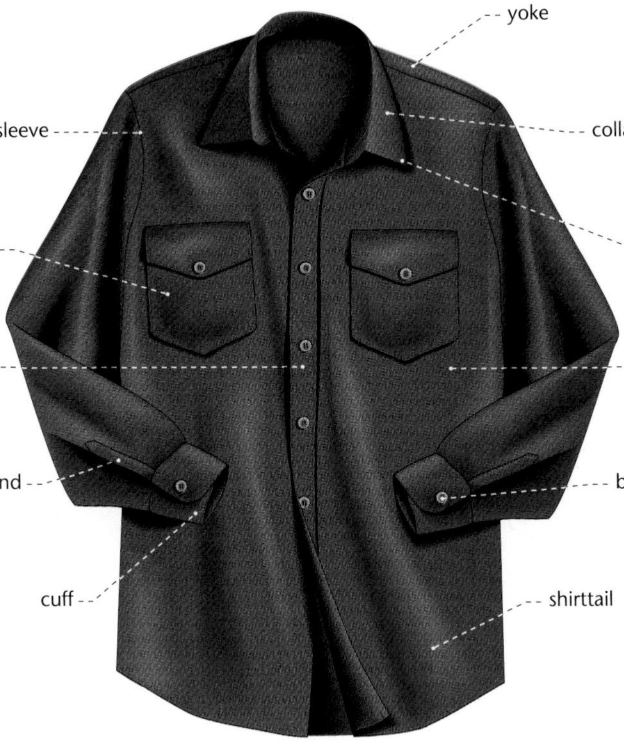

yoke

set-in sleeve

collar

collar point

breast pocket

buttoned placket

front

pointed tab end

button

cuff

shirttail

buttondown collar

spread collar

ascot tie

collar stay

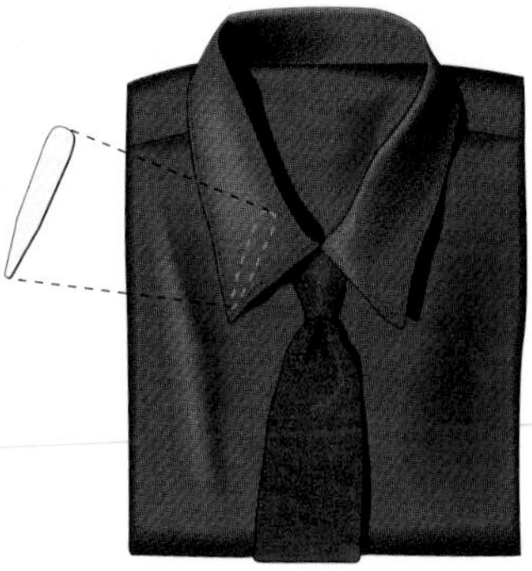

bow tie

NECKTIE

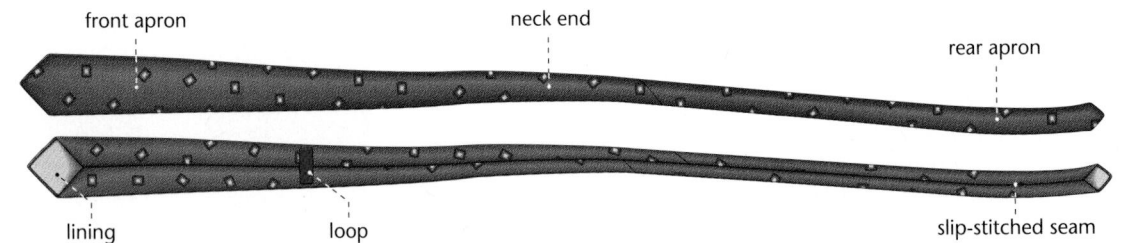

front apron

neck end

rear apron

lining

loop

slip-stitched seam

athletic shirt

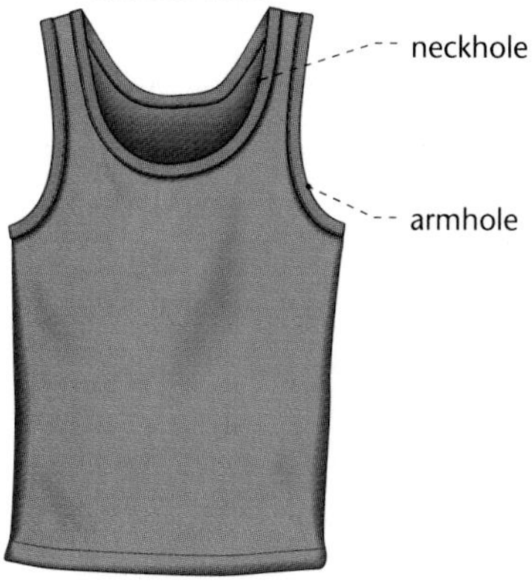

- - - - - - - neckhole

- - - - - - - armhole

briefs

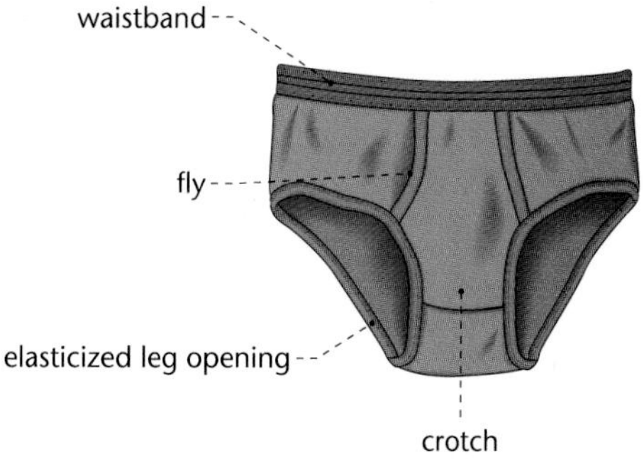

waistband - - -

fly - - -

elasticized leg opening - - -

crotch

union suit

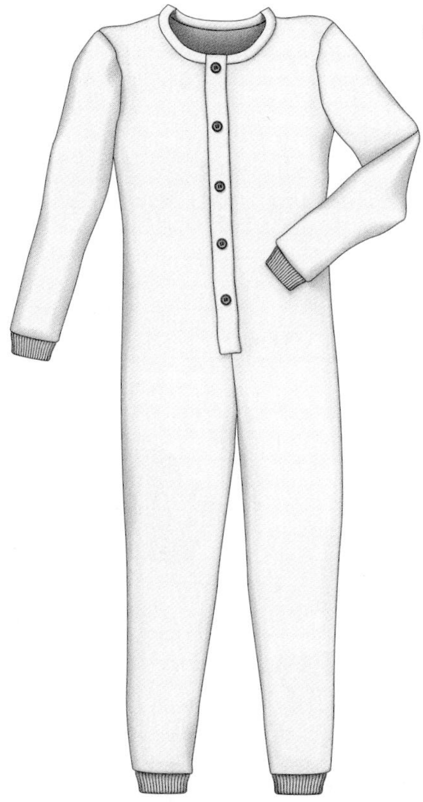

drawers

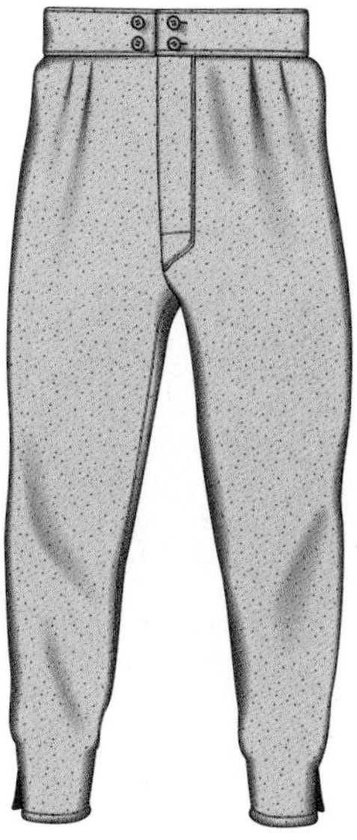

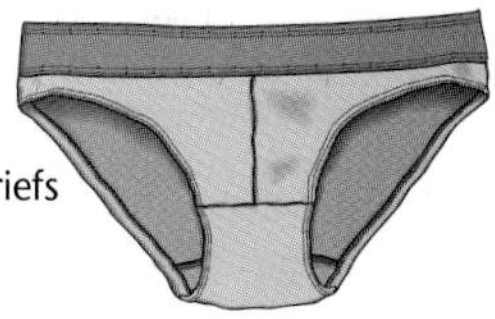

bikini briefs

boxer shorts

SOCKS

executive length

mid-calf length

- - - straight-up ribbed top

ankle length

- - - leg

heel - - -

- - - instep

sole - - -

toe - - -

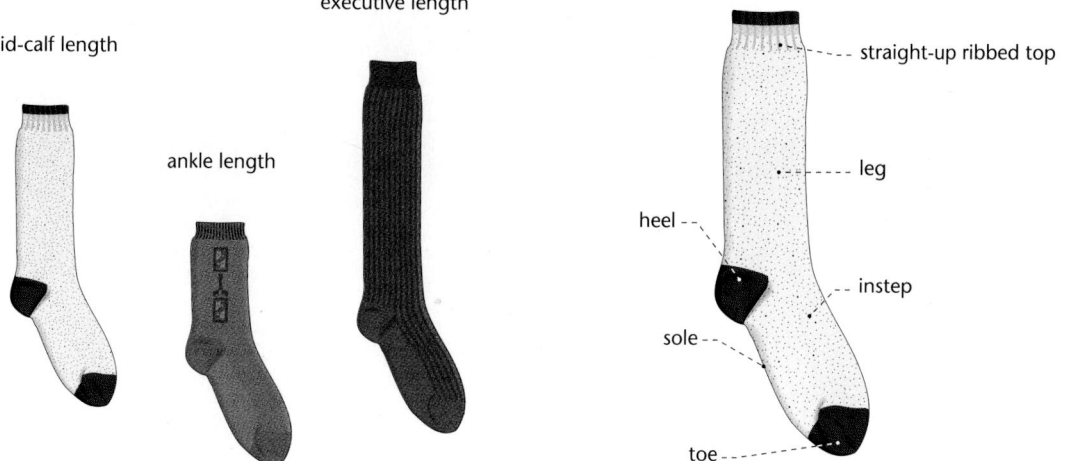

CLOTHING

V-NECK CARDIGAN

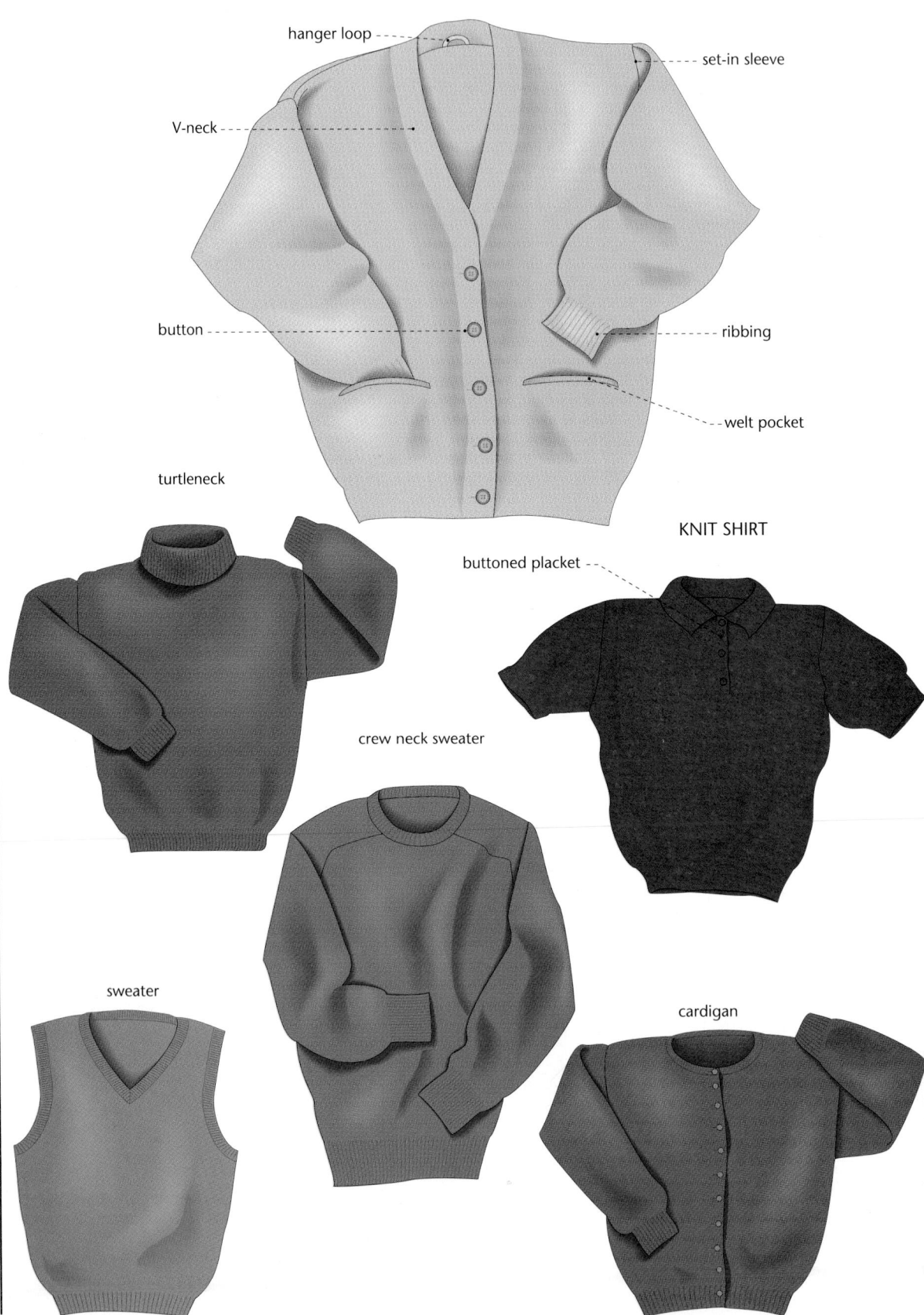

hanger loop

set-in sleeve

V-neck

button

ribbing

welt pocket

turtleneck

KNIT SHIRT

buttoned placket

crew neck sweater

sweater

cardigan

GLOVES

thumb

fourchette

glove finger

palm

snap fastener

stitching

seam

DRIVING GLOVE

perforation

opening

mitten

MITT

gauntlet

evening glove

wrist-length glove

gauntlet

short glove

327

CLOTHING

FELT HAT

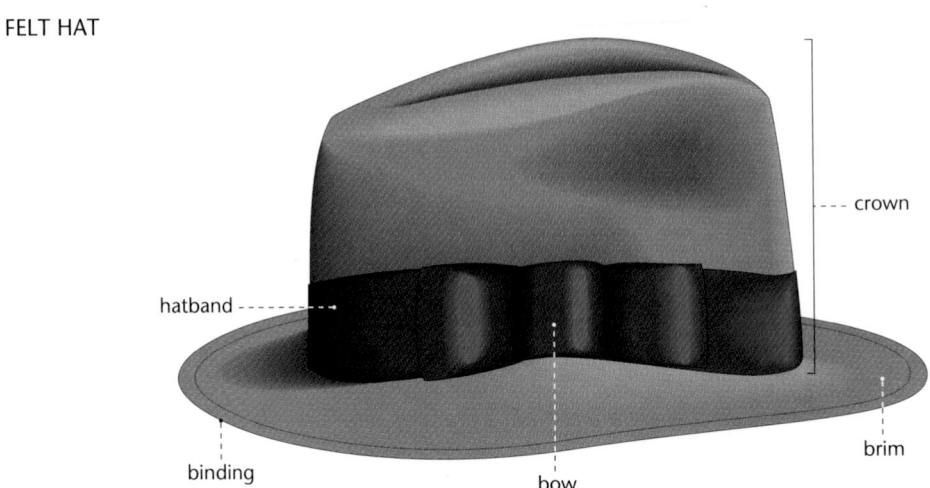

crown

hatband

binding

bow

brim

boater

top hat

derby

HUNTING CAP

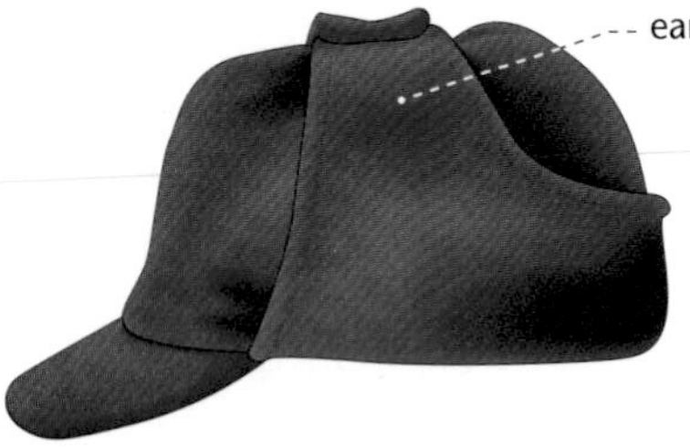

ear flap

shapka

CAP

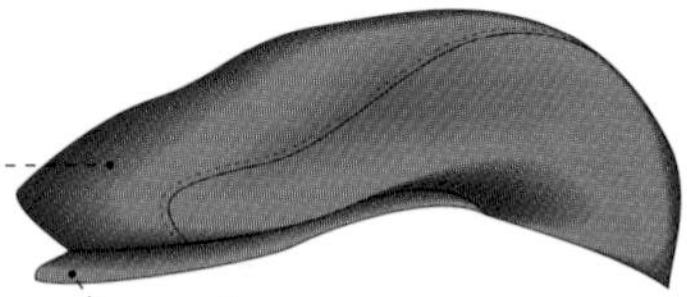

crown

peak

garrison cap

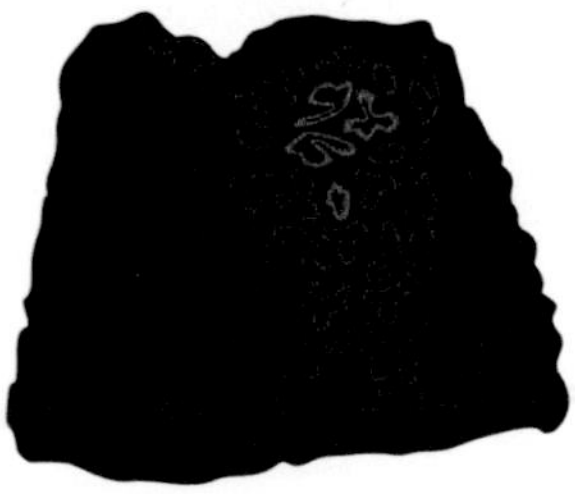

skullcap

panama

toque

pillbox hat

beret

turban

cloche

felt hat

southwester

BALACLAVA

peak

stocking cap

knit cap

GOB HAT

cartwheel hat

crown

brim

TYPES OF COATS

CLOTHING

pea jacket

tailored collar

hand warmer pocket

mock pocket

car coat

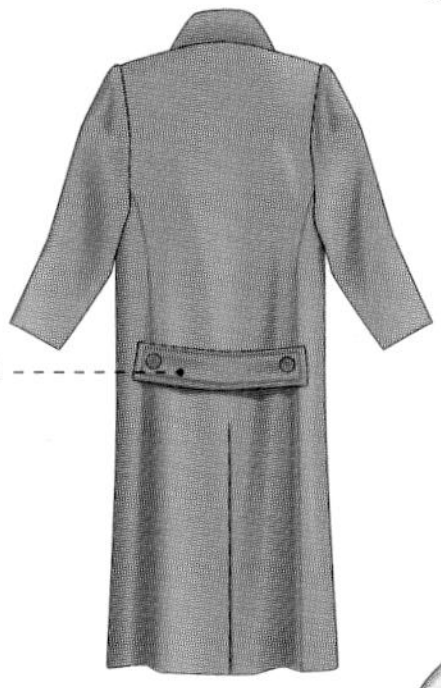

back belt

raglan

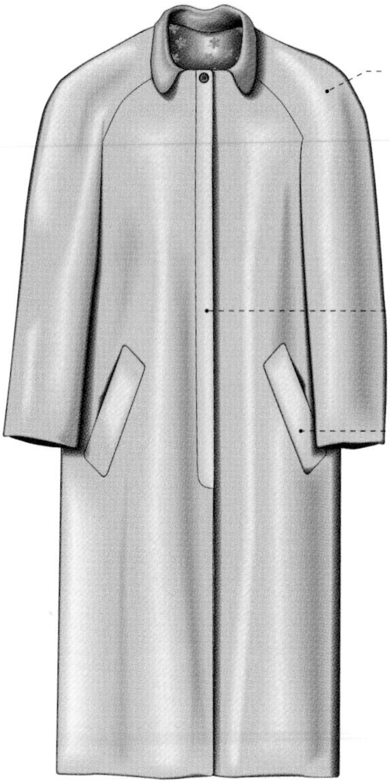

raglan sleeve

fly front closing

broad welt side pocket

pelerine

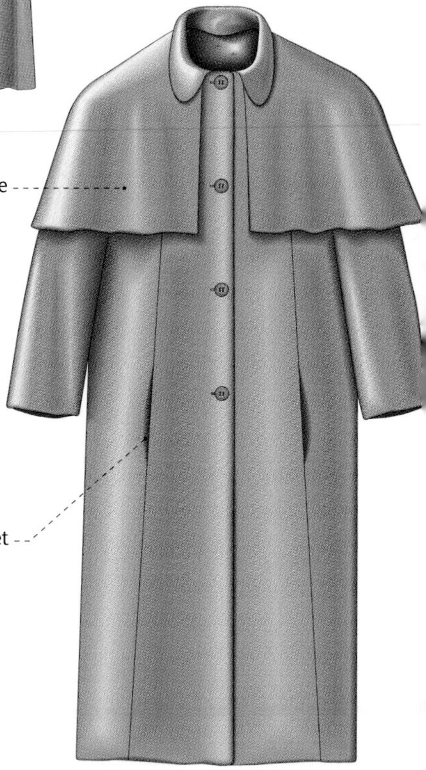

pelerine

seam pocket

cape

arm slit

overcoat

top coat

poncho

suit

jacket

skirt

jacket

TYPES OF DRESSES

CLOTHING

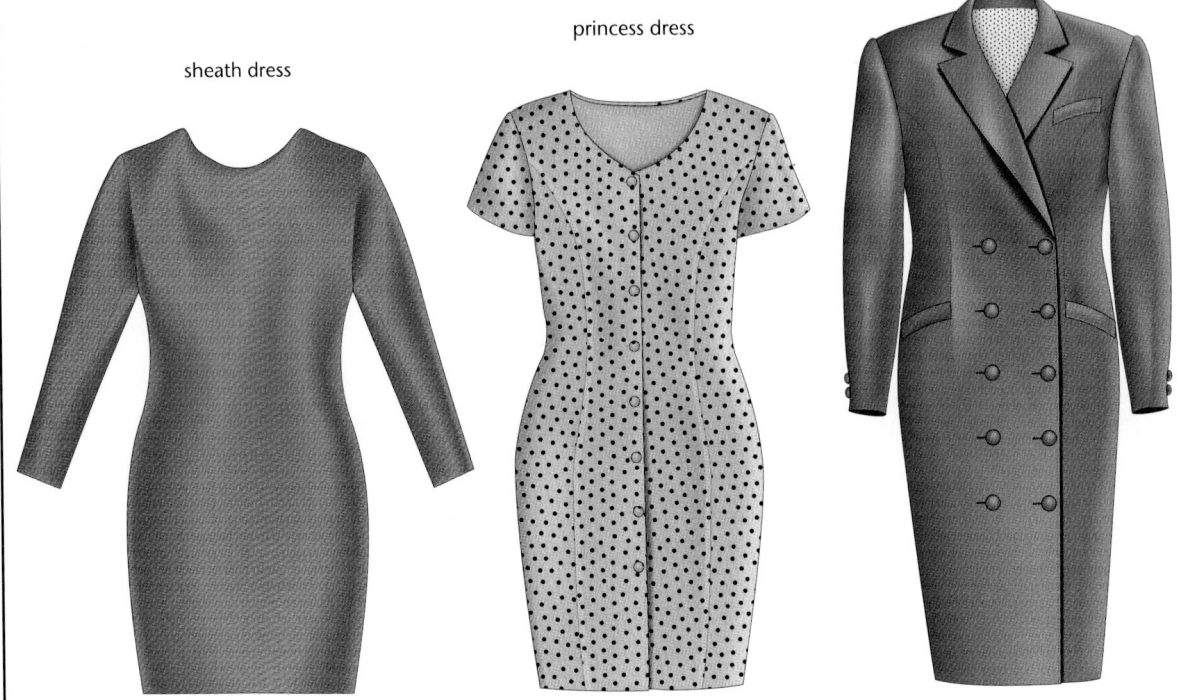

sheath dress

princess dress

coat dress

drop waist dress

trapeze dress

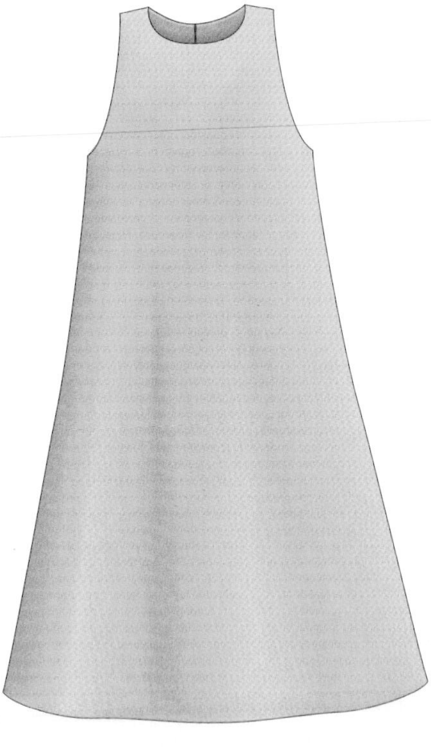

sundress

332

polo dress

house dress

shirtwaist dress

jumper

wraparound dress

tunic dress

TYPES OF SKIRTS

sheath skirt

yoke skirt

gored skirt

ruffled skirt

sarong

wraparound skirt

straight skirt

culotte

kilt

gather skirt

TYPES OF PLEATS

inverted pleat

kick pleat

accordion pleat

knife pleat

top stitched pleat

TYPES OF PANTS

jeans

Bermuda shorts

shorts

ski pants

knickers

pedal pushers

footstrap

jumpsuit

bell bottoms

overalls

classic blouse

middy

polo shirt

smock

yoke

gather

tunic

wrap-over top

mini shirtdress

body shirt

over-blouse

shirttail

crotch piece

JACKETS, VEST AND SWEATERS

CLOTHING

safari jacket

blazer

gusset pocket

bolero

spencer

vest

twin-set

turtleneck

V-neck cardigan

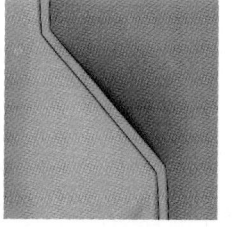

inset pocket

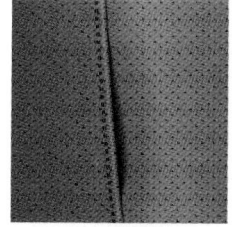

seam pocket

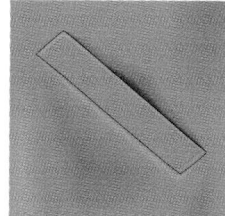

broad welt side pocket

hand warmer pouch

gusset pocket

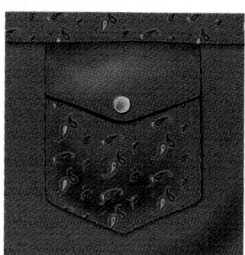

flap pocket

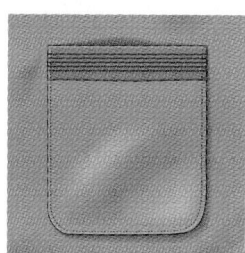

patch pocket

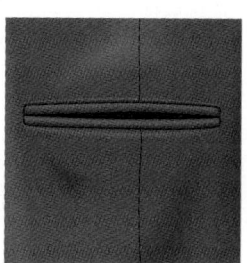

welt pocket

CLOTHING

TYPES OF SLEEVES

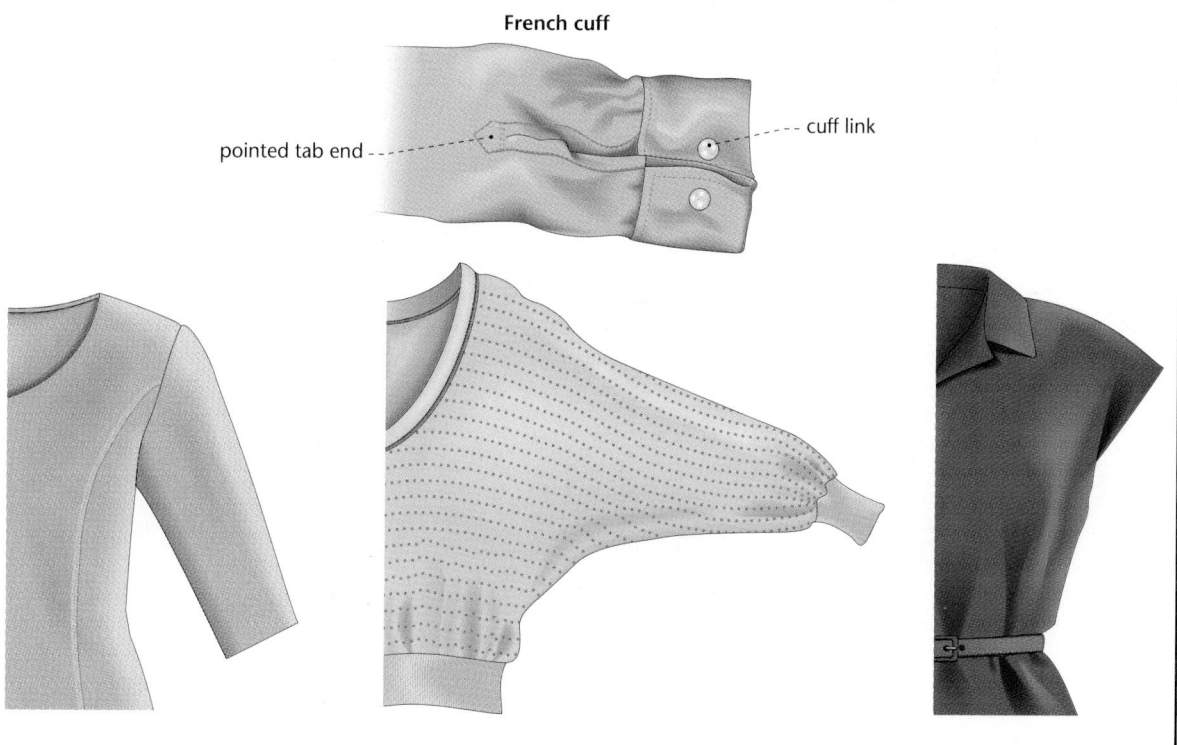

French cuff

pointed tab end

cuff link

three-quarter sleeve

batwing sleeve

cap sleeve

TYPES OF SLEEVES

CLOTHING

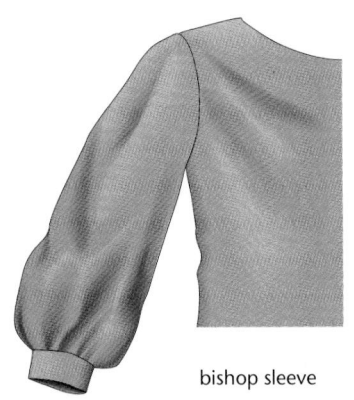
bishop sleeve

leg-of-mutton sleeve

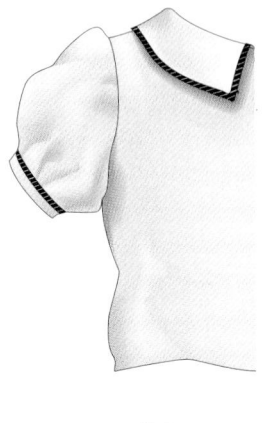
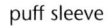
puff sleeve

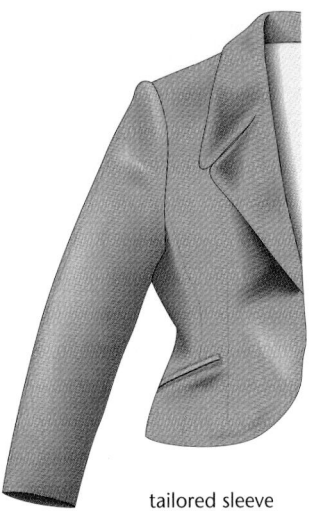
tailored sleeve

epaulet sleeve

kimono sleeve

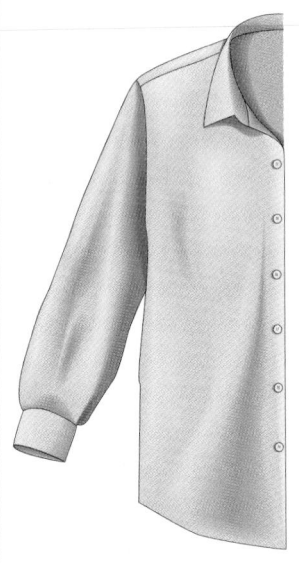

shirt sleeve

raglan sleeve

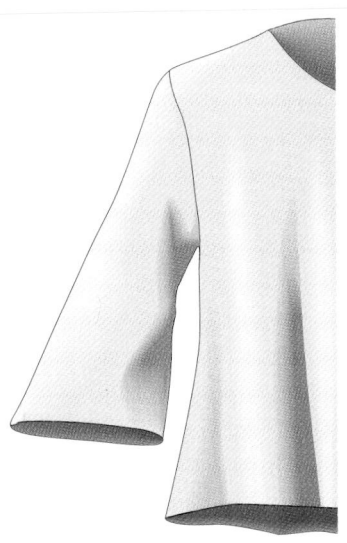
pagoda sleeve

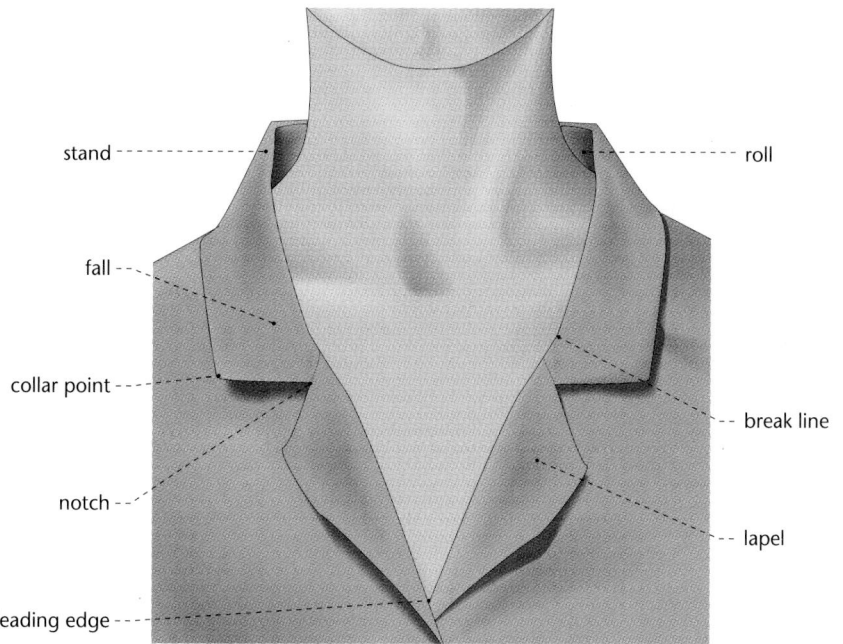

stand

roll

fall

collar point

break line

notch

lapel

leading edge

TYPES OF COLLARS

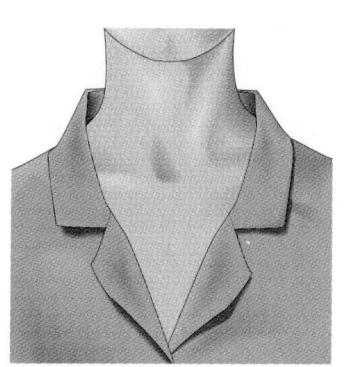

shirt collar

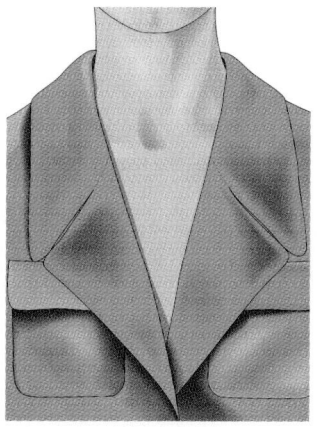

tailored collar

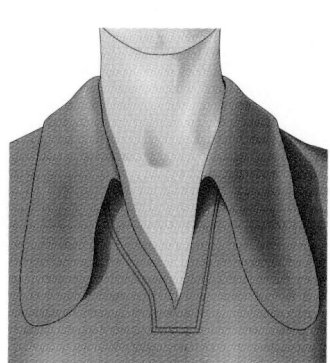

dog ear collar

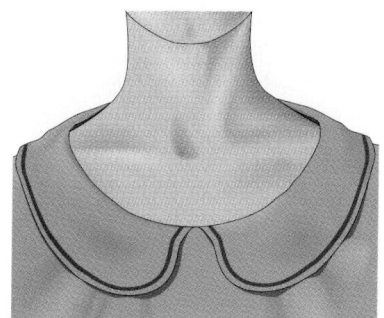

Peter Pan collar

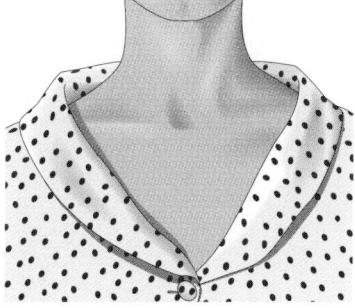

shawl collar

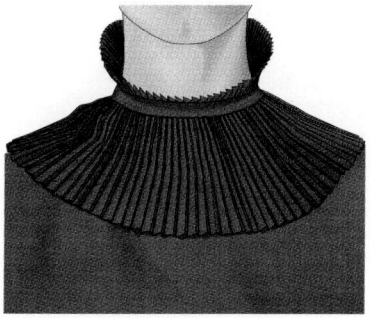

collaret

TYPES OF COLLARS

CLOTHING

bertha collar

bow collar

sailor collar

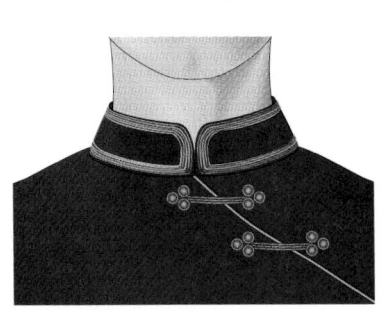

mandarin collar

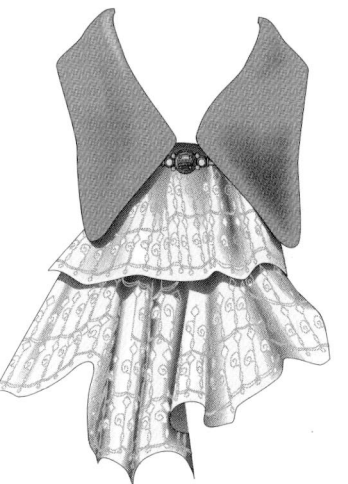

jabot

stand-up collar

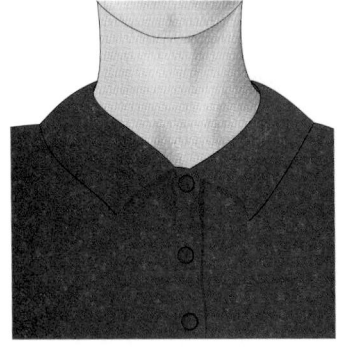

polo collar

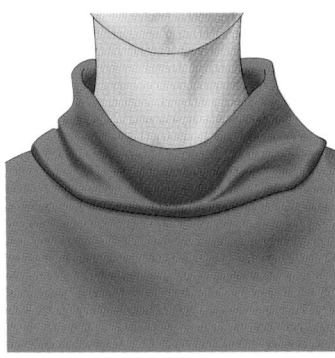

cowl neck

turtleneck

plunging neckline

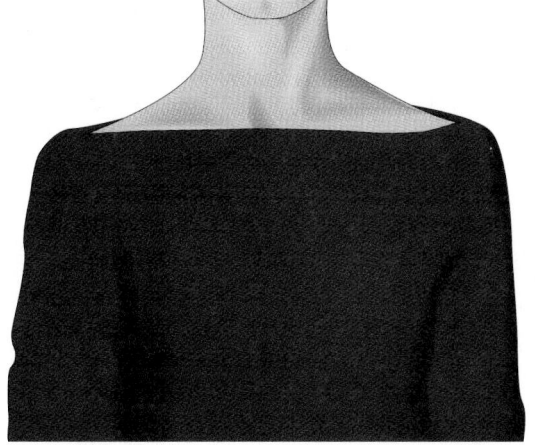

bateau neck

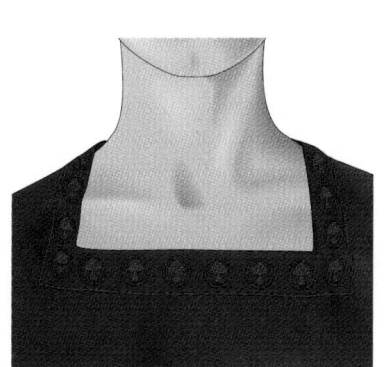

square neck

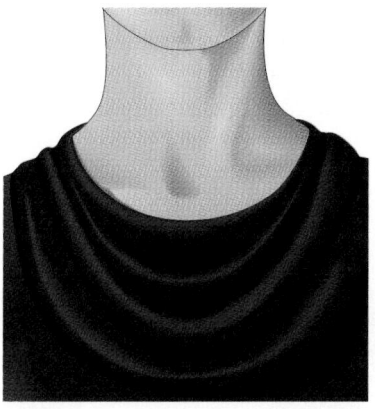

draped neck

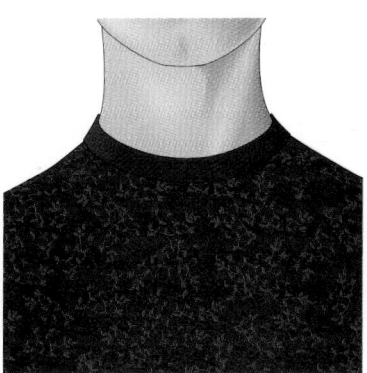

round neck

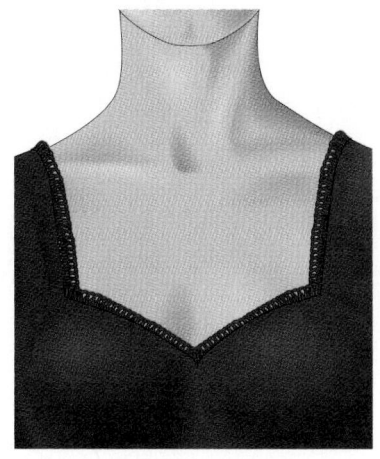

sweetheart neckline

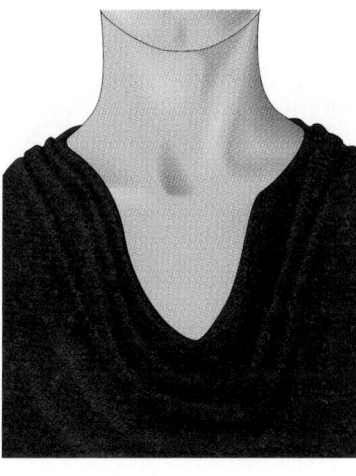

draped neckline

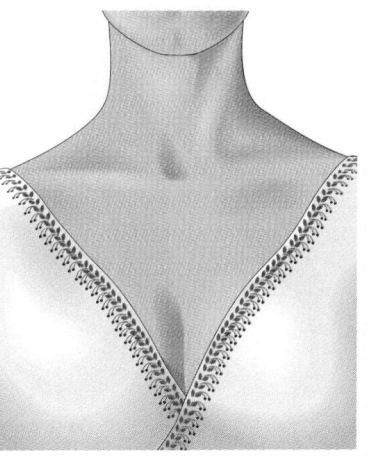

V-shaped neck

343

HOSE

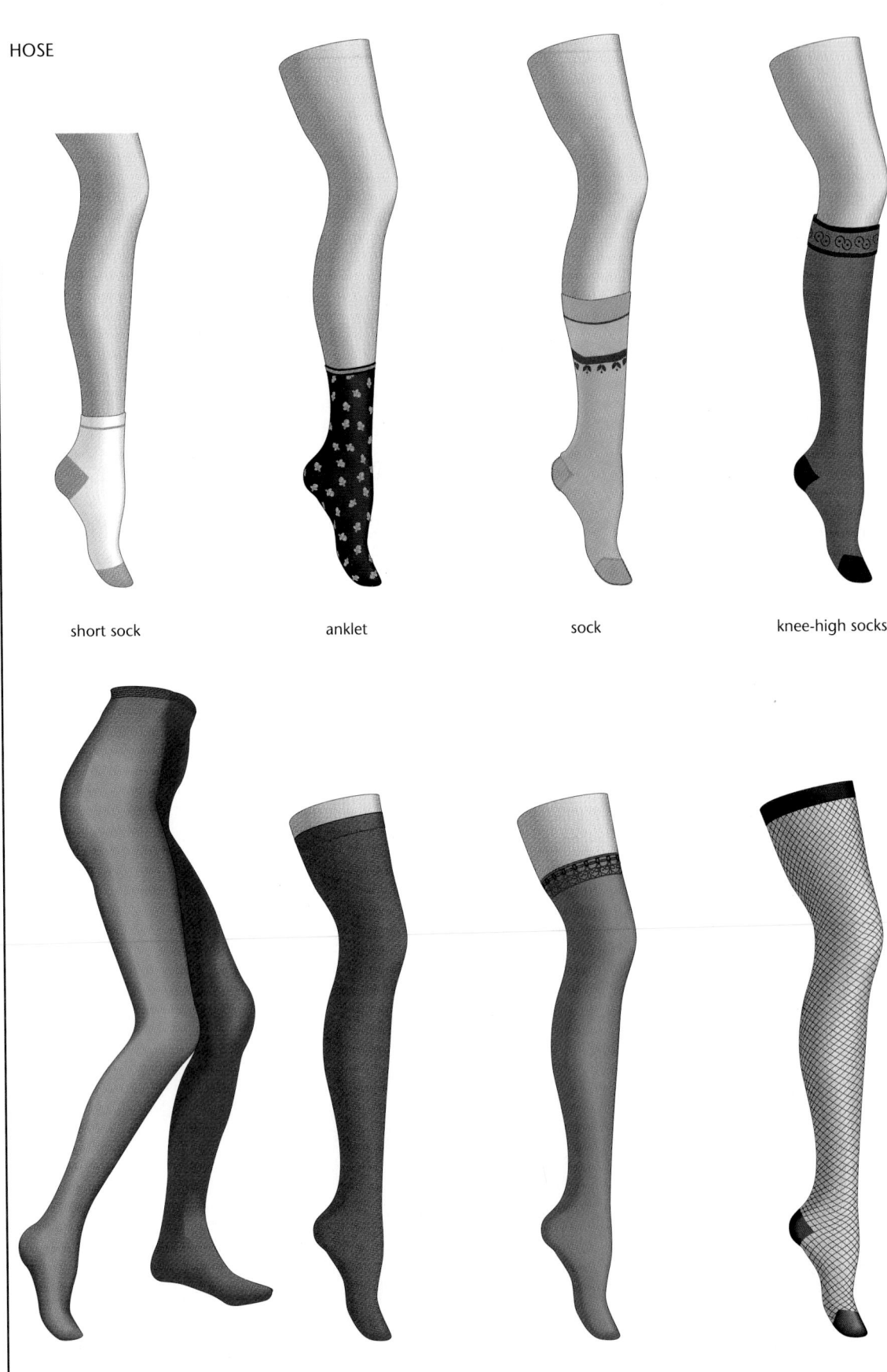

short sock

anklet

sock

knee-high socks

panty hose

hose

thigh-high stocking

net stocking

CLOTHING

344

CLOTHING

body suit

teddy

camisole

foundation slip

slip

princess seaming

half-slip

UNDERWEAR

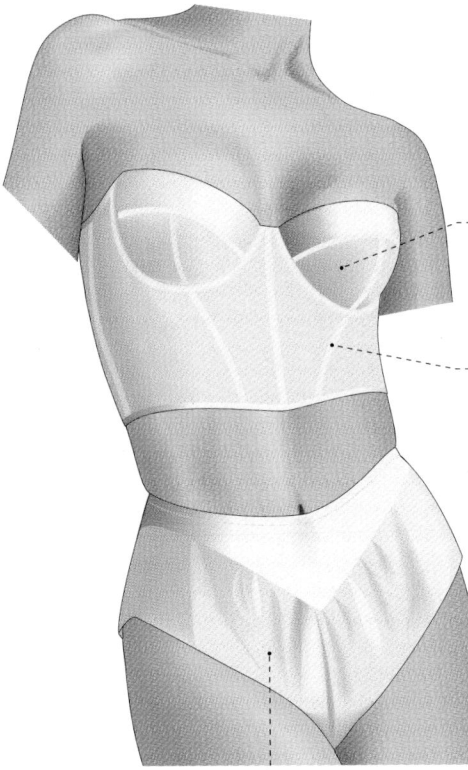

décolleté bra

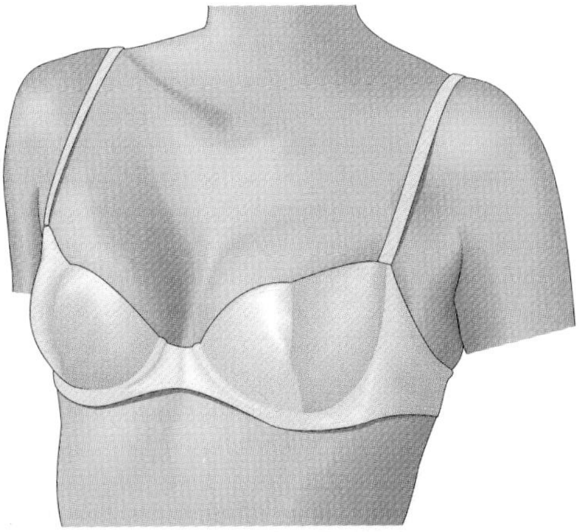

strapless brassiere

steel

bra

shoulder strap

brassiere cup

midriff band

briefs

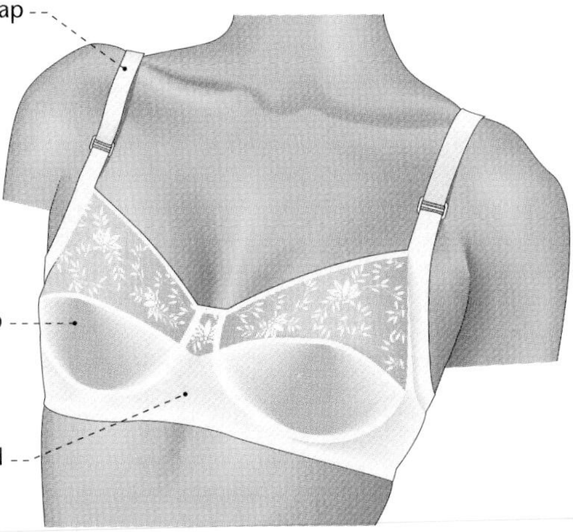

girdle

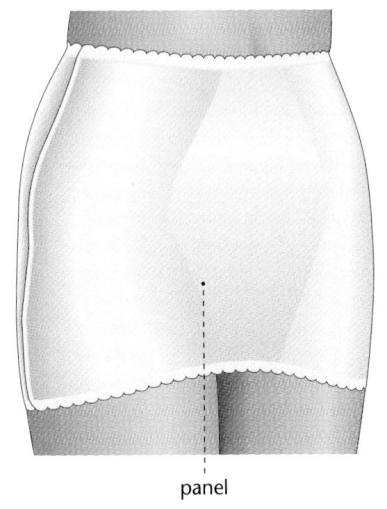

panty girdle

corset

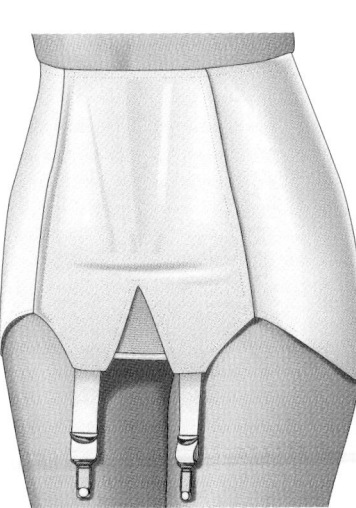

panel

CLOTHING

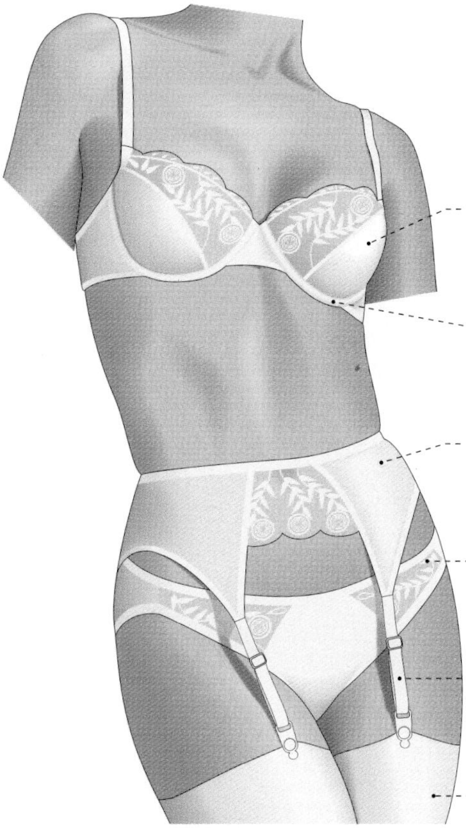

corselette

push-up bra

underwiring

garter belt

bikini

garter

hose

panty corselette

wasp-waisted corset

NIGHTWEAR

kimono

nightgown

baby doll

pajamas

negligee

bathrobe

348

CHILDREN'S CLOTHING

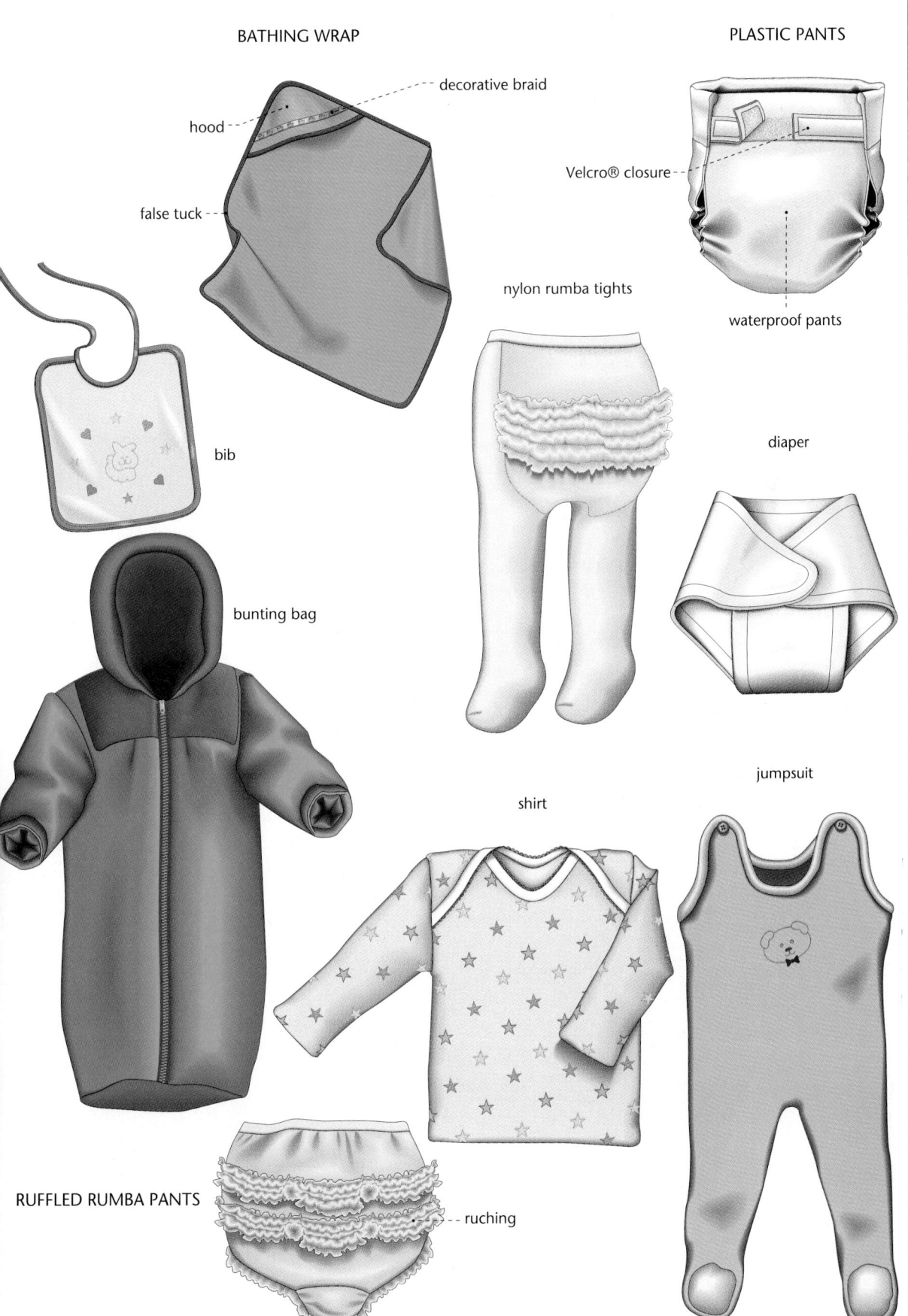

BATHING WRAP

decorative braid

hood

false tuck

PLASTIC PANTS

Velcro® closure

waterproof pants

nylon rumba tights

bib

diaper

bunting bag

jumpsuit

shirt

RUFFLED RUMBA PANTS

ruching

349

CLOTHING

BLANKET SLEEPERS

SLEEPERS

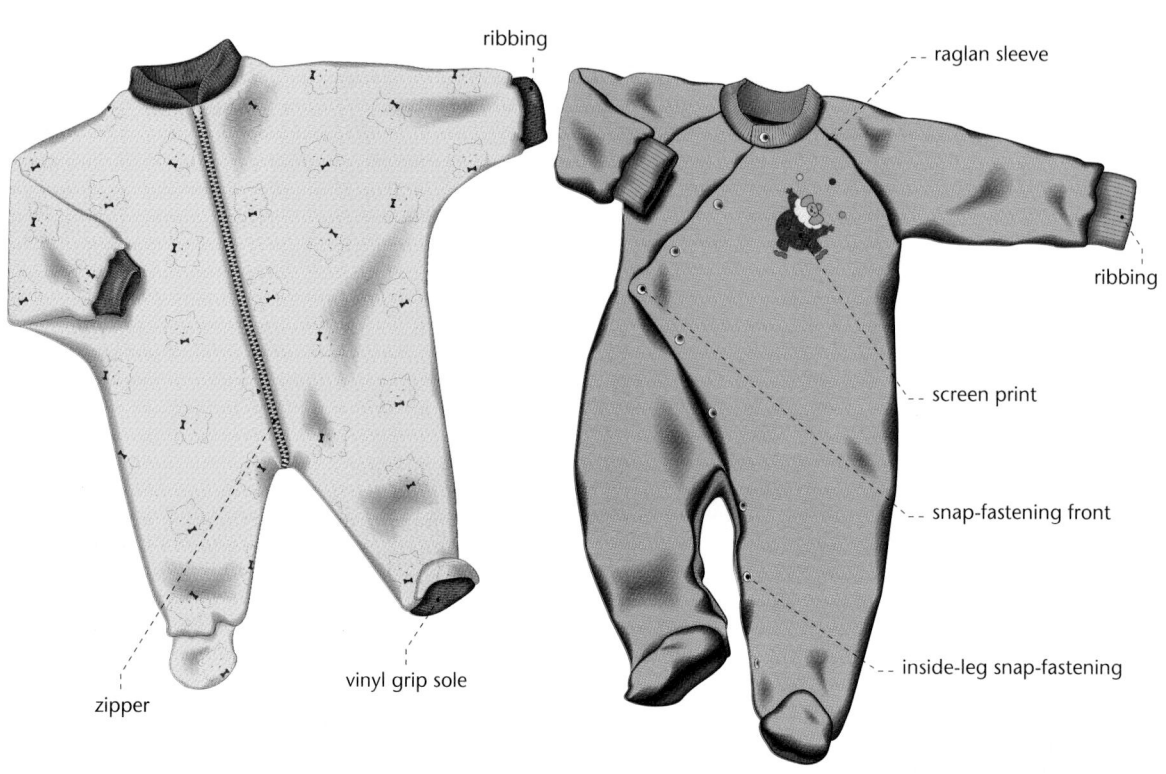

ribbing

raglan sleeve

ribbing

screen print

snap-fastening front

inside-leg snap-fastening

zipper

vinyl grip sole

HIGH-BACK OVERALLS

GROW SLEEPERS

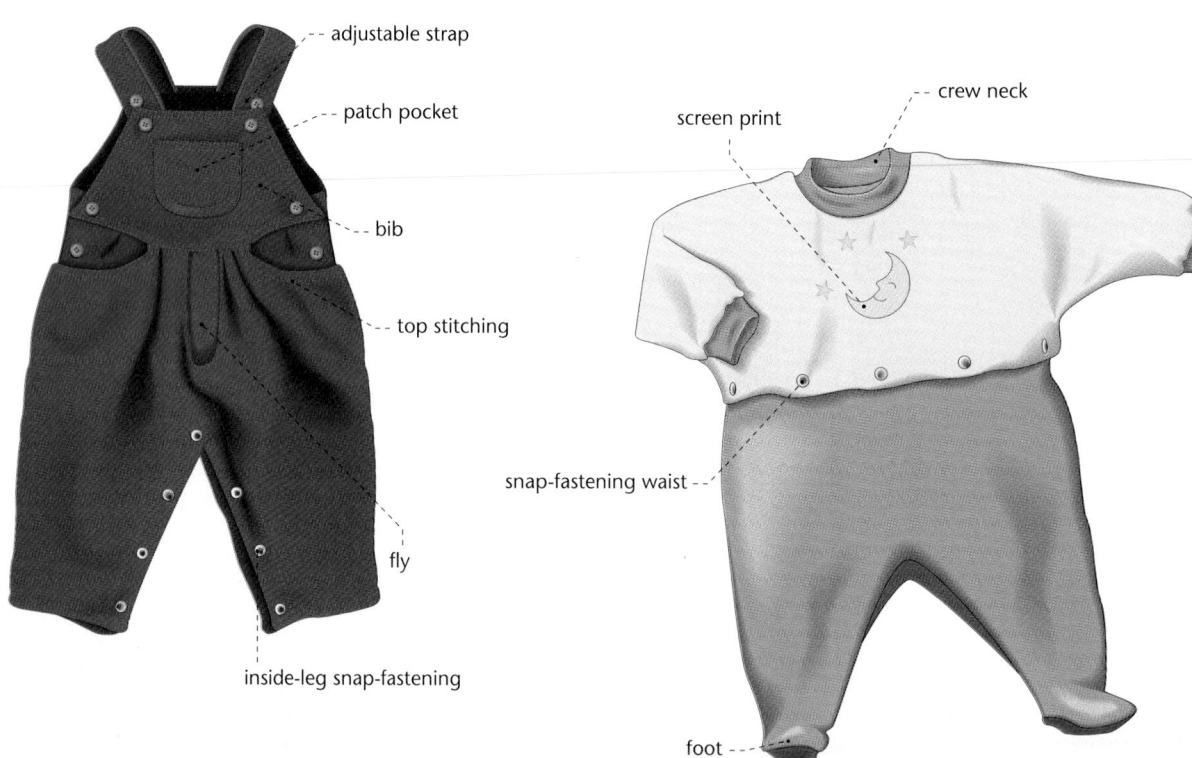

adjustable strap

crew neck

patch pocket

screen print

bib

top stitching

snap-fastening waist

fly

inside-leg snap-fastening

foot

350

TRAINING SET

- - - tank top

- - - shorts

CROSSOVER BACK STRAPS OVERALLS

button strap - - - -

bib - -

polojama

SNOWSUIT

- - - drawstring hood

- - - fly front closing

rompers

jumpsuit

T-shirt dress

351

CLOTHING

RUNNING SHOE

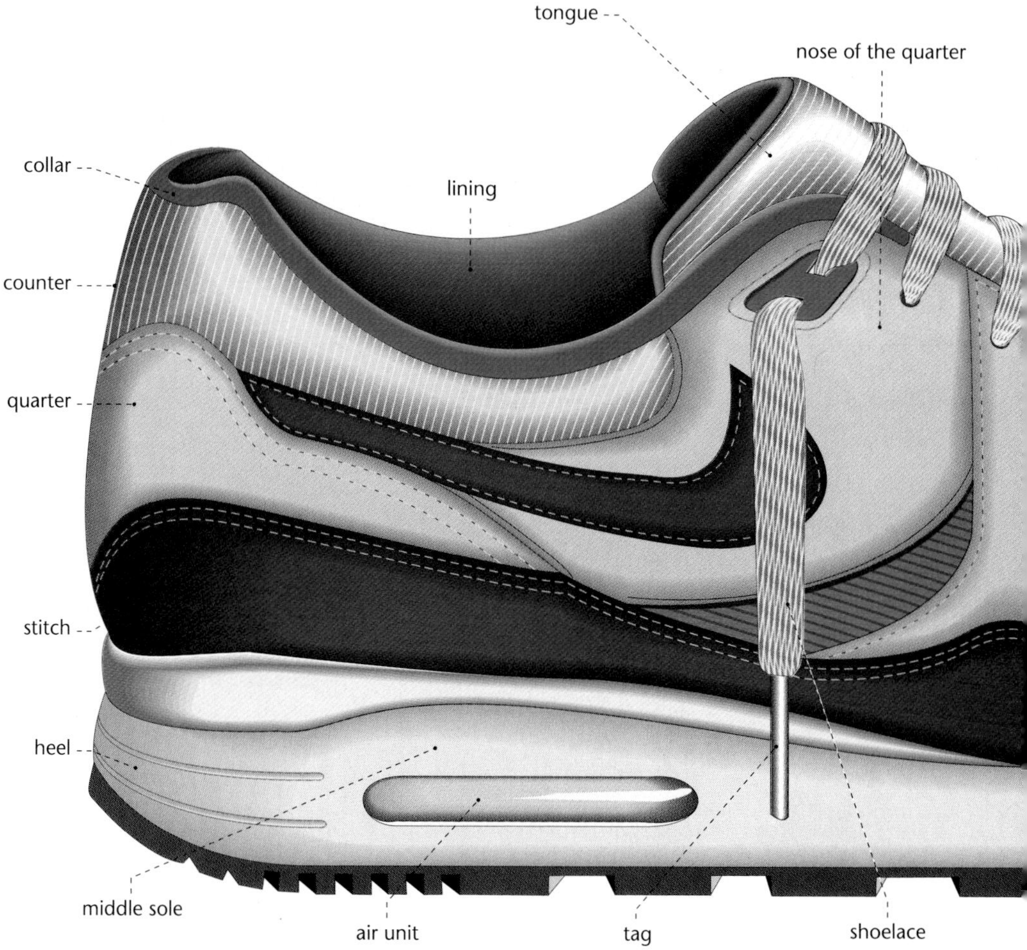

tongue

nose of the quarter

collar

lining

counter

quarter

stitch

heel

middle sole

air unit

tag

shoelace

TRAINING SUIT

hooded sweat shirt

sweat pants

sweat shirt

swimming trunks

swimsuit

eyelet

vamp

punch hole

leotard

outsole

stud

footless tights

leg-warmer

boxer shorts

pants

anorak

tank top

PARTS OF A SHOE

cuff

lining

tongue

shoelace

heel grip

quarter

outside counter

heel

top lift

waist

nose of the quarter

tag

eyelet

eyelet tab

MAJOR TYPES OF SHOES

oxford shoe

chukka

bootee

tennis shoe

blucher oxford

vamp

stitch

moccasin

punch hole

perforated toe cap

welt

loafer

outsole

mule

heavy duty boot

rubber

MAJOR TYPES OF SHOES

sling back shoe

pump

sandal

T-strap shoe

one-bar shoe

ballerina

casual shoe

boot

sandal

thong

ankle boot

clog

espadrille

thigh-boot

sandal

ACCESSORIES

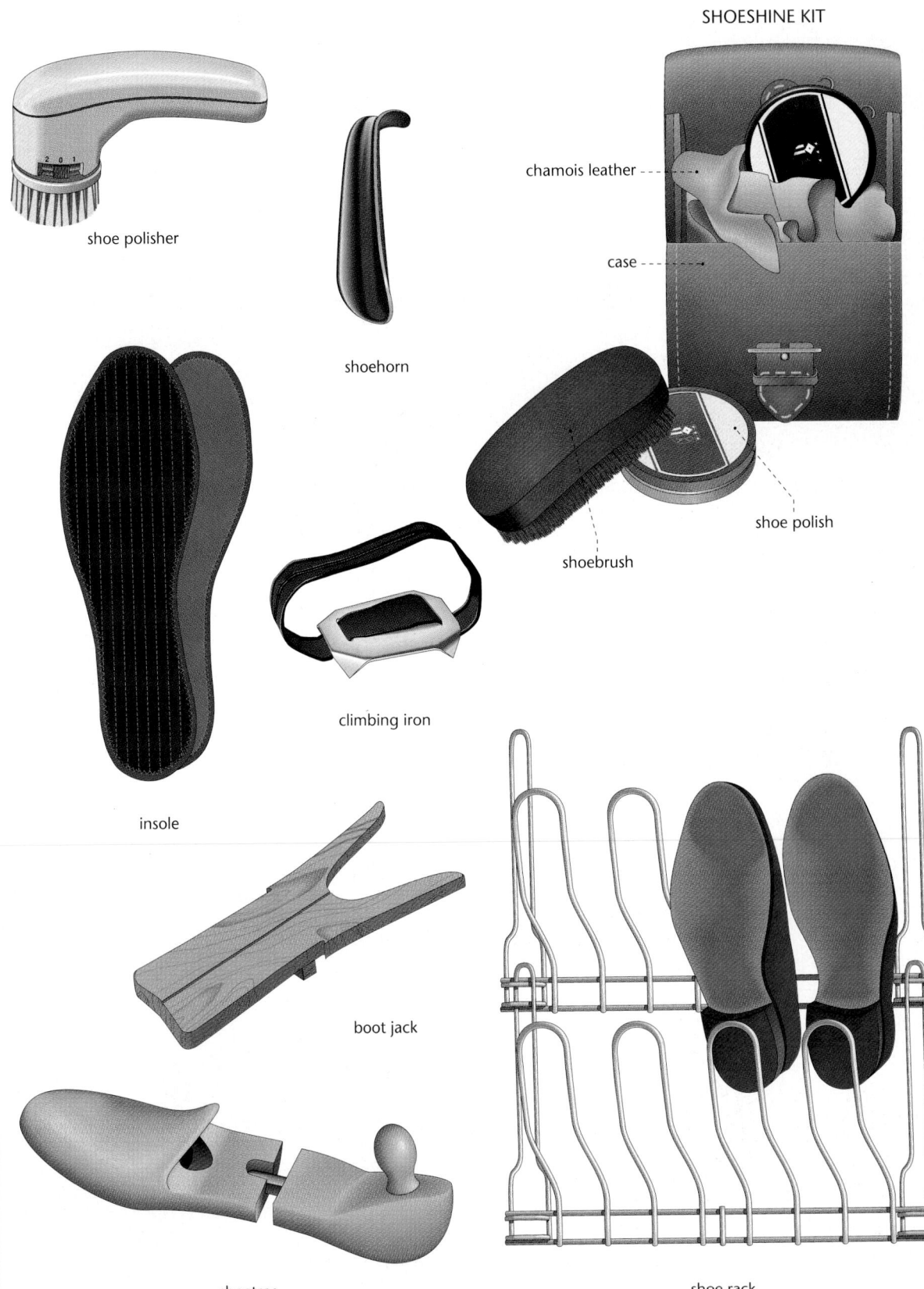

shoe polisher

shoehorn

SHOESHINE KIT

chamois leather

case

shoe polish

shoebrush

insole

climbing iron

boot jack

shoetree

shoe rack

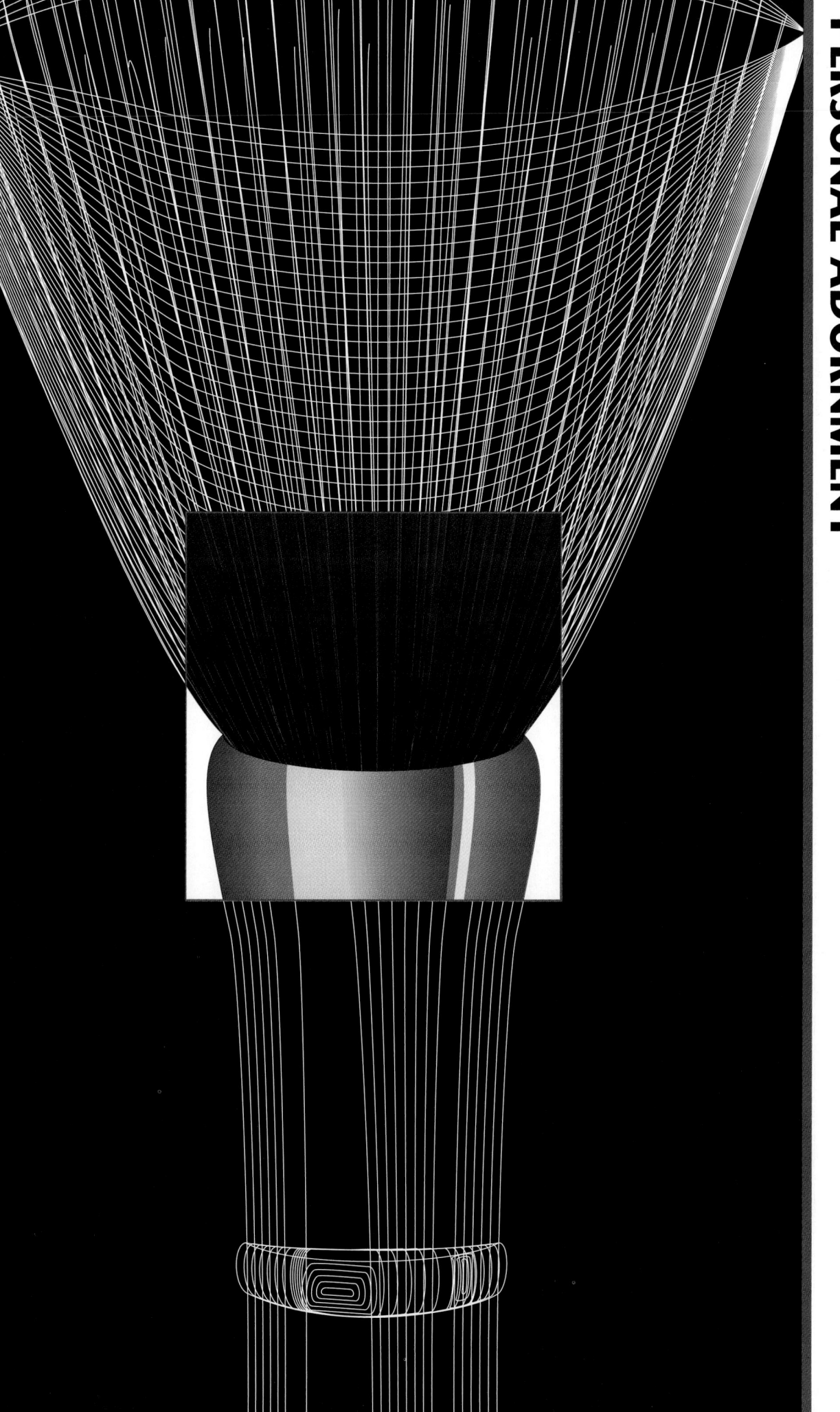

CONTENTS

JEWELRY 361

MANICURE..365

MAKEUP..366

HAIRDRESSING..368

PERSONAL ADORNMENT

JEWELRY

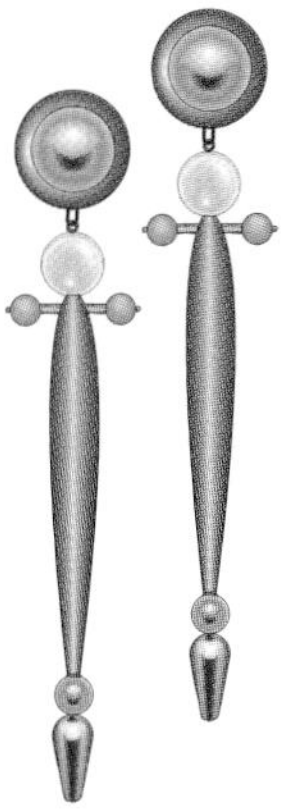

drop earrings

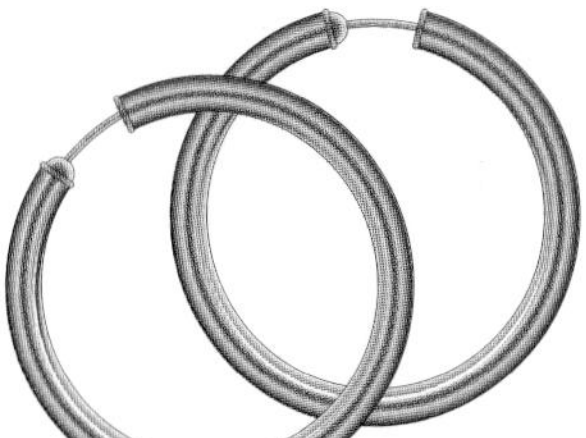

hoop earrings

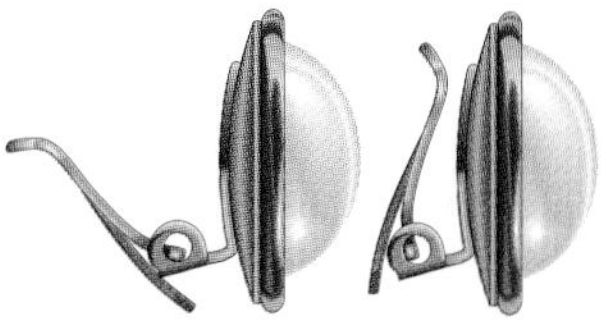

clip earrings

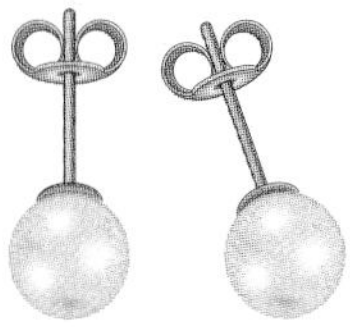

pierced earrings

screw earrings

NECKLACES

pendant

locket

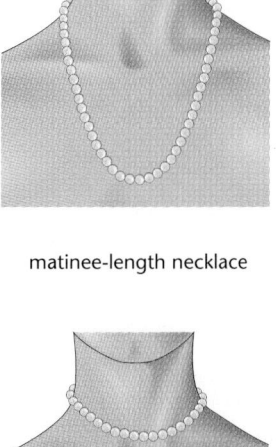

matinee-length necklace

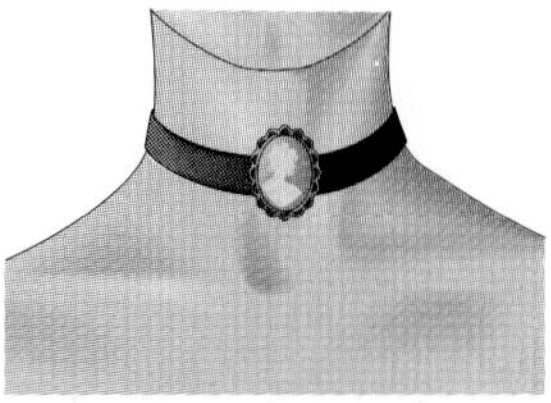

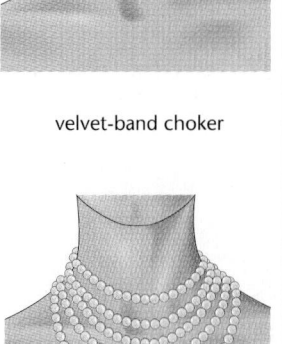

velvet-band choker

opera-length necklace

rope

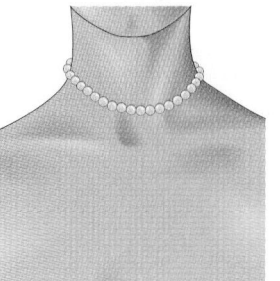

choker

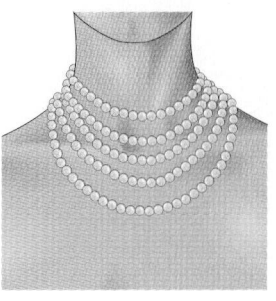

bib necklace

PERSONAL ADORNMENT

361

CUT FOR GEMSTONES

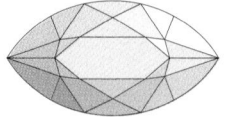

navette cut

baguette cut

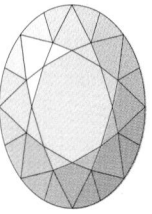

oval cut

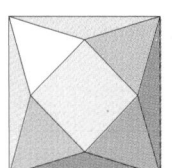

French cut

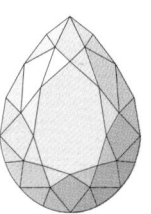

pear-shaped cut

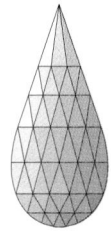

briolette cut

table cut

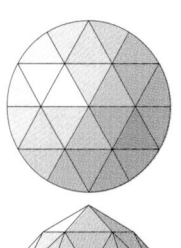

rose cut

cabochon cut

step cut

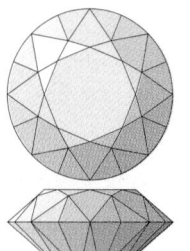

brilliant full cut

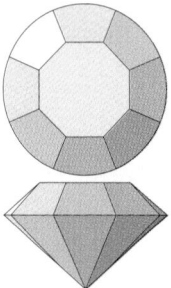

eight cut

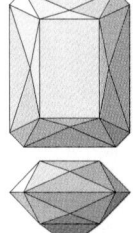

scissors cut

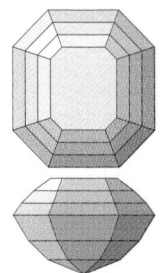

emerald cut

BOTTOM FACE

pavilion facet (8)

culet

lower girdle facet (16)

TOP FACE

star facet (8)

table

bezel facet (8)

upper girdle facet (16)

SIDE FACE

table

girdle

crown

pavilion

culet

PRECIOUS STONES

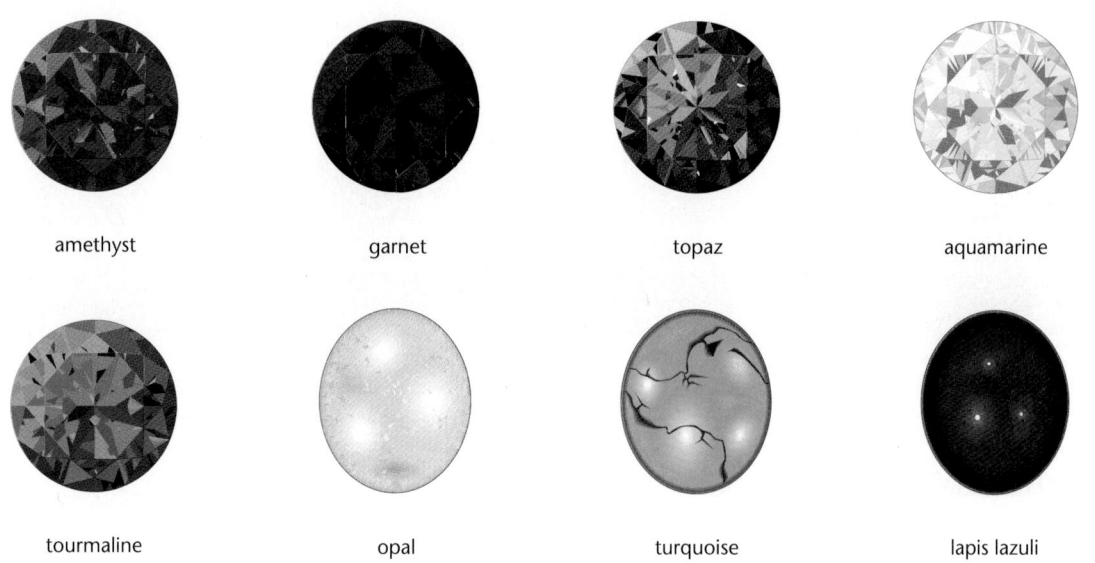

emerald

ruby

sapphire

diamond

SEMIPRECIOUS STONES

amethyst

garnet

topaz

aquamarine

tourmaline

opal

turquoise

lapis lazuli

PERSONAL ADORNMENT

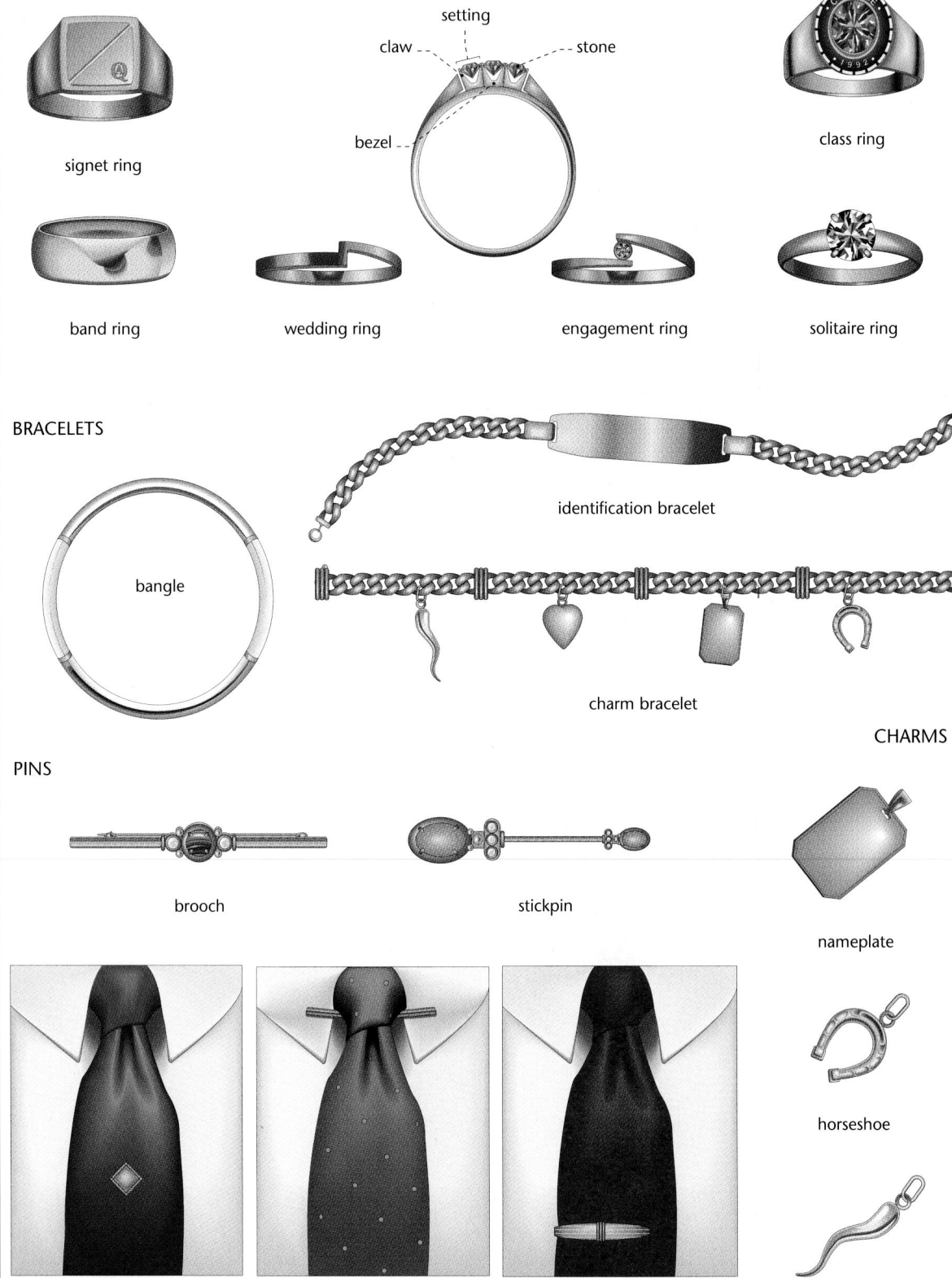

RINGS

signet ring

setting
claw
stone
bezel

class ring

band ring

wedding ring

engagement ring

solitaire ring

BRACELETS

bangle

identification bracelet

charm bracelet

CHARMS

PINS

brooch

stickpin

nameplate

horseshoe

tiepin

collar bar

tie bar

horn

MANICURE

MANICURE SET

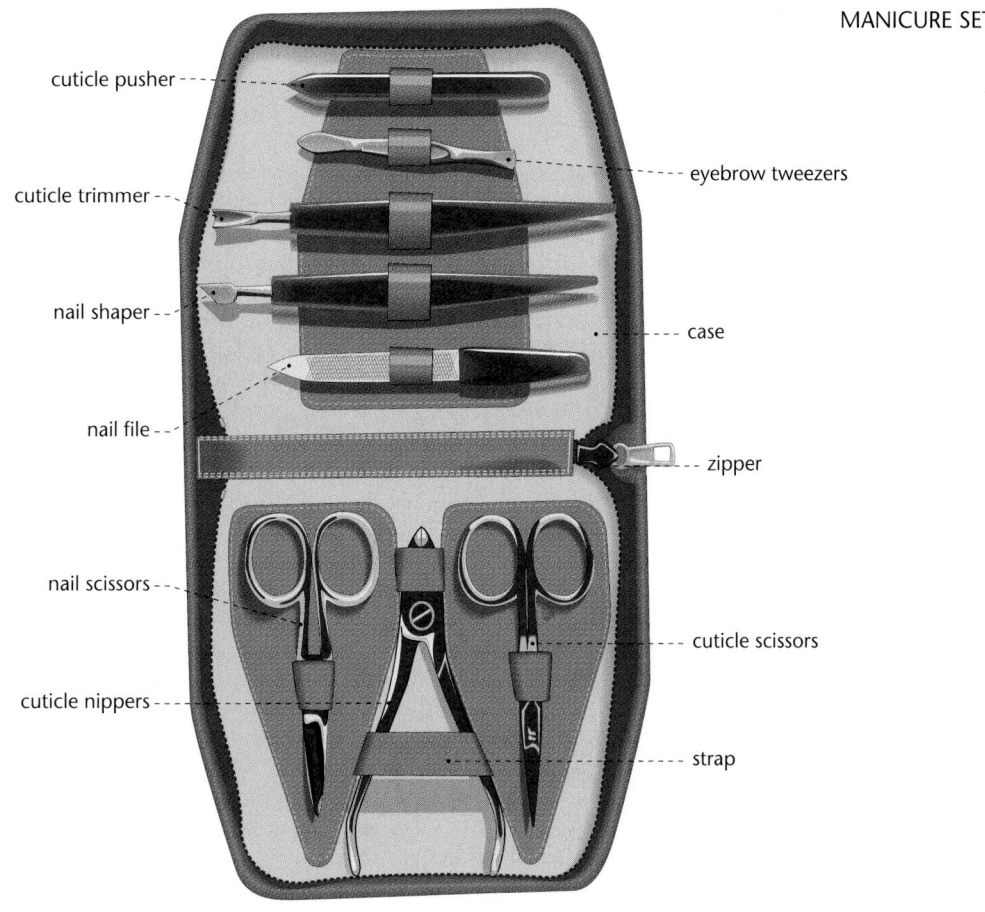

cuticle pusher

eyebrow tweezers

cuticle trimmer

nail shaper

case

nail file

zipper

nail scissors

cuticle scissors

cuticle nippers

strap

NAIL CLIPPERS

MANICURING IMPLEMENTS

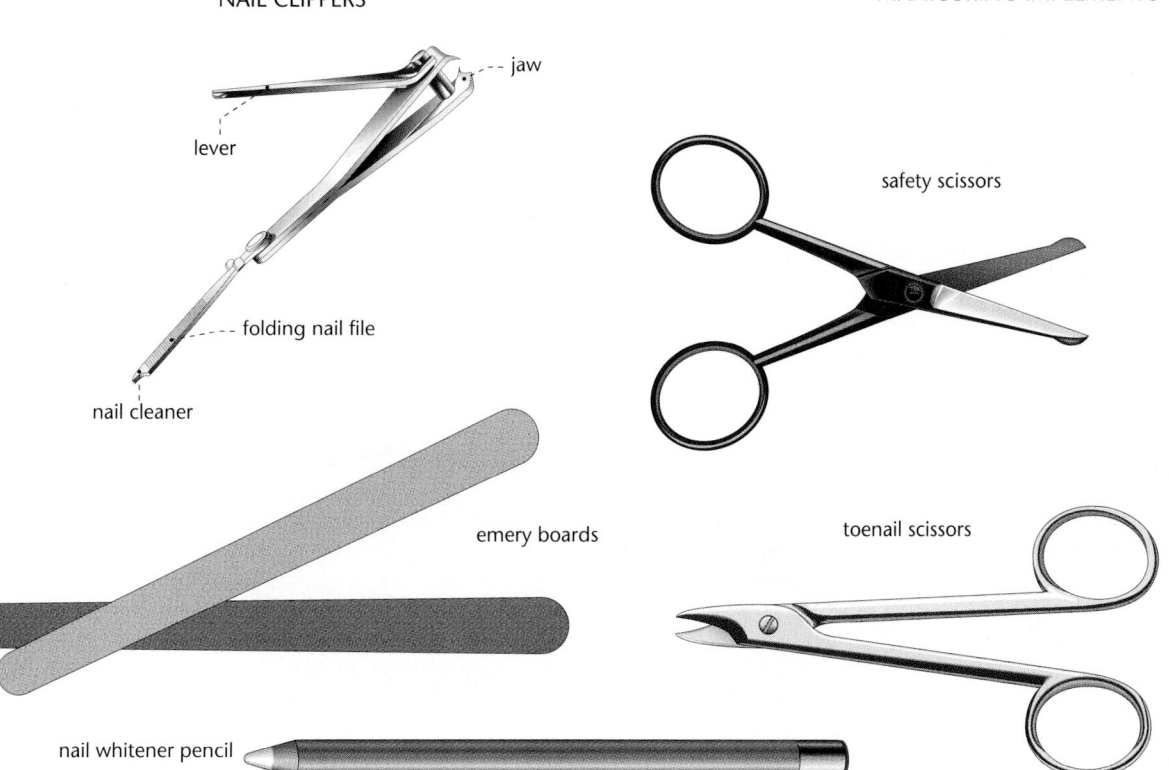

jaw

lever

safety scissors

folding nail file

nail cleaner

emery boards

toenail scissors

nail whitener pencil

FACIAL MAKEUP

fan brush

loose powder brush

loose powder

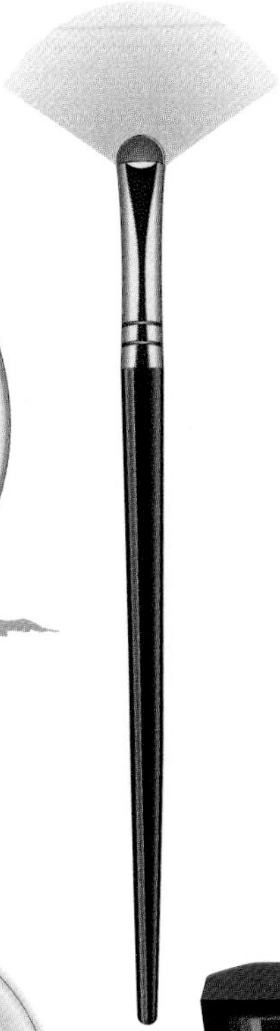

liquid foundation

powder puff

blusher brush

compact

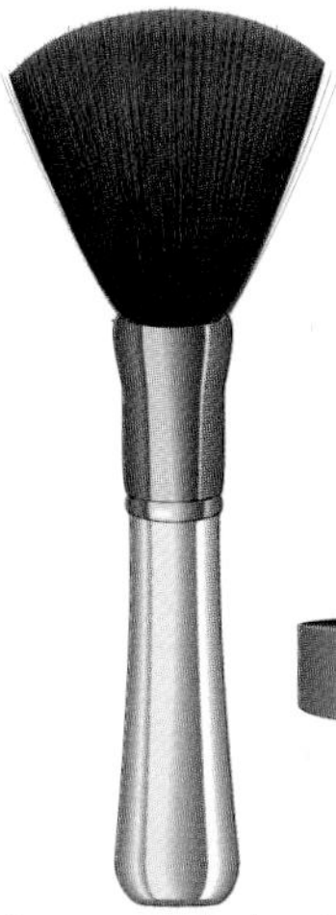

pressed powder

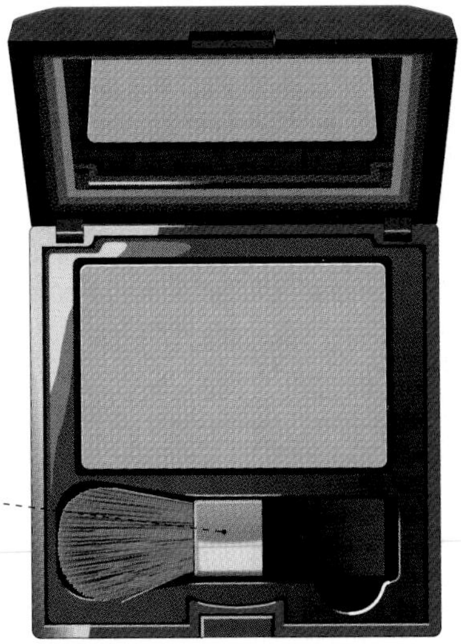

powder blusher

LIP MAKEUP

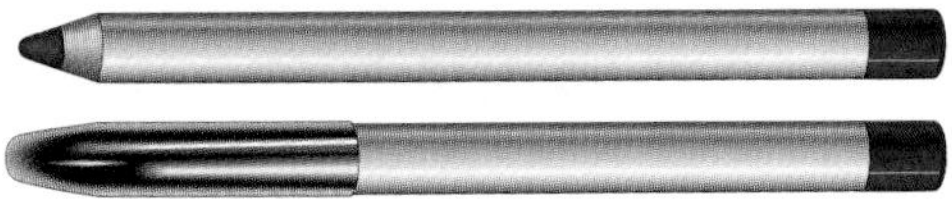

lipbrush

lipstick

lipliner

PERSONAL ADORNMENT

eyebrow pencil

brow brush and lash comb

liquid eyeliner

liquid mascara

eyelash curler

mascara brush

sponge-tipped applicator

cake mascara

eyeshadow

SPONGES

vegetable sponge

natural sponge

synthetic sponge

PERSONAL ADORNMENT

LIGHTED MIRROR

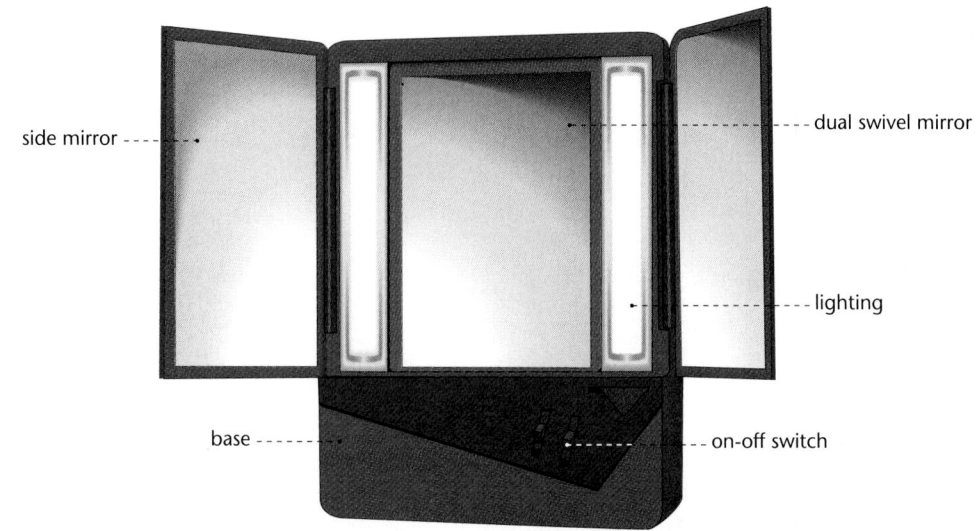

side mirror

dual swivel mirror

lighting

base

on-off switch

HAIRBRUSHES

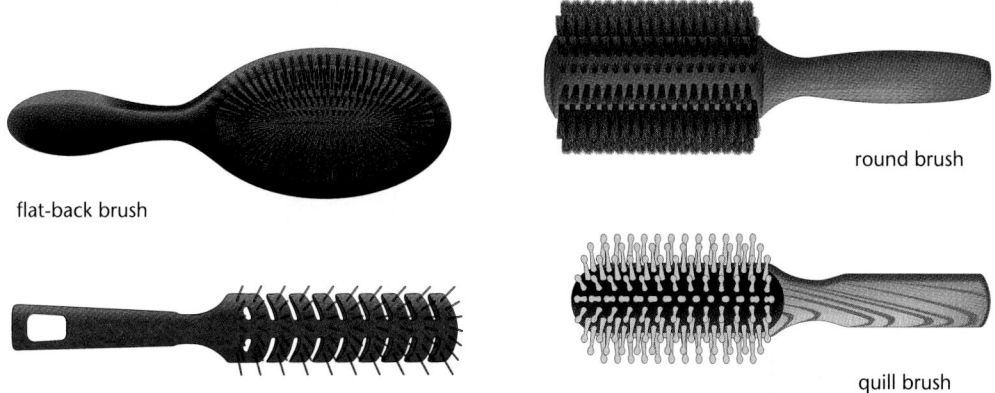

flat-back brush

round brush

vent brush

quill brush

COMBS

teaser comb

rake comb

tail comb

pitchfork comb

Afro pick

barber comb

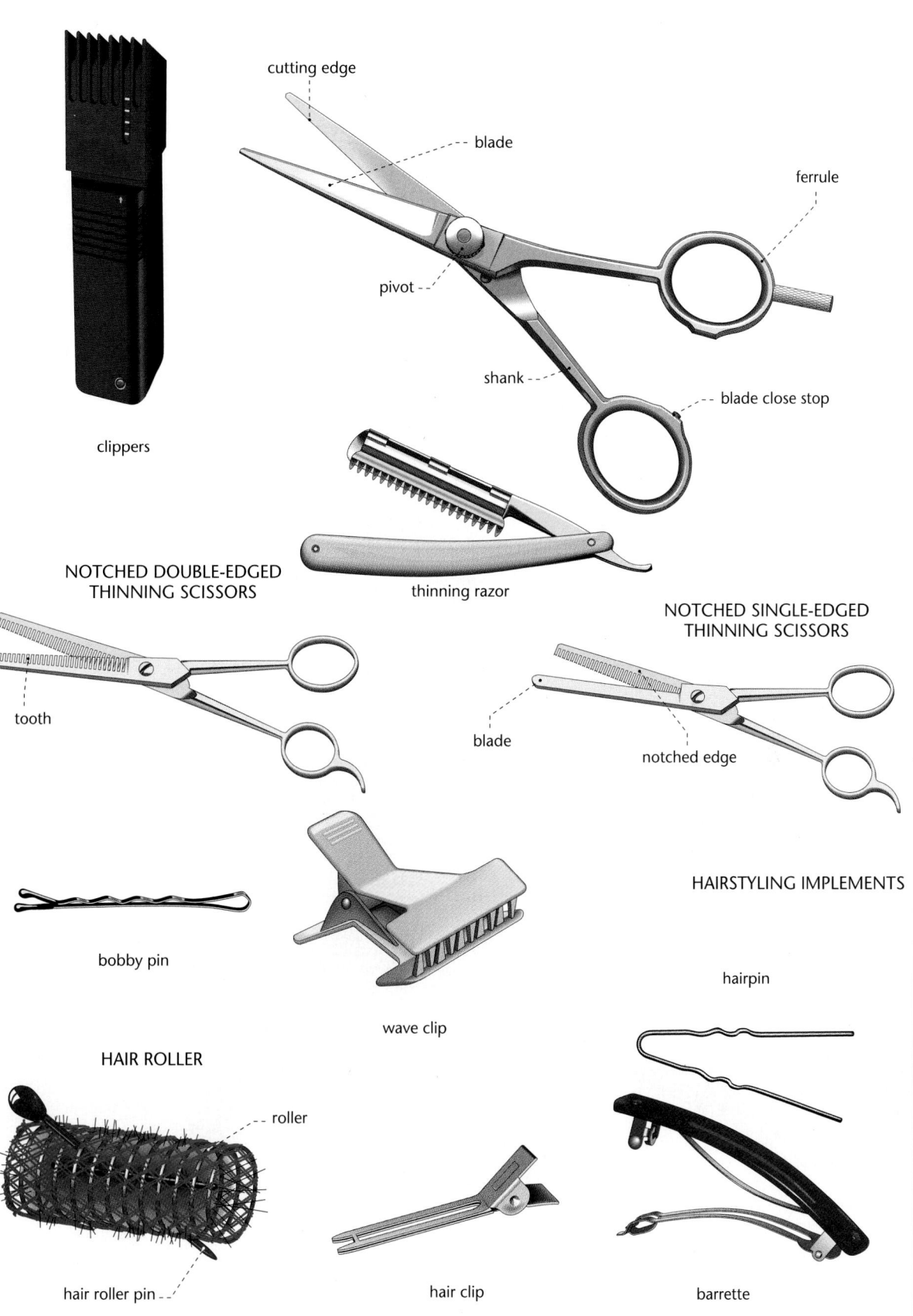

cutting edge

blade

ferrule

pivot

shank

blade close stop

clippers

thinning razor

NOTCHED DOUBLE-EDGED
THINNING SCISSORS

NOTCHED SINGLE-EDGED
THINNING SCISSORS

tooth

blade

notched edge

HAIRSTYLING IMPLEMENTS

bobby pin

hairpin

wave clip

HAIR ROLLER

roller

hair roller pin

hair clip

barrette

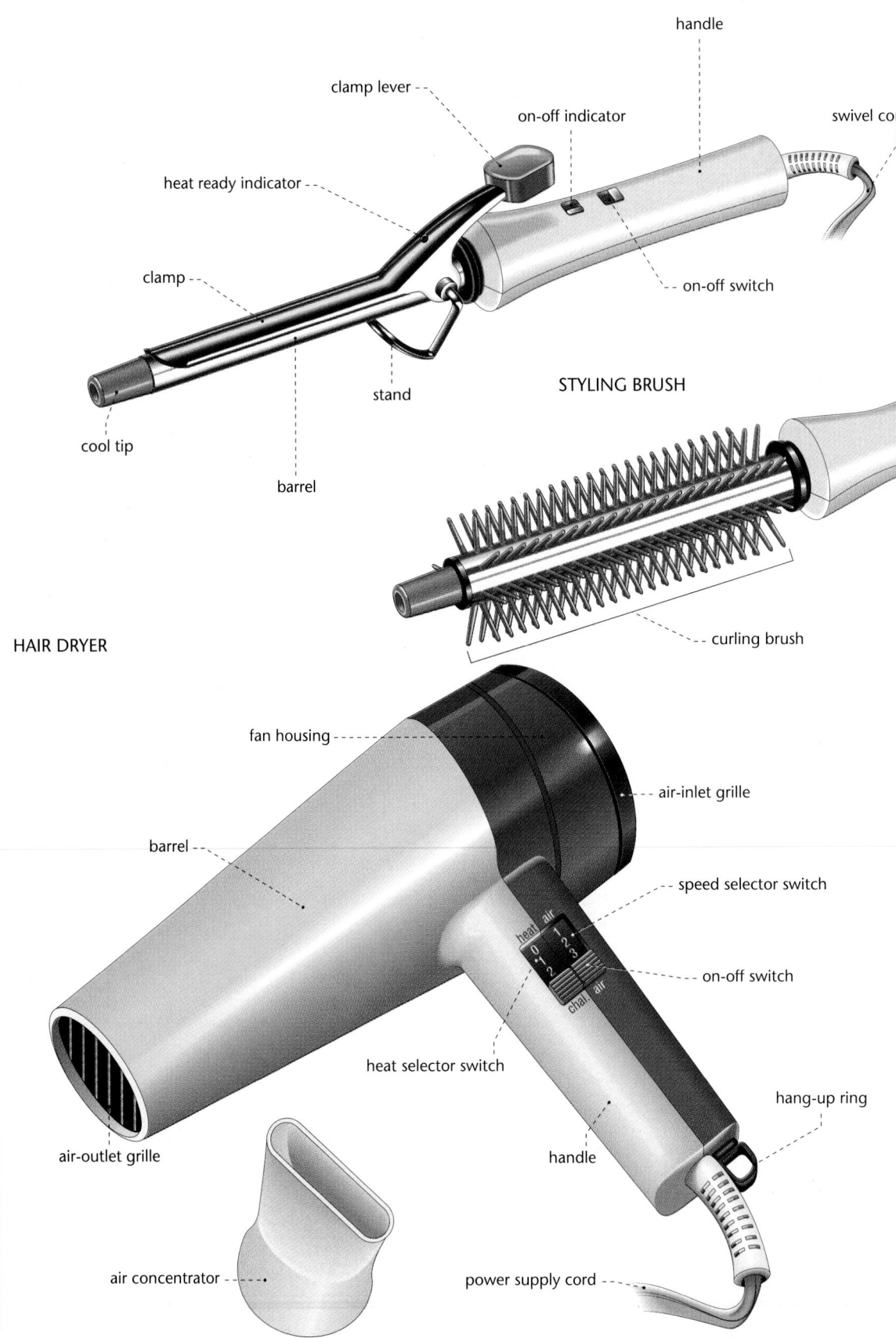

CURLING IRON

clamp lever

on-off indicator

handle

heat ready indicator

swivel cord

clamp

on-off switch

stand

STYLING BRUSH

cool tip

barrel

curling brush

HAIR DRYER

fan housing

air-inlet grille

barrel

speed selector switch

on-off switch

heat selector switch

hang-up ring

air-outlet grille

handle

air concentrator

power supply cord

PERSONAL ARTICLES

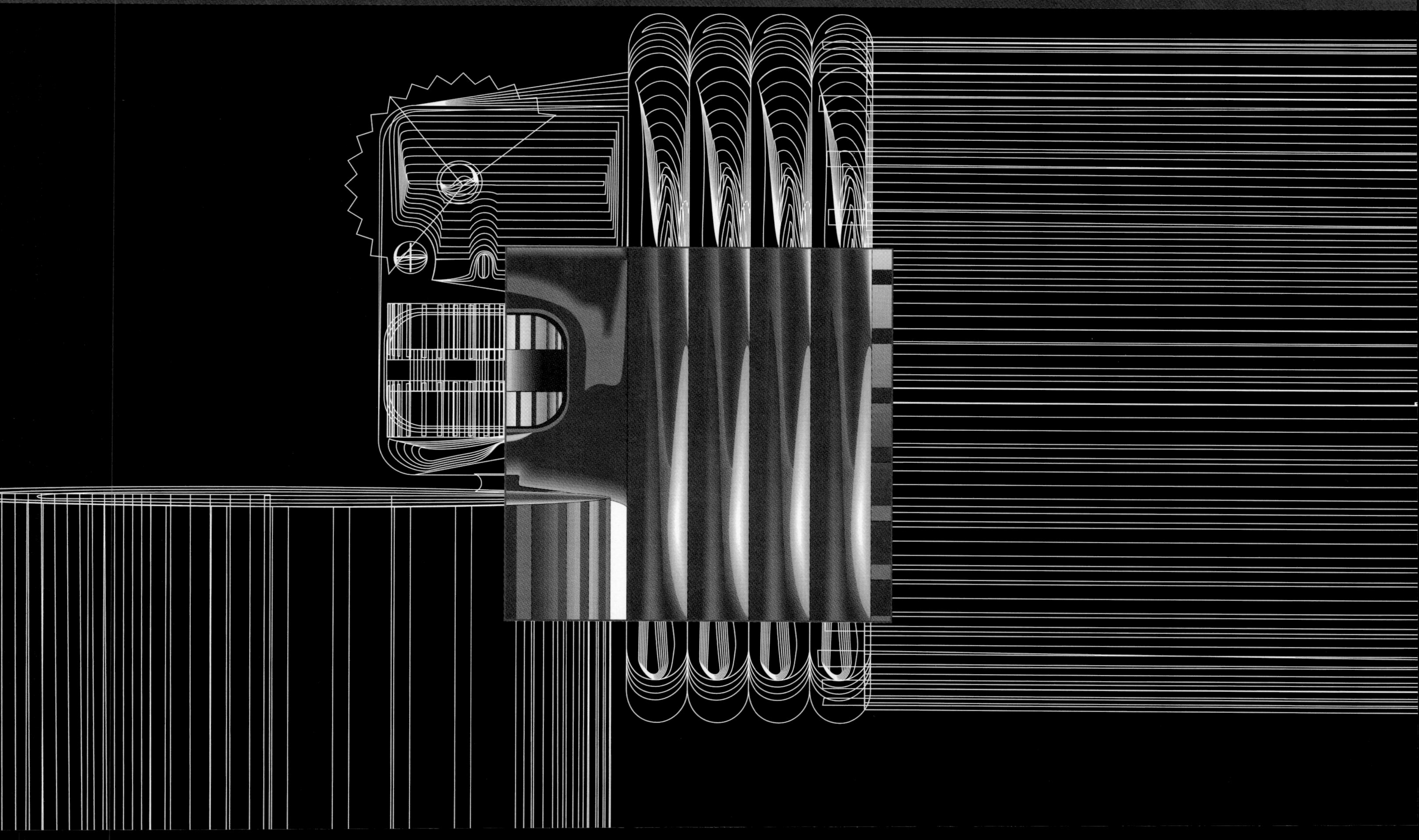

CONTENTS

DENTAL CARE 373

RAZORS 374

UMBRELLA AND STICK...375

EYEGLASSES 376

LEATHER GOODS..378

HANDBAGS..380

LUGGAGE 382

SMOKING ACCESSORIES...384

PERSONAL ARTICLES

DENTAL CARE

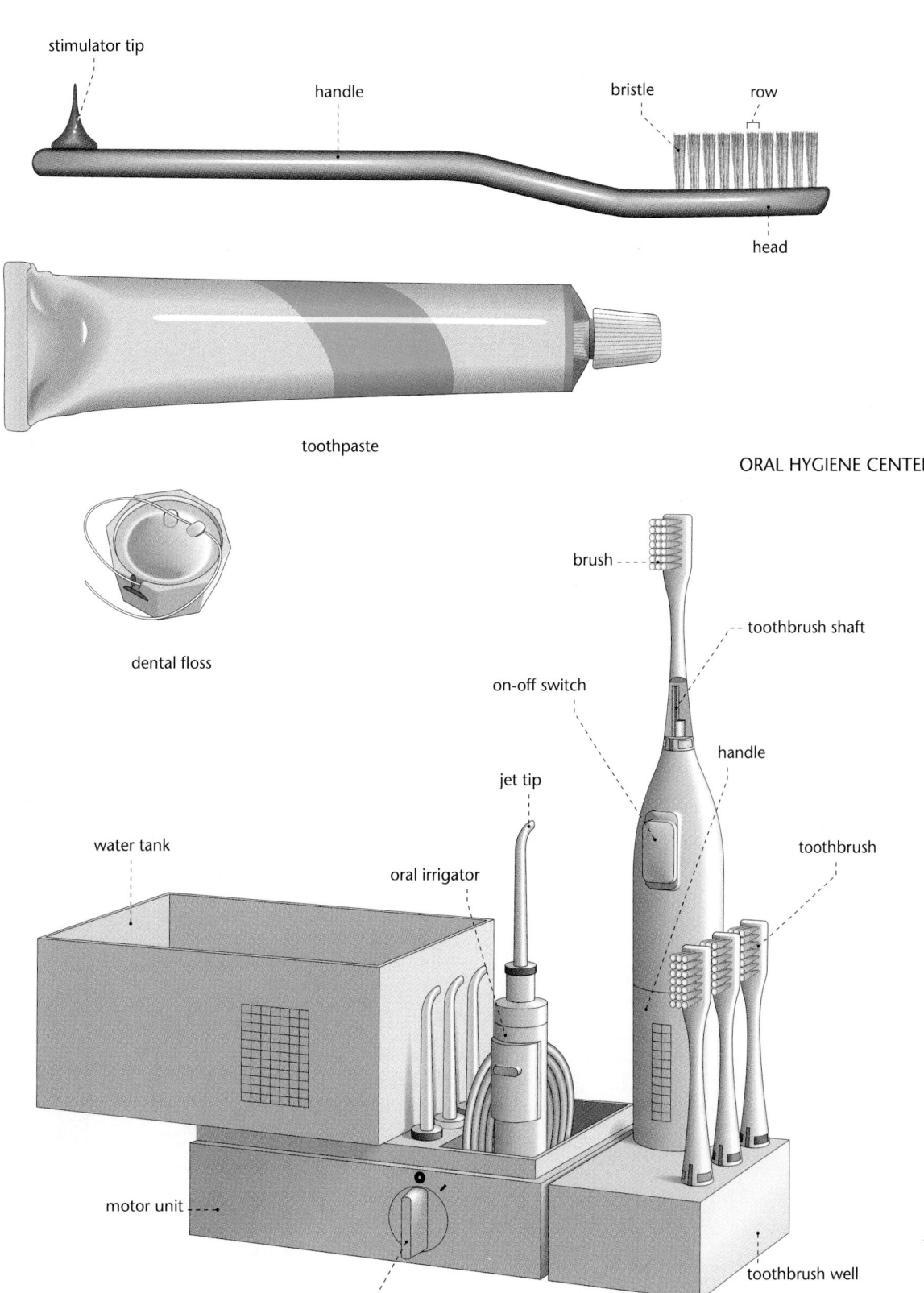

stimulator tip

handle

bristle

row

head

toothpaste

dental floss

ORAL HYGIENE CENTER

brush

toothbrush shaft

on-off switch

handle

jet tip

toothbrush

water tank

oral irrigator

motor unit

toothbrush well

pressure control

ELECTRIC RAZOR

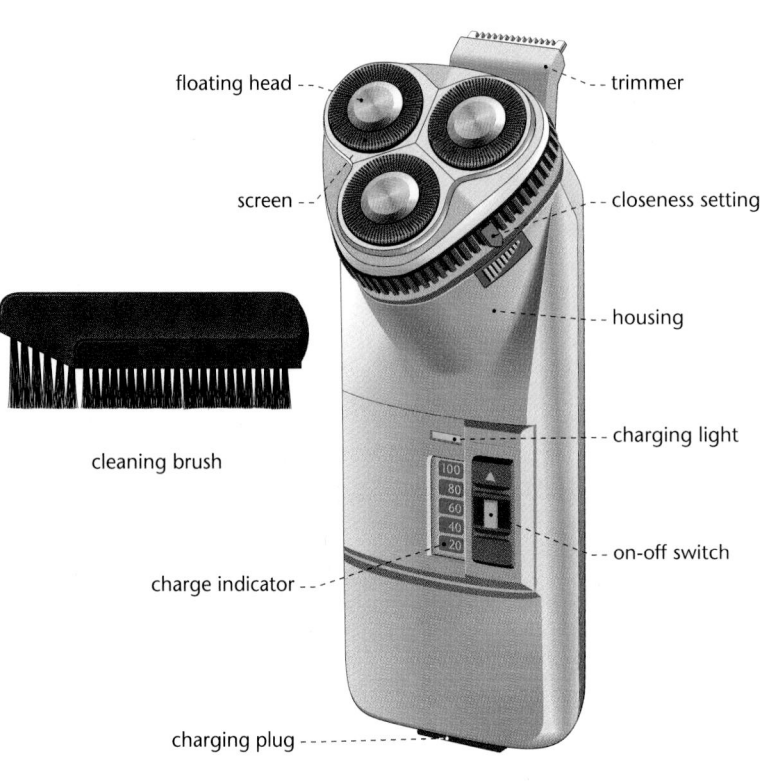

floating head --- --- trimmer

screen --- closeness setting

housing

charging light

charge indicator

on-off switch

100
80
60
40
20

charging plug

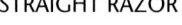

cleaning brush

power cord

plug adapter

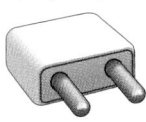

STRAIGHT RAZOR

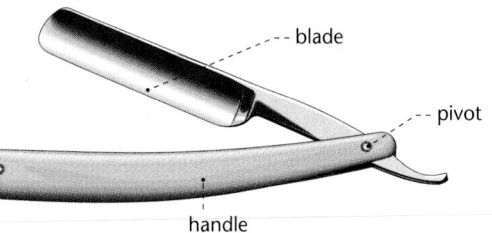

blade

pivot

handle

DOUBLE-EDGE RAZOR

head ---

collar ---

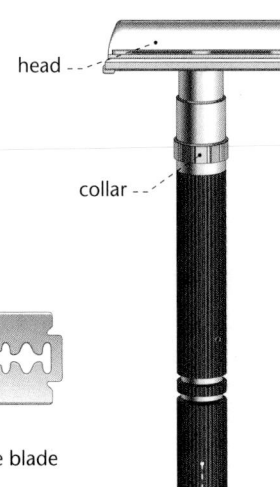

handle

disposable razor

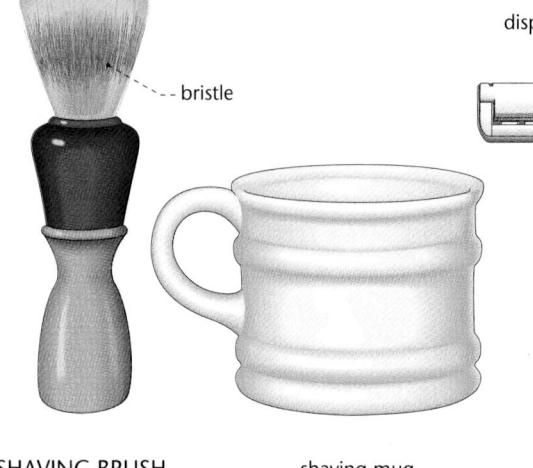

bristle

double-edge blade

5   5

blade injector

SHAVING BRUSH   shaving mug

UMBRELLA AND STICK

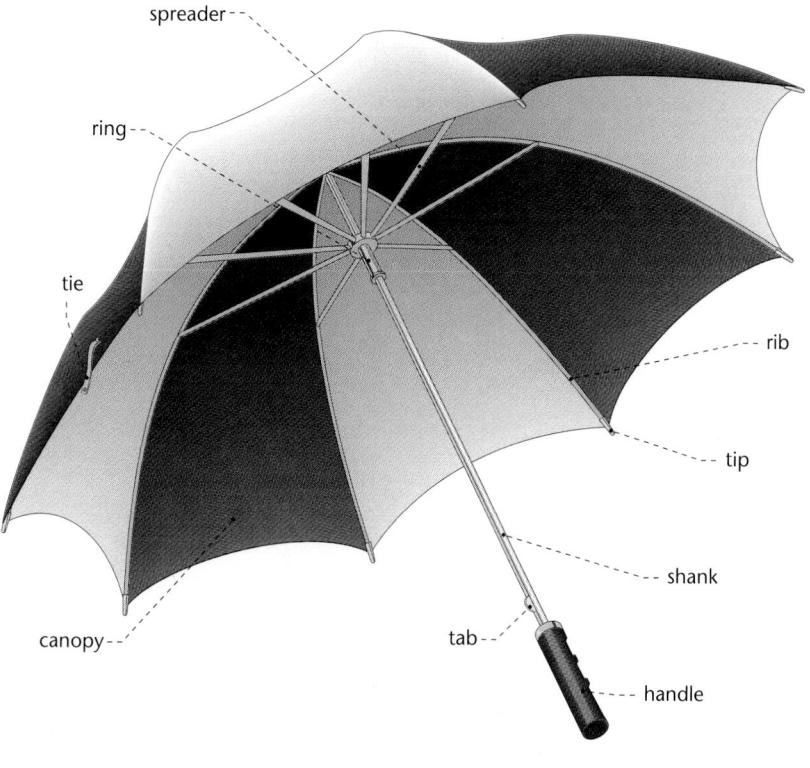

UMBRELLA

spreader
ring
tie
rib
tip
shank
canopy
tab
handle

TELESCOPIC UMBRELLA

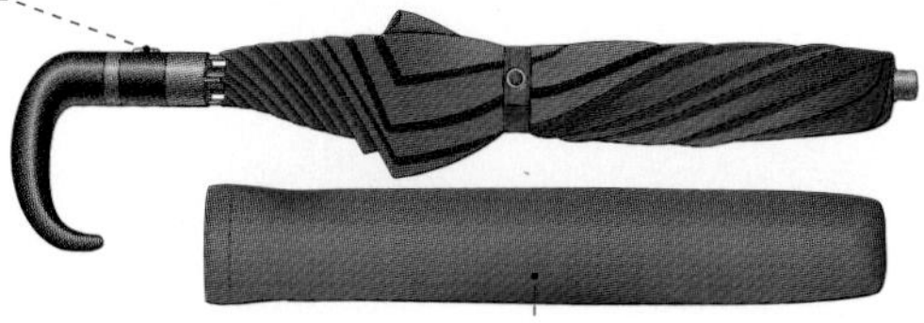

push button
cover

STICK UMBRELLA

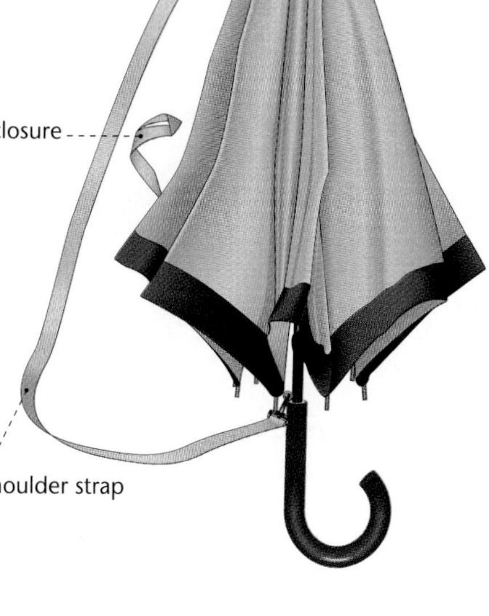

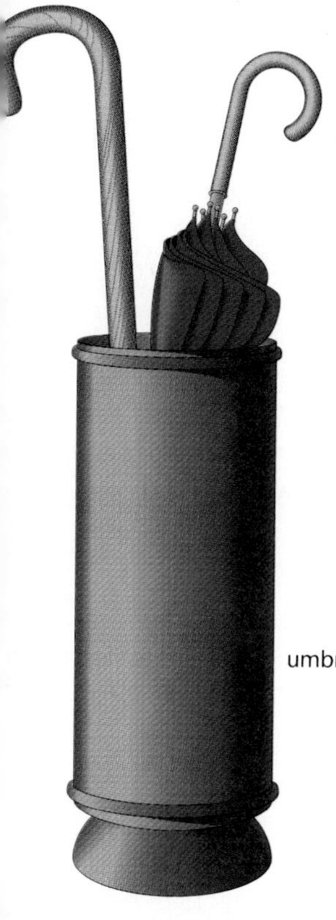

ferrule
tie closure
shoulder strap

umbrella stand

swagger stick

walking stick

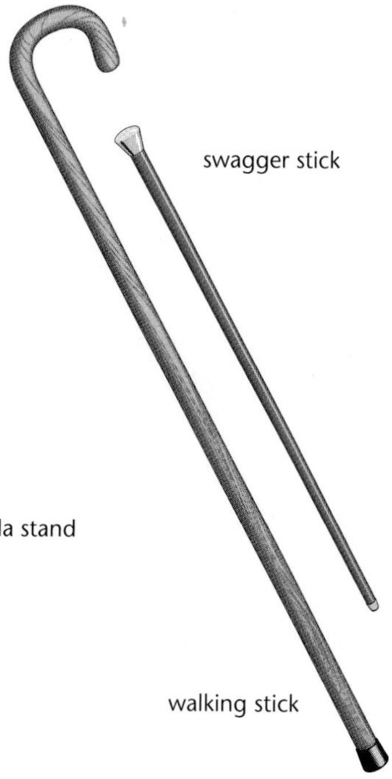

EYEGLASSES PARTS

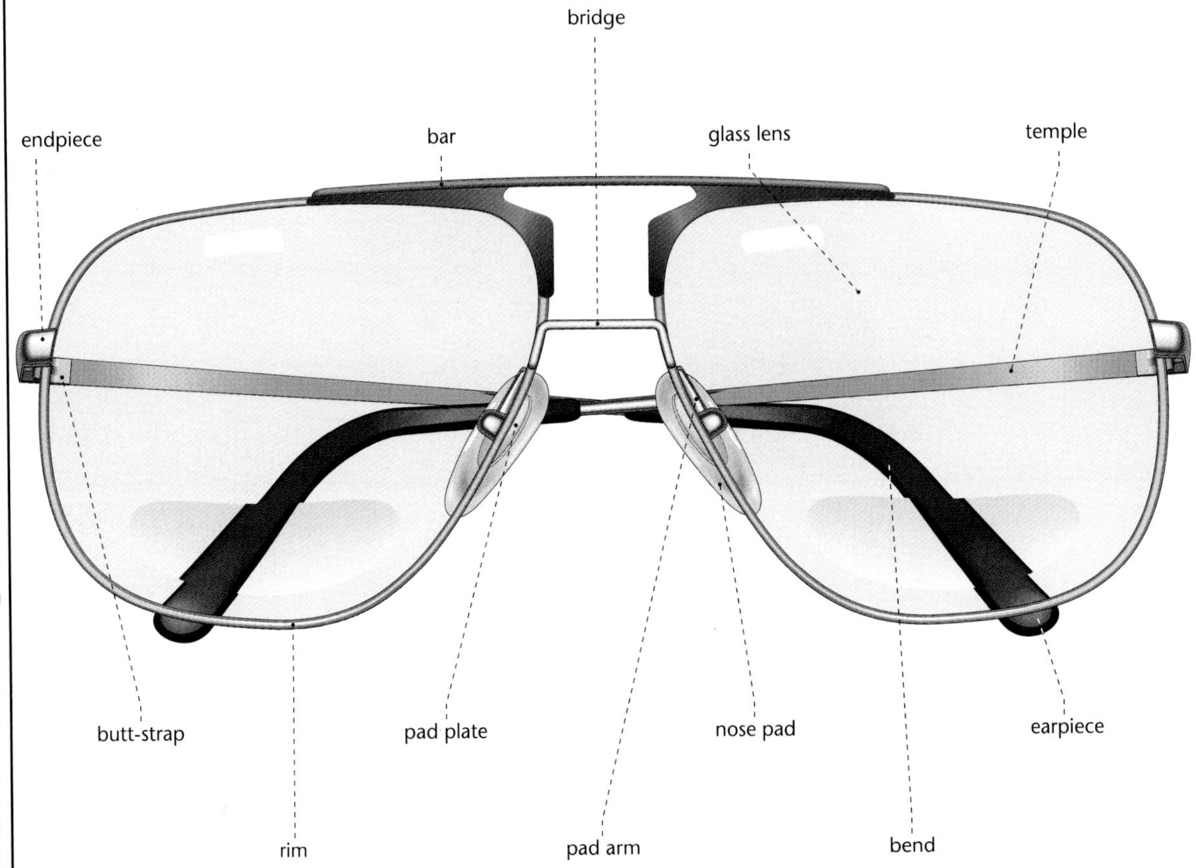

bridge

endpiece

bar

glass lens

temple

butt-strap

pad plate

nose pad

earpiece

rim

pad arm

bend

BIFOCAL LENS

distance

rim

reading

FRAMES

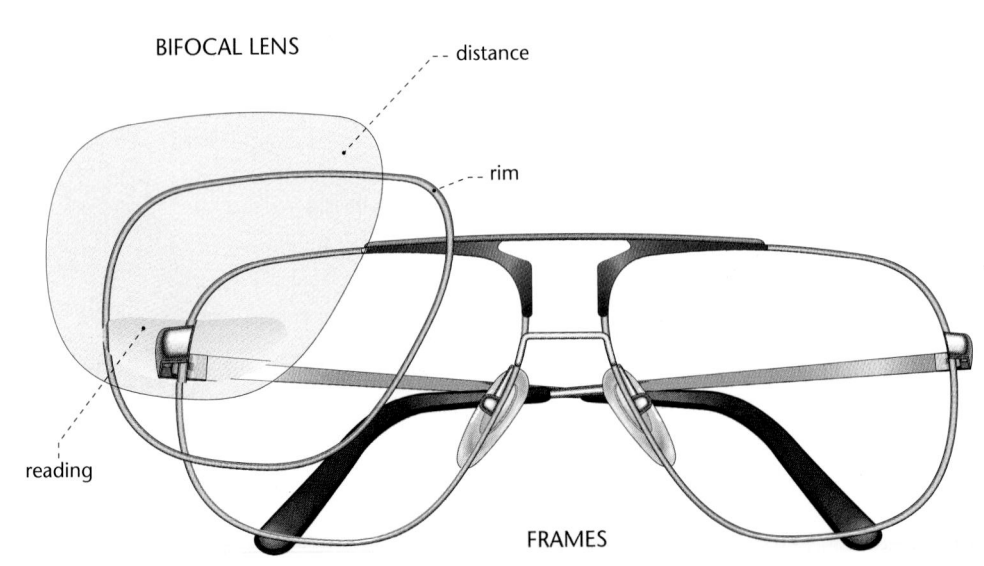

half-glasses

scissors-glasses

sunglasses

pince-nez

lorgnette

monocle

opera glasses

LEATHER GOODS

ATTACHÉ CASE

clasp

divider

expandable file pouch

pocket

hinge

pen holder

lining

frame

handle

combination lock

BRIEFCASE

BOTTOM-FOLD PORTFOLIO

retractable handle

tab

exterior pocket

gusset

key lock

underarm portfolio

writing case

378

eyeglasses case

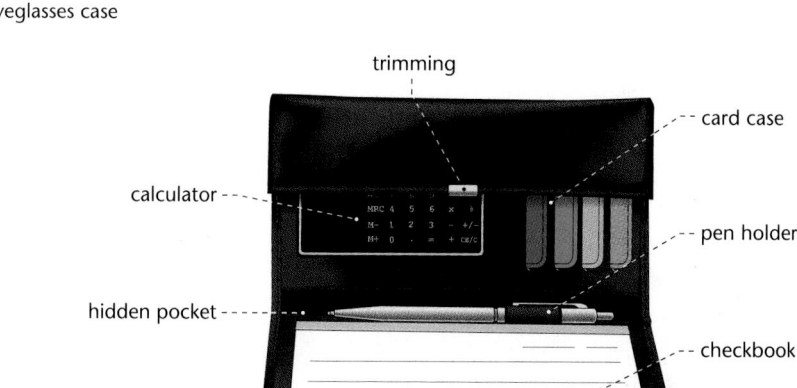

trimming

calculator

hidden pocket

card case

pen holder

checkbook

CARD CASE

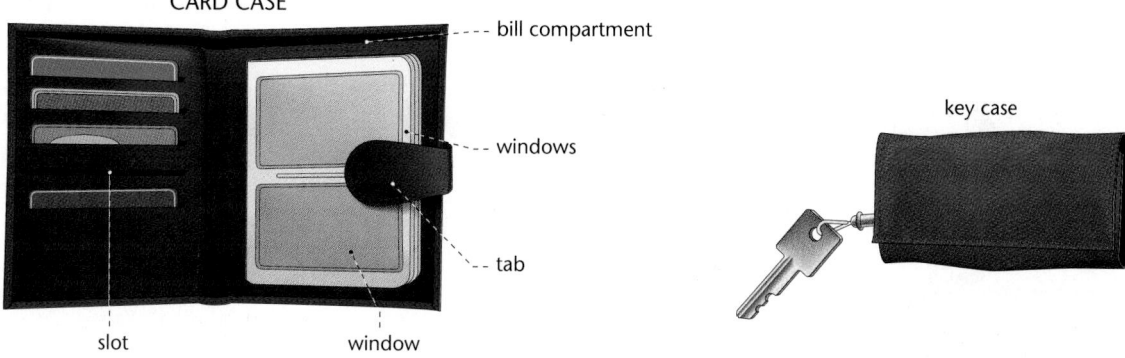

bill compartment

windows

tab

slot

window

key case

billfold

purse

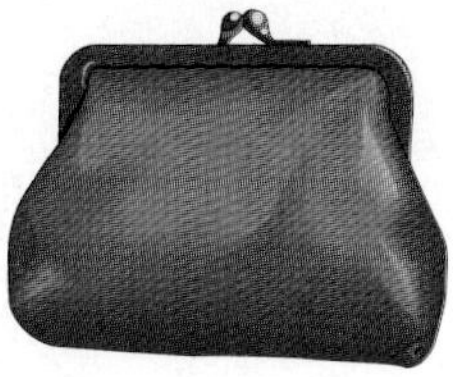

wallet

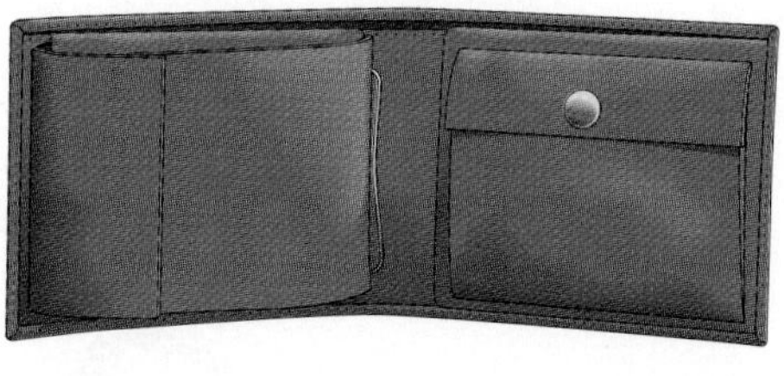

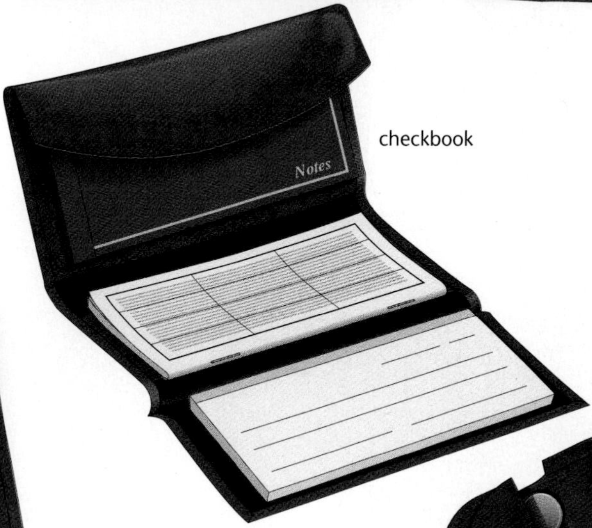

checkbook

Notes

passport case

PASS

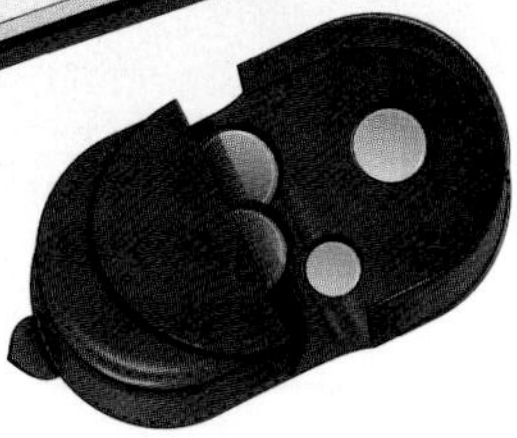

coin purse

PERSONAL ARTICLES

379

HANDBAGS

SATCHEL BAG

men's bag

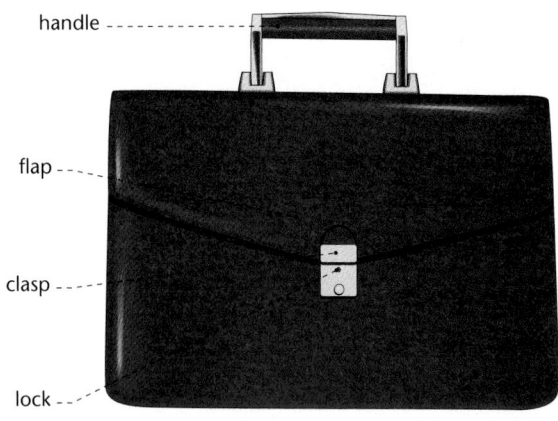

handle

flap

clasp

lock

pouch

SHOULDER BAG

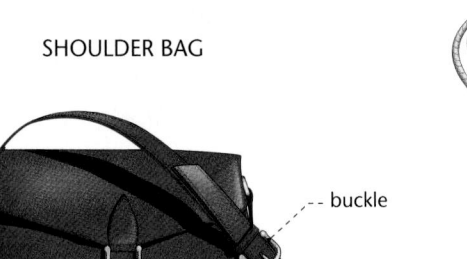

buckle

shoulder strap

pouch

ACCORDION BAG

gusset

tote bag

duffel bag

hobo bag

sea bag

box bag

clutch bag

DRAWSTRING BAG

eyelet

drawstring

front pocket

duffel bag

muff

shopping bag

carrier bag

LUGGAGE

CARRY-ON BAG

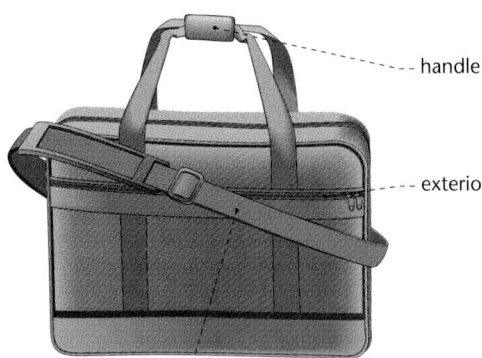

tote bag

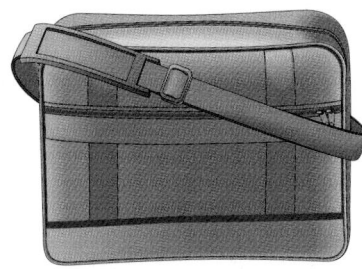

handle

exterior pocket

shoulder strap

VANITY CASE

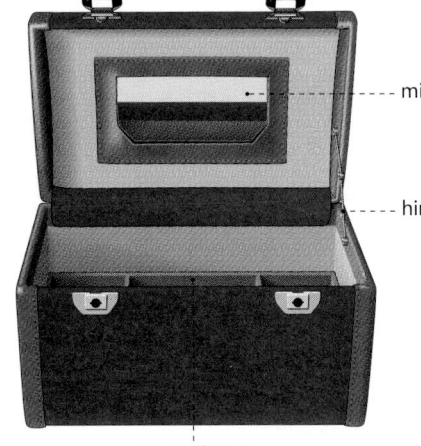

mirror

hinge

cosmetic tray

GARMENT BAG

zipper

LUGGAGE CARRIER

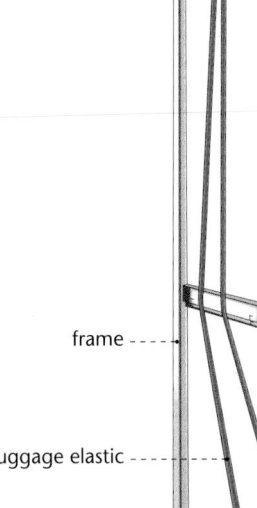

utility case

frame

luggage elastic

stand

382

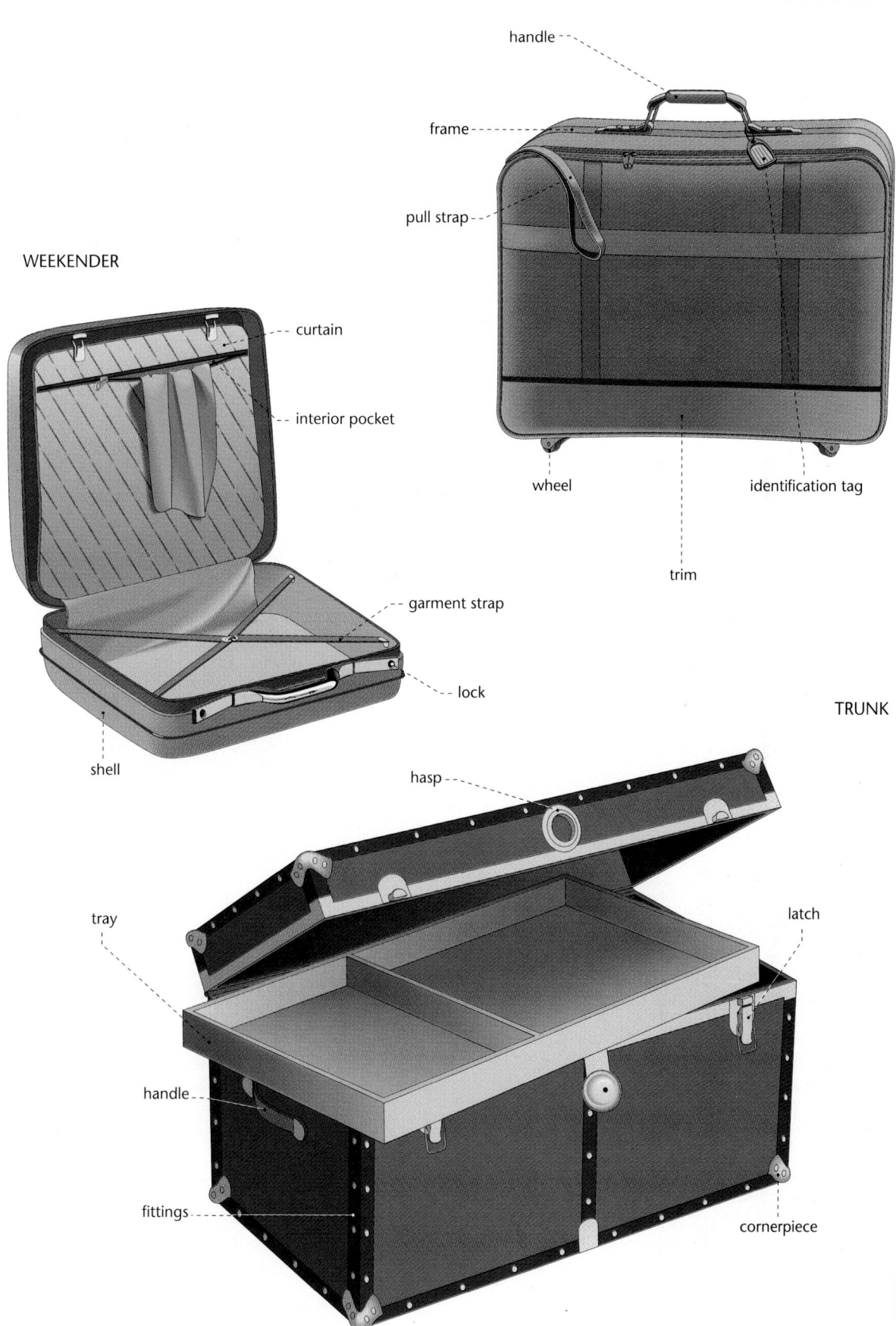

PULLMAN CASE

handle

frame

pull strap

wheel

identification tag

trim

WEEKENDER

curtain

interior pocket

garment strap

lock

shell

TRUNK

hasp

tray

latch

handle

fittings

cornerpiece

SMOKING ACCESSORIES

CIGAR

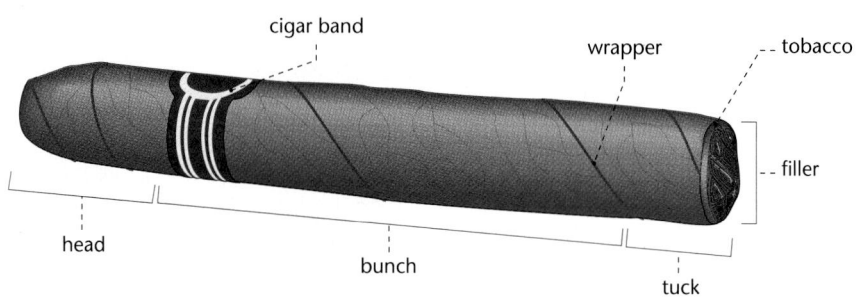

cigar band
wrapper
tobacco
filler
head
bunch
tuck

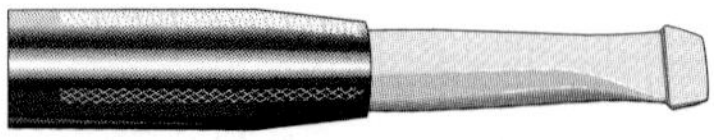

cigarette holder

CIGARETTE

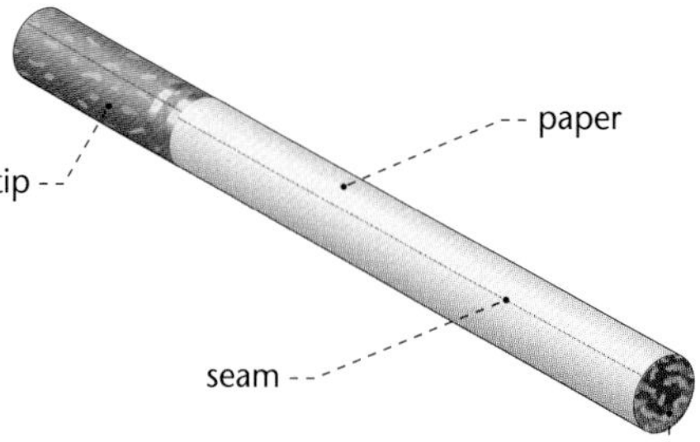

paper
filter tip
seam
tobacco

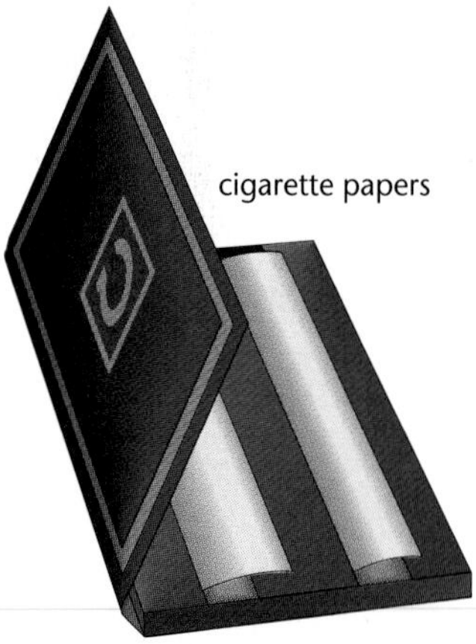

cigarette papers

CIGARETTE PACK

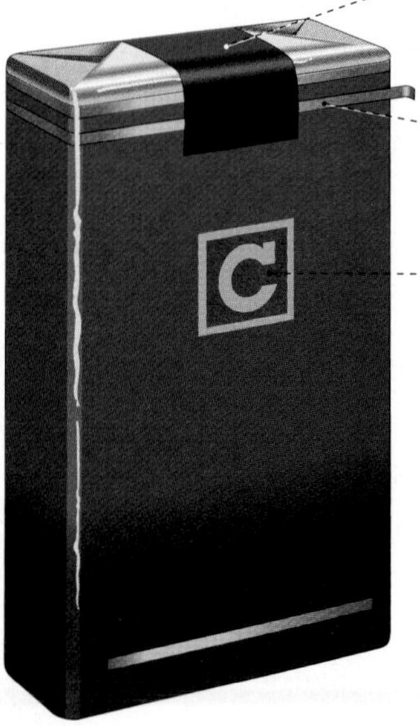

stamp
tear tape
trade name

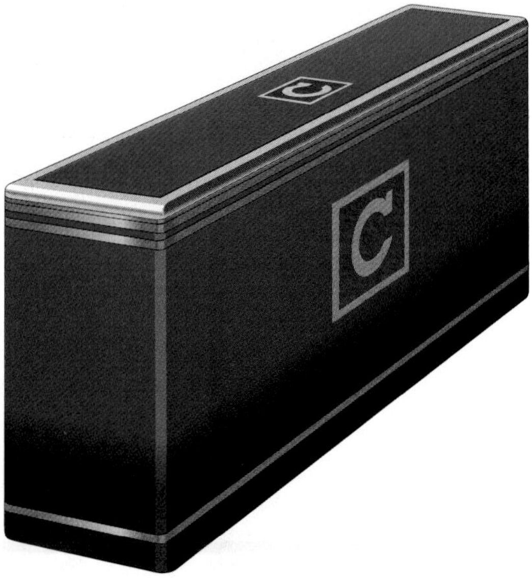

carton

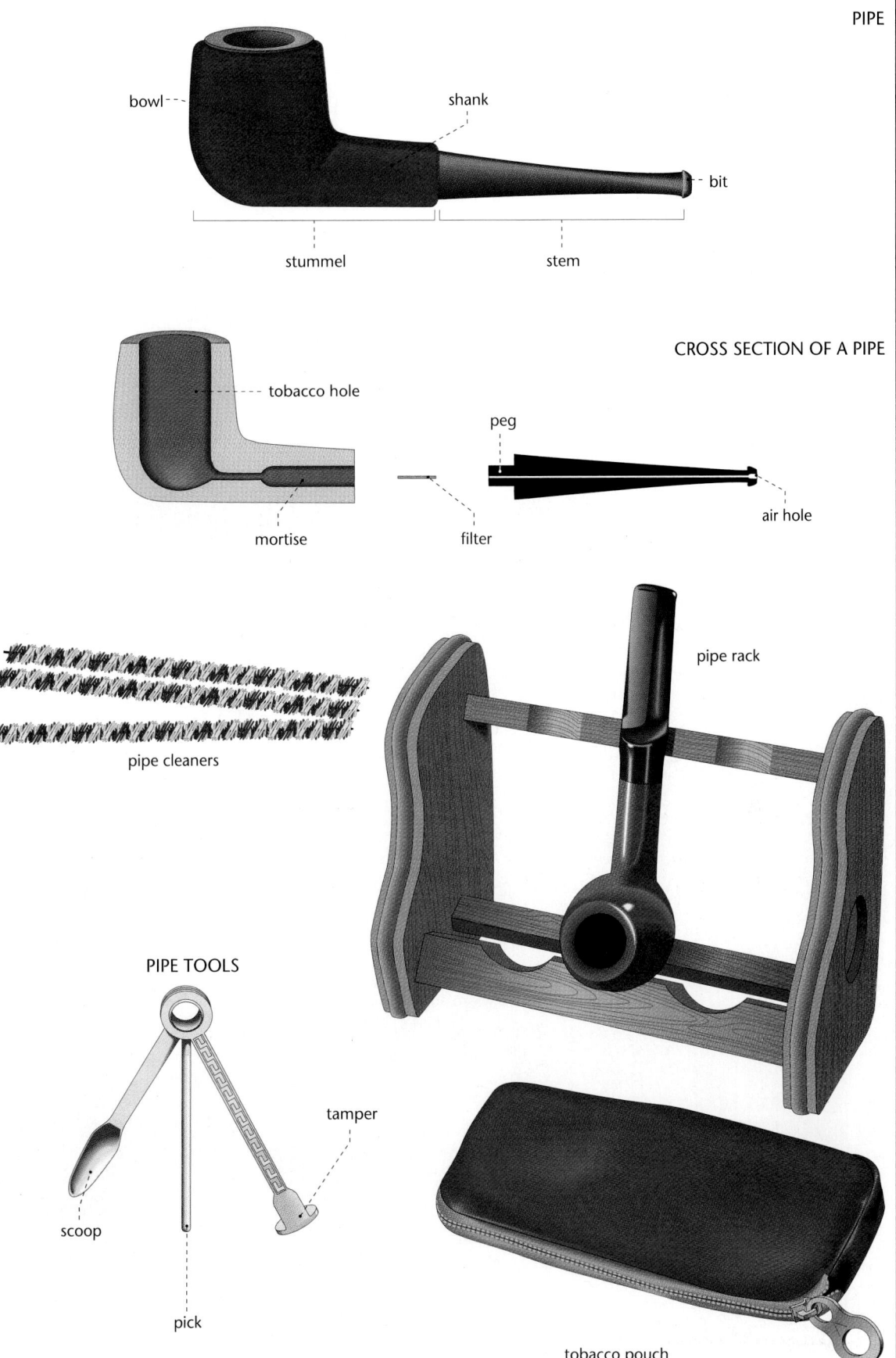

PIPE

bowl

shank

bit

stummel

stem

CROSS SECTION OF A PIPE

tobacco hole

peg

air hole

mortise

filter

pipe cleaners

pipe rack

PIPE TOOLS

tamper

scoop

pick

tobacco pouch

MATCHBOOK

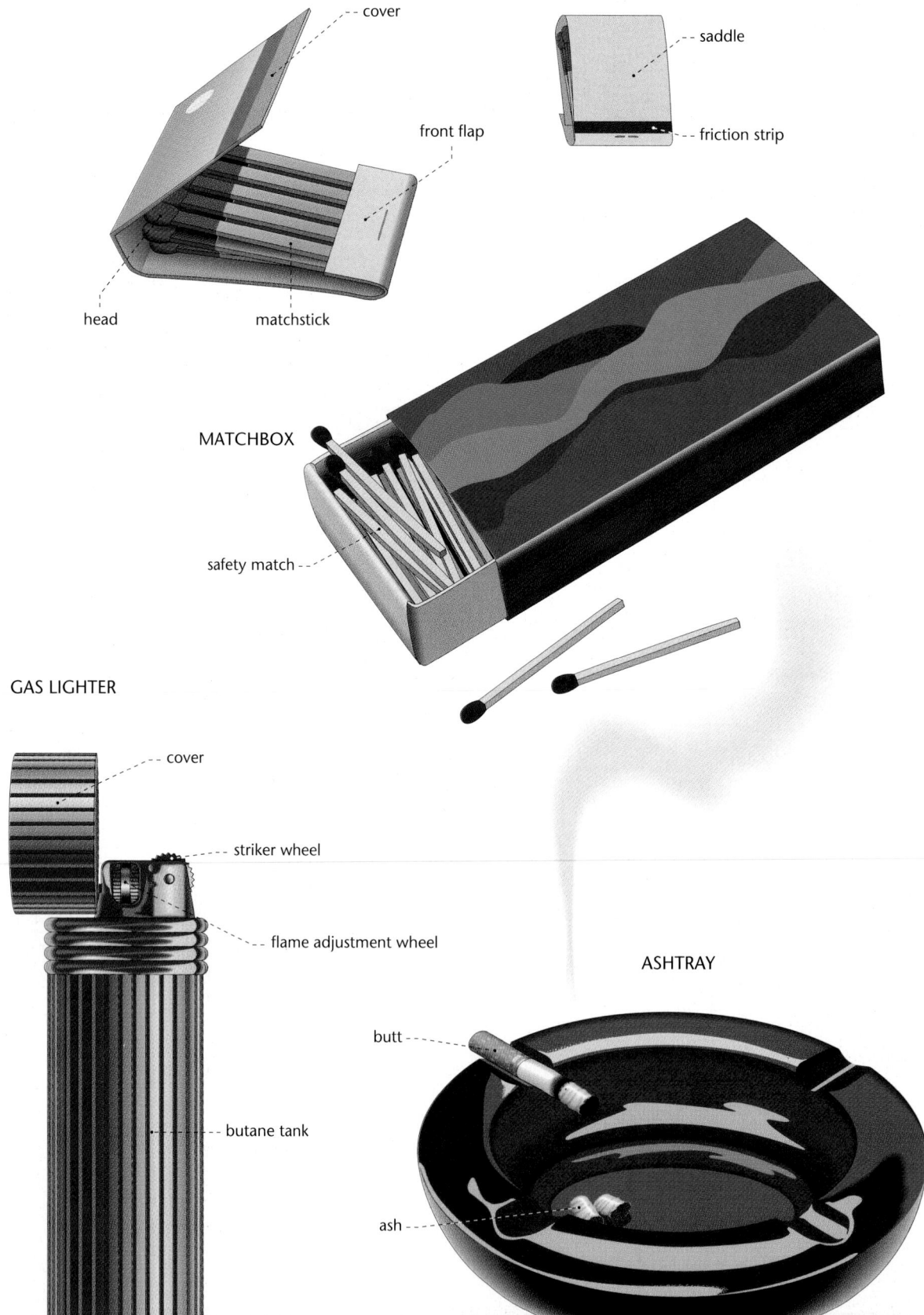

cover

saddle

front flap

friction strip

head

matchstick

MATCHBOX

safety match

GAS LIGHTER

cover

striker wheel

flame adjustment wheel

ASHTRAY

butt

butane tank

ash

CONTENTS

WRITING INSTRUMENTS..389

PHOTOGRAPHY 390

SOUND REPRODUCING SYSTEM...400

DYNAMIC MICROPHONE 406

HEADPHONE...406

RADIO: STUDIO AND CONTROL ROOM 407

PORTABLE SOUND SYSTEMS 408

VIDEO CAMERA 409

TELEVISION...410

MOBILE UNIT..415

BROADCAST SATELLITE COMMUNICATION 416

TELECOMMUNICATIONS BY SATELLITE 417

TELECOMMUNICATION SATELLITES 418

COMMUNICATION BY TELEPHONE 420

COMMUNICATIONS

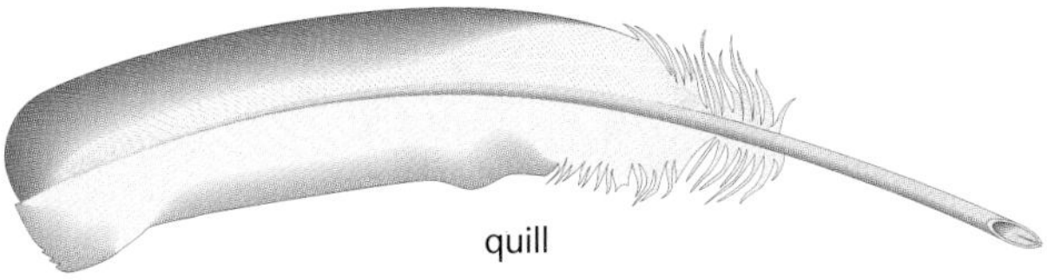

WRITING INSTRUMENTS

quill

Roman metal pen

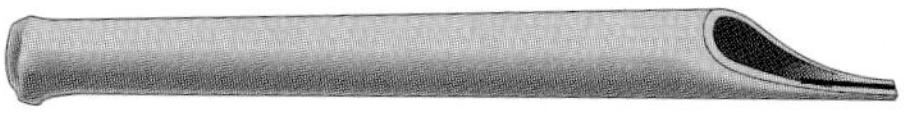

cane pen

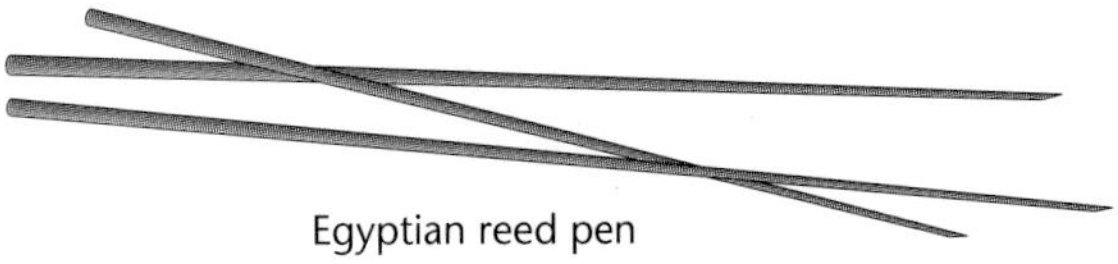

Egyptian reed pen

writing brush

stylus

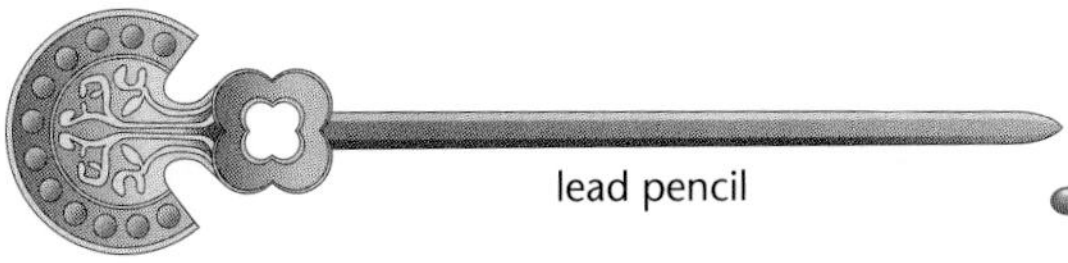

lead pencil

steel pen

pencil

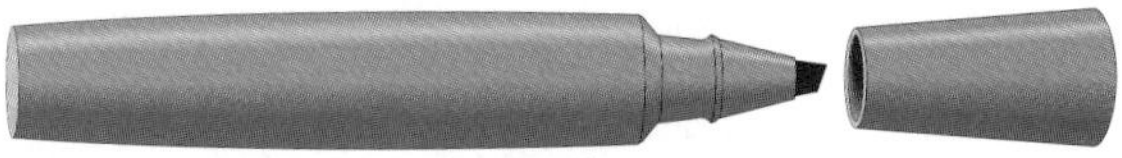

marker

FOUNTAIN PEN

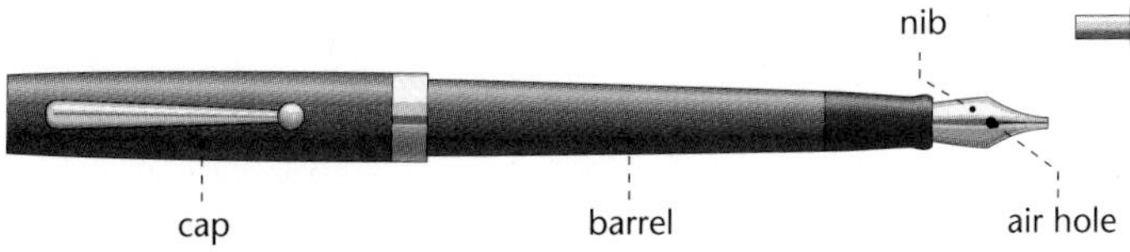

nib

mechanical pencil

cap

barrel

air hole

BALLPOINT PEN

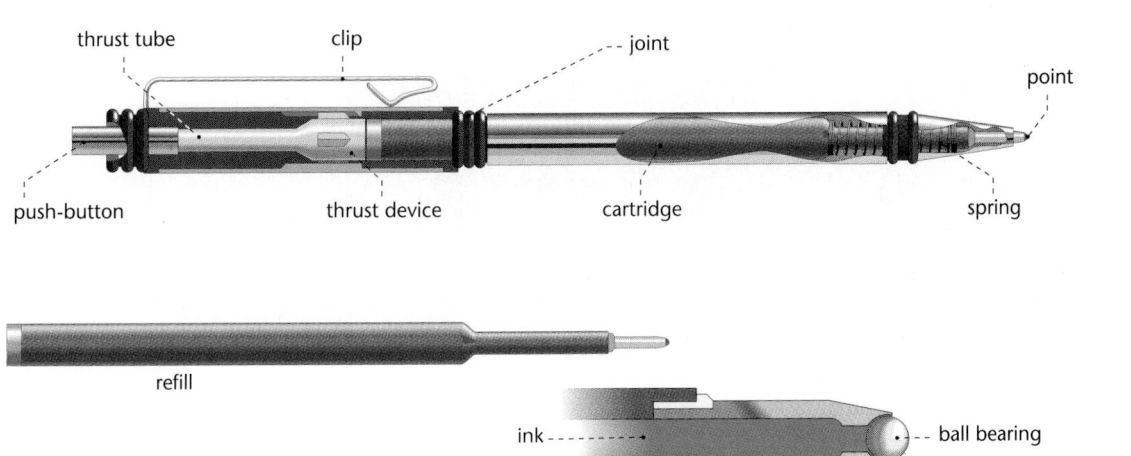

thrust tube

clip

joint

point

push-button

thrust device

cartridge

spring

refill

ink

ball bearing

CROSS SECTION OF A REFLEX CAMERA

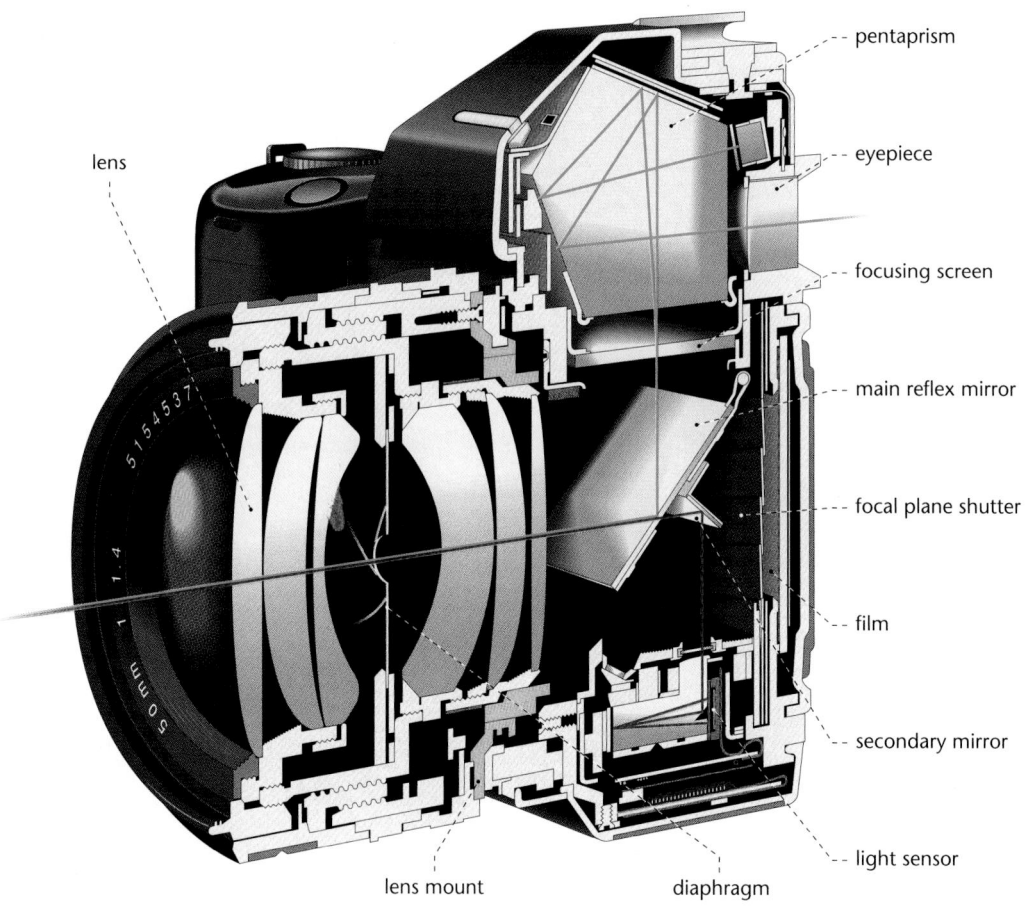

pentaprism

lens

eyepiece

focusing screen

main reflex mirror

focal plane shutter

film

secondary mirror

light sensor

lens mount

diaphragm

CAMERA BACK

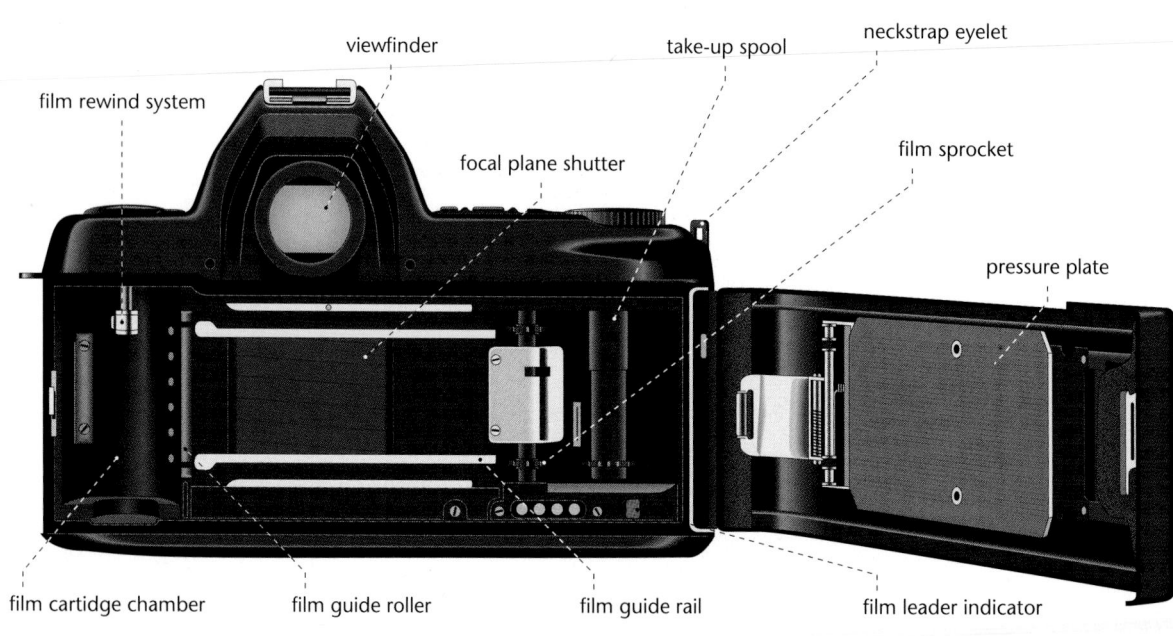

viewfinder

take-up spool

neckstrap eyelet

film rewind system

focal plane shutter

film sprocket

pressure plate

film cartridge chamber

film guide roller

film guide rail

film leader indicator

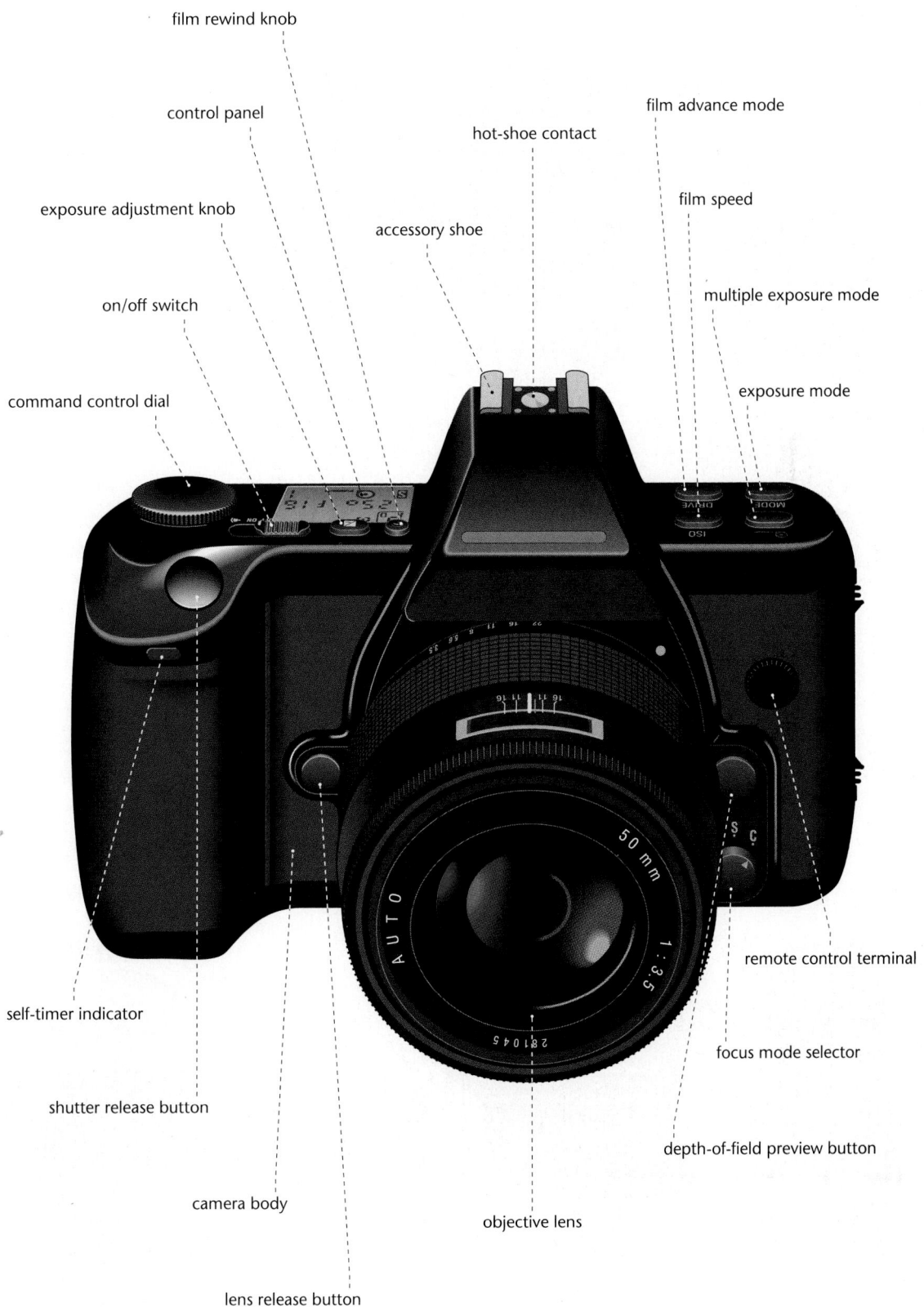

film rewind knob

control panel

exposure adjustment knob

on/off switch

command control dial

hot-shoe contact

accessory shoe

film advance mode

film speed

multiple exposure mode

exposure mode

self-timer indicator

shutter release button

camera body

lens release button

objective lens

remote control terminal

focus mode selector

depth-of-field preview button

LENSES

standard lens

lens

focus setting ring

depth-of-field scale

distance scale

lens aperture scale

wide-angle lens

bayonet mount

LENS ACCESSORIES

lens cap

lens hood

zoom lens

semi-fisheye lens

color filter

close-up lens

polarizing filter

objective lens

telephoto lens

fisheye lens

tele-converter

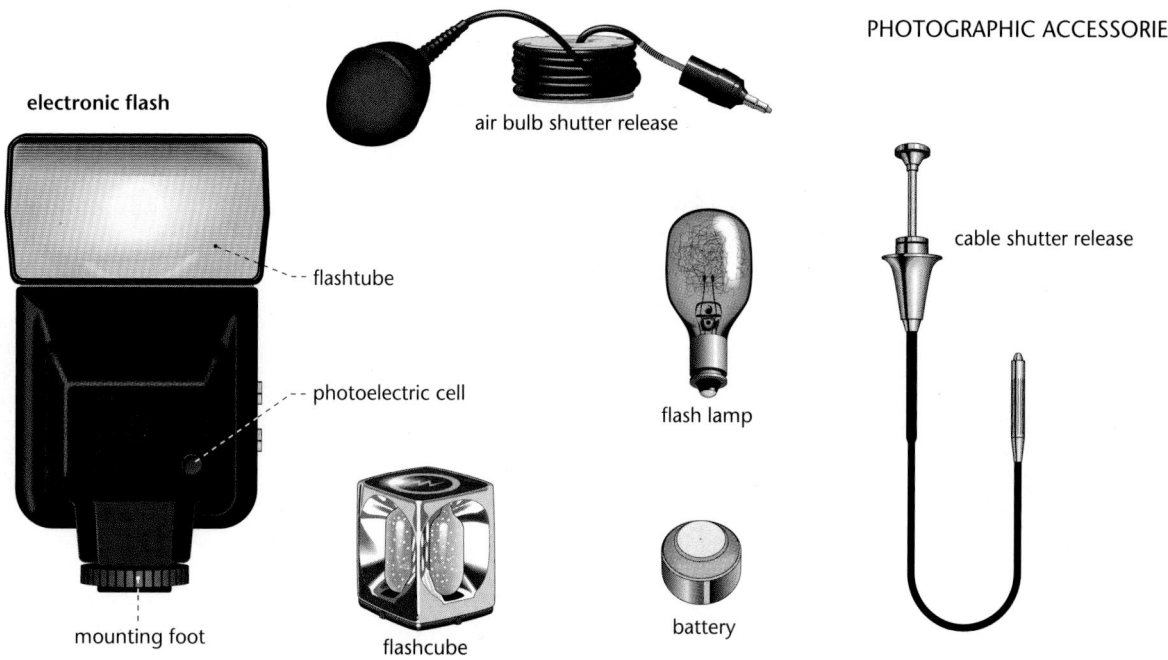

PHOTOGRAPHIC ACCESSORIES

electronic flash
flashtube
photoelectric cell
mounting foot
air bulb shutter release
flash lamp
flashcube
battery

cable shutter release

TRIPOD

camera screw
plate
quick release system
side-tilt lock
horizontal motion lock
column
camera platform
panoramic head
camera platform lock
column lock
column crank
collet
telescoping leg

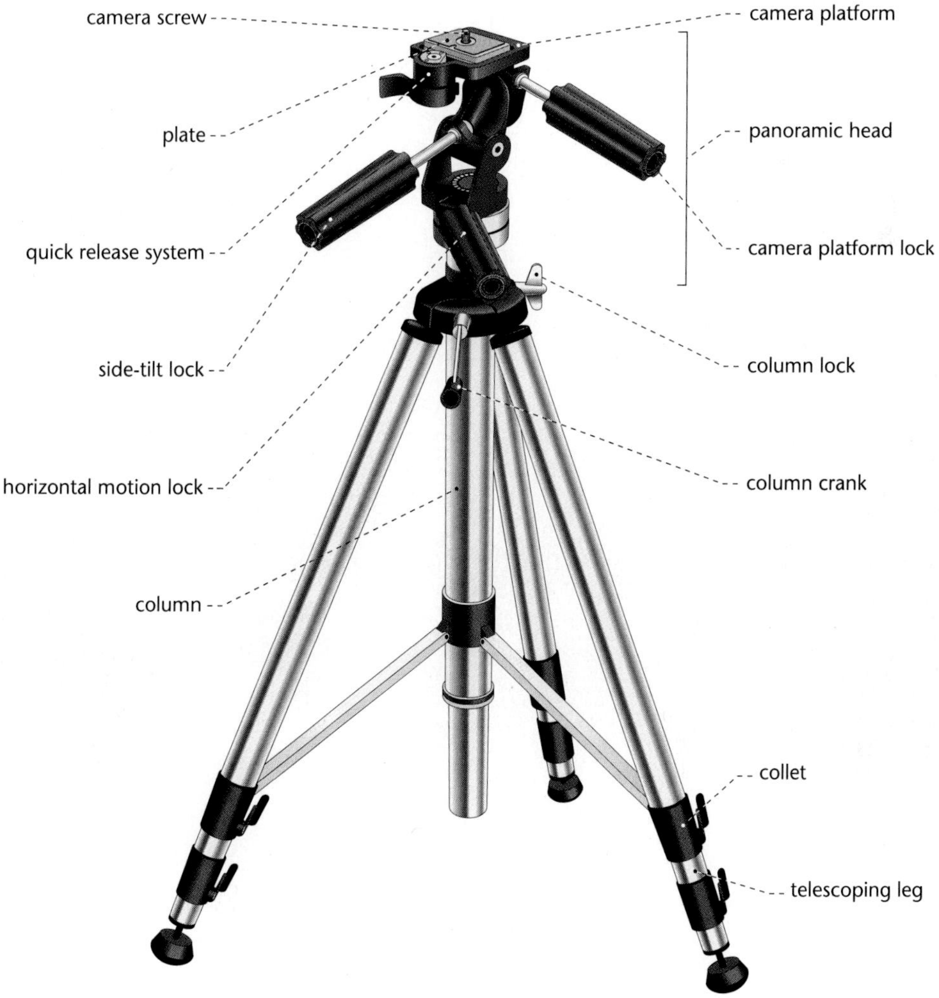

STILL CAMERAS

rangefinder

Polaroid® Land camera

underwater camera

single-lens reflex camera

disposable camera

twin-lens reflex camera

view camera

medium format SLR (6 x 6)

pocket camera

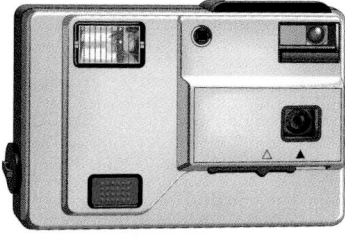

disk camera

stereo camera

still video camera

film leader   perforation

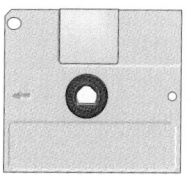

still video film disk

cassette film

film disk

cartridge film

sheet film

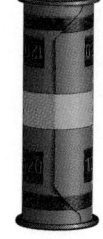

roll film

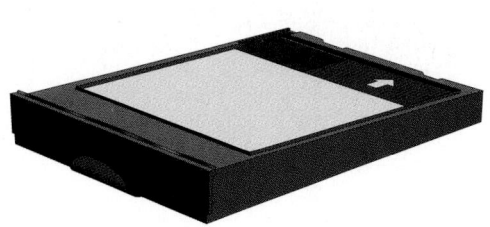

film pack

EXPOSURE METER

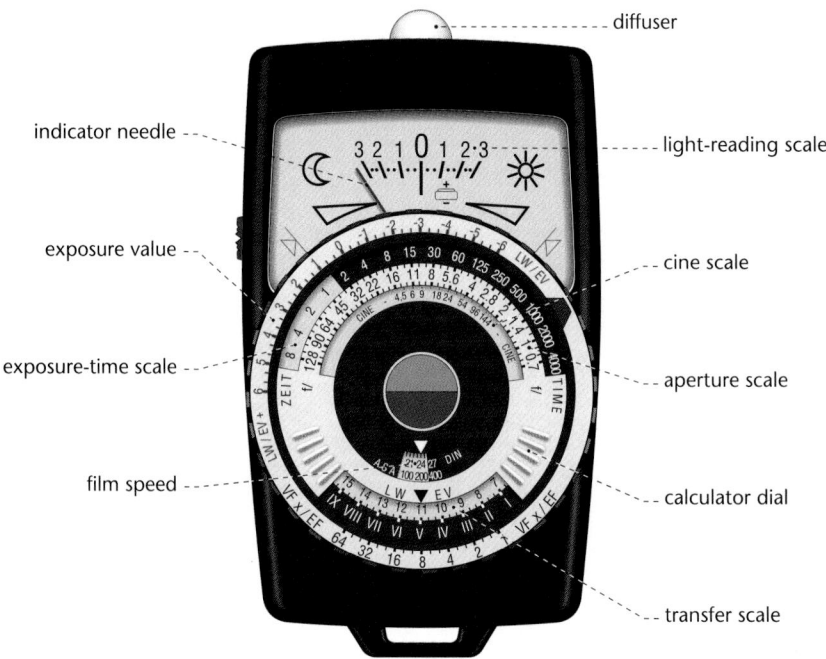

diffuser

indicator needle

light-reading scale

exposure value

cine scale

exposure-time scale

aperture scale

film speed

calculator dial

transfer scale

SPOTMETER

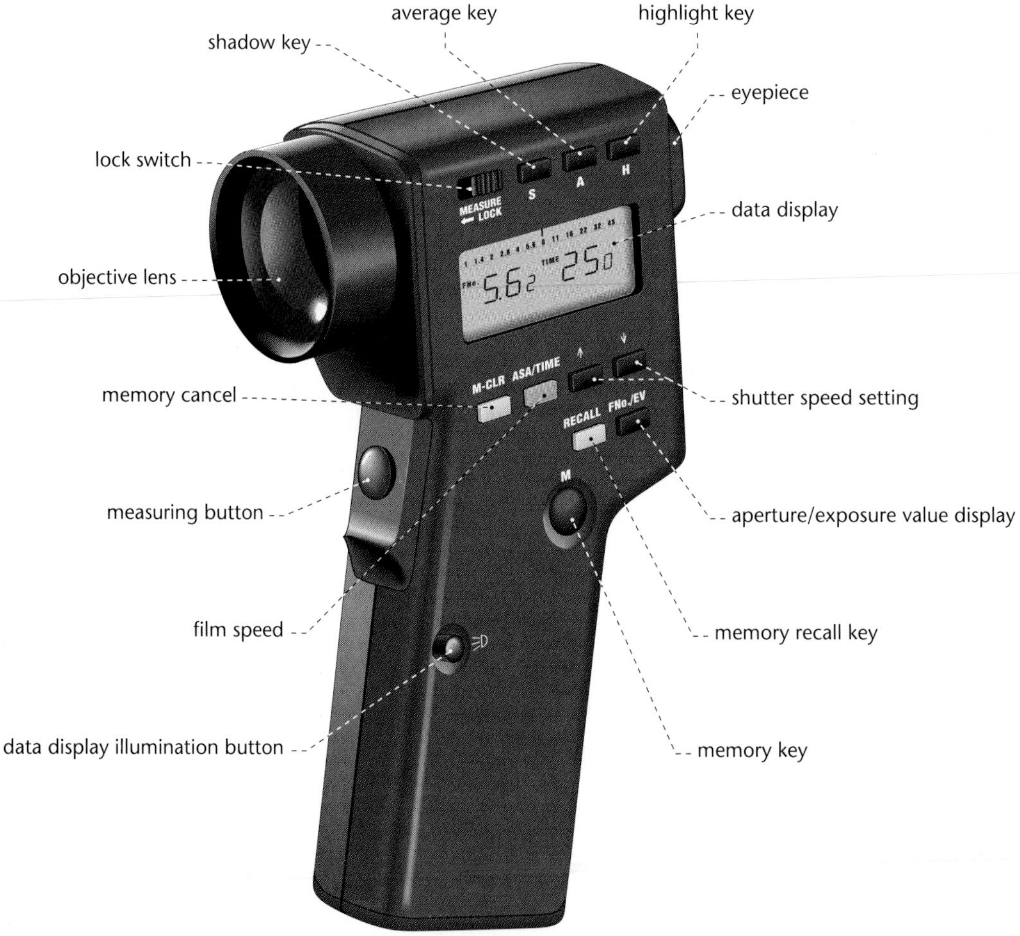

average key

highlight key

shadow key

eyepiece

lock switch

data display

objective lens

memory cancel

shutter speed setting

measuring button

aperture/exposure value display

film speed

memory recall key

data display illumination button

memory key

SLIDE PROJECTOR

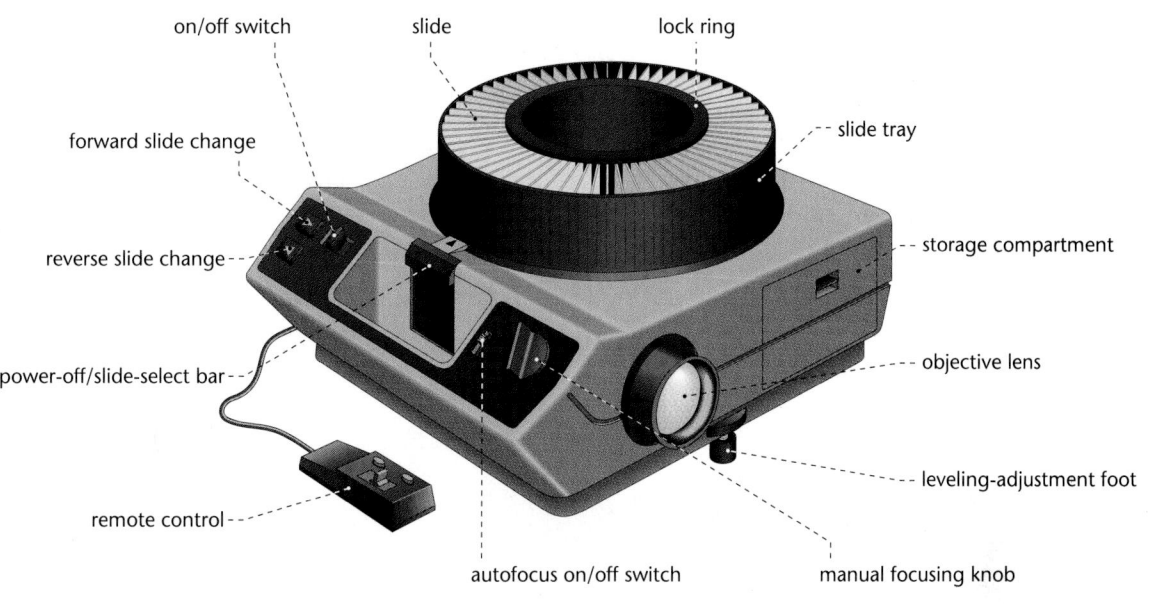

on/off switch
slide
lock ring
forward slide change
slide tray
reverse slide change
storage compartment
objective lens
power-off/slide-select bar
leveling-adjustment foot
remote control
autofocus on/off switch
manual focusing knob

PROJECTION SCREEN

hanger
saddle
push-button
pull bail
tube
screen
screen case
tripod
shoe

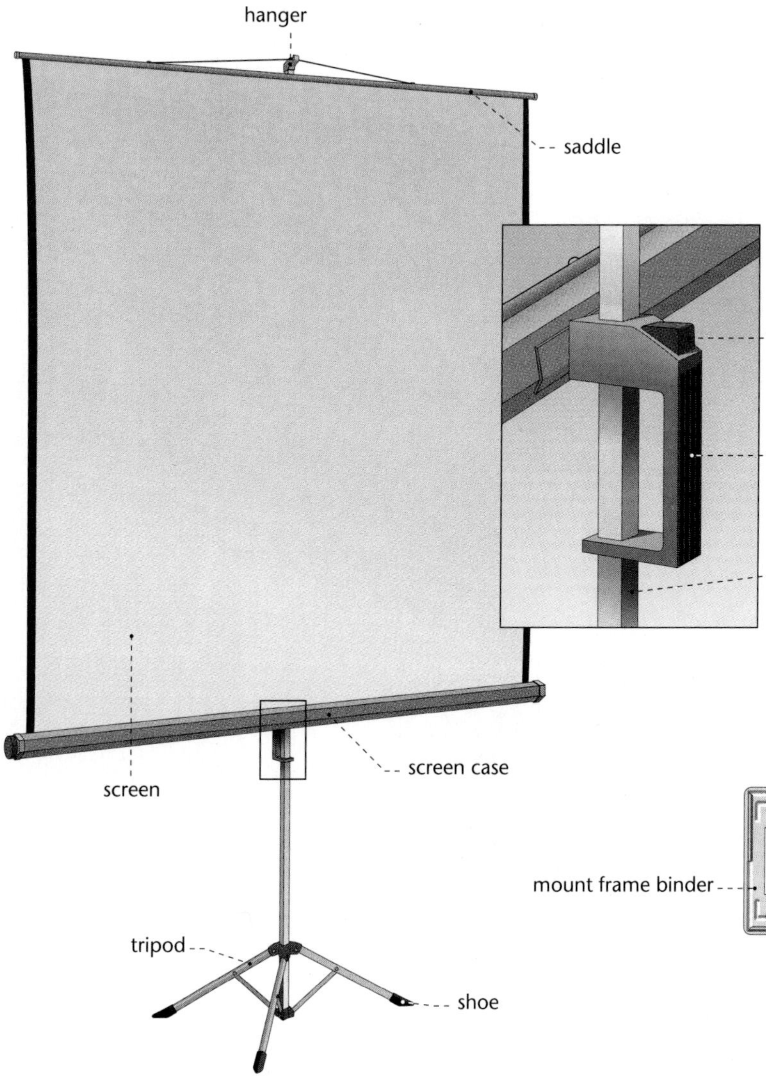

TRANSPARENCY SLIDE

mount frame binder
photographic picture

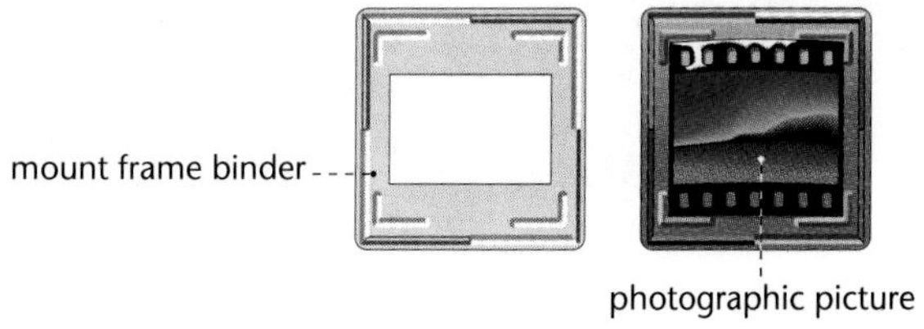

DEVELOPING TANK

cap

lid

reel

tank

lightbox

timer

guillotine trimmer

safelight

film drying cabinet

easel

contact printer

COMMUNICATIONS

NEGATIVE CARRIER

window
negative

ENLARGER

column
lamphouse head
lamphouse elevation control
negative carrier
height control
bellows
red safelight filter
enlarging lens
height scale
baseboard

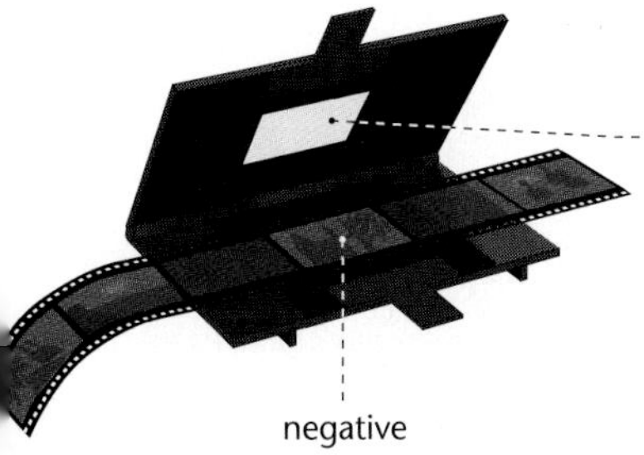

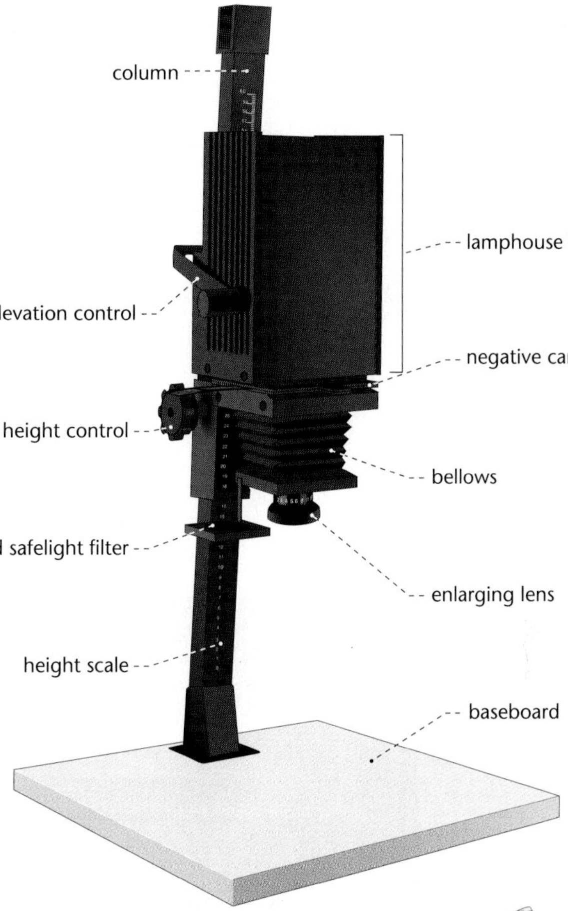

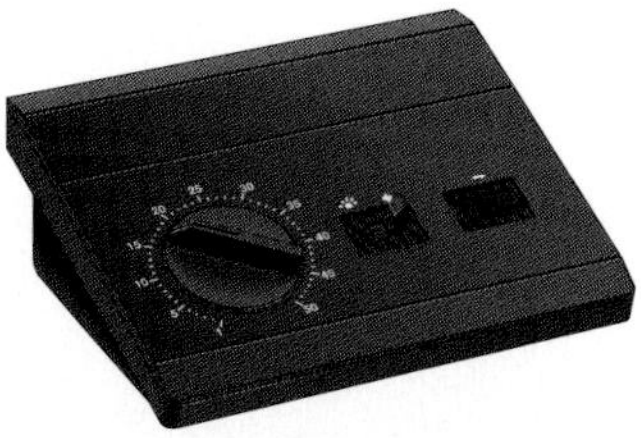

enlarger timer

DEVELOPING BATHS

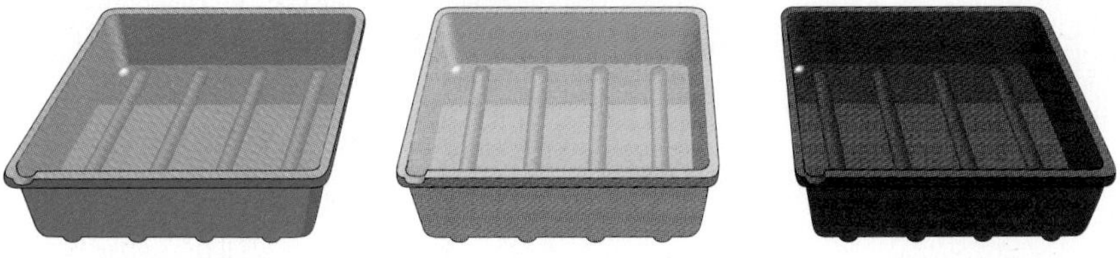

developer bath
stop bath
fixing bath

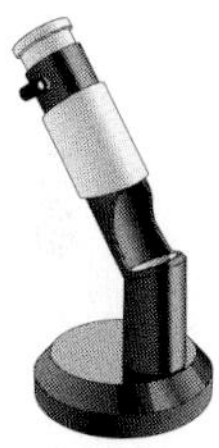

focusing magnifier

PRINT WASHER

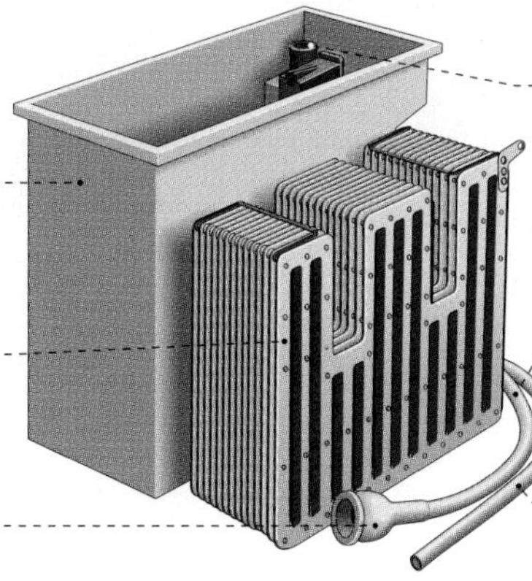

overflow tube
tank
cradle
inlet hose
adaptor
outlet hose

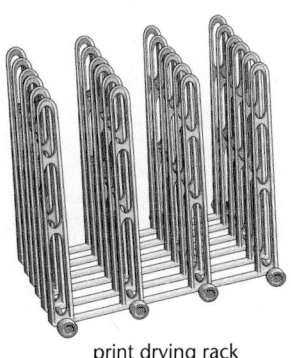

print drying rack

SYSTEM COMPONENTS

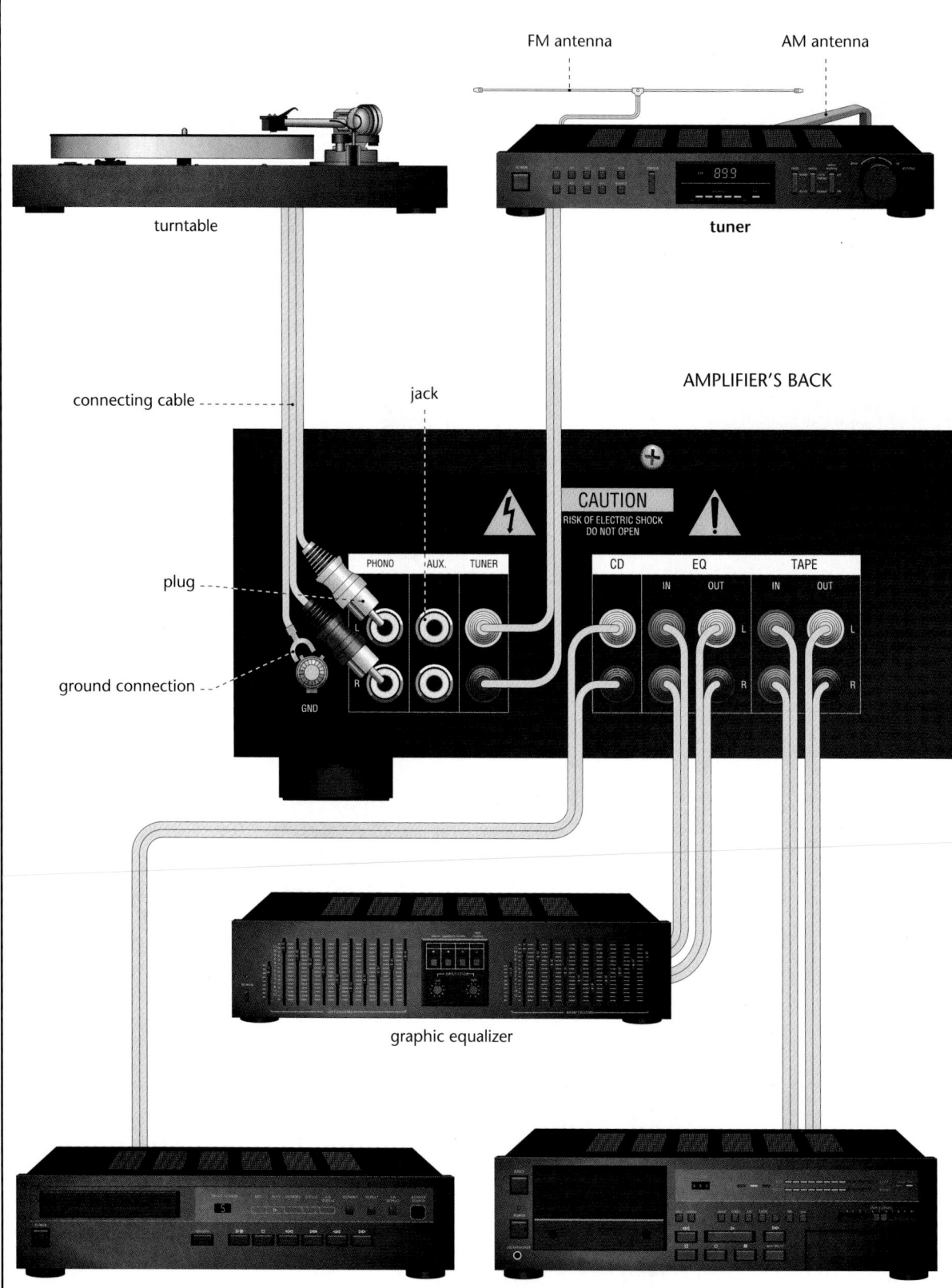

FM antenna   AM antenna

turntable   **tuner**

connecting cable   jack   AMPLIFIER'S BACK

CAUTION
RISK OF ELECTRIC SHOCK
DO NOT OPEN

PHONO   AUX.   TUNER   CD   EQ   TAPE

IN   OUT   IN   OUT

plug   L   L

R   R

ground connection

GND

graphic equalizer

compact disk player   cassette tape deck

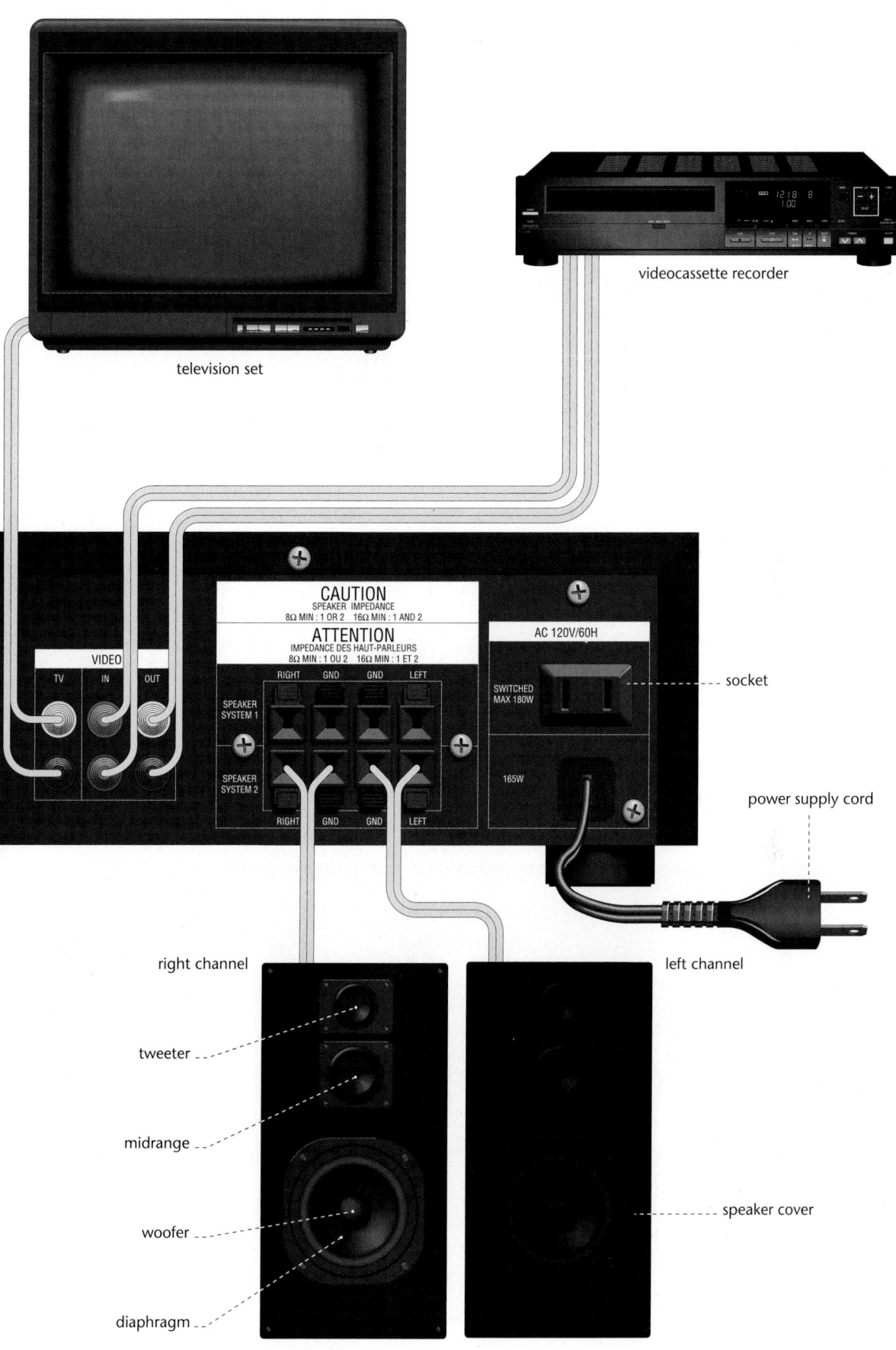

videocassette recorder

television set

CAUTION
SPEAKER IMPEDANCE
8Ω MIN : 1 OR 2   16Ω MIN : 1 AND 2
ATTENTION
IMPEDANCE DES HAUT-PARLEURS
8Ω MIN : 1 OU 2   16Ω MIN : 1 ET 2

AC 120V/60H

VIDEO

TV   IN   OUT

RIGHT   GND   GND   LEFT

SPEAKER
SYSTEM 1

SPEAKER
SYSTEM 2

RIGHT   GND   GND   LEFT

SWITCHED
MAX 180W

165W

socket

power supply cord

right channel

left channel

tweeter

midrange

woofer

diaphragm

speaker cover

loudspeakers

SOUND REPRODUCING SYSTEM

TUNER

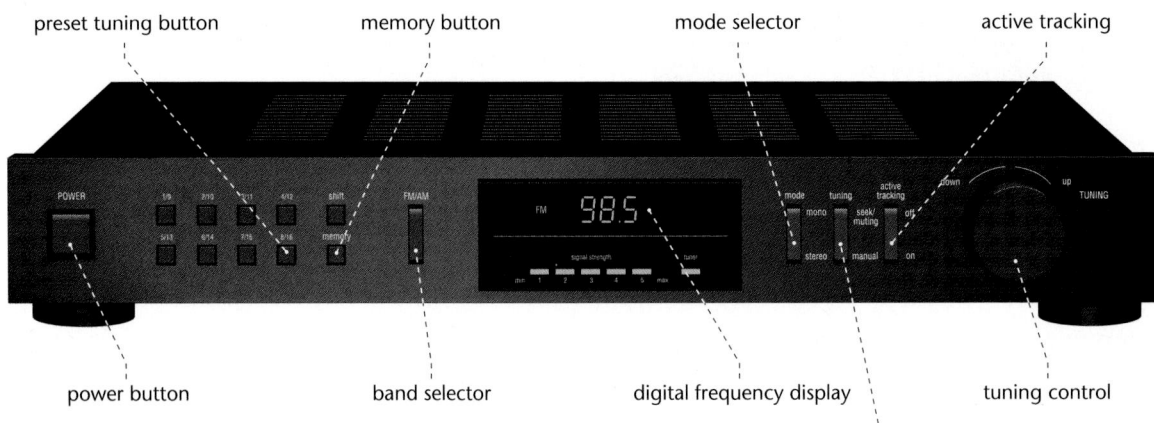

preset tuning button   memory button   mode selector   active tracking

FM   98.5

power button   band selector   digital frequency display   tuning control

tuning mode

AMPLIFIER

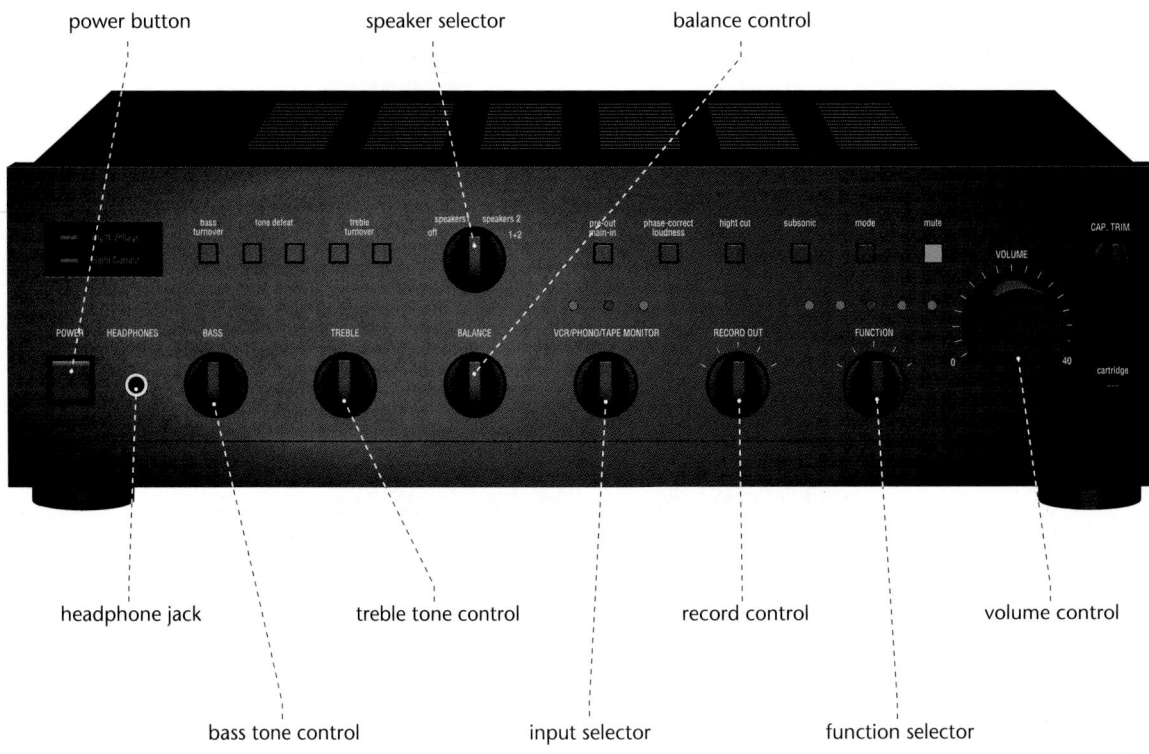

power button   speaker selector   balance control

headphone jack   treble tone control   record control   volume control

bass tone control   input selector   function selector

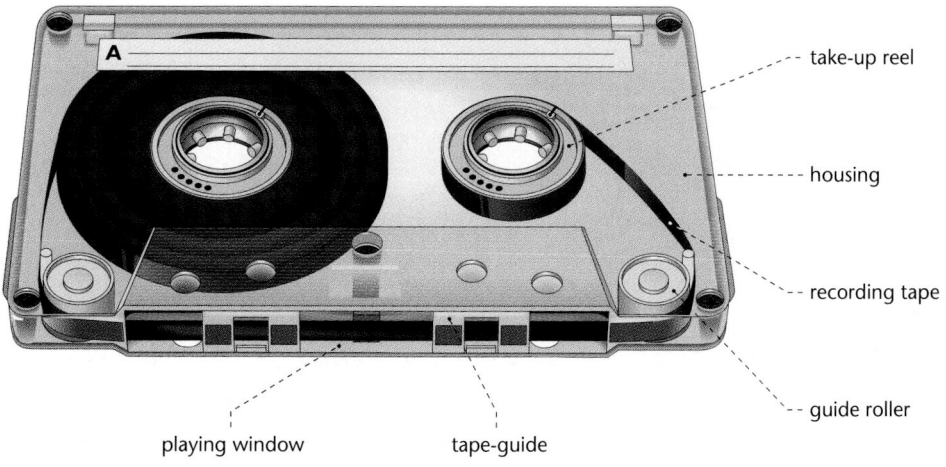

CASSETTE

A
take-up reel
housing
recording tape
guide roller
playing window
tape-guide

CASSETTE TAPE DECK

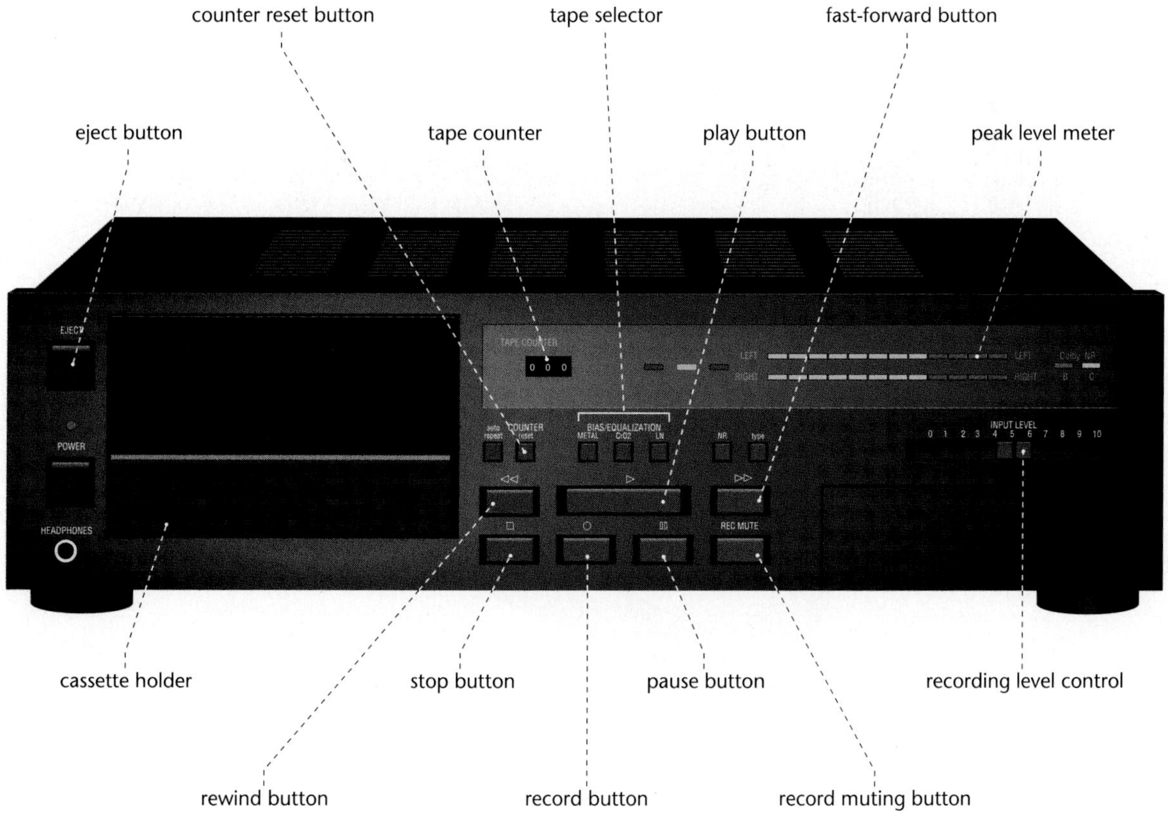

counter reset button
tape selector
fast-forward button
eject button
tape counter
play button
peak level meter
EJECT
POWER
HEADPHONES
TAPE COUNTER
0 0 0
COUNTER
reset
BIAS/EQUALIZATION
METAL
CrO2
LN
NR
type
INPUT LEVEL
0 1 2 3 4 5 6 7 8 9 10
REC MUTE
cassette holder
stop button
pause button
recording level control
rewind button
record button
record muting button

RECORD

TURNTABLE

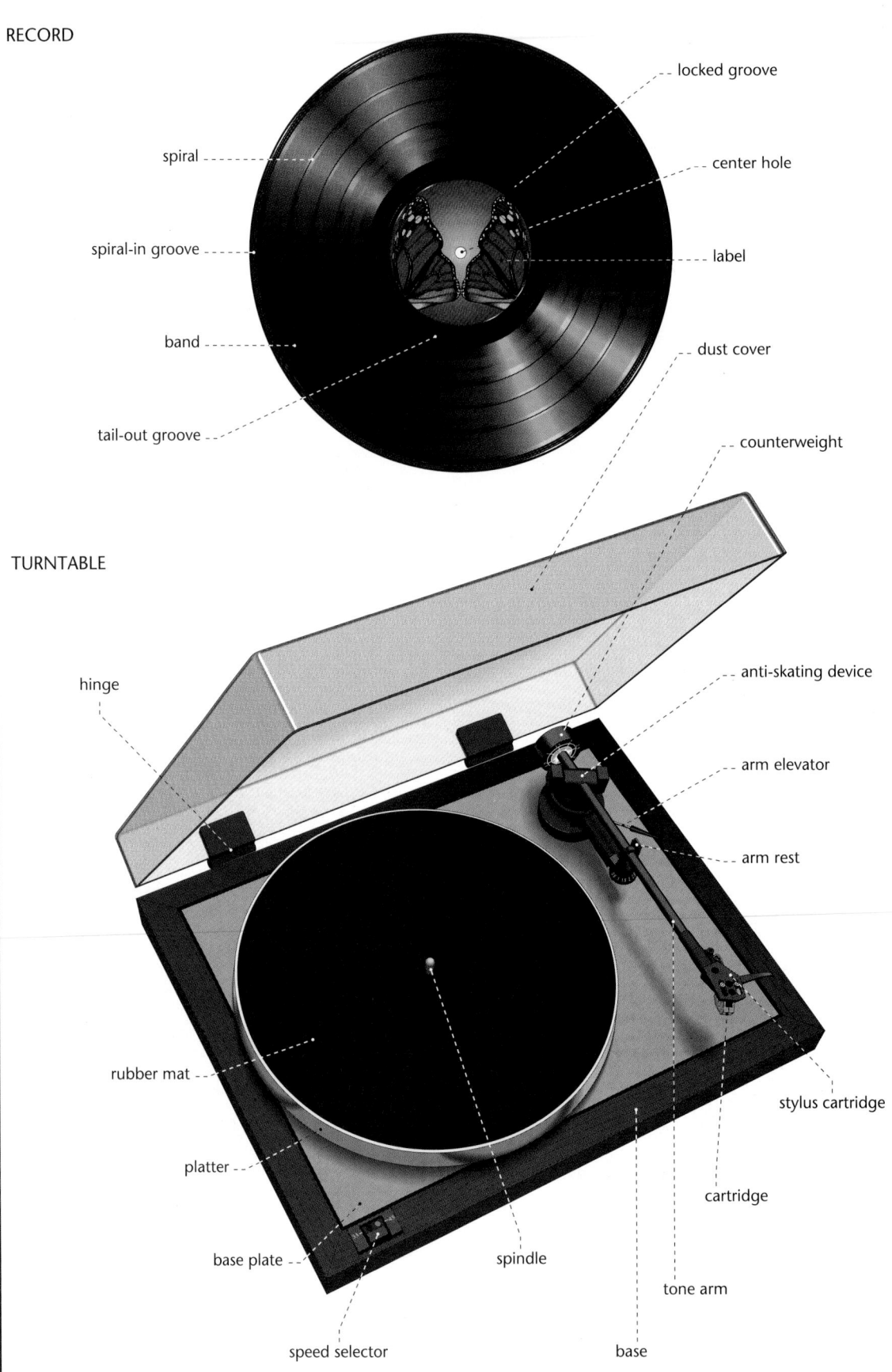

locked groove

center hole

spiral

label

spiral-in groove

band

dust cover

tail-out groove

counterweight

hinge

anti-skating device

arm elevator

arm rest

rubber mat

stylus cartridge

platter

cartridge

base plate

spindle

tone arm

speed selector

base

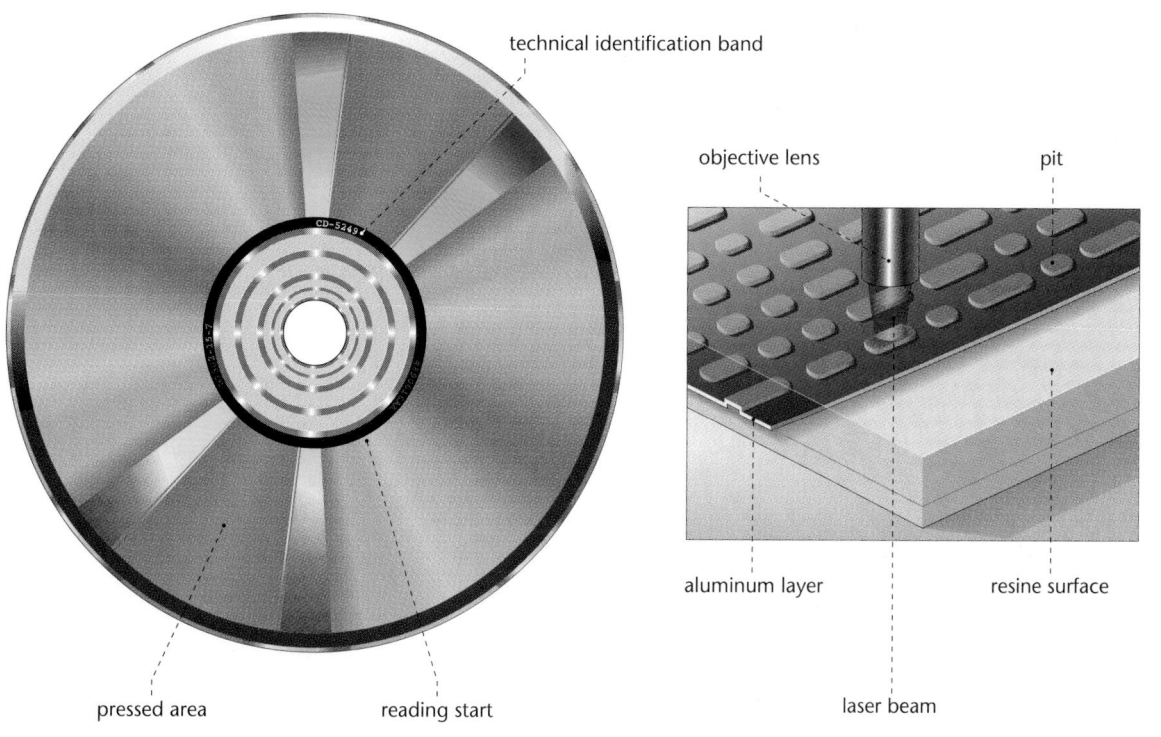

technical identification band

objective lens

pit

aluminum layer

resine surface

pressed area

reading start

laser beam

COMMUNICATIONS

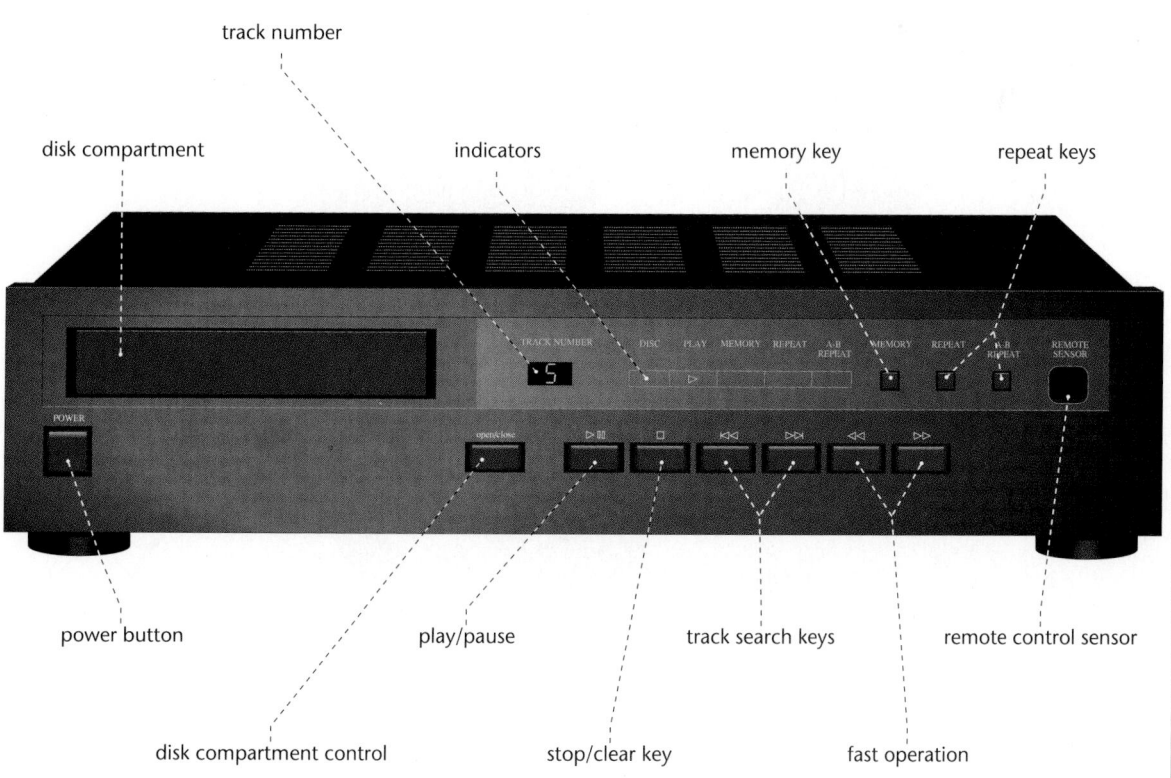

track number

disk compartment

indicators

memory key

repeat keys

TRACK NUMBER   DISC   PLAY MEMORY REPEAT A-B REPEAT   MEMORY   REPEAT   A-B REPEAT   REMOTE SENSOR

POWER

open/close

power button

play/pause

track search keys

remote control sensor

disk compartment control

stop/clear key

fast operation

DYNAMIC MICROPHONE

windscreen

diaphragm

moving coil

magnet

on/off switch

housing

connector

plug

cable

HEADPHONE

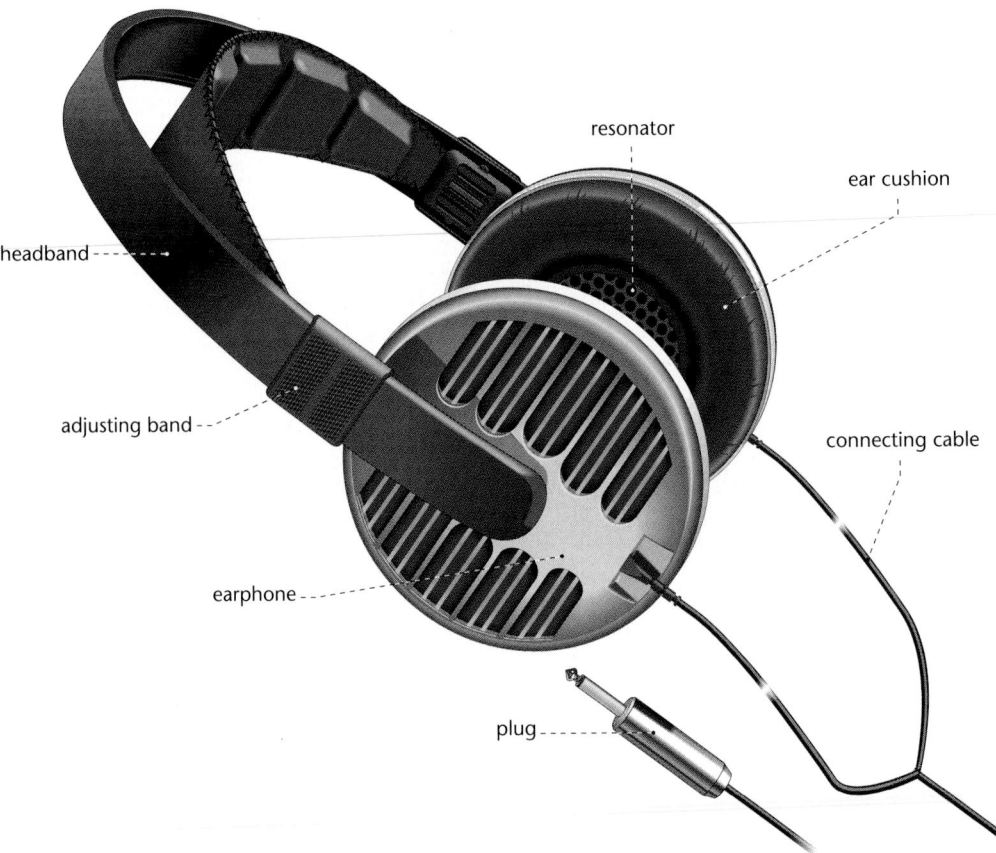

resonator

ear cushion

headband

adjusting band

connecting cable

earphone

plug

studio

microphone

announcer turret

on-air warning light

tone leader generator

clock

volume unit meters

audio monitor

cartridge tape recorder

digital audio tape recorder

compact disk player

cassette deck

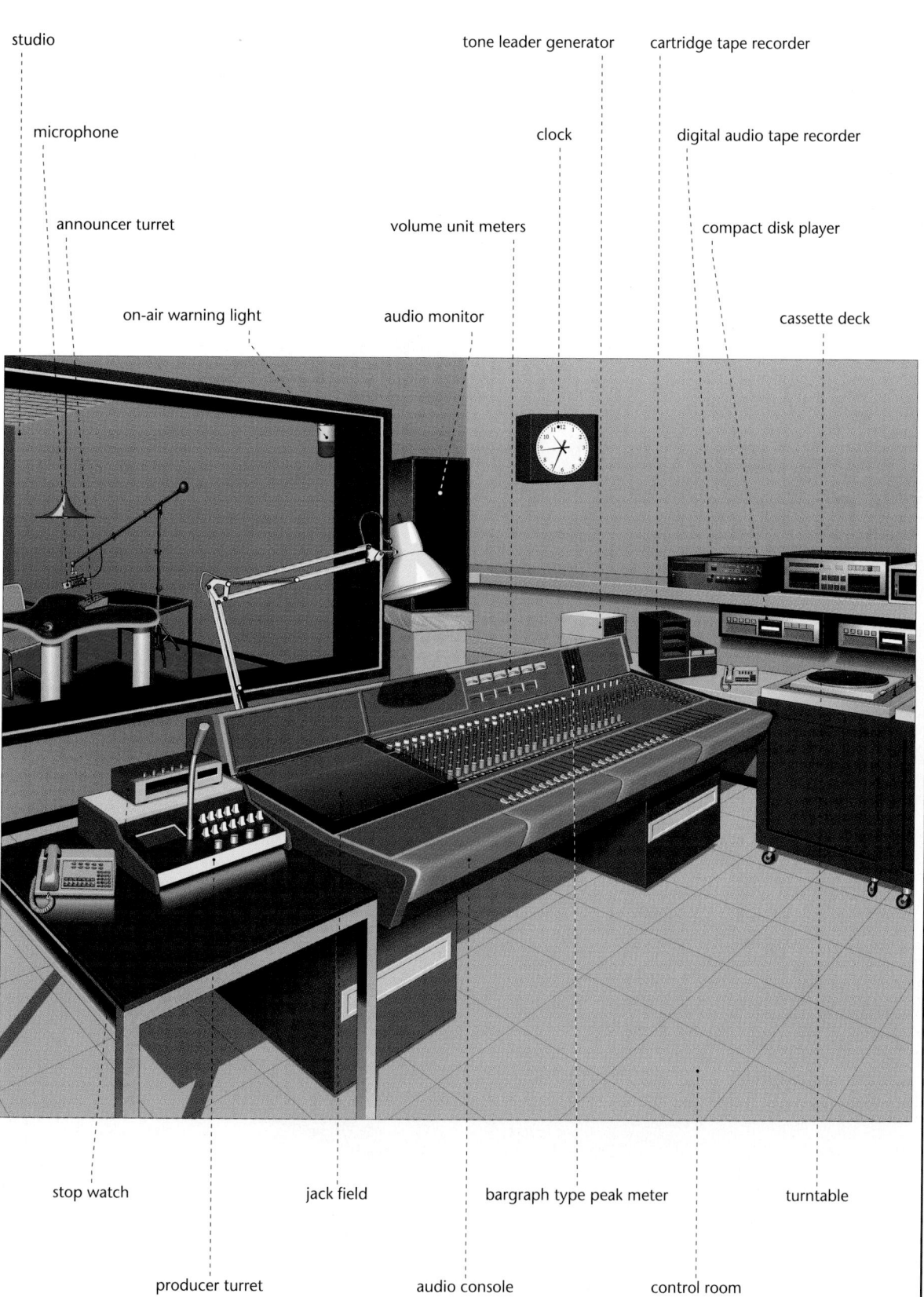

stop watch

jack field

bargraph type peak meter

turntable

producer turret

audio console

control room

COMMUNICATIONS

PERSONAL AM-FM CASSETTE
PLAYER

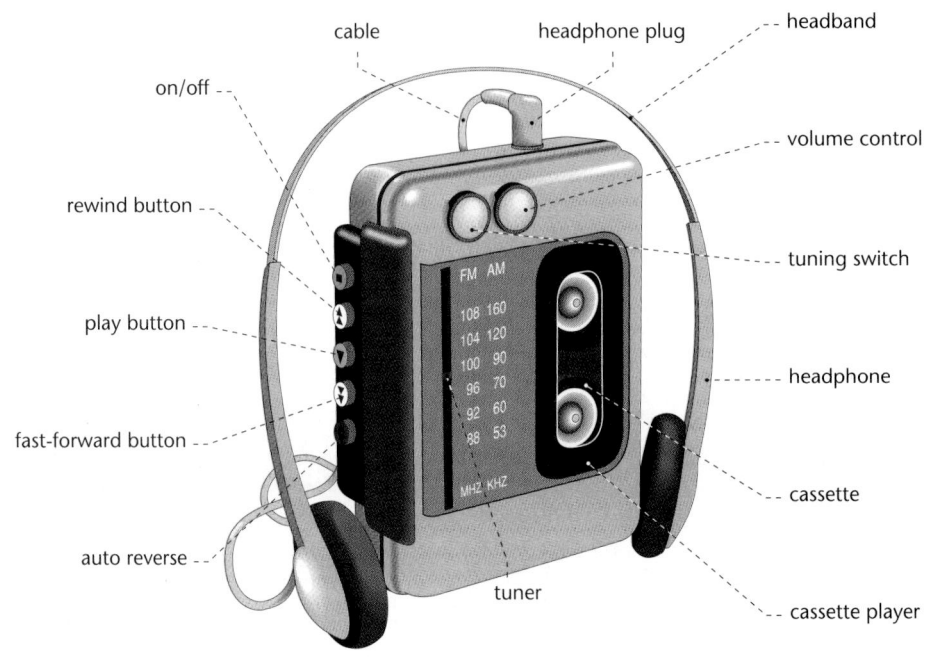

cable

headphone plug

headband

on/off

volume control

rewind button

tuning switch

play button

FM AM
108 160
104 120
100 90
96 70
92 60
88 53

MHZ KHZ

headphone

fast-forward button

auto reverse

cassette

tuner

cassette player

PORTABLE AM-FM CASSETTE
RECORDER

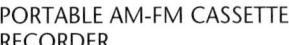

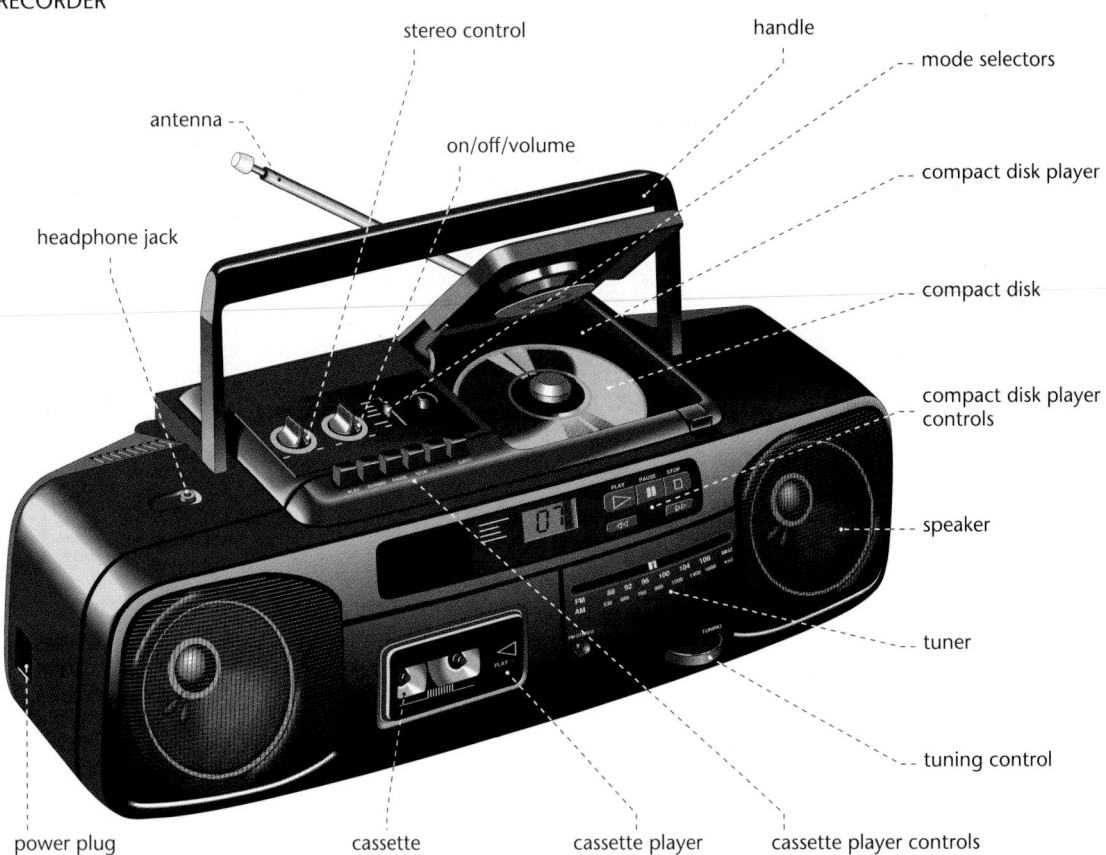

stereo control

handle

mode selectors

antenna

compact disk player

on/off/volume

headphone jack

compact disk

compact disk player
controls

PLAY   PAUSE   STOP

speaker

tuner

tuning control

power plug

cassette

cassette player

cassette player controls

eyepiece

power zoom button

electronic viewfinder

white balance sensor

accessory shoe

cassette eject switch

videotape operation controls

viewfinder adjustment keys

built-in microphone

DATA SET

ZERO MEM.

ADJUST

RESET

SELECT

SPEED

EXPOSURE

EDIT SEARCH

AUTO LOCK

FOCUS

WHITE BAL.

FADER

BATT

macro set button

cassette compartment

zoom lens

data display

battery eject switch

lens hood

shooting adjustment keys

battery

edit/search buttons

TELEVISION SET

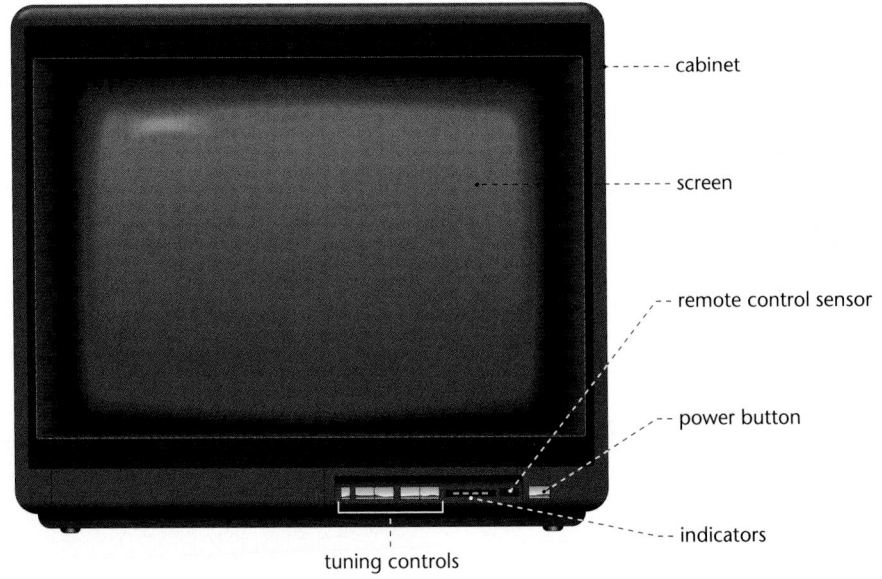

cabinet

screen

remote control sensor

power button

indicators

tuning controls

PICTURE TUBE

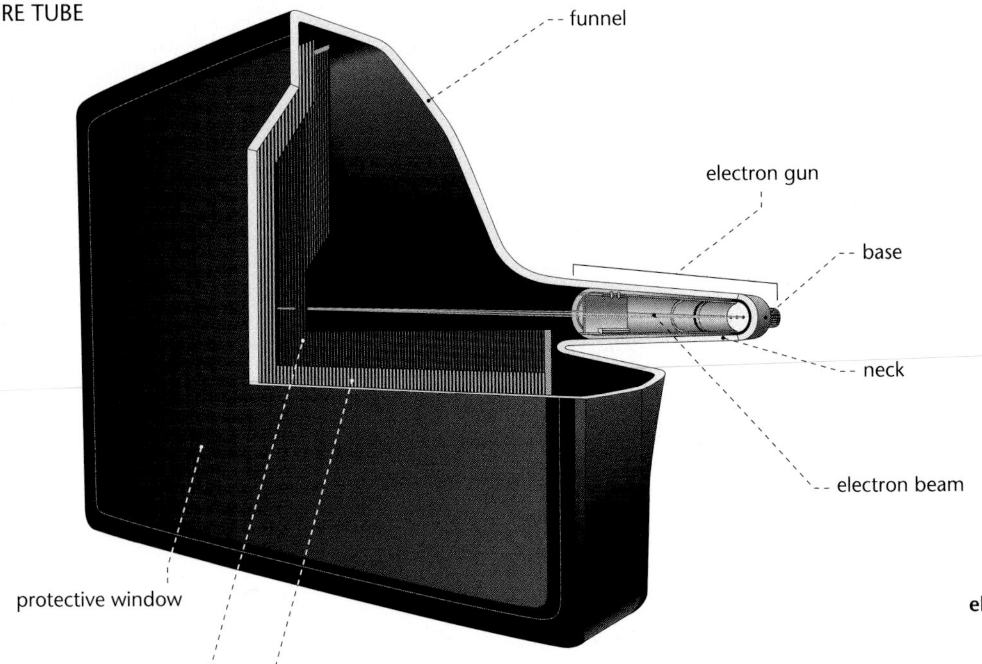

funnel

electron gun

base

neck

electron beam

protective window

color selection filter

screen

electron gun

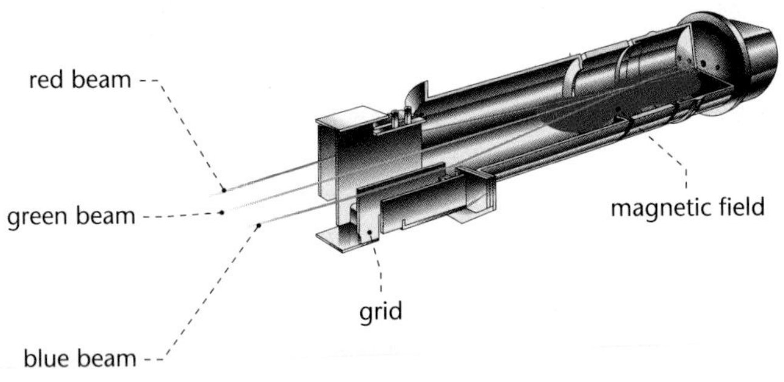

red beam

green beam

magnetic field

grid

blue beam

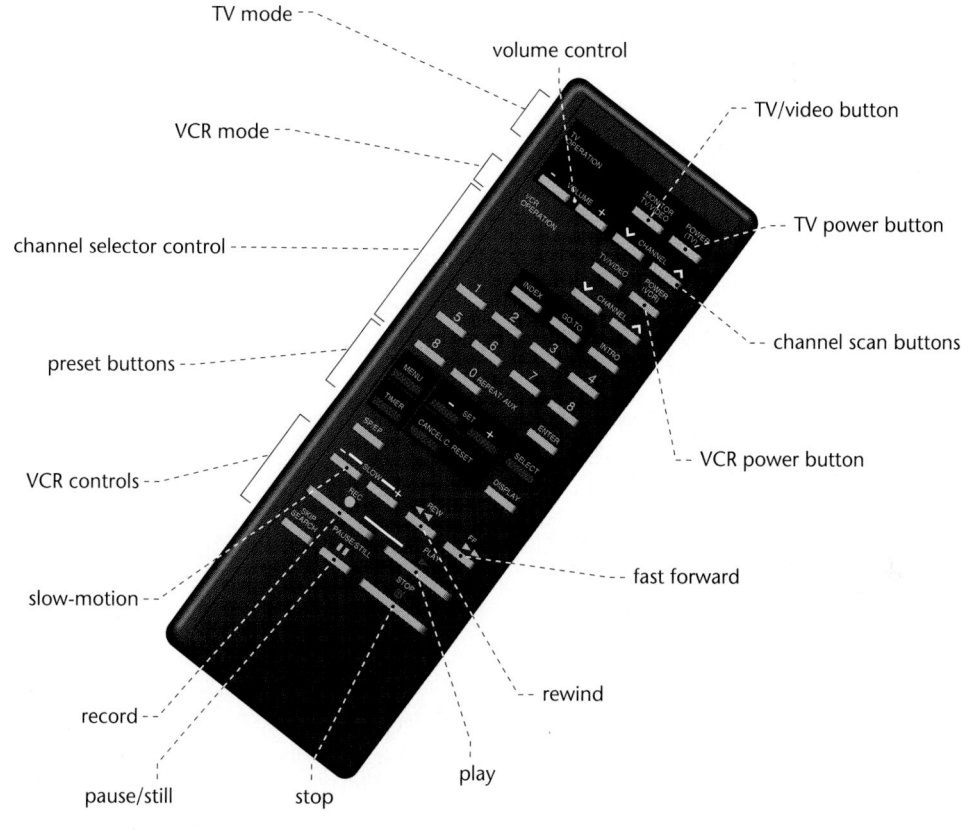

TV mode

volume control

VCR mode

TV/video button

channel selector control

TV power button

preset buttons

channel scan buttons

VCR controls

VCR power button

slow-motion

fast forward

record

rewind

pause/still

play

stop

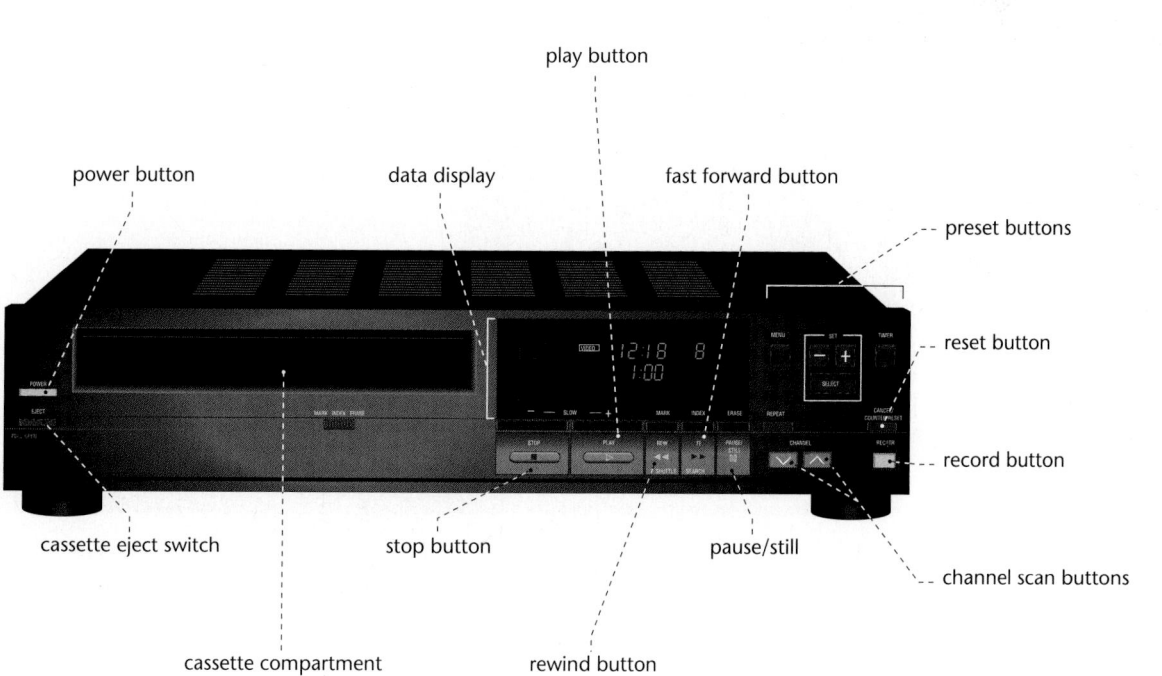

play button

power button

data display

fast forward button

preset buttons

reset button

record button

cassette eject switch

stop button

pause/still

channel scan buttons

cassette compartment

rewind button

COMMUNICATIONS

STUDIO AND CONTROL ROOMS

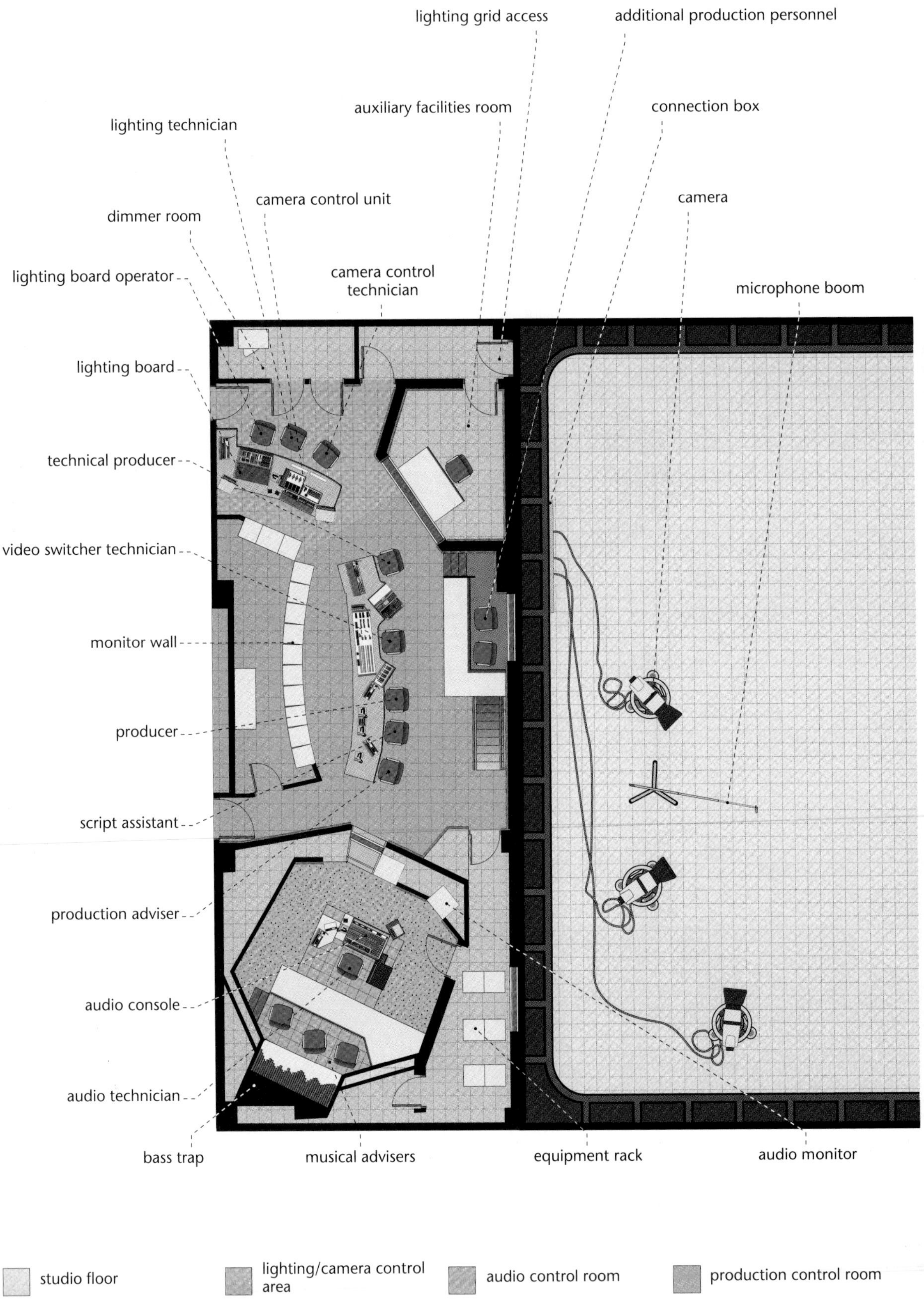

lighting grid access

additional production personnel

auxiliary facilities room

connection box

lighting technician

camera control unit

camera

dimmer room

camera control technician

microphone boom

lighting board operator

lighting board

technical producer

video switcher technician

monitor wall

producer

script assistant

production adviser

audio console

audio technician

bass trap

musical advisers

equipment rack

audio monitor

studio floor

lighting/camera control area

audio control room

production control room

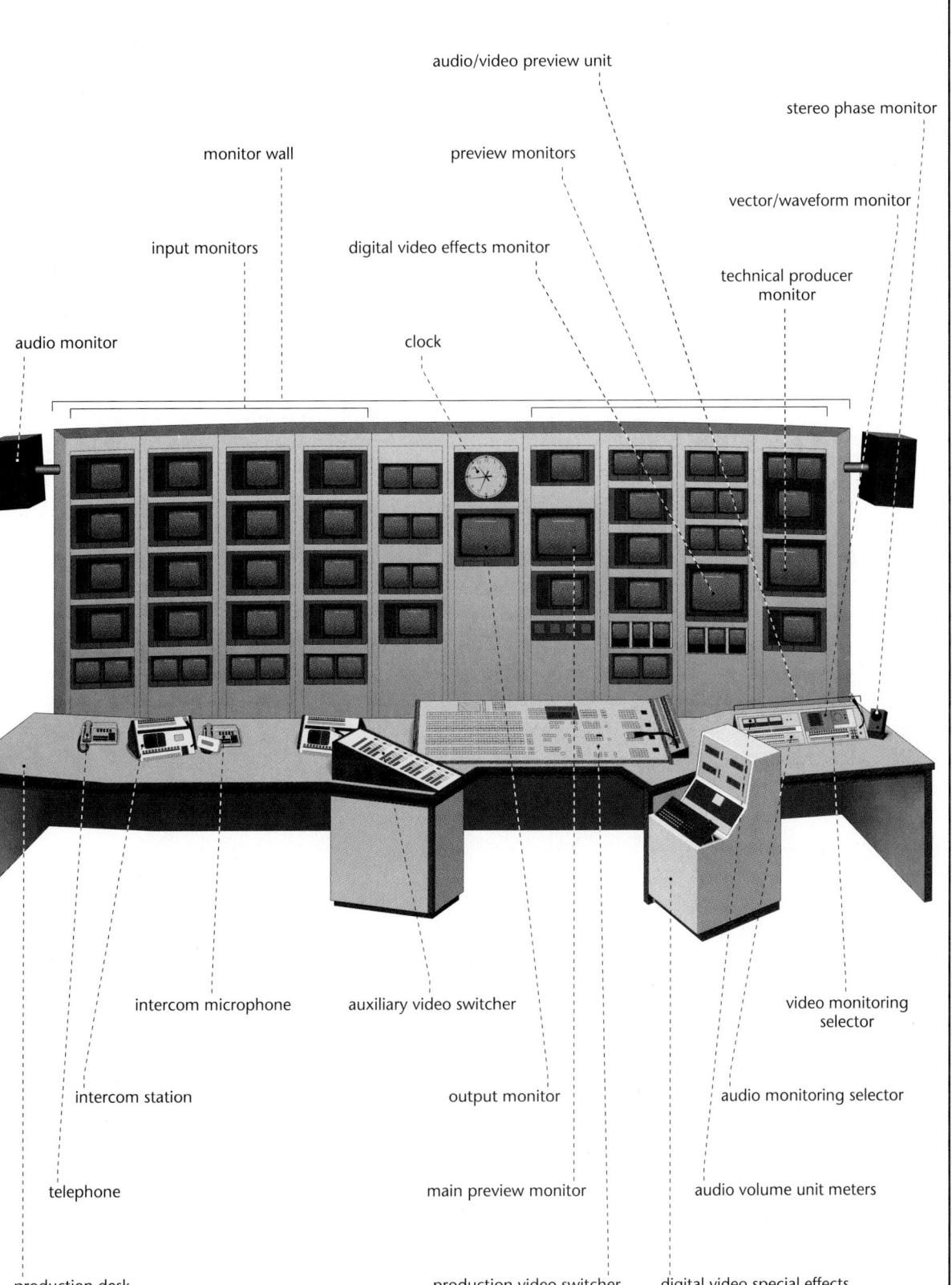

audio/video preview unit

stereo phase monitor

monitor wall

preview monitors

vector/waveform monitor

input monitors

digital video effects monitor

technical producer
monitor

audio monitor

clock

intercom microphone

auxiliary video switcher

video monitoring
selector

intercom station

output monitor

audio monitoring selector

telephone

main preview monitor

audio volume unit meters

production desk

production video switcher

digital video special effects

TELEVISION

STUDIO FLOOR

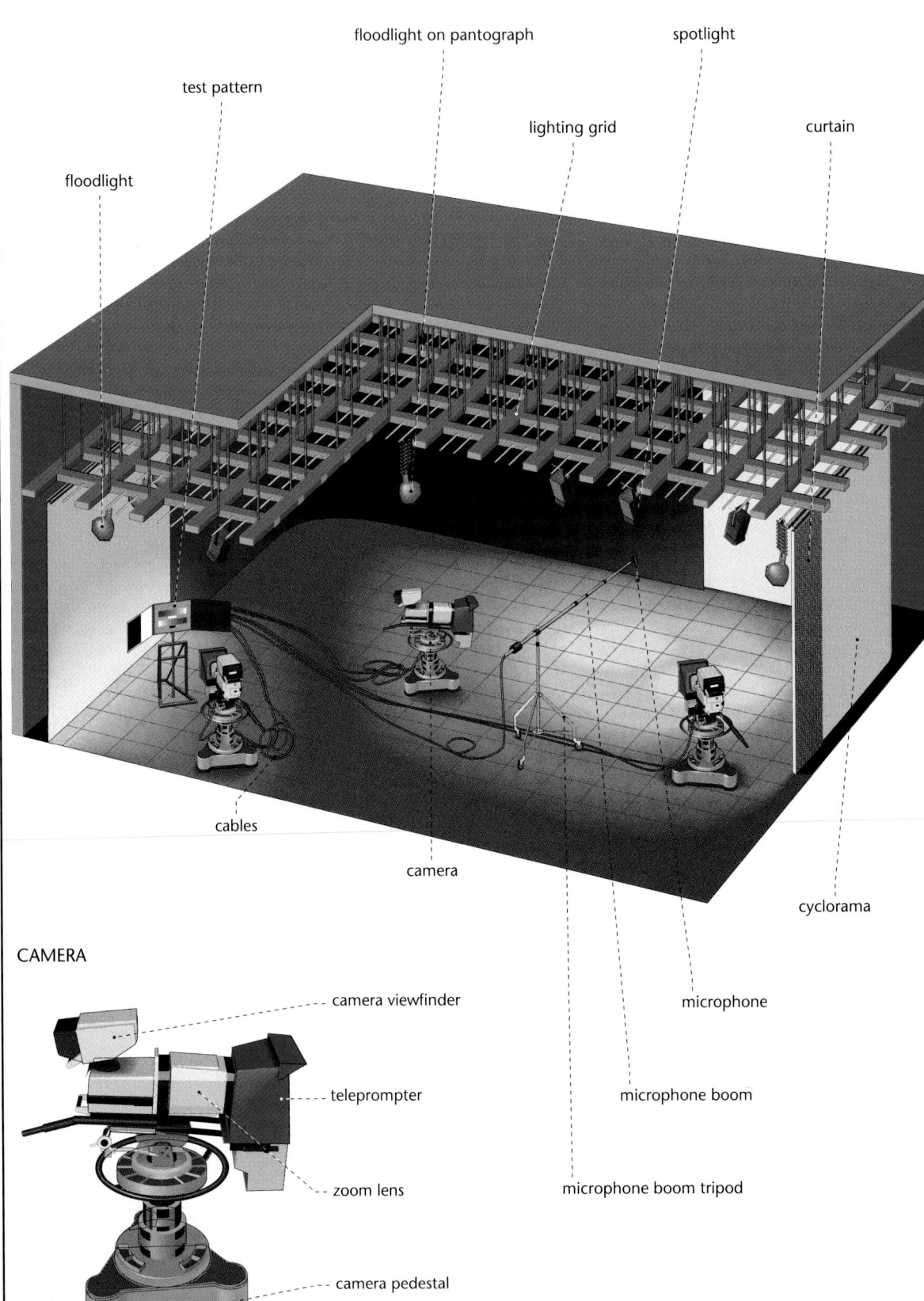

floodlight on pantograph

spotlight

test pattern

lighting grid

curtain

floodlight

camera viewfinder

cables

camera

cyclorama

CAMERA

camera viewfinder

microphone

teleprompter

microphone boom

zoom lens

microphone boom tripod

camera pedestal

MOBILE UNIT

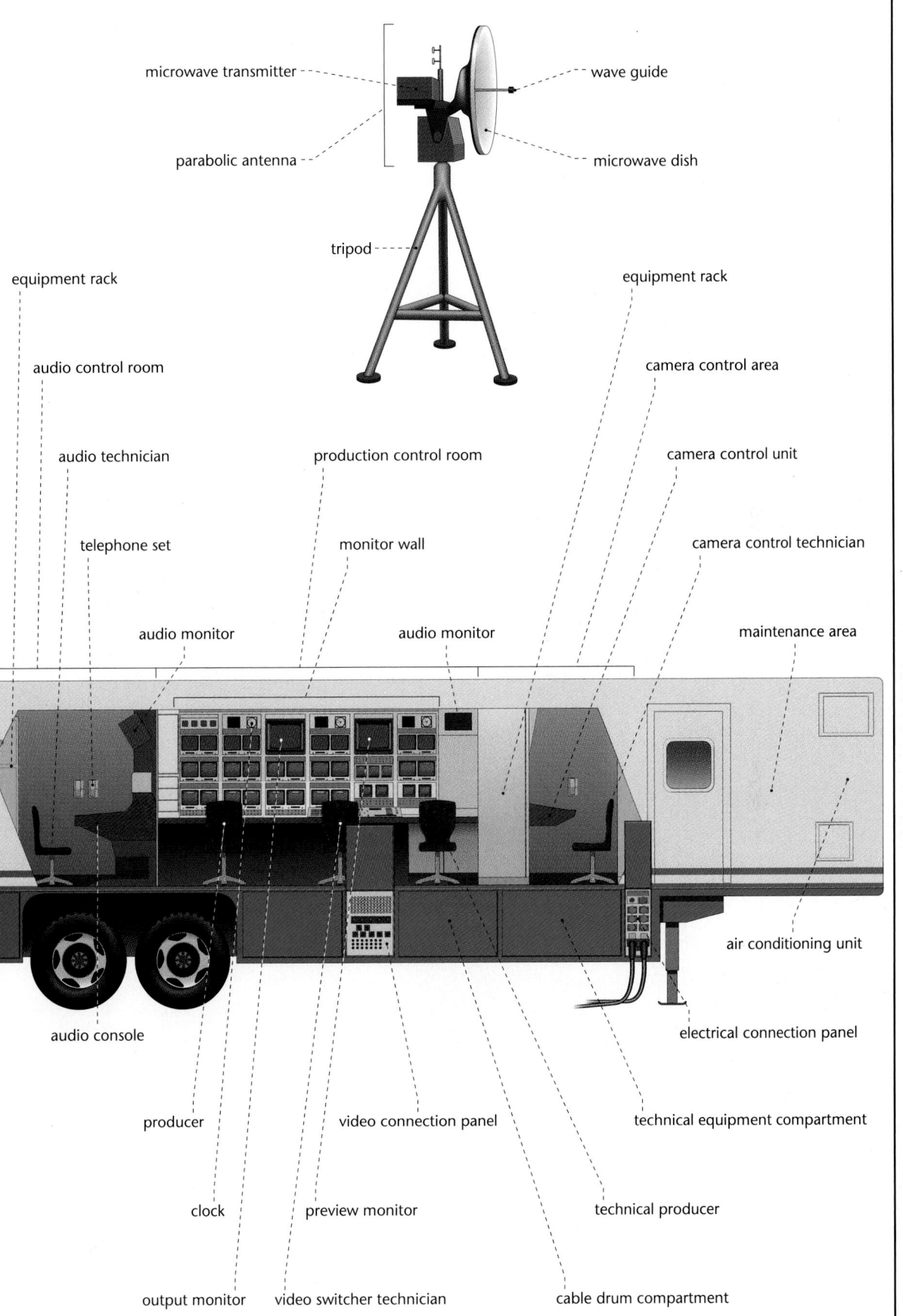

microwave transmitter

parabolic antenna

wave guide

microwave dish

tripod

equipment rack

audio control room

audio technician

telephone set

audio monitor

production control room

monitor wall

audio monitor

equipment rack

camera control area

camera control unit

camera control technician

maintenance area

air conditioning unit

electrical connection panel

audio console

producer

clock

output monitor

video connection panel

preview monitor

video switcher technician

technical equipment compartment

technical producer

cable drum compartment

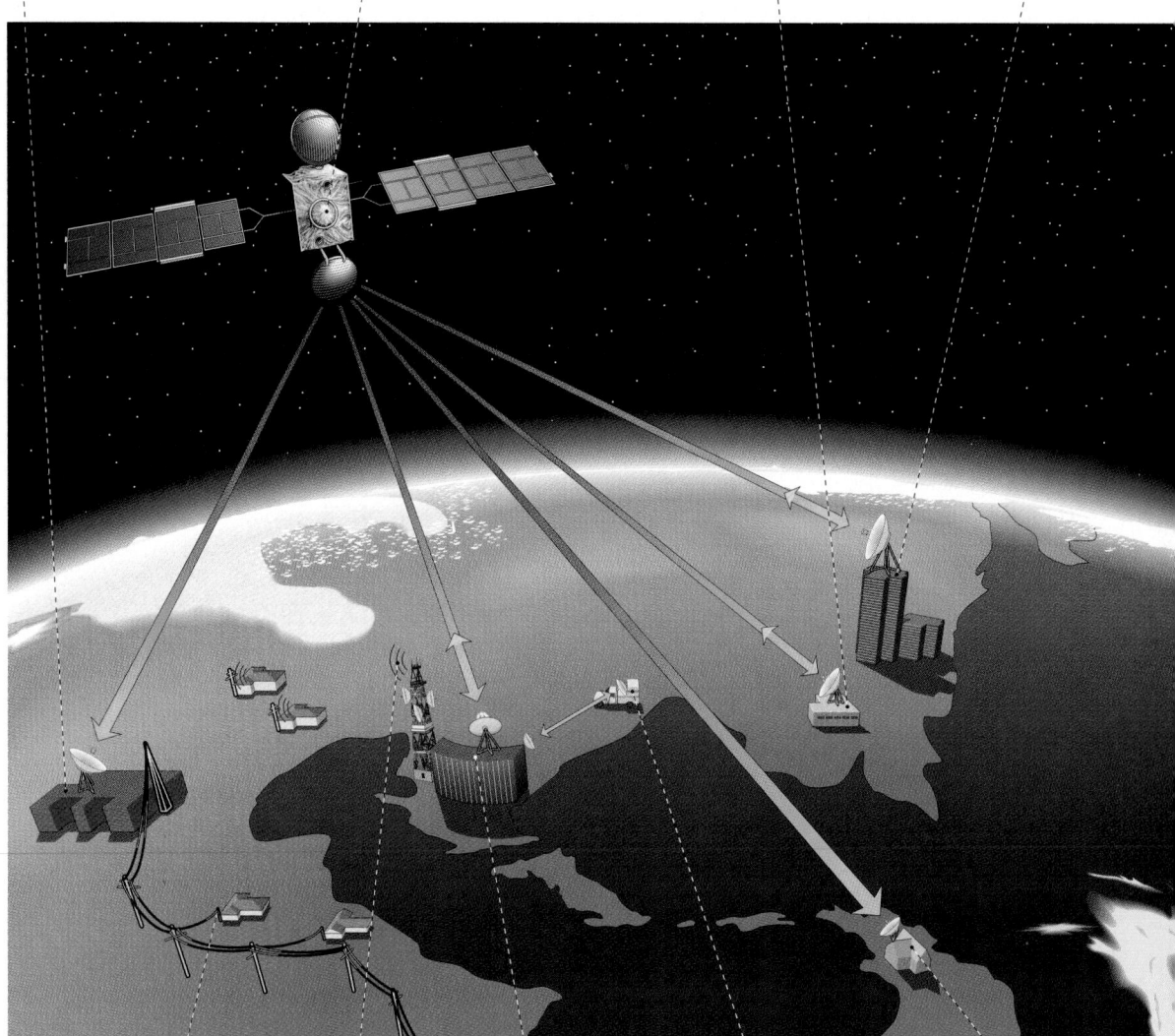

satellite

local station

cable distributor

private broadcasting network

distribution by cable network

direct home reception

Hertzian wave transmission

mobile unit

national broadcasting network

TELECOMMUNICATIONS BY SATELLITE

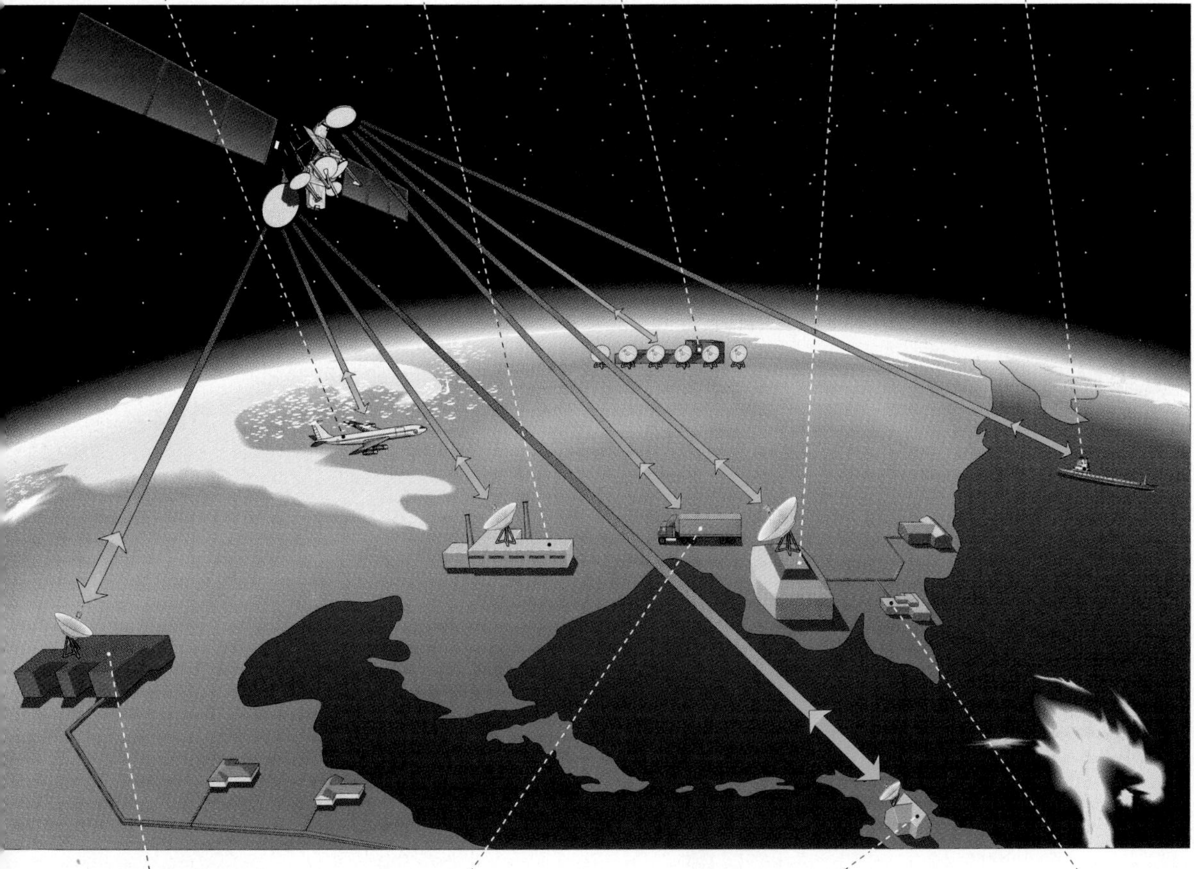

industrial communications

teleport

air communications

military communications

maritime communications

telephone network

road communications

personal communications

consumer

TELECOMMUNICATIONS BY TELEPHONE NETWORK

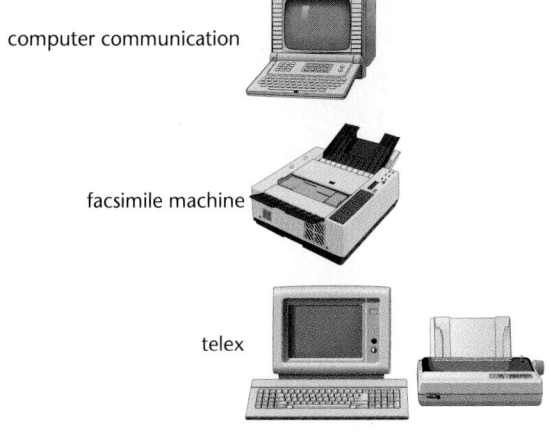

computer communication

facsimile machine

telex

cellular telephone

telephone set

417

TELECOMMUNICATION SATELLITES

EXAMPLES OF SATELLITES

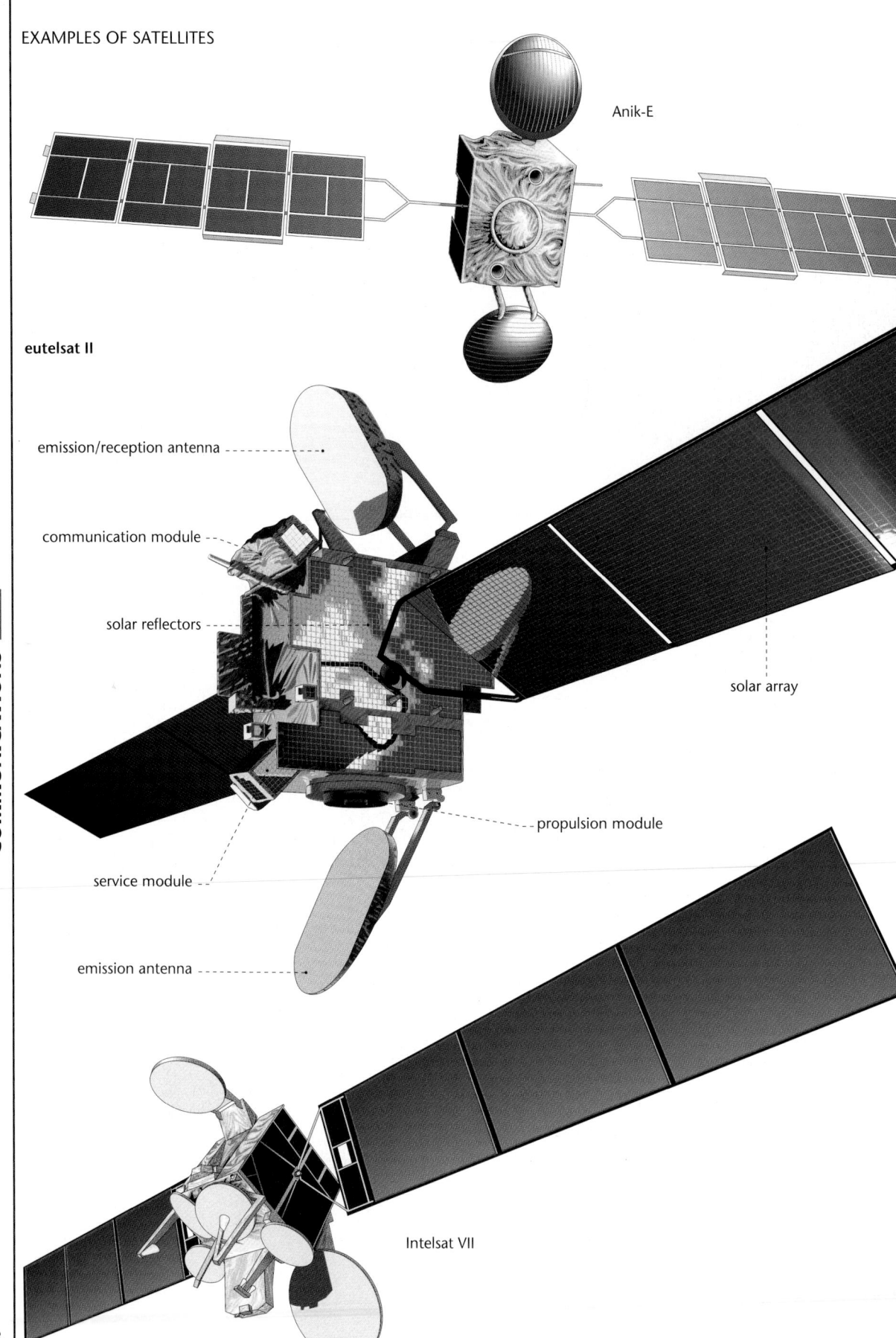

Anik-E

eutelsat II

emission/reception antenna

communication module

solar reflectors

solar array

propulsion module

service module

emission antenna

Intelsat VII

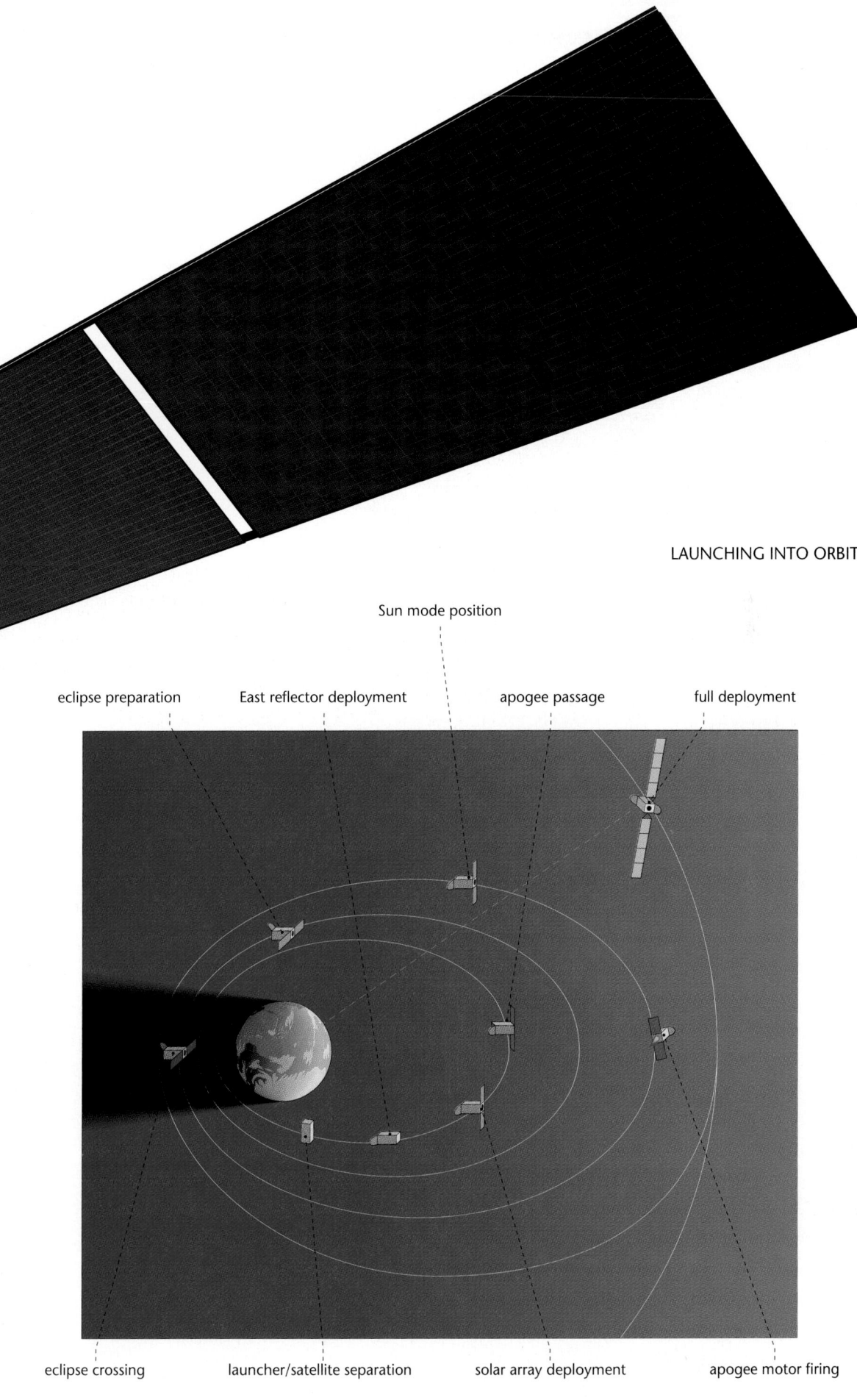

Sun mode position

eclipse preparation   East reflector deployment   apogee passage   full deployment

eclipse crossing   launcher/satellite separation   solar array deployment   apogee motor firing

TELEPHONE ANSWERING MACHINE

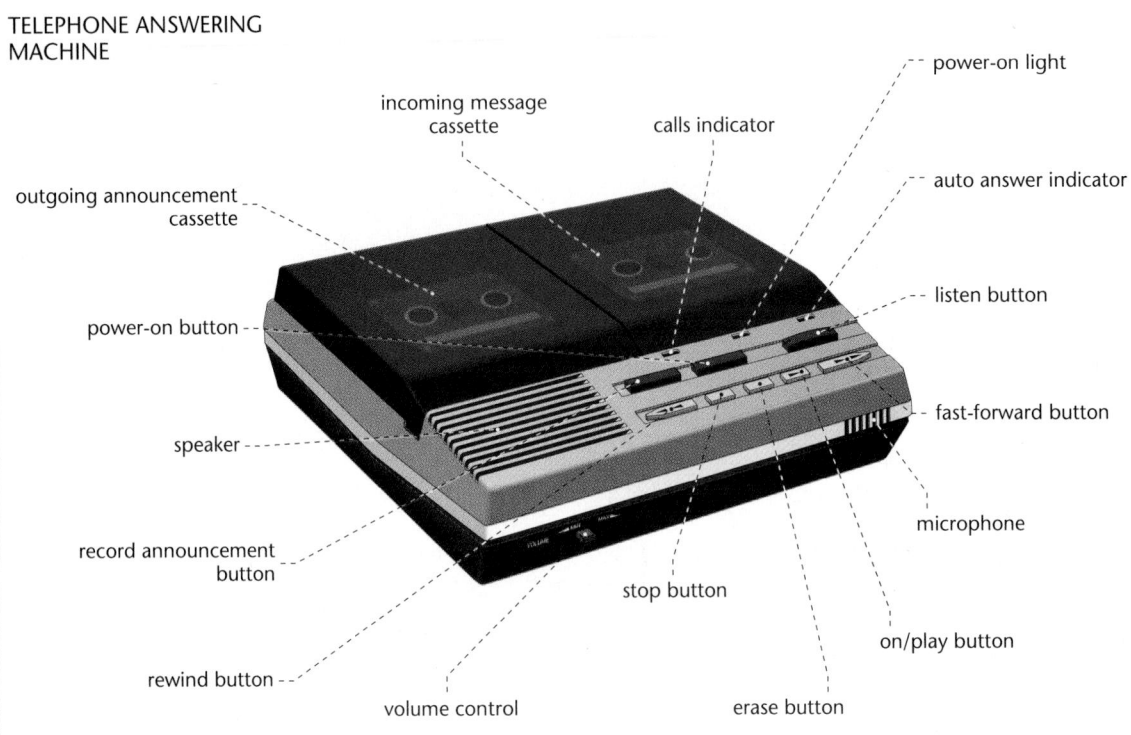

incoming message cassette

calls indicator

power-on light

auto answer indicator

outgoing announcement cassette

listen button

power-on button

fast-forward button

speaker

microphone

record announcement button

stop button

on/play button

rewind button

volume control

erase button

TELEPHONE SET

receiver

display

handset

on/off light

receiver volume control

transmitter

display setting

handset cord

ringing volume control

push buttons

telephone index

memory button

automatic dialer index

function selectors

terminal

printer

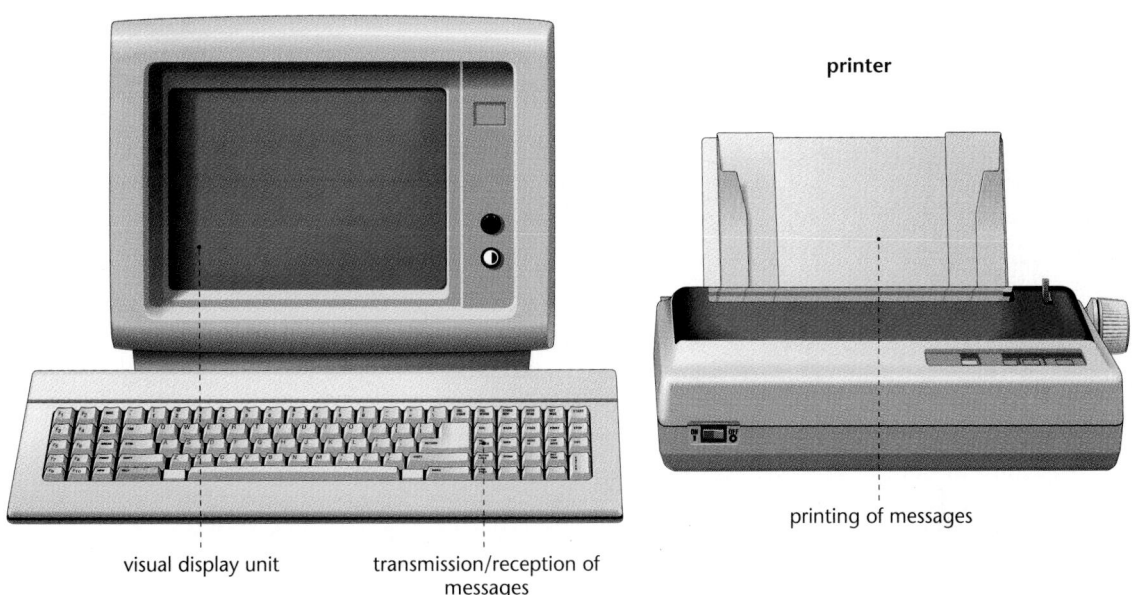

printing of messages

visual display unit | transmission/reception of messages

FACSIMILE MACHINE

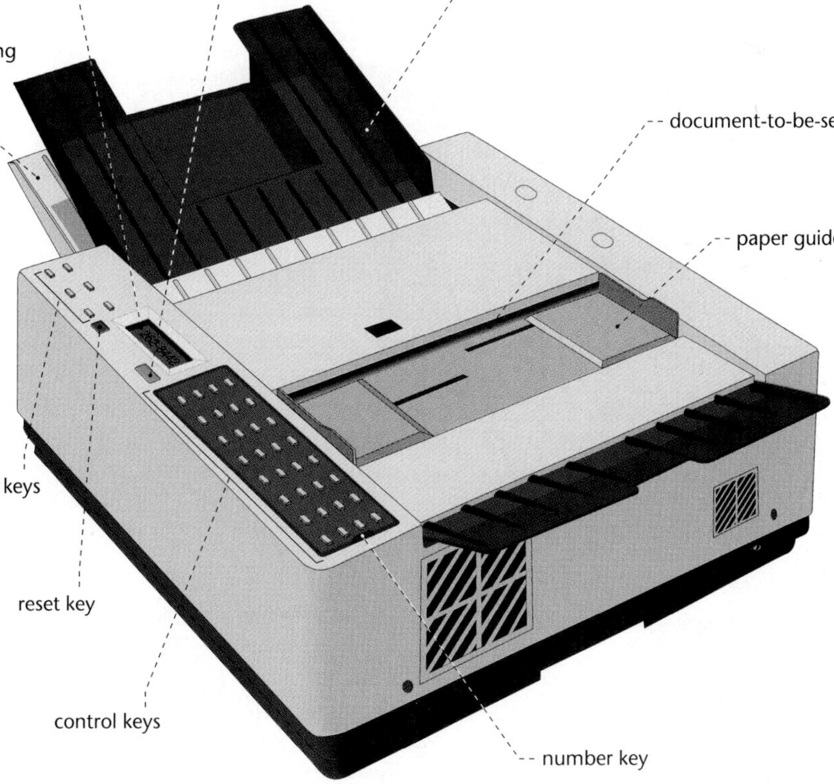

document receiving

data display | start key | sent document recovery

document-to-be-sent position

paper guide

function keys

reset key

control keys

number key

TYPES OF TELEPHONES

cordless telephone

telecommunication terminal

housing

visual display unit

function keys

numeric keyboard

call director telephone

operation keys

alphanumeric keyboard

keyboard

portable cellular telephone

volume control

handset

armored cord

pay phone

coin slot

display

next call

language display button

push buttons

card reader

coin return bucket

push-button telephone

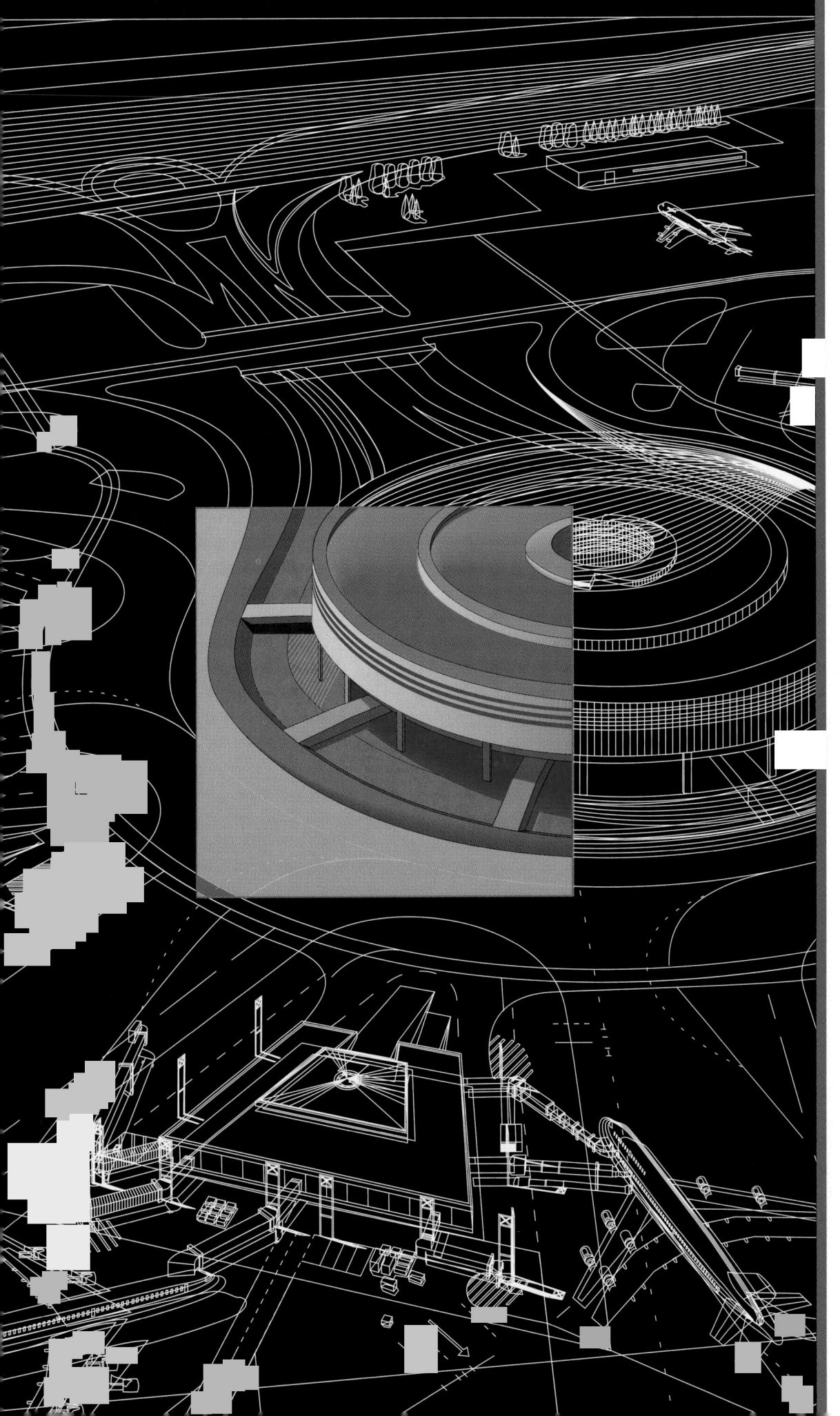

CONTENTS

ROAD TRANSPORT

AUTOMOBILE 425

TRUCKING 440

MOTORCYCLE 442

SNOWMOBILE 445

BICYCLE 446

CARAVAN 449

ROAD SYSTEM 450

SERVICE STATION 453

FIXED BRIDGES 454

MOVABLE BRIDGES 457

RAIL TRANSPORT

HIGH-SPEED TRAIN 458

TYPES OF PASSENGER CARS 460

PASSENGER STATION 462

RAILROAD STATION 464

YARD 465

RAILROAD TRACK 466

DIESEL-ELECTRIC LOCOMOTIVE 468

CAR 470

TYPES OF FREIGHT CARS 472

SUBWAY TRANSPORT

SUBWAY 474

MARITIME TRANSPORT

FOUR-MASTED BARK 478

TYPES OF SAILS 482

TYPES OF RIGS 482

ANCHOR 483

NAVIGATION DEVICES 484

MARITIME SIGNALS 486

MARITIME BUOYAGE SYSTEM 488

HARBOR 490

CANAL LOCK 492

HOVERCRAFT 492

FERRY 494

CONTAINER SHIP 494

HYDROFOIL BOAT 495

PASSENGER LINER 496

AIR TRANSPORT

LONG-RANGE JET 498

TYPES OF TAIL SHAPES 498

TYPES OF WING SHAPES 499

FLIGHT DECK 500

TURBOFAN ENGINE 501

AIRPORT 502

HELICOPTER 508

SPACE TRANSPORT

ROCKET 509

SPACE SHUTTLE 510

SPACESUIT 512

TRANSPORT

AUTOMOBILE

sports car

two-door sedan

hatchback

station wagon

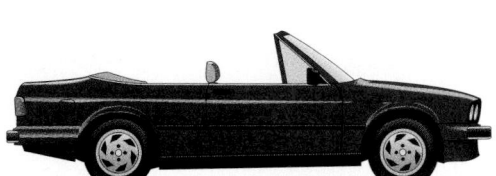

convertible

pickup truck

four-door sedan

minivan

multipurpose vehicle

limousine

ROAD TRANSPORT

425

BODY

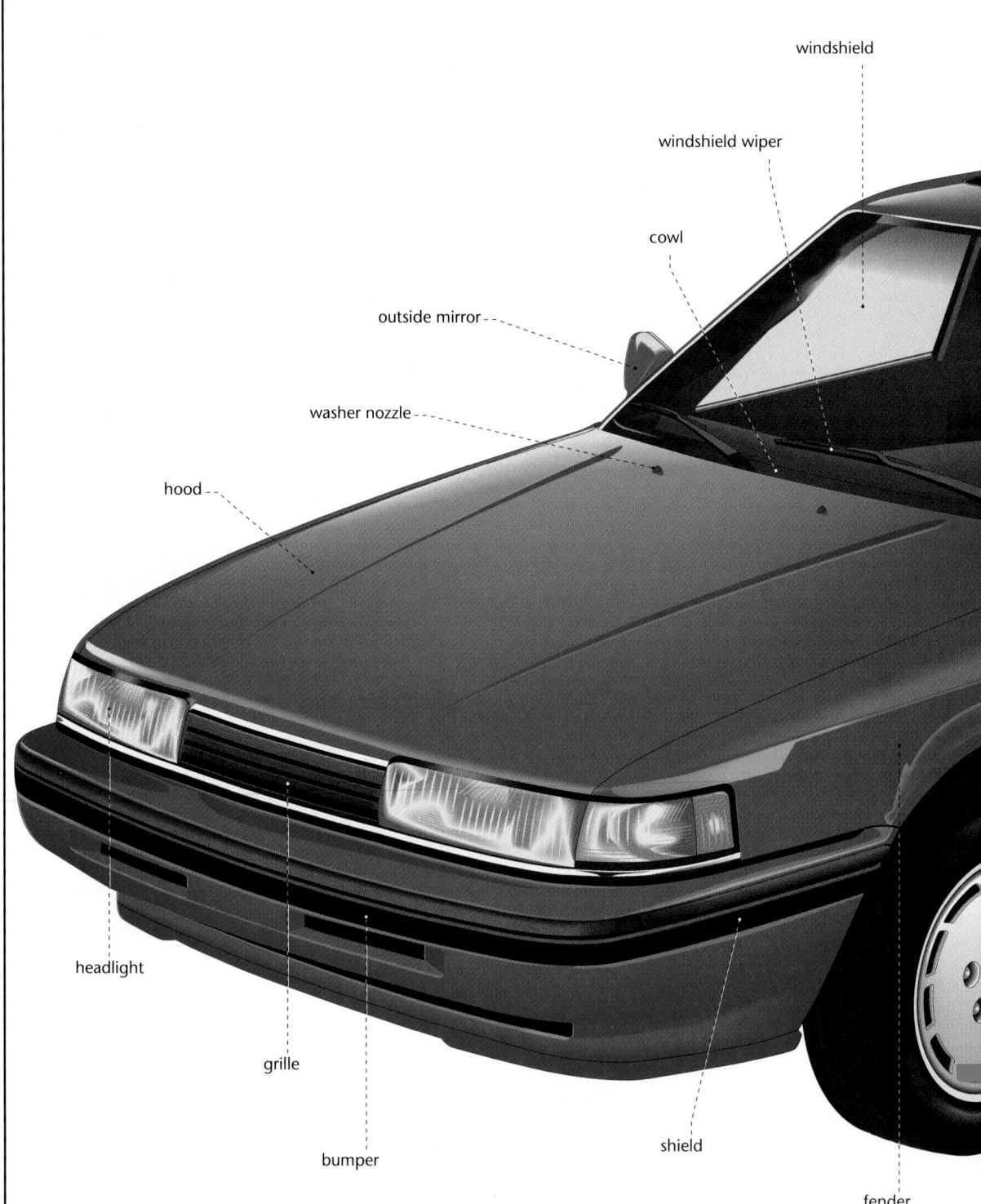

windshield

windshield wiper

cowl

outside mirror

washer nozzle

hood

headlight

grille

bumper

shield

fender

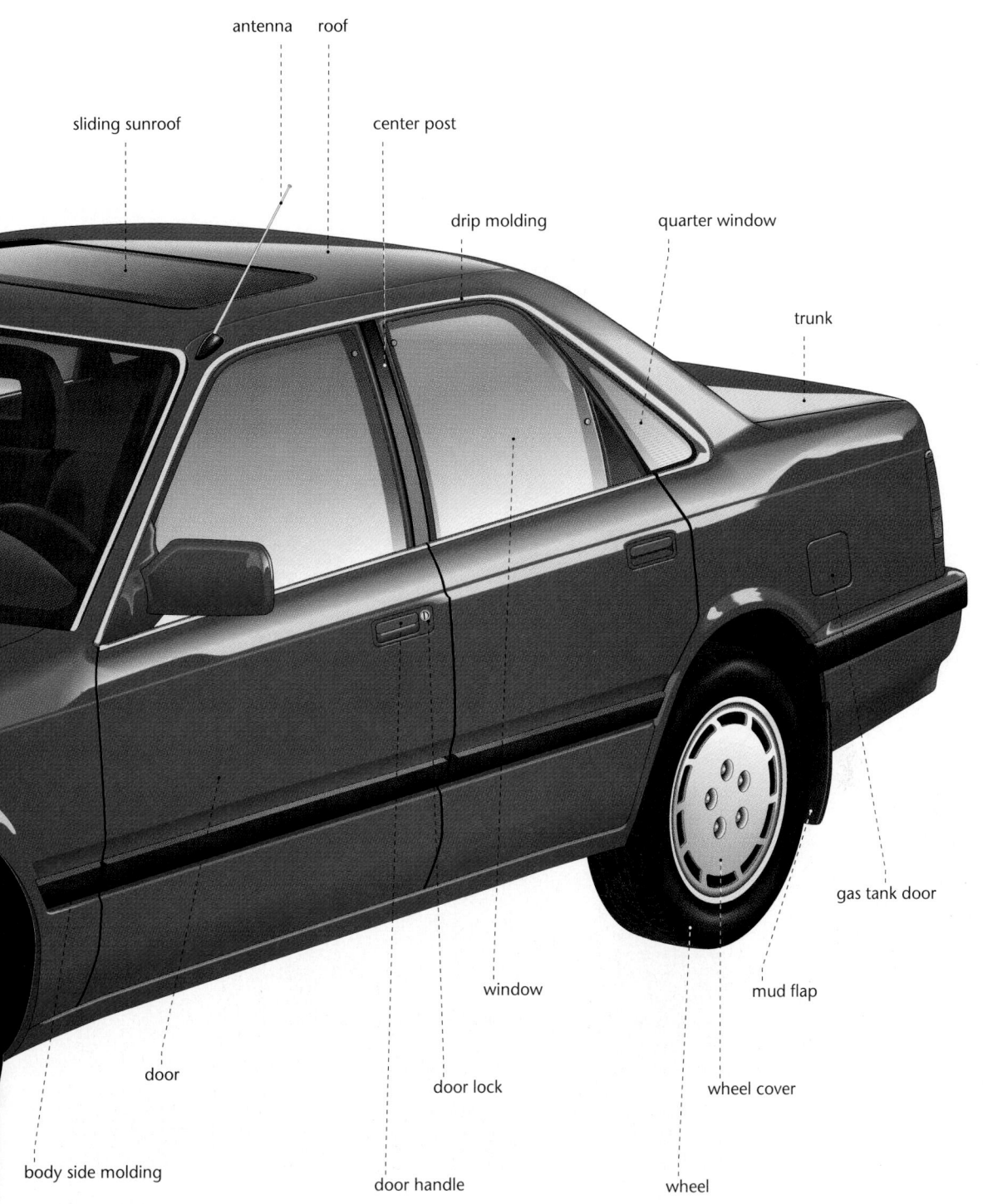

antenna   roof

sliding sunroof

center post

drip molding

quarter window

trunk

window

door

door lock

gas tank door

mud flap

wheel cover

body side molding

door handle

wheel

ROAD TRANSPORT

BUCKET SEAT

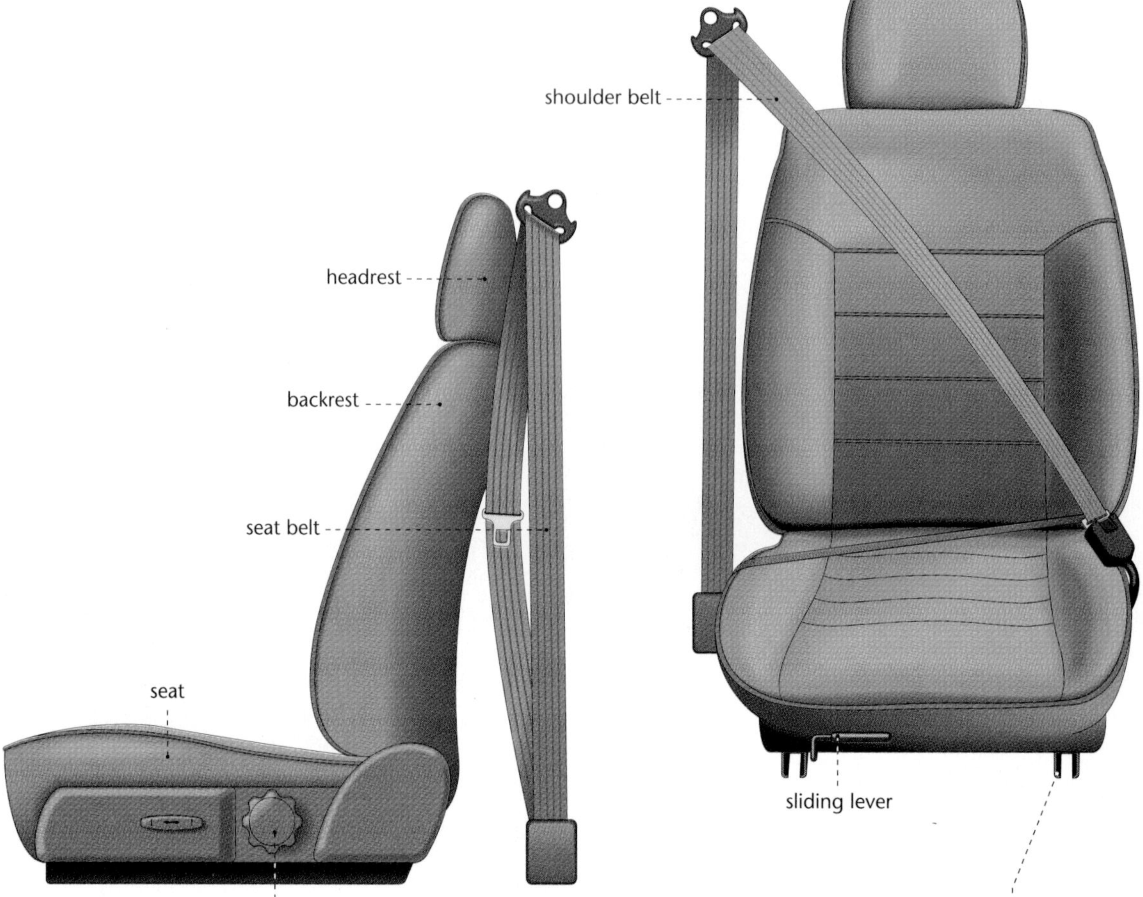

shoulder belt - - - - -

headrest - - - - -

backrest - - - - -

seat belt - - - -

seat

adjustment knob

sliding lever

sliding rail

REAR SEAT

armrest - - - -

webbing - - -

buckle - - - -

bench seat - - - -

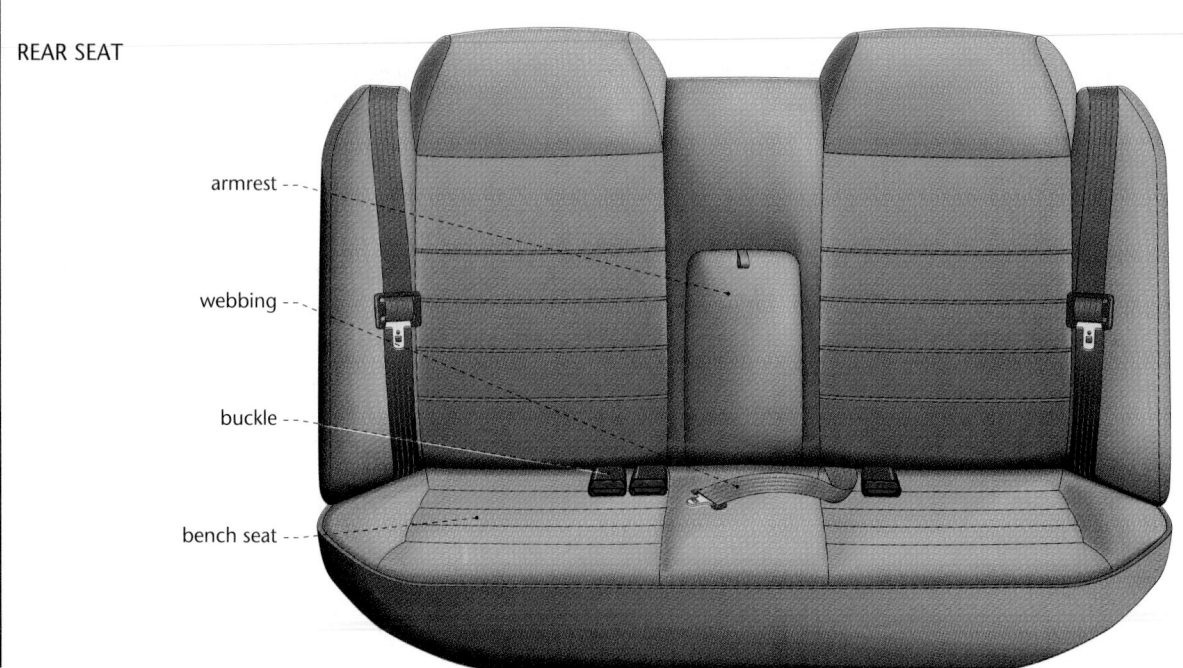

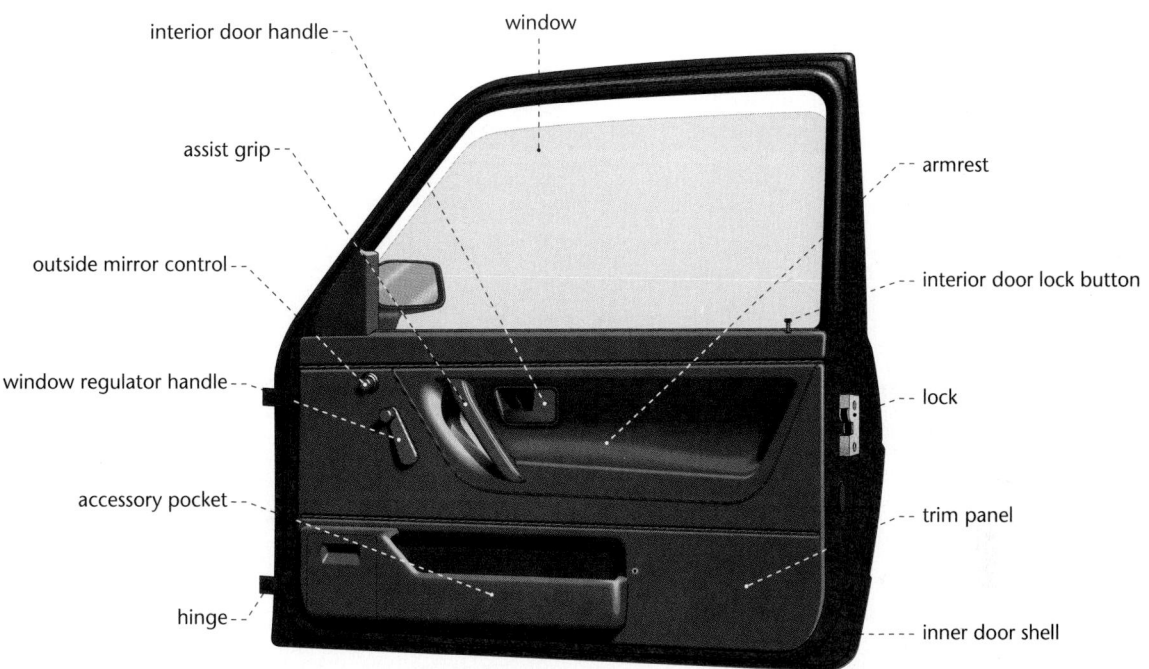

interior door handle

window

assist grip

armrest

outside mirror control

interior door lock button

window regulator handle

lock

accessory pocket

trim panel

hinge

inner door shell

headlights

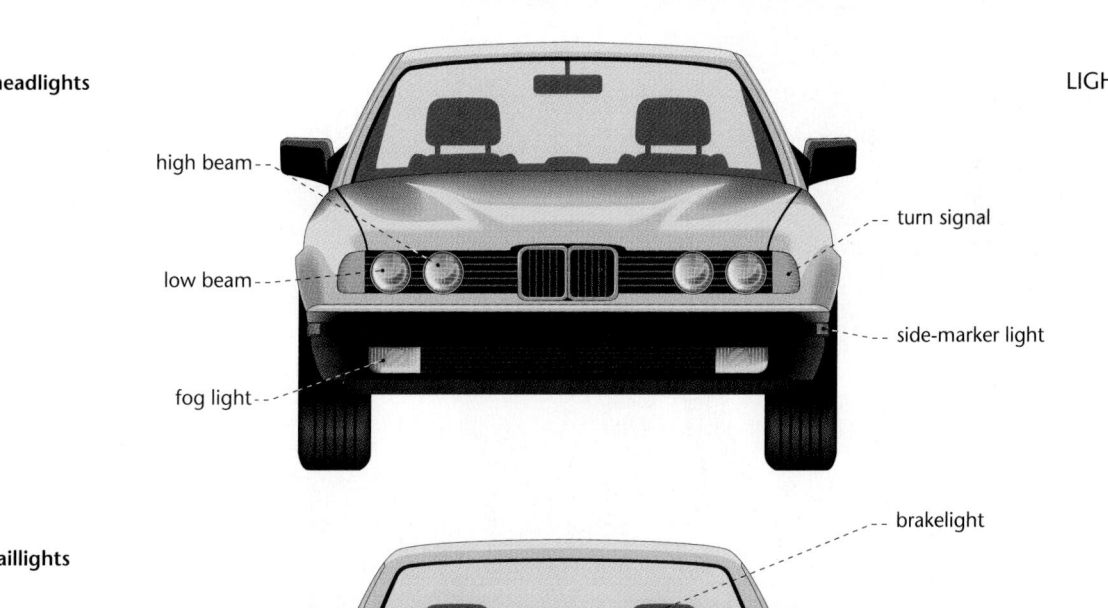

high beam

turn signal

low beam

side-marker light

fog light

taillights

brakelight

turn signal

license plate light

brakelight

taillight

backup light

side-marker light

ROAD TRANSPORT

DASHBOARD

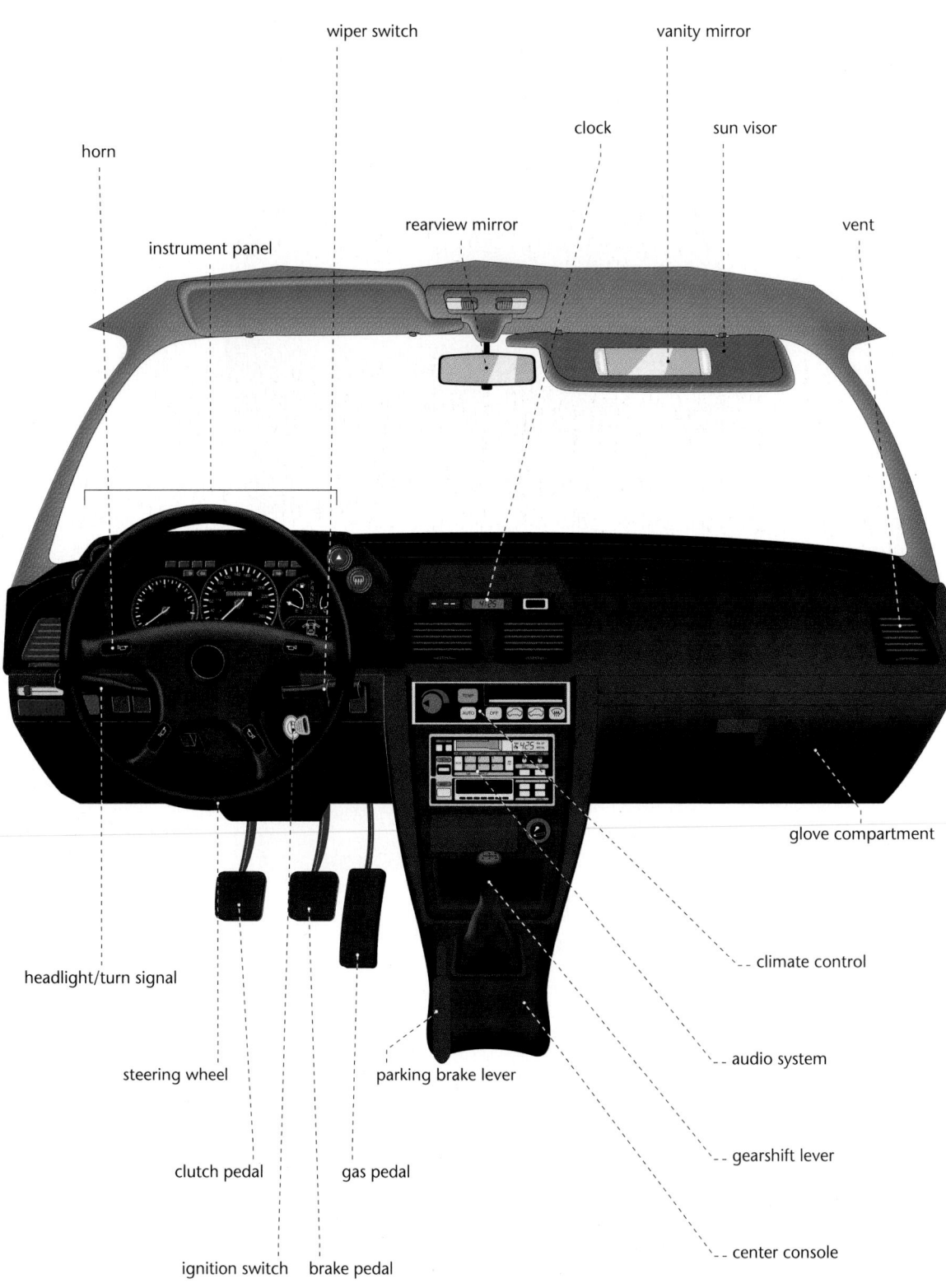

wiper switch

vanity mirror

horn

clock

sun visor

instrument panel

rearview mirror

vent

glove compartment

climate control

headlight/turn signal

audio system

steering wheel

parking brake lever

gearshift lever

clutch pedal

gas pedal

center console

ignition switch

brake pedal

INSTRUMENT PANEL

alternator warning light
high beam indicator light
oil warning light
low fuel warning light
fuel indicator
warning lights
turn signal indicator
temperature indicator
ENGINE
MOTEUR
ALB
CRUISE
CONTROL
tachometer
odometer
trip odometer
door open warning light
seat-belt warning light
speedometer

WINDSHIELD WIPER

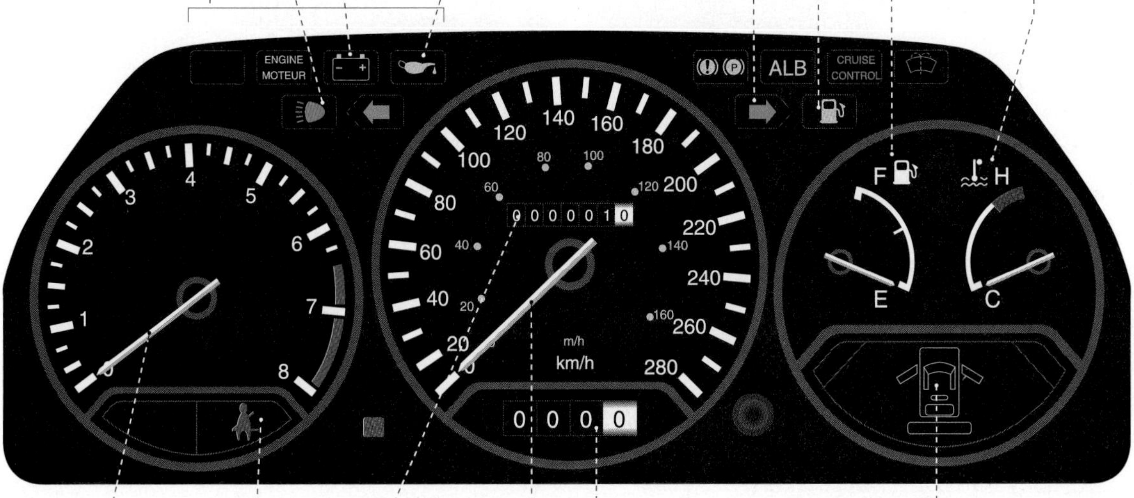

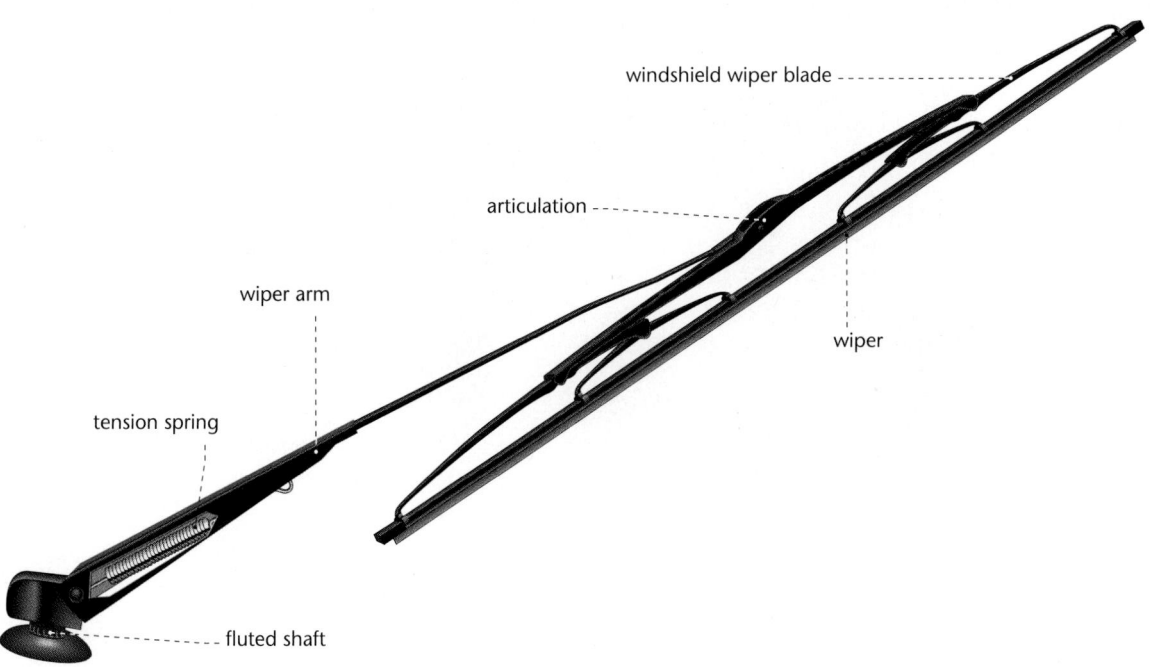

windshield wiper blade
articulation
wiper arm
wiper
tension spring
fluted shaft

ROAD TRANSPORT

DISK BRAKE

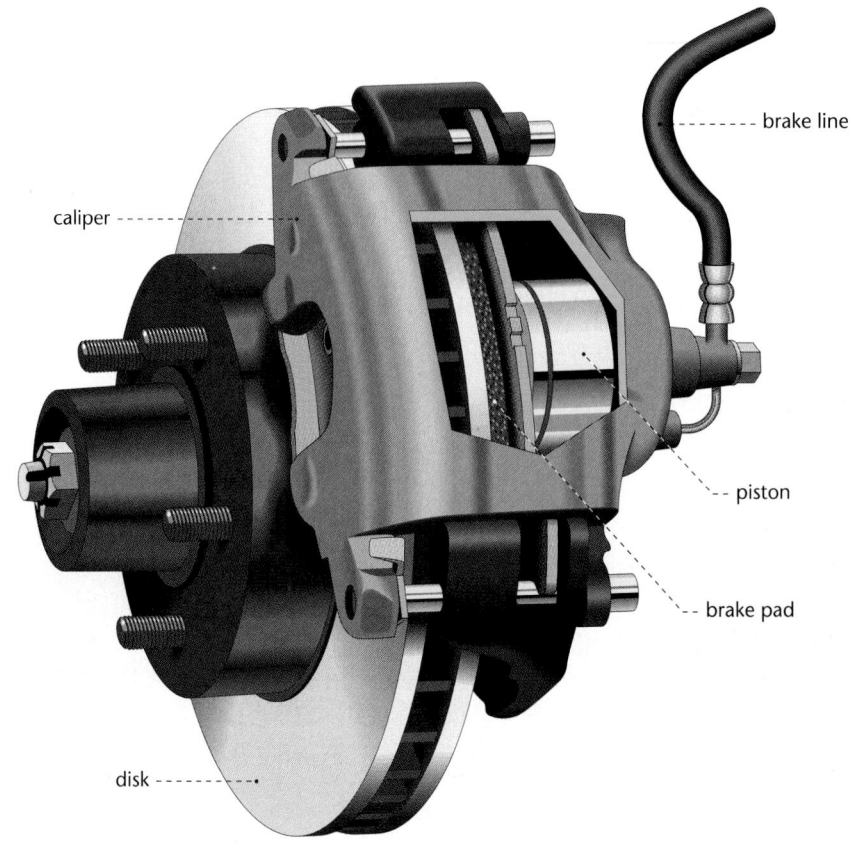

brake line

caliper

piston

brake pad

disk

DRUM BRAKE

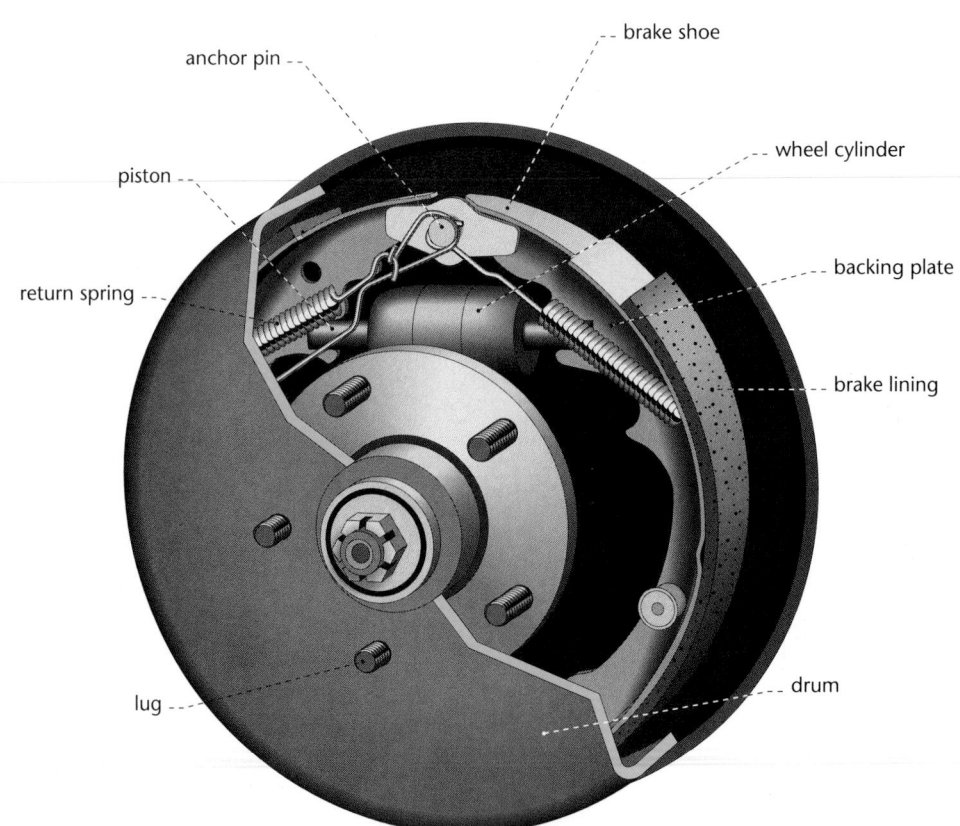

brake shoe

anchor pin

wheel cylinder

piston

backing plate

return spring

brake lining

lug

drum

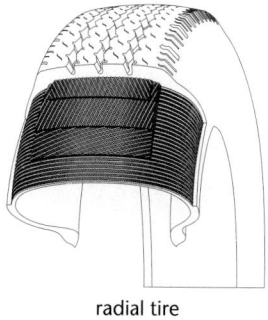

bias-ply tire

radial tire

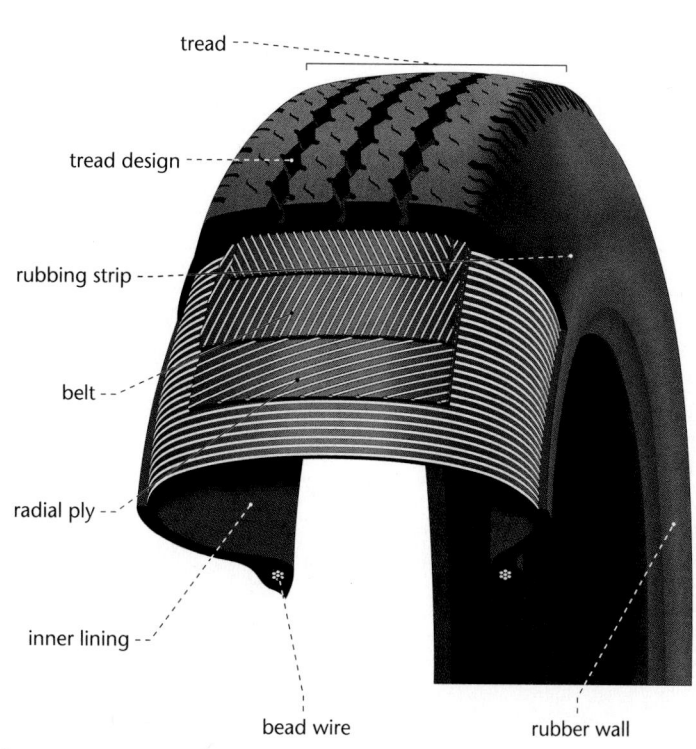

tread

tread design

rubbing strip

belt

radial ply

inner lining

bead wire

rubber wall

TIRE

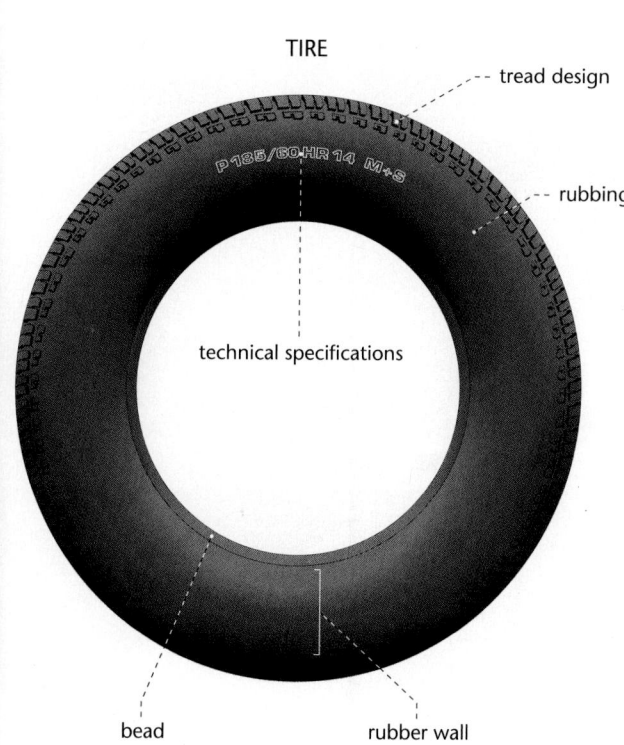

tread design

rubbing strip

technical specifications

P185/60HR14 M+S

bead

rubber wall

WHEEL

disk

rim

rim flange

GASOLINE ENGINE

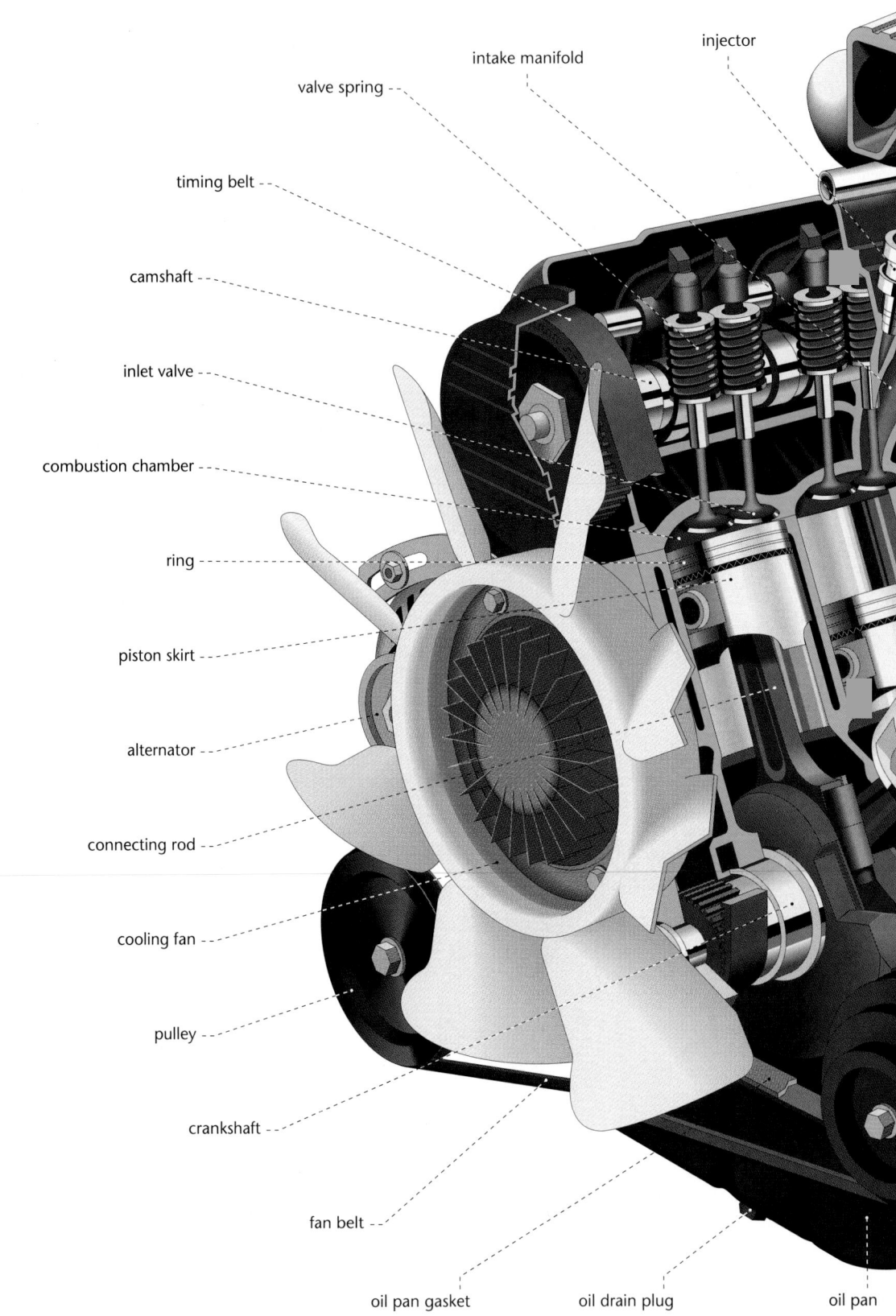

intake manifold

injector

valve spring

timing belt

camshaft

inlet valve

combustion chamber

ring

piston skirt

alternator

connecting rod

cooling fan

pulley

crankshaft

fan belt

oil pan gasket

oil drain plug

oil pan

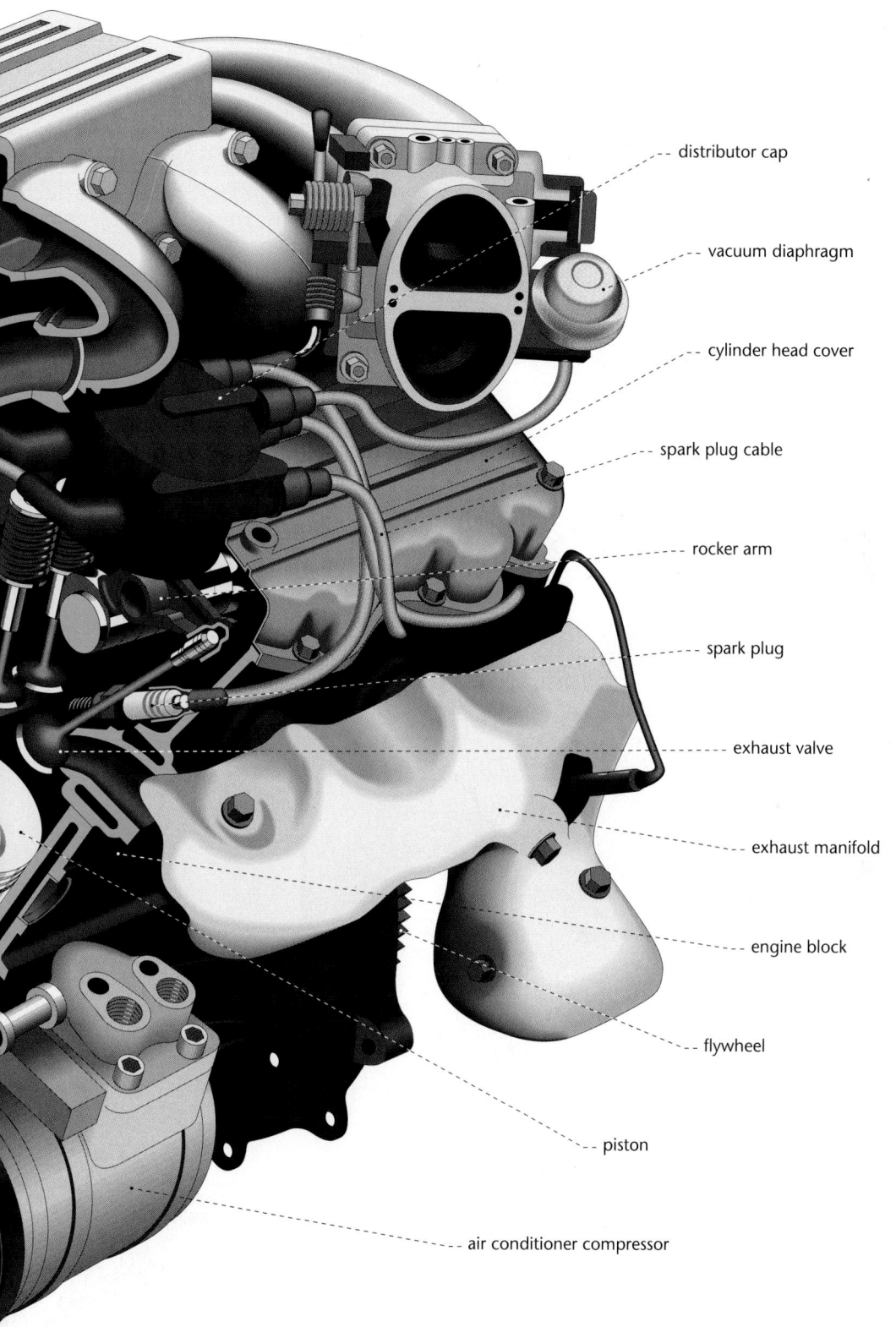

distributor cap

vacuum diaphragm

cylinder head cover

spark plug cable

rocker arm

spark plug

exhaust valve

exhaust manifold

engine block

flywheel

piston

air conditioner compressor

TYPES OF ENGINES

FOUR-STROKE-CYCLE
ENGINE

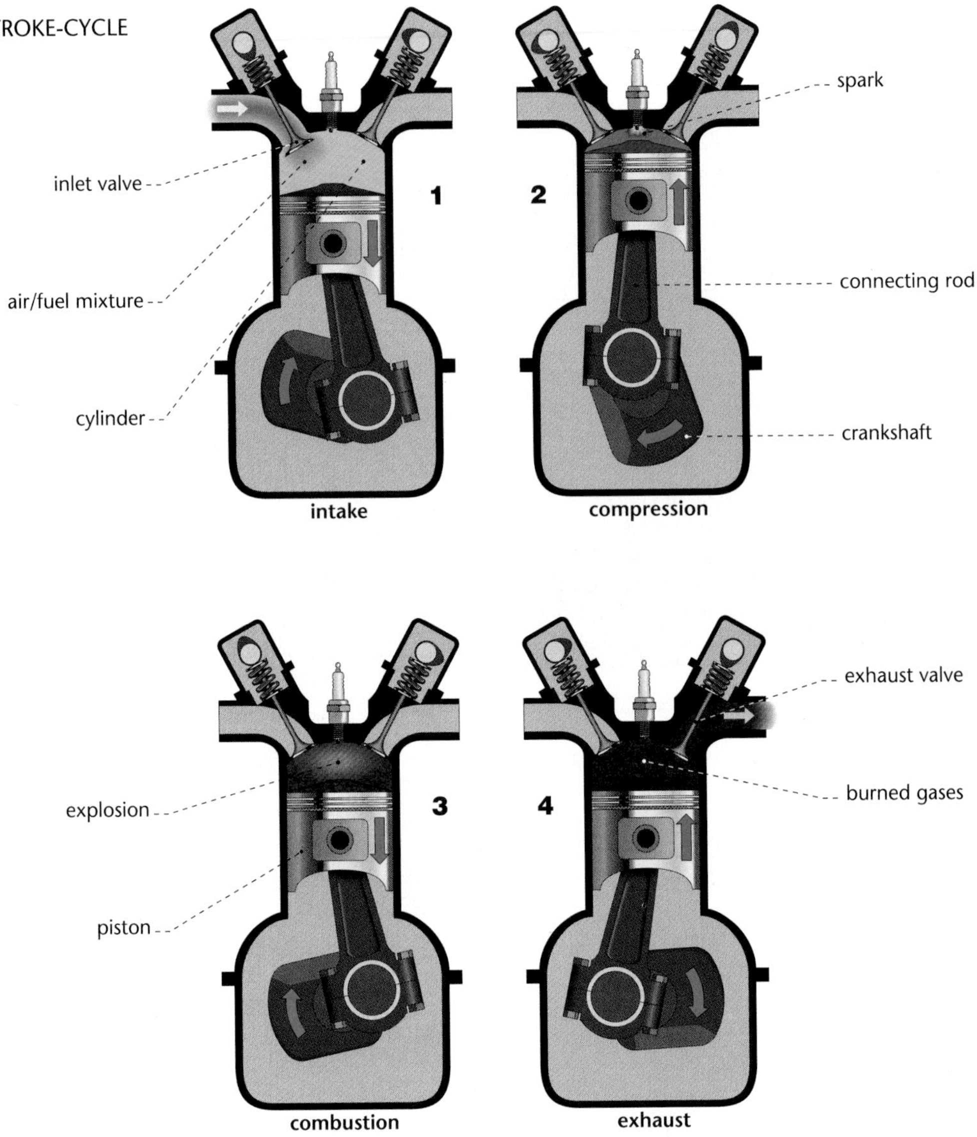

spark

inlet valve

connecting rod

air/fuel mixture

1 **2**

crankshaft

cylinder

intake

compression

exhaust valve

explosion

burned gases

3 **4**

piston

combustion

exhaust

TWO-STROKE-CYCLE ENGINE

exhaust port

transfer port

intake port

crankcase

compression/admission

combustion

exhaust

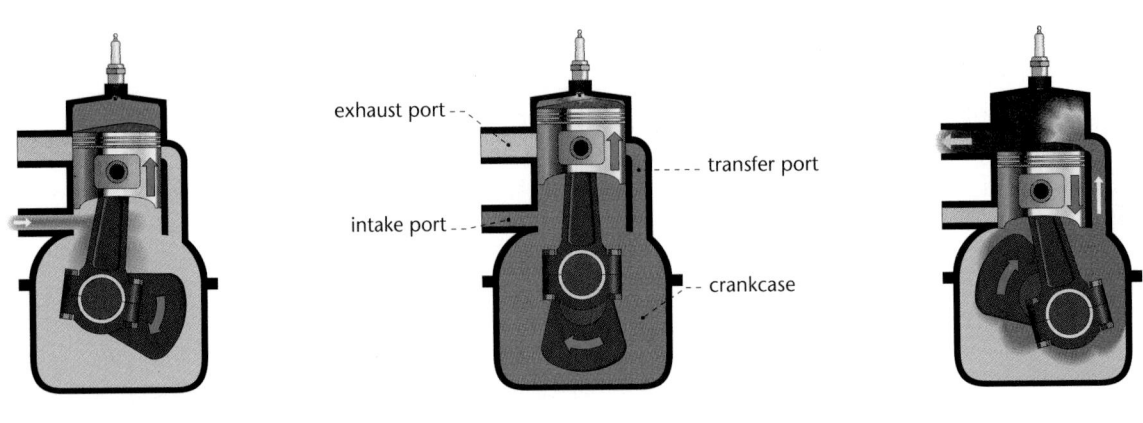

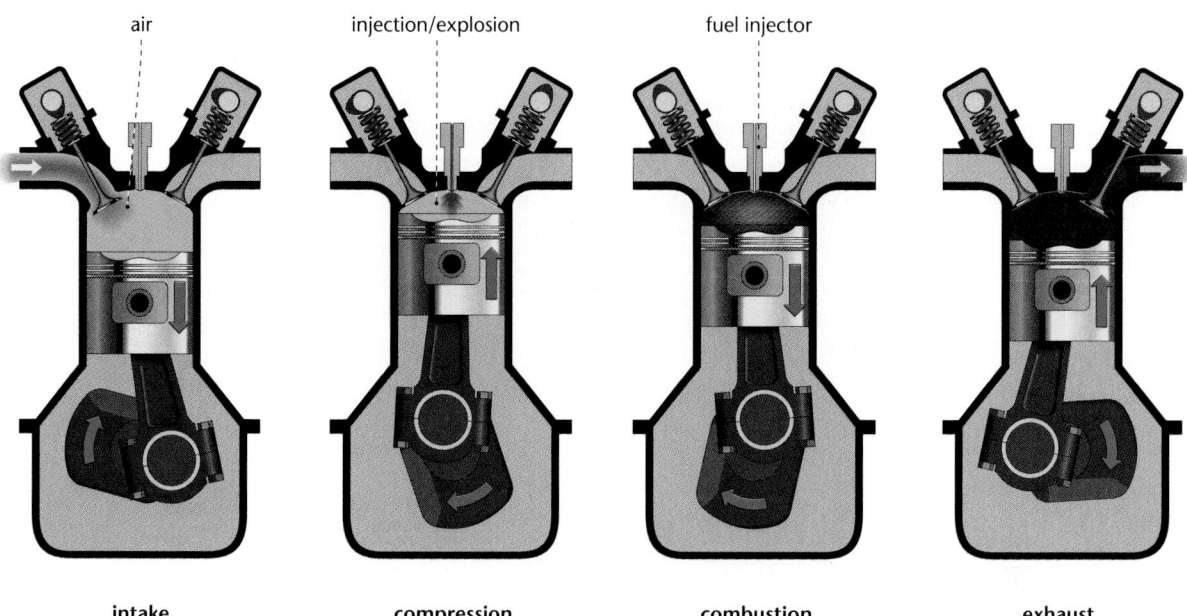

DIESEL ENGINE

air
injection/explosion
fuel injector
intake
compression
combustion
exhaust

ROTARY ENGINE

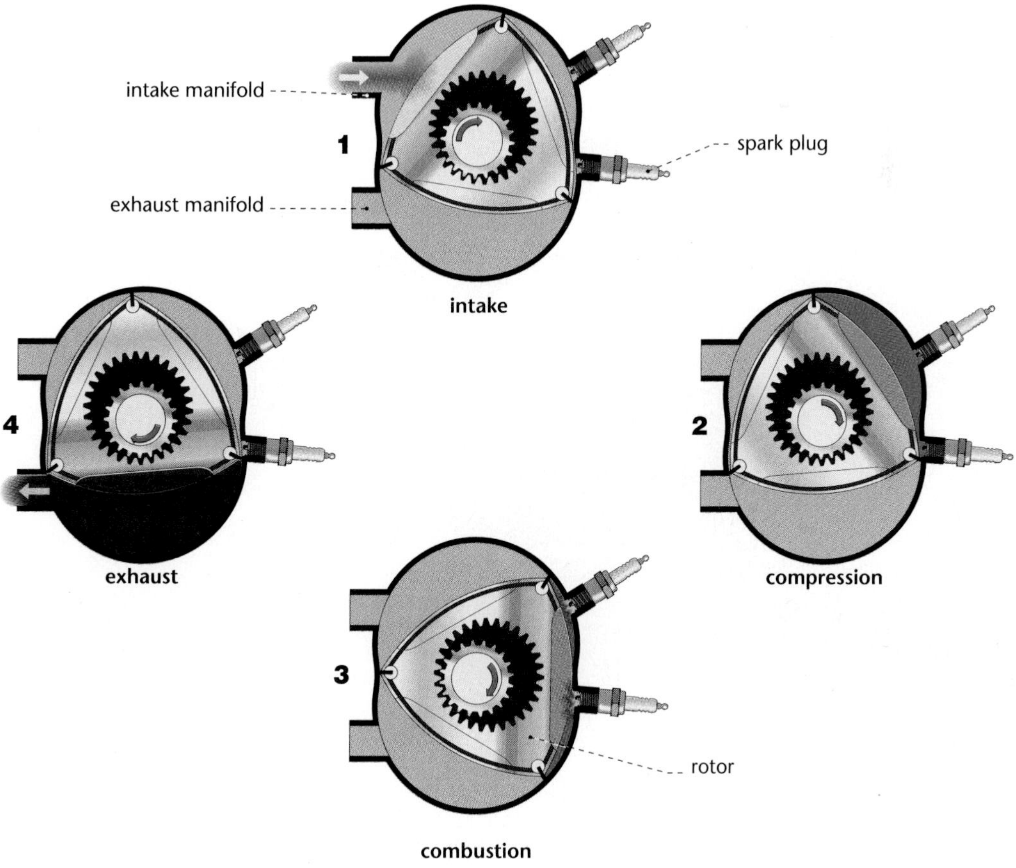

intake manifold
1
spark plug
exhaust manifold
intake
4
2
exhaust
compression
3
rotor
combustion

RADIATOR

filler cap

cooling fan

fan thermostat

radiator hose

grille

electric motor

TURBO-COMPRESSOR ENGINE

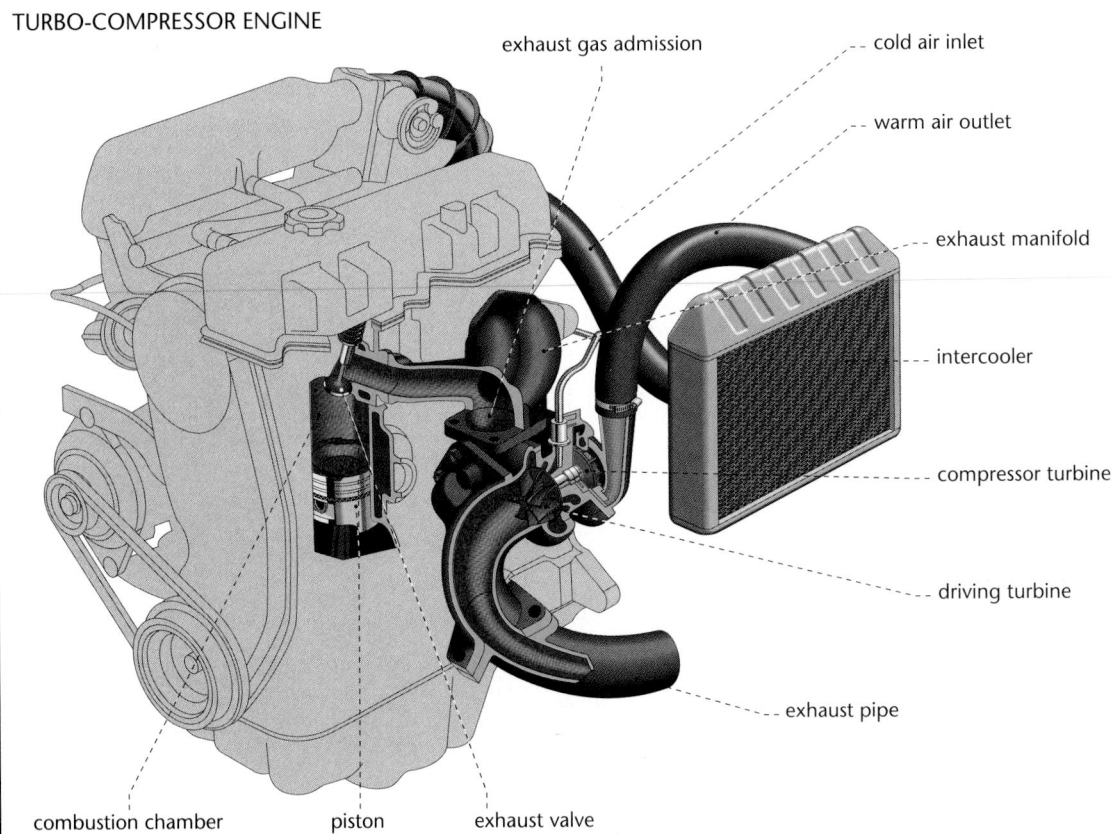

exhaust gas admission

cold air inlet

warm air outlet

exhaust manifold

intercooler

compressor turbine

driving turbine

exhaust pipe

combustion chamber   piston   exhaust valve

SPARK PLUG

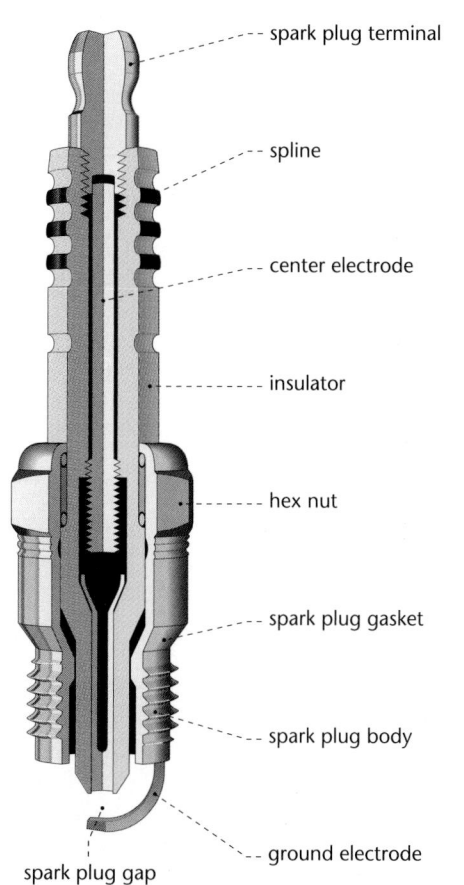

- spark plug terminal
- spline
- center electrode
- insulator
- hex nut
- spark plug gasket
- spark plug body
- ground electrode
- spark plug gap

EXHAUST SYSTEM

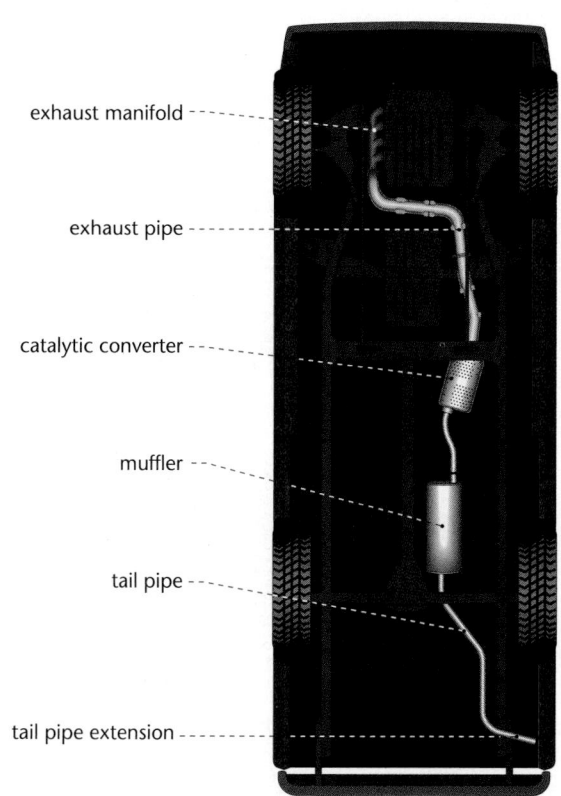

- exhaust manifold
- exhaust pipe
- catalytic converter
- muffler
- tail pipe
- tail pipe extension

BATTERY

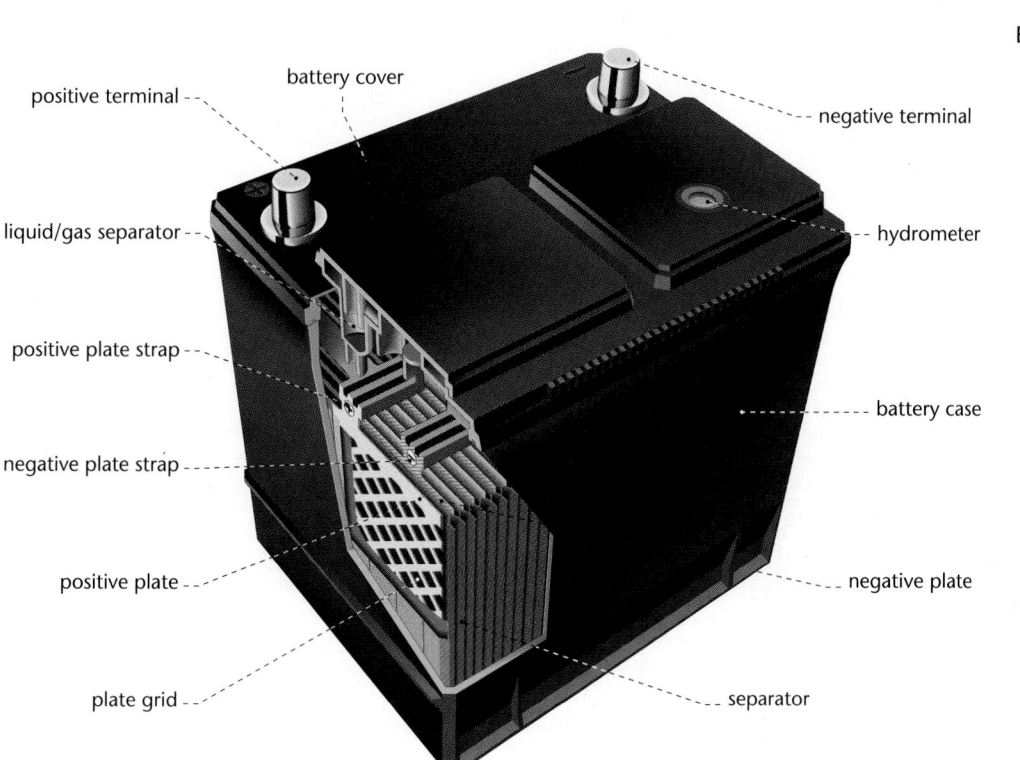

- positive terminal
- battery cover
- negative terminal
- liquid/gas separator
- hydrometer
- positive plate strap
- negative plate strap
- battery case
- positive plate
- negative plate
- plate grid
- separator

TRUCK TRACTOR

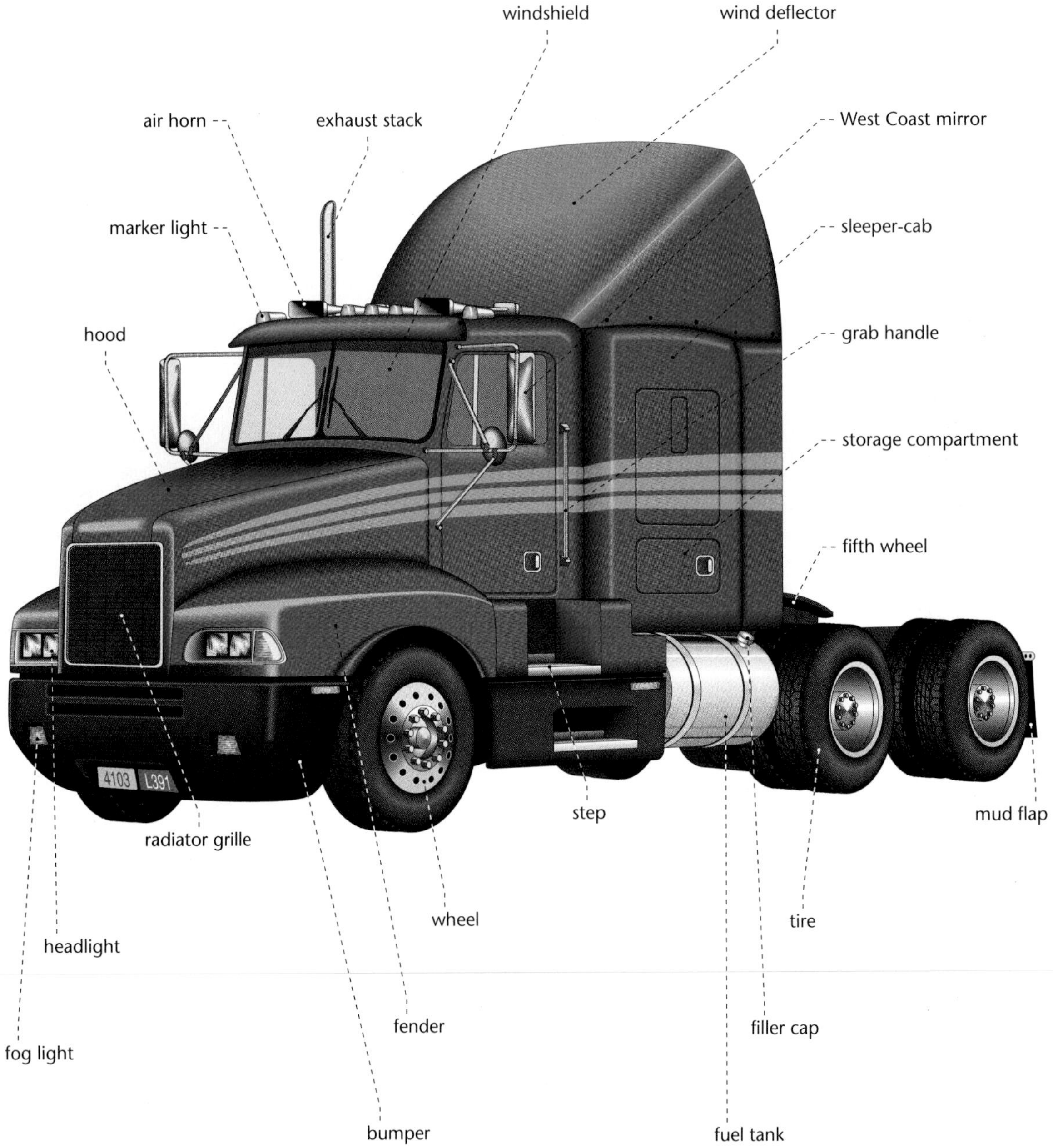

windshield

wind deflector

air horn

exhaust stack

West Coast mirror

marker light

sleeper-cab

hood

grab handle

storage compartment

fifth wheel

radiator grille

step

mud flap

headlight

wheel

tire

fog light

fender

filler cap

bumper

fuel tank

4103 L391

TANDEM TRACTOR TRAILER

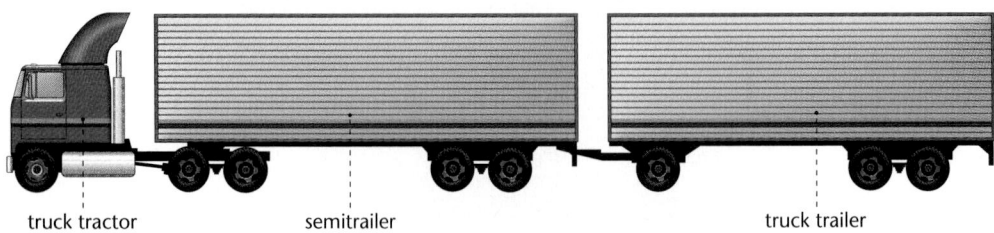

truck tractor

semitrailer

truck trailer

SEMITRAILER

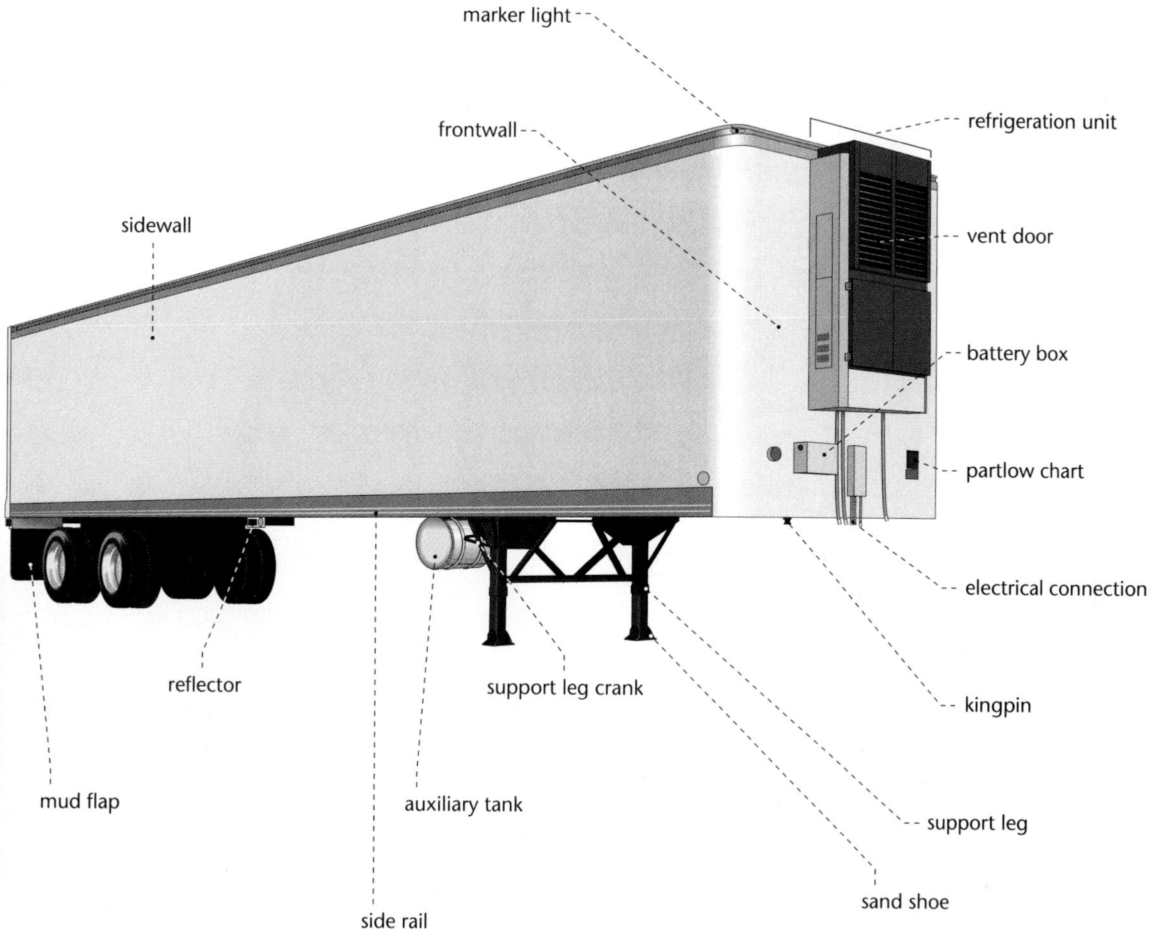

marker light

frontwall

sidewall

refrigeration unit

vent door

battery box

partlow chart

electrical connection

reflector

kingpin

mud flap

auxiliary tank

support leg crank

support leg

side rail

sand shoe

FLATBED

stake pocket

bulkhead

deck

taillight

turn signal

mud flap

bumper

rub rail

support leg crank

marker light

441

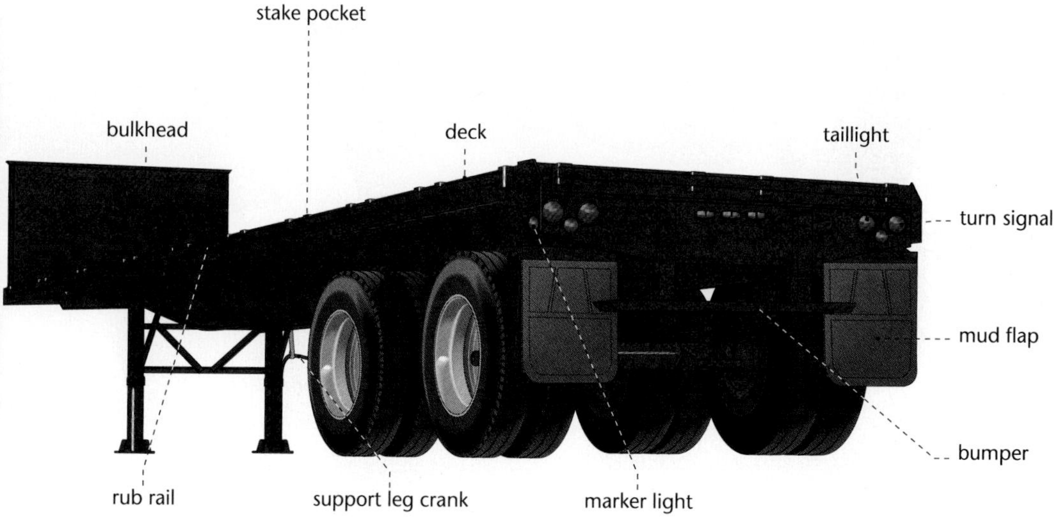

SIDE VIEW

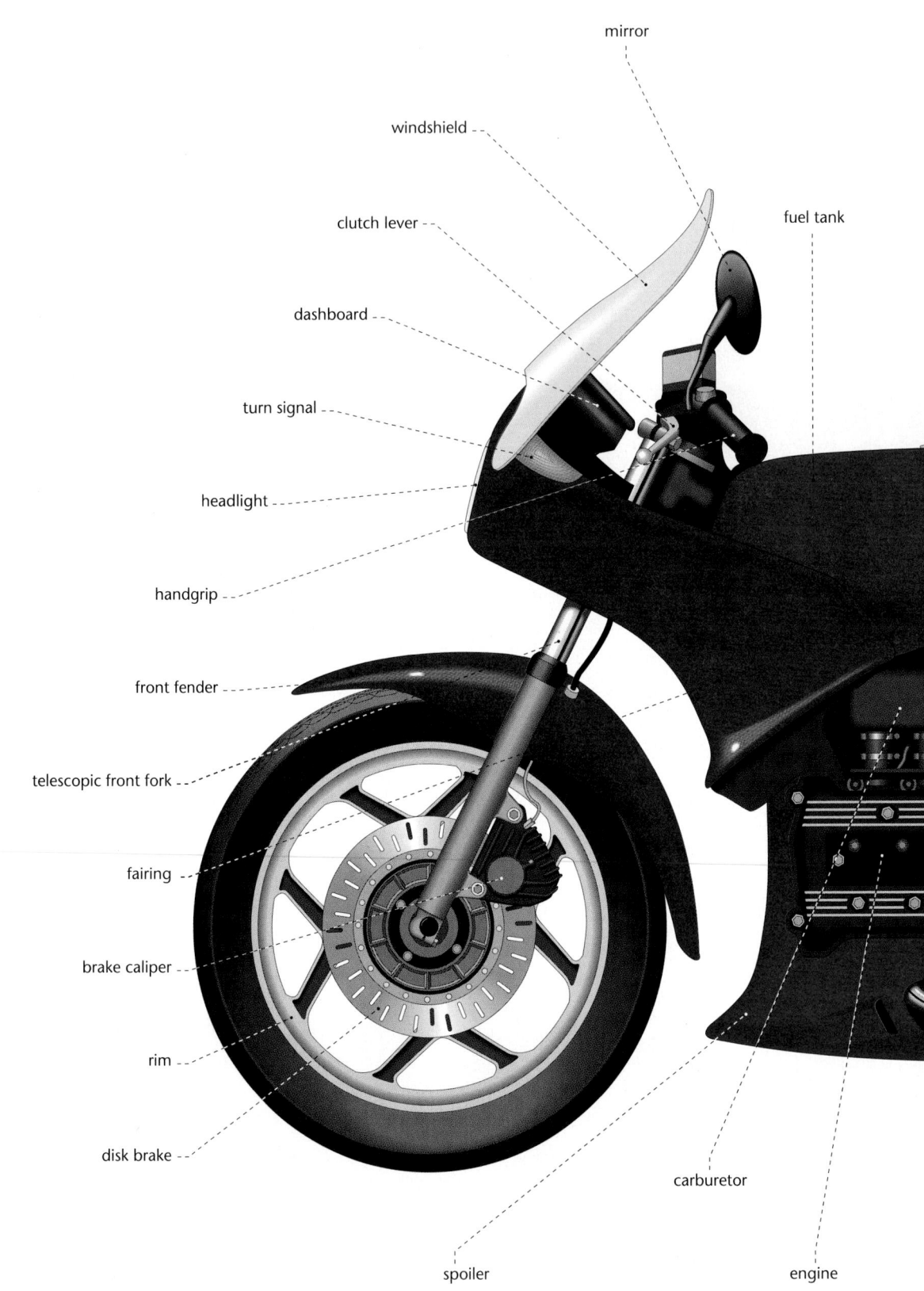

mirror

windshield

clutch lever

fuel tank

dashboard

turn signal

headlight

handgrip

front fender

telescopic front fork

fairing

brake caliper

rim

disk brake

carburetor

spoiler

engine

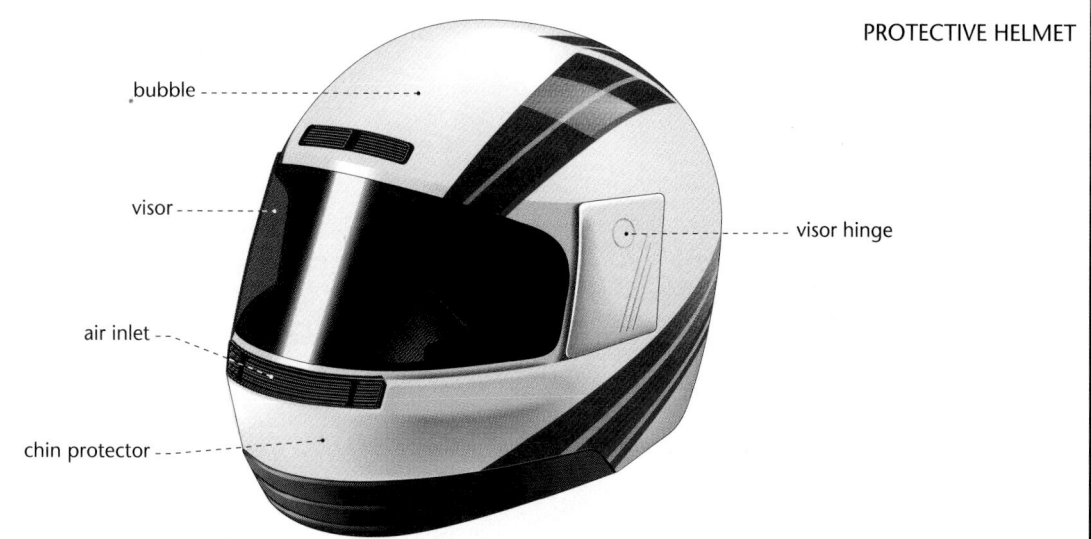

PROTECTIVE HELMET

bubble
visor
visor hinge
air inlet
chin protector

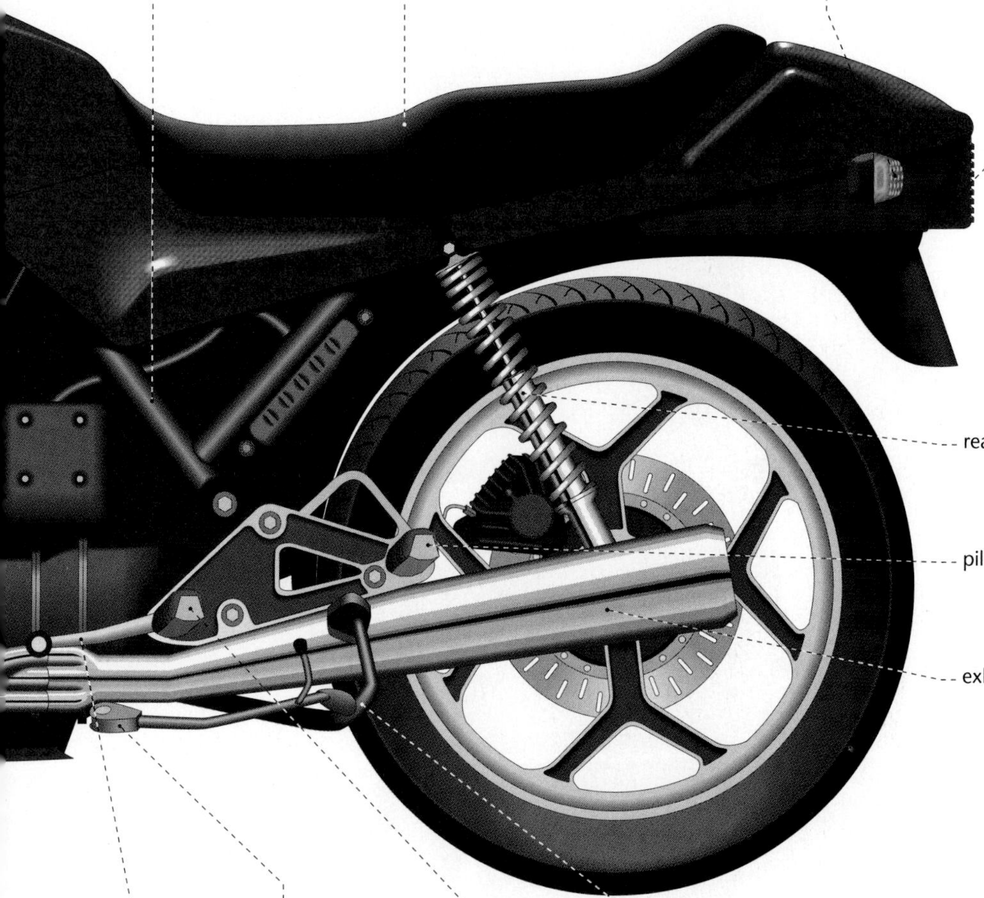
frame
dual seat
turn signal
taillight
rear shock absorber
pillion footrest
exhaust pipe
kickstand
main stand
gearshift lever
front footrest

VIEW FROM ABOVE

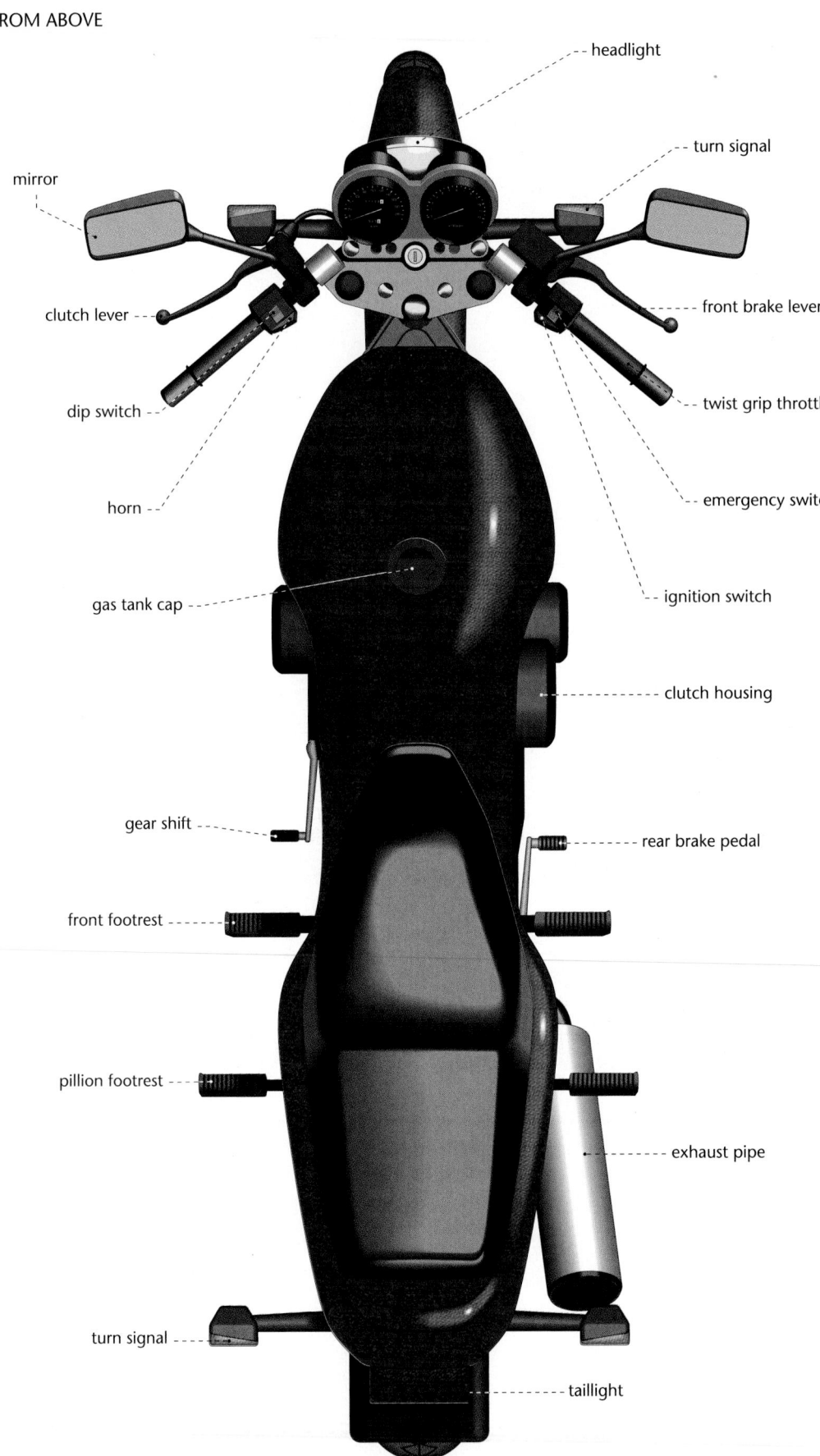

headlight

turn signal

mirror

clutch lever

front brake lever

dip switch

twist grip throttle

horn

emergency switch

gas tank cap

ignition switch

clutch housing

gear shift

rear brake pedal

front footrest

pillion footrest

exhaust pipe

turn signal

taillight

MOTORCYCLE DASHBOARD

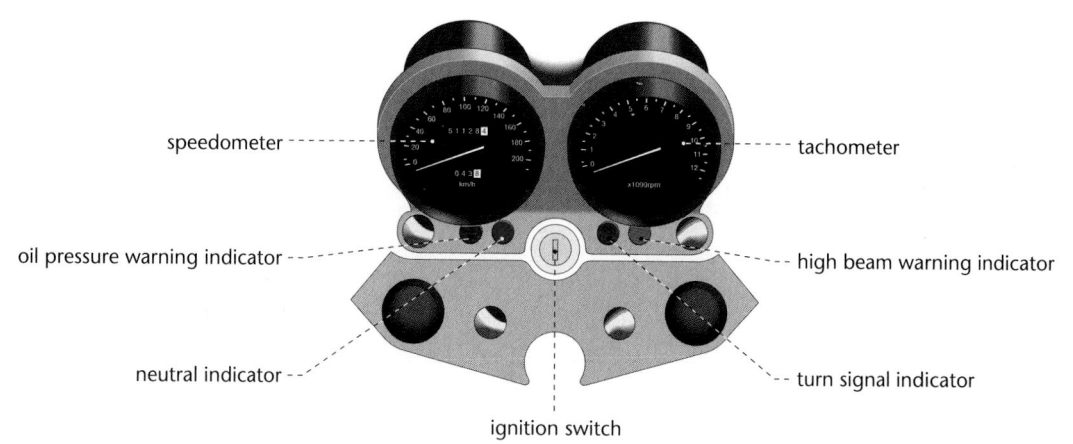

speedometer

tachometer

oil pressure warning indicator

high beam warning indicator

neutral indicator

turn signal indicator

ignition switch

SNOWMOBILE

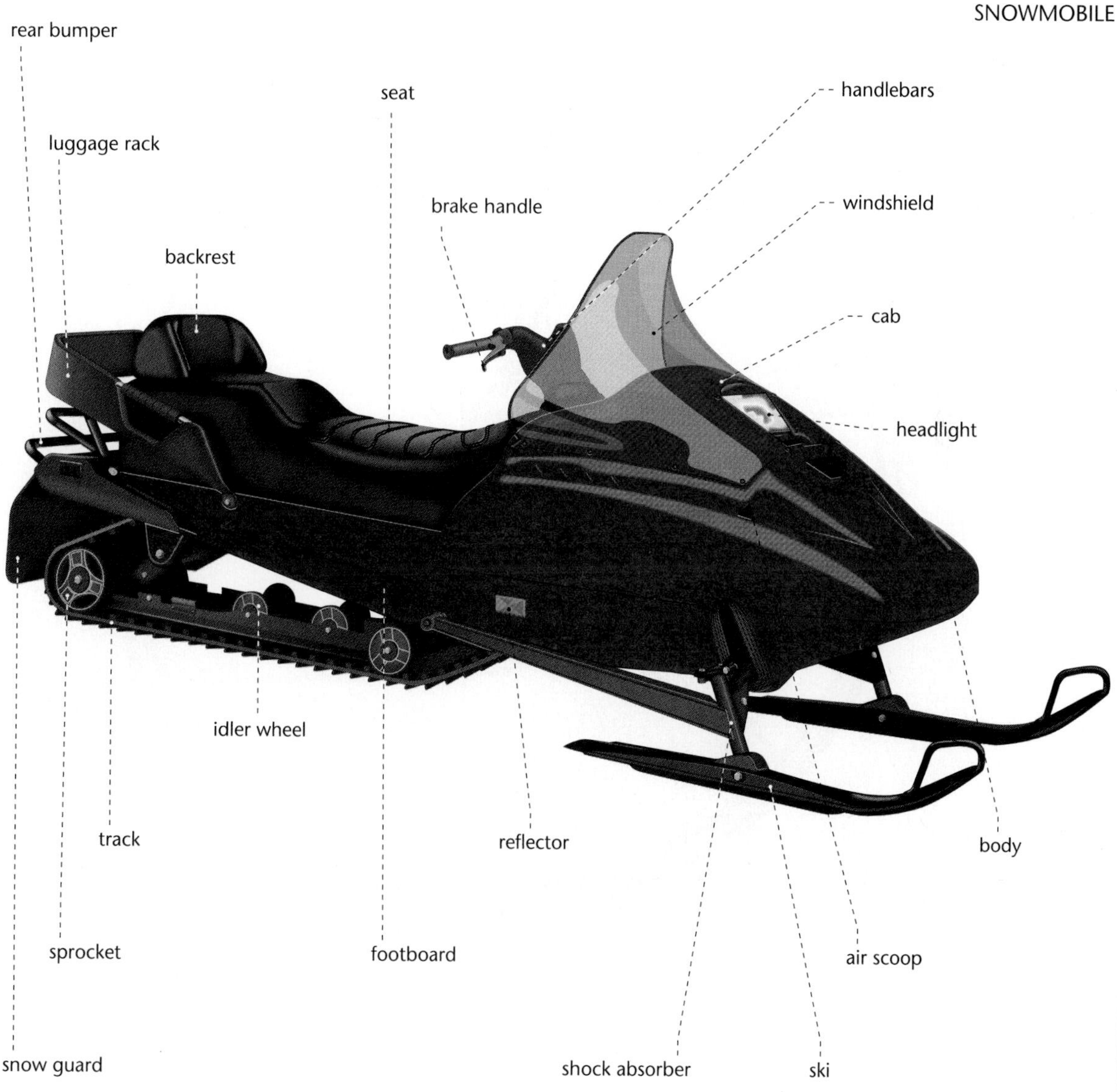

rear bumper

seat

handlebars

luggage rack

brake handle

windshield

backrest

cab

headlight

idler wheel

track

reflector

body

sprocket

footboard

air scoop

snow guard

shock absorber

ski

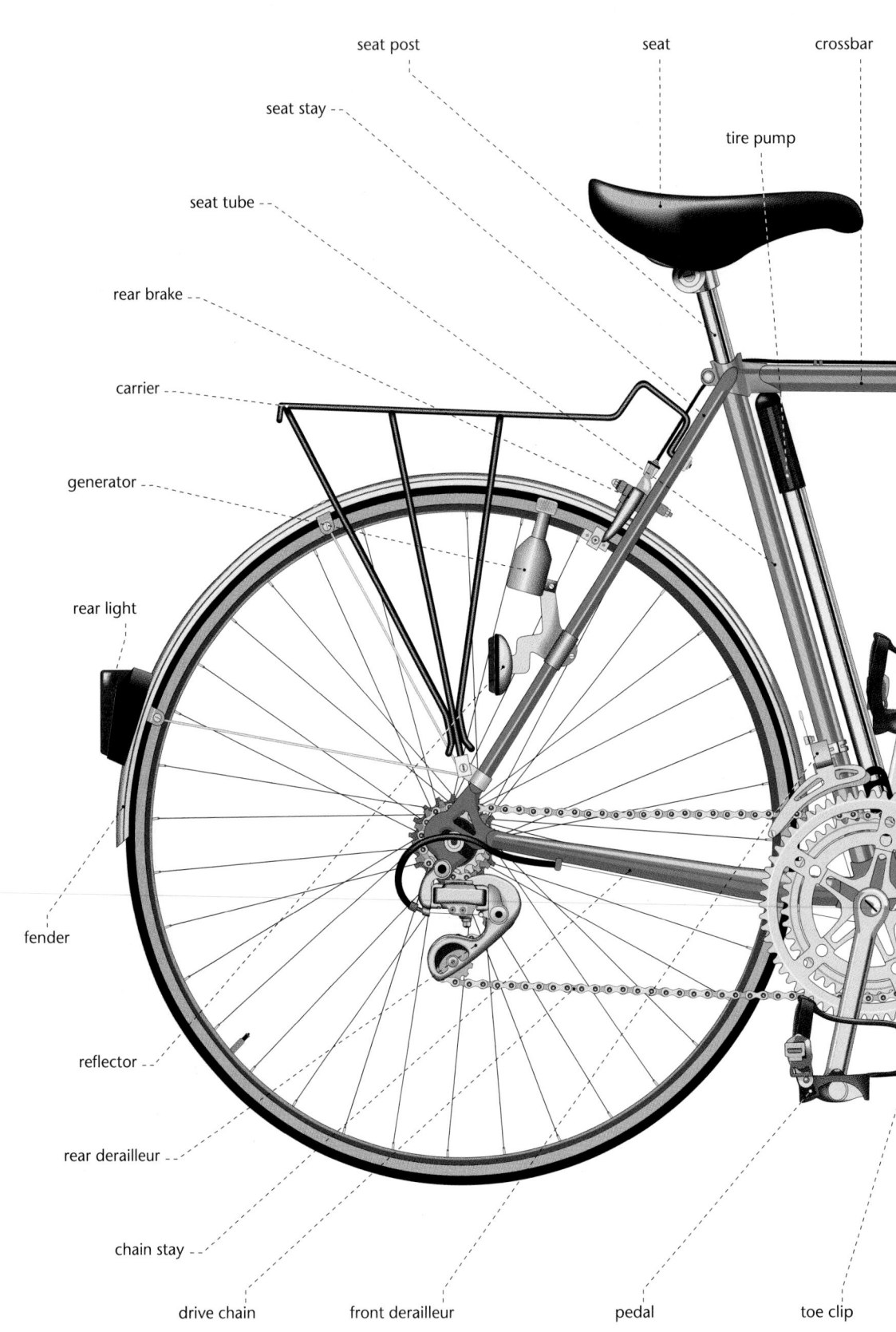

seat post

seat

crossbar

seat stay

tire pump

seat tube

rear brake

carrier

generator

rear light

fender

reflector

rear derailleur

chain stay

drive chain

front derailleur

pedal

toe clip

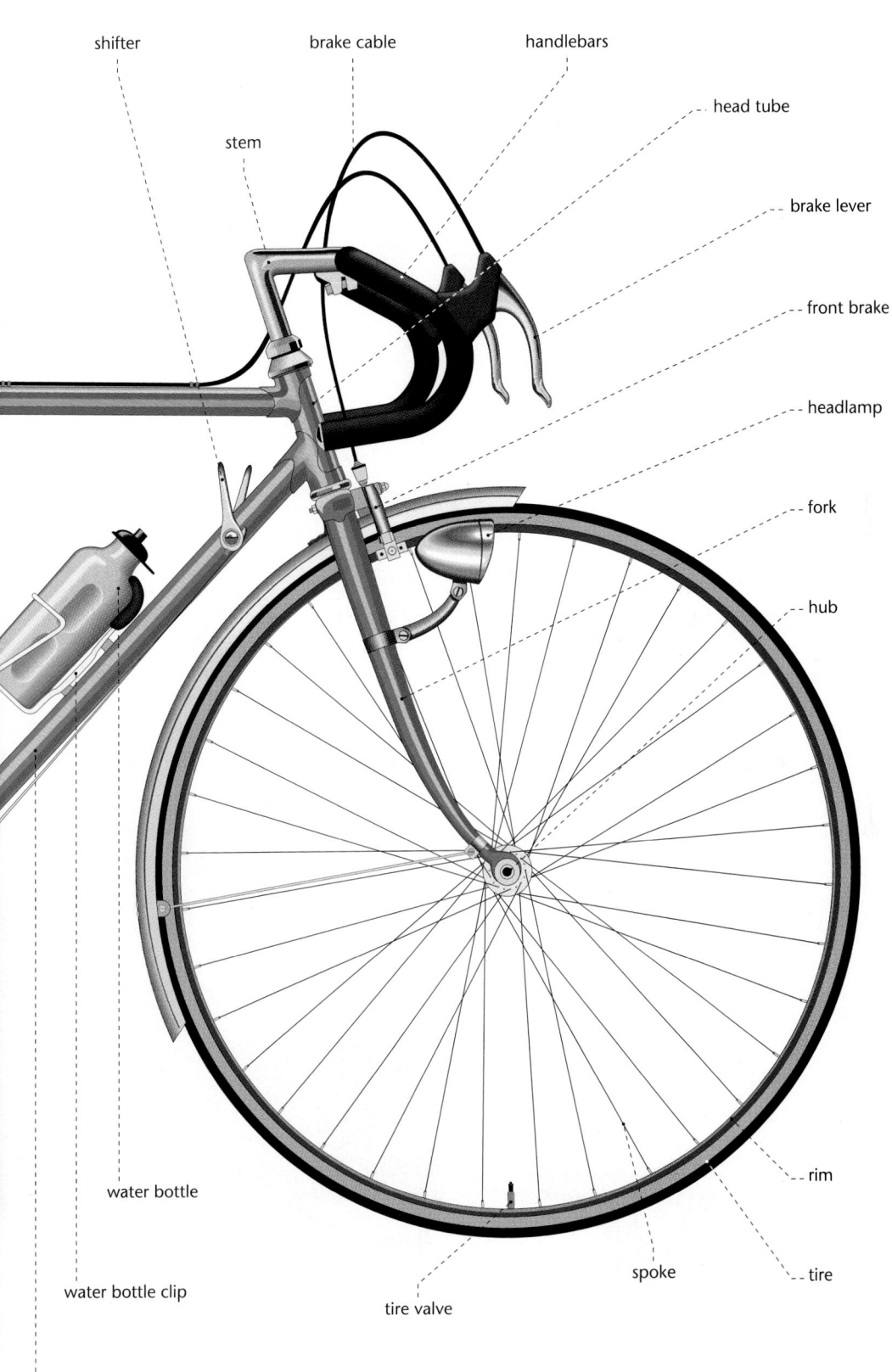

shifter

stem

brake cable

handlebars

head tube

brake lever

front brake

headlamp

fork

hub

water bottle

water bottle clip

down tube

tire valve

spoke

rim

tire

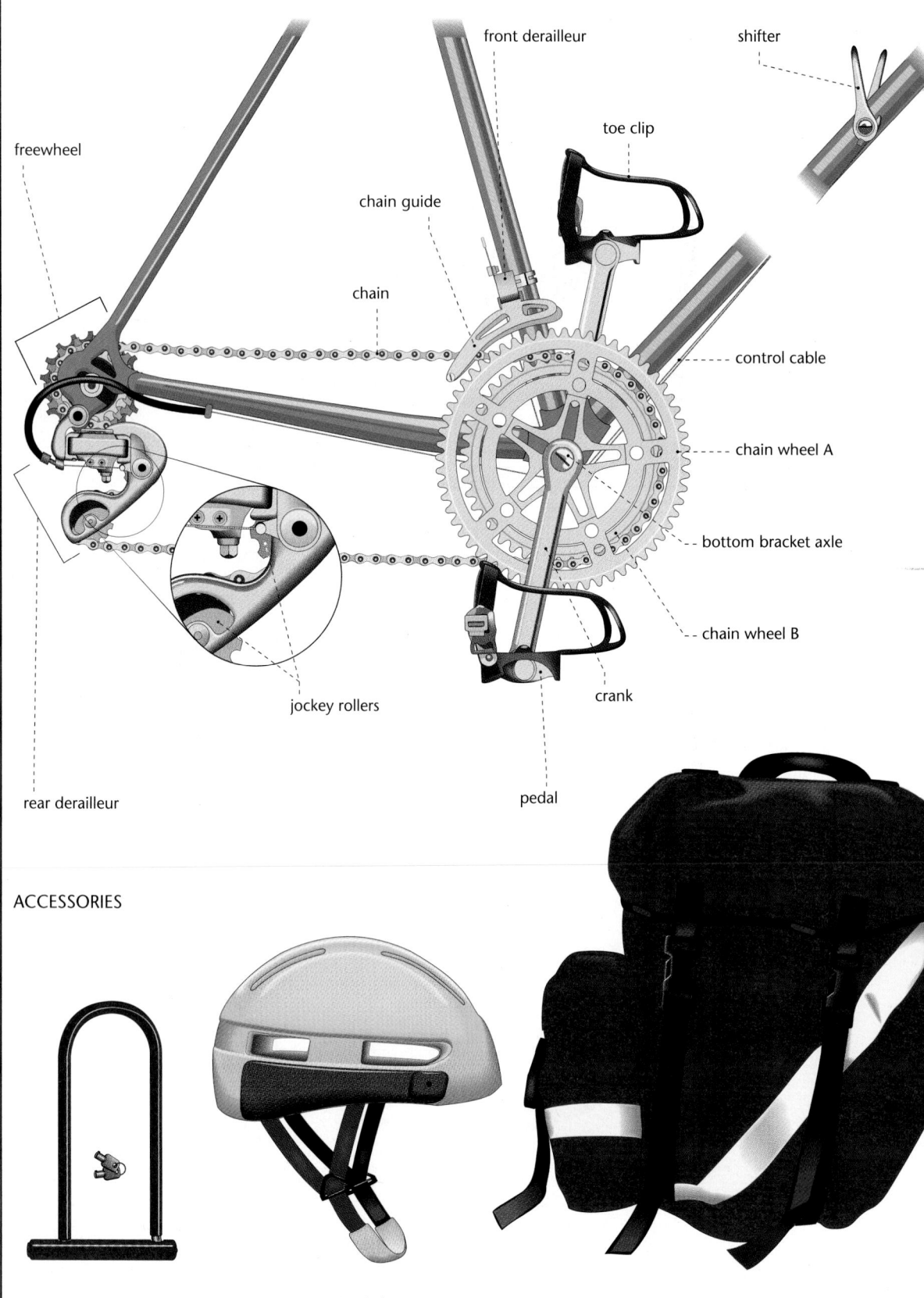

POWER TRAIN

ROAD TRANSPORT

front derailleur

shifter

toe clip

freewheel

chain guide

chain

control cable

chain wheel A

bottom bracket axle

chain wheel B

jockey rollers

crank

rear derailleur

pedal

ACCESSORIES

lock

protective helmet

bicycle bag

CARAVAN

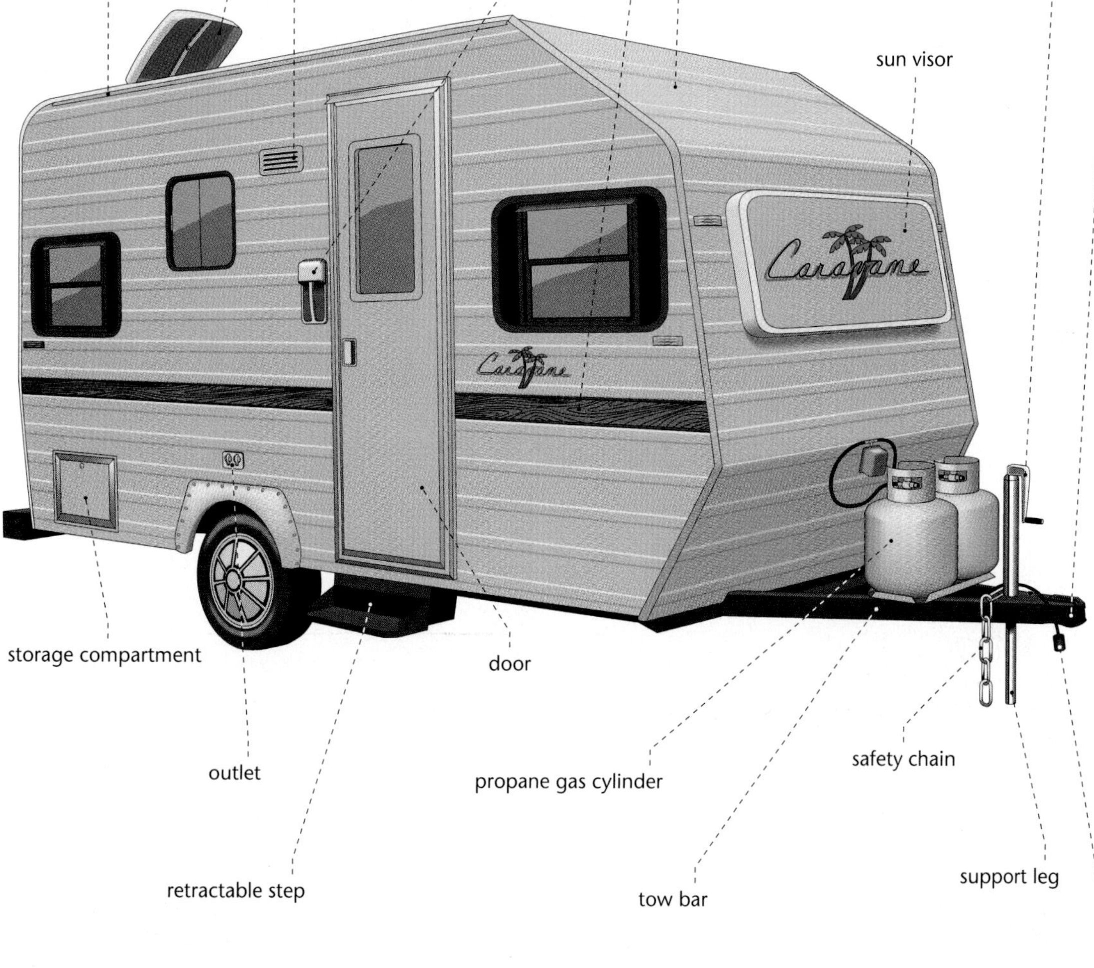

side vent

body

roof vent

body guard molding

towing hitch

awning channel

grab handle

hydraulic jack

sun visor

Caravane

Caravane

storage compartment

door

safety chain

outlet

propane gas cylinder

support leg

retractable step

tow bar

lighting cable

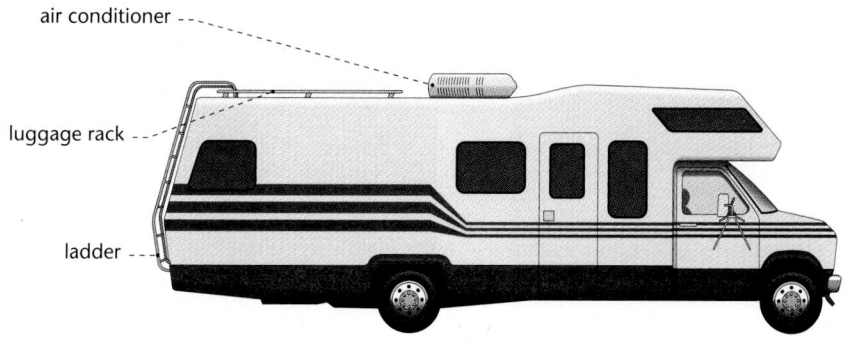

air conditioner

MOTOR HOME

luggage rack

ladder

CROSS SECTION OF A ROAD

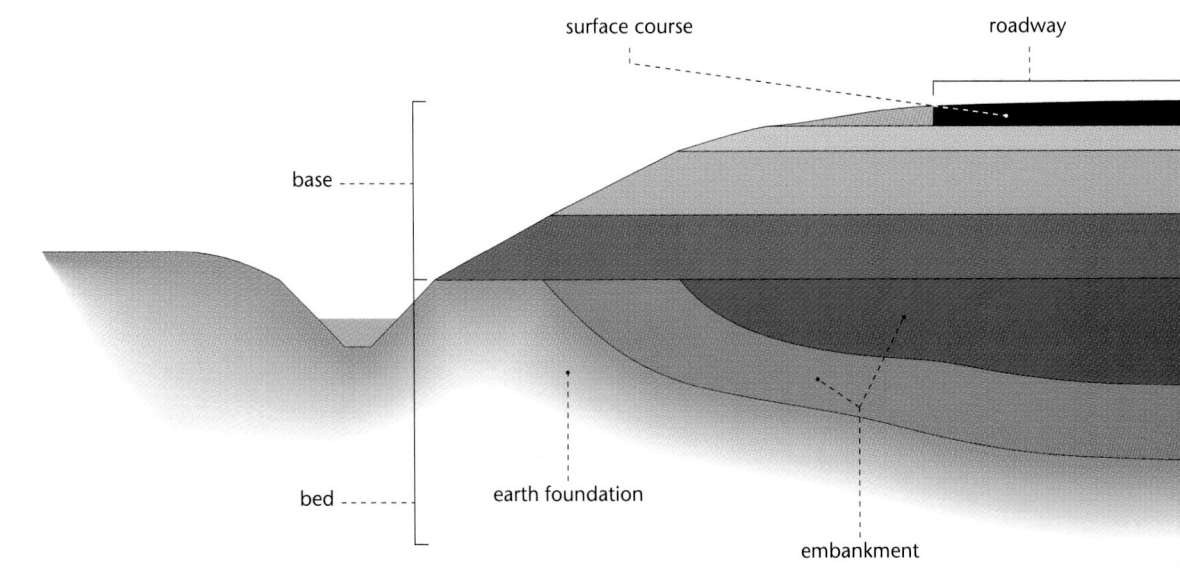

surface course

roadway

base

bed

earth foundation

embankment

MAJOR TYPES OF INTERCHANGES

cloverleaf

traffic circle

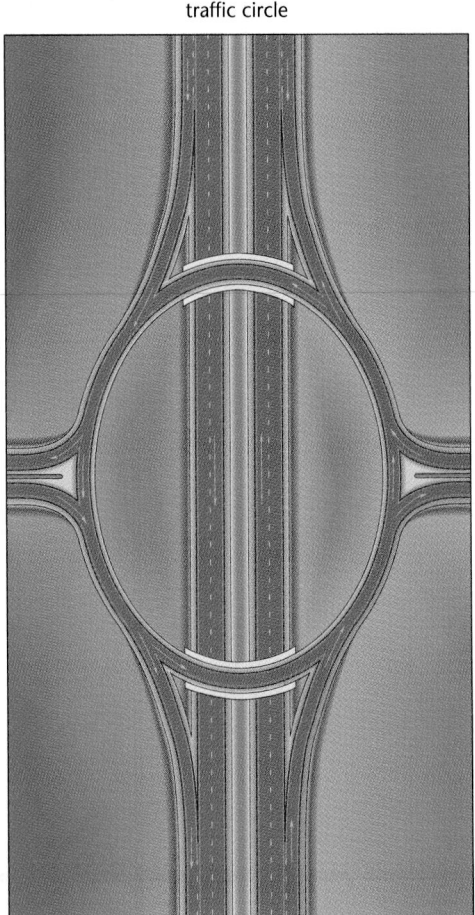

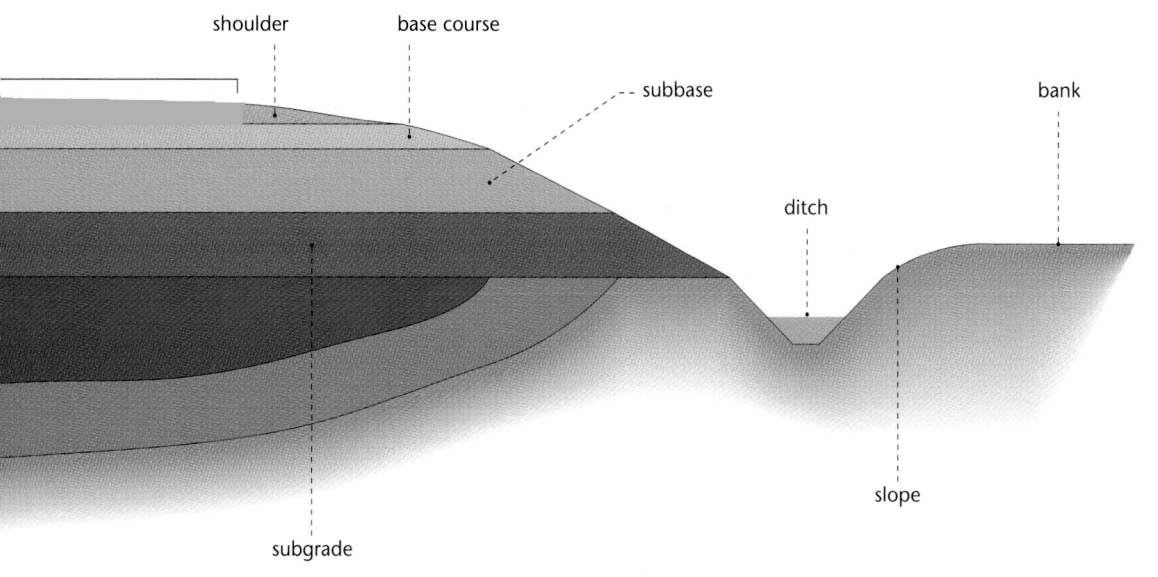

shoulder   base course   subbase   bank

ditch

slope

subgrade

diamond interchange

trumpet interchange

CLOVERLEAF

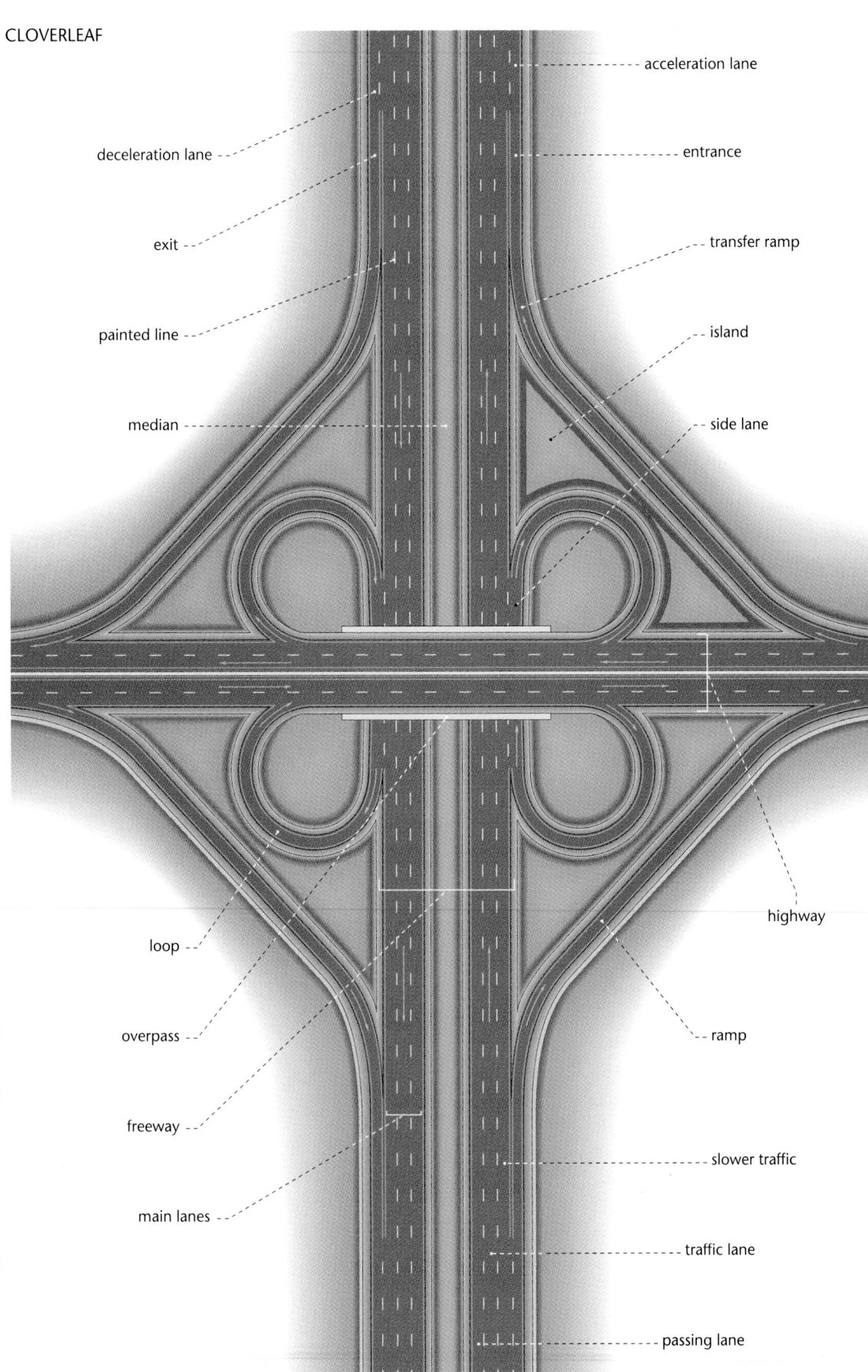

acceleration lane

deceleration lane

exit

entrance

transfer ramp

painted line

island

median

side lane

loop

highway

overpass

ramp

freeway

main lanes

slower traffic

traffic lane

passing lane

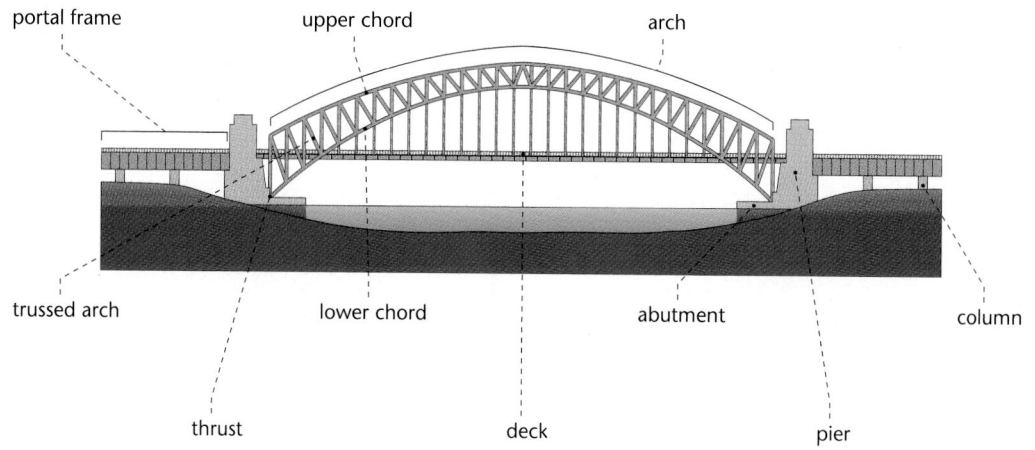

portal frame

upper chord

arch

trussed arch

lower chord

abutment

column

thrust

deck

pier

TYPES OF ARCH BRIDGES

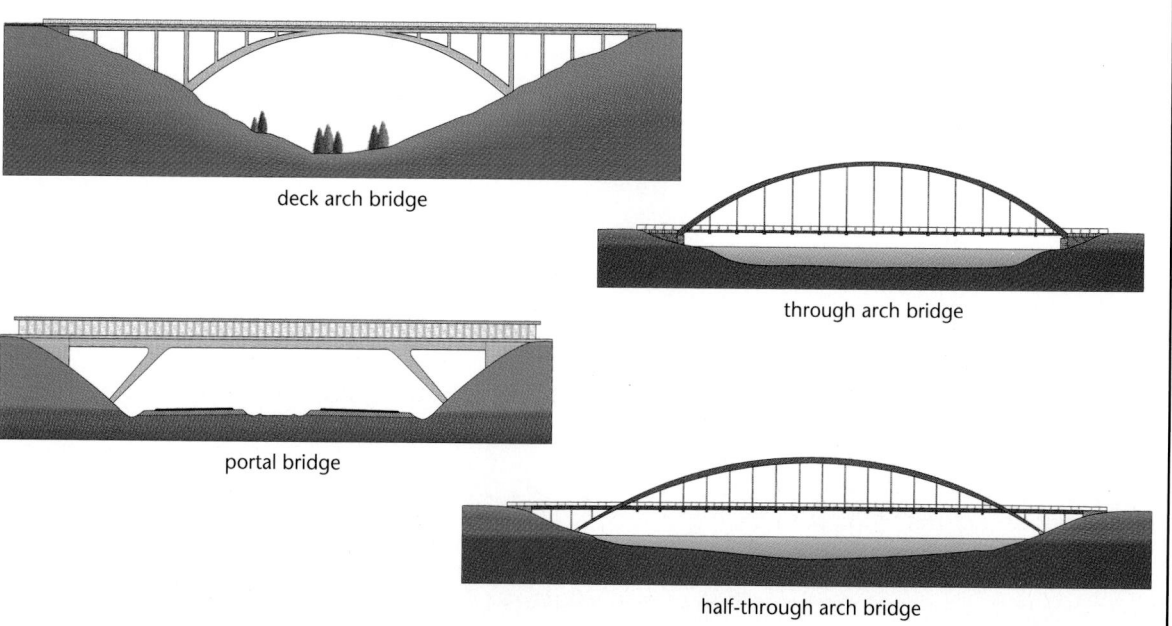

deck arch bridge

through arch bridge

portal bridge

half-through arch bridge

TYPES OF ARCHES

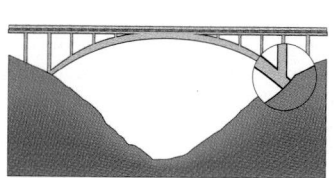

fixed arch

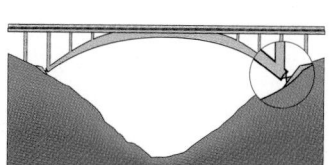

two-hinged arch

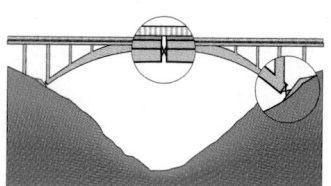

three-hinged arch

FIXED BRIDGES

SUSPENSION BRIDGE

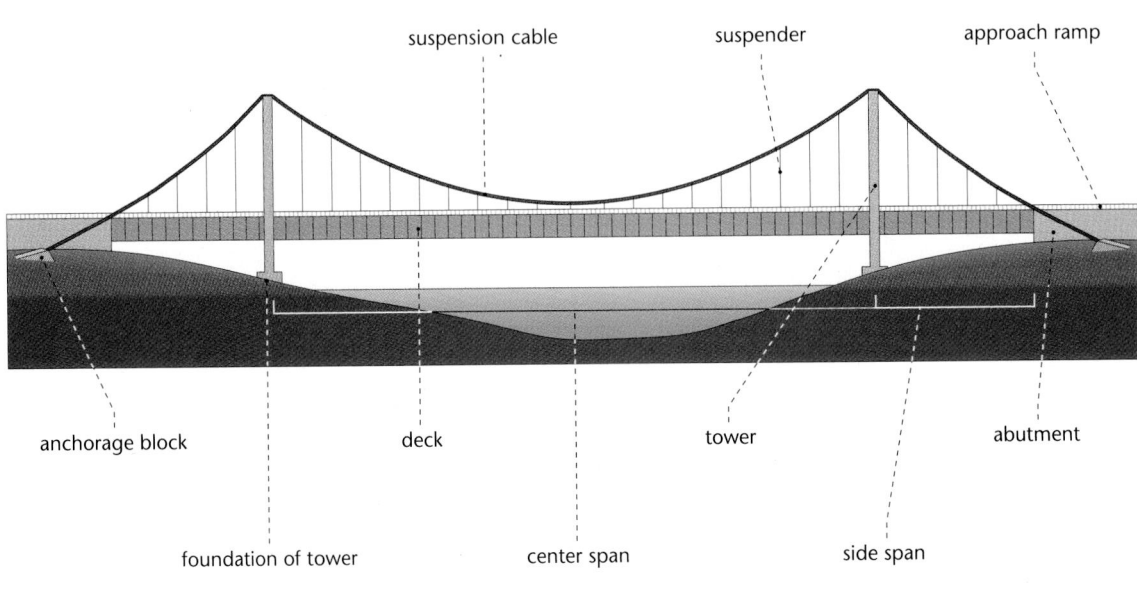

suspension cable

suspender

approach ramp

anchorage block

deck

tower

abutment

foundation of tower

center span

side span

CABLE-STAYED BRIDGES

fan cable stays

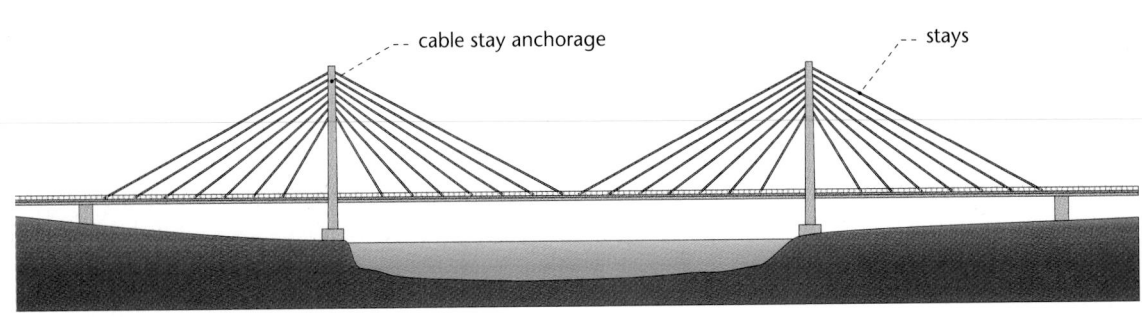

cable stay anchorage

stays

harp cable stays

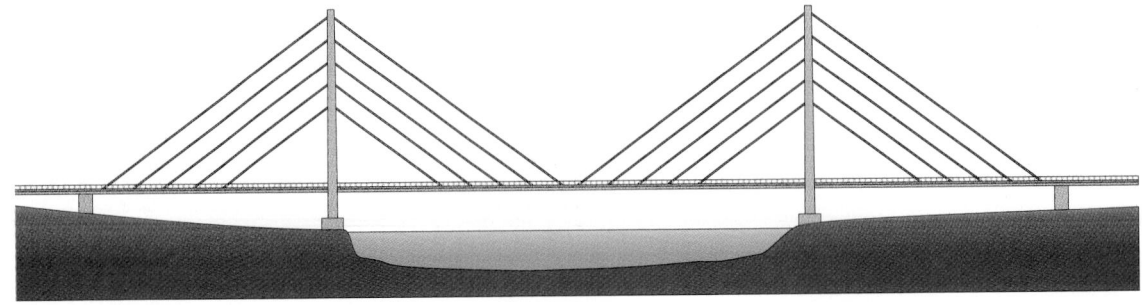

MOVABLE BRIDGES

turntable

SWING BRIDGE

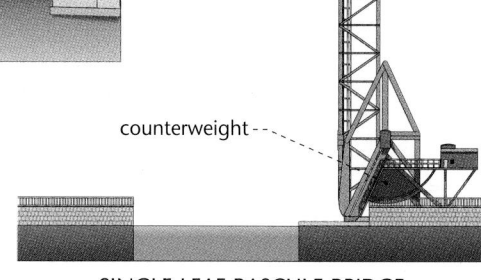

counterweight

SINGLE-LEAF BASCULE BRIDGE

FLOATING BRIDGE

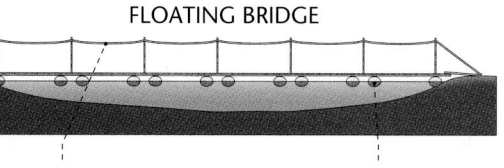

manrope   pontoon

Bailey bridge

double-leaf bascule bridge

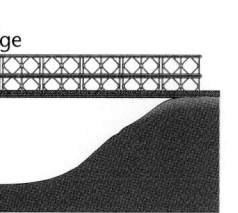

LIFT BRIDGE

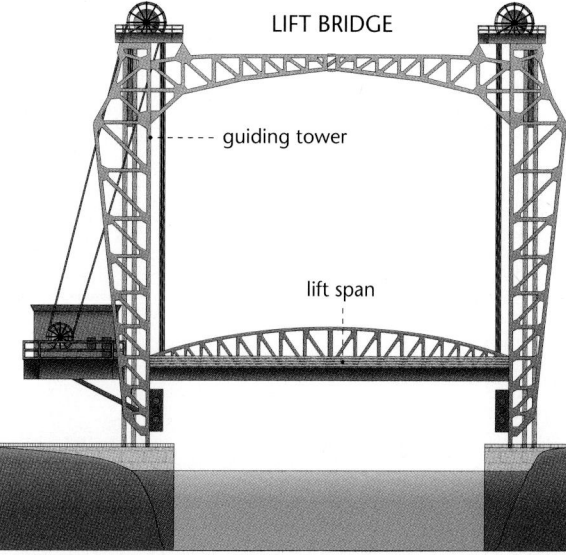

guiding tower

lift span

TRANSPORTER BRIDGE

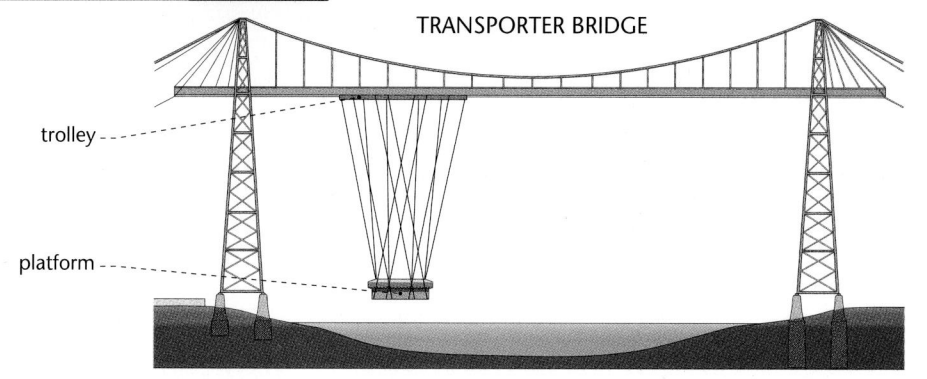

trolley

platform

HIGH-SPEED TRAIN

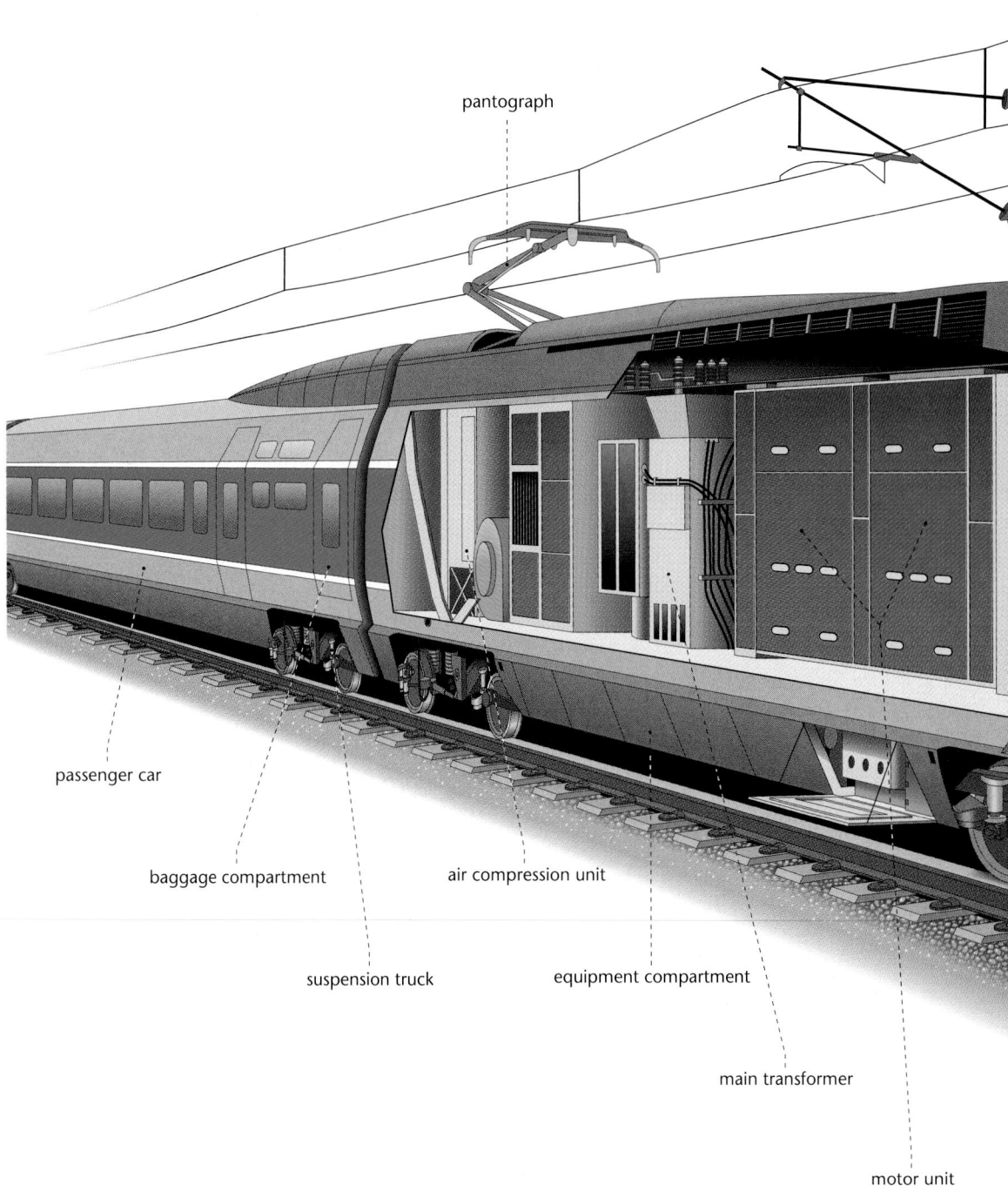

pantograph

passenger car

baggage compartment

air compression unit

suspension truck

equipment compartment

main transformer

motor unit

catenary

headlight

driver's cab

power car

headlight

position light

motor truck

pilot

coupling guide device

TYPES OF PASSENGER CARS

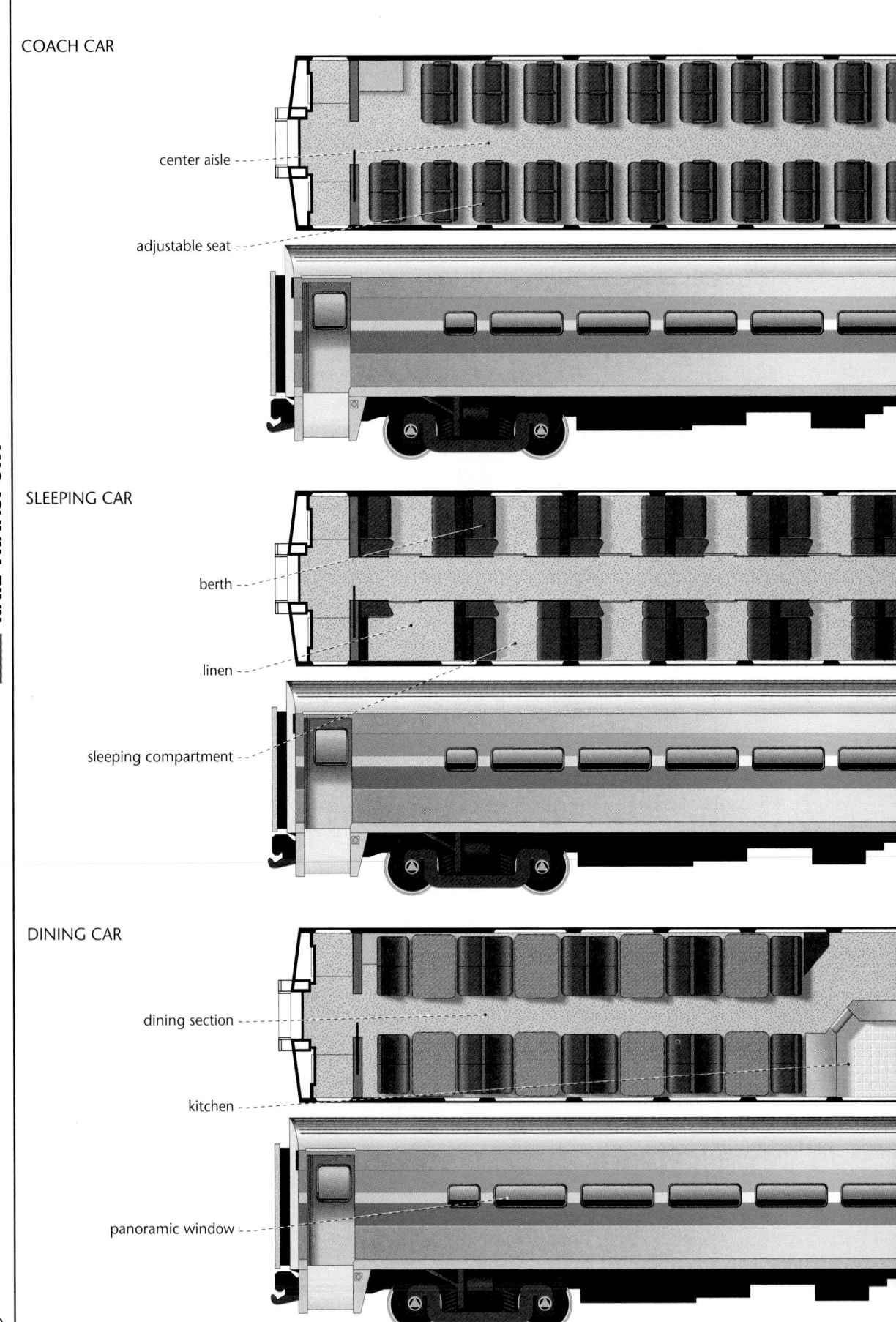

COACH CAR

center aisle

adjustable seat

SLEEPING CAR

berth

linen

sleeping compartment

DINING CAR

dining section

kitchen

panoramic window

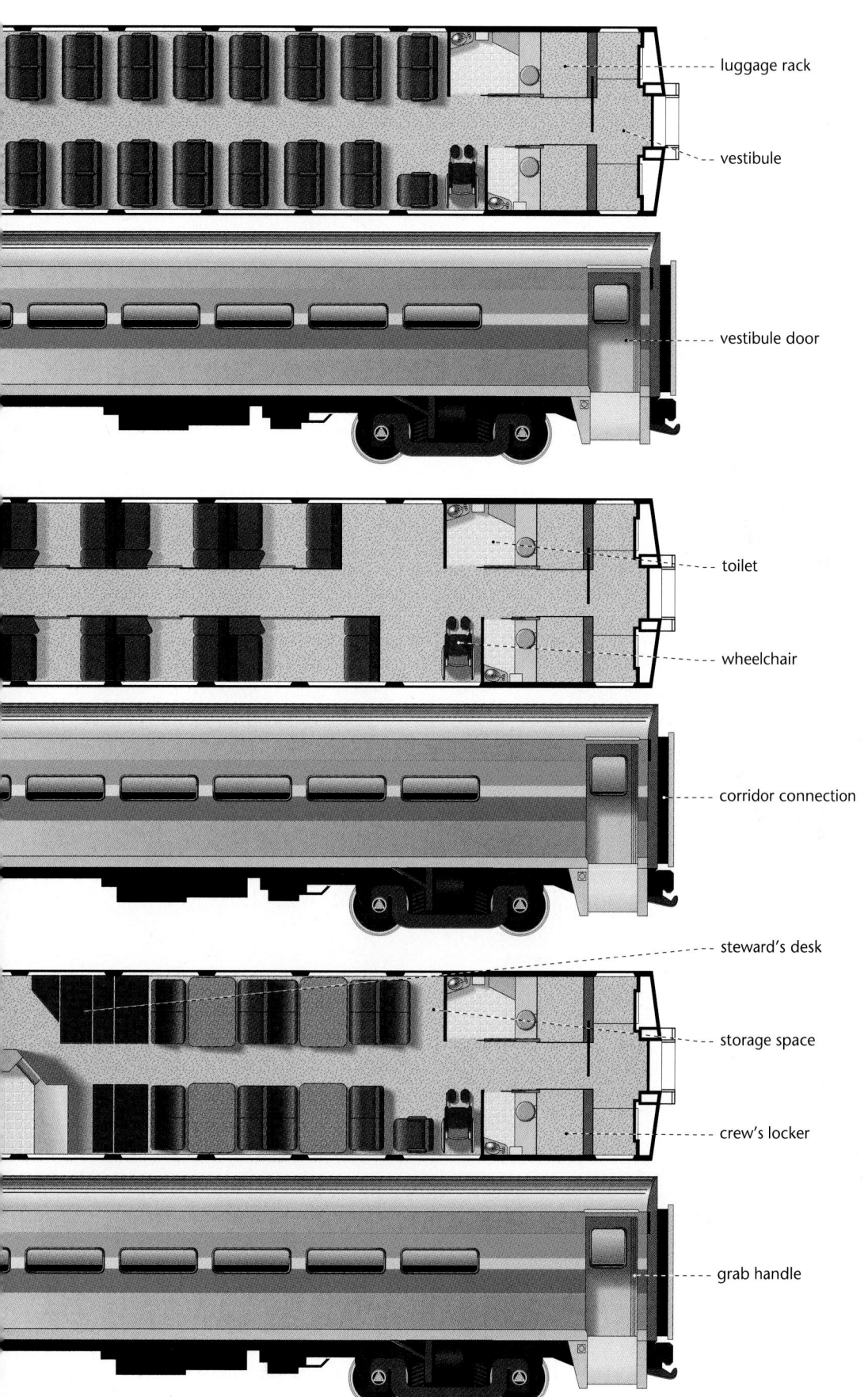

luggage rack

vestibule

vestibule door

toilet

wheelchair

corridor connection

steward's desk

storage space

crew's locker

grab handle

office

glassed roof

indicator board

parcels office

baggage room

passenger train

platform edge

passenger platform

gate

booking hall

platform number

metal structure

baggage cart

departure time indicator

ticket collector

baggage lockers

destination

platform entrance

track

schedules

ticket control

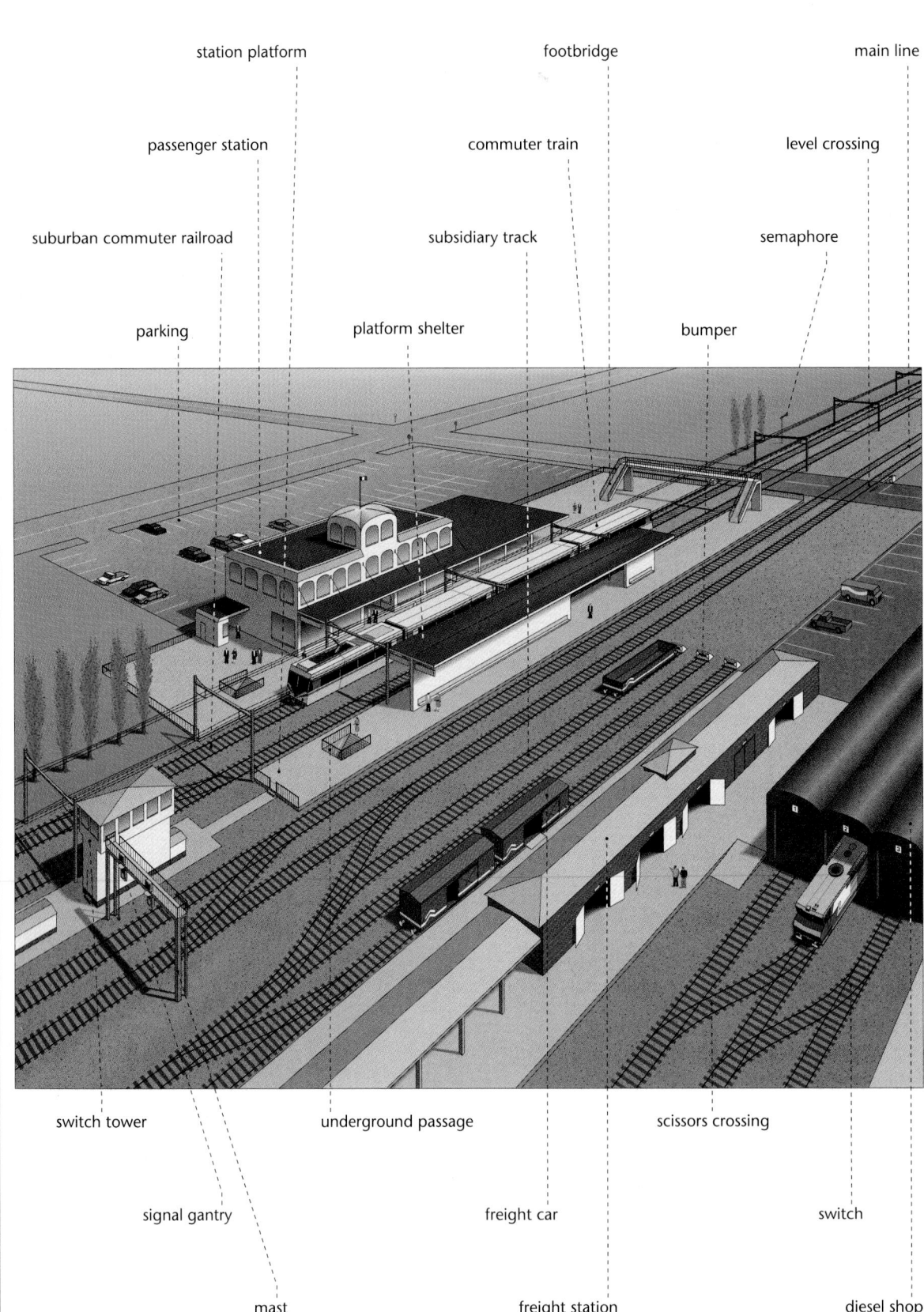

station platform

footbridge

main line

passenger station

commuter train

level crossing

suburban commuter railroad

subsidiary track

semaphore

parking

platform shelter

bumper

switch tower

underground passage

scissors crossing

signal gantry

freight car

switch

mast

freight station

diesel shop

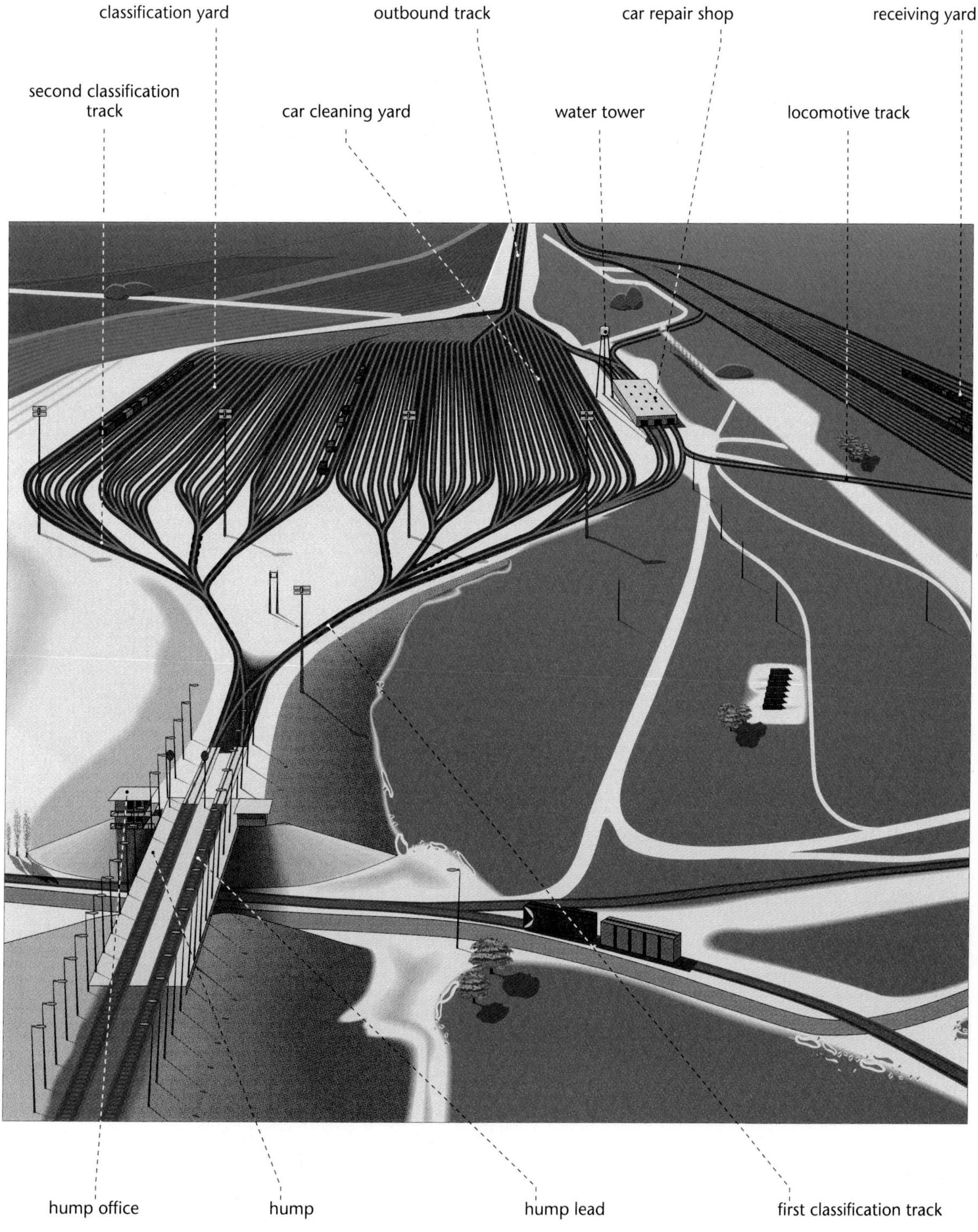

RAIL TRANSPORT

classification yard

outbound track

car repair shop

receiving yard

second classification track

car cleaning yard

water tower

locomotive track

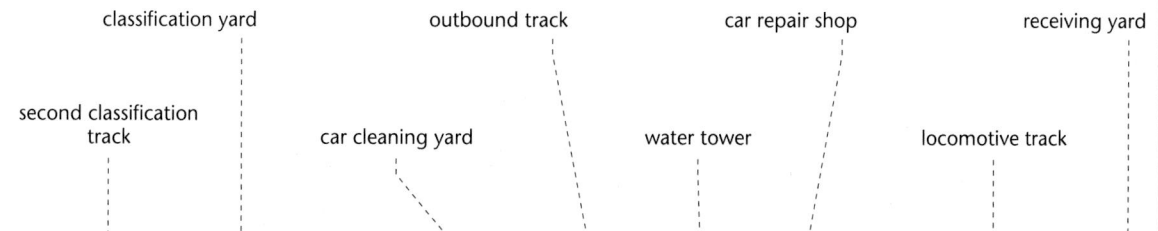

hump office

hump

hump lead

first classification track

RAILROAD TRACK

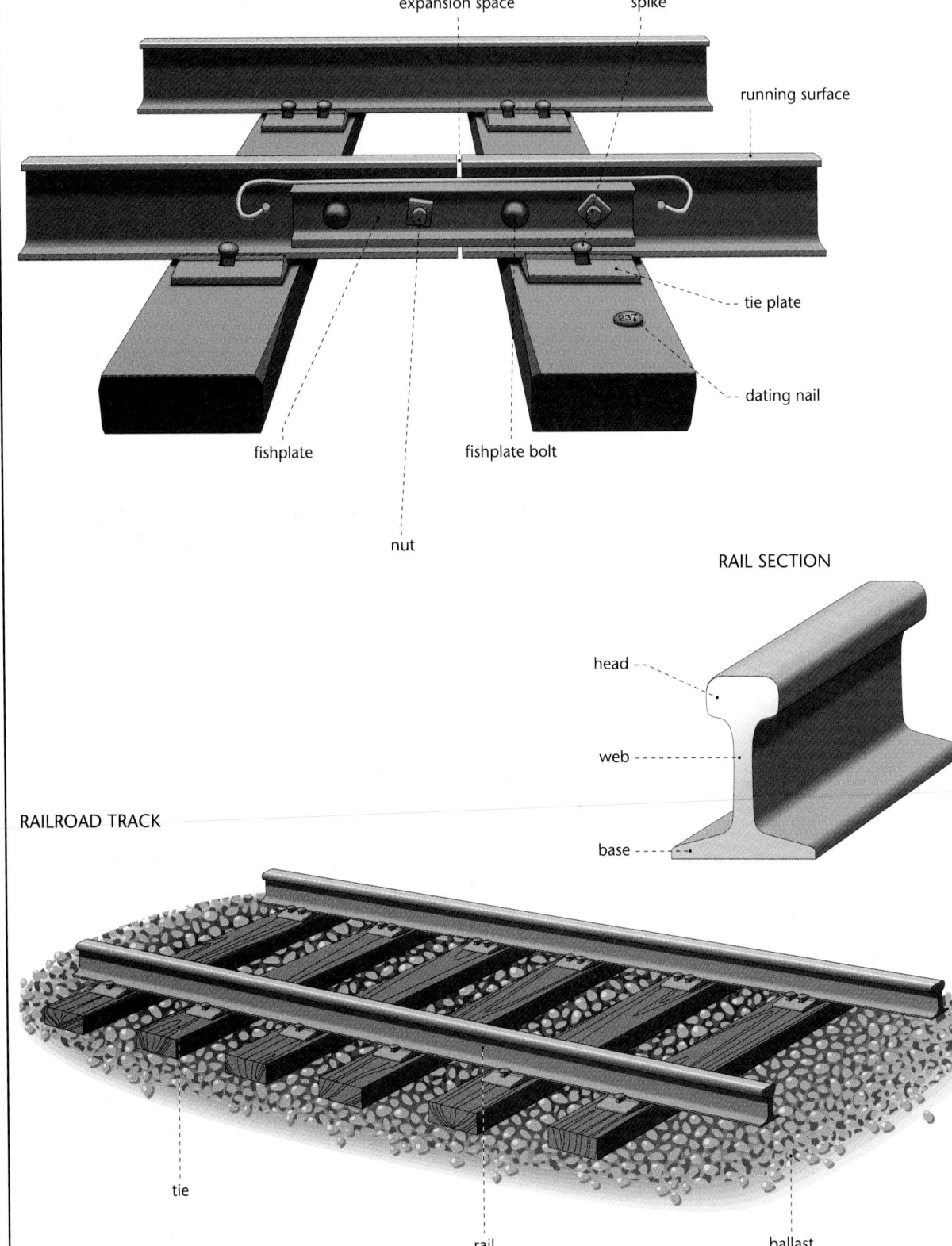

RAIL JOINT

expansion space

spike

running surface

tie plate

dating nail

fishplate

fishplate bolt

nut

RAIL SECTION

head

web

base

RAILROAD TRACK

tie

rail

ballast

466

REMOTE-CONTROLLED SWITCH

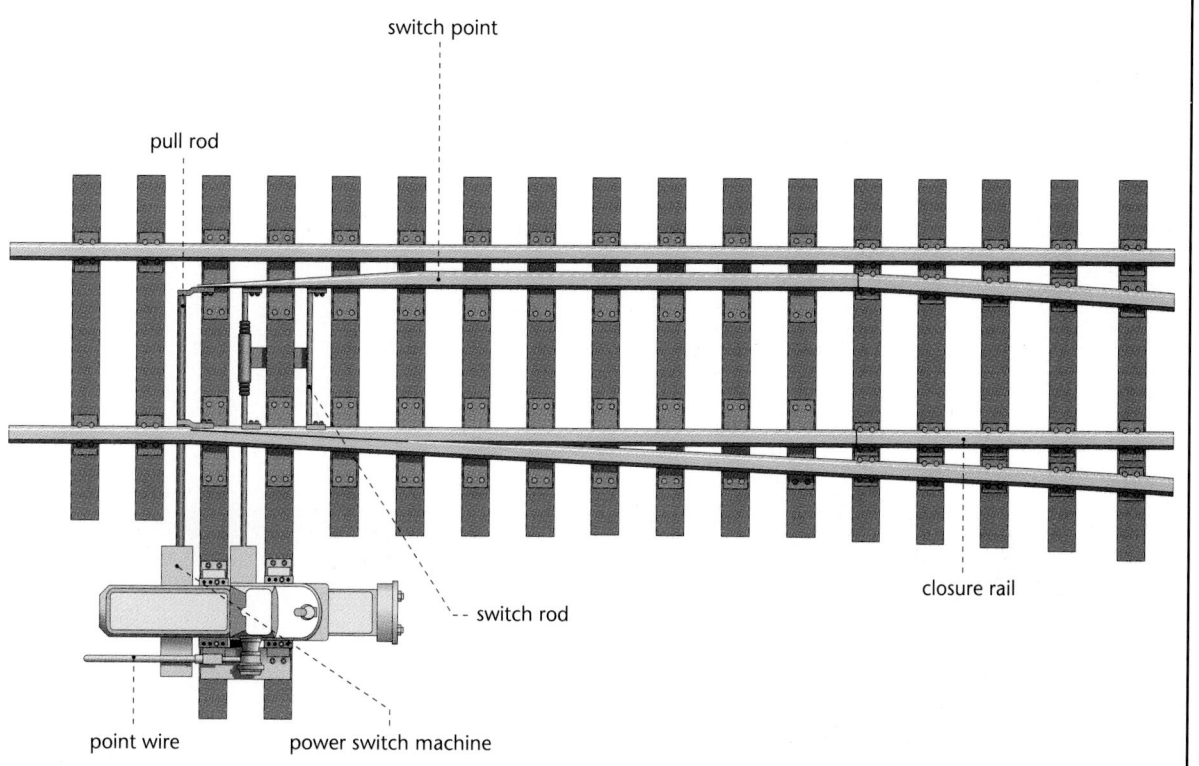

switch point
pull rod
closure rail
switch rod
point wire
power switch machine

MANUALLY-OPERATED SWITCH

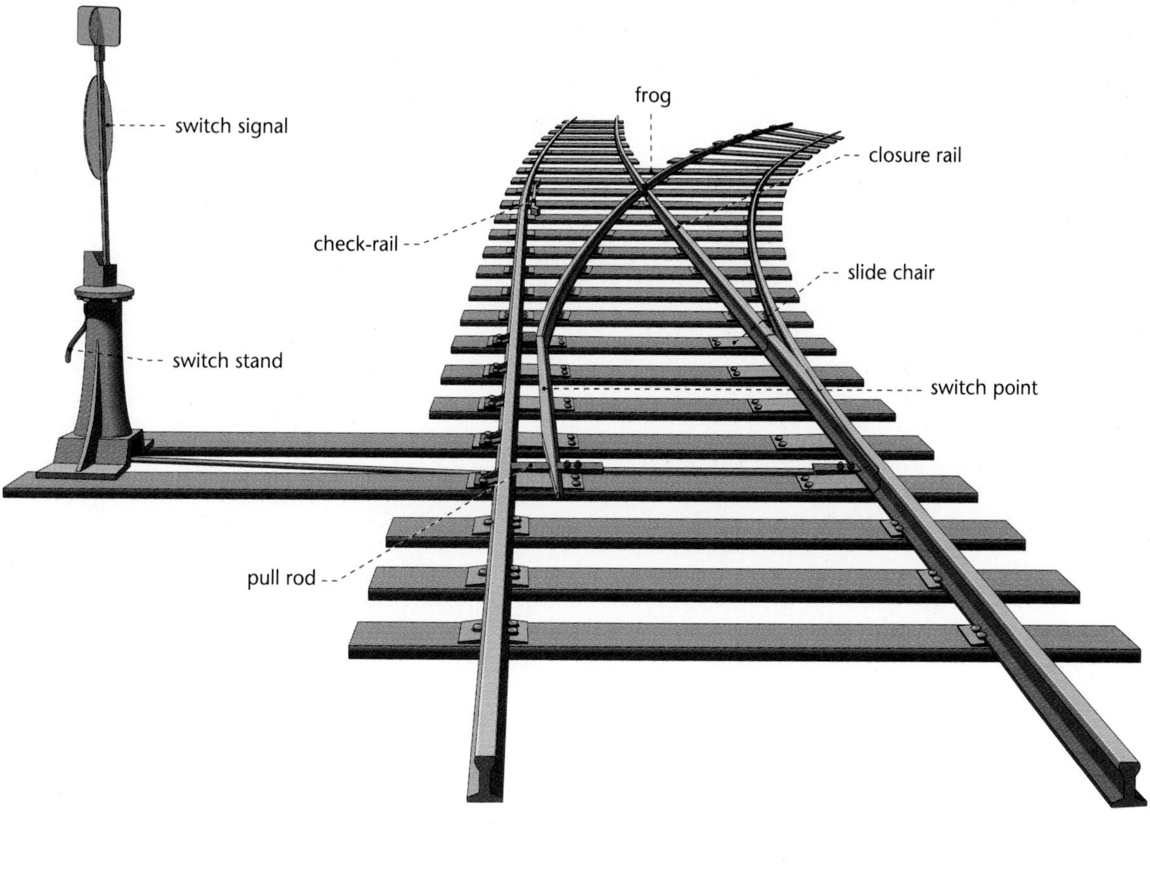

frog
switch signal
closure rail
check-rail
slide chair
switch stand
switch point
pull rod

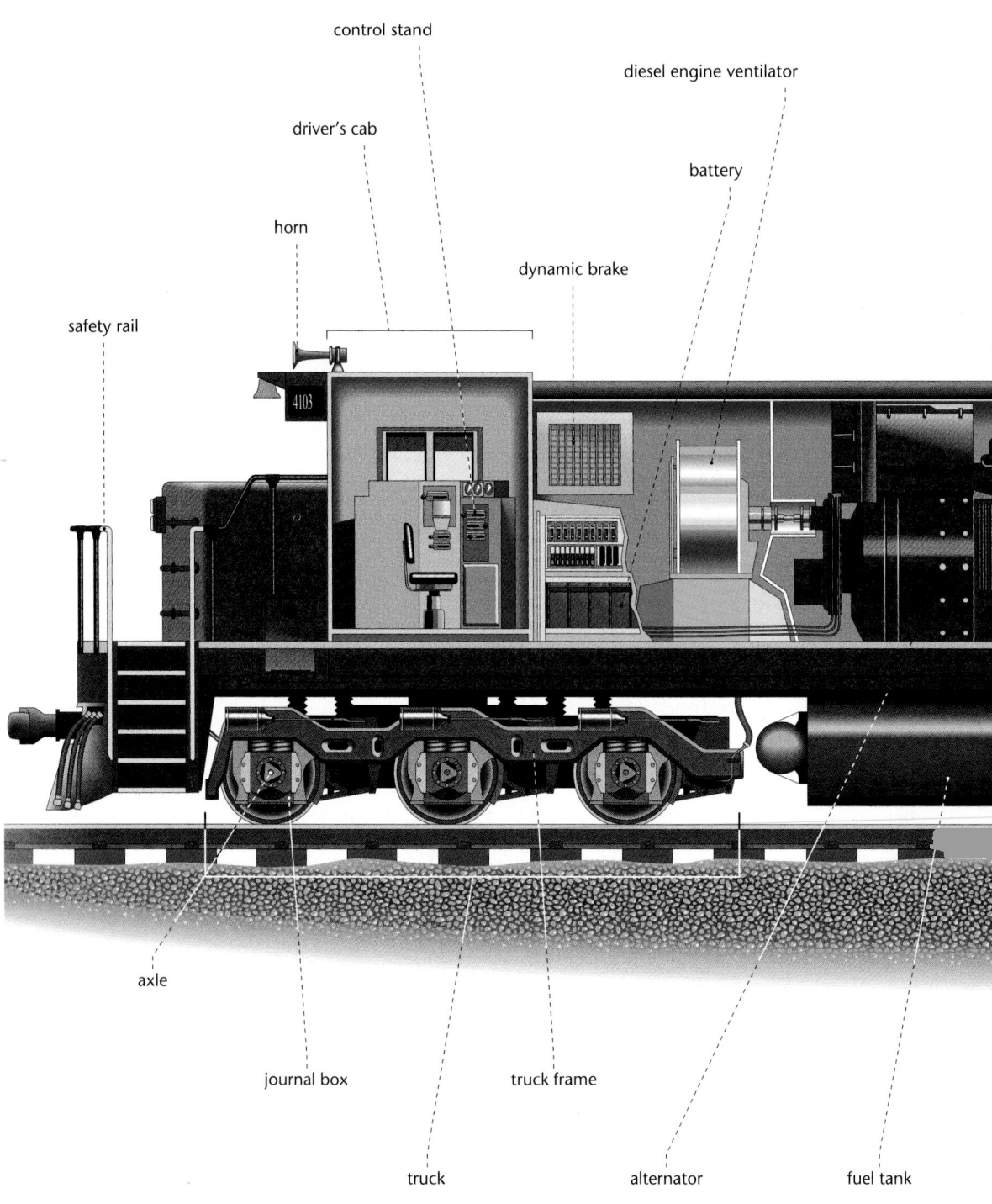

control stand

diesel engine ventilator

driver's cab

battery

horn

dynamic brake

safety rail

4103

axle

journal box

truck frame

truck

alternator

fuel tank

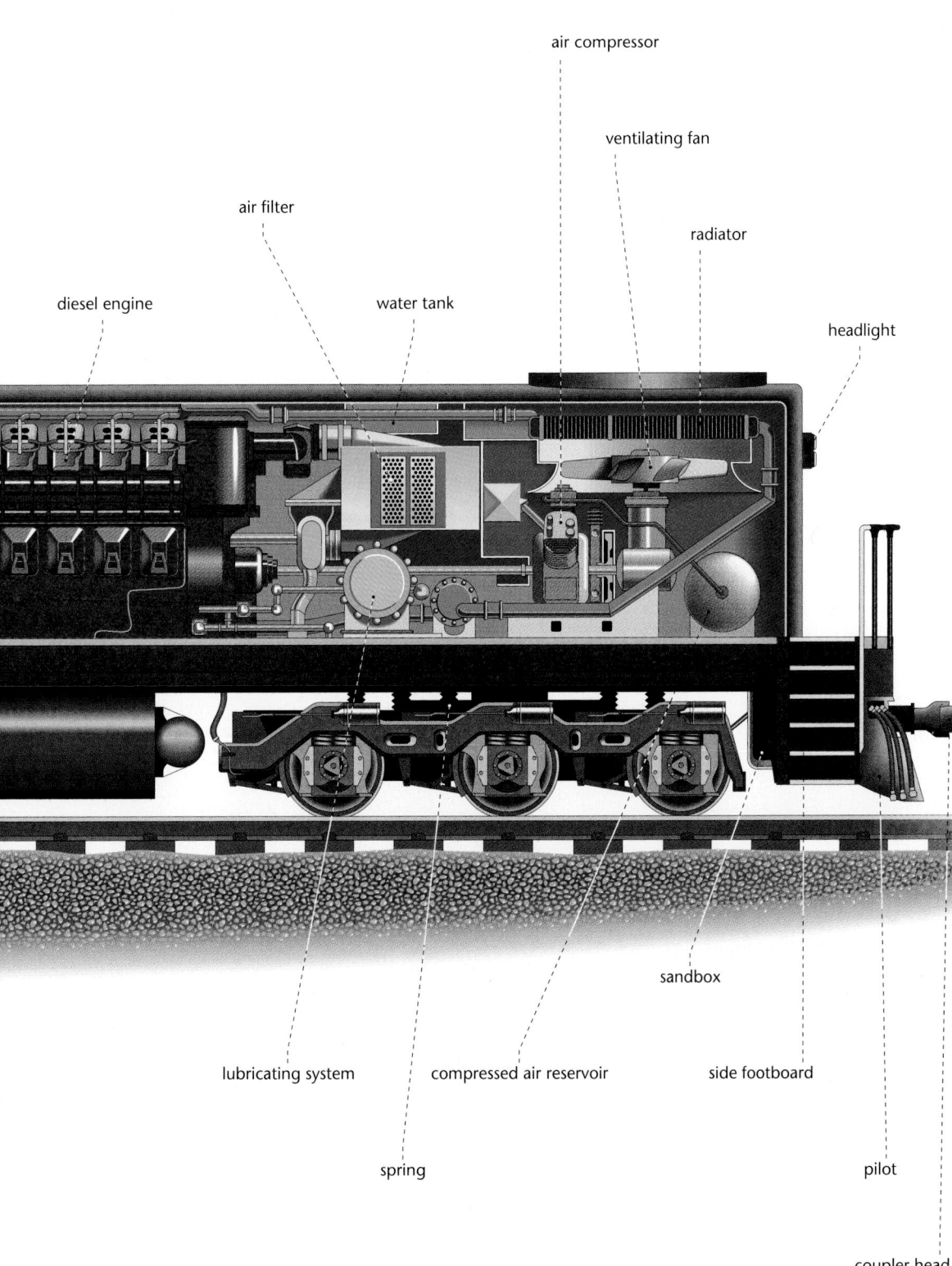

air compressor

ventilating fan

air filter

radiator

diesel engine

water tank

headlight

sandbox

lubricating system

compressed air reservoir

side footboard

spring

pilot

coupler head

BOX CAR

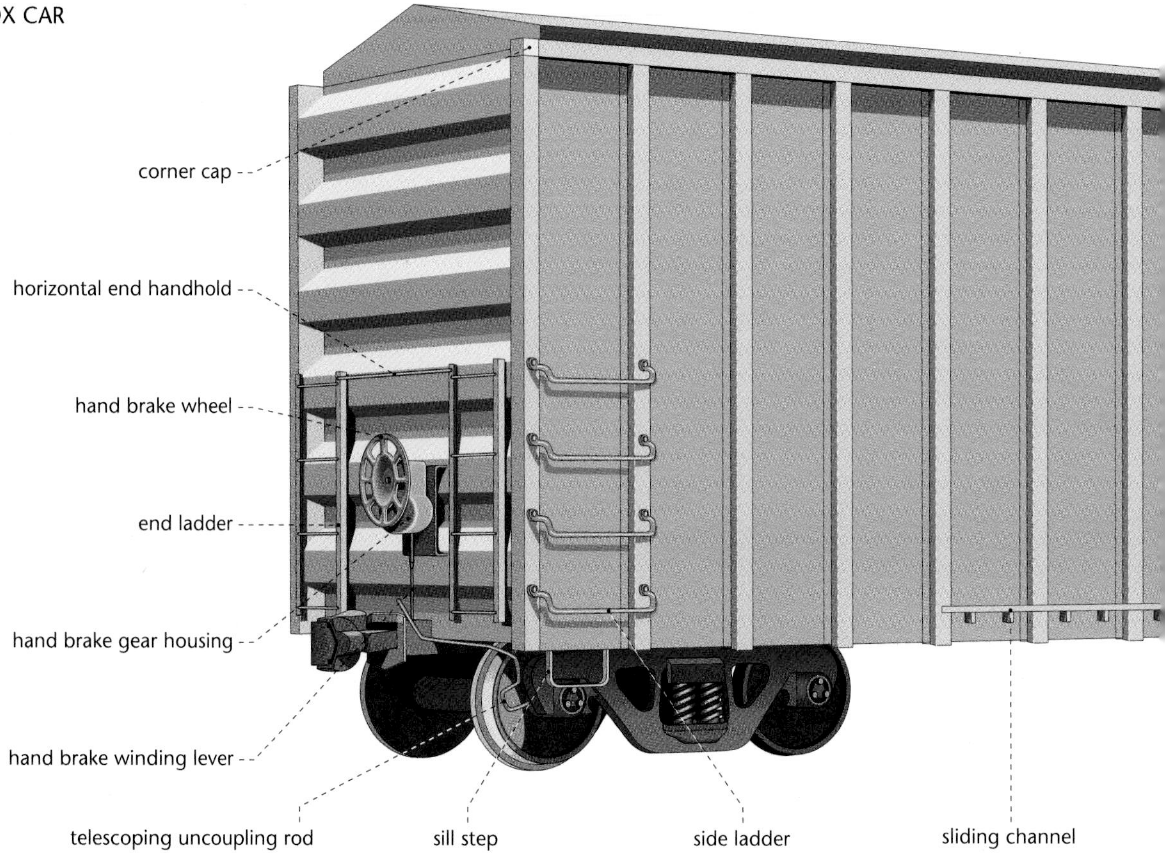

corner cap

horizontal end handhold

hand brake wheel

end ladder

hand brake gear housing

hand brake winding lever

telescoping uncoupling rod

sill step

side ladder

sliding channel

CONTAINER

roof

corner fitting

top-end transverse member

side wall

end door

corner structure

fork pocket

bottom side rail

bottom-end transverse member

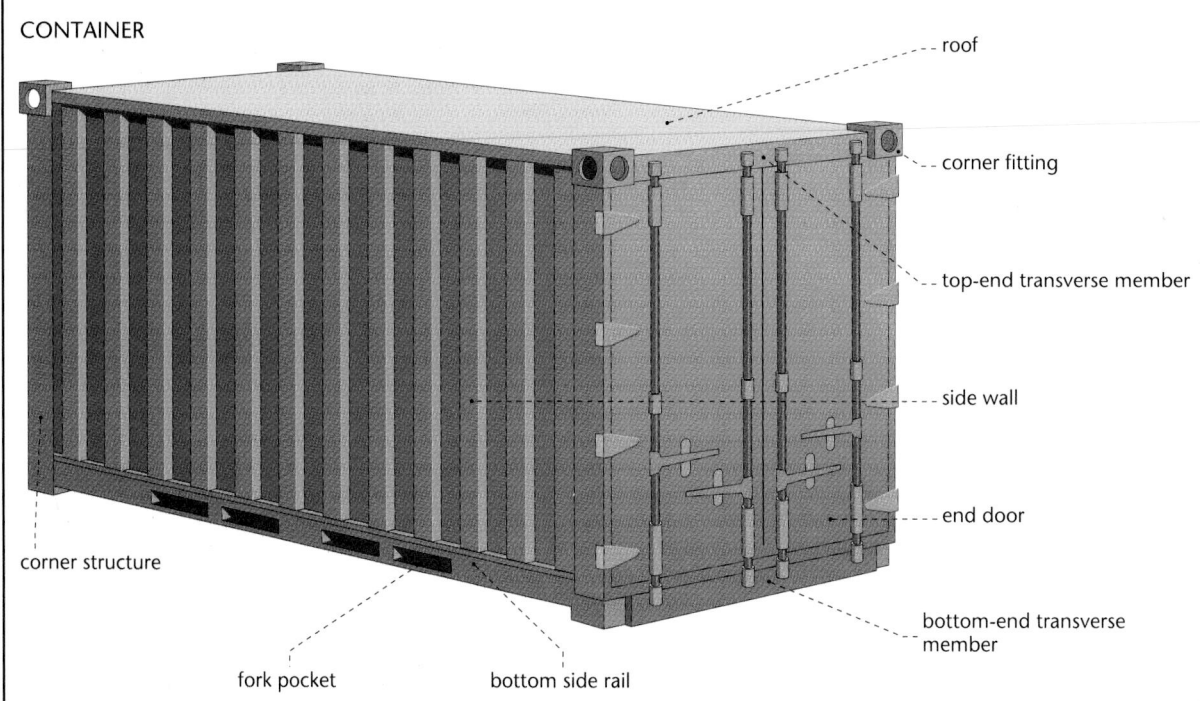

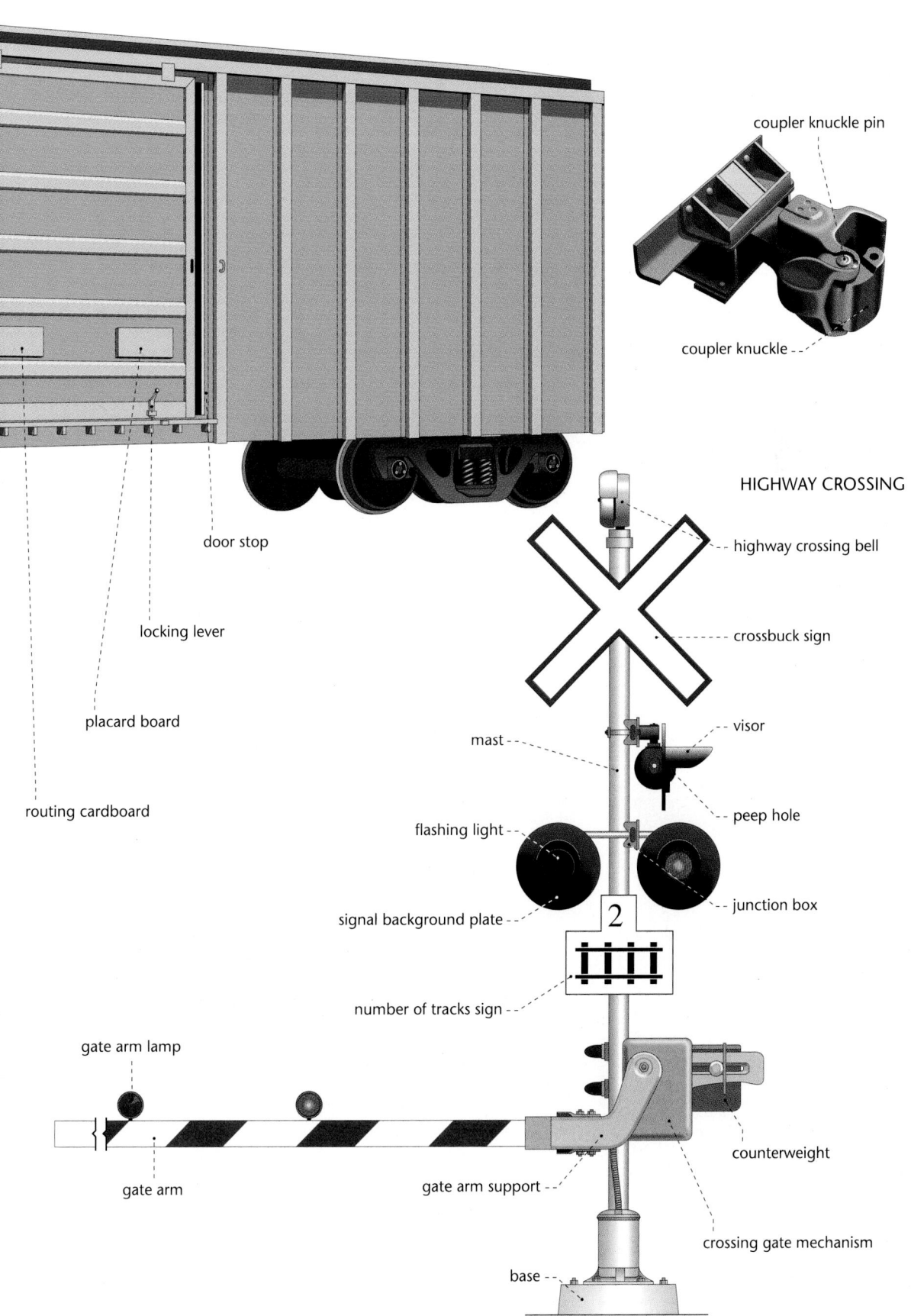

COUPLER HEAD

coupler knuckle pin

coupler knuckle

door stop

locking lever

placard board

routing cardboard

HIGHWAY CROSSING

highway crossing bell

crossbuck sign

visor

mast

peep hole

flashing light

junction box

signal background plate

2

number of tracks sign

gate arm lamp

gate arm

gate arm support

counterweight

crossing gate mechanism

base

TYPES OF FREIGHT CARS

box car   tank car

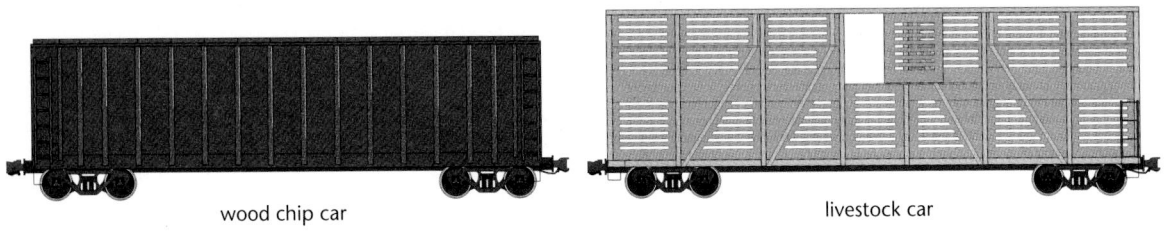

wood chip car   livestock car

hopper car   hard top gondola

hopper ore car   refrigerator car

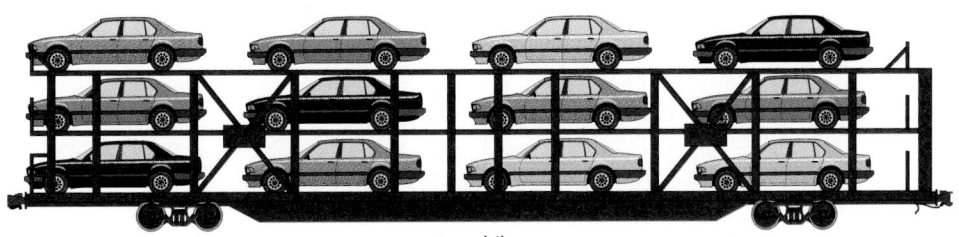
automobile car

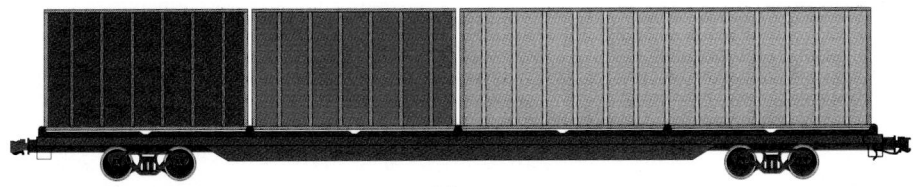
container car

piggyback car

flat car

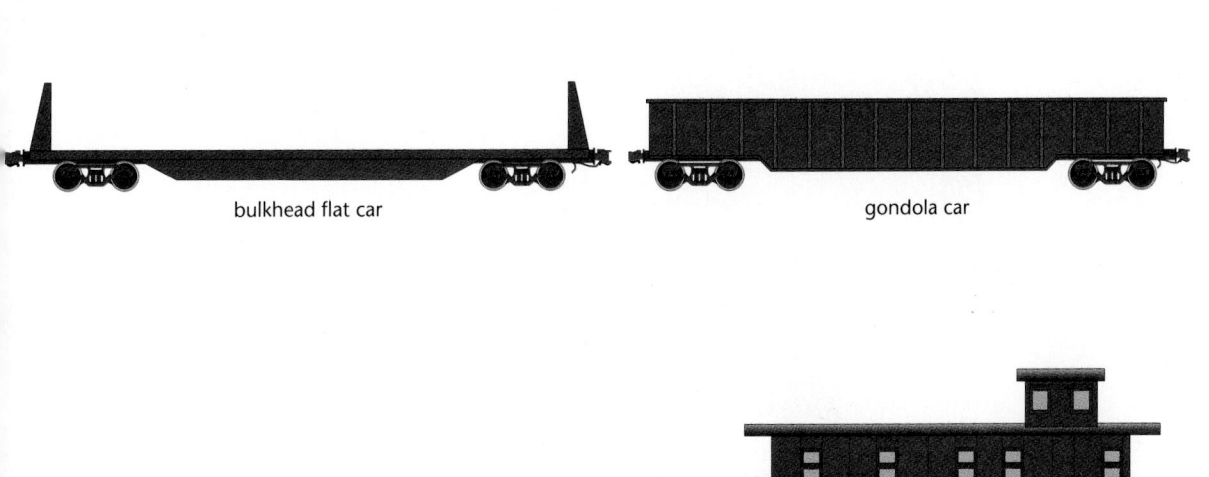

bulkhead flat car

gondola car

depressed-center flat car

caboose

SUBWAY STATION

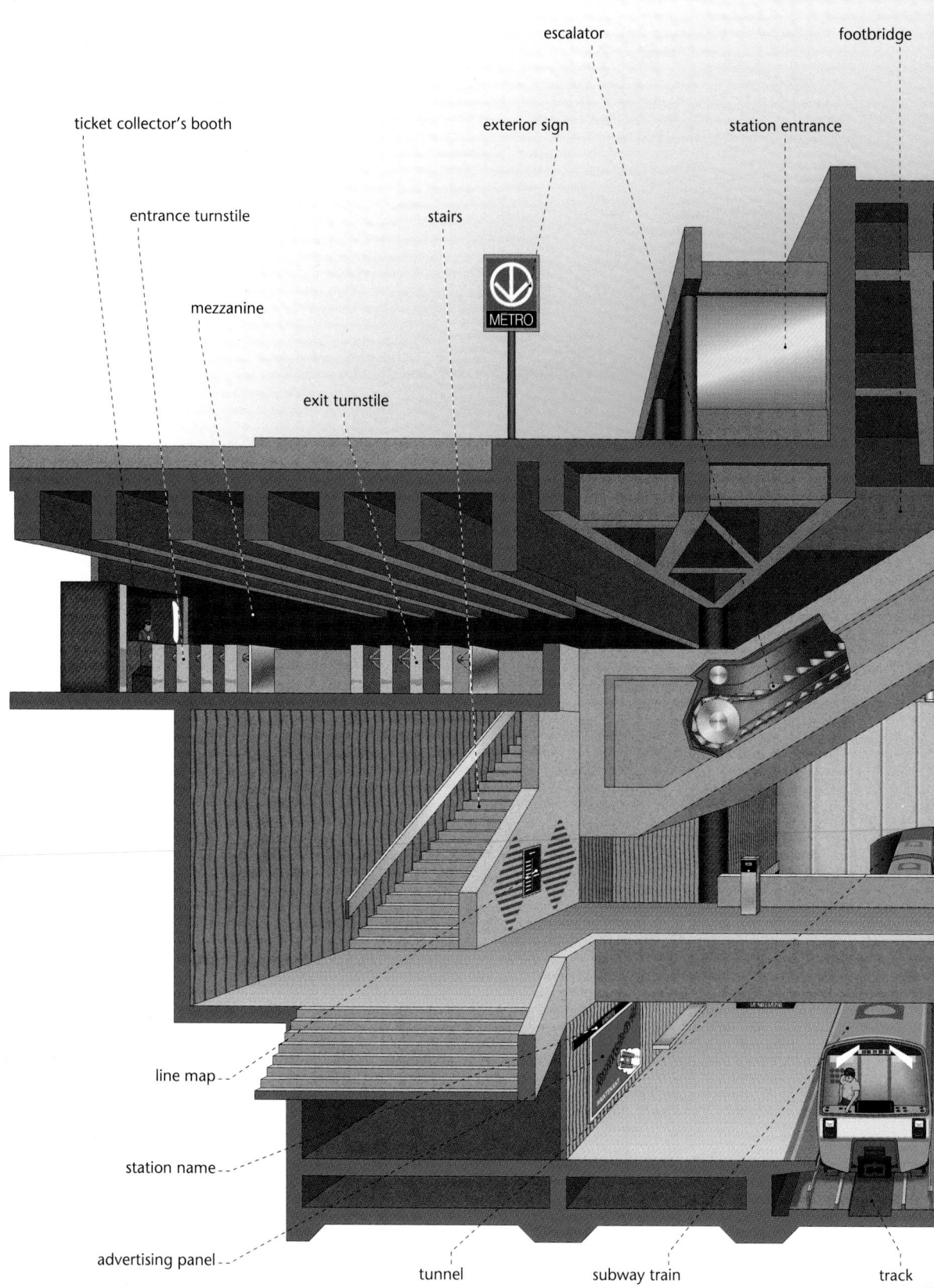

escalator

footbridge

ticket collector's booth

exterior sign

station entrance

entrance turnstile

stairs

mezzanine

exit turnstile

METRO

line map

station name

advertising panel

tunnel

subway train

track

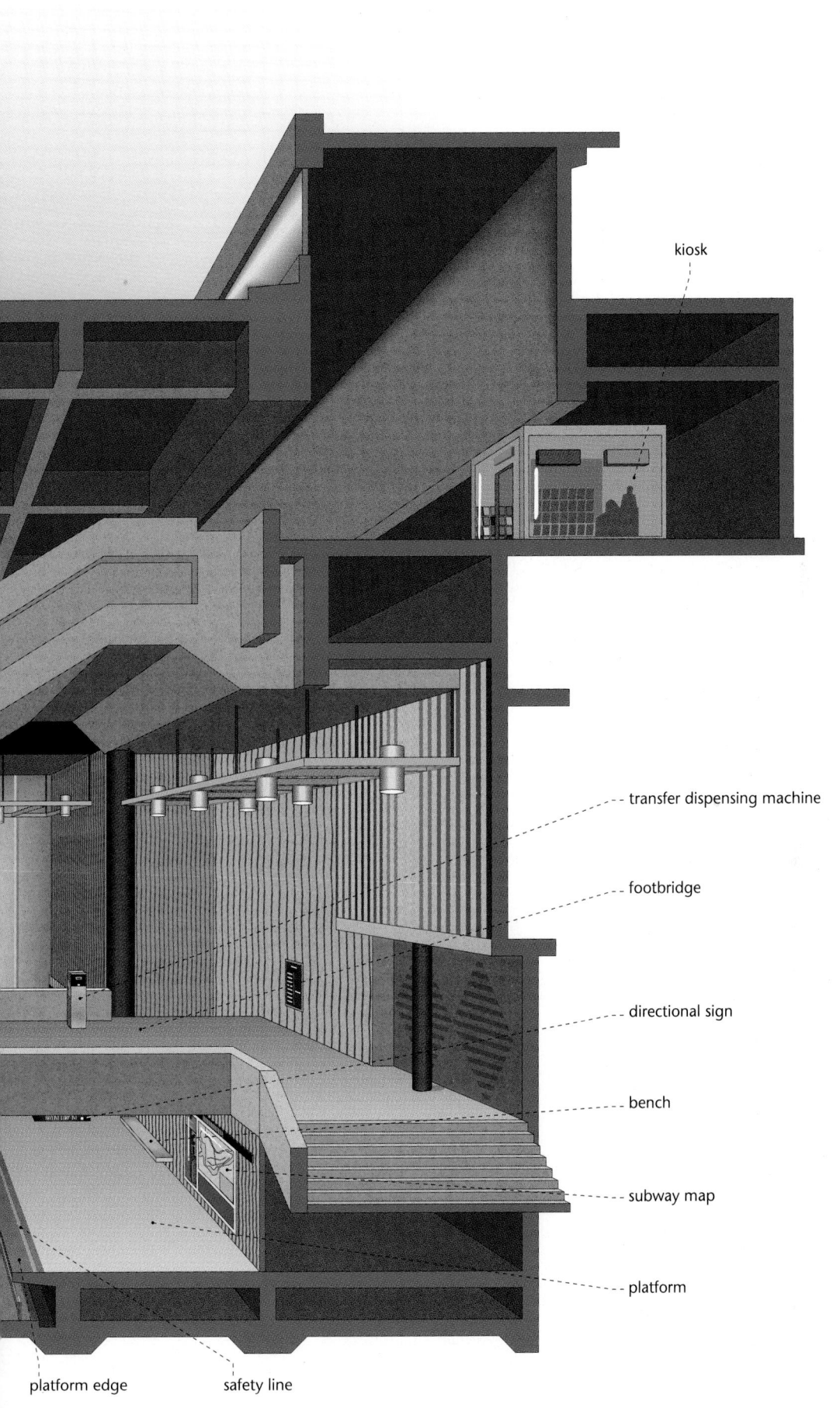

kiosk

transfer dispensing machine

footbridge

directional sign

bench

subway map

platform

platform edge   safety line

SUBWAY TRANSPORT

TRUCK AND TRACK

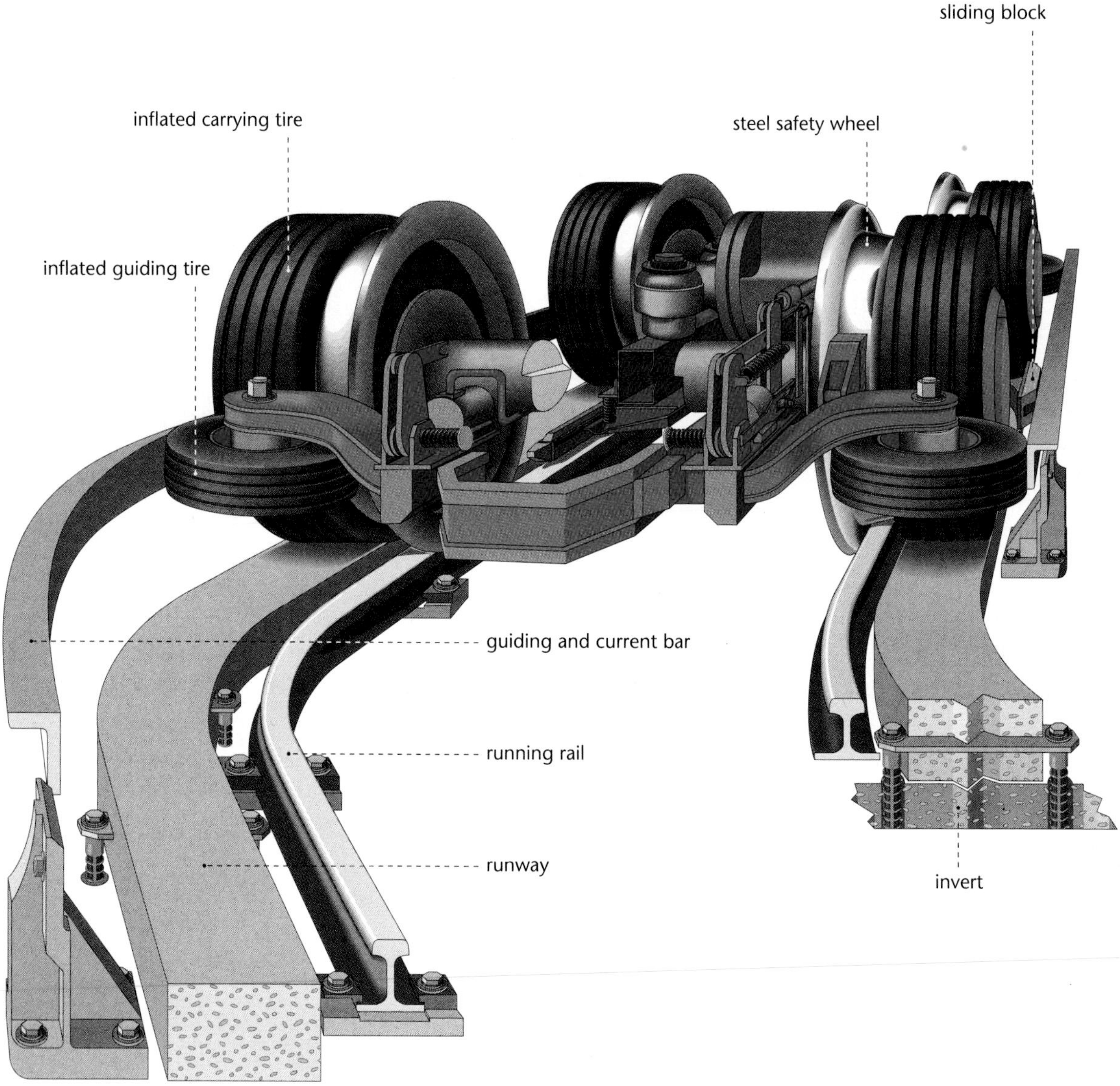

inflated carrying tire

inflated guiding tire

steel safety wheel

sliding block

guiding and current bar

running rail

runway

invert

SUBWAY TRAIN

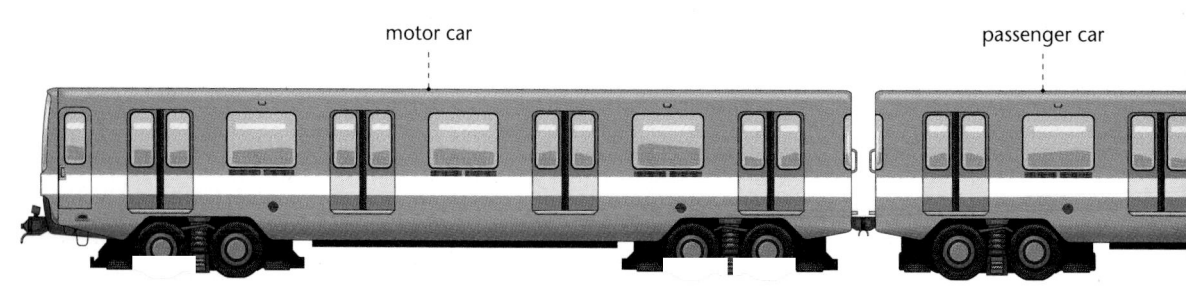

motor car

passenger car

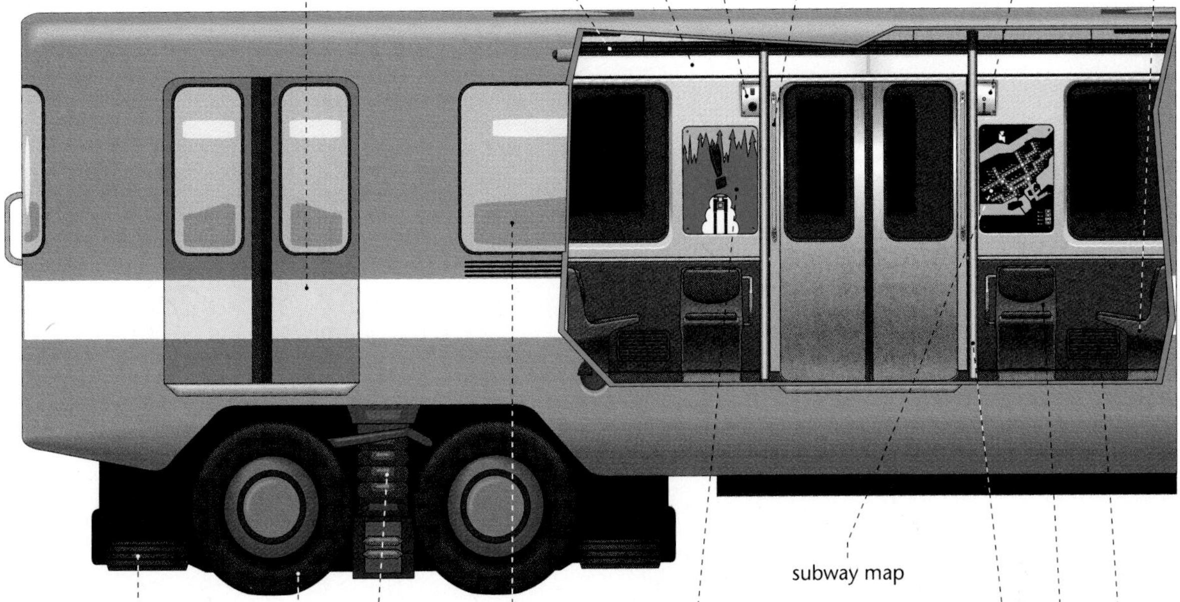

communication set

light

side handrail

double seat

side door

ventilator

emergency brake

subway map

inflated guiding tire

window

handrail

inflated carrying tire

single seat

advertising sign

suspension

heating grille

motor car

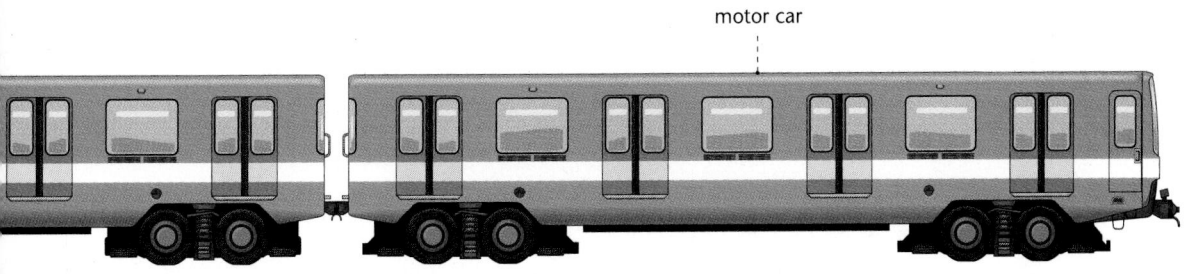

MASTING AND RIGGING

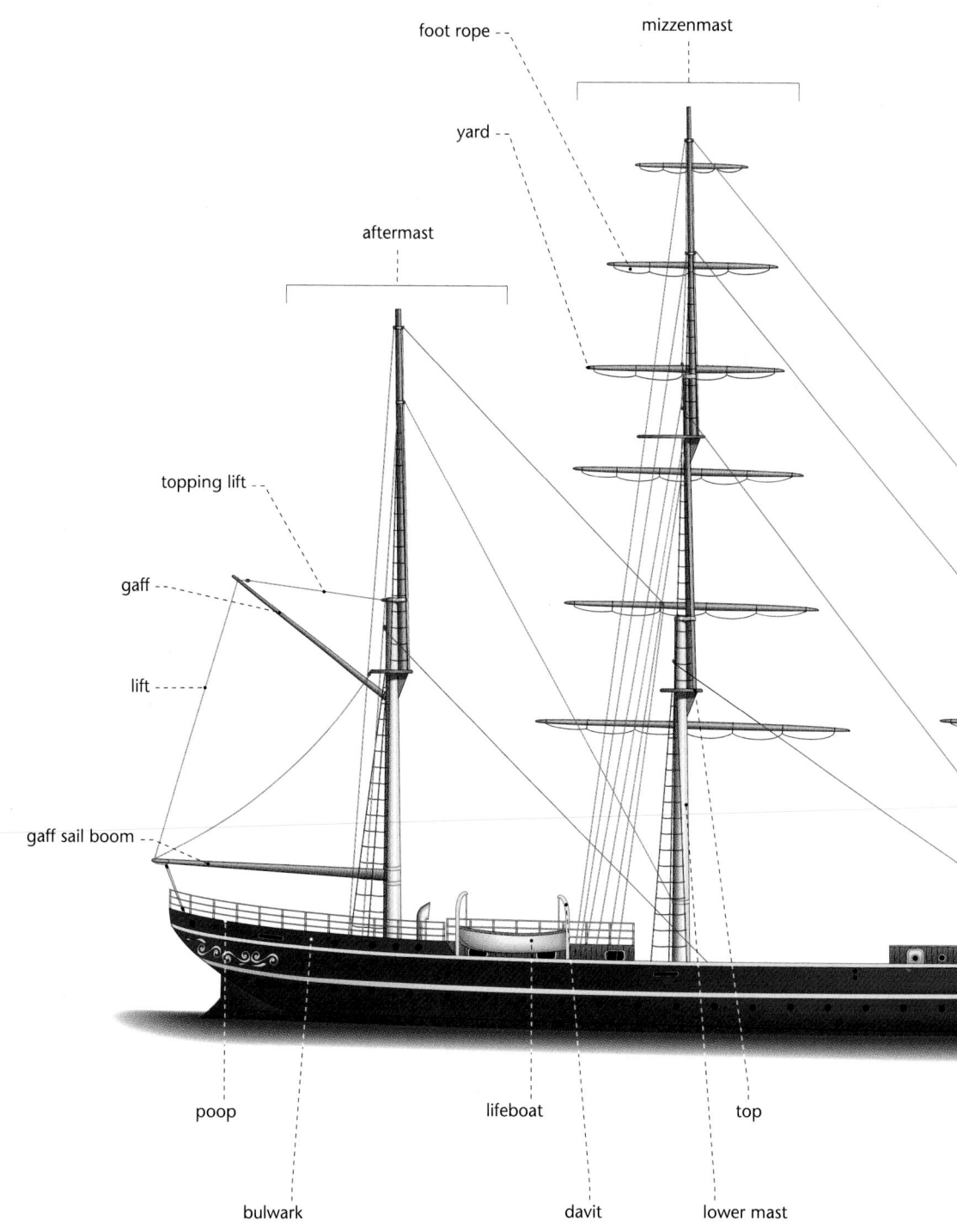

foot rope

mizzenmast

yard

aftermast

topping lift

gaff

lift

gaff sail boom

poop

lifeboat

top

bulwark

davit

lower mast

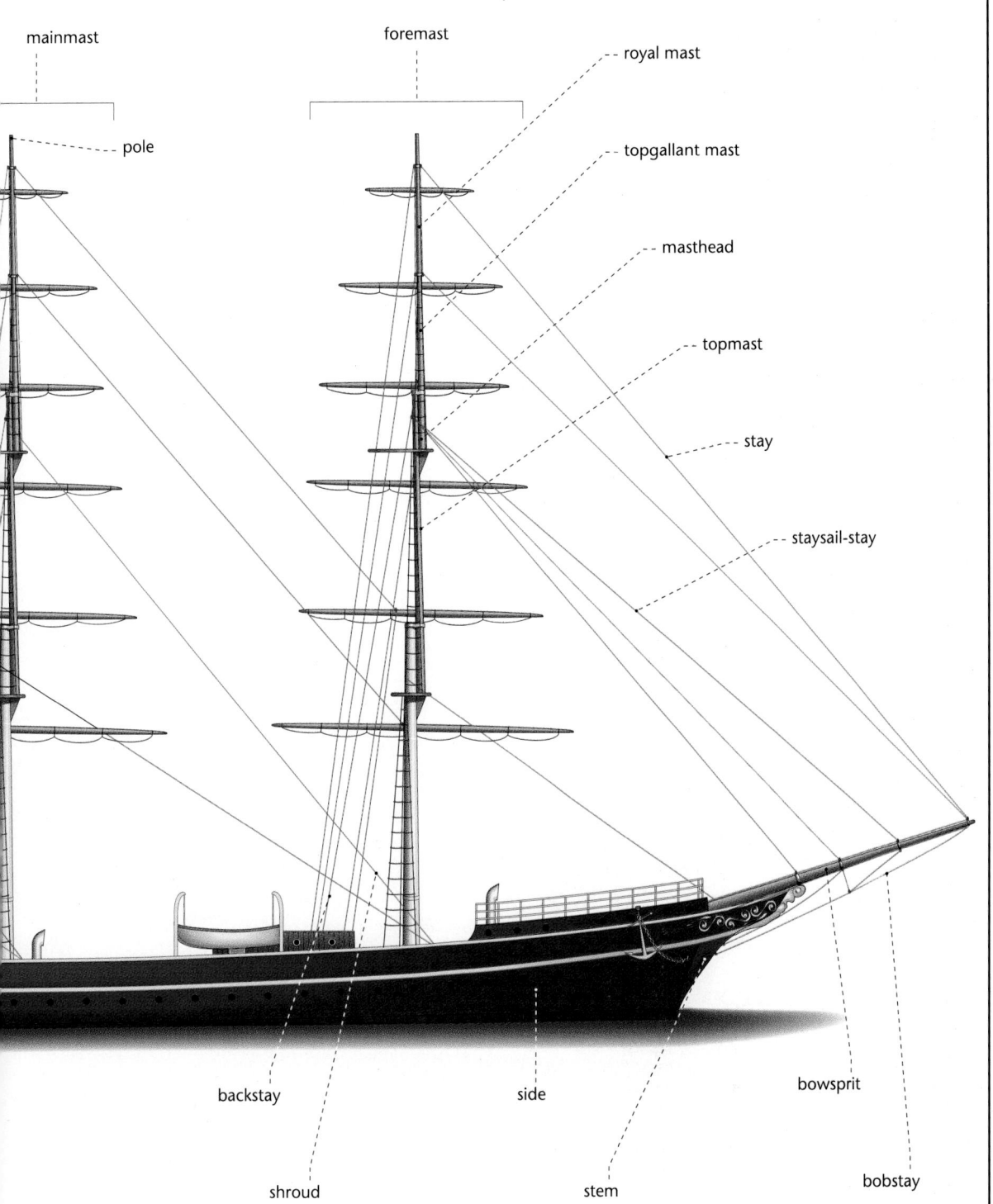

mainmast

foremast

royal mast

pole

topgallant mast

masthead

topmast

stay

staysail-stay

backstay

side

bowsprit

shroud

stem

bobstay

FOUR-MASTED BARK

SAILS

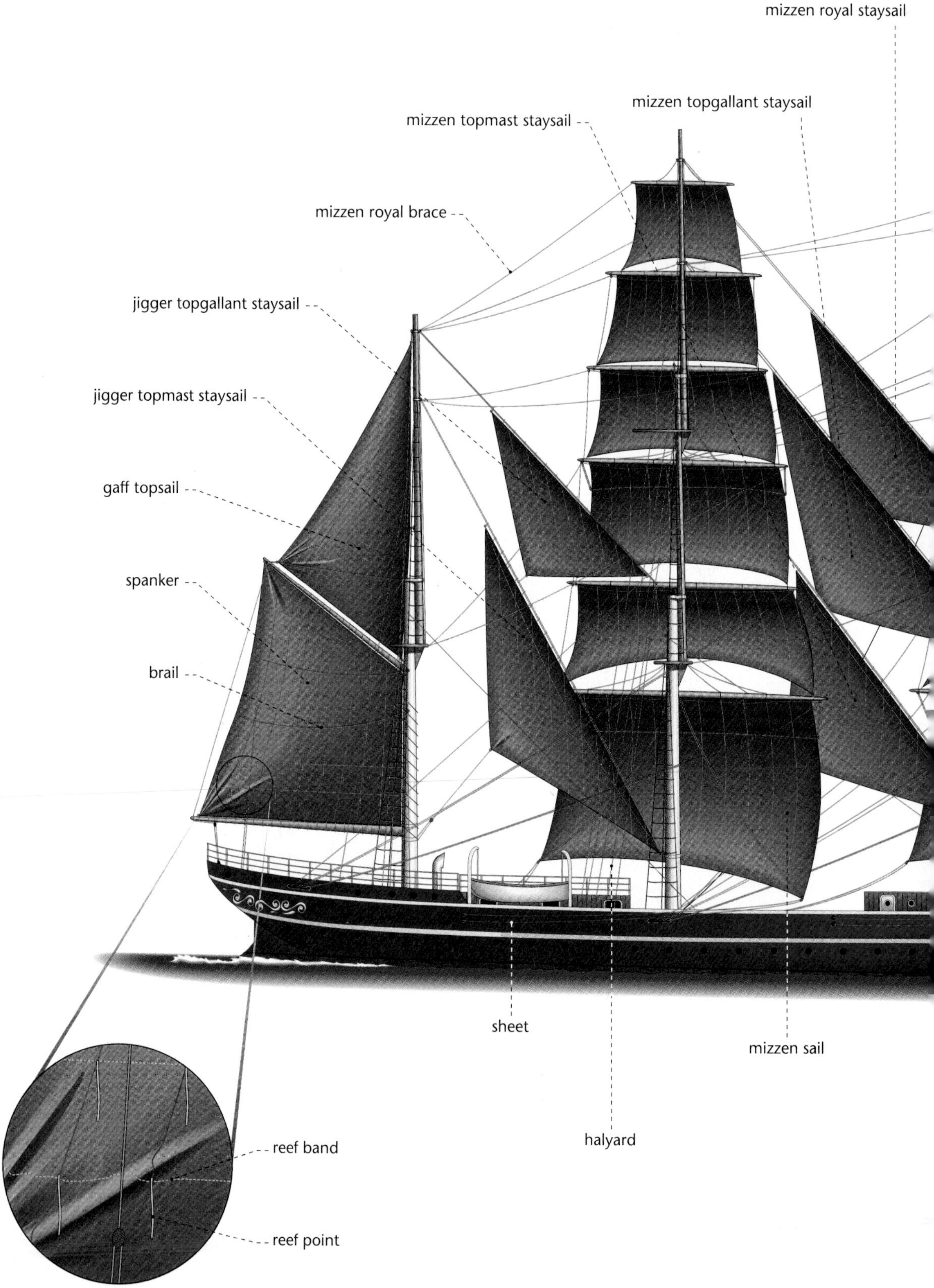
mizzen royal staysail
mizzen topgallant staysail
mizzen topmast staysail
mizzen royal brace
jigger topgallant staysail
jigger topmast staysail
gaff topsail
spanker
brail
sheet
mizzen sail
halyard
reef band
reef point

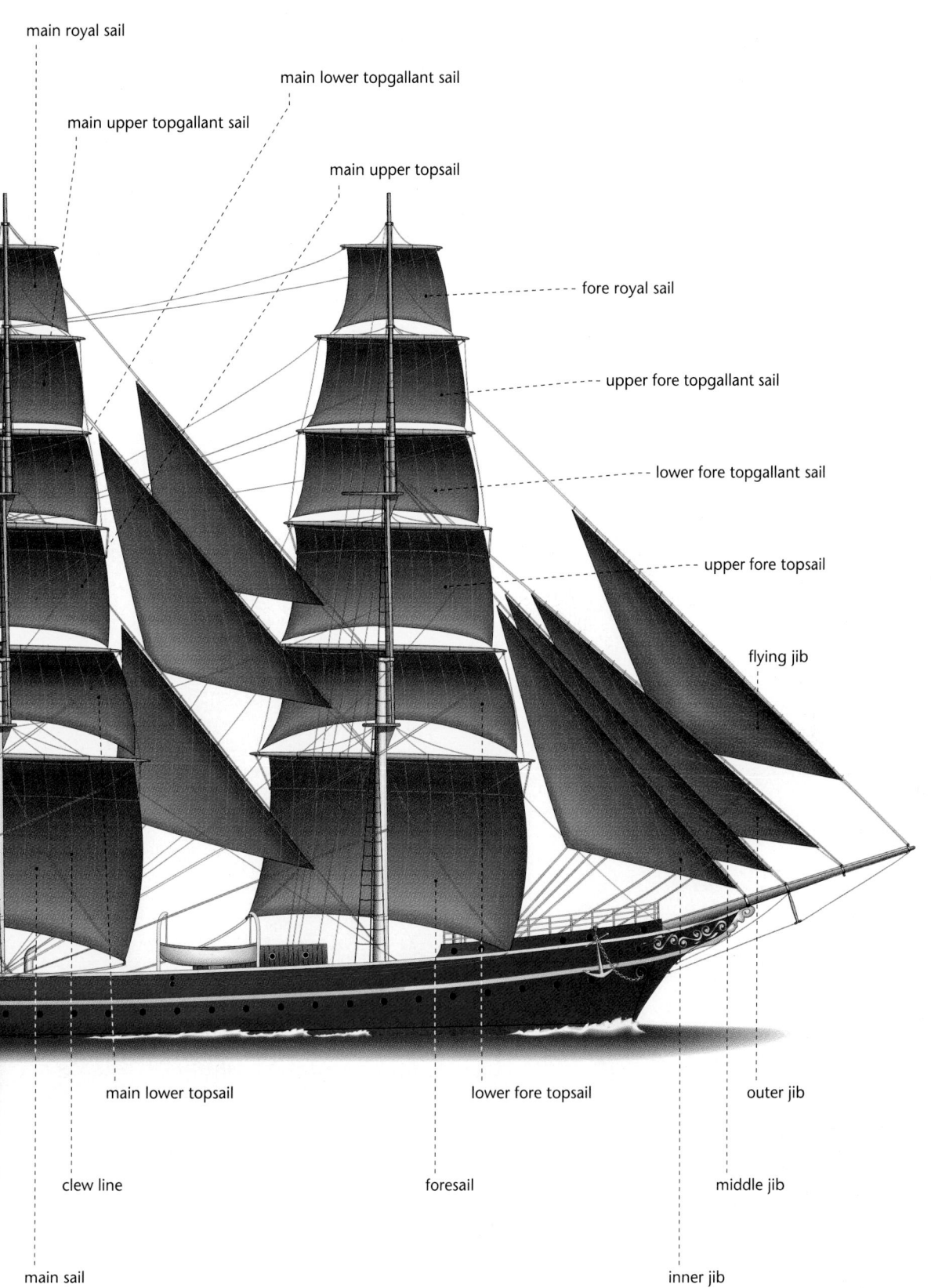

main royal sail

main upper topgallant sail

main lower topgallant sail

main upper topsail

fore royal sail

upper fore topgallant sail

lower fore topgallant sail

upper fore topsail

flying jib

main lower topsail

lower fore topsail

outer jib

clew line

foresail

middle jib

main sail

inner jib

TYPES OF SAILS

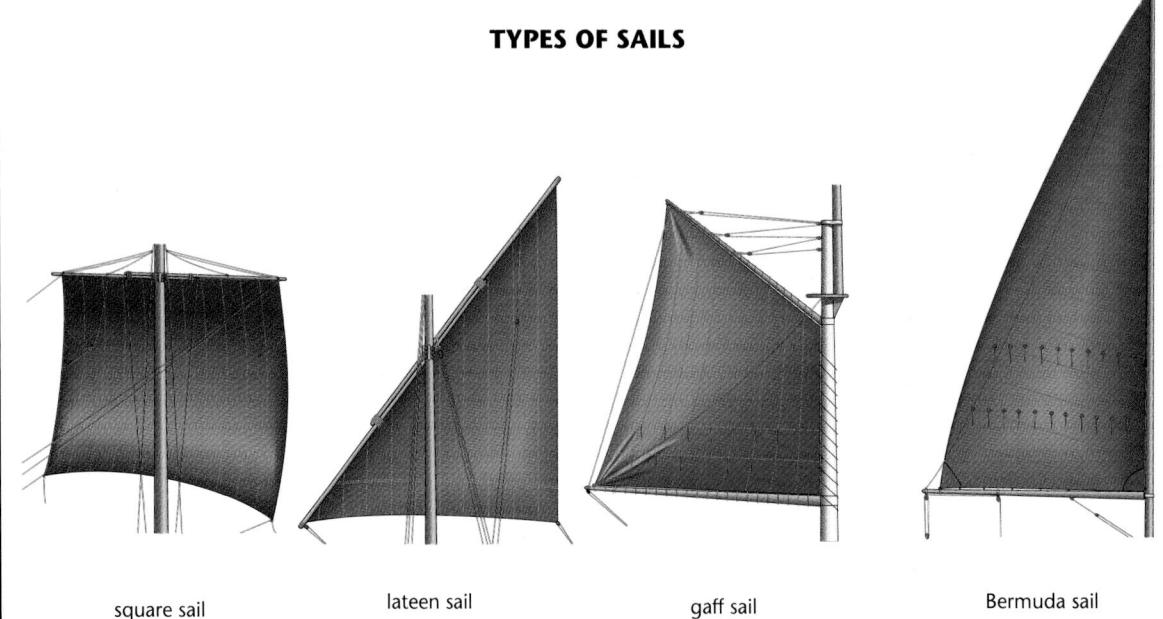

square sail

lateen sail

gaff sail

Bermuda sail

TYPES OF RIGS

whale boat

ketch

brigantine

Marconi cutter

brig

schooner

ANCHOR

SHIP'S ANCHOR

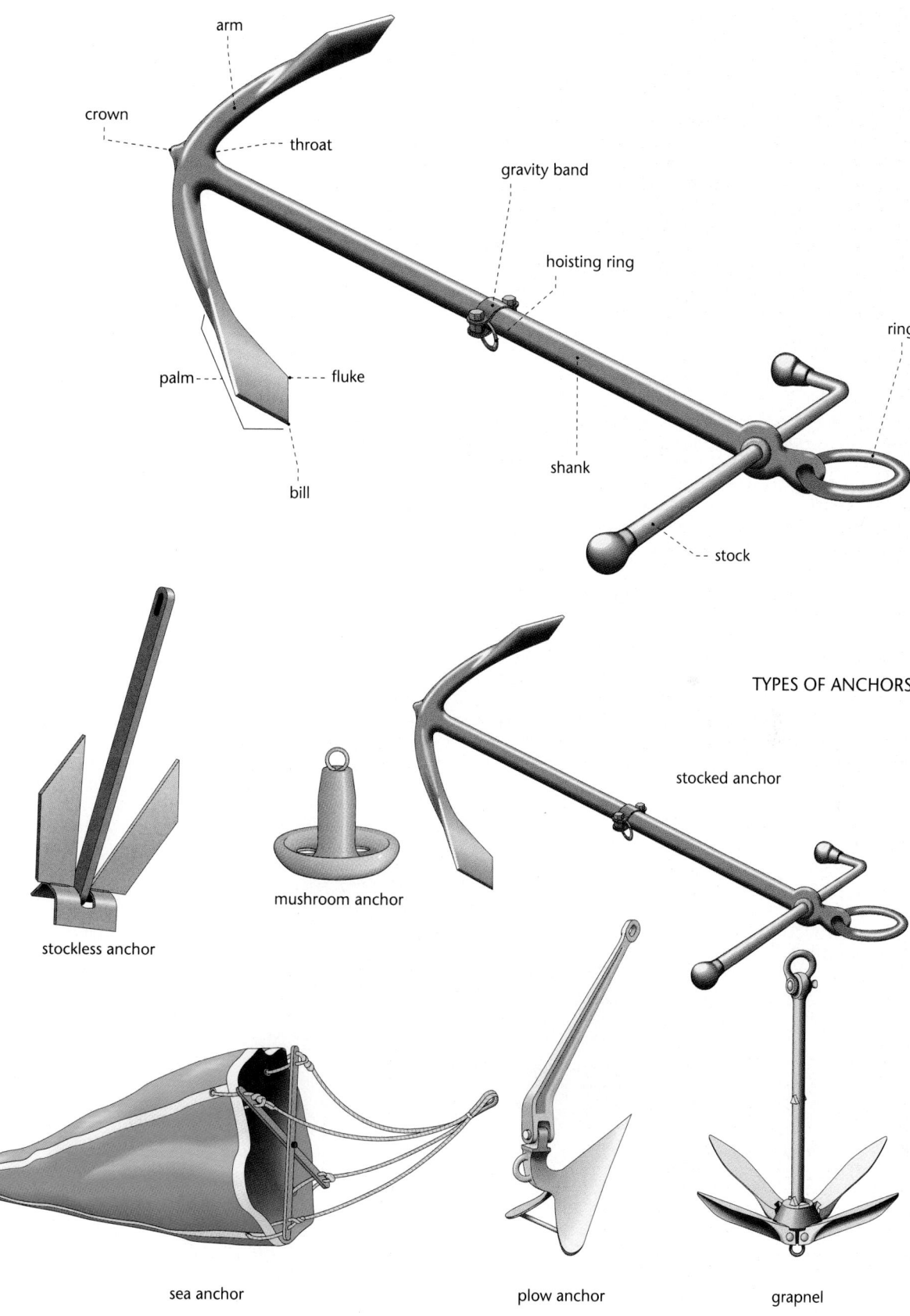

arm

crown

throat

gravity band

hoisting ring

ring

palm

fluke

shank

bill

stock

TYPES OF ANCHORS

stocked anchor

stockless anchor

mushroom anchor

sea anchor

plow anchor

grapnel

483

SEXTANT

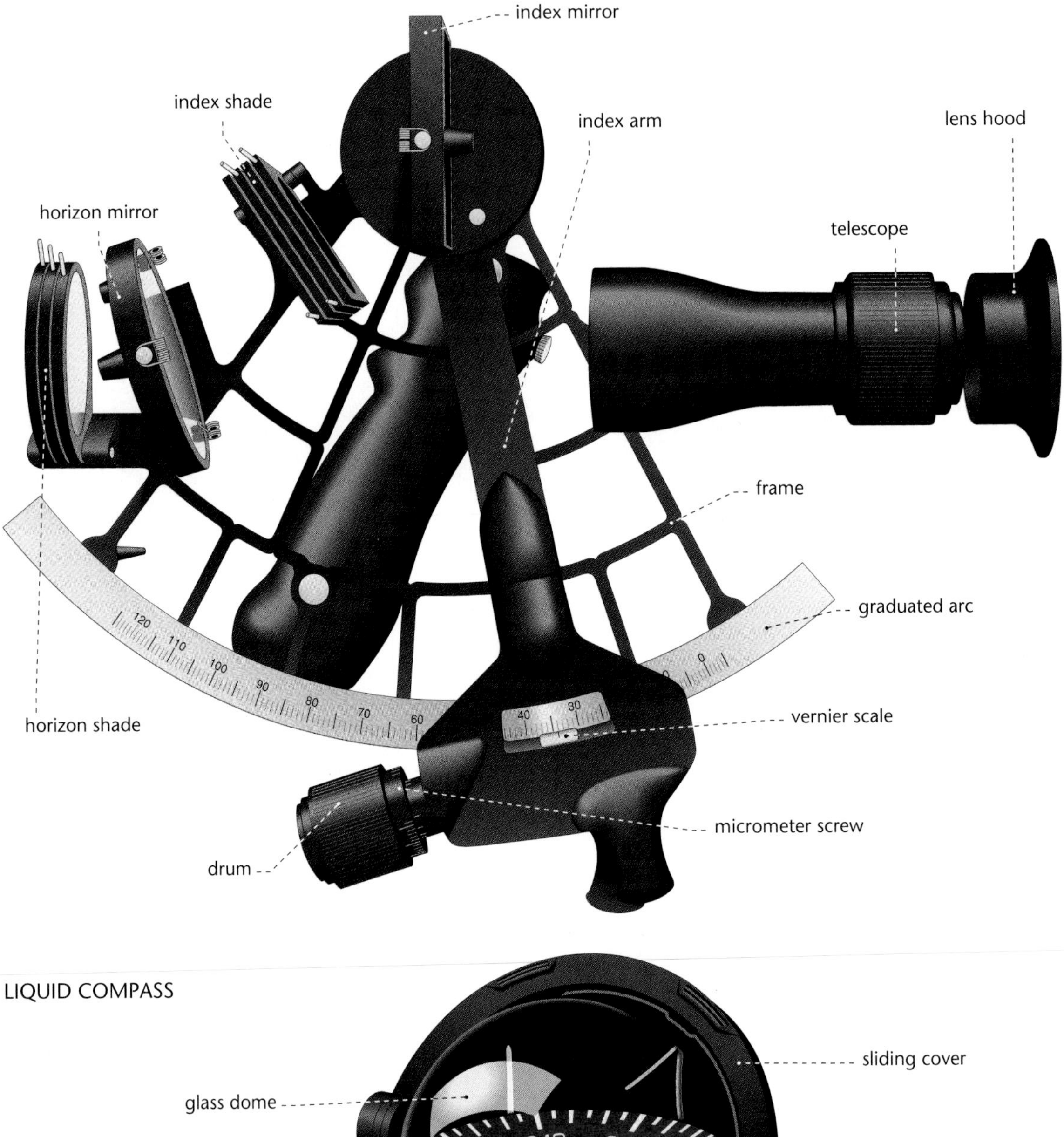

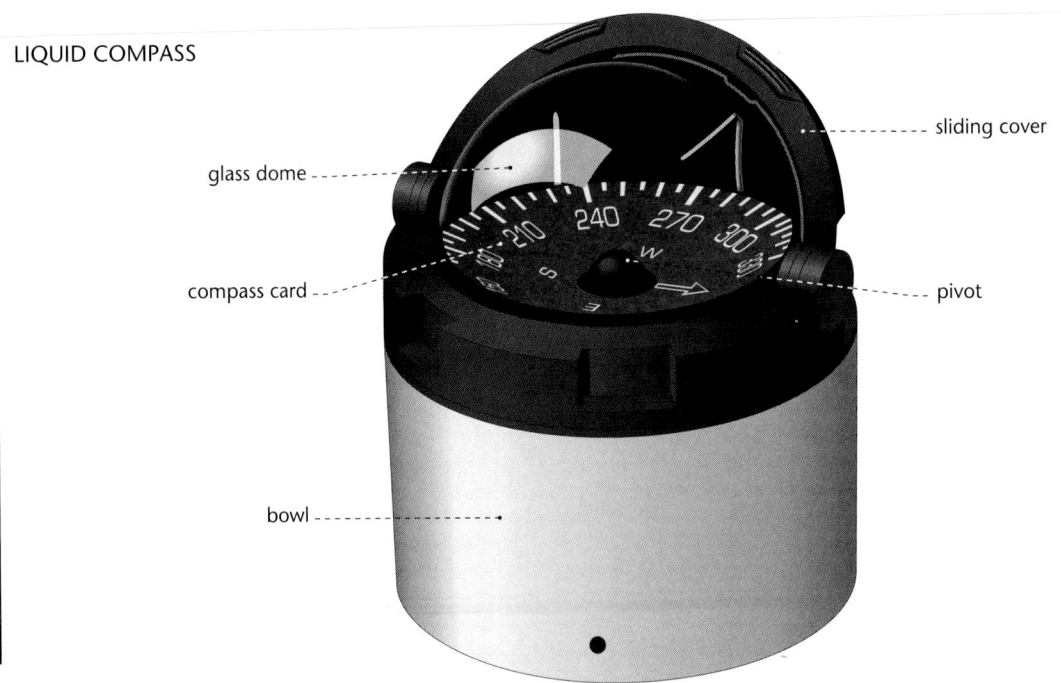

index mirror

index shade

index arm

lens hood

horizon mirror

telescope

frame

graduated arc

horizon shade

vernier scale

micrometer screw

drum

LIQUID COMPASS

sliding cover

glass dome

compass card

pivot

bowl

240   270   300

W

ECHO SOUNDER

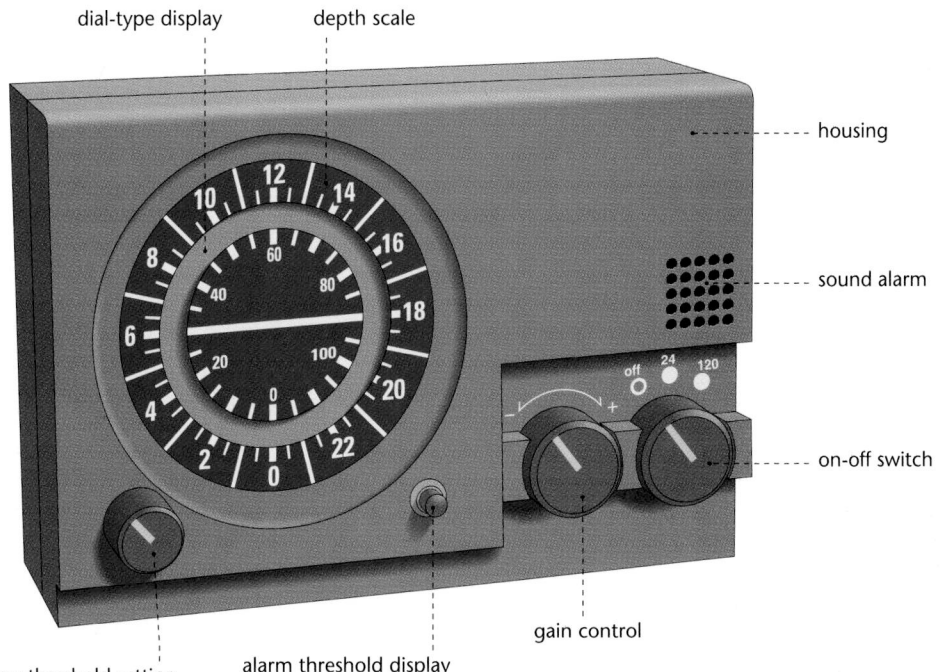

dial-type display

depth scale

housing

sound alarm

off 24 120

on-off switch

gain control

alarm threshold setting

alarm threshold display button

ECHO SOUNDER PROBE

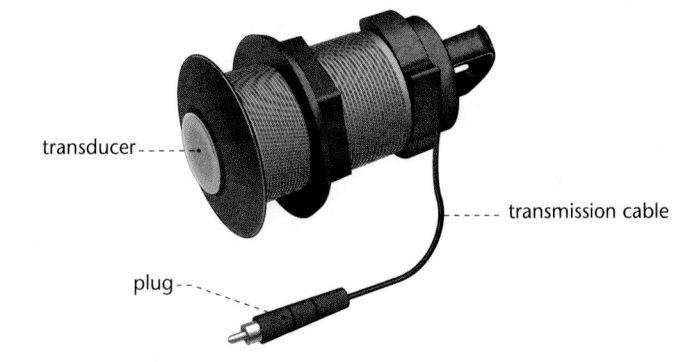

transducer

transmission cable

plug

CROSS SECTION OF A LIQUID COMPASS

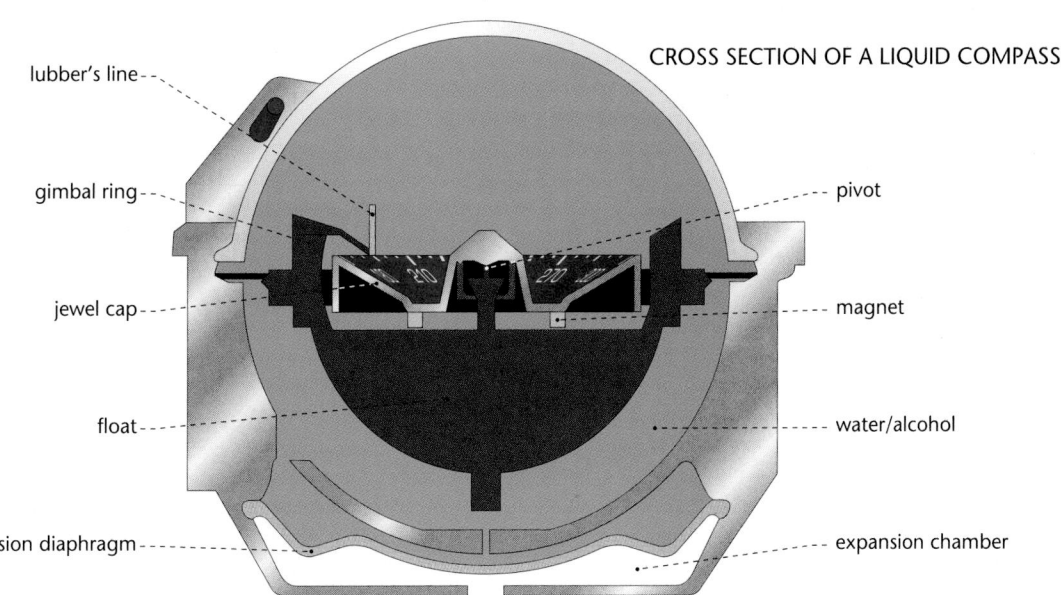

lubber's line

gimbal ring

jewel cap

float

expansion diaphragm

pivot

magnet

water/alcohol

expansion chamber

MARITIME TRANSPORT

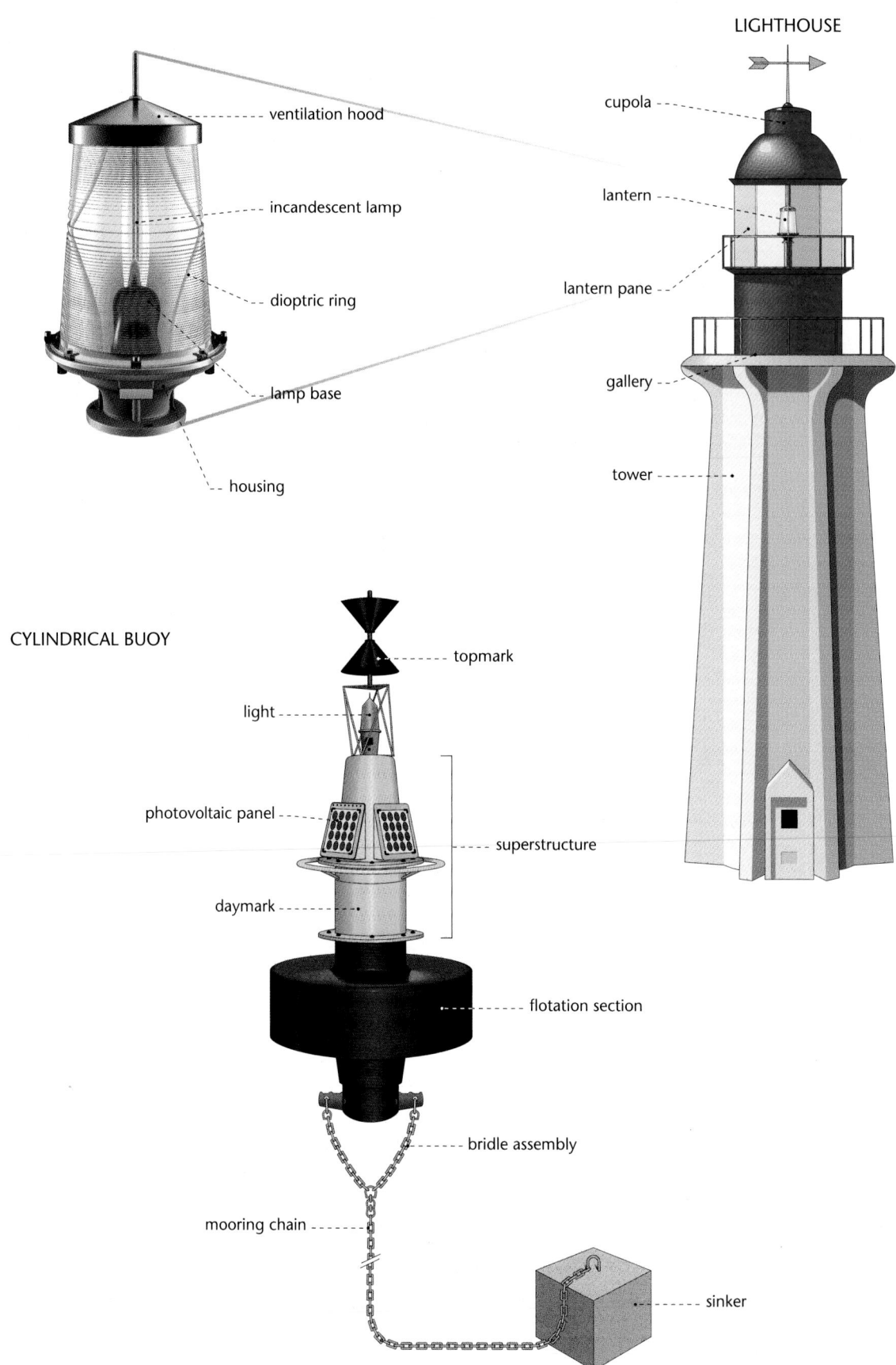

LIGHTHOUSE LANTERN

ventilation hood

incandescent lamp

dioptric ring

lamp base

housing

LIGHTHOUSE

cupola

lantern

lantern pane

gallery

tower

CYLINDRICAL BUOY

topmark

light

photovoltaic panel

superstructure

daymark

flotation section

bridle assembly

mooring chain

sinker

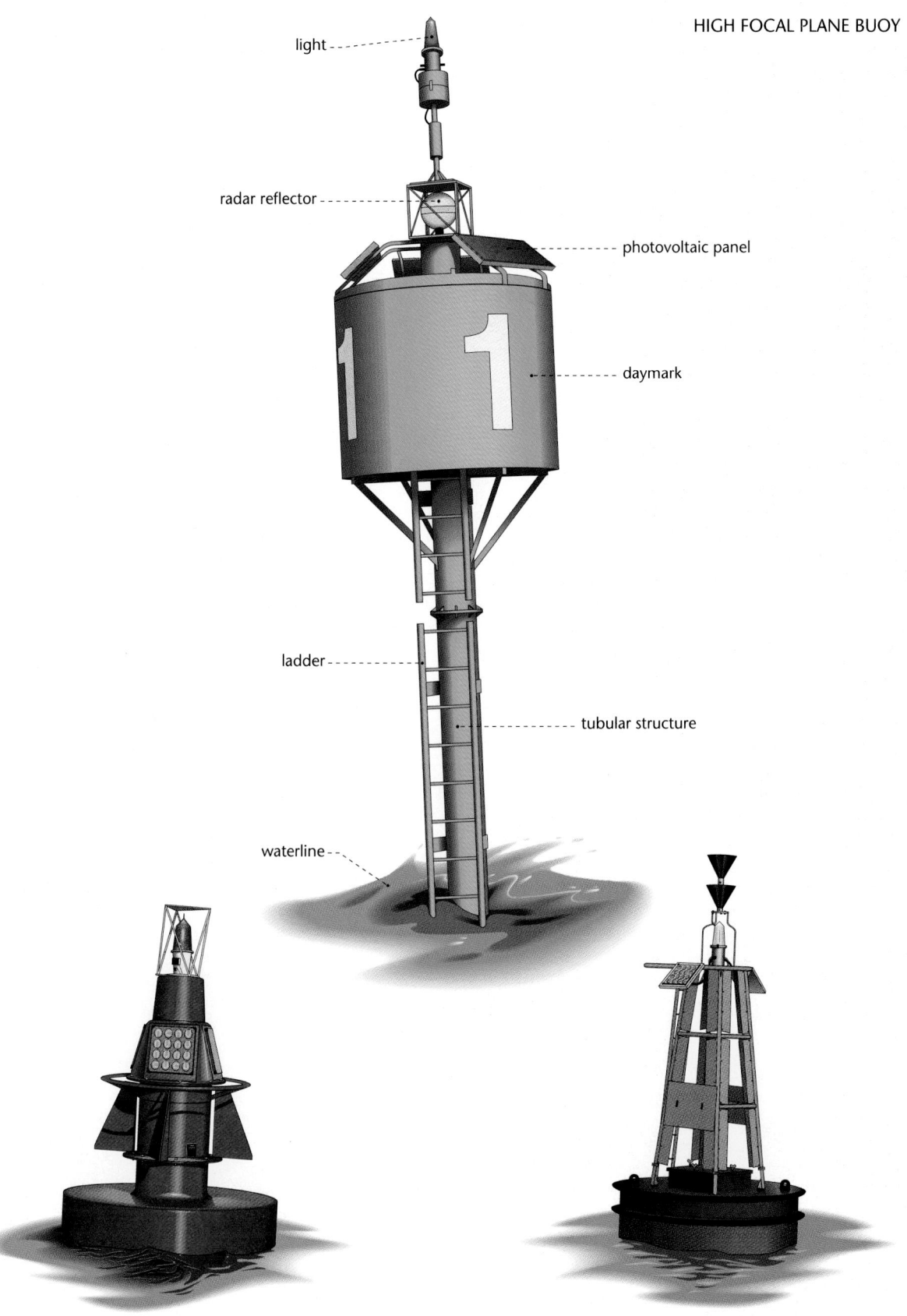

light

radar reflector

photovoltaic panel

daymark

ladder

tubular structure

waterline

conical buoy

pillar buoy

MARITIME BUOYAGE SYSTEM

CARDINAL MARKS

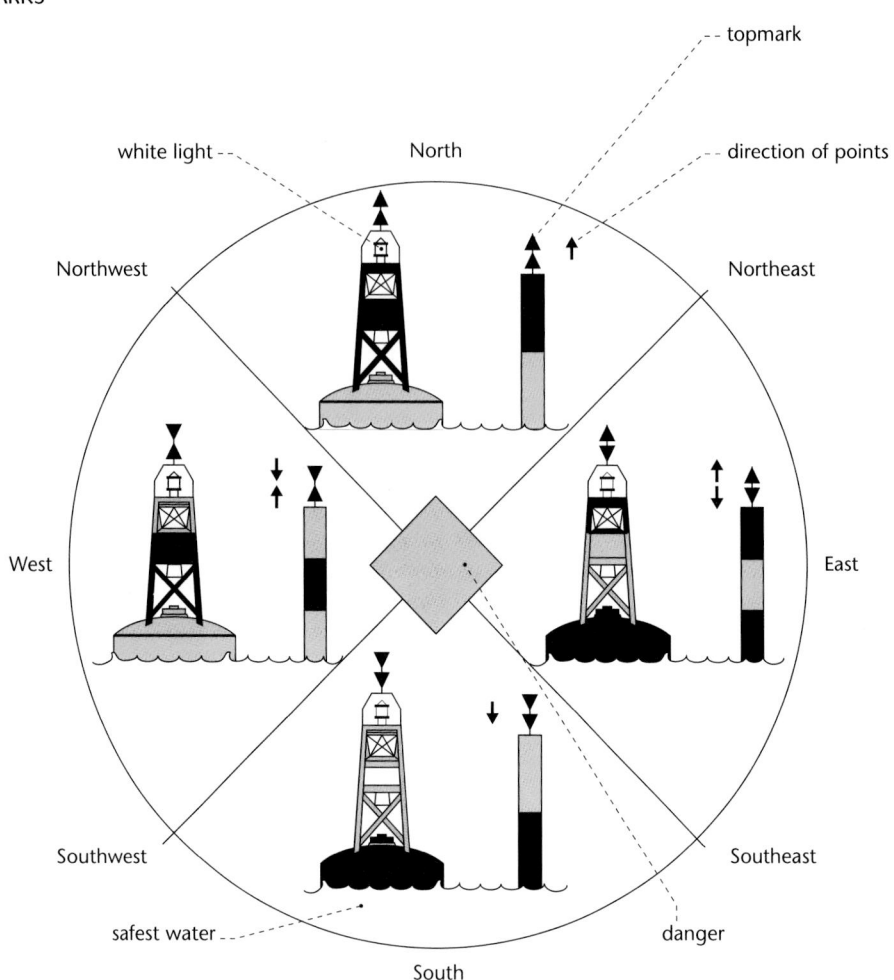

topmark

white light

direction of points

North

Northwest

Northeast

West

East

Southwest

Southeast

safest water

danger

South

BUOYAGE REGIONS

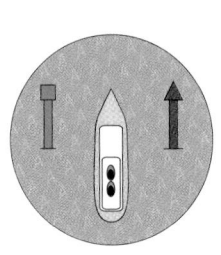

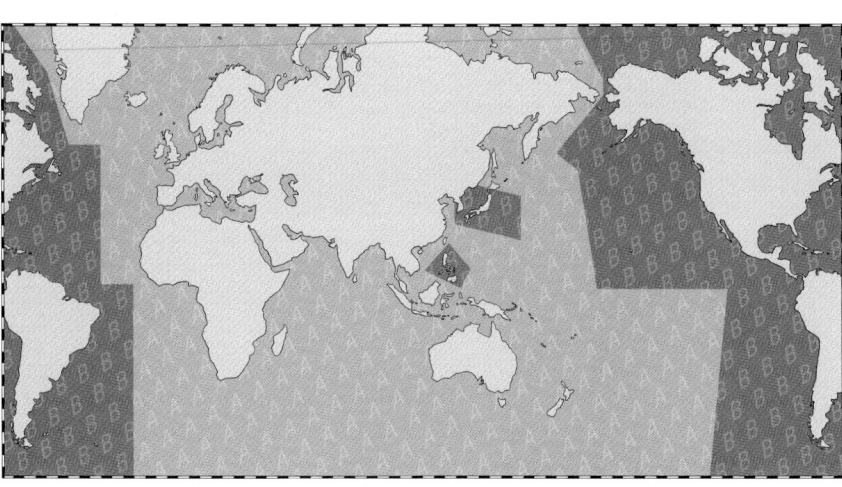

port hand

starboard hand

RHYTHM OF MARKS BY NIGHT

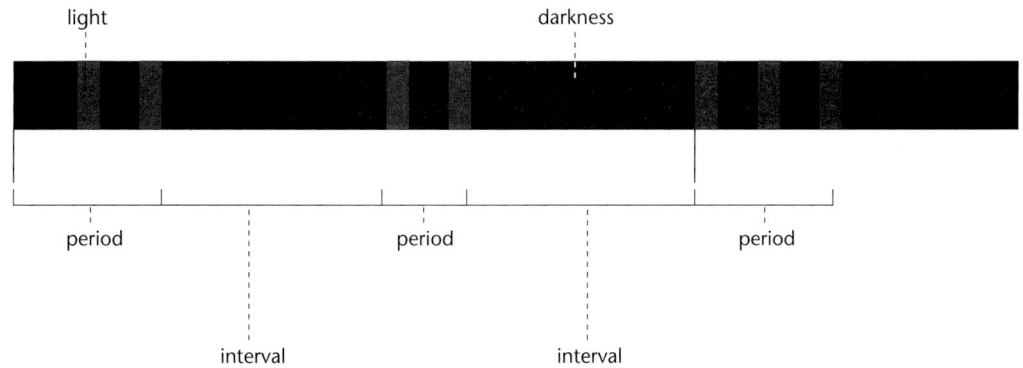

light

darkness

period

period

period

interval

interval

DAYMARKS (REGION B)

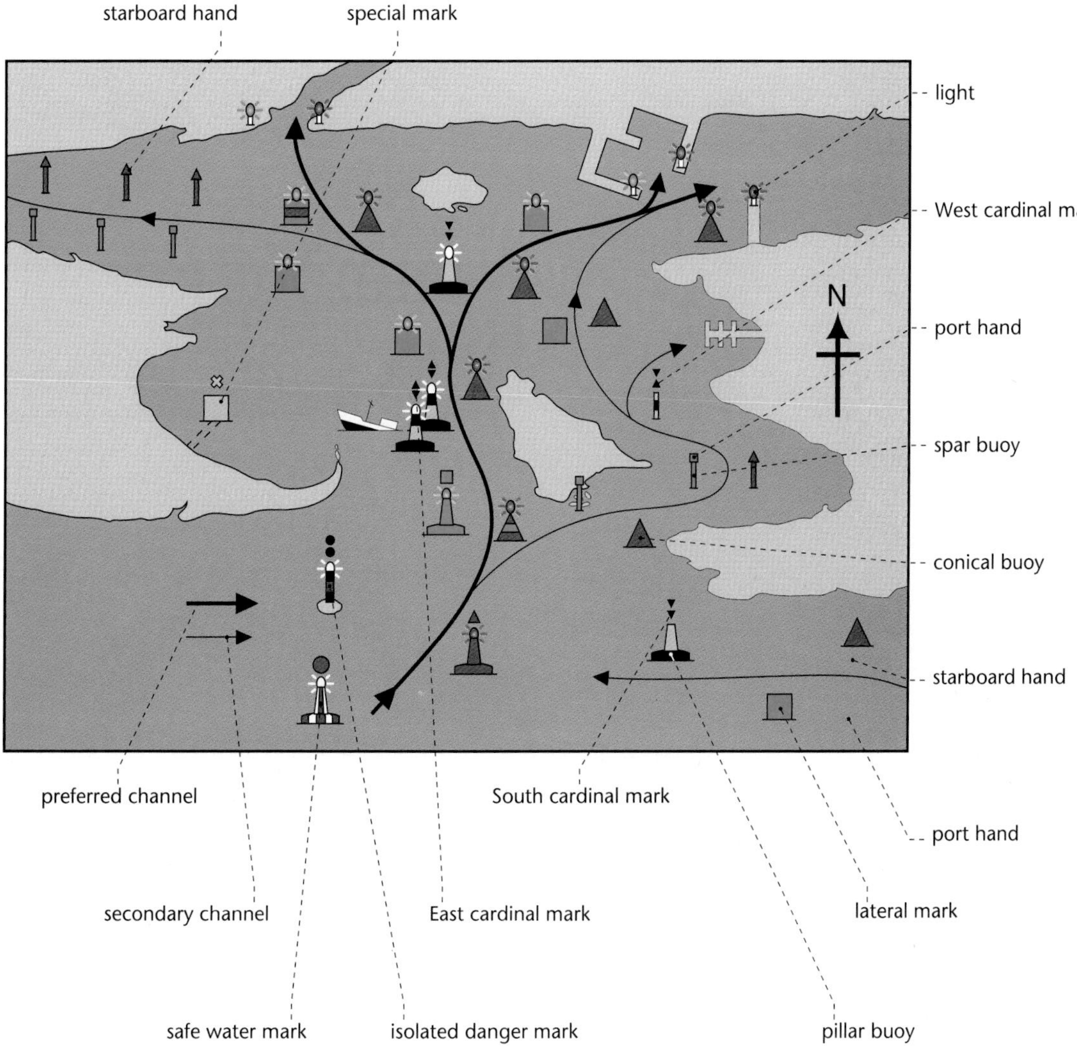

starboard hand

special mark

- light

- West cardinal mark

N

- port hand

- spar buoy

- conical buoy

- starboard hand

South cardinal mark

- port hand

preferred channel

secondary channel

East cardinal mark

lateral mark

safe water mark

isolated danger mark

pillar buoy

gate

transit shed

dry dock

quayside crane

quay

bulk terminal

canal lock

floating crane

container-loading bridge

silos

dock

quay ramp

grain terminal

container ship

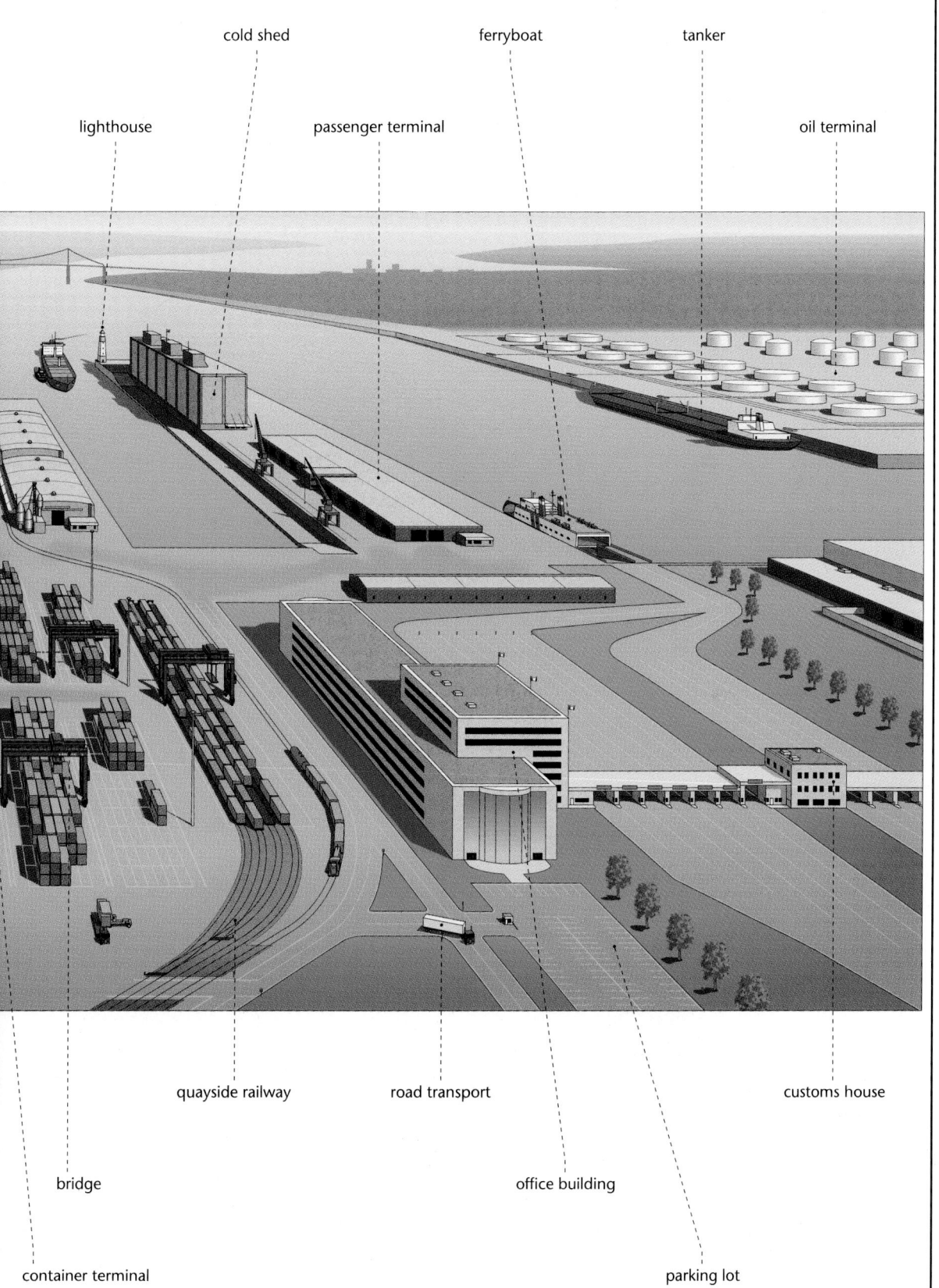

cold shed

ferryboat

tanker

lighthouse

passenger terminal

oil terminal

quayside railway

road transport

customs house

bridge

office building

container terminal

parking lot

CANAL LOCK

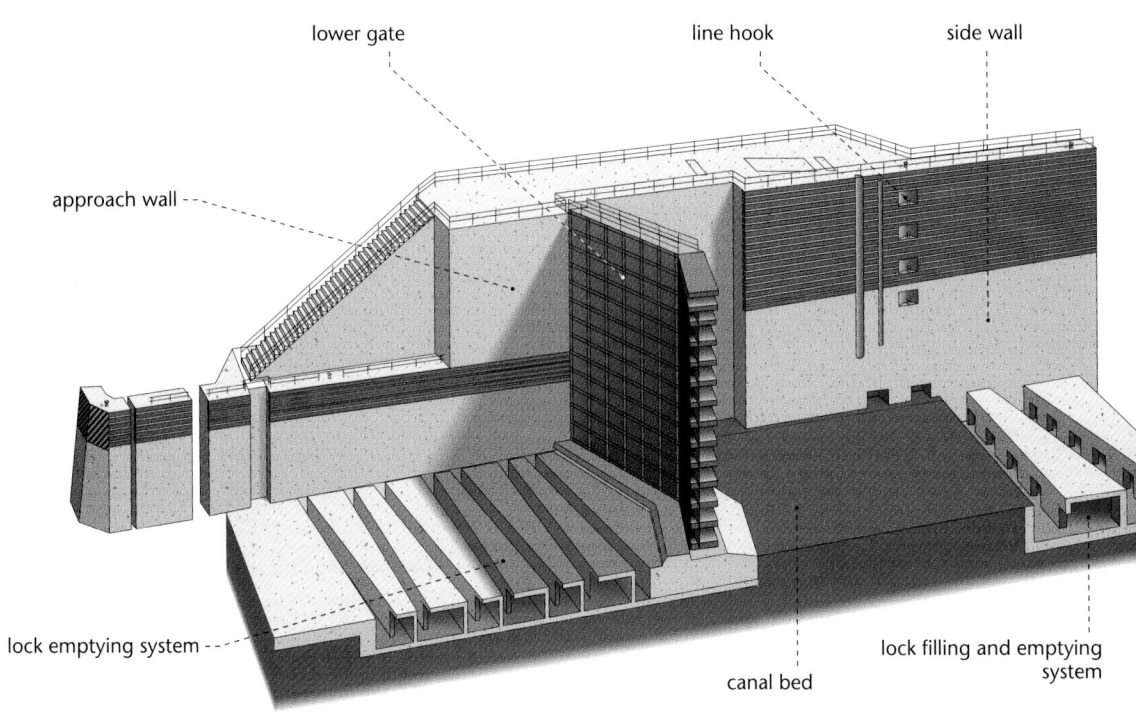

lower gate

line hook

side wall

approach wall

lock emptying system

canal bed

lock filling and emptying system

HOVERCRAFT

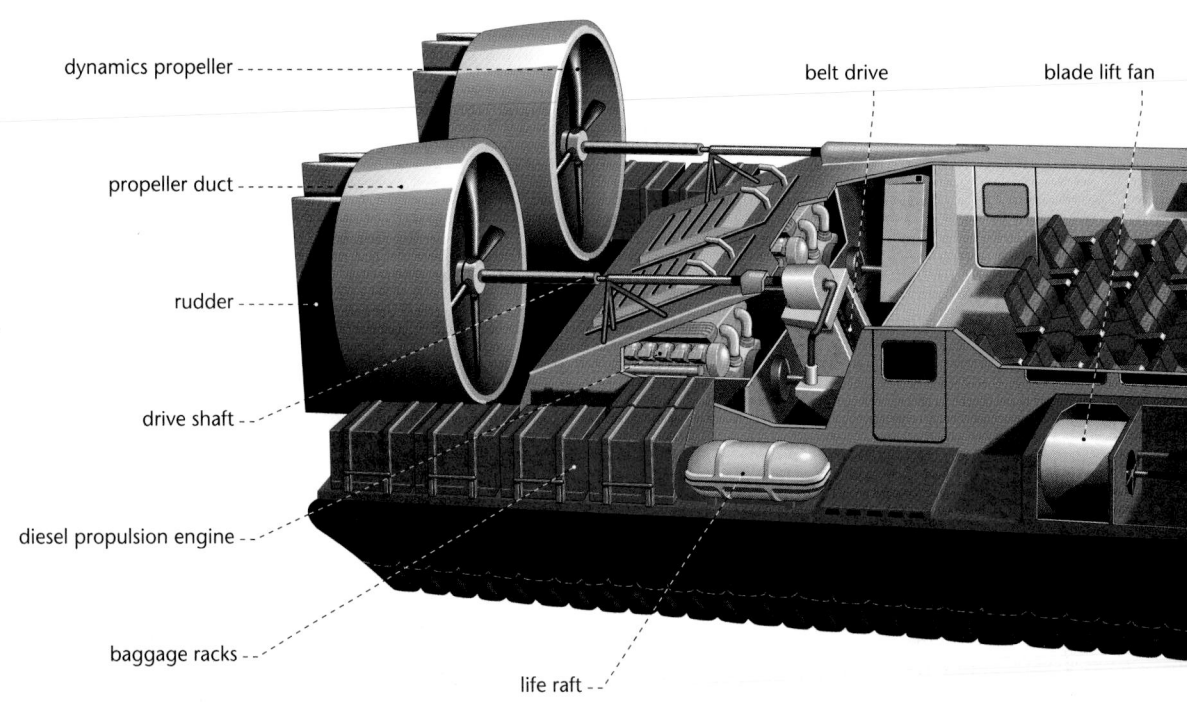

dynamics propeller

belt drive

blade lift fan

propeller duct

rudder

drive shaft

diesel propulsion engine

baggage racks

life raft

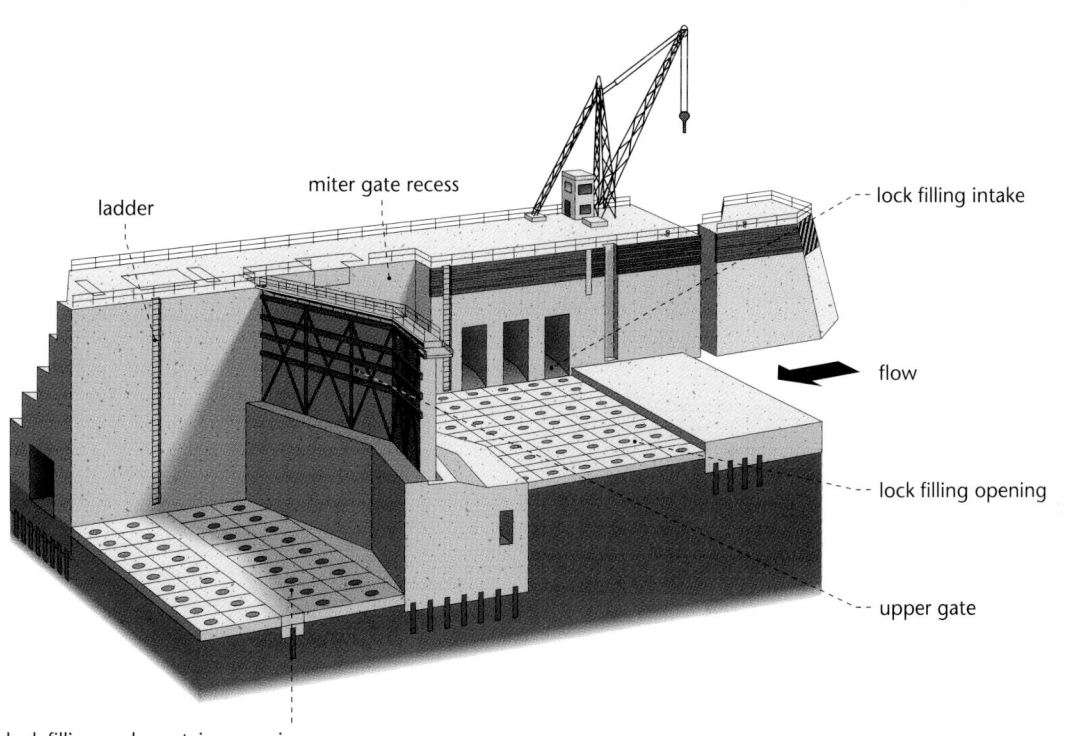

ladder　　　miter gate recess

lock filling intake

flow

lock filling opening

upper gate

lock filling and emptying opening

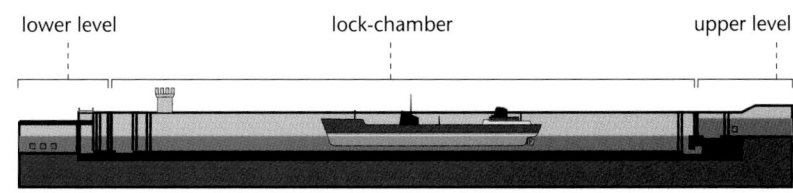

lower level

lock-chamber

upper level

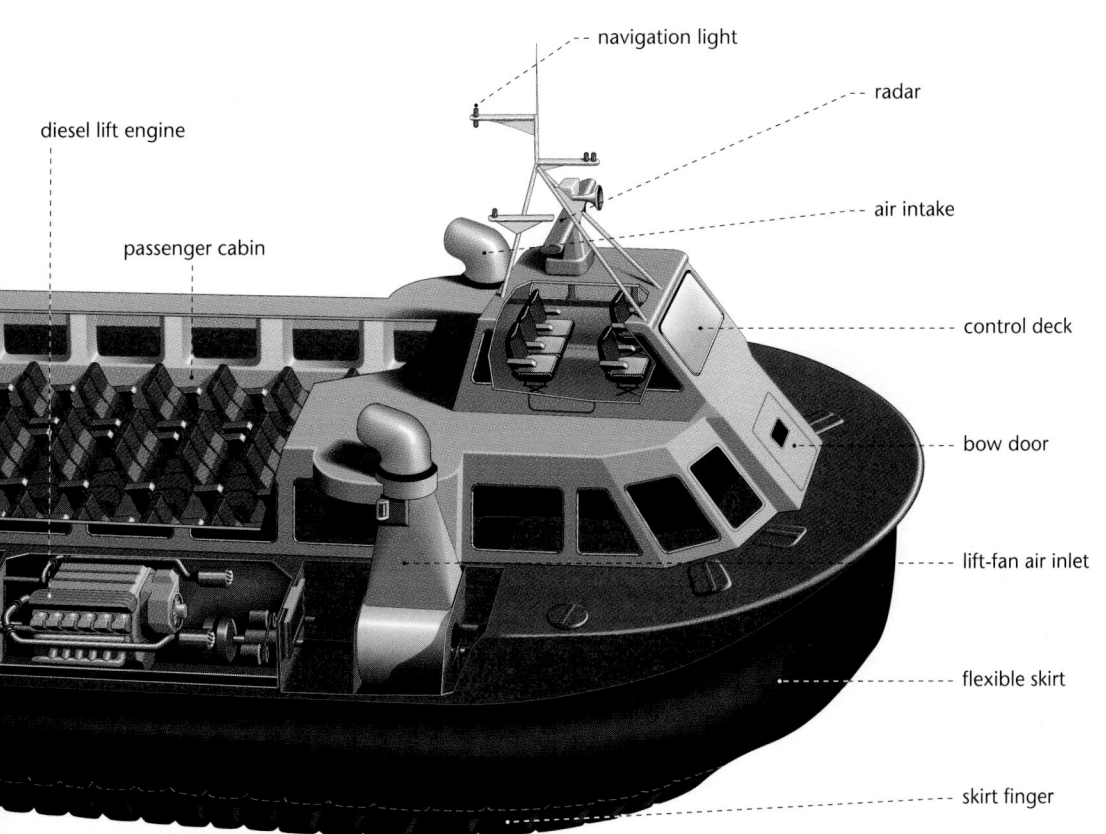

diesel lift engine

passenger cabin

navigation light

radar

air intake

control deck

bow door

lift-fan air inlet

flexible skirt

skirt finger

FERRY

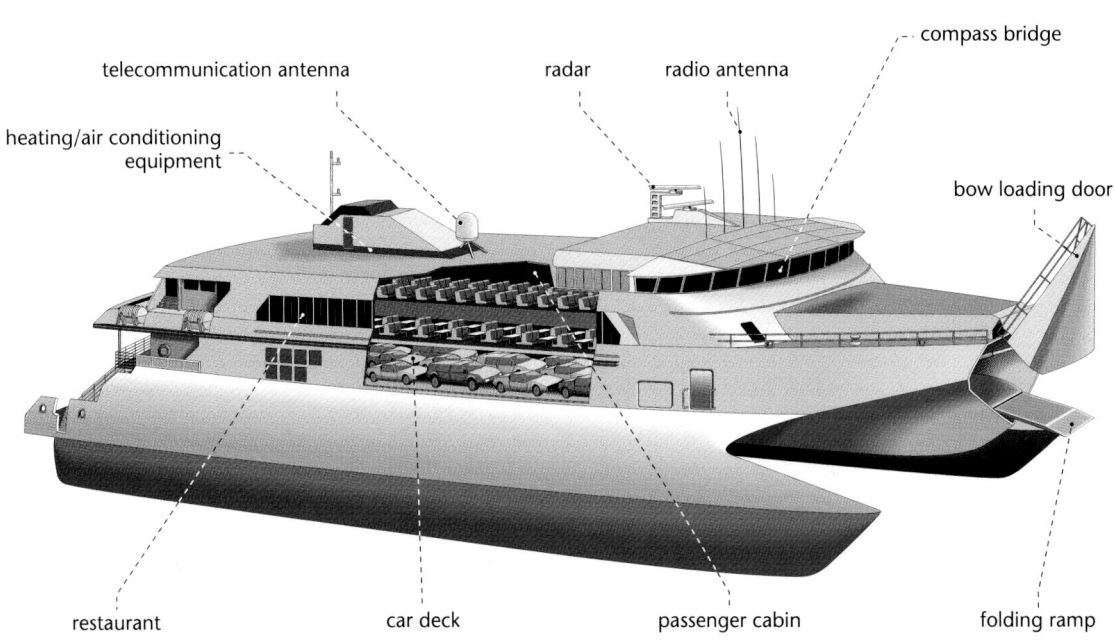

telecommunication antenna

radar

radio antenna

compass bridge

heating/air conditioning equipment

bow loading door

restaurant

car deck

passenger cabin

folding ramp

CONTAINER SHIP

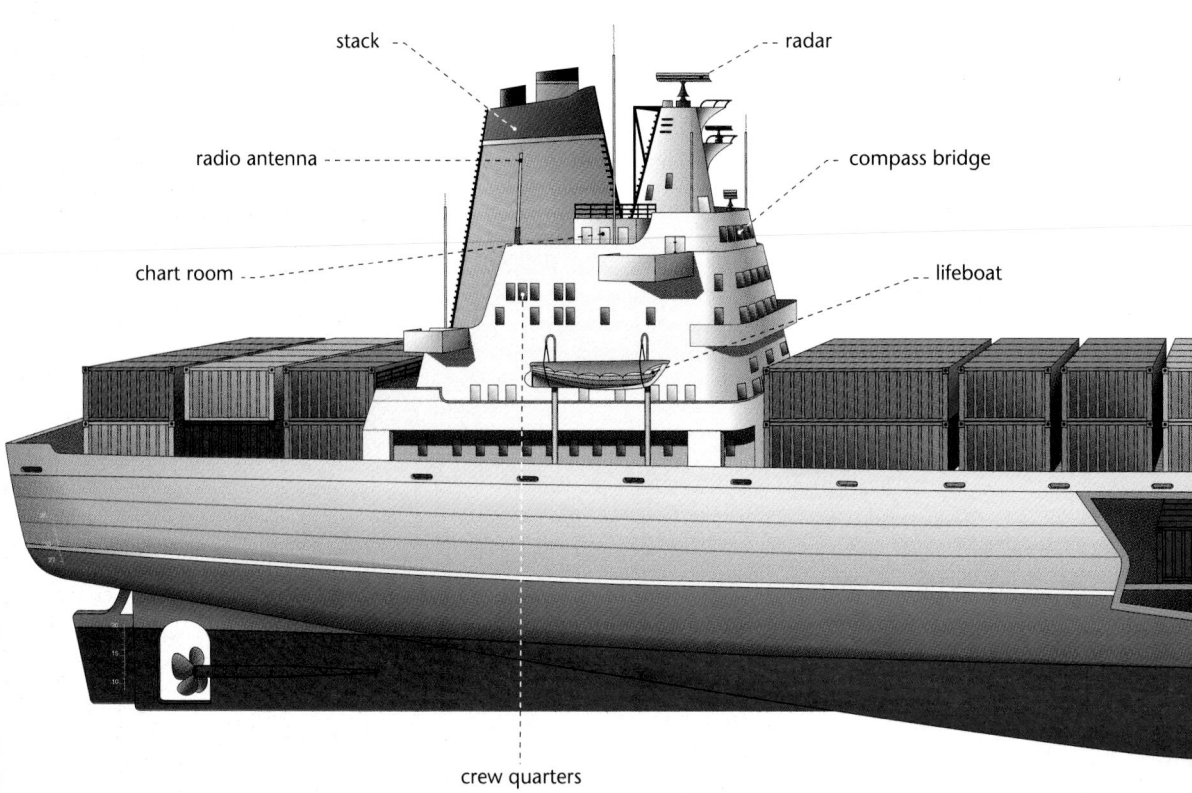

stack

radar

radio antenna

compass bridge

chart room

lifeboat

crew quarters

HYDROFOIL BOAT

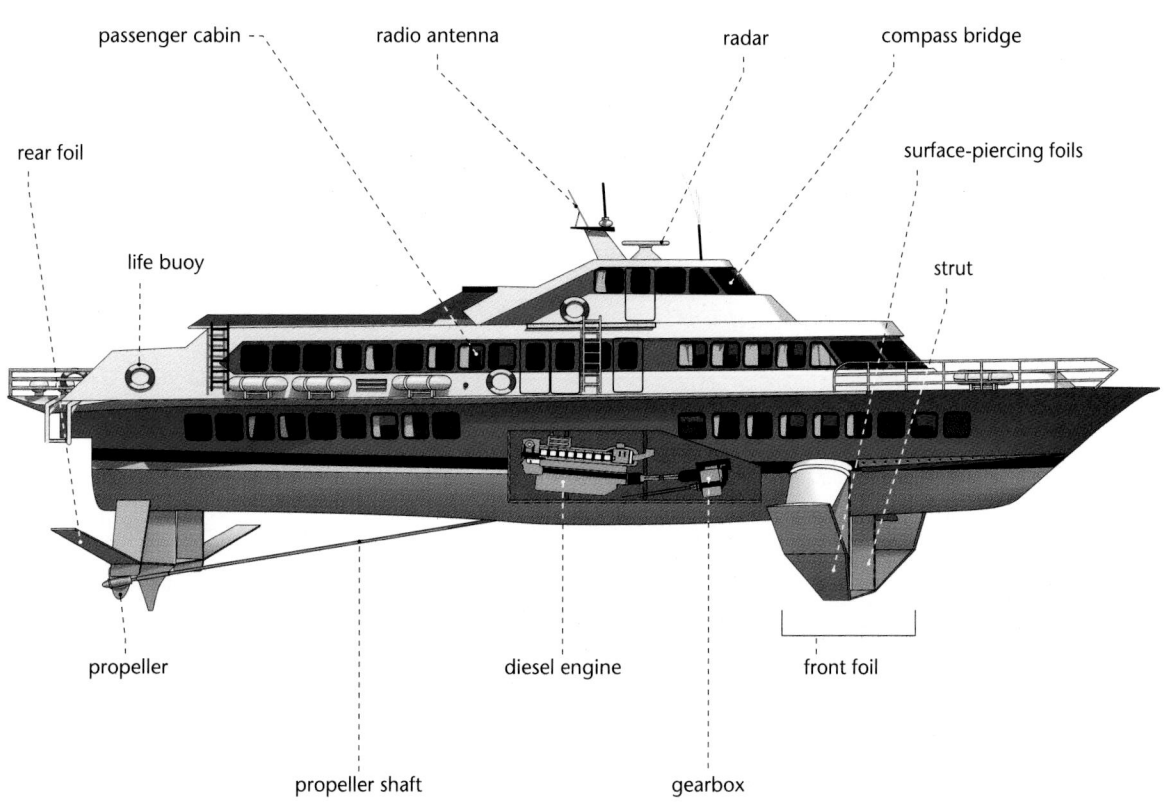

passenger cabin

radio antenna

radar

compass bridge

rear foil

surface-piercing foils

life buoy

strut

propeller

diesel engine

front foil

propeller shaft

gearbox

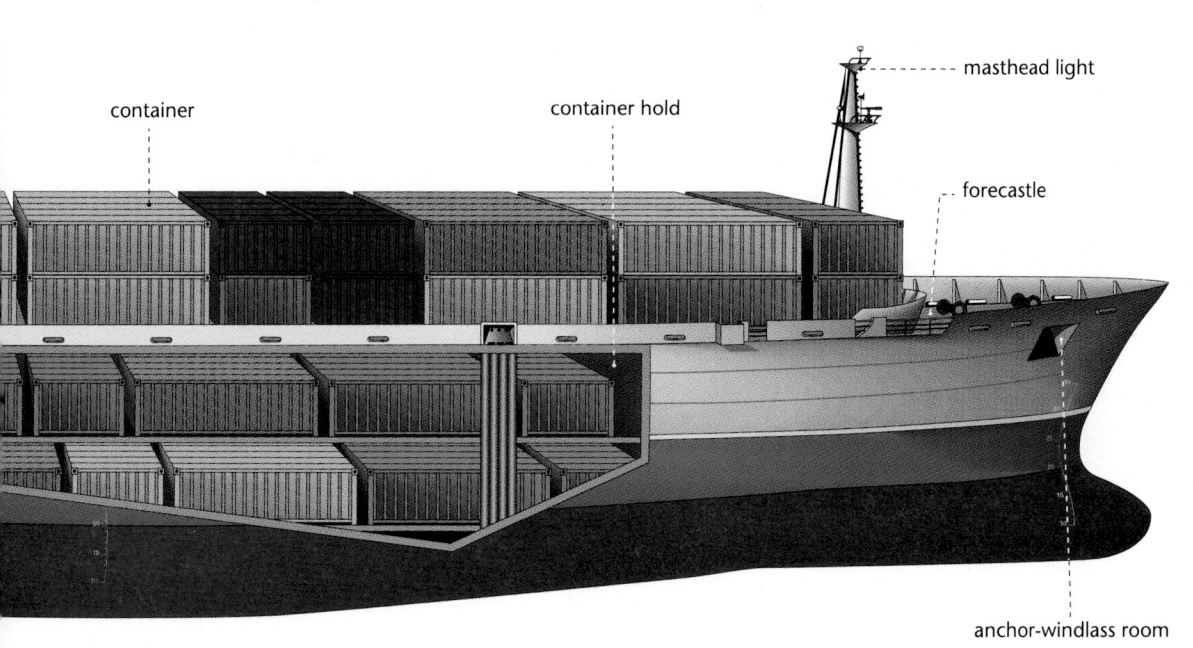

masthead light

container

container hold

forecastle

anchor-windlass room

MARITIME TRANSPORT

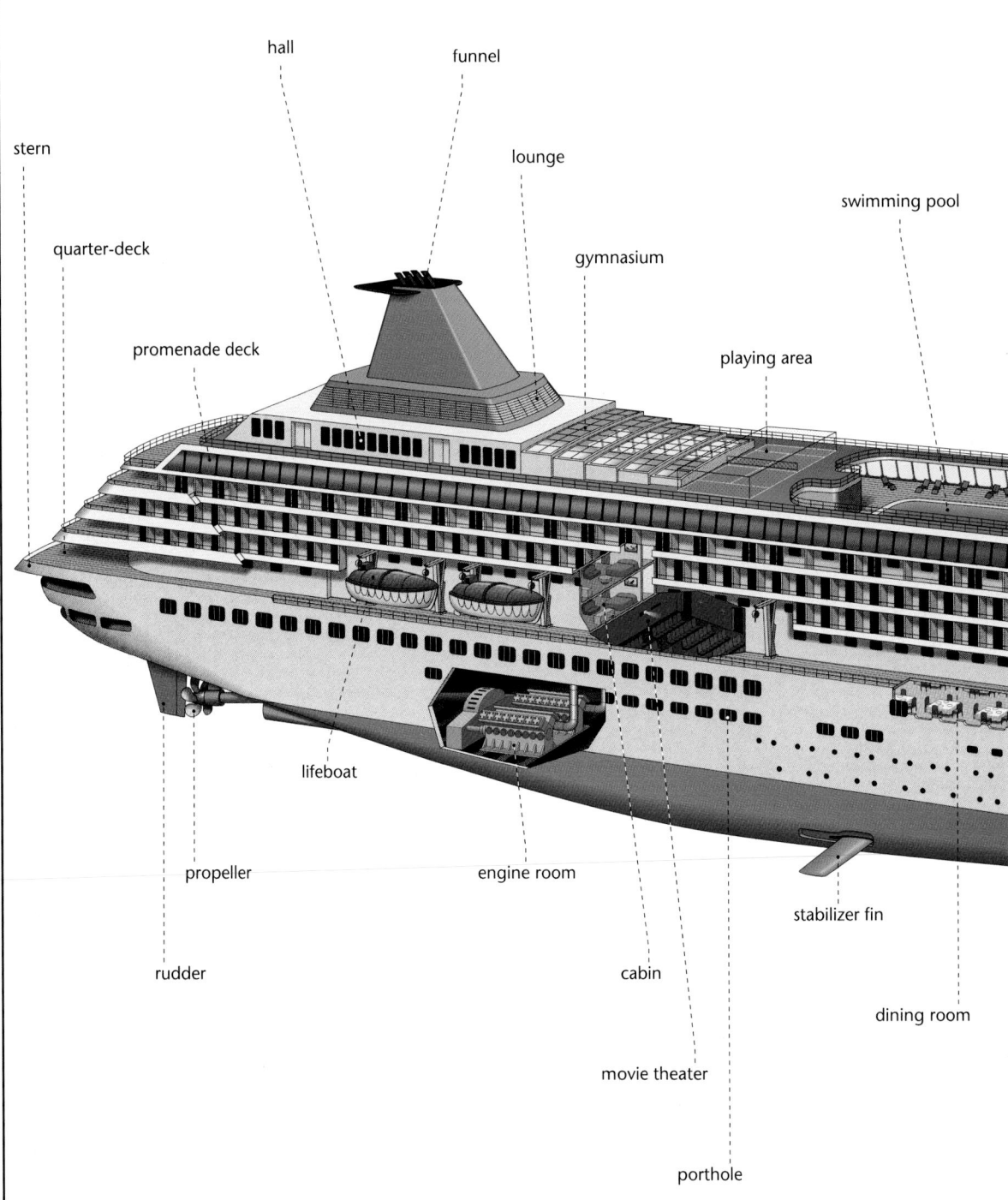

hall

funnel

stern

lounge

quarter-deck

swimming pool

gymnasium

promenade deck

playing area

lifeboat

propeller

engine room

stabilizer fin

rudder

cabin

dining room

movie theater

porthole

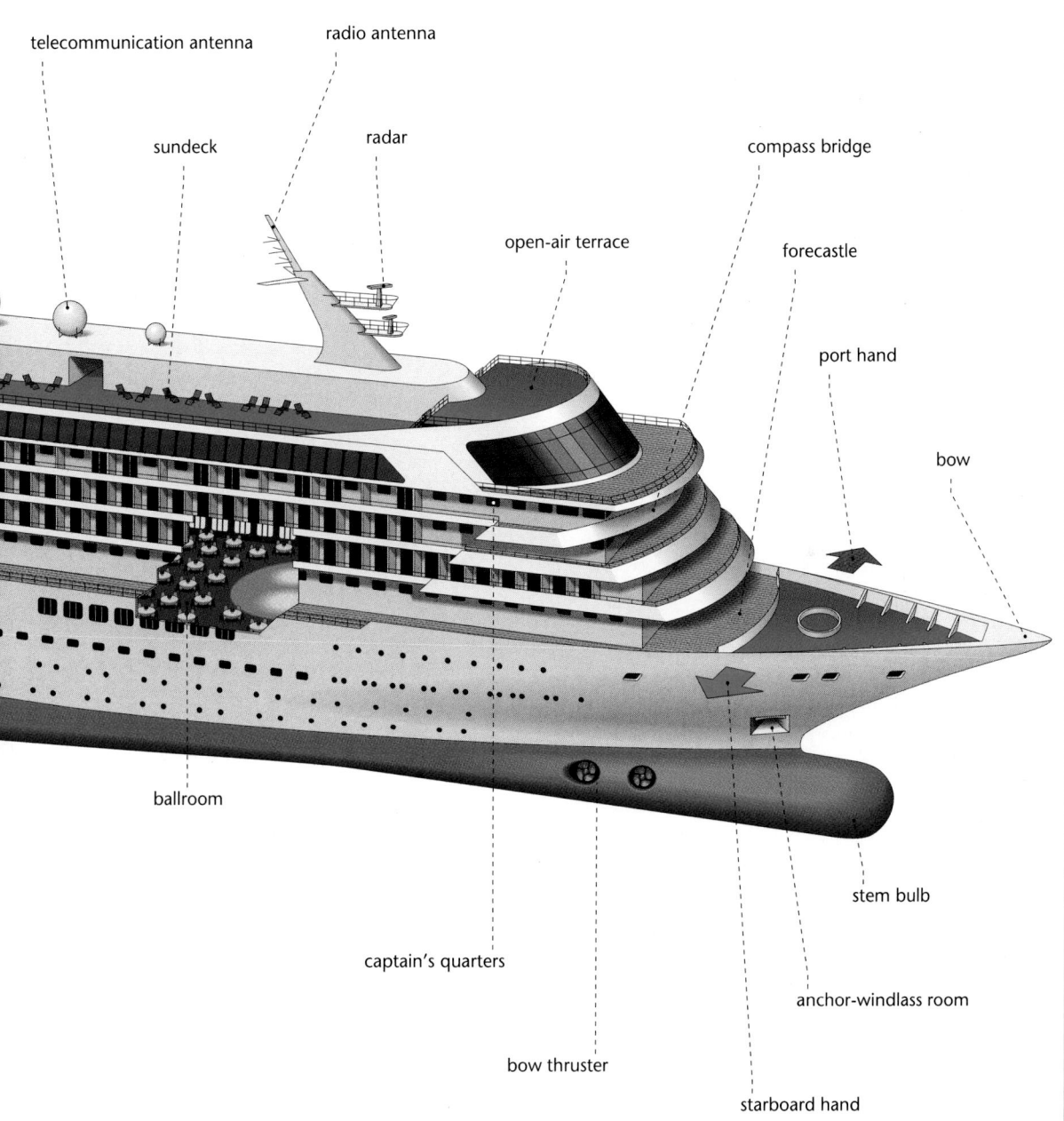

telecommunication antenna

radio antenna

sundeck

radar

compass bridge

open-air terrace

forecastle

port hand

bow

ballroom

stem bulb

captain's quarters

anchor-windlass room

bow thruster

starboard hand

LONG-RANGE JET

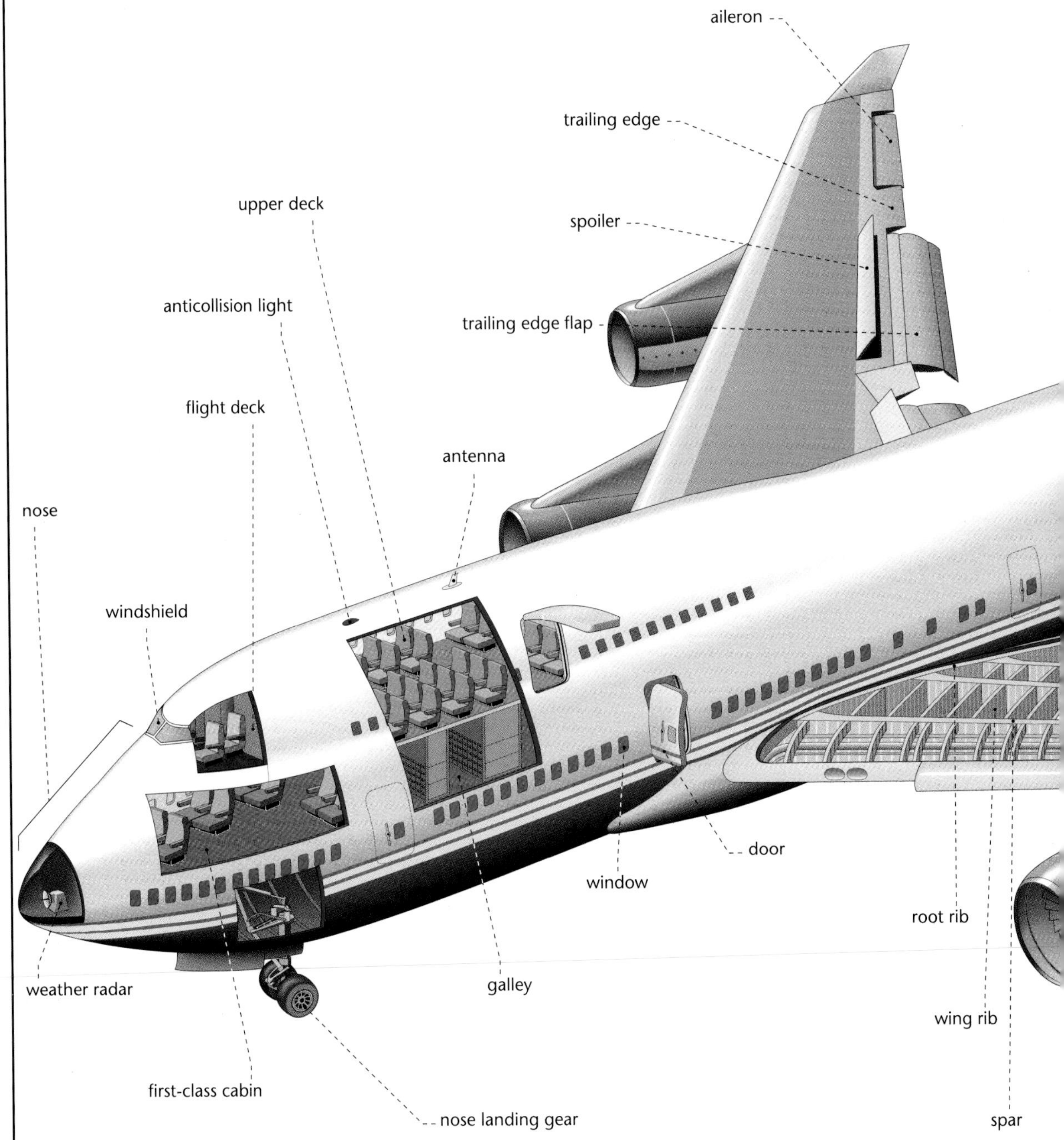

aileron

trailing edge

upper deck

spoiler

anticollision light

trailing edge flap

flight deck

antenna

nose

windshield

weather radar

first-class cabin

nose landing gear

galley

window

door

root rib

wing rib

spar

TYPES OF TAIL SHAPES

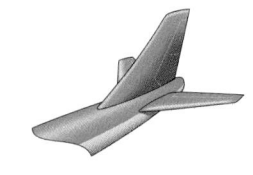

fuselage mounted tail
unit

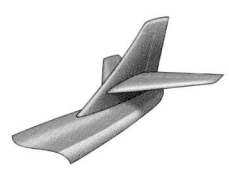

fin-mounted tail unit

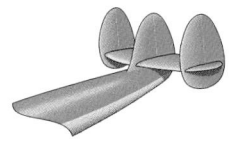

triple tail unit

T-tail unit

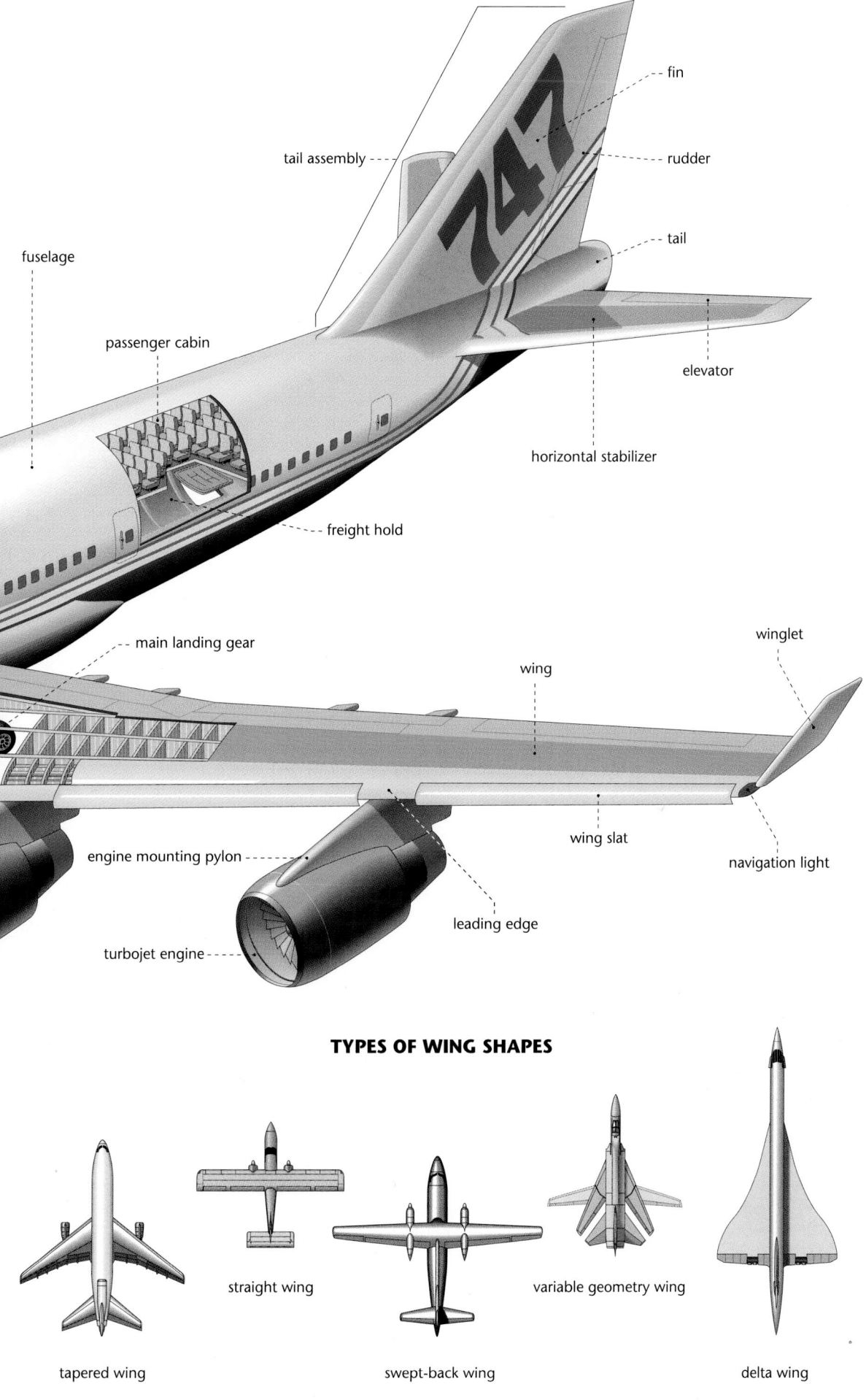

fin

tail assembly

rudder

fuselage

tail

passenger cabin

elevator

horizontal stabilizer

freight hold

main landing gear

winglet

wing

engine mounting pylon

wing slat

navigation light

leading edge

turbojet engine

TYPES OF WING SHAPES

straight wing

variable geometry wing

tapered wing

swept-back wing

delta wing

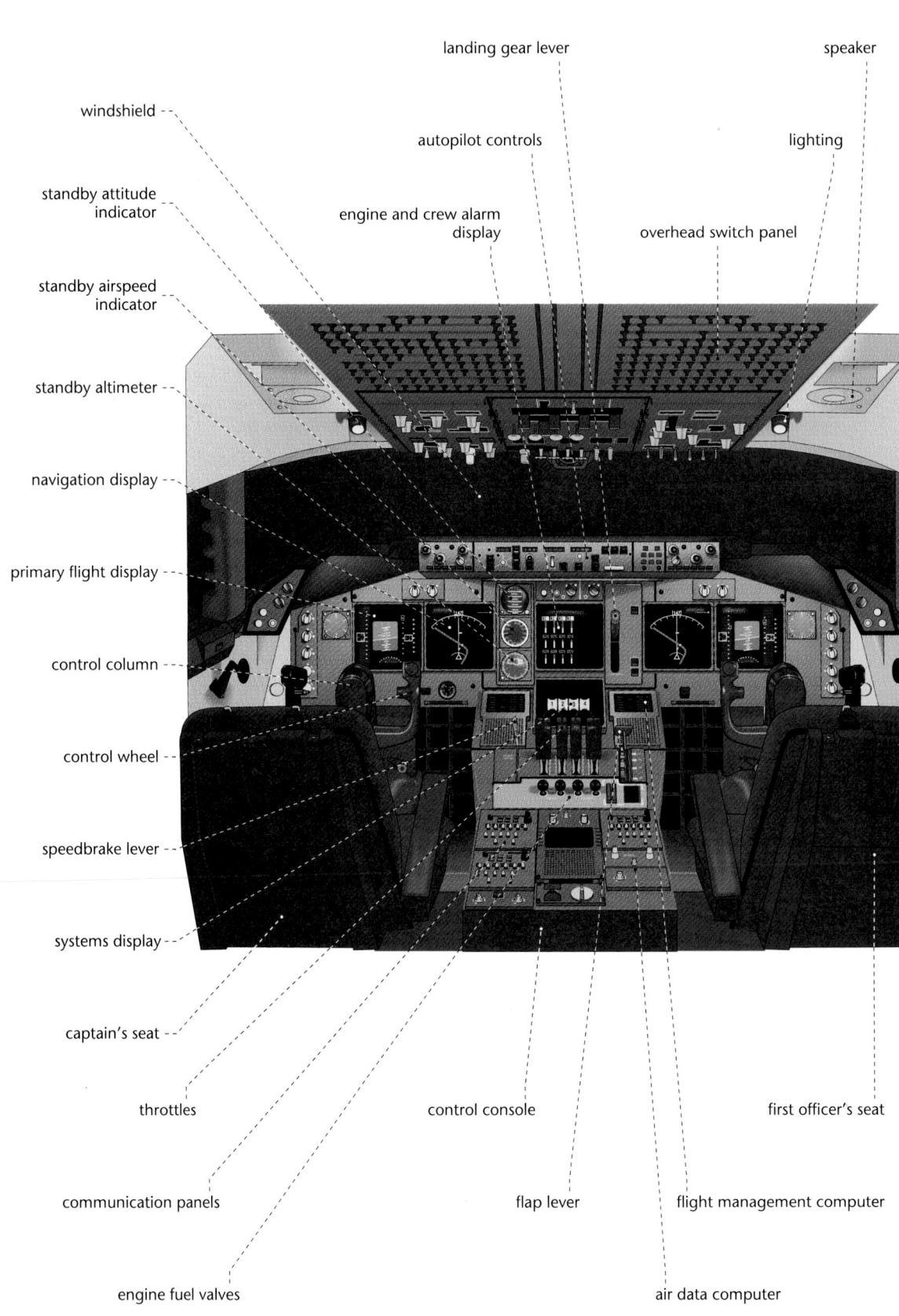

landing gear lever

speaker

windshield

autopilot controls

lighting

standby attitude
indicator

engine and crew alarm
display

overhead switch panel

standby airspeed
indicator

standby altimeter

navigation display

primary flight display

control column

control wheel

speedbrake lever

systems display

captain's seat

throttles

control console

first officer's seat

communication panels

flap lever

flight management computer

engine fuel valves

air data computer

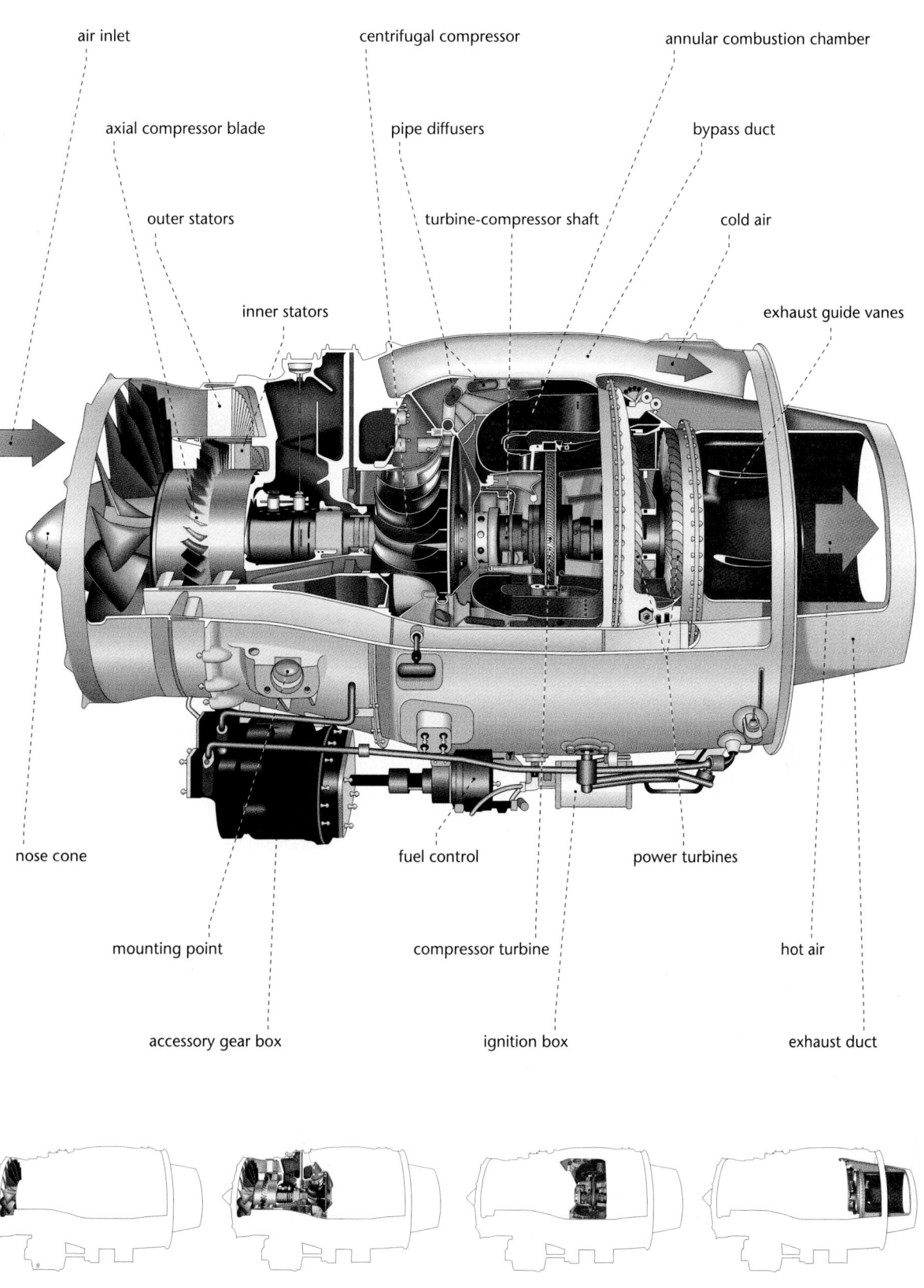

air inlet

centrifugal compressor

annular combustion chamber

axial compressor blade

pipe diffusers

bypass duct

outer stators

turbine-compressor shaft

cold air

inner stators

exhaust guide vanes

nose cone

fuel control

power turbines

hot air

mounting point

compressor turbine

accessory gear box

ignition box

exhaust duct

fan

compression

combustion

exhaust

control tower cab

access road

high-speed exit taxiway

control tower

taxiway

by-pass taxiway

apron

apron

taxiway

service road

maintenance hangar

passenger terminal

parking area

telescopic corridor

boarding walkway

radial passenger loading area

service area

taxiway line

AIR TRANSPORT

PASSENGER TERMINAL

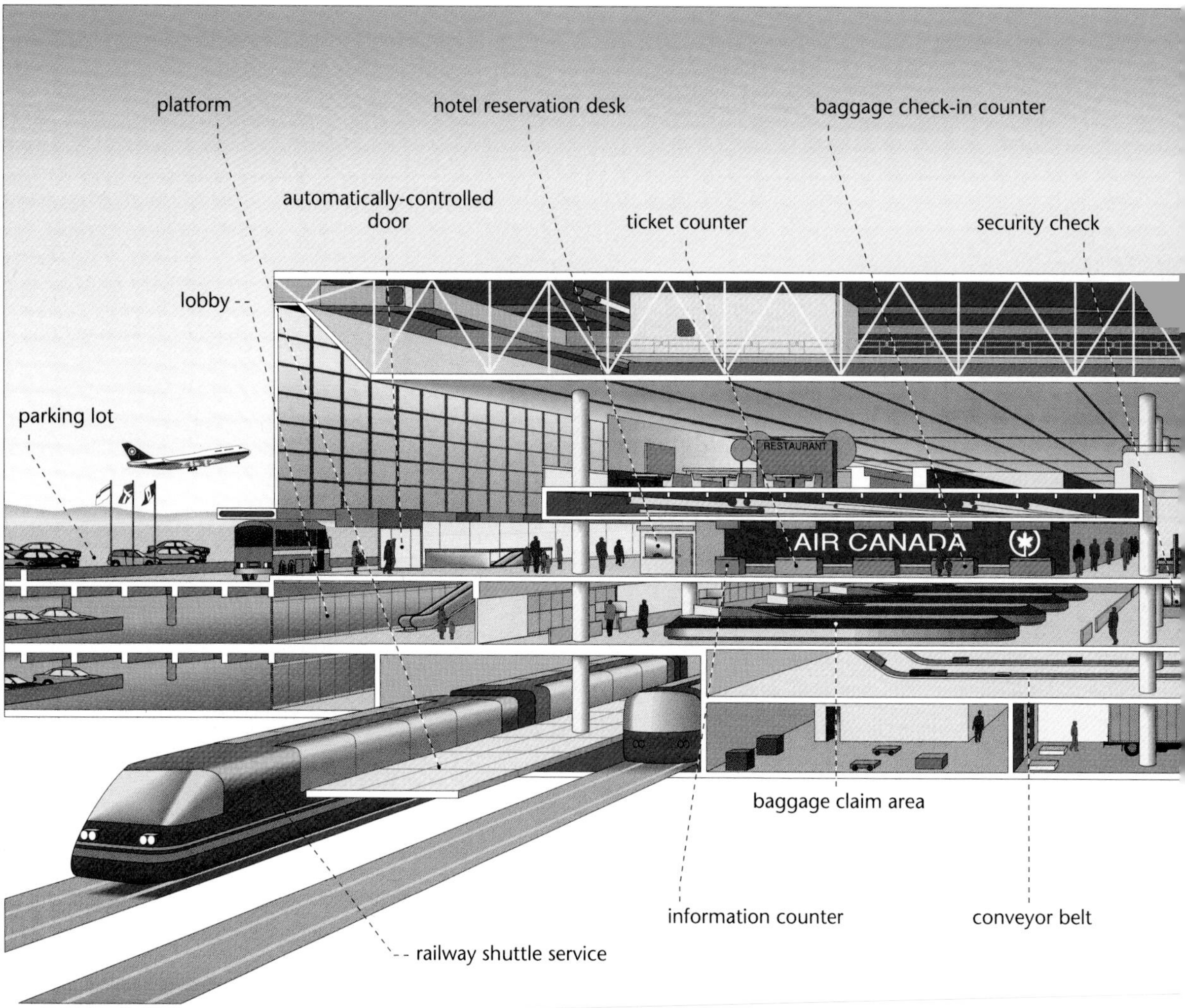

platform

hotel reservation desk

baggage check-in counter

automatically-controlled
door

ticket counter

security check

lobby

parking lot

RESTAURANT

AIR CANADA

baggage claim area

information counter

conveyor belt

railway shuttle service

RUNWAY

runway center line markings

runway designation marking

holding area marking

runway side stripe markings

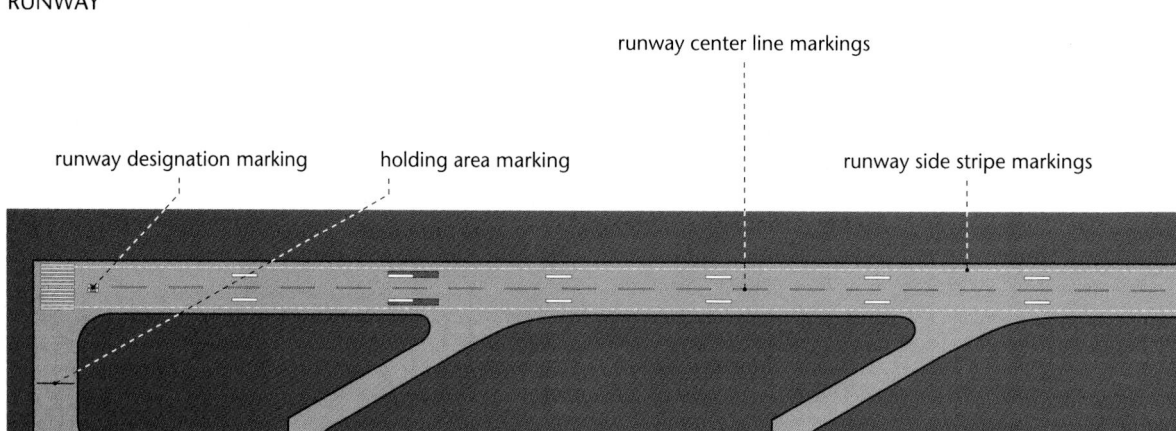

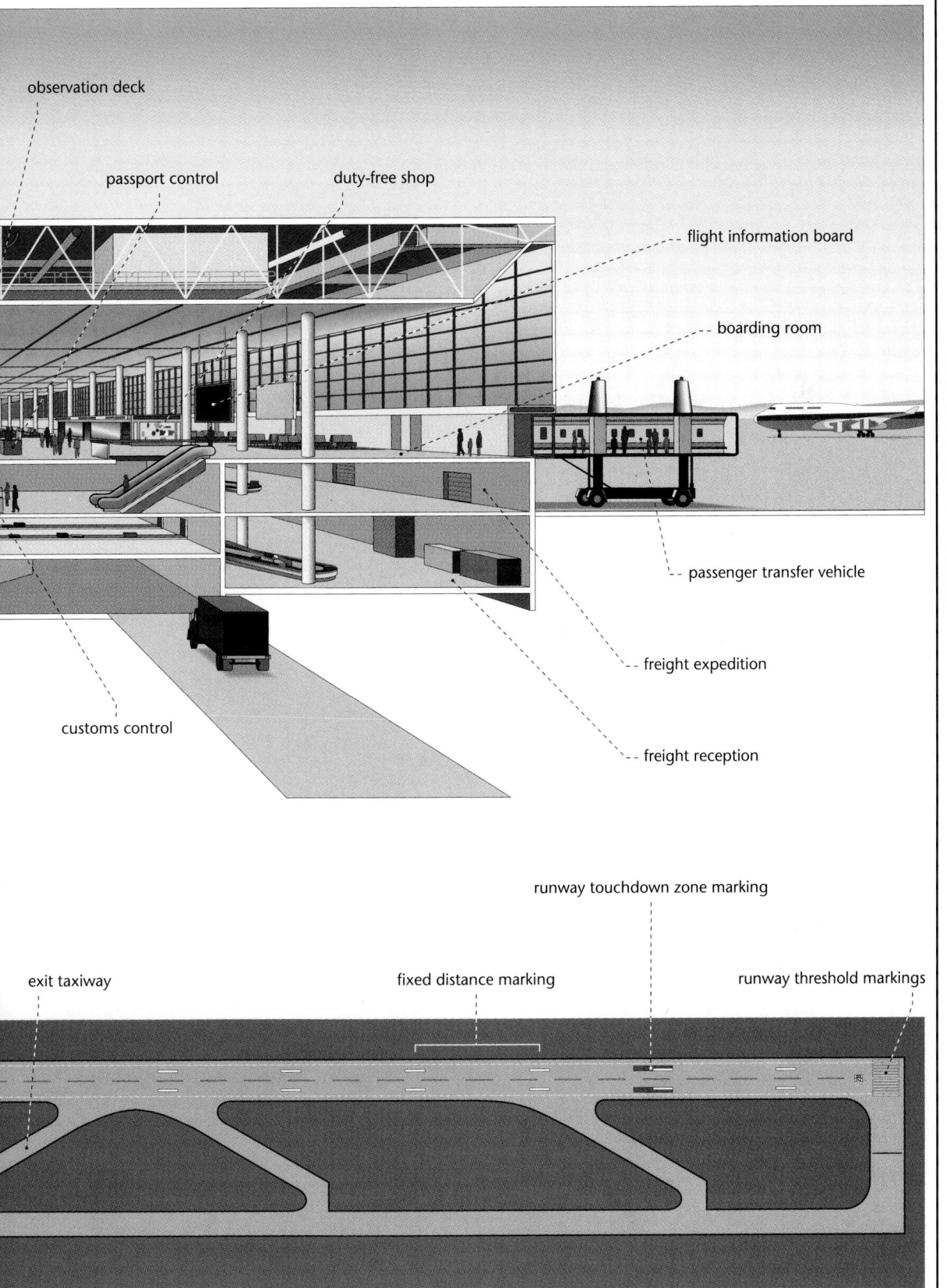

observation deck

passport control

duty-free shop

flight information board

boarding room

passenger transfer vehicle

freight expedition

customs control

freight reception

runway touchdown zone marking

exit taxiway

fixed distance marking

runway threshold markings

AIR TRANSPORT

GROUND AIRPORT EQUIPMENT

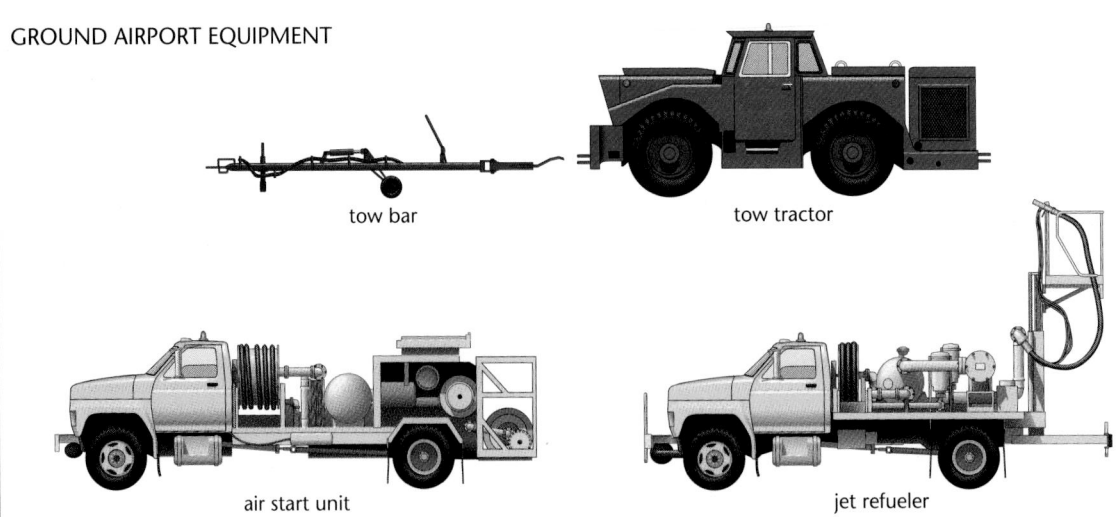

tow bar

tow tractor

air start unit

jet refueler

electrical power unit

ground air conditioner

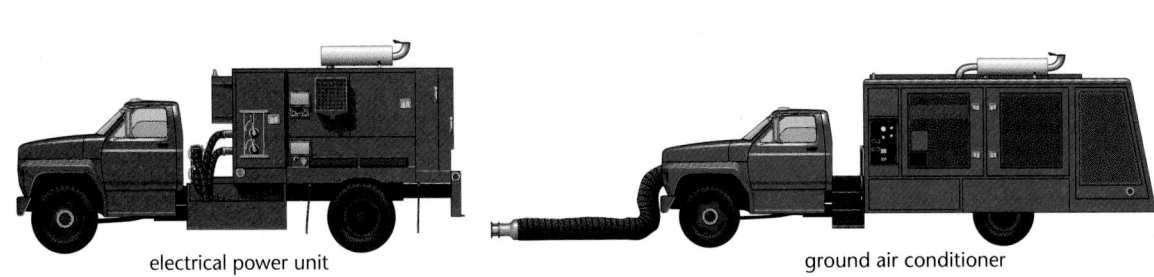

lavatory truck

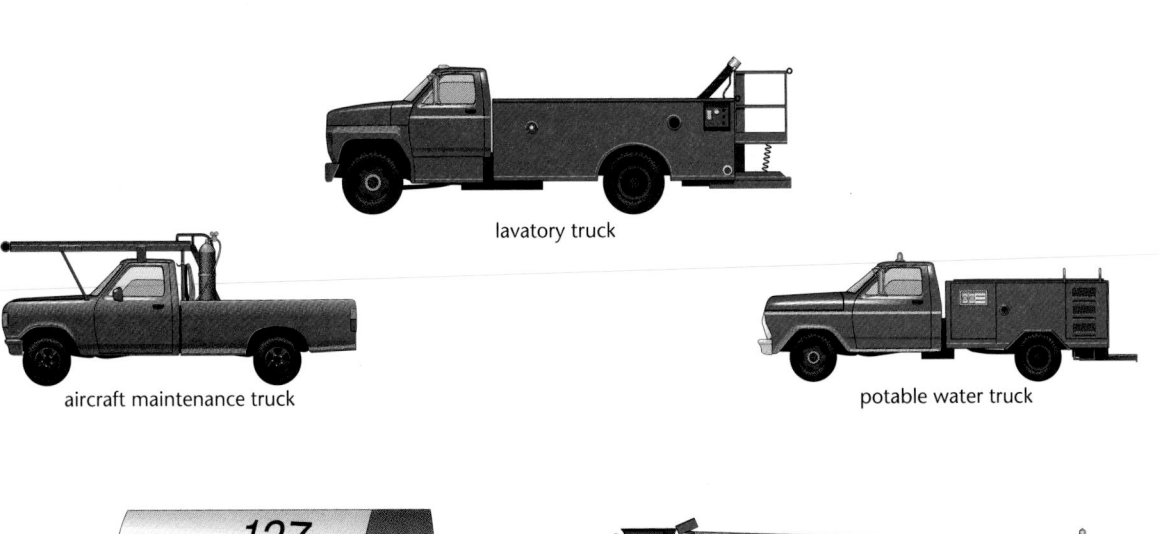

aircraft maintenance truck

potable water truck

127

wheel chock

boom truck

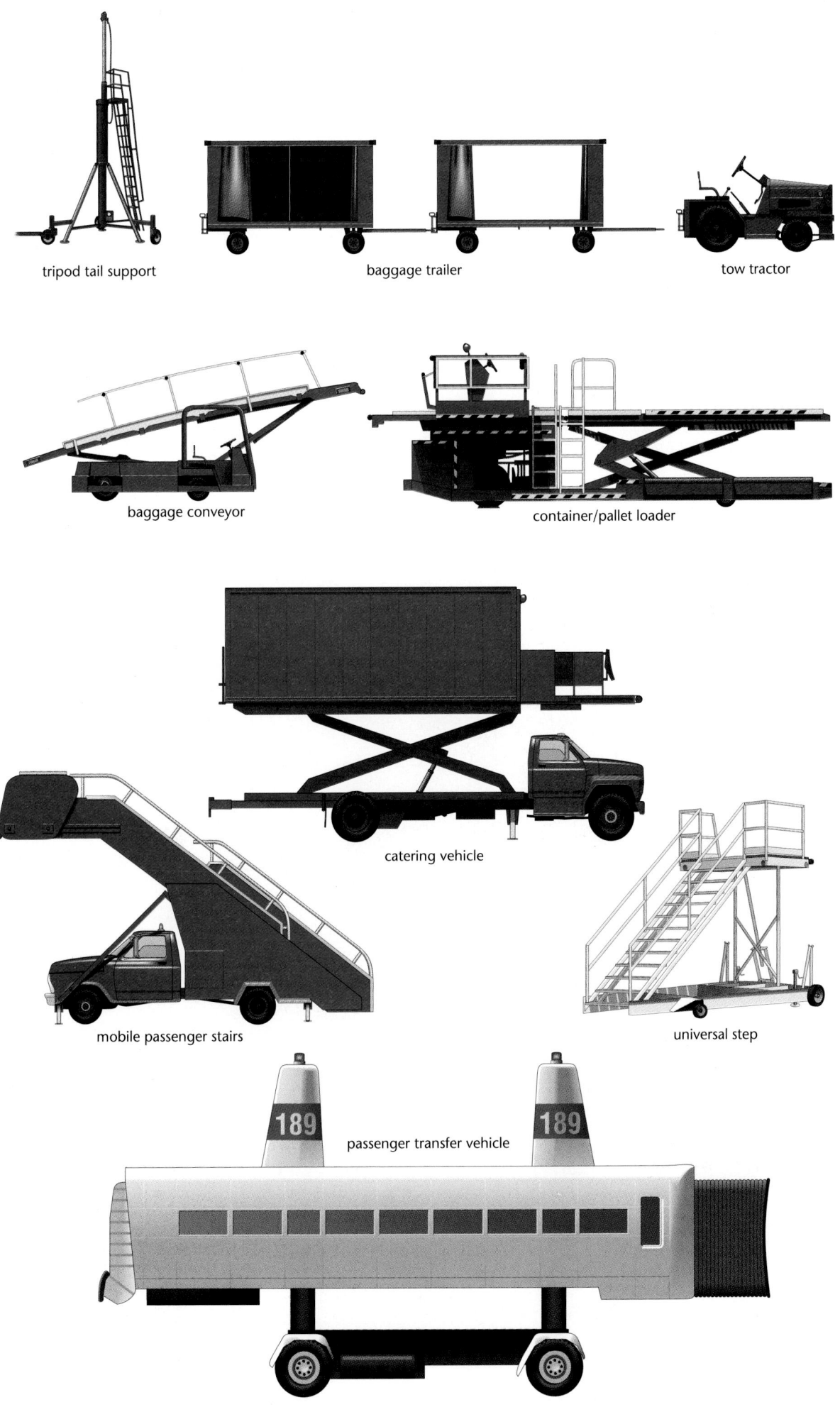

tripod tail support

baggage trailer

tow tractor

baggage conveyor

container/pallet loader

catering vehicle

mobile passenger stairs

universal step

passenger transfer vehicle

189

189

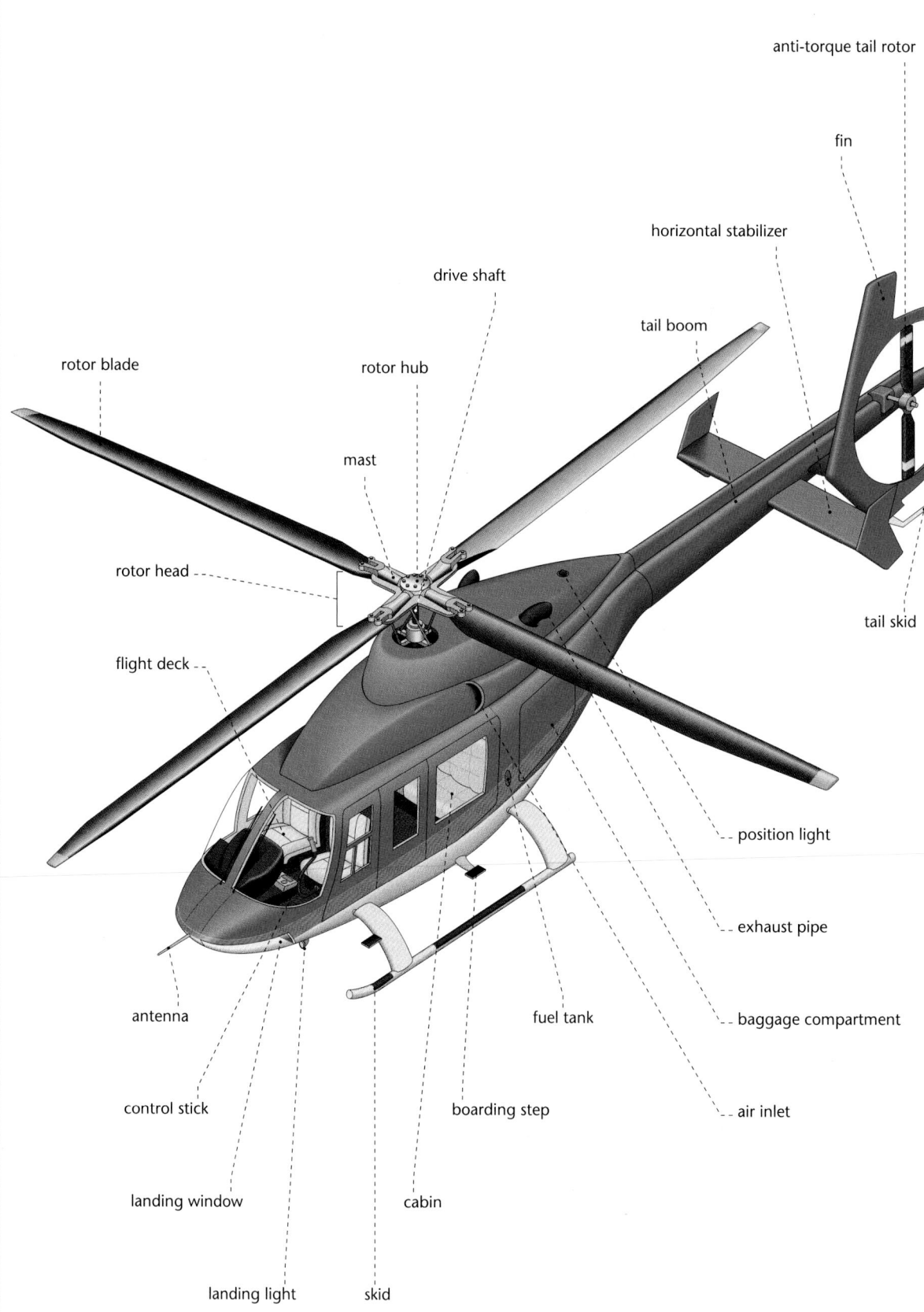

anti-torque tail rotor

fin

horizontal stabilizer

drive shaft

tail boom

rotor blade

rotor hub

mast

rotor head

tail skid

flight deck

position light

exhaust pipe

antenna

fuel tank

baggage compartment

control stick

boarding step

air inlet

landing window

cabin

landing light

skid

ROCKET

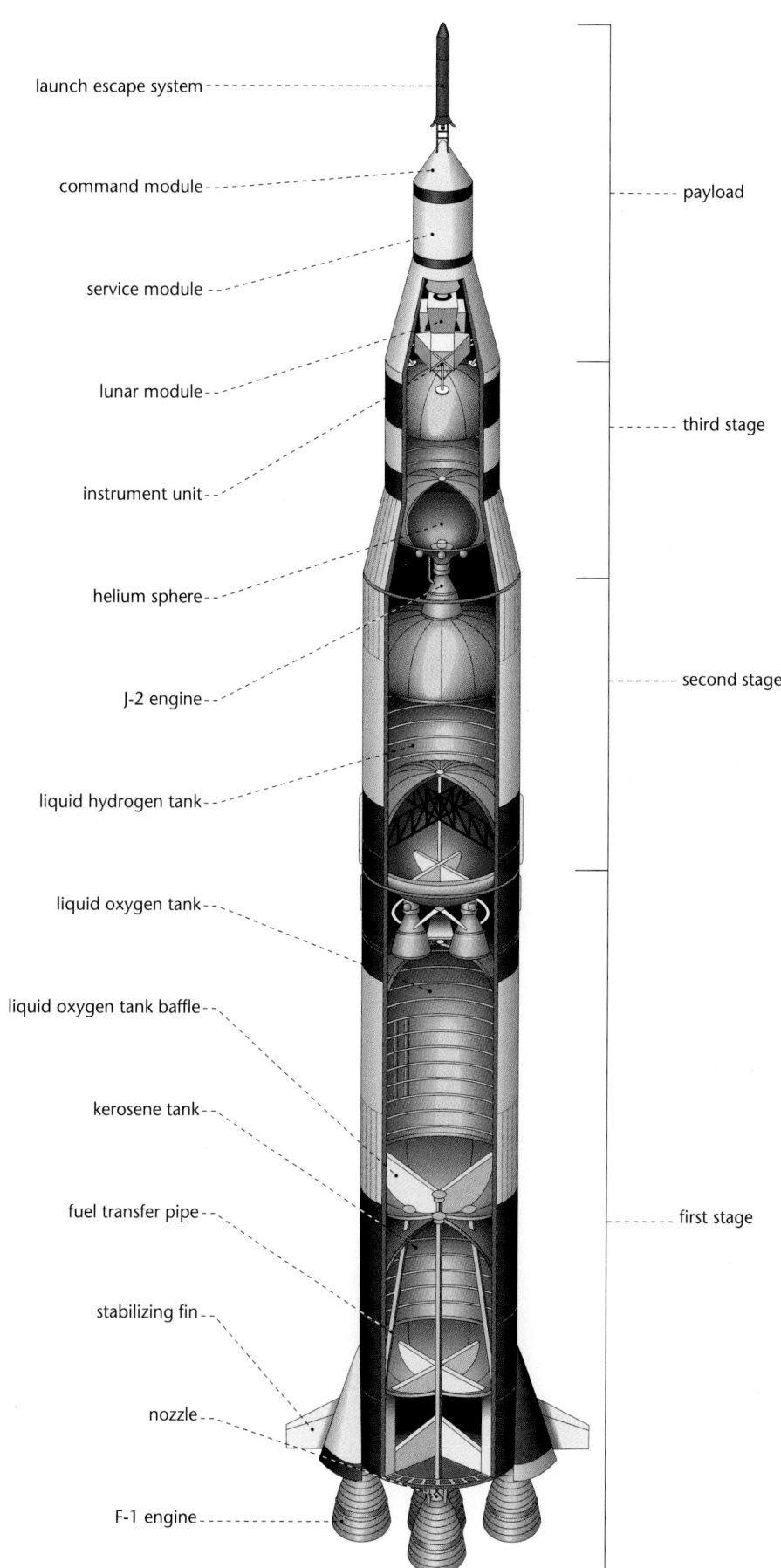

launch escape system

command module

service module

lunar module

instrument unit

helium sphere

J-2 engine

liquid hydrogen tank

liquid oxygen tank

liquid oxygen tank baffle

kerosene tank

fuel transfer pipe

stabilizing fin

nozzle

F-1 engine

payload

third stage

second stage

first stage

SPACE SHUTTLE

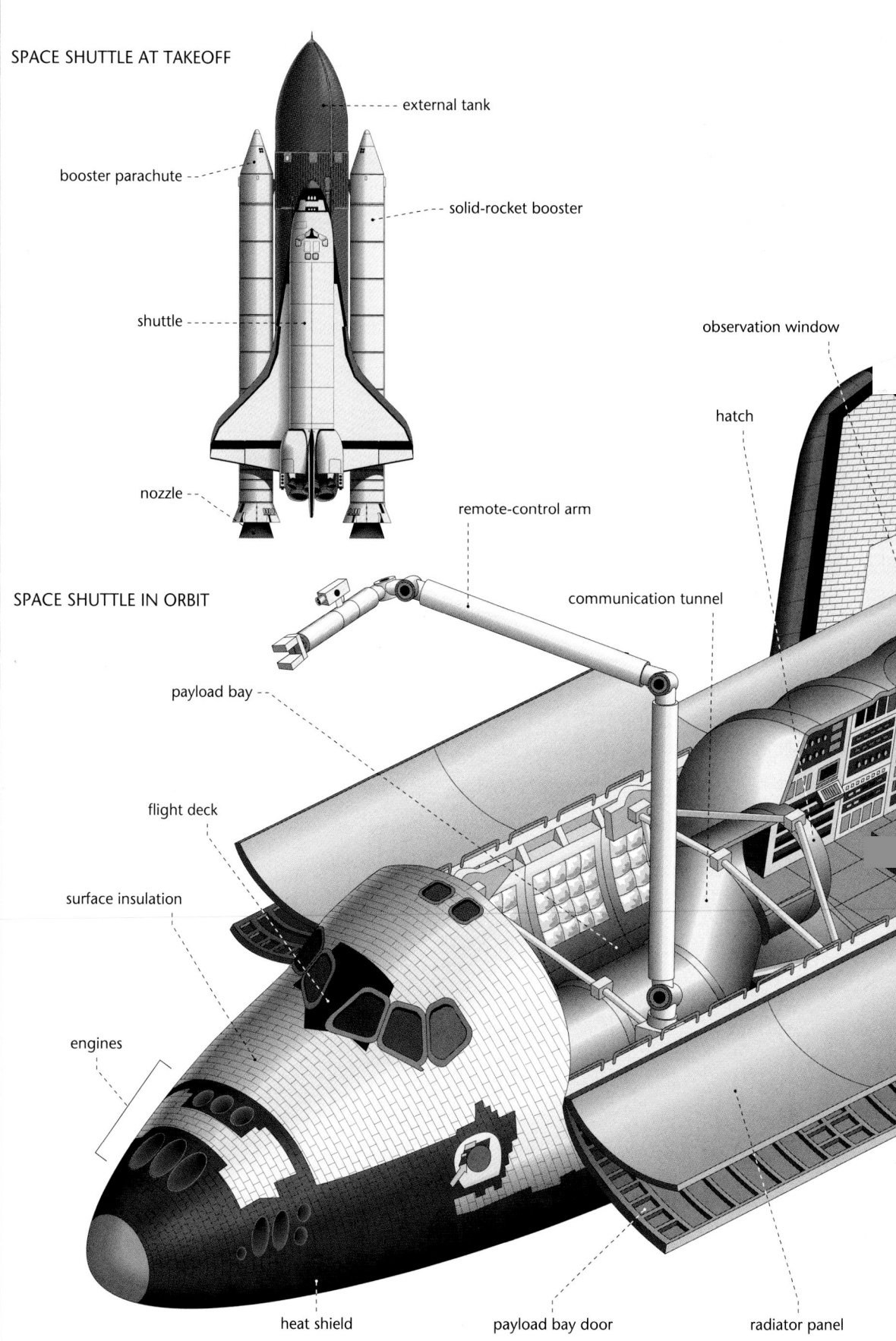

SPACE SHUTTLE AT TAKEOFF

external tank

booster parachute

solid-rocket booster

shuttle

nozzle

SPACE SHUTTLE IN ORBIT

observation window

hatch

remote-control arm

communication tunnel

payload bay

flight deck

surface insulation

engines

heat shield

payload bay door

radiator panel

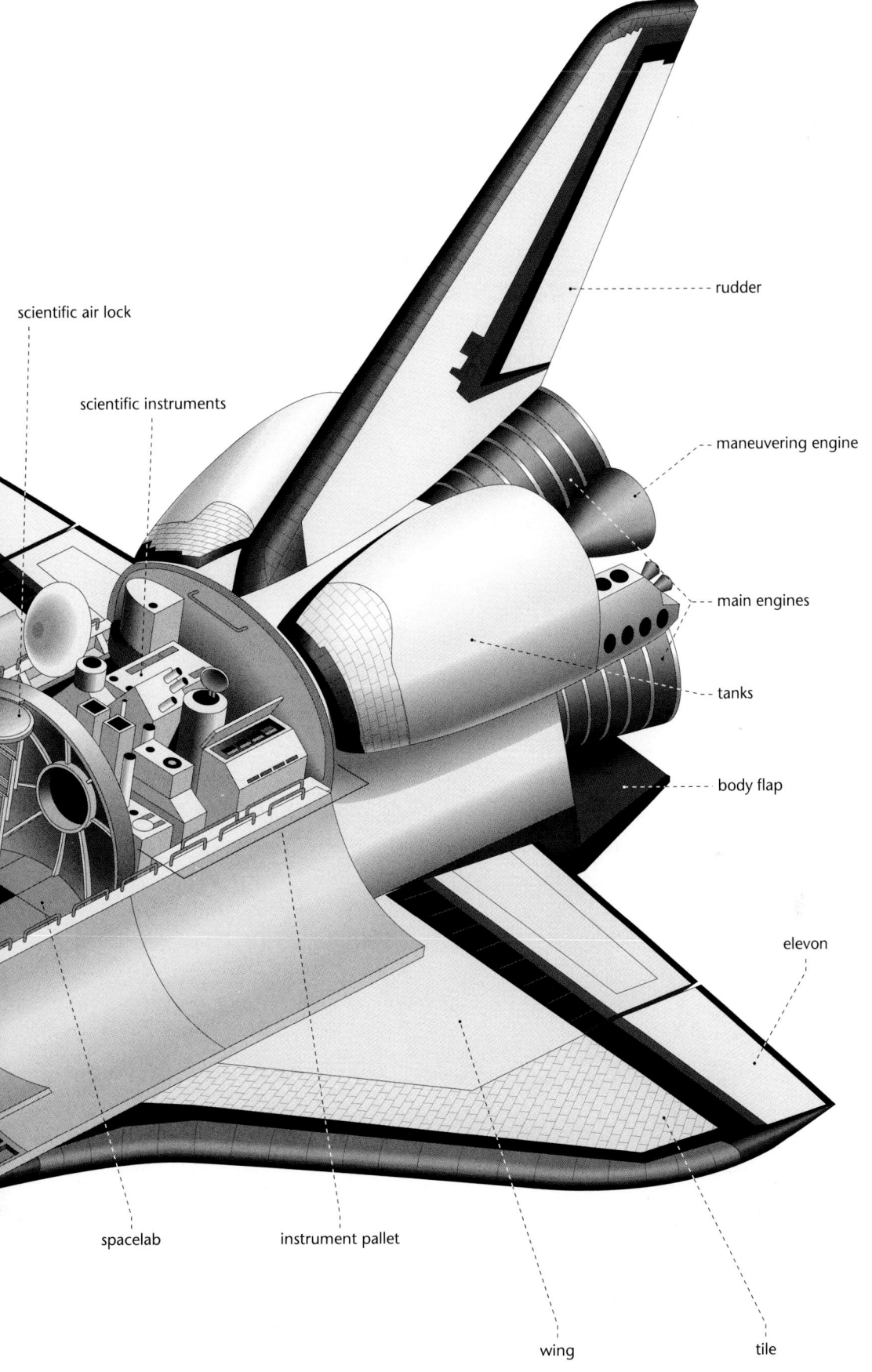

scientific air lock

scientific instruments

rudder

maneuvering engine

main engines

tanks

body flap

elevon

spacelab

instrument pallet

wing

tile

SPACESUIT

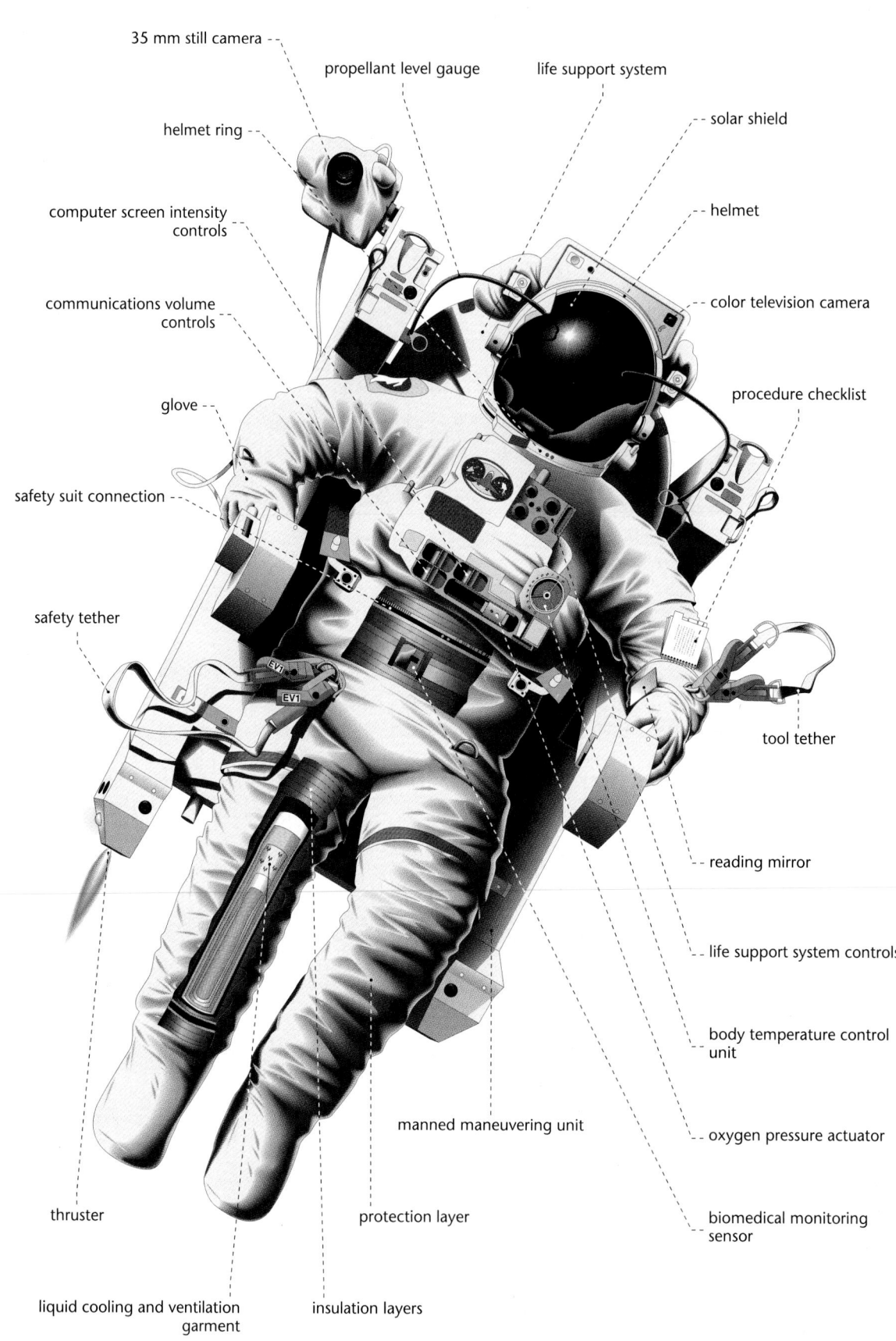

35 mm still camera

propellant level gauge

life support system

solar shield

helmet ring

helmet

computer screen intensity
controls

color television camera

communications volume
controls

procedure checklist

glove

safety suit connection

safety tether

tool tether

reading mirror

life support system controls

body temperature control
unit

manned maneuvering unit

oxygen pressure actuator

thruster

protection layer

biomedical monitoring
sensor

liquid cooling and ventilation
garment

insulation layers

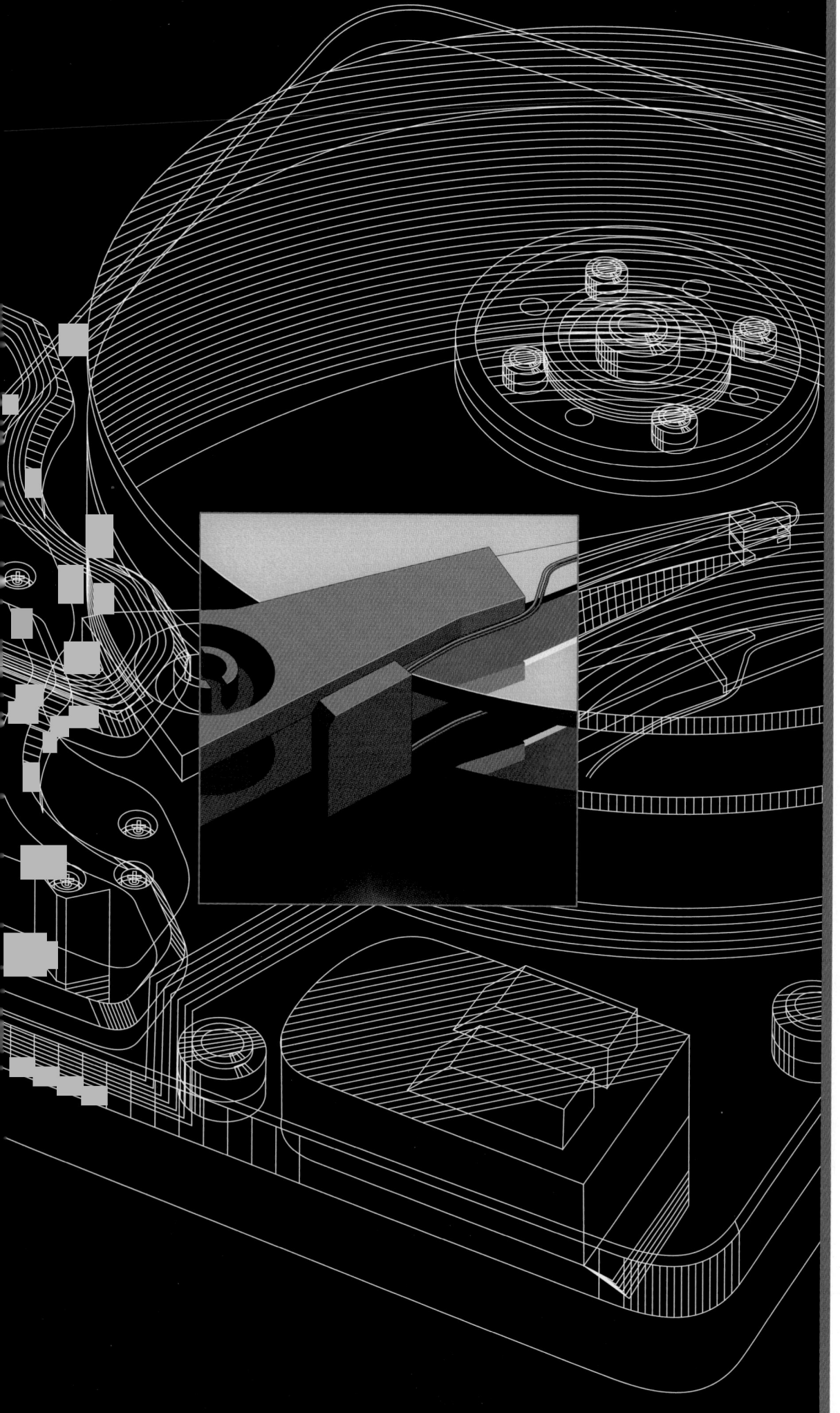

CONTENTS

OFFICE SUPPLIES

STATIONERY 515

OFFICE FURNITURE 520

CALCULATOR..523

ELECTRONIC TYPEWRITER...524

OFFICE AUTOMATION

CONFIGURATION OF AN OFFICE AUTOMATION SYSTEM 526

BASIC COMPONENTS..528

PHOTOCOPIER...532

OFFICE SUPPLIES

STATIONERY

ballpoint pen

mechanical pencil

fountain pen

pencil

eraser holder

stick eraser

marker

glue stick

eraser

correction fluid

highlighter pen

clip

paper clips

stapler

letter opener

paper fasteners

staples

thumb tacks

pencil sharpener

correction paper

staple remover

515

OFFICE SUPPLIES

rubber stamp

stamp pad

tape dispenser

numbering machine

dater

stamp rack

bill-file

label maker

paper punch

moistener

rotary file

letter scale

pencil sharpener

telephone index

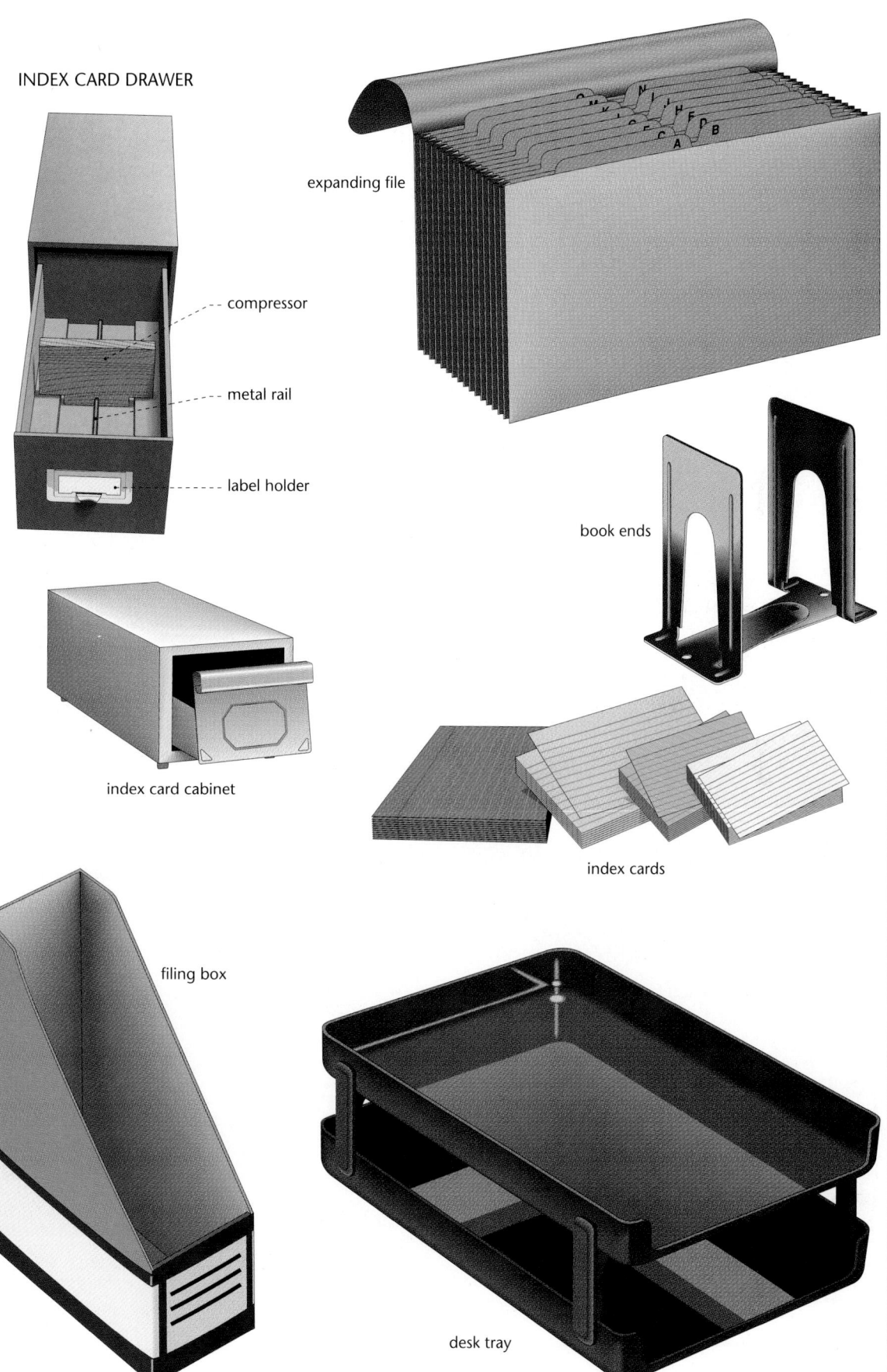

INDEX CARD DRAWER

compressor

metal rail

label holder

index card cabinet

expanding file

book ends

index cards

filing box

desk tray

tear-off calendar

appointment book

calendar pad

account book

memo pad

self-adhesive labels

tab

archboard

window tab

folder

file guides

hanging file

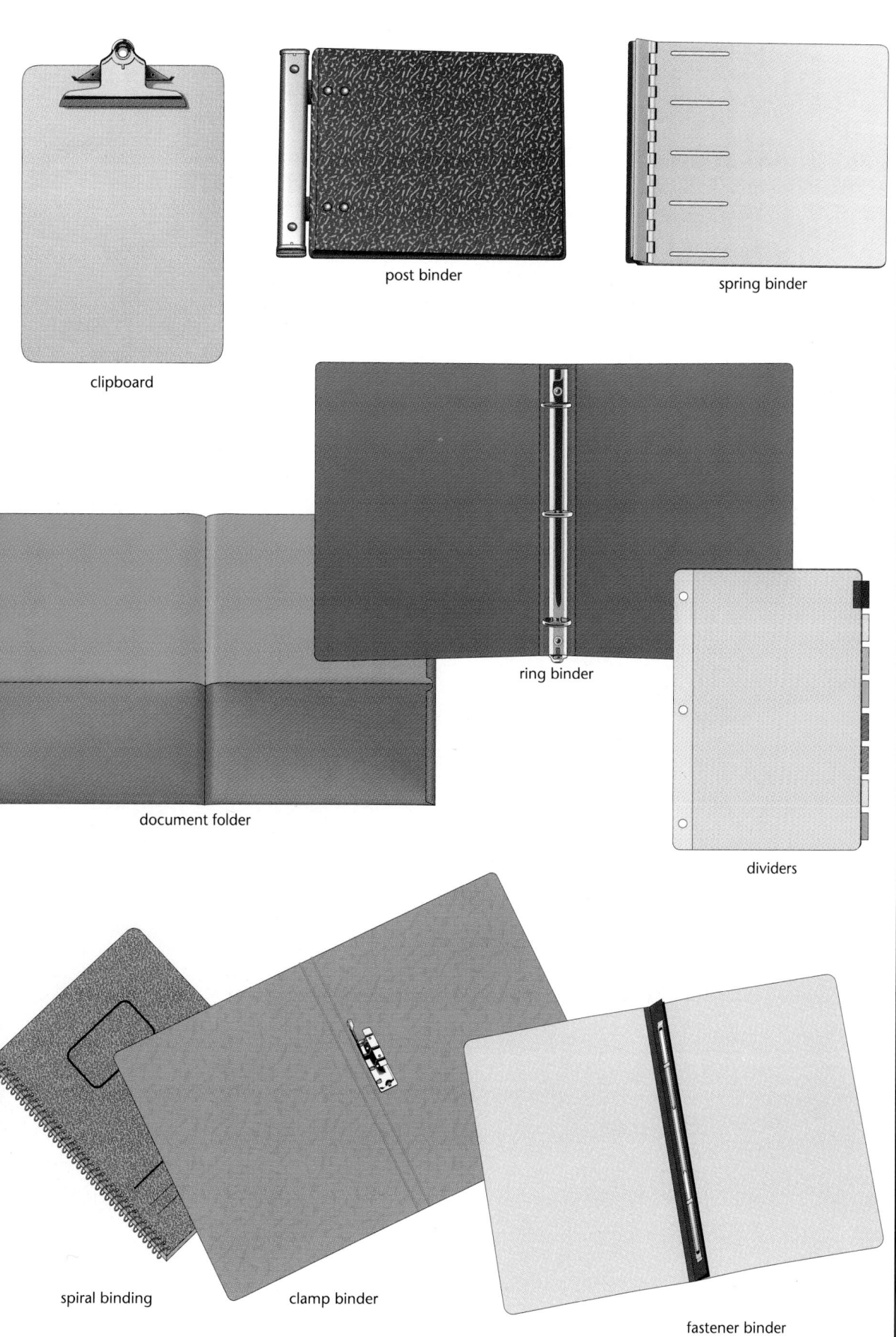

clipboard

post binder

spring binder

document folder

ring binder

dividers

spiral binding

clamp binder

fastener binder

executive desk

swivel-tilter armchair

credenza

desk mat

partition

lateral filing cabinet

COMPUTER TABLE

PRINTER TABLE

paper catcher

adjustable platen

modesty panel

paper tray

paper feed channel

mobile filing unit

mobile drawer unit

typist's chair

return

SECRETARIAL DESK

display cabinet

coat hook

stationery cabinet

coat tree

locker

coat rack

CALCULATOR

POCKET CALCULATOR

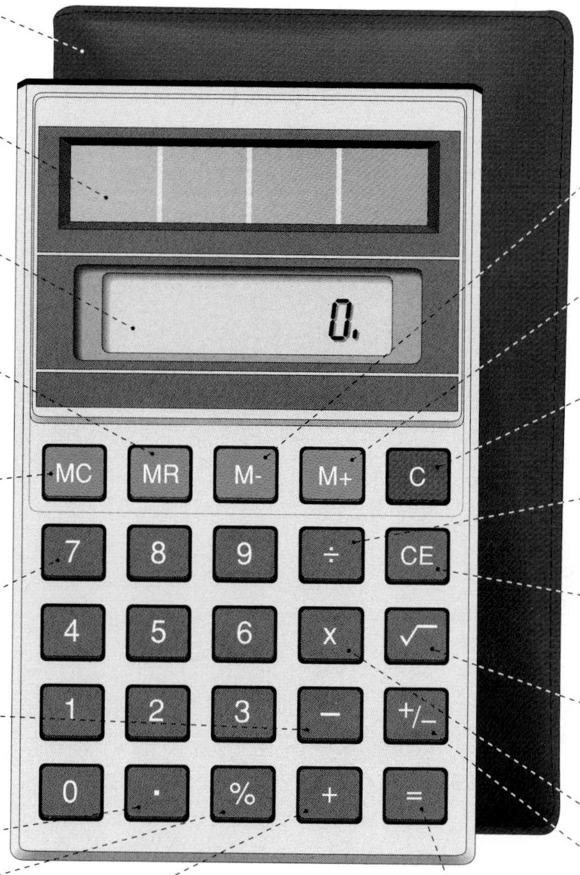

wallet

solar cell

display

memory recall

memory cancel

number key

subtract key

decimal key

percent key

add key

equal key

subtract from memory

add in memory

clear key

divide key

clear-entry key

square root key

multiply key

change sign key

PRINTING CALCULATOR

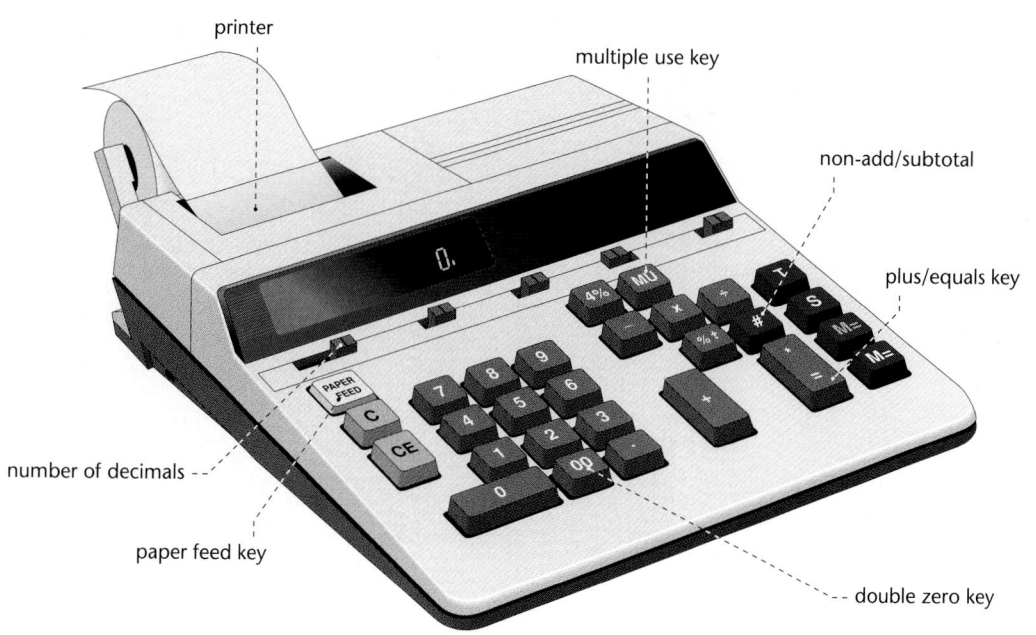

printer

multiple use key

non-add/subtotal

plus/equals key

number of decimals

paper feed key

double zero key

platen

paper bail

printing unit

pitch scale

text display

margin release

tabulator

indent

decimal tab

shift lock key

centering

shift key

spelling corrector

text

code

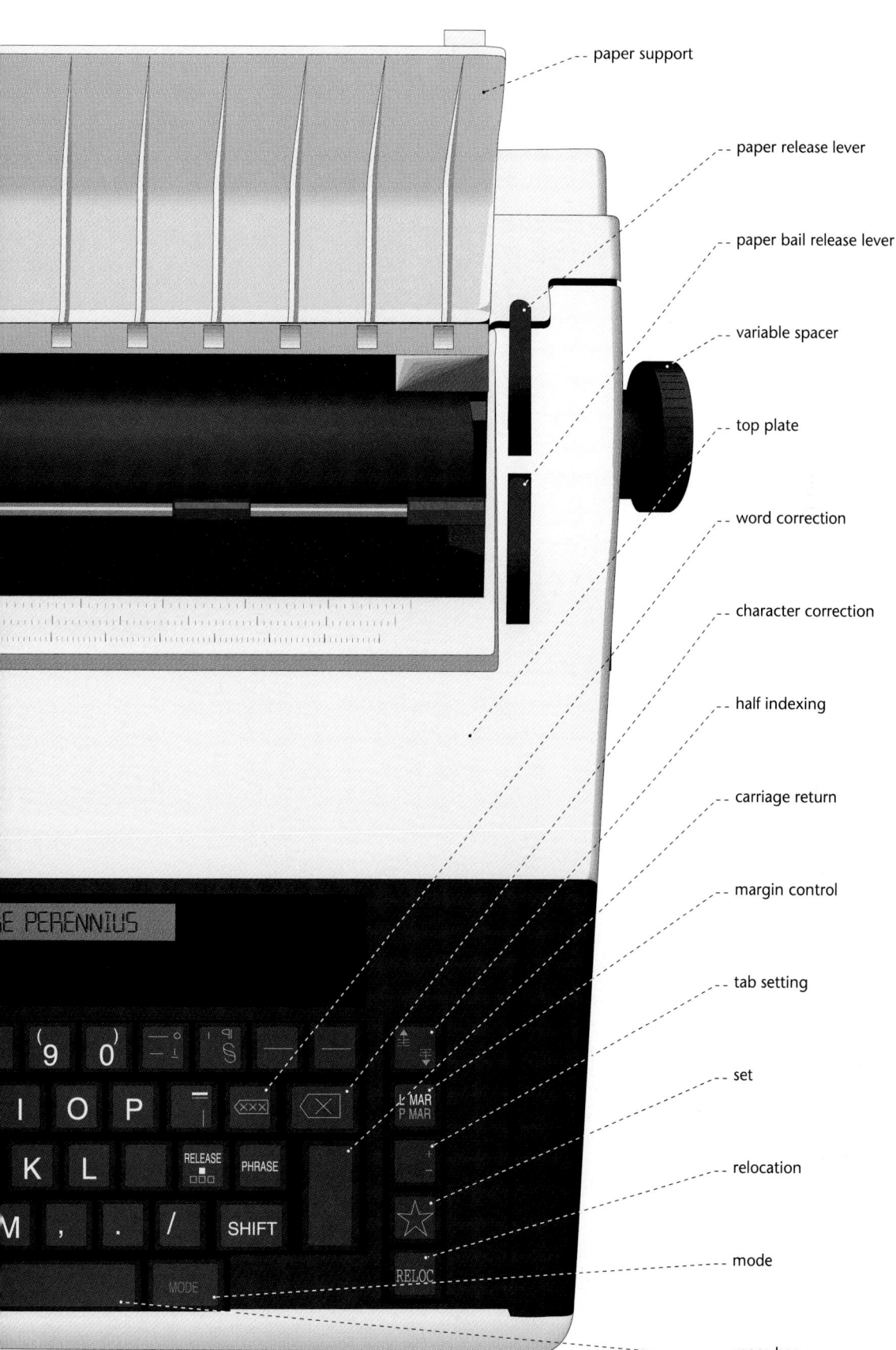

paper support

paper release lever

paper bail release lever

variable spacer

top plate

word correction

character correction

half indexing

carriage return

margin control

tab setting

set

relocation

mode

space bar

OFFICE AUTOMATION

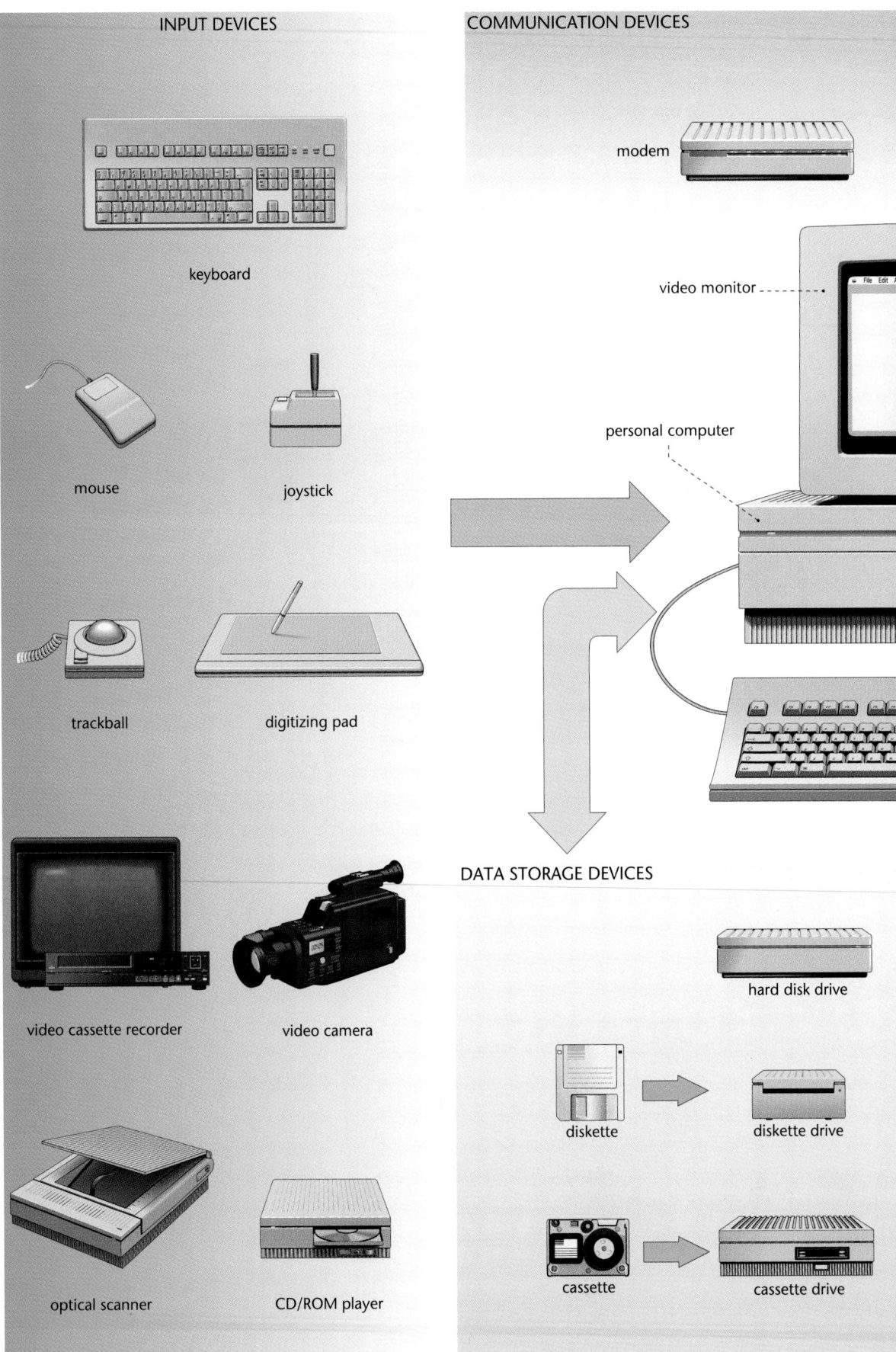

INPUT DEVICES

keyboard

mouse

joystick

trackball

digitizing pad

video cassette recorder

video camera

optical scanner

CD/ROM player

COMMUNICATION DEVICES

modem

video monitor

personal computer

DATA STORAGE DEVICES

hard disk drive

diskette

diskette drive

cassette

cassette drive

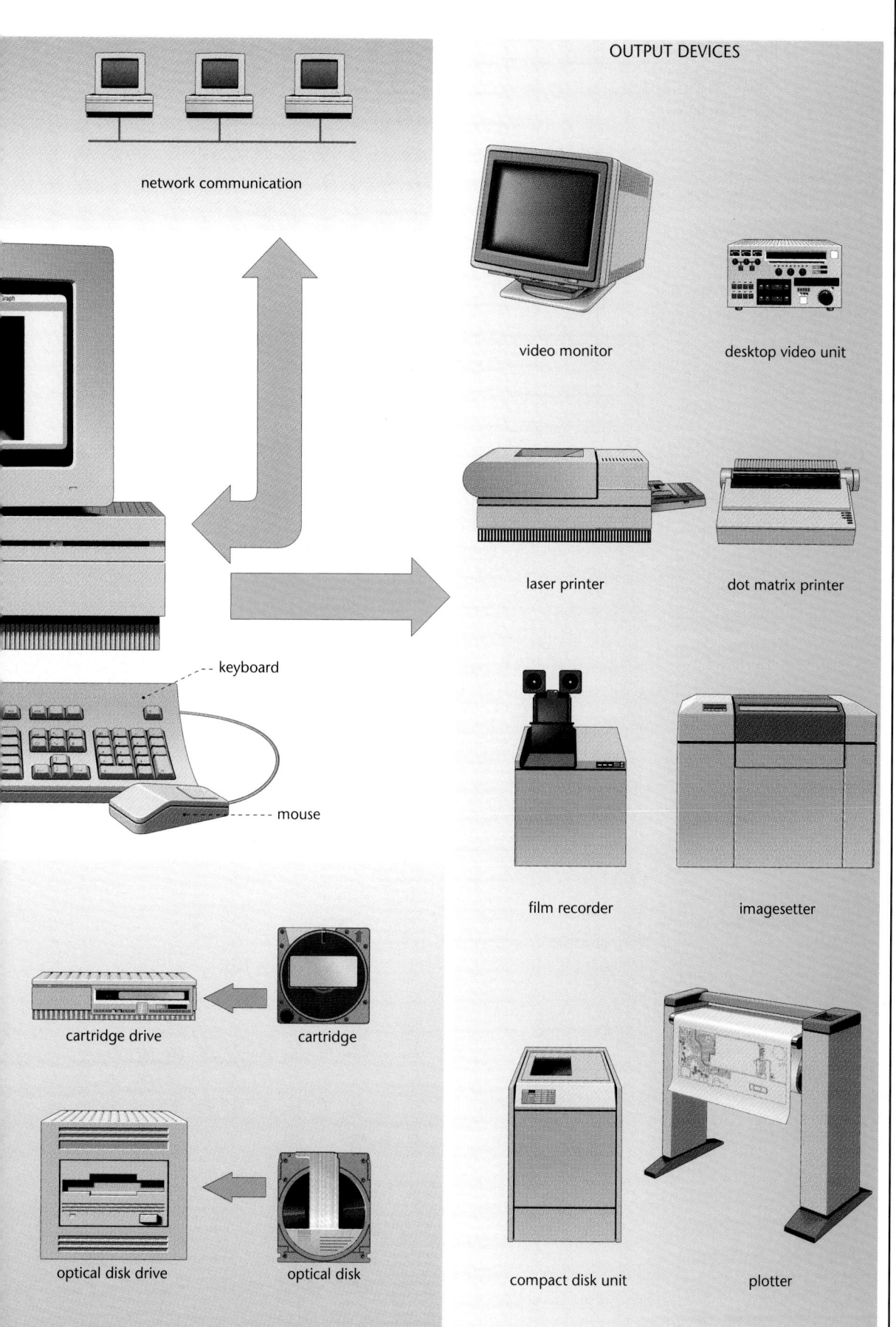

network communication

keyboard

mouse

video monitor

desktop video unit

laser printer

dot matrix printer

film recorder

imagesetter

cartridge drive

cartridge

optical disk drive

optical disk

compact disk unit

plotter

OFFICE AUTOMATION

PERSONAL COMPUTER (VIEW FROM ABOVE)

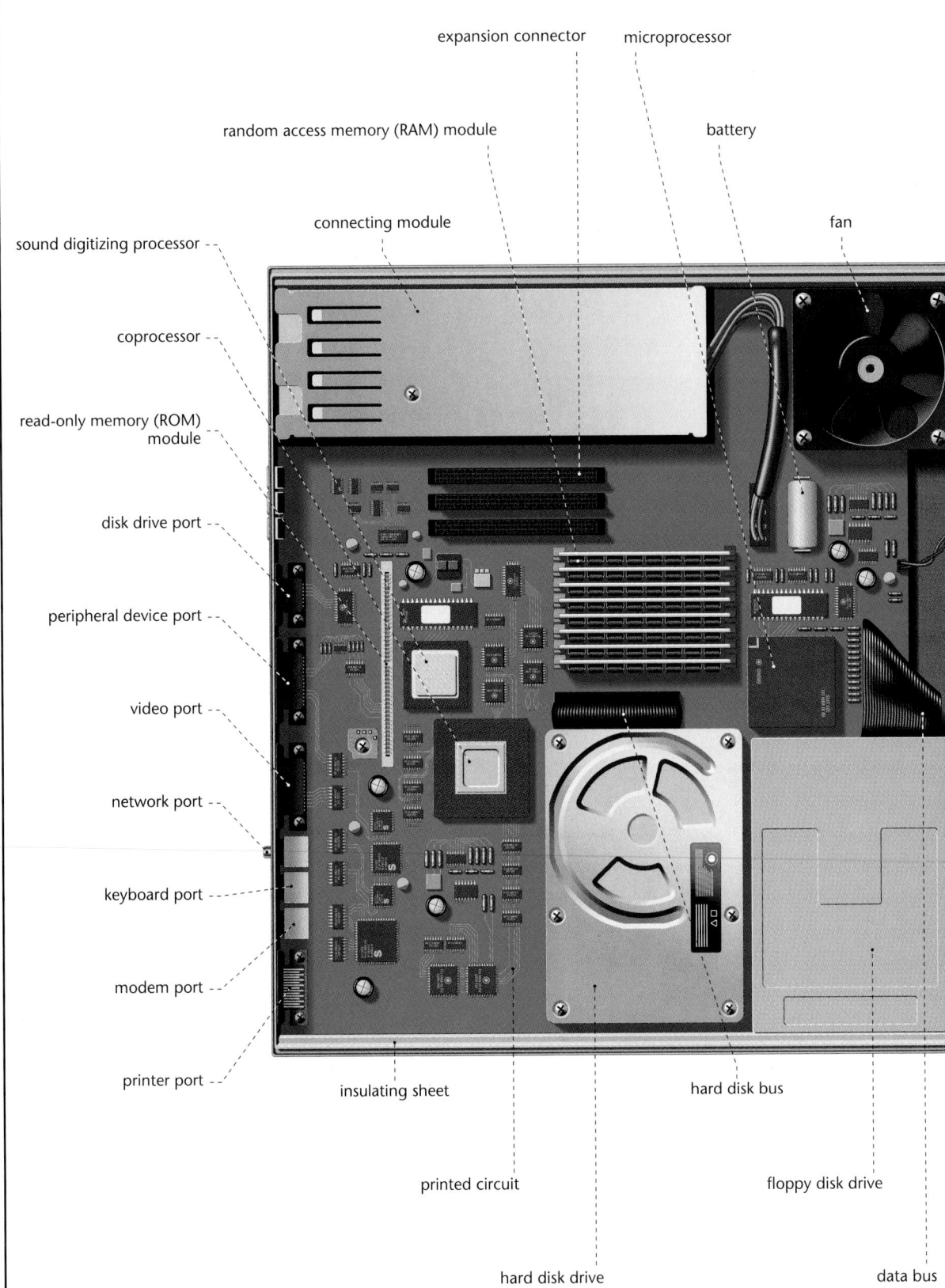

expansion connector

microprocessor

random access memory (RAM) module

battery

connecting module

fan

sound digitizing processor

coprocessor

read-only memory (ROM) module

disk drive port

peripheral device port

video port

network port

keyboard port

modem port

printer port

insulating sheet

hard disk bus

printed circuit

floppy disk drive

hard disk drive

data bus

VIDEO MONITOR

vertical control

horizontal control

centering control

power indicator

power switch

contrast control

brightness control

FLOPPY DISK

MINI-FLOPPY DISK

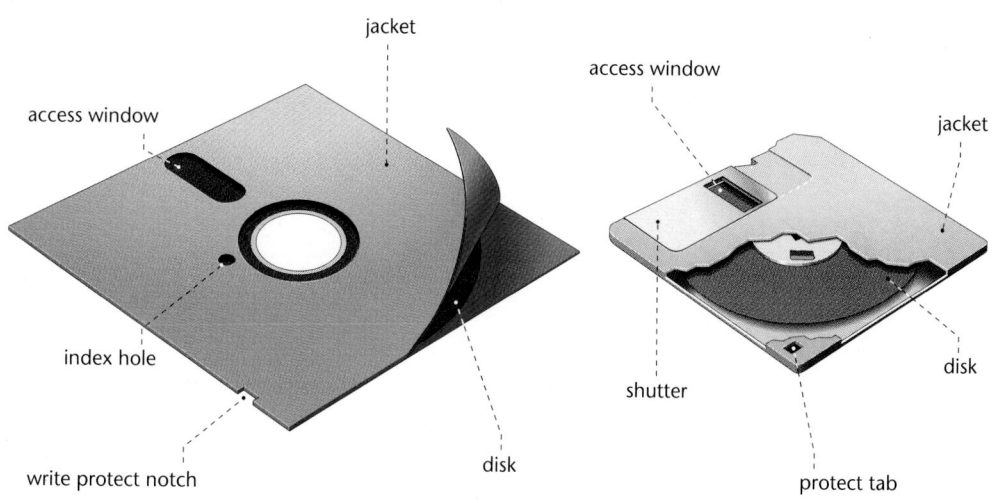

jacket

access window

jacket

access window

disk

index hole

shutter

write protect notch

disk

protect tab

HARD DISK DRIVE

actuator arm

disk

actuator arm motor

disk motor

read/write head

OFFICE AUTOMATION

KEYBOARD

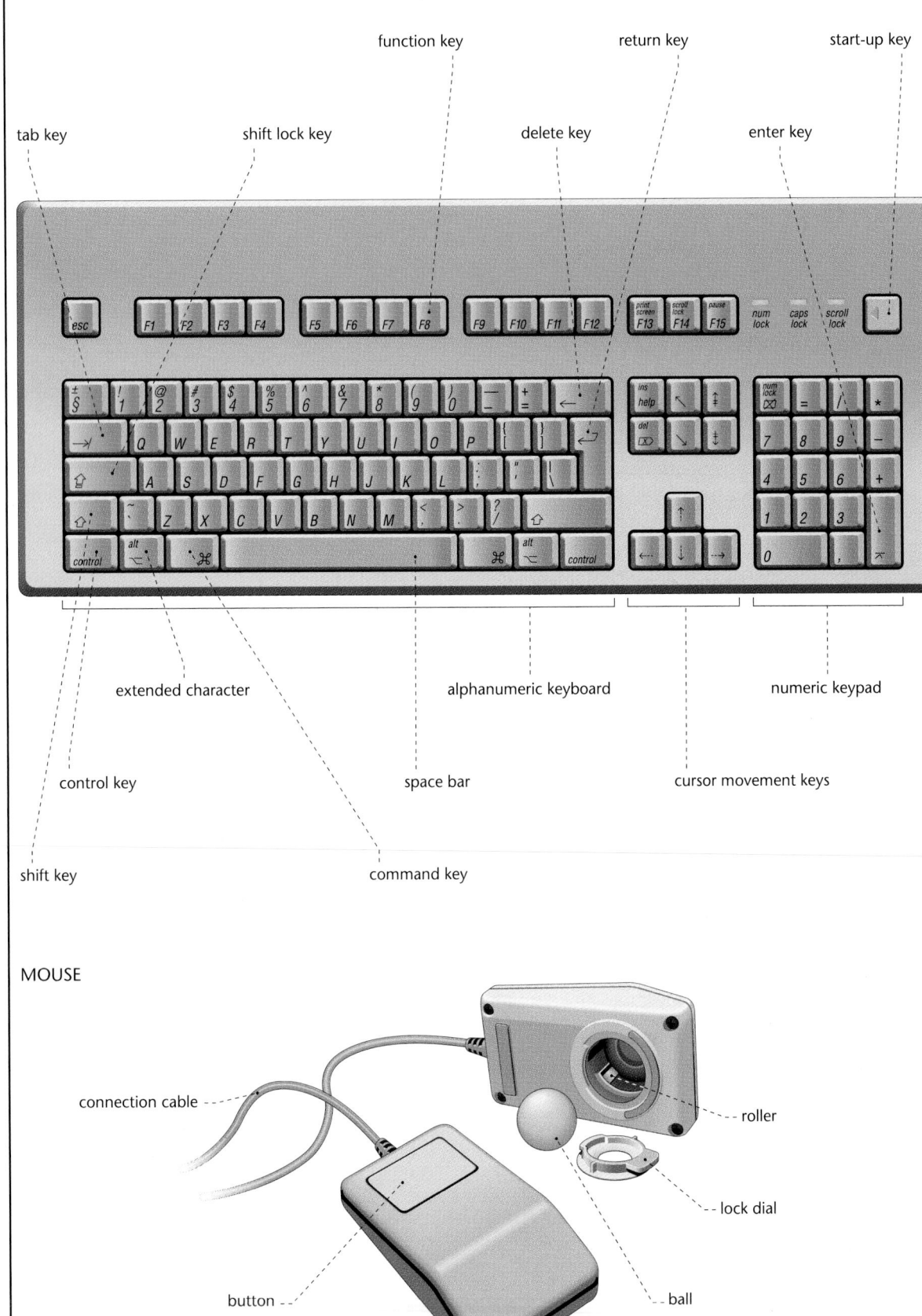

function key

return key

start-up key

tab key

shift lock key

delete key

enter key

esc

extended character

alphanumeric keyboard

numeric keypad

control key

space bar

cursor movement keys

shift key

command key

MOUSE

connection cable

roller

lock dial

button

ball

platen

paper bail

paper clamp

paper bail roller

platen knob

feed pin

paper advance setting

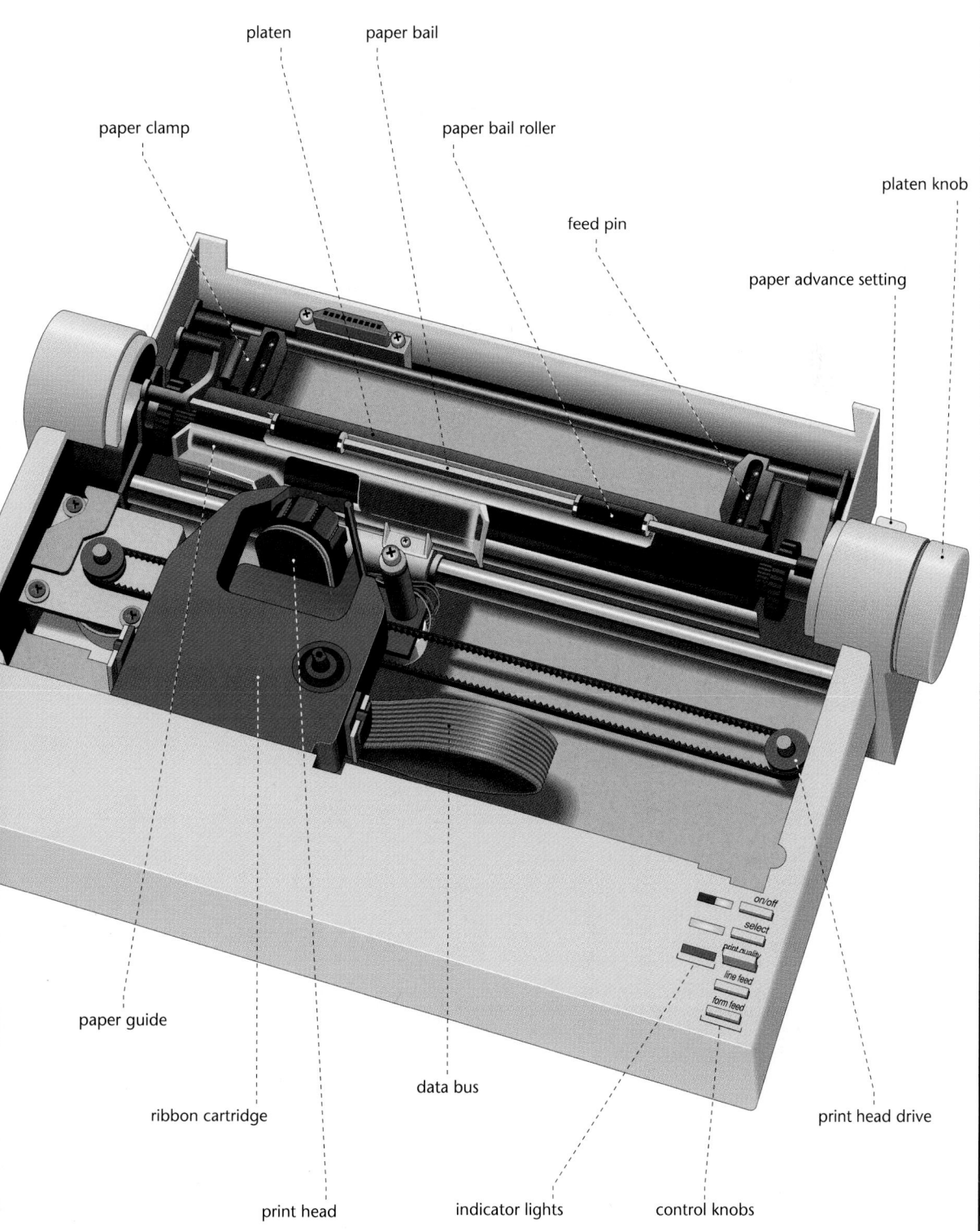

on/off

select

print quality

line feed

form feed

paper guide

data bus

ribbon cartridge

print head drive

print head

indicator lights

control knobs

PHOTOCOPIER

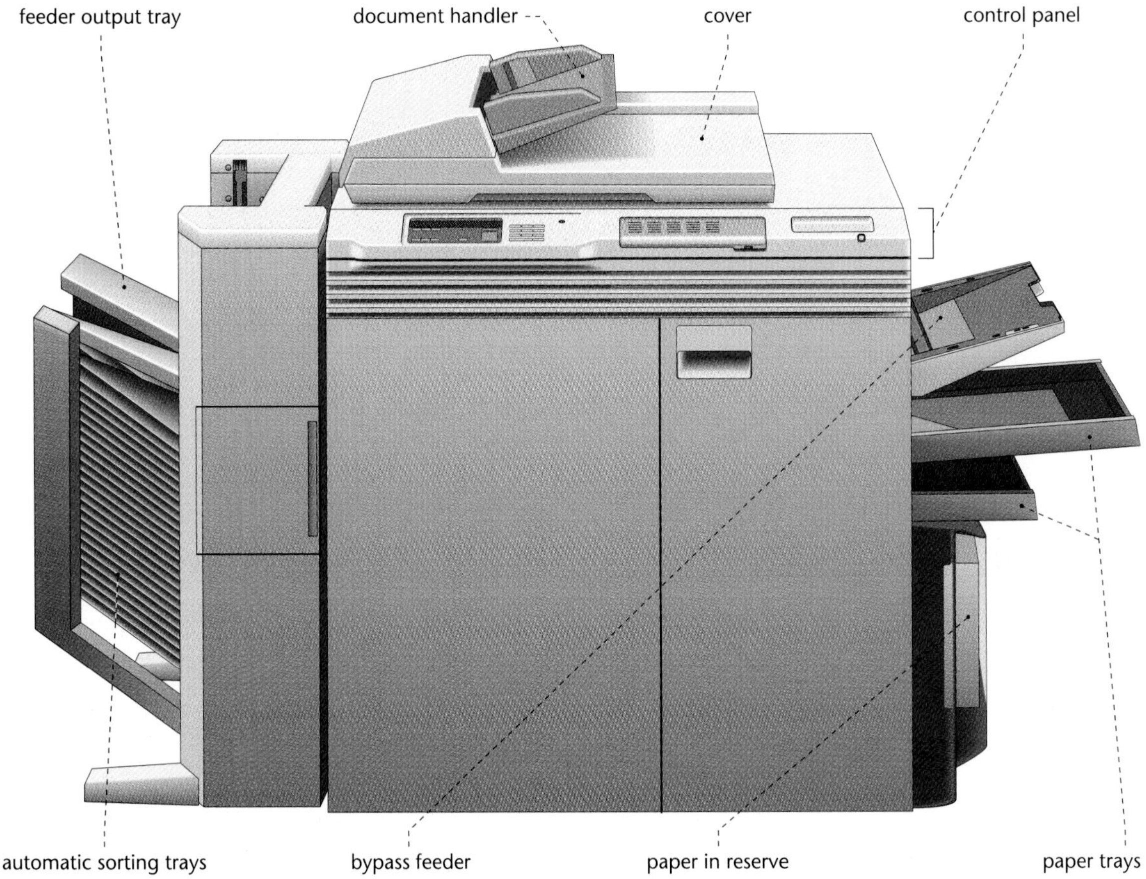

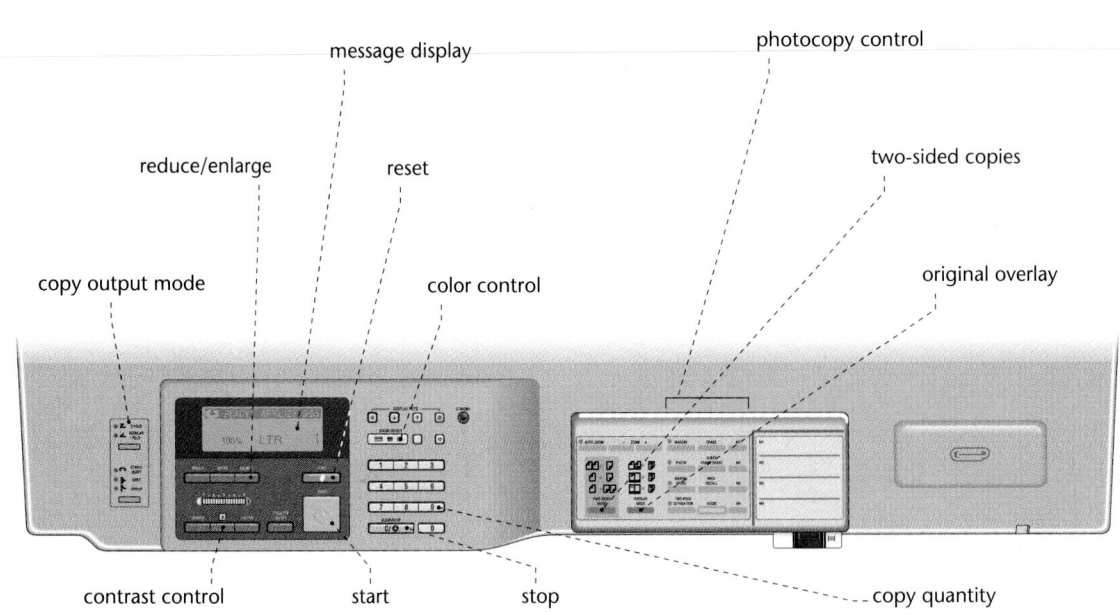

feeder output tray
document handler
cover
control panel
automatic sorting trays
bypass feeder
paper in reserve
paper trays

CONTROL PANEL

message display
photocopy control
reduce/enlarge
reset
two-sided copies
copy output mode
color control
original overlay
contrast control
start
stop
copy quantity

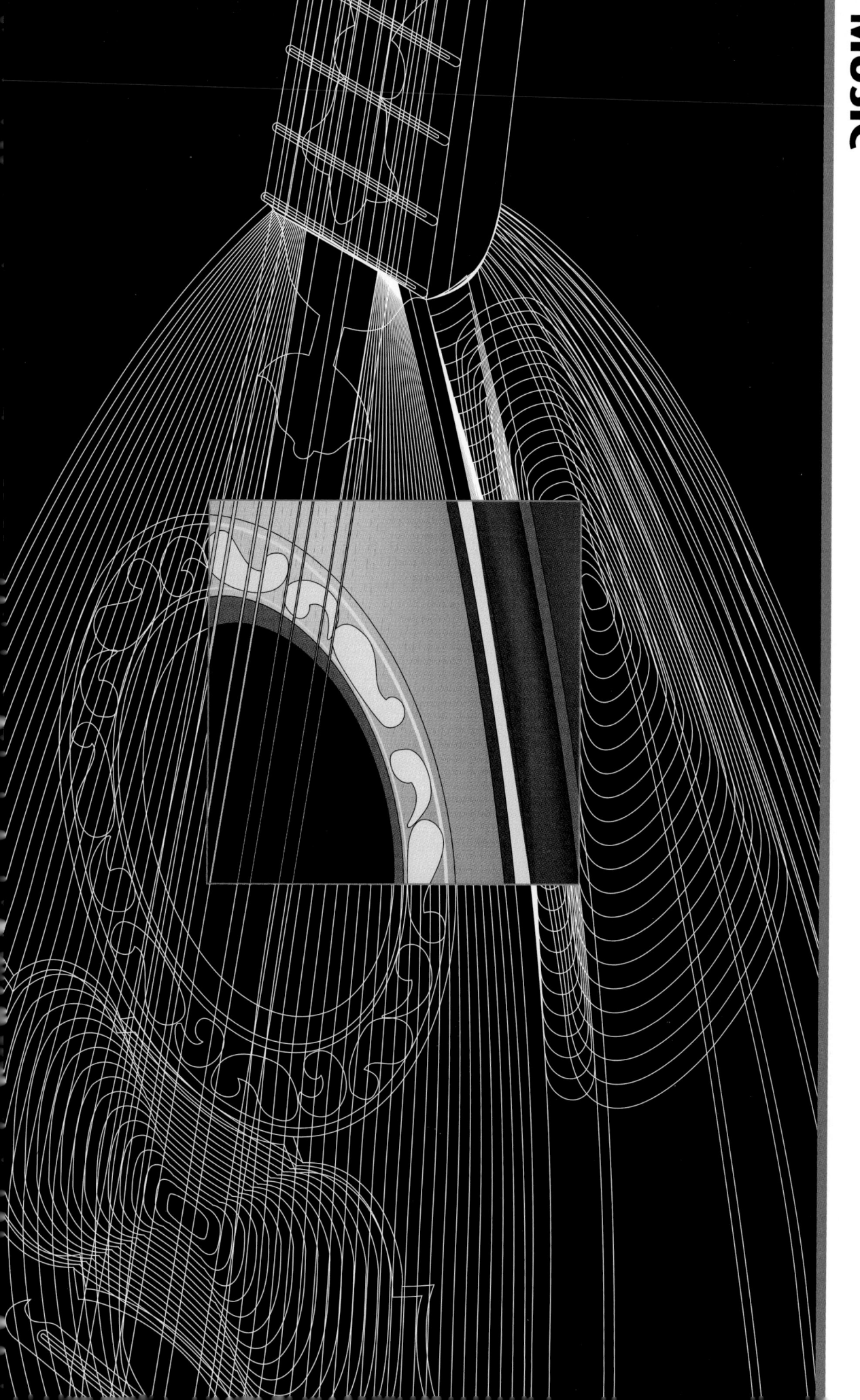

CONTENTS

TRADITIONAL MUSICAL INSTRUMENTS..535

MUSICAL NOTATION...537

MUSICAL ACCESSORIES 539

KEYBOARD INSTRUMENTS...540

ORGAN 542

STRINGED INSTRUMENTS..544

WIND INSTRUMENTS 548

PERCUSSION INSTRUMENTS...552

ELECTRONIC INSTRUMENTS...555

SYMPHONY ORCHESTRA 556

EXAMPLES OF INSTRUMENTAL GROUPS..558

MUSIC

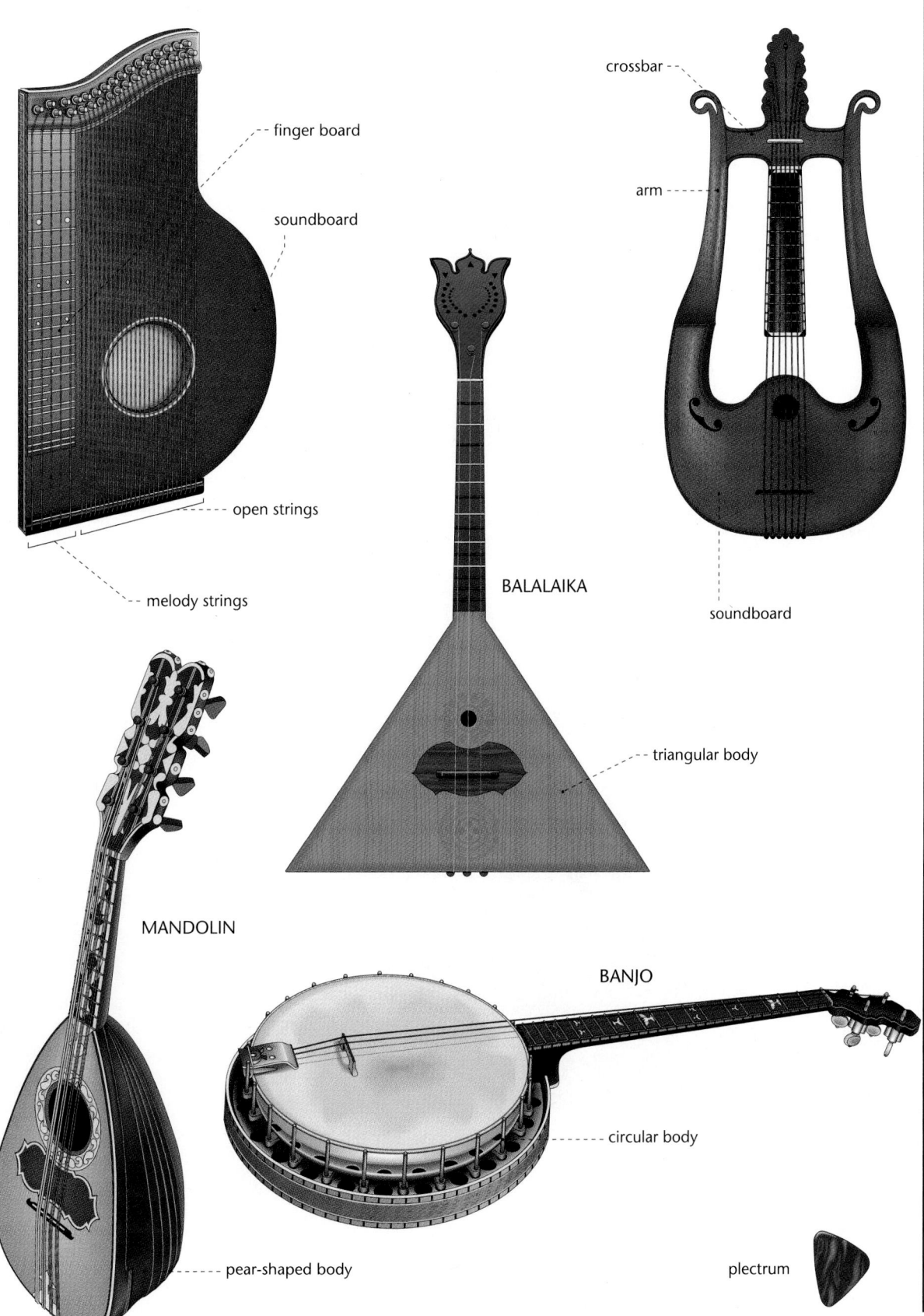

ZITHER

LYRE

finger board

soundboard

crossbar

arm

open strings

soundboard

melody strings

BALALAIKA

triangular body

MANDOLIN

BANJO

circular body

pear-shaped body

plectrum

MUSIC

535

ACCORDION

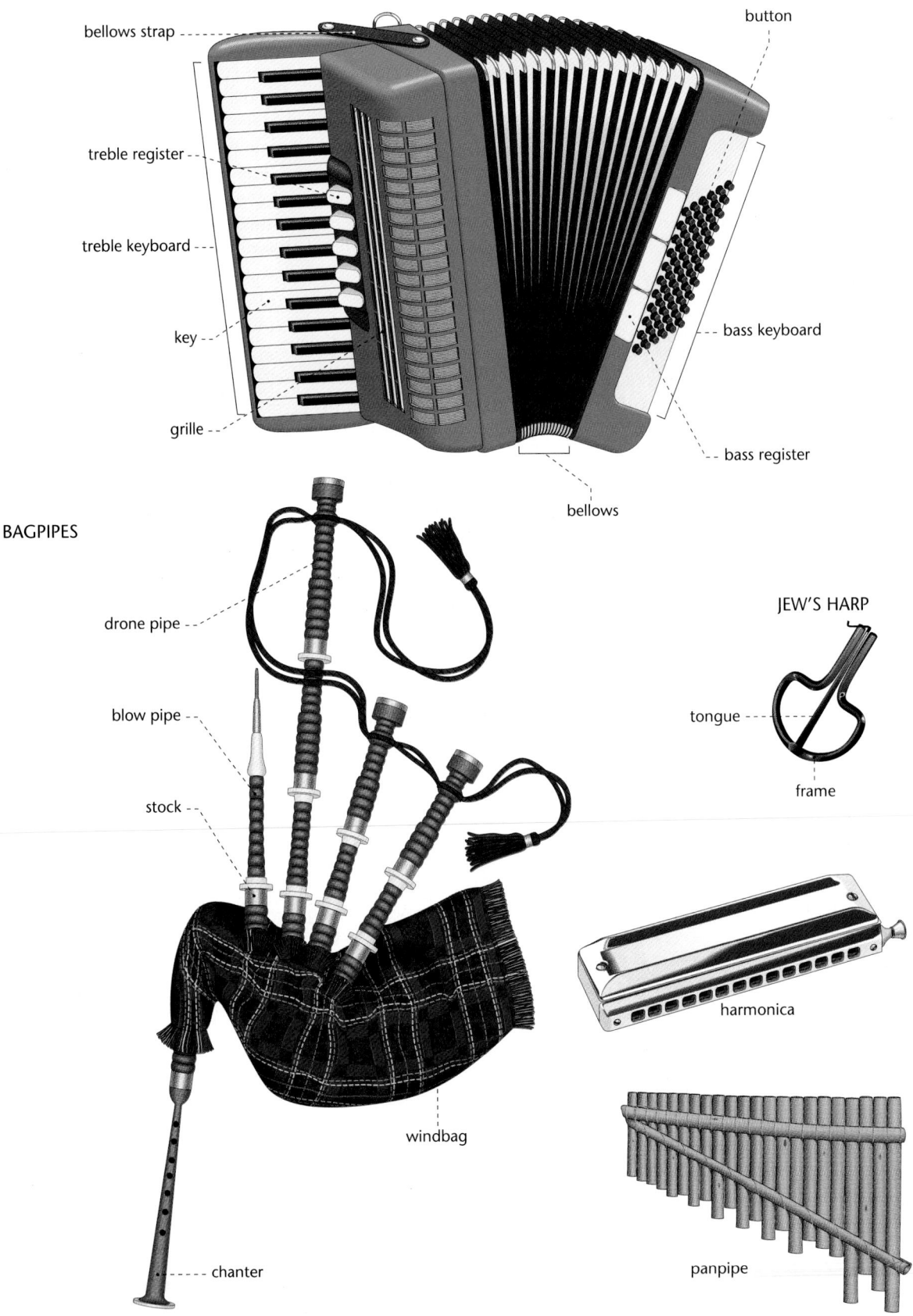

bellows strap

button

treble register

treble keyboard

key

grille

bass keyboard

bass register

bellows

BAGPIPES

drone pipe

blow pipe

stock

JEW'S HARP

tongue

frame

harmonica

windbag

chanter

panpipe

536

MUSICAL NOTATION

STAFF

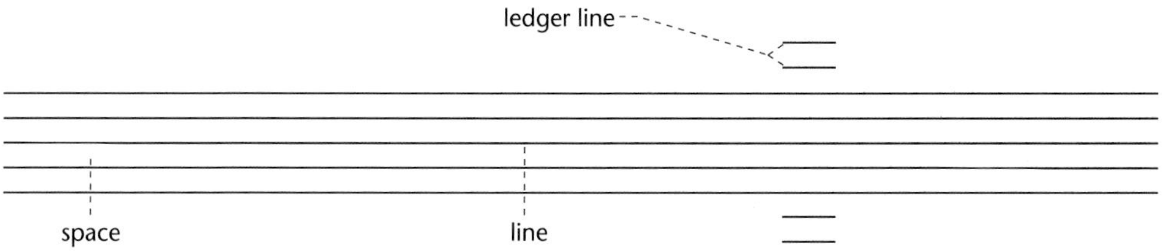

ledger line

space   line

CLEFS

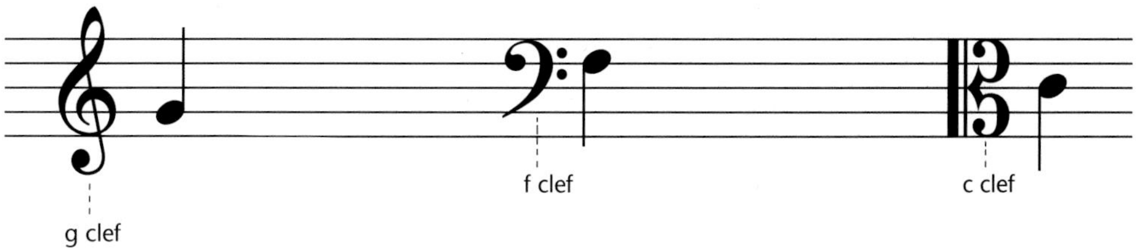

g clef   f clef   c clef

TIME SIGNATURES

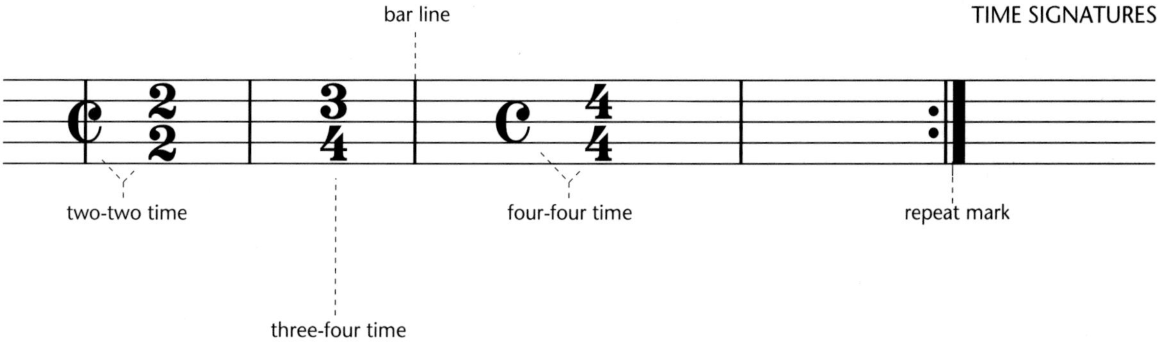

bar line

two-two time   four-four time   repeat mark

three-four time

SCALE

c   d   e   f   g   a   b   c

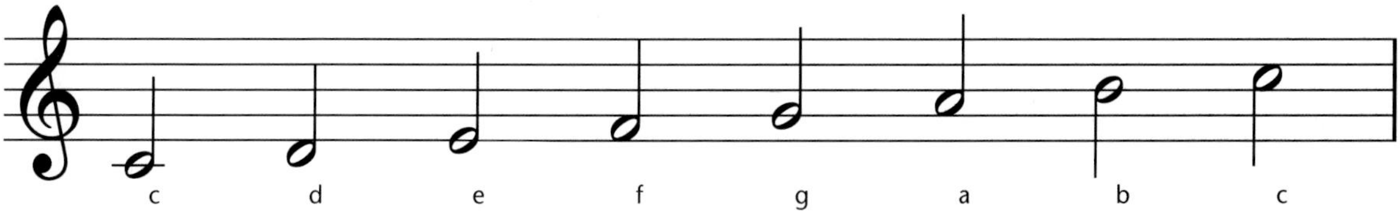

INTERVALS

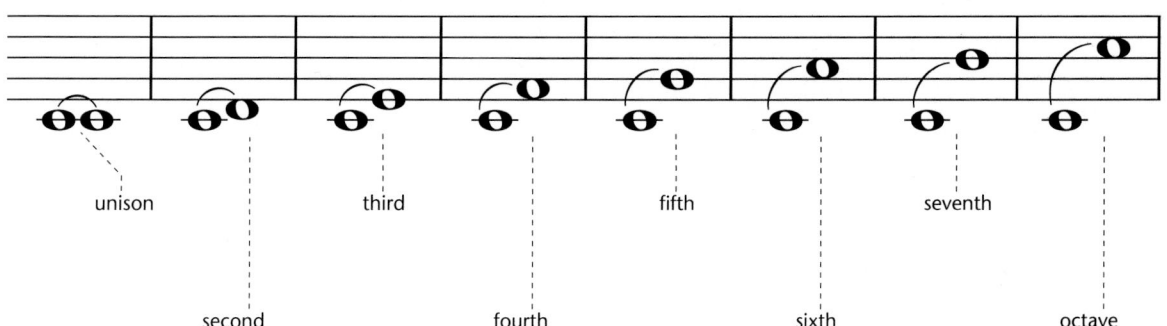

unison   third   fifth   seventh

second   fourth   sixth   octave

MUSICAL NOTATION

NOTE SYMBOLS

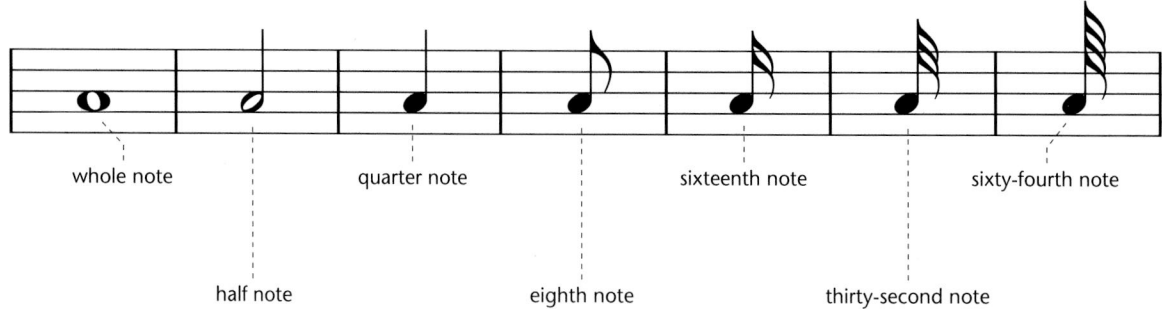

whole note

half note

quarter note

eighth note

sixteenth note

thirty-second note

sixty-fourth note

REST SYMBOLS

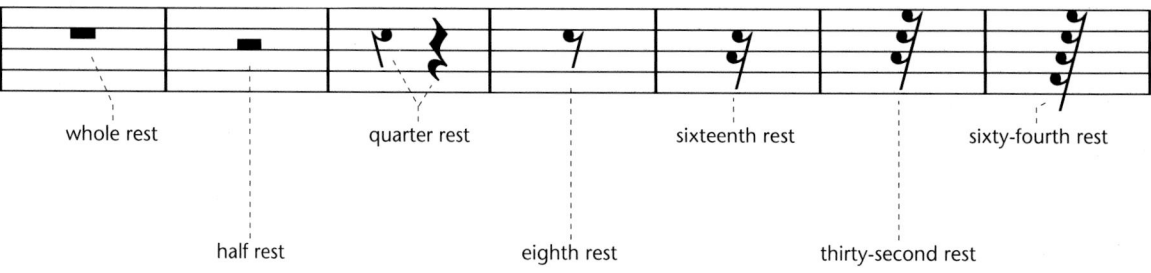

whole rest

half rest

quarter rest

eighth rest

sixteenth rest

thirty-second rest

sixty-fourth rest

ACCIDENTALS

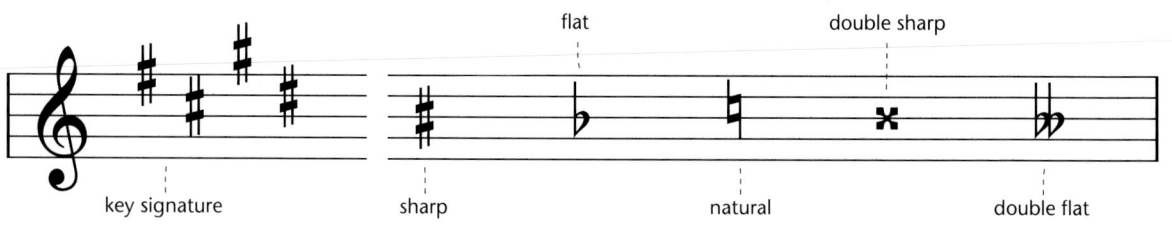

key signature

sharp

flat

natural

double sharp

double flat

ORNAMENTS

appoggiatura

trill

turn

mordent

CHORD

OTHER SIGNS

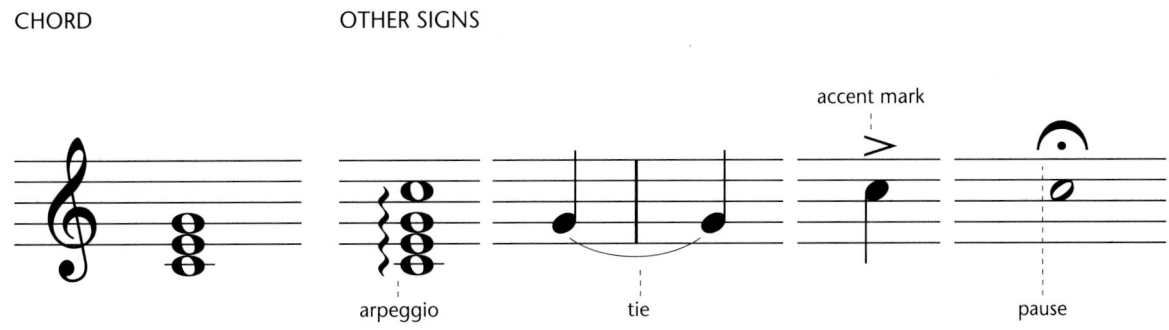

accent mark

arpeggio

tie

pause

MUSICAL ACCESSORIES

MUSIC STAND

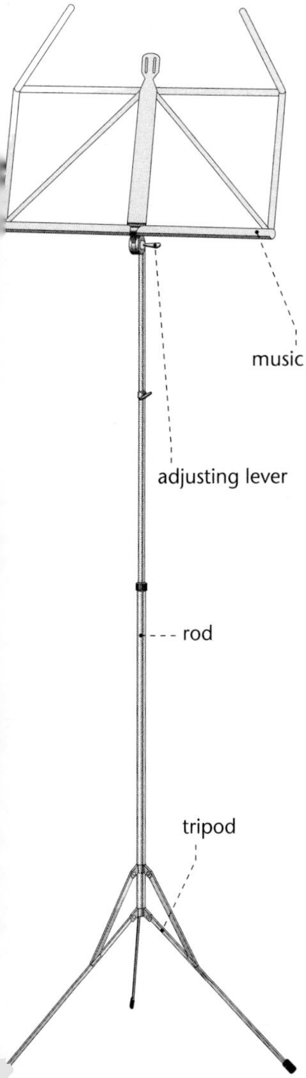

tuning fork

QUARTZ METRONOME

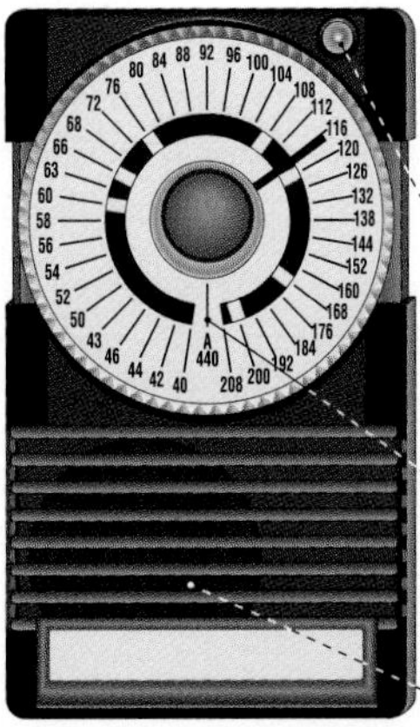

light signal

standard A

sound signal

music rest

adjusting lever

rod

tripod

case

METRONOME

pendulum bar

tempo scale

key

sliding weight

escapement mechanism

pivot

fixed weight

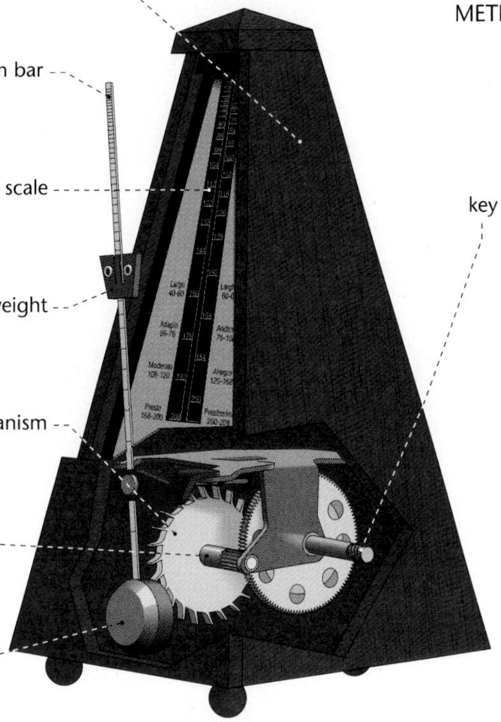

UPRIGHT PIANO

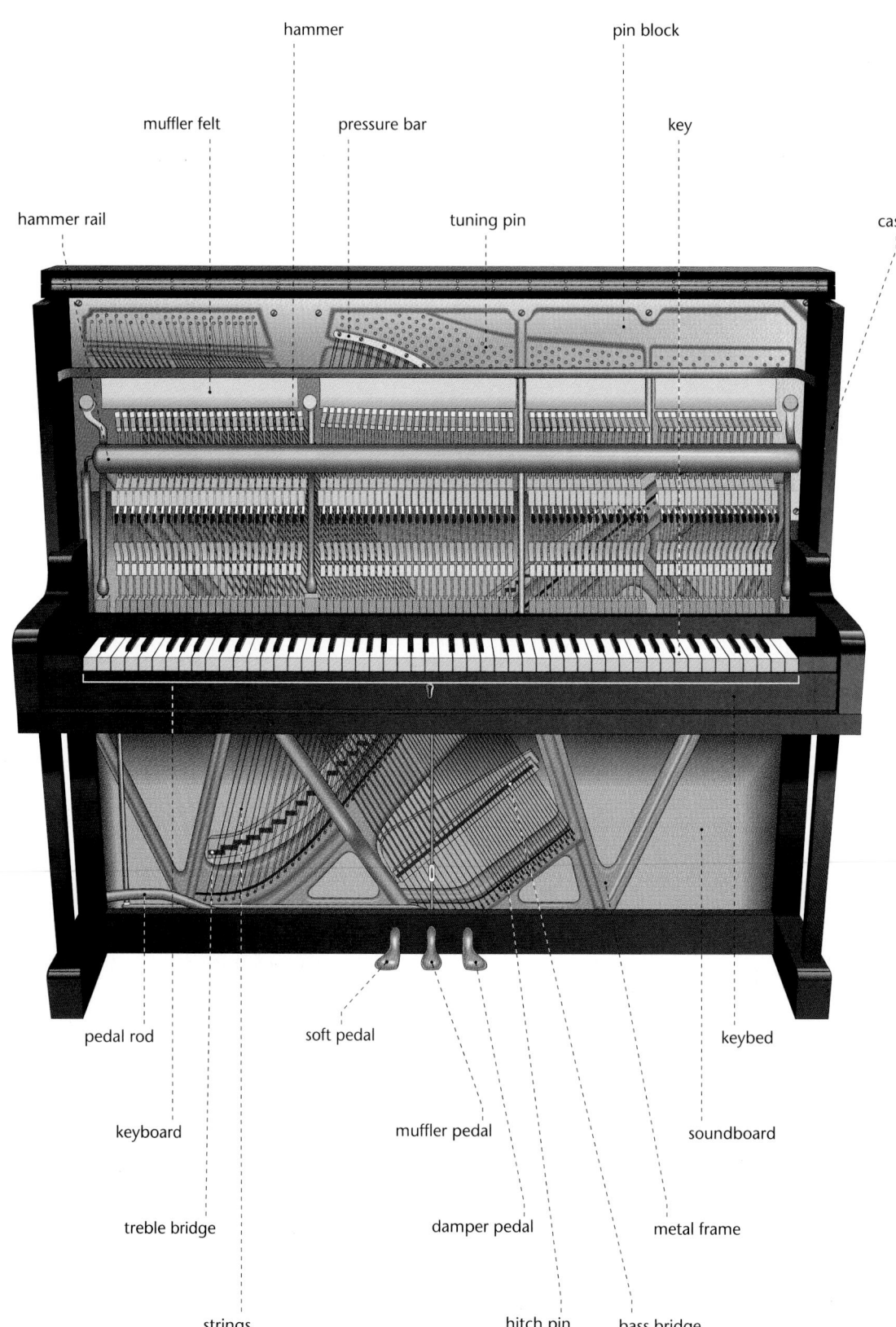

hammer

pin block

muffler felt

pressure bar

key

hammer rail

tuning pin

case

MUSIC

pedal rod

soft pedal

keybed

keyboard

muffler pedal

soundboard

treble bridge

damper pedal

metal frame

strings

hitch pin

bass bridge

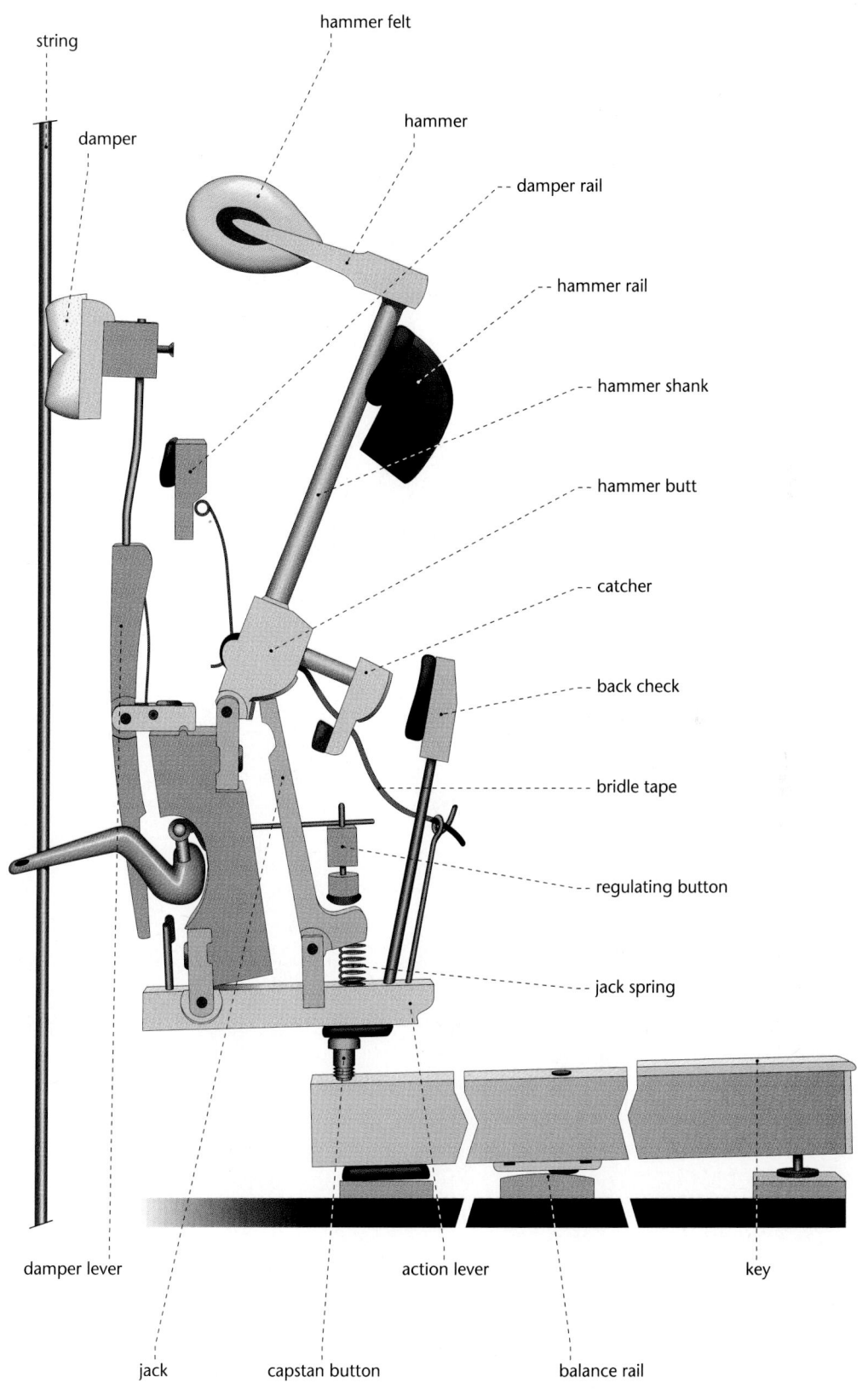

string

hammer felt

damper

hammer

damper rail

hammer rail

hammer shank

hammer butt

catcher

back check

bridle tape

regulating button

jack spring

damper lever

action lever

key

jack

capstan button

balance rail

MUSIC

ORGAN

ORGAN CONSOLE

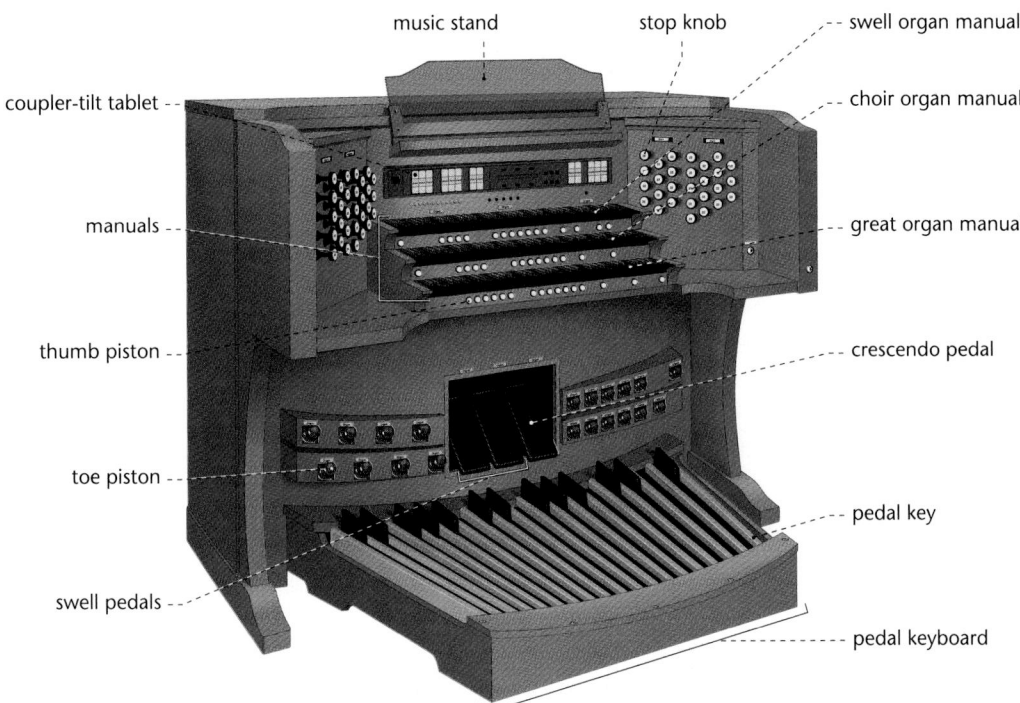

music stand · stop knob · swell organ manual · coupler-tilt tablet · choir organ manual · manuals · great organ manual · thumb piston · crescendo pedal · toe piston · pedal key · swell pedals · pedal keyboard

FLUE PIPE

REED PIPE

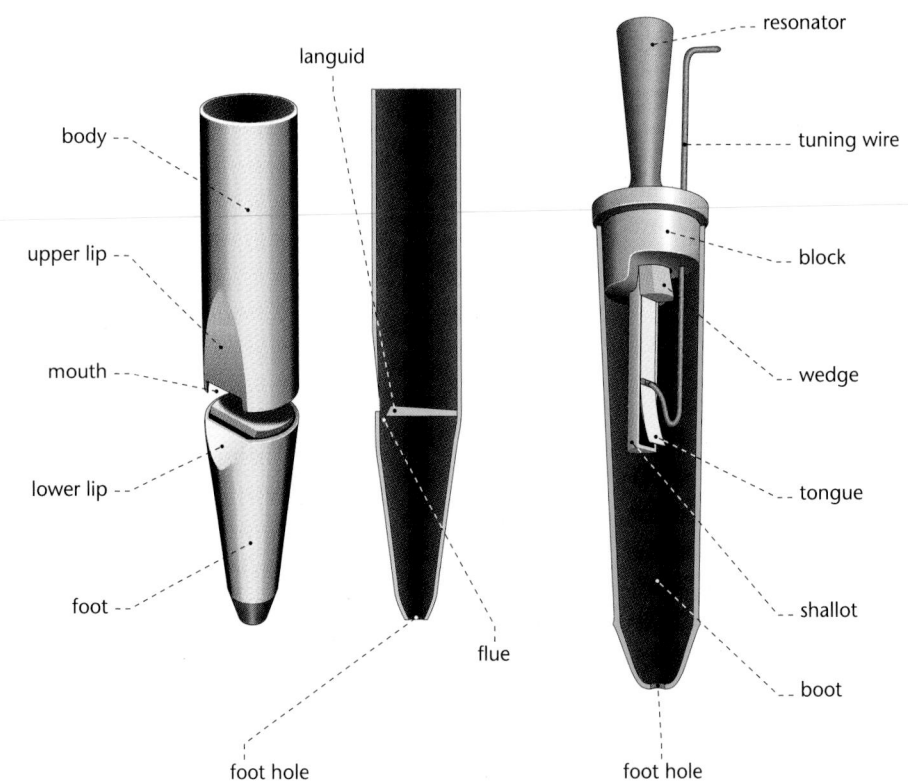

languid · resonator · body · tuning wire · upper lip · block · mouth · wedge · lower lip · tongue · foot · shallot · flue · boot · foot hole · foot hole

542

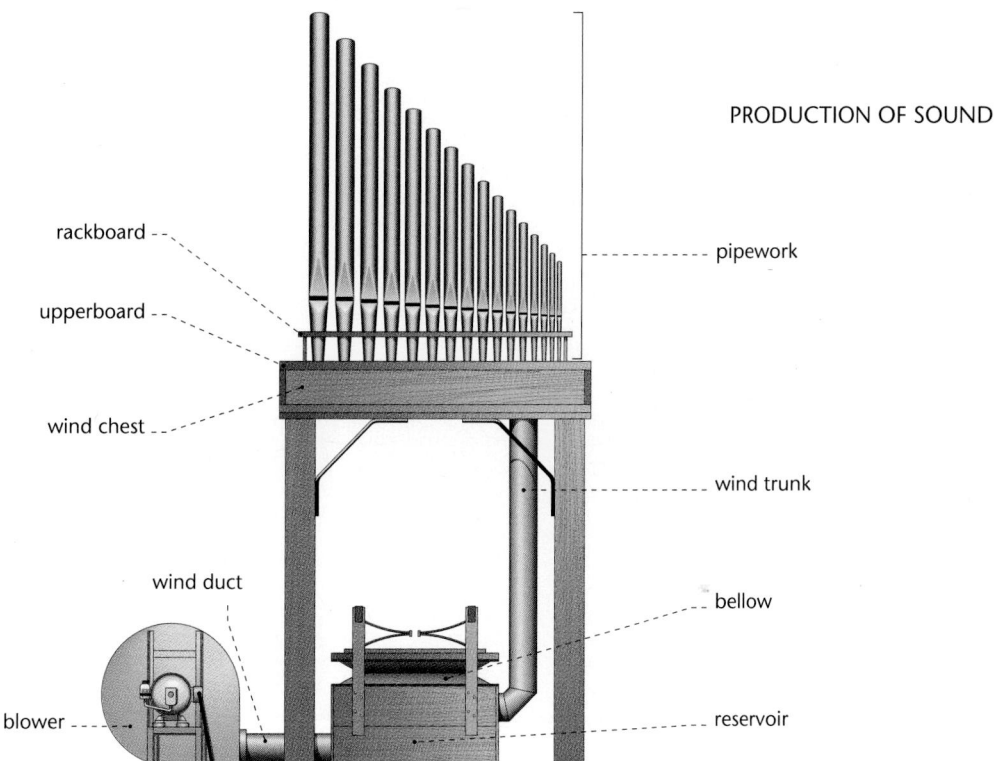

MECHANISM OF THE ORGAN

rackboard
pipe
wind chest table
upperboard
pallet
rackboard support
air sealing gland
slider
manual
bearer
key
bottomboard
roller board and arms
wind supply
tracker
wind trunk
pallet spring
stop rod
stop knob

PRODUCTION OF SOUND

pipework
rackboard
upperboard
wind chest
wind trunk
wind duct
bellow
blower
reservoir

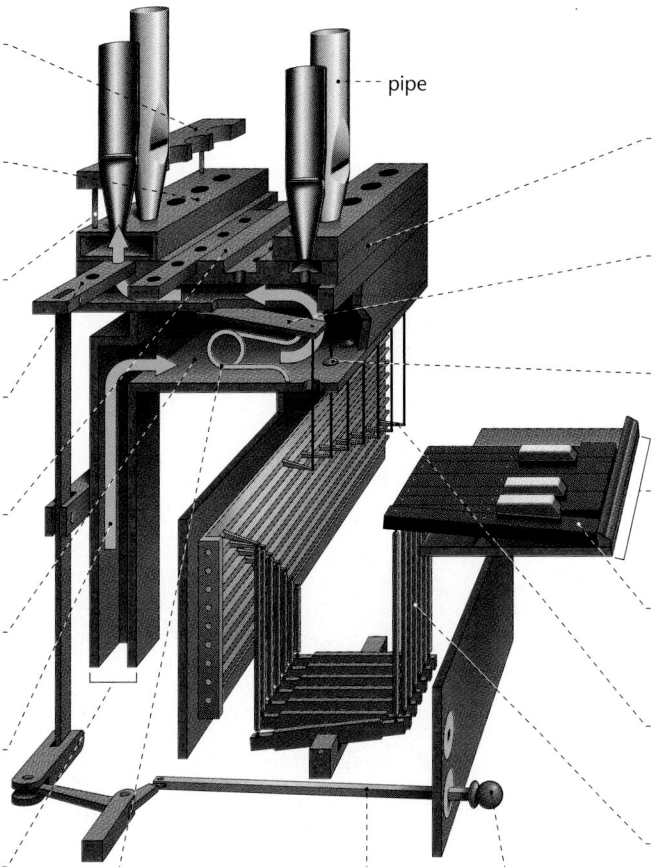

VIOLIN

BOW

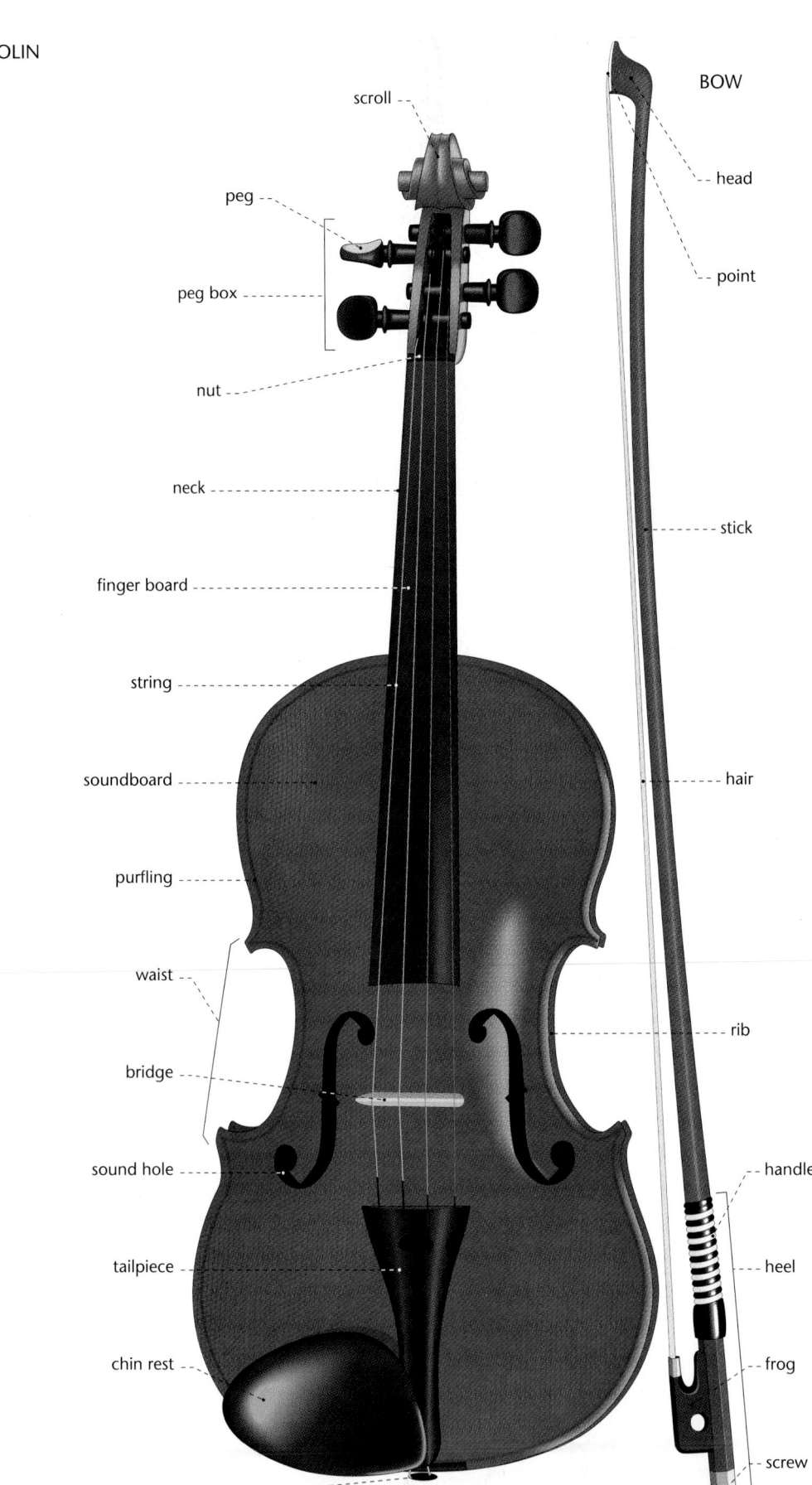

scroll

peg

peg box

nut

neck

finger board

string

soundboard

purfling

waist

bridge

sound hole

tailpiece

chin rest

end button

head

point

stick

hair

rib

handle

heel

frog

screw

MUSIC

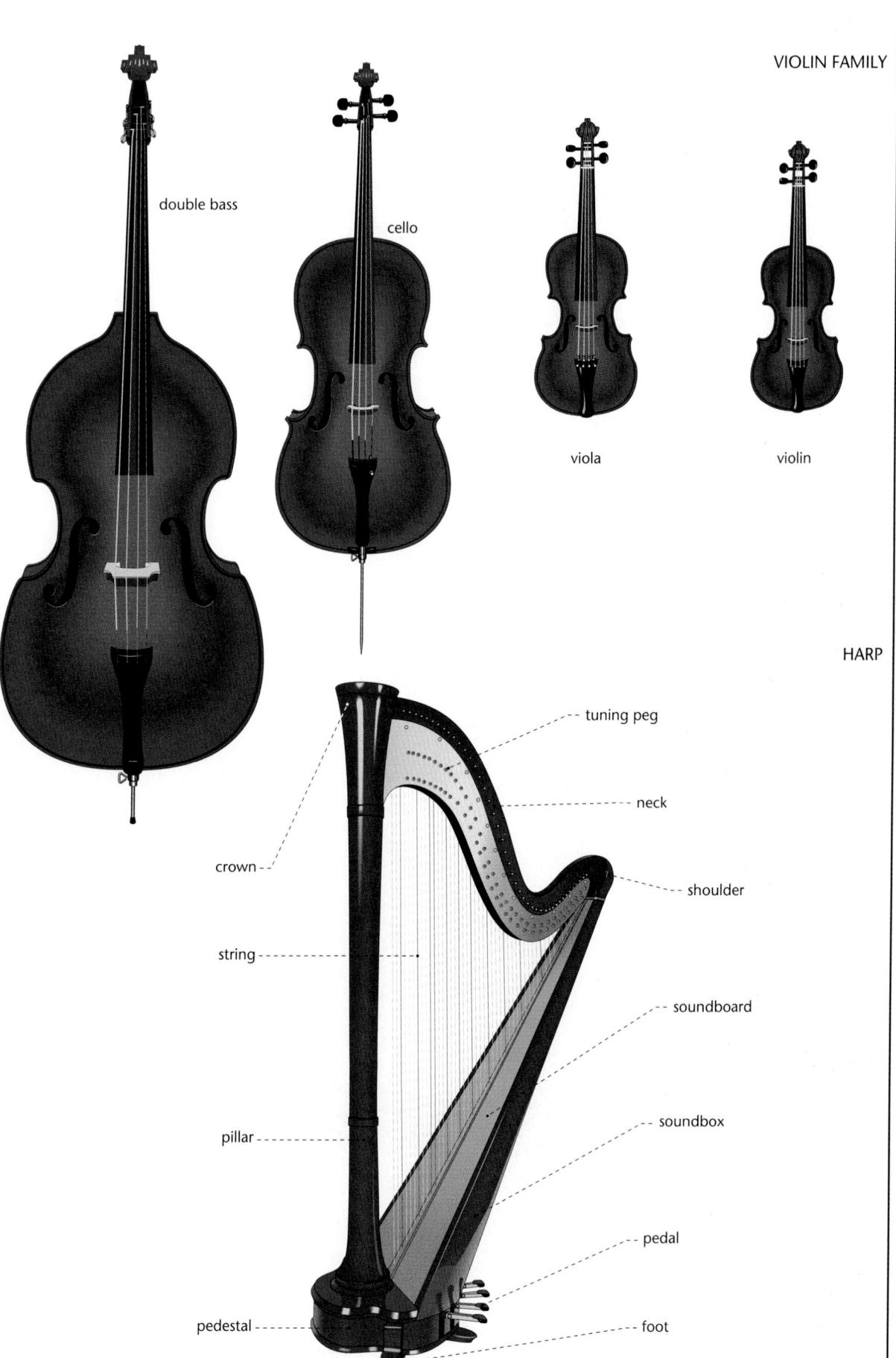

double bass

cello

viola

violin

tuning peg

neck

crown

shoulder

string

soundboard

pillar

soundbox

pedal

pedestal

foot

ACOUSTIC GUITAR

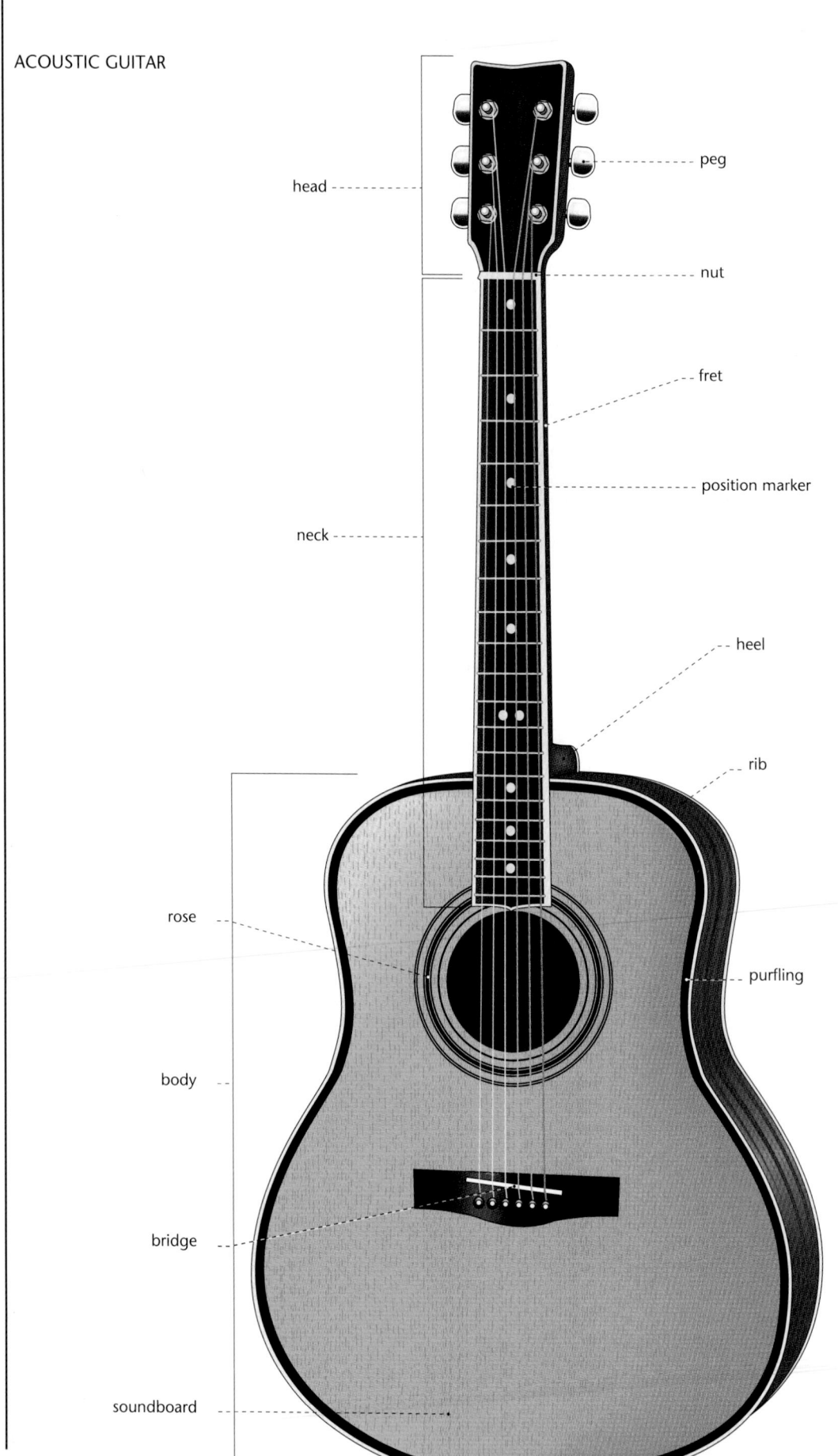

head

peg

nut

fret

position marker

neck

heel

rib

rose

purfling

body

bridge

soundboard

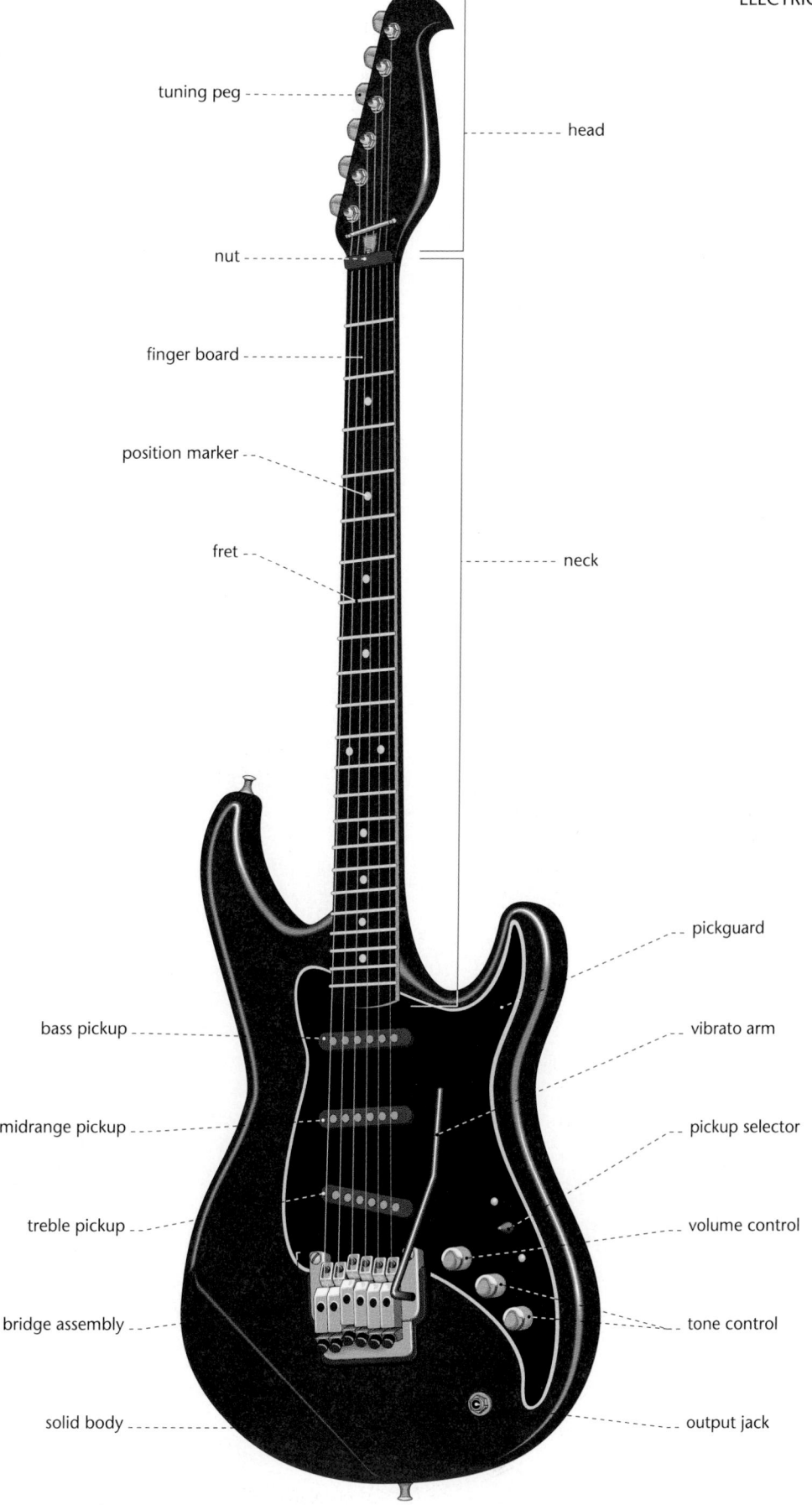

tuning peg

head

nut

finger board

position marker

fret

neck

bass pickup

pickguard

midrange pickup

vibrato arm

treble pickup

pickup selector

volume control

bridge assembly

tone control

solid body

output jack

WIND INSTRUMENTS

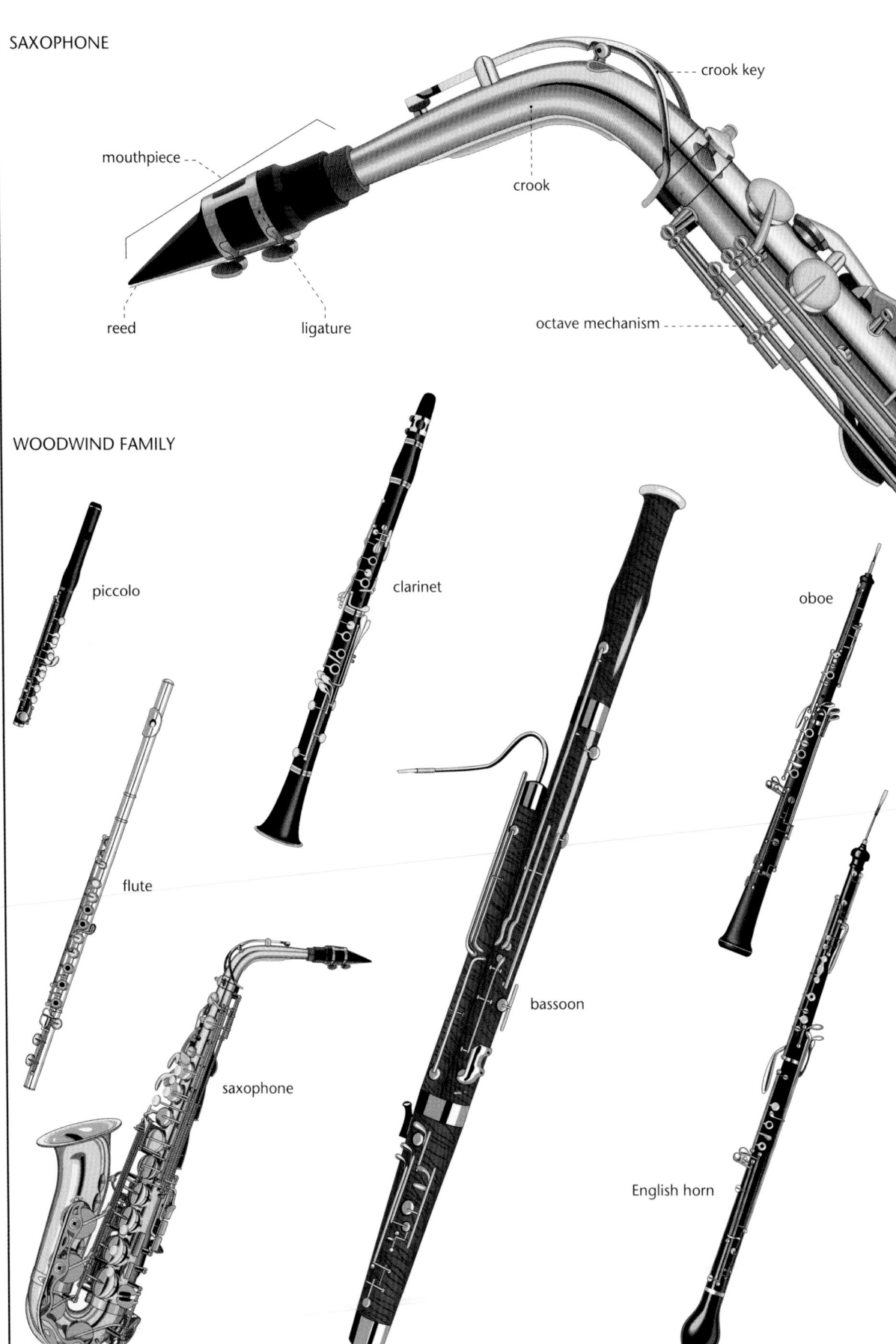

SAXOPHONE

crook key

mouthpiece

crook

reed

ligature

octave mechanism

WOODWIND FAMILY

piccolo

clarinet

oboe

flute

bassoon

saxophone

English horn

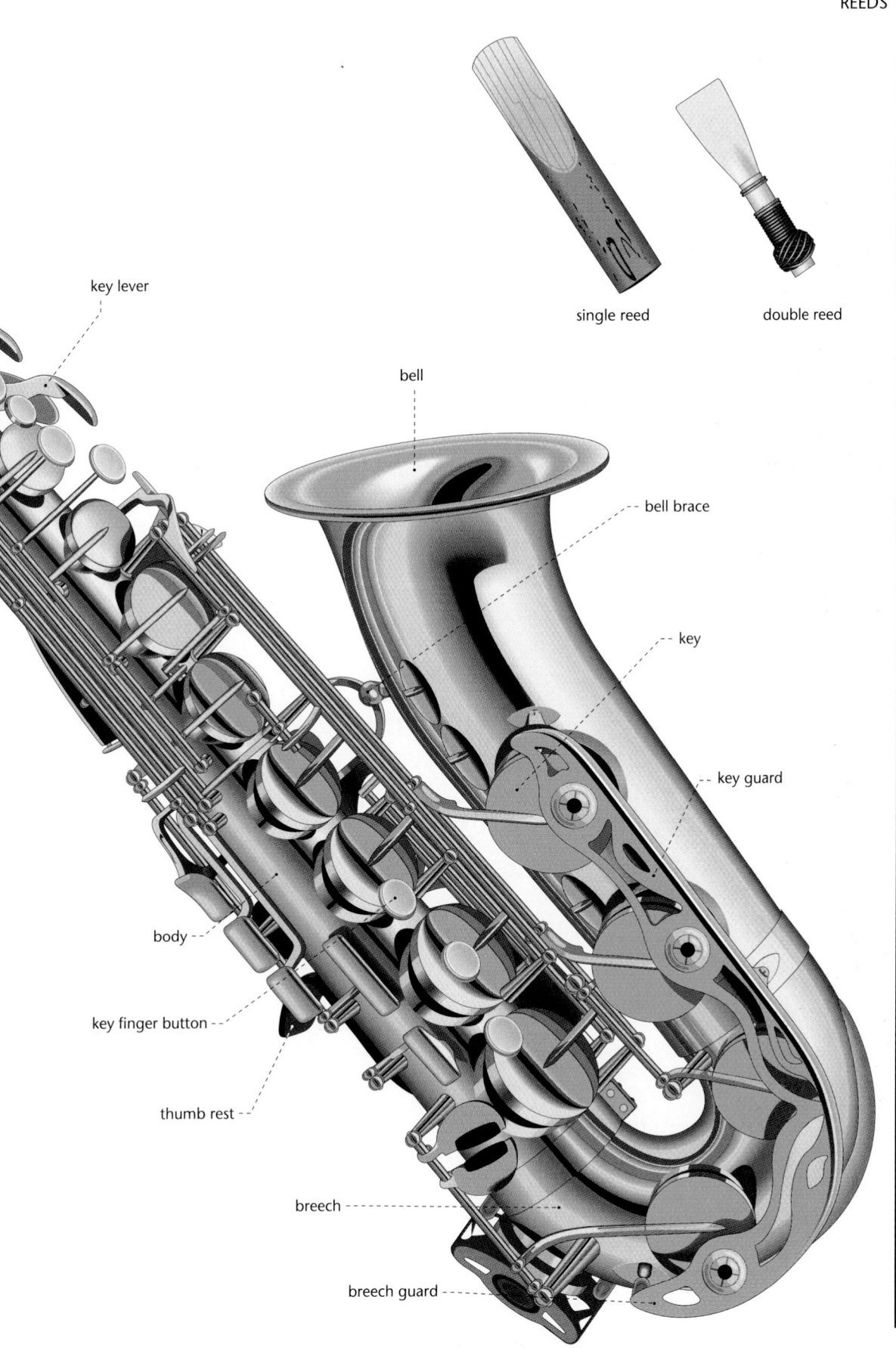

single reed

double reed

key lever

bell

bell brace

key

key guard

body

key finger button

thumb rest

breech

breech guard

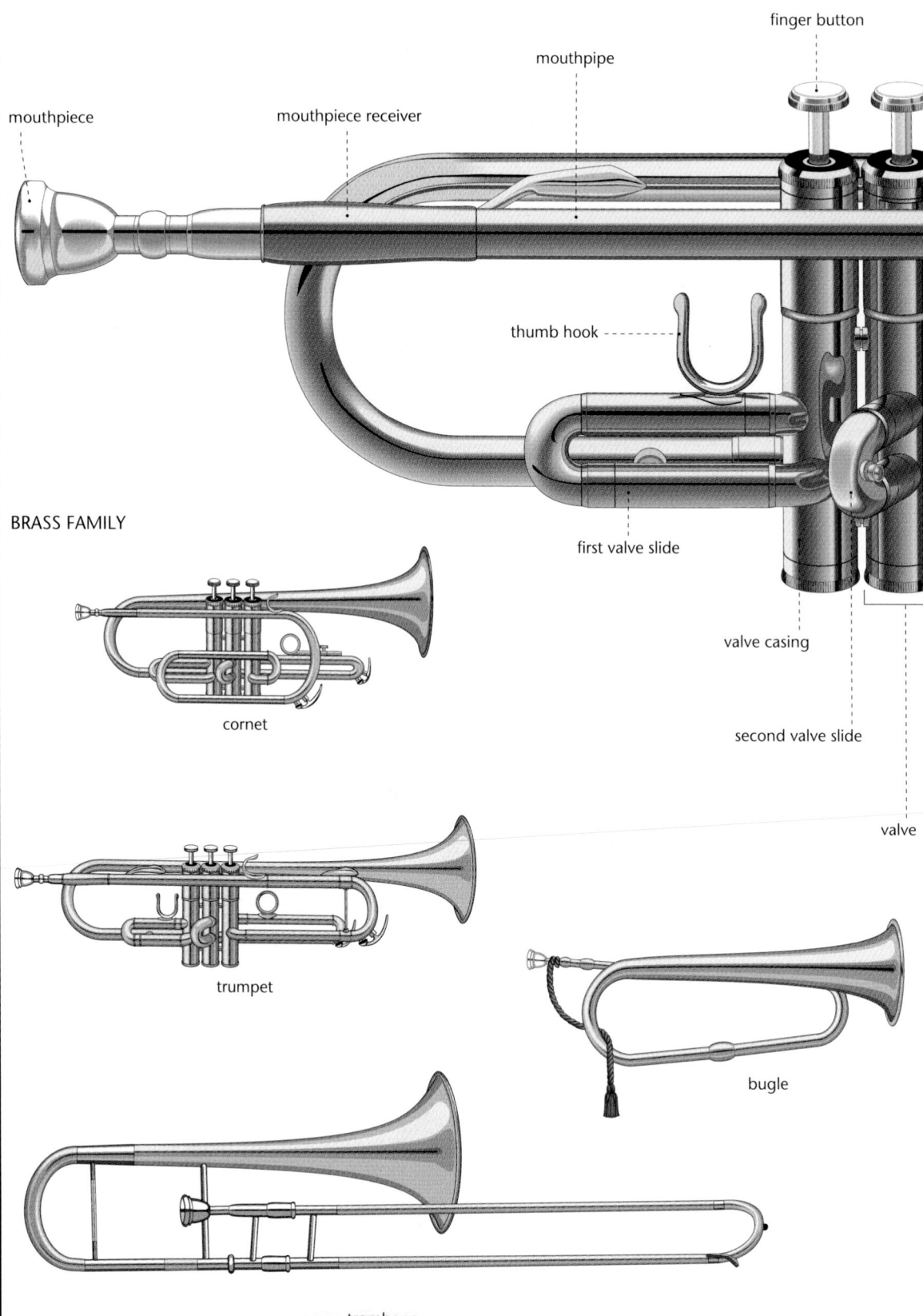

TRUMPET

finger button

mouthpipe

mouthpiece

mouthpiece receiver

thumb hook

first valve slide

BRASS FAMILY

valve casing

second valve slide

valve

cornet

trumpet

bugle

trombone

MUSIC

little finger hook

ring

bell

tuning slide

third valve slide

water key

mute

tuba

saxhorn

French horn

DRUMS

cymbal

tom-tom

Charleston cymbal

superior cymbal

inferior cymbal

batter head

snare drum

tripod stand

bass drum

tension screw

stand

mallet

pedal

spur

MUSIC

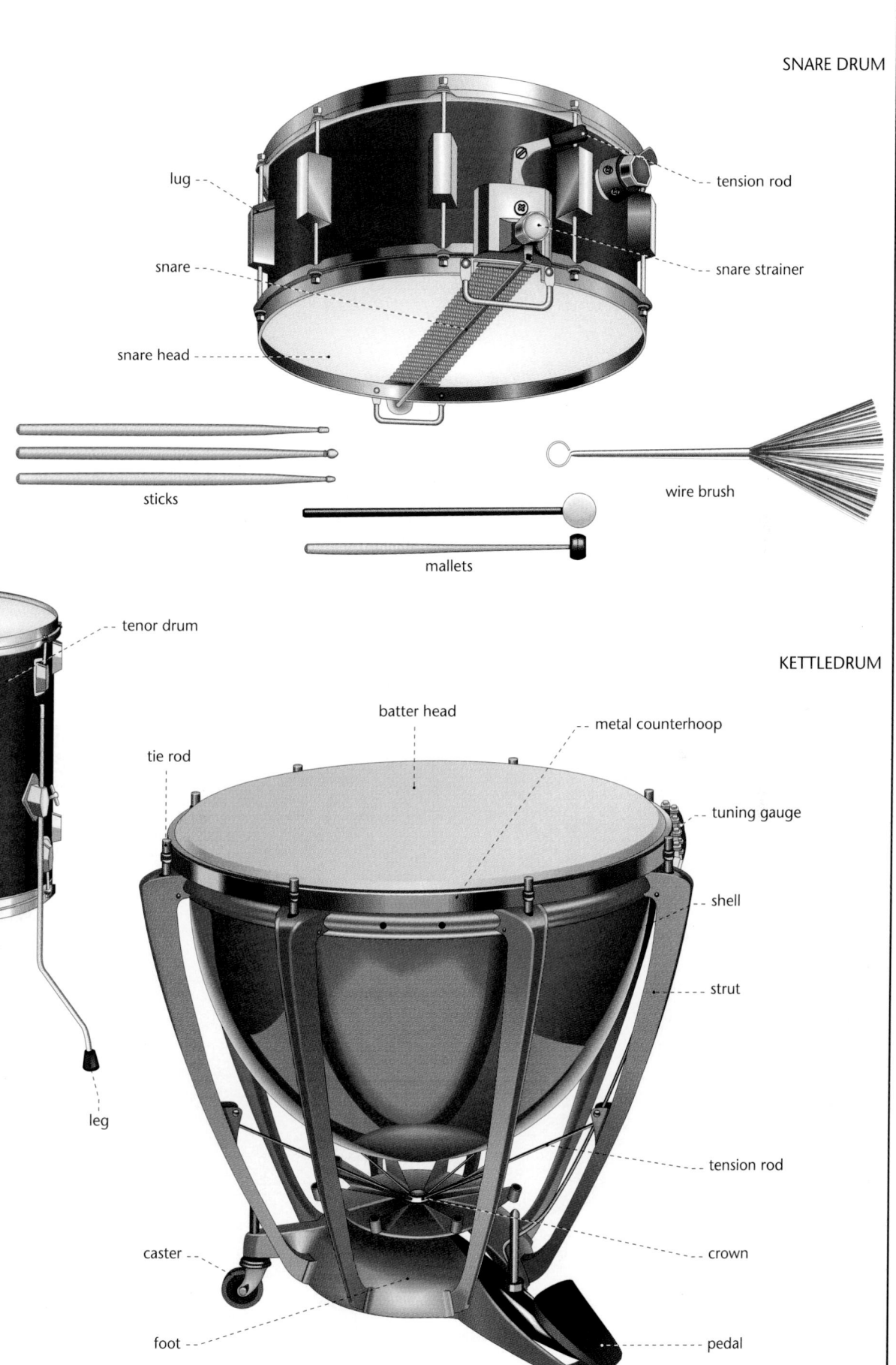

lug

tension rod

snare

snare strainer

snare head

sticks

wire brush

mallets

tenor drum

batter head

metal counterhoop

tie rod

tuning gauge

shell

strut

leg

tension rod

caster

crown

foot

pedal

MUSIC

PERCUSSION INSTRUMENTS

TRIANGLE

metal rod

castanets

TAMBOURINE

jingle

head

cymbals

XYLOPHONE

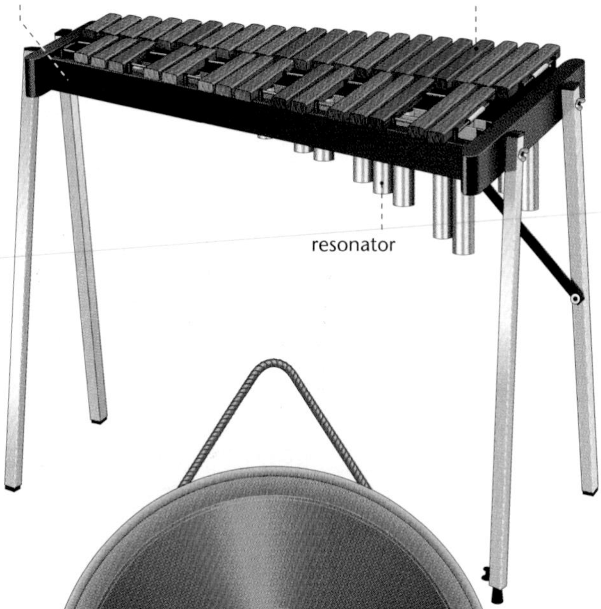

tubular bells

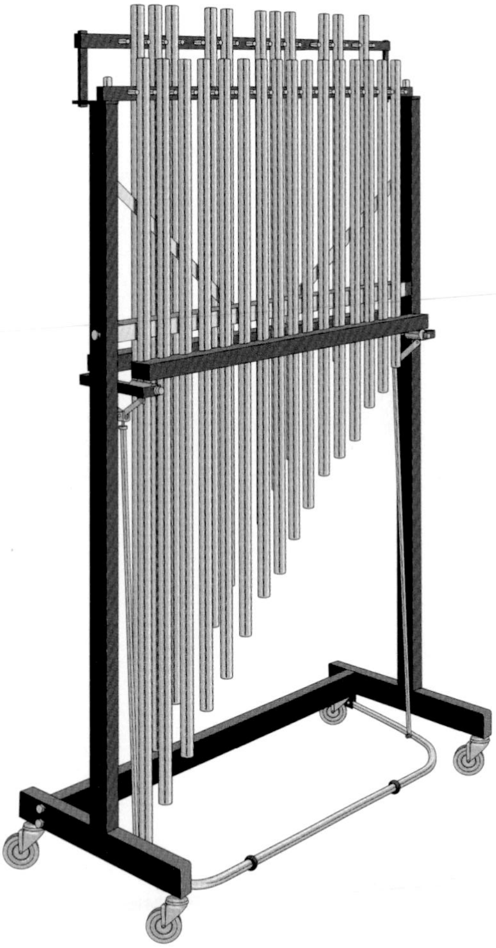

frame

bar

resonator

gong

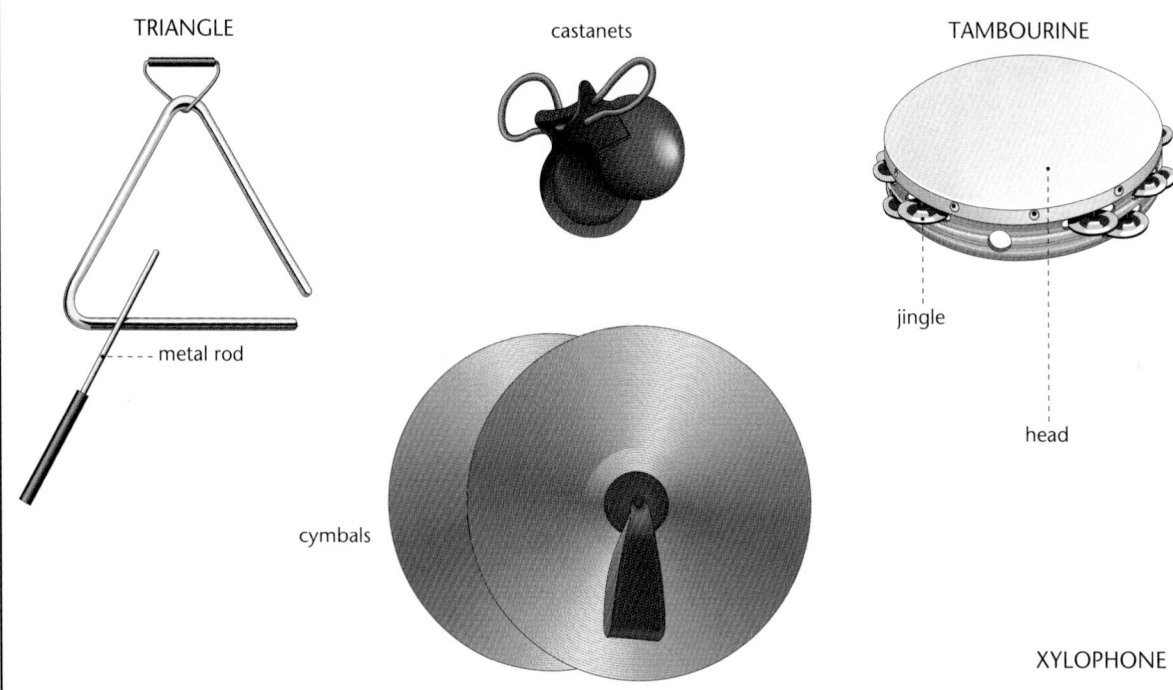

ELECTRONIC INSTRUMENTS

SYNTHESIZER

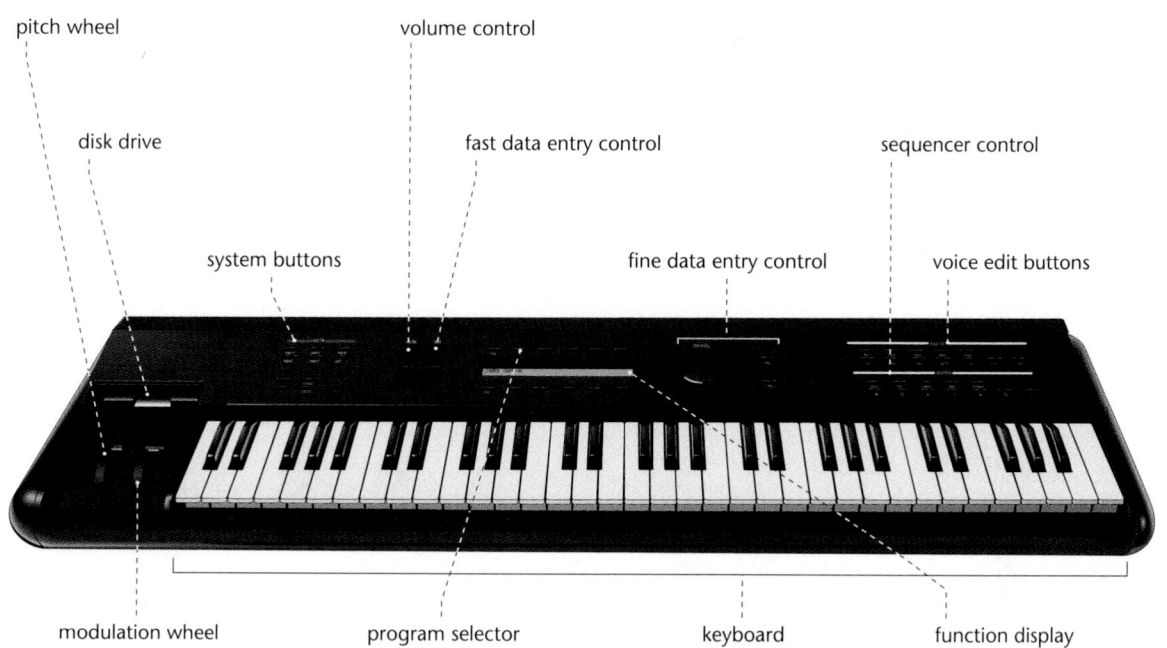

pitch wheel

volume control

disk drive

fast data entry control

sequencer control

system buttons

fine data entry control

voice edit buttons

modulation wheel

program selector

keyboard

function display

ELECTRONIC PIANO

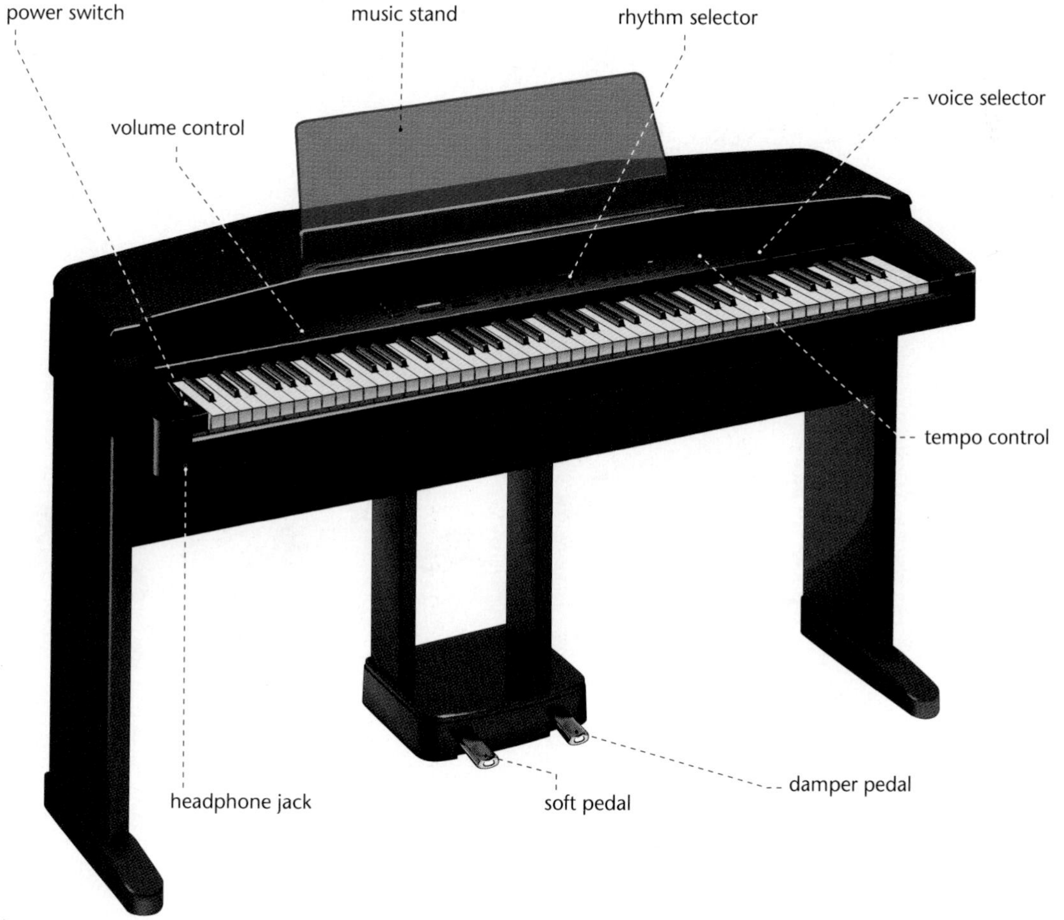

power switch

music stand

rhythm selector

voice selector

volume control

tempo control

headphone jack

soft pedal

damper pedal

SYMPHONY ORCHESTRA

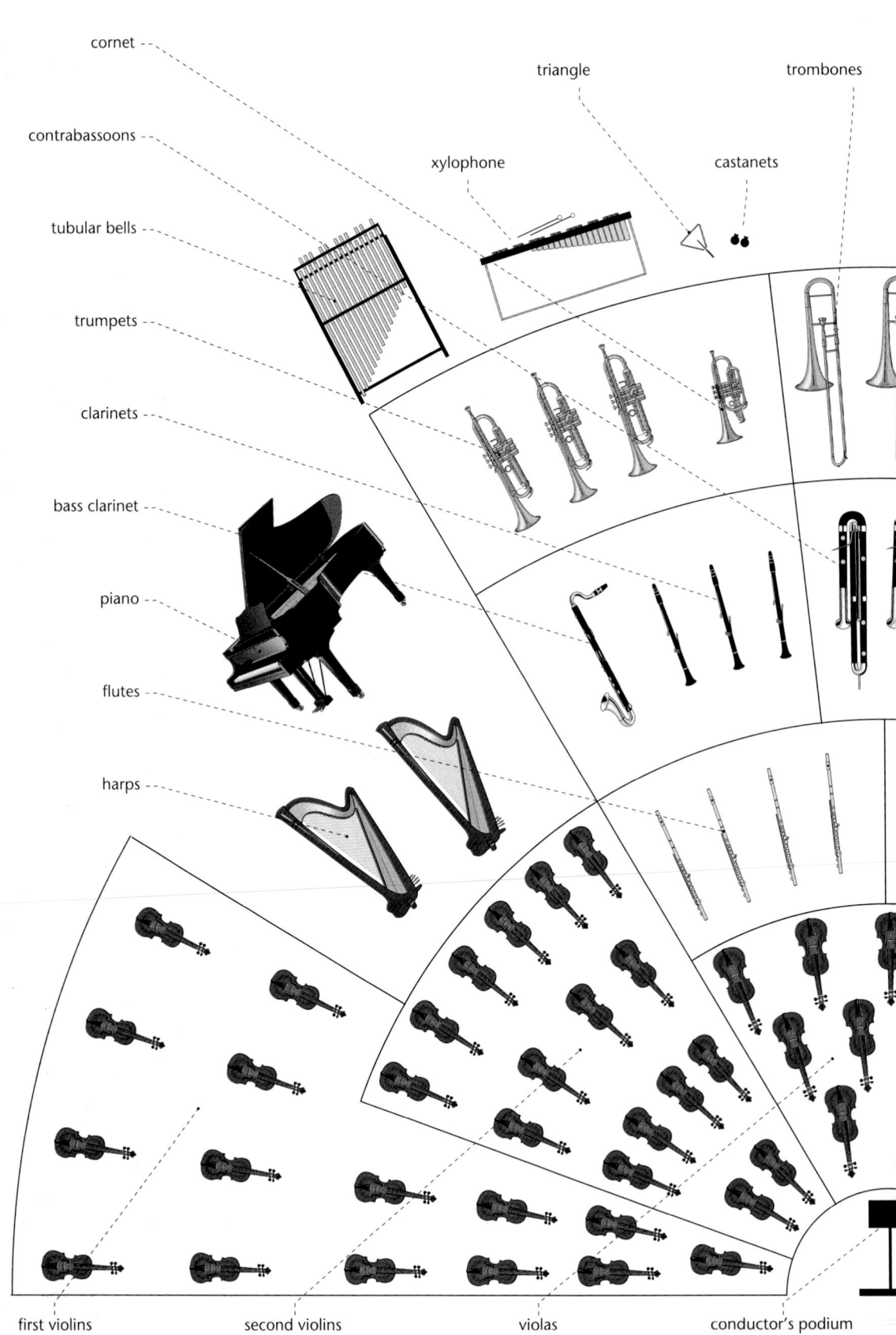

cornet

contrabassoons

tubular bells

trumpets

clarinets

bass clarinet

piano

flutes

harps

triangle

xylophone

castanets

trombones

first violins

second violins

violas

conductor's podium

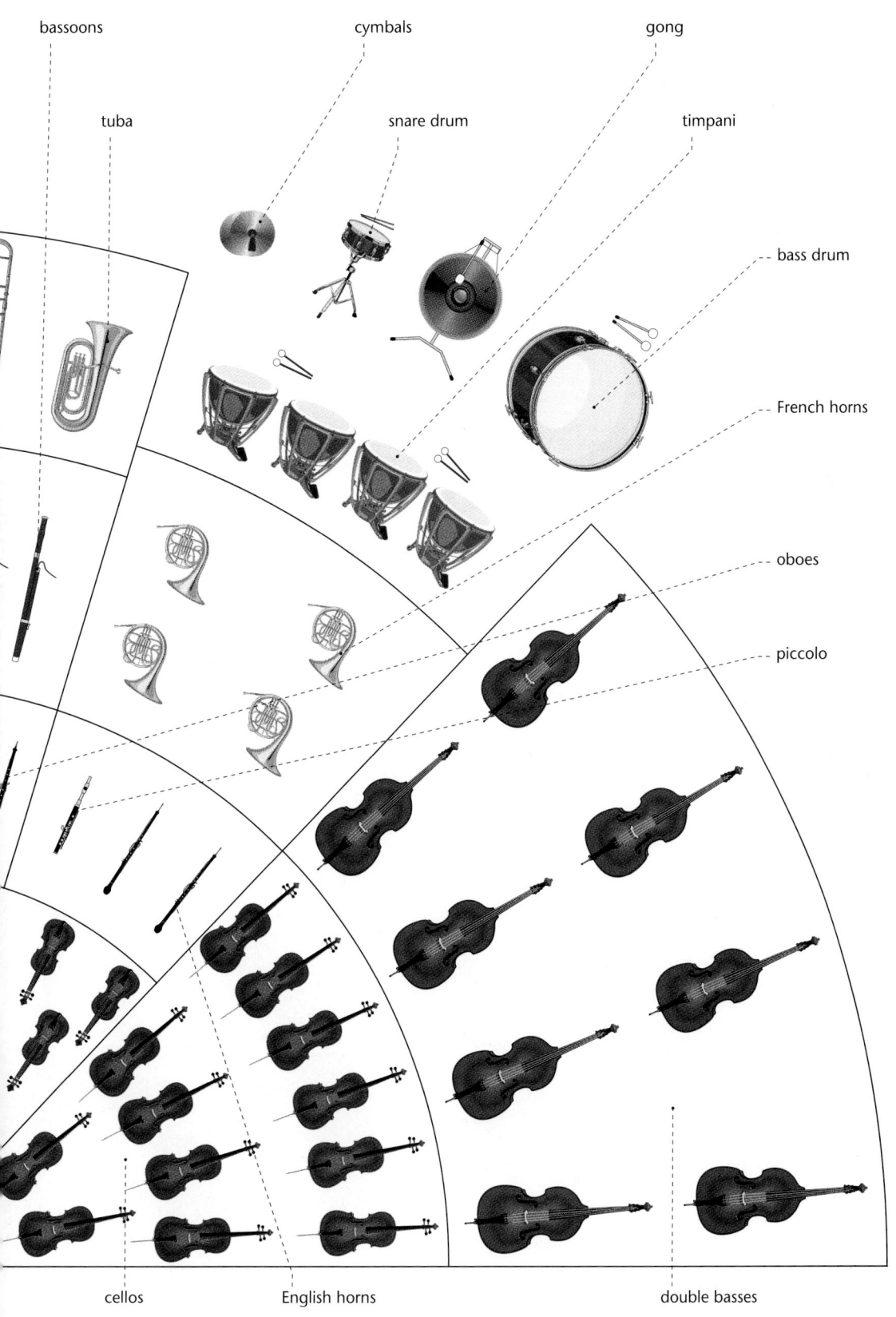

bassoons

tuba

cymbals

snare drum

gong

timpani

bass drum

French horns

oboes

piccolo

cellos

English horns

double basses

duo

trio

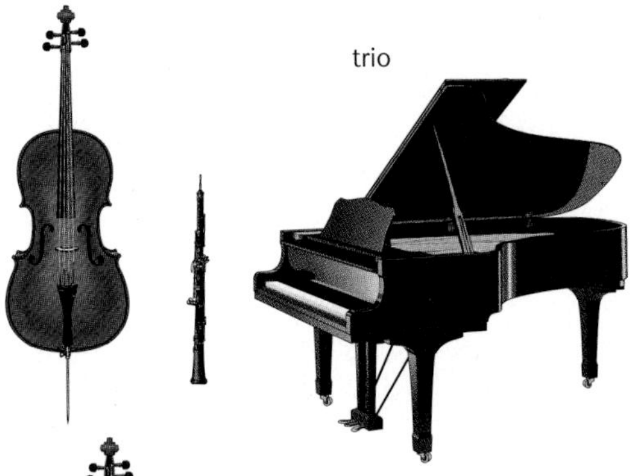

quartet

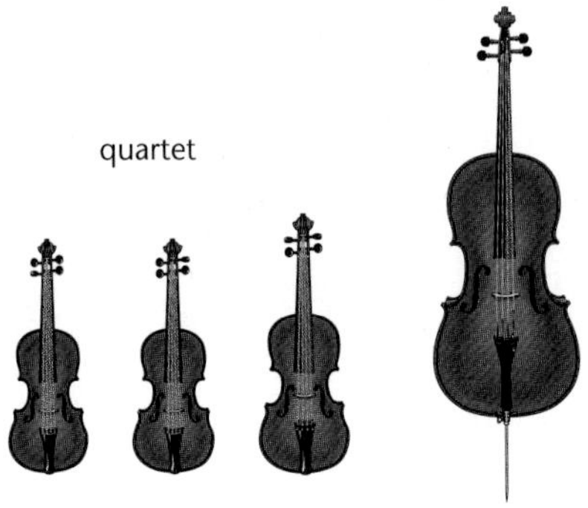

quintet

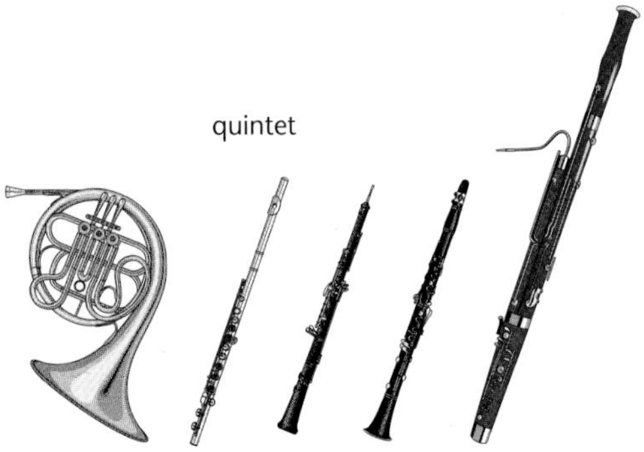

sextet

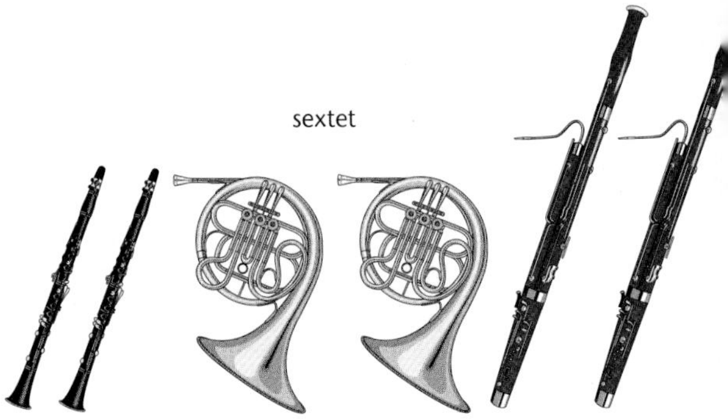

jazz band

CONTENTS

SEWING 561

KNITTING 567

KNITTING MACHINE..568

BOBBIN LACE...570

EMBROIDERY 571

WEAVING..572

FINE BOOKBINDING...577

PRINTING 580

RELIEF PRINTING PROCESS 581

INTAGLIO PRINTING PROCESS 582

LITHOGRAPHY 583

POTTERY 584

WOOD CARVING..586

PAINTING AND DRAWING...588

SEWING

SEWING MACHINE

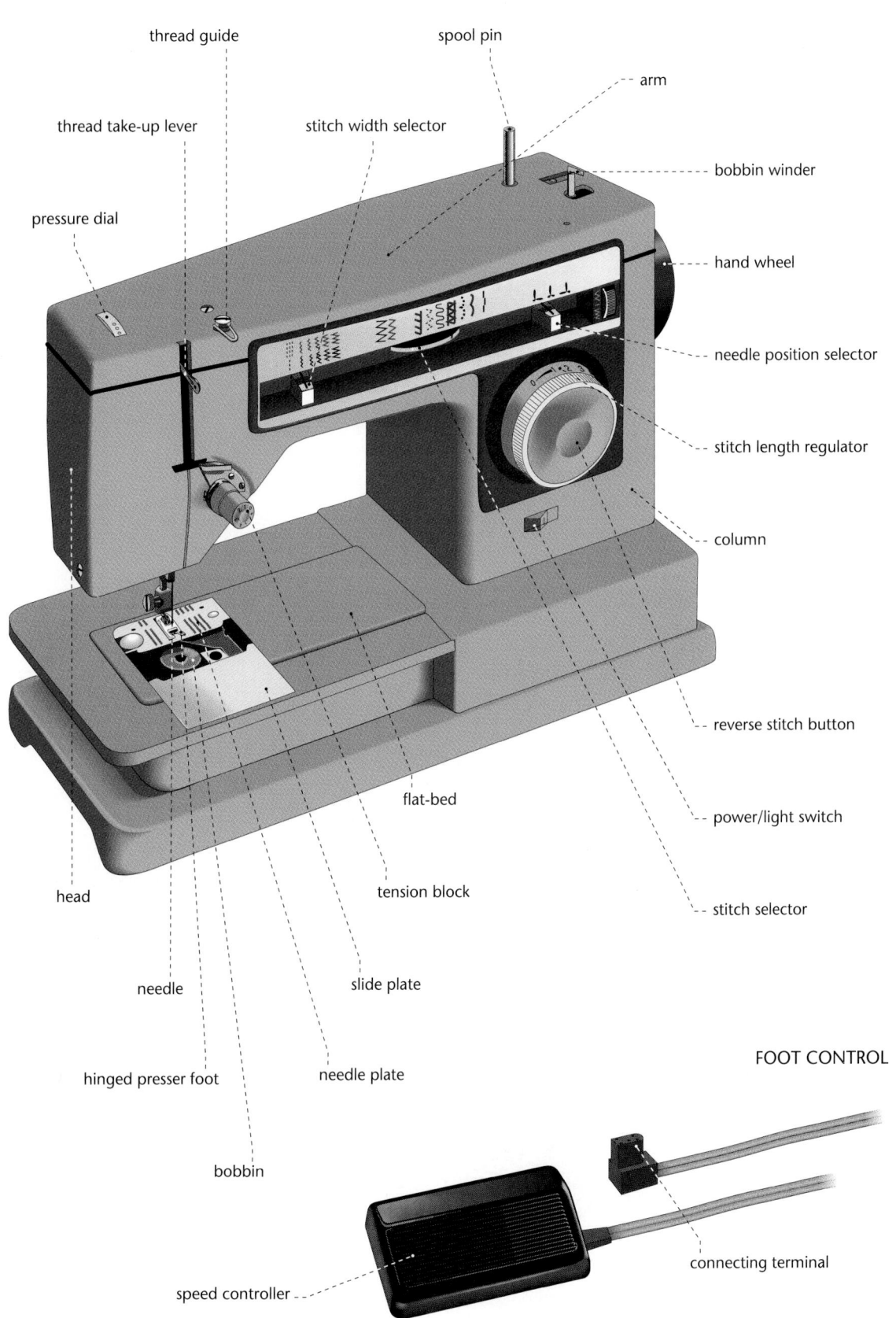

thread guide

spool pin

arm

thread take-up lever

stitch width selector

bobbin winder

pressure dial

hand wheel

needle position selector

stitch length regulator

column

reverse stitch button

flat-bed

power/light switch

head

tension block

stitch selector

needle

slide plate

hinged presser foot

needle plate

bobbin

FOOT CONTROL

connecting terminal

speed controller

SEWING

PRESSER FOOT

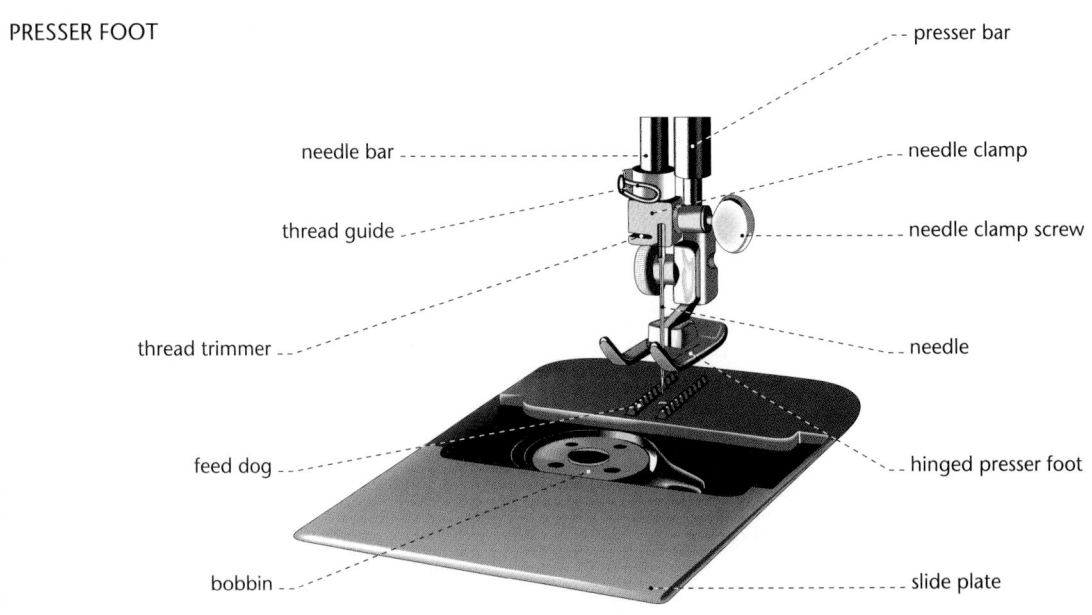

presser bar

needle bar

needle clamp

thread guide

needle clamp screw

thread trimmer

needle

feed dog

hinged presser foot

bobbin

slide plate

NEEDLE

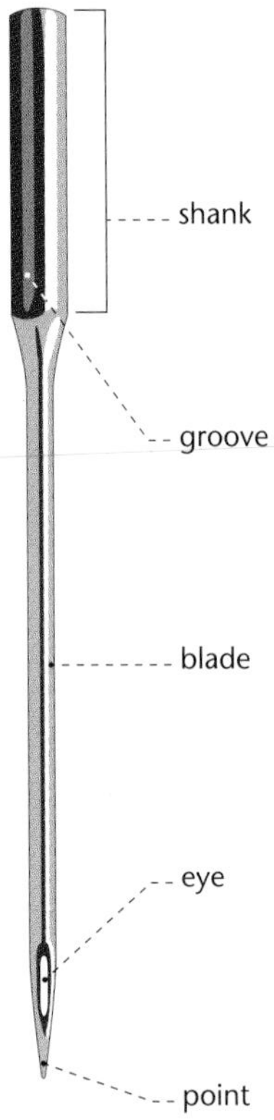

shank

groove

blade

eye

point

TENSION BLOCK

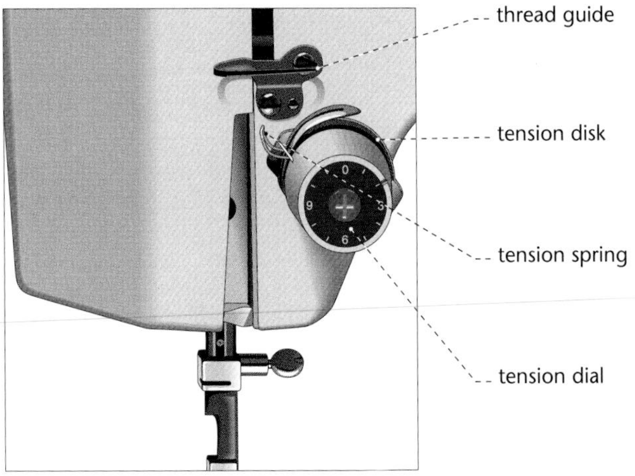

thread guide

tension disk

tension spring

tension dial

BOBBIN CASE

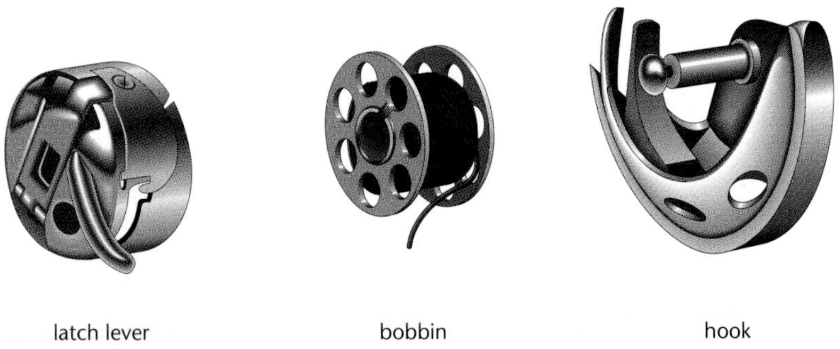

latch lever

bobbin

hook

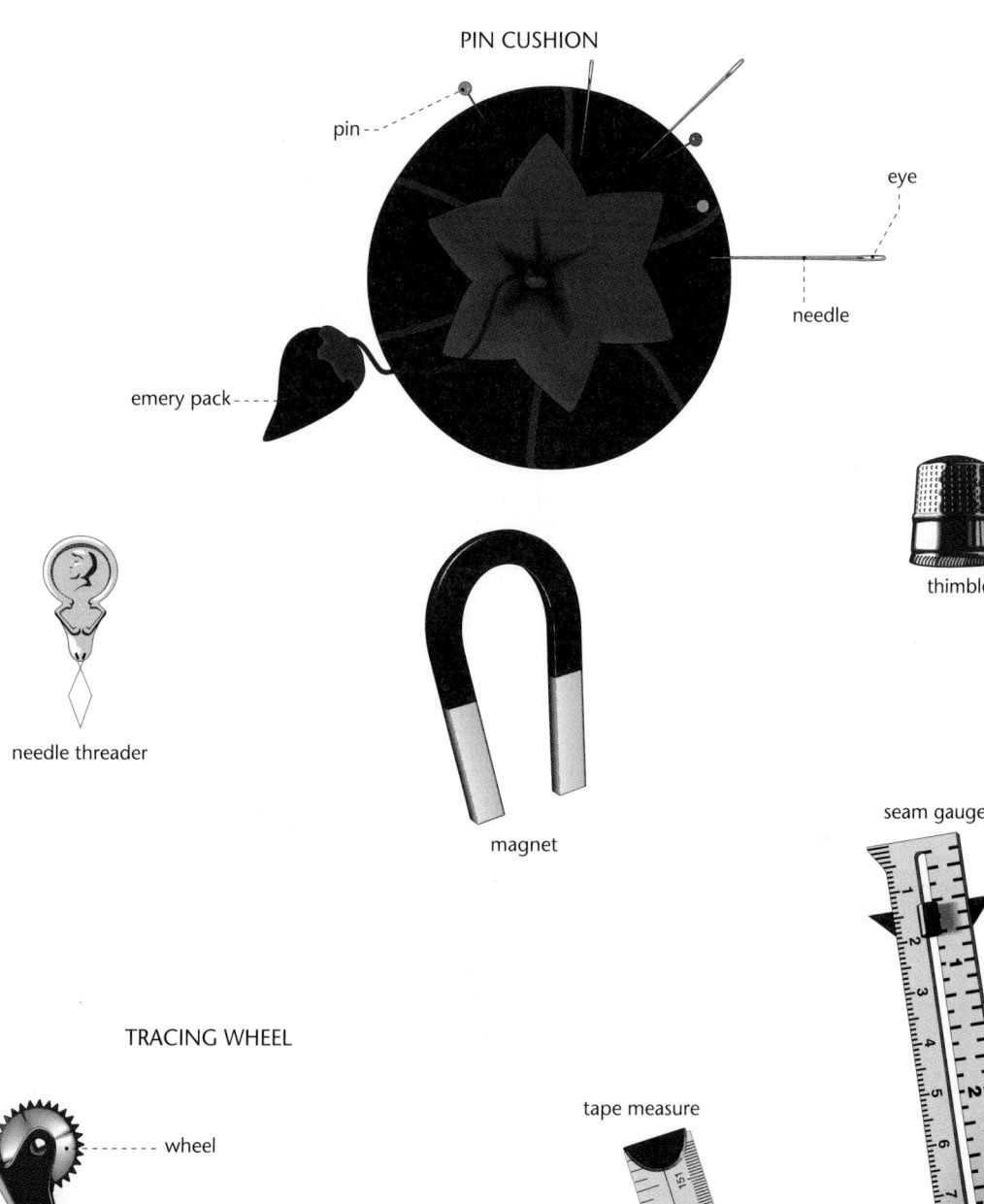

PIN CUSHION

pin

eye

needle

emery pack

thimble

needle threader

magnet

seam gauge

TRACING WHEEL

wheel

shank

handle

tape measure

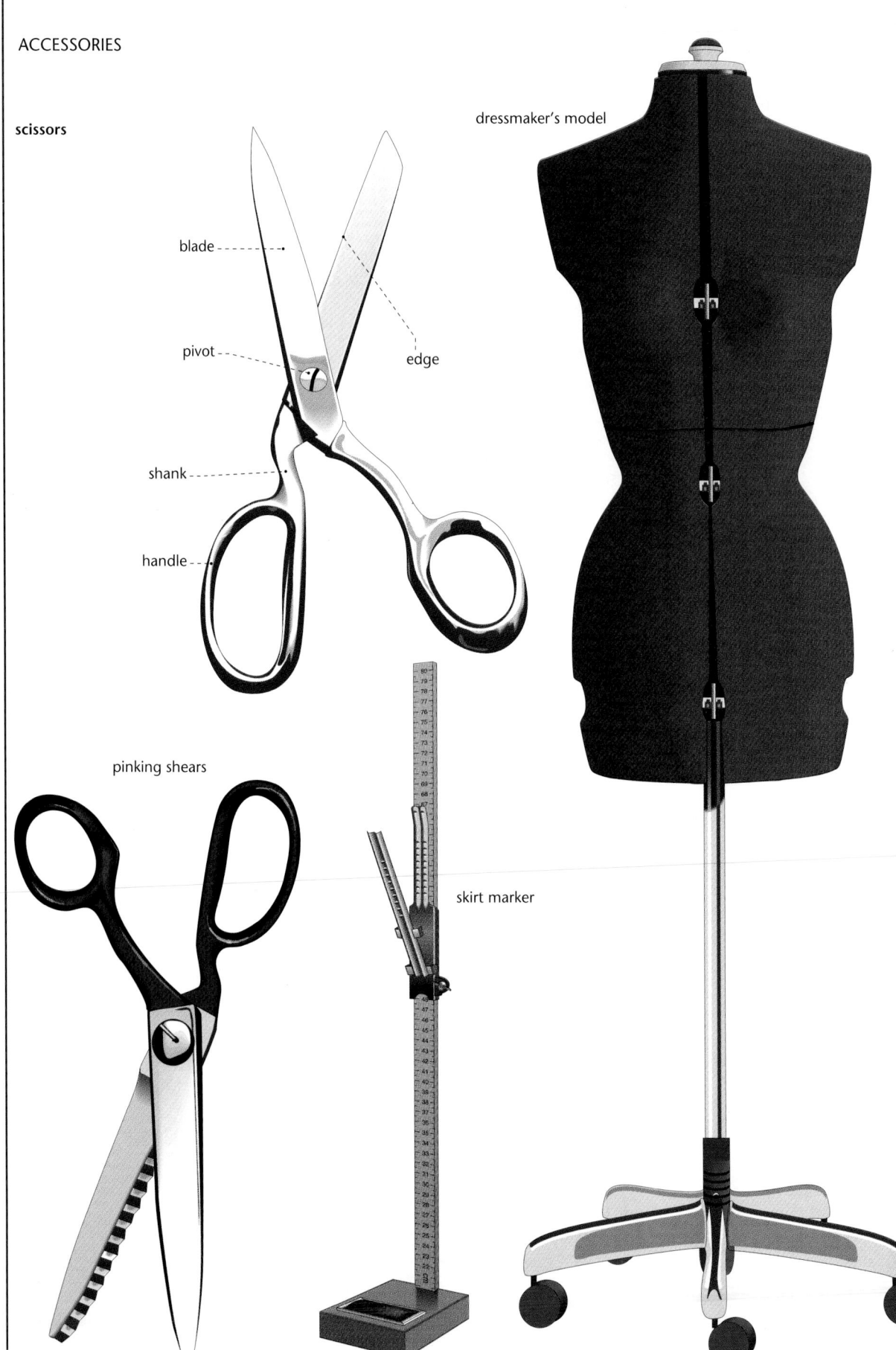

ACCESSORIES

scissors

blade

pivot

edge

shank

handle

dressmaker's model

pinking shears

skirt marker

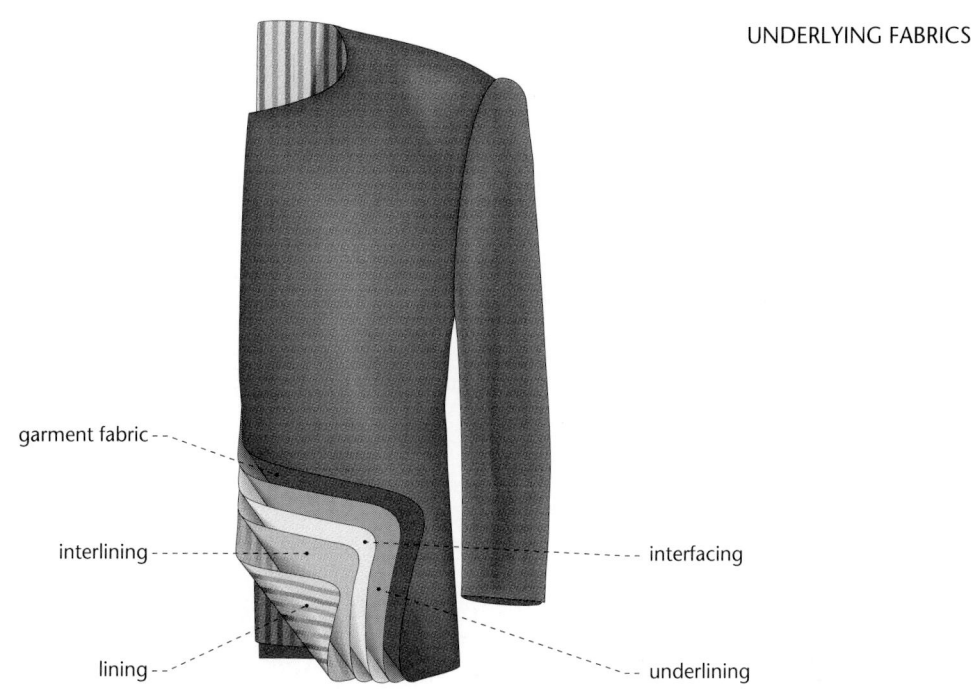

garment fabric

interlining

lining

interfacing

underlining

PATTERN

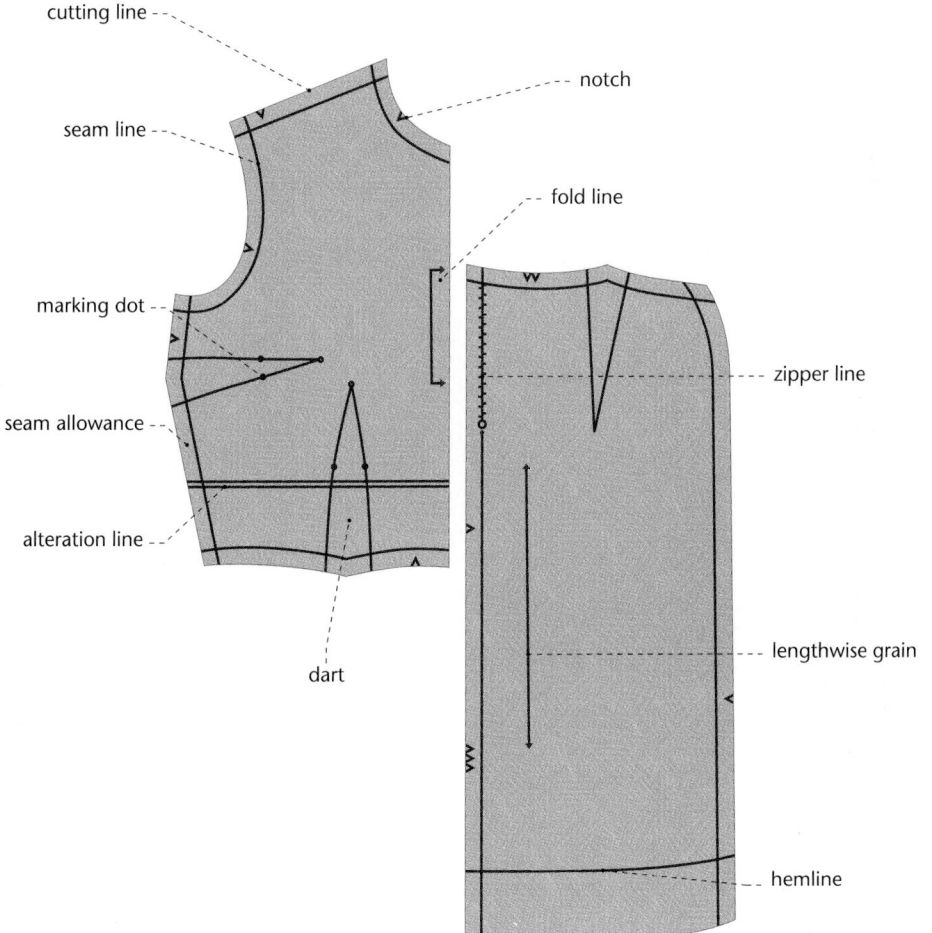

cutting line

seam line

notch

fold line

marking dot

zipper line

seam allowance

alteration line

dart

lengthwise grain

hemline

CREATIVE LEISURE ACTIVITIES

FASTENERS

shank button

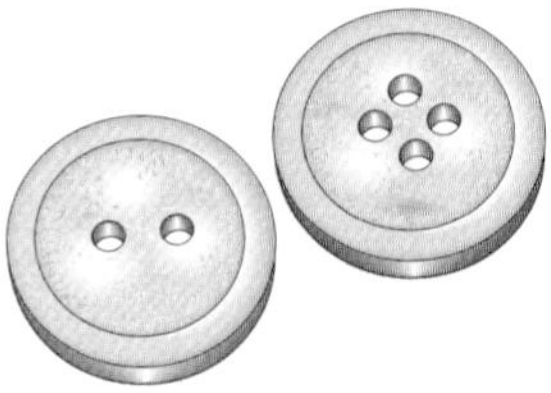

sew-through buttons

snap

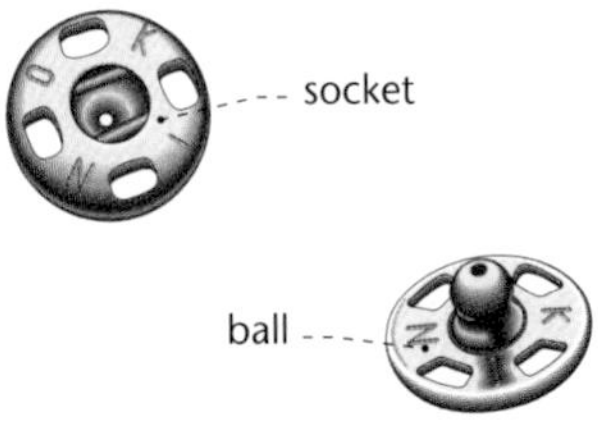

socket

ball

hook and eyes

hook

round eye

ring

straight eye

buckle

tongue

safety pin

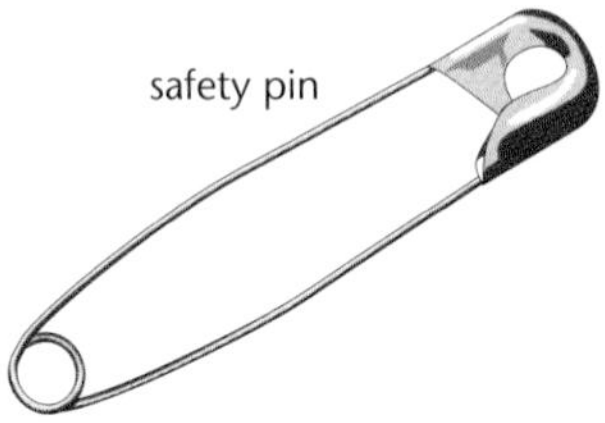

zipper

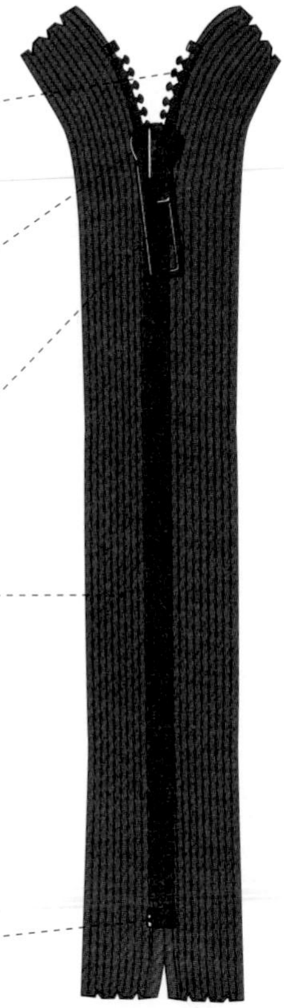

teeth

slide

tab

tape

stop

FABRIC STRUCTURE

bias

selvage

crosswise grain

lengthwise grain

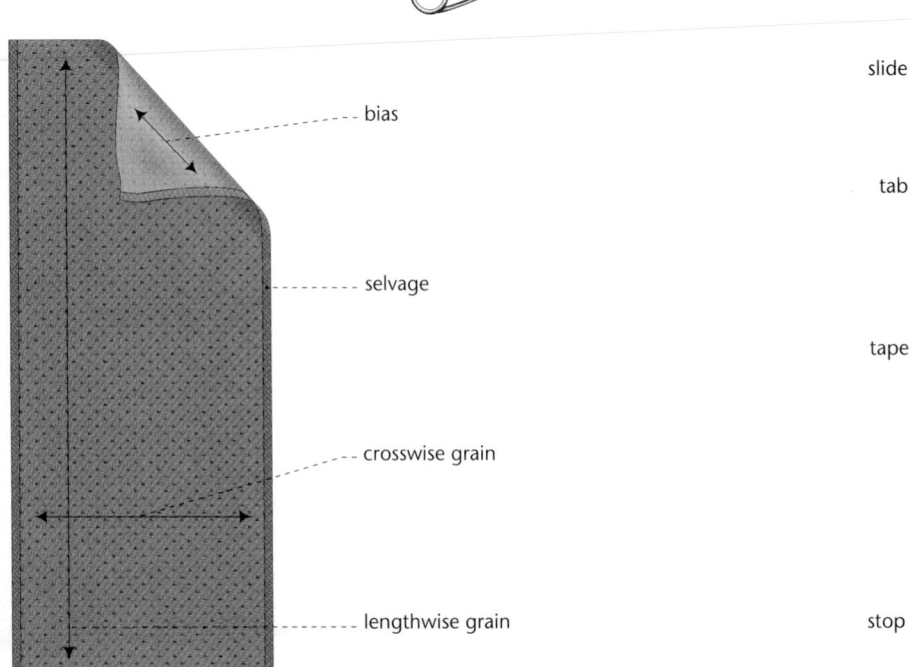

KNITTING

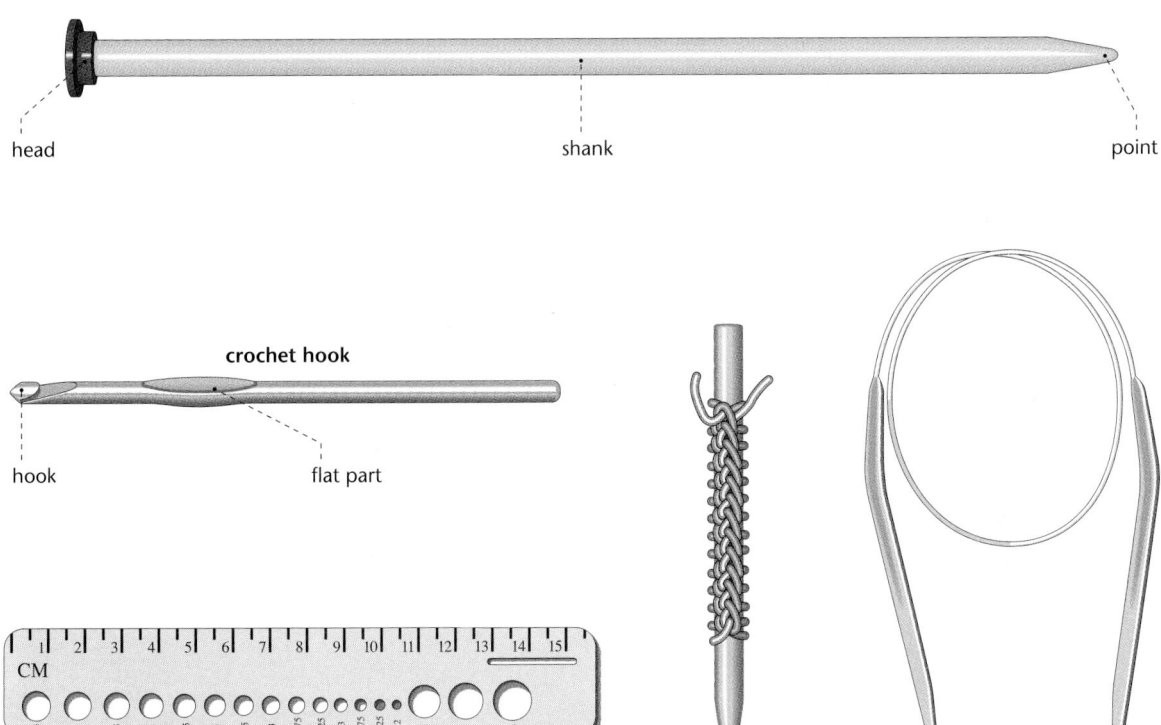

head

shank

point

crochet hook

hook

flat part

knitting measure

cast-on stitches

circular needle

CREATIVE LEISURE ACTIVITIES

STITCH PATTERNS

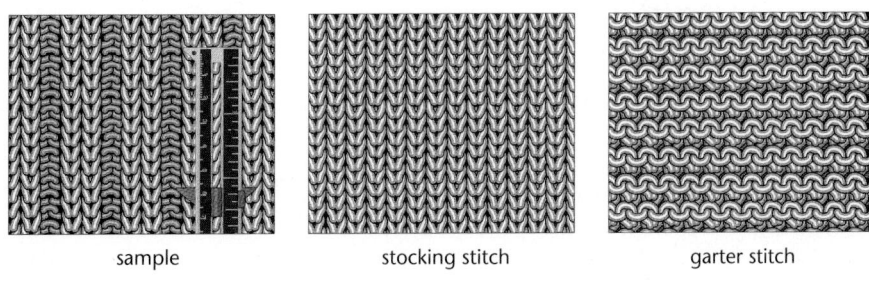

sample

stocking stitch

garter stitch

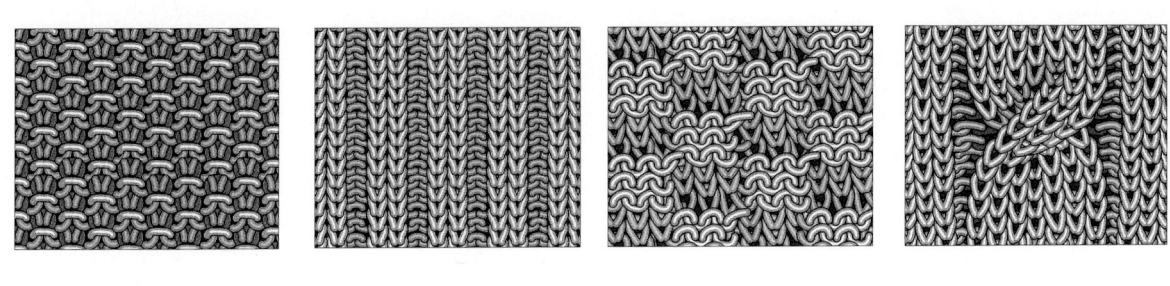

moss stitch

rib stitch

basket stitch

cable stitch

KNITTING MACHINE

NEEDLE BED AND CARRIAGES

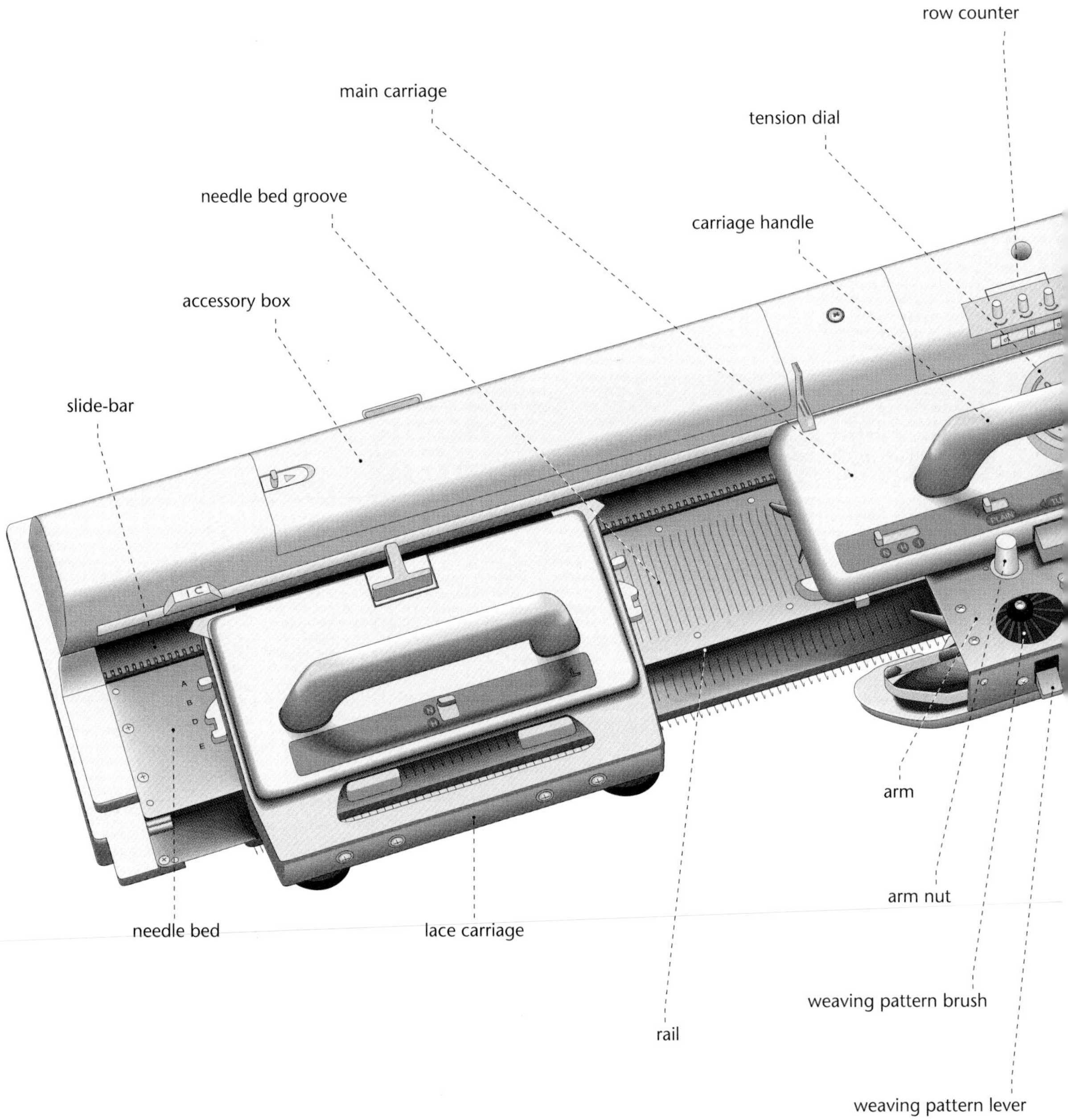

row counter
main carriage
tension dial
needle bed groove
carriage handle
accessory box
slide-bar
arm
arm nut
needle bed
lace carriage
weaving pattern brush
rail
weaving pattern lever

LATCH NEEDLE

latch
butt
shank
hook

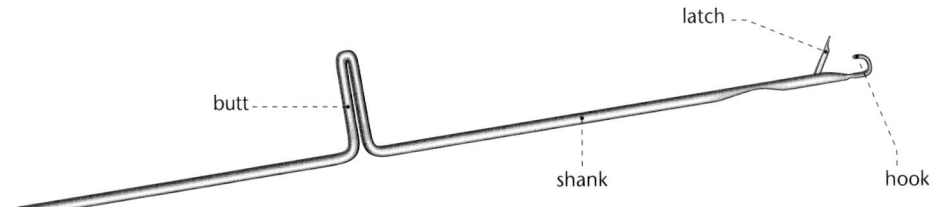

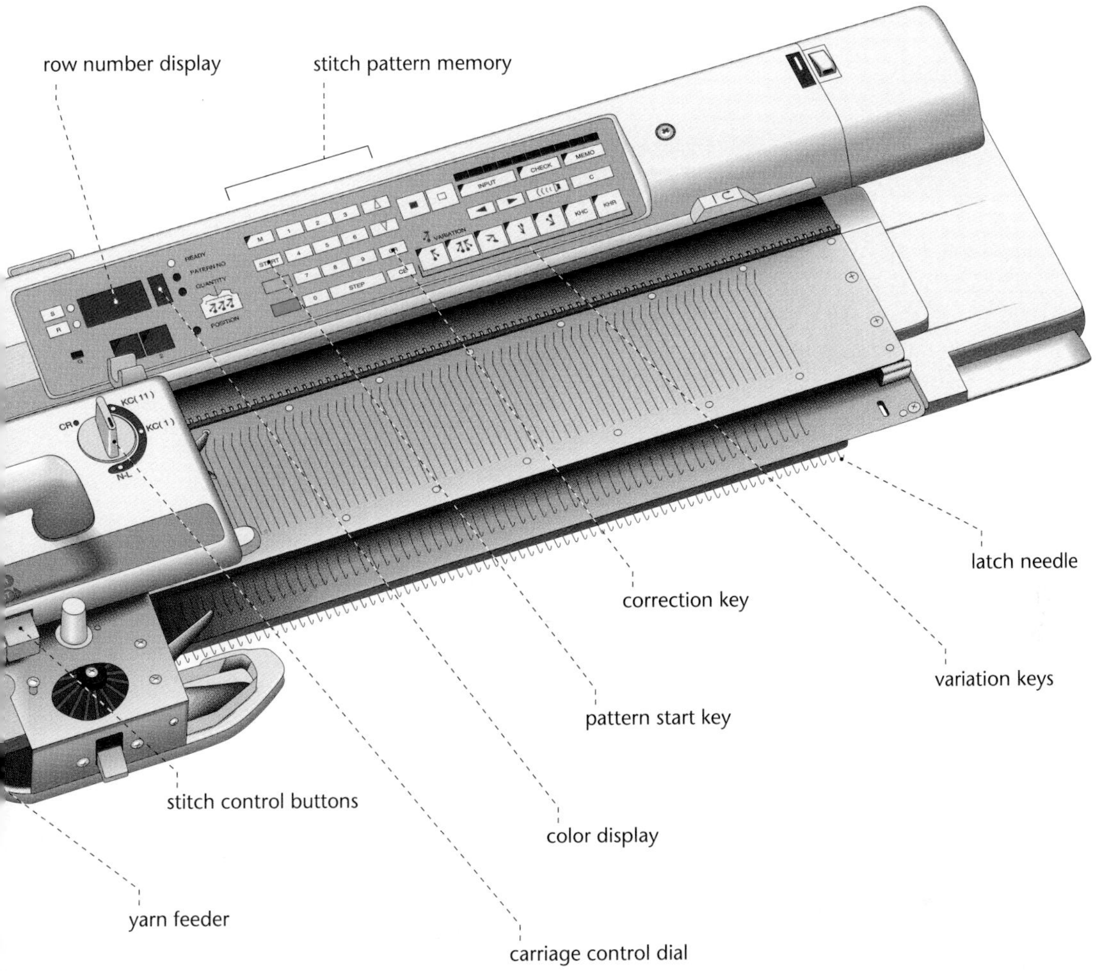

row number display

stitch pattern memory

latch needle

variation keys

correction key

pattern start key

color display

stitch control buttons

yarn feeder

carriage control dial

TENSION BLOCK

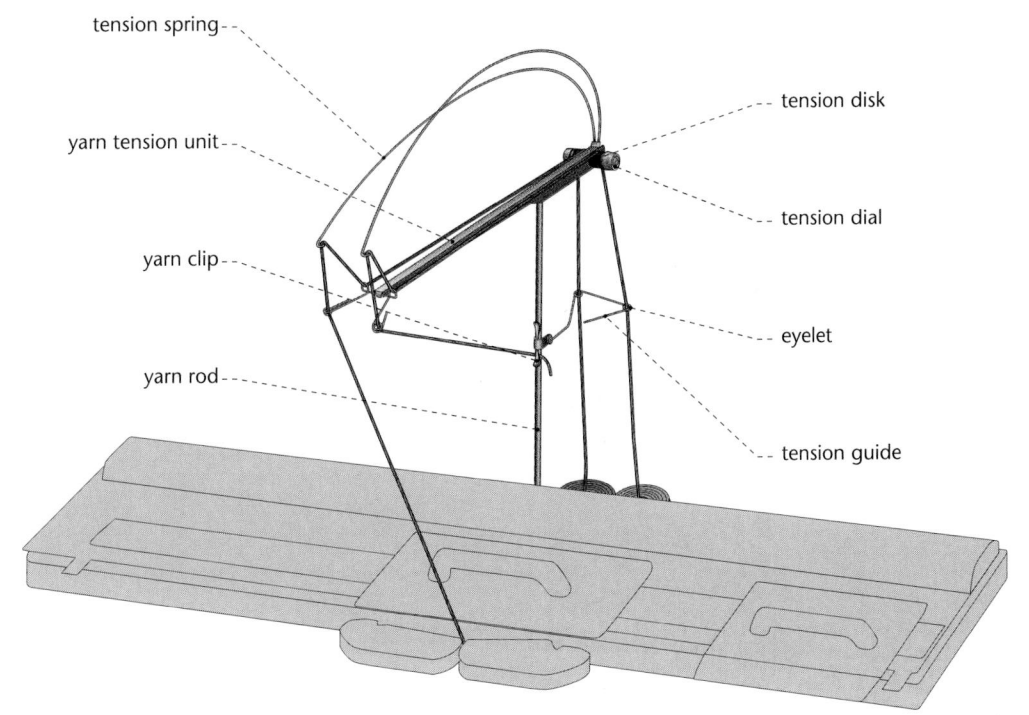

tension spring

tension disk

yarn tension unit

tension dial

yarn clip

eyelet

yarn rod

tension guide

BOBBIN LACE

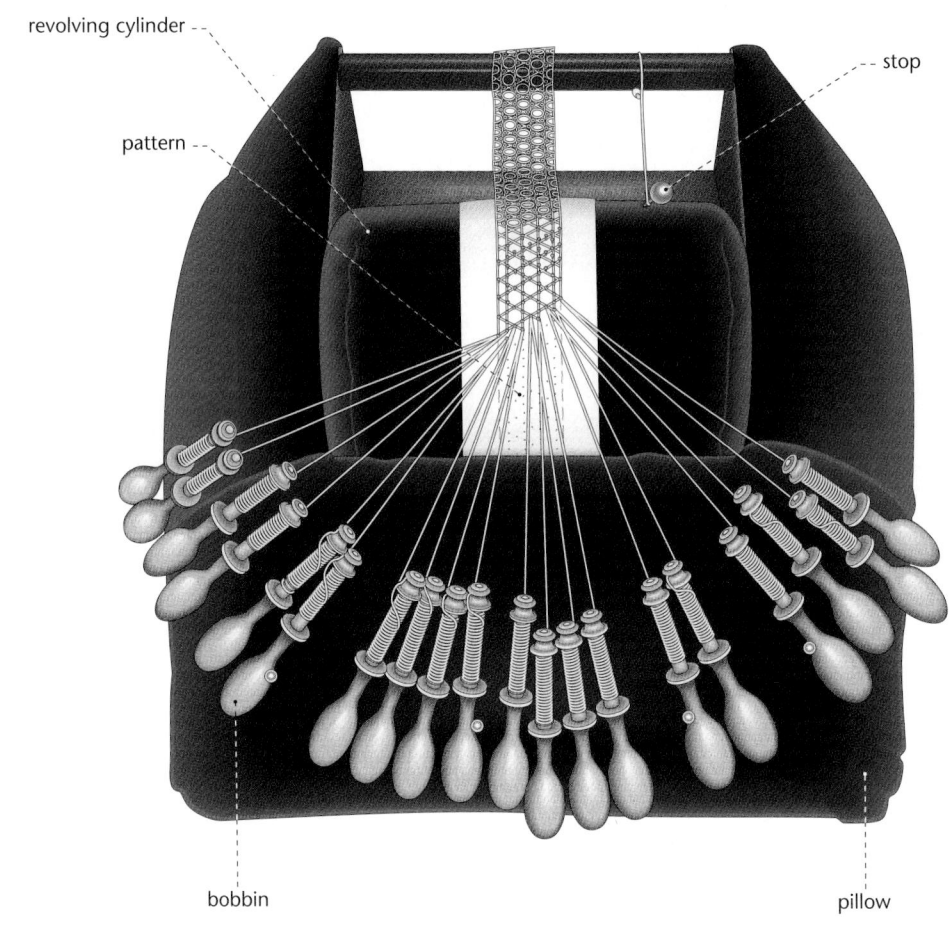

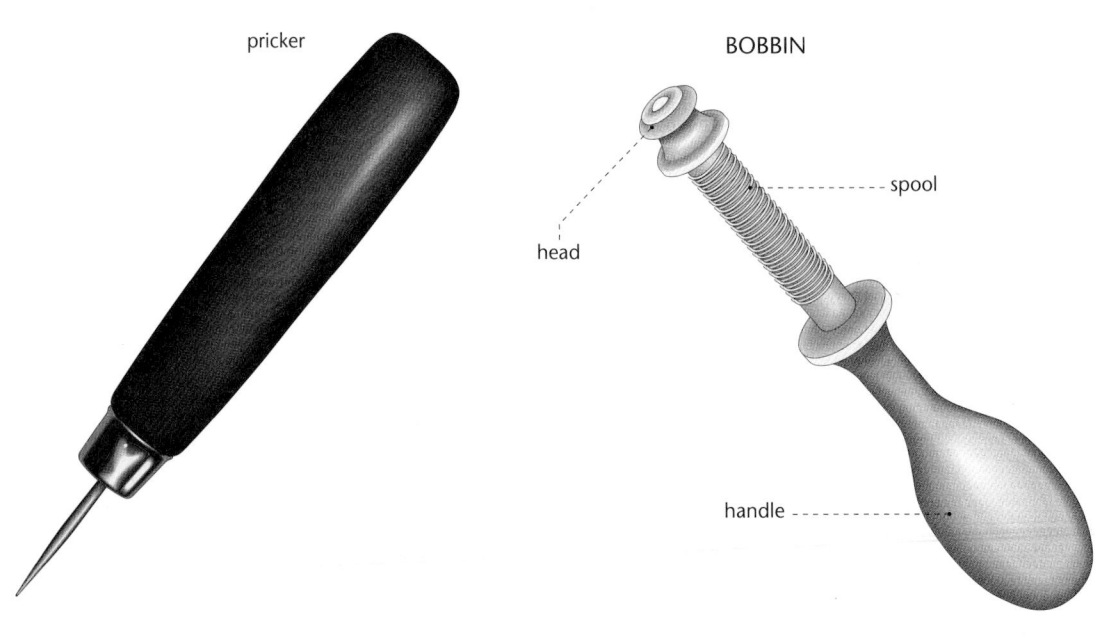

PILLOW

revolving cylinder

pattern

stop

bobbin

pillow

pricker

BOBBIN

head

spool

handle

EMBROIDERY

embroidered fabric

peg

tape

slat

webbing

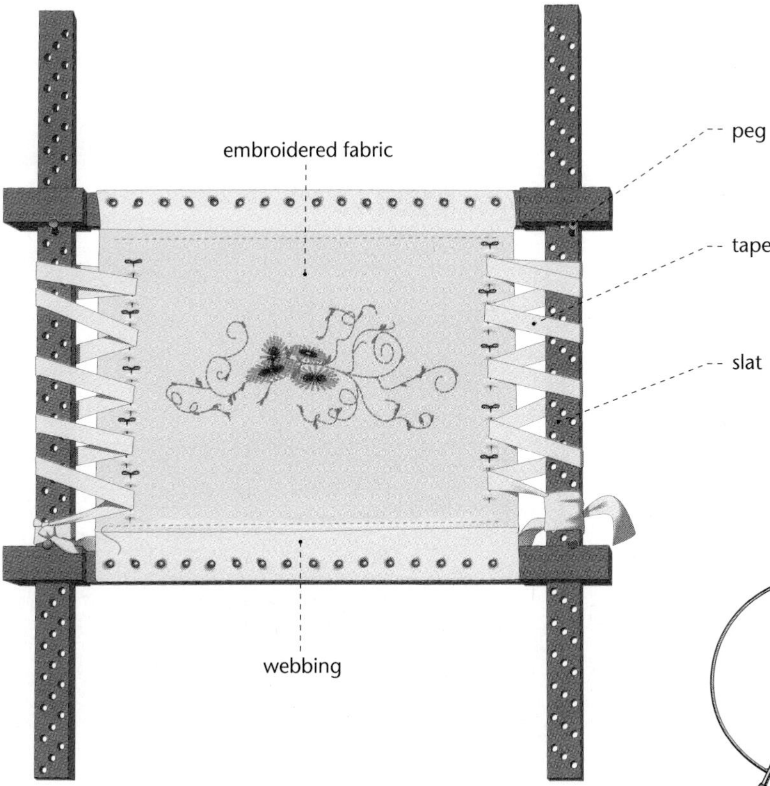

hoop

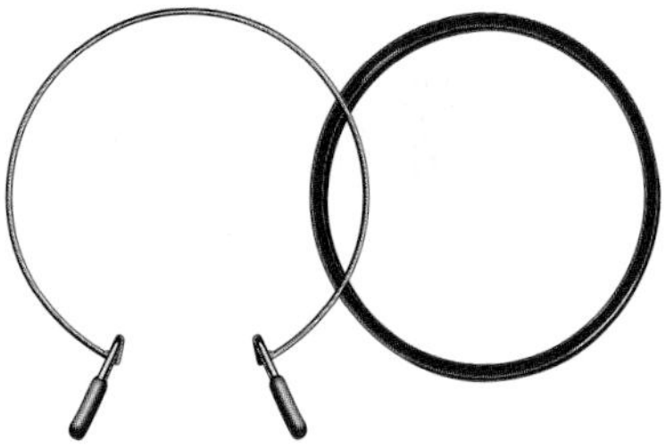

STITCHES

cross stitches

herringbone stitch

chevron stitch

flat stitches

couched stitches

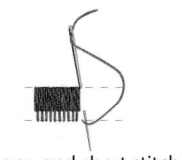

long and short stitch

fishbone stitch

Romanian couching stitch

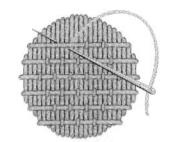

Oriental couching stitch

knot stitches

loop stitches

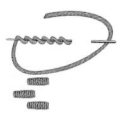

bullion stitch

French knot stitch

chain stitch

feather stitch

571

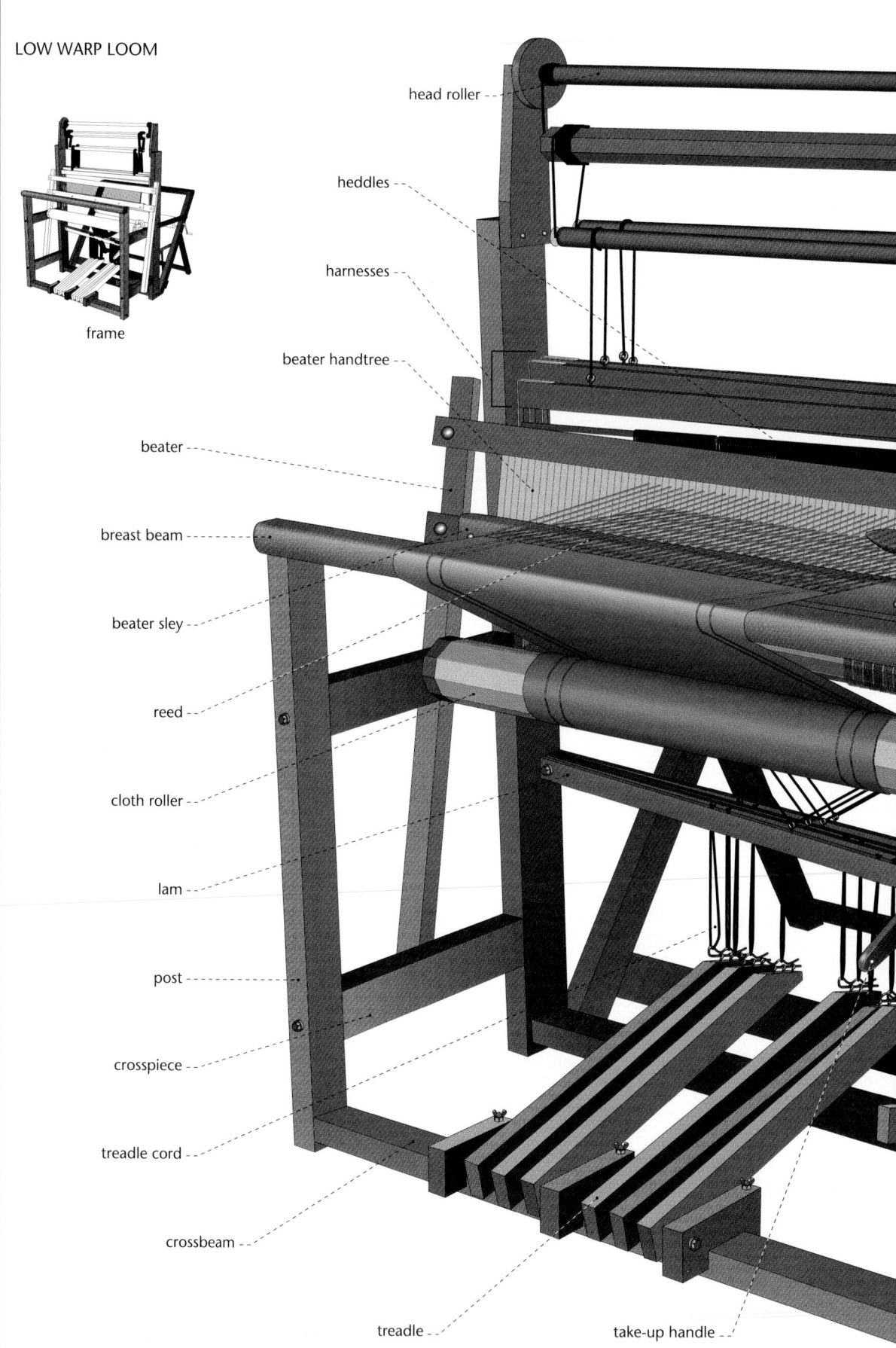

LOW WARP LOOM

frame

head roller

heddles

harnesses

beater handtree

beater

breast beam

beater sley

reed

cloth roller

lam

post

crosspiece

treadle cord

crossbeam

treadle

take-up handle

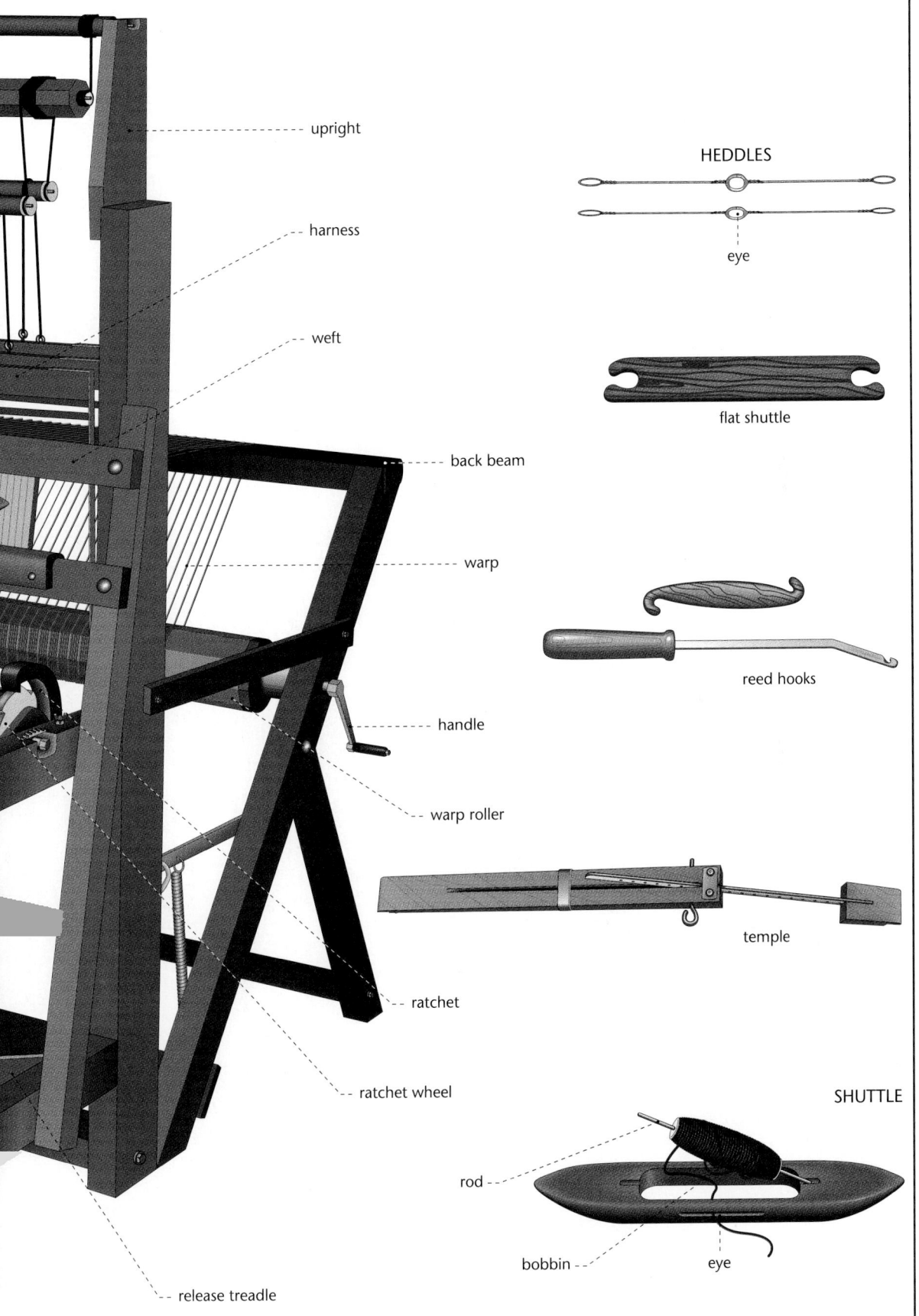

upright

harness

weft

back beam

warp

handle

warp roller

ratchet

ratchet wheel

release treadle

HEDDLES

eye

flat shuttle

reed hooks

temple

SHUTTLE

rod

bobbin

eye

HIGH WARP LOOM

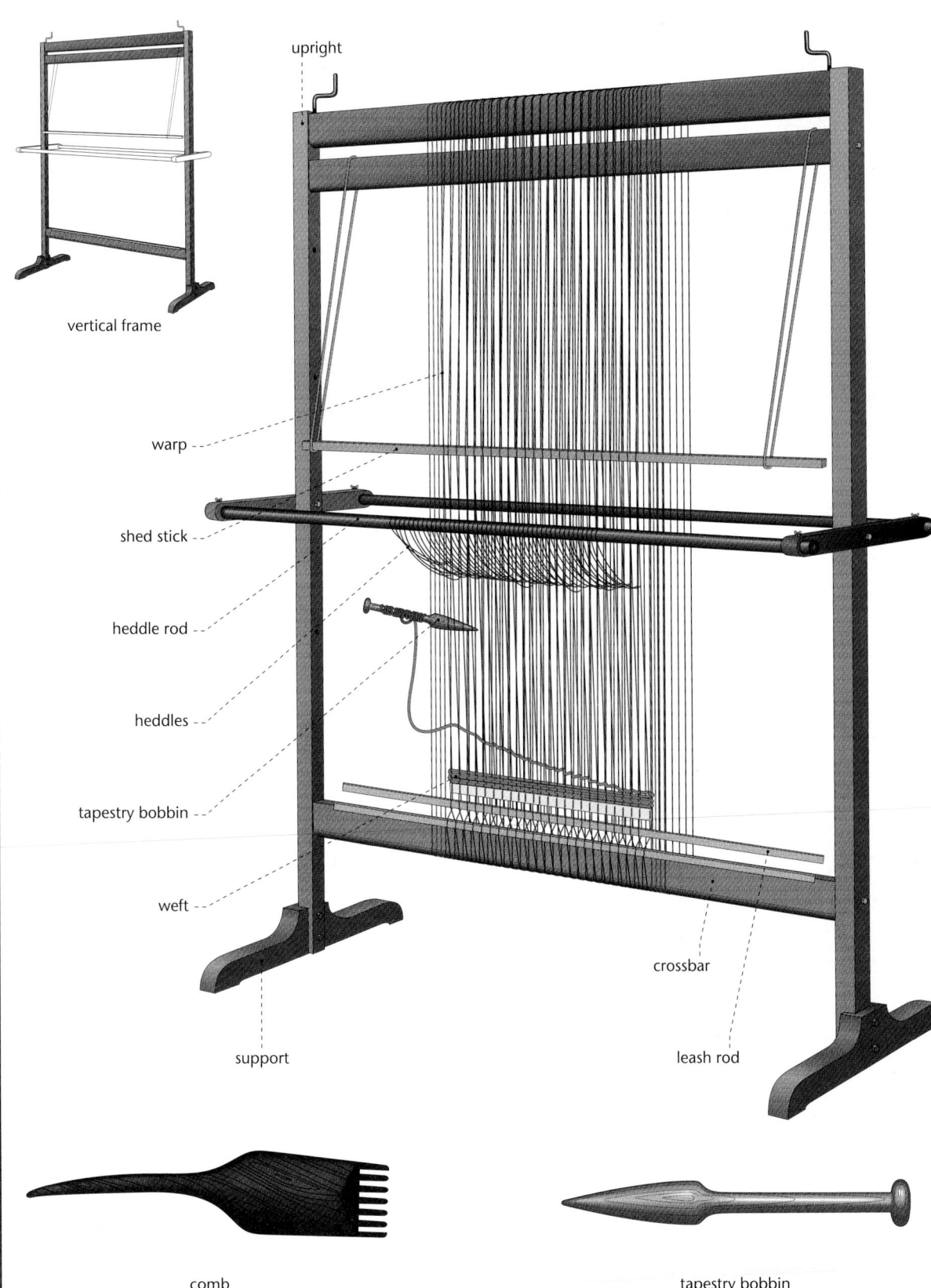

vertical frame

upright

warp

shed stick

heddle rod

heddles

tapestry bobbin

weft

support

crossbar

leash rod

comb

tapestry bobbin

bobbin winder

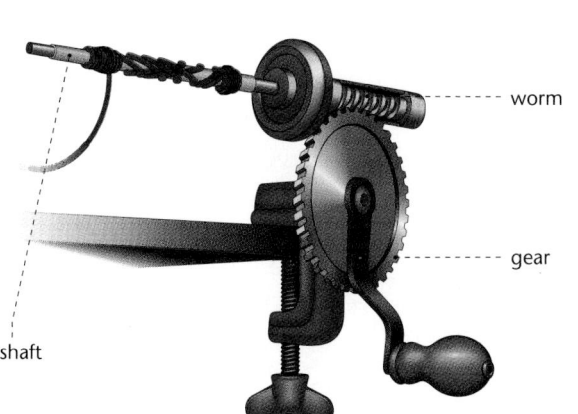

worm

gear

shaft

ball winder

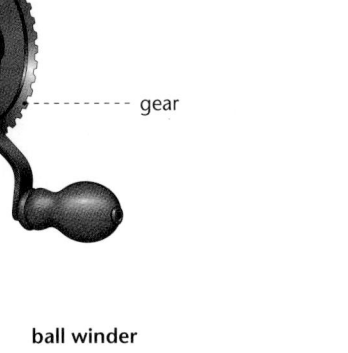

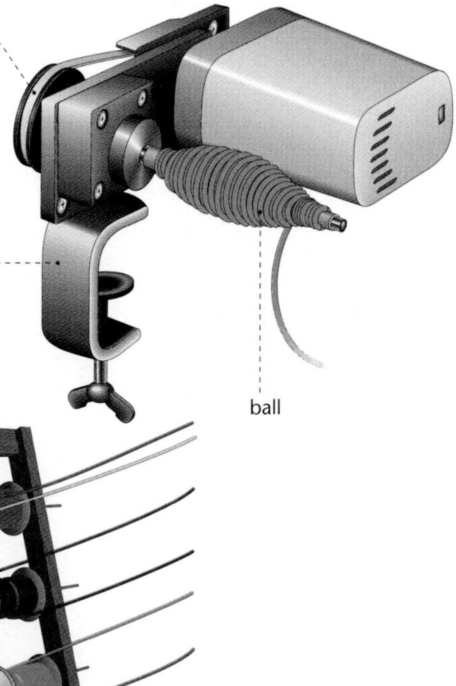

driving wheel

clamp

ball

swift

warping frame

peg

spool rack

575

CREATIVE LEISURE ACTIVITIES

DIAGRAM OF WEAVING PRINCIPLE

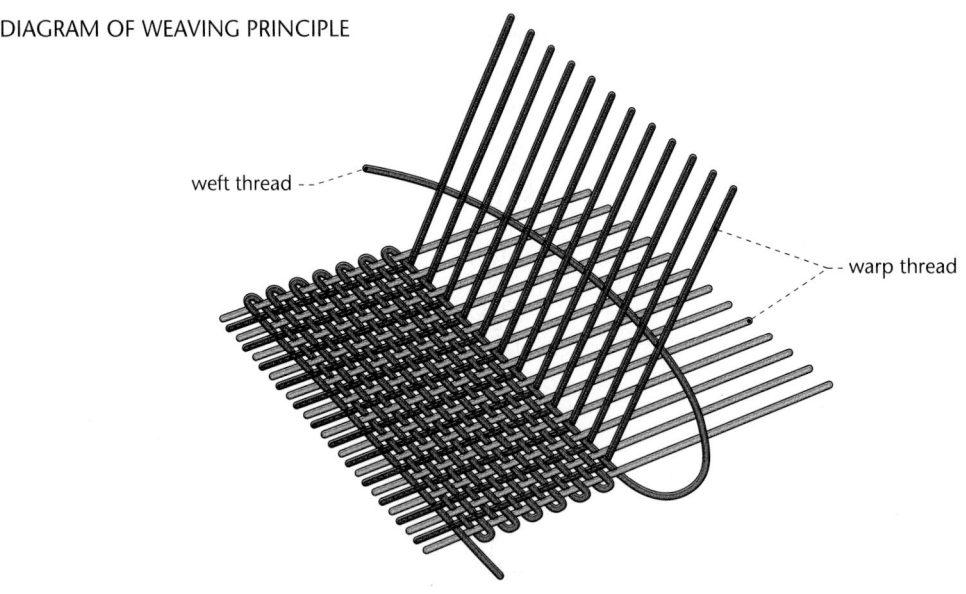

weft thread

warp thread

BASIC WEAVES

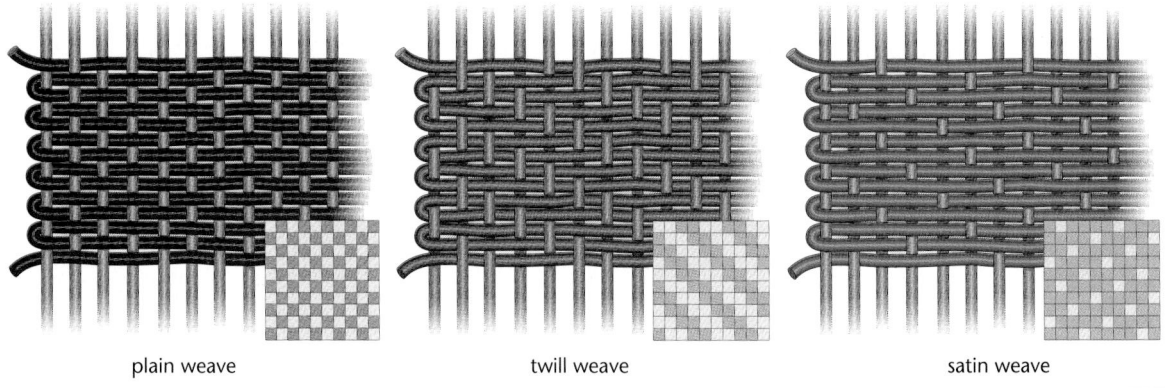

plain weave

twill weave

satin weave

OTHER TECHNIQUES

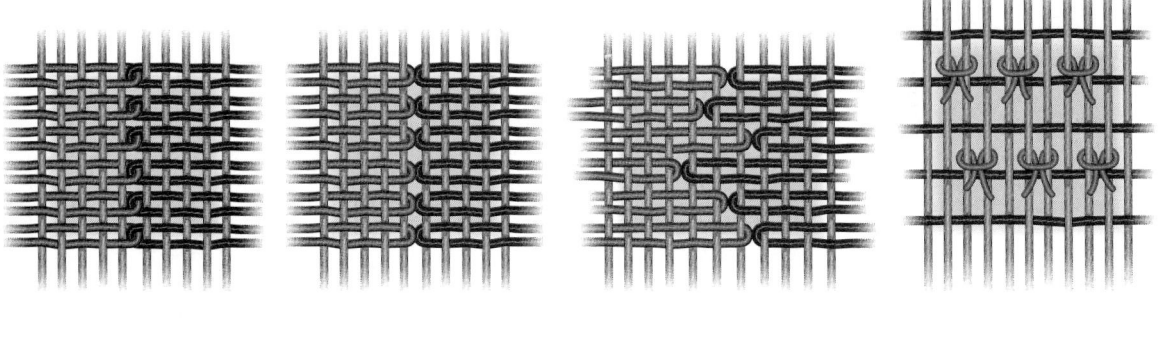

interlock

slit

hatching

knot

FINE BOOKBINDING

headcap

headband

square

top edge

joint

flyleaf

spine

corner

raised band

back board

front board

fore edge

tail edge

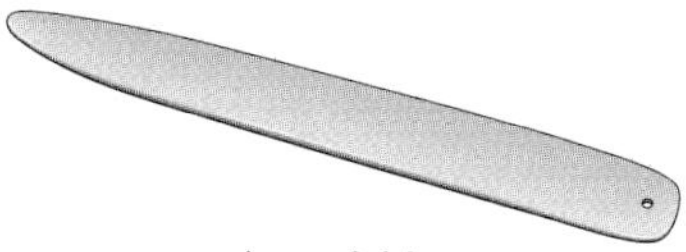

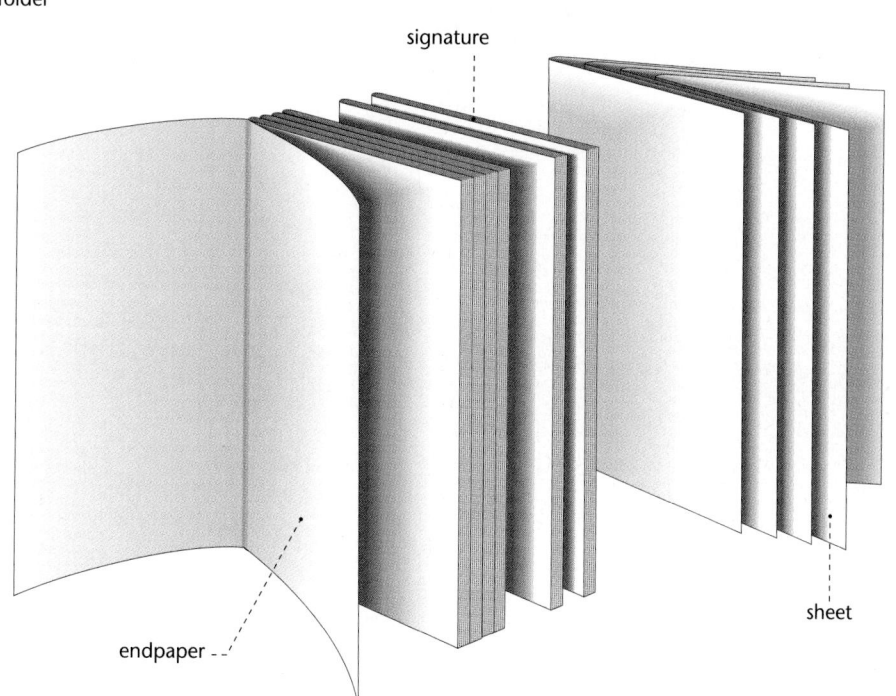

bone folder

signature

sheet

endpaper

TRIMMING

board cutter

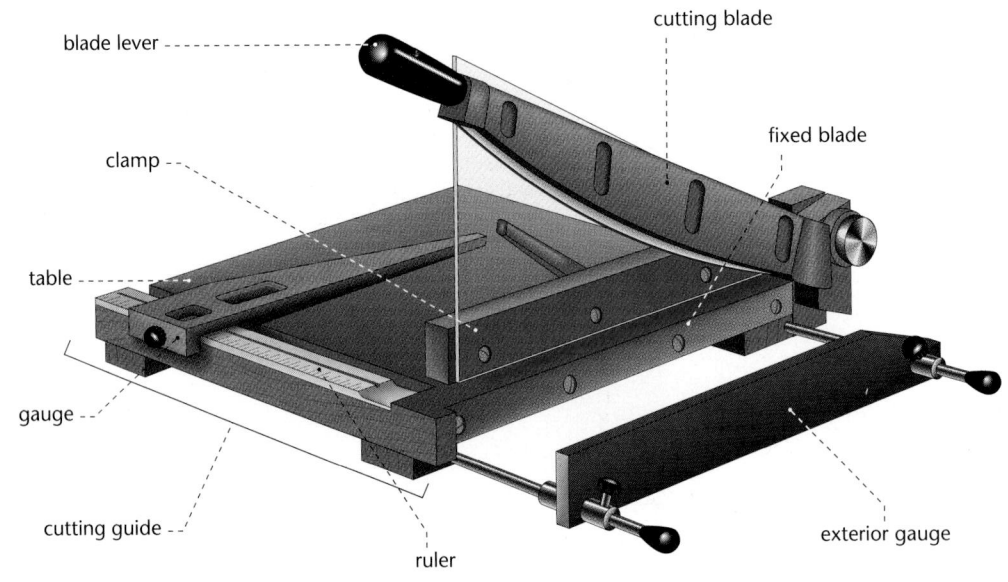

blade lever

cutting blade

clamp

fixed blade

table

gauge

cutting guide

ruler

exterior gauge

SAWING-IN

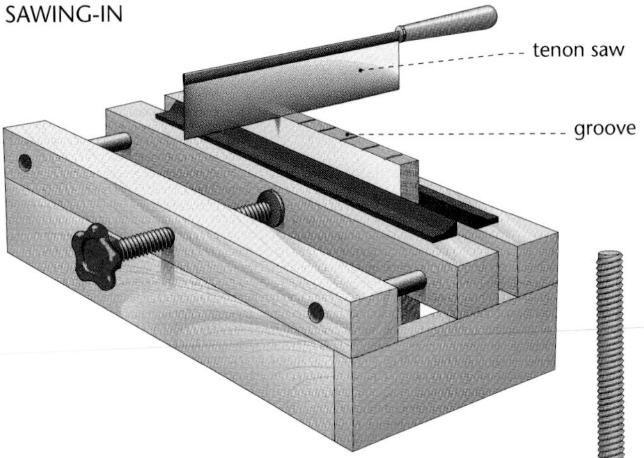

tenon saw

groove

SEWING

sewing frame

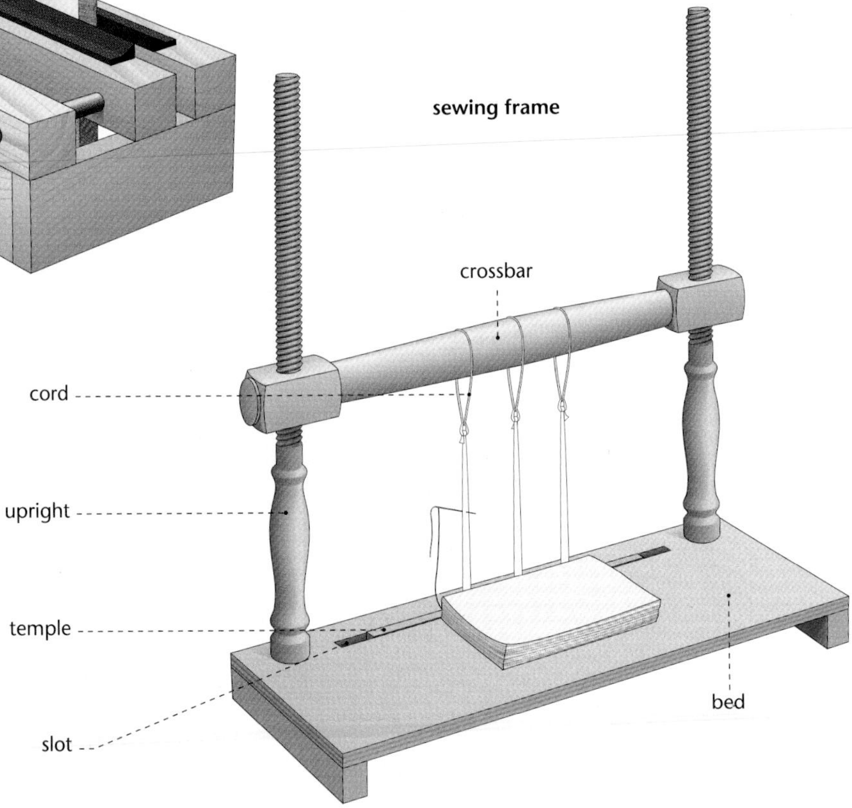

crossbar

cord

upright

temple

bed

slot

BACKING PRESS

backing board

spine of the book

PRESSING

standing press

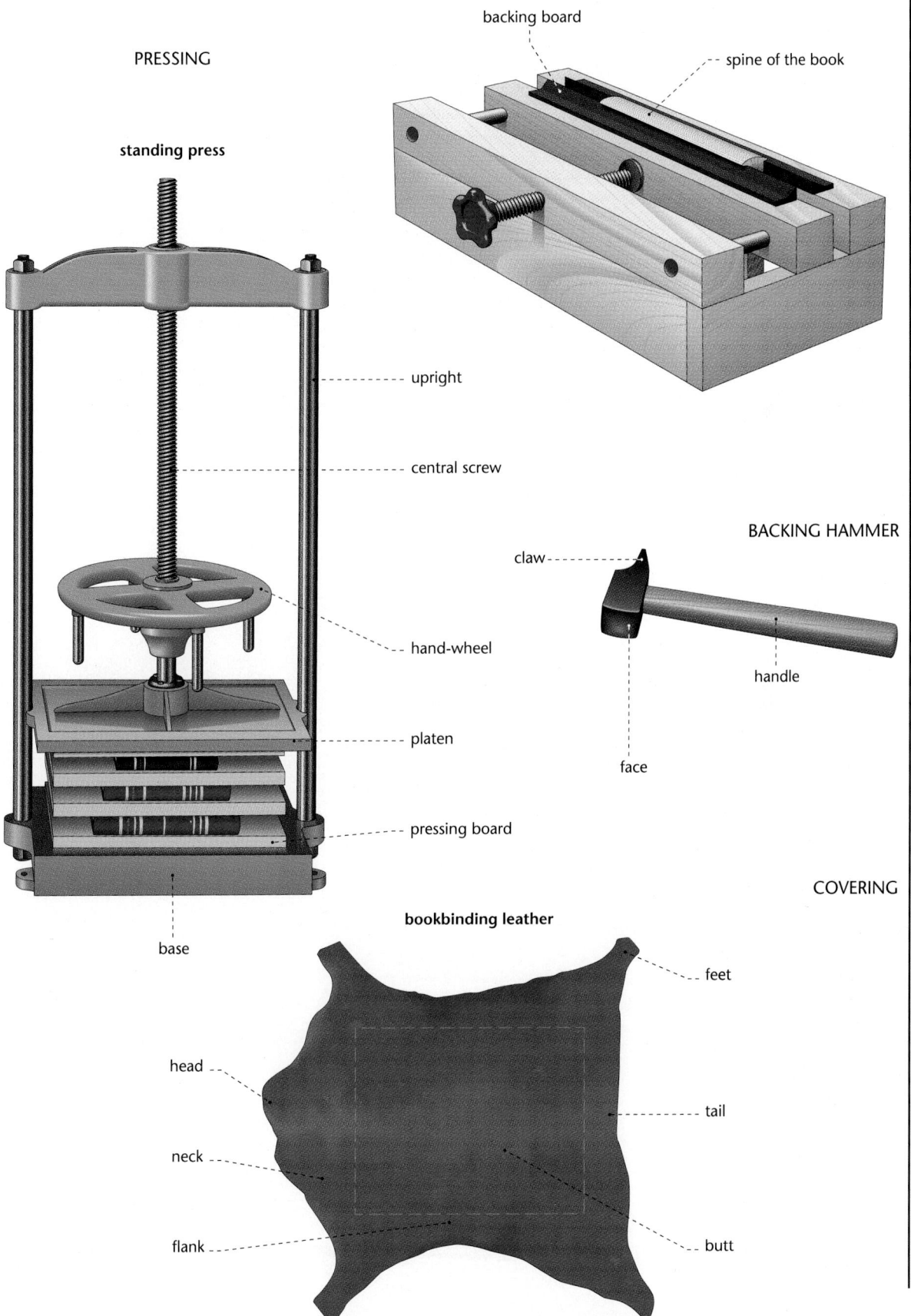

upright

central screw

hand-wheel

platen

pressing board

base

BACKING HAMMER

claw

handle

face

COVERING

bookbinding leather

feet

head

tail

neck

flank

butt

RELIEF PRINTING

paper

printed image

inked surface

raised figure

INTAGLIO PRINTING

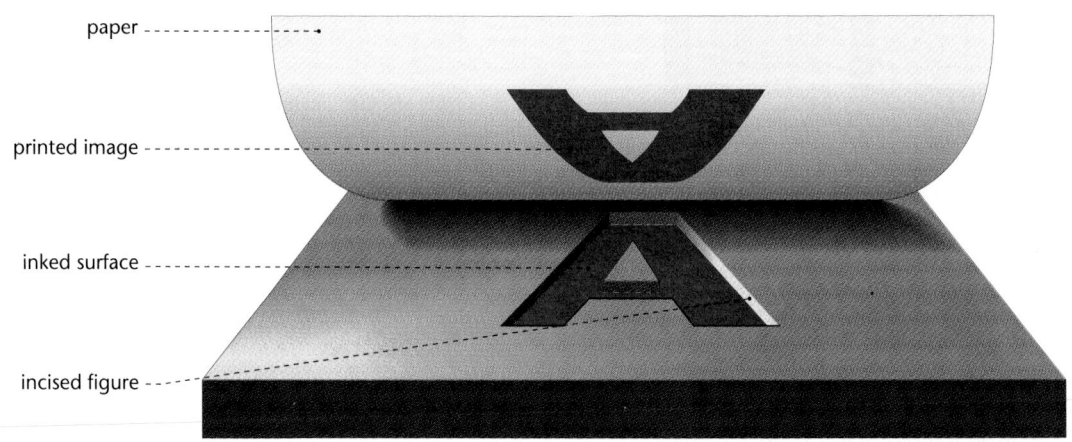

paper

printed image

inked surface

incised figure

LITHOGRAPHIC PRINTING

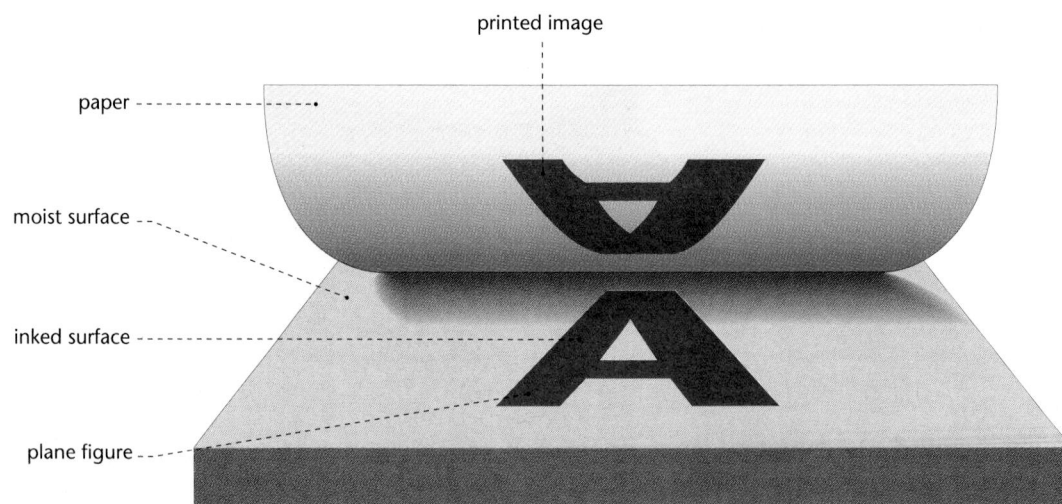

printed image

paper

moist surface

inked surface

plane figure

RELIEF PRINTING PROCESS

EQUIPMENT

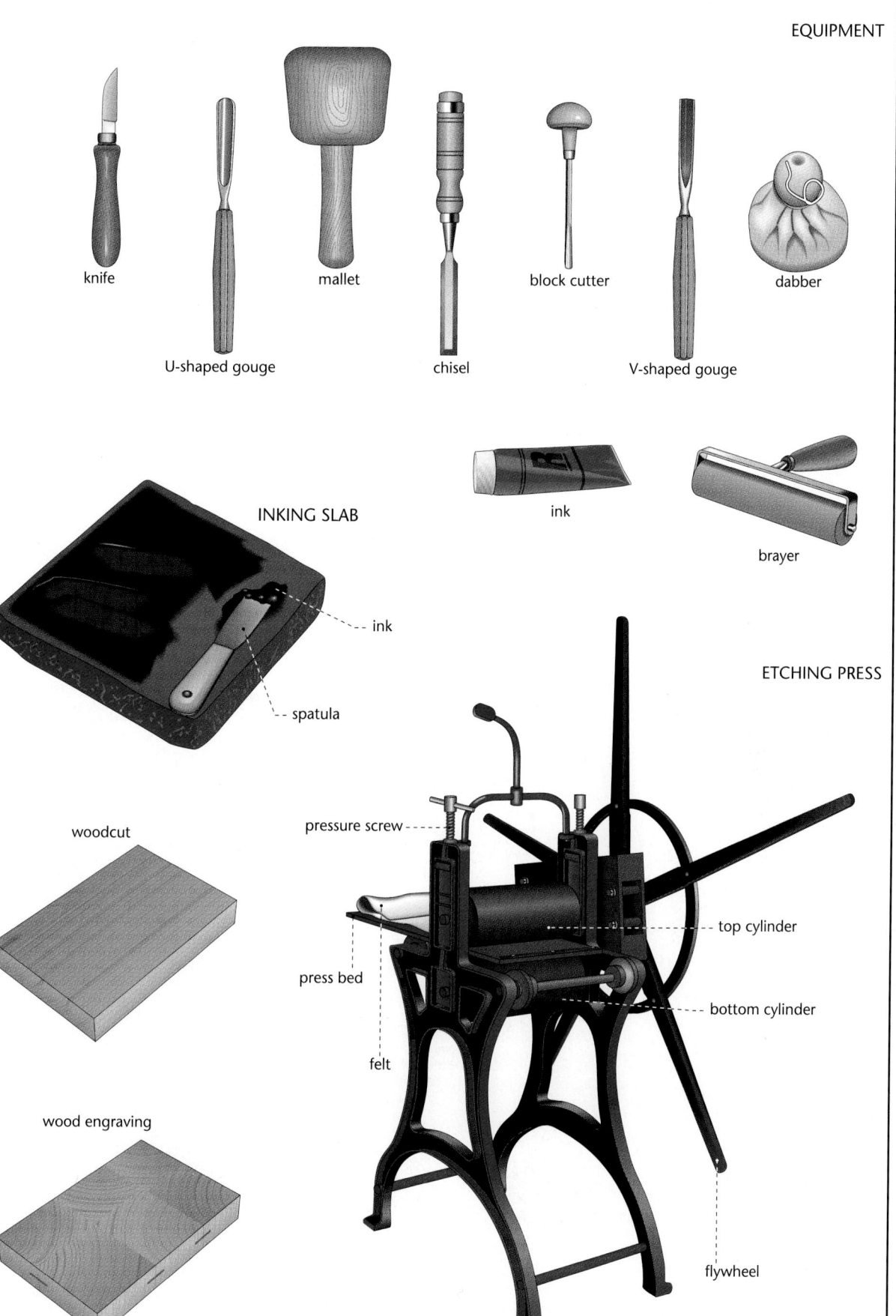

knife

U-shaped gouge

mallet

chisel

block cutter

V-shaped gouge

dabber

INKING SLAB

ink

brayer

ink

spatula

ETCHING PRESS

woodcut

pressure screw

top cylinder

press bed

bottom cylinder

felt

wood engraving

flywheel

581

EQUIPMENT

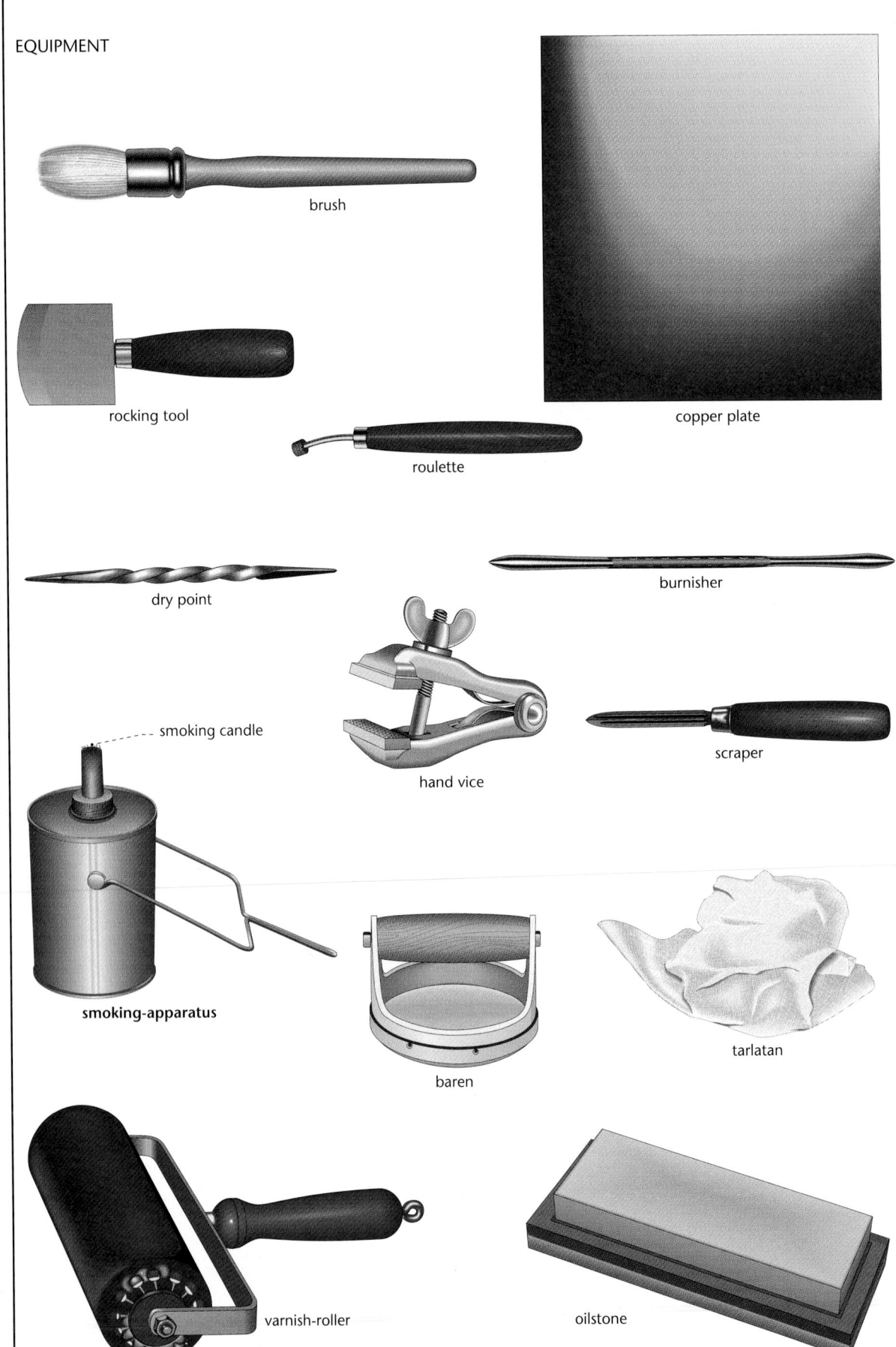

brush

rocking tool

copper plate

roulette

dry point

burnisher

smoking candle

hand vice

scraper

smoking-apparatus

baren

tarlatan

varnish-roller

oilstone

LITHOGRAPHY

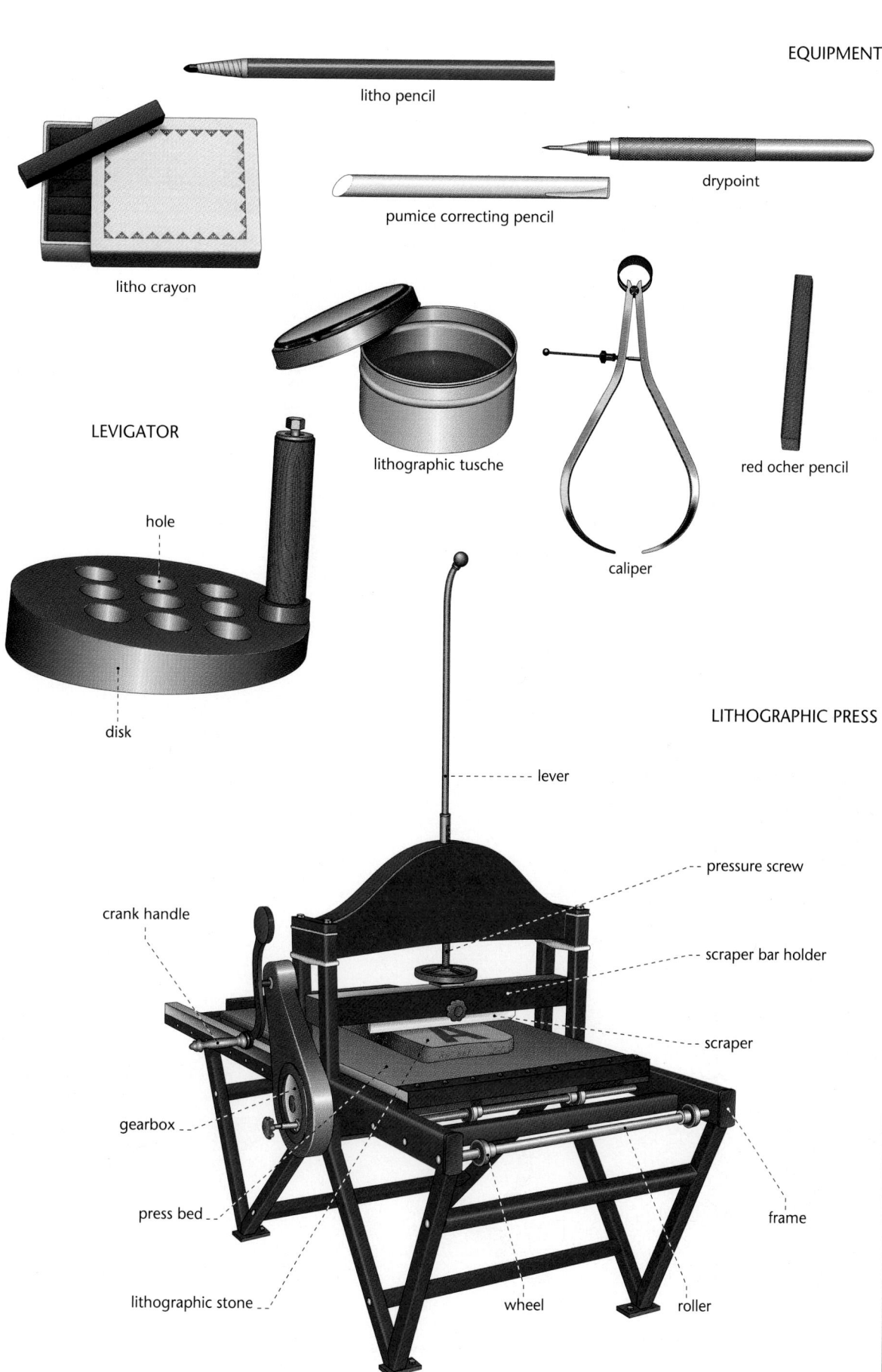

EQUIPMENT

litho pencil

drypoint

pumice correcting pencil

litho crayon

LEVIGATOR

lithographic tusche

red ocher pencil

caliper

hole

disk

LITHOGRAPHIC PRESS

lever

crank handle

pressure screw

scraper bar holder

scraper

gearbox

press bed

frame

lithographic stone

wheel

roller

POTTERY

CREATIVE LEISURE ACTIVITIES

TURNING

turning wheel — ball of clay

plaster bat

wheel head

shaft

seat

flywheel

footrest

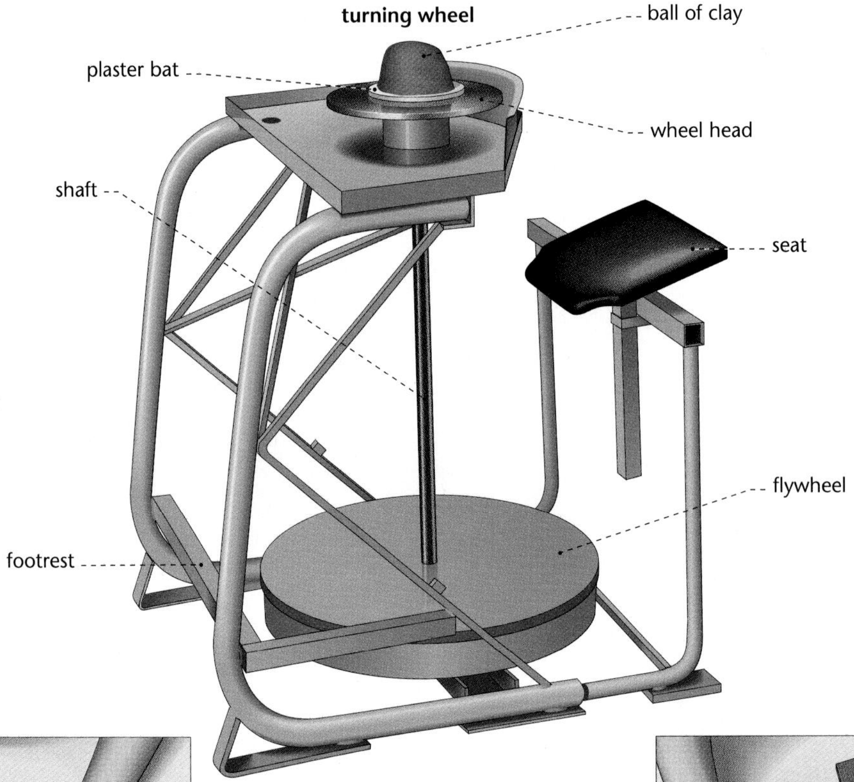

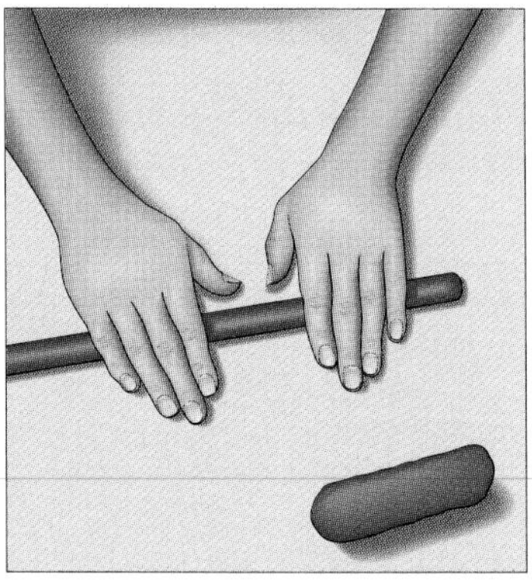

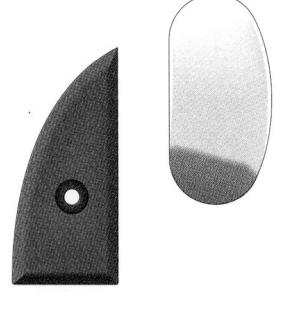

coiling

slab building

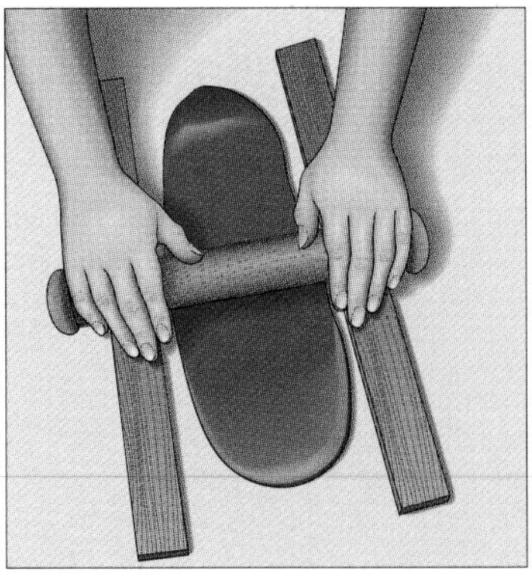

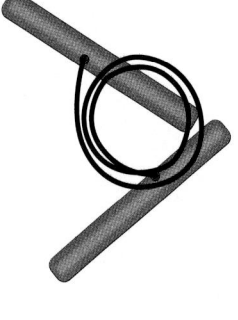

TOOLS

ribs

cutting wire

banding wheel

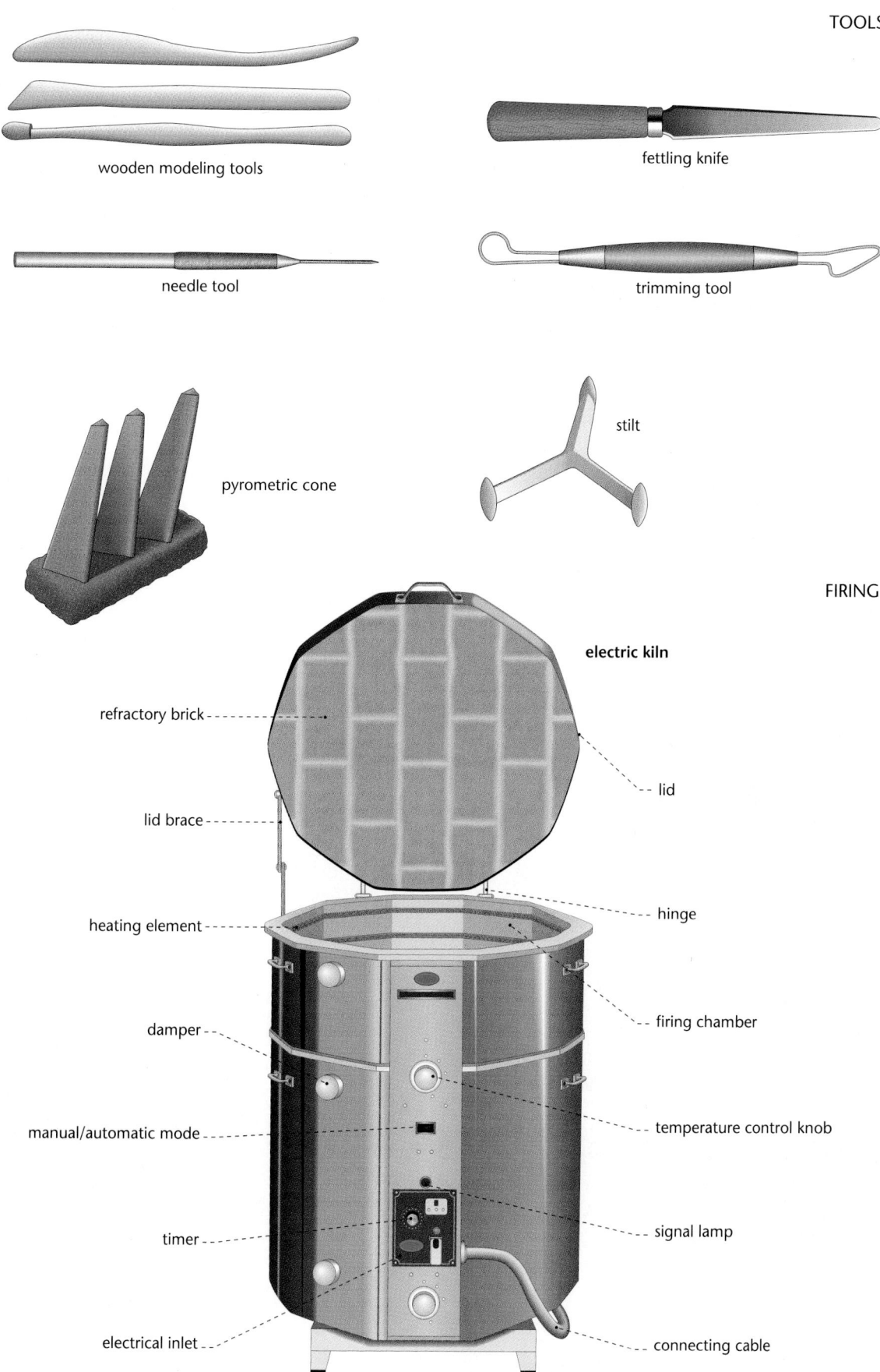

wooden modeling tools

fettling knife

needle tool

trimming tool

pyrometric cone

stilt

electric kiln

refractory brick

lid

lid brace

heating element

hinge

firing chamber

damper

manual/automatic mode

temperature control knob

timer

signal lamp

electrical inlet

connecting cable

STEPS

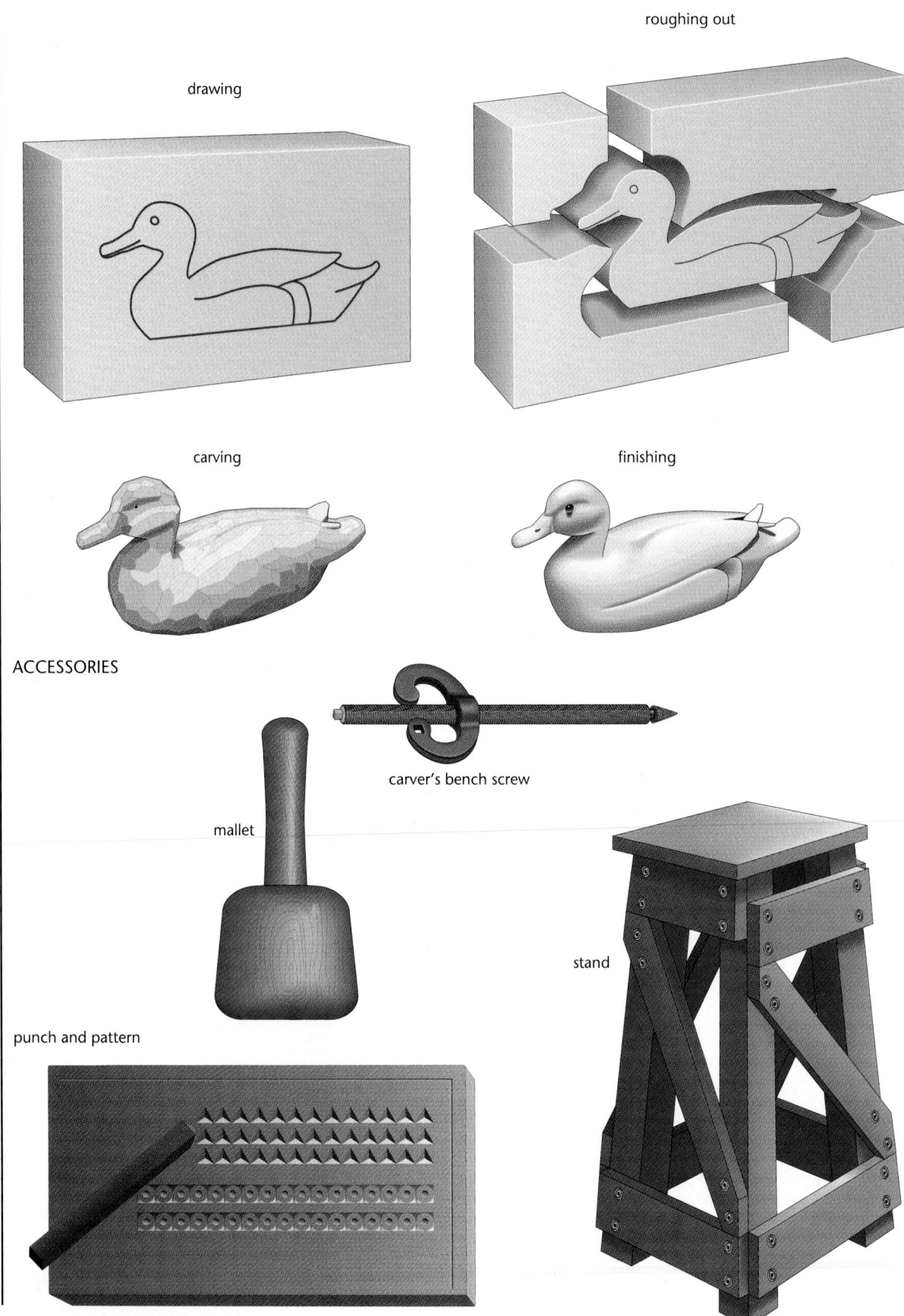

roughing out

drawing

carving

finishing

ACCESSORIES

carver's bench screw

mallet

stand

punch and pattern

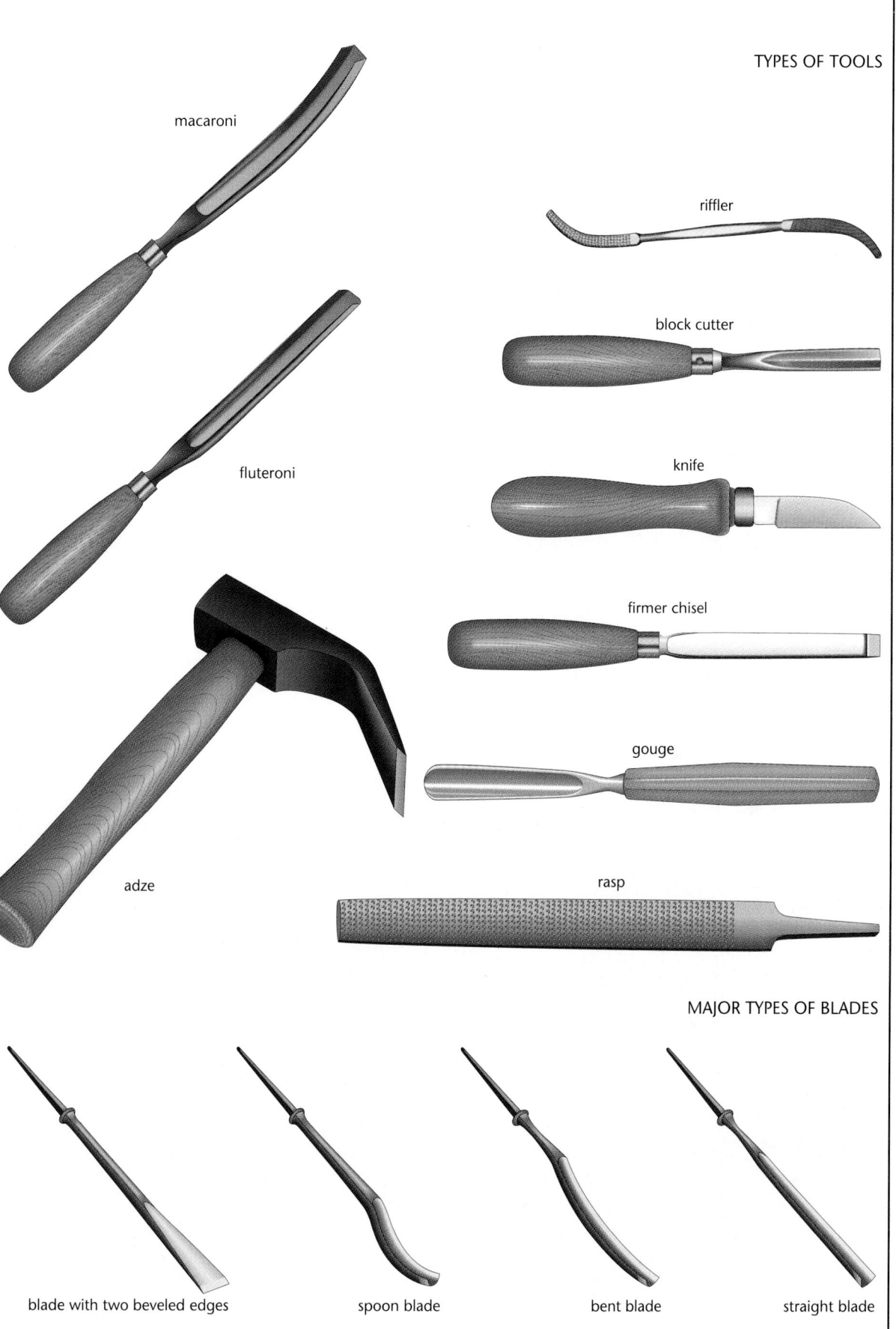

macaroni

riffler

block cutter

fluteroni

knife

firmer chisel

gouge

adze

rasp

MAJOR TYPES OF BLADES

blade with two beveled edges

spoon blade

bent blade

straight blade

MAJOR TECHNIQUES

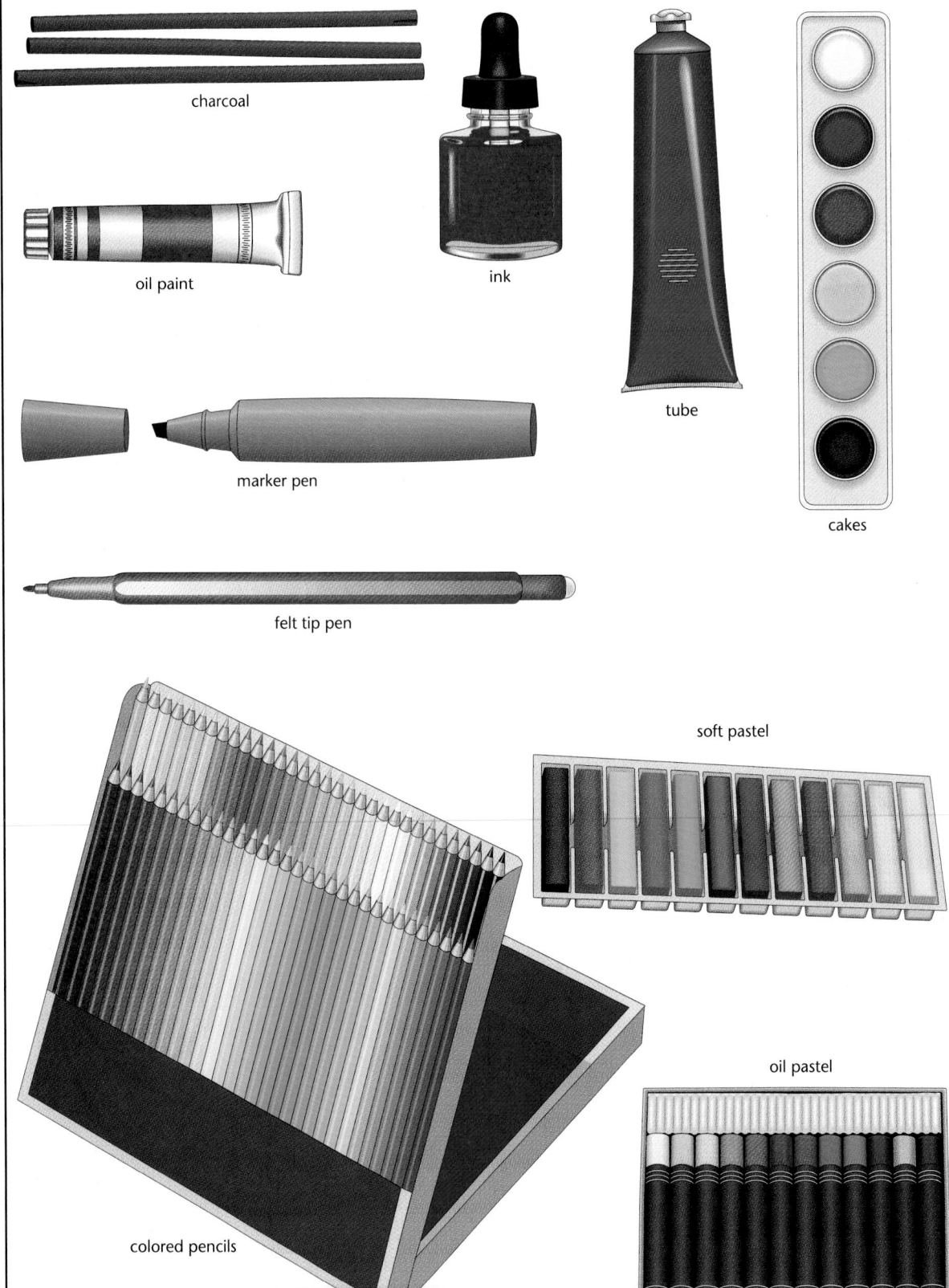

charcoal

oil paint

ink

watercolor and gouache

tube

cakes

marker pen

felt tip pen

soft pastel

oil pastel

colored pencils

EQUIPMENT

reservoir-nib pen
sumie
brush
painting knife
flat brush
fan brush
spatula

SUPPORTS

paper
cardboard
canvas
panel

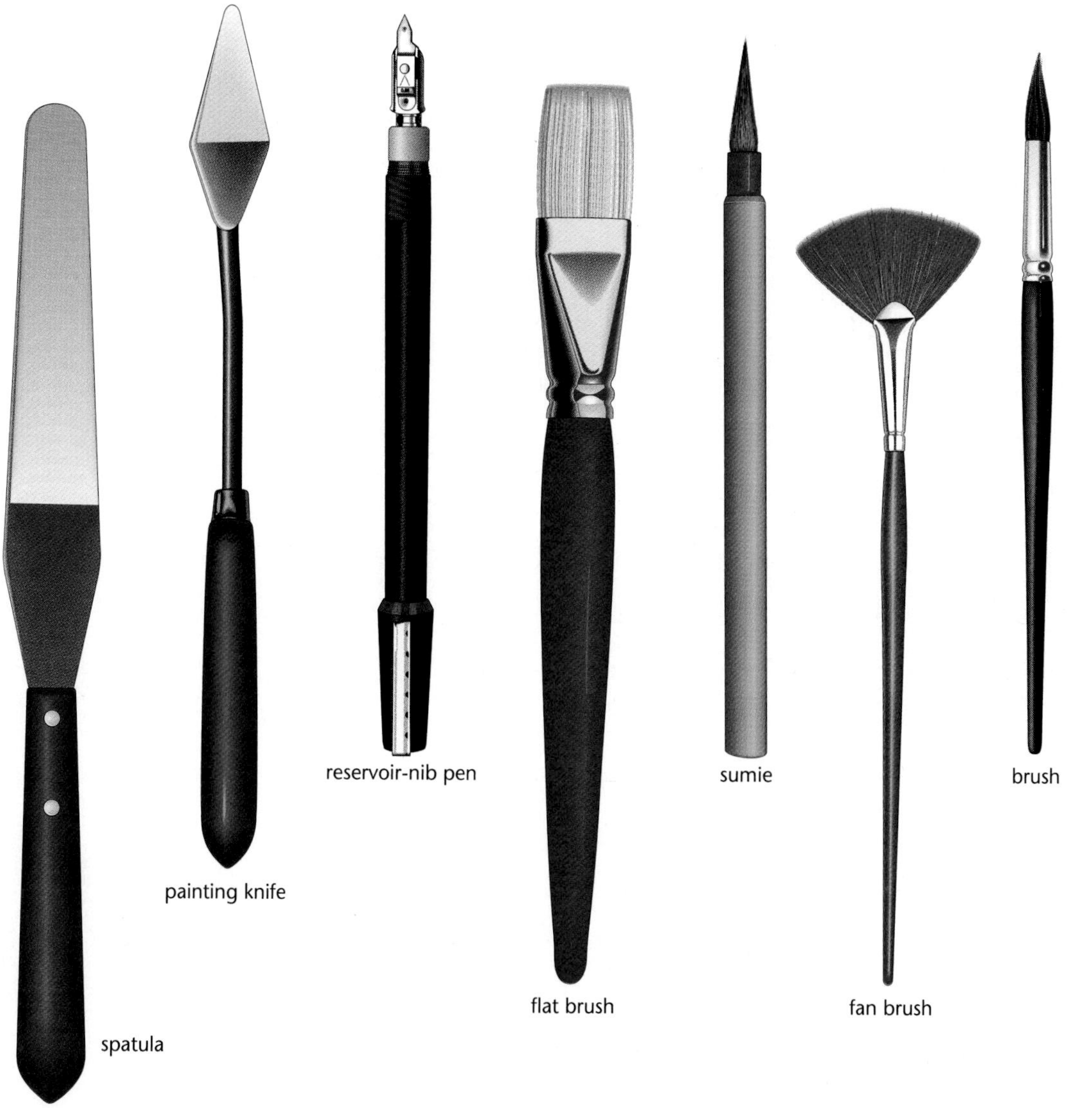

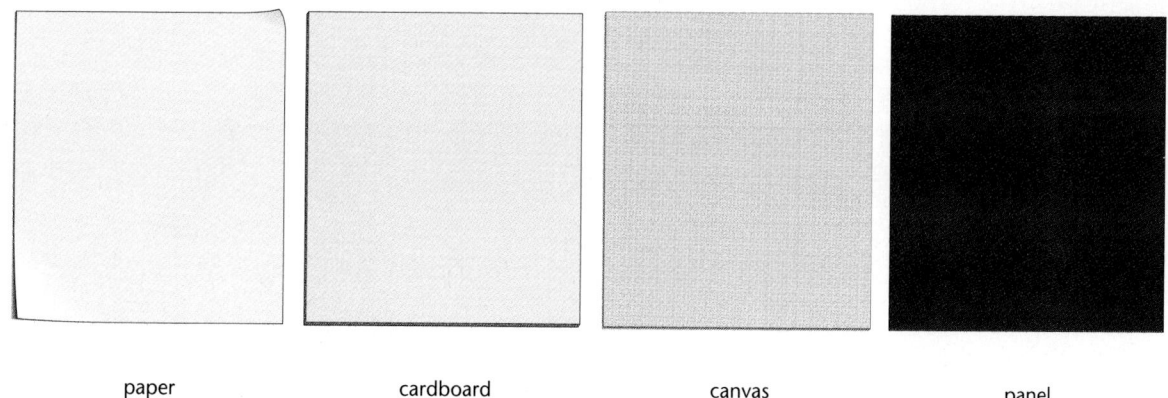

AIRBRUSH

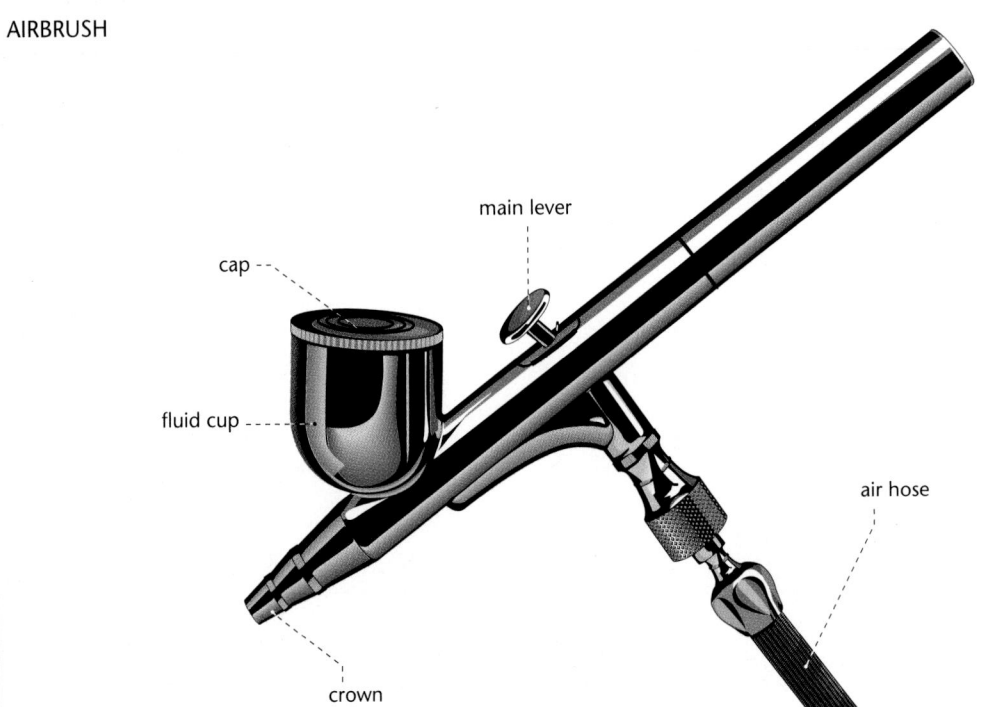

main lever

cap

fluid cup

air hose

crown

CROSS SECTION OF AN AIRBRUSH

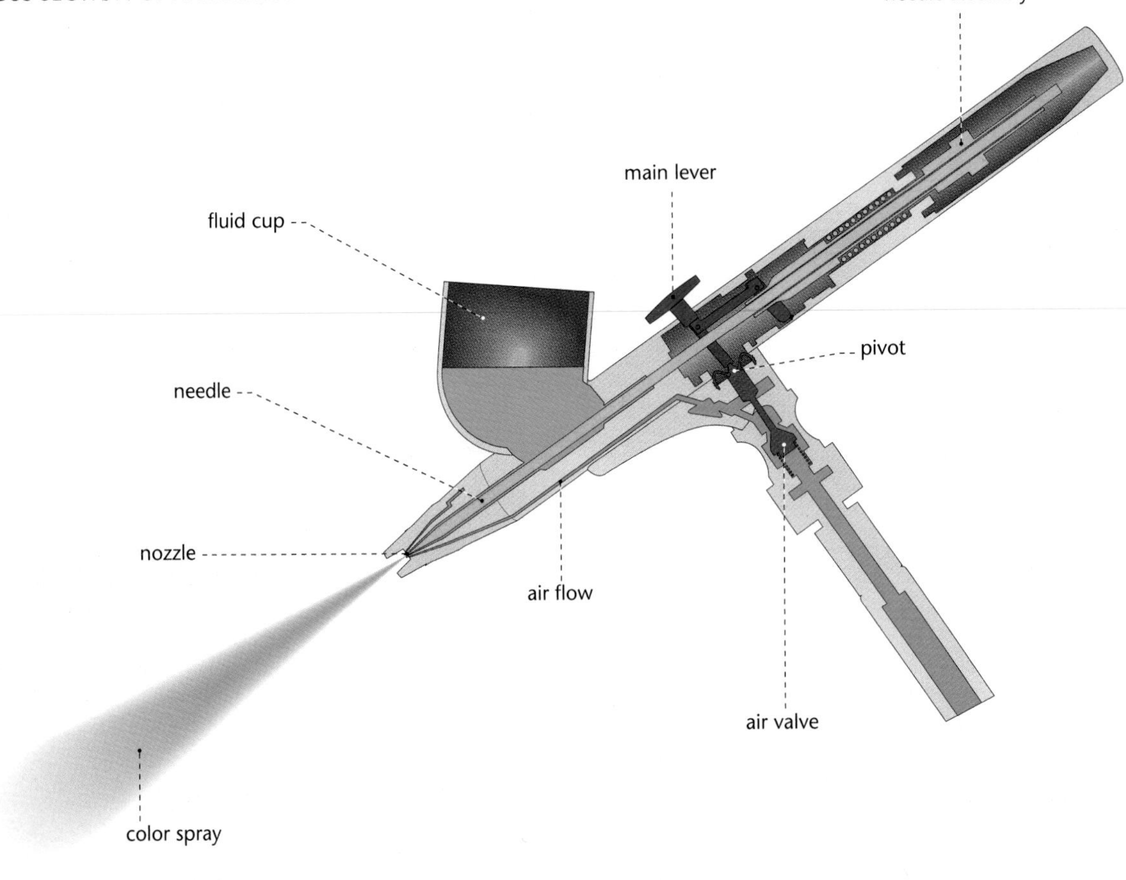

needle assembly

fluid cup

main lever

pivot

needle

nozzle

air flow

air valve

color spray

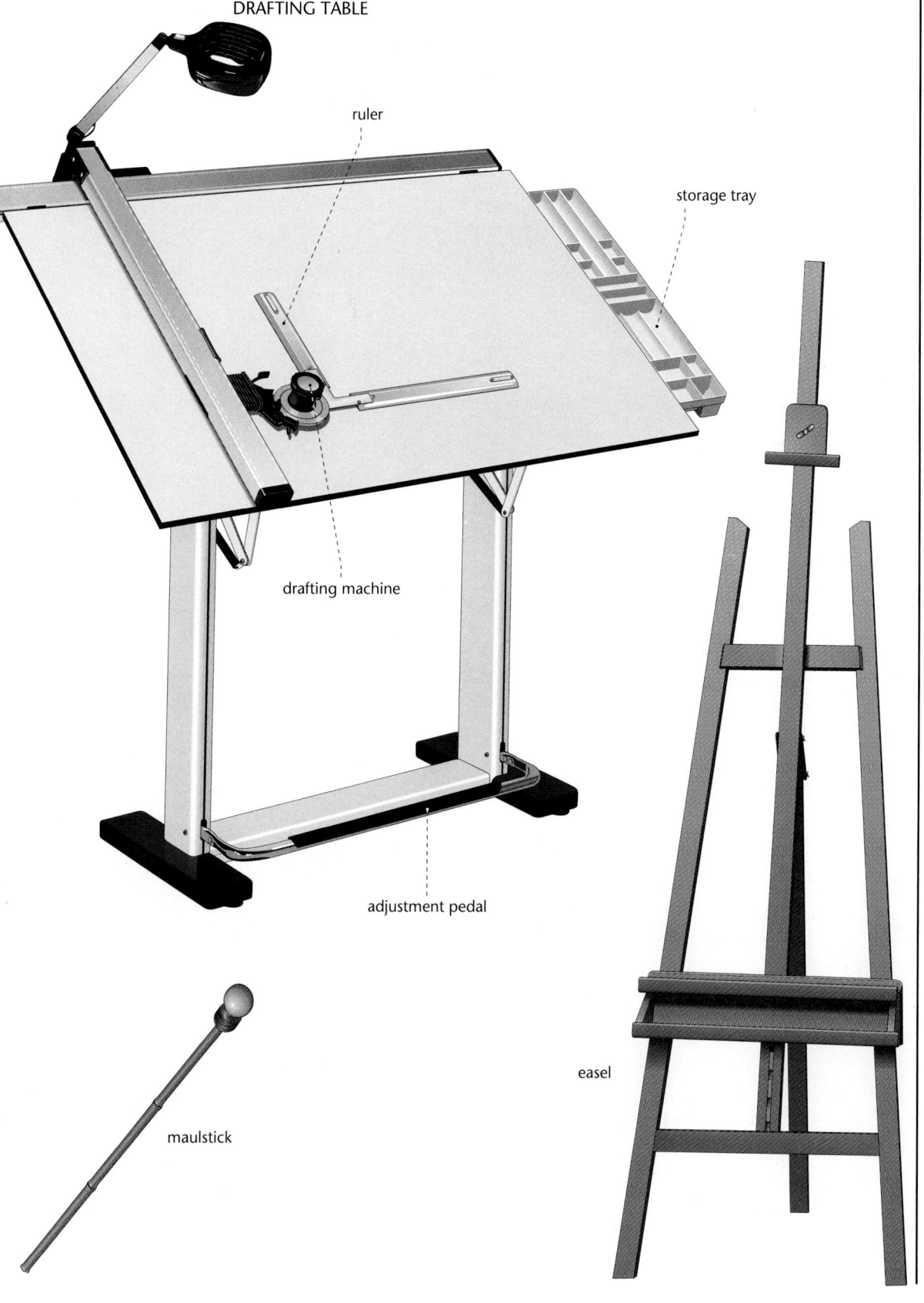

DRAFTING TABLE

ruler

storage tray

drafting machine

adjustment pedal

maulstick

easel

CREATIVE LEISURE ACTIVITIES

ACCESSORIES

color chart

palette with hollows

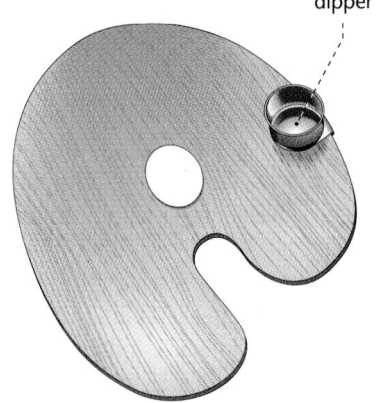

dipper

palette with dipper

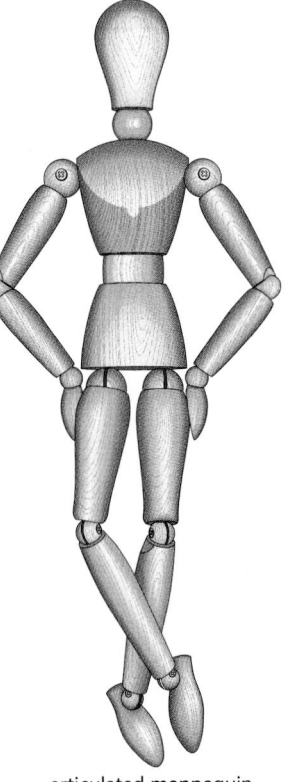

articulated mannequin

UTILITY LIQUIDS

varnish

linseed oil

turpentine

fixative

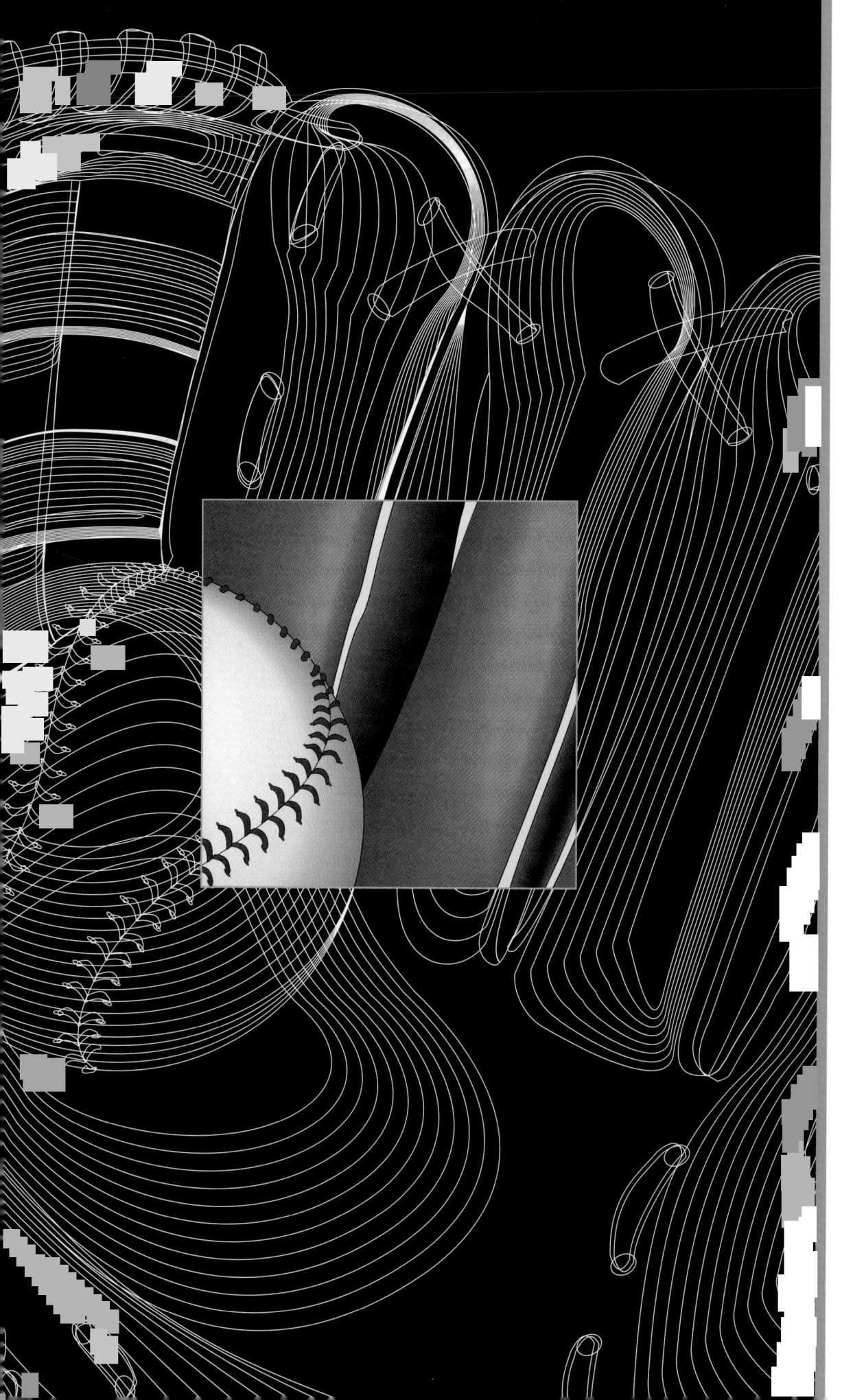

CONTENTS

TEAM GAMES

BASEBALL 595
CRICKET 598
SOCCER 600
FOOTBALL 602
RUGBY 606
FIELD HOCKEY 607
ICE HOCKEY 608
BASKETBALL 610
NETBALL 611
HANDBALL 612
VOLLEYBALL 613
TENNIS 614
SQUASH 616
RACQUETBALL 617
BADMINTON 618
TABLE TENNIS 619
CURLING 620

WATER SPORTS

SWIMMING 621
DIVING 624
WATER POLO 626
SKIN DIVING 627
SAILING 628
SAILBOARD 631
ROWING AND SCULLING 632
WATER SKIING 633

AERIAL SPORTS

MONTGOLFIER 634
FREE FALL 635
PARAGLIDING 636
HANG GLIDING 637
GLIDING 638

WINTER SPORTS

ALPINE SKIING 640
CROSS-COUNTRY SKIING 642
BOBSLED 643
LUGE 643
SKATING 644
ROLLER SKATE 645
SNOWSHOE 645

EQUESTRIAN SPORTS

RIDING 646
TYPES OF BITS 650
HORSE-RACING 651
HARNESS RACING 652

ATHLETICS

TRACK AND FIELD ATHLETICS 654
GYMNASTICS 659
WEIGHTLIFTING 662
FITNESS EQUIPMENT 663

COMBAT SPORTS

FENCING 666
JUDO 668
BOXING 669

LEISURE SPORTS

FISHING 670
BILLIARDS 673
GOLF 676
MOUNTAINEERING 680
BOWLS AND PETANQUE 682
BOWLING 683
ARCHERY 684

CAMPING

CAMPING 685
KNOTS 691
CABLE 692

SPORTS

BATTER

CATCHER

frame

batter's helmet

bat

mask

team shirt

batting glove

throat protector

undershirt

catcher's glove

stirrup sock

shin guard

chest protector

pants

toe guard

knee pad

spiked shoe

BAT

BASEBALL

$2^{13}/_{16} - 2^{29}/_{32}$ in

knob

handle

BASEBALL, CROSS SECTION

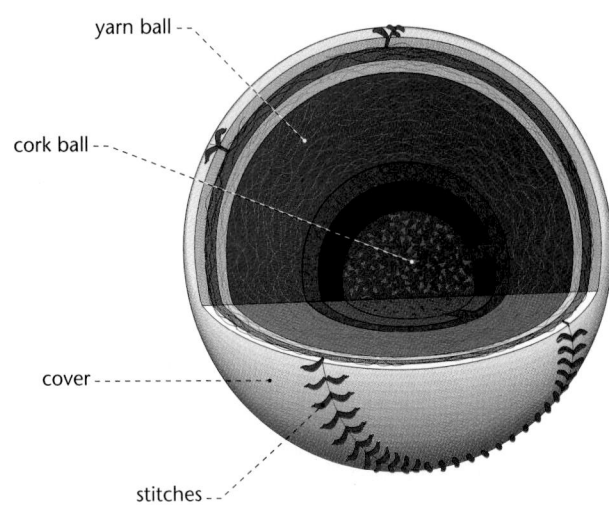

yarn ball

cork ball

cover

stitches

web

FIELDER'S GLOVE

crest

finger

strap

thumb

hitting area

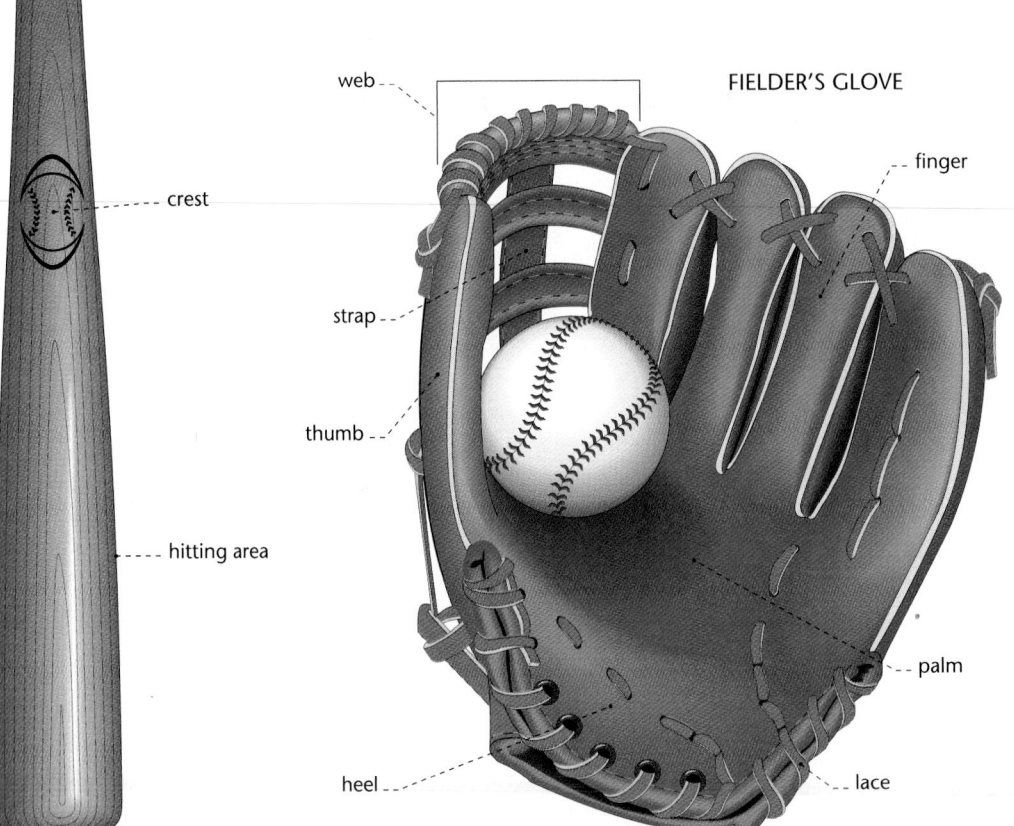

palm

heel

lace

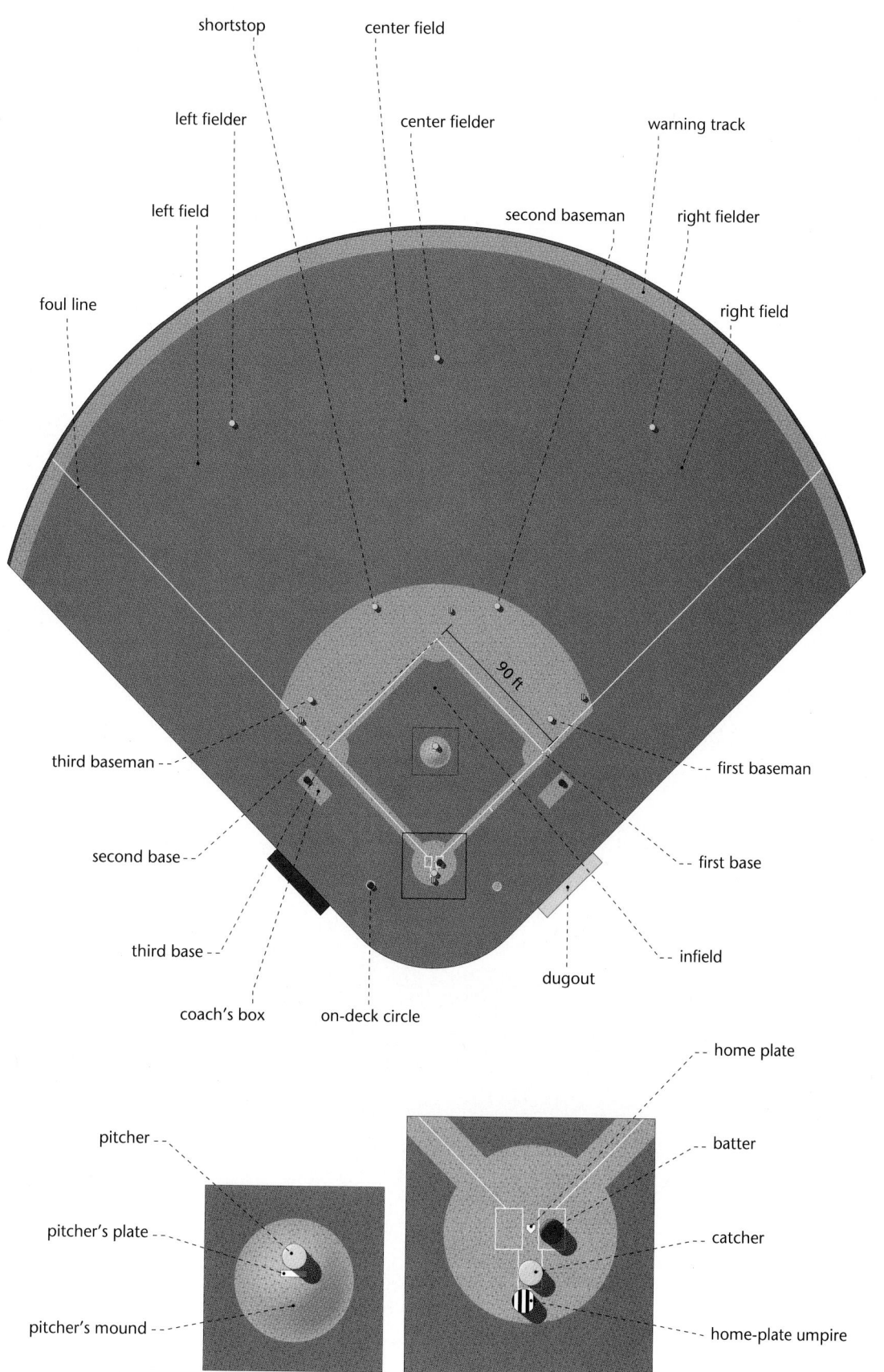

shortstop

center field

left fielder

center fielder

warning track

left field

second baseman

right fielder

right field

foul line

90 ft

third baseman

first baseman

second base

first base

third base

infield

coach's box

dugout

on-deck circle

home plate

pitcher

batter

pitcher's plate

catcher

pitcher's mound

home-plate umpire

CRICKET

CRICKET PLAYER

bat

glove

stump

pad

cricket shoe

studs

BAT

handle

ball

willow

groove

CRICKET BALL

seam

leather skin

2 $^{13}/_{16}$ – 2 $^{7}/_{8}$ in

WICKET

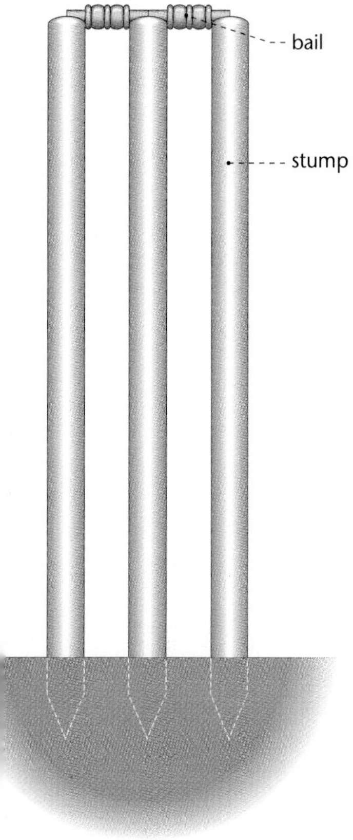

FIELD

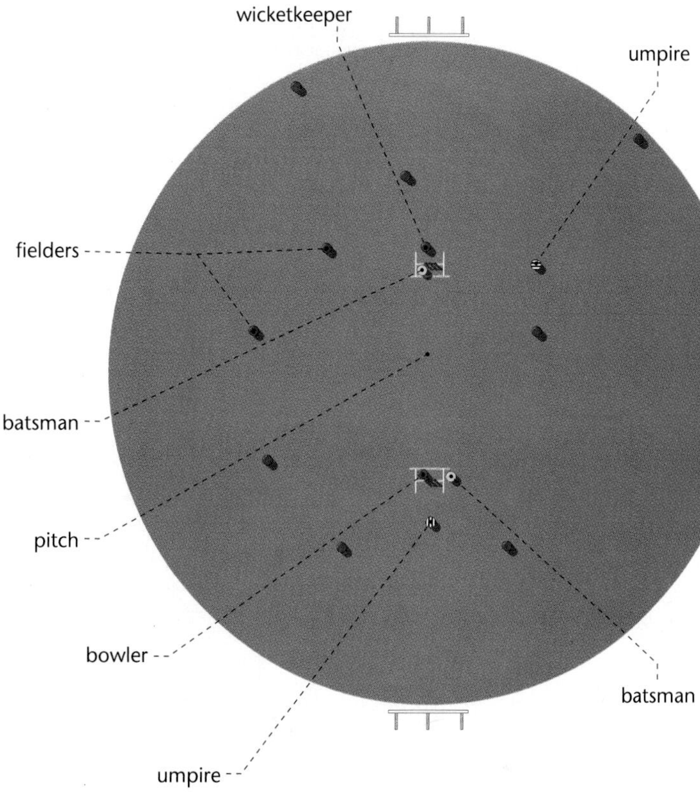

bail

stump

wicketkeeper

umpire

fielders

batsman

pitch

bowler

batsman

umpire

PITCH

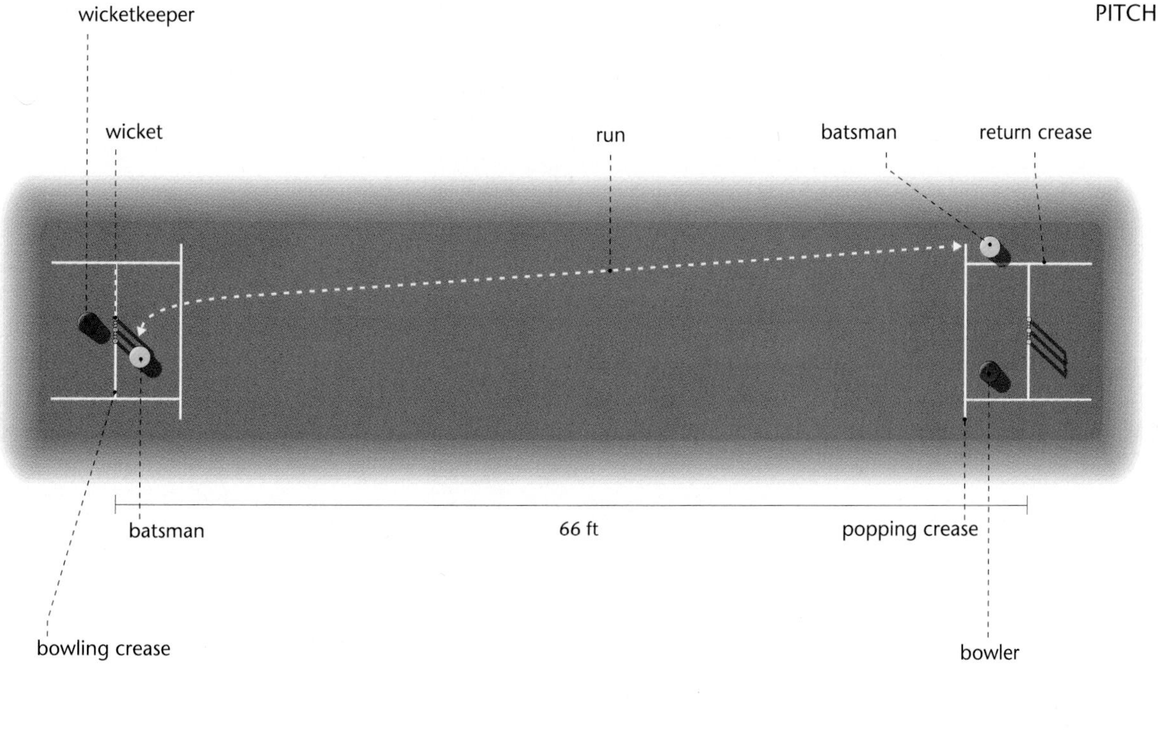

wicketkeeper

wicket

run

batsman

return crease

batsman

66 ft

popping crease

bowling crease

bowler

SOCCER PLAYER

SOCCER BALL

team shirt

8 $\frac{1}{2}$ in

shorts

shin guard

soccer shoe

interchangeable studs

600

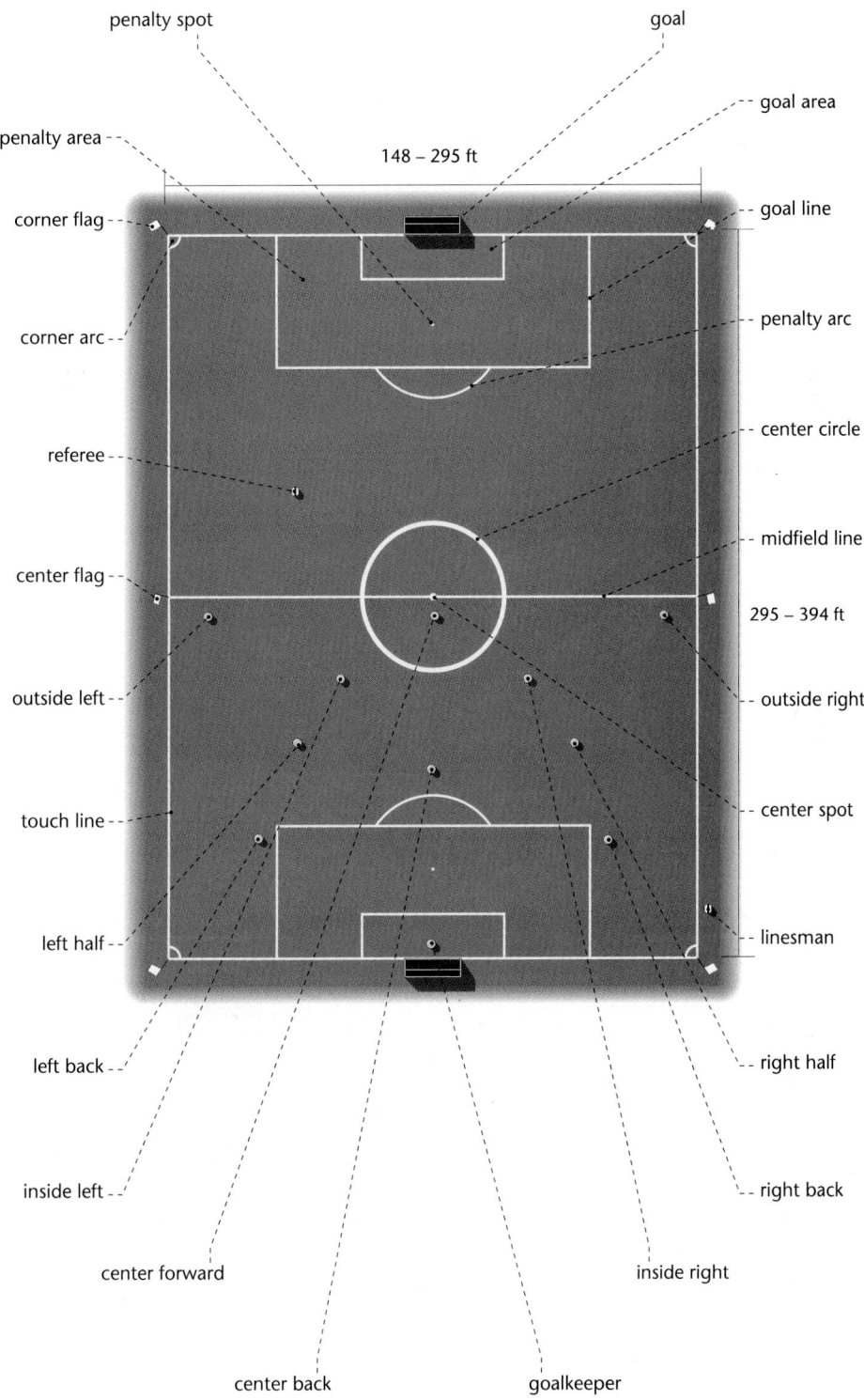

penalty spot

goal

goal area

penalty area

148 – 295 ft

goal line

corner flag

corner arc

penalty arc

referee

center circle

center flag

midfield line

295 – 394 ft

outside left

outside right

touch line

center spot

left half

linesman

left back

right half

inside left

right back

center forward

inside right

center back

goalkeeper

FOOTBALL

FOOTBALL PLAYER

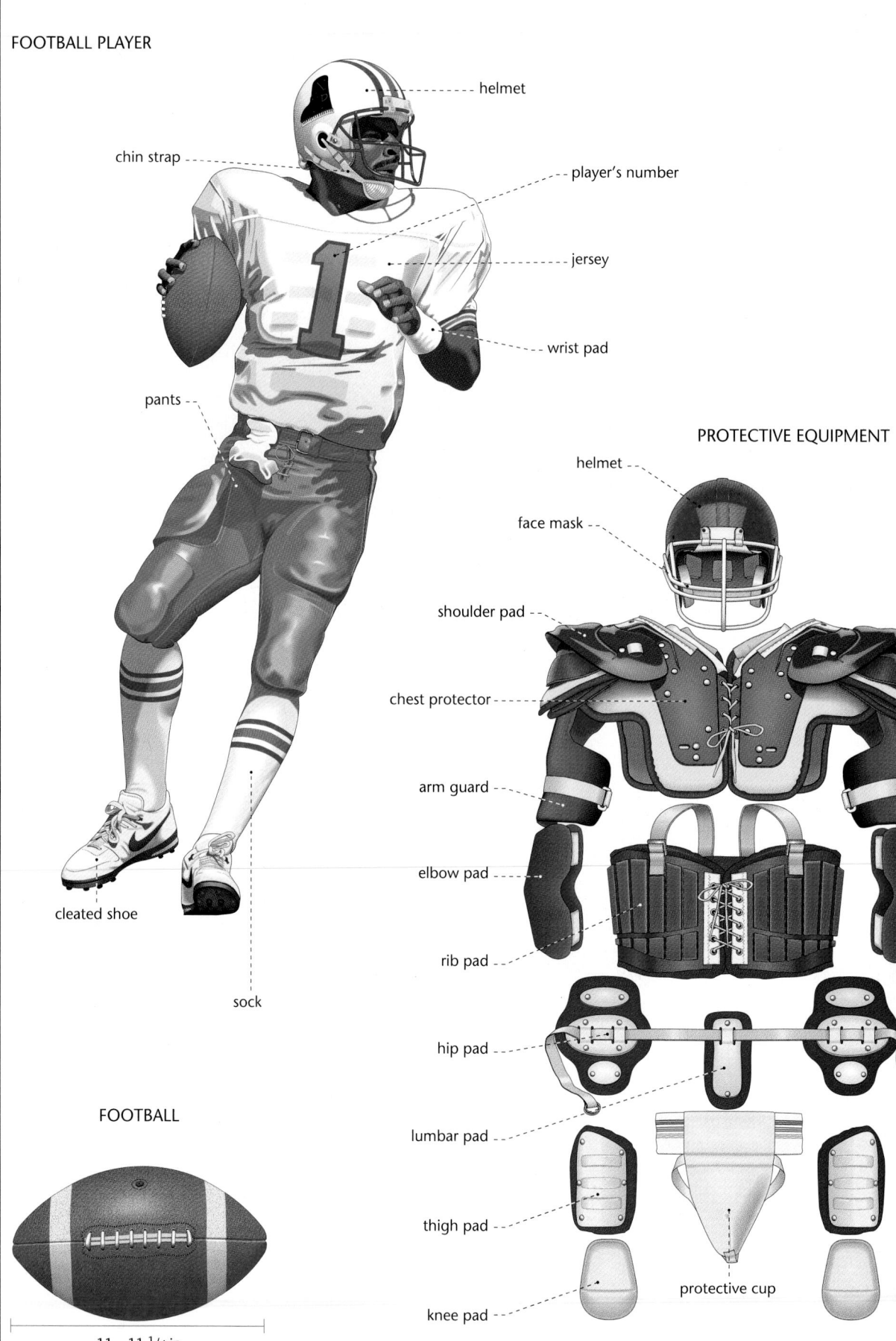

helmet

chin strap

player's number

jersey

wrist pad

pants

PROTECTIVE EQUIPMENT

helmet

face mask

shoulder pad

chest protector

arm guard

elbow pad

rib pad

hip pad

lumbar pad

thigh pad

cleated shoe

sock

FOOTBALL

protective cup

knee pad

11 – 11 ¹/₄ in

TEAM GAMES

602

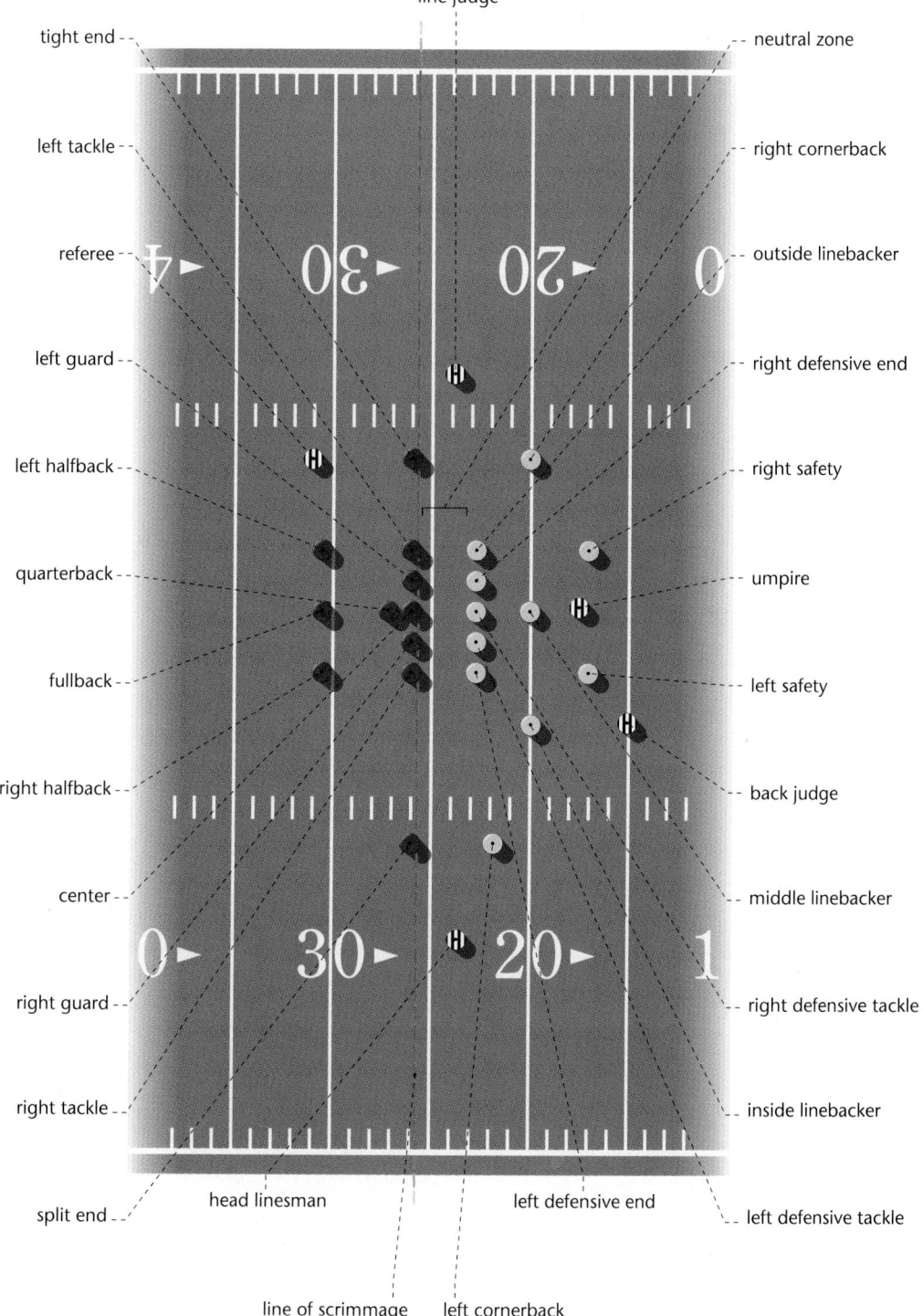

OFFENSE

DEFENSE

line judge

tight end -- -- neutral zone

left tackle -- -- right cornerback

referee -- -- outside linebacker

left guard -- -- right defensive end

left halfback -- -- right safety

quarterback -- -- umpire

fullback -- -- left safety

right halfback -- -- back judge

center -- -- middle linebacker

right guard -- -- right defensive tackle

right tackle -- -- inside linebacker

split end -- -- left defensive tackle

head linesman   left defensive end

line of scrimmage   left cornerback

PLAYING FIELD FOR AMERICAN FOOTBALL

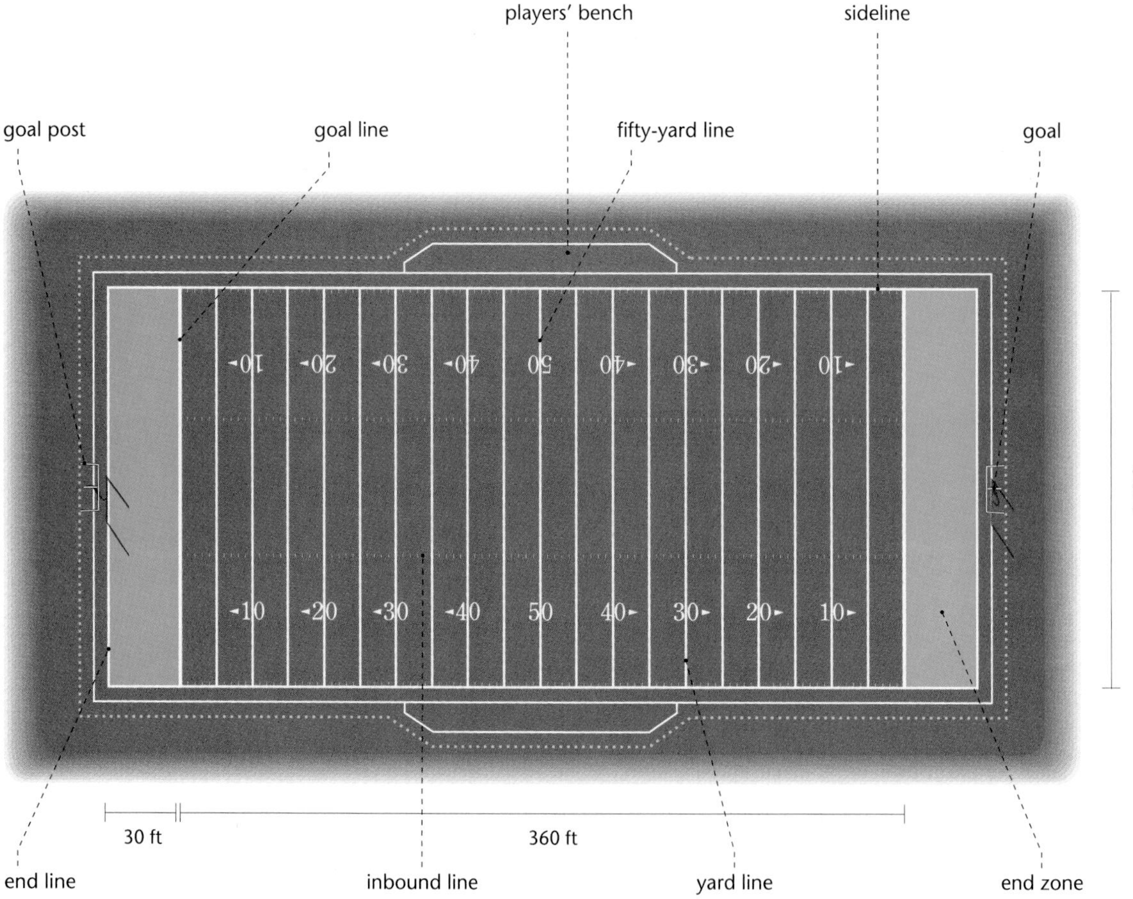

players' bench
sideline
goal post
goal line
fifty-yard line
goal
10
20
30
40
50
40
30
20
10
160 ft
30 ft
360 ft
end line
inbound line
yard line
end zone

PLAYING FIELD FOR CANADIAN FOOTBALL

C
10
20
30
40
50
50
40
30
20
10
197 ft
60 ft
450 ft

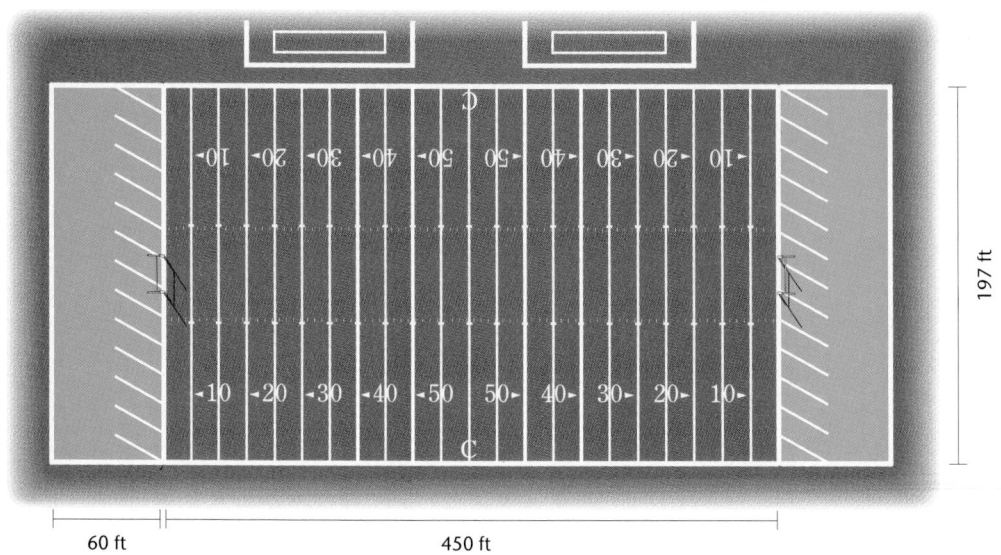

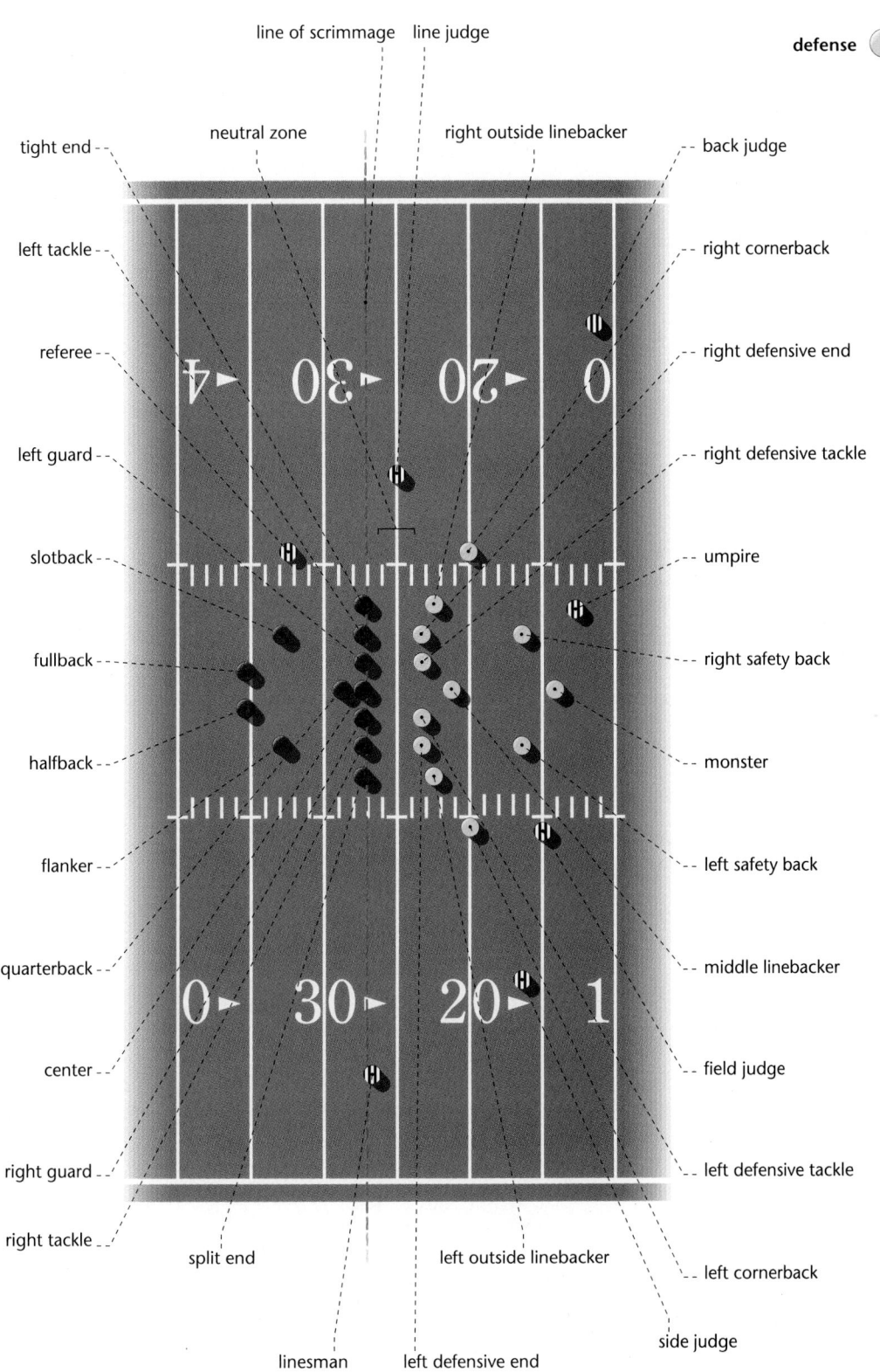

offense

defense

tight end

left tackle

referee

left guard

slotback

fullback

halfback

flanker

quarterback

center

right guard

right tackle

split end

linesman

line of scrimmage   line judge

neutral zone

right outside linebacker

left defensive end

left outside linebacker

back judge

right cornerback

right defensive end

right defensive tackle

umpire

right safety back

monster

left safety back

middle linebacker

field judge

left defensive tackle

left cornerback

side judge

RUGBY

FIELD

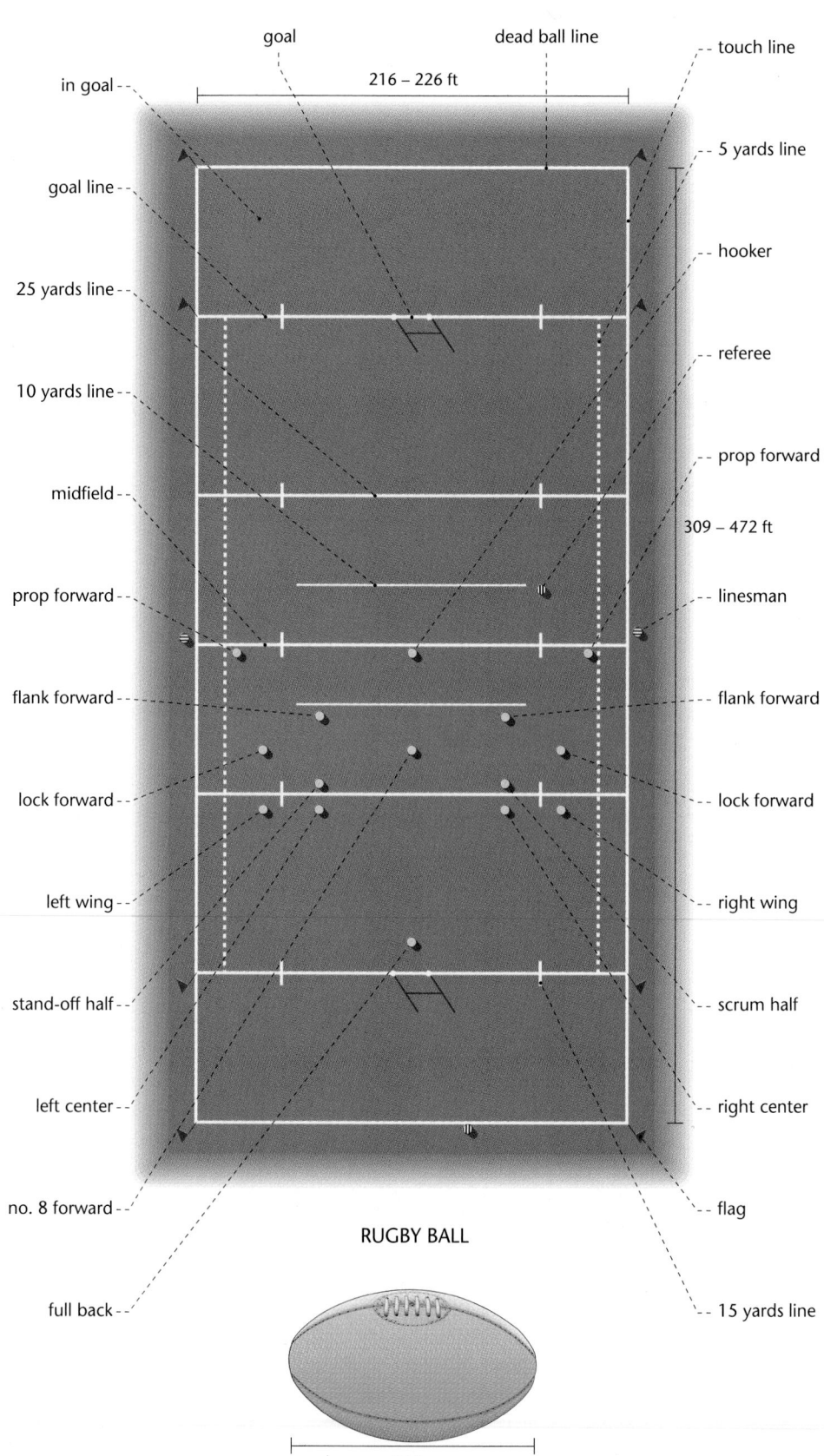

goal   dead ball line   touch line

216 – 226 ft

in goal

5 yards line

goal line

hooker

25 yards line

referee

10 yards line

prop forward

midfield

309 – 472 ft

prop forward

linesman

flank forward

flank forward

lock forward

lock forward

left wing

right wing

stand-off half

scrum half

left center

right center

no. 8 forward

flag

RUGBY BALL

full back

15 yards line

11 in

FIELD HOCKEY

180 ft

goal line

25 yards line

center line

left inner

300 ft

left wing

left half

center half

left back

goalkeeper

corner flag

goal

striking circle

sideline

right wing

right inner

center forward

right half

right back

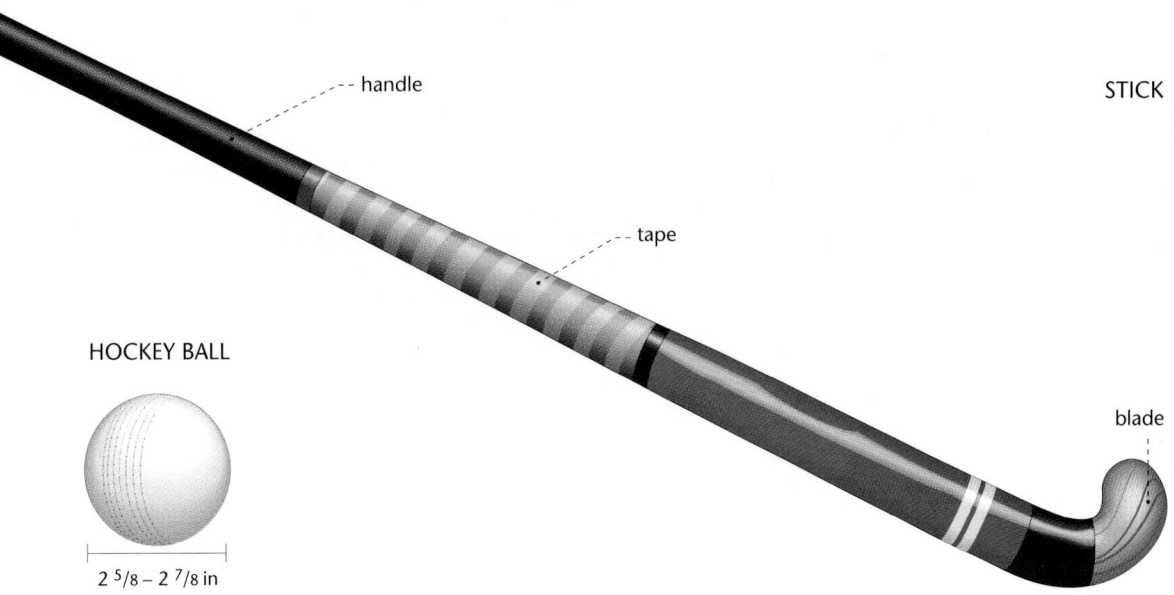

handle

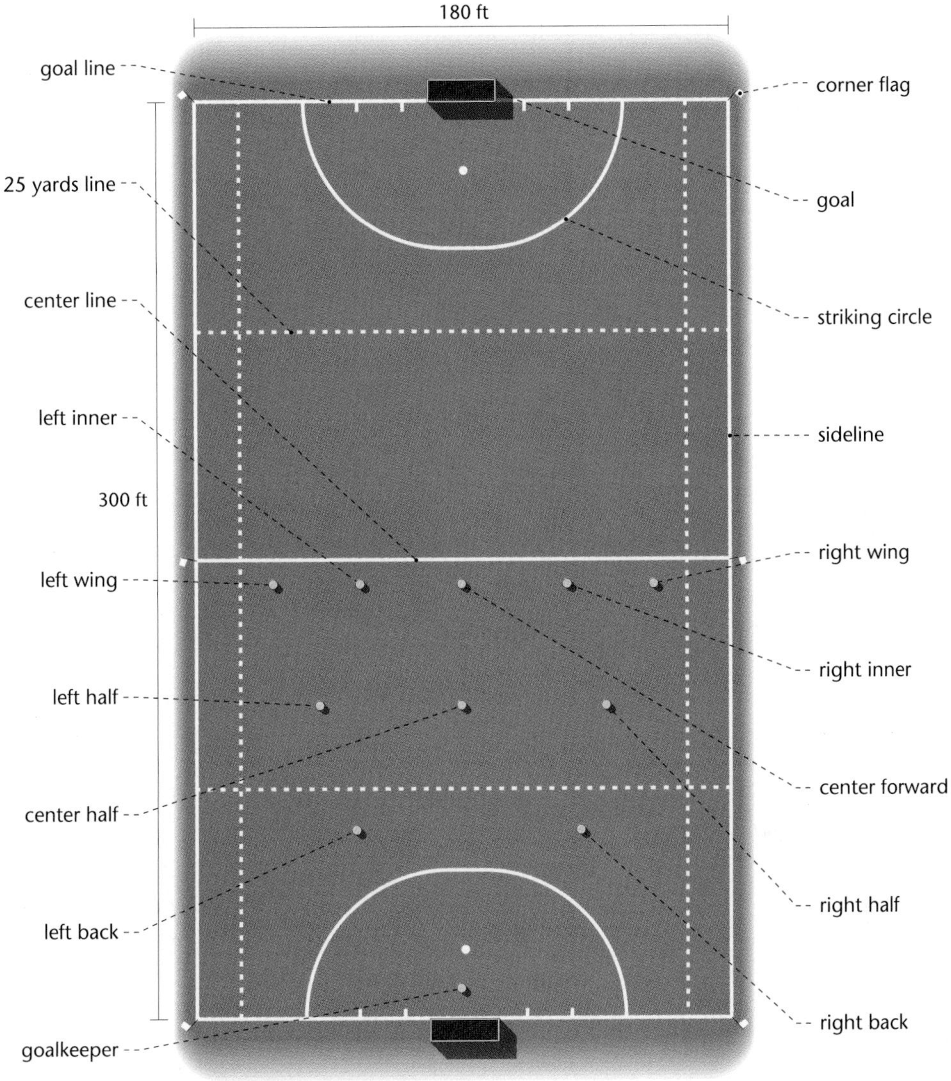

STICK

tape

HOCKEY BALL

blade

2 $\frac{5}{8}$ – 2 $\frac{7}{8}$ in

RINK

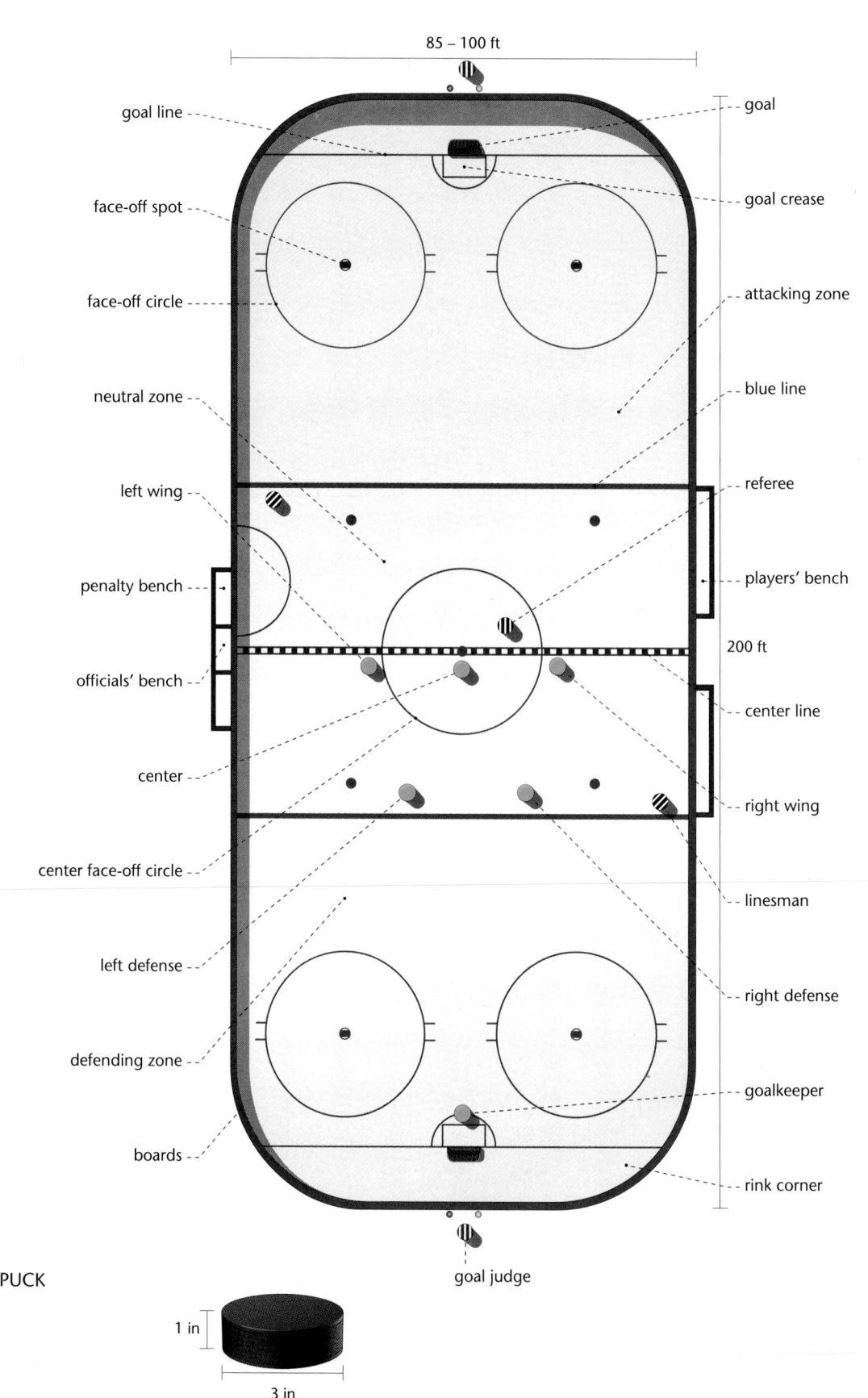

85 – 100 ft

goal line

goal

face-off spot

goal crease

face-off circle

attacking zone

neutral zone

blue line

left wing

referee

penalty bench

players' bench

200 ft

officials' bench

center line

center

right wing

center face-off circle

linesman

left defense

right defense

defending zone

goalkeeper

boards

rink corner

PUCK

goal judge

1 in

3 in

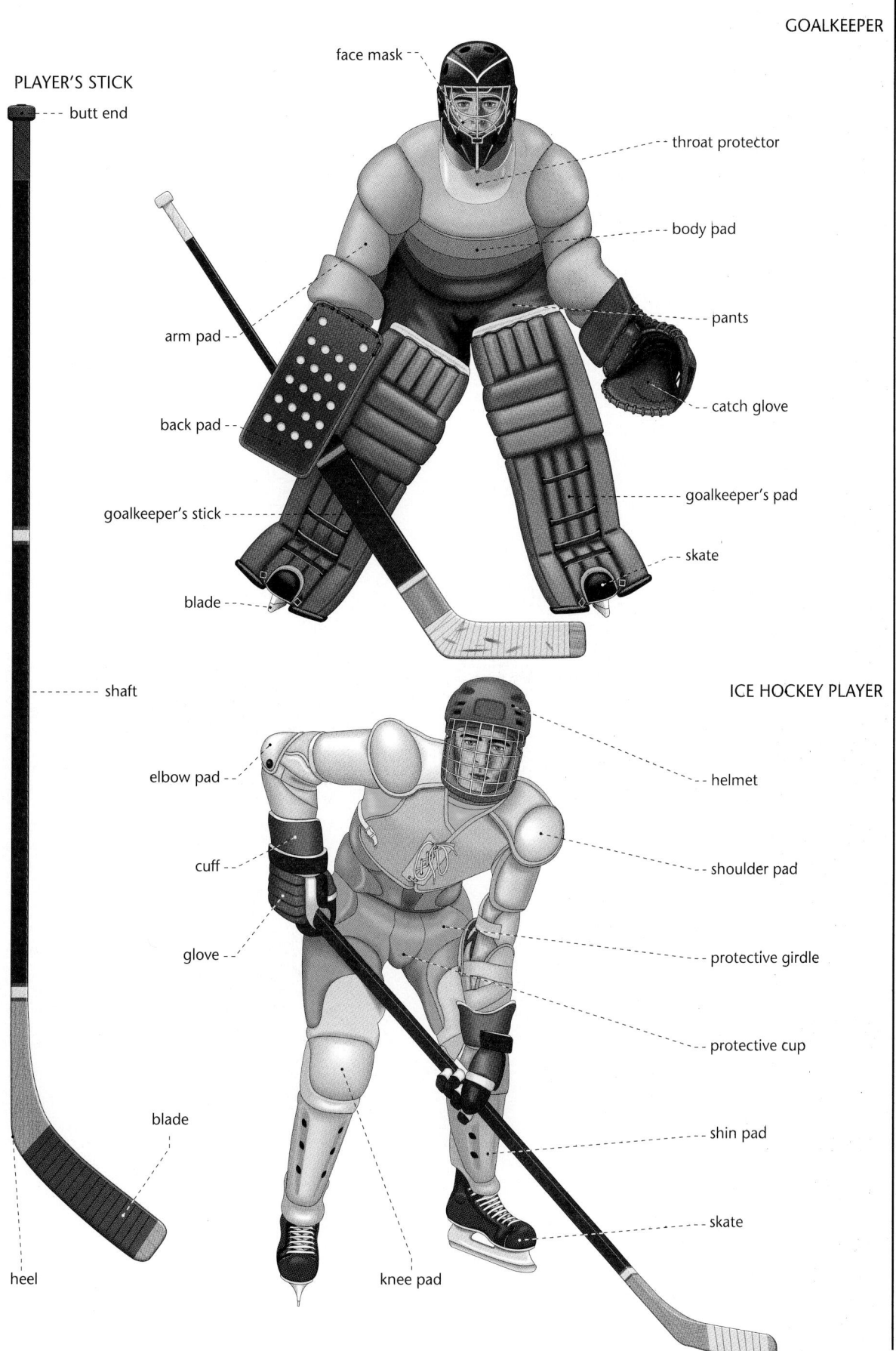

PLAYER'S STICK

butt end

face mask

throat protector

body pad

arm pad

pants

back pad

catch glove

goalkeeper's stick

goalkeeper's pad

blade

skate

shaft

elbow pad

helmet

cuff

shoulder pad

glove

protective girdle

protective cup

shin pad

blade

skate

heel

knee pad

TEAM GAMES

BASKETBALL

COURT

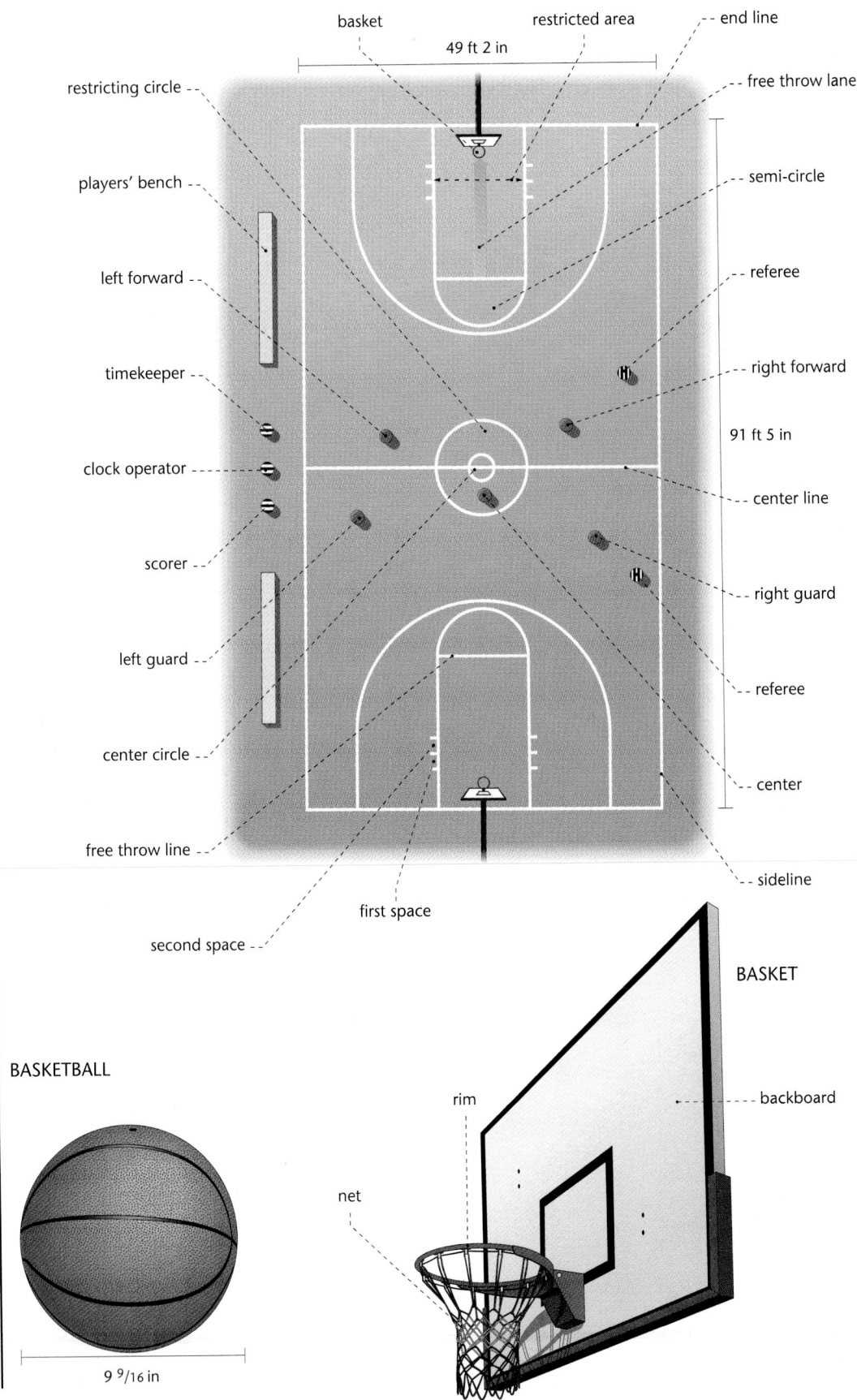

basket

restricted area

end line

49 ft 2 in

restricting circle

free throw lane

players' bench

semi-circle

left forward

referee

timekeeper

right forward

91 ft 5 in

clock operator

center line

scorer

right guard

left guard

referee

center circle

center

free throw line

sideline

first space

second space

BASKET

BASKETBALL

rim

backboard

net

9 9/16 in

NETBALL

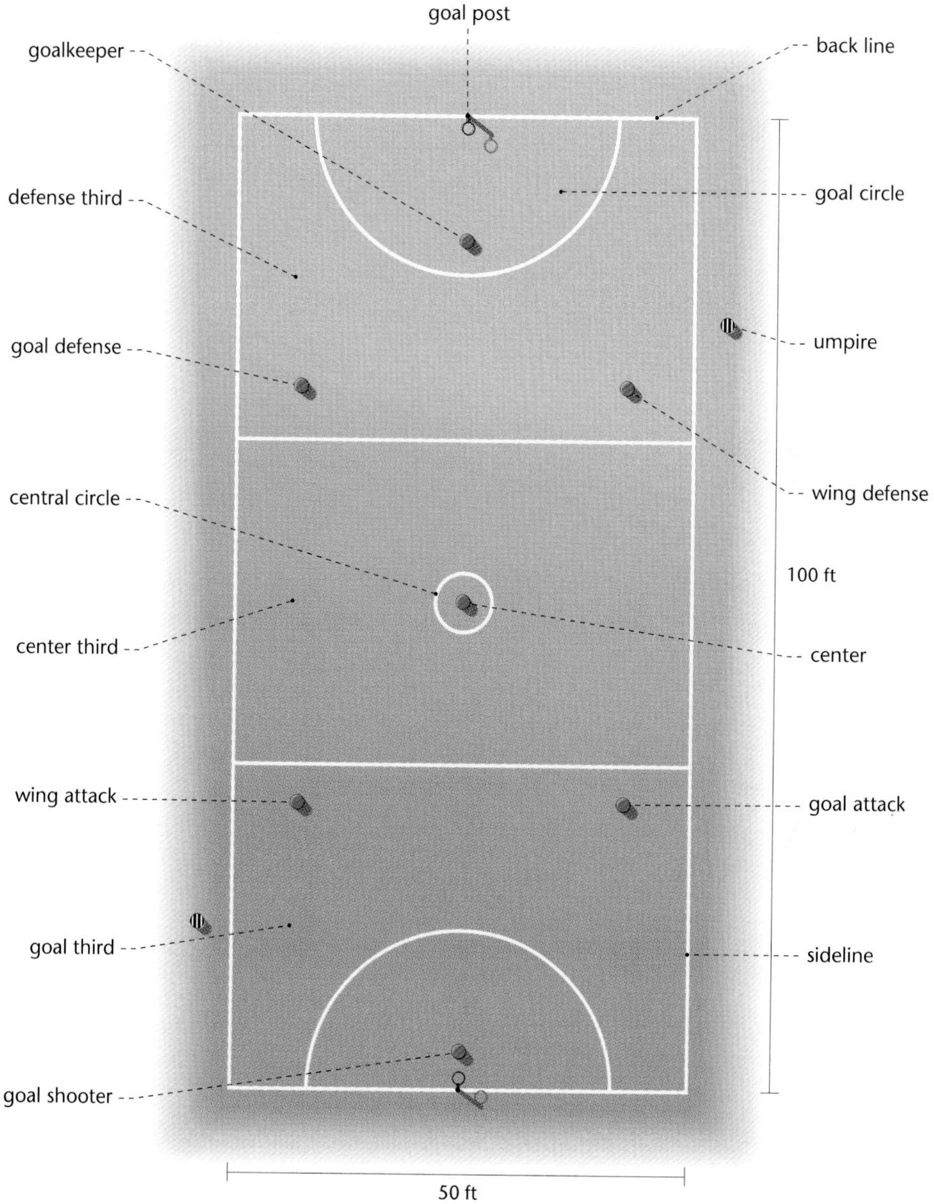

goal post

goalkeeper

back line

defense third

goal circle

goal defense

umpire

central circle

wing defense

center third

100 ft

center

wing attack

goal attack

goal third

sideline

goal shooter

50 ft

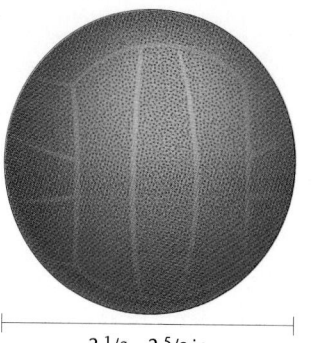

2 1/2 – 2 5/8 in

HANDBALL

COURT

goalkeeper

penalty line

65.6 ft

guide mark

center back

right back

left back

goal line referee

substitute corridor

right winger

secretary

131 ft

timekeeper

center line

players' bench

court referee

left winger

free throw line

center forward

goal area line

sideline

goal line

goal

net

goal area

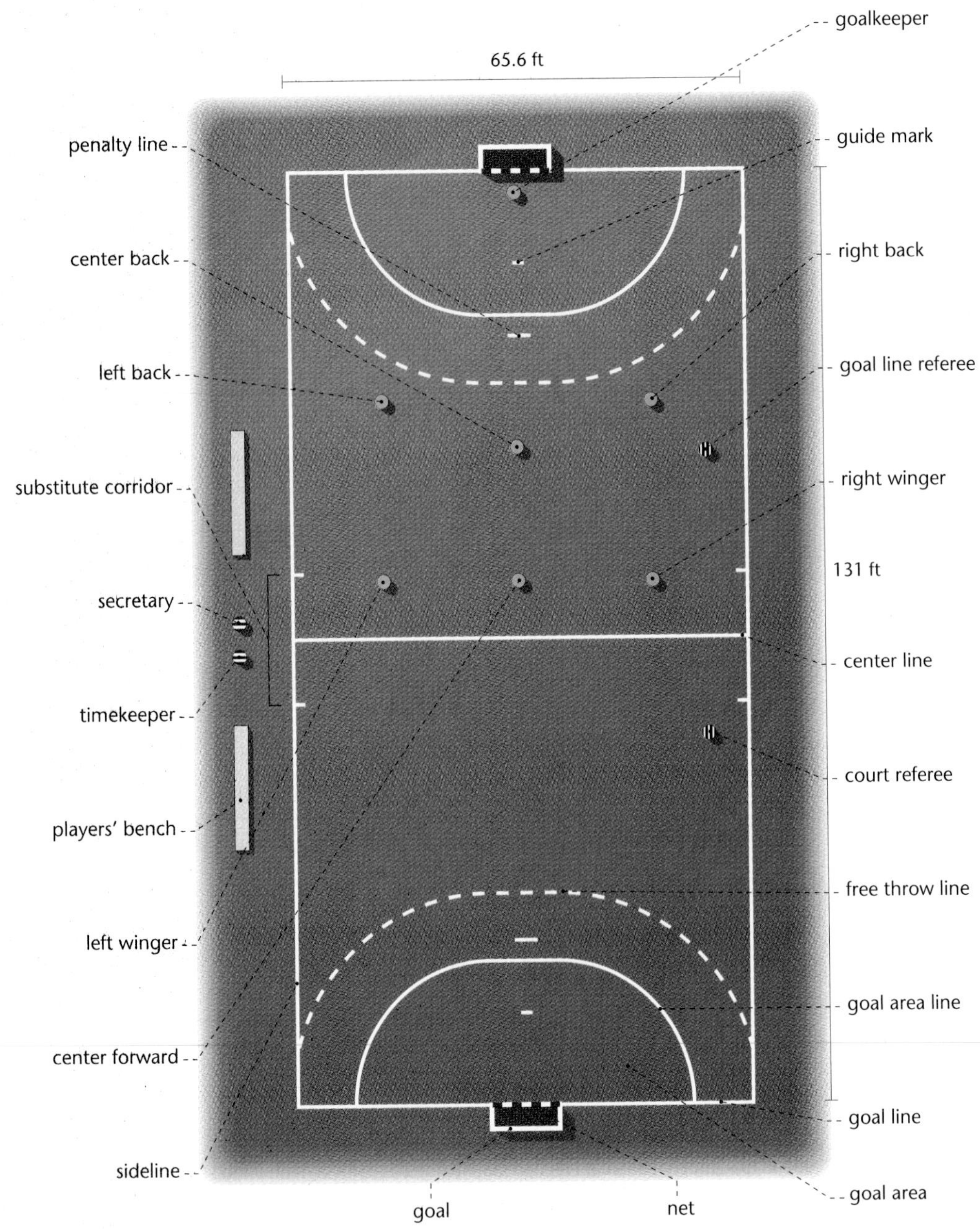

HANDBALL

♀

6 $\frac{11}{16}$ – 7 in

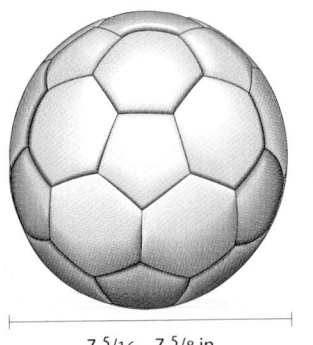

♂

7 $\frac{5}{16}$ – 7 $\frac{5}{8}$ in

VOLLEYBALL

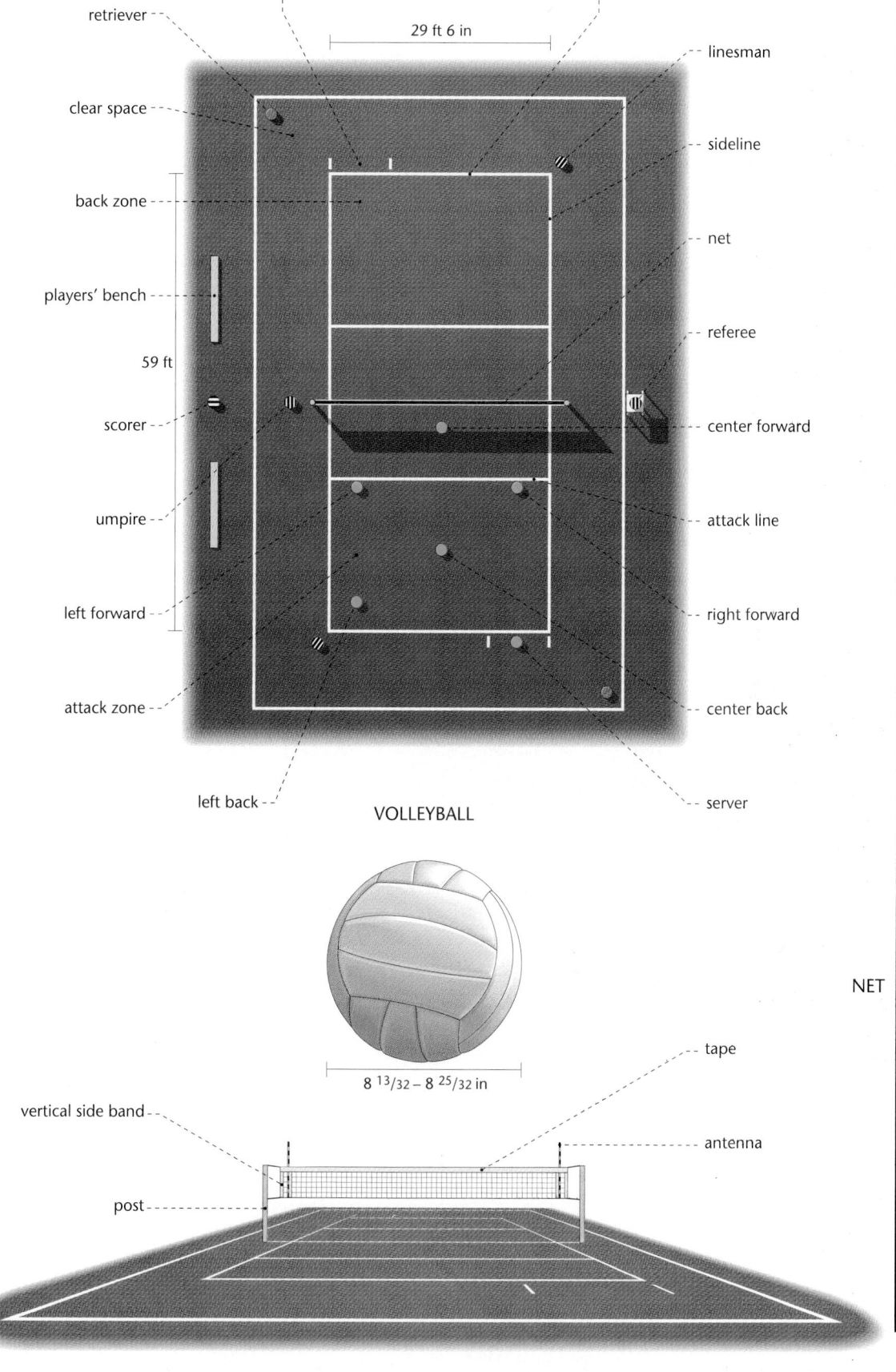

service area

end line

retriever

29 ft 6 in

linesman

clear space

sideline

back zone

net

players' bench

referee

59 ft

scorer

center forward

umpire

attack line

left forward

right forward

attack zone

center back

left back

server

VOLLEYBALL

8 $^{13}/_{32}$ – 8 $^{25}/_{32}$ in

tape

vertical side band

antenna

post

TENNIS

COURT

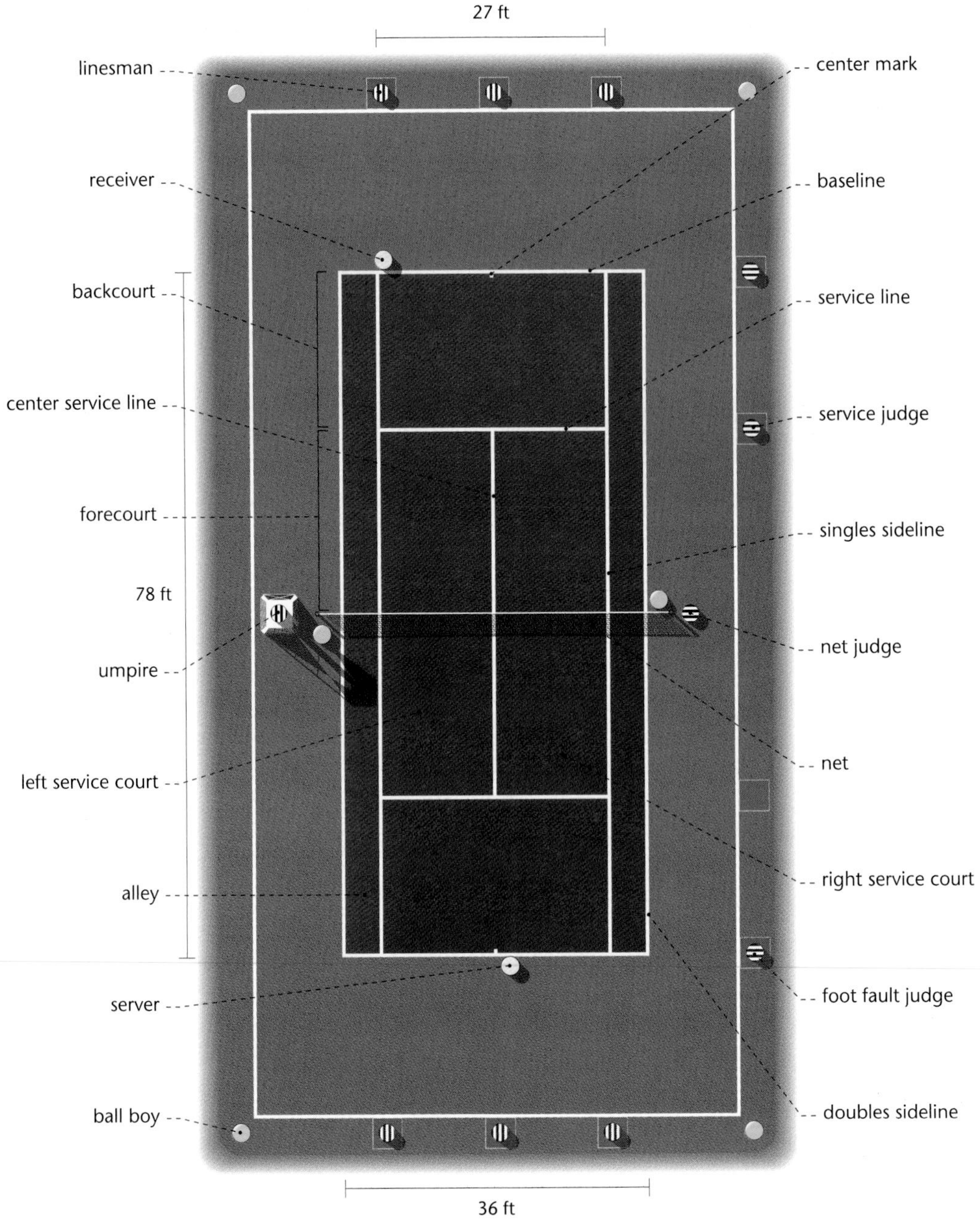

27 ft

linesman

center mark

receiver

baseline

backcourt

service line

center service line

service judge

forecourt

singles sideline

78 ft

umpire

net judge

left service court

net

right service court

alley

server

foot fault judge

ball boy

doubles sideline

36 ft

NET

net band

center strap

singles pole

doubles pole

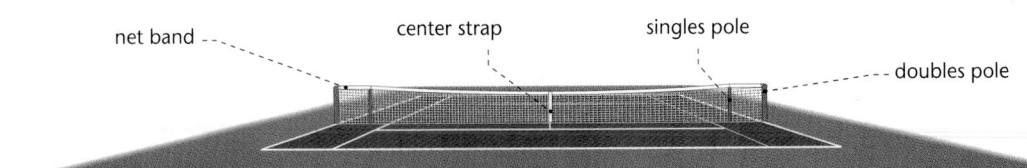

headband

polo shirt

wristband

skirt

frame

head

stringing

shoulder

throat

shaft

handle

butt

sock

tennis shoe

TENNIS BALL

2 $^1/_2$ – 2 $^5/_8$ in

TEAM GAMES

615

SQUASH

SQUASH BALL

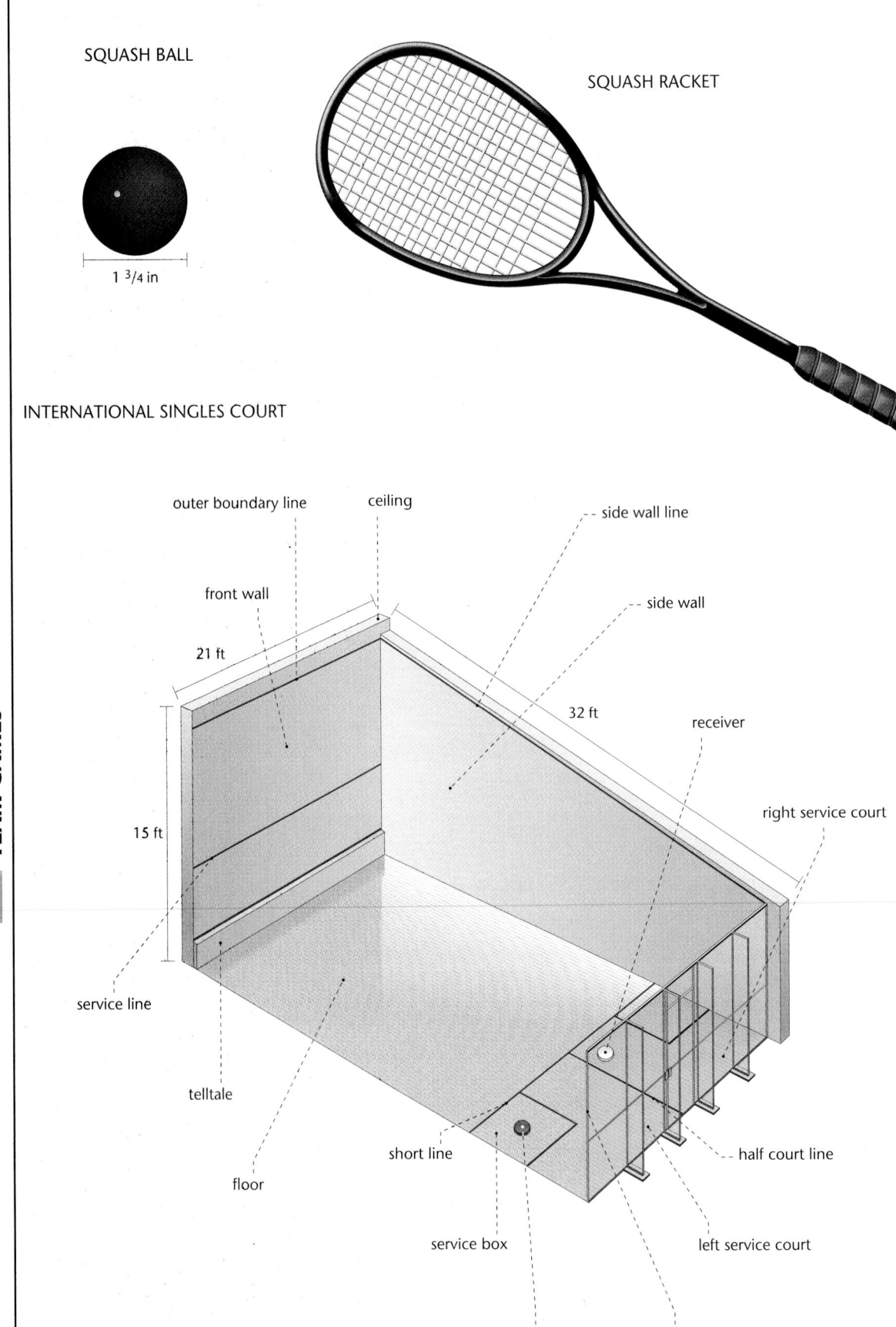

1 3/4 in

SQUASH RACKET

INTERNATIONAL SINGLES COURT

outer boundary line

ceiling

side wall line

front wall

side wall

21 ft

32 ft

receiver

15 ft

right service court

service line

telltale

short line

half court line

floor

service box

left service court

server

back wall

RACQUETBALL

RACQUETBALL RACKET

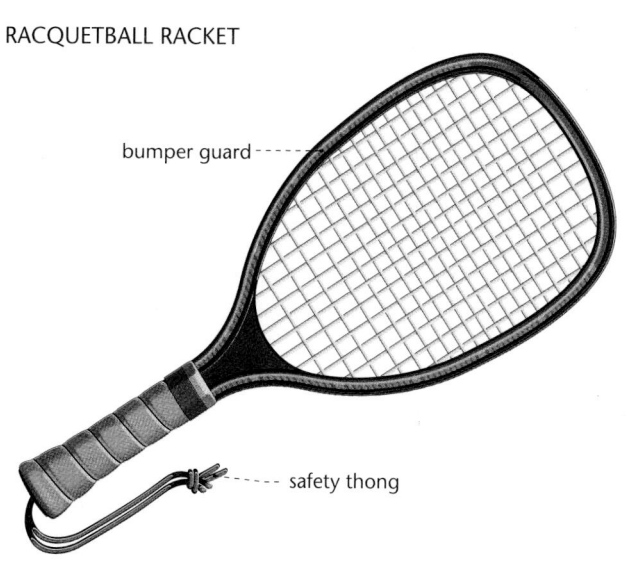

bumper guard ---------

safety thong

RACQUETBALL

1 7/8 in

COURT

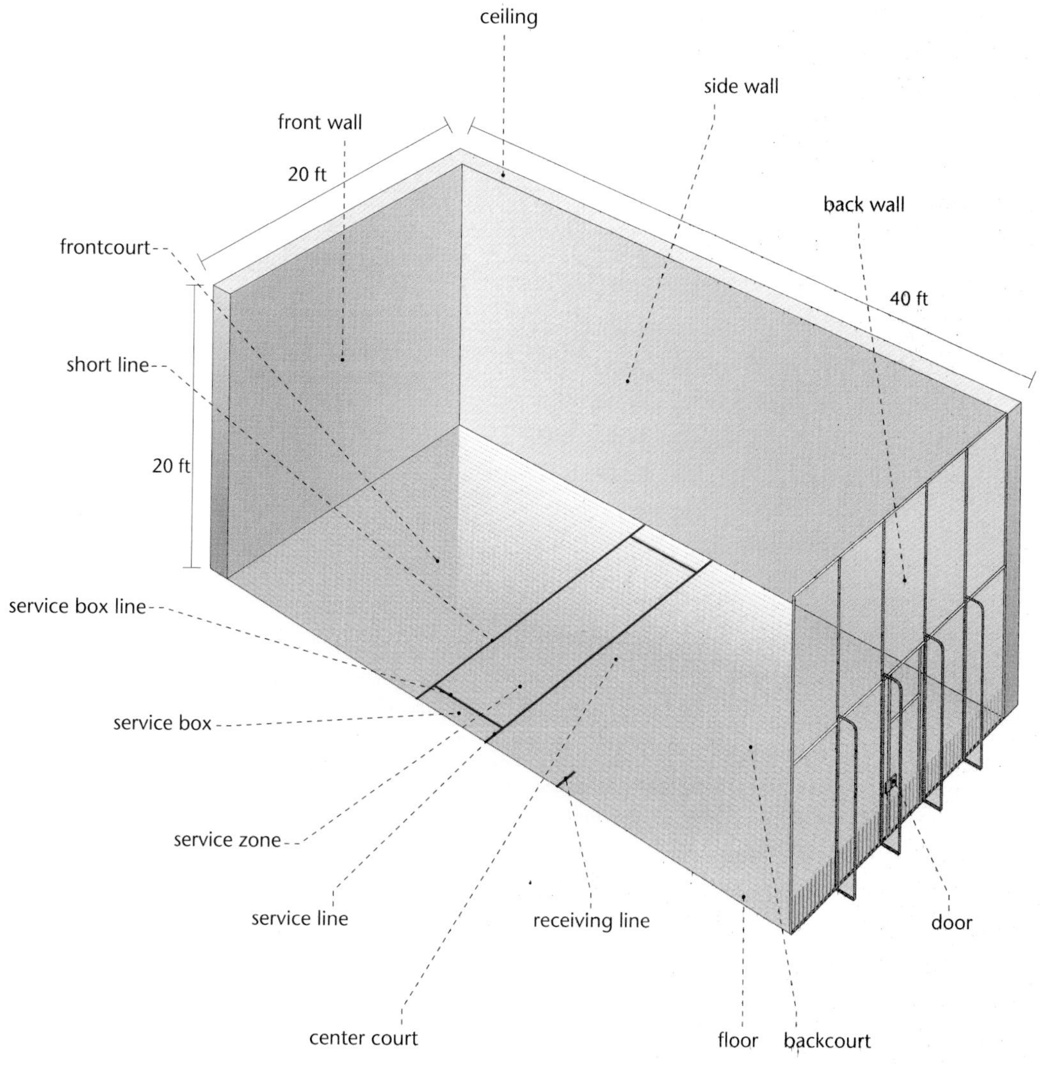

ceiling

side wall

front wall

20 ft

back wall

frontcourt---

40 ft

short line---

20 ft

service box line---

service box---

service zone---

service line

receiving line

center court

floor   backcourt

door

BADMINTON

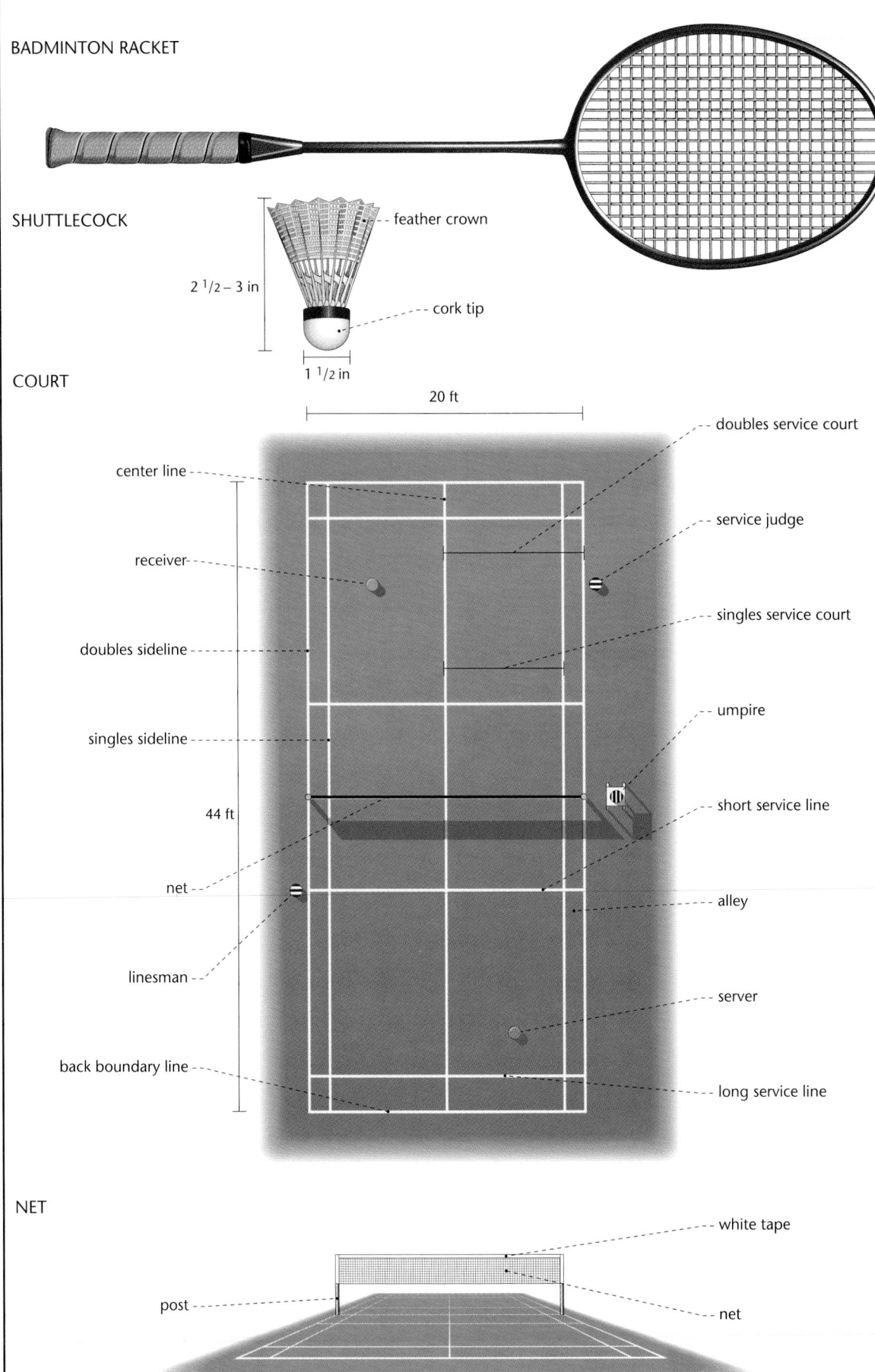

BADMINTON RACKET

SHUTTLECOCK

- feather crown

$2\,^{1}/_{2} - 3$ in

- cork tip

$1\,^{1}/_{2}$ in

COURT

20 ft

center line

doubles service court

receiver

service judge

doubles sideline

singles service court

singles sideline

umpire

44 ft

short service line

net

alley

linesman

server

back boundary line

long service line

NET

white tape

post

net

TABLE TENNIS

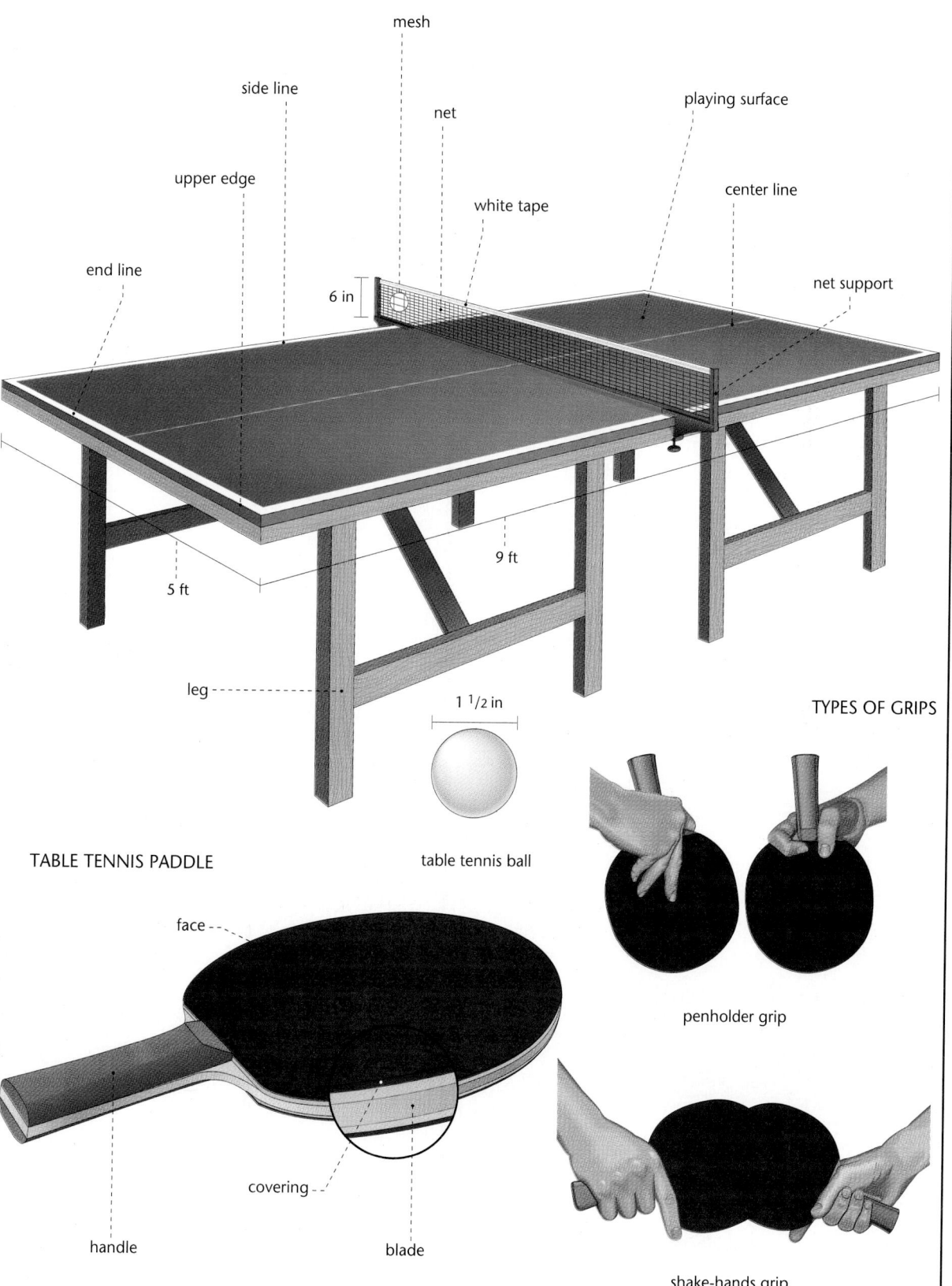

mesh

side line

net

upper edge

white tape

playing surface

end line

center line

net support

6 in

9 ft

5 ft

leg

1 1/2 in

table tennis ball

TYPES OF GRIPS

TABLE TENNIS PADDLE

face

penholder grip

covering

handle

blade

shake-hands grip

CURLING STONE

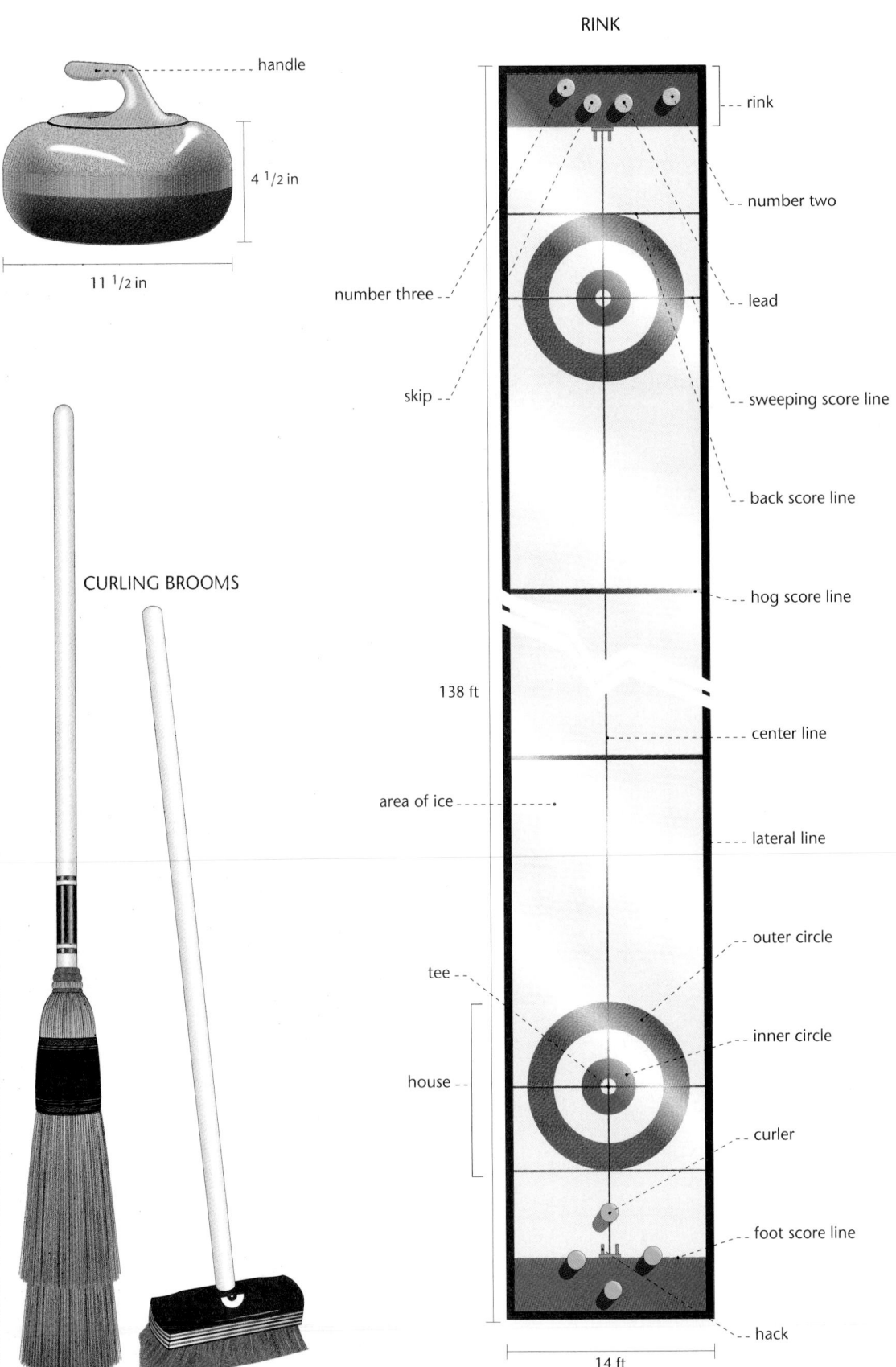

handle

4 1/2 in

11 1/2 in

CURLING BROOMS

RINK

rink

number two

number three

lead

skip

sweeping score line

back score line

hog score line

138 ft

center line

area of ice

lateral line

outer circle

tee

inner circle

house

curler

foot score line

hack

14 ft

SWIMMING

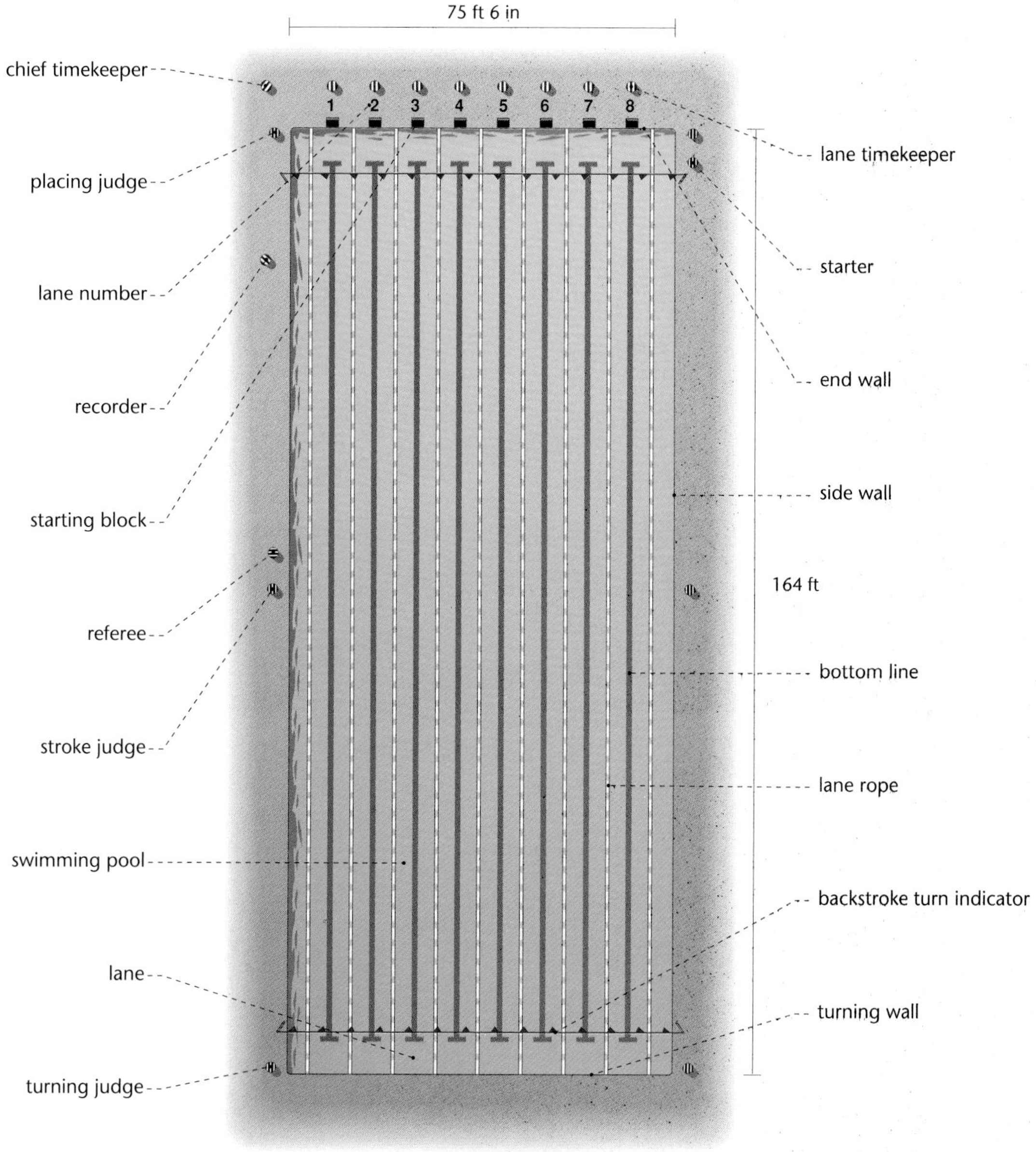

75 ft 6 in

chief timekeeper

1 2 3 4 5 6 7 8

lane timekeeper

placing judge

starter

lane number

end wall

recorder

side wall

starting block

164 ft

referee

bottom line

stroke judge

lane rope

swimming pool

backstroke turn indicator

lane

turning wall

turning judge

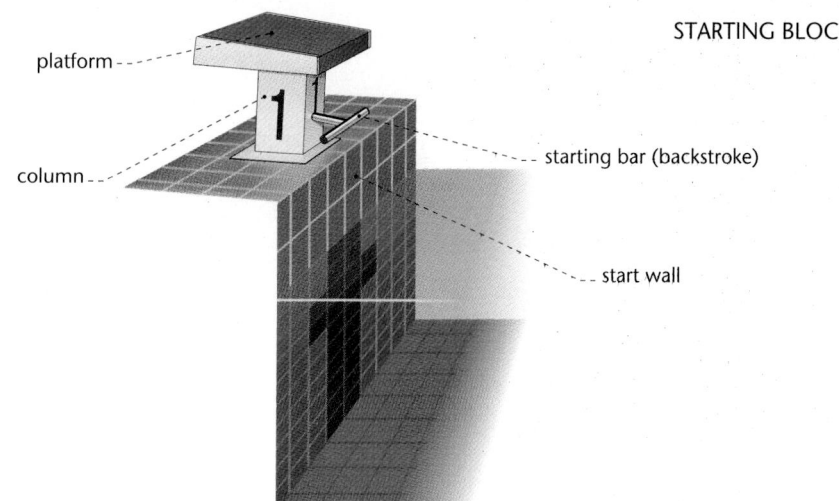

platform

starting bar (backstroke)

column

start wall

SWIMMING

TYPES OF STROKES

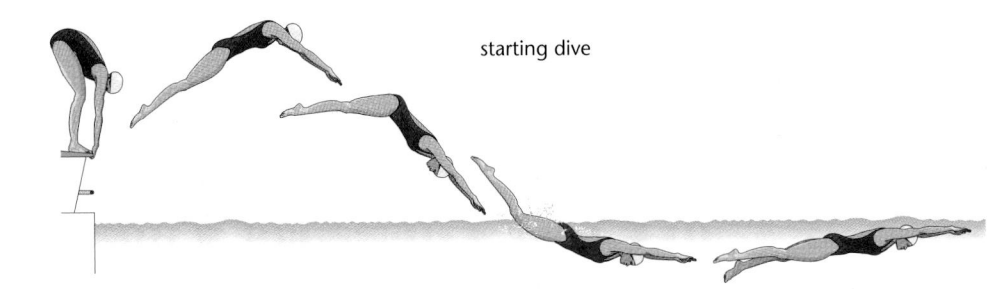

starting dive

FRONT CRAWL STROKE

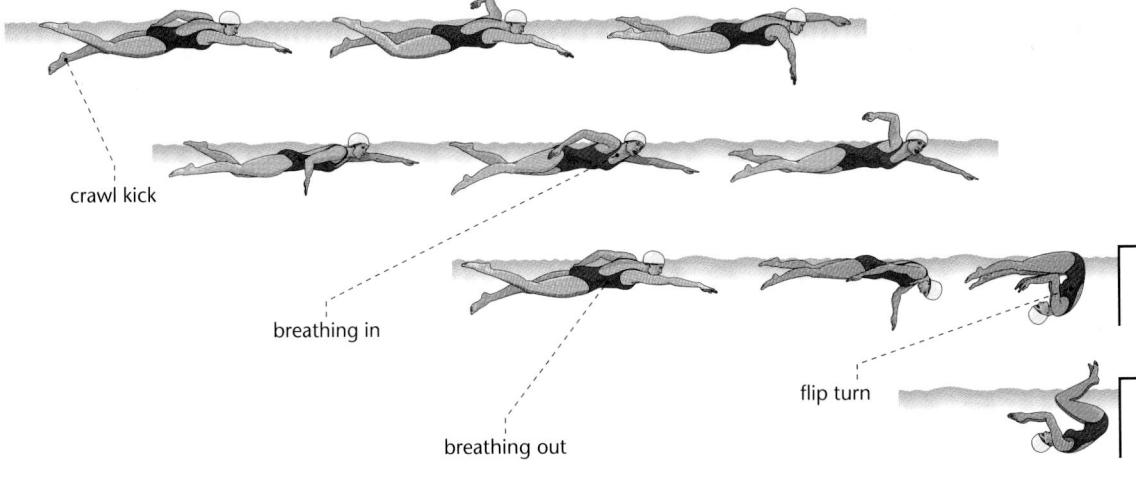

crawl kick

breathing in

breathing out

flip turn

turning wall

WATER SPORTS

BREASTSTROKE

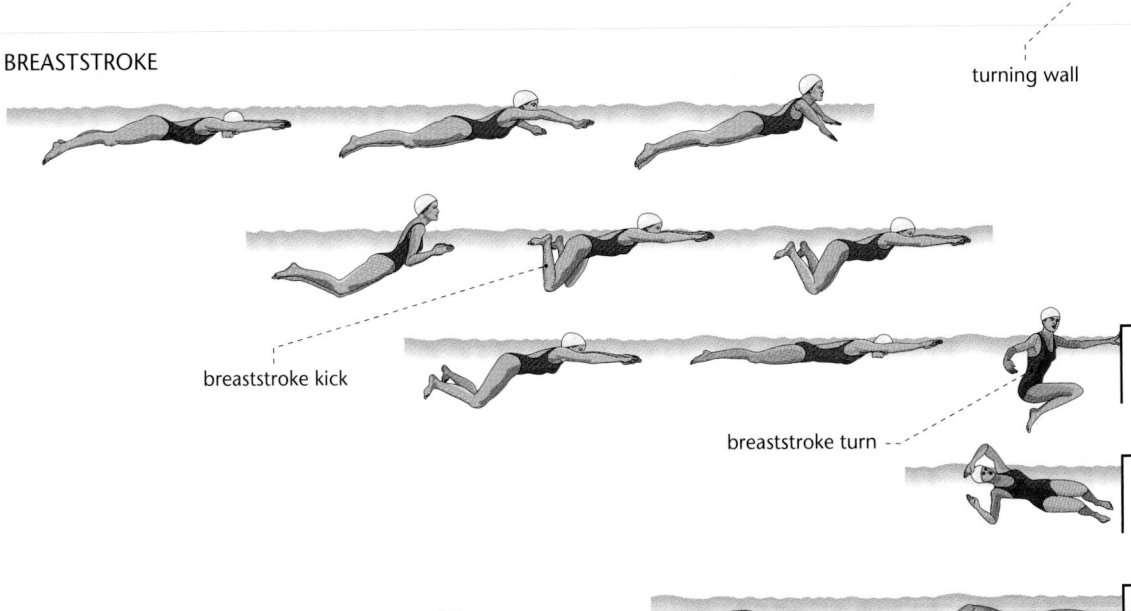

breaststroke kick

breaststroke turn

BUTTERFLY STROKE

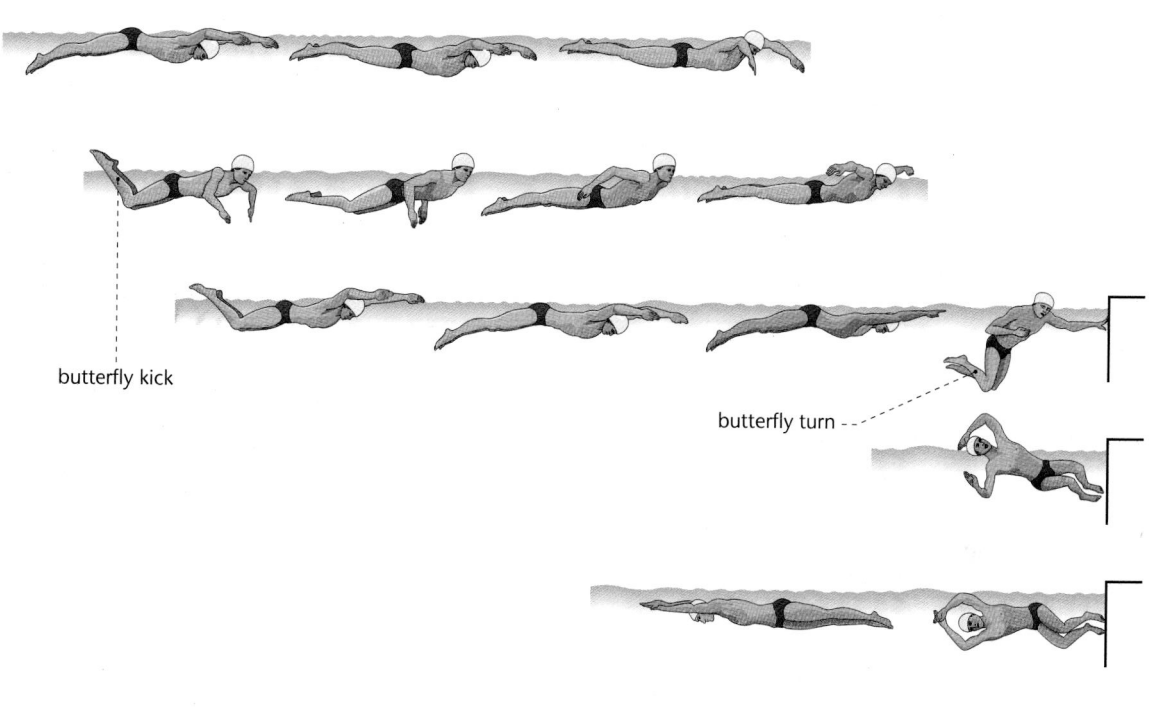

butterfly kick

butterfly turn

BACKSTROKE START

BACKSTROKE

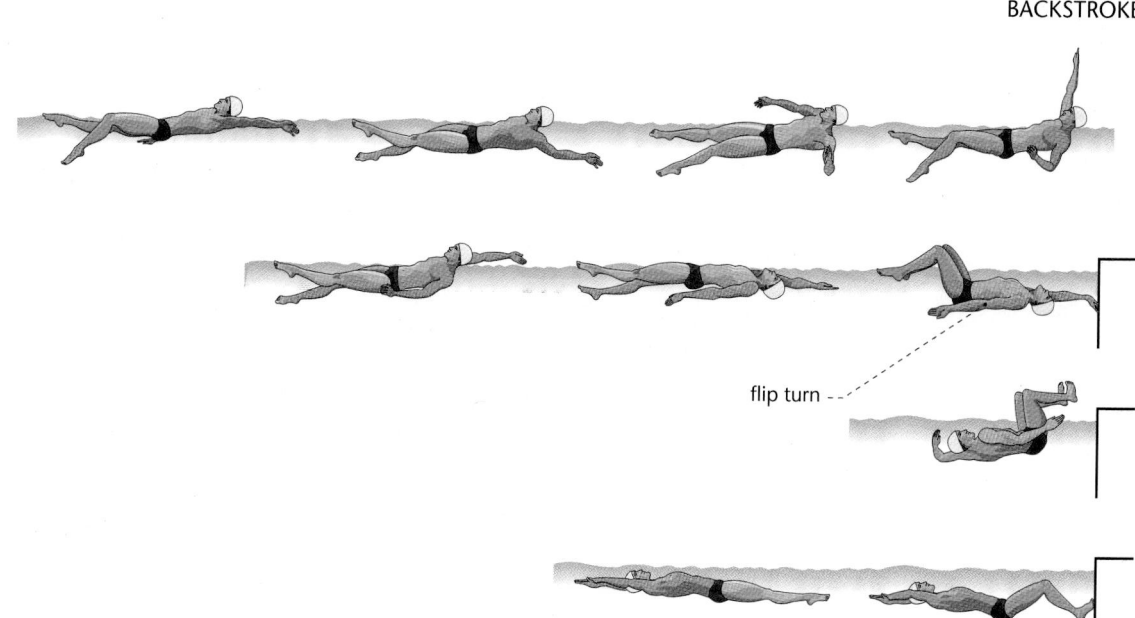

flip turn

DIVING

DIVING INSTALLATIONS

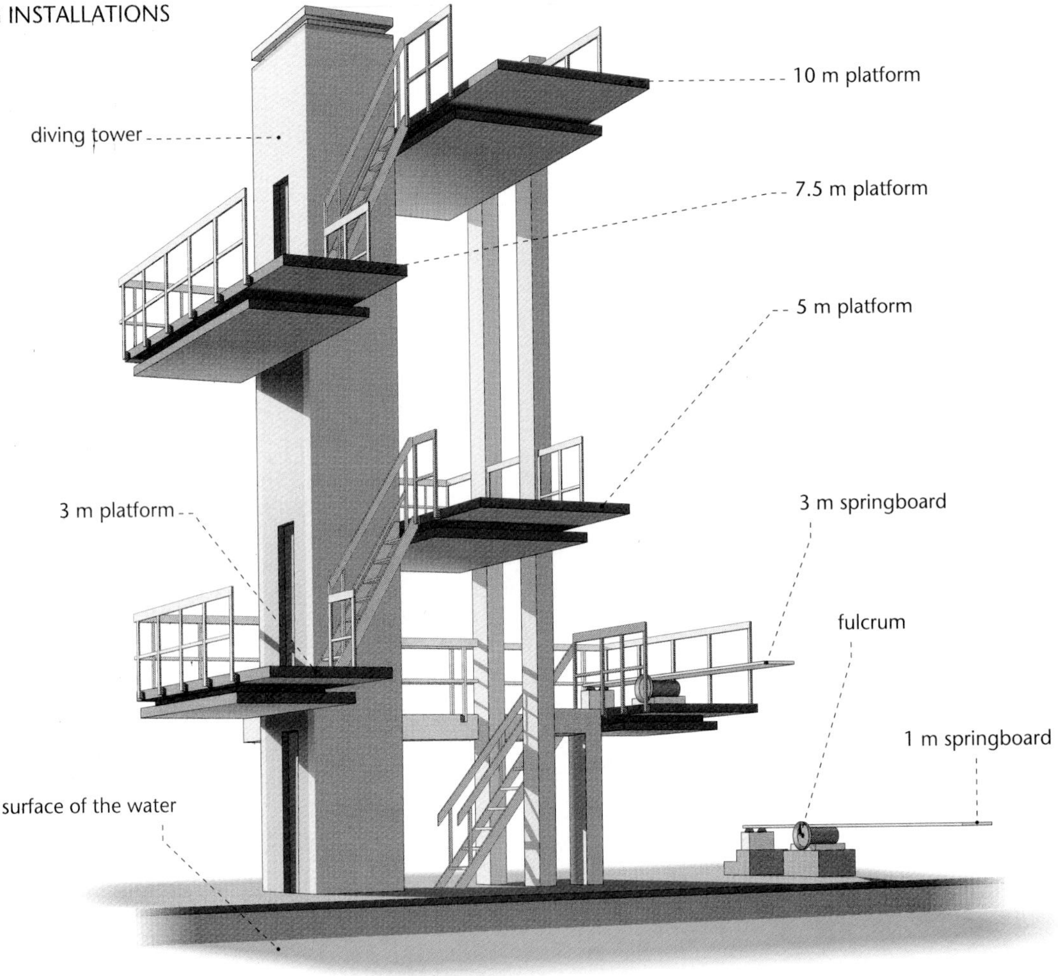

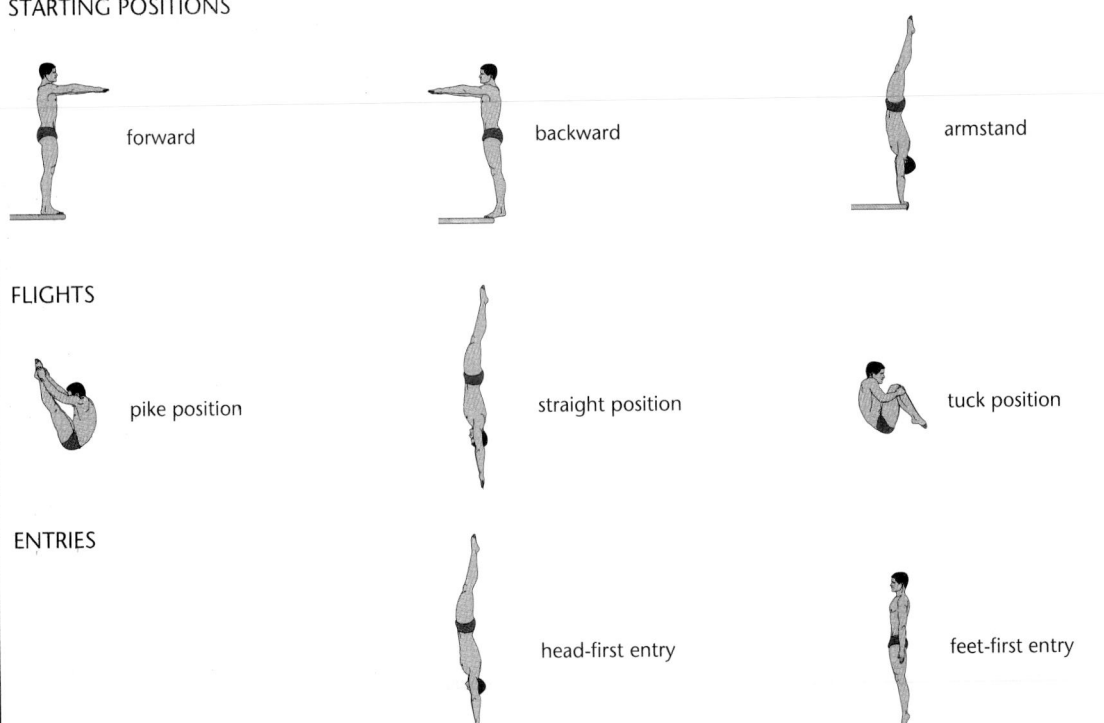

diving tower

10 m platform

7.5 m platform

5 m platform

3 m springboard

fulcrum

1 m springboard

3 m platform

surface of the water

STARTING POSITIONS

forward

backward

armstand

FLIGHTS

pike position

straight position

tuck position

ENTRIES

head-first entry

feet-first entry

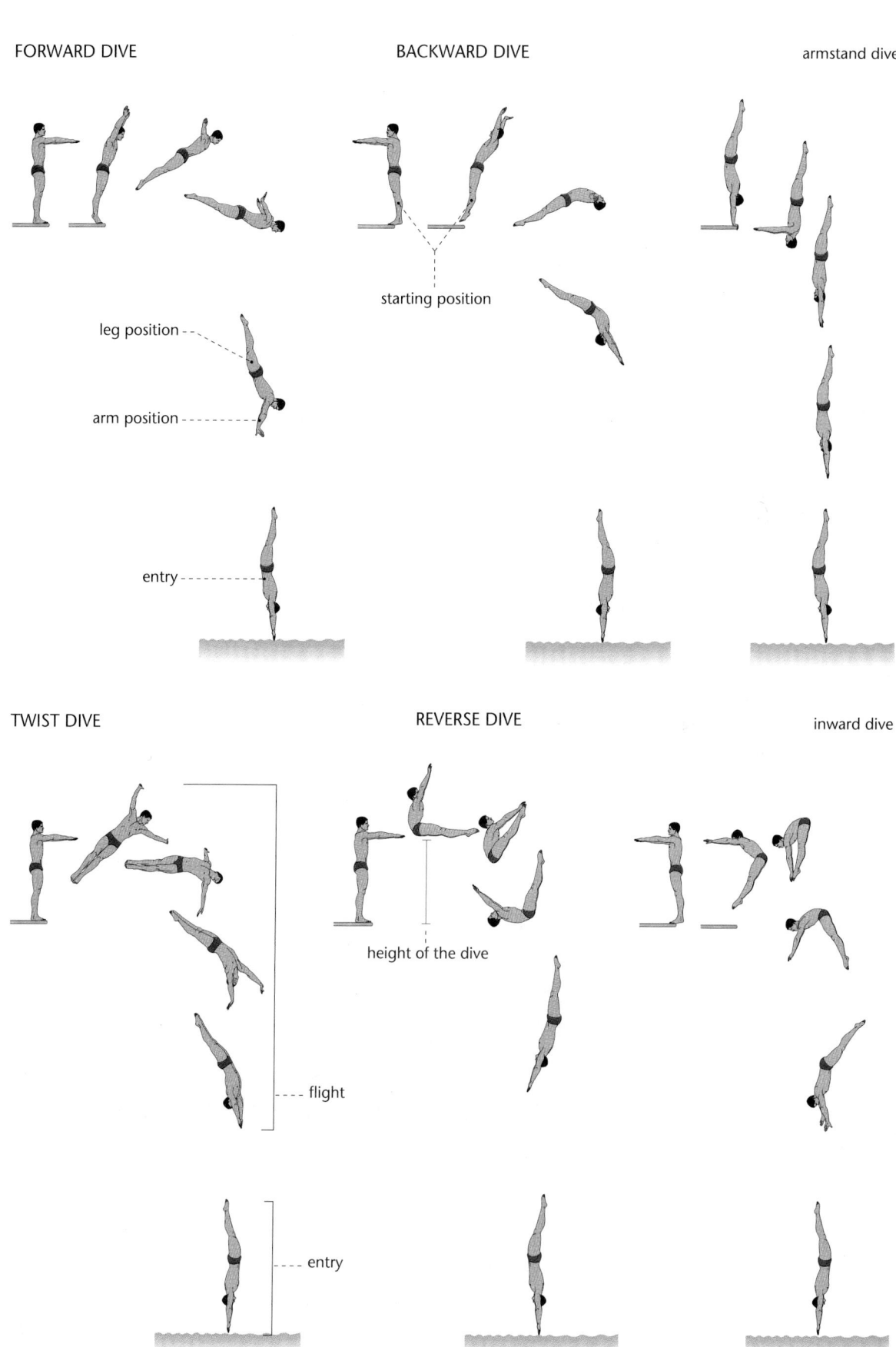

FORWARD DIVE

BACKWARD DIVE

armstand dive

starting position

leg position

arm position

entry

TWIST DIVE

REVERSE DIVE

inward dive

height of the dive

flight

entry

WATER POLO

PLAYING AREA

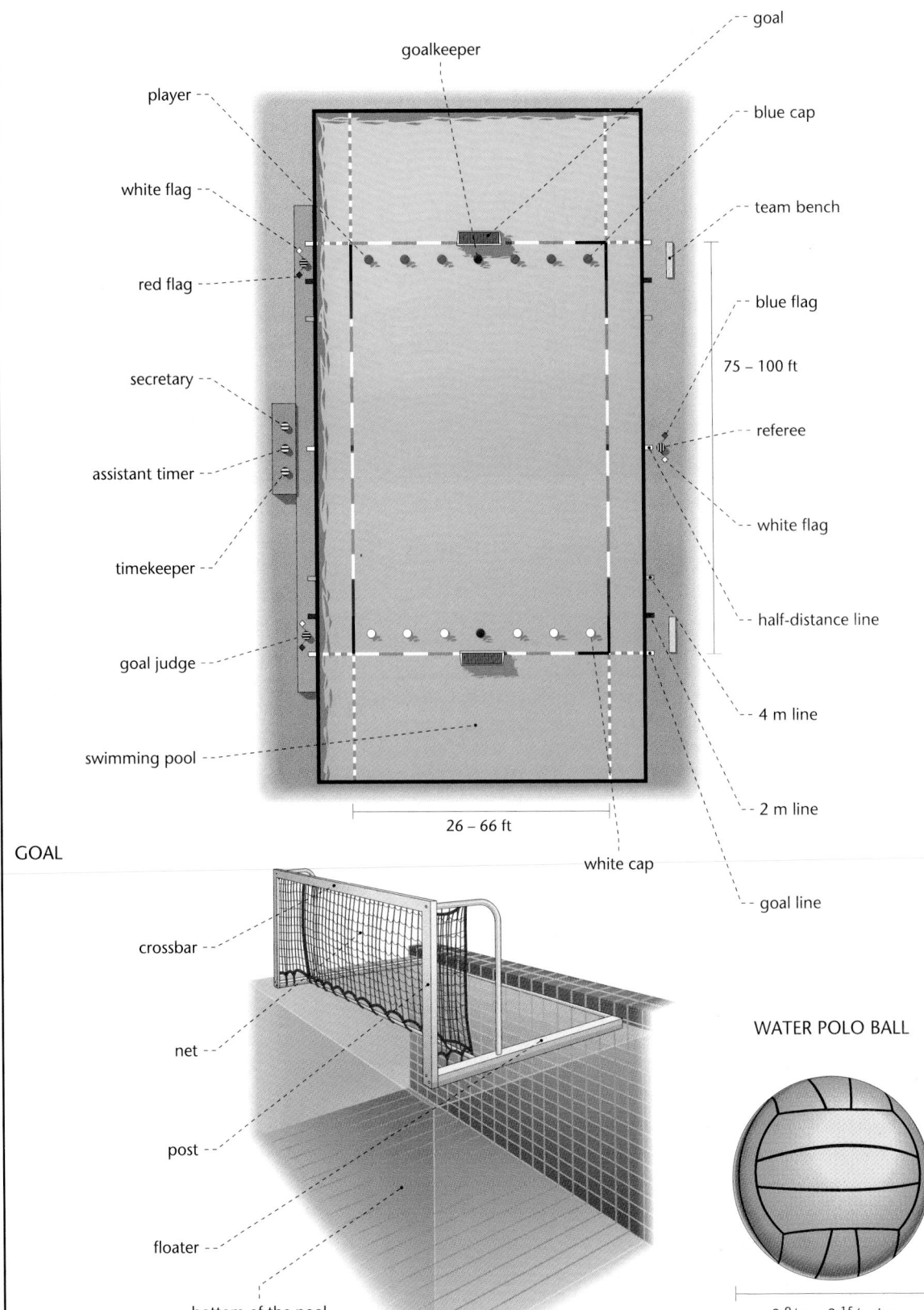

goal

goalkeeper

player

blue cap

white flag

team bench

red flag

blue flag

secretary

75 – 100 ft

assistant timer

referee

timekeeper

white flag

half-distance line

goal judge

4 m line

swimming pool

2 m line

26 – 66 ft

white cap

goal line

GOAL

crossbar

net

post

WATER POLO BALL

floater

bottom of the pool

8 9/16 – 8 15/16 in

SCUBA DIVING

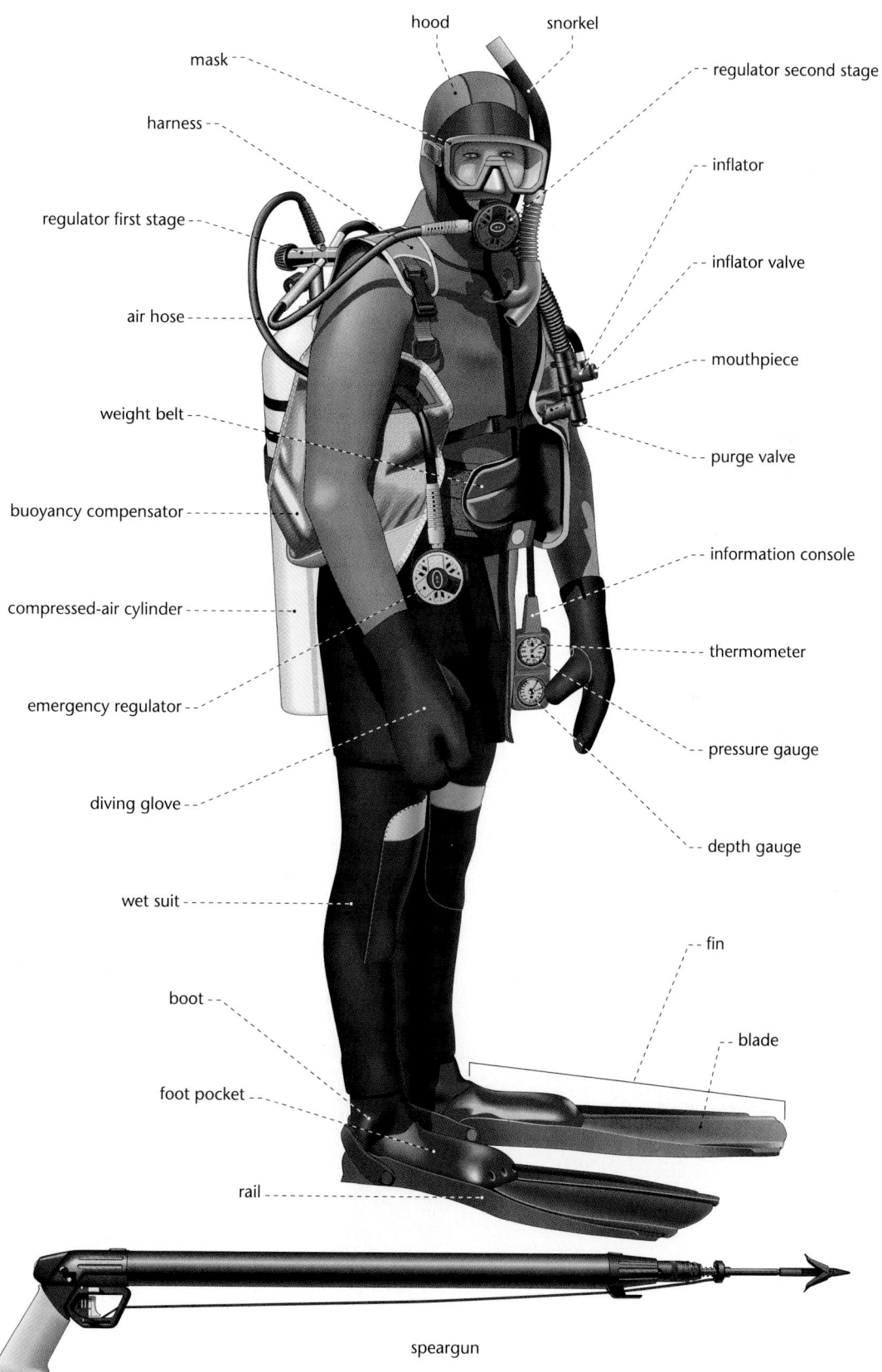

hood

snorkel

mask

regulator second stage

harness

inflator

regulator first stage

inflator valve

air hose

mouthpiece

weight belt

purge valve

buoyancy compensator

information console

compressed-air cylinder

thermometer

emergency regulator

pressure gauge

diving glove

depth gauge

wet suit

fin

boot

blade

foot pocket

rail

speargun

SAILBOAT

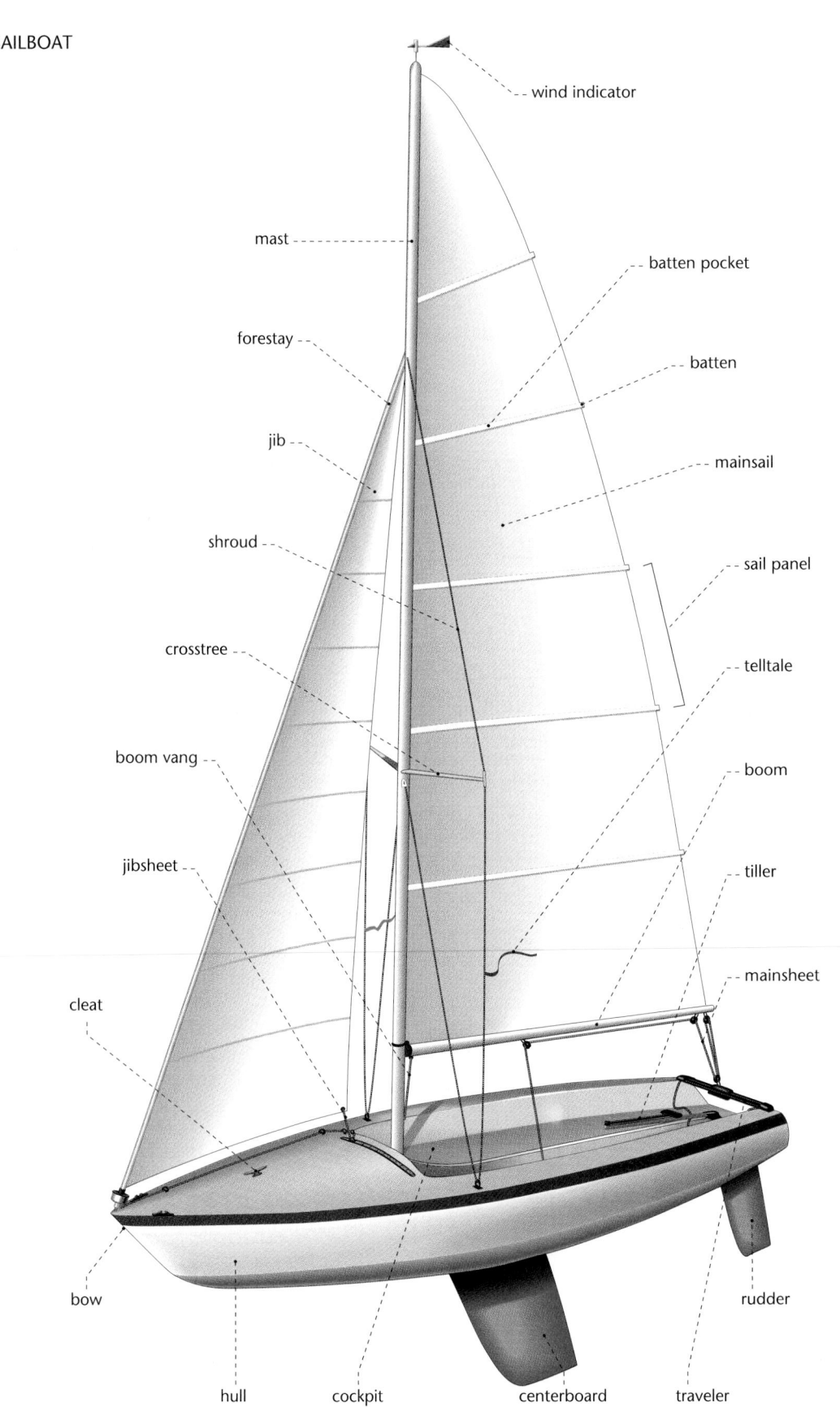

wind indicator

mast

batten pocket

forestay

batten

jib

mainsail

shroud

sail panel

crosstree

telltale

boom vang

boom

jibsheet

tiller

cleat

mainsheet

bow

rudder

hull   cockpit   centerboard   traveler

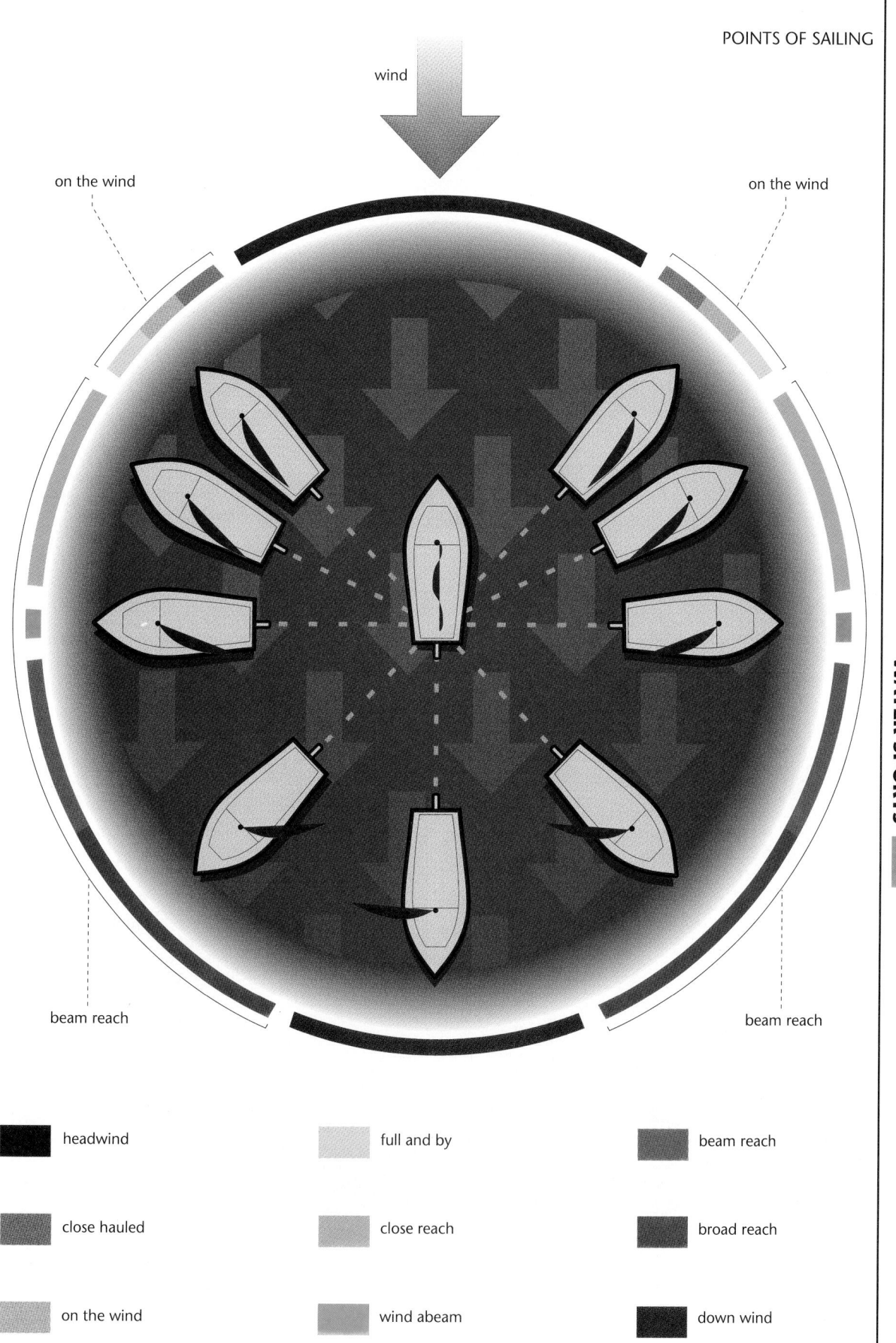

wind

on the wind

on the wind

beam reach

beam reach

WATER SPORTS

	headwind		full and by		beam reach
	close hauled		close reach		broad reach
	on the wind		wind abeam		down wind

WATER SPORTS

UPPERWORKS

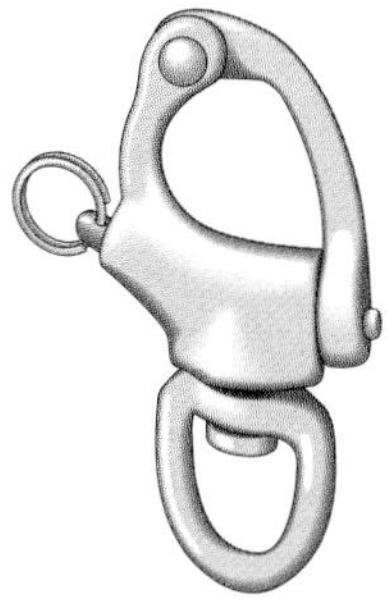

hank

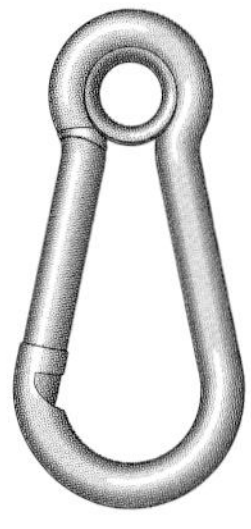

snap shackle

shackle

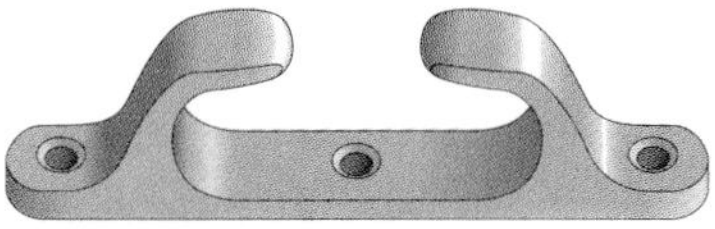

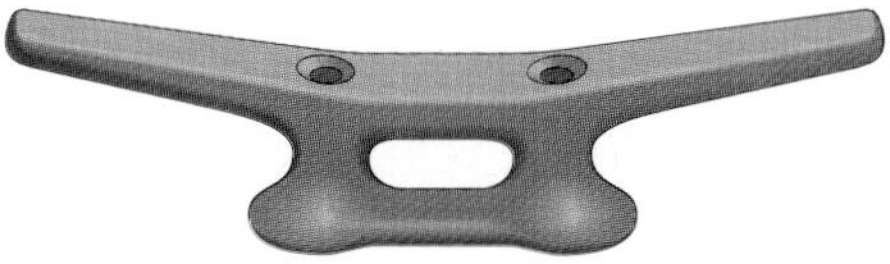

cleat

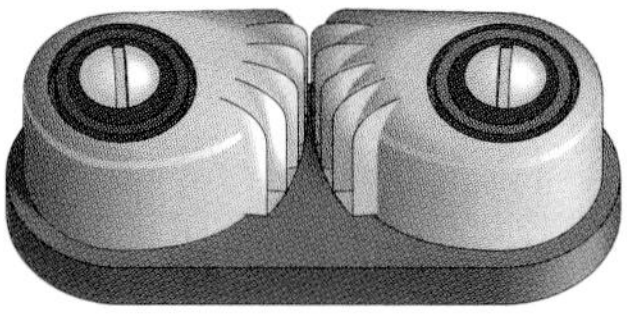

fairlead

clam cleat

turnbuckle

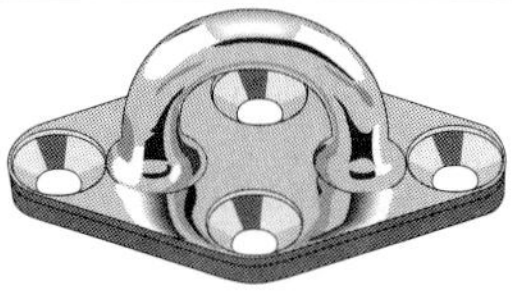

sheet lead

winch

TRAVELER

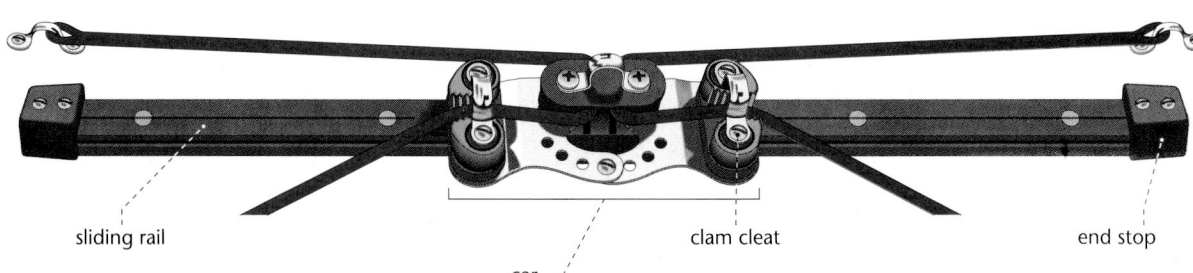

sliding rail

clam cleat

car

end stop

SAILBOARD

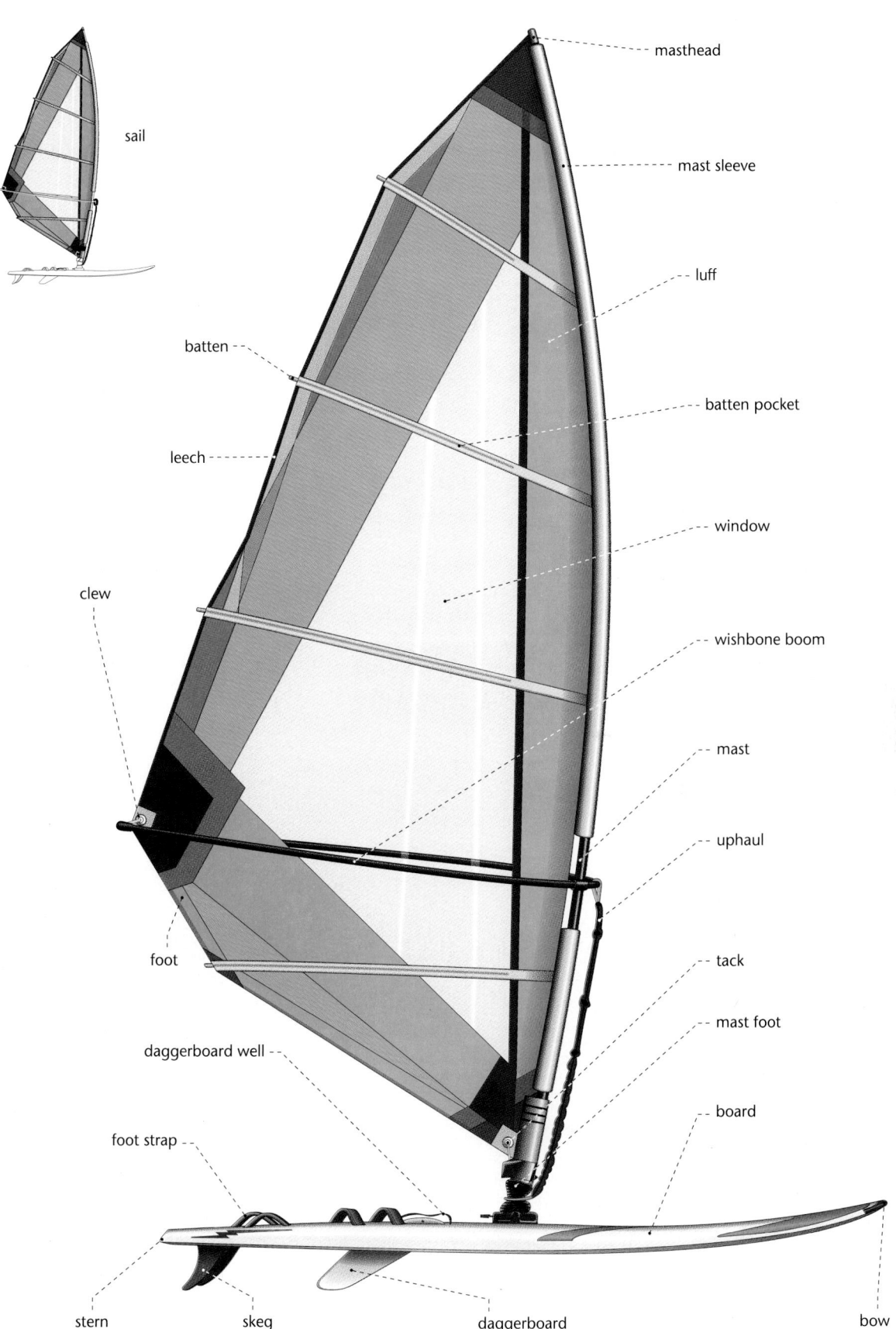

sail

masthead

mast sleeve

luff

batten

batten pocket

leech

window

clew

wishbone boom

mast

uphaul

foot

tack

mast foot

daggerboard well

board

foot strap

stern   skeg   daggerboard   bow

ROWING AND SCULLING

SCULLING (TWO OARS)

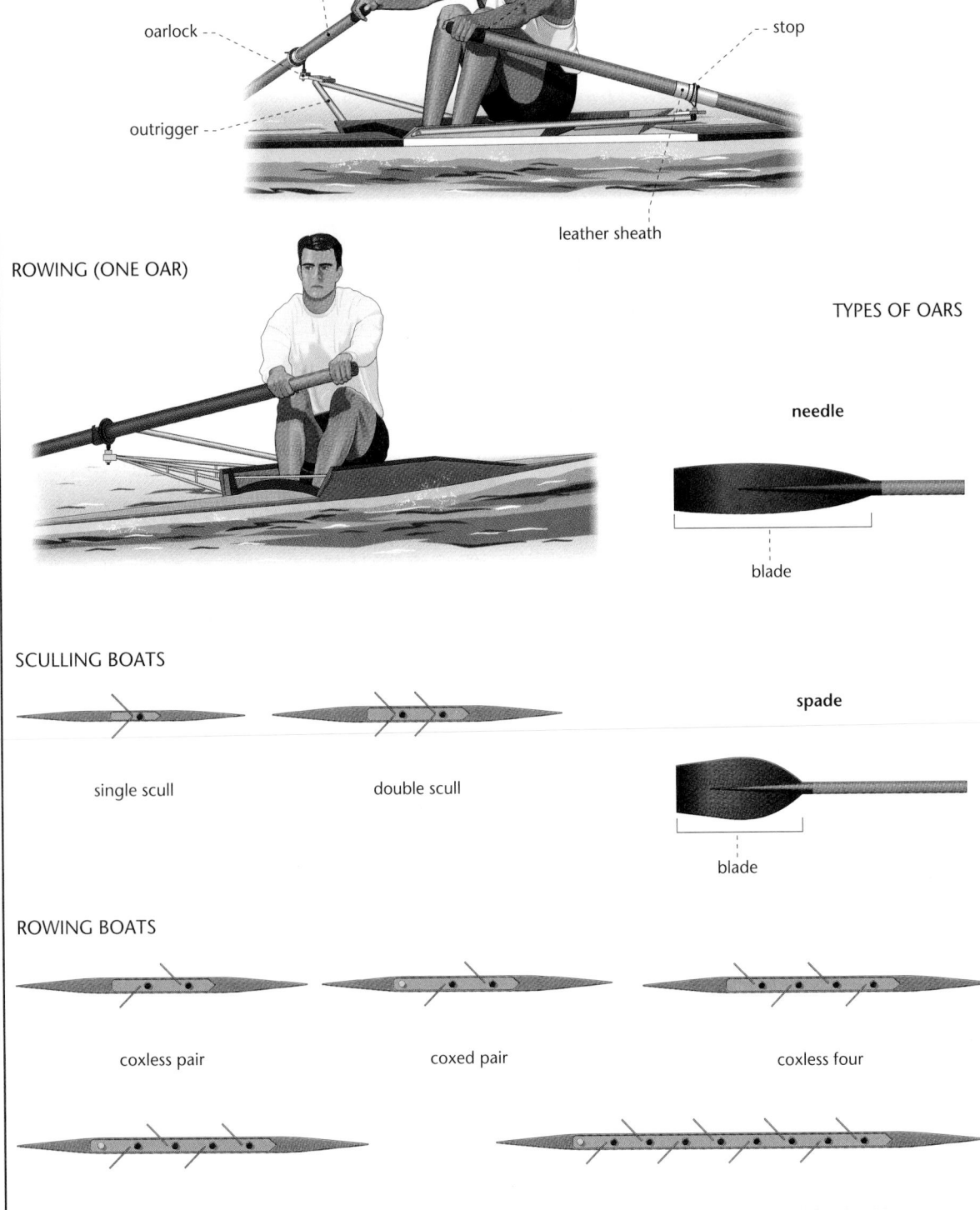

grip

shaft

oarlock

stop

outrigger

leather sheath

ROWING (ONE OAR)

TYPES OF OARS

needle

blade

SCULLING BOATS

spade

single scull

double scull

blade

ROWING BOATS

coxless pair

coxed pair

coxless four

coxed four

eight

632

WATER SKIING

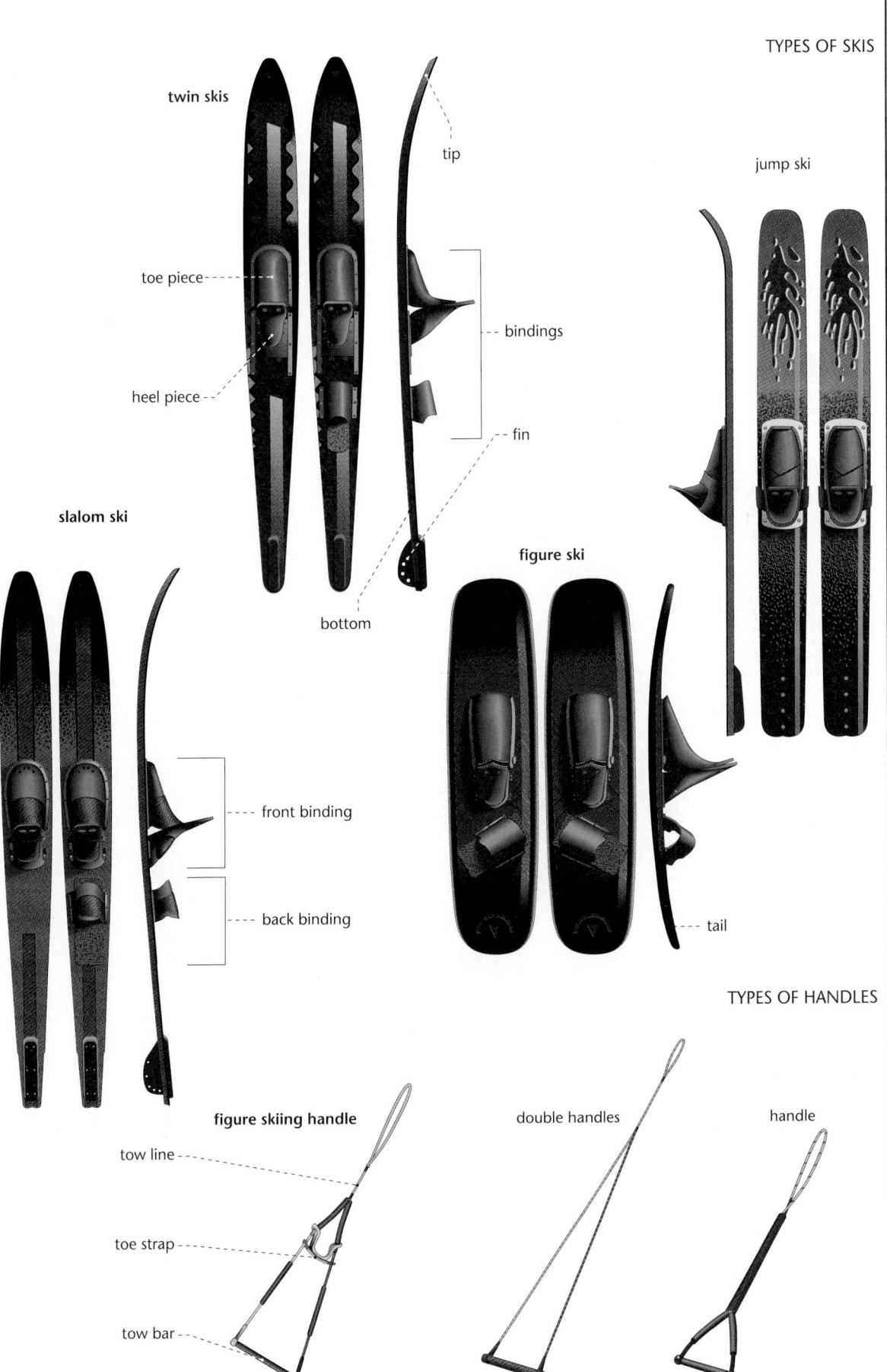

twin skis

jump ski

tip

toe piece

bindings

heel piece

fin

slalom ski

figure ski

bottom

front binding

back binding

tail

figure skiing handle

double handles

handle

tow line

toe strap

tow bar

633

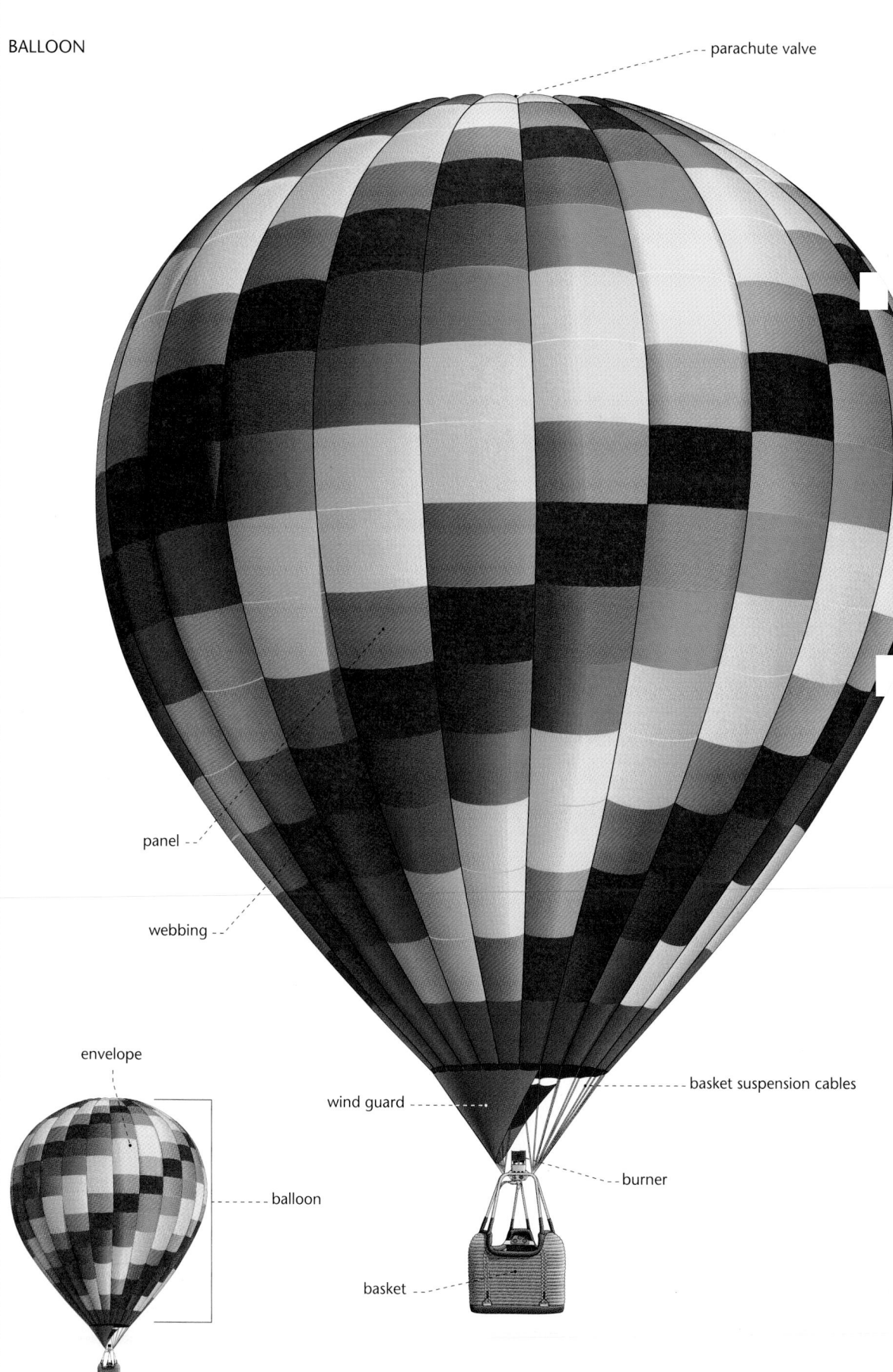

BALLOON

parachute valve

panel

webbing

envelope

balloon

wind guard

basket suspension cables

burner

basket

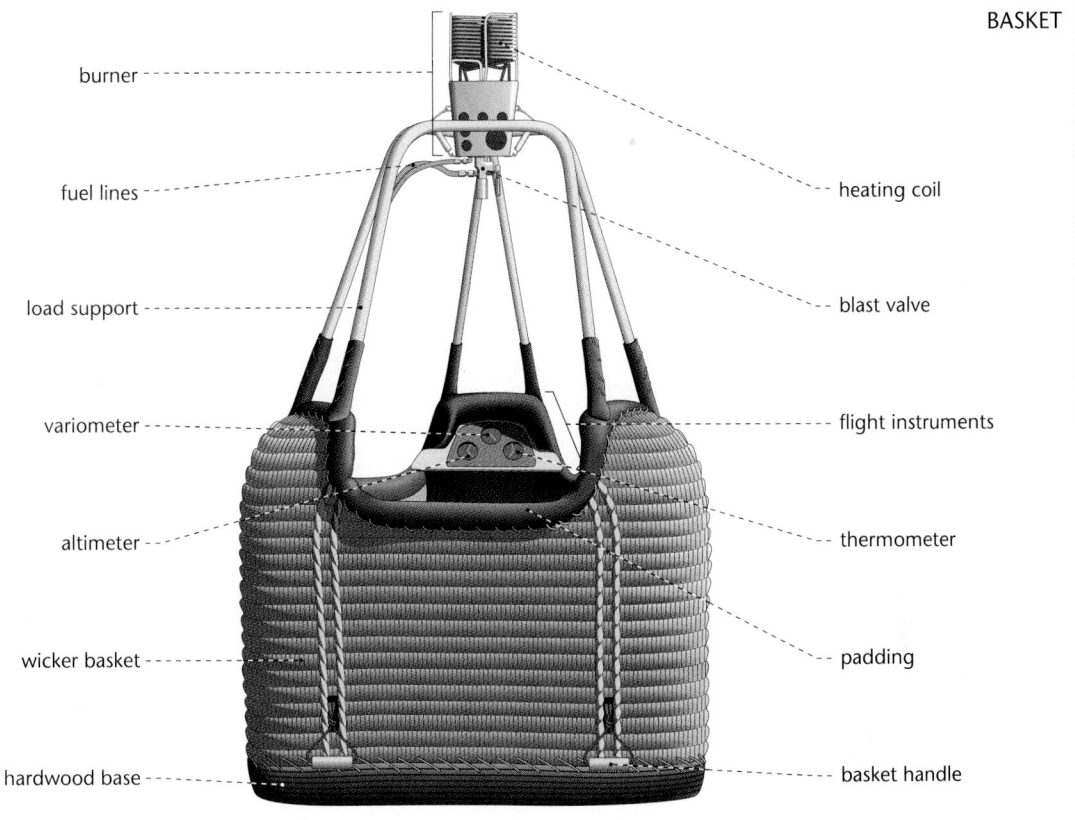

burner

fuel lines

load support

variometer

altimeter

wicker basket

hardwood base

heating coil

blast valve

flight instruments

thermometer

padding

basket handle

SKY DIVING

SKY DIVER

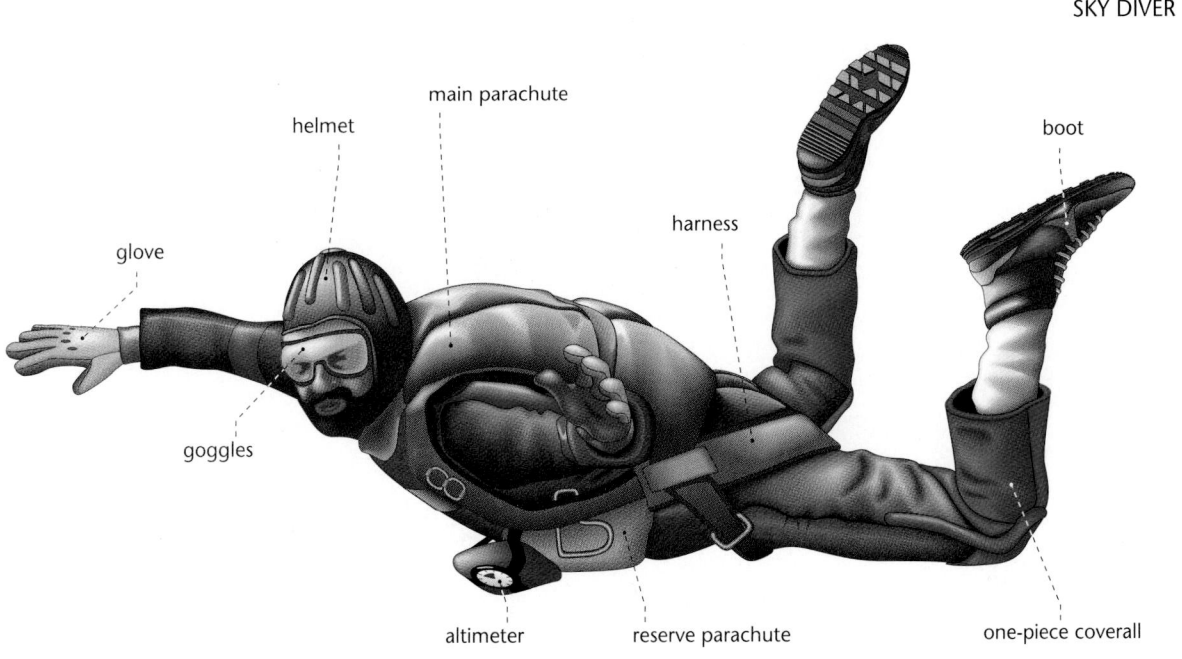

helmet

main parachute

glove

goggles

altimeter

reserve parachute

harness

boot

one-piece coverall

CANOPY

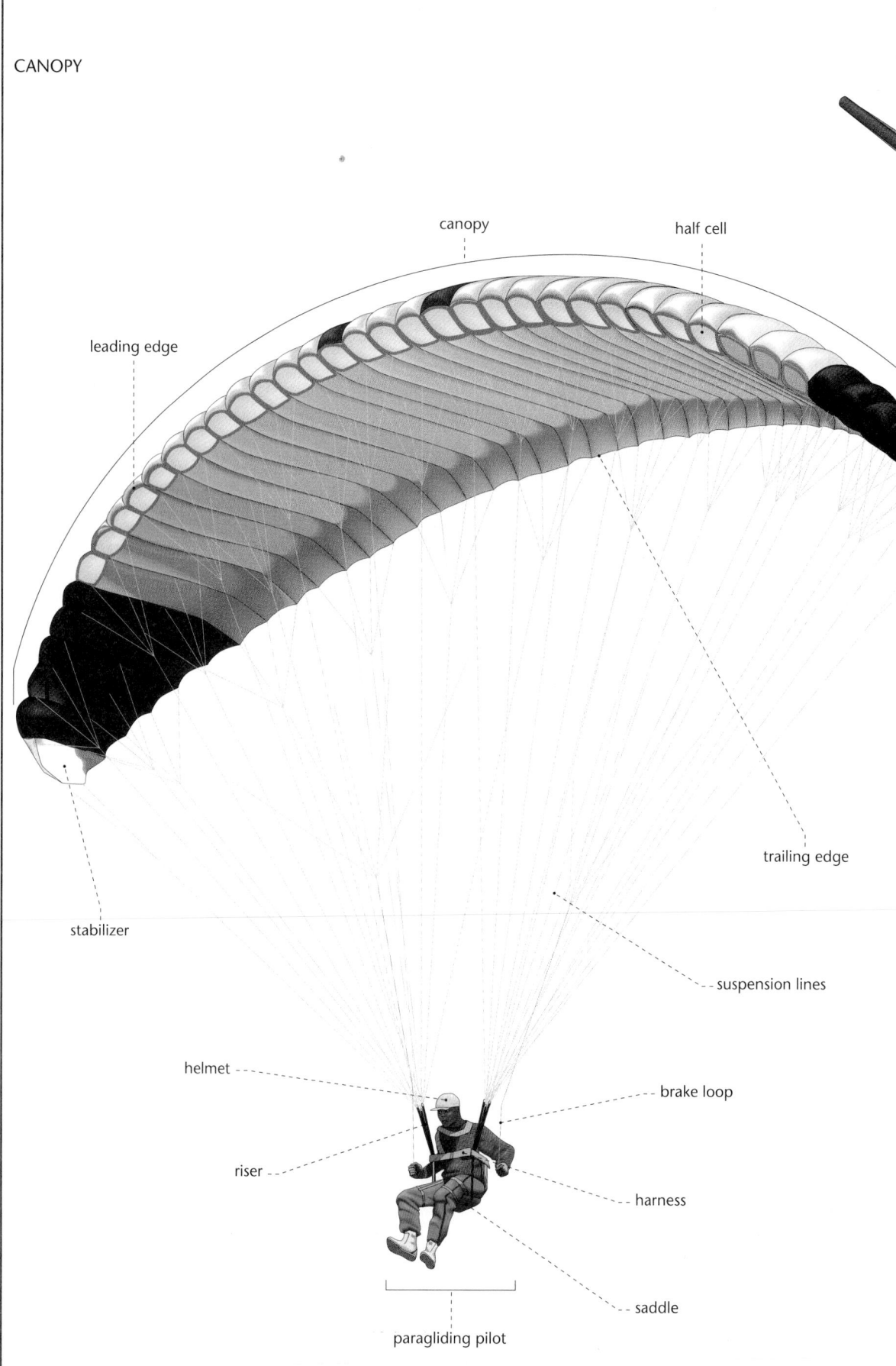

canopy

half cell

leading edge

trailing edge

stabilizer

suspension lines

helmet

brake loop

riser

harness

saddle

paragliding pilot

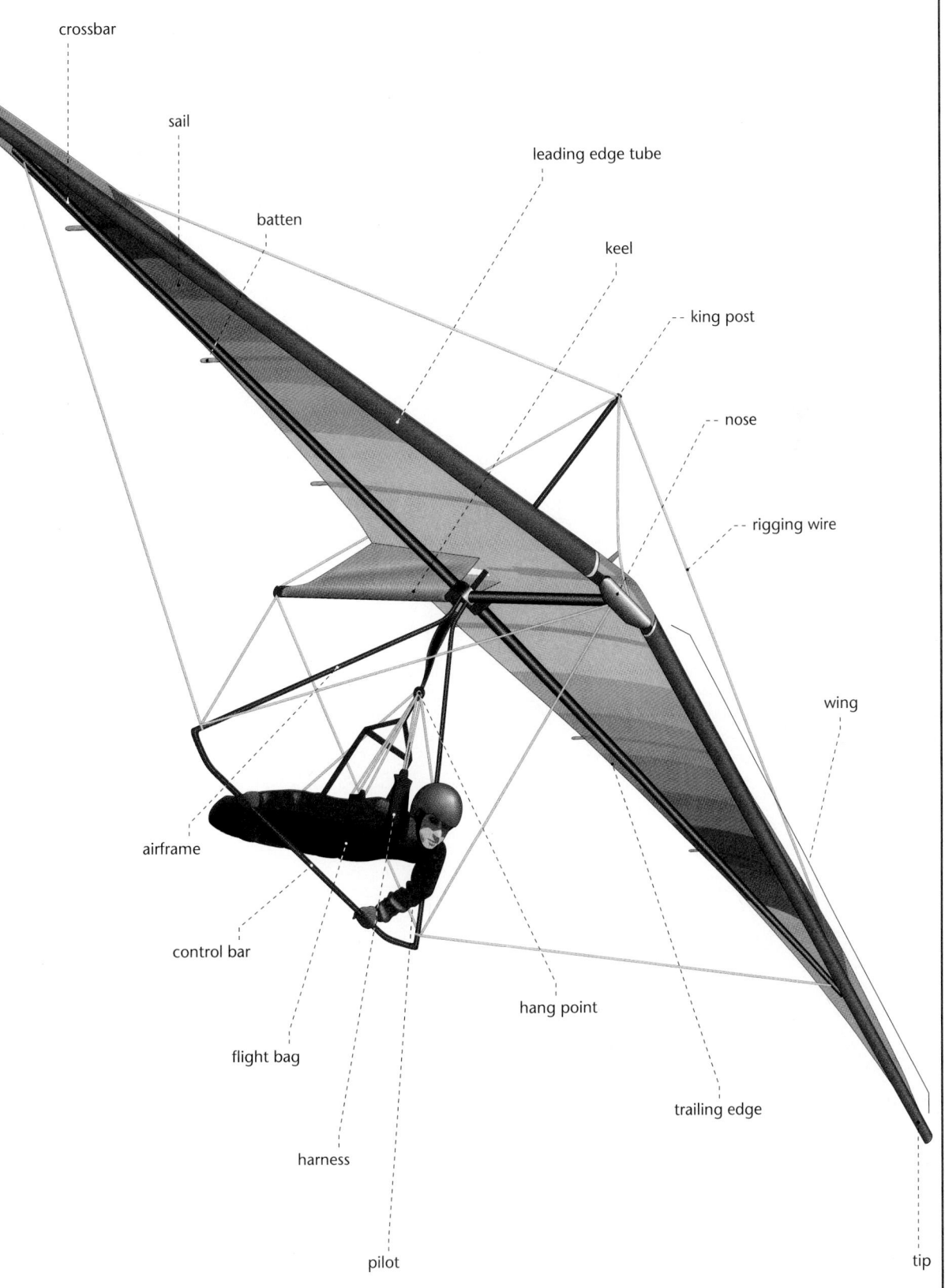

crossbar

sail

batten

leading edge tube

keel

king post

nose

rigging wire

wing

airframe

control bar

hang point

flight bag

trailing edge

harness

pilot

tip

GLIDER

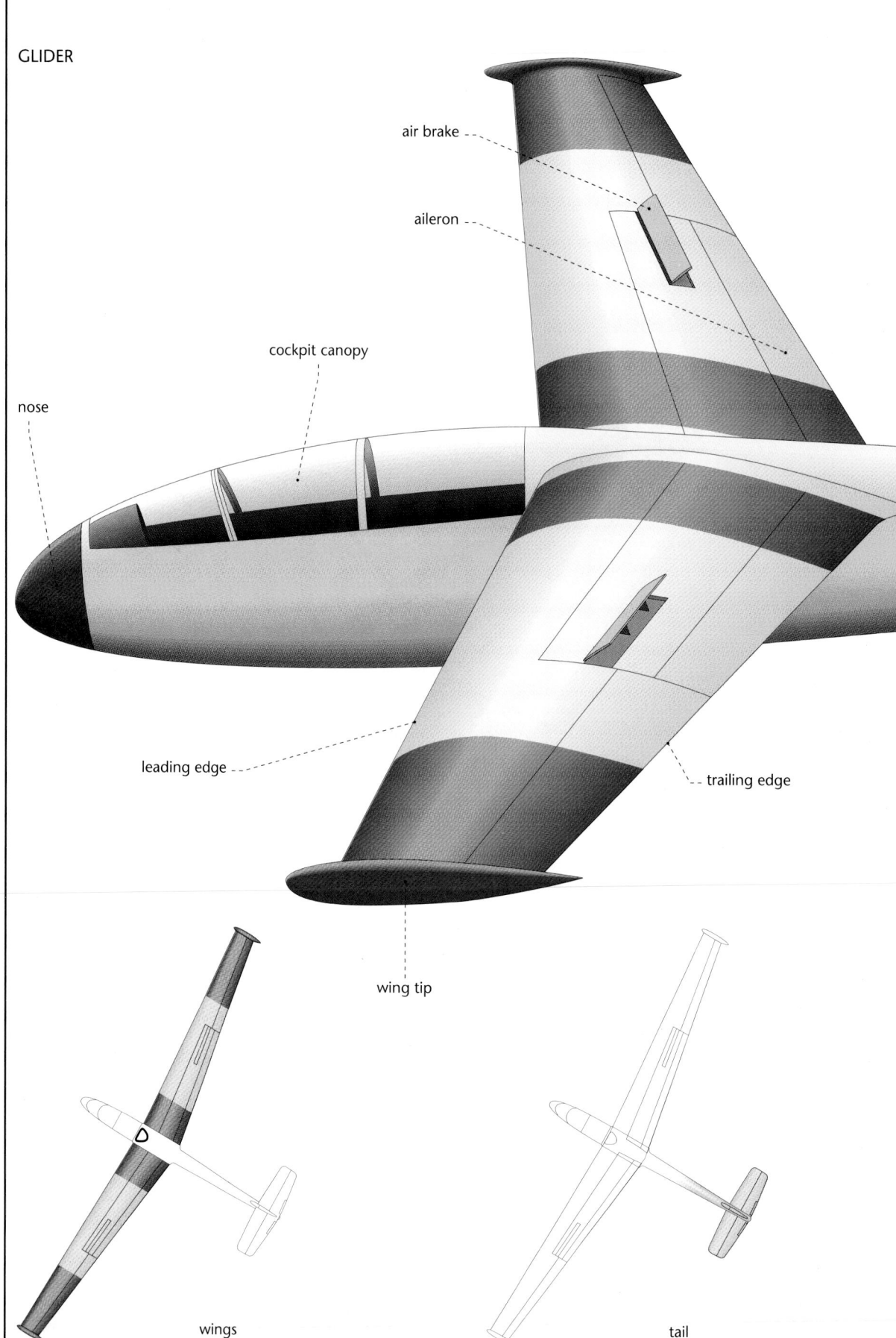

air brake

aileron

cockpit canopy

nose

leading edge

trailing edge

wing tip

wings

tail

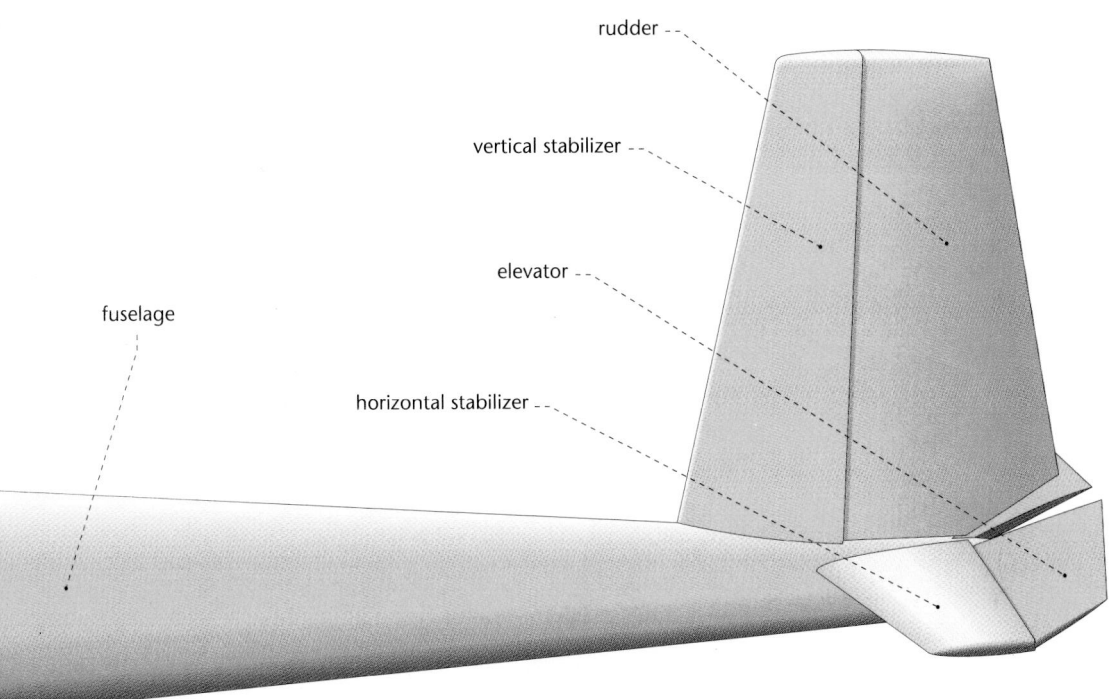

rudder

vertical stabilizer

elevator

fuselage

horizontal stabilizer

COCKPIT

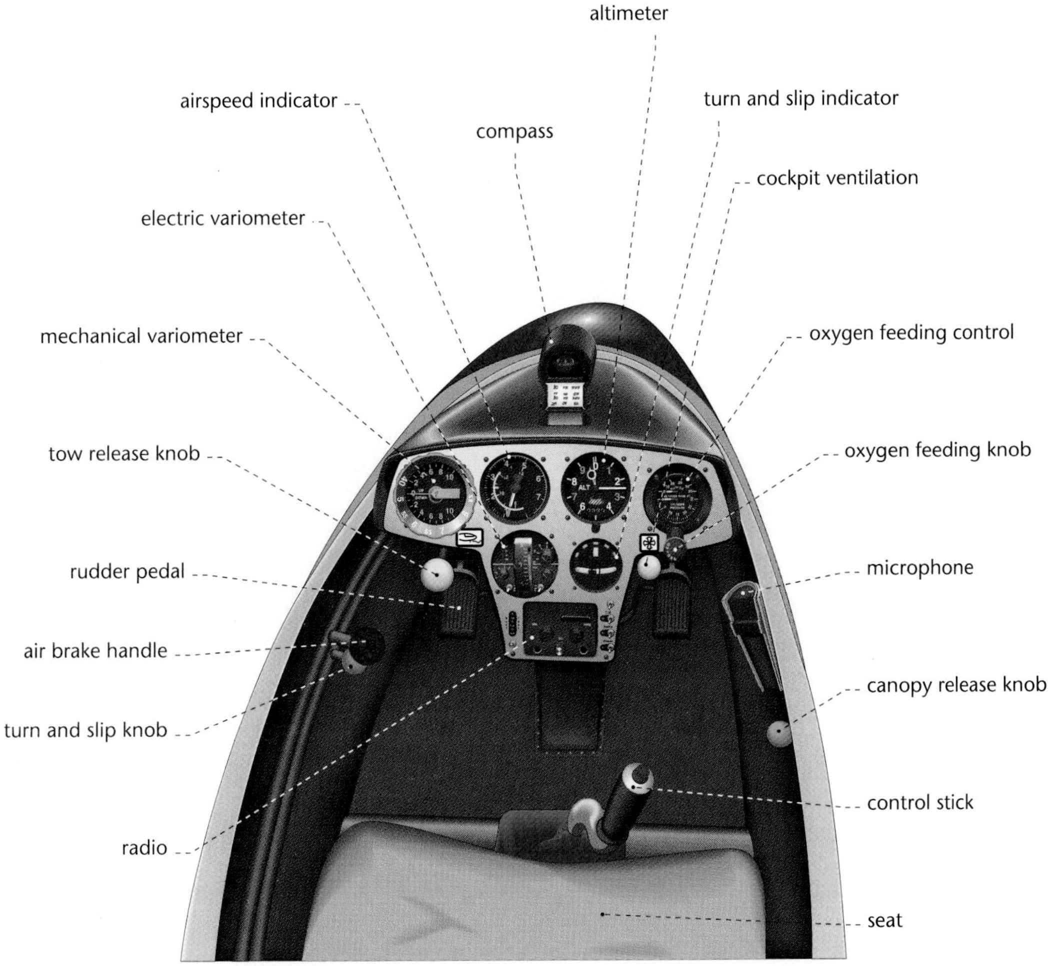

altimeter

airspeed indicator

turn and slip indicator

compass

cockpit ventilation

electric variometer

mechanical variometer

oxygen feeding control

tow release knob

oxygen feeding knob

rudder pedal

microphone

air brake handle

turn and slip knob

canopy release knob

control stick

radio

seat

ALPINE SKIER

ski hat

ski goggles

ski suit

ski glove

handle

wrist strap

ski pole

bottom

ski stop

shovel

edge

heel piece

ski boot

tip

toe piece

SAFETY BINDING

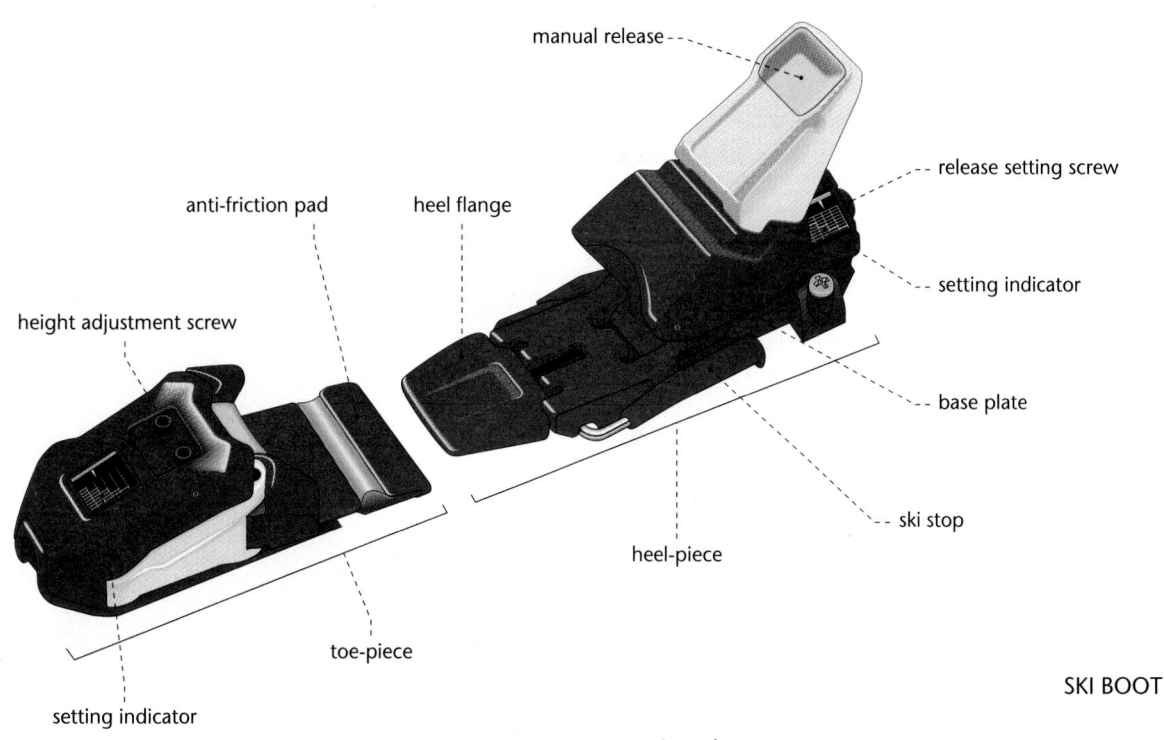

manual release
release setting screw
anti-friction pad
heel flange
setting indicator
height adjustment screw
base plate
ski stop
heel-piece
toe-piece
setting indicator

SKI BOOT

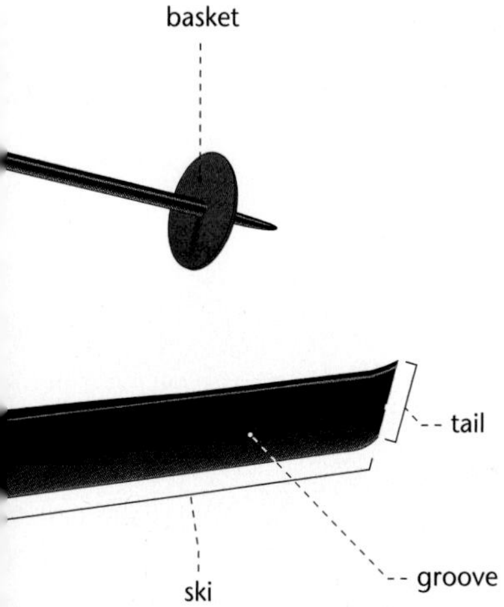

basket
tail
ski
groove

inner boot
upper cuff
tongue
upper
upper strap
buckle
upper shell
wire
adjusting catch
hinge
lower shell
sole

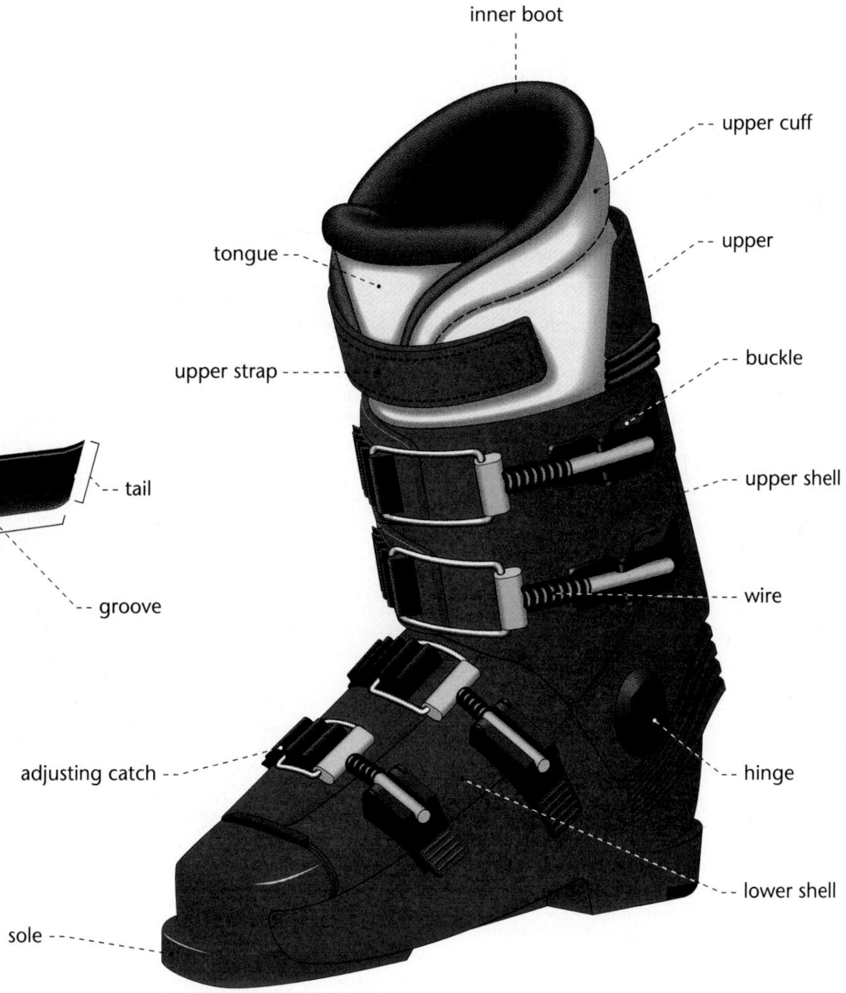

CROSS-COUNTRY SKIER

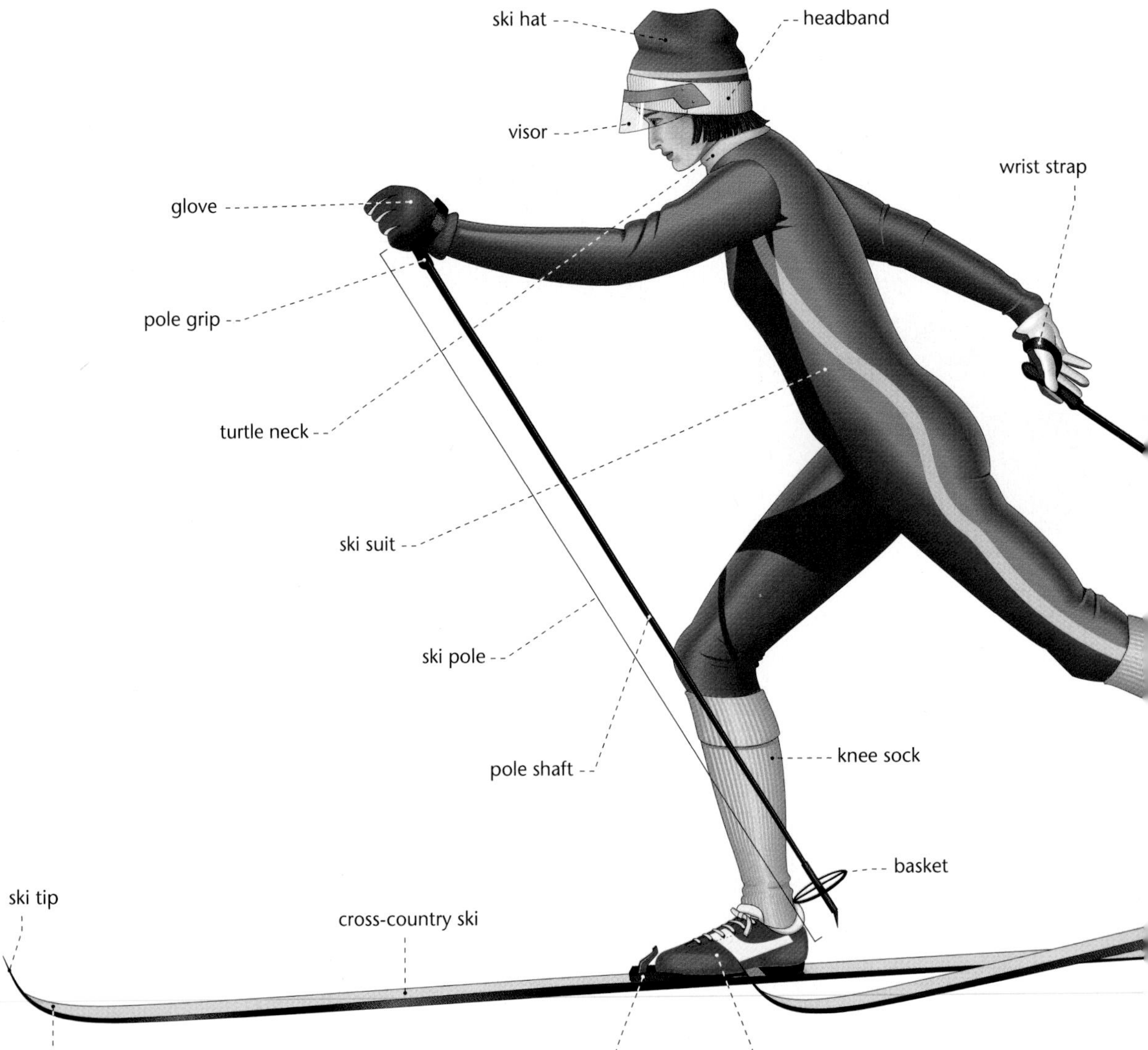

ski hat

headband

visor

wrist strap

glove

pole grip

turtle neck

ski suit

ski pole

knee sock

pole shaft

basket

ski tip

cross-country ski

shovel

binding

touring boot

WINTER SPORTS

CROSS-COUNTRY SKI

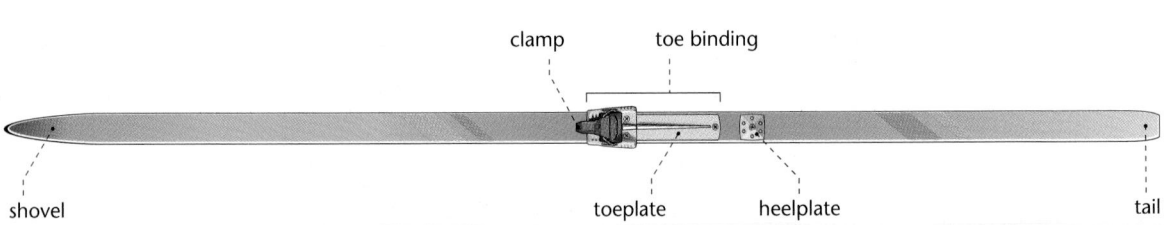

clamp

toe binding

shovel

toeplate

heelplate

tail

642

LUGE

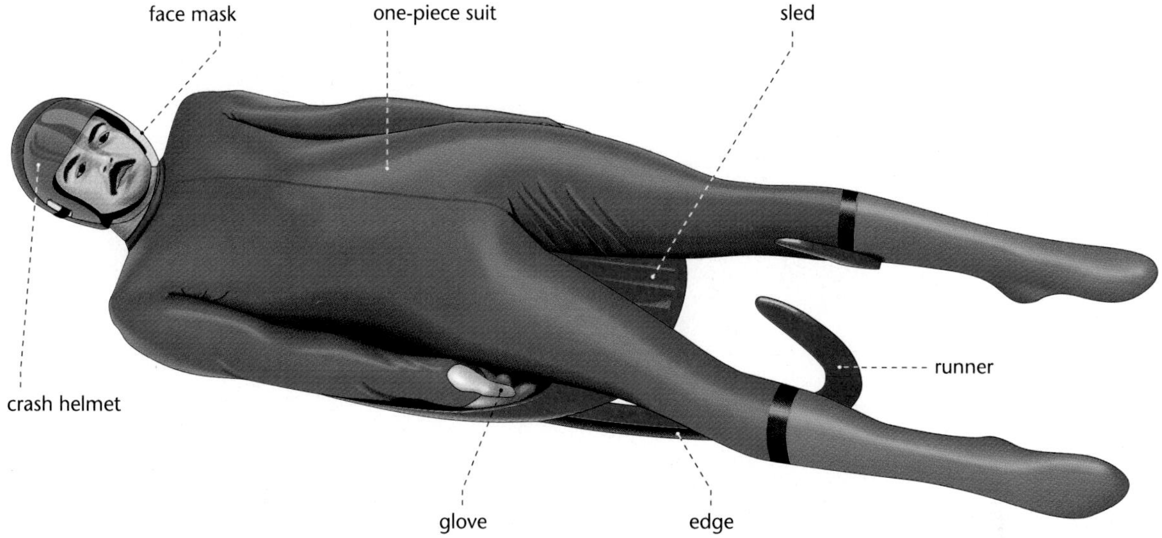

face mask

one-piece suit

sled

crash helmet

glove

edge

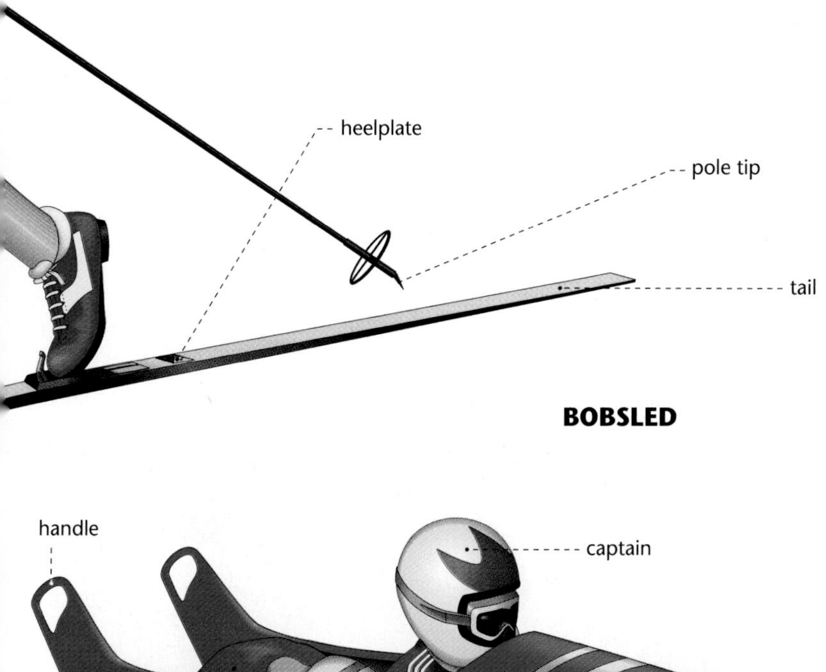

runner

heelplate

pole tip

tail

BOBSLED

handle

captain

shell

brakeman

rear runner

front runner

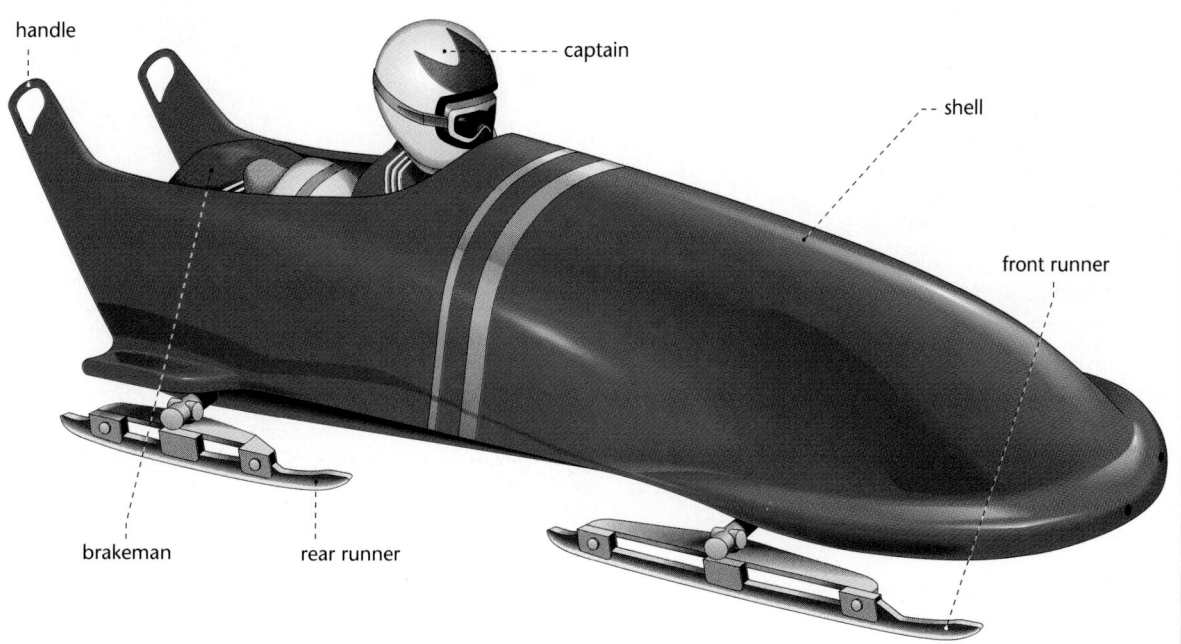

SKATING

FIGURE SKATE

tongue

lining

hook

backstay

lace

boot

heel

eyelet

sole

stanchion

edge

toe pick

blade

HOCKEY SKATE

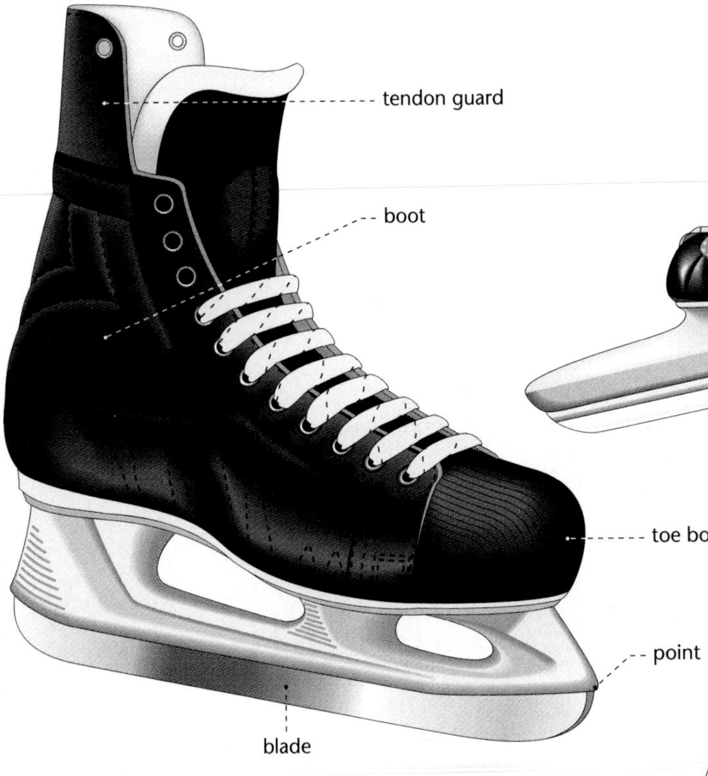

speed skate

tendon guard

boot

toe box

point

skate guard

blade

644

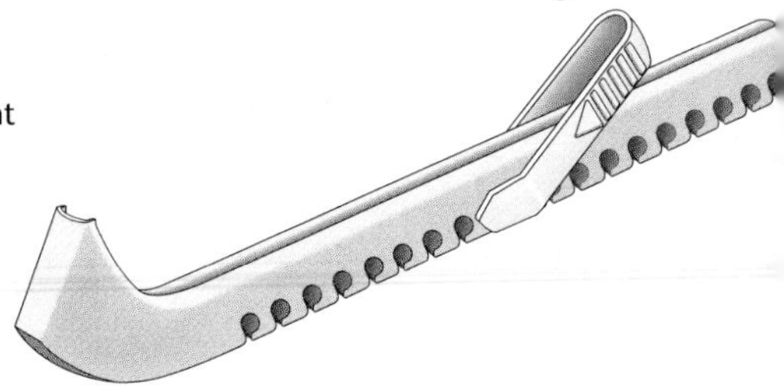

SNOWSHOE

MICHIGAN SNOWSHOE

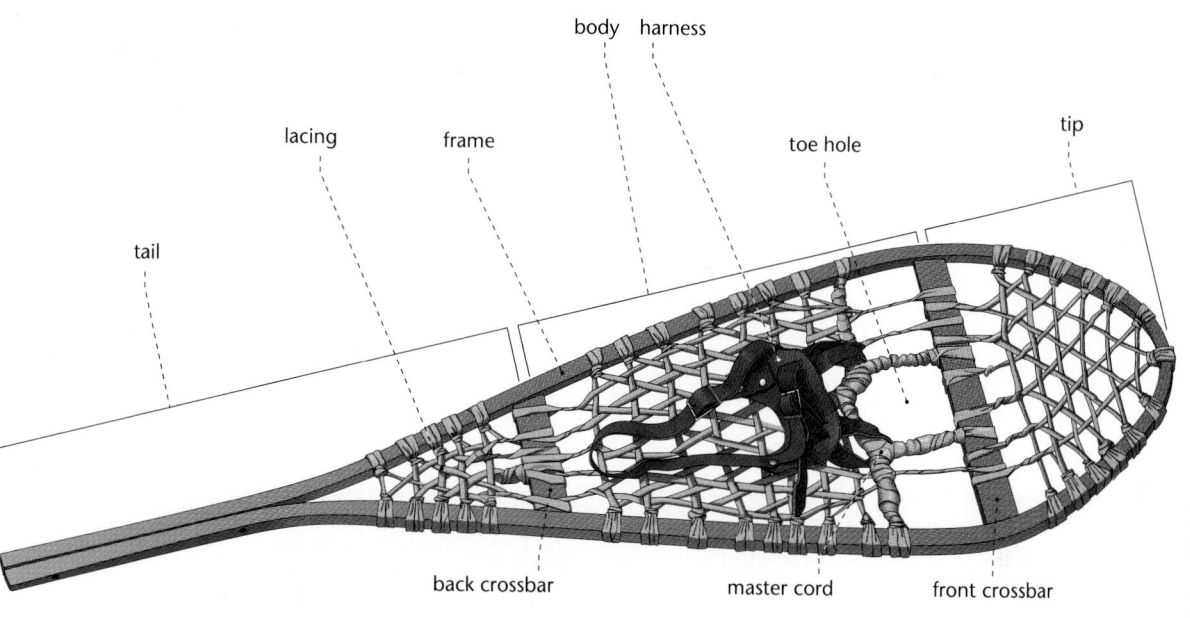

body   harness

lacing   frame   toe hole   tip

tail

back crossbar   master cord   front crossbar

ROLLER SKATE

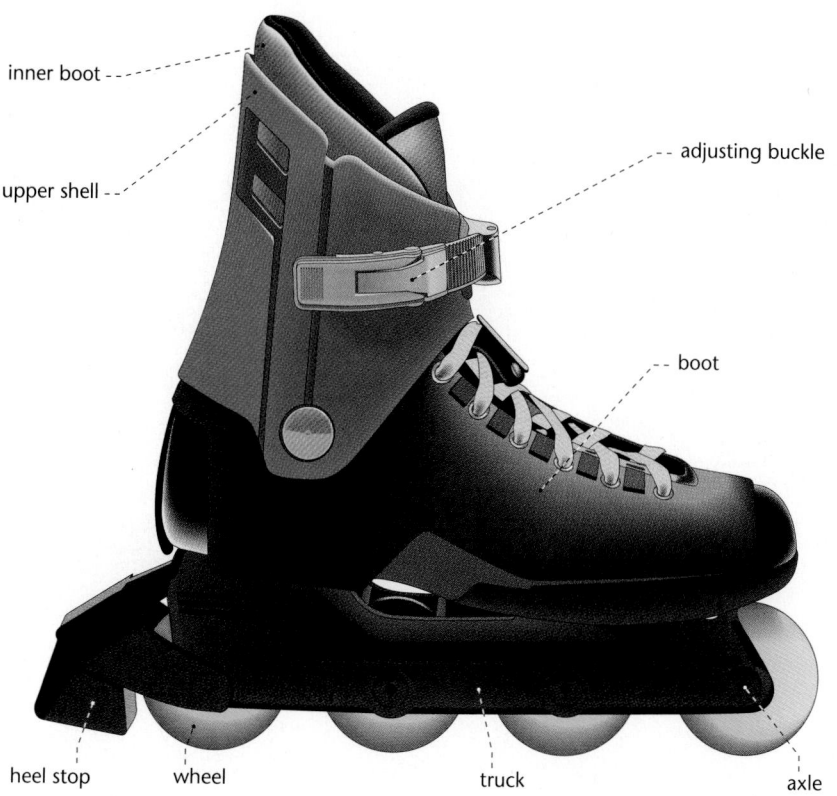

inner boot

adjusting buckle

upper shell

boot

heel stop   wheel   truck   axle

645

COMPETITION RING

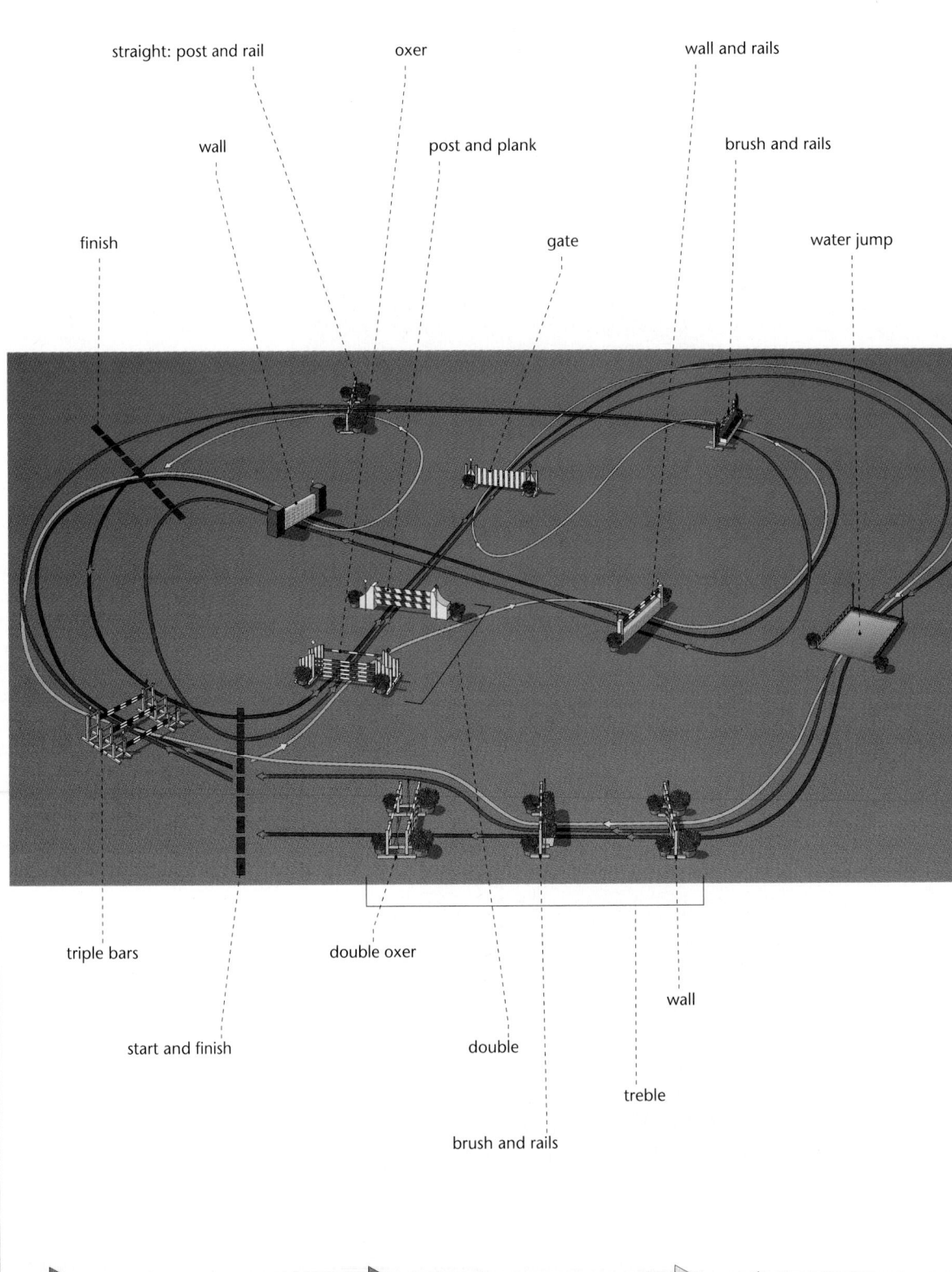

straight: post and rail

oxer

wall and rails

wall

post and plank

brush and rails

finish

gate

water jump

triple bars

double oxer

wall

start and finish

double

treble

brush and rails

expert drivers course   beginner's course   speed course

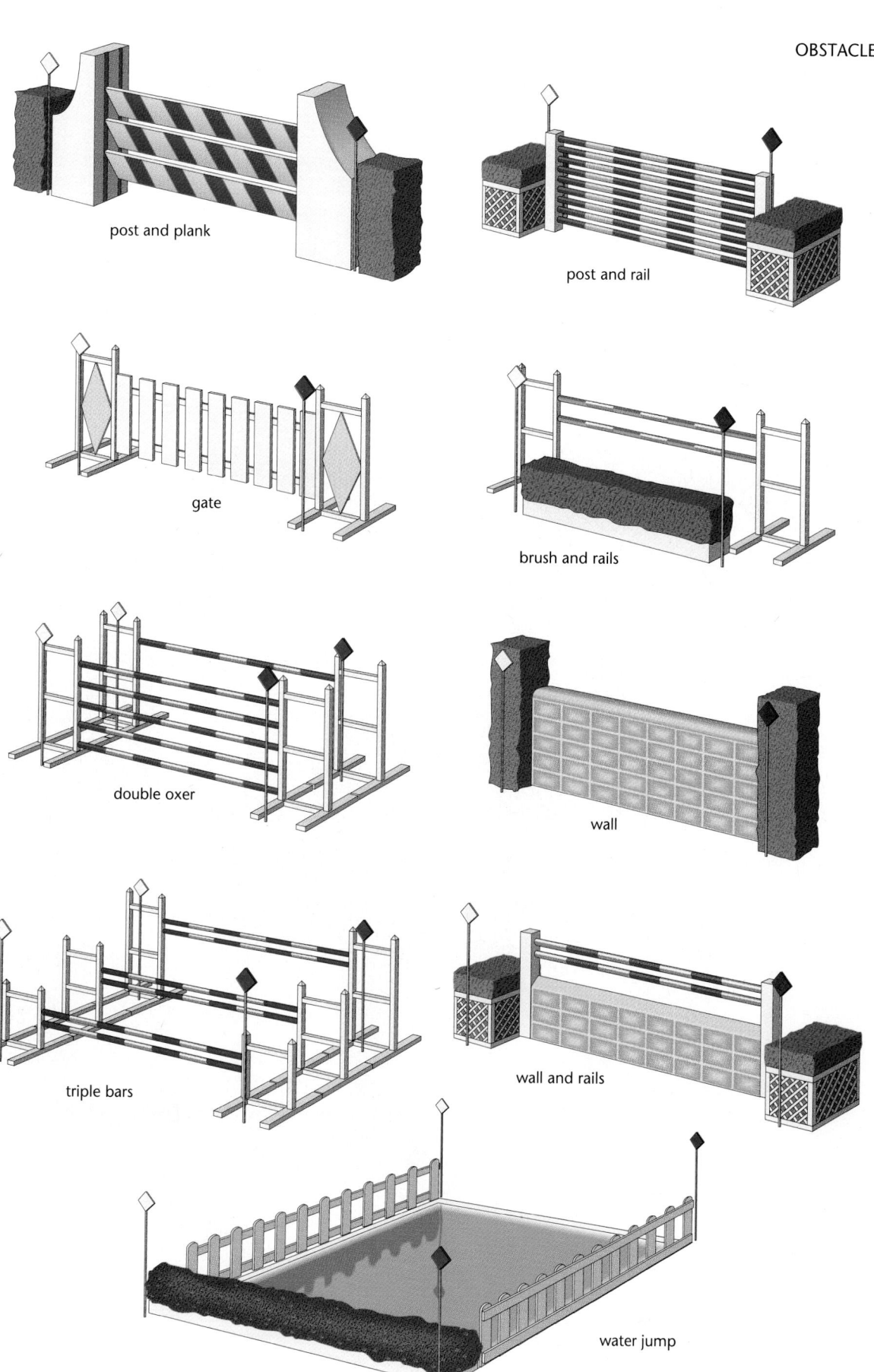

post and plank

post and rail

gate

brush and rails

double oxer

wall

triple bars

wall and rails

water jump

647

RIDER

EQUESTRIAN SPORTS

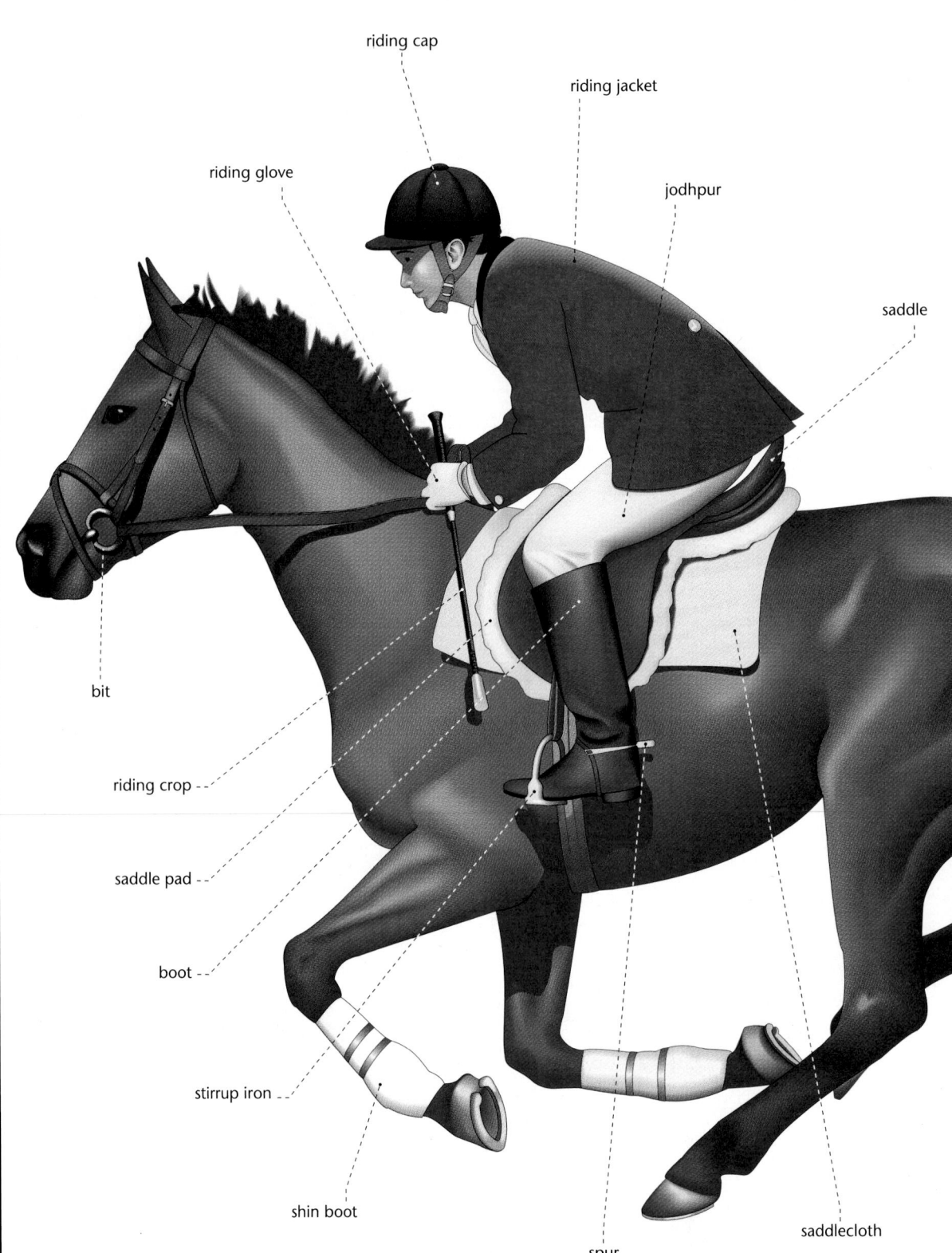

riding cap

riding jacket

jodhpur

riding glove

saddle

bit

riding crop

saddle pad

boot

stirrup iron

shin boot

spur

saddlecloth

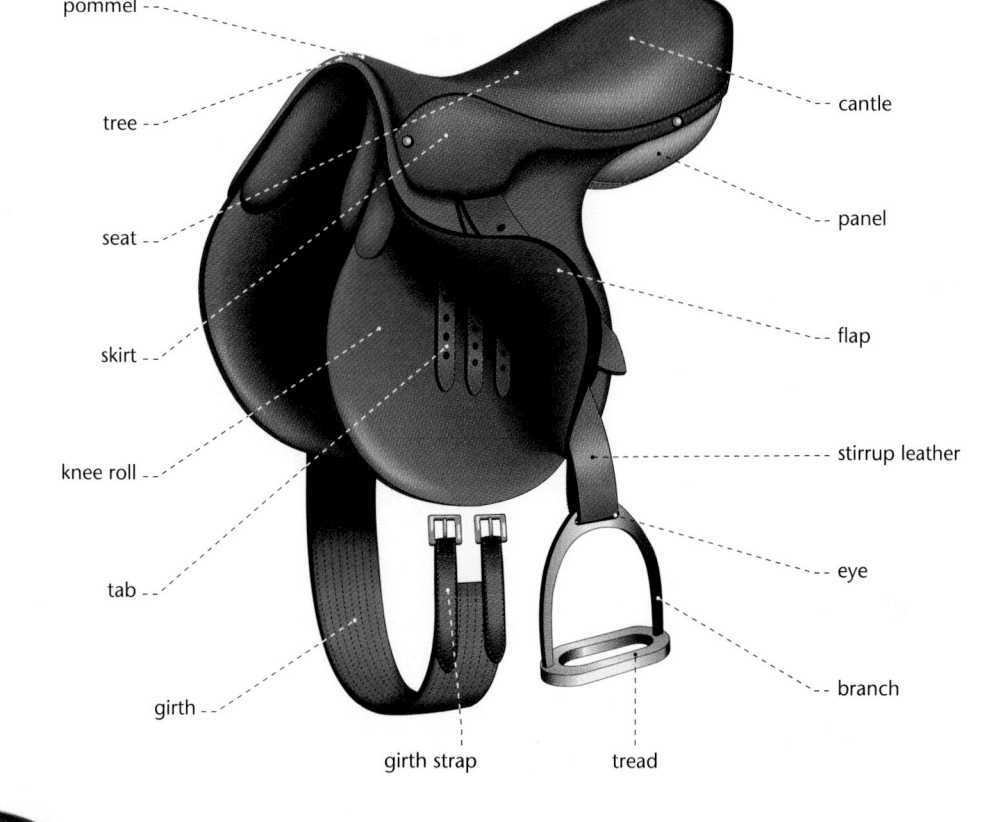

pommel

tree

seat

skirt

knee roll

tab

girth

cantle

panel

flap

stirrup leather

eye

branch

girth strap

tread

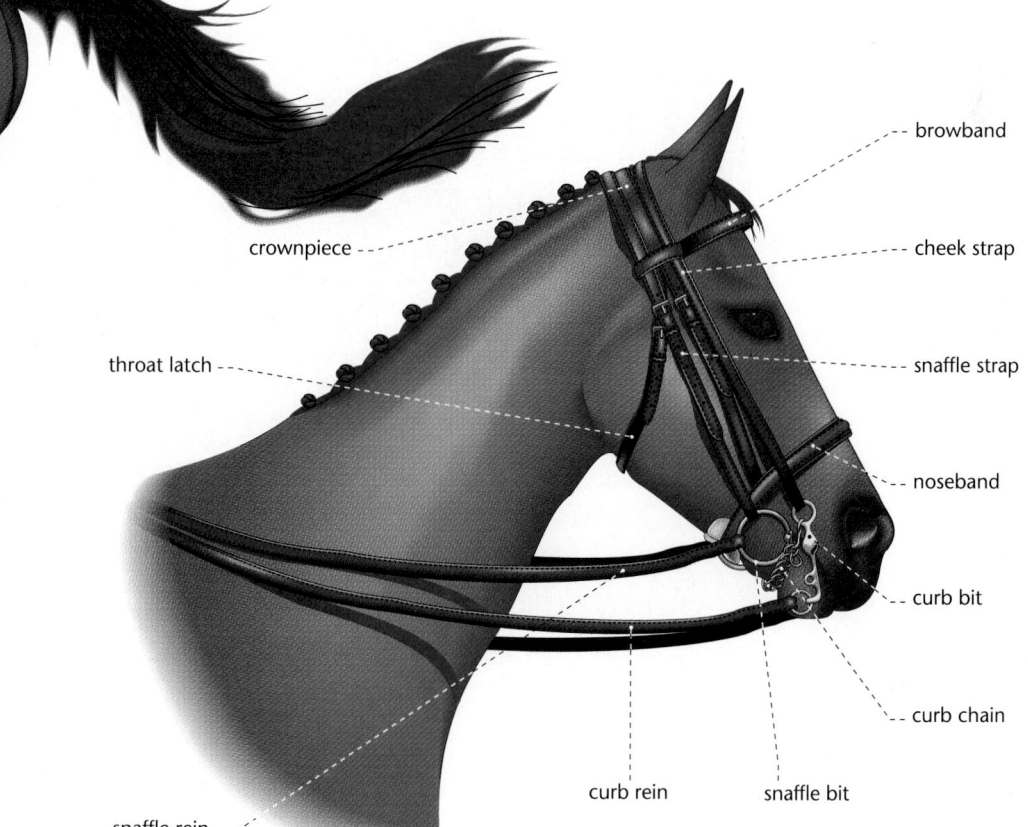

crownpiece

throat latch

snaffle rein

browband

cheek strap

snaffle strap

noseband

curb bit

curb chain

curb rein

snaffle bit

EQUESTRIAN SPORTS

649

TYPES OF BITS

SNAFFLE BIT

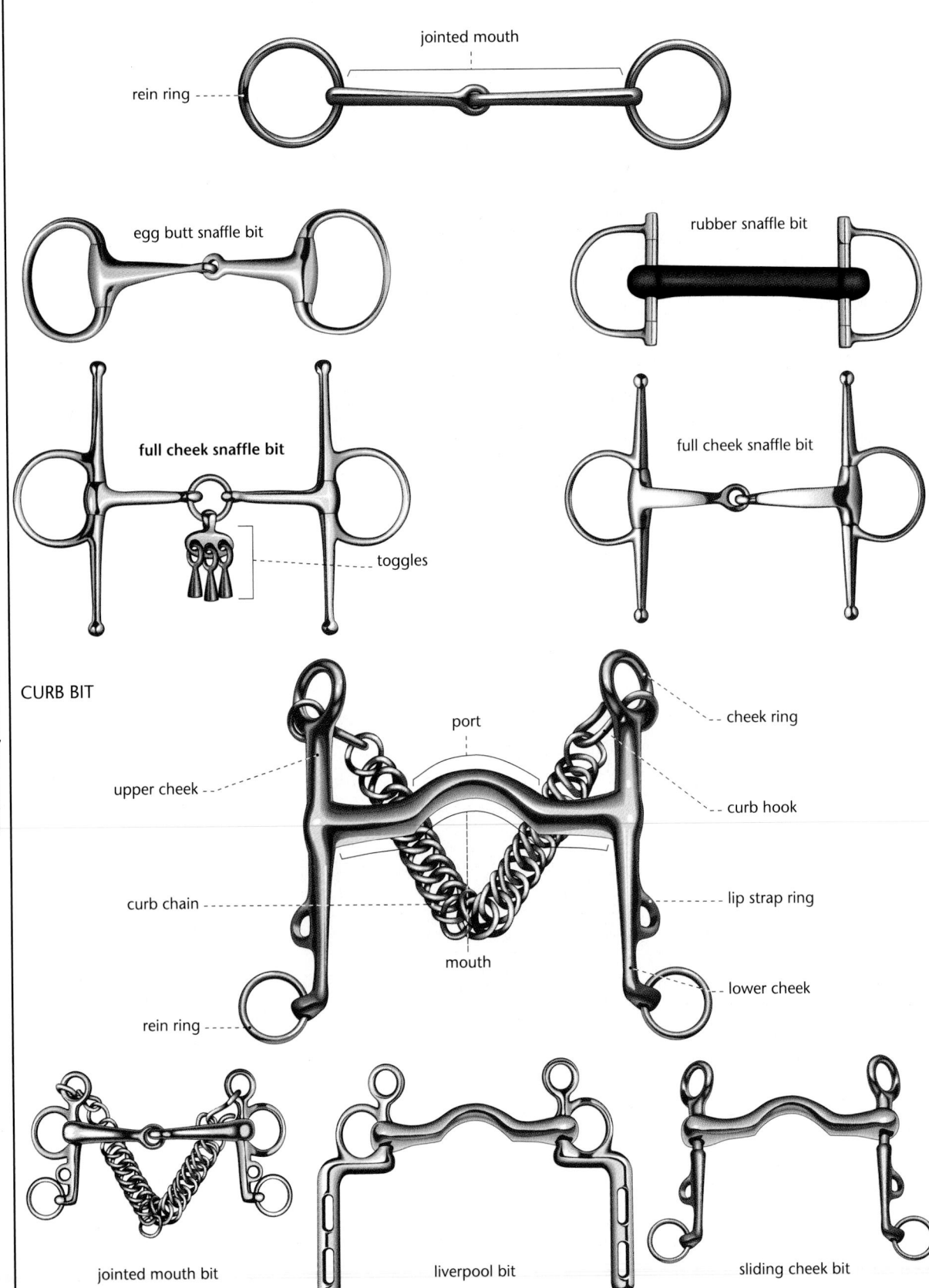

jointed mouth

rein ring

egg butt snaffle bit

rubber snaffle bit

full cheek snaffle bit

full cheek snaffle bit

toggles

CURB BIT

port

cheek ring

upper cheek

curb hook

curb chain

lip strap ring

mouth

lower cheek

rein ring

jointed mouth bit

liverpool bit

sliding cheek bit

HORSE RACING

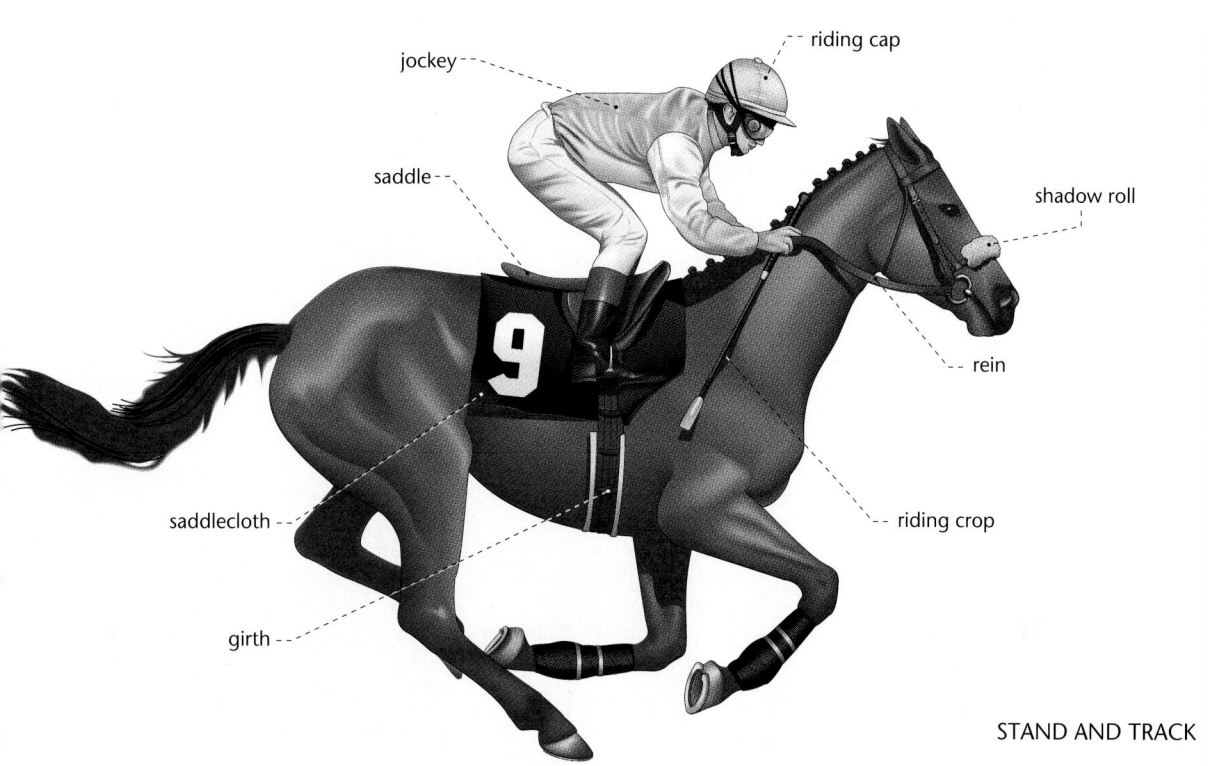

jockey

riding cap

saddle

shadow roll

rein

saddlecloth

riding crop

girth

STAND AND TRACK

far turn

length post

backstretch

stable

clubhouse

clubhouse turn

tote board

judge's stand

finishing line

paddock

grandstand

homestretch

furlong chute

STANDARDBRED PACER

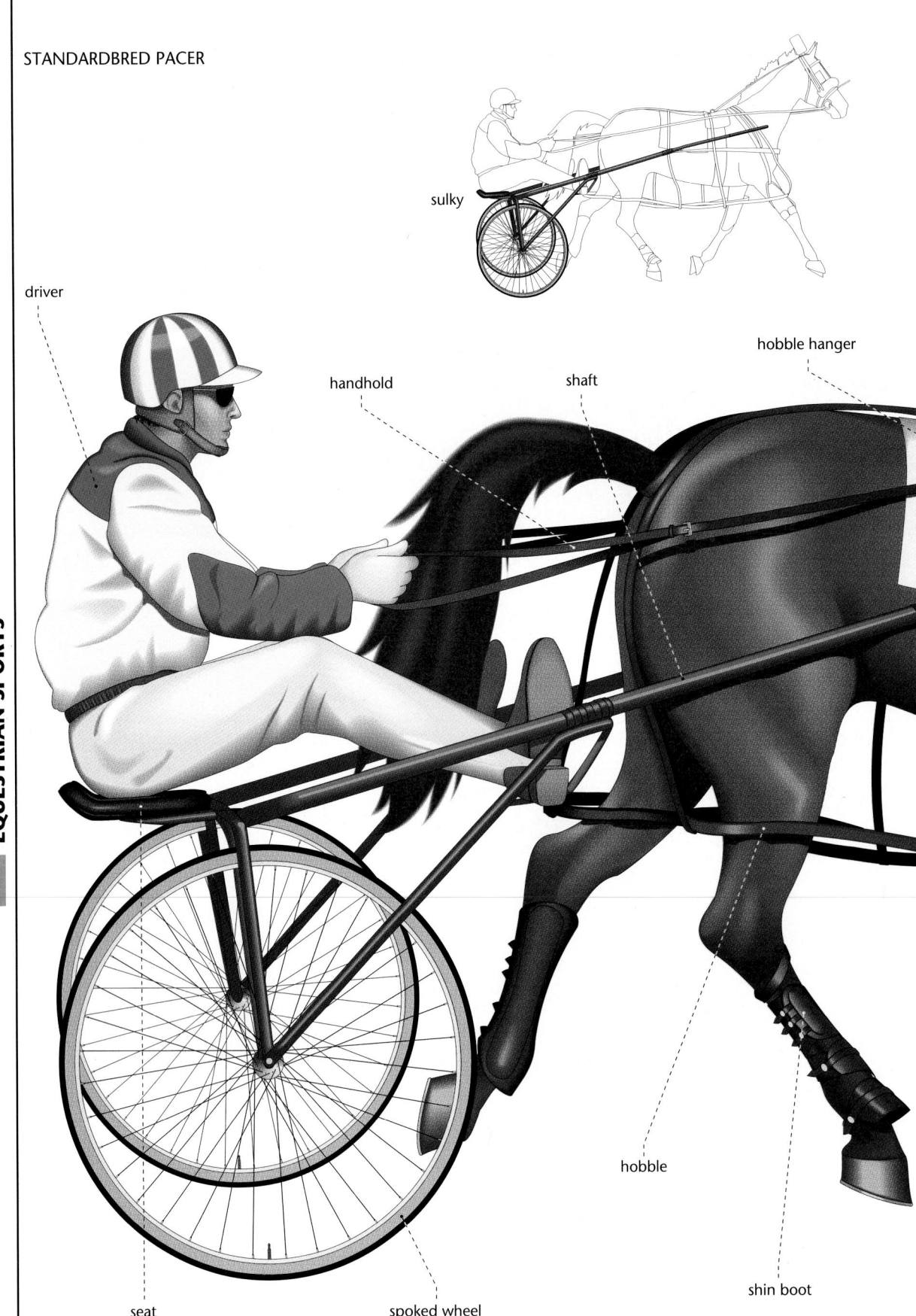

sulky

driver

hobble hanger

handhold

shaft

hobble

shin boot

seat

spoked wheel

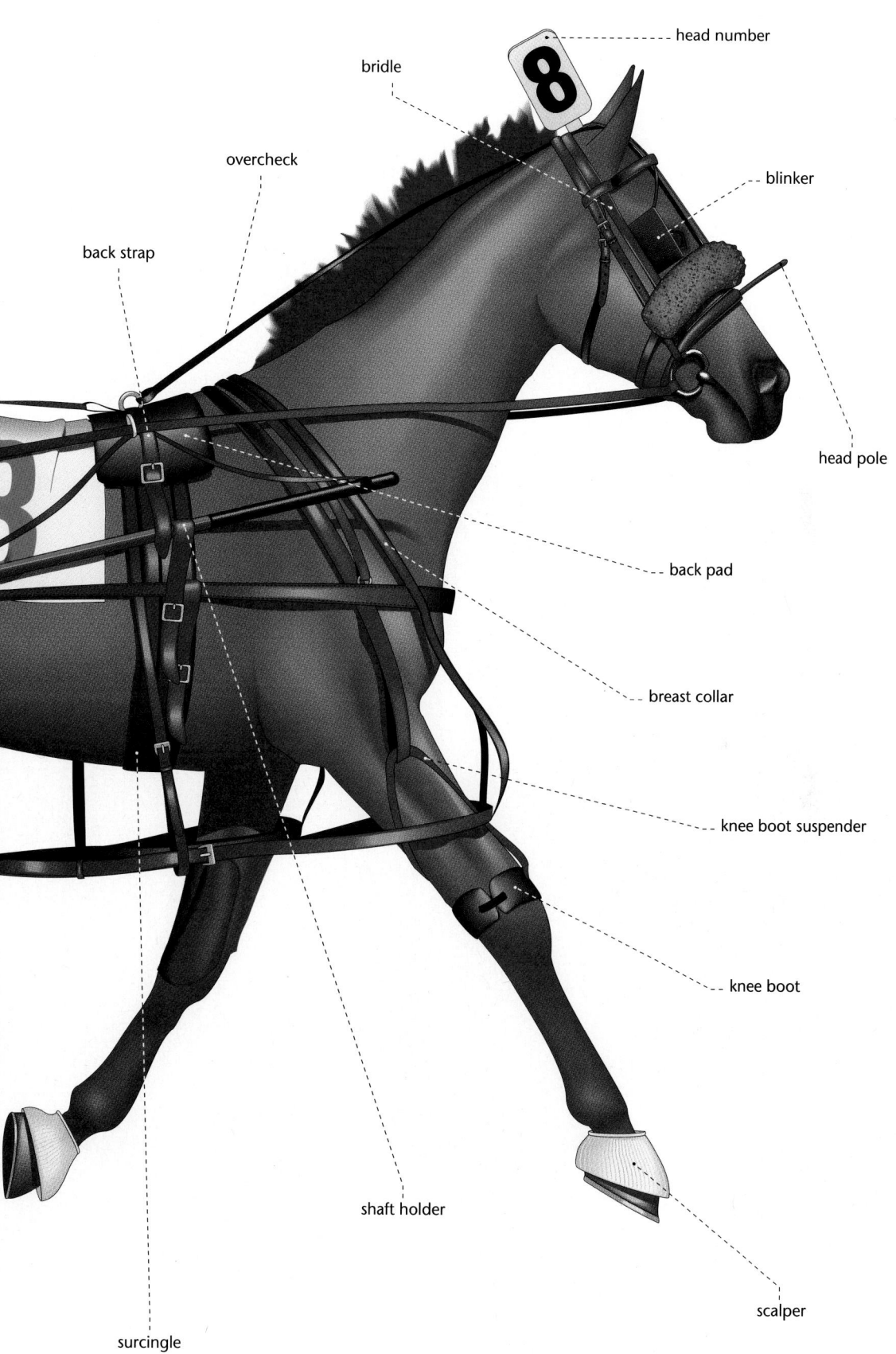

head number

bridle

overcheck

blinker

back strap

head pole

back pad

breast collar

knee boot suspender

knee boot

shaft holder

scalper

surcingle

ARENA

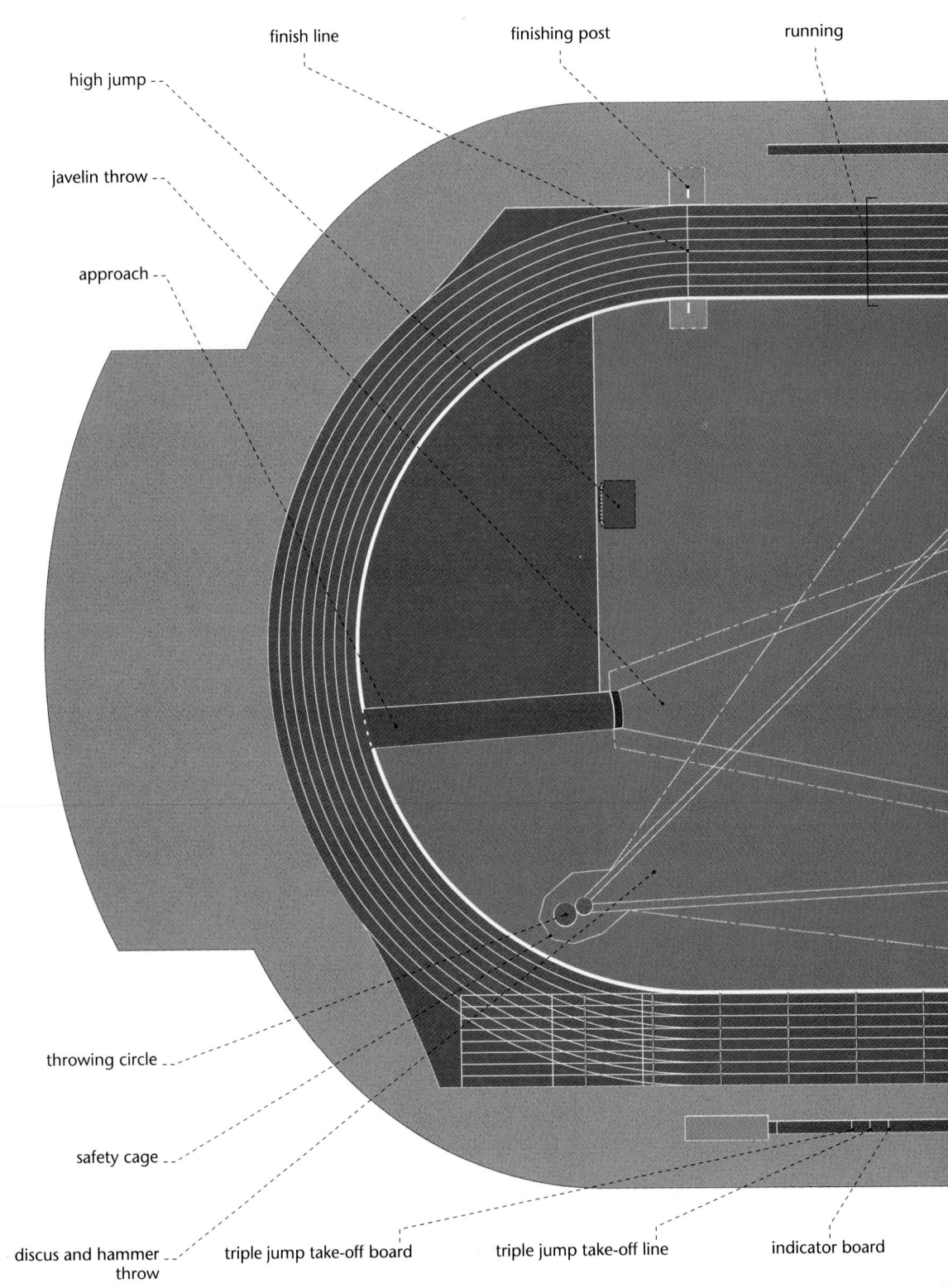

finish line

finishing post

running

high jump

javelin throw

approach

throwing circle

safety cage

discus and hammer throw

triple jump take-off board

triple jump take-off line

indicator board

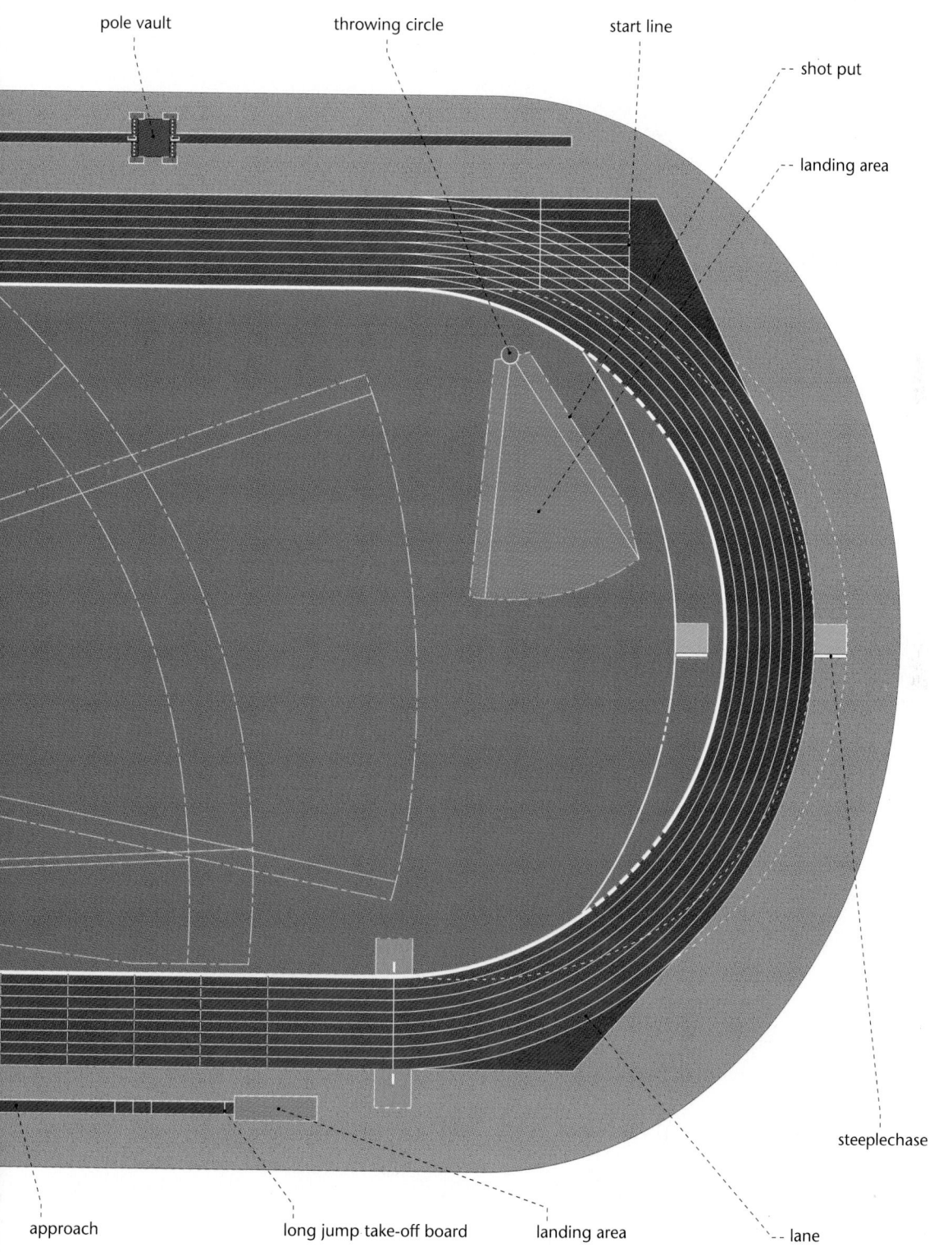

pole vault

throwing circle

start line

shot put

landing area

ATHLETICS

steeplechase

approach

long jump take-off board

landing area

lane

ATHLETICS

STARTING BLOCK

shirt

number

shorts

track shoe

anchor

start line

rack

base

lane line

notch

pedal

spike

block

hurdle

steeple hurdle

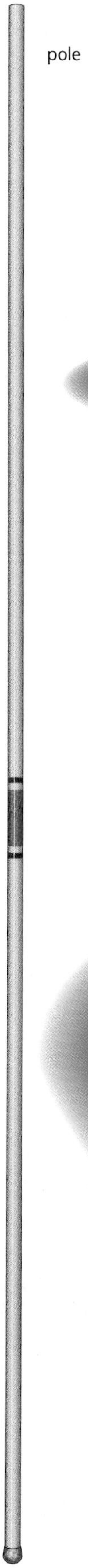

pole

HIGH JUMP

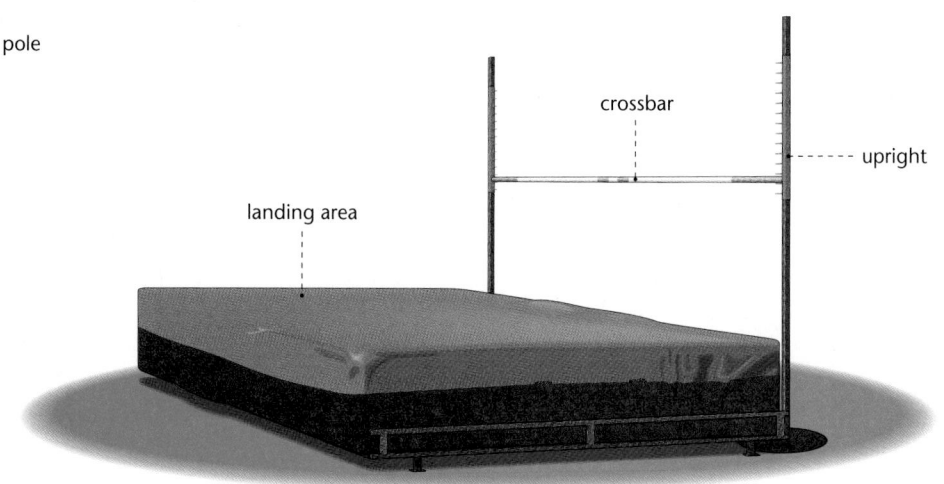

crossbar
upright
landing area

POLE VAULT

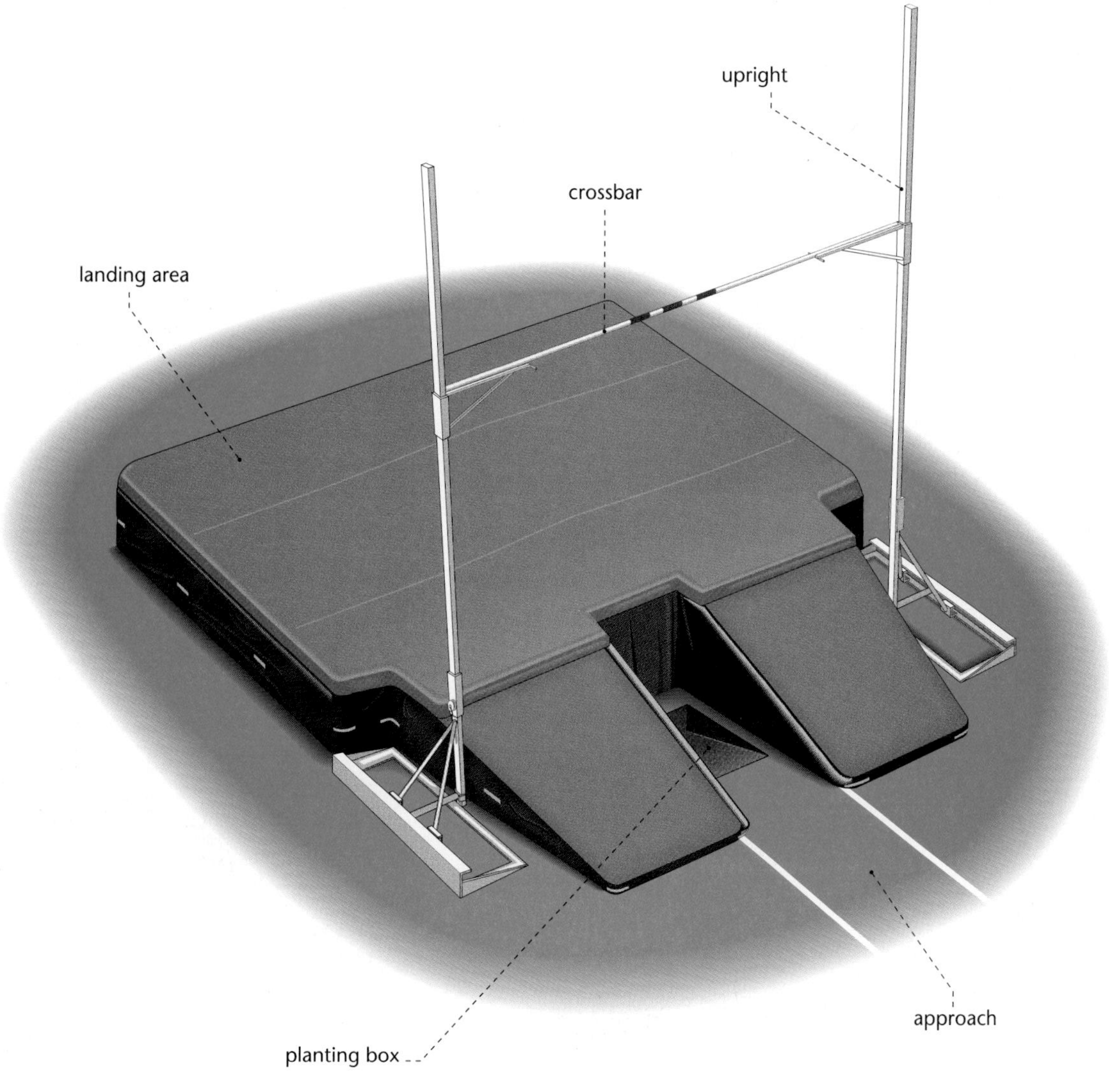

upright
crossbar
landing area
approach
planting box

THROWINGS

ATHLETICS

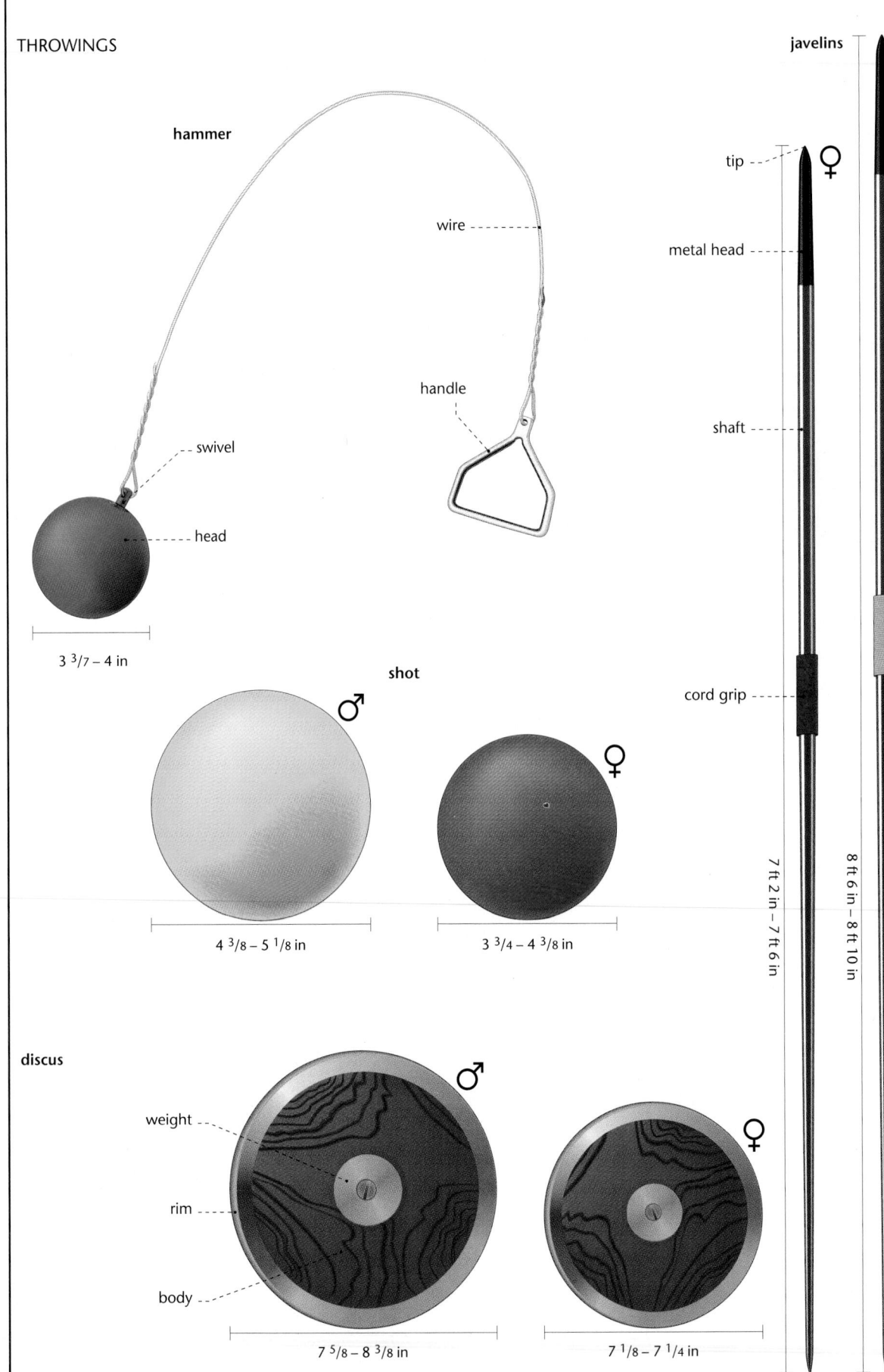

hammer

wire

handle

swivel

head

3 $^3/_7$ – 4 in

shot

♂

♀

4 $^3/_8$ – 5 $^1/_8$ in

3 $^3/_4$ – 4 $^3/_8$ in

discus

weight

rim

body

♂

♀

7 $^5/_8$ – 8 $^3/_8$ in

7 $^1/_8$ – 7 $^1/_4$ in

javelins

♂

♀

tip

metal head

shaft

cord grip

7 ft 2 in – 7 ft 6 in

8 ft 6 in – 8 ft 10 in

GYMNASTICS

vaulting horse

ASYMMETRICAL BARS

top bar

low bar

adjusting tube

springboard

BALANCE BEAM

beam

upright

height adjustment

TRAMPOLINE

safety pad

bed

spring

frame

leg

RINGS

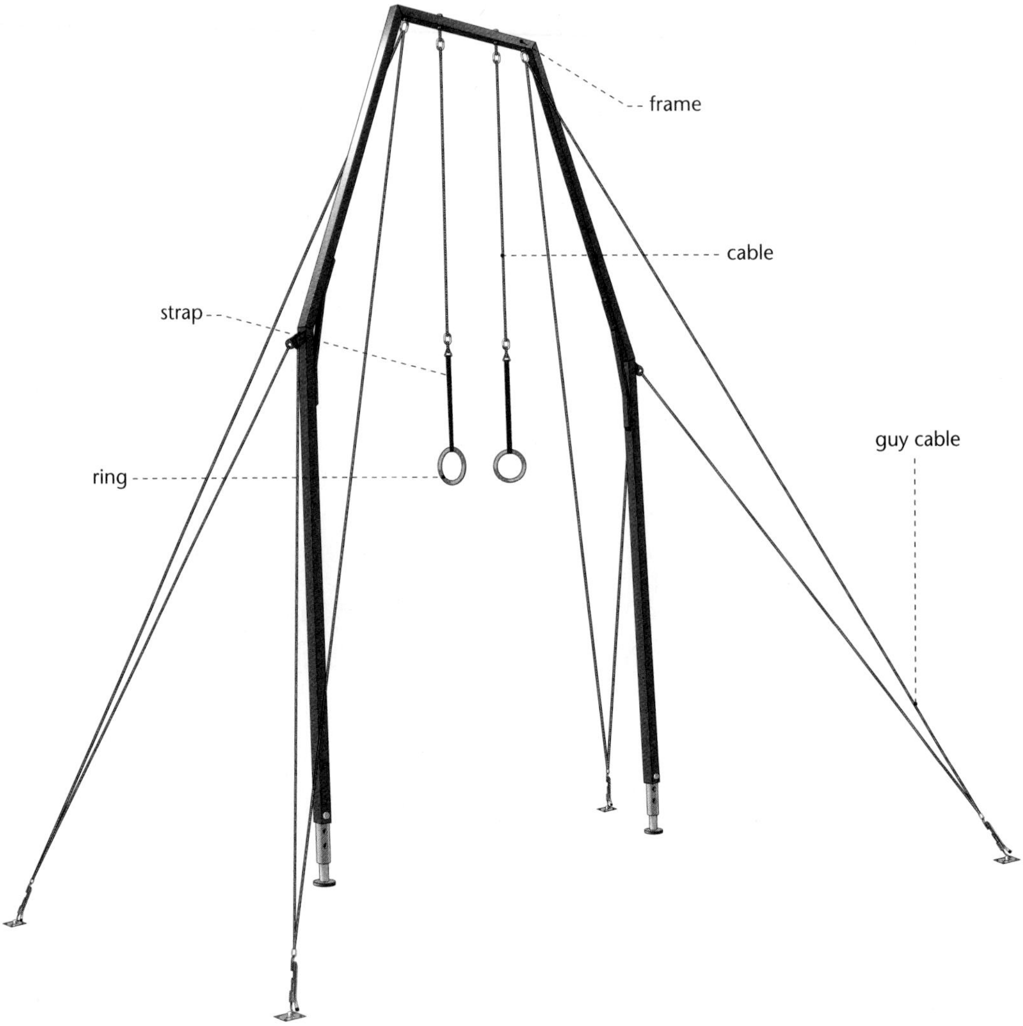

frame

cable

strap

ring

guy cable

HORIZONTAL BAR

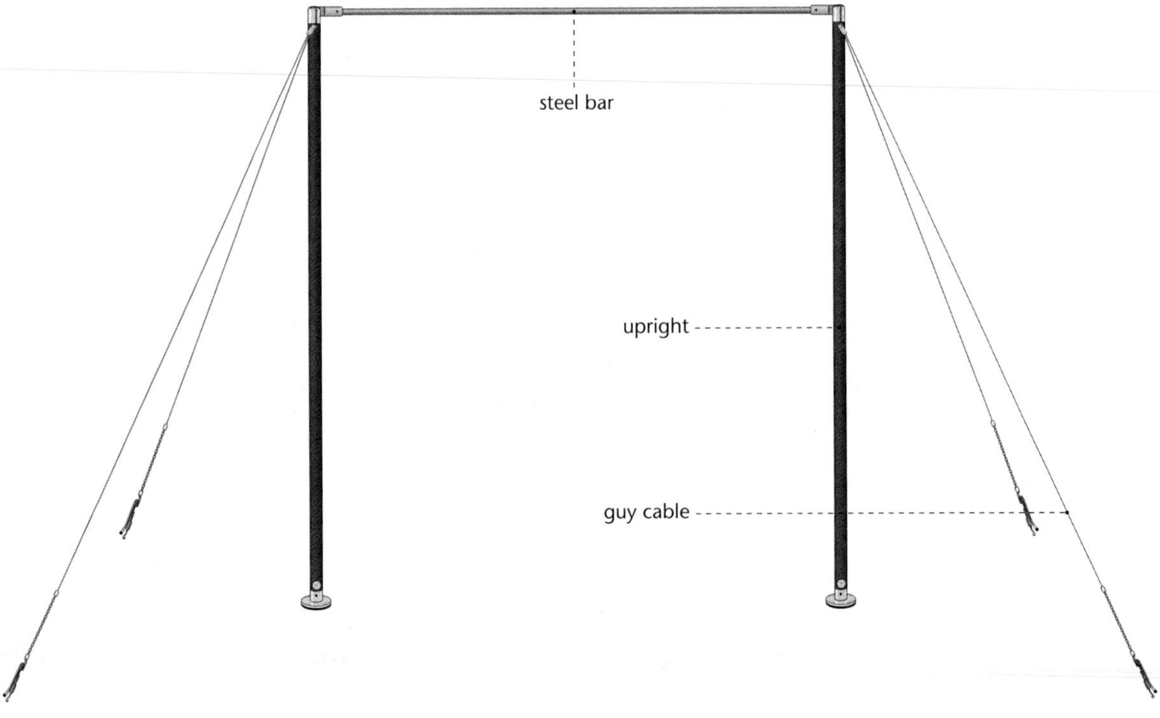

steel bar

upright

guy cable

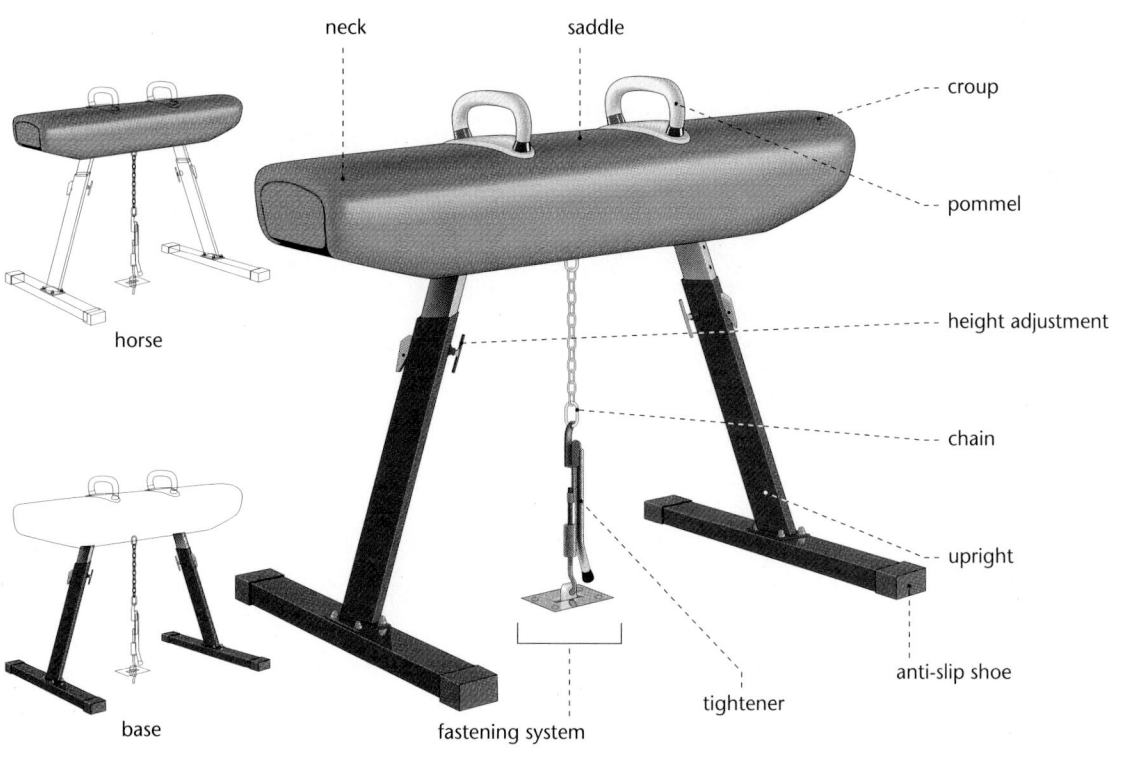

neck

saddle

croup

pommel

height adjustment

chain

upright

anti-slip shoe

tightener

horse

base

fastening system

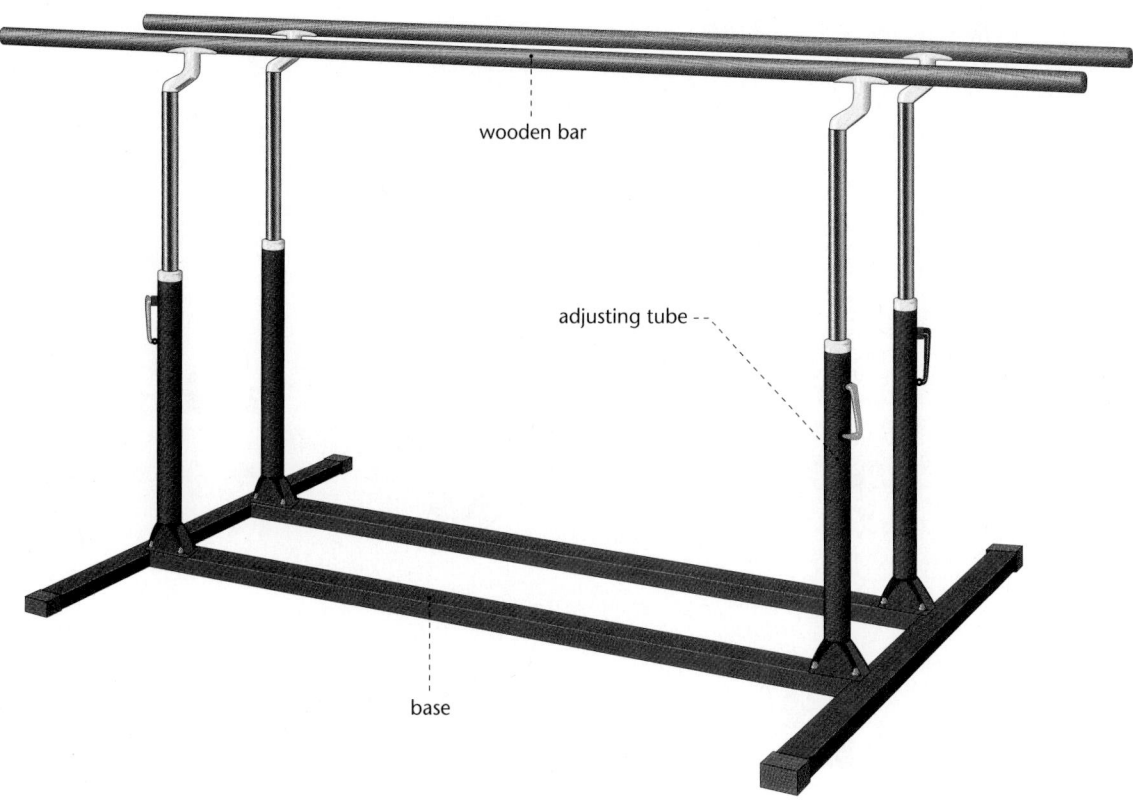

wooden bar

adjusting tube

base

WEIGHTLIFTING

WEIGHTLIFTER

sleeve

gauze bandage

sleeveless jersey

weightlifting belt

trunks

weightlifting shoe

strap

TWO-HAND SNATCH

TWO-HAND CLEAN AND JERK

FITNESS EQUIPMENT

WEIGHT STACK EXERCISE UNIT

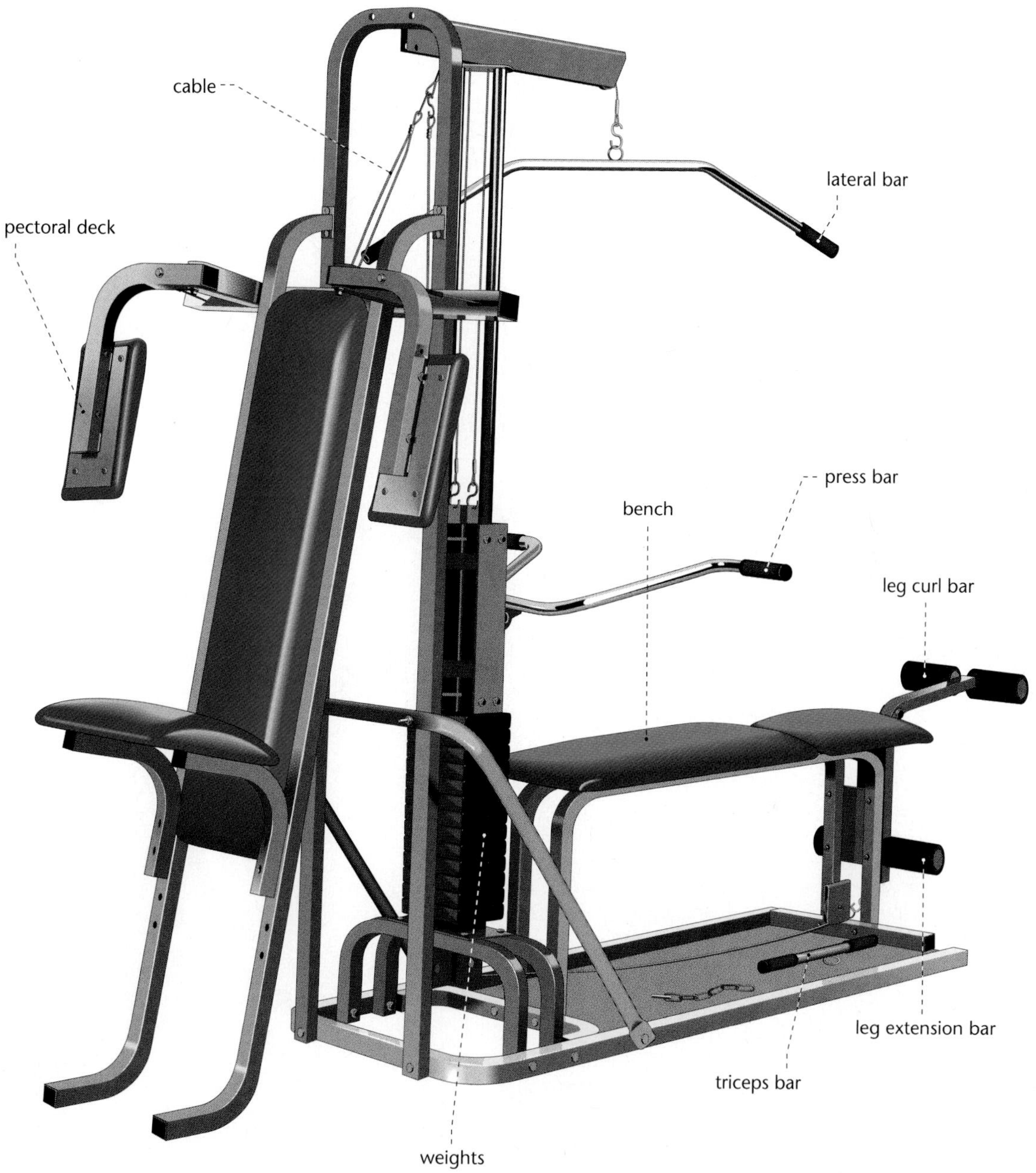

cable

lateral bar

pectoral deck

press bar

bench

leg curl bar

leg extension bar

triceps bar

weights

BARBELL

bar

disk

collar

sleeve

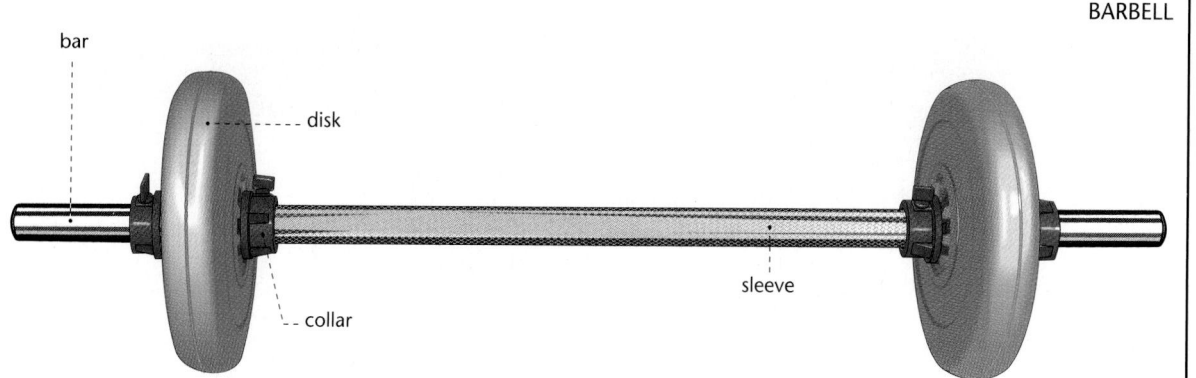

FITNESS EQUIPMENT

STATIONARY BICYCLE

resistance adjustment

handlebar

seat

timer

speedometer

height adjustment

footstrap

pedal

climber

brake

flywheel

ROWER

push-up stand

oar

hydraulic resistance

foot support

free-rolling seat

DUMBBELL

handgrips

weight

bar

ankle/wrist weight

jump rope

TWIST BAR

grip

tension spring

chest expander

FENCING

PARTS OF THE WEAPON

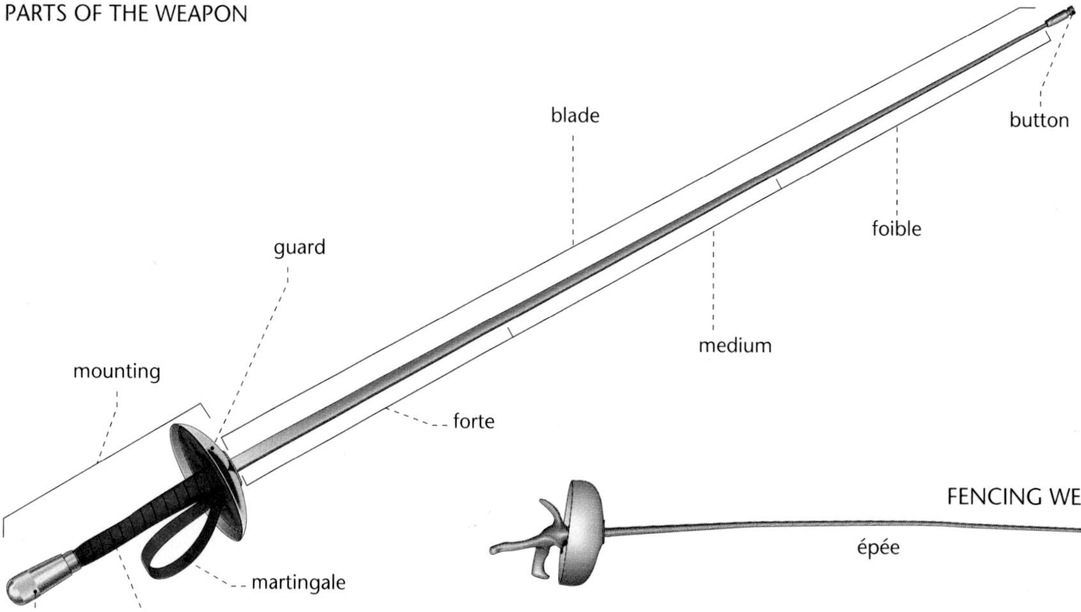

blade

button

guard

foible

mounting

medium

forte

martingale

handle

pommel

FENCING WEAPONS

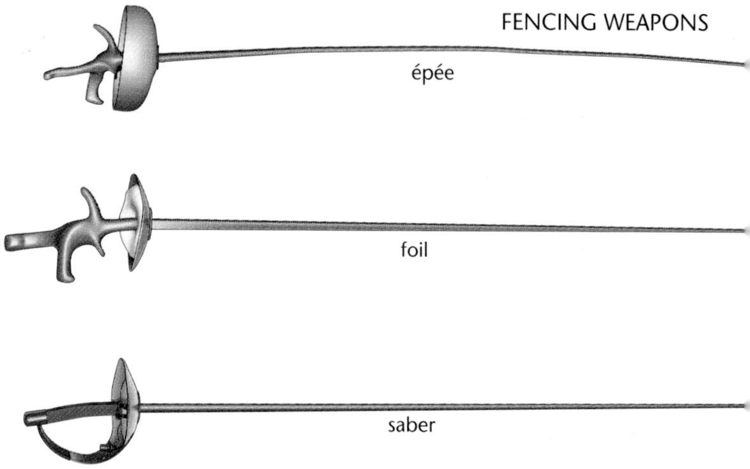

épée

foil

saber

PISTE

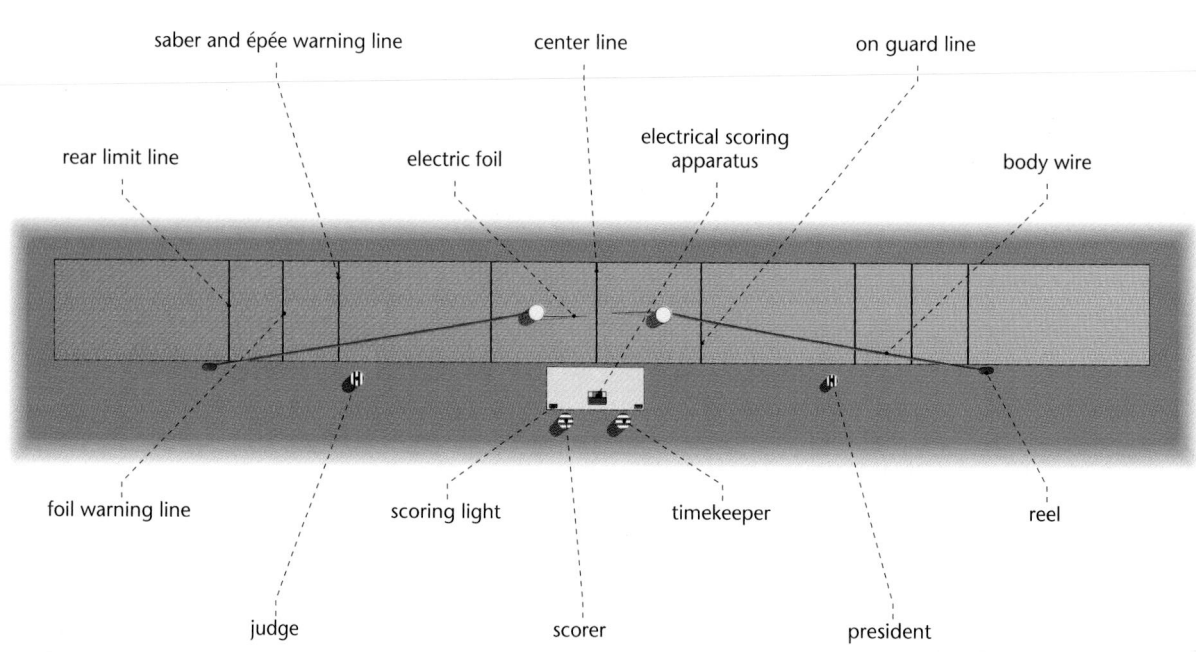

saber and épée warning line

center line

on guard line

rear limit line

electric foil

electrical scoring apparatus

body wire

foil warning line

scoring light

timekeeper

reel

judge

scorer

president

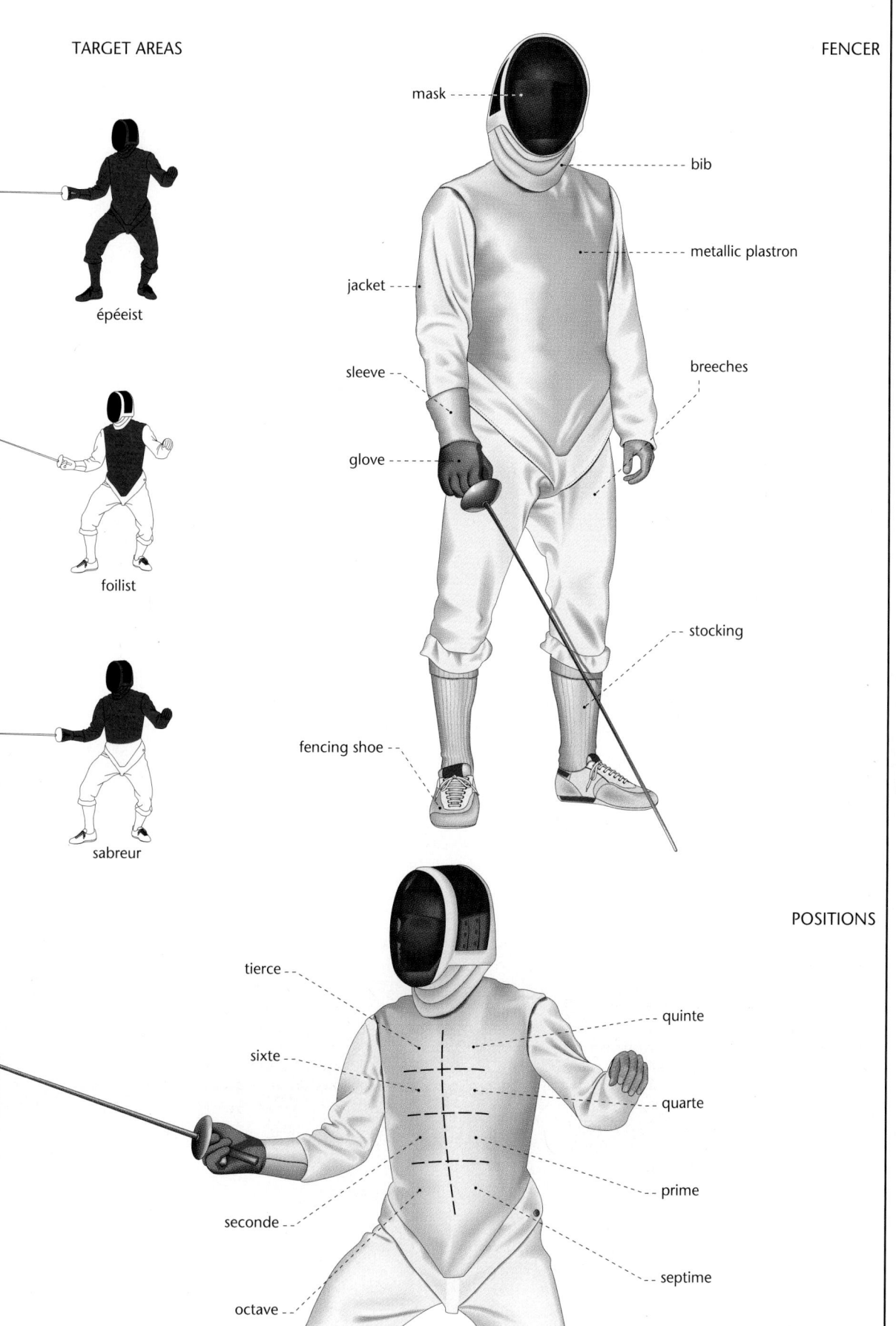

TARGET AREAS

épéeist

foilist

sabreur

FENCER

mask

bib

metallic plastron

jacket

sleeve

glove

breeches

stocking

fencing shoe

POSITIONS

tierce

quinte

sixte

quarte

prime

seconde

septime

octave

JUDO

JUDO SUIT

- jacket
- belt
- trousers

EXAMPLES OF HOLDS

arm lock

holding

major outer reaping throw

one-arm shoulder throw

major inner reaping throw

naked strangle

stomach throw

sweeping hip throw

COMBAT SPORTS

MAT

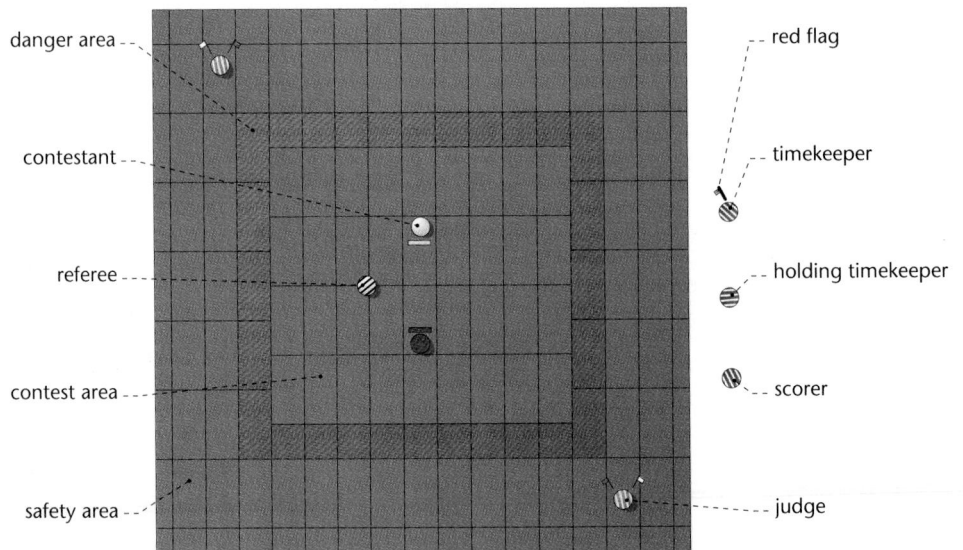

- danger area
- contestant
- referee
- contest area
- safety area
- red flag
- timekeeper
- holding timekeeper
- scorer
- judge

BOXING

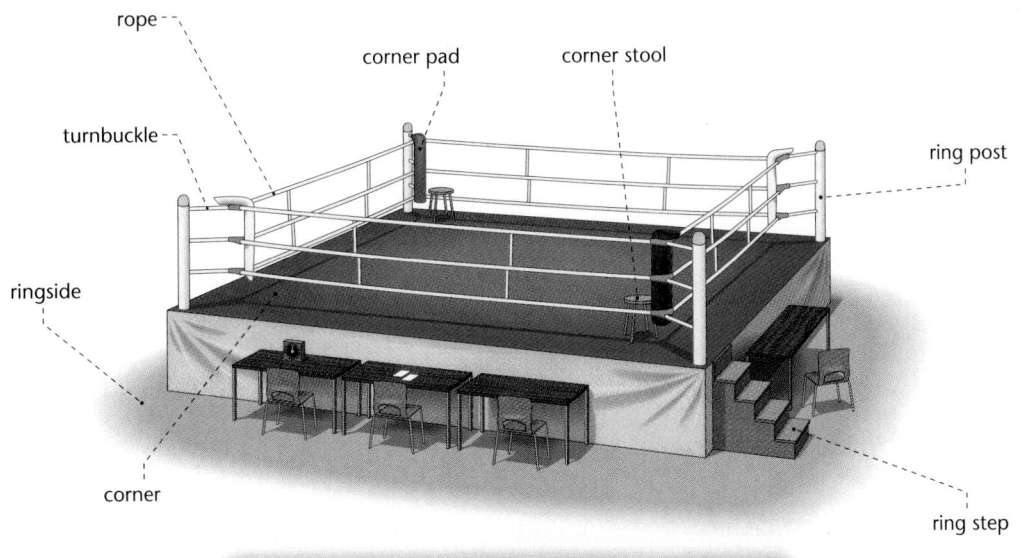

rope

corner pad   corner stool

turnbuckle

ring post

ringside

corner

ring step

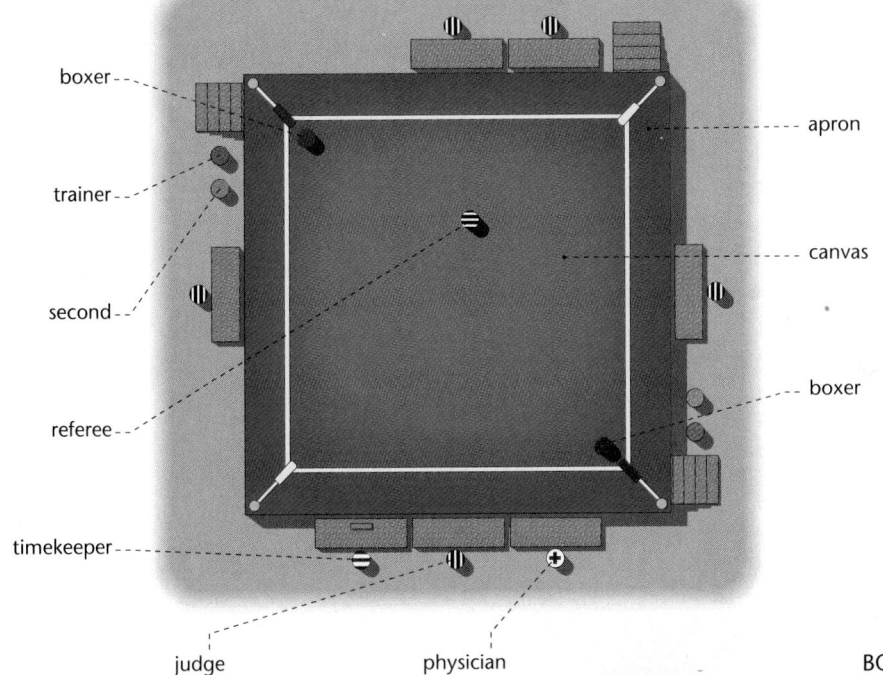

boxer

trainer

second

referee

timekeeper

judge   physician

apron

canvas

boxer

bandage

mouthpiece

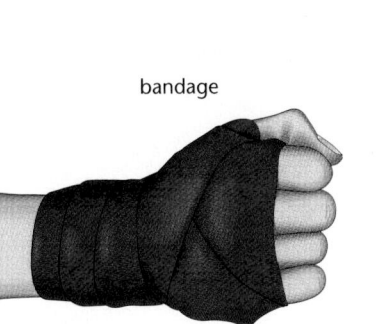

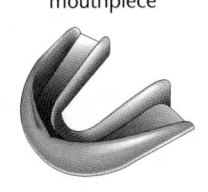

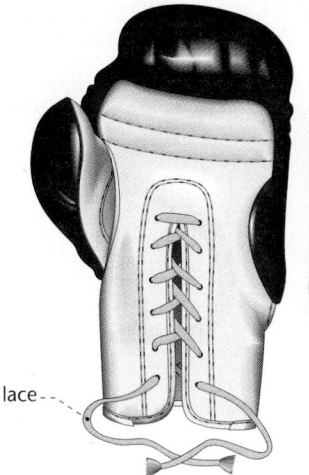

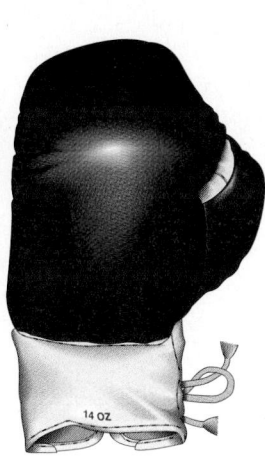

lace

14 OZ

FLY ROD

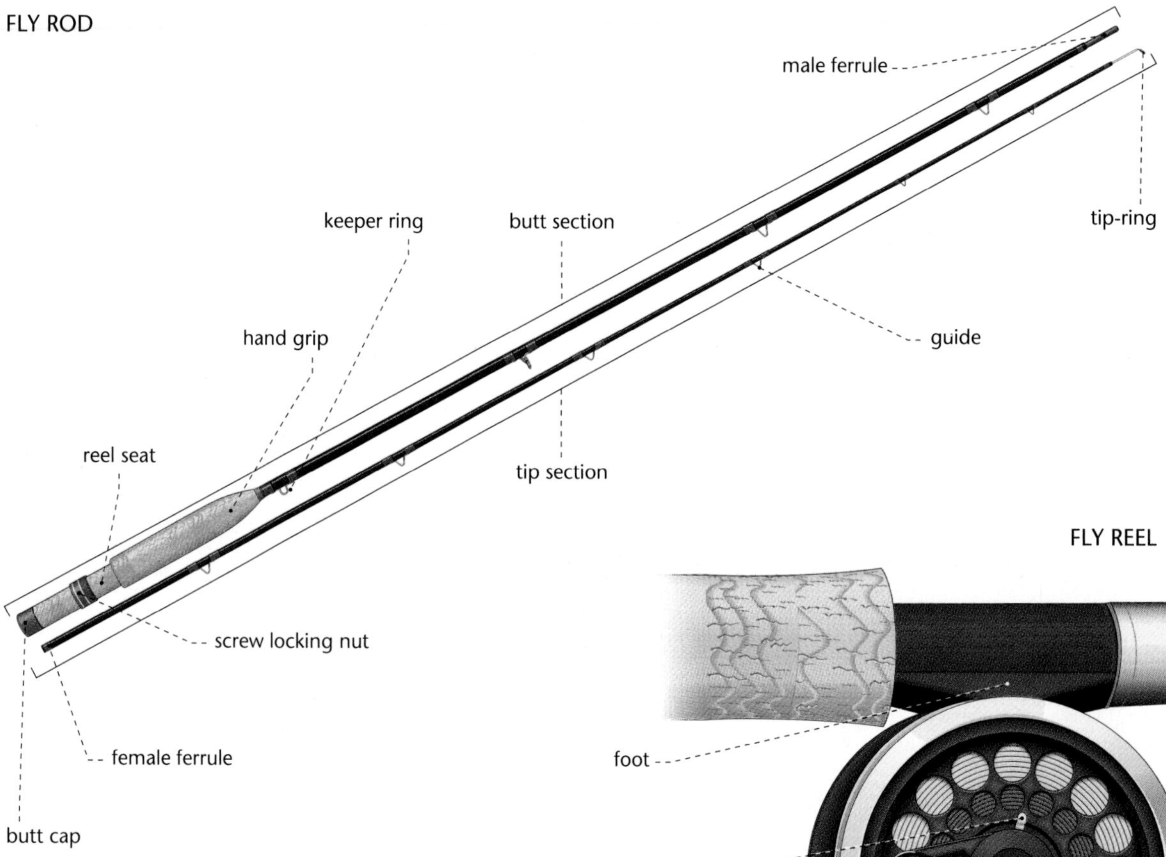

male ferrule

keeper ring   butt section

tip-ring

hand grip

guide

reel seat

tip section

screw locking nut

FLY REEL

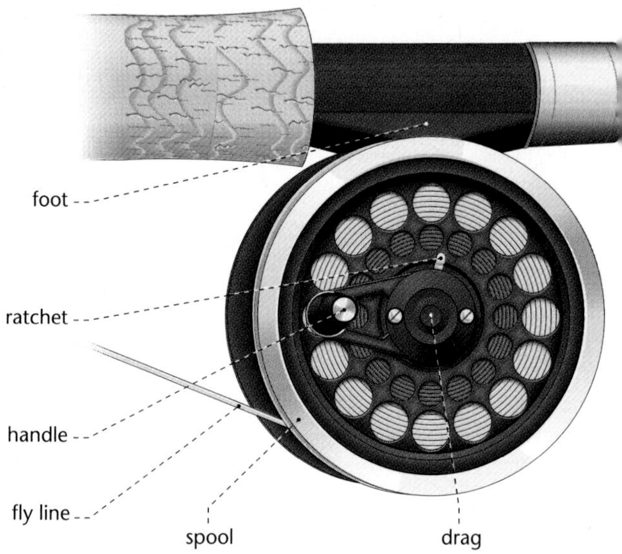

female ferrule

foot

butt cap

ratchet

handle

fly line

spool   drag

ARTIFICIAL FLY

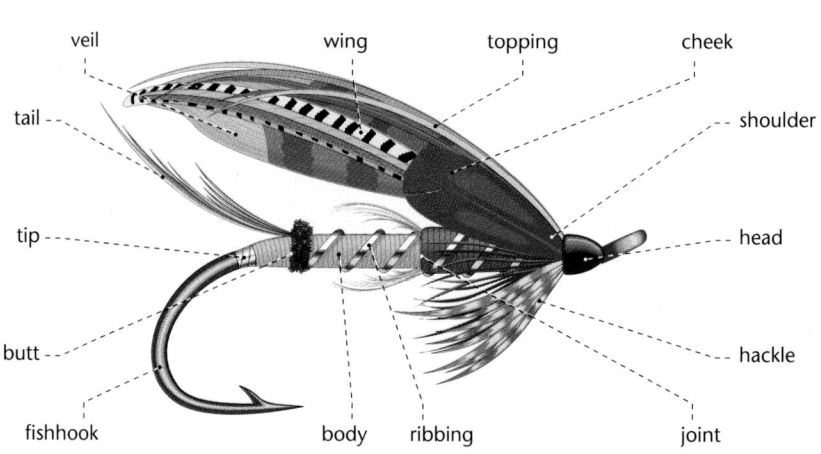

veil   wing   topping   cheek

tail

shoulder

tip

head

butt

hackle

fishhook   body   ribbing   joint

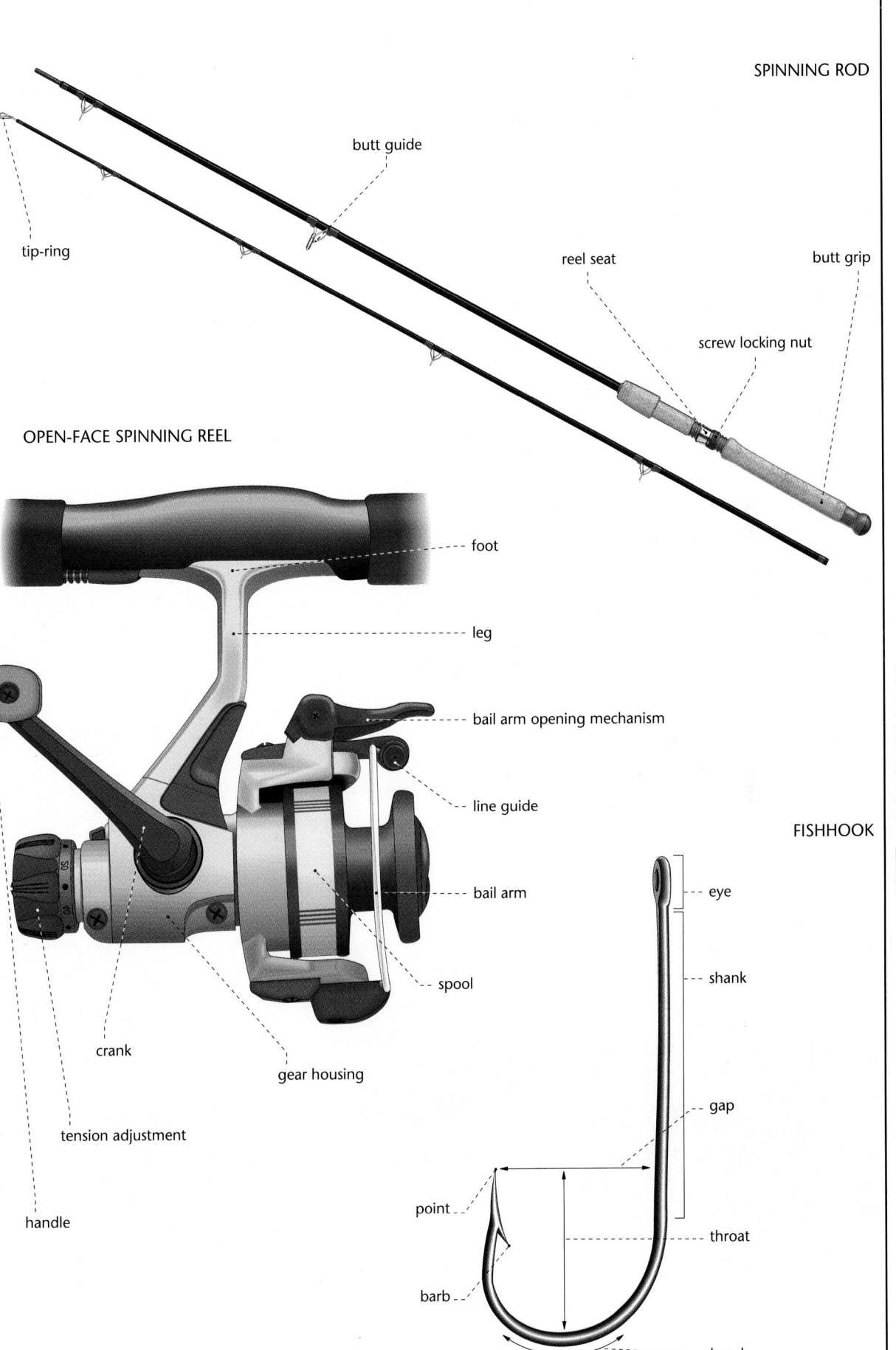

SPINNING ROD

butt guide

tip-ring

reel seat

butt grip

screw locking nut

OPEN-FACE SPINNING REEL

foot

leg

bail arm opening mechanism

line guide

FISHHOOK

bail arm

eye

spool

shank

gap

crank

gear housing

point

throat

tension adjustment

barb

handle

bend

FISHING

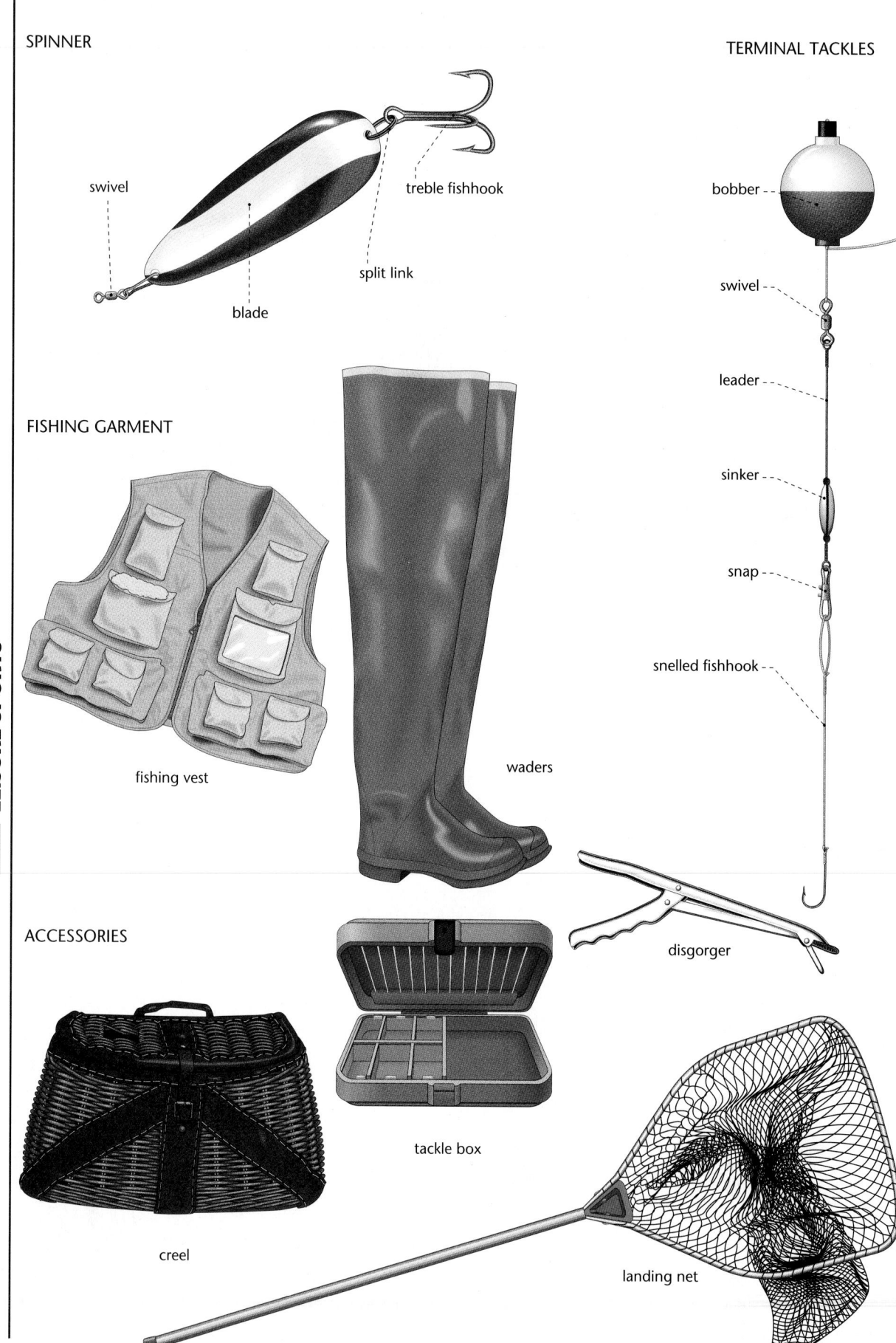

SPINNER

swivel

treble fishhook

split link

blade

TERMINAL TACKLES

bobber

swivel

leader

sinker

snap

snelled fishhook

FISHING GARMENT

fishing vest

waders

disgorger

ACCESSORIES

creel

tackle box

landing net

BILLIARDS

CAROM BILLIARDS

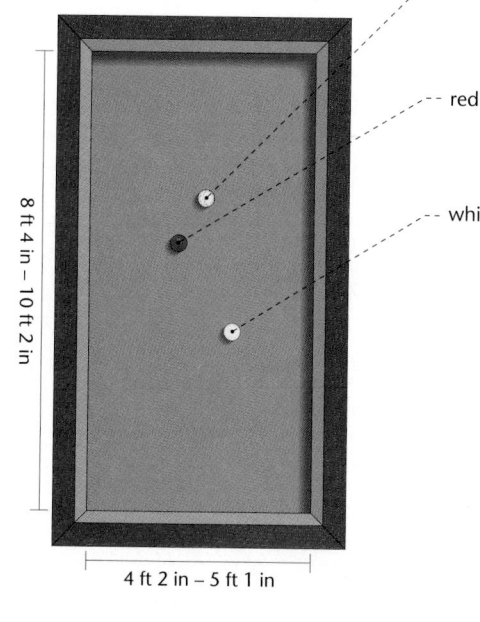

cue ball

red ball

white spot ball

8 ft 4 in – 10 ft 2 in

4 ft 2 in – 5 ft 1 in

POOL

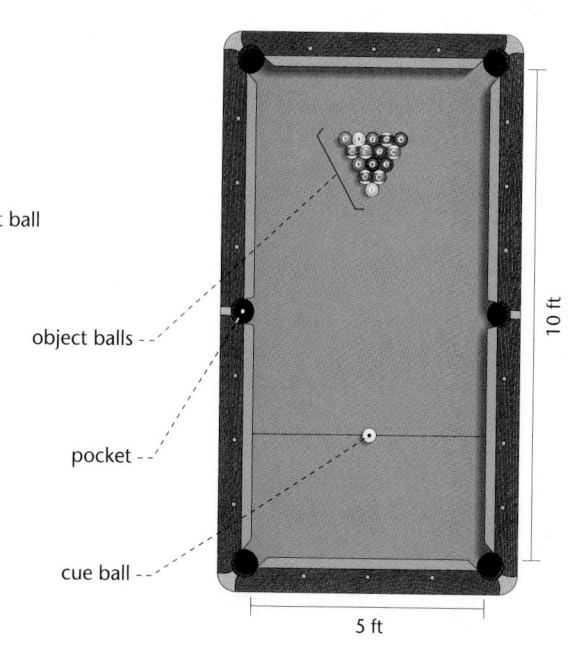

object balls

pocket

cue ball

10 ft

5 ft

ENGLISH BILLIARDS

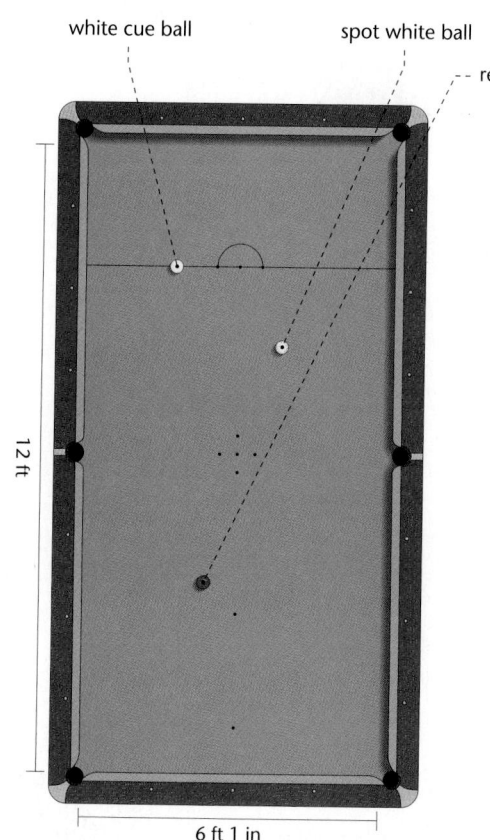

white cue ball

spot white ball

red ball

12 ft

6 ft 1 in

SNOOKER

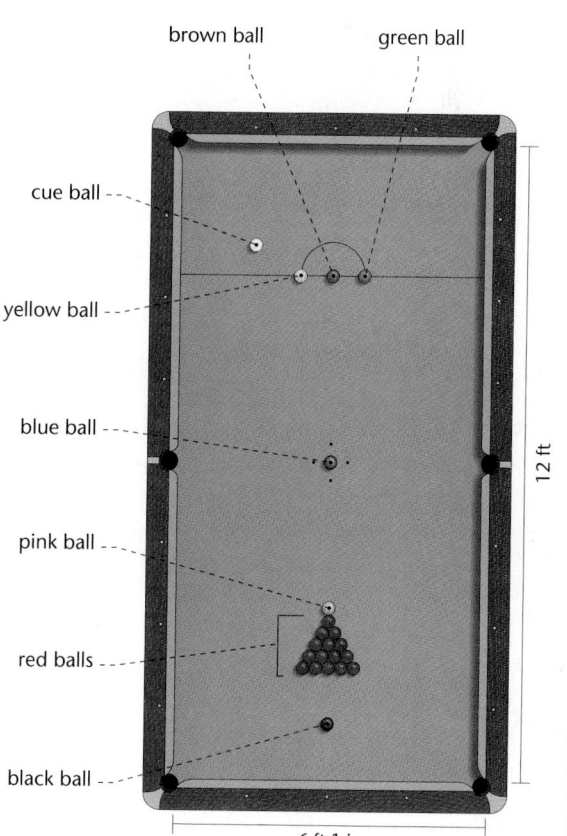

brown ball

green ball

cue ball

yellow ball

blue ball

pink ball

red balls

black ball

12 ft

6 ft 1 in

TABLE

balk line spot

center spot

balk area

«D»

top pocket

head cushion

balk line

hook

center pocket

BRIDGE

shaft

notch

end-piece

rack

baize

pyramid spot

billiard spot

foot cushion

bottom pocket

tip

ferrule

shaft

rail

joint

butt

chalk

LEISURE SPORTS

COURSE

hole

clubhouse

cart path

practice green

putting green

fairway

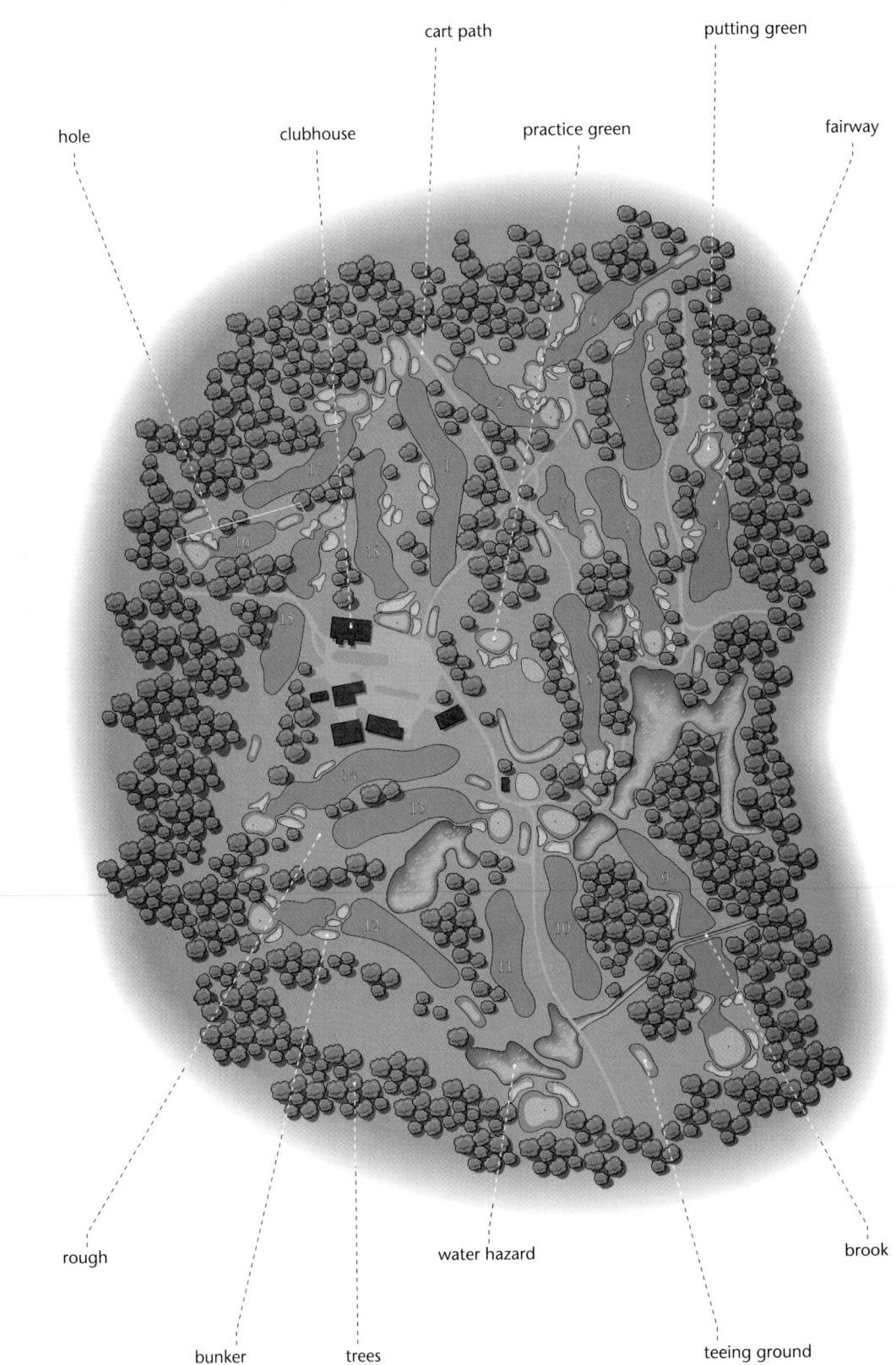

rough

bunker

trees

water hazard

teeing ground

brook

CROSS SECTION OF A GOLF BALL

GOLF BALL

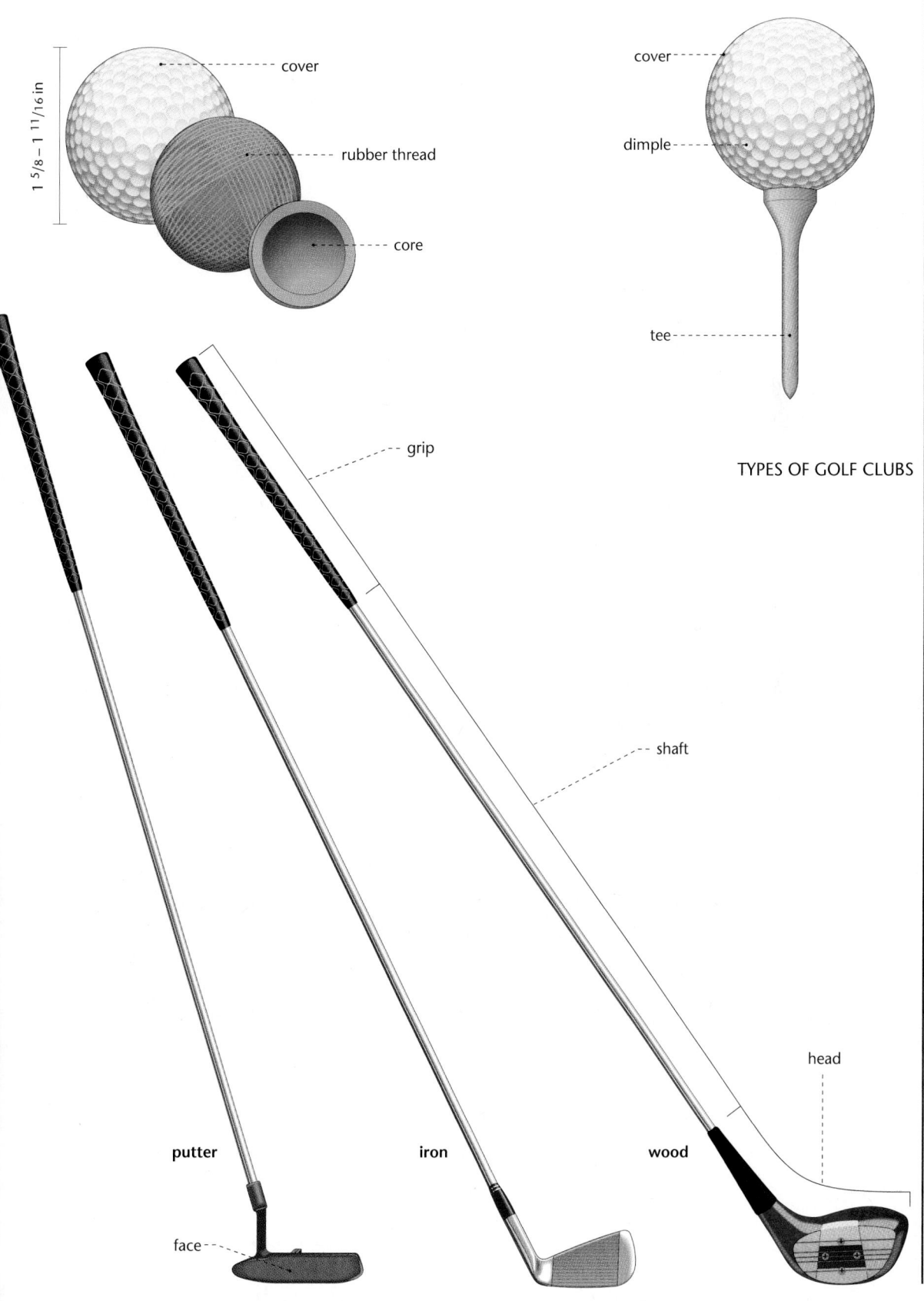

cover

rubber thread

core

$1^{5}/_{8} - 1^{11}/_{16}$ in

cover

dimple

tee

TYPES OF GOLF CLUBS

grip

shaft

head

putter

iron

wood

face

677

GOLF

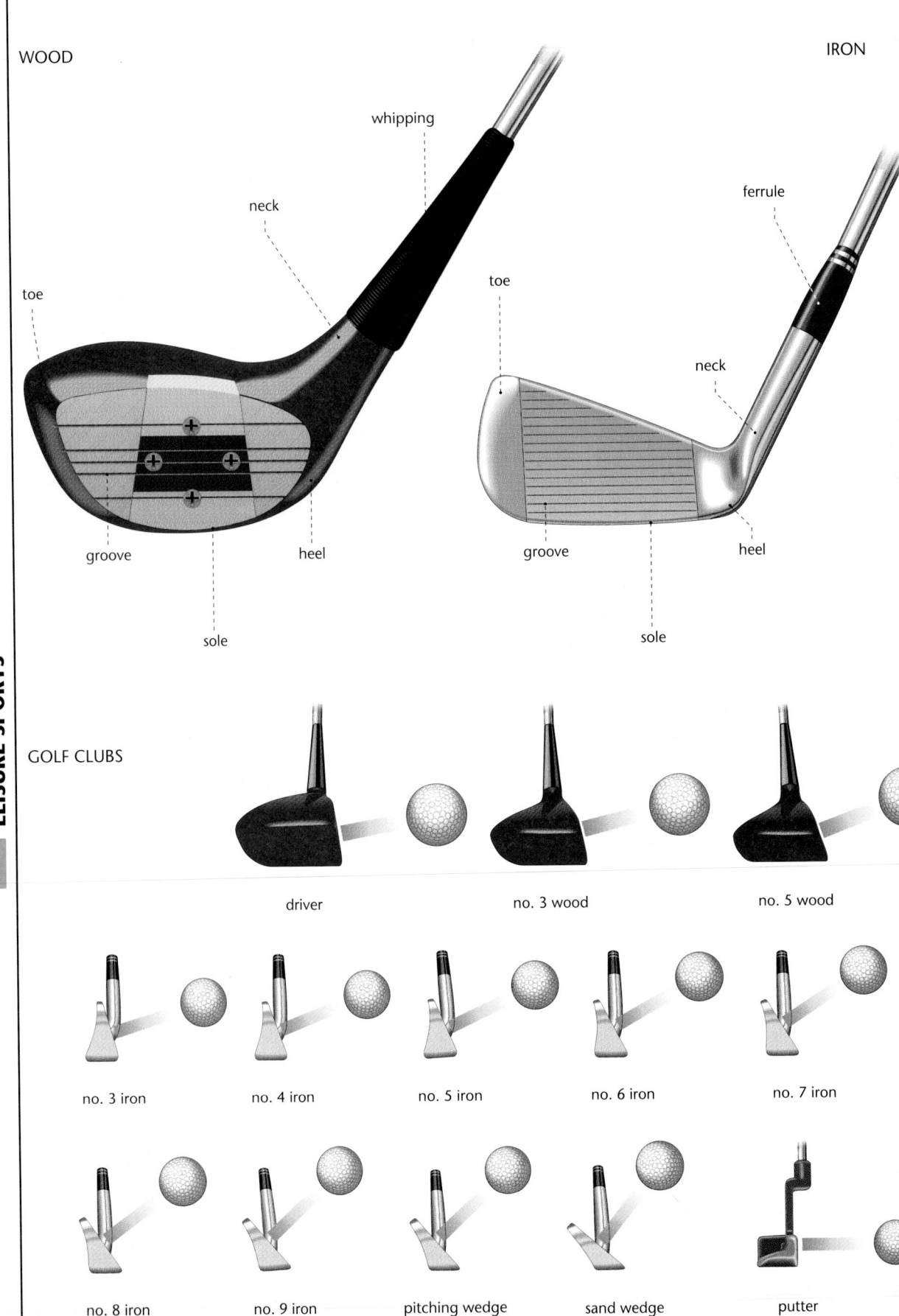

WOOD

IRON

whipping

neck

toe

groove

sole

heel

ferrule

toe

neck

groove

heel

sole

GOLF CLUBS

driver

no. 3 wood

no. 5 wood

no. 3 iron

no. 4 iron

no. 5 iron

no. 6 iron

no. 7 iron

no. 8 iron

no. 9 iron

pitching wedge

sand wedge

putter

LEISURE SPORTS

678

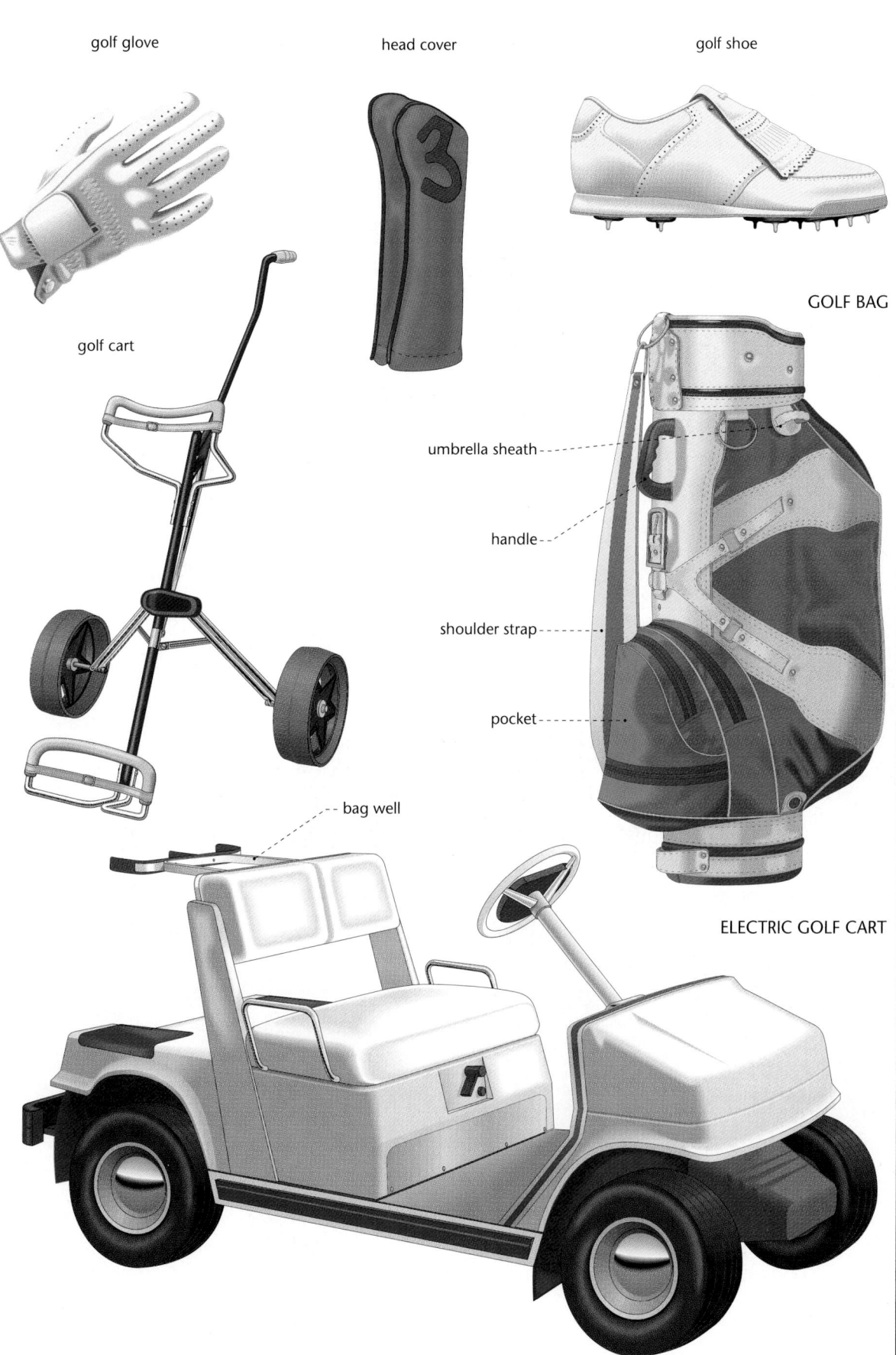

golf glove

head cover

golf shoe

golf cart

GOLF BAG

umbrella sheath

handle

shoulder strap

pocket

bag well

ELECTRIC GOLF CART

MOUNTAINEER

helmet lamp

helmet

hood

knapsack

rope

parka

carabiner

climbing harness

piton-carrier

chock

mountaineering shovel

mitten

hammer ax

ice ax

ice piton

ice screw

pants

crampon strap

legging

front point

spike

mountaineering boot

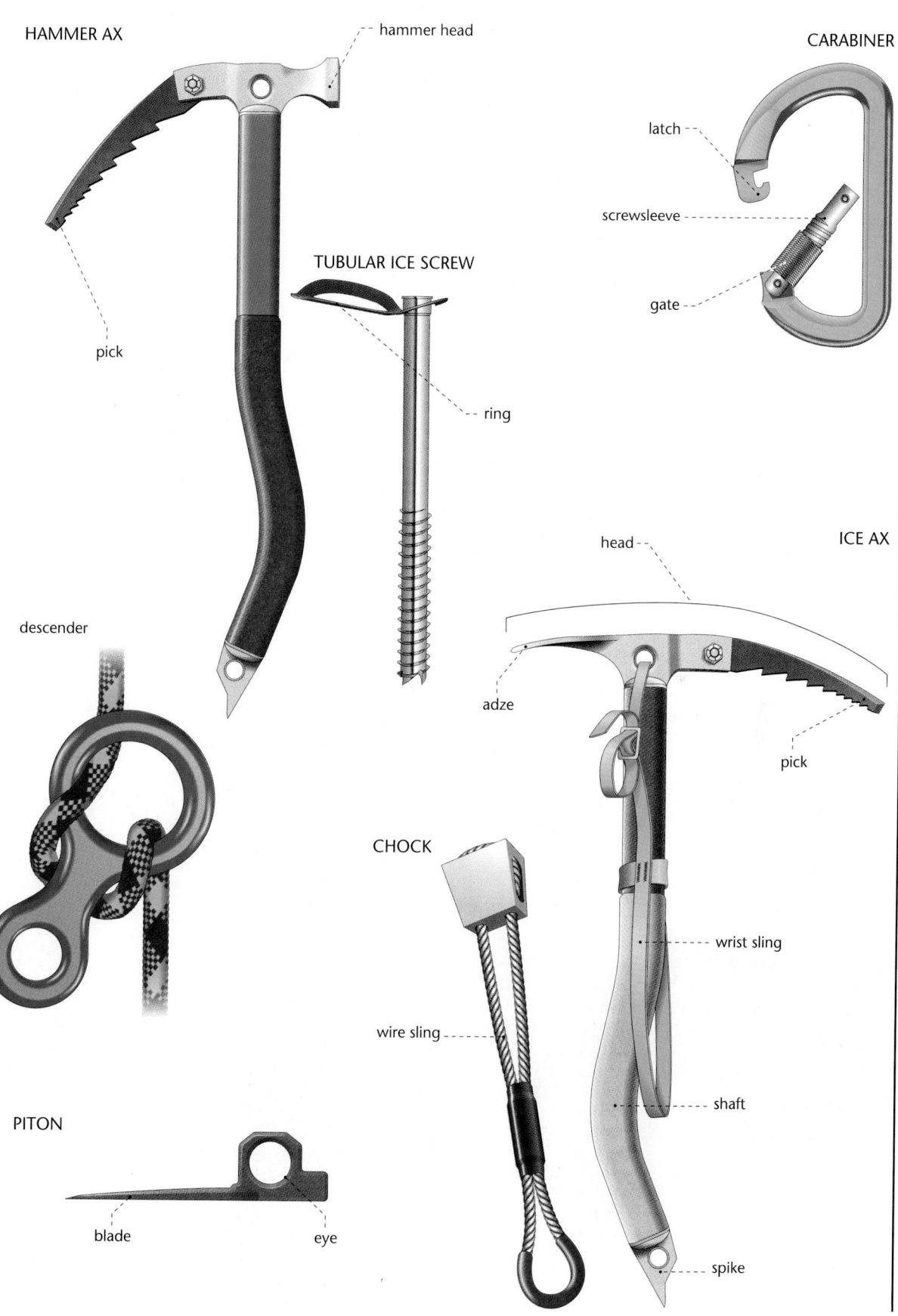

HAMMER AX

hammer head

pick

CARABINER

latch

screwsleeve

gate

TUBULAR ICE SCREW

ring

descender

head

ICE AX

adze

pick

CHOCK

wrist sling

wire sling

shaft

PITON

blade

eye

spike

GREEN

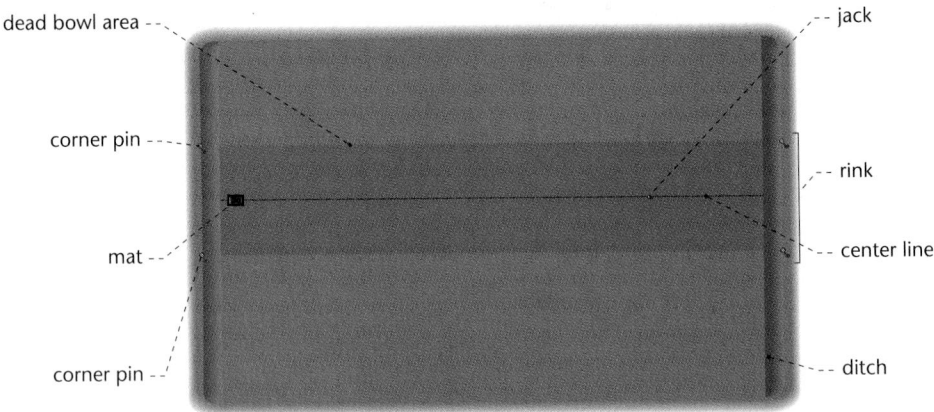

dead bowl area

corner pin

mat

corner pin

jack

rink

center line

ditch

DELIVERY

forward swing

delivery

follow-through

bowl

petanque bowl

jack

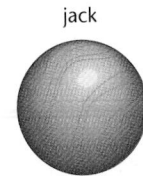

BOWLING

TYPES OF PINS

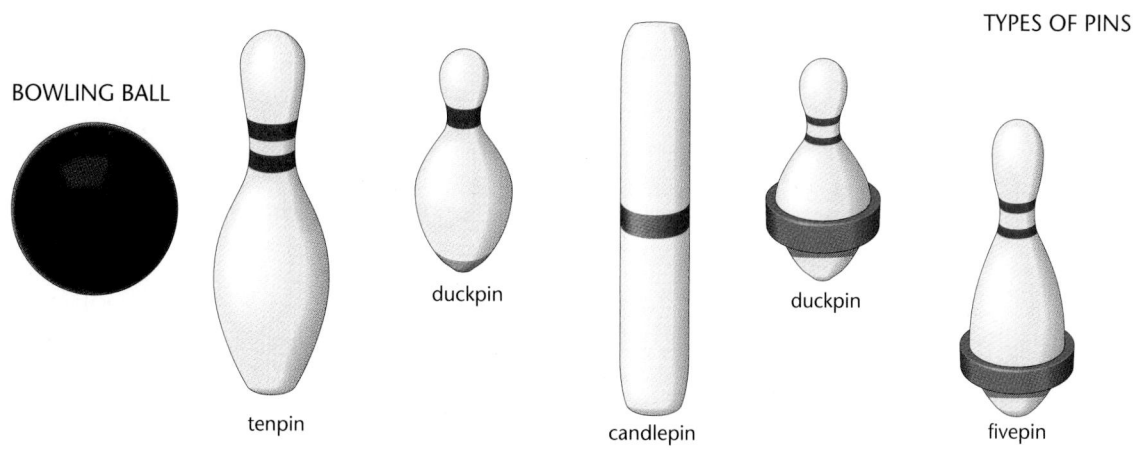

BOWLING BALL

tenpin

duckpin

candlepin

duckpin

fivepin

SETUP

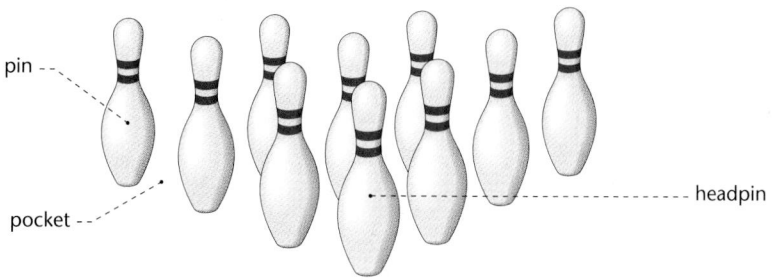

pin

pocket

headpin

LANE

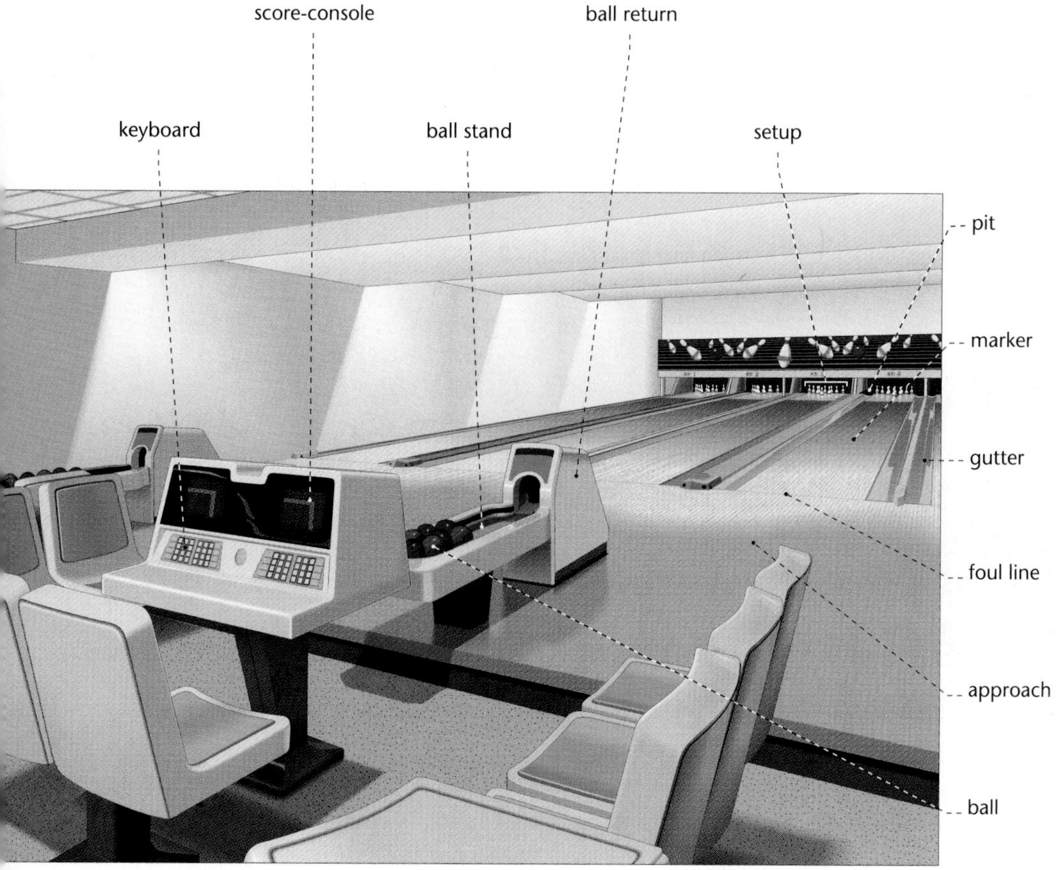

score-console

ball return

keyboard

ball stand

setup

pit

marker

gutter

foul line

approach

ball

683

ARCHERY

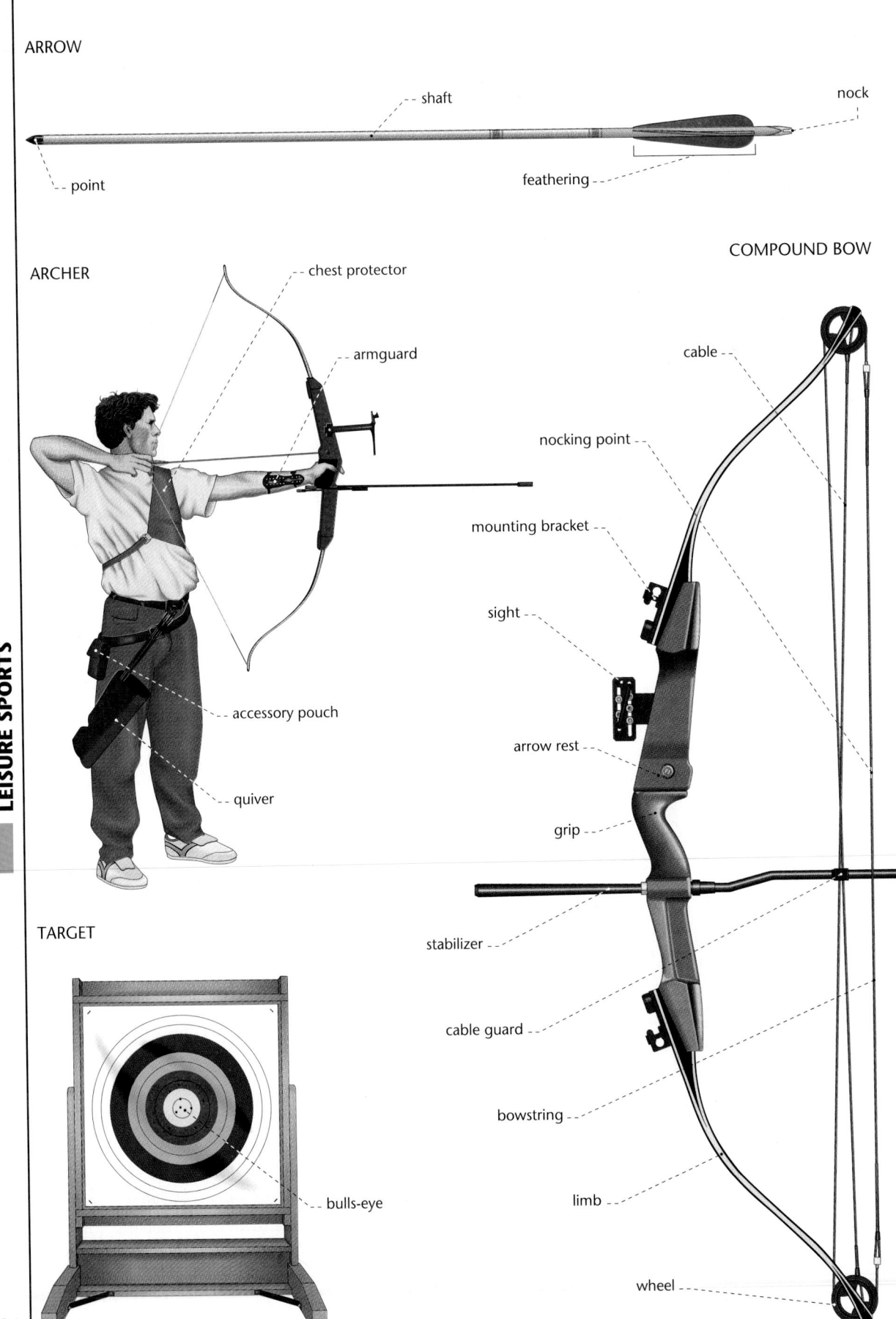

ARROW

point

shaft

feathering

nock

ARCHER

chest protector

armguard

accessory pouch

quiver

COMPOUND BOW

cable

nocking point

mounting bracket

sight

arrow rest

grip

stabilizer

cable guard

bowstring

limb

wheel

TARGET

bulls-eye

CAMPING

TWO-PERSON TENT

rainfly

door

canopy

strainer

zipper

inner tent

elastic strainer

guy line

stake

FAMILY TENT

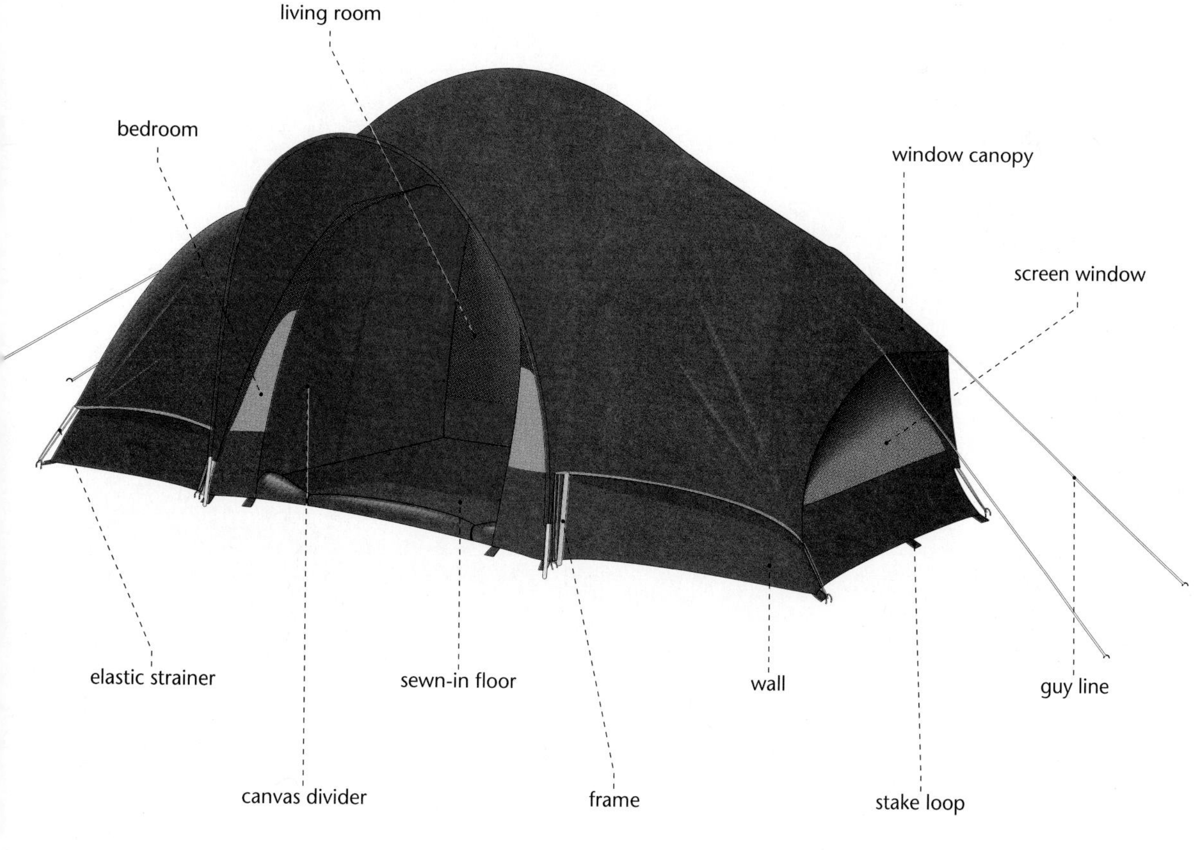

living room

bedroom

window canopy

screen window

elastic strainer

sewn-in floor

wall

guy line

canvas divider

frame

stake loop

CAMPING

685

PUP TENT

rainfly

inner tent

roof pole

door

elastic strainer

sewn-in floor

stake loop

stake

MAJOR TYPES OF TENTS

wall tent

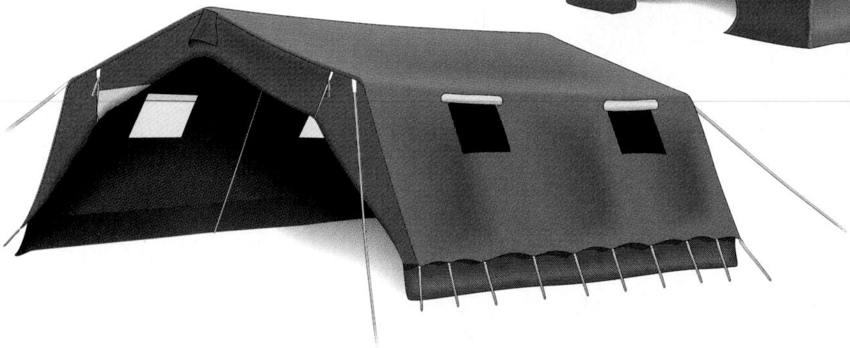

wagon tent

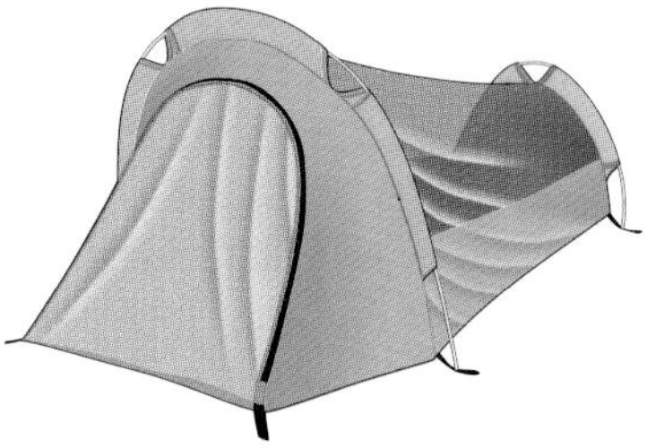

dome tent

one-person tent

pop-up tent

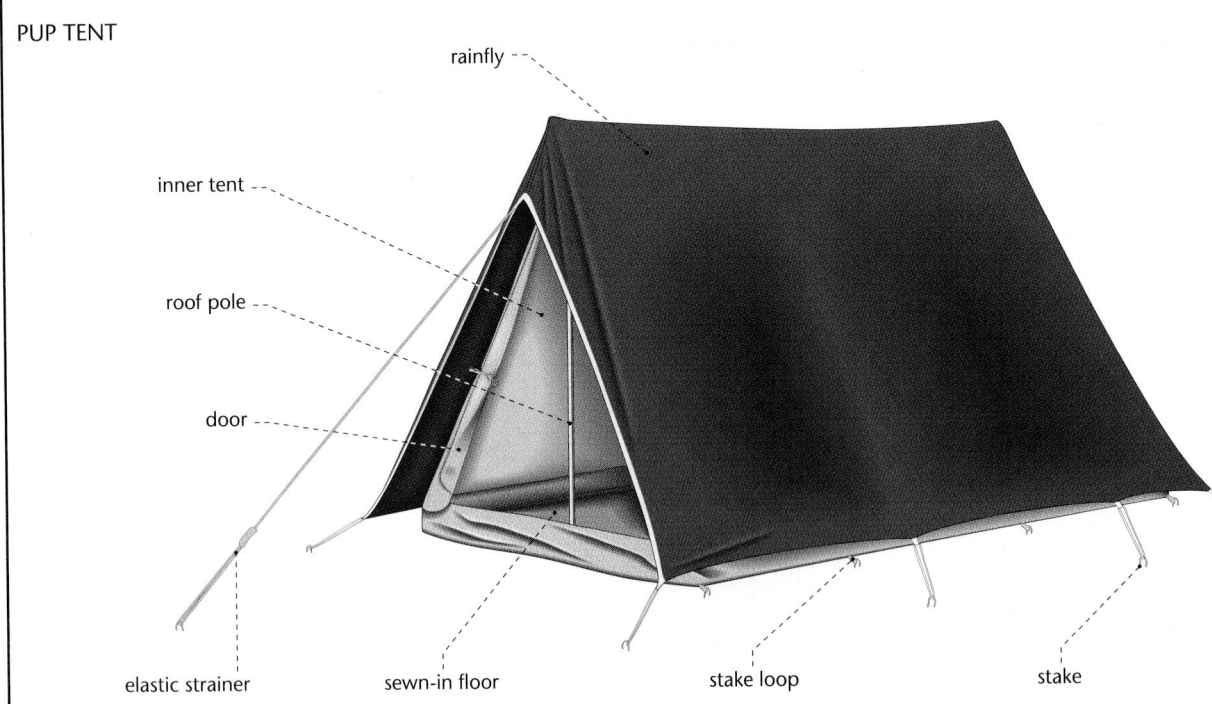

686

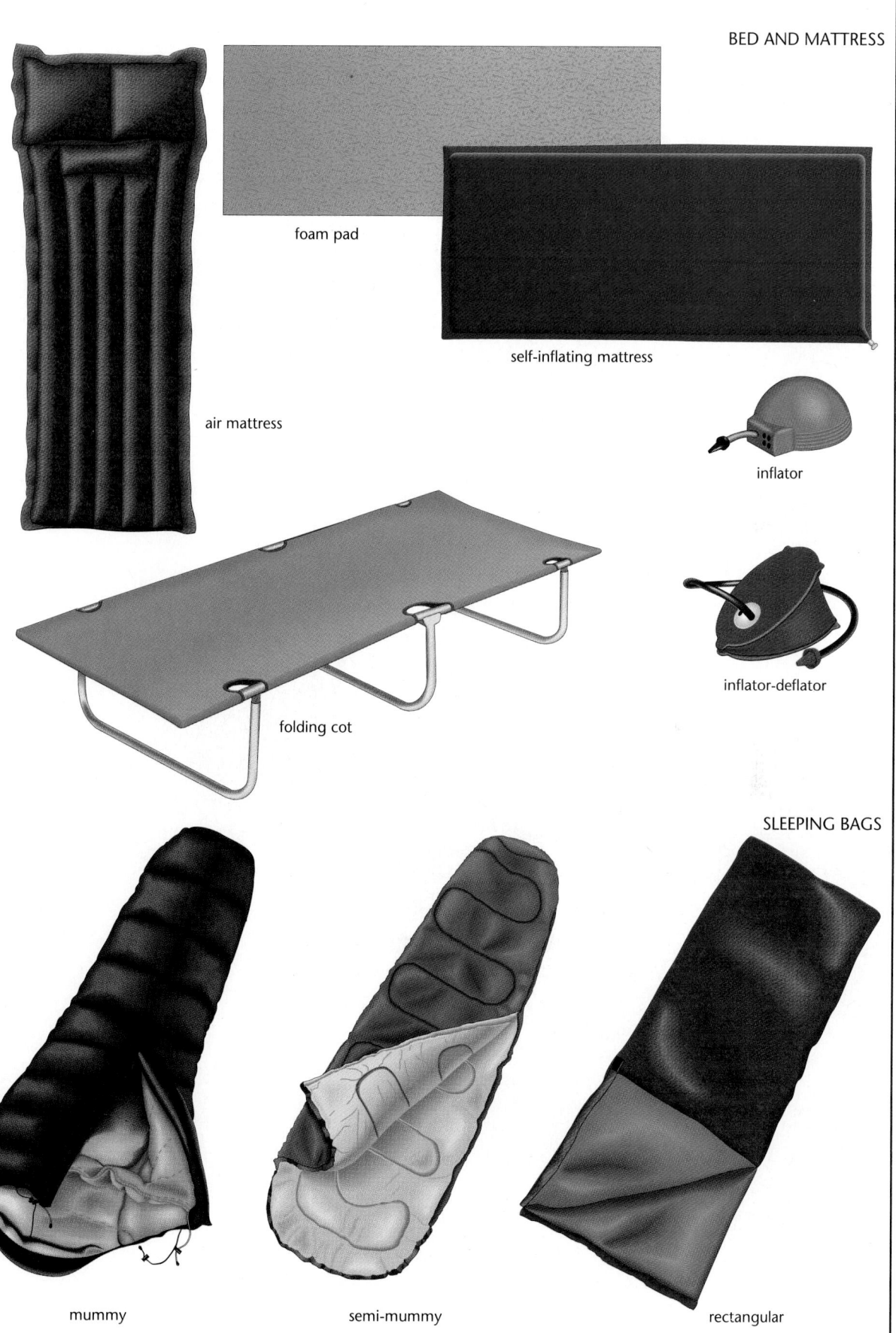

foam pad

self-inflating mattress

air mattress

inflator

inflator-deflator

folding cot

SLEEPING BAGS

CAMPING

mummy

semi-mummy

rectangular

CAMPING EQUIPMENT

SWISS ARMY KNIFE

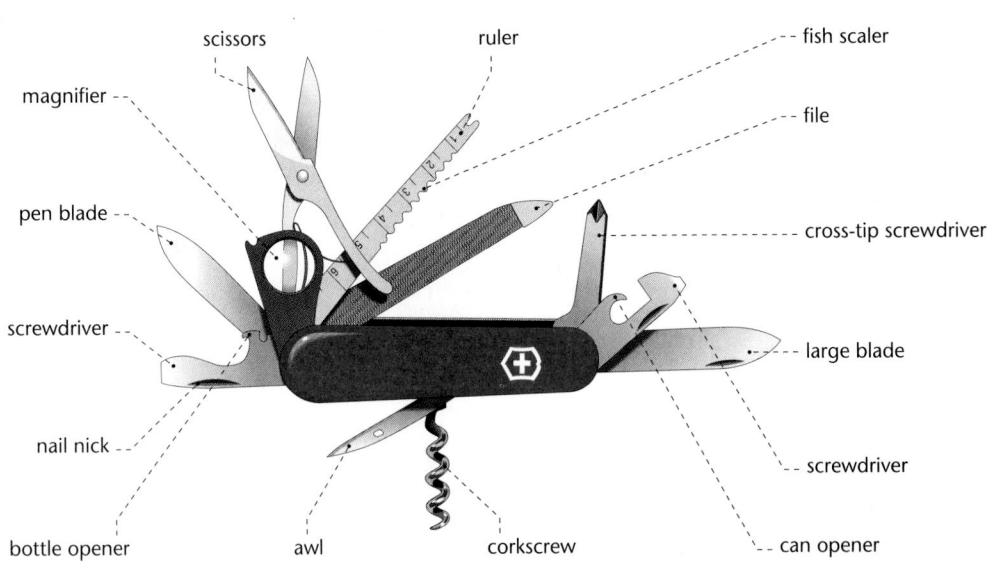

scissors

ruler

fish scaler

magnifier

file

pen blade

cross-tip screwdriver

screwdriver

large blade

nail nick

screwdriver

bottle opener

awl

corkscrew

can opener

COOKING SET

cup

coffee pot

sauce pan

frying pan

plate

handle

CUTLERY SET

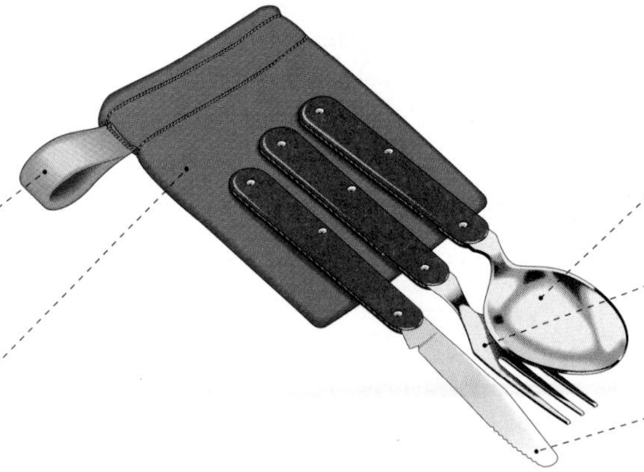

spoon

belt loop

fork

sheath

knife

lantern

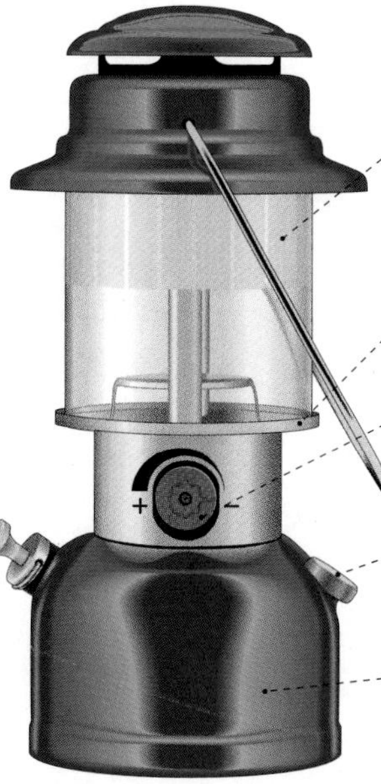

globe

burner frame

pressure regulator

leakproof cap

tank

pump

heater

single-burner camp stove

two-burner camp stove

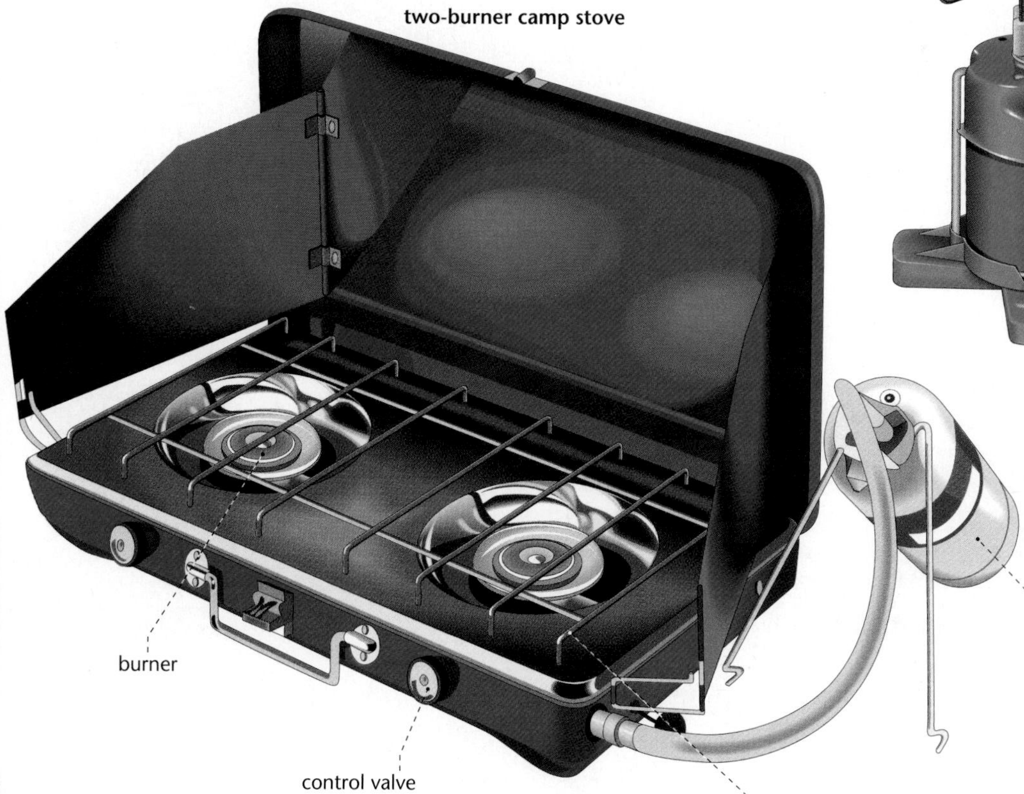

burner

control valve

wire support

tank

CAMPING

CAMPING EQUIPMENT

thermos

water carrier

canteen

hurricane lamp

cooler

folding grill

TOOLS

hatchet

leather sheath

sheath

knife

folding shovel

bow saw

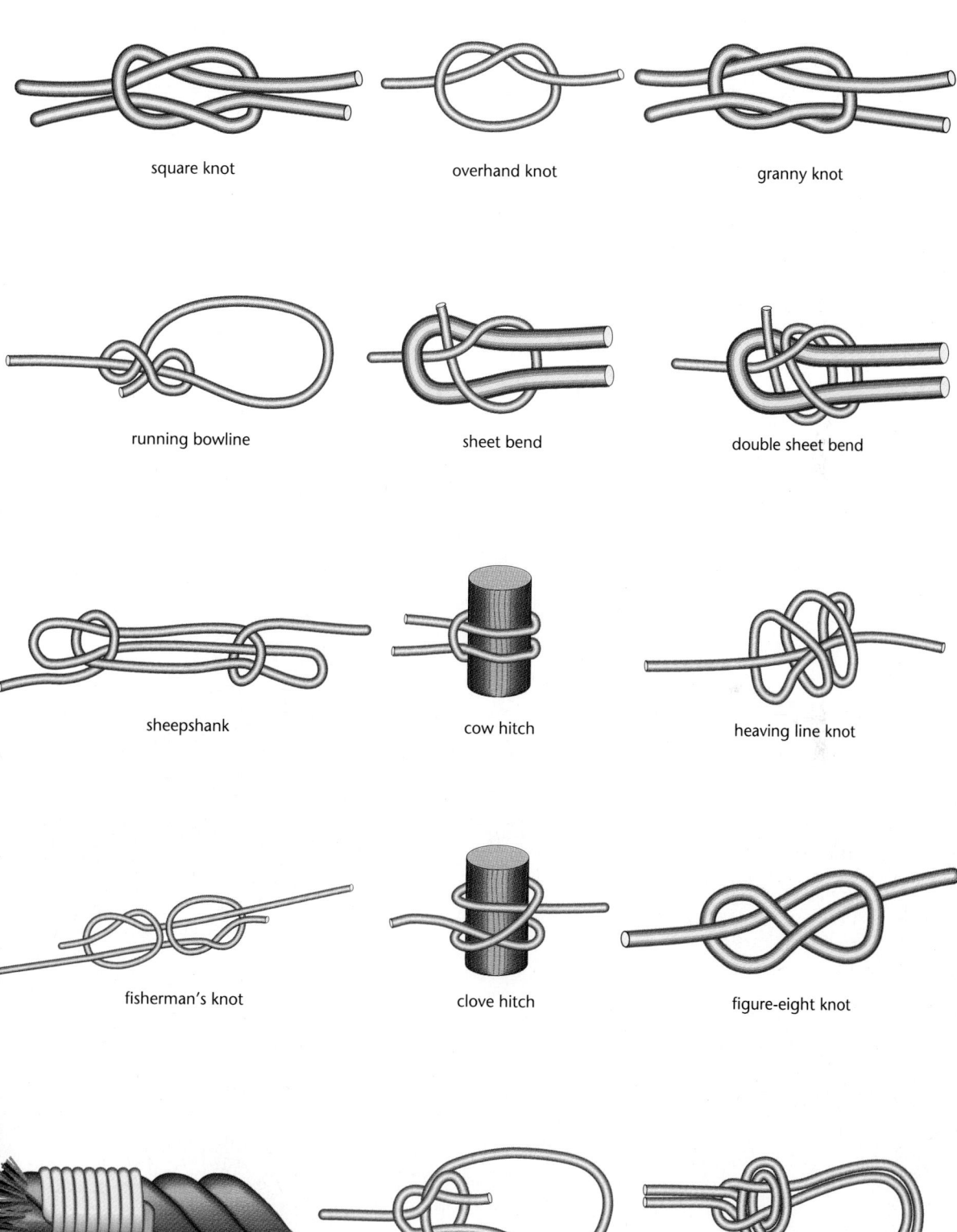

square knot

overhand knot

granny knot

running bowline

sheet bend

double sheet bend

sheepshank

cow hitch

heaving line knot

fisherman's knot

clove hitch

figure-eight knot

common whipping

bowline

bowline on a bight

KNOTS

SHORT SPLICE

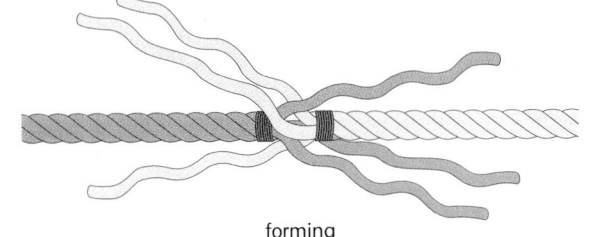

forming

completion

CABLE

TWISTED ROPE

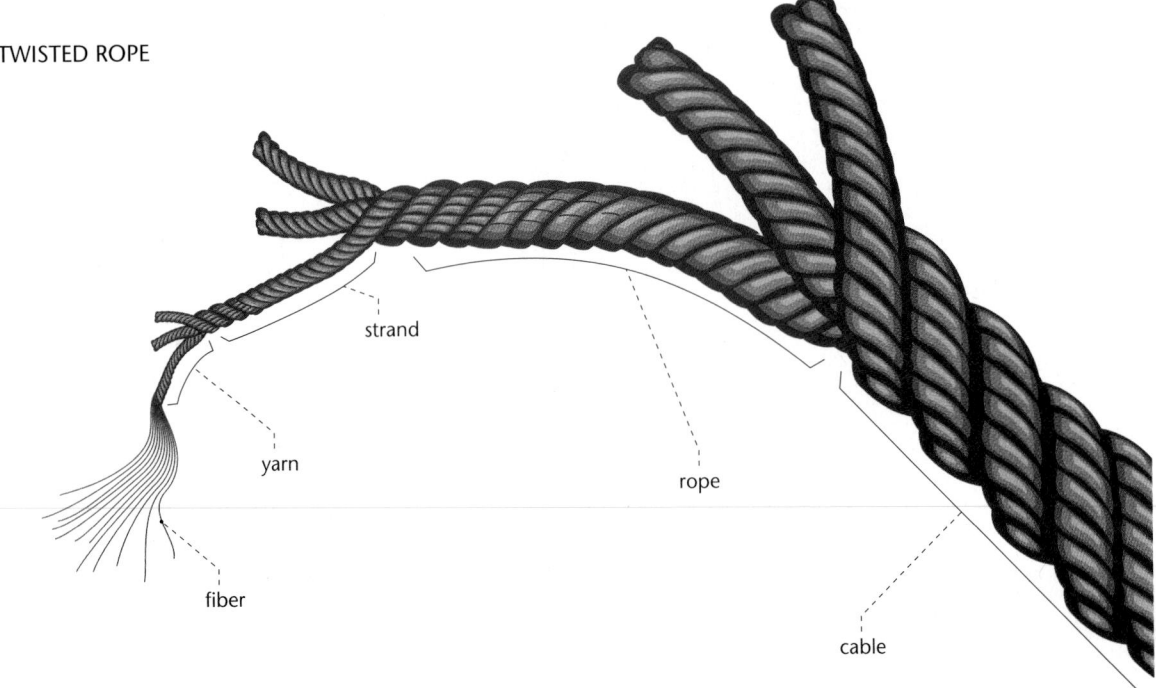

strand

yarn

rope

fiber

cable

BRAIDED ROPE

core

sheath

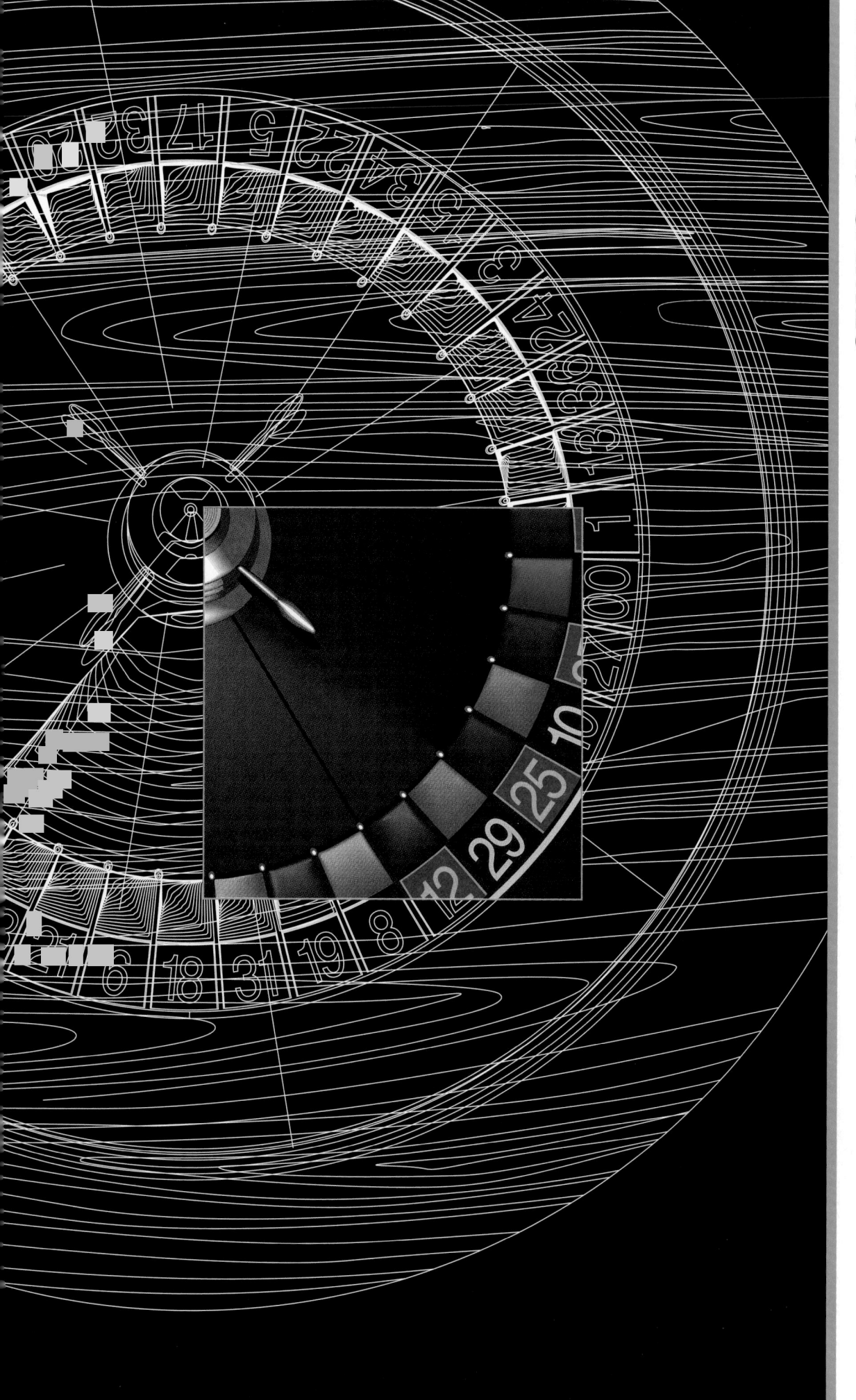

CONTENTS

CARD GAMES...695

DOMINOES..695

CHESS 696

BACKGAMMON 697

GO...697

GAME OF DARTS..698

VIDEO ENTERTAINMENT SYSTEM 699

DICE 699

ROULETTE TABLE 700

SLOT MACHINE 702

INDOOR GAMES

CARD GAMES

heart

diamond

club

spade

Joker

Ace

King

Queen

Jack

STANDARD POKER HANDS

royal flush

straight flush

four-of-a-kind

full house

flush

straight

three-of-a-kind

two pairs

one pair

high card

DOMINOES

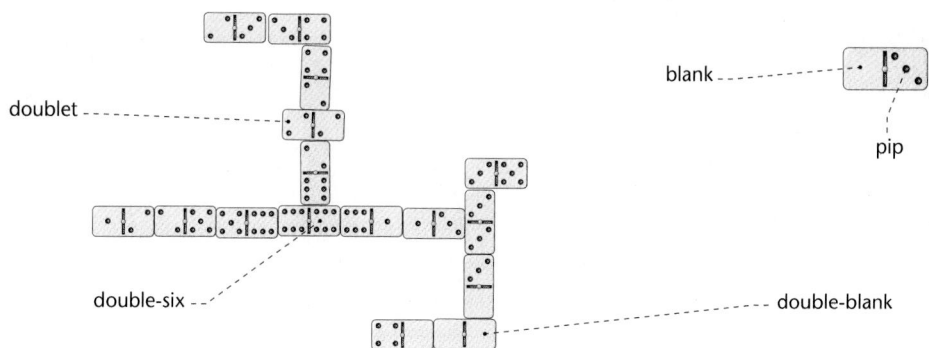

doublet

blank

pip

double-six

double-blank

INDOOR GAMES

695

CHESS

CHESSBOARD

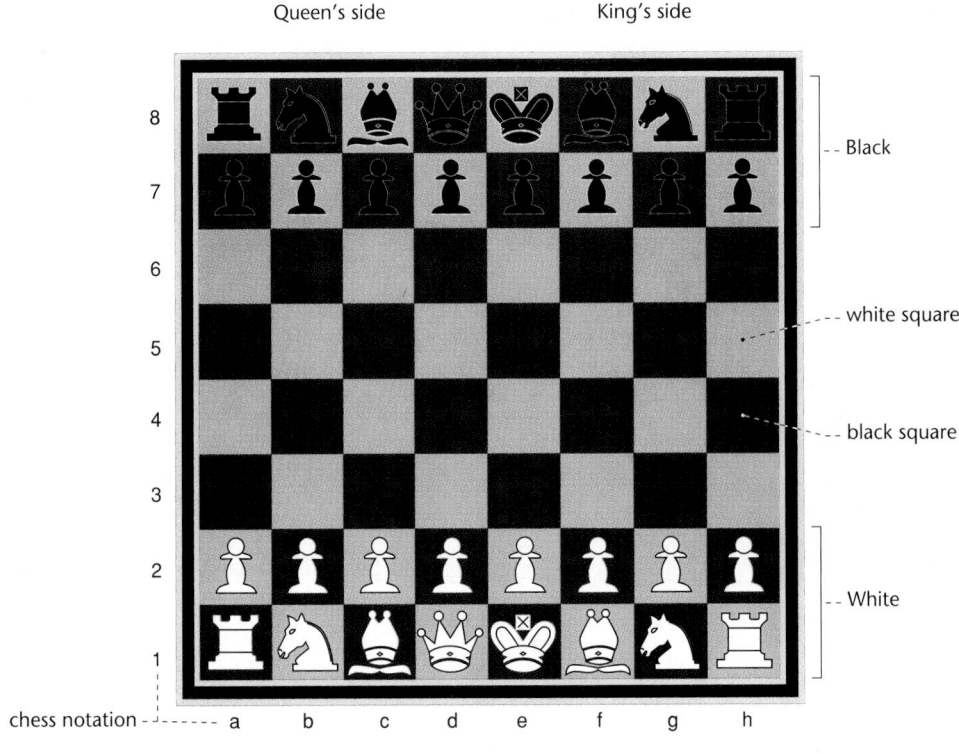

Queen's side   King's side

8

7

6 · · · white square

5

4 · · · black square

3

2 · · White

1

chess notation · · · a   b   c   d   e   f   g   h

Black

White

TYPES OF MOVEMENTS

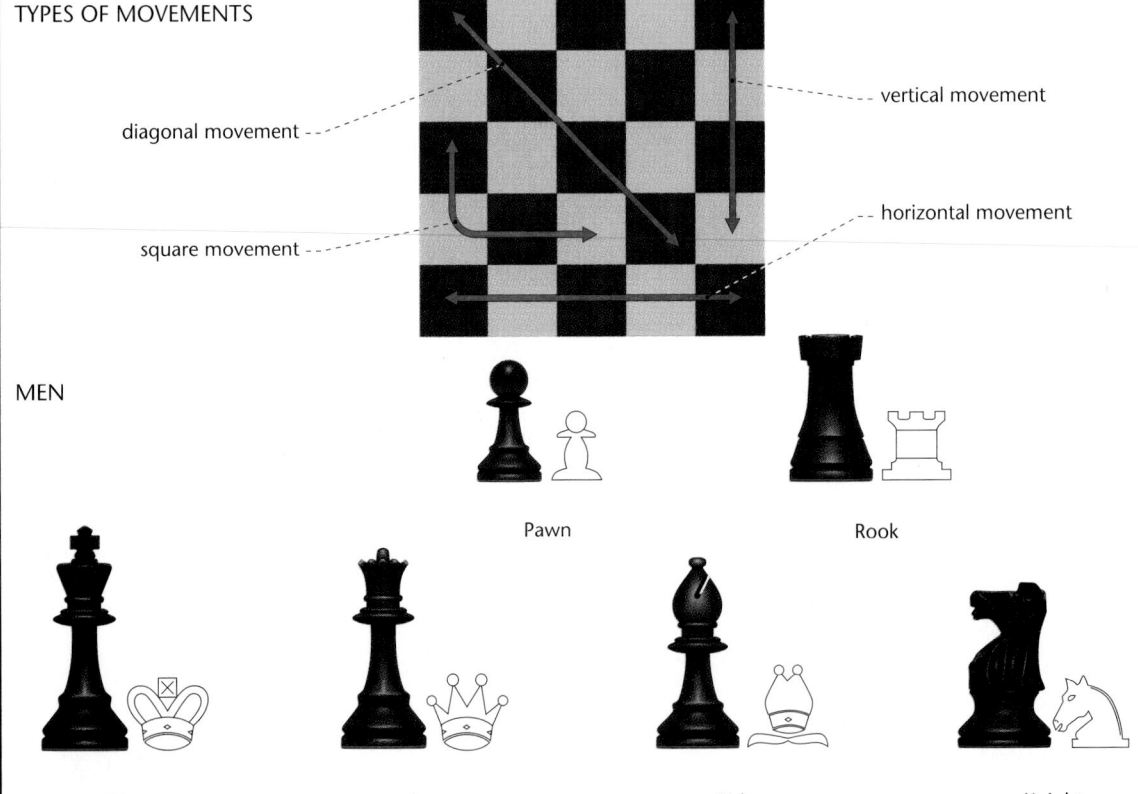

diagonal movement

square movement

vertical movement

horizontal movement

MEN

Pawn

Rook

King

Queen

Bishop

Knight

BACKGAMMON

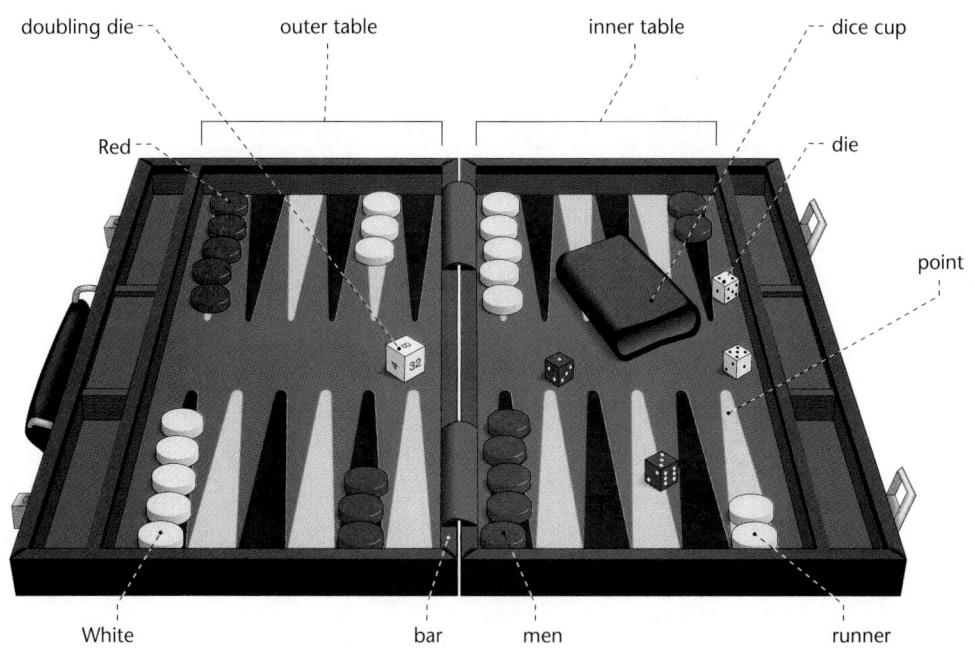

doubling die

outer table

inner table

dice cup

Red

die

point

White

bar

men

runner

GO

BOARD

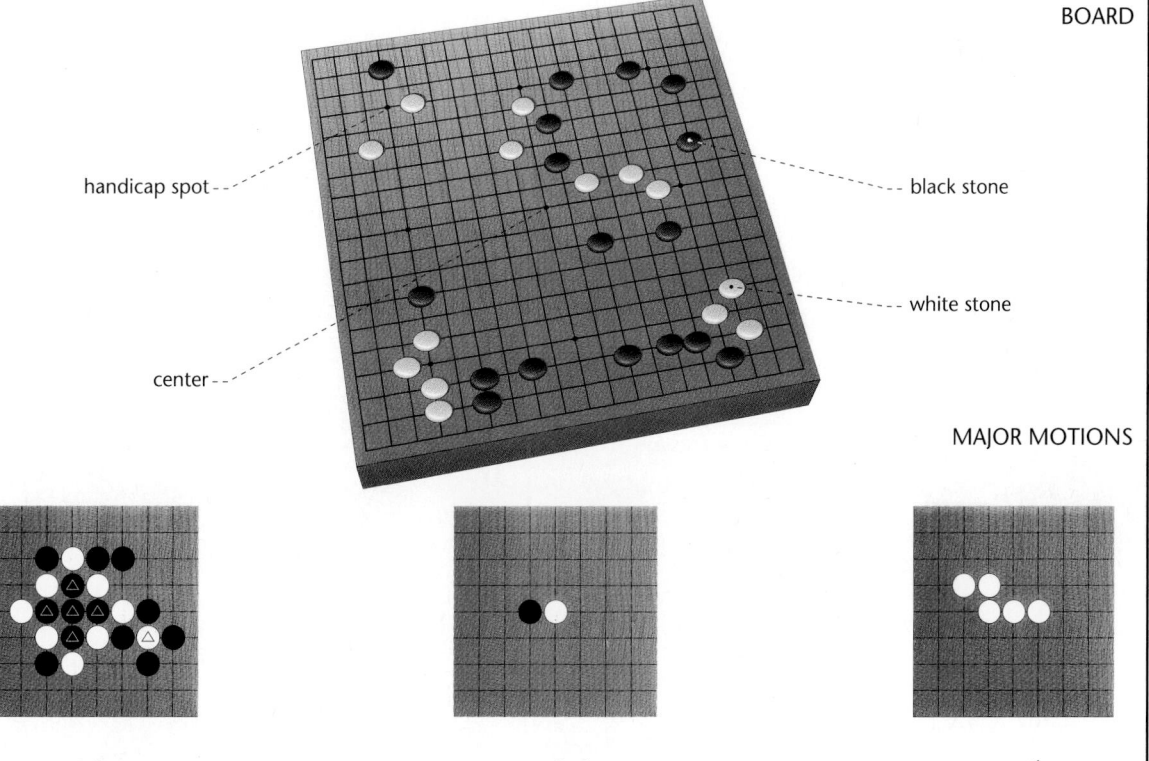

handicap spot

black stone

white stone

center

MAJOR MOTIONS

capture

contact

connection

GAME OF DARTS

INDOOR GAMES

DARTBOARD

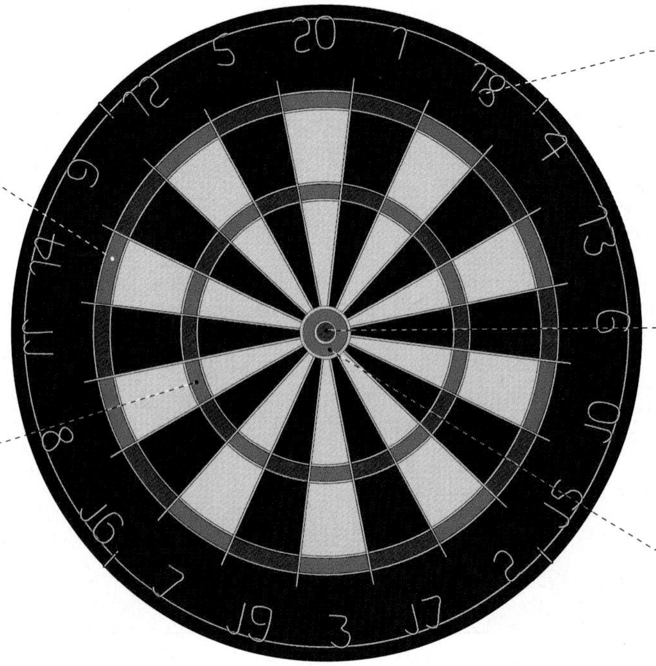

segment score number

double ring

bull's-eye

triple ring

25 ring

DART

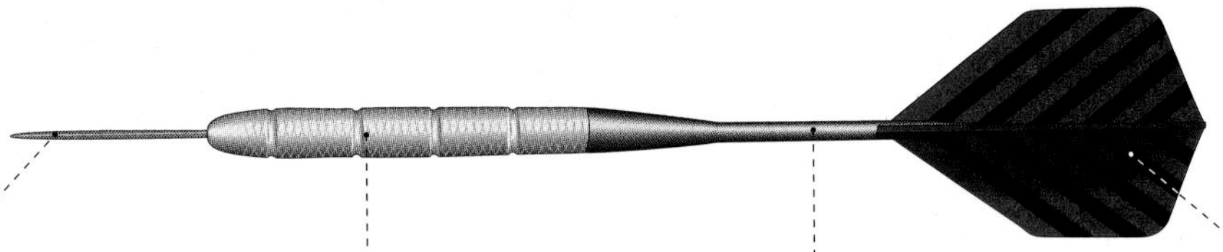

point

barrel

shaft

flight

PLAYING AREA

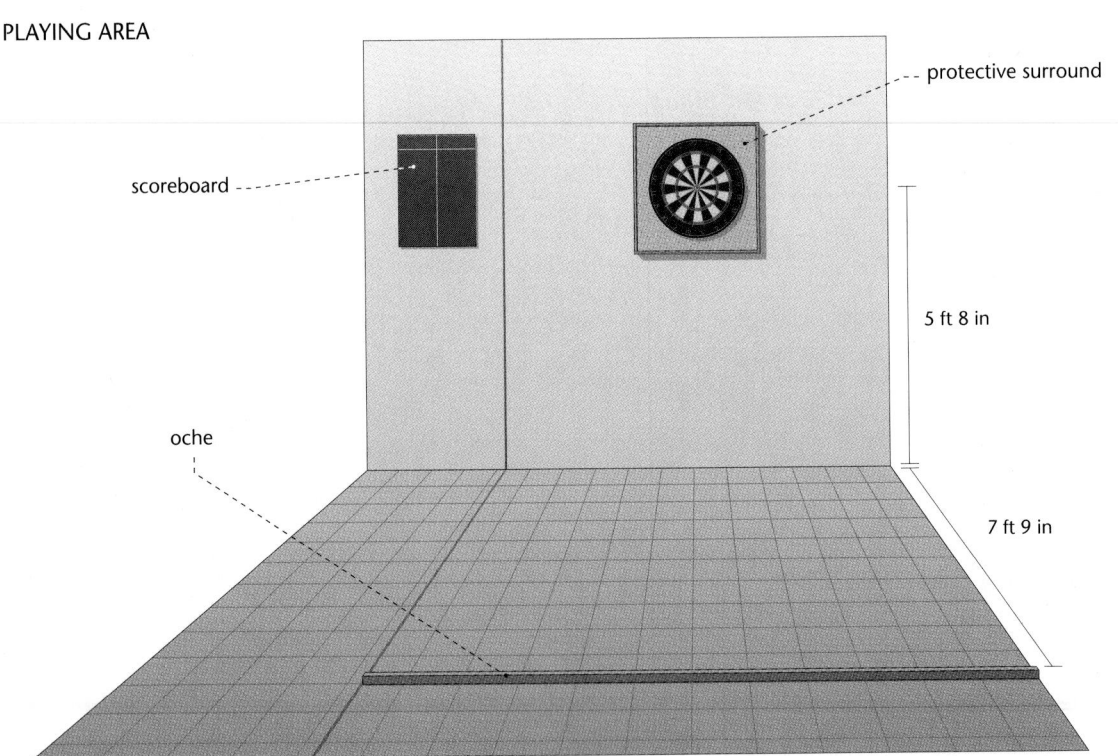

protective surround

scoreboard

5 ft 8 in

oche

7 ft 9 in

VIDEO ENTERTAINMENT SYSTEM

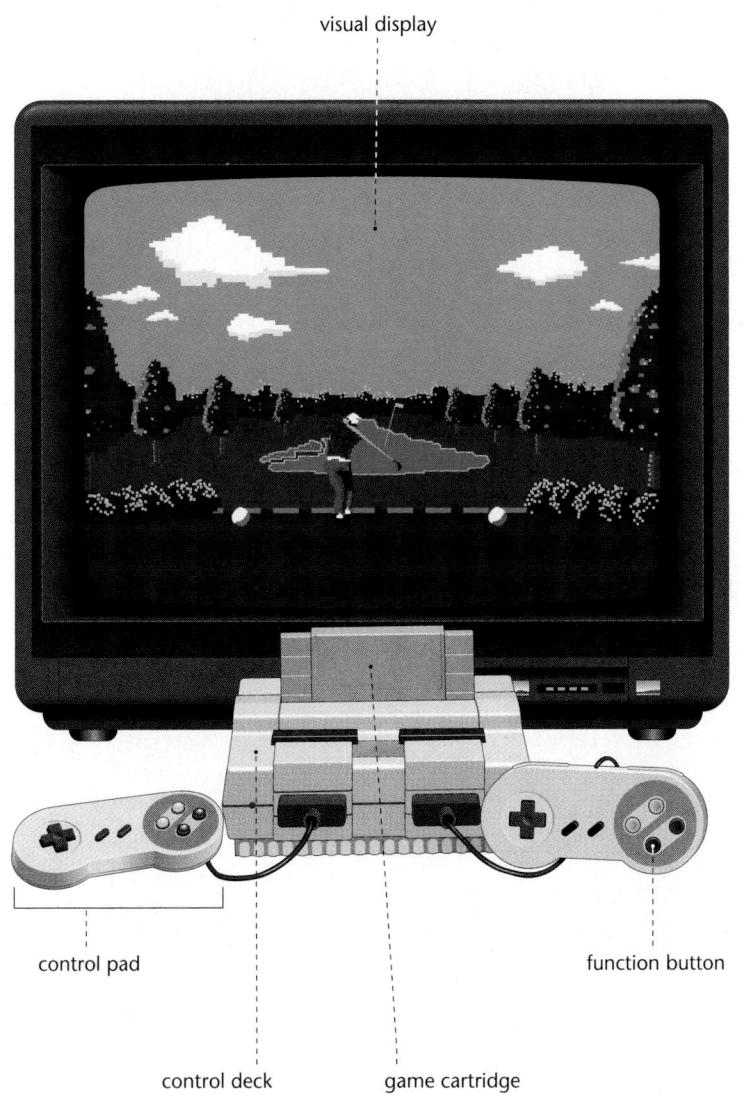

visual display

control pad

control deck

game cartridge

function button

DICE

poker die

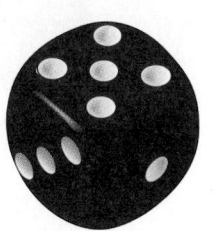

ordinary die

AMERICAN ROULETTE WHEEL

AMERICAN BETTING LAYOUT

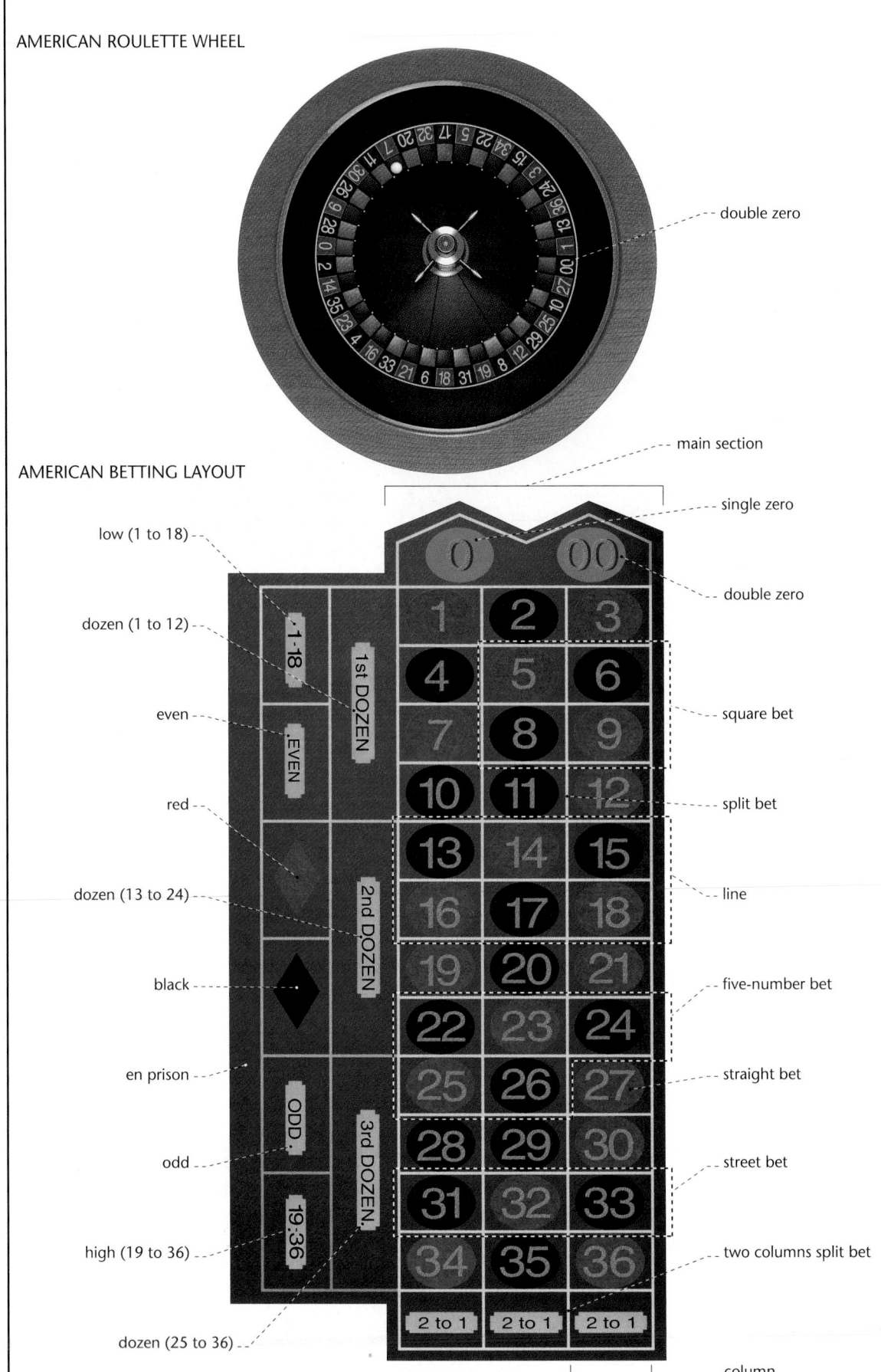

double zero

main section

single zero

double zero

low (1 to 18)

dozen (1 to 12)

even

red

dozen (13 to 24)

black

en prison

odd

high (19 to 36)

dozen (25 to 36)

square bet

split bet

line

five-number bet

straight bet

street bet

two columns split bet

column

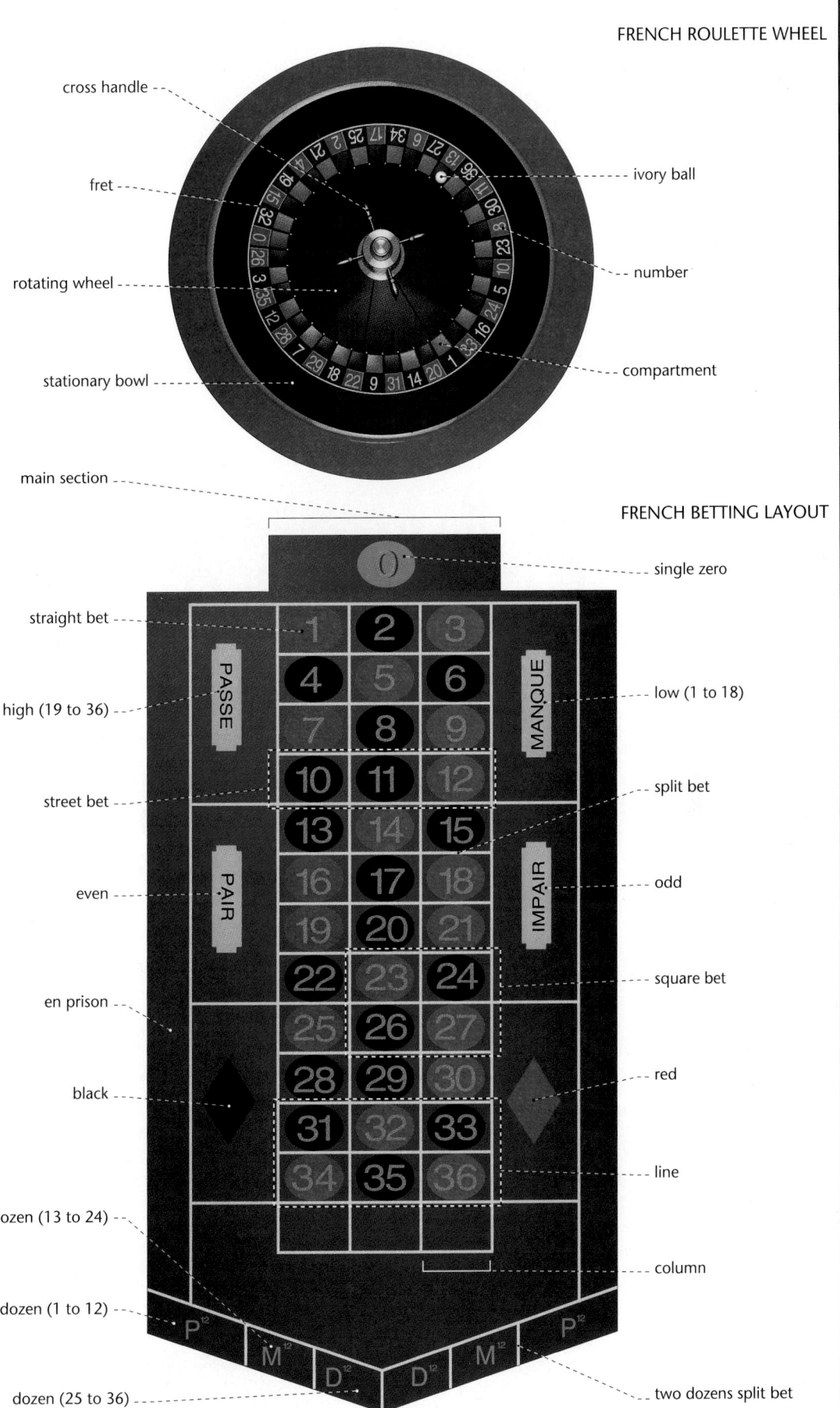

FRENCH ROULETTE WHEEL

cross handle

fret

rotating wheel

stationary bowl

ivory ball

number

compartment

main section

FRENCH BETTING LAYOUT

single zero

straight bet

high (19 to 36)

PASSE

MANQUE

low (1 to 18)

street bet

split bet

even

PAIR

IMPAIR

odd

en prison

square bet

black

red

line

dozen (13 to 24)

dozen (1 to 12)

column

dozen (25 to 36)

two dozens split bet

SLOT MACHINE

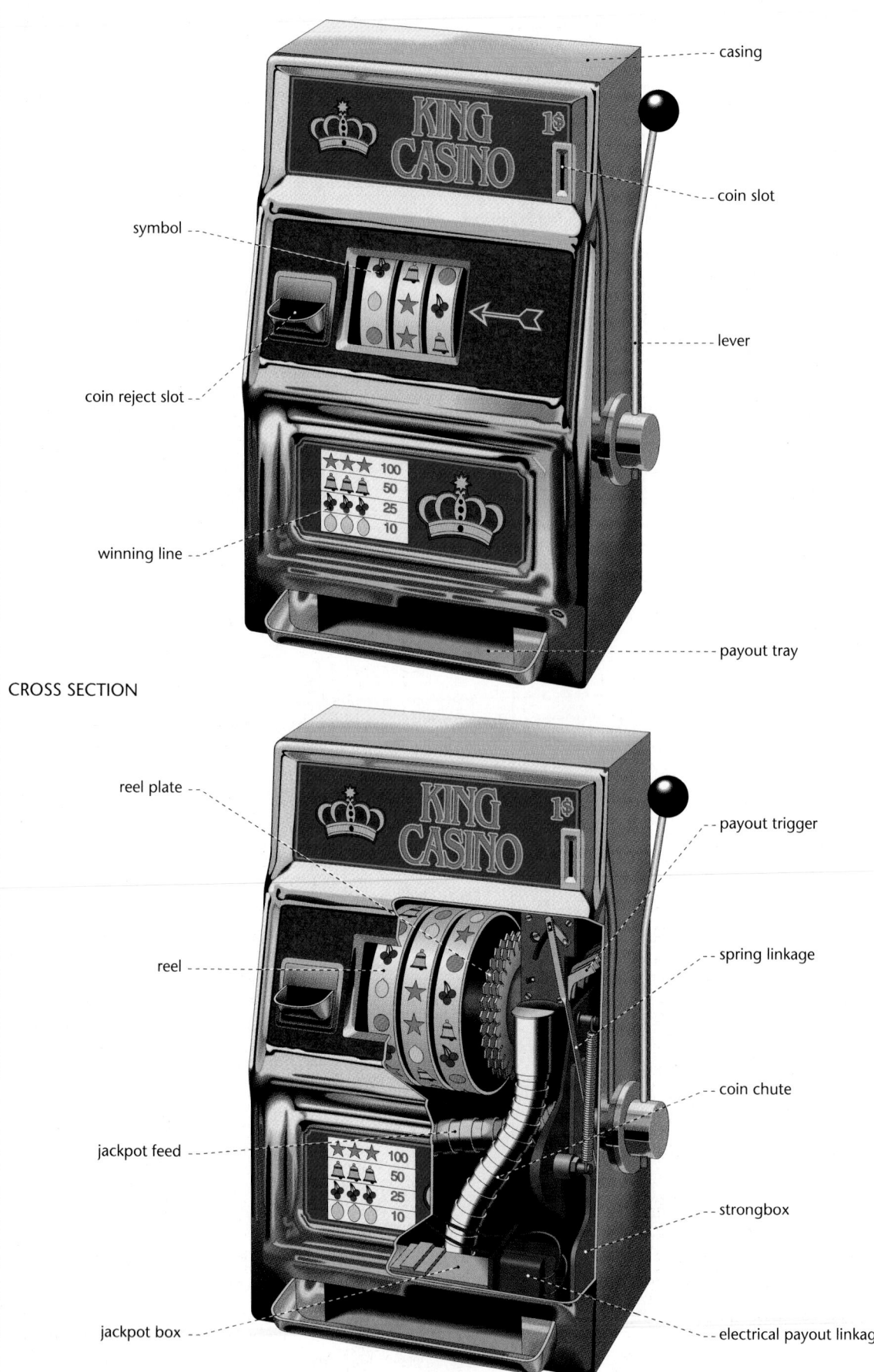

casing

coin slot

symbol

coin reject slot

lever

winning line

payout tray

CROSS SECTION

reel plate

payout trigger

spring linkage

reel

coin chute

jackpot feed

strongbox

jackpot box

electrical payout linkage

CONTENTS

MEASURE OF TEMPERATURE 705

MEASURE OF TIME..706

MEASURE OF WEIGHT..708

MEASURE OF PRESSURE 710

MEASURE OF LENGTH...711

MEASURE OF DISTANCE 711

MEASURE OF THICKNESS...711

WATT-HOUR METER..712

MEASURE OF ANGLES...713

MEASURE OF SEISMIC WAVES..714

MEASURING DEVICES

MEASURE OF TEMPERATURE

THERMOMETER

CLINICAL THERMOMETER

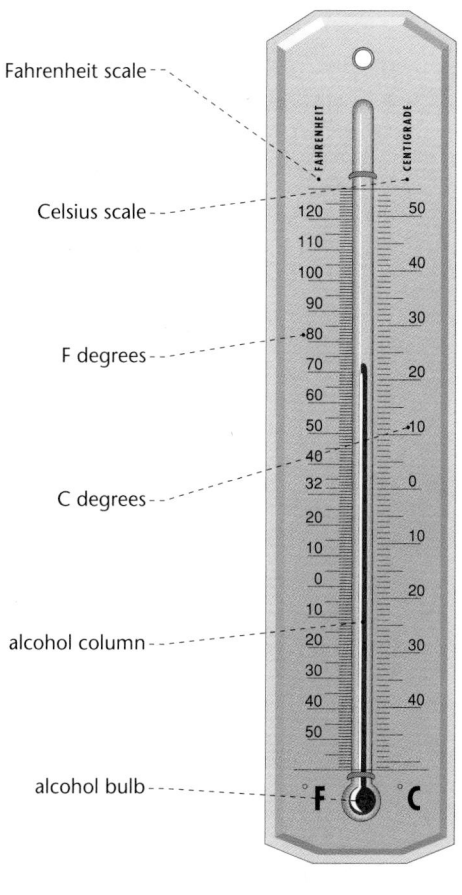

Fahrenheit scale

Celsius scale

F degrees

C degrees

alcohol column

alcohol bulb

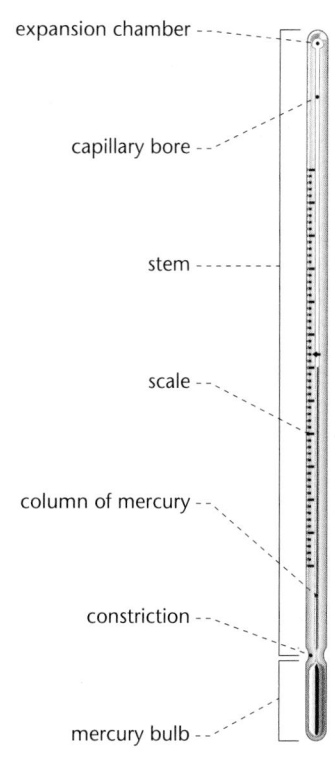

expansion chamber

capillary bore

stem

scale

column of mercury

constriction

mercury bulb

BIMETALLIC THERMOMETER

ROOM THERMOSTAT

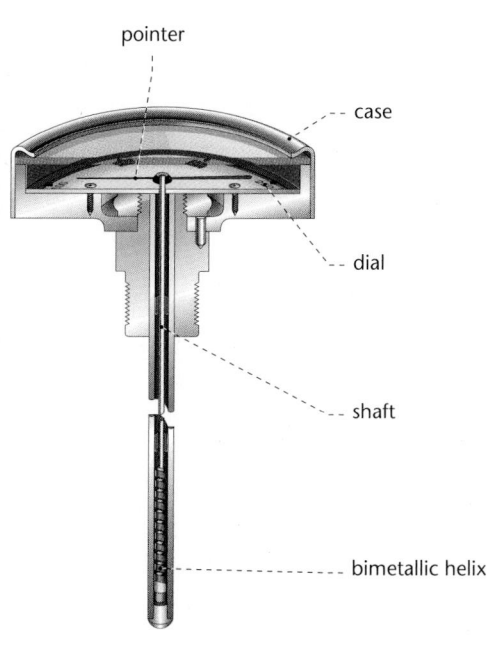

pointer

case

dial

shaft

bimetallic helix

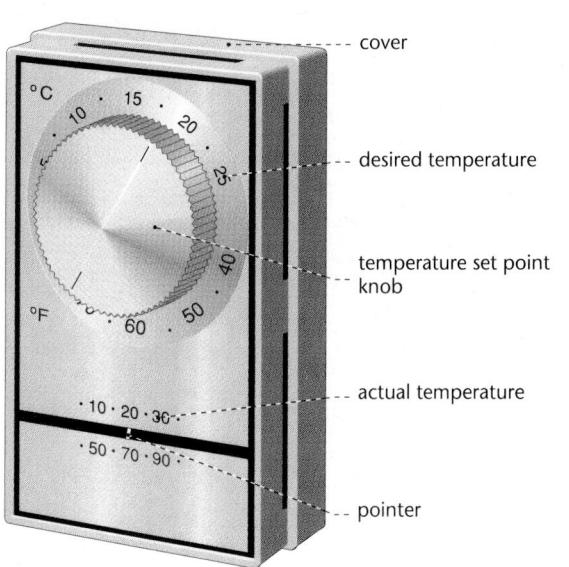

cover

desired temperature

temperature set point knob

actual temperature

pointer

STOPWATCH

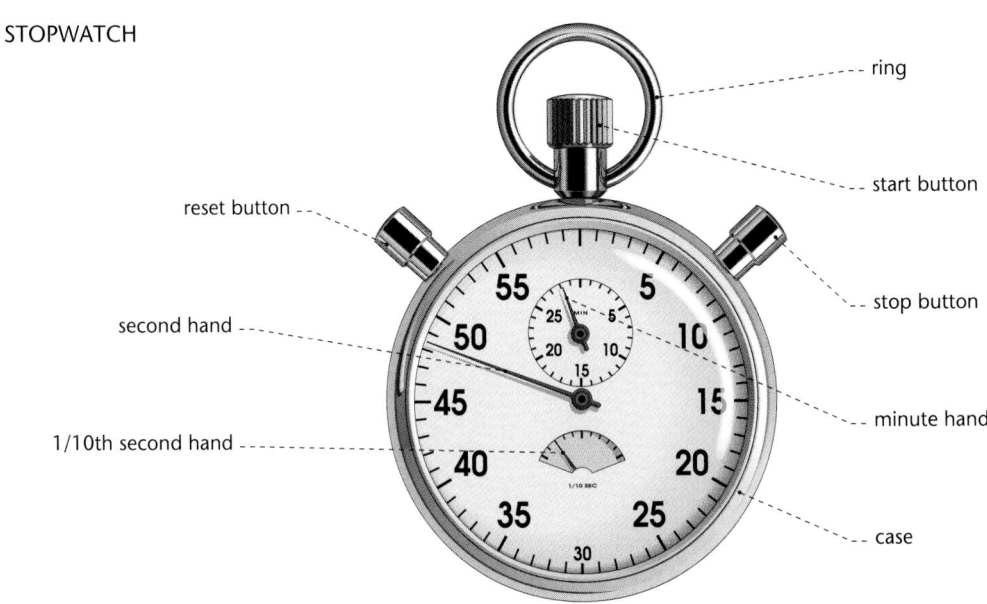

ring

start button

reset button

stop button

second hand

1/10th second hand

minute hand

case

MECHANICAL WATCH

ANALOG WATCH

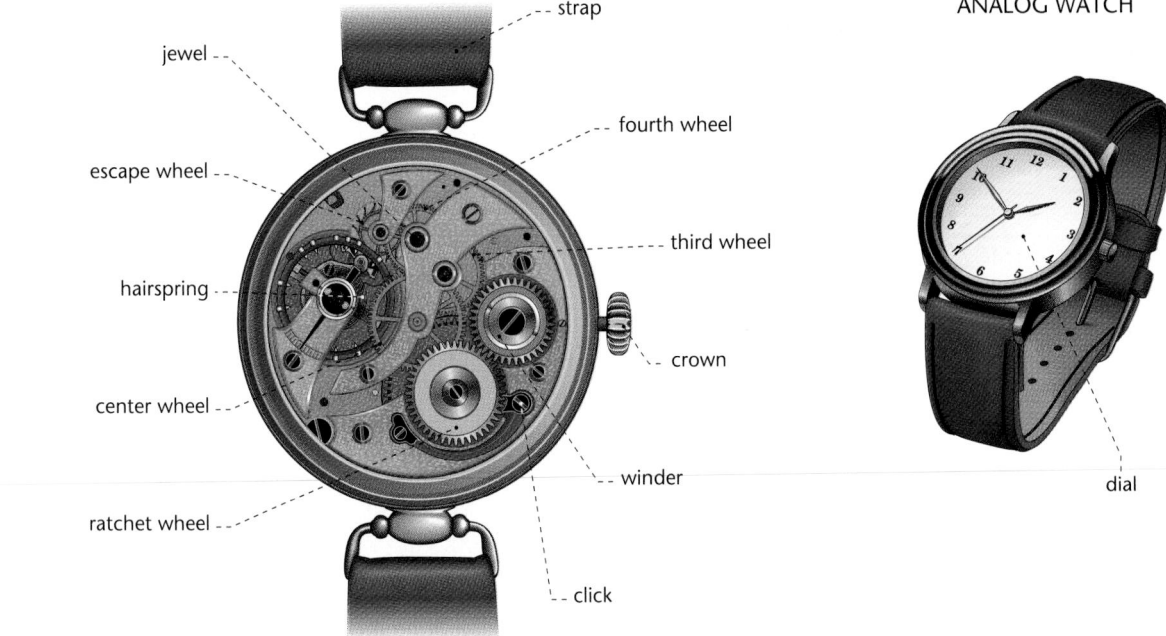

strap

jewel

fourth wheel

escape wheel

third wheel

hairspring

crown

center wheel

winder

ratchet wheel

click

dial

SUNDIAL

DIGITAL WATCH

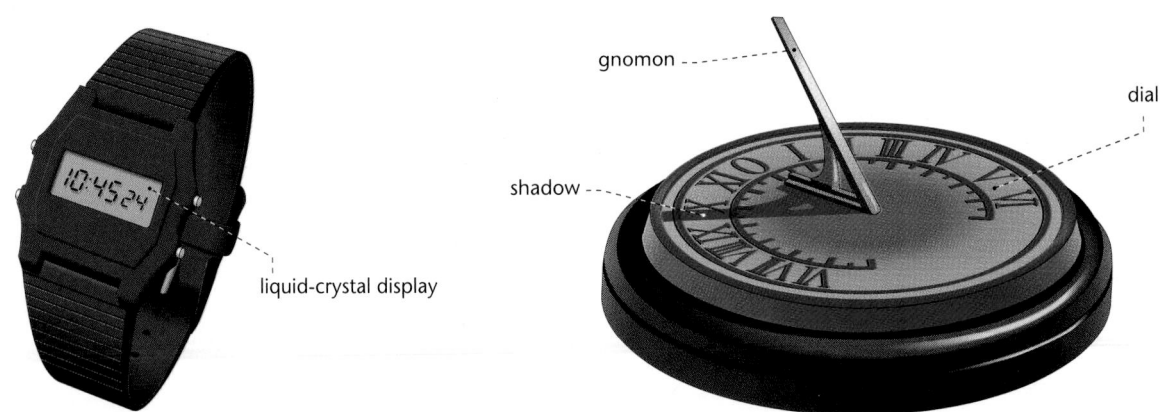

gnomon

dial

shadow

liquid-crystal display

GRANDFATHER CLOCK

pediment
body
hour hand
dial
plinth
Moon dial
minute hand
weight
pendulum
chain

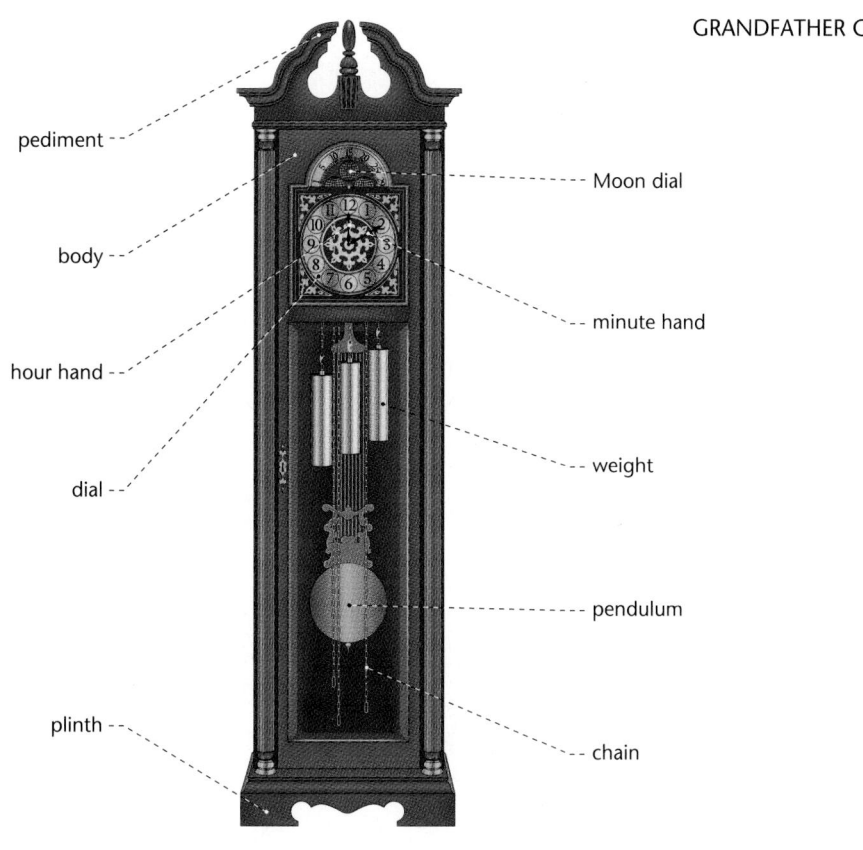

WEIGHT-DRIVEN CLOCK MECHANISM

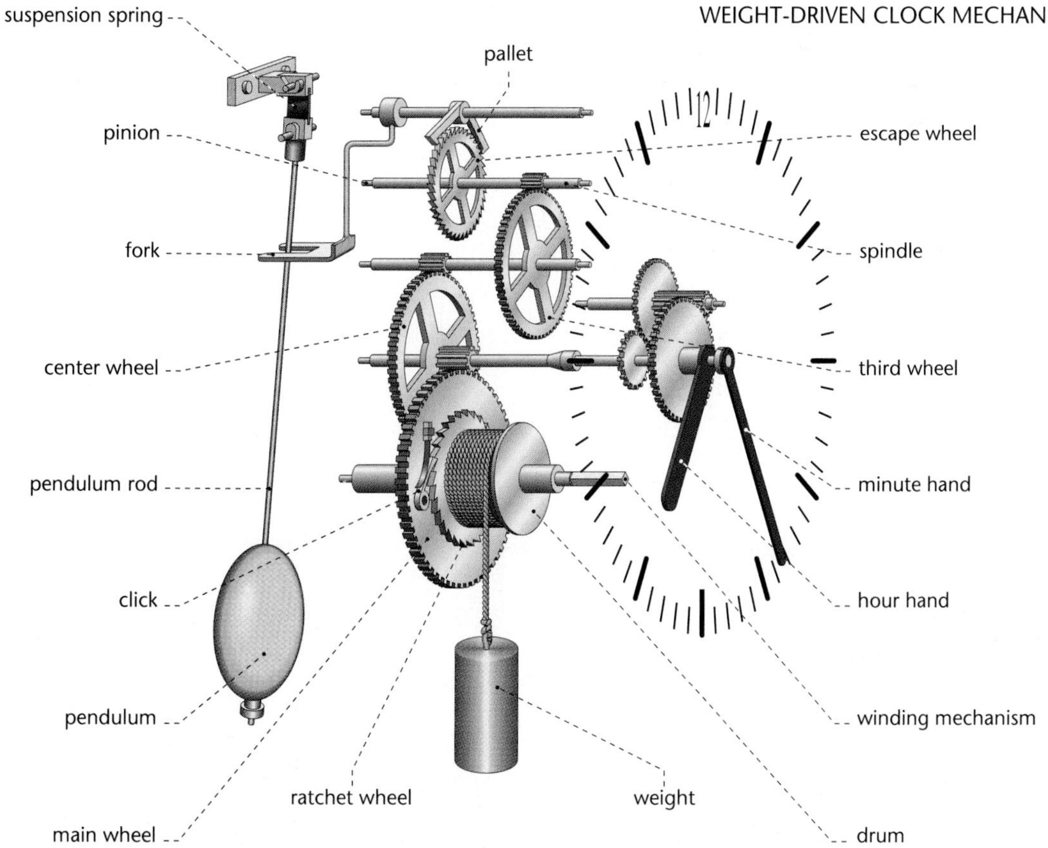

suspension spring
pallet
pinion
fork
center wheel
pendulum rod
click
pendulum
main wheel
ratchet wheel
weight
escape wheel
spindle
third wheel
minute hand
hour hand
winding mechanism
drum

MEASURE OF WEIGHT

BEAM BALANCE

beam

pan

weight

STEELYARD

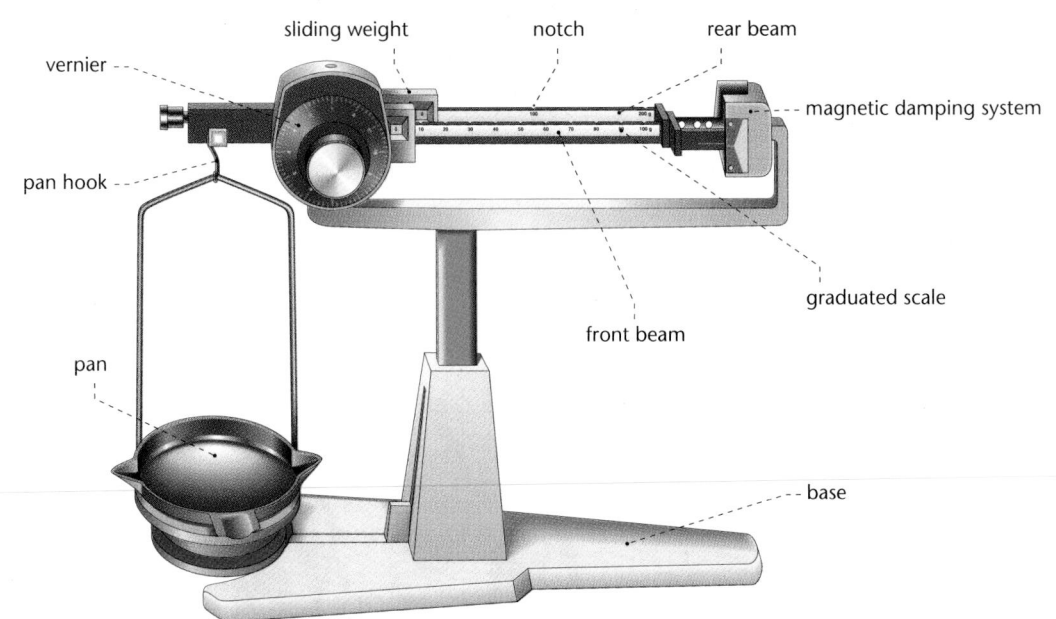

sliding weight

notch

rear beam

vernier

magnetic damping system

pan hook

graduated scale

front beam

pan

base

ROBERVAL'S BALANCE

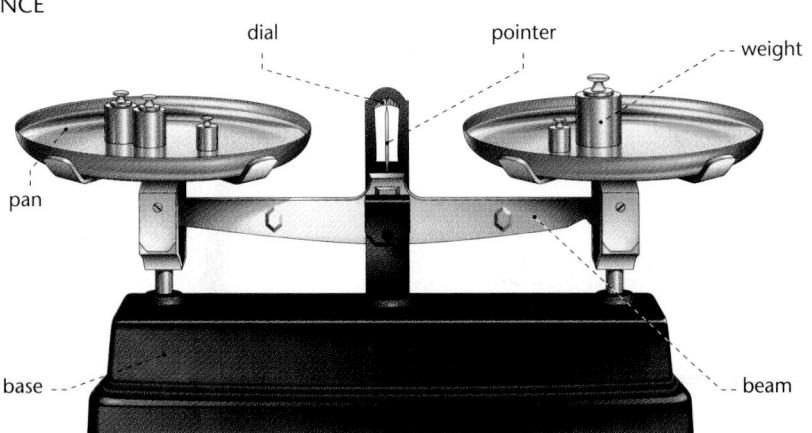

dial

pointer

weight

pan

base

beam

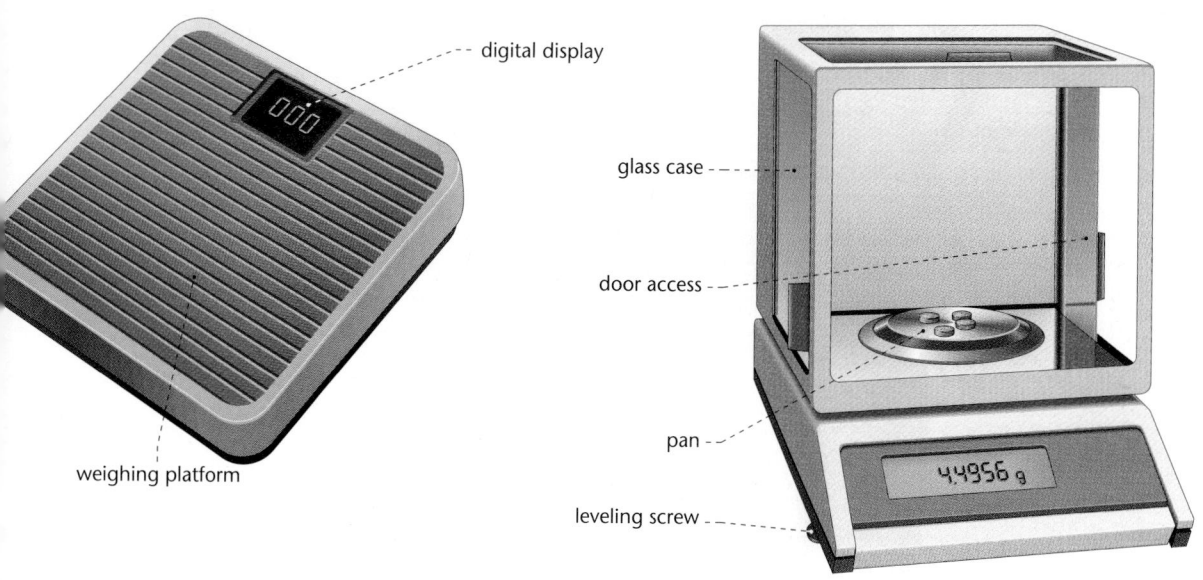

SPRING BALANCE

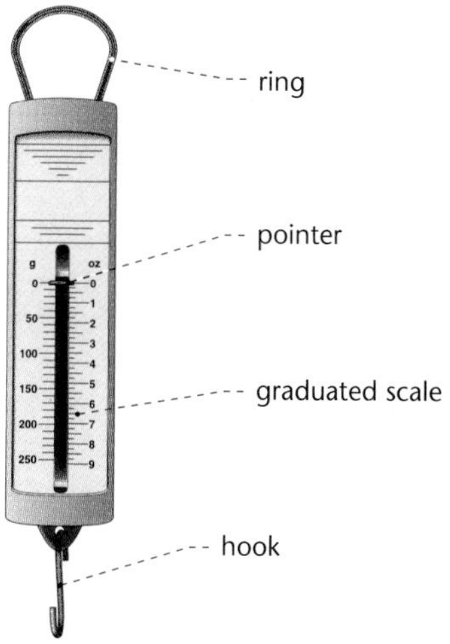

ring

pointer

graduated scale

hook

ELECTRONIC SCALE

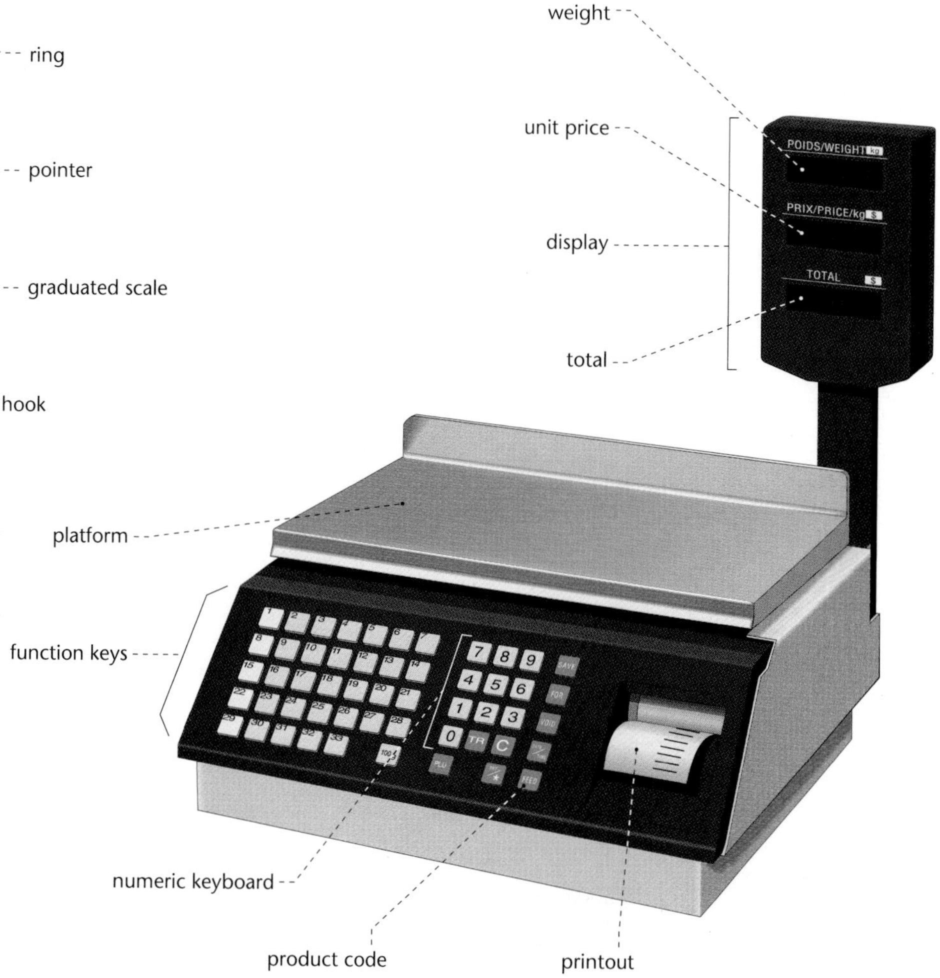

weight

unit price

display

total

POIDS/WEIGHT

PRIX/PRICE/kg

TOTAL

platform

function keys

numeric keyboard

product code

printout

BATHROOM SCALE

digital display

weighing platform

ANALYTICAL BALANCE

glass case

door access

pan

leveling screw

MEASURING DEVICES

MEASURING DEVICES

BAROMETER/THERMOMETER

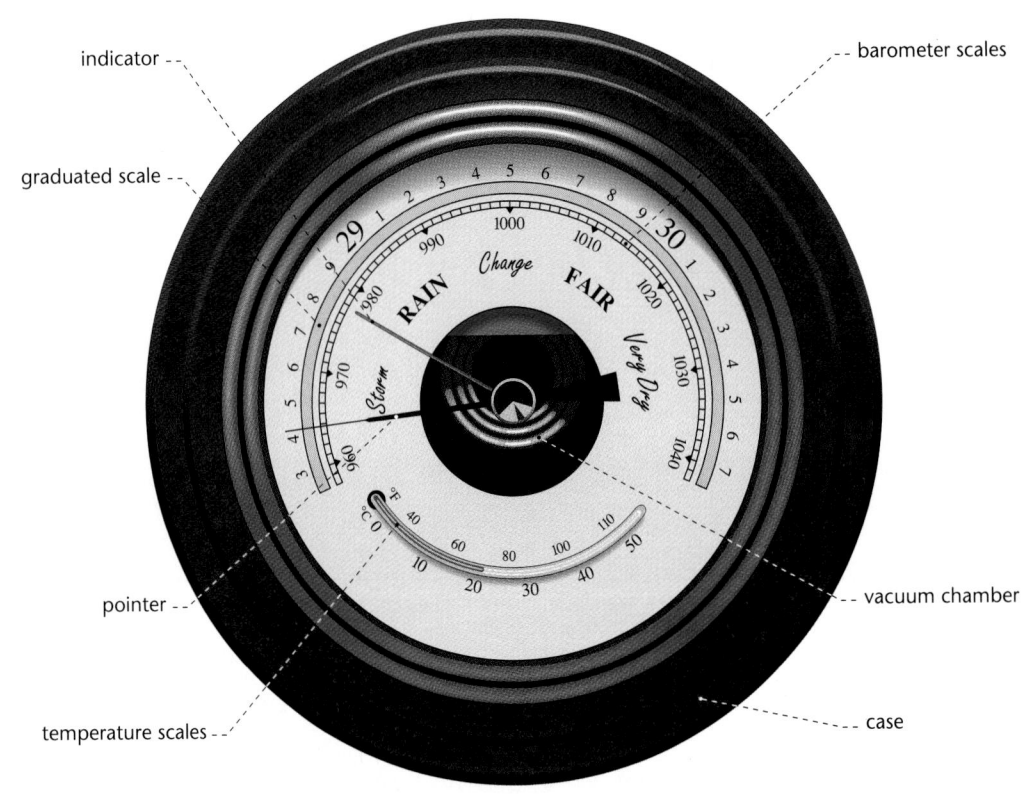

indicator

barometer scales

graduated scale

pointer

vacuum chamber

temperature scales

case

TENSIOMETER

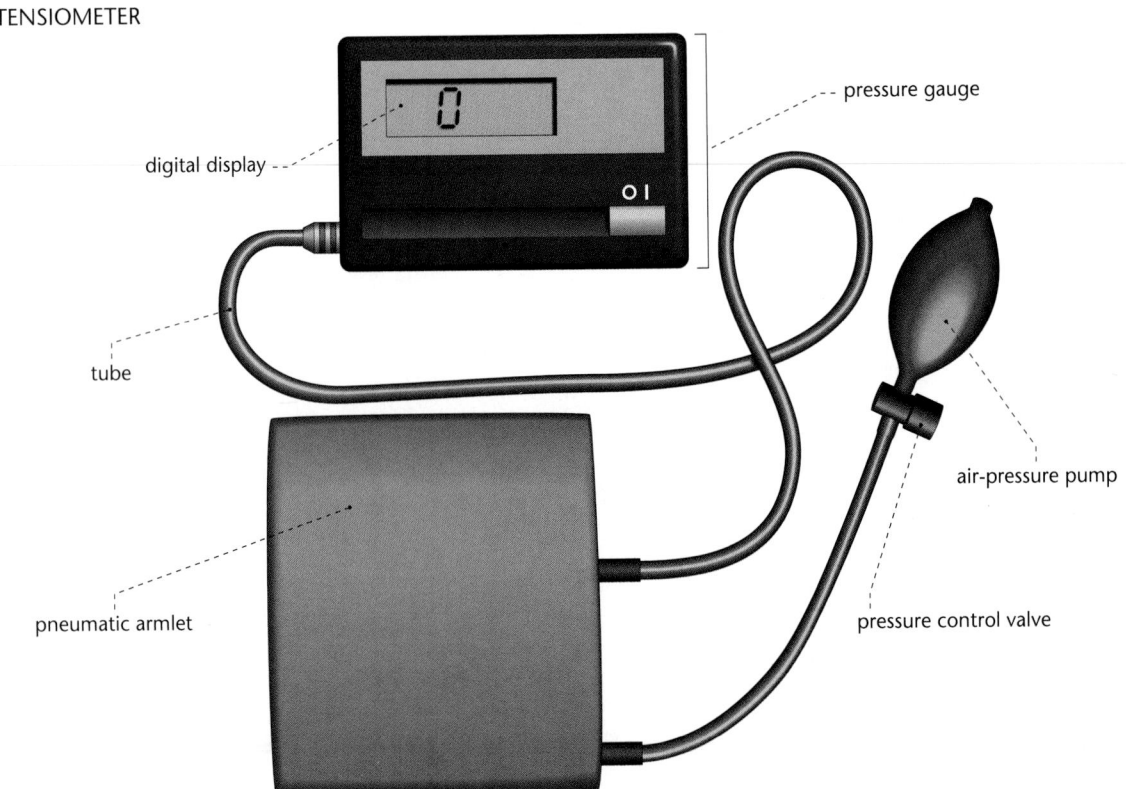

pressure gauge

digital display

tube

air-pressure pump

pneumatic armlet

pressure control valve

MEASURE OF LENGTH

TAPE MEASURE

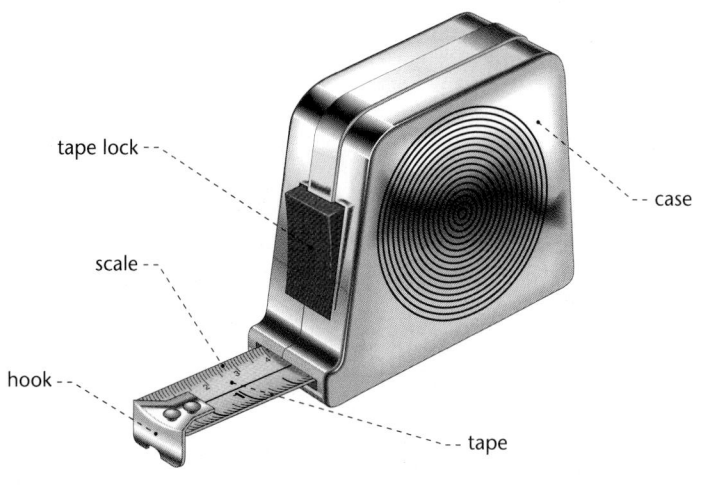

tape lock

scale

hook

case

tape

MEASURE OF DISTANCE

PEDOMETER

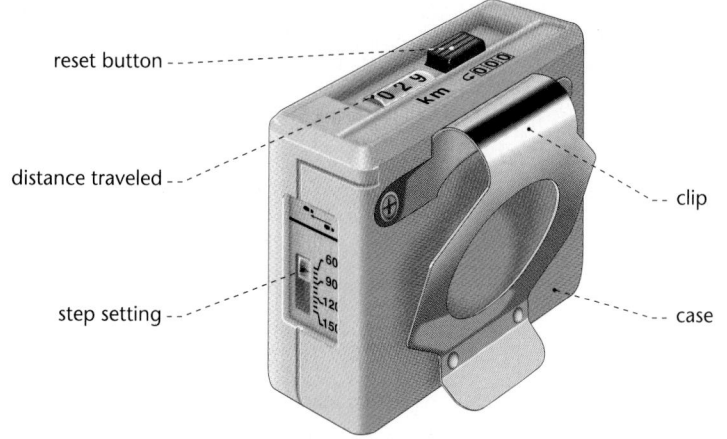

reset button

distance traveled

step setting

clip

case

MEASURE OF THICKNESS

MICROMETER CALIPER

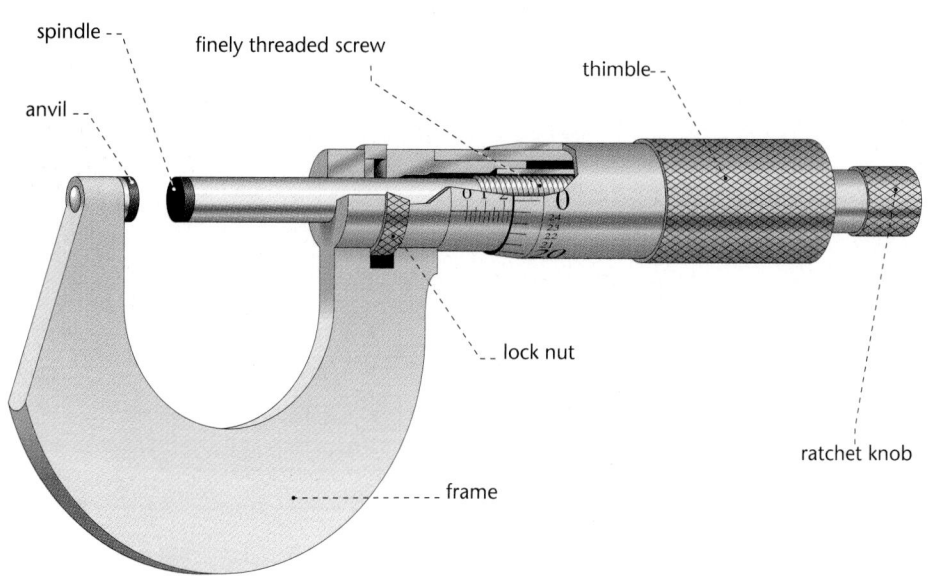

spindle

finely threaded screw

thimble

anvil

lock nut

ratchet knob

frame

711

WATT-HOUR METER

EXTERIOR VIEW

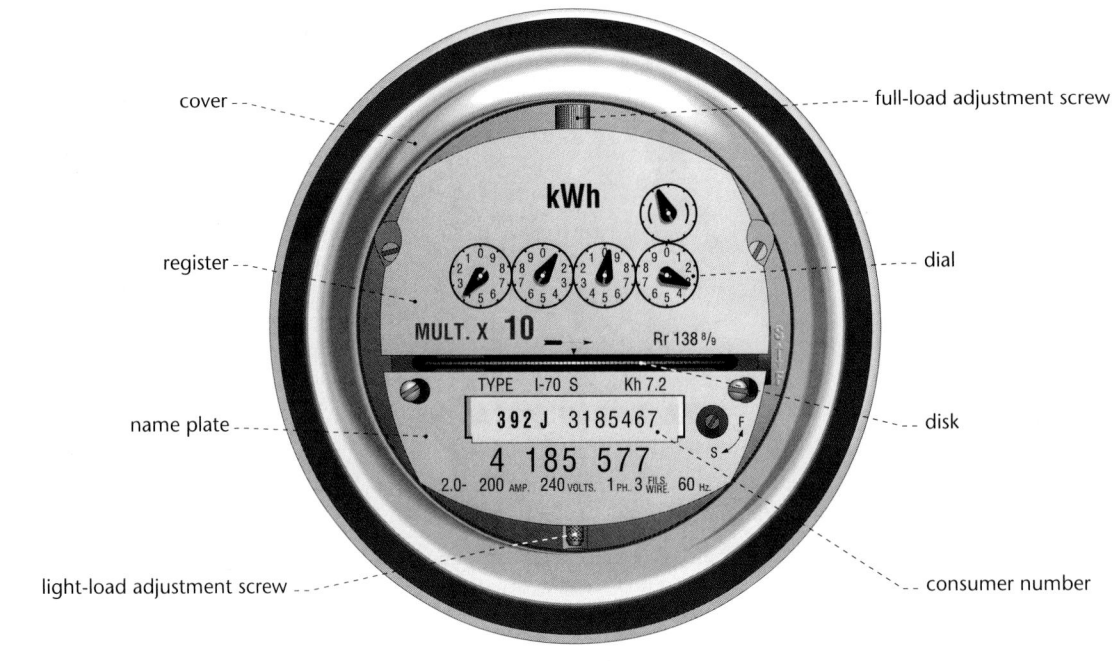

cover

full-load adjustment screw

register

dial

name plate

disk

light-load adjustment screw

consumer number

MECHANISM

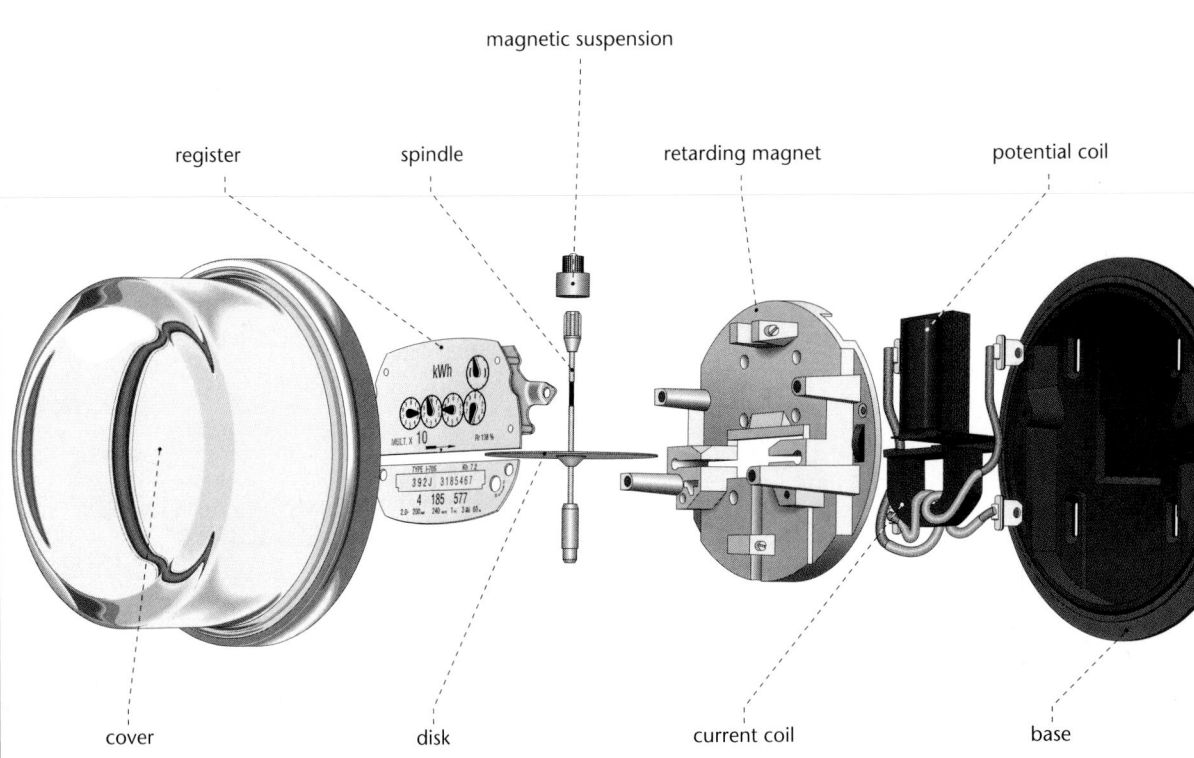

magnetic suspension

register

spindle

retarding magnet

potential coil

cover

disk

current coil

base

MEASURE OF ANGLES

alidade

optical sight

adjustment for vertical-circle image

telescope

illumination mirror

micrometer screw

adjustment for horizontal-circle image

alidade level

horizontal clamp

leveling head level

leveling screw

leveling head

base plate

leveling head locking knob

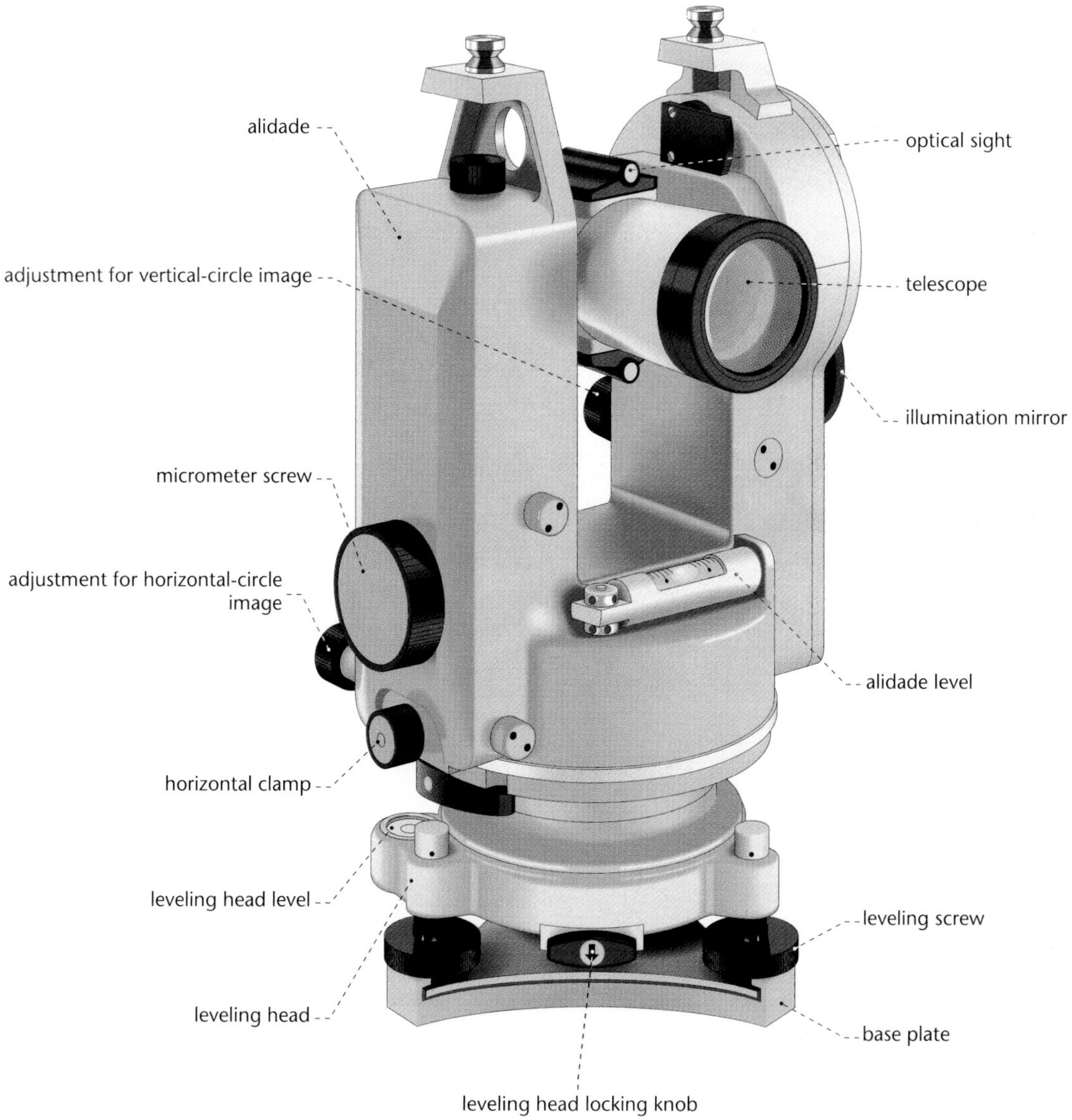

bevel square

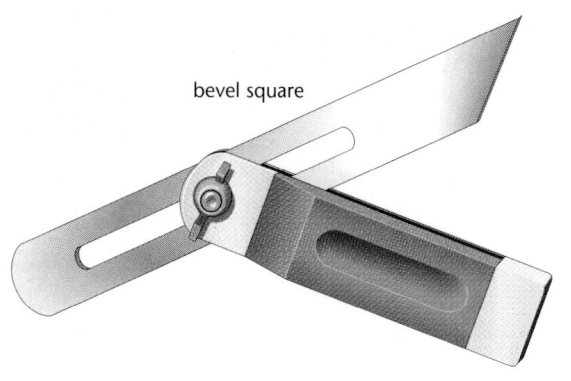

protractor

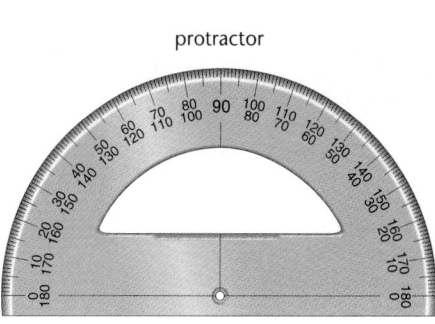

MEASURE OF SEISMIC WAVES

DETECTION OF SEISMIC WAVES

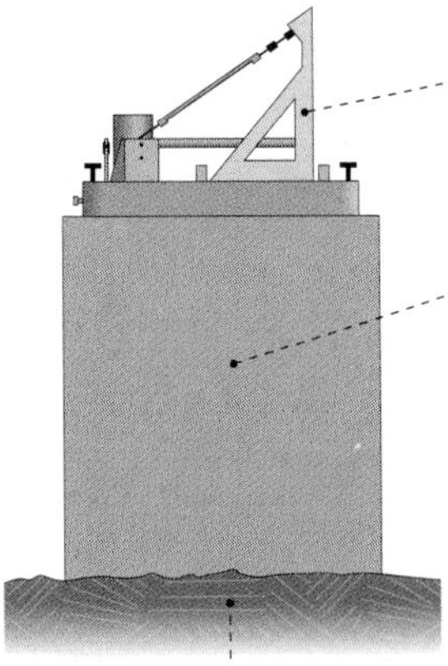

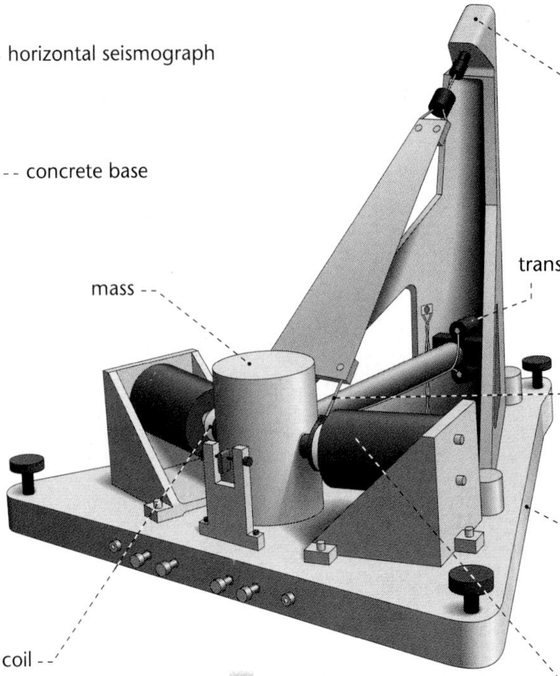

horizontal seismograph

pillar

concrete base

transmission of the electrical current

mass

wire

stand

bedrock

coil

magnet

AMPLIFICATION OF SEISMIC WAVES

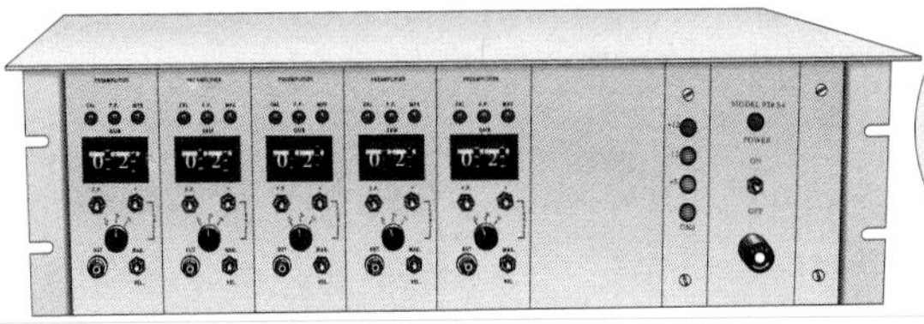

amplifier

clock

TRANSCRIPTION OF SEISMIC WAVES

visualization of seismic waves

seismogram

rotating drum

pen

drum

sheet of paper

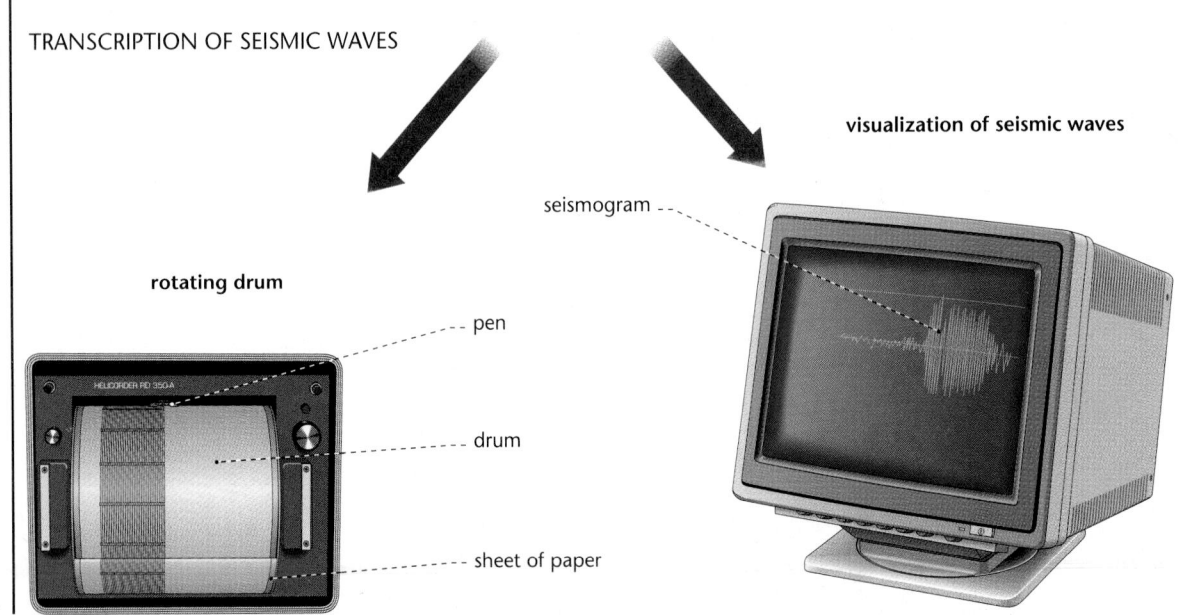

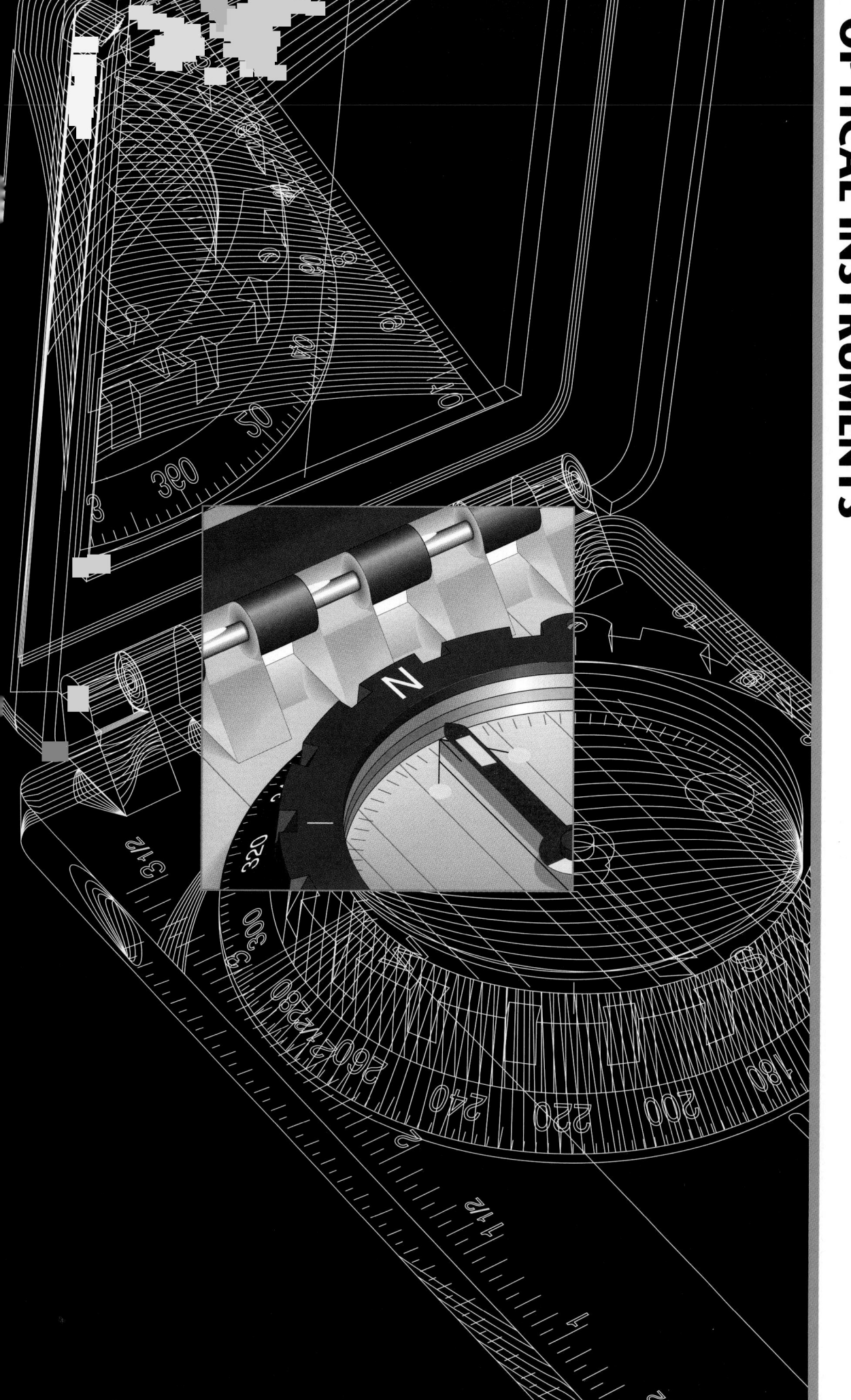

CONTENTS

ELECTRON MICROSCOPE 717

BINOCULAR MICROSCOPE 718

TELESCOPIC SIGHT 718

PRISM BINOCULARS...719

MAGNETIC COMPASS 719

REFLECTING TELESCOPE 720

REFRACTING TELESCOPE 721

RADAR 722

LENSES...722

OPTICAL INSTRUMENTS

ELECTRON MICROSCOPE

CROSS SECTION OF AN ELECTRON MICROSCOPE

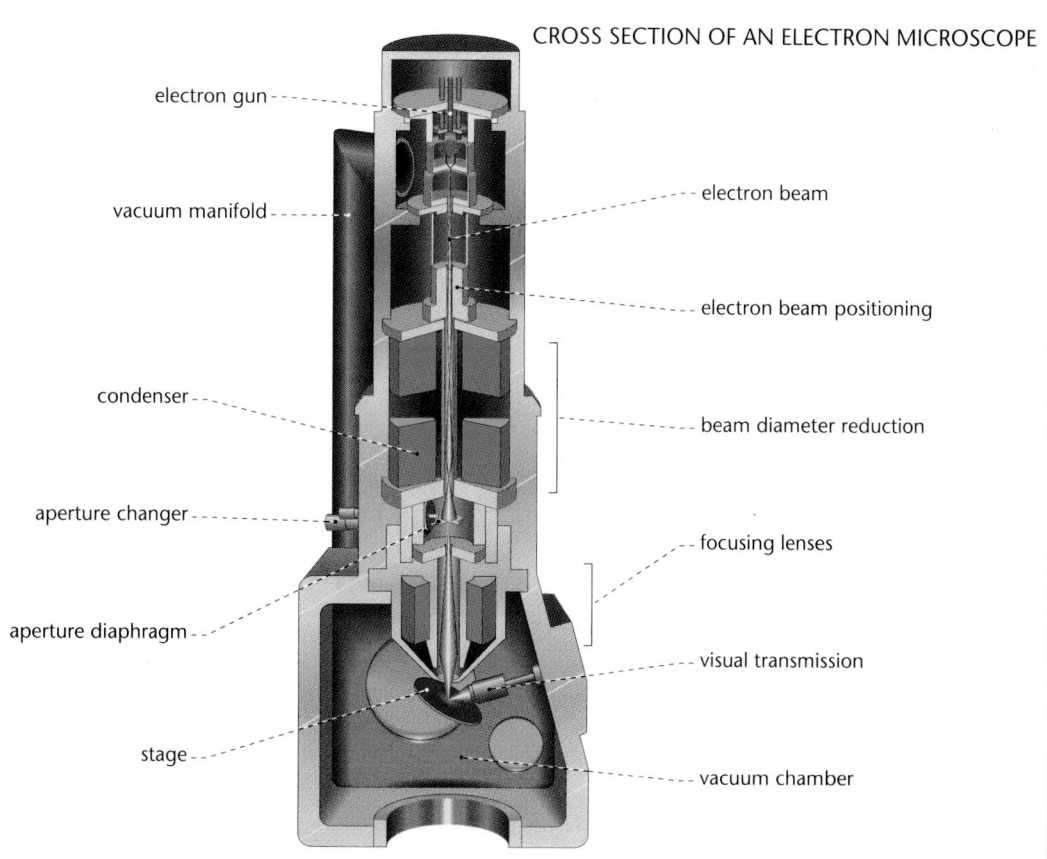

electron gun

vacuum manifold

condenser

aperture changer

aperture diaphragm

stage

electron beam

electron beam positioning

beam diameter reduction

focusing lenses

visual transmission

vacuum chamber

ELECTRON MICROSCOPE ELEMENTS

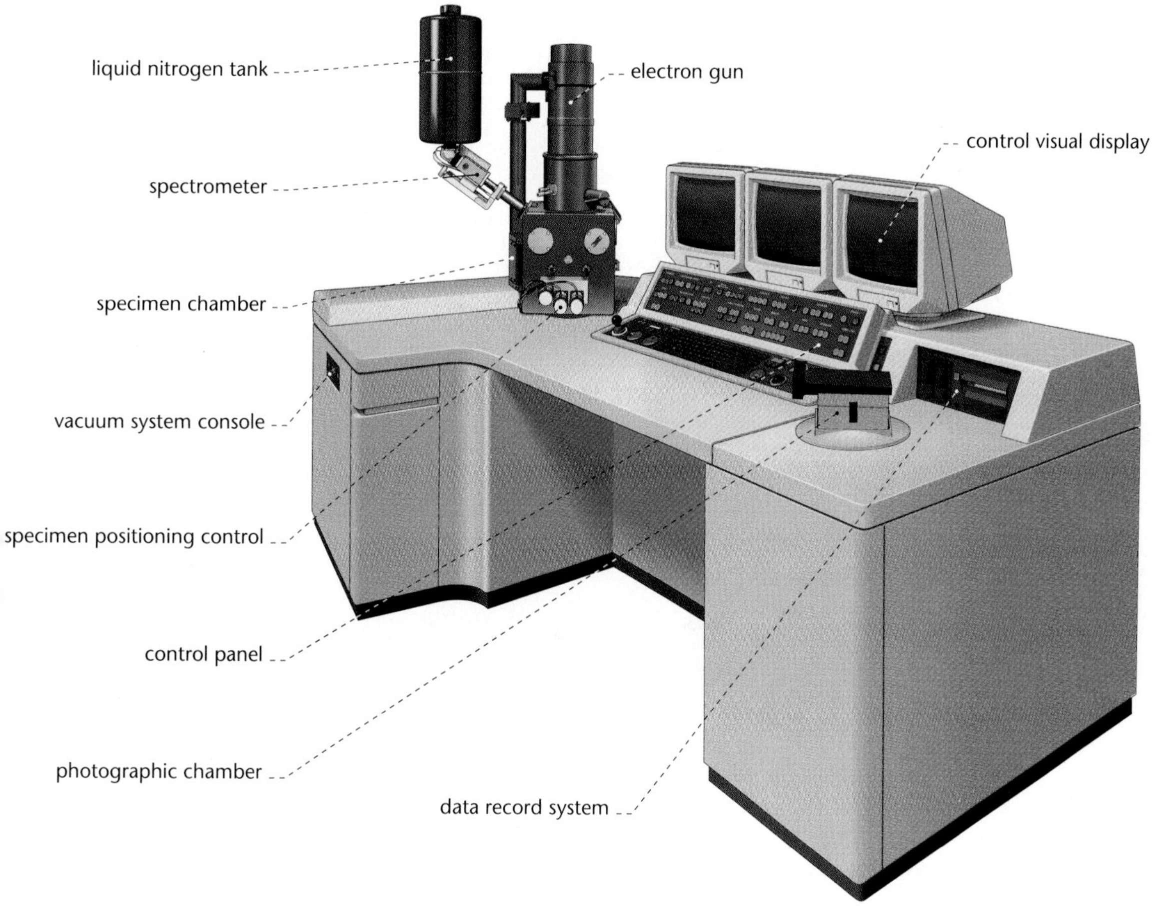

liquid nitrogen tank

spectrometer

specimen chamber

vacuum system console

specimen positioning control

control panel

photographic chamber

data record system

electron gun

control visual display

717

BINOCULAR MICROSCOPE

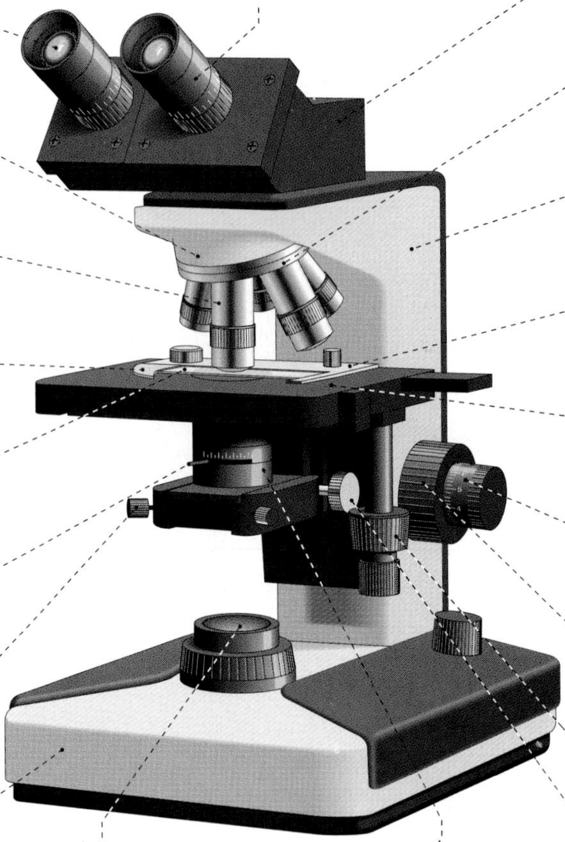

eyepiece

draw tube

body tube

revolving nosepiece

limb top

arm

objective

mechanical stage

stage clip

stage

glass slide

fine adjustment knob

field lens adjustment

condenser adjustment knob

coarse adjustment knob

base

lamp

condenser

mechanical stage control

condenser height adjustment

TELESCOPIC SIGHT

elevation adjustment

main scope tube

reticle

erecting lenses

objective lens

eyepiece

field lens

dovetail

turret cap

winding adjustment

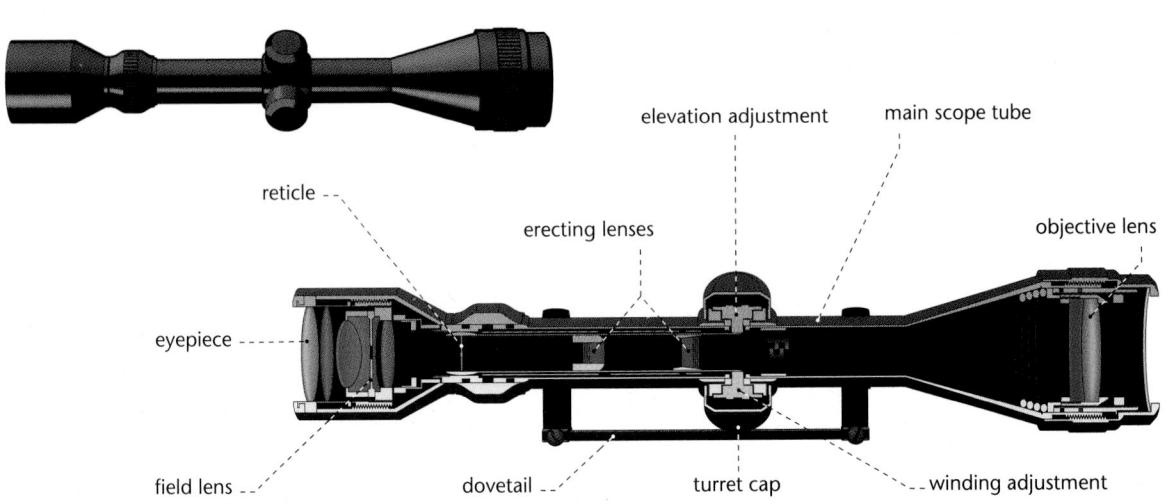

PRISM BINOCULARS

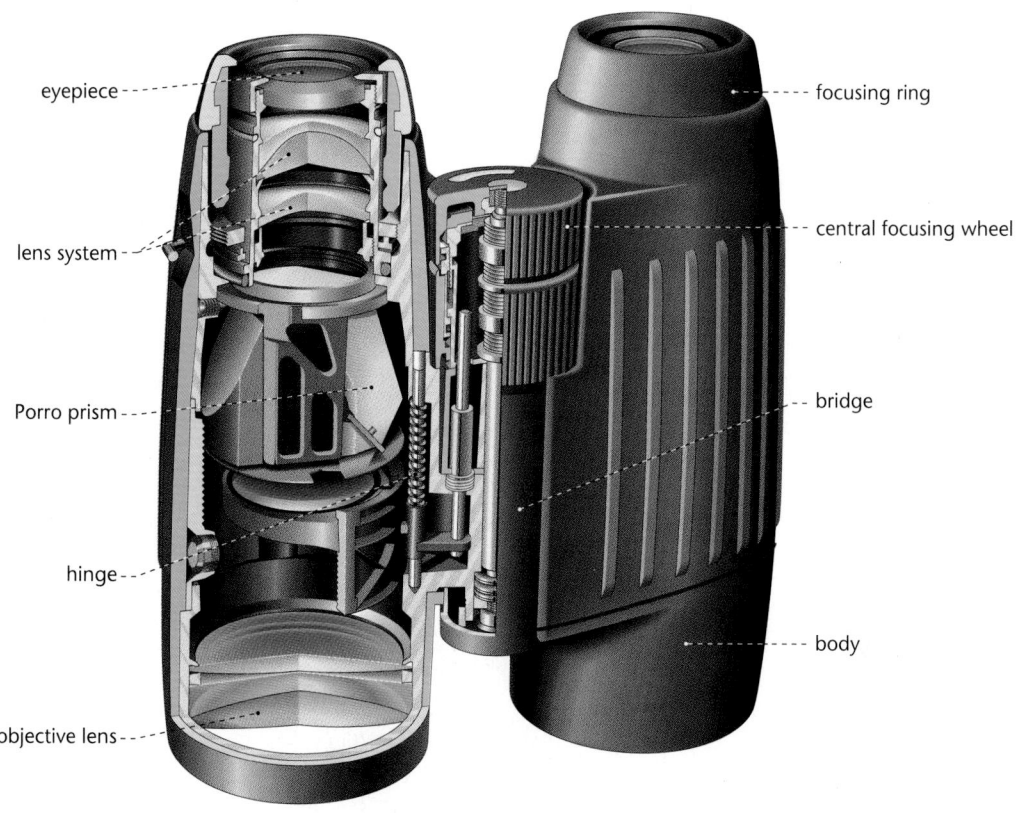

eyepiece

lens system

Porro prism

hinge

objective lens

focusing ring

central focusing wheel

bridge

body

MAGNETIC COMPASS

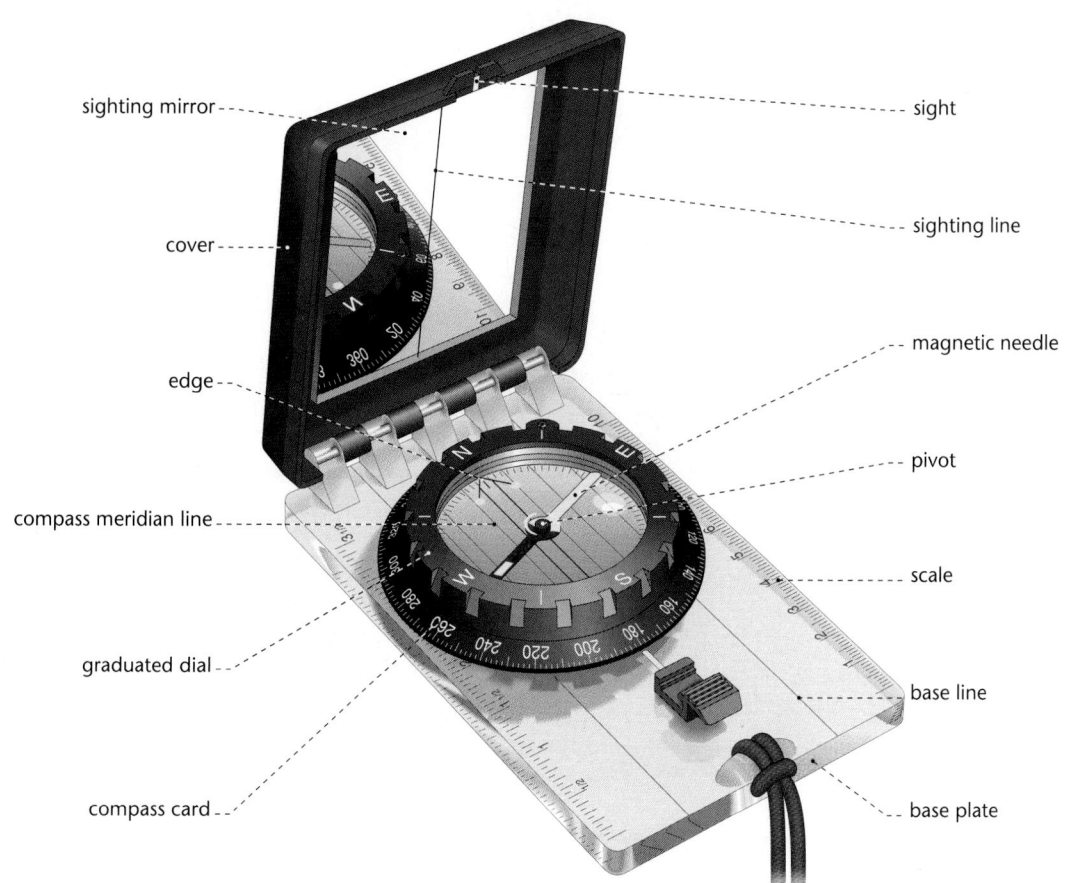

sighting mirror

cover

edge

compass meridian line

graduated dial

compass card

sight

sighting line

magnetic needle

pivot

scale

base line

base plate

REFLECTING TELESCOPE

support
finderscope
eyepiece
cradle
main tube
focusing knob
declination setting scale
right ascension setting scale
azimuth clamp
azimuth fine adjustment
altitude clamp
altitude fine adjustment

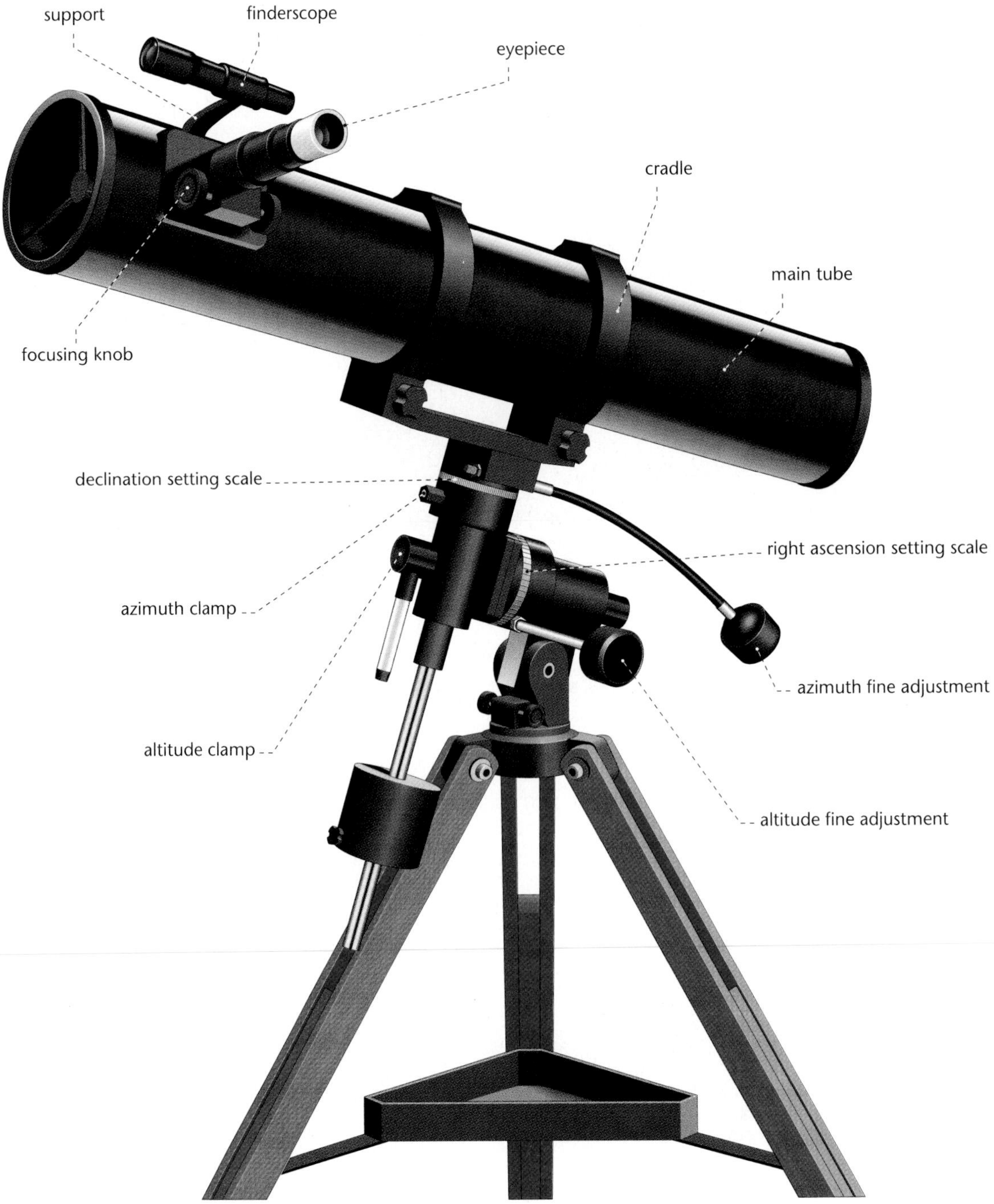

CROSS SECTION OF A REFLECTING TELESCOPE

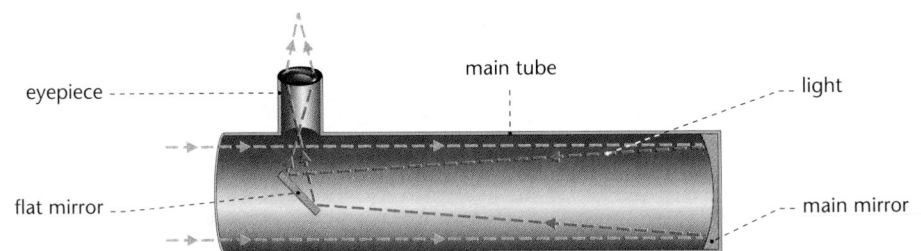

eyepiece
main tube
light
flat mirror
main mirror

REFRACTING TELESCOPE

dew shield

cradle

main tube

objective lens

finderscope

eyepiece

eyepiece holder

star diagonal

focusing knob

azimuth fine adjustment

altitude fine adjustment

fork

declination setting scale

azimuth clamp

altitude clamp

right ascension setting scale

counterweight

tripod

tripod accessories shelf

CROSS SECTION OF A REFRACTING TELESCOPE

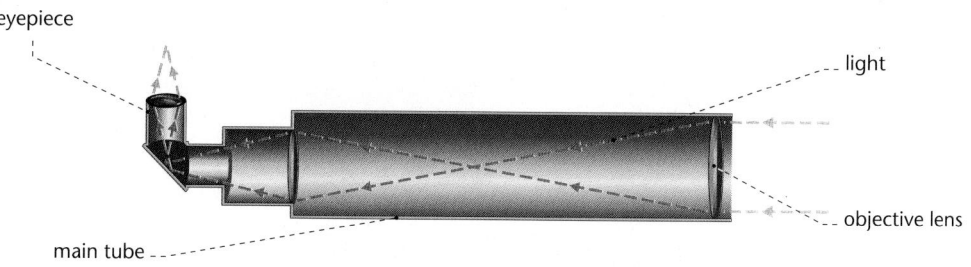

eyepiece

light

main tube

objective lens

LENSES

CONVERGING LENSES

convex lens ---------- positive meniscus

biconvex lens ---------- plano-convex lens

DIVERGING LENSES

concave lens ---------- negative meniscus

biconcave lens ---------- plano-concave lens

RADAR

transmitted pulse ---

airplane

echo ---

adjustable antenna ---

transmitting station

receiving station

information processing

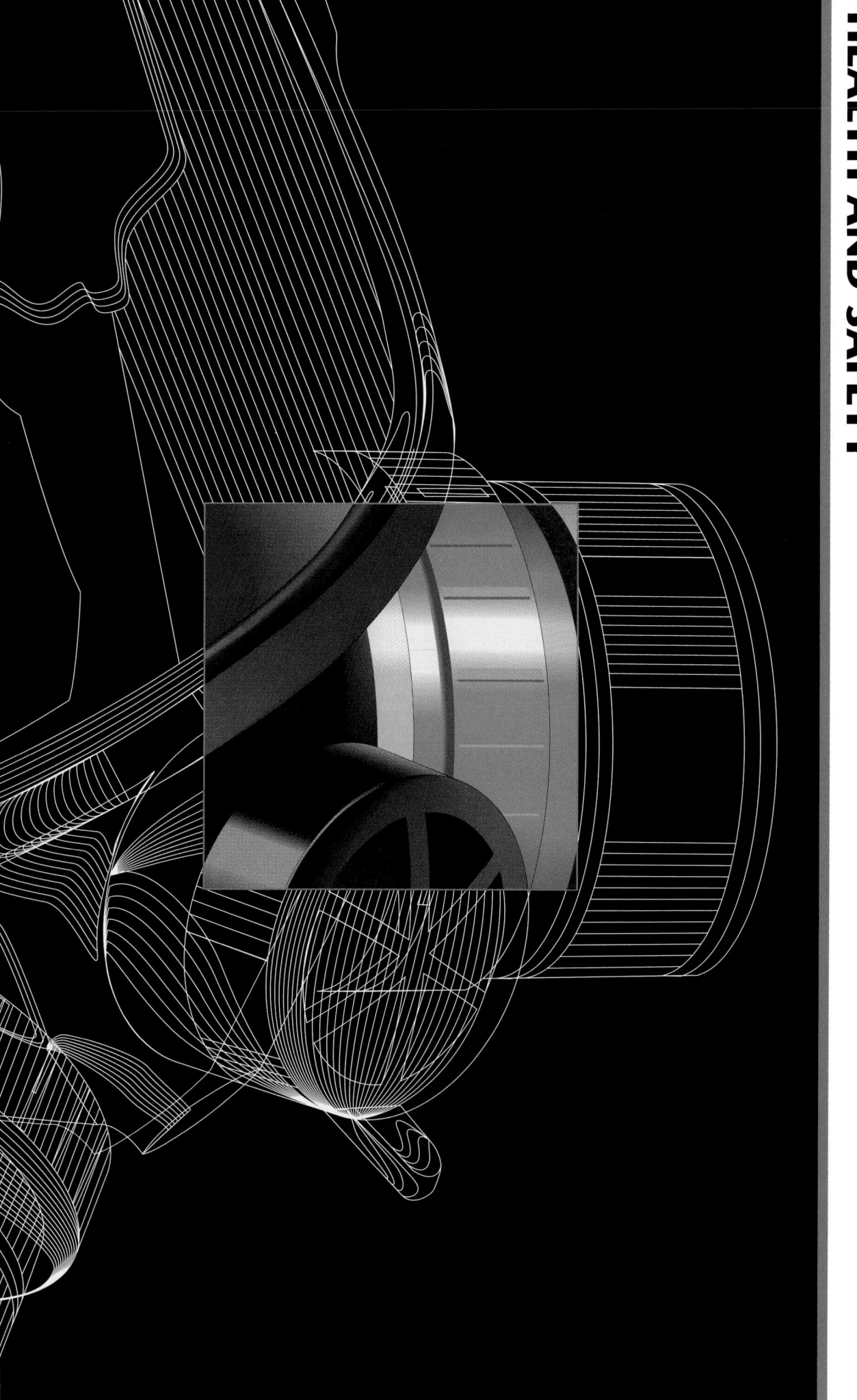

CONTENTS

FIRST AID KIT 725

FIRST AID EQUIPMENT 726

WHEELCHAIR 727

WALKING AIDS 728

EAR PROTECTION 729

EYE PROTECTION 729

HEAD PROTECTION 729

RESPIRATORY SYSTEM PROTECTION 730

SAFETY VEST 730

FEET PROTECTION 730

HEALTH AND SAFETY

FIRST AID KIT

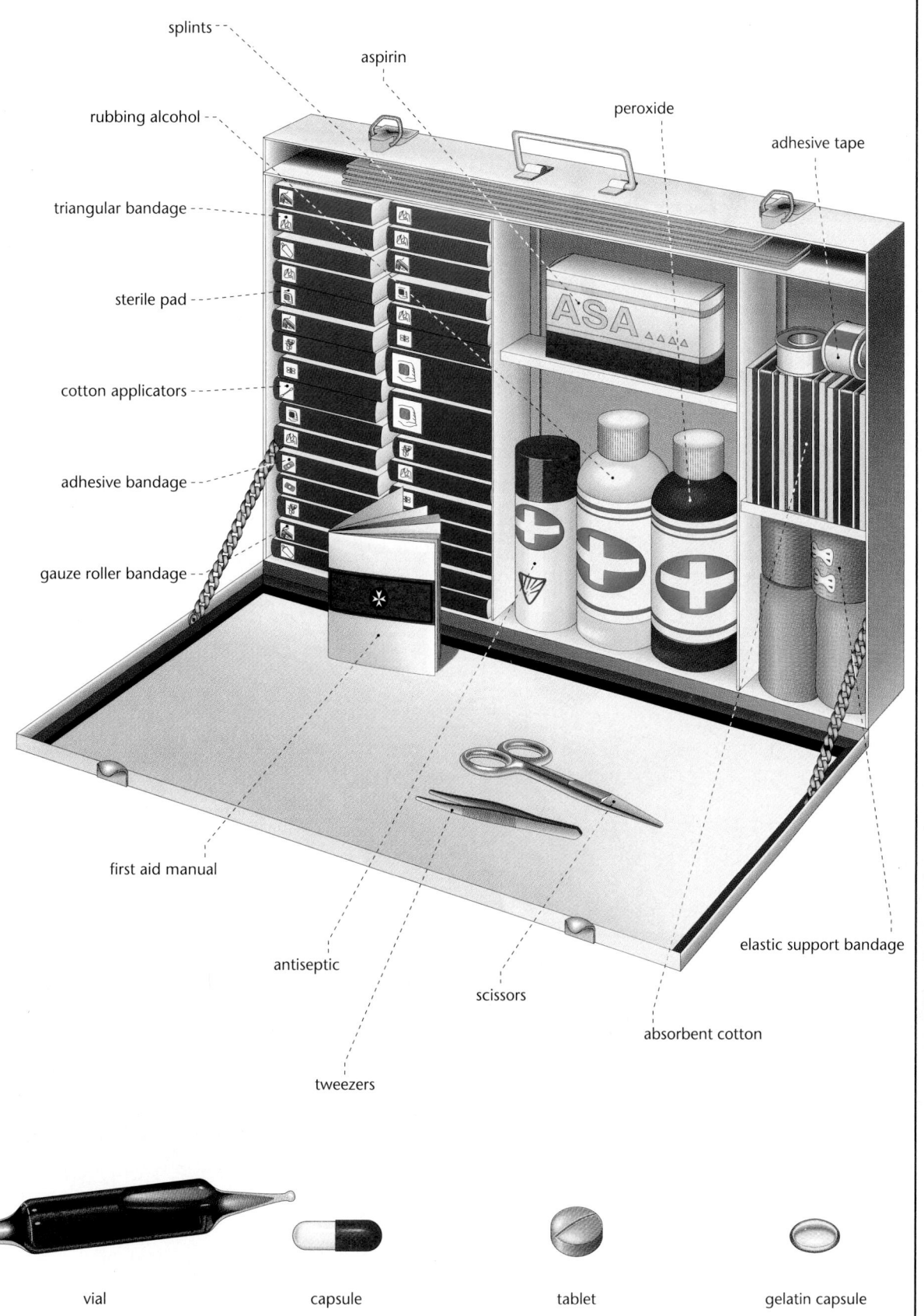

splints

aspirin

peroxide

adhesive tape

rubbing alcohol

triangular bandage

sterile pad

cotton applicators

adhesive bandage

gauze roller bandage

first aid manual

antiseptic

scissors

tweezers

absorbent cotton

elastic support bandage

vial

capsule

tablet

gelatin capsule

FIRST AID EQUIPMENT

STETHOSCOPE

SYRINGE

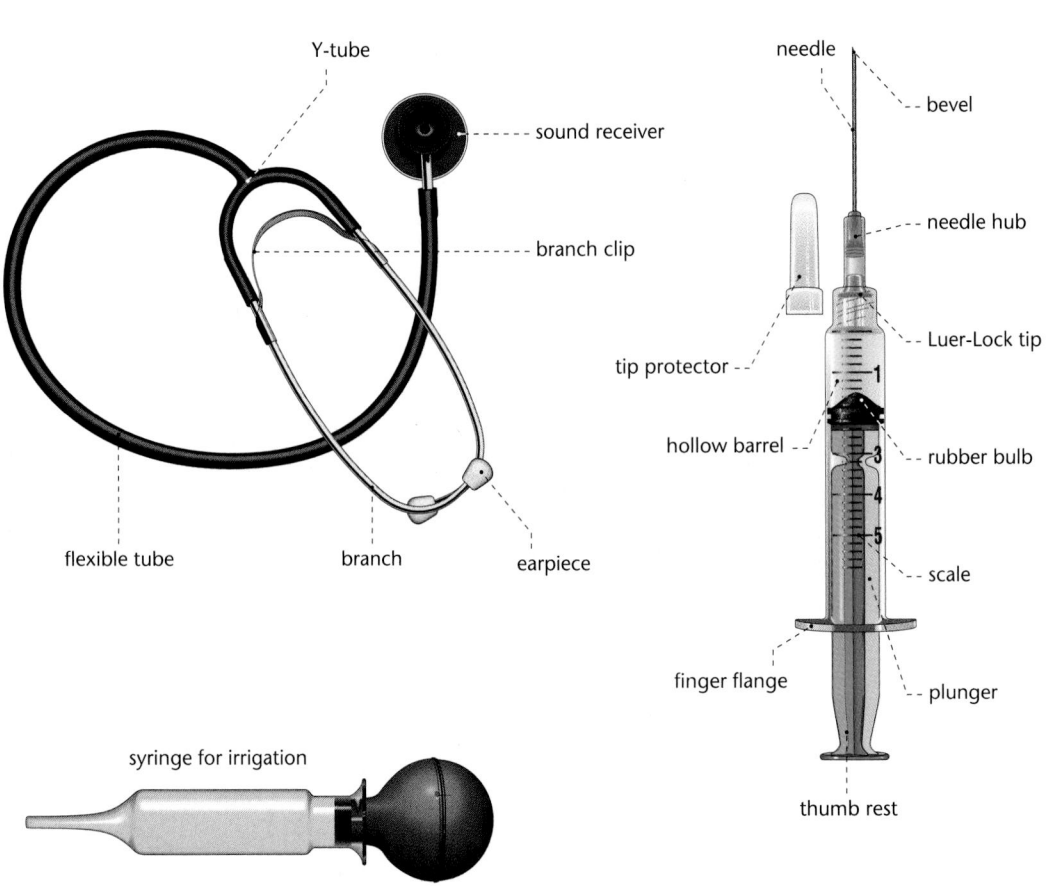

Y-tube

sound receiver

branch clip

flexible tube

branch

earpiece

needle

bevel

needle hub

Luer-Lock tip

tip protector

hollow barrel

rubber bulb

finger flange

plunger

scale

thumb rest

syringe for irrigation

COT

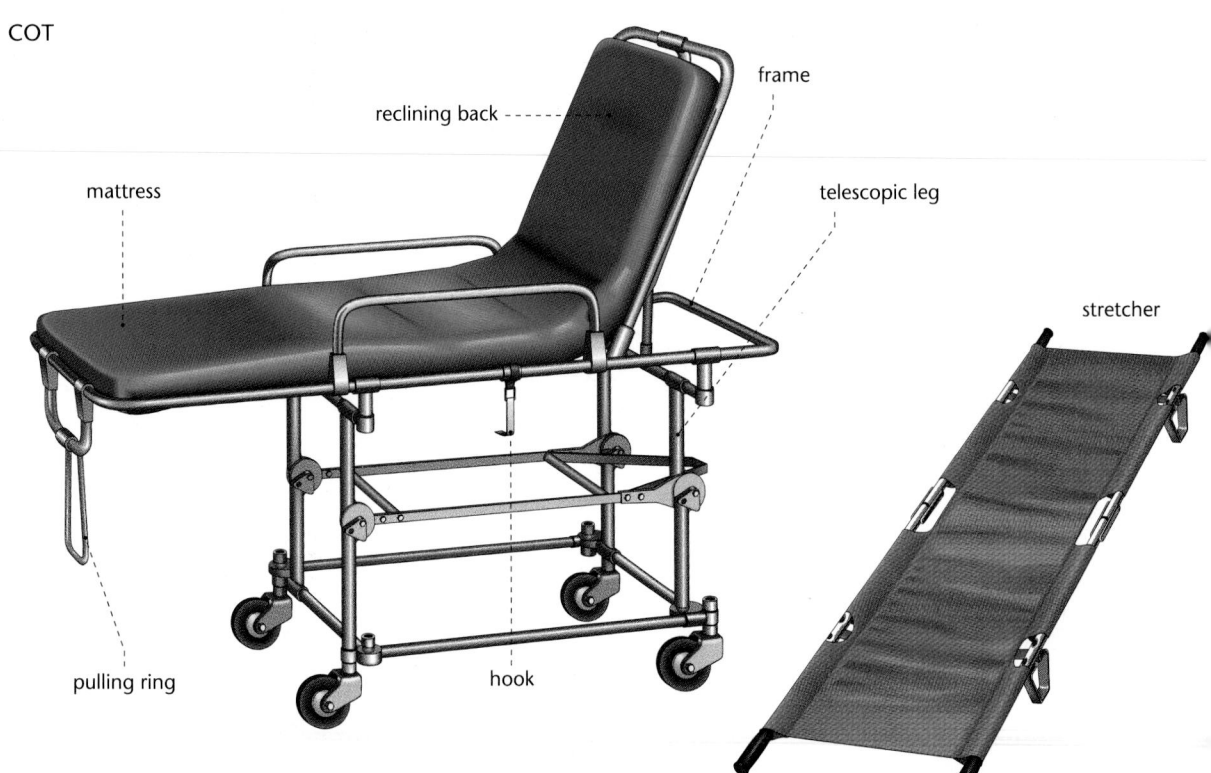

frame

reclining back

telescopic leg

mattress

stretcher

pulling ring

hook

WHEELCHAIR

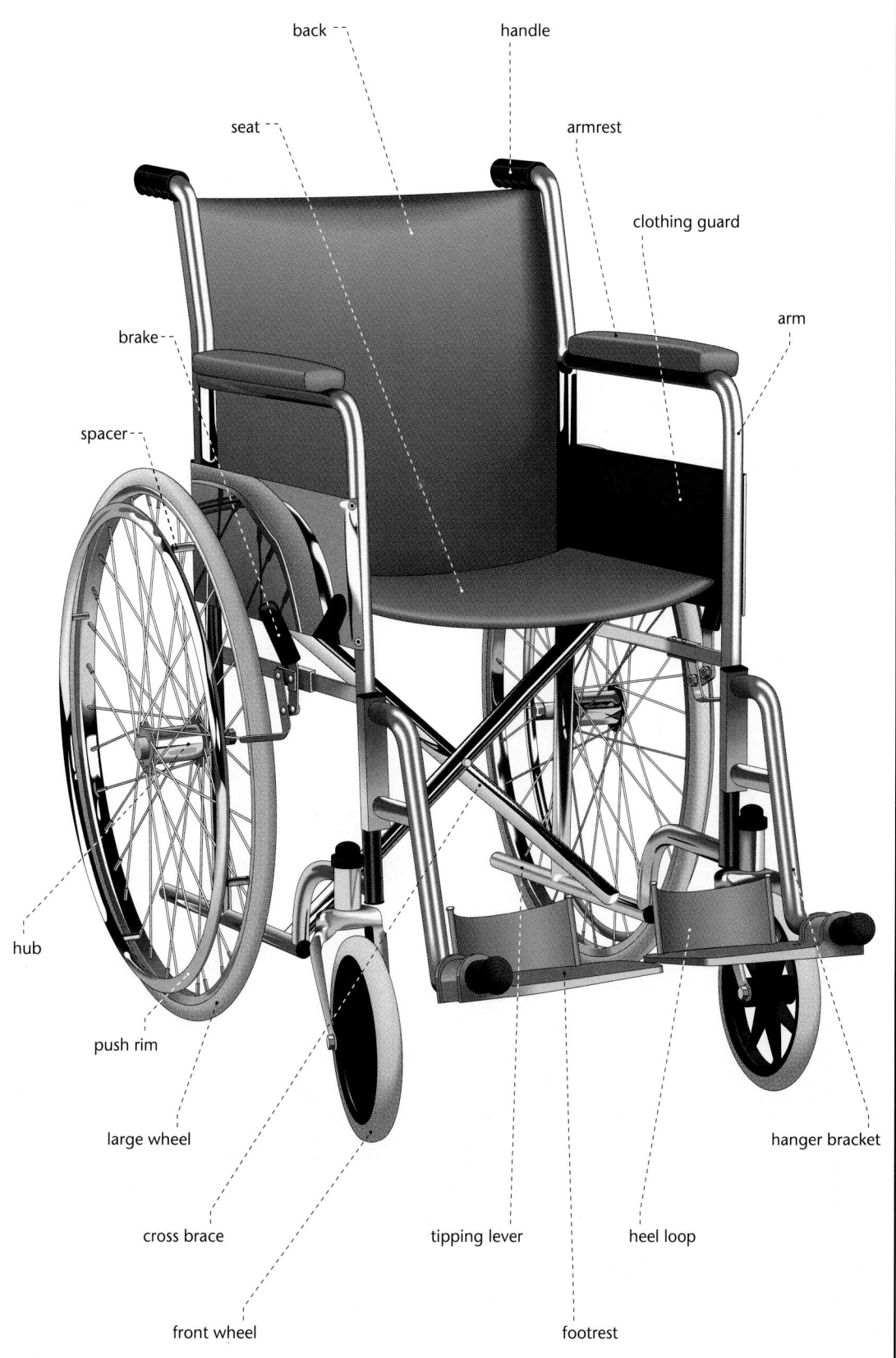

back

handle

seat

armrest

clothing guard

arm

brake

spacer

hub

push rim

large wheel

cross brace

front wheel

tipping lever

footrest

heel loop

hanger bracket

WALKING AIDS

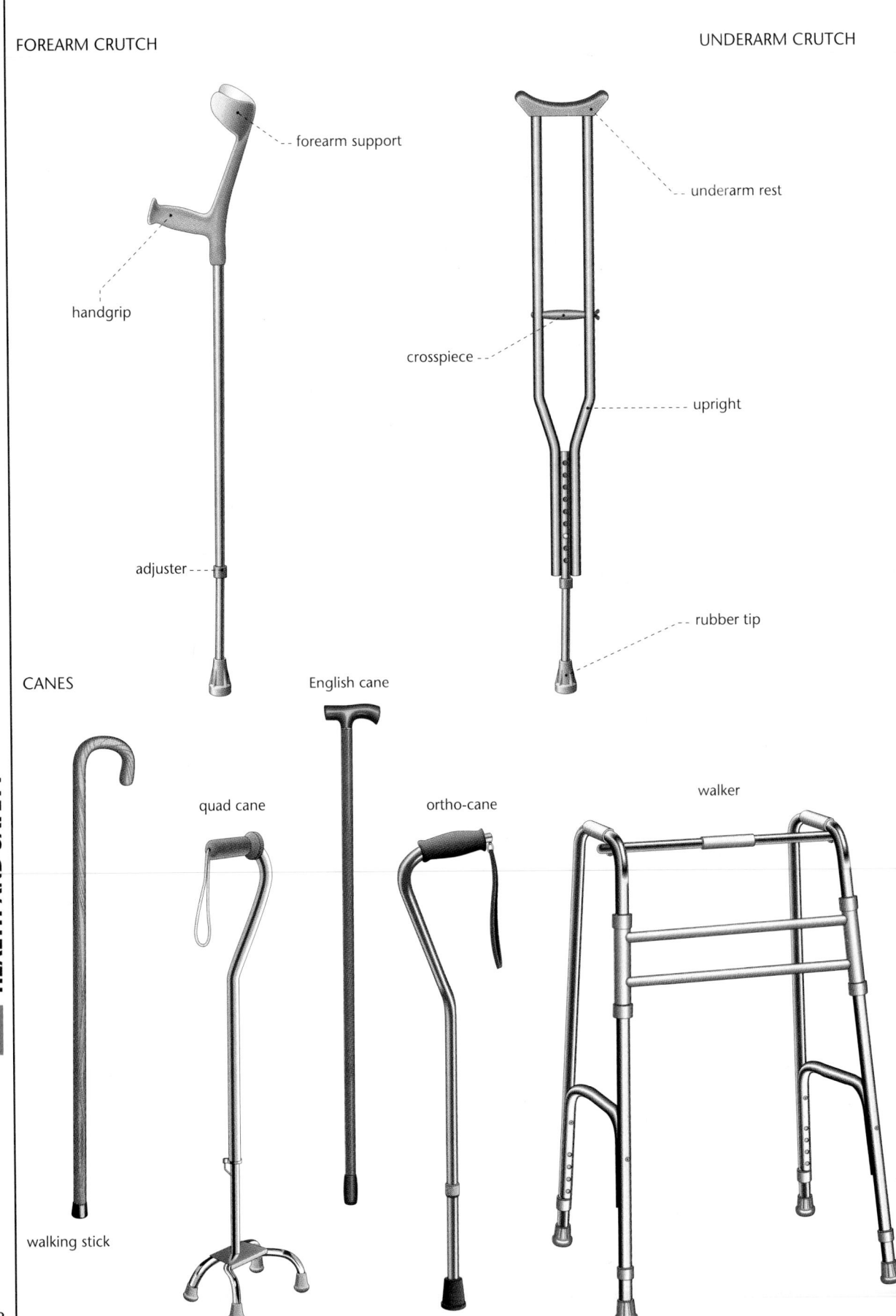

FOREARM CRUTCH

UNDERARM CRUTCH

forearm support

underarm rest

handgrip

crosspiece

upright

adjuster

rubber tip

CANES

English cane

quad cane

ortho-cane

walker

walking stick

EAR PROTECTION

SAFETY EARMUFF

ear plugs

headband

foam cushion

EYE PROTECTION

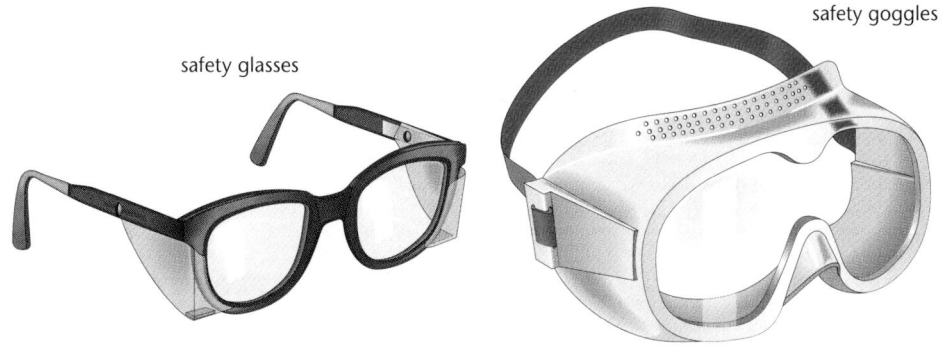

safety glasses

safety goggles

HEAD PROTECTION

SAFETY CAP

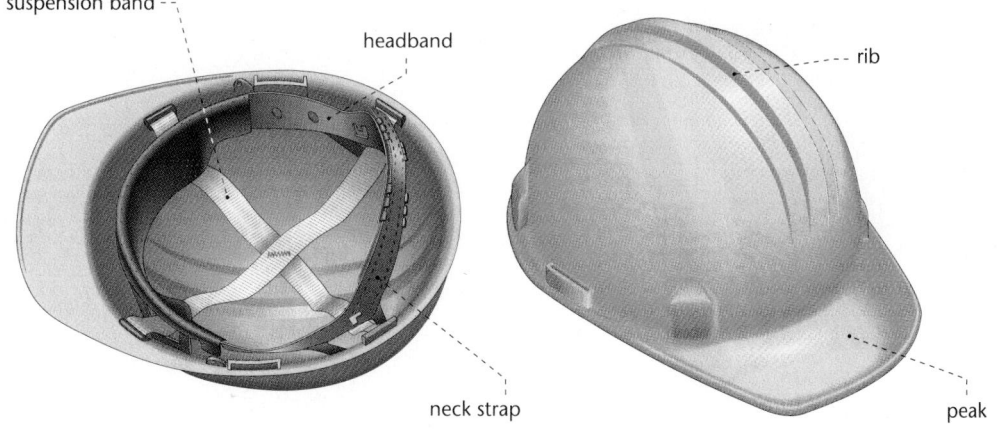

suspension band

headband

rib

neck strap

peak

RESPIRATORY SYSTEM PROTECTION

RESPIRATOR

facepiece

visor

cartridge

head harness

inhalation valve

filter cover

exhalation valve

HALF-MASK RESPIRATOR

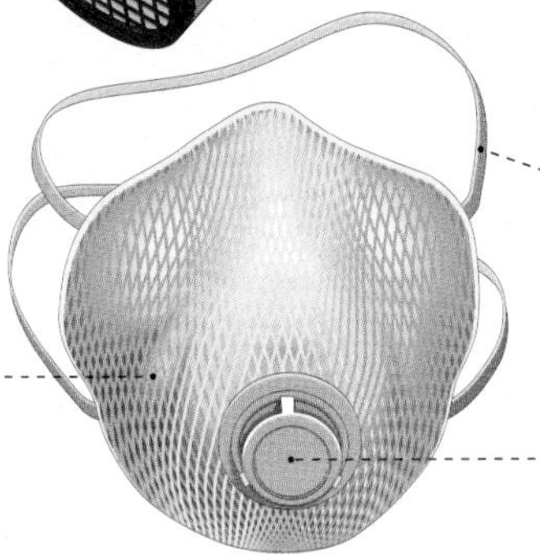

headband

cup gasket

exhalation valve

SAFETY VEST

FEET PROTECTION

toe guard

reflective stripe

SAFETY BOOT

reinforced toe

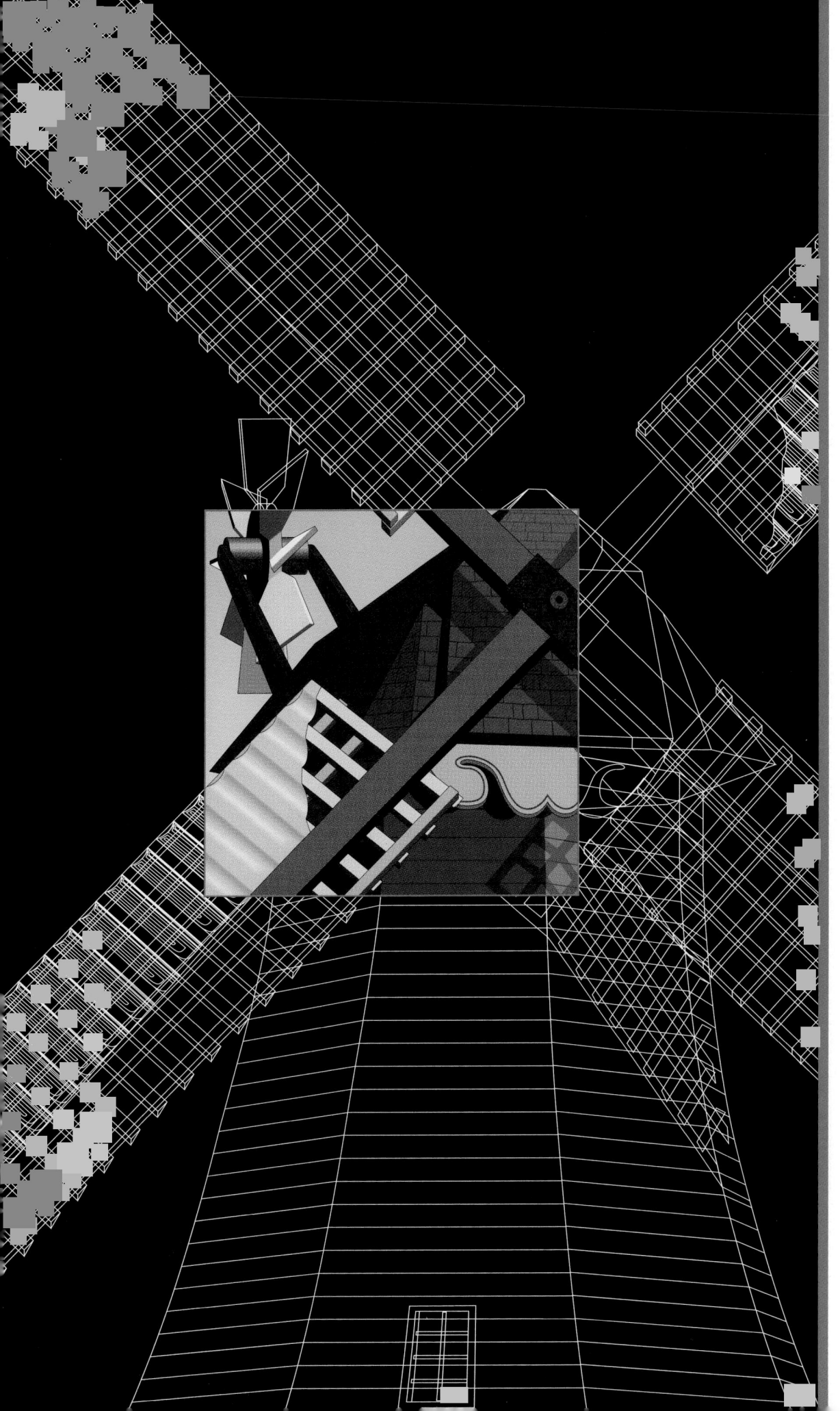

CONTENTS

COAL MINE 733

OIL...737

ELECTRICITY..746

NUCLEAR ENERGY 758

SOLAR ENERGY 768

WIND ENERGY 773

ENERGY

COAL MINE

face   bench

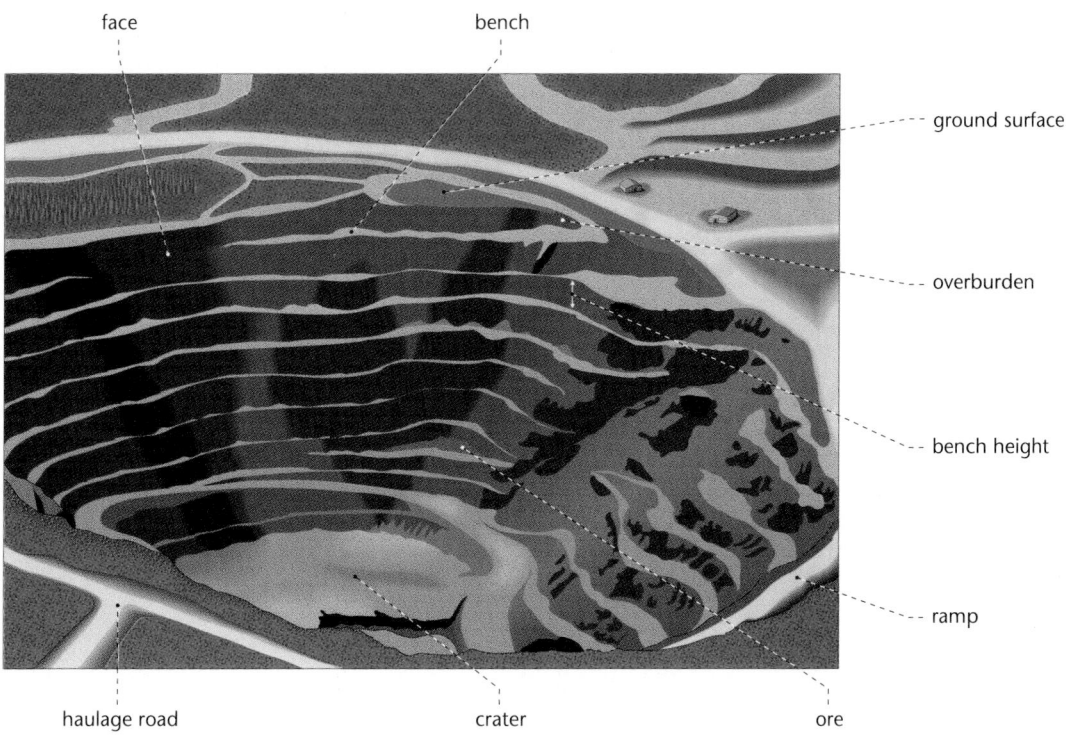

ground surface

overburden

bench height

ramp

haulage road   crater   ore

dump   conveyor

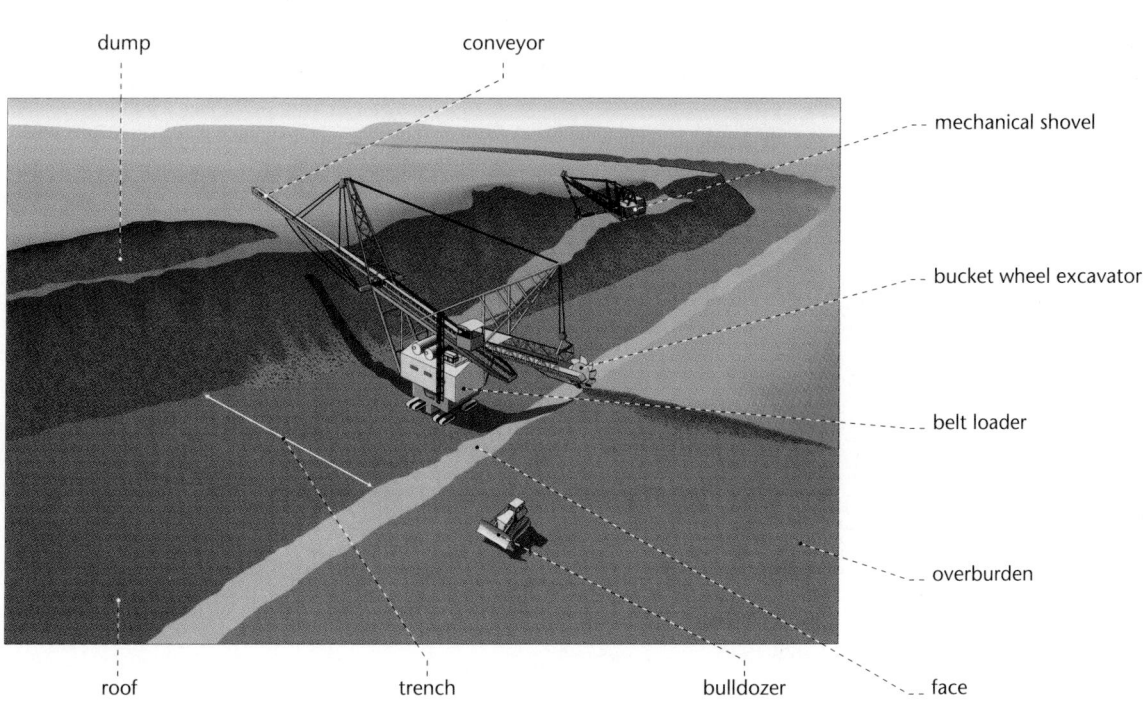

mechanical shovel

bucket wheel excavator

belt loader

overburden

roof   trench   bulldozer   face

ENERGY

COAL MINE

JACKLEG DRILL

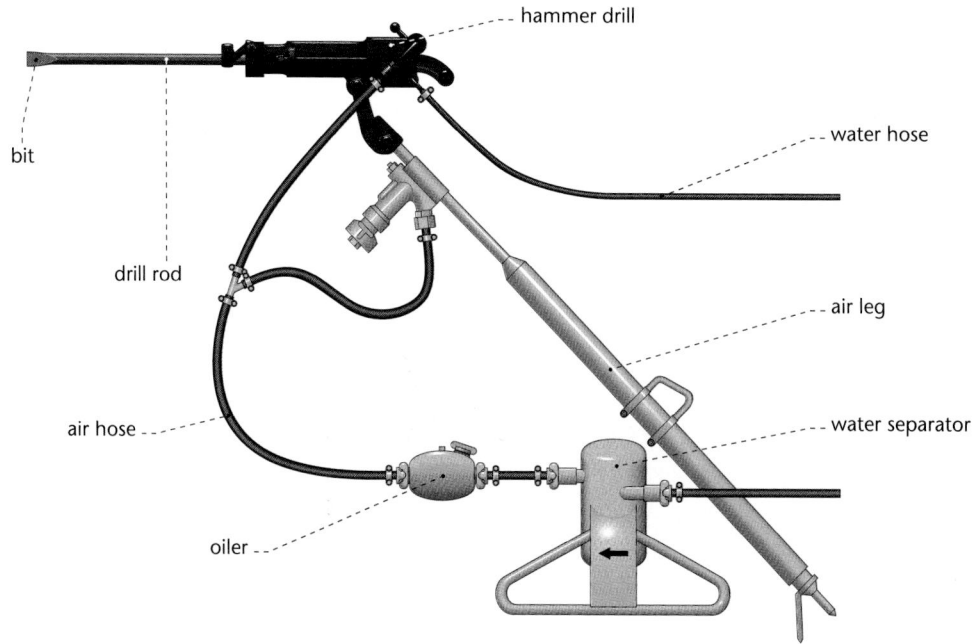

hammer drill

bit

water hose

drill rod

air leg

air hose

water separator

oiler

PITHEAD

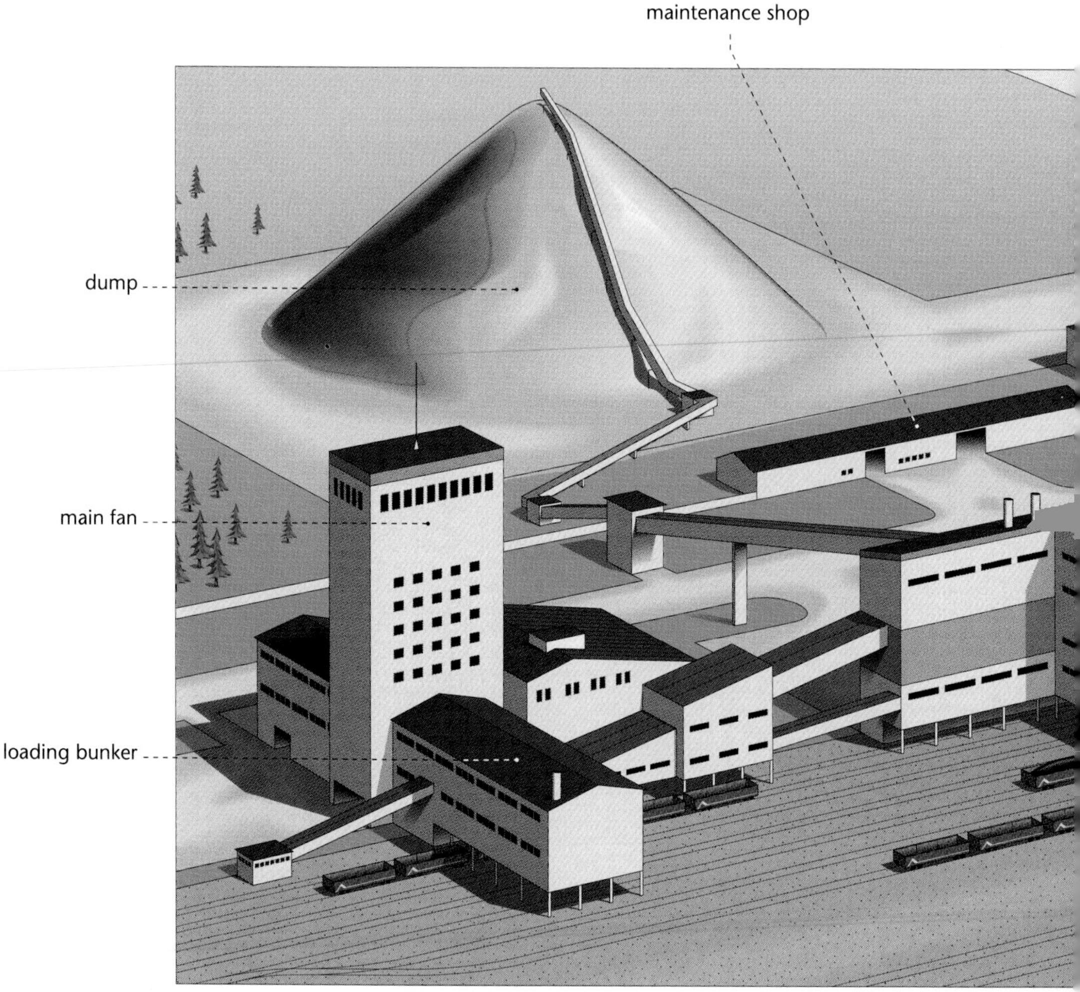

maintenance shop

dump

main fan

loading bunker

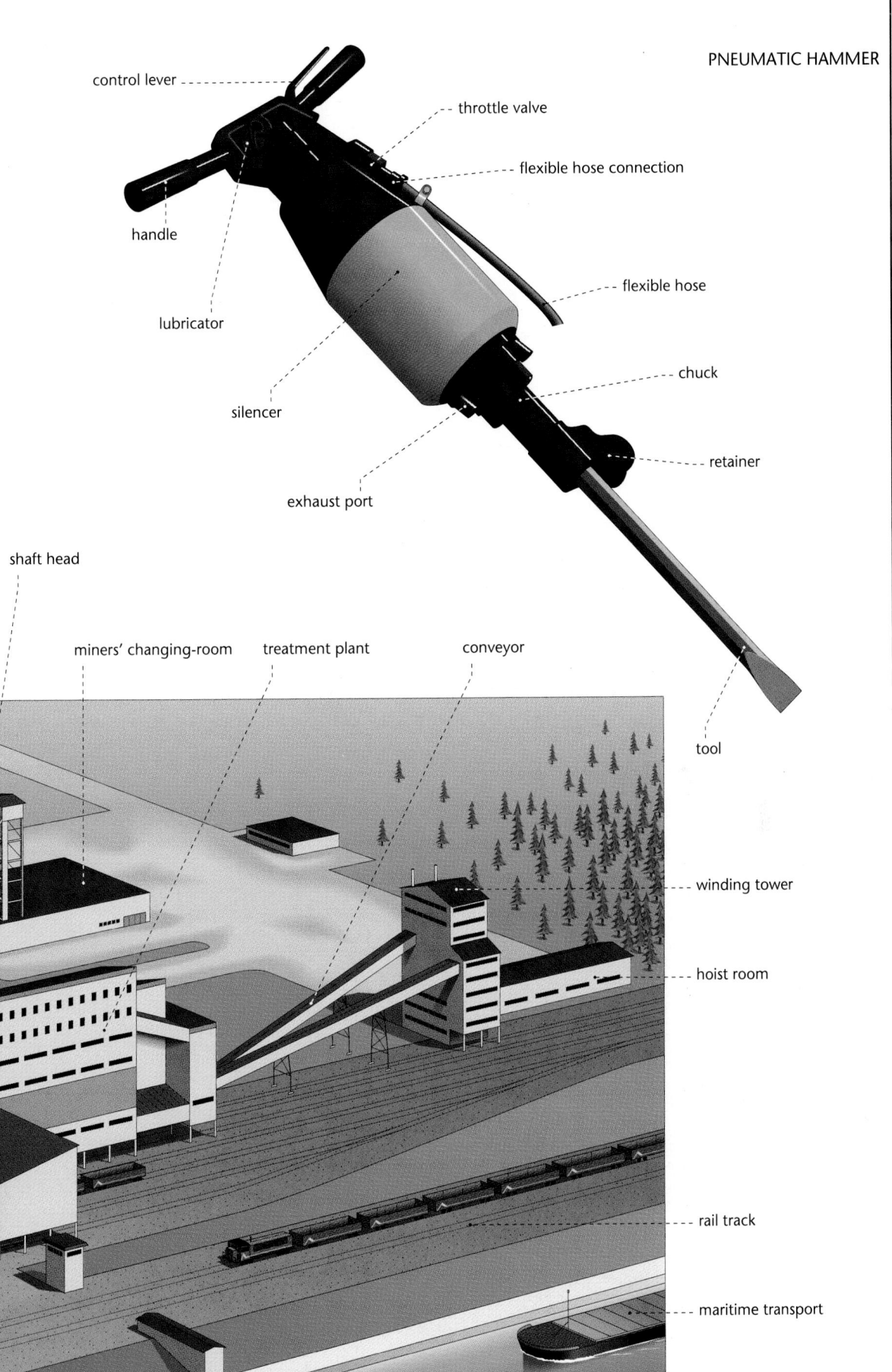

control lever

throttle valve

flexible hose connection

handle

lubricator

flexible hose

silencer

chuck

retainer

exhaust port

tool

shaft head

miners' changing-room

treatment plant

conveyor

winding tower

hoist room

rail track

maritime transport

UNDERGROUND MINE

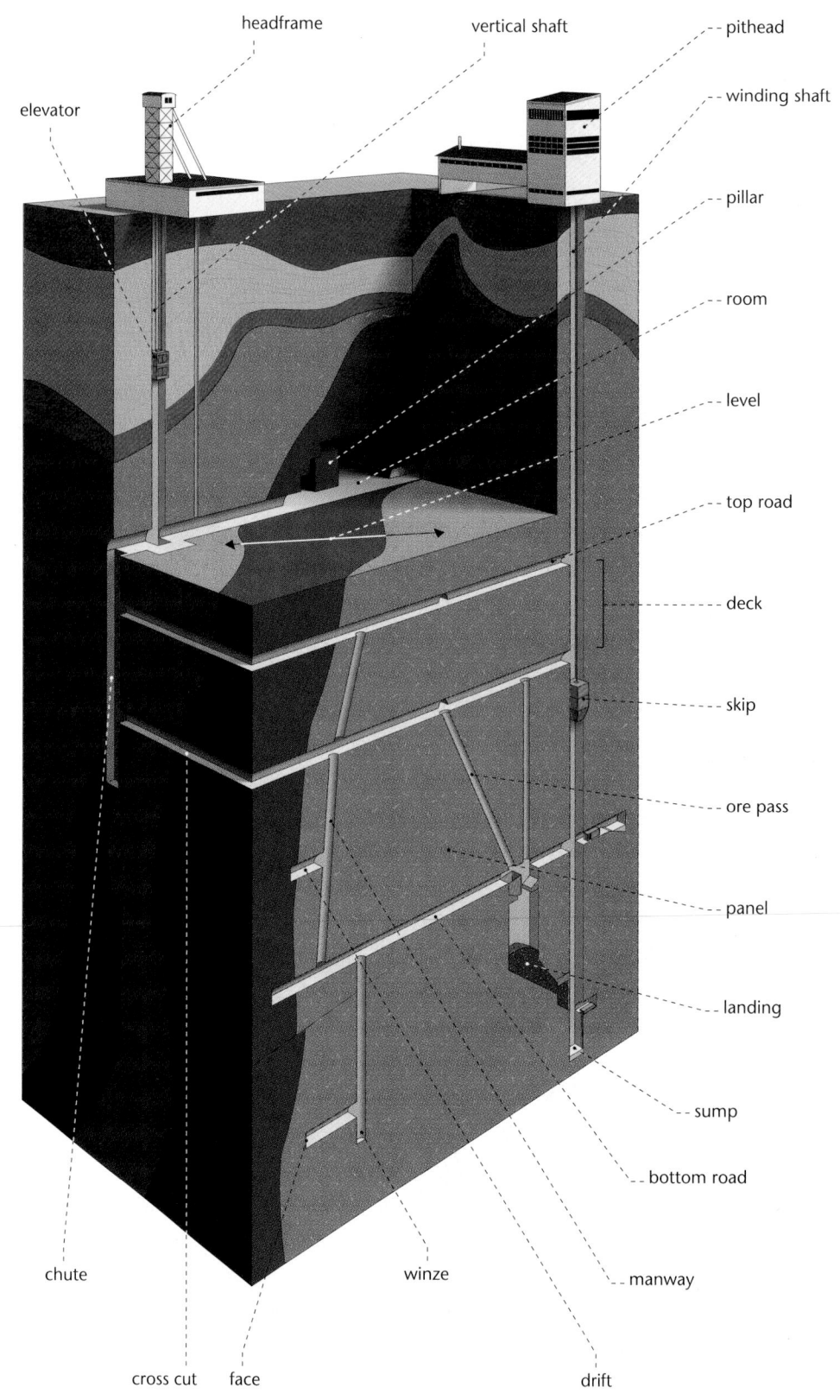

headframe

vertical shaft

pithead

winding shaft

elevator

pillar

room

level

top road

deck

skip

ore pass

panel

landing

sump

bottom road

chute

winze

manway

cross cut   face

drift

OIL

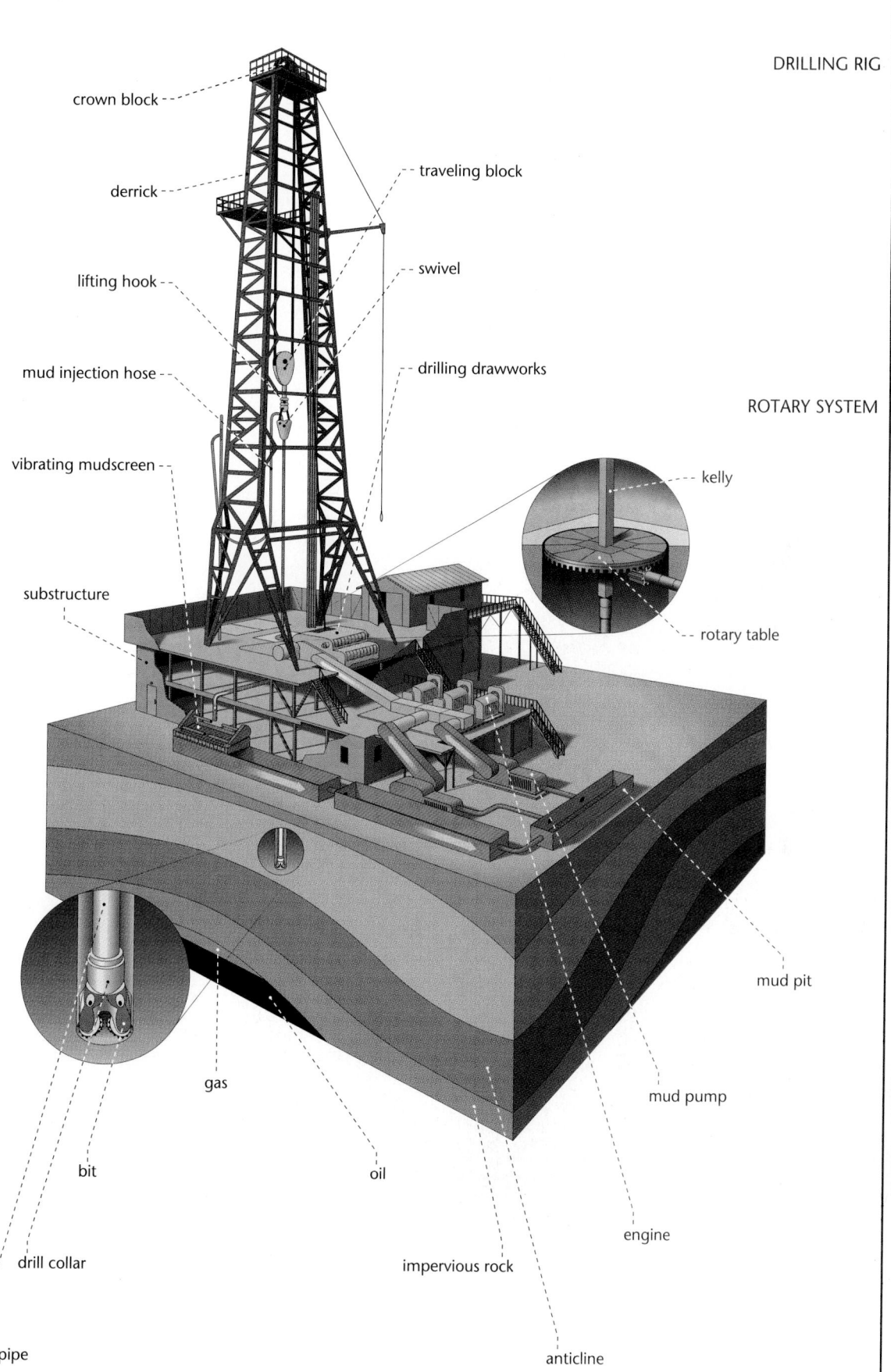

crown block

derrick

lifting hook

mud injection hose

vibrating mudscreen

substructure

traveling block

swivel

drilling drawworks

kelly

rotary table

mud pit

mud pump

engine

anticline

impervious rock

oil

gas

bit

drill collar

drill pipe

PRODUCTION PLATFORM

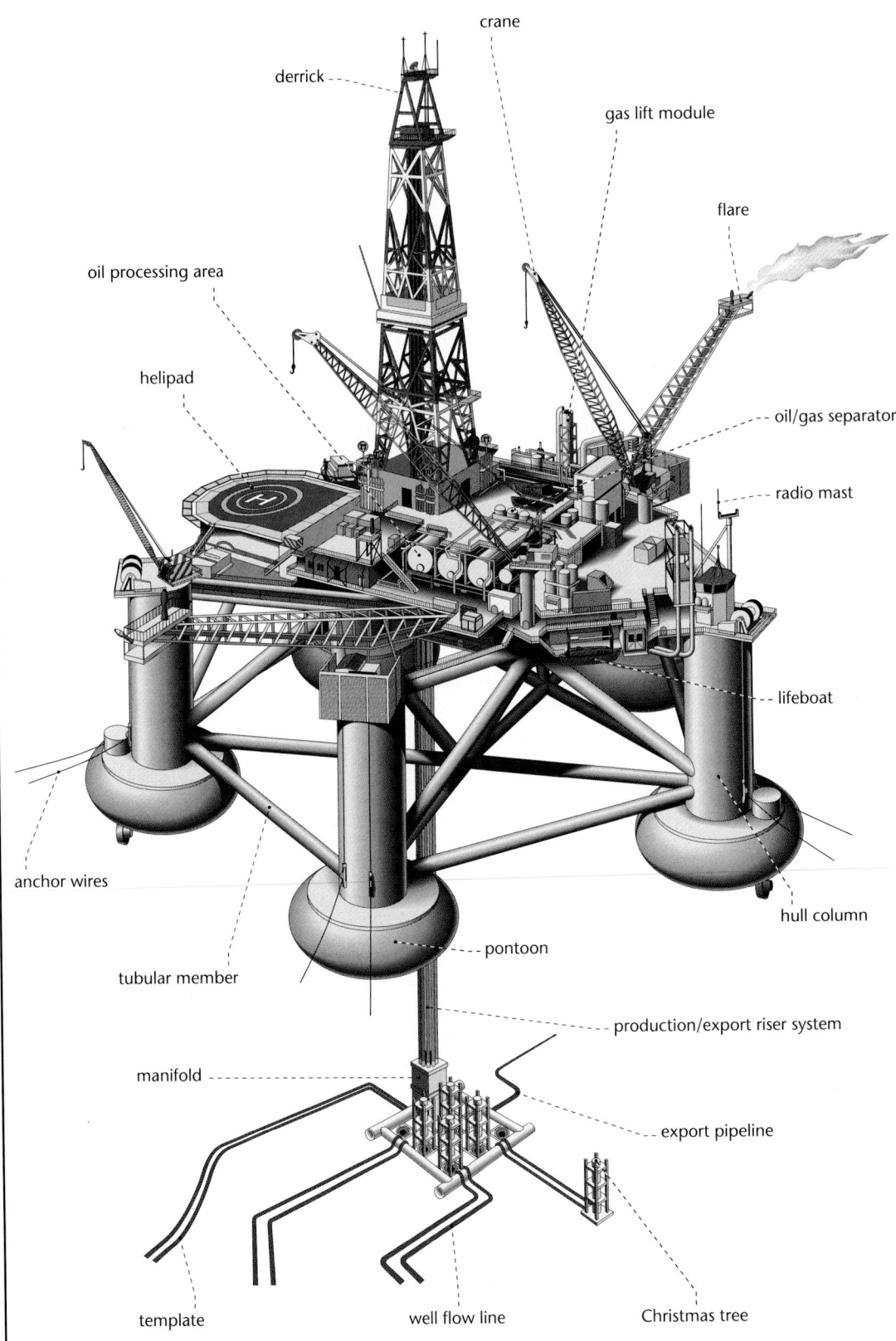

crane

derrick

gas lift module

flare

oil processing area

helipad

oil/gas separator

radio mast

lifeboat

anchor wires

hull column

tubular member

pontoon

production/export riser system

manifold

export pipeline

template

well flow line

Christmas tree

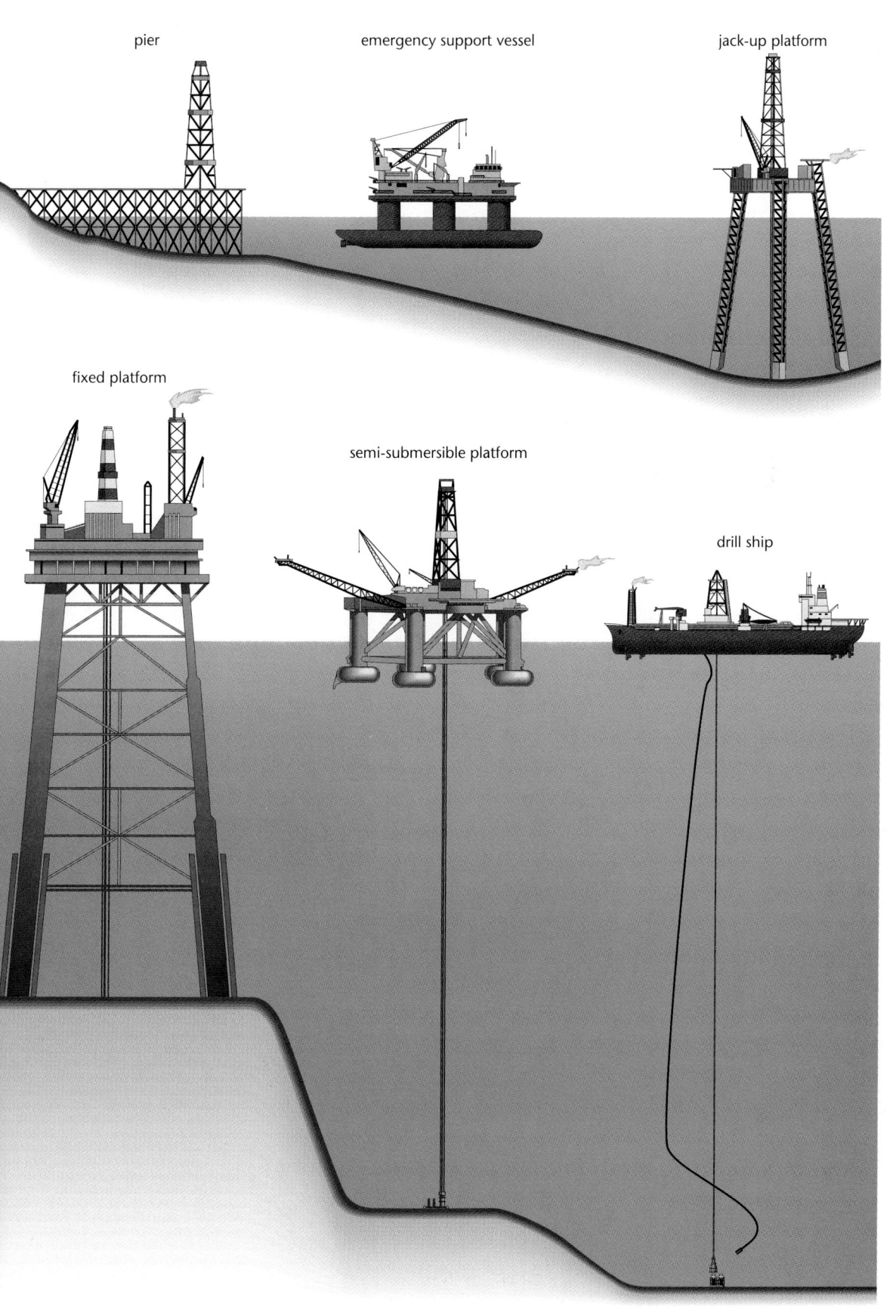

pier

emergency support vessel

jack-up platform

fixed platform

semi-submersible platform

drill ship

OIL

CHRISTMAS TREE

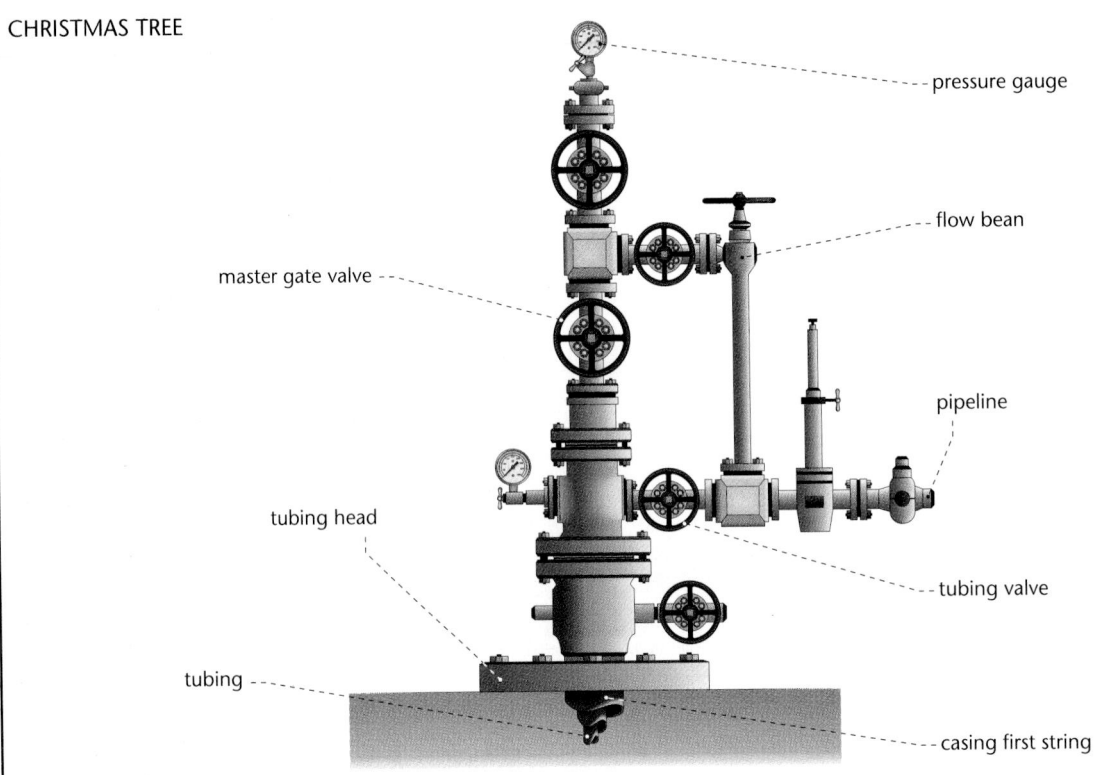

pressure gauge

flow bean

master gate valve

pipeline

tubing head

tubing valve

tubing

casing first string

CRUDE-OIL PIPELINE

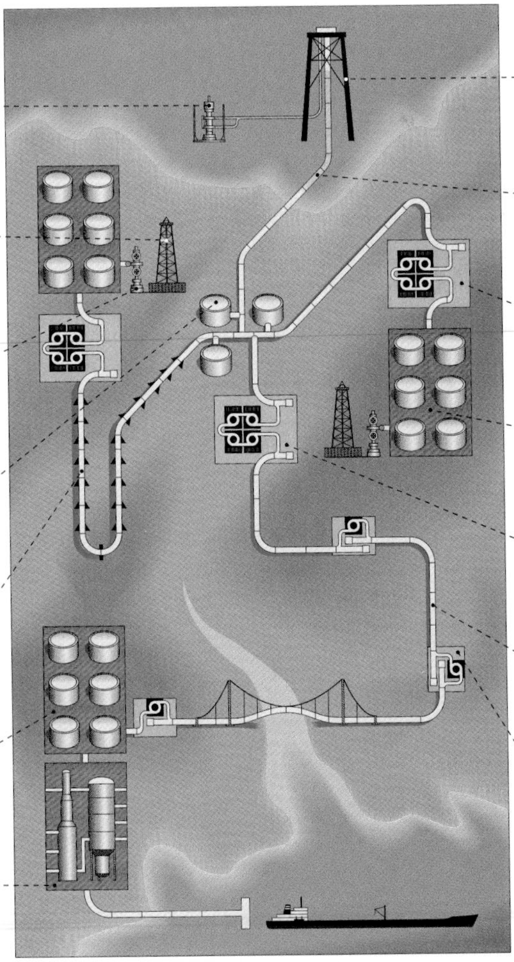

offshore well

production platform

submarine pipeline

derrick

pumping station

Christmas tree

buffer tank

tank farm

central pumping station

aboveground pipeline

pipeline

terminal

booster intermediate station

refinery

ENERGY

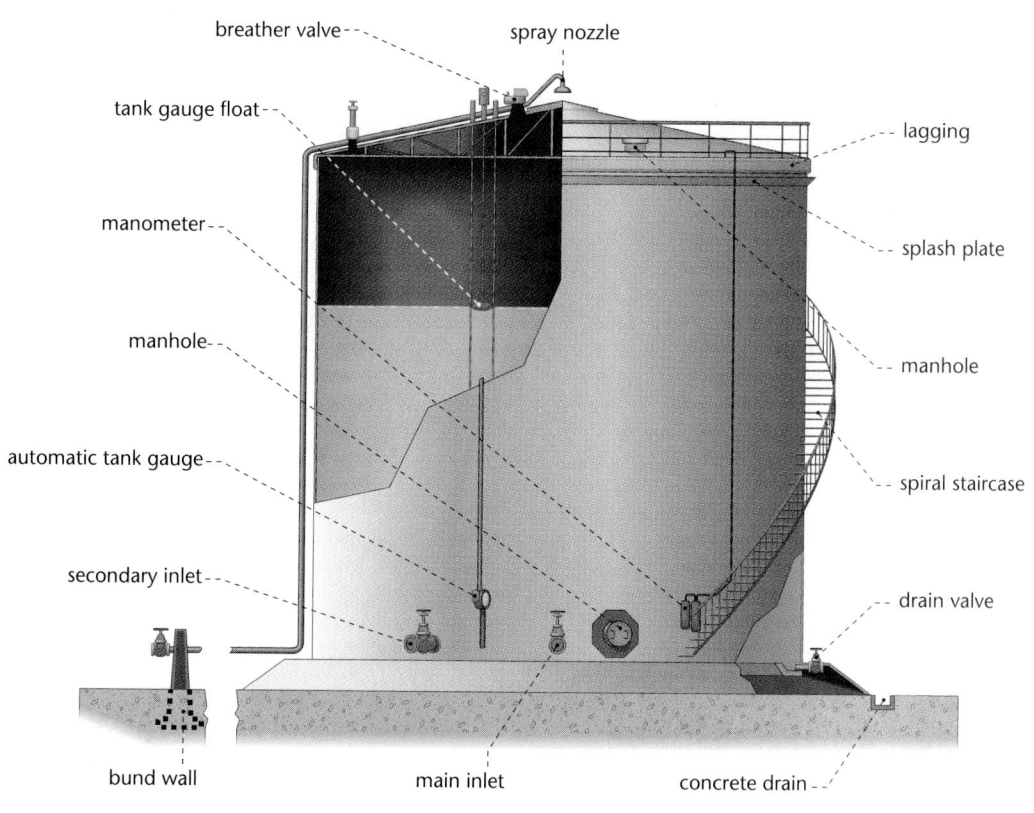

breather valve

spray nozzle

tank gauge float

lagging

manometer

splash plate

manhole

manhole

automatic tank gauge

spiral staircase

secondary inlet

drain valve

bund wall

main inlet

concrete drain

FLOATING-ROOF TANK

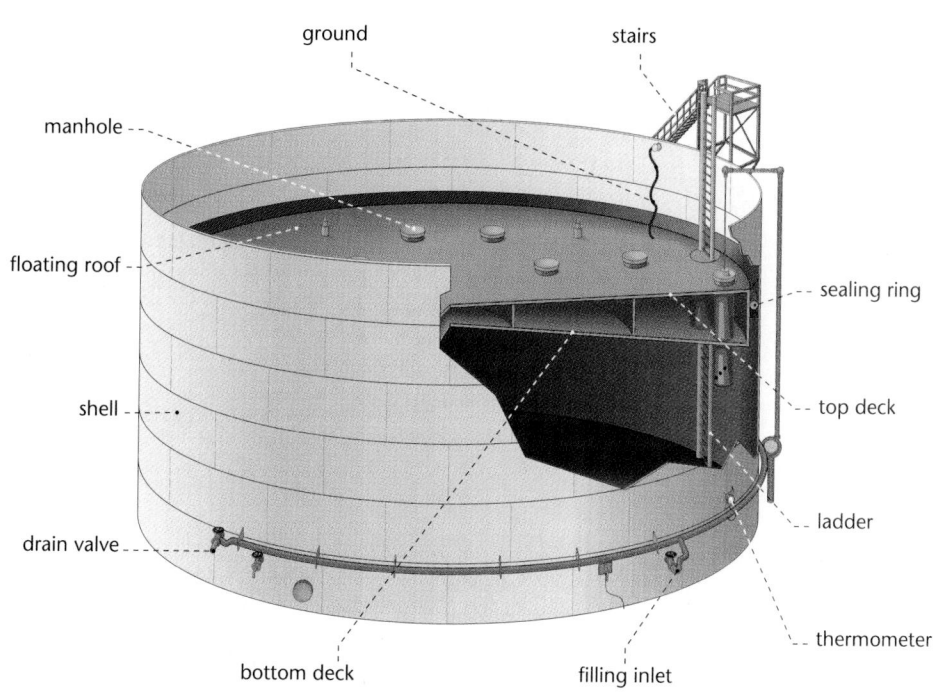

ground

stairs

manhole

floating roof

sealing ring

shell

top deck

drain valve

ladder

bottom deck

filling inlet

thermometer

ENERGY

TANK TRAILER

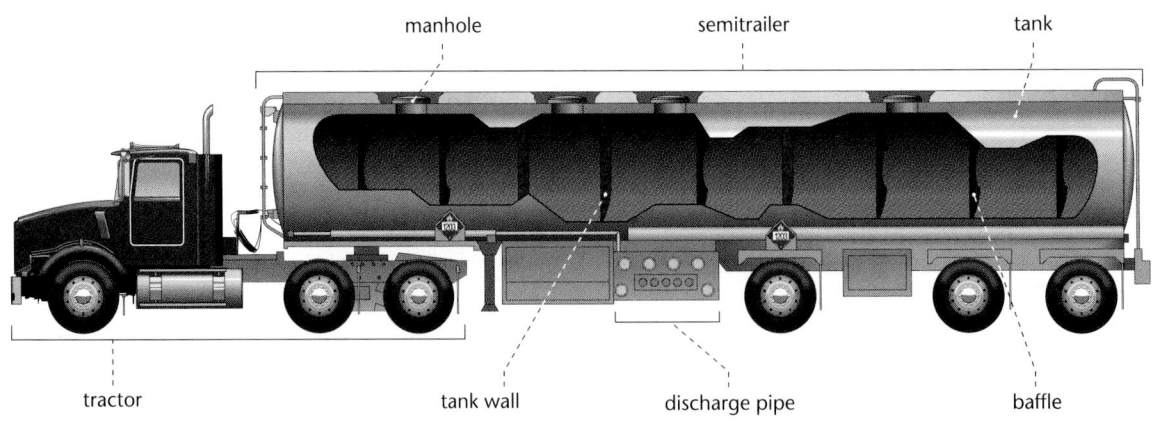

manhole semitrailer tank

tractor tank wall discharge pipe baffle

TANKER

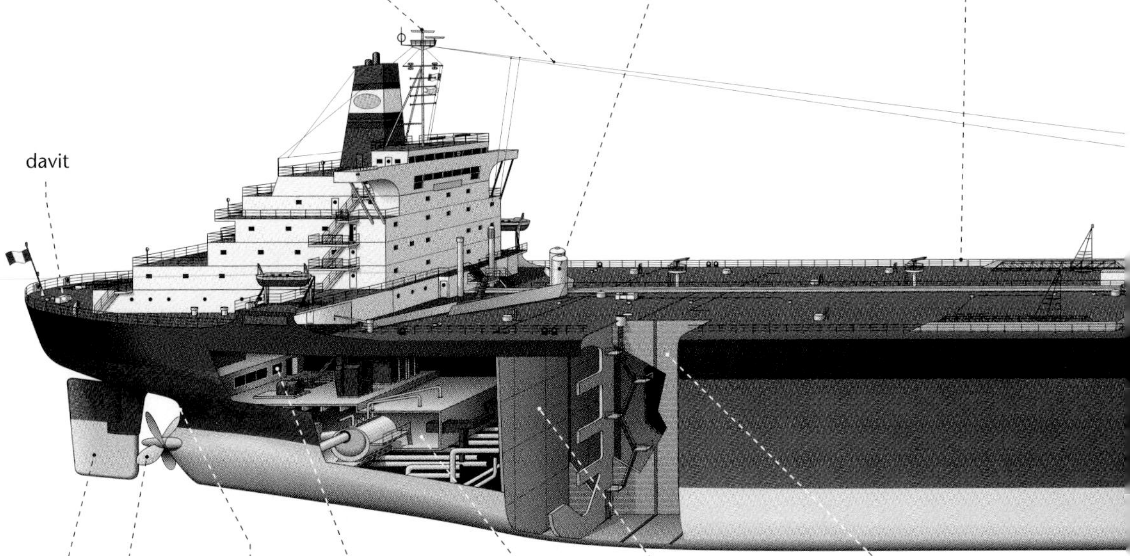

radio antenna separator

gangway

radar mast

davit

stern post

propeller

rudder engine control room transverse bulkhead

pump room lengthwise bulkhead

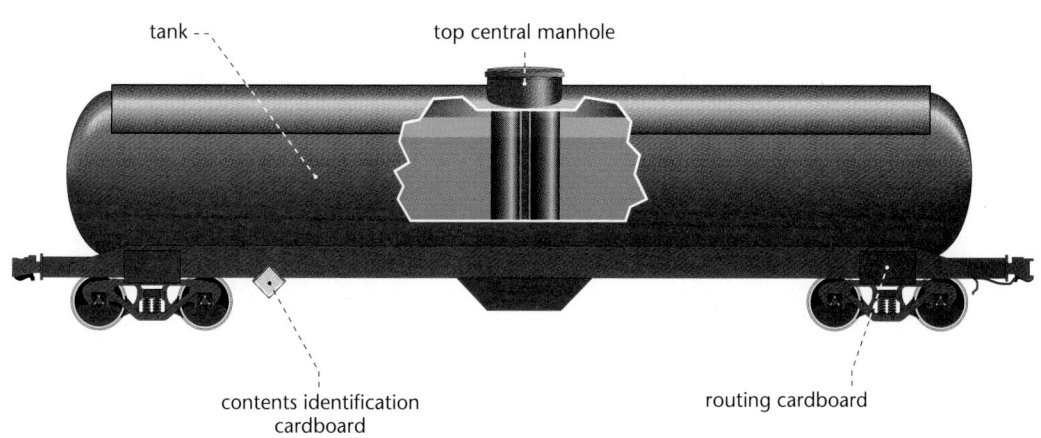

tank

top central manhole

contents identification
cardboard

routing cardboard

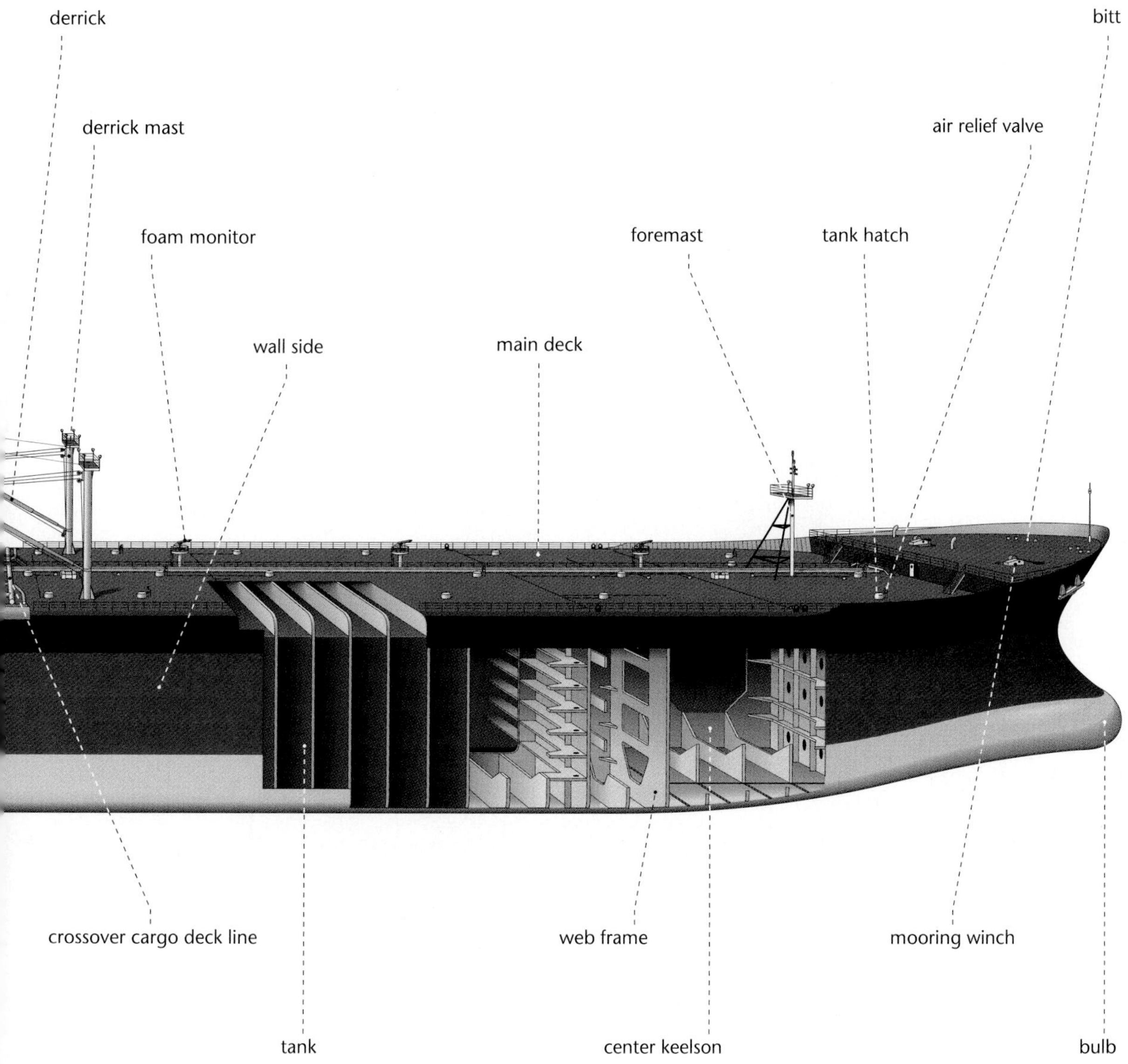

derrick

bitt

derrick mast

air relief valve

foam monitor

foremast

tank hatch

wall side

main deck

crossover cargo deck line

web frame

mooring winch

tank

center keelson

bulb

REFINERY PRODUCTS

petrochemical industry

gas

cooling

catalytic reforming plant

gasoline

fractionating tower

kerosene

heavy gasoline

fractionating tower

fuel oil

tubular heater

solvent extraction unit

long residue

vacuum distillation

storage tank

crude oil

asphalt still

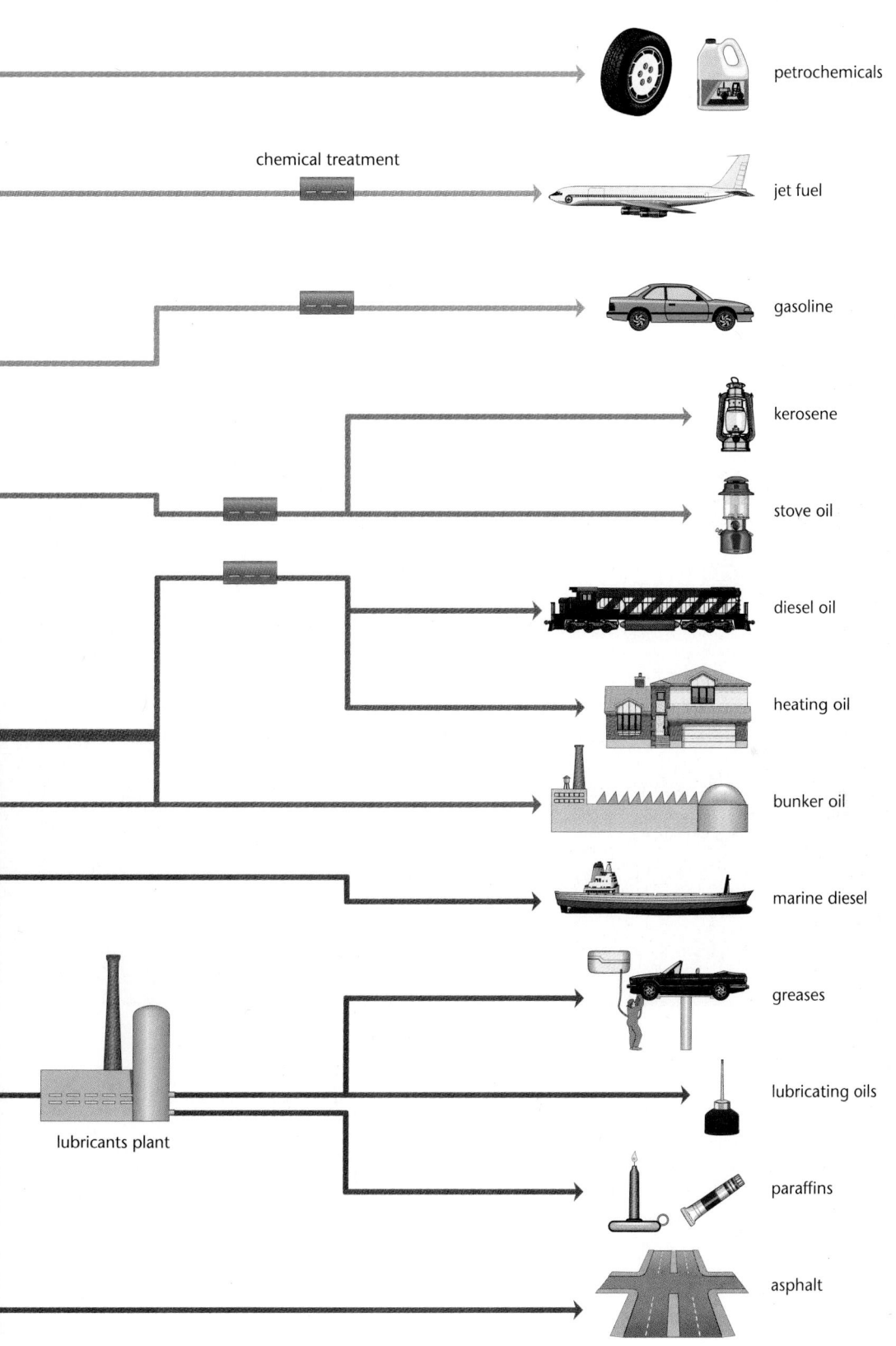

petrochemicals

chemical treatment

jet fuel

gasoline

kerosene

stove oil

diesel oil

heating oil

bunker oil

marine diesel

greases

lubricating oils

lubricants plant

paraffins

asphalt

HYDROELECTRIC COMPLEX

crest of spillway

spillway gate

top of dam

penstock

headbay

spillway

reservoir

gantry crane

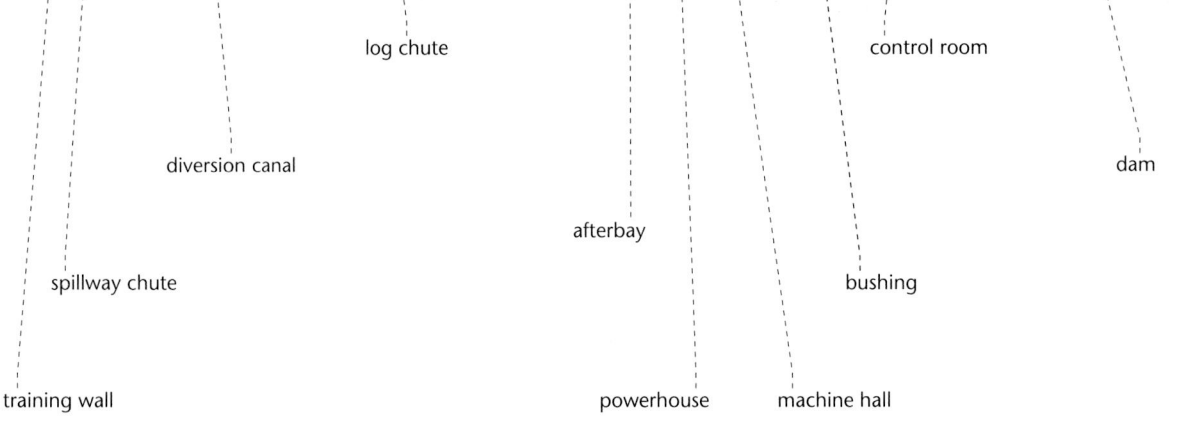

log chute

control room

diversion canal

dam

afterbay

spillway chute

bushing

training wall

powerhouse

machine hall

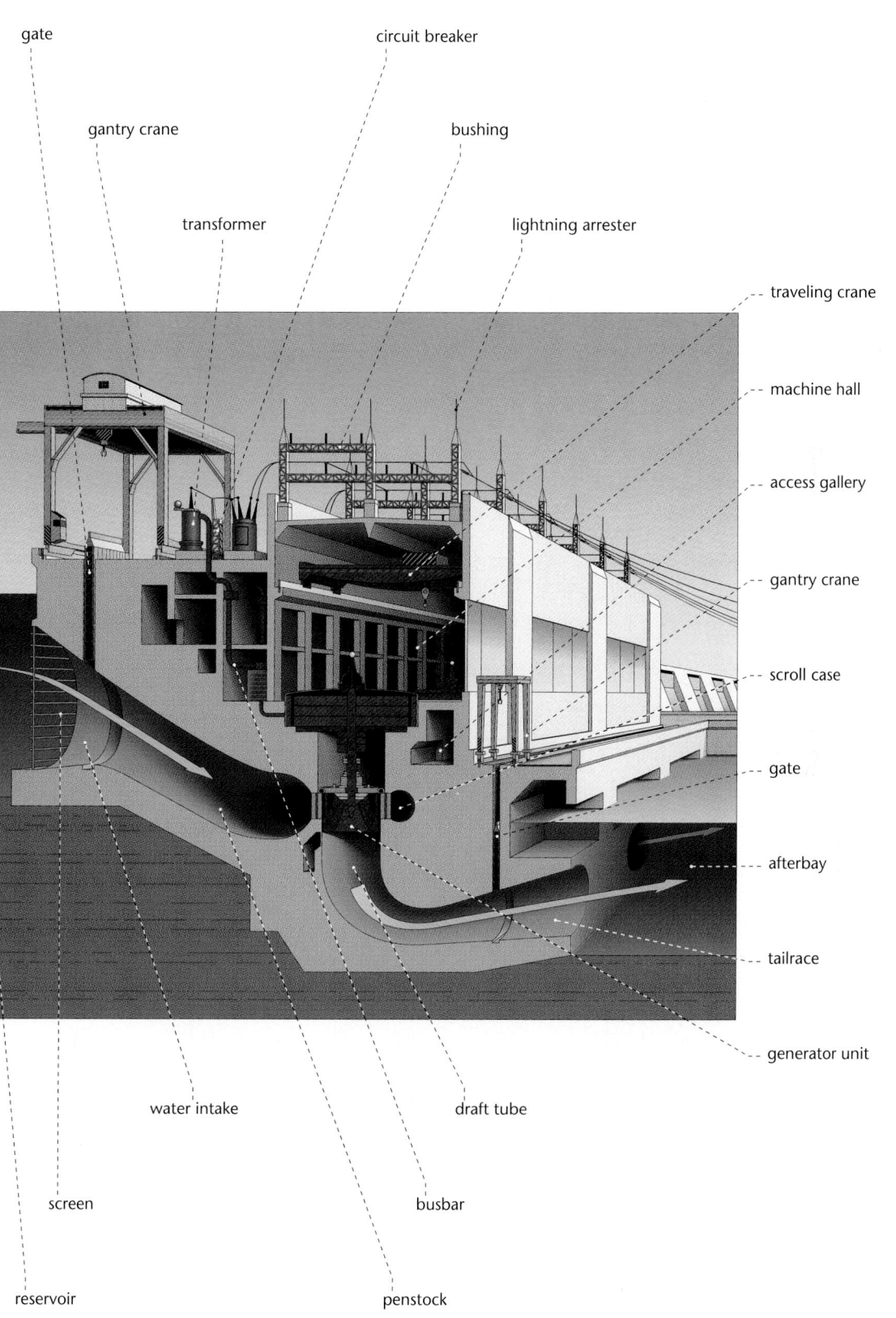

gate

circuit breaker

gantry crane

bushing

transformer

lightning arrester

traveling crane

machine hall

access gallery

gantry crane

scroll case

gate

afterbay

tailrace

generator unit

water intake

draft tube

screen

busbar

reservoir

penstock

ENERGY

embankment dam

CROSS SECTION OF AN EMBANKMENT DAM

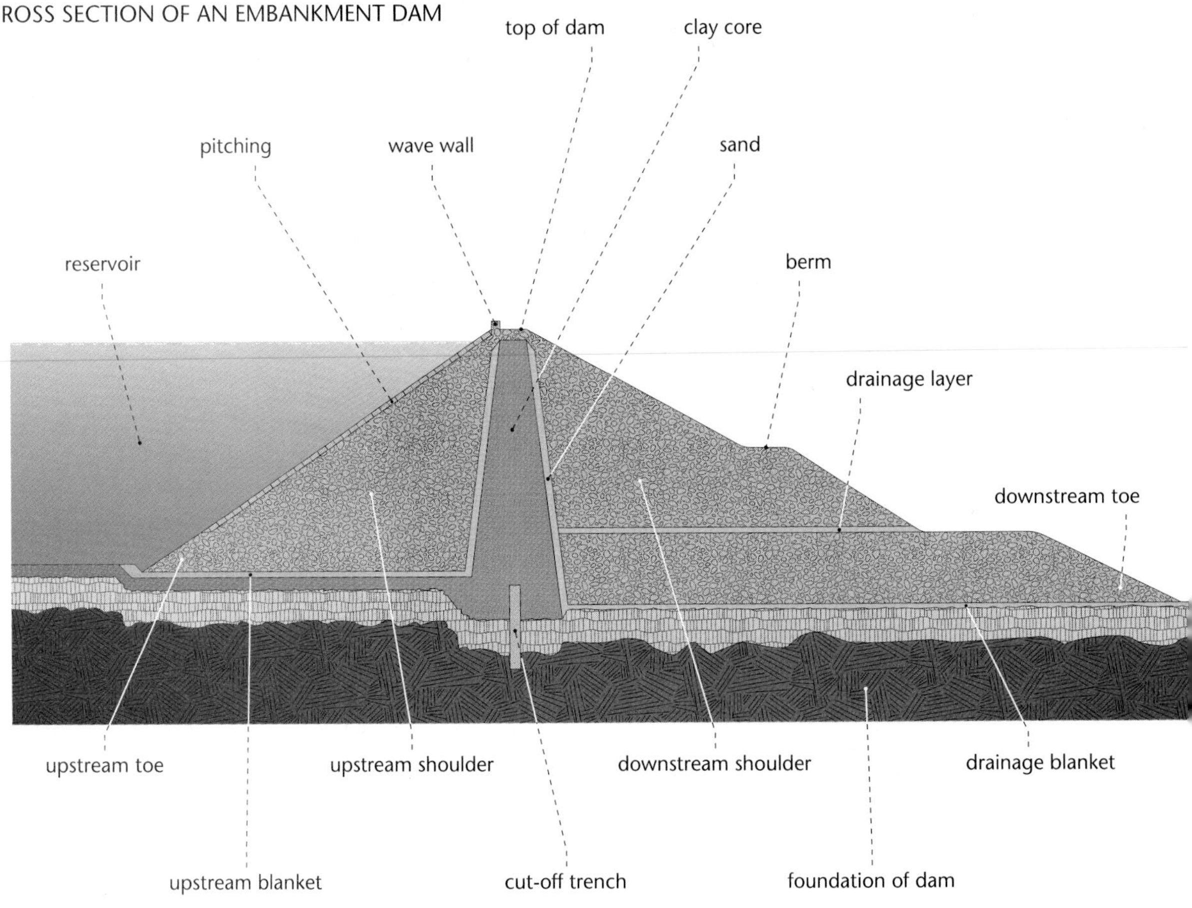

top of dam   clay core

pitching   wave wall   sand

reservoir   berm

drainage layer

downstream toe

upstream toe   upstream shoulder   downstream shoulder   drainage blanket

upstream blanket   cut-off trench   foundation of dam

CROSS SECTION OF A GRAVITY DAM

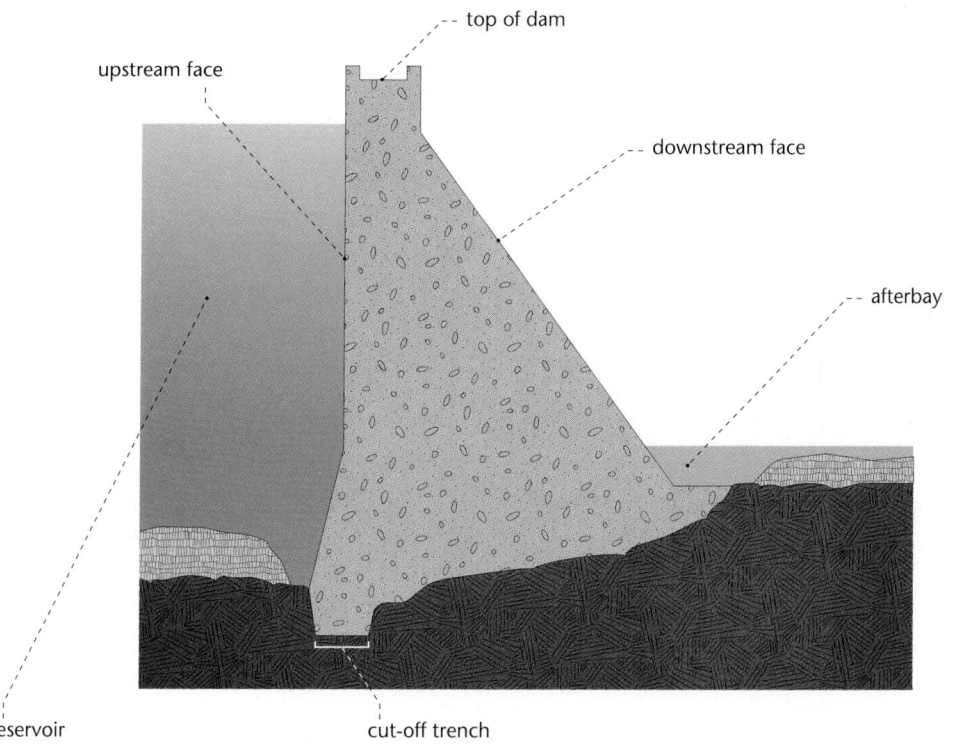

upstream face

top of dam

downstream face

afterbay

reservoir

cut-off trench

ENERGY

749

arch dam

CROSS SECTION OF AN ARCH DAM

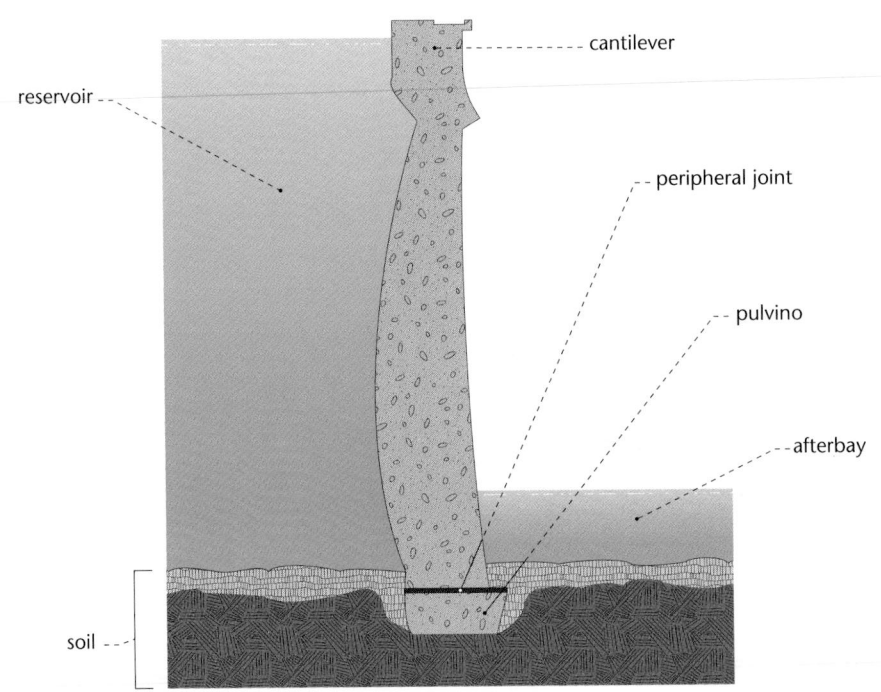

reservoir

cantilever

peripheral joint

pulvino

afterbay

soil

CROSS SECTION OF A BUTTRESS DAM

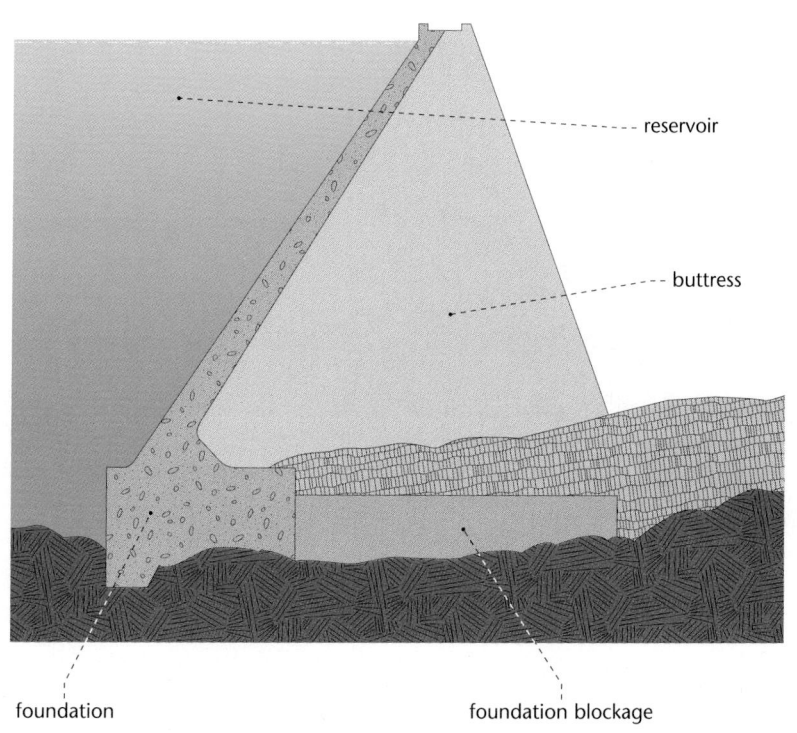

reservoir

buttress

foundation

foundation blockage

ELECTRICITY

TIDAL POWER PLANT

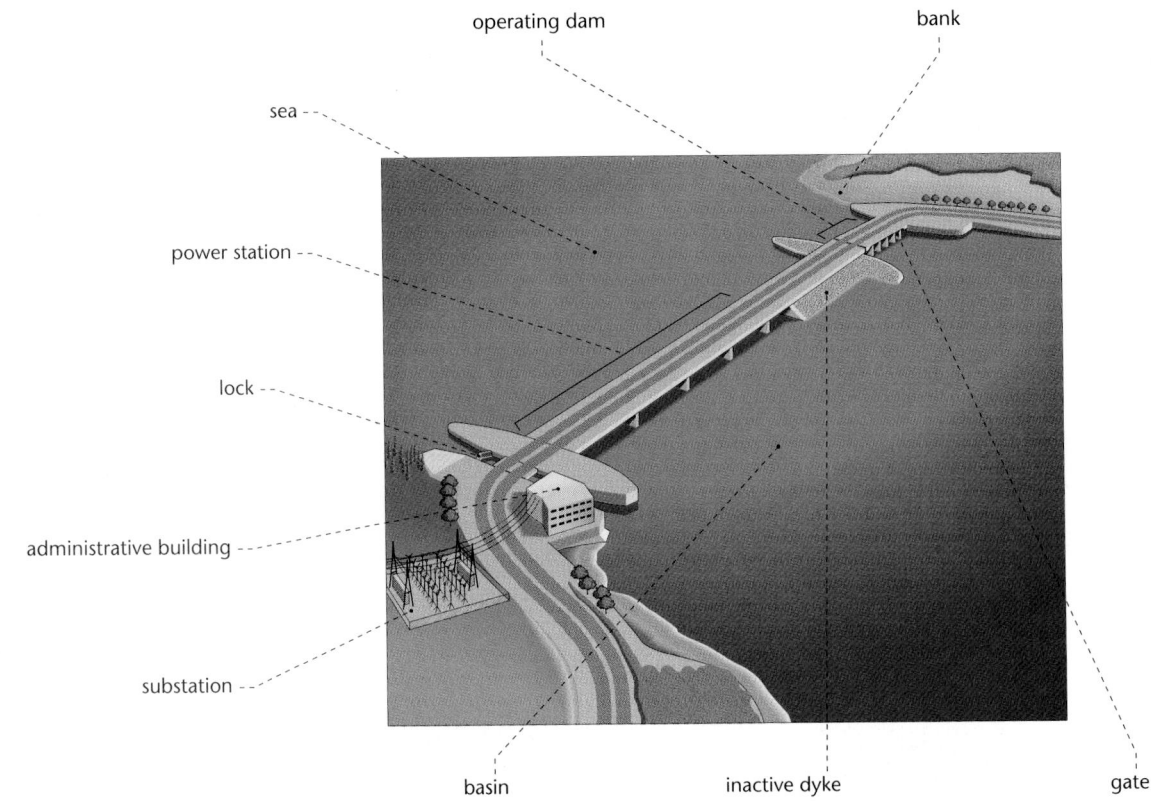

operating dam

bank

sea

power station

lock

administrative building

substation

basin

inactive dyke

gate

CROSS SECTION OF POWER PLANT

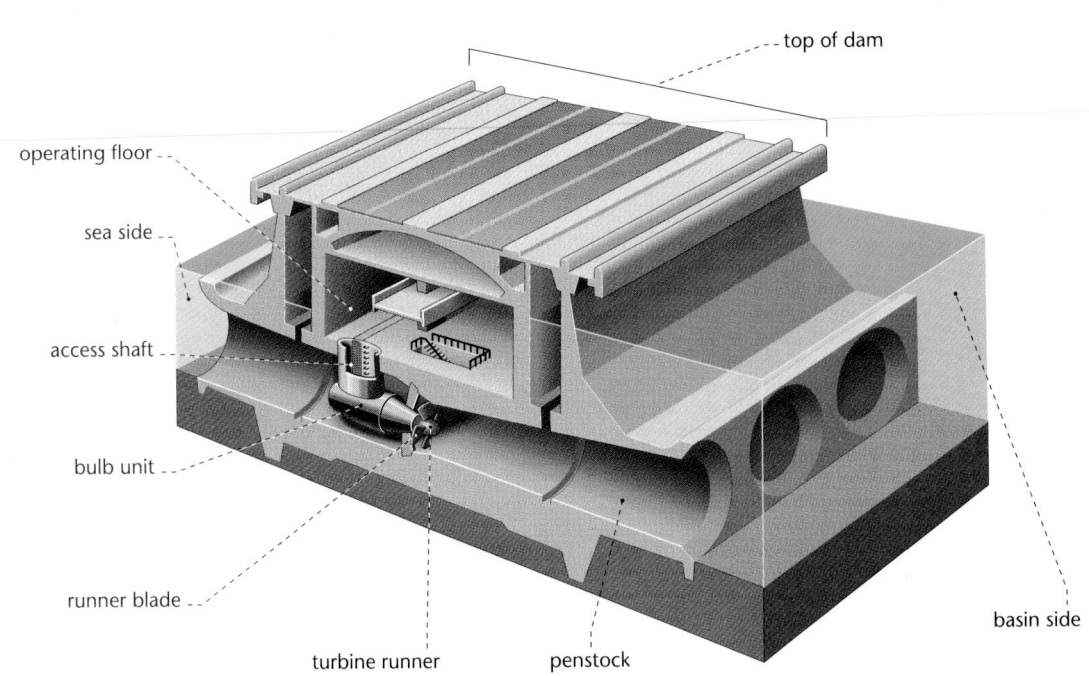

top of dam

operating floor

sea side

access shaft

bulb unit

runner blade

turbine runner

penstock

basin side

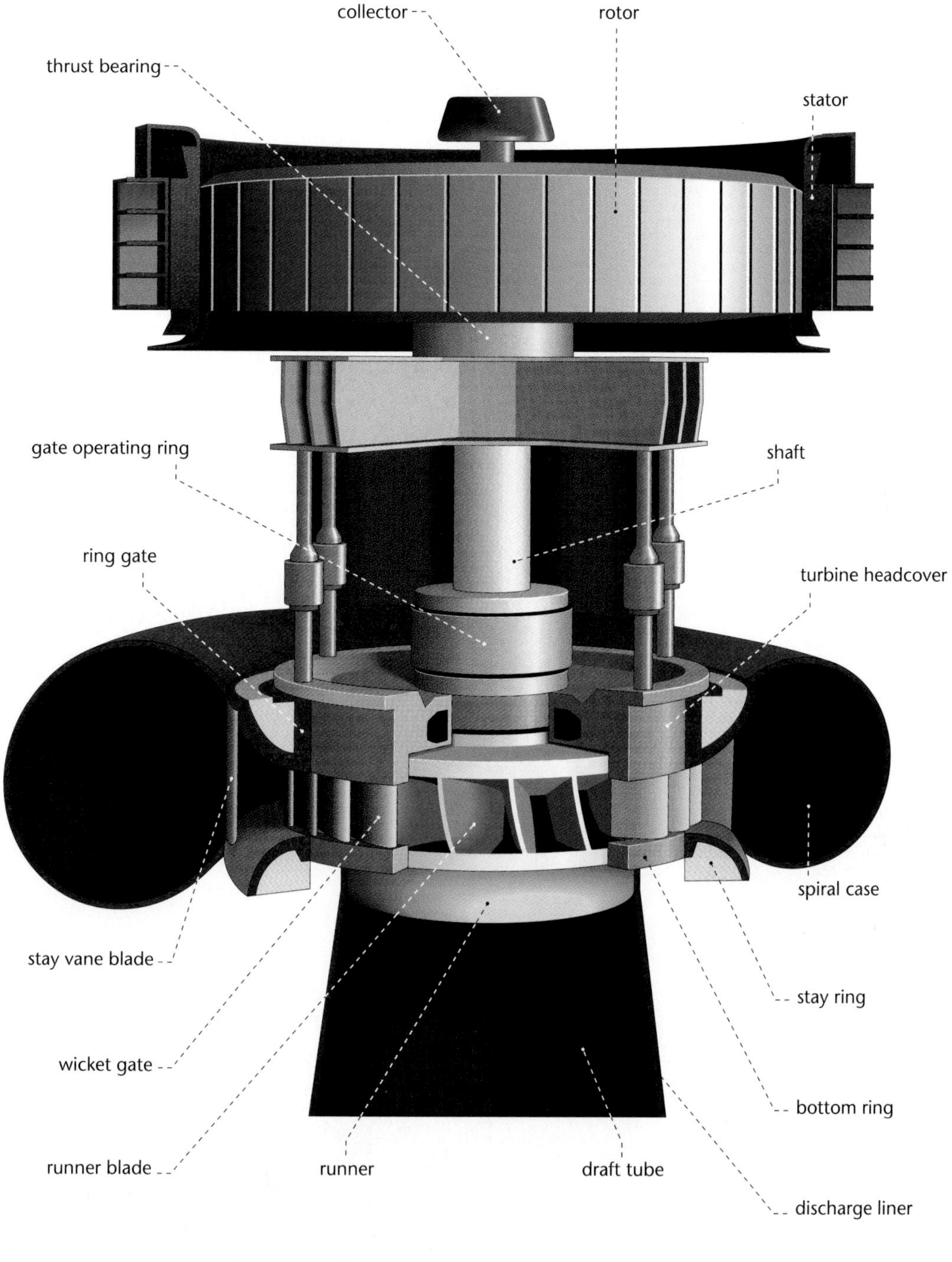

collector

rotor

thrust bearing

stator

gate operating ring

shaft

ring gate

turbine headcover

stay vane blade

spiral case

wicket gate

stay ring

runner blade

bottom ring

runner

draft tube

discharge liner

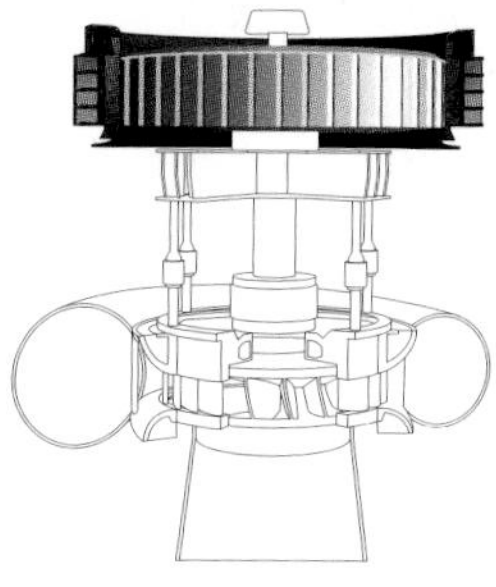

generator

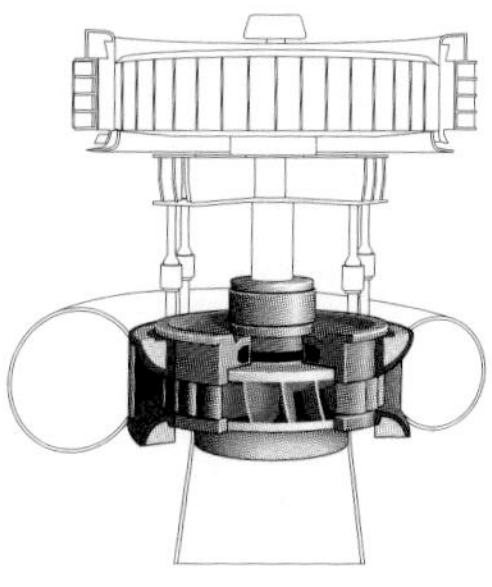

turbine

FRANCIS TURBINE

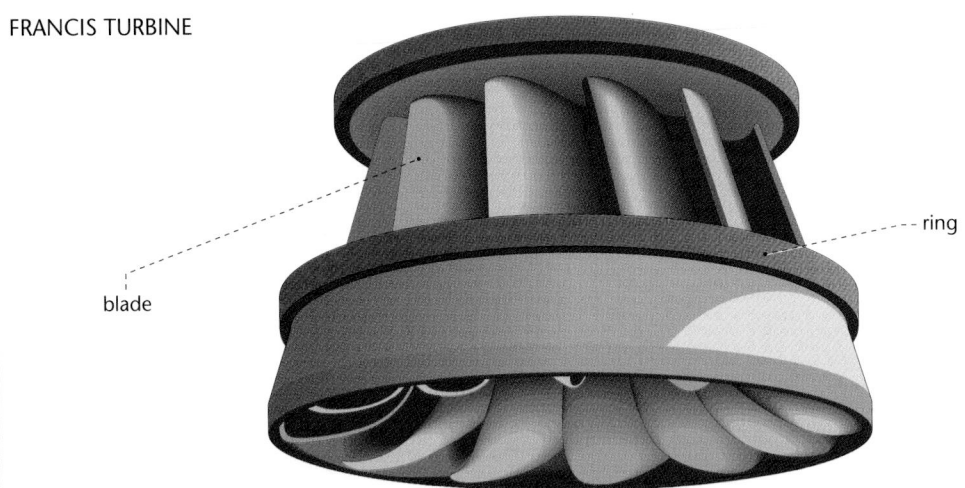

blade

ring

KAPLAN TURBINE

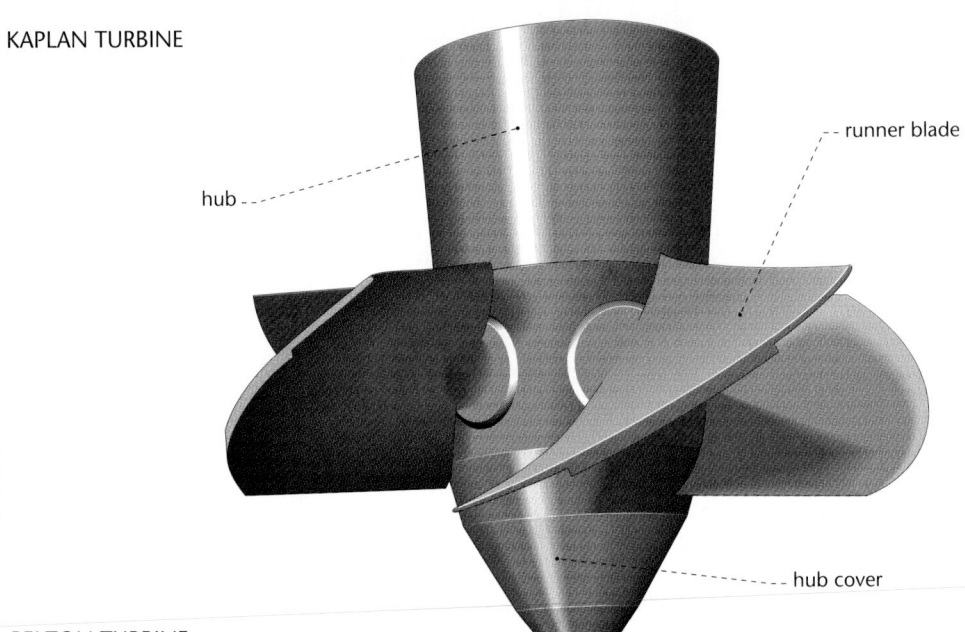

hub

runner blade

hub cover

PELTON TURBINE

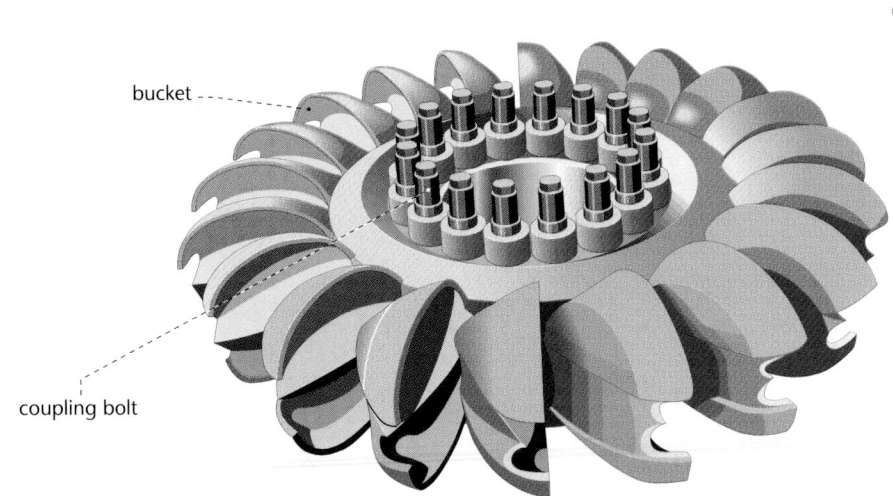

bucket

coupling bolt

bucket ring

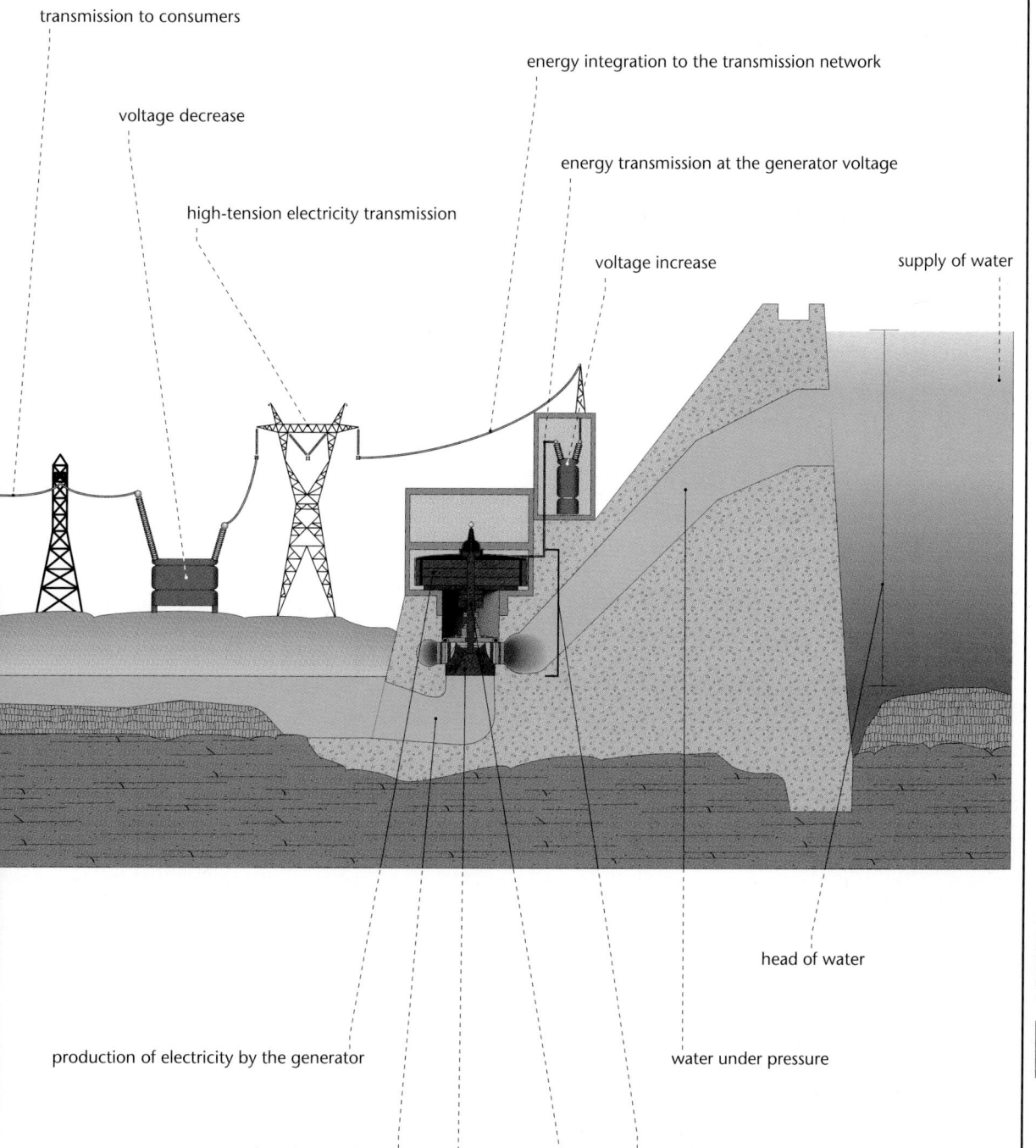

transmission to consumers

voltage decrease

high-tension electricity transmission

energy integration to the transmission network

energy transmission at the generator voltage

voltage increase

supply of water

head of water

production of electricity by the generator

water under pressure

turbined water draining

transformation of mechanical work into electricity

rotation of the turbine

transmission of the rotative movement to the rotor

ENERGY

755

TOWER

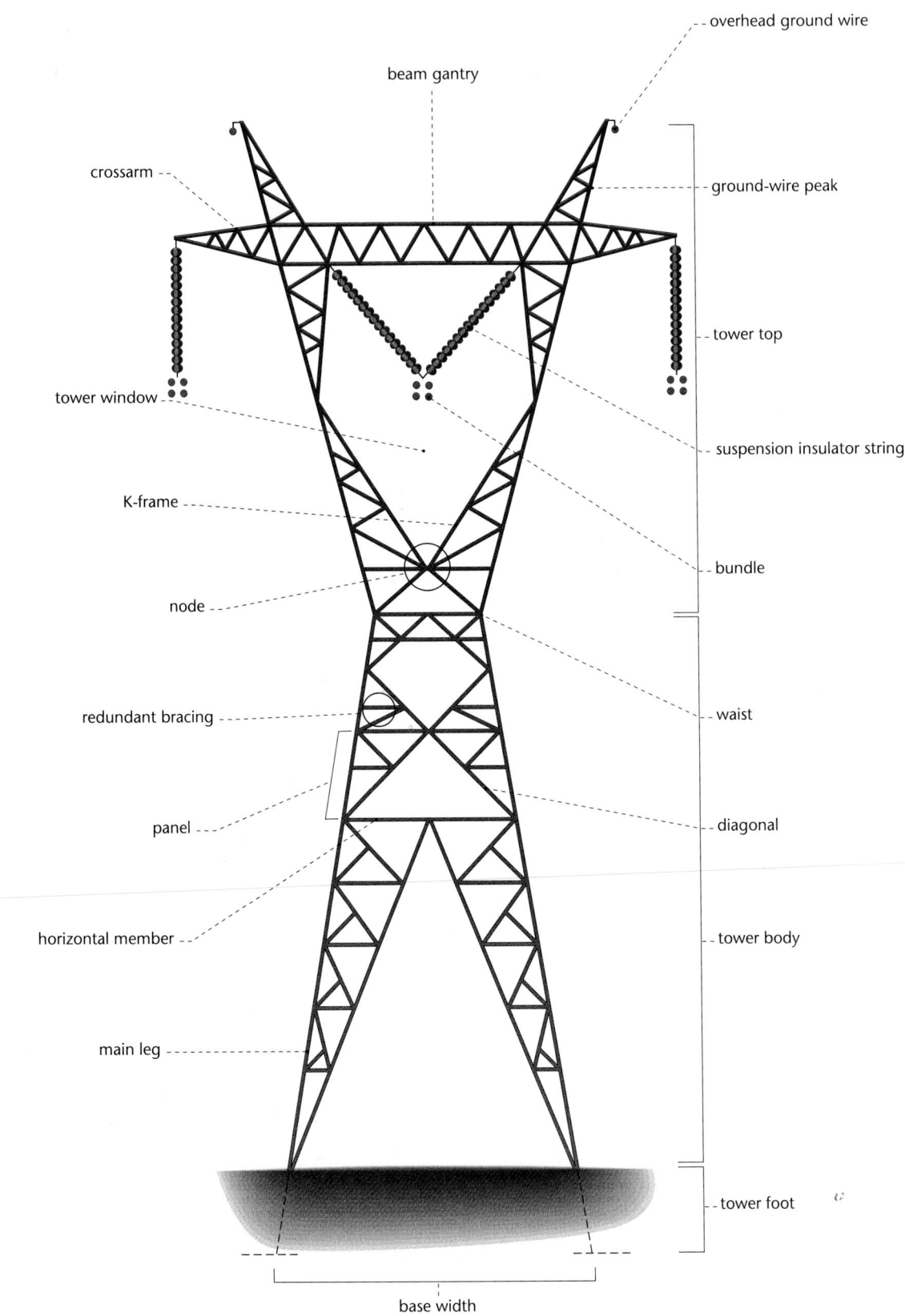

beam gantry

overhead ground wire

crossarm

ground-wire peak

tower top

tower window

suspension insulator string

K-frame

node

bundle

redundant bracing

waist

panel

diagonal

horizontal member

tower body

main leg

tower foot

base width

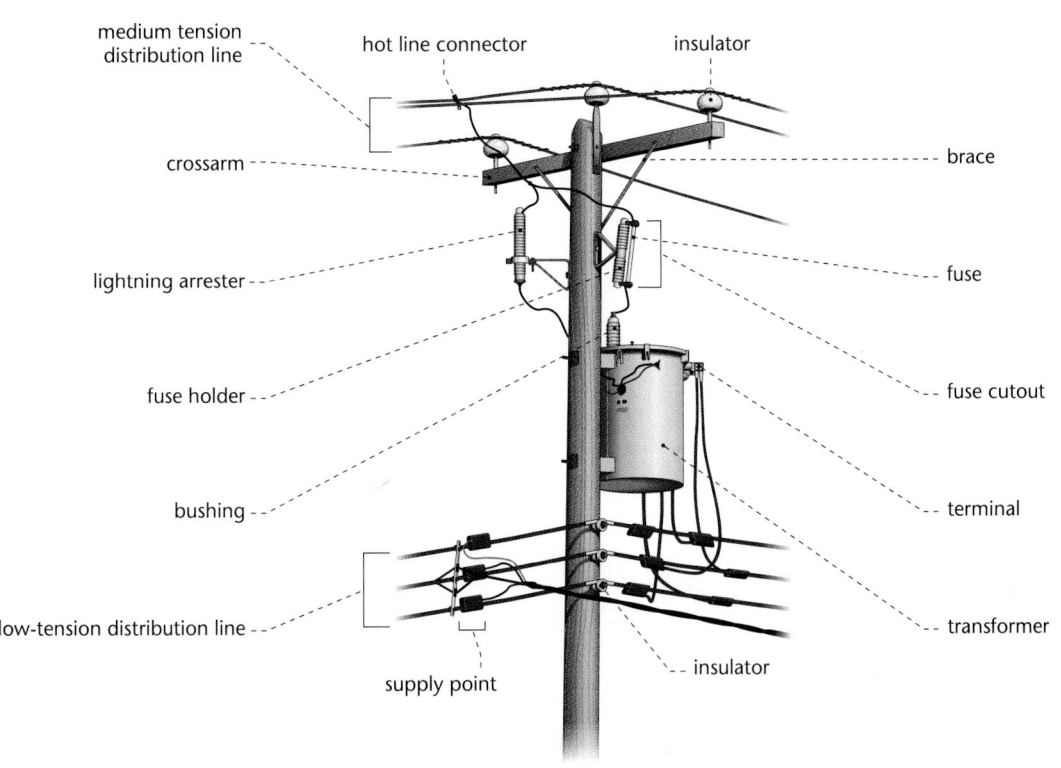

medium tension
distribution line

hot line connector

insulator

crossarm

brace

lightning arrester

fuse

fuse holder

fuse cutout

bushing

terminal

low-tension distribution line

transformer

supply point

insulator

OVERHEAD CONNECTION

supply point

customer's service entrance

connection point

phase conductor

medium tension
distribution line

neutral conductor

low-tension distribution line

ground wire

distributor service loop

electricity meter

main switch

service box

distribution board

fuse

ENERGY

757

NUCLEAR GENERATING STATION

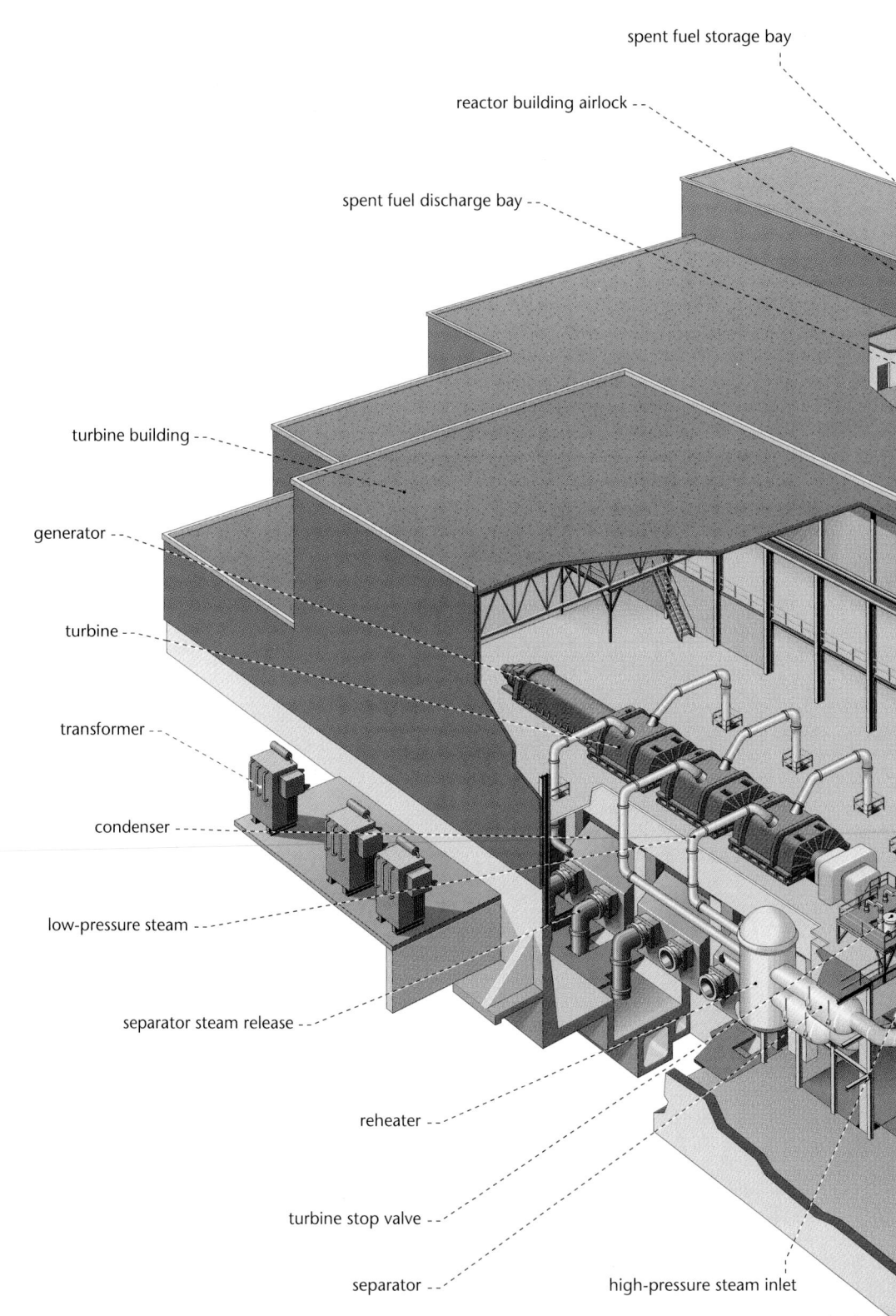

spent fuel storage bay

reactor building airlock

spent fuel discharge bay

turbine building

generator

turbine

transformer

condenser

low-pressure steam

separator steam release

reheater

turbine stop valve

separator

high-pressure steam inlet

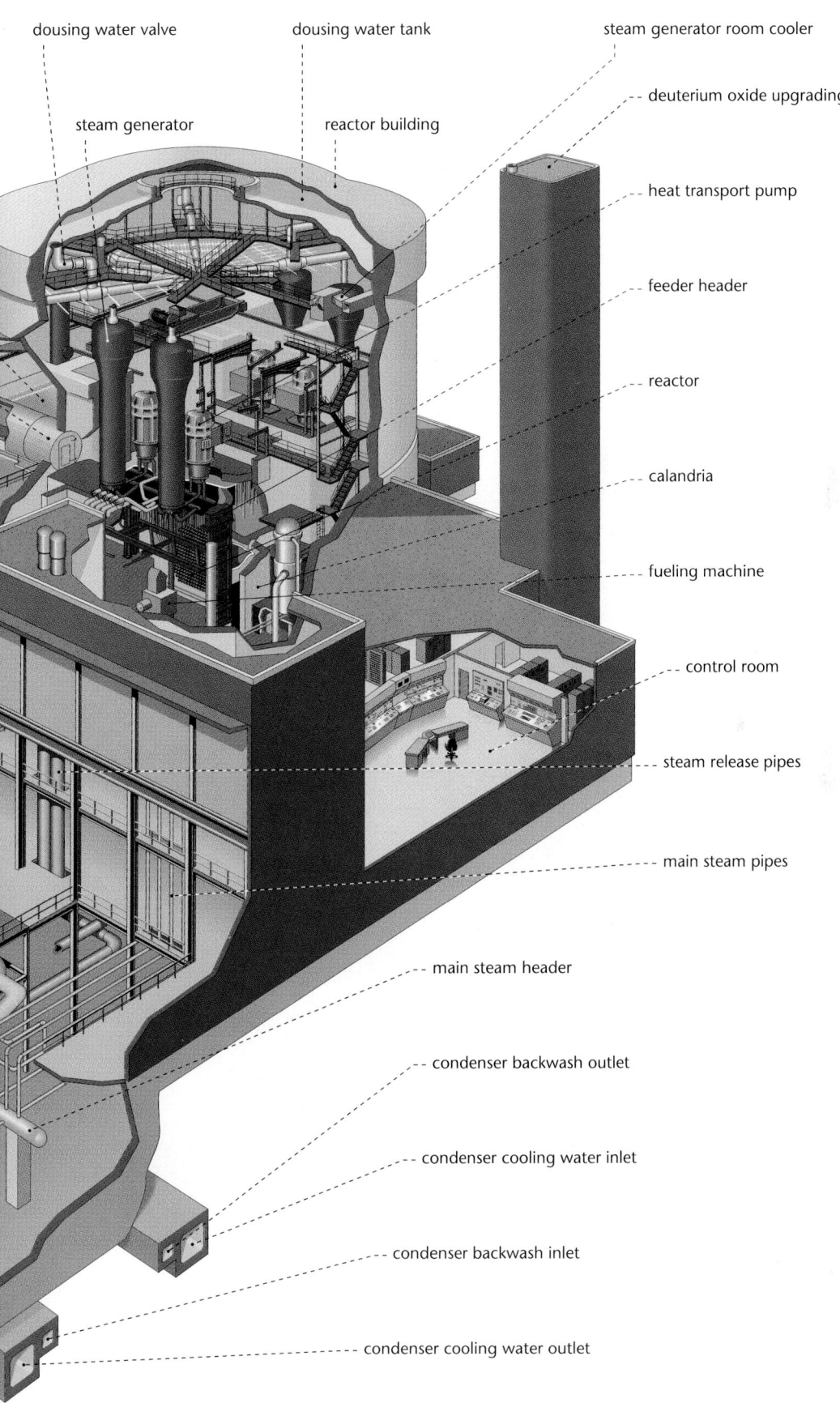

dousing water valve

dousing water tank

steam generator room cooler

steam generator

reactor building

deuterium oxide upgrading

heat transport pump

feeder header

reactor

calandria

fueling machine

control room

steam release pipes

main steam pipes

main steam header

condenser backwash outlet

condenser cooling water inlet

condenser backwash inlet

condenser cooling water outlet

CARBON DIOXIDE REACTOR

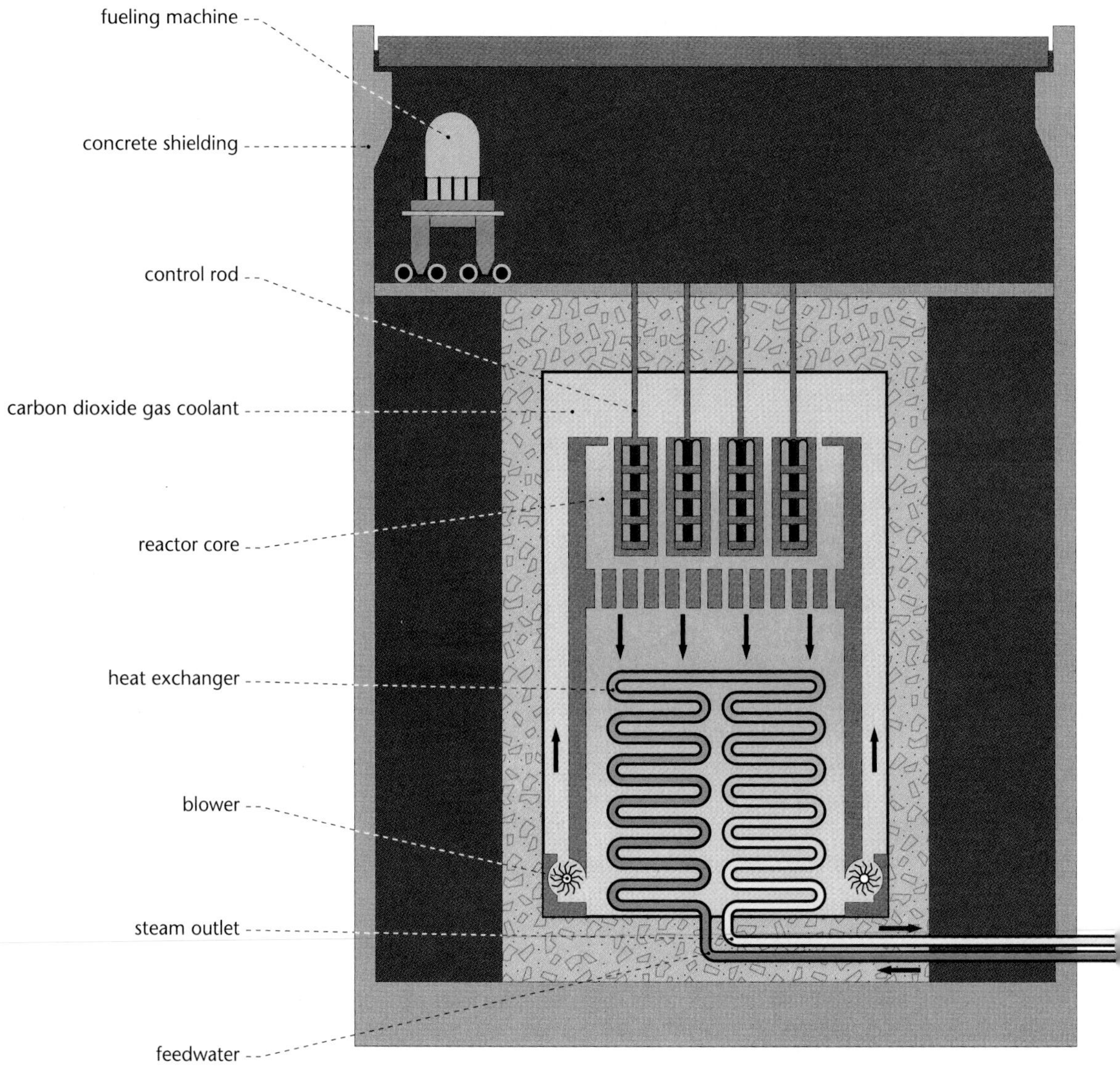

fueling machine

concrete shielding

control rod

carbon dioxide gas coolant

reactor core

heat exchanger

blower

steam outlet

feedwater

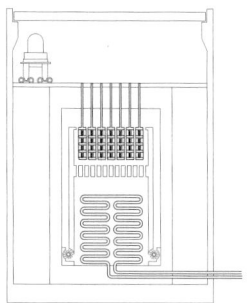

fuel: natural uranium

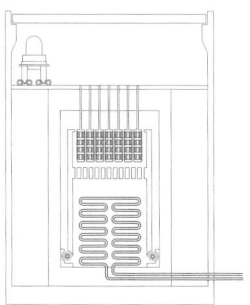

moderator: graphite

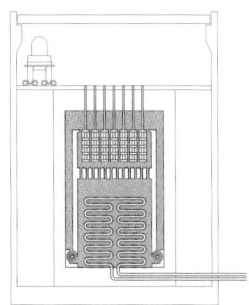

coolant: carbon dioxide

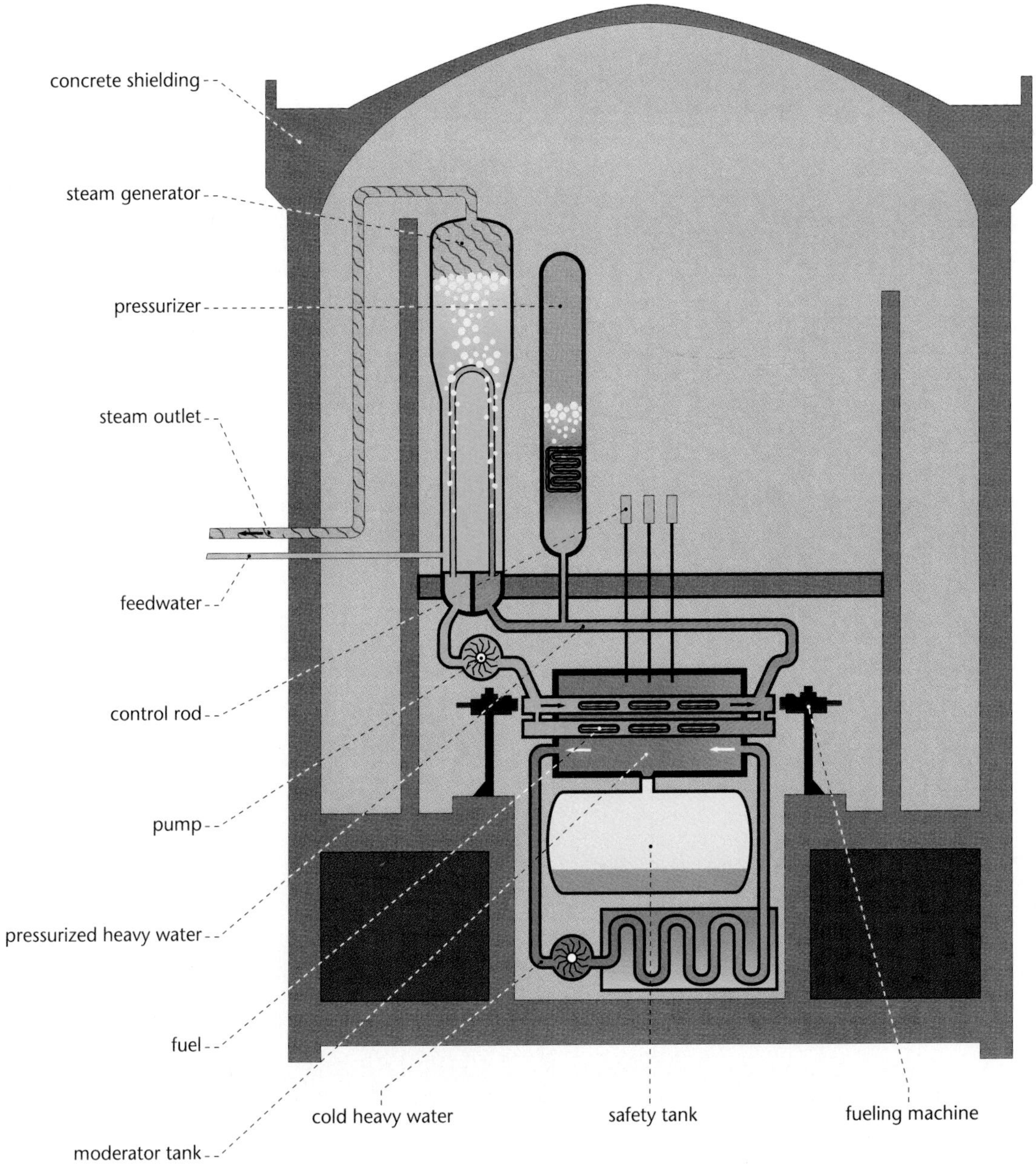

concrete shielding

steam generator

pressurizer

steam outlet

feedwater

control rod

pump

pressurized heavy water

fuel

moderator tank

cold heavy water

safety tank

fueling machine

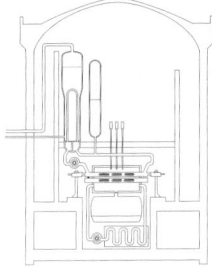

fuel: natural uranium

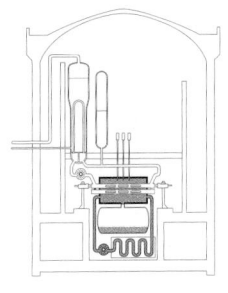

moderator: heavy water

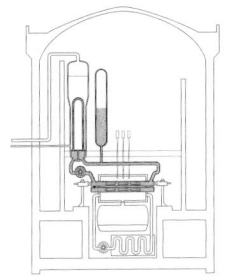

coolant: pressurized heavy water

PRESSURIZED-WATER REACTOR

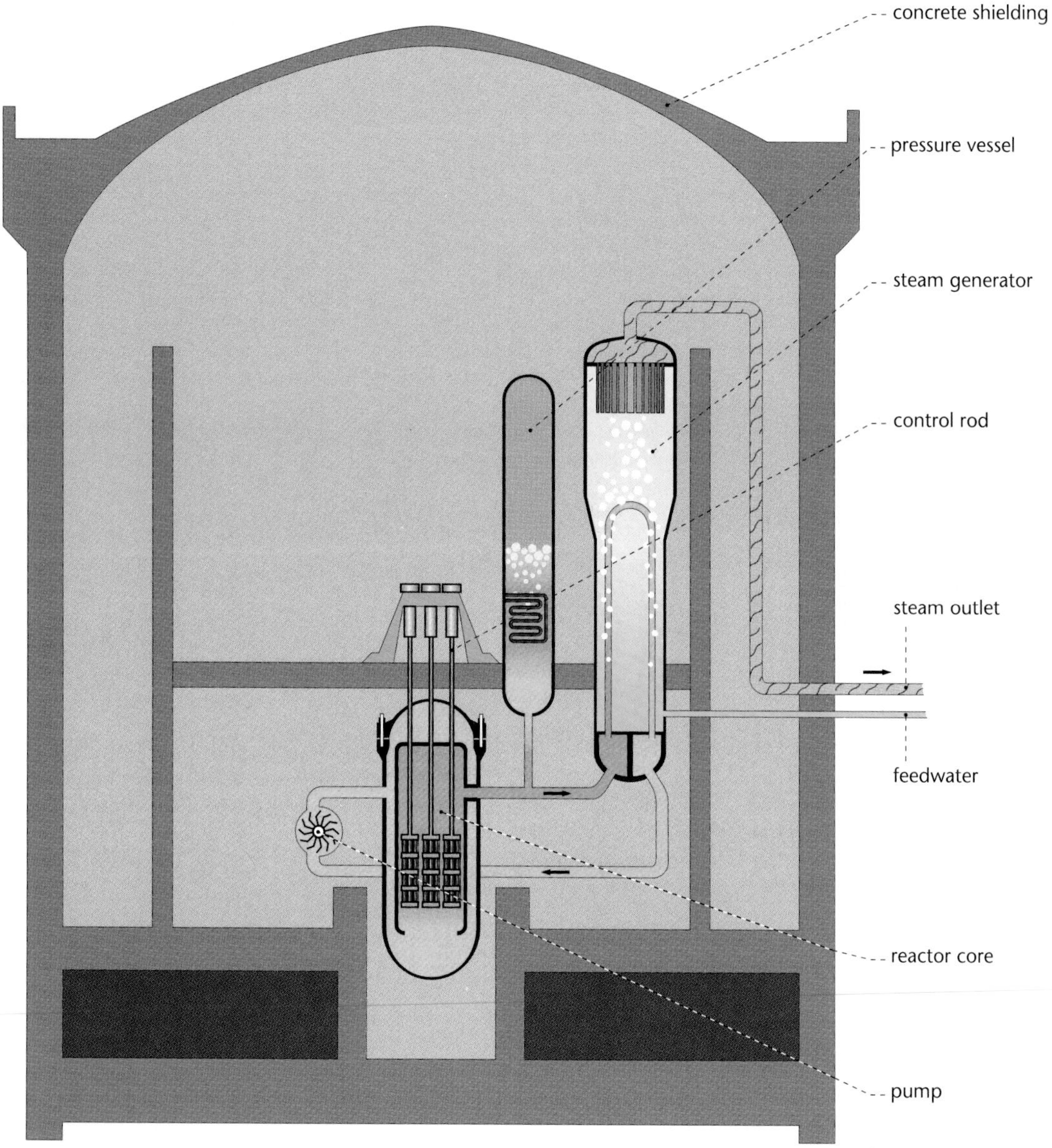

concrete shielding

pressure vessel

steam generator

control rod

steam outlet

feedwater

reactor core

pump

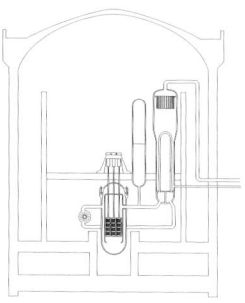

fuel: enriched uranium

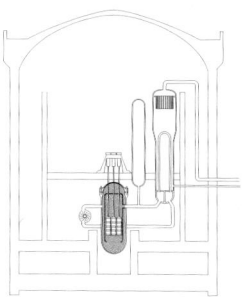

moderator: natural water

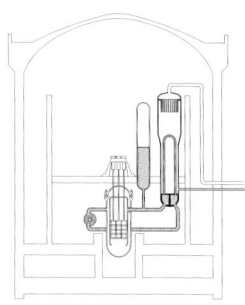

coolant: pressurized water

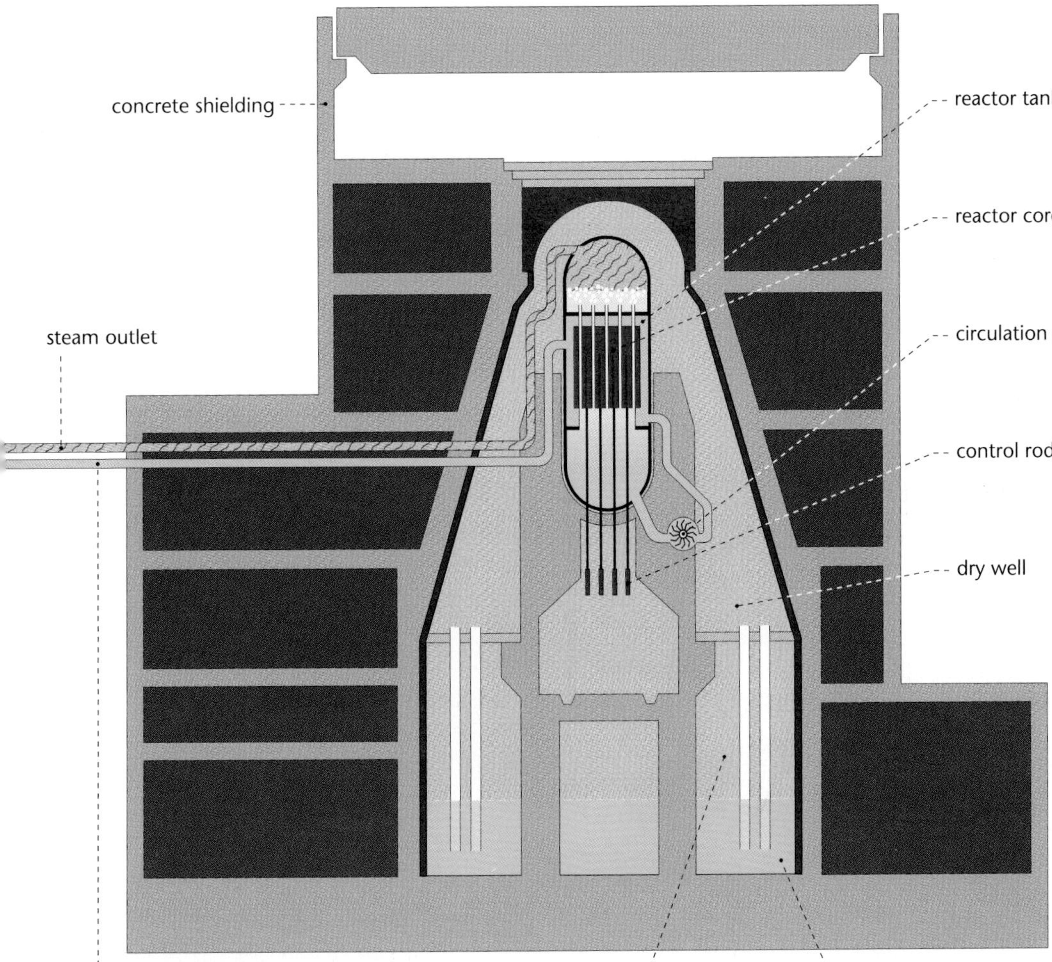

concrete shielding

reactor tank

reactor core

circulation pump

steam outlet

control rod

dry well

feedwater

wet well

condensation pool

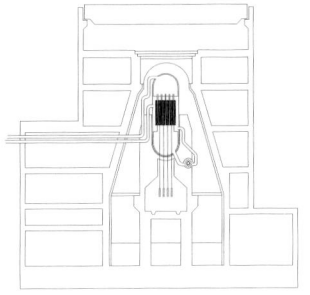

fuel: enriched uranium

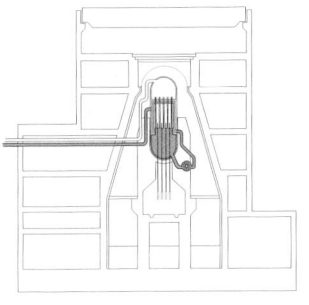

moderator: natural water

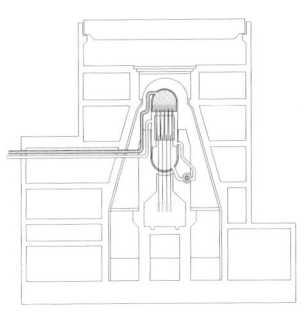

coolant: boiling water

FUEL HANDLING SEQUENCE

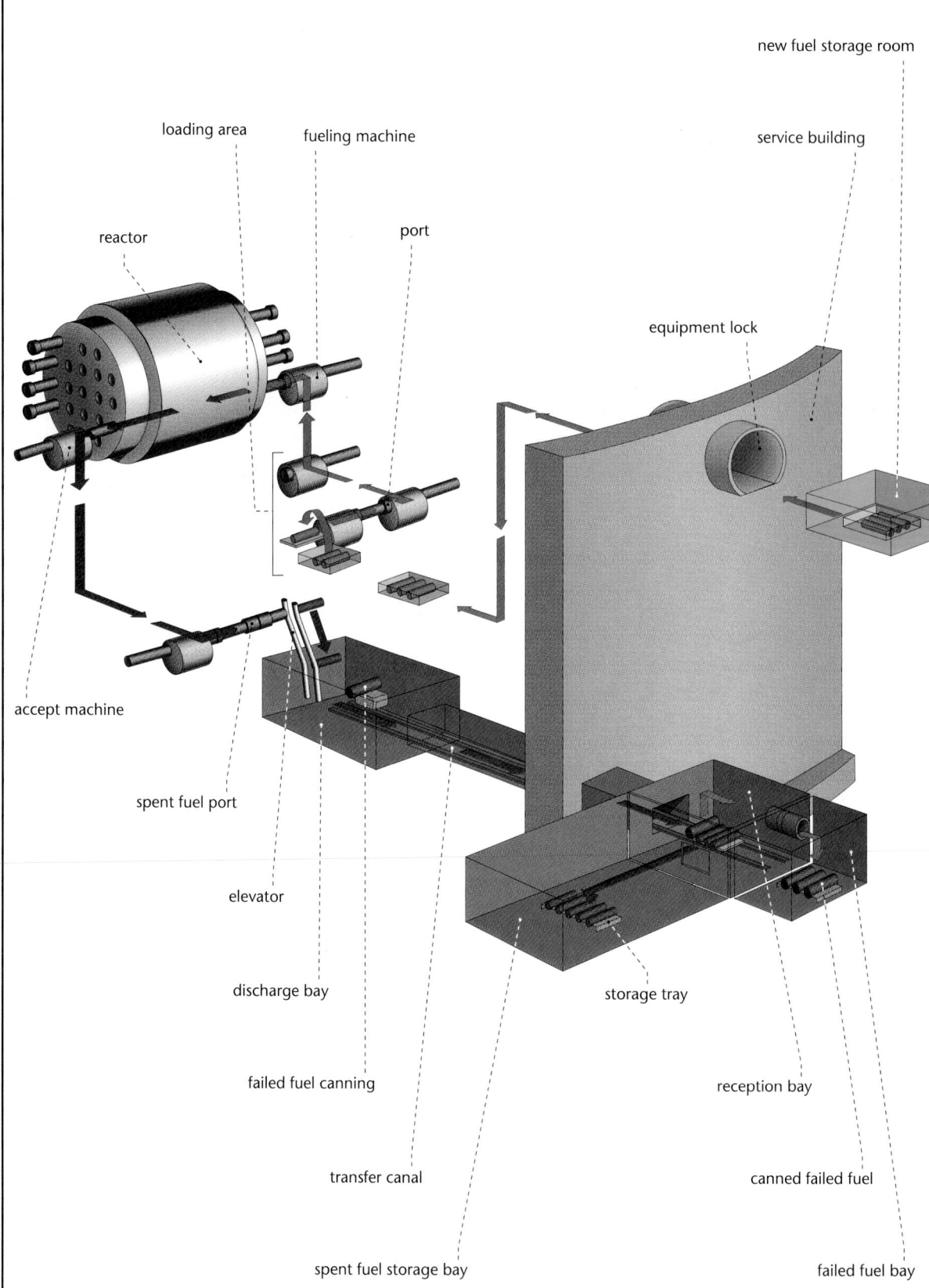

new fuel storage room

loading area   fueling machine

service building

reactor   port

equipment lock

accept machine

spent fuel port

elevator

discharge bay

storage tray

failed fuel canning

reception bay

transfer canal

canned failed fuel

spent fuel storage bay

failed fuel bay

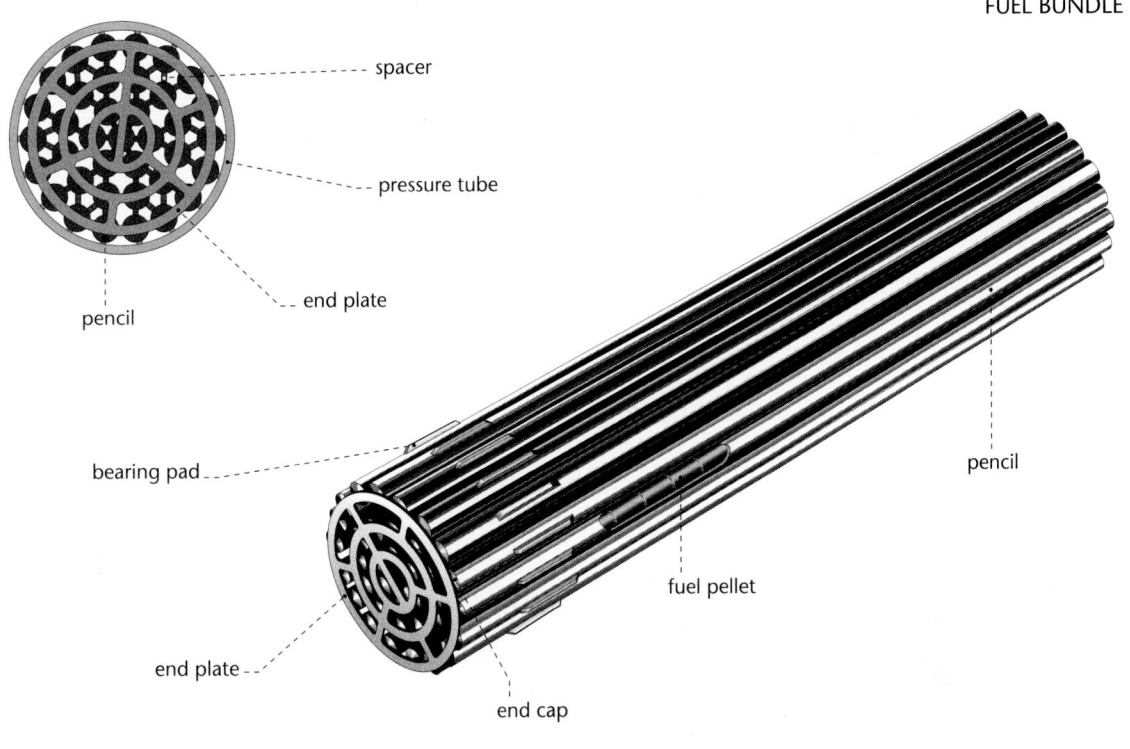

spacer

pressure tube

end plate

pencil

bearing pad

end plate

end cap

pencil

fuel pellet

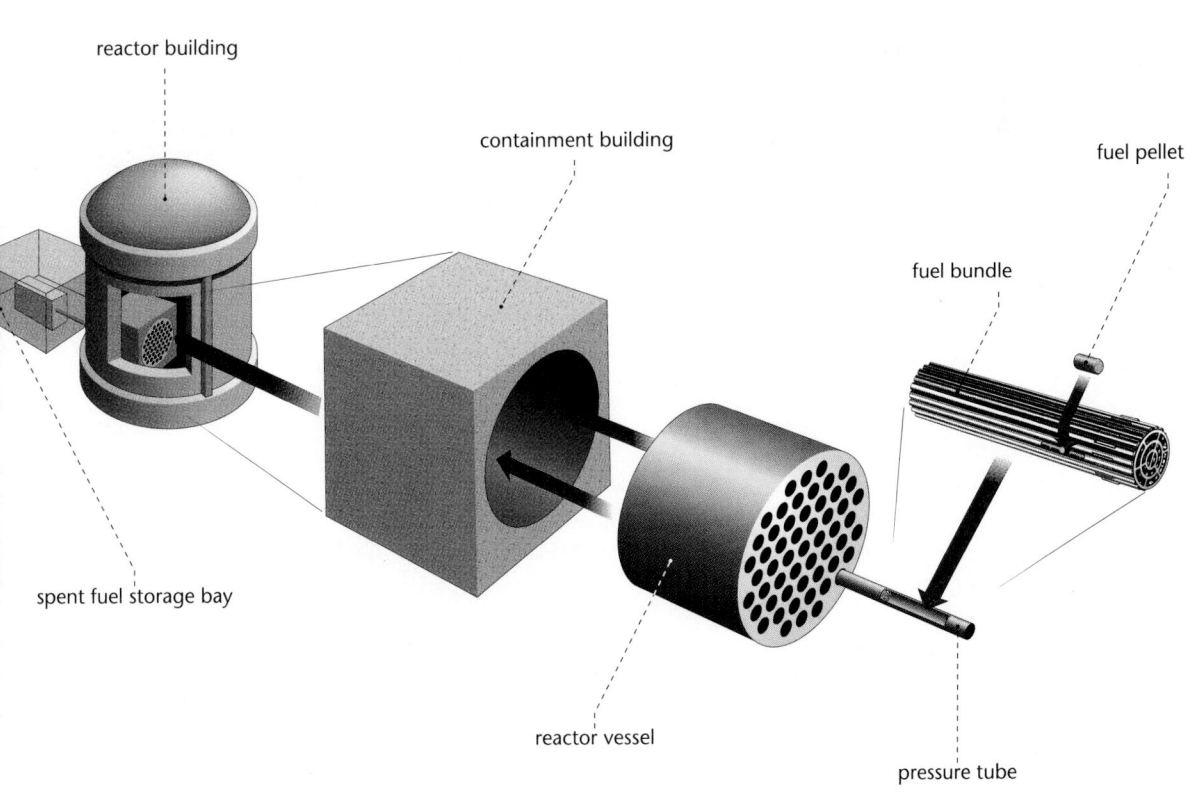

reactor building

containment building

fuel pellet

fuel bundle

spent fuel storage bay

reactor vessel

pressure tube

ENERGY

PRODUCTION OF ELECTRICITY FROM NUCLEAR ENERGY

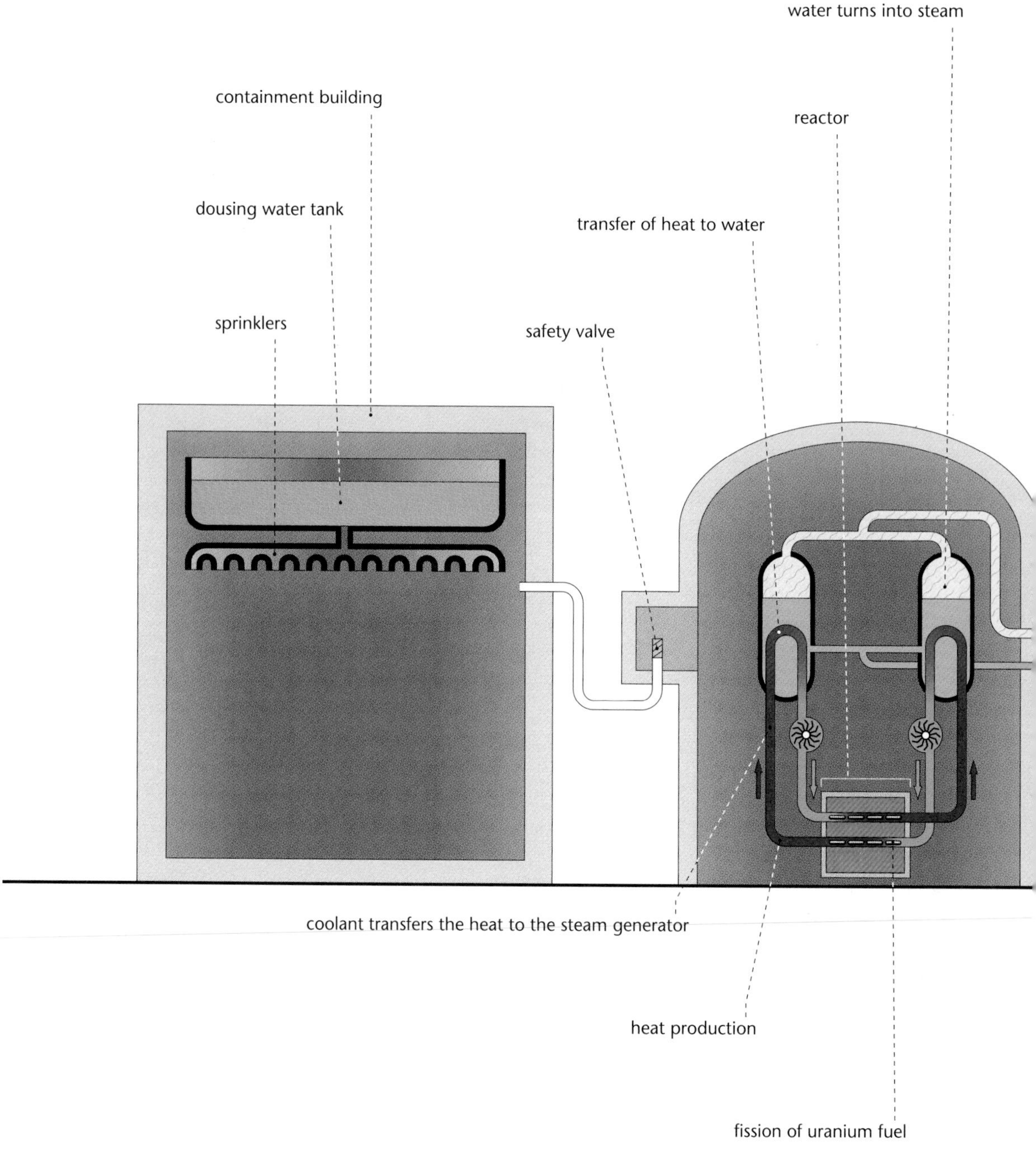

water turns into steam

containment building

reactor

dousing water tank

transfer of heat to water

sprinklers

safety valve

coolant transfers the heat to the steam generator

heat production

fission of uranium fuel

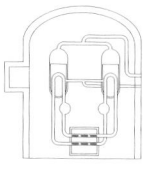

fuel

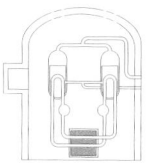

moderator

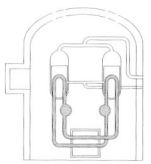

coolant

ENERGY

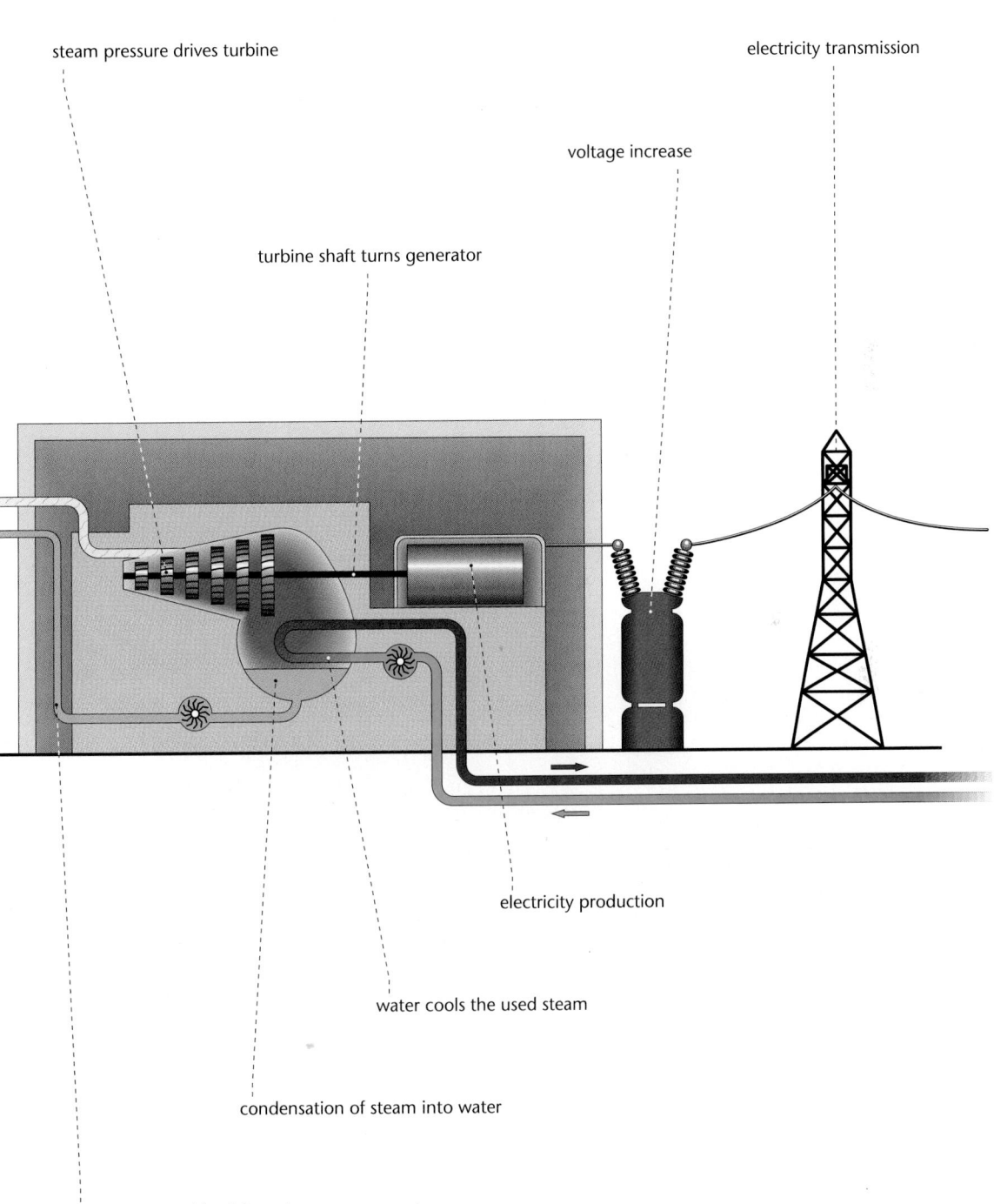

steam pressure drives turbine

electricity transmission

voltage increase

turbine shaft turns generator

electricity production

water cools the used steam

condensation of steam into water

water is pumped back into the steam generator

SOLAR ENERGY

SOLAR CELL

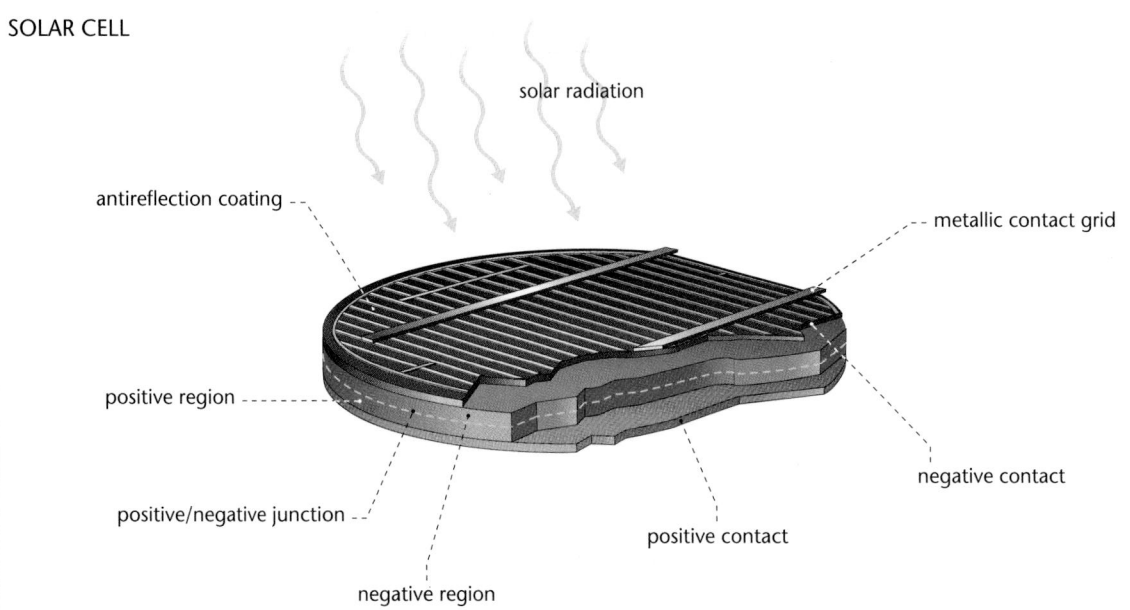

solar radiation

antireflection coating

metallic contact grid

positive region

negative contact

positive/negative junction

positive contact

negative region

FLAT-PLATE SOLAR COLLECTOR

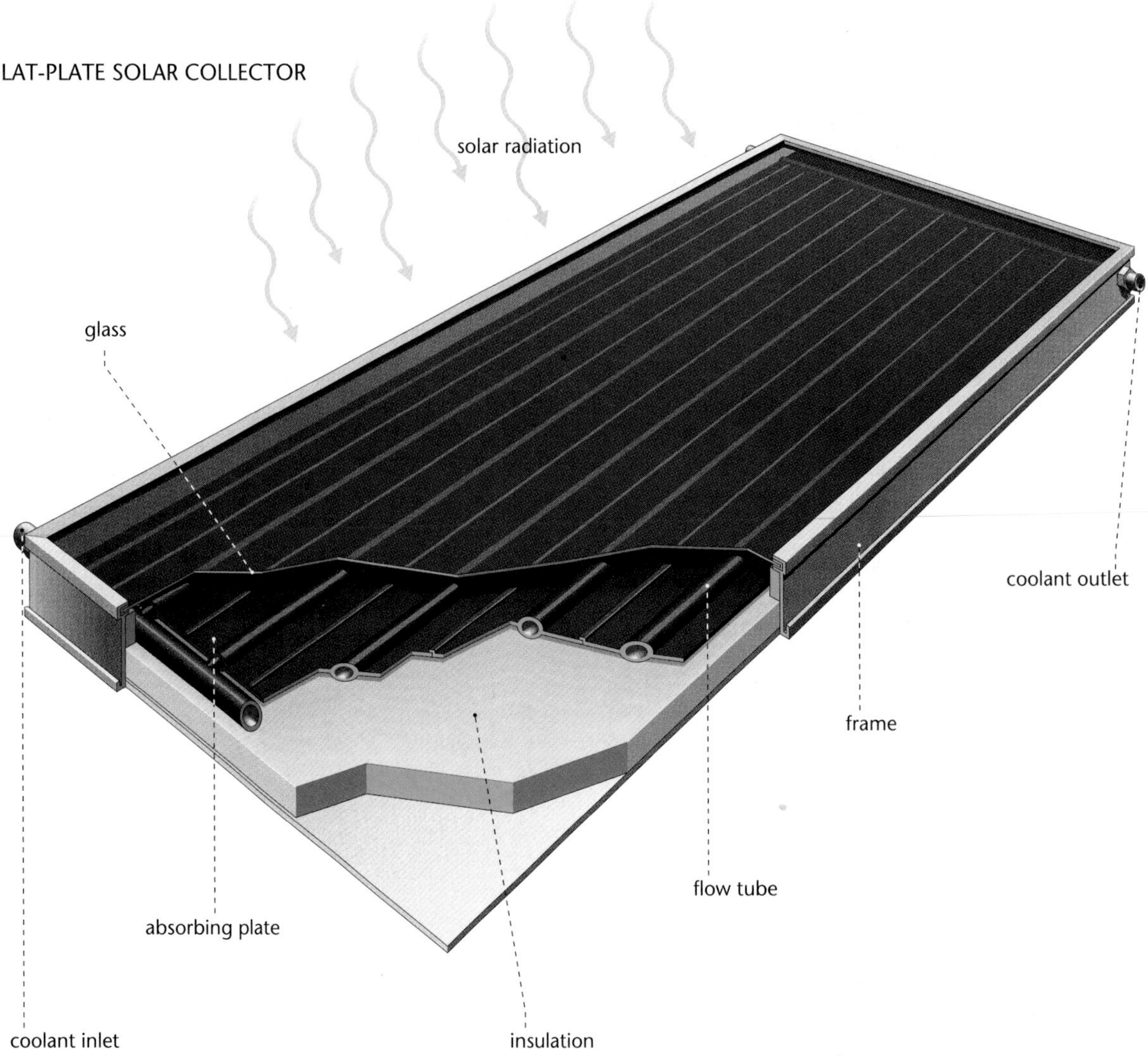

solar radiation

glass

coolant outlet

frame

flow tube

absorbing plate

coolant inlet

insulation

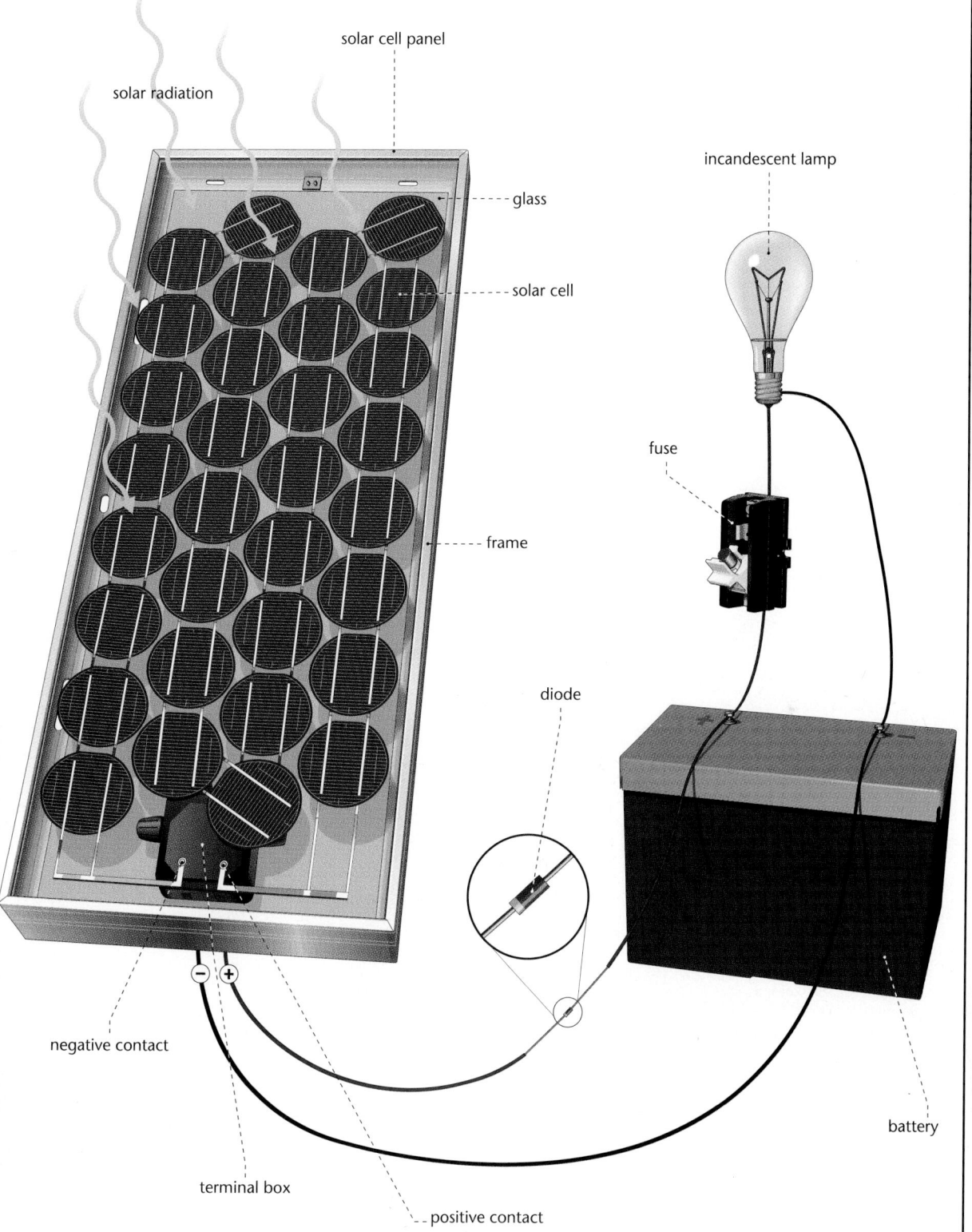

solar cell panel

solar radiation

glass

solar cell

incandescent lamp

frame

fuse

diode

negative contact

positive contact

terminal box

battery

SOLAR FURNACE

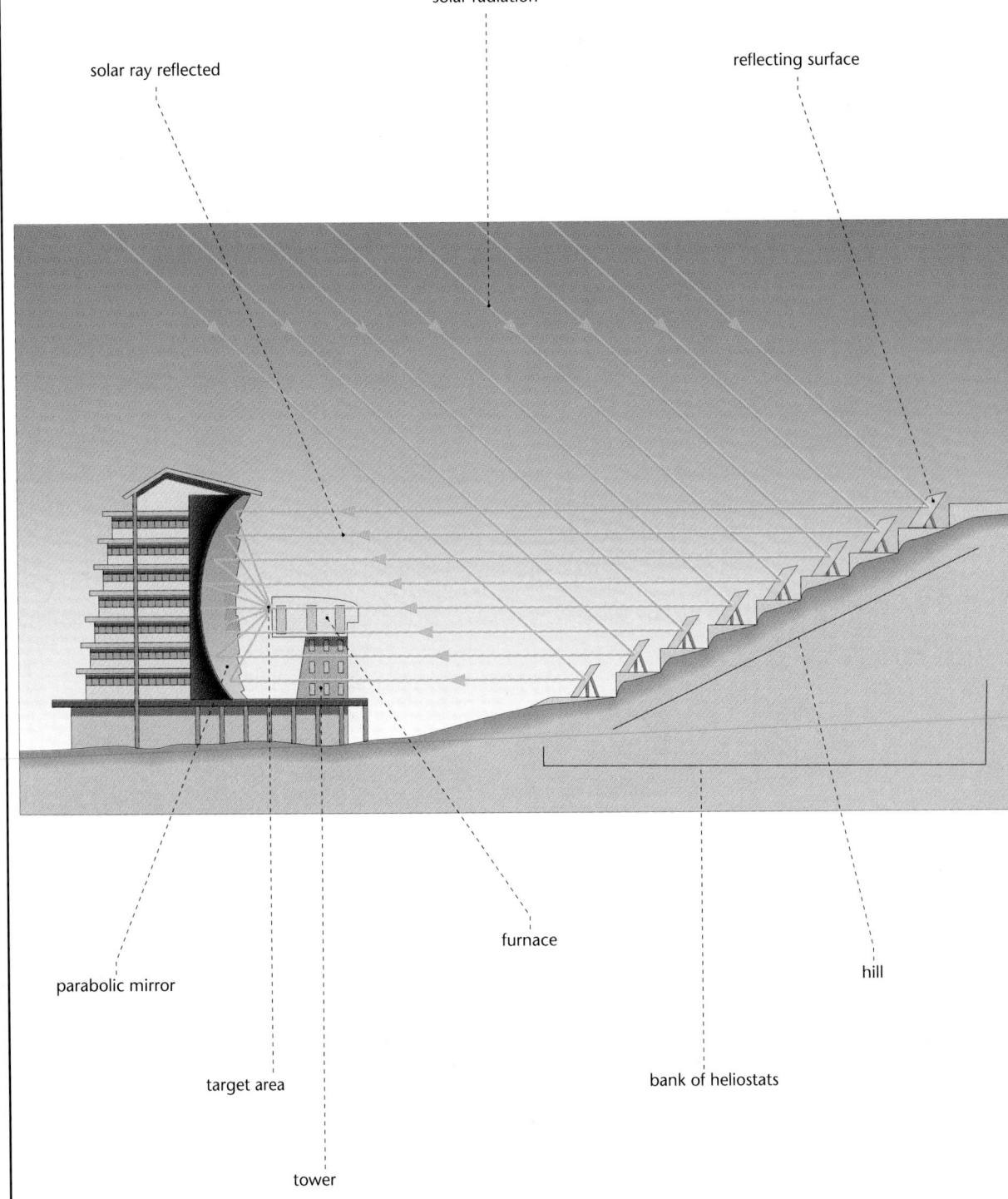

solar radiation

reflecting surface

solar ray reflected

furnace

hill

parabolic mirror

bank of heliostats

target area

tower

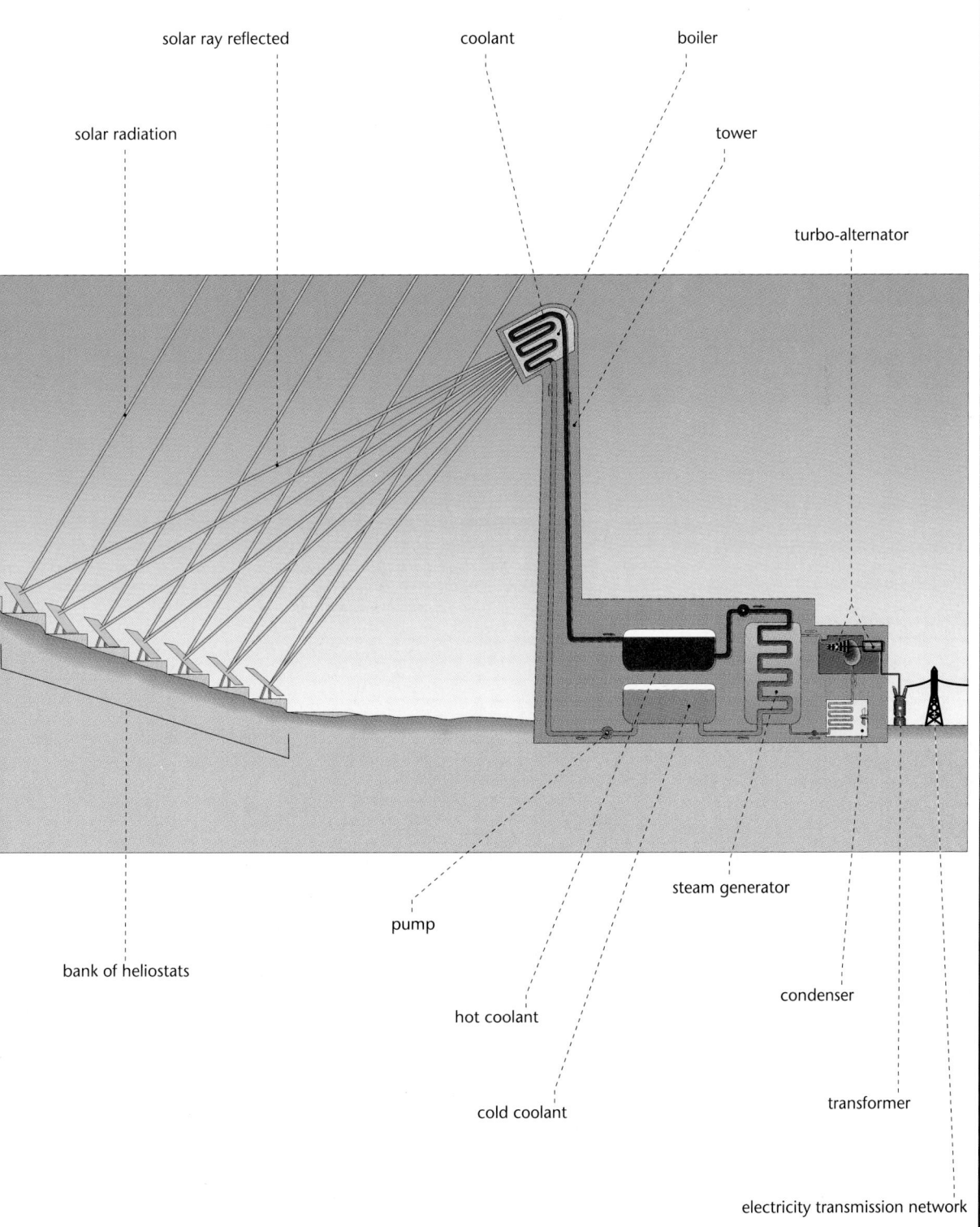

solar ray reflected

coolant

boiler

solar radiation

tower

turbo-alternator

bank of heliostats

pump

hot coolant

cold coolant

steam generator

condenser

transformer

electricity transmission network

SOLAR HOUSE

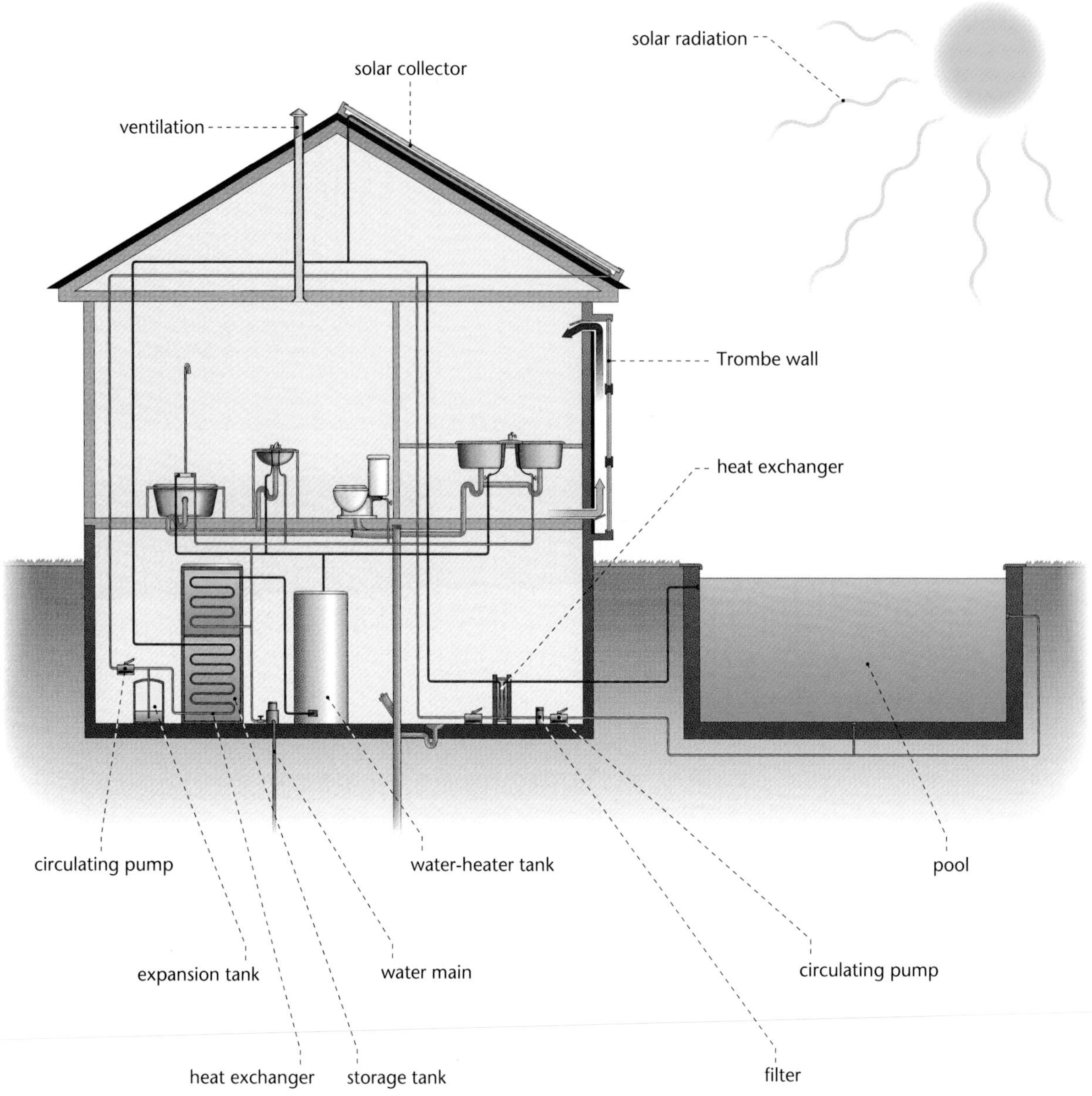

solar radiation

solar collector

ventilation

Trombe wall

heat exchanger

circulating pump

water-heater tank

pool

expansion tank

water main

circulating pump

heat exchanger

storage tank

filter

TROMBE WALL

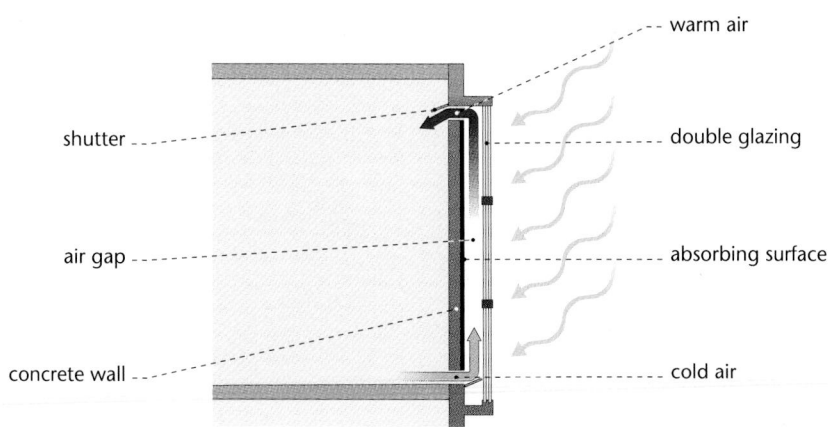

warm air

shutter

double glazing

air gap

absorbing surface

concrete wall

cold air

WIND ENERGY

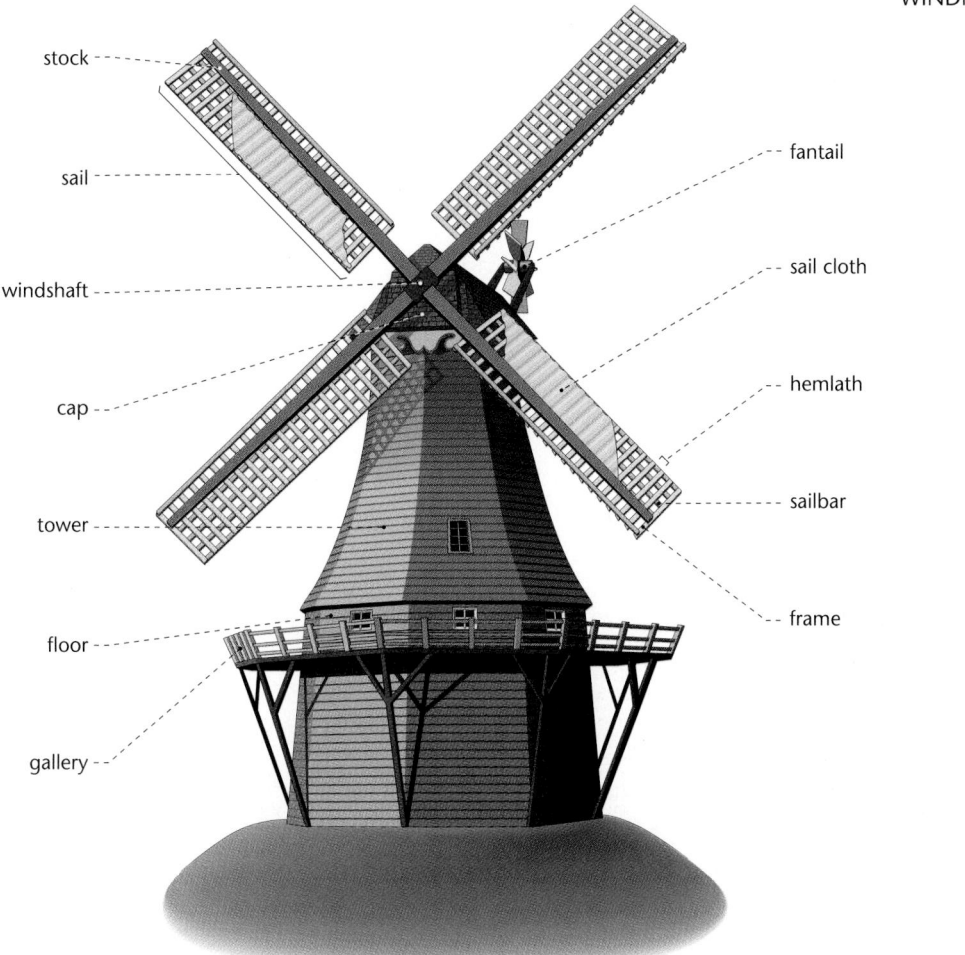

stock

sail

windshaft

cap

tower

floor

gallery

fantail

sail cloth

hemlath

sailbar

frame

rotor

ladder

tail pole

post

ENERGY

HORIZONTAL-AXIS WIND TURBINE

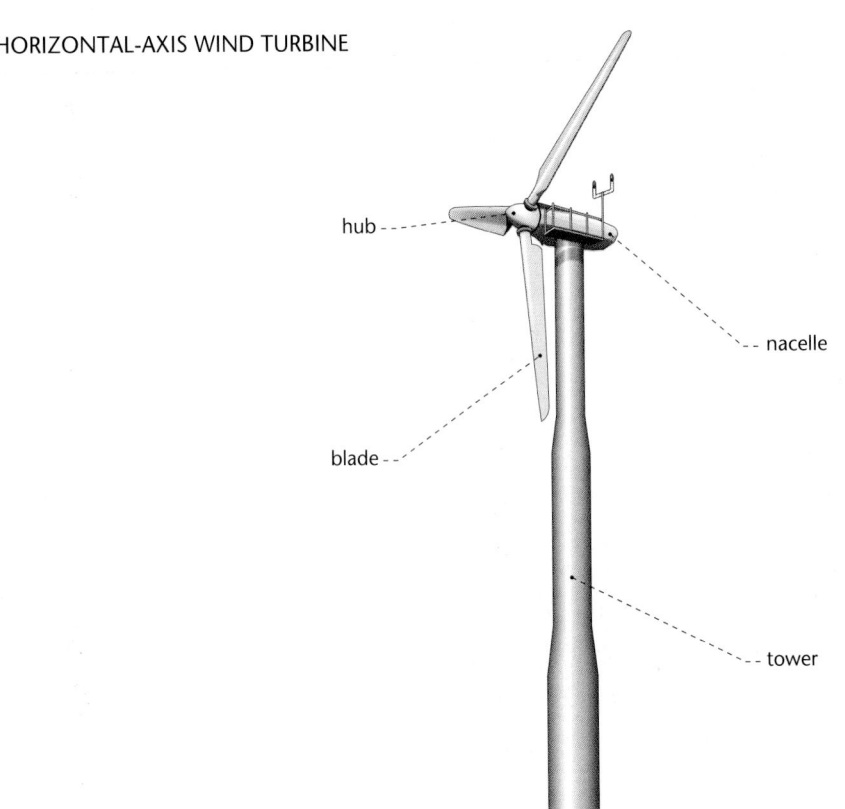

hub

nacelle

blade

tower

VERTICAL-AXIS WIND TURBINE

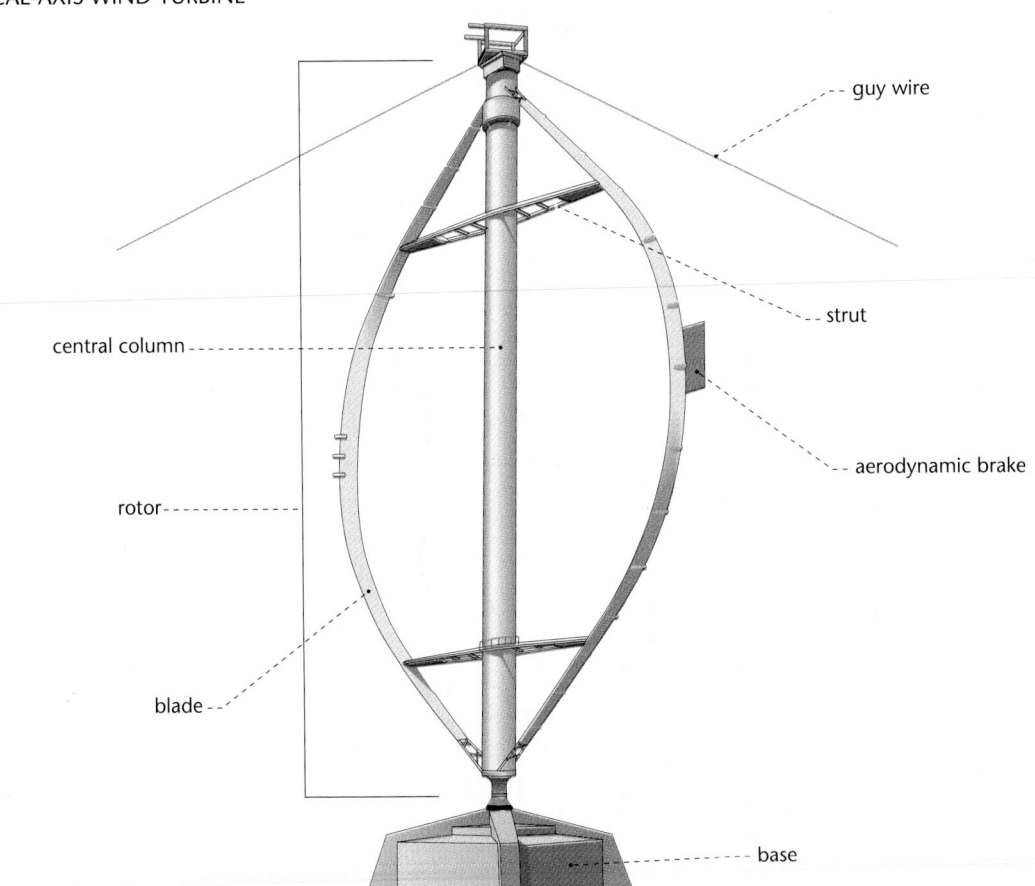

guy wire

strut

central column

aerodynamic brake

rotor

blade

base

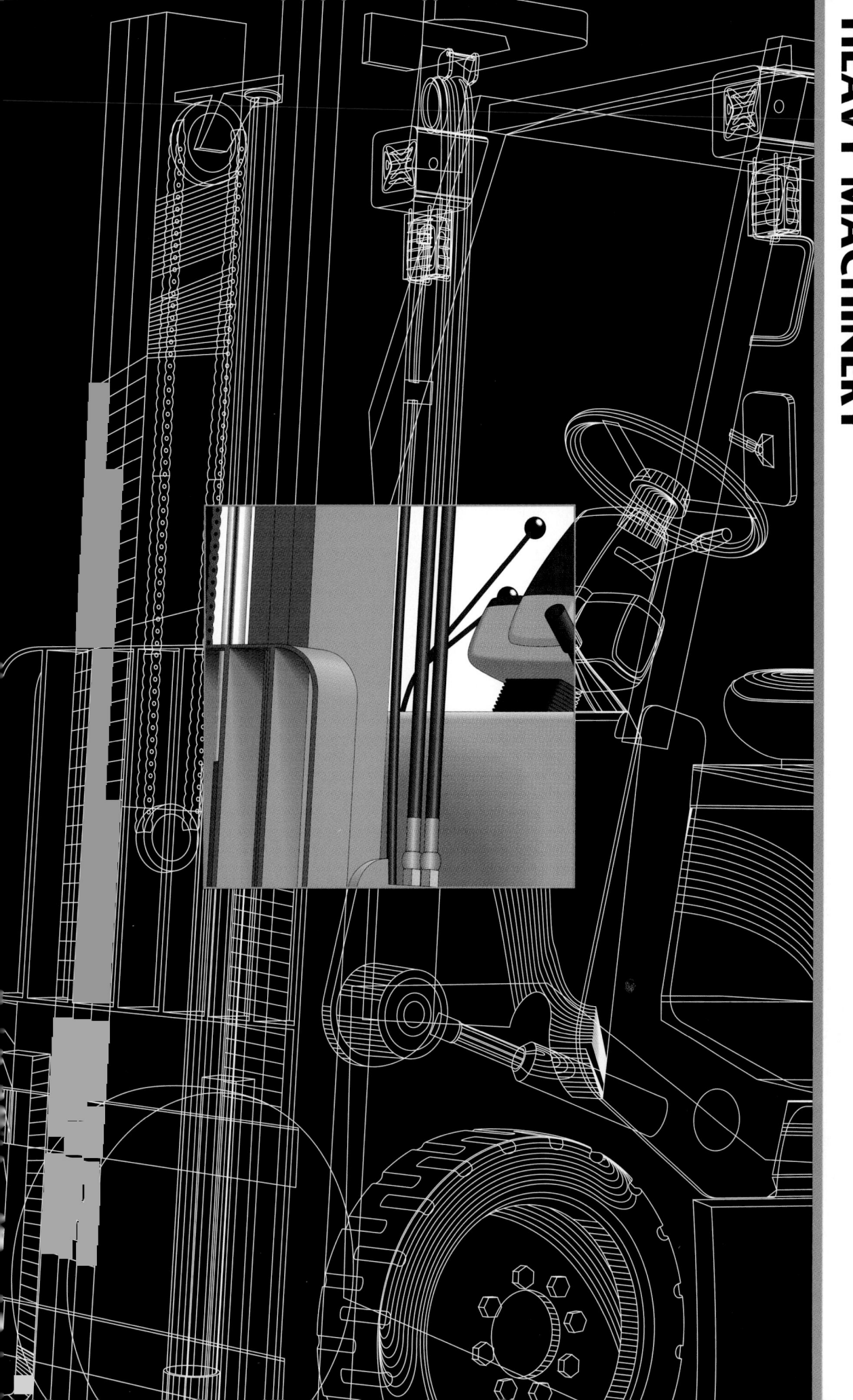

CONTENTS

FIRE PREVENTION 777

FIRE ENGINE 778

MATERIAL HANDLING..786

HEAVY MACHINERY

FIRE PREVENTION

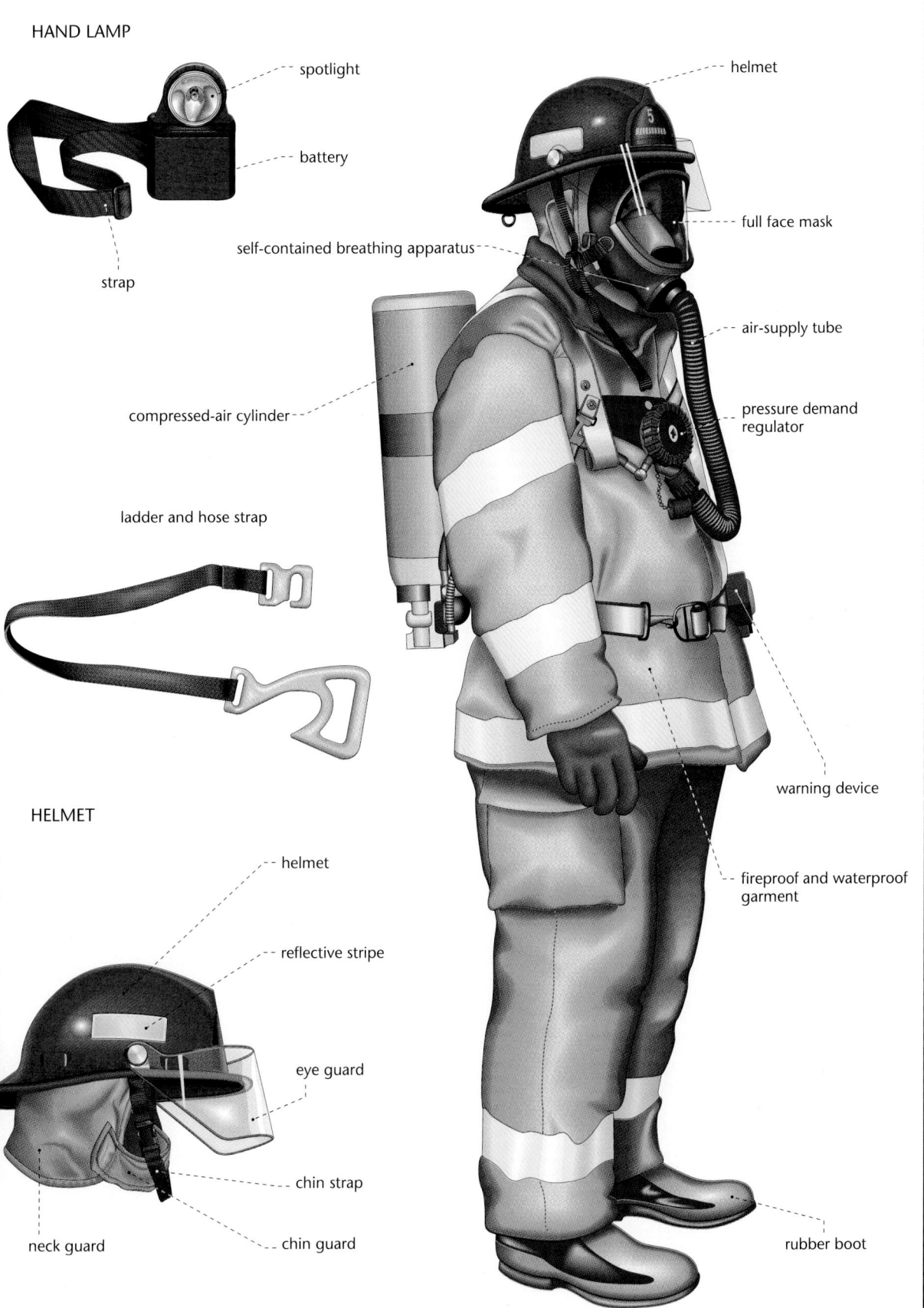

HAND LAMP

- spotlight
- battery
- strap

helmet

full face mask

self-contained breathing apparatus

air-supply tube

pressure demand regulator

compressed-air cylinder

ladder and hose strap

warning device

fireproof and waterproof garment

HELMET

- helmet
- reflective stripe
- eye guard
- chin strap
- neck guard
- chin guard

rubber boot

HEAVY MACHINERY

FIRE ENGINE

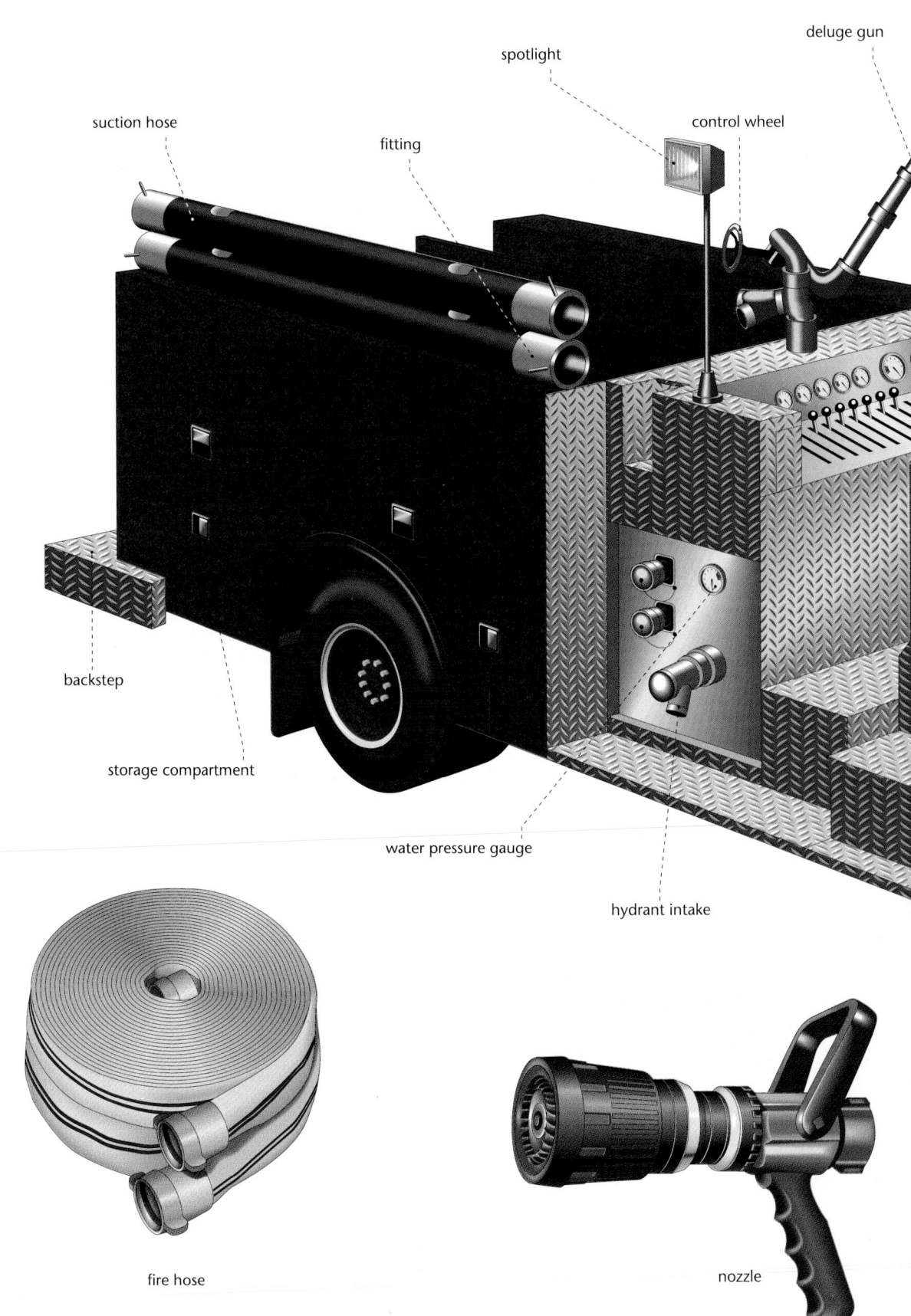

suction hose

fitting

spotlight

control wheel

deluge gun

backstep

storage compartment

water pressure gauge

hydrant intake

fire hose

nozzle

dividing breeching

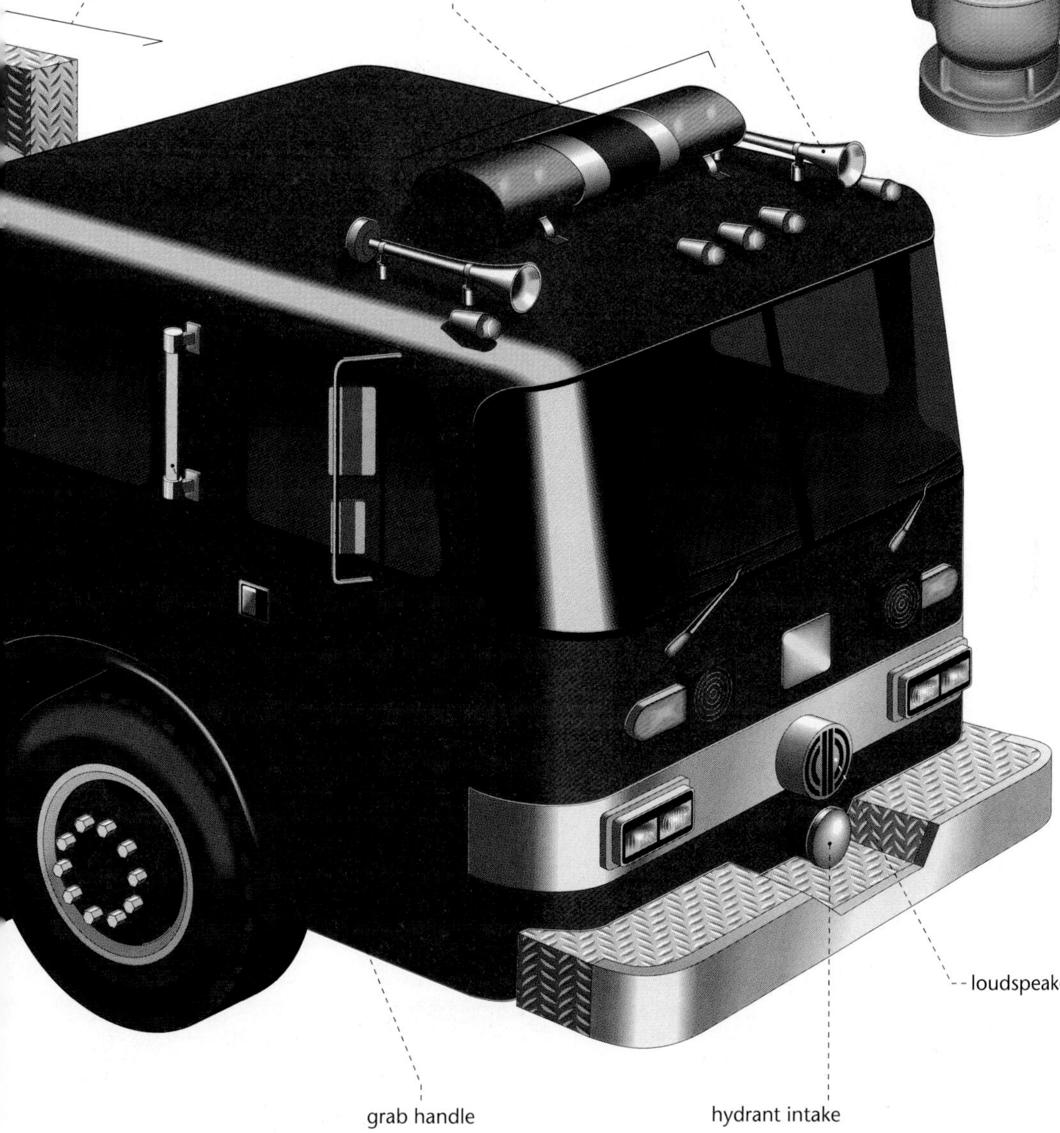

control panel

horn

light bar

loudspeaker

grab handle

hydrant intake

fire hydrant wrench

FIRE ENGINE

AERIAL LADDER TRUCK

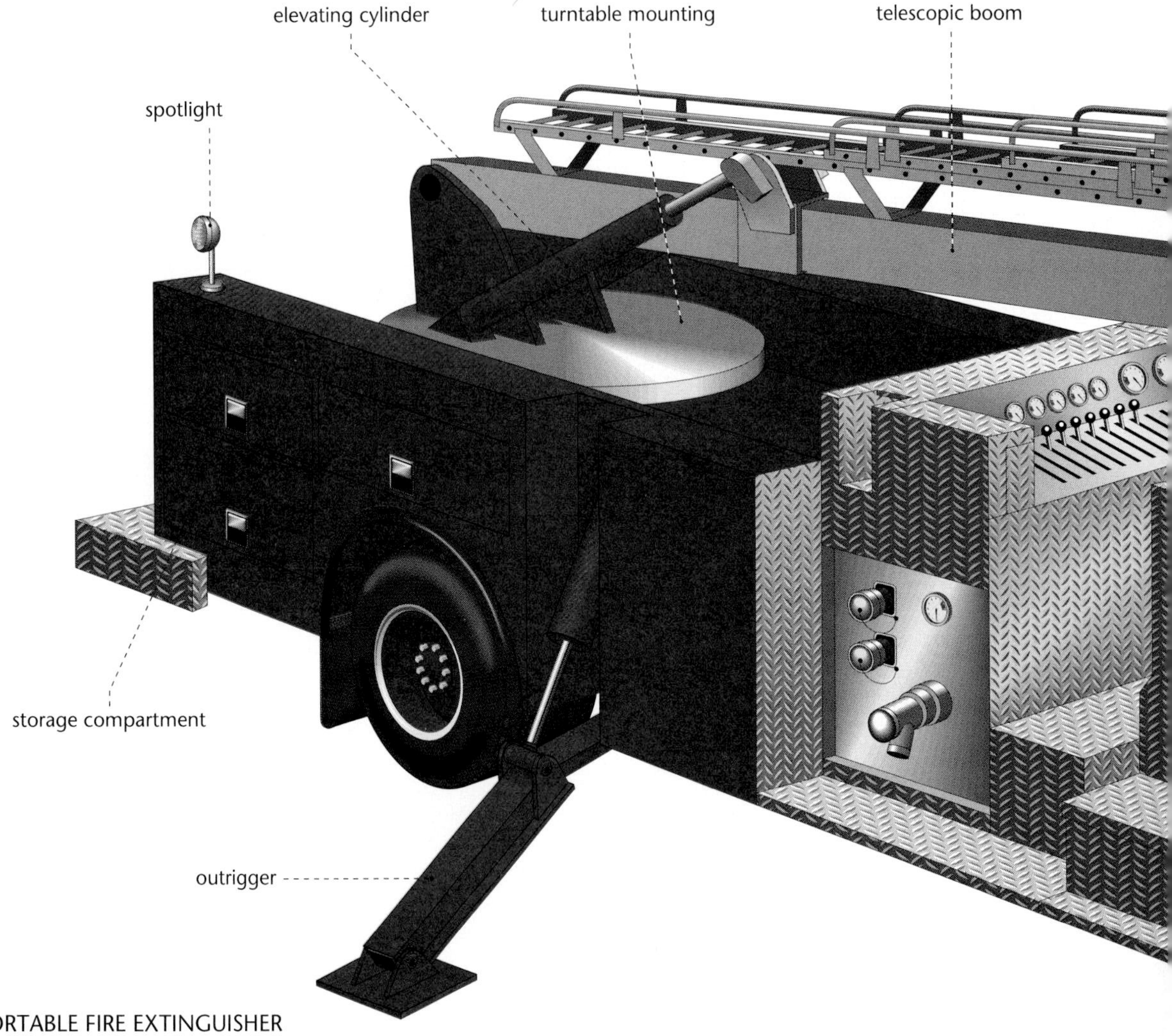

elevating cylinder

turntable mounting

telescopic boom

spotlight

storage compartment

outrigger

PORTABLE FIRE EXTINGUISHER

trigger

pin

hose

tank

pike pole

percussion bar

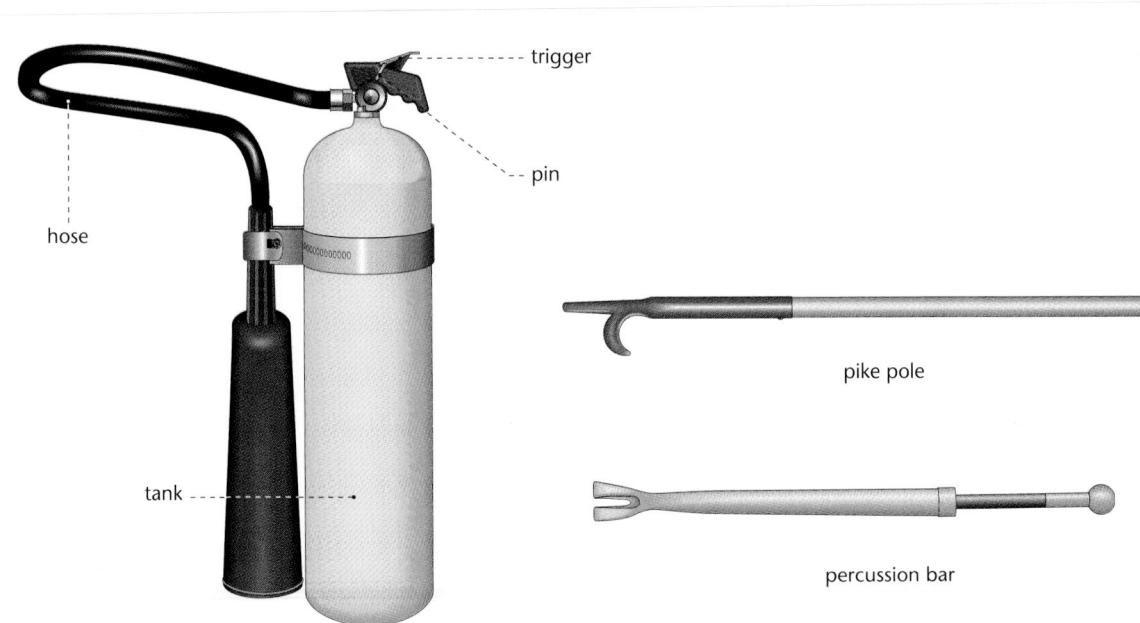

tower ladder

mars light

top ladder

ladder pipe nozzle

hook ladder

fireman's hatchet

WHEEL LOADER

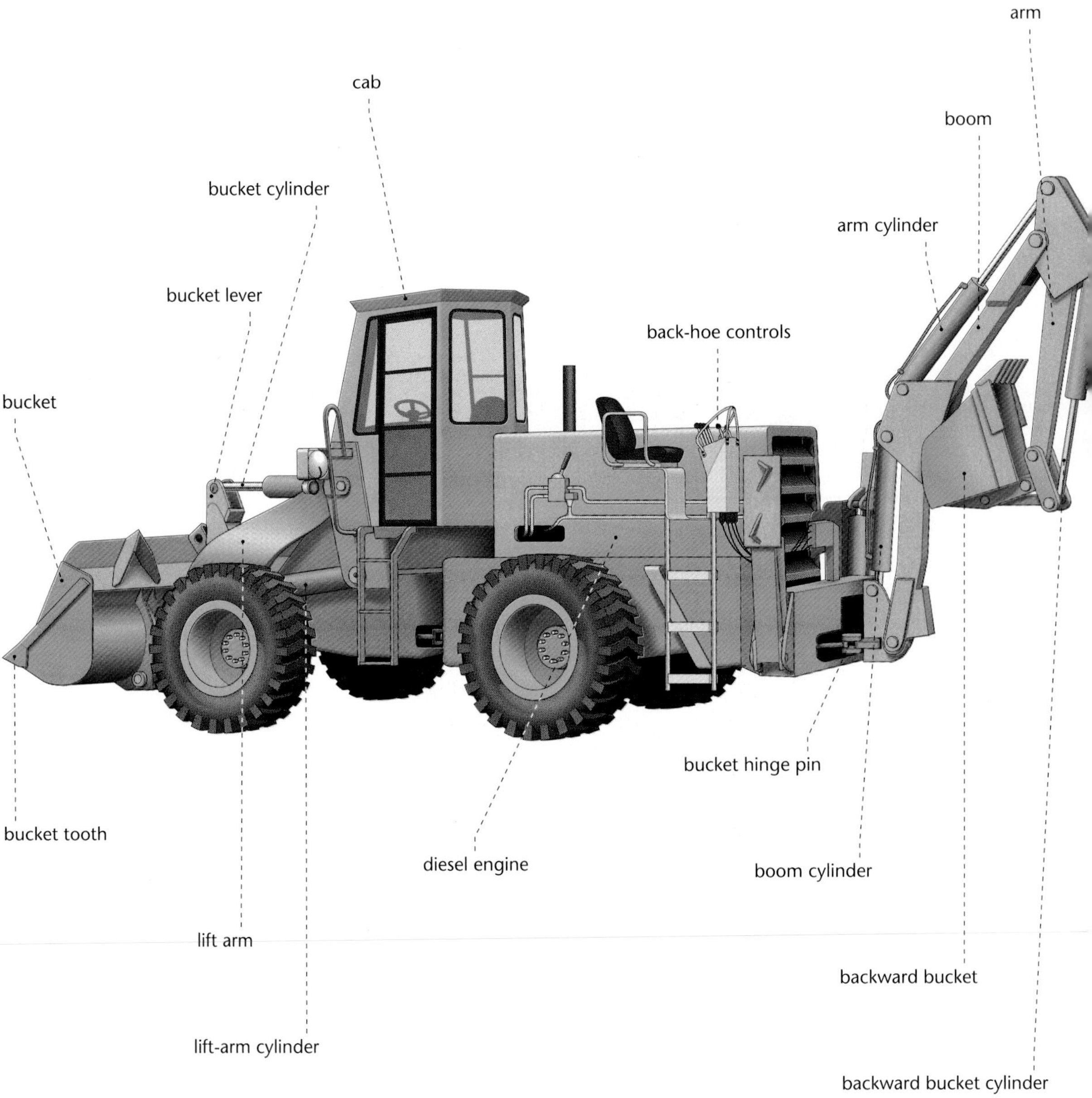

arm

cab

boom

bucket cylinder

arm cylinder

bucket lever

back-hoe controls

bucket

bucket hinge pin

bucket tooth

diesel engine

boom cylinder

lift arm

backward bucket

lift-arm cylinder

backward bucket cylinder

front-end loader

wheel tractor

back-hoe

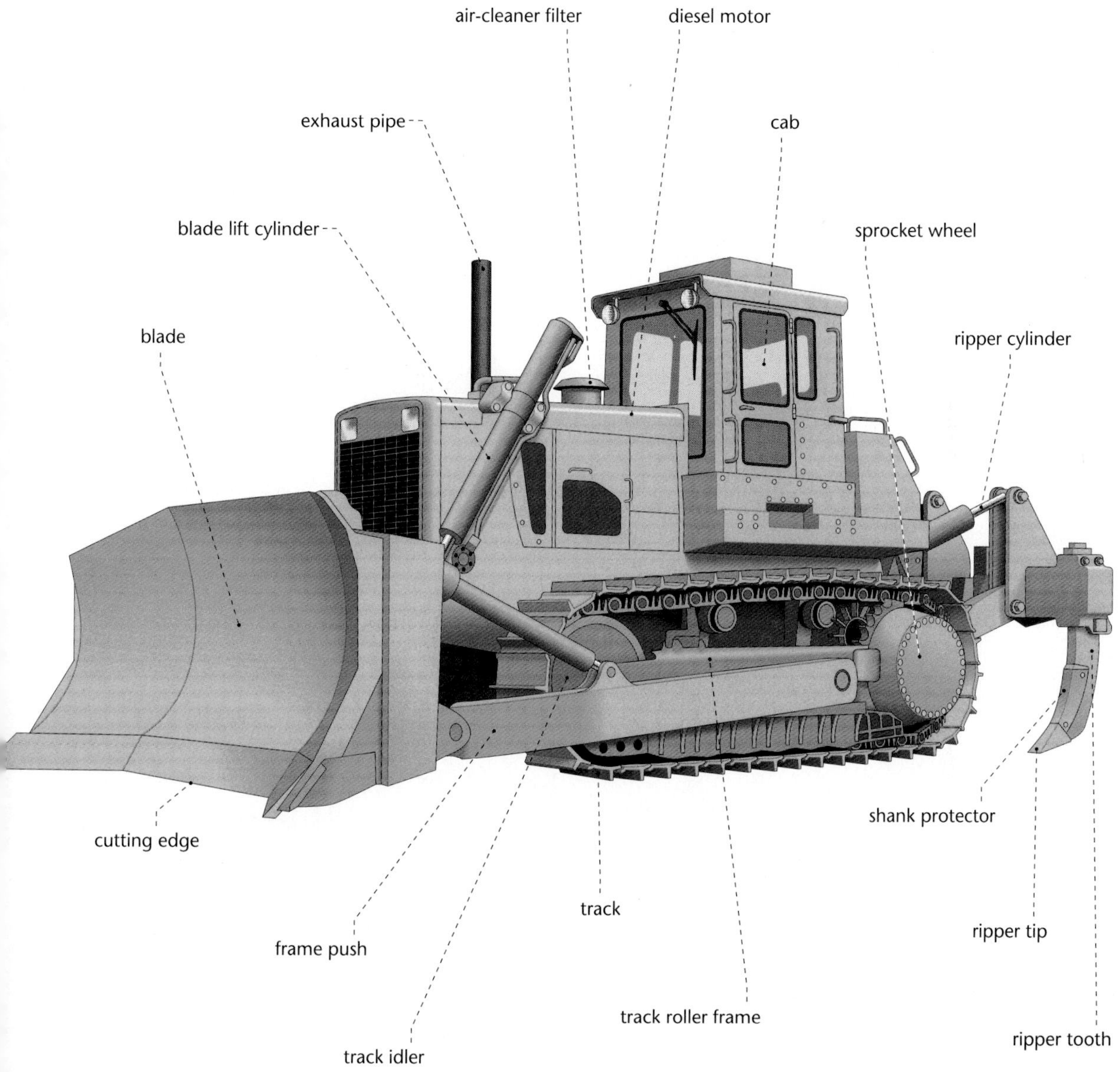

air-cleaner filter

diesel motor

exhaust pipe

cab

blade lift cylinder

sprocket wheel

blade

ripper cylinder

cutting edge

shank protector

frame push

track

ripper tip

track roller frame

track idler

ripper tooth

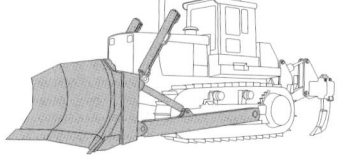

blade

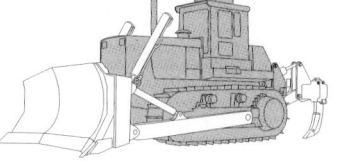

crawler tractor

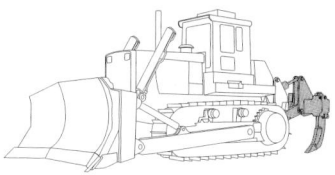

ripper

SCRAPER

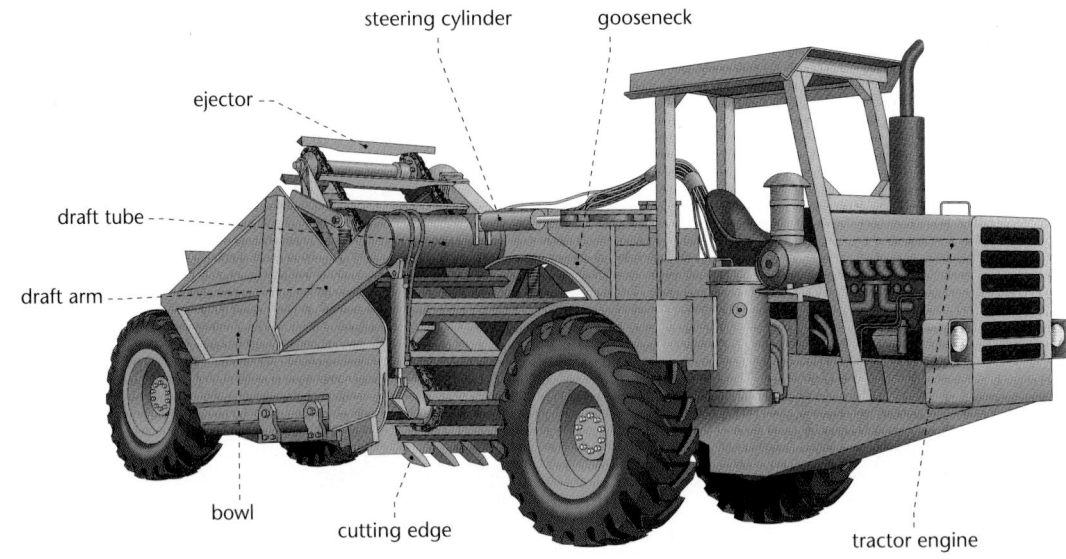

steering cylinder

gooseneck

ejector

draft tube

draft arm

bowl

cutting edge

tractor engine

GRADER

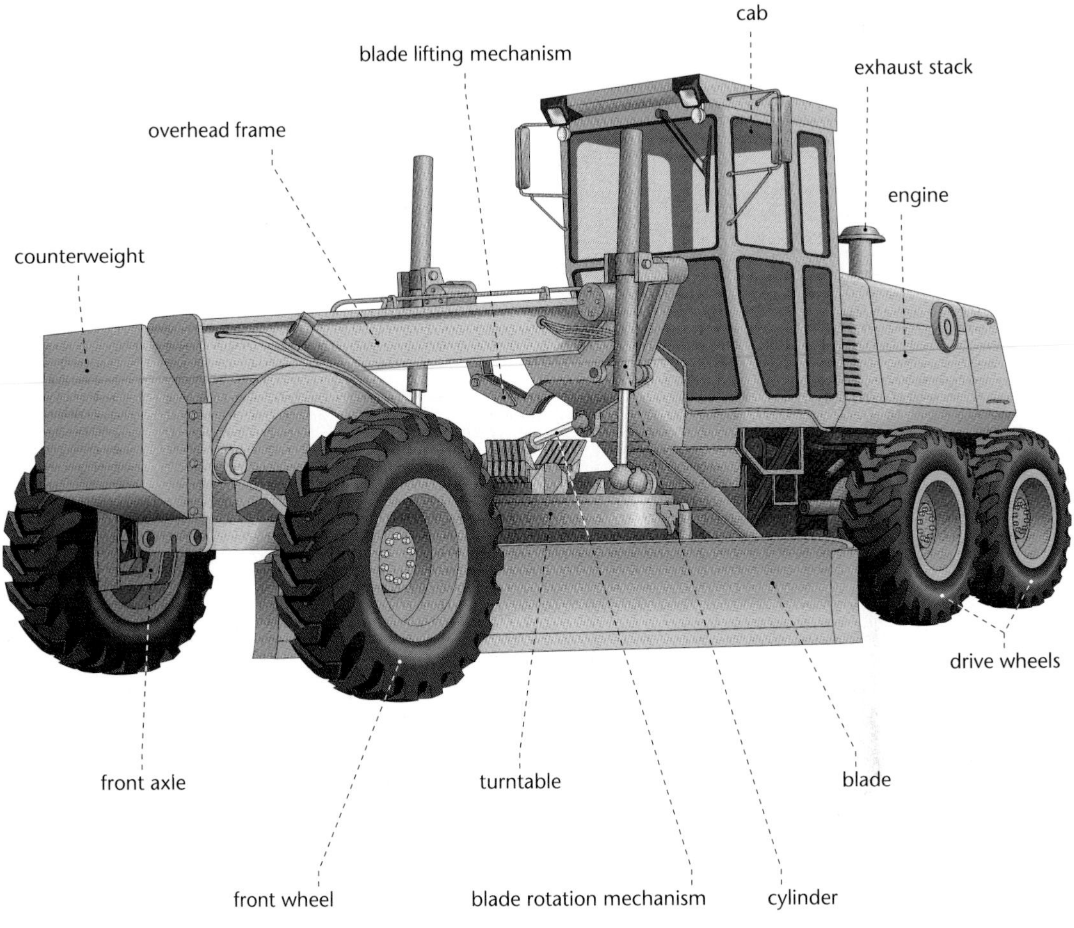

cab

blade lifting mechanism

exhaust stack

overhead frame

engine

counterweight

drive wheels

front axle

turntable

blade

front wheel

blade rotation mechanism

cylinder

DUMP TRUCK

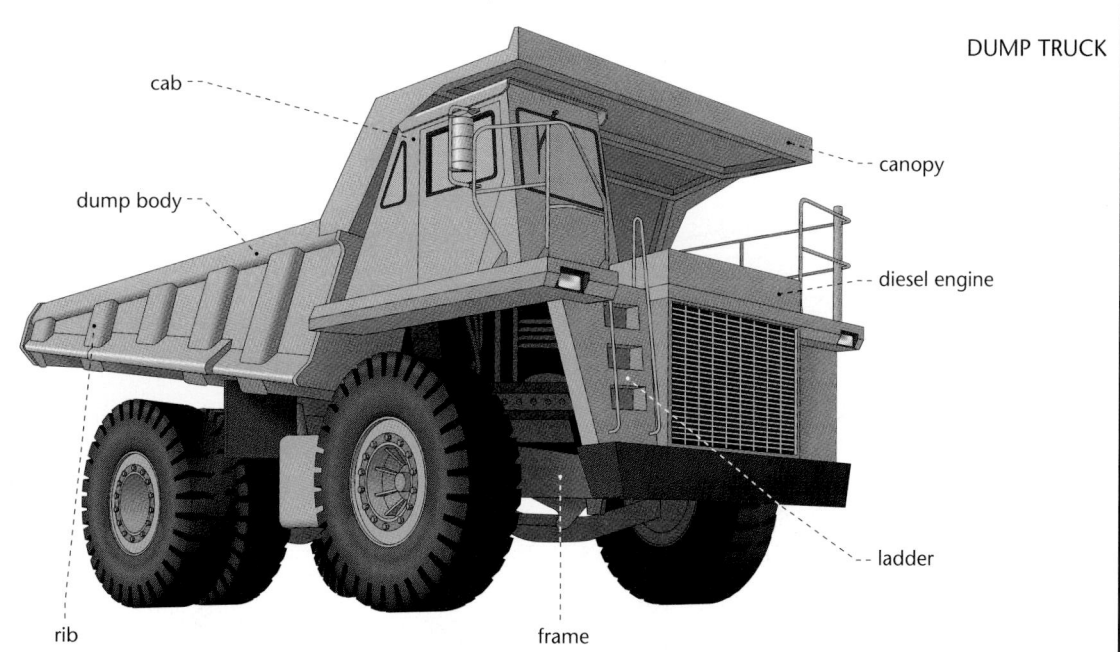

cab

canopy

dump body

diesel engine

ladder

rib

frame

HYDRAULIC SHOVEL

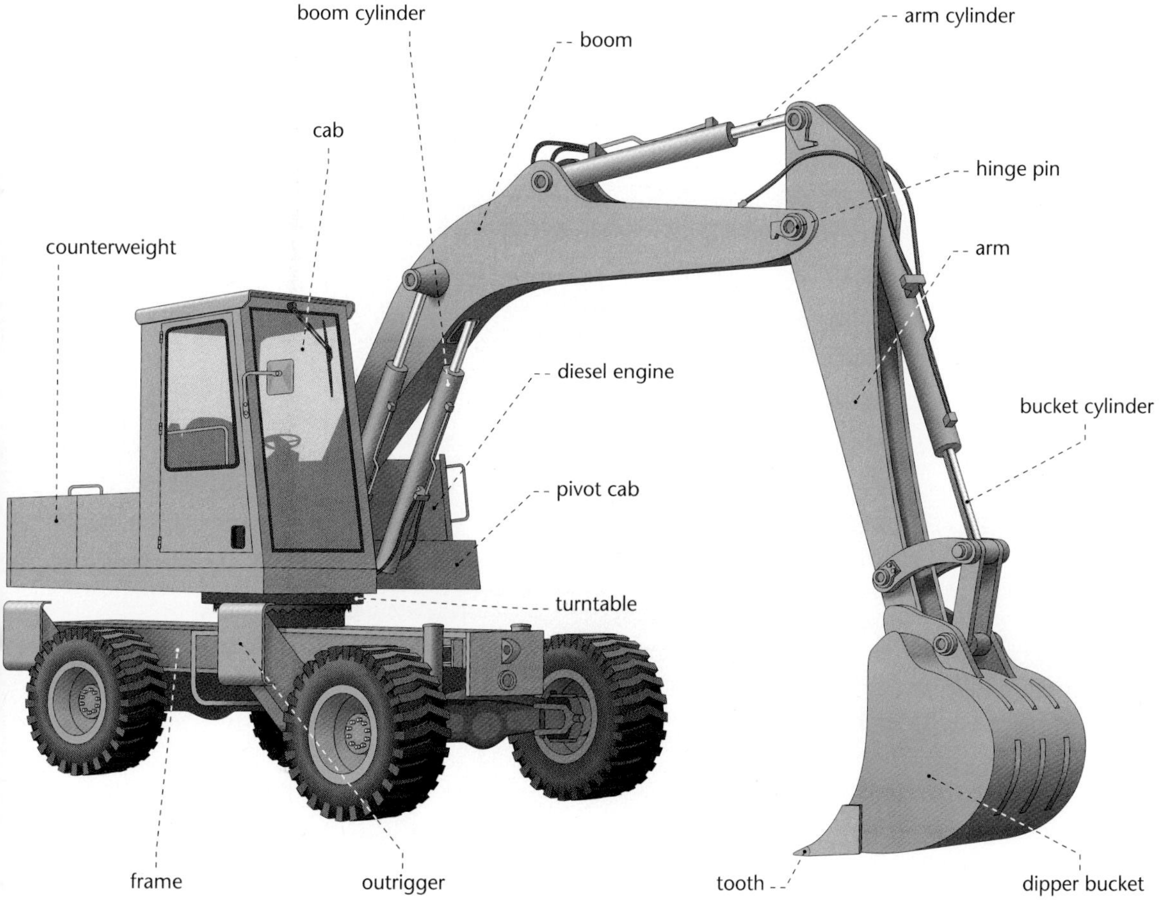

boom cylinder

boom

arm cylinder

cab

hinge pin

counterweight

arm

diesel engine

bucket cylinder

pivot cab

turntable

frame

outrigger

tooth

dipper bucket

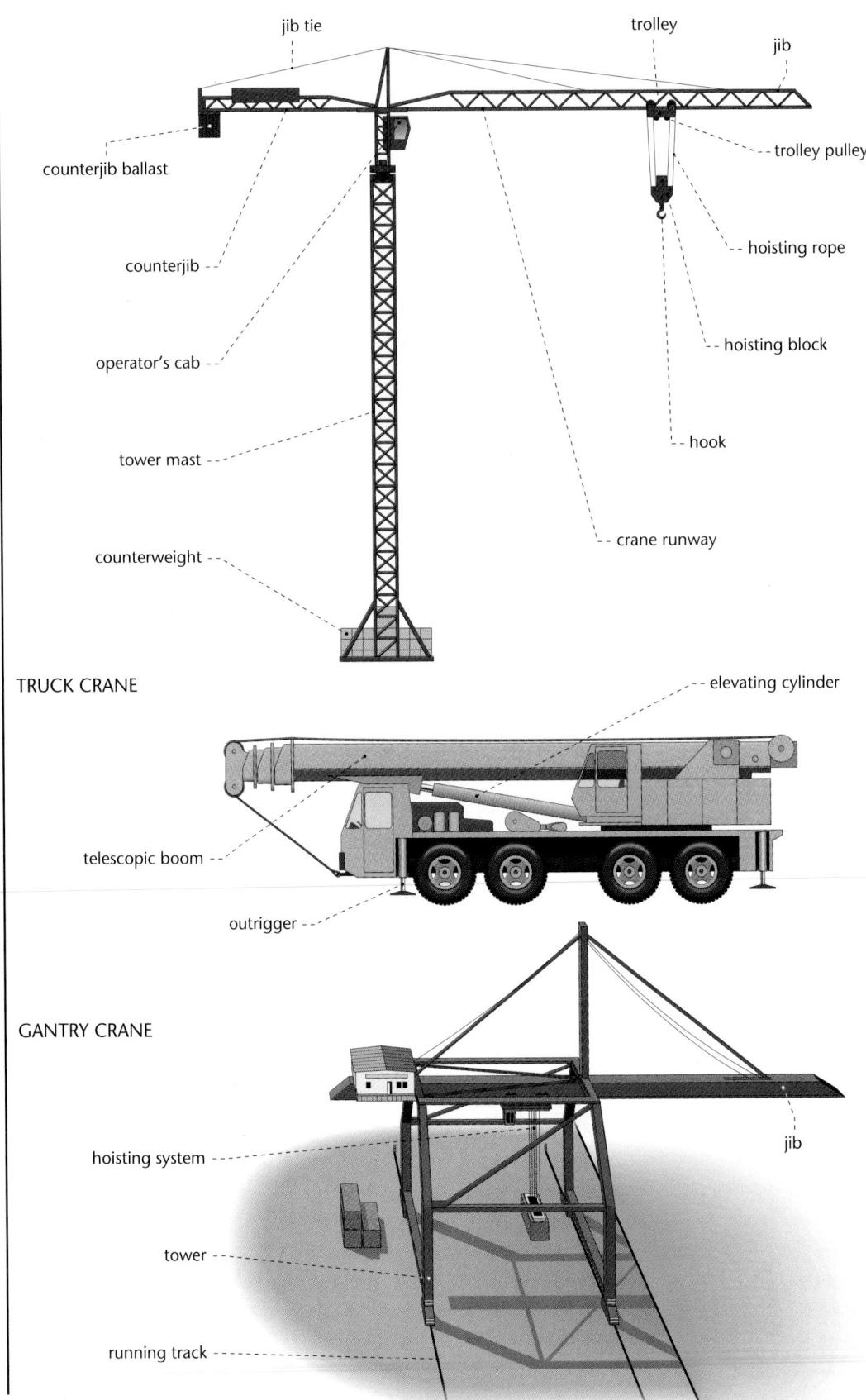

TOWER CRANE

jib tie

trolley

jib

counterjib ballast

trolley pulley

counterjib

hoisting rope

operator's cab

hoisting block

tower mast

hook

crane runway

counterweight

TRUCK CRANE

elevating cylinder

telescopic boom

outrigger

GANTRY CRANE

jib

hoisting system

tower

running track

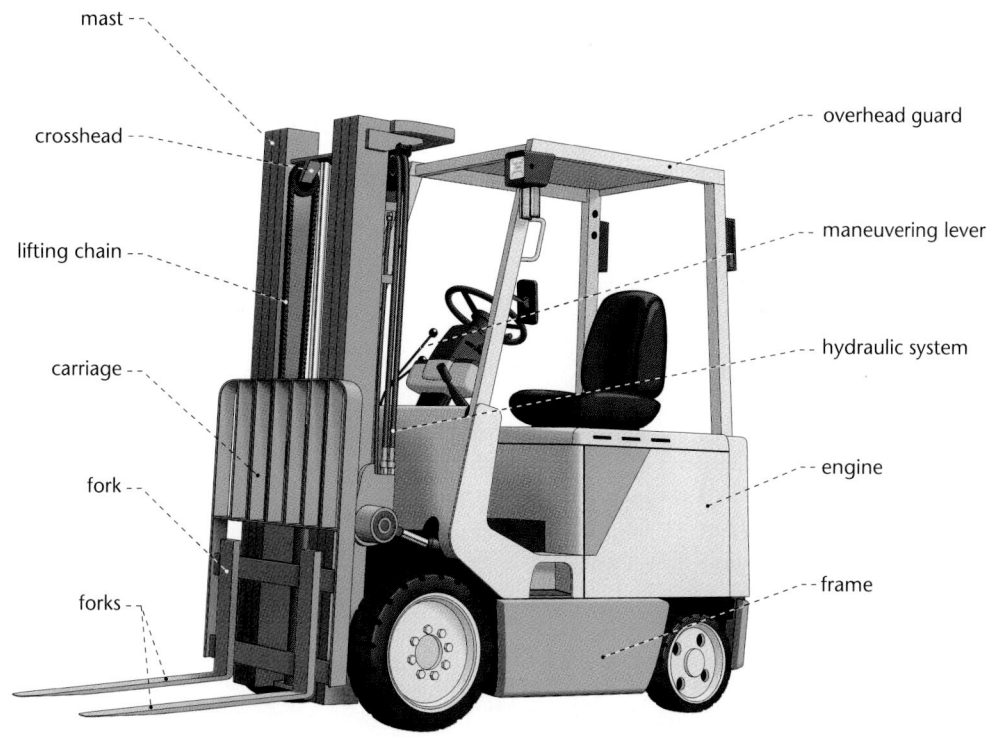

mast

crosshead

lifting chain

carriage

fork

forks

overhead guard

maneuvering lever

hydraulic system

engine

frame

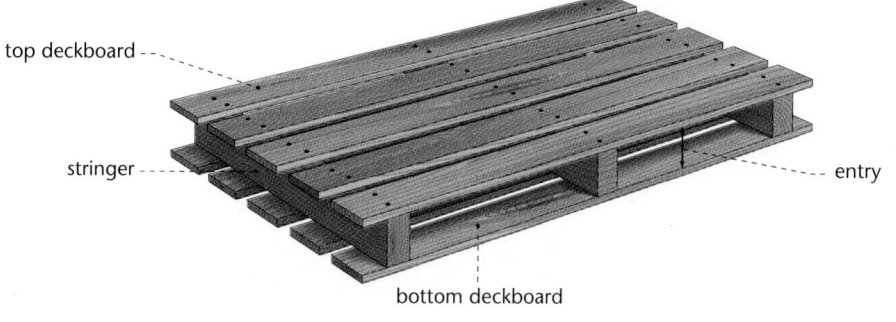

top deckboard

stringer

entry

bottom deckboard

double-decked pallet

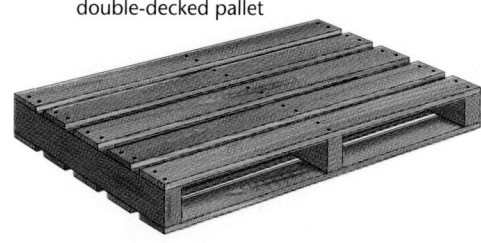

single-decked pallet

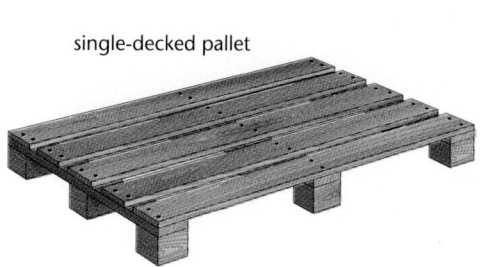

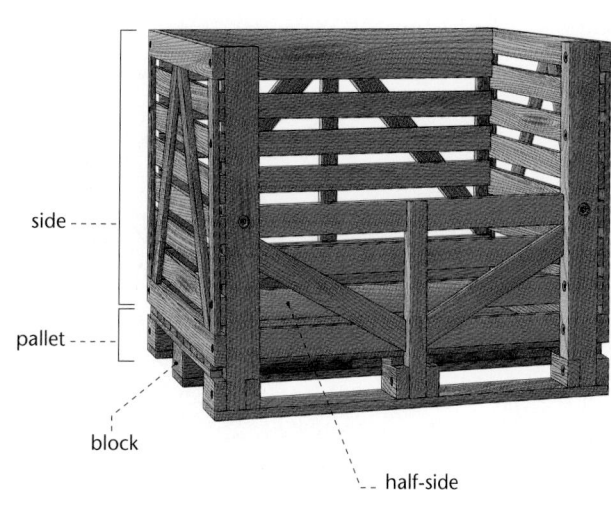

side

pallet

block

half-side

HEAVY MACHINERY

787

HYDRAULIC PALLET TRUCK

pallet truck

maneuvering lever

steering lever

mast

hydraulic cylinder

hand truck

forks

solid rubber tire

stabilizing shaft

steering axle

frame

roller

platform pallet truck

flatbed pushcart

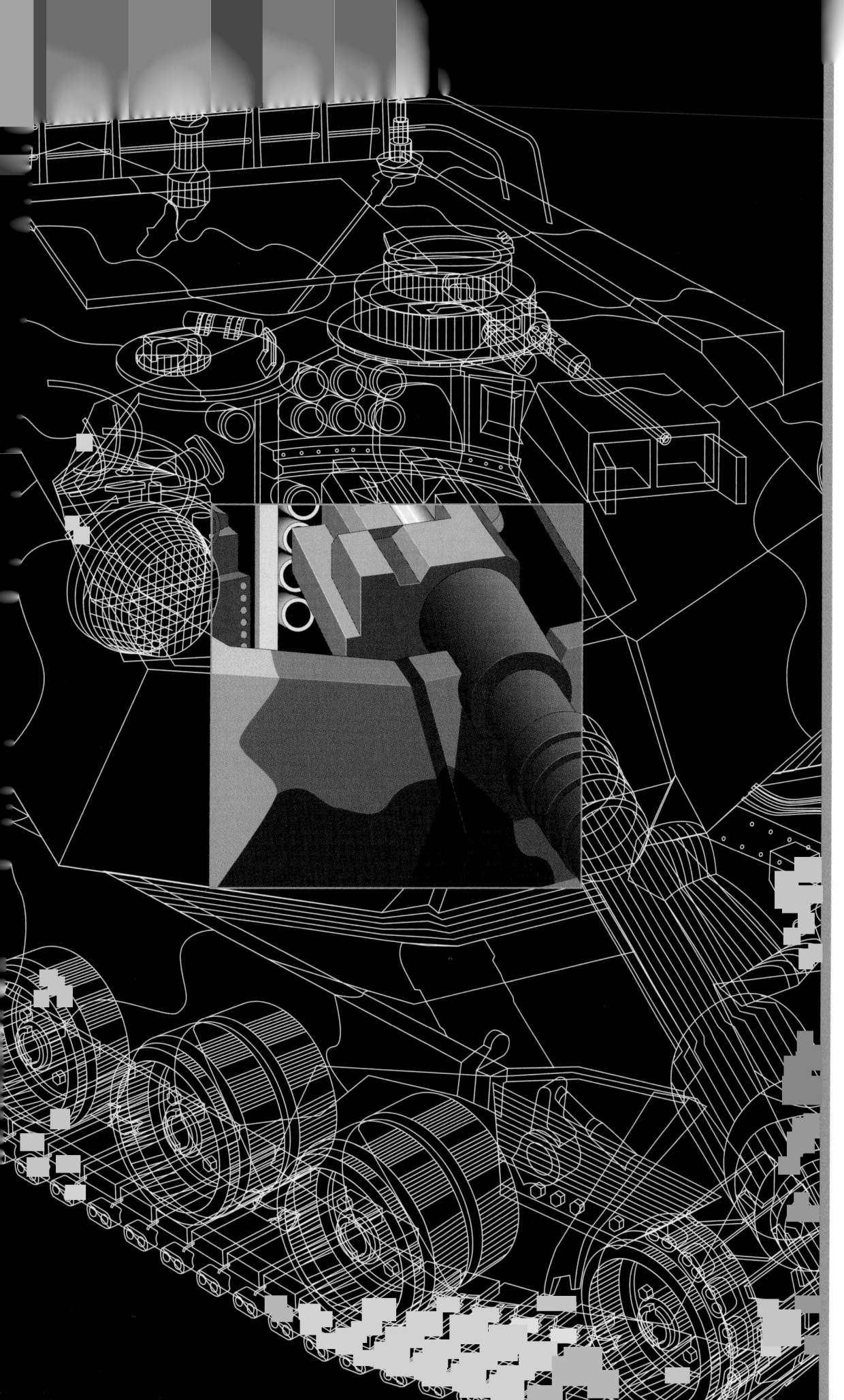

CONTENTS

STONE AGE ARMS..791

WEAPONS IN THE AGE OF THE ROMANS 791

ARMOR 792

BOWS AND CROSSBOW 793

THRUSTING AND CUTTING WEAPONS...794

HARQUEBUS 795

SUBMACHINE GUN..795

AUTOMATIC RIFLE 796

LIGHT MACHINE GUN 796

PISTOL 797

REVOLVER 797

HUNTING WEAPONS 798

SEVENTEENTH CENTURY CANNON 800

MODERN HOWITZER 802

MORTAR 803

HAND GRENADE 804

BAZOOKA 804

RECOILLESS RIFLE...804

TANK 805

SUBMARINE 806

FRIGATE 808

AIRCRAFT CARRIER...810

COMBAT AIRCRAFT..812

MISSILES 814

WEAPONS

STONE AGE ARMS

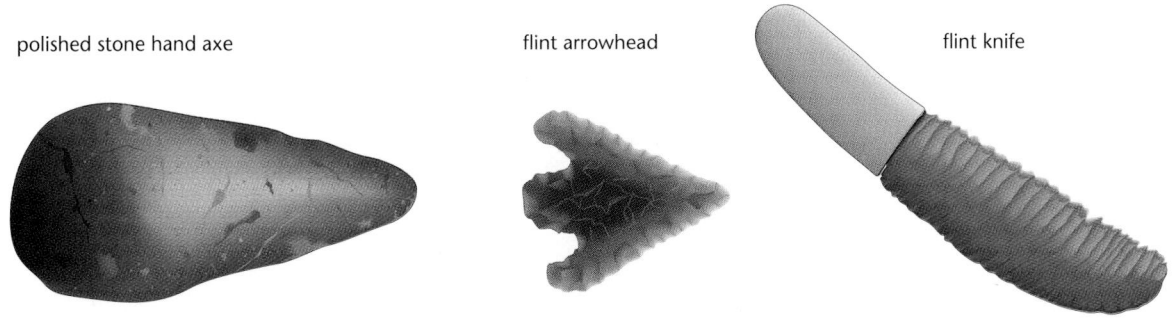

polished stone hand axe

flint arrowhead

flint knife

WEAPONS IN THE AGE OF THE ROMANS

GALLIC WARRIOR

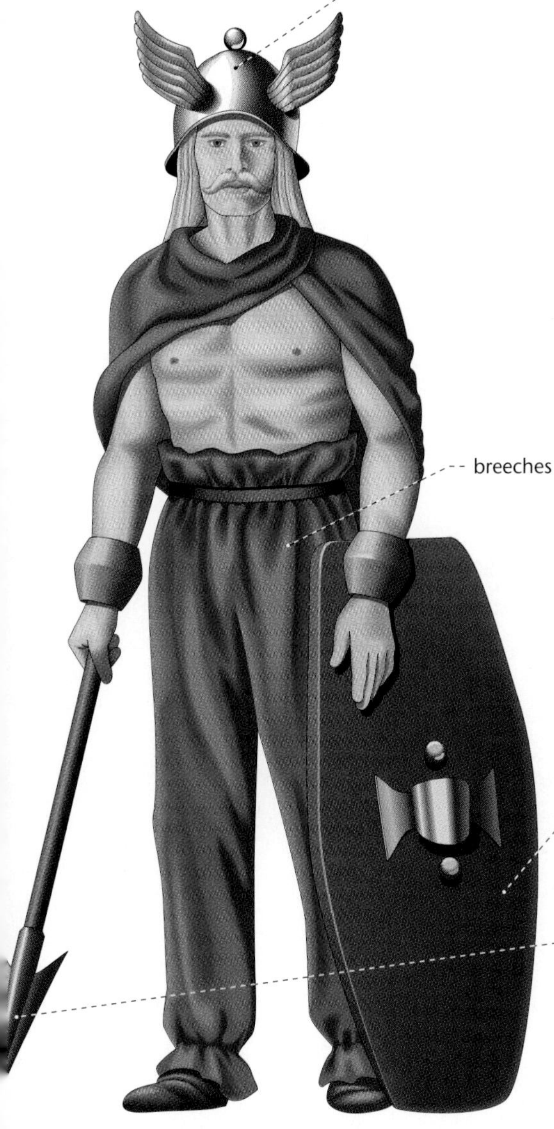

ROMAN LEGIONARY

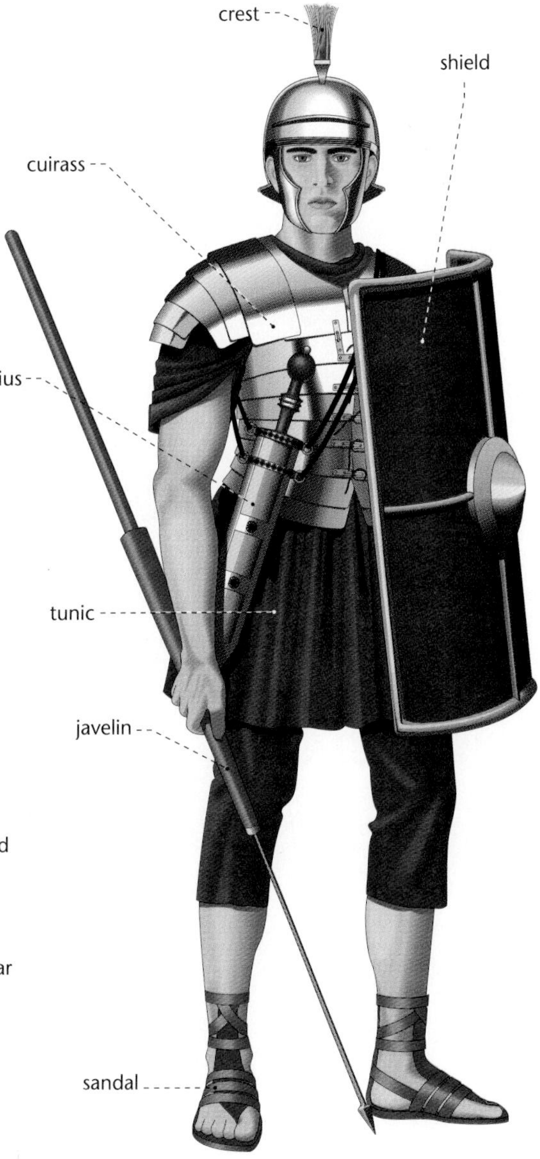

helmet

crest

shield

cuirass

gladius

breeches

tunic

javelin

shield

spear

sandal

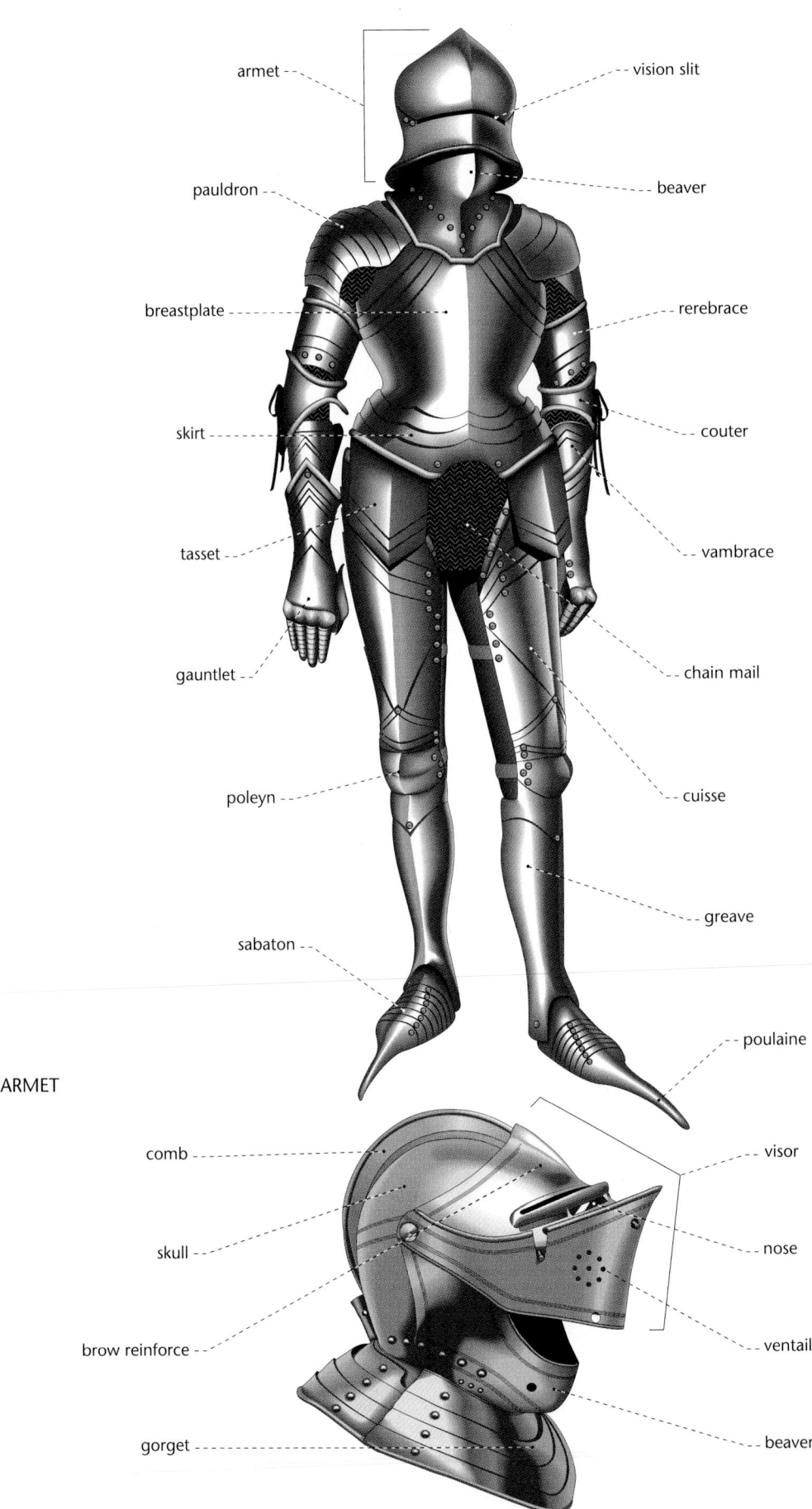

armet

vision slit

pauldron

beaver

breastplate

rerebrace

skirt

couter

tasset

vambrace

gauntlet

chain mail

poleyn

cuisse

greave

sabaton

poulaine

ARMET

comb

visor

skull

nose

brow reinforce

ventail

gorget

beaver

BOWS AND CROSSBOW

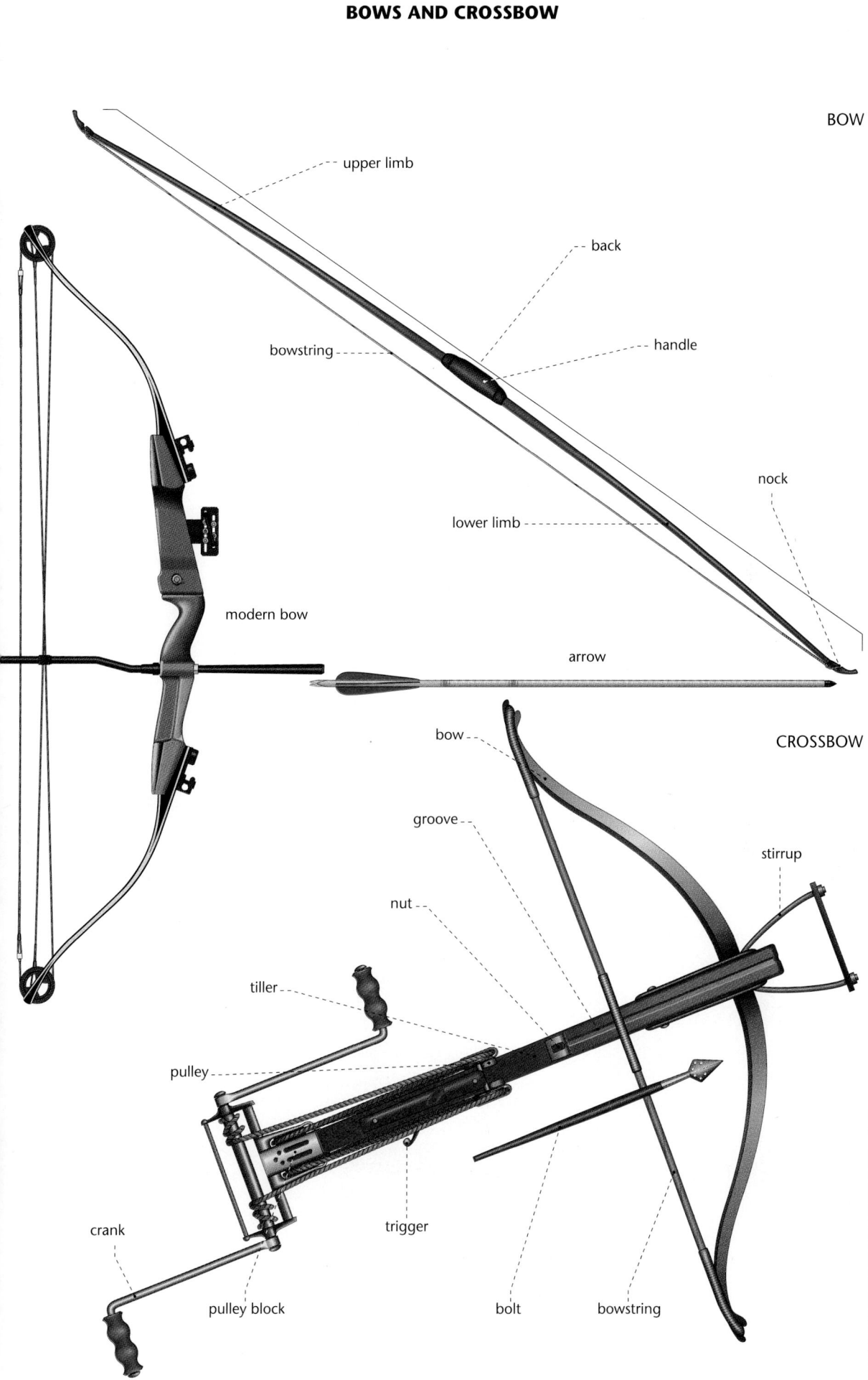

BOW

upper limb

back

handle

bowstring

nock

lower limb

modern bow

arrow

CROSSBOW

bow

groove

stirrup

nut

tiller

pulley

crank

trigger

pulley block

bolt

bowstring

saber

rapier

broadsword

poniard

stiletto

dagger

machete

hilted bayonet

commando knife

integral bayonet

plug bayonet

socket bayonet

HARQUEBUS

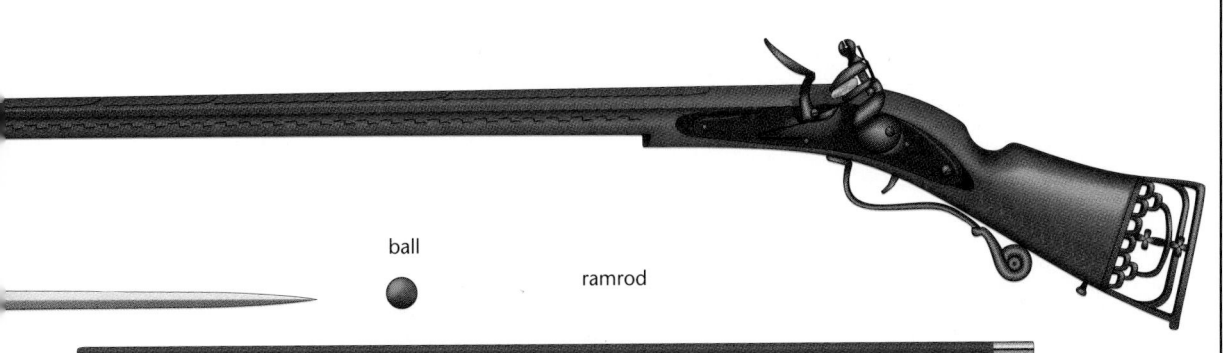

ball

ramrod

powder flask

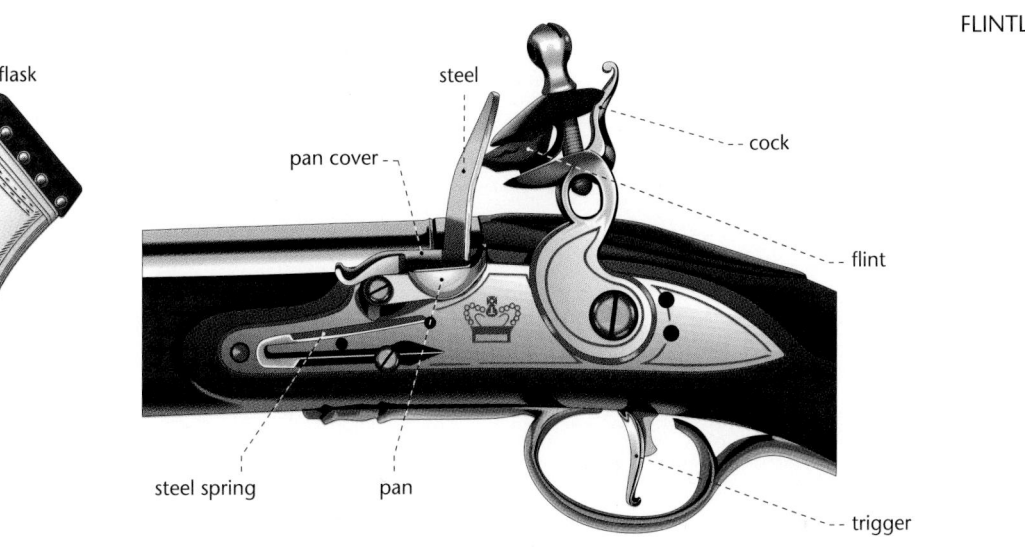

steel

pan cover

cock

flint

steel spring

pan

trigger

SUBMACHINE GUN

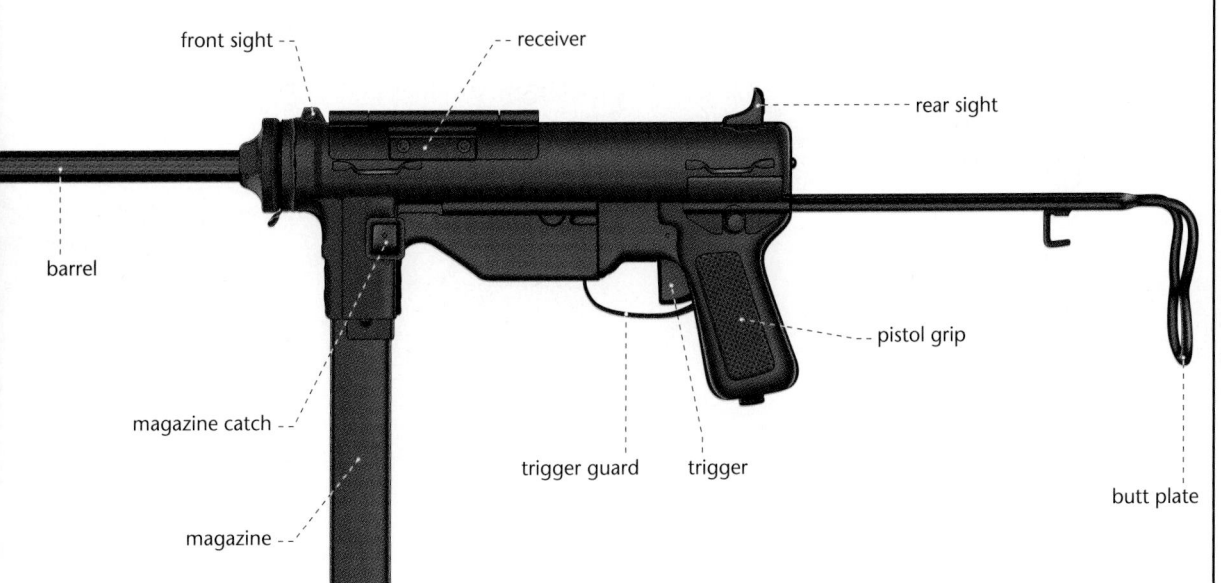

front sight

receiver

rear sight

barrel

pistol grip

magazine catch

trigger guard

trigger

butt plate

magazine

WEAPONS

AUTOMATIC RIFLE

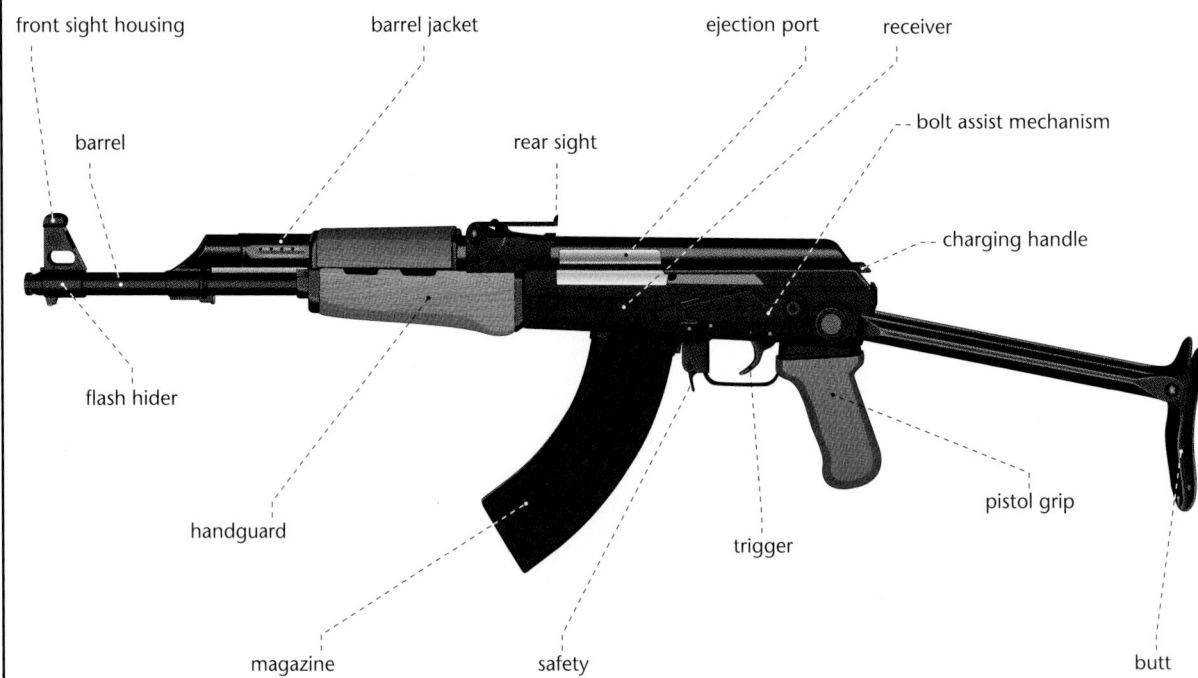

front sight housing

barrel jacket

ejection port

receiver

bolt assist mechanism

barrel

rear sight

charging handle

flash hider

handguard

pistol grip

trigger

magazine

safety

butt

LIGHT MACHINE GUN

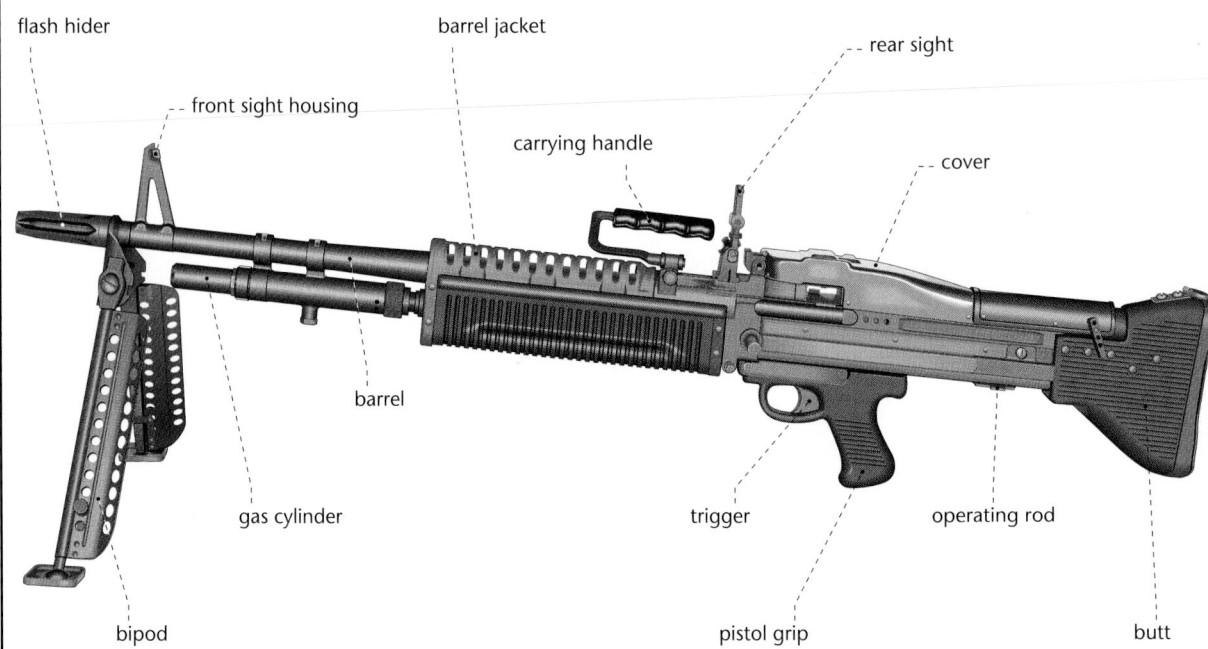

flash hider

barrel jacket

rear sight

front sight housing

carrying handle

cover

barrel

gas cylinder

trigger

operating rod

bipod

pistol grip

butt

REVOLVER

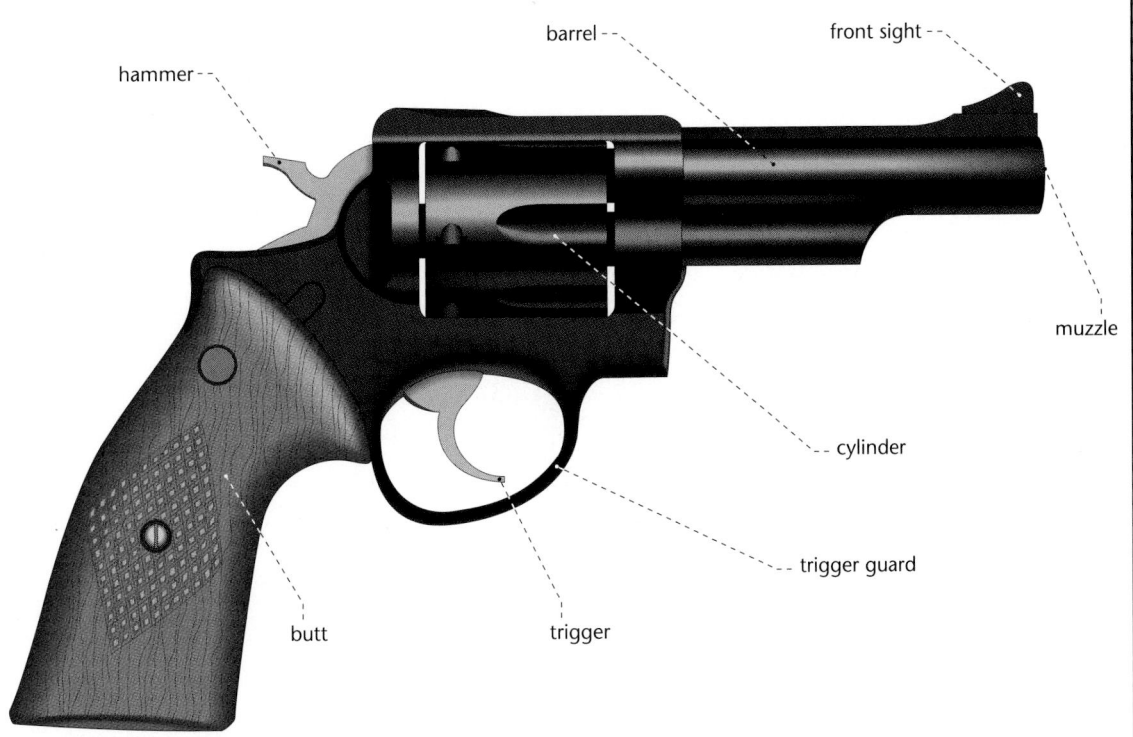

hammer

barrel

front sight

muzzle

cylinder

trigger guard

butt

trigger

PISTOL

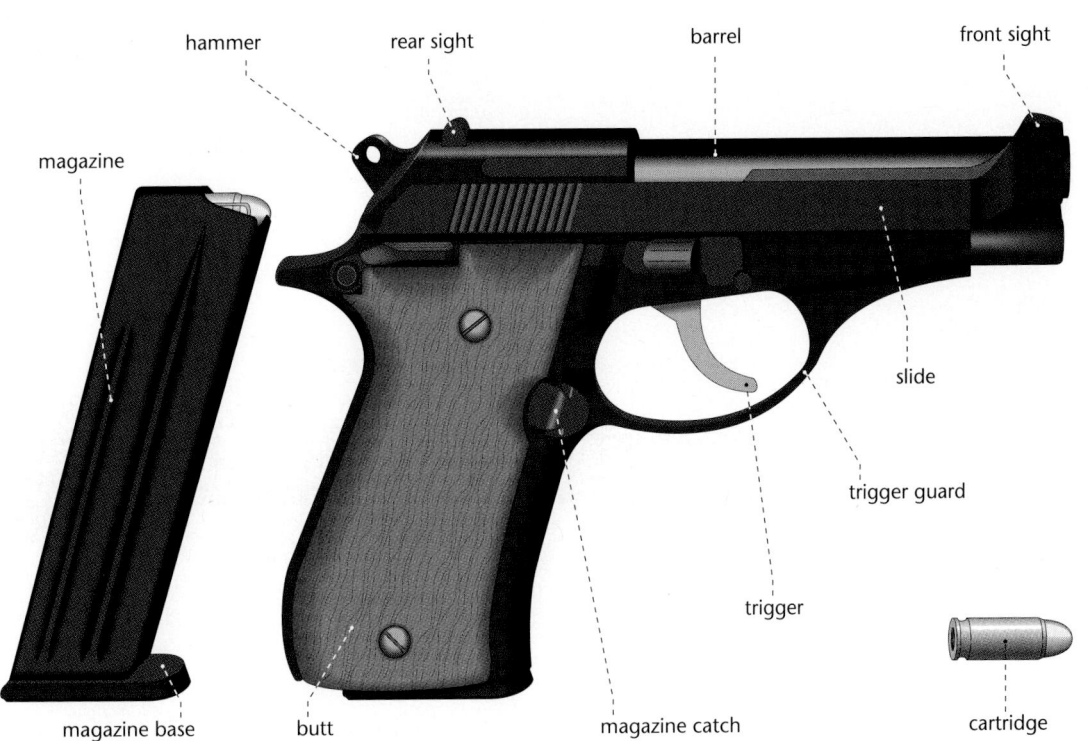

hammer

rear sight

barrel

front sight

magazine

slide

trigger guard

trigger

magazine base

butt

magazine catch

cartridge

HUNTING WEAPONS

CARTRIDGE (RIFLE)

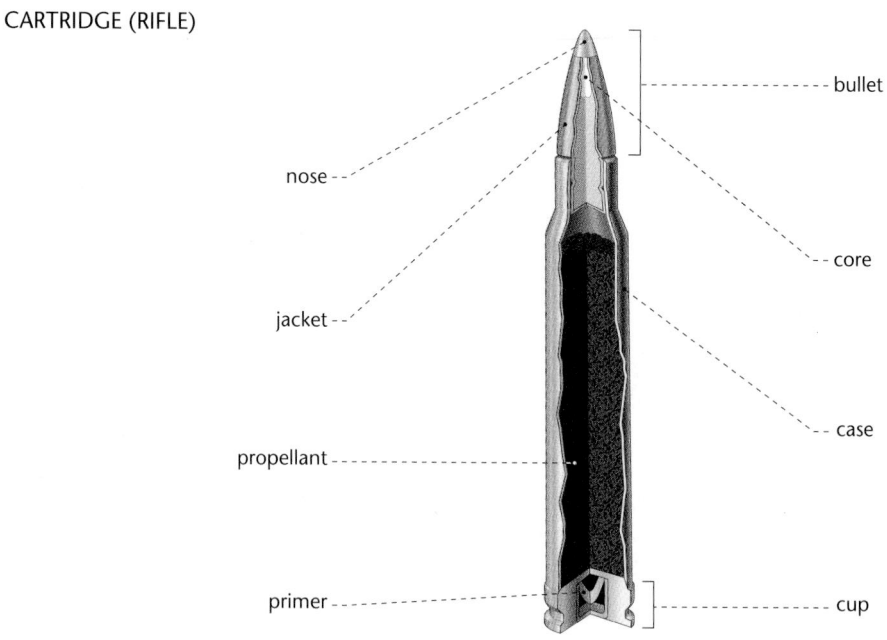

nose

jacket

propellant

primer

bullet

core

case

cup

RIFLE (RIFLED BORE)

hammer

breechblock

telescopic sight

pistol grip

stock

rear sight

butt plate

trigger guard

lever

trigger

front sight

muzzle

ventilated rib

barrel

forearm

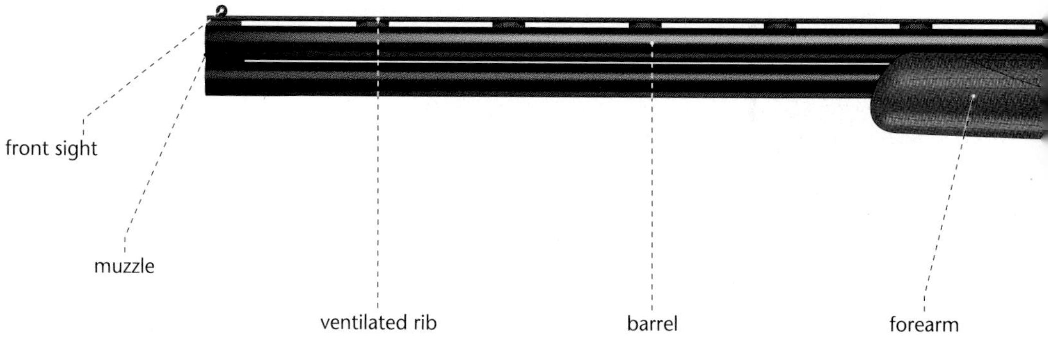

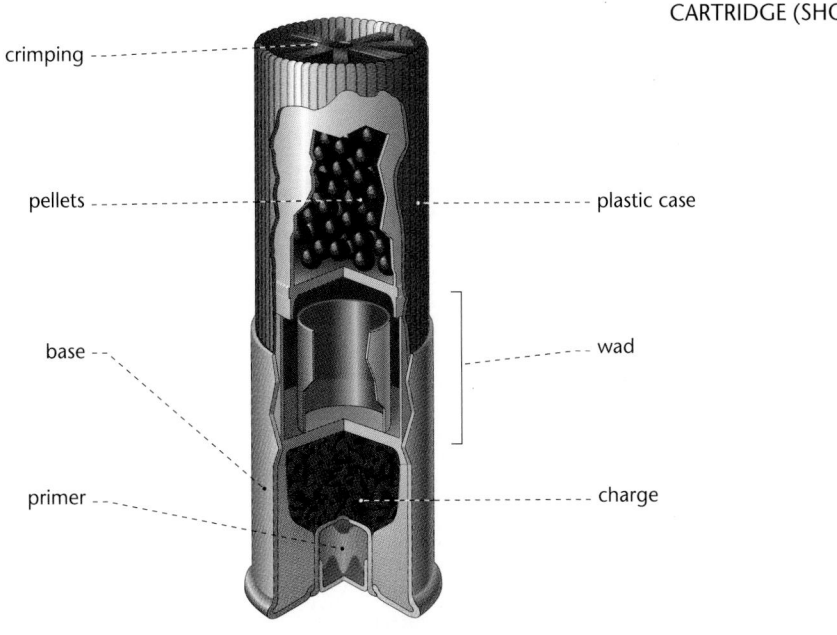

crimping

pellets — plastic case

base — wad

primer — charge

front sight

muzzle

barrel

SHOTGUN (SMOOTH-BORE)

pistol grip

hammer

stock

butt plate

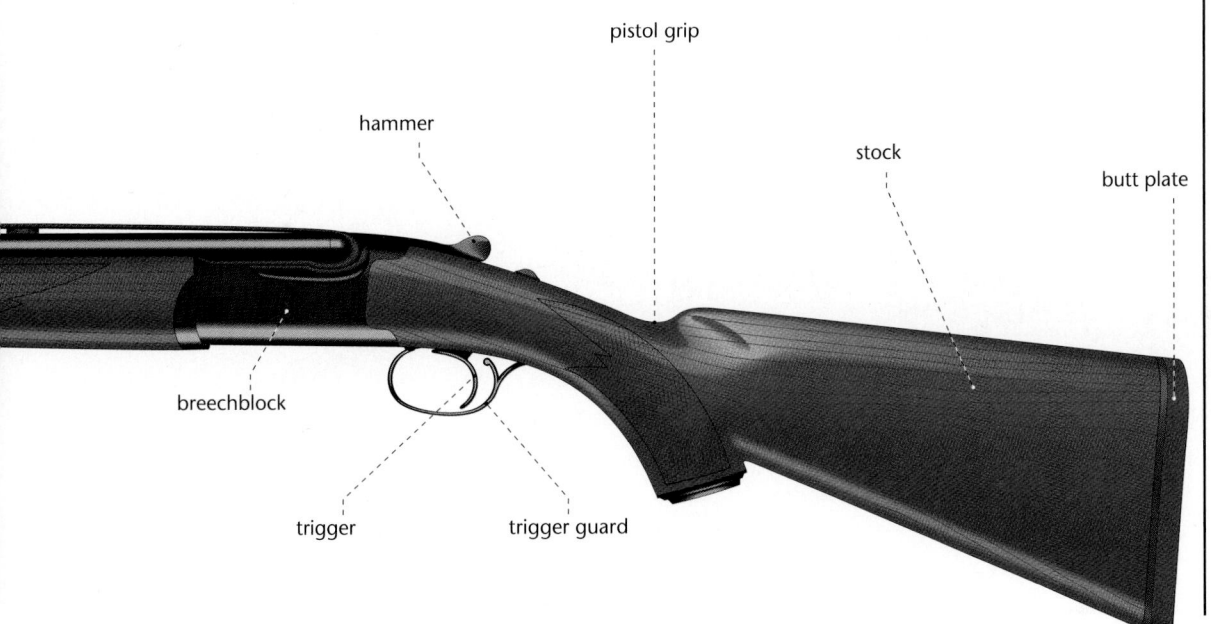

breechblock

trigger

trigger guard

MUZZLE LOADING

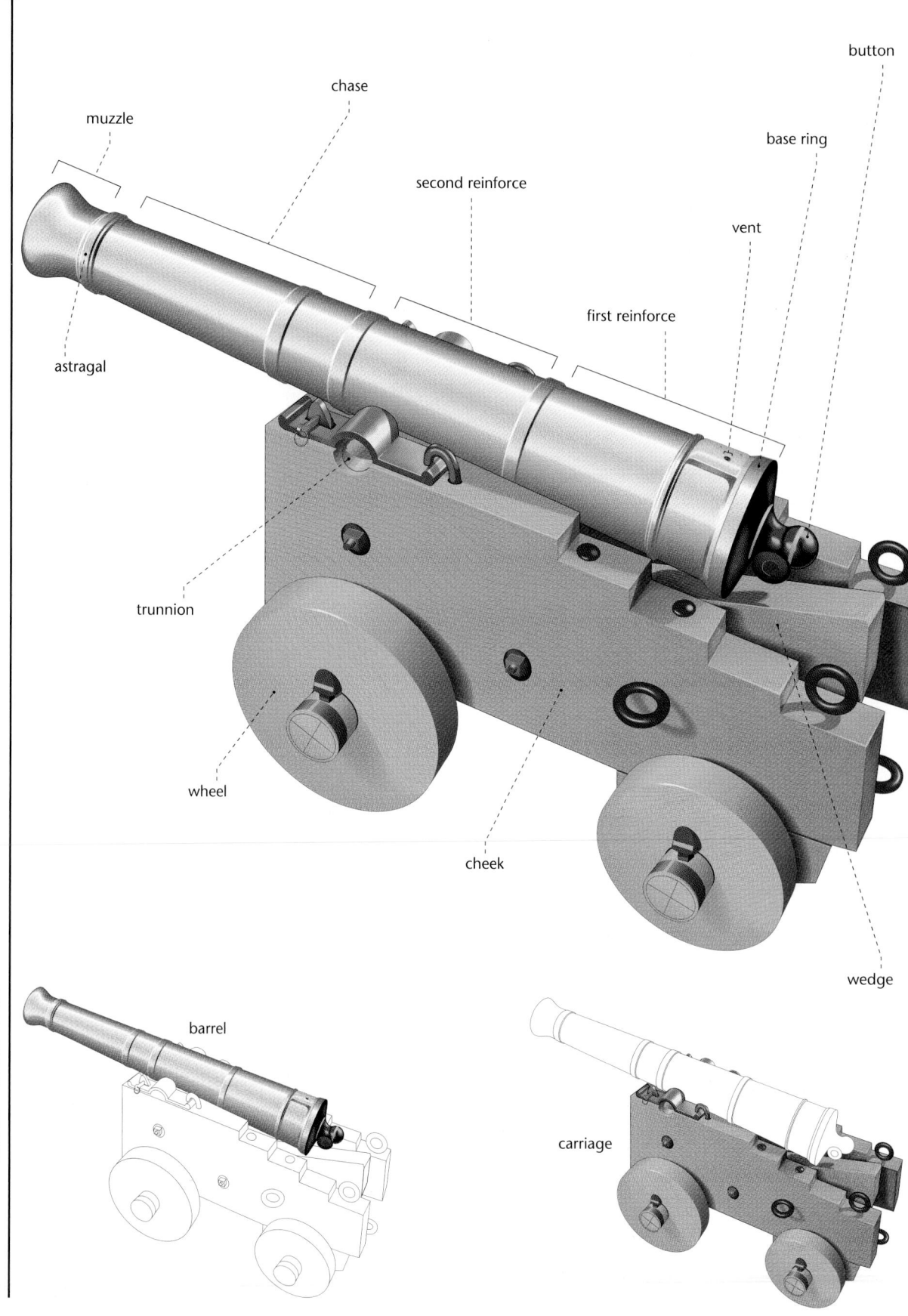

button

base ring

vent

chase

muzzle

second reinforce

first reinforce

astragal

trunnion

wheel

cheek

wedge

barrel

carriage

CROSS SECTION OF A MUZZLE LOADING

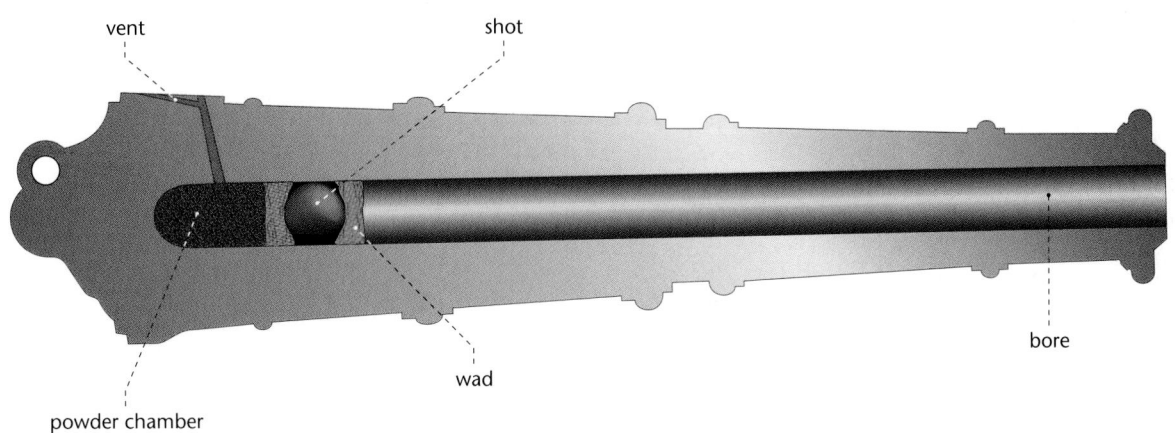

vent

shot

powder chamber

wad

bore

FIRING ACCESSORIES

rammer

linstock

worm

ladle

sponge

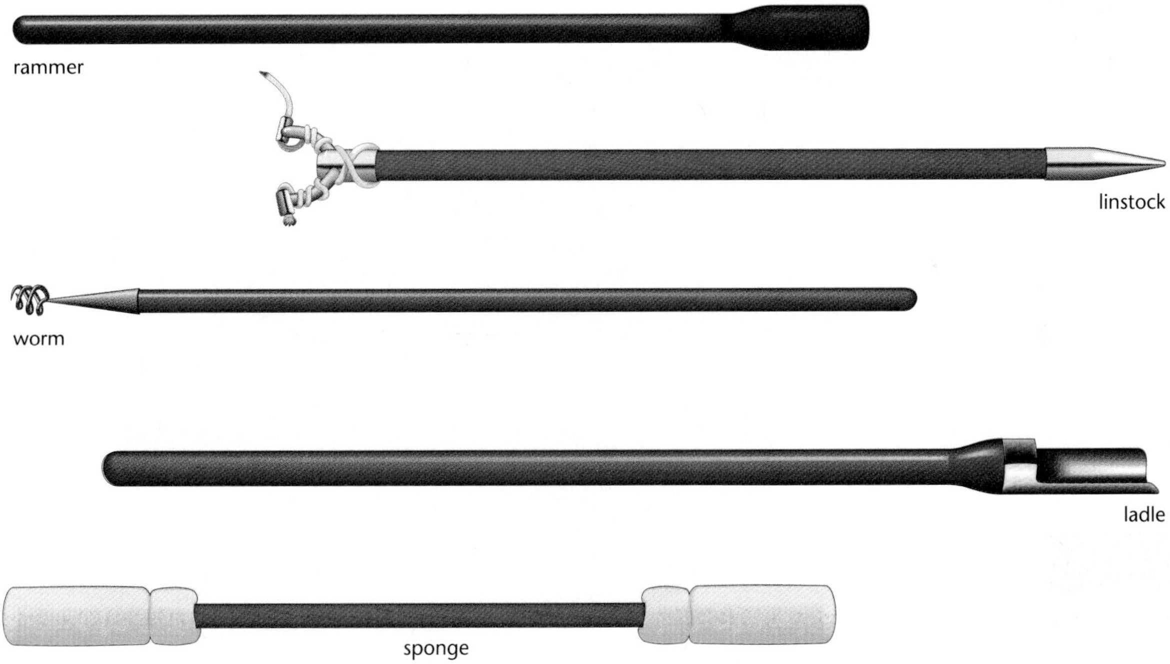

PROJECTILES

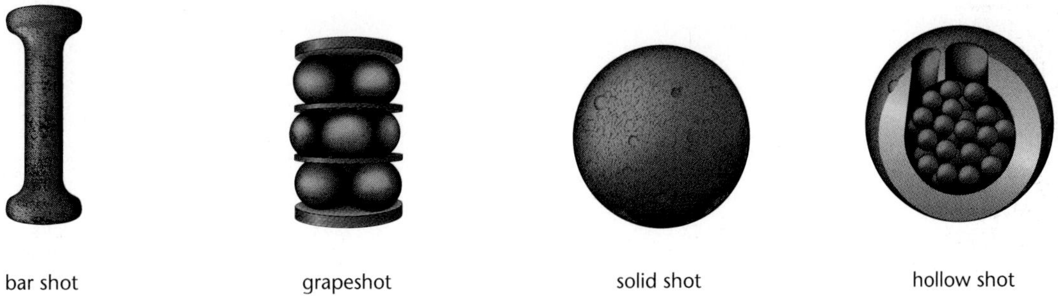

bar shot

grapeshot

solid shot

hollow shot

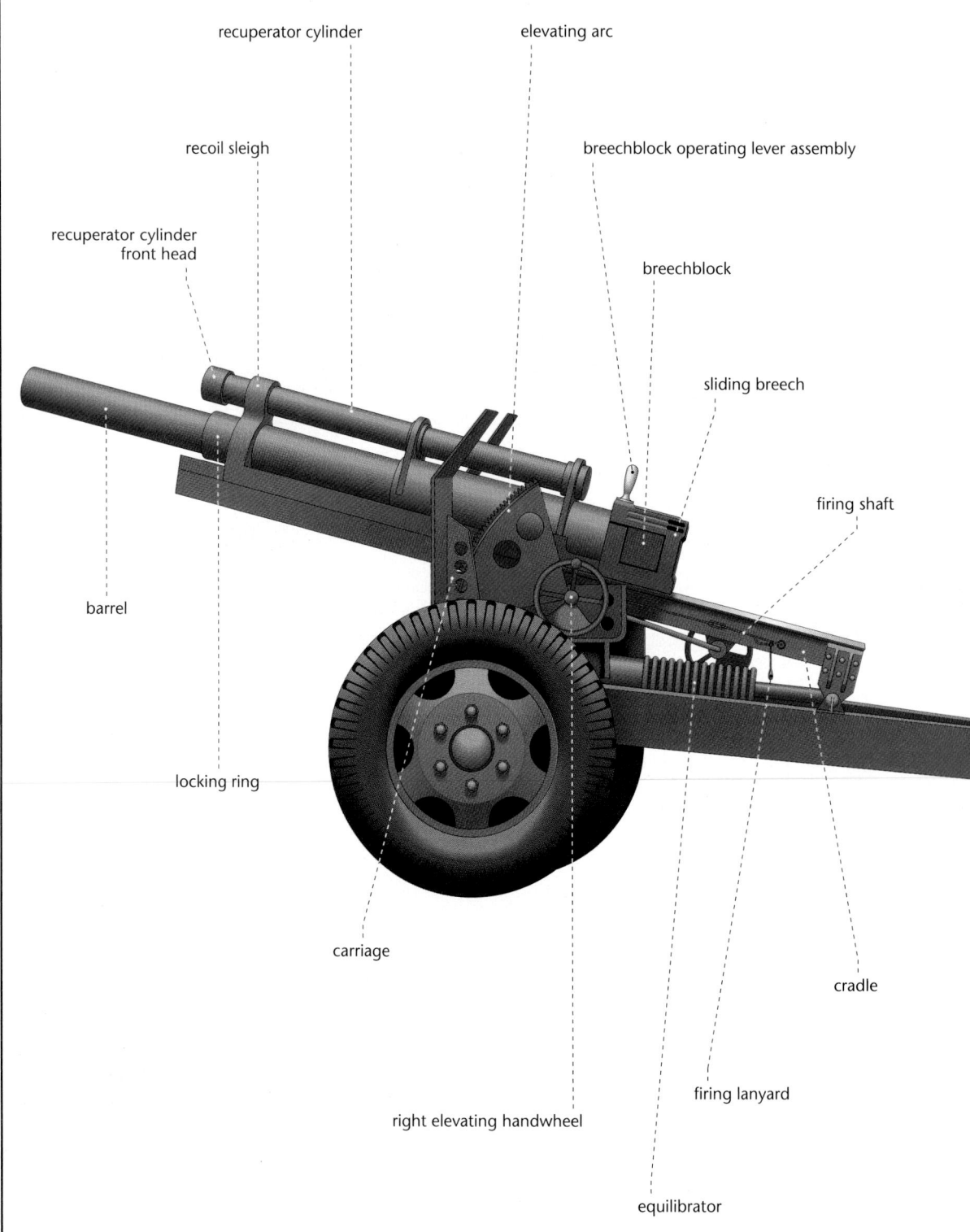

recuperator cylinder

elevating arc

recoil sleigh

breechblock operating lever assembly

recuperator cylinder
front head

breechblock

sliding breech

firing shaft

barrel

locking ring

carriage

cradle

right elevating handwheel

firing lanyard

equilibrator

MORTAR

MODERN MORTAR

muzzle

sight

elevating handle

traversing handle

tube

bipod

baseplate

drawbar

drawbar lock

towing eye

right trail

SEVENTEENTH-CENTURY MORTAR

lifting handle

spade

float

HAND GRENADE

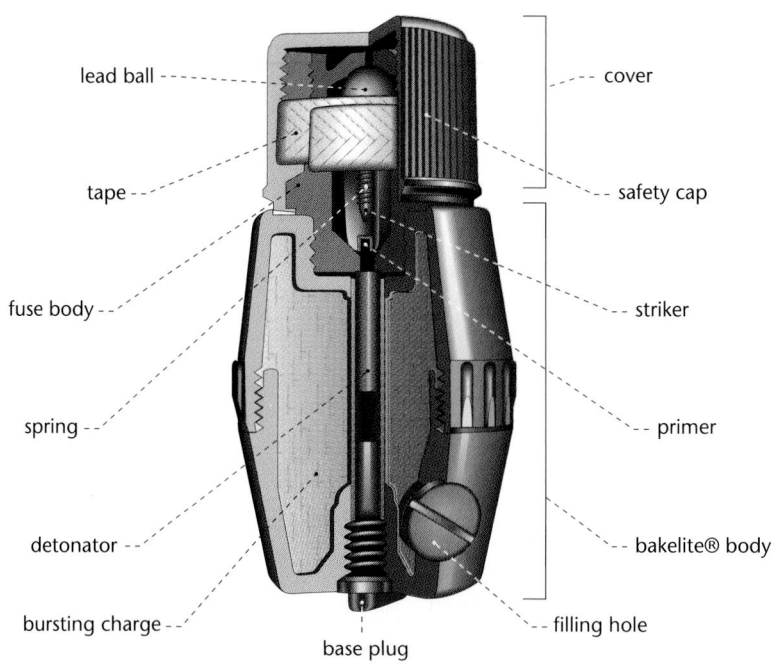

lead ball

tape

fuse body

spring

detonator

bursting charge

base plug

cover

safety cap

striker

primer

bakelite® body

filling hole

BAZOOKA

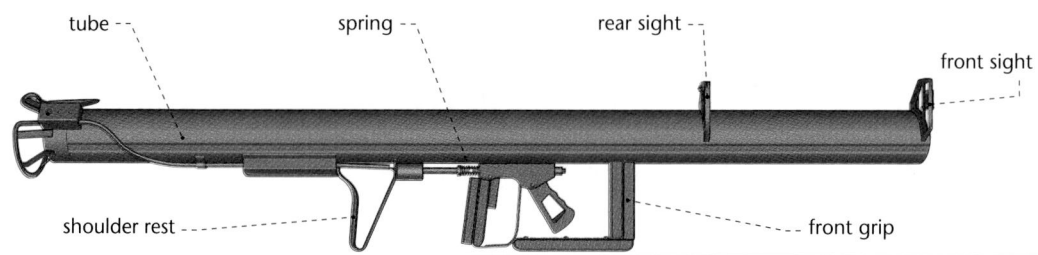

tube

spring

rear sight

front sight

shoulder rest

front grip

RECOILLESS RIFLE

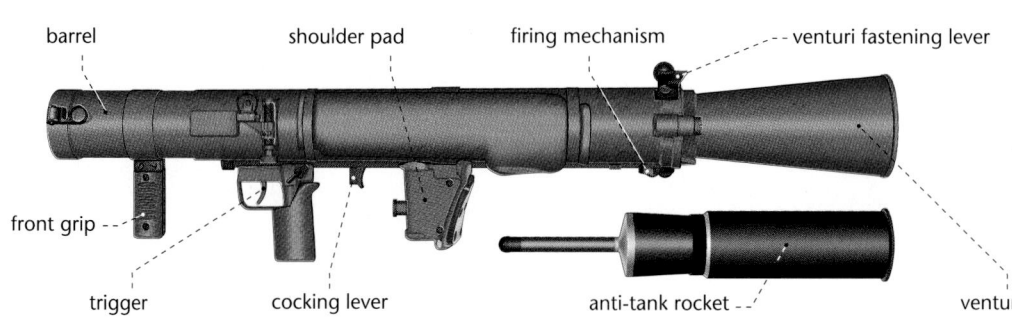

barrel

shoulder pad

firing mechanism

venturi fastening lever

front grip

trigger

cocking lever

anti-tank rocket

venturi

TANK

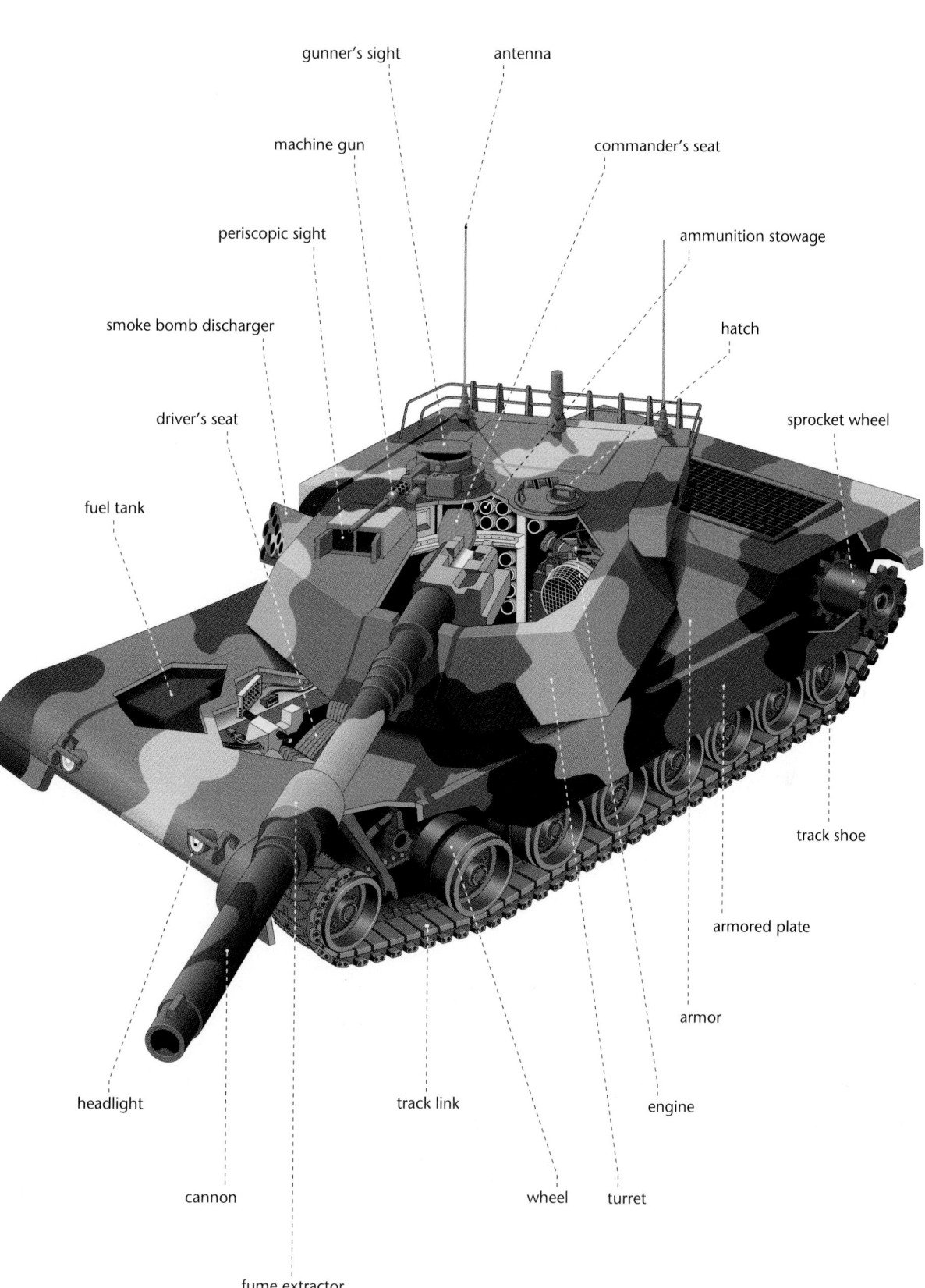

gunner's sight

antenna

machine gun

commander's seat

periscopic sight

ammunition stowage

smoke bomb discharger

hatch

driver's seat

sprocket wheel

fuel tank

track shoe

armored plate

armor

headlight

track link

engine

cannon

wheel

turret

fume extractor

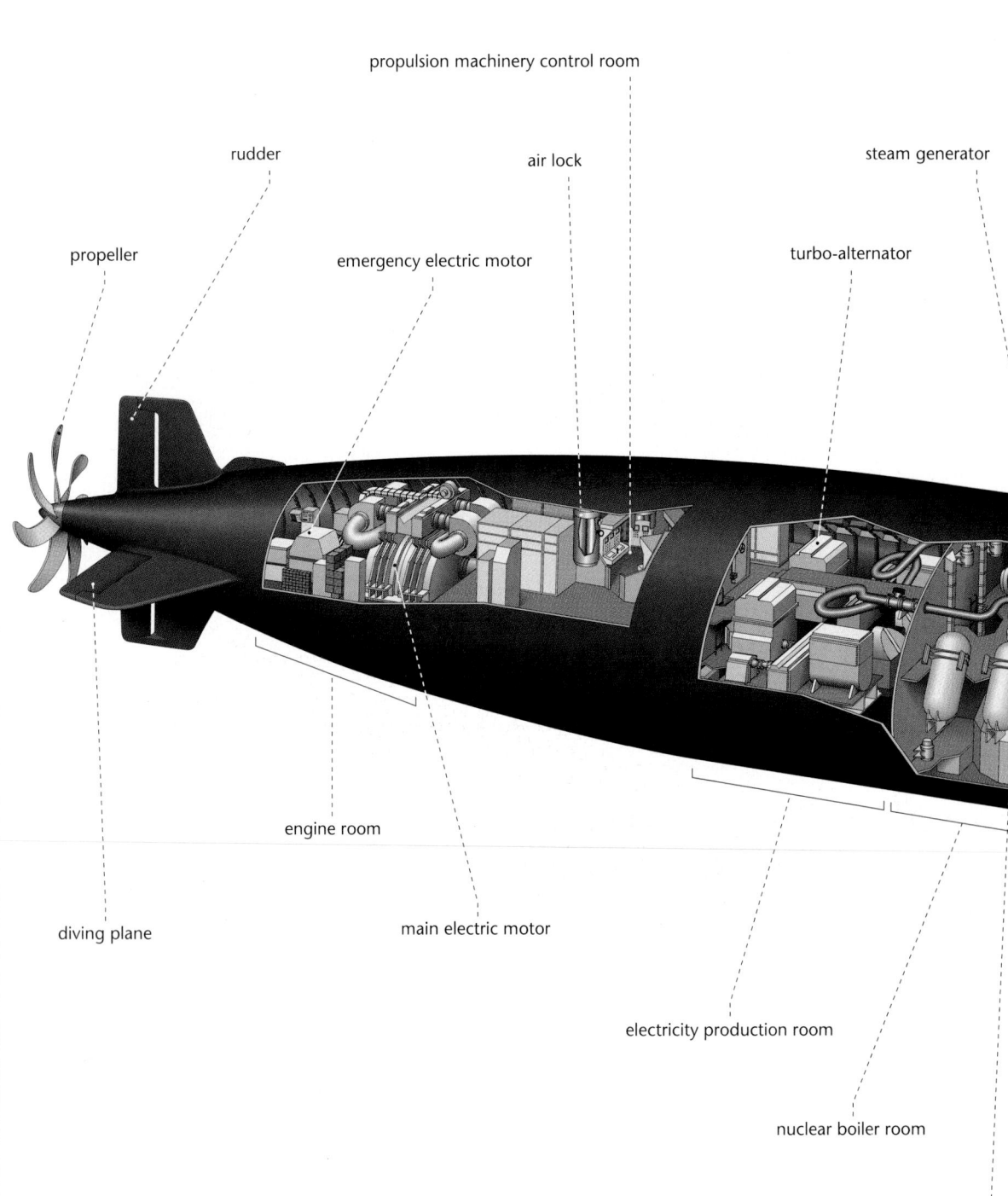

propulsion machinery control room

rudder

air lock

steam generator

propeller

emergency electric motor

turbo-alternator

engine room

main electric motor

diving plane

electricity production room

nuclear boiler room

reactor

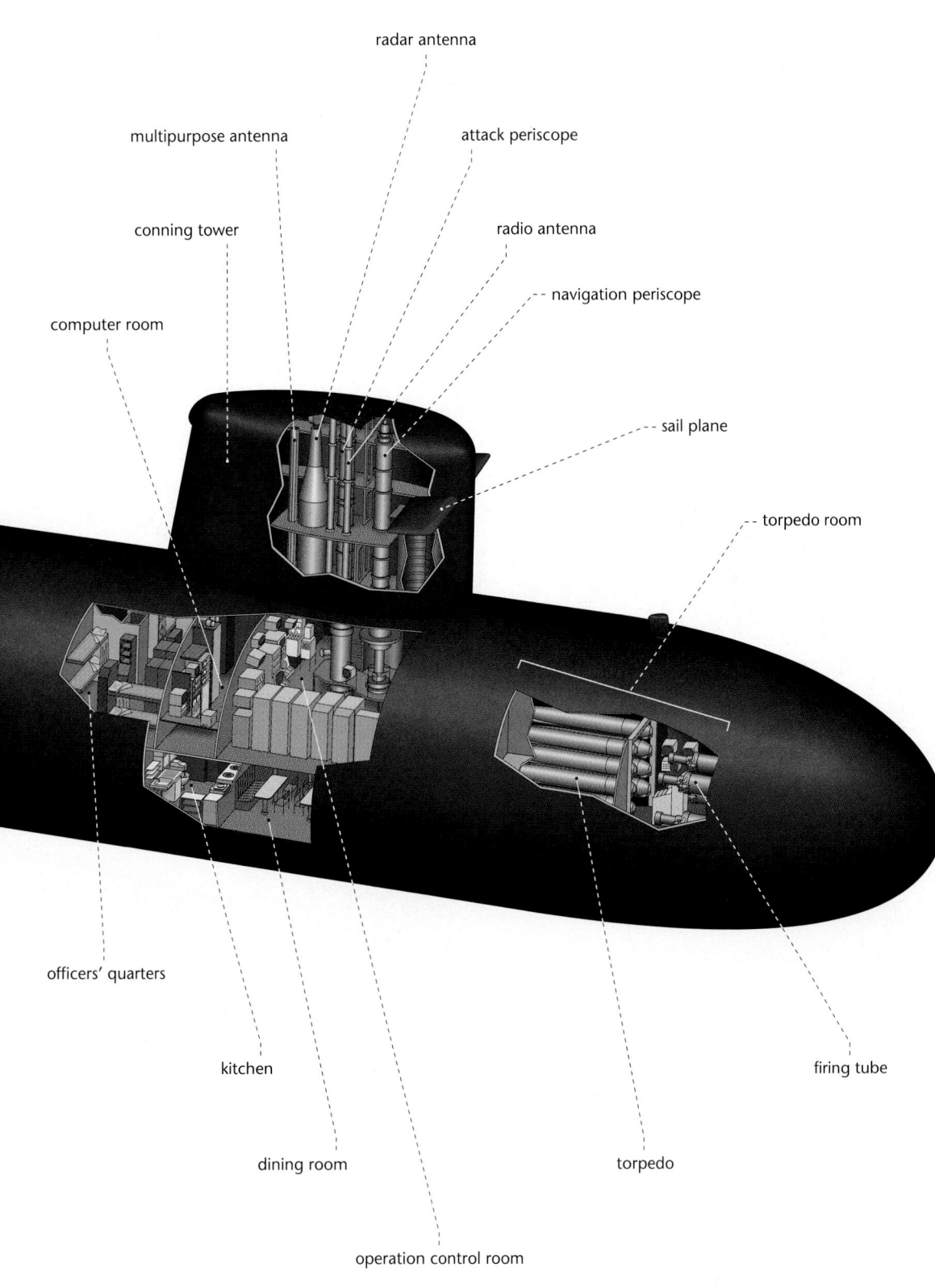

radar antenna

multipurpose antenna

attack periscope

conning tower

radio antenna

computer room

navigation periscope

sail plane

torpedo room

officers' quarters

kitchen

dining room

torpedo

firing tube

operation control room

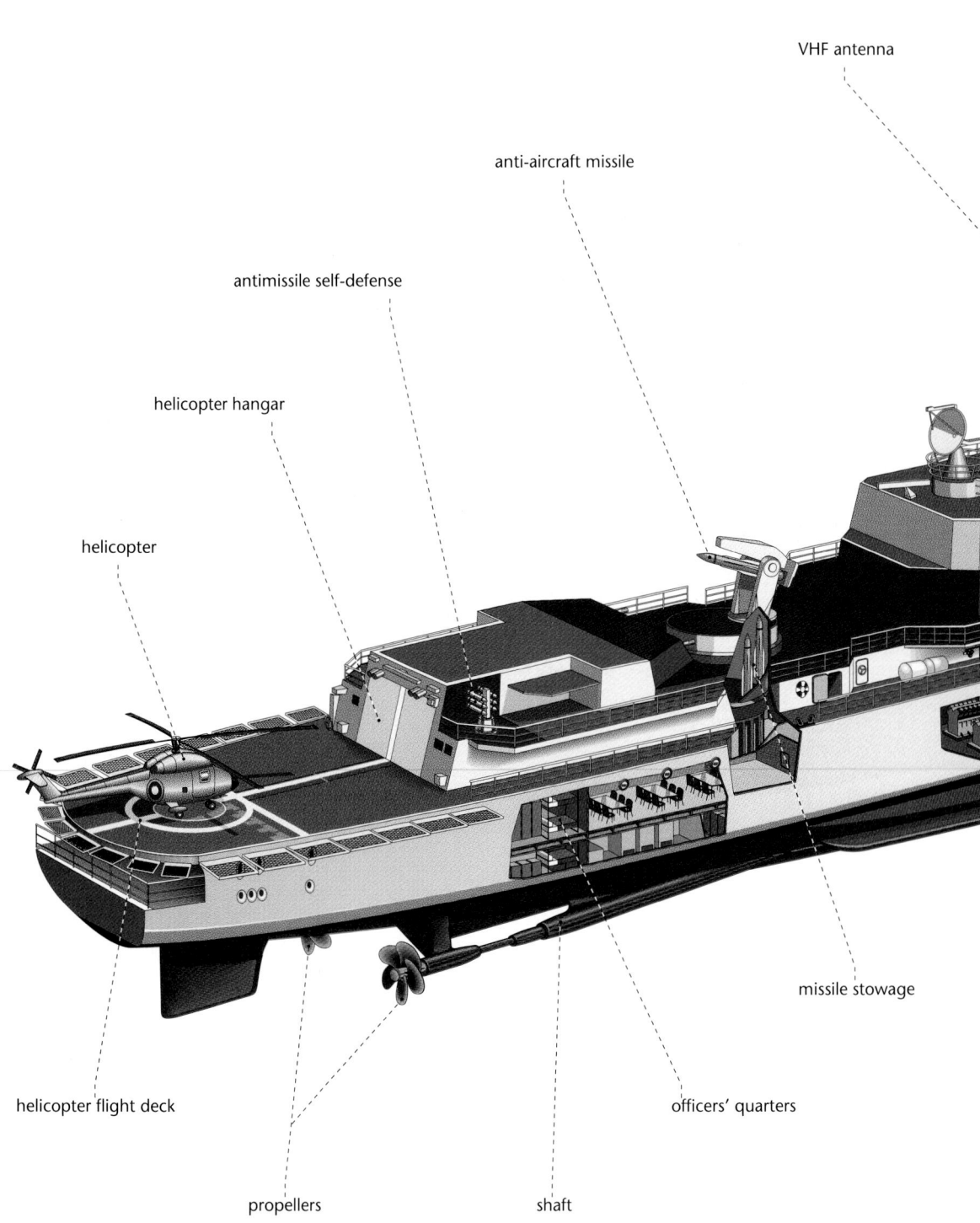

VHF antenna

anti-aircraft missile

antimissile self-defense

helicopter hangar

helicopter

missile stowage

helicopter flight deck

officers' quarters

propellers

shaft

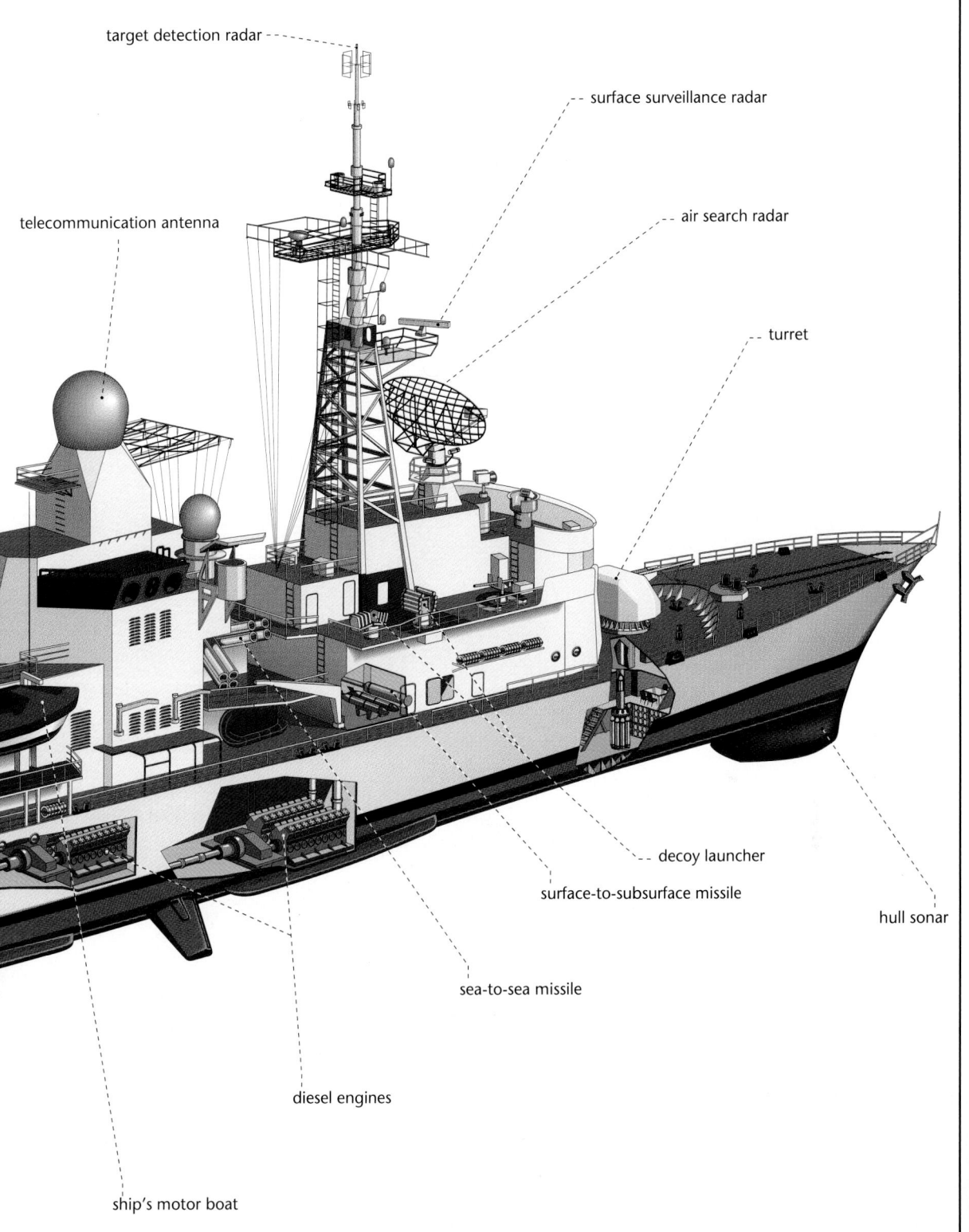

target detection radar

surface surveillance radar

air search radar

telecommunication antenna

turret

decoy launcher

surface-to-subsurface missile

hull sonar

sea-to-sea missile

diesel engines

ship's motor boat

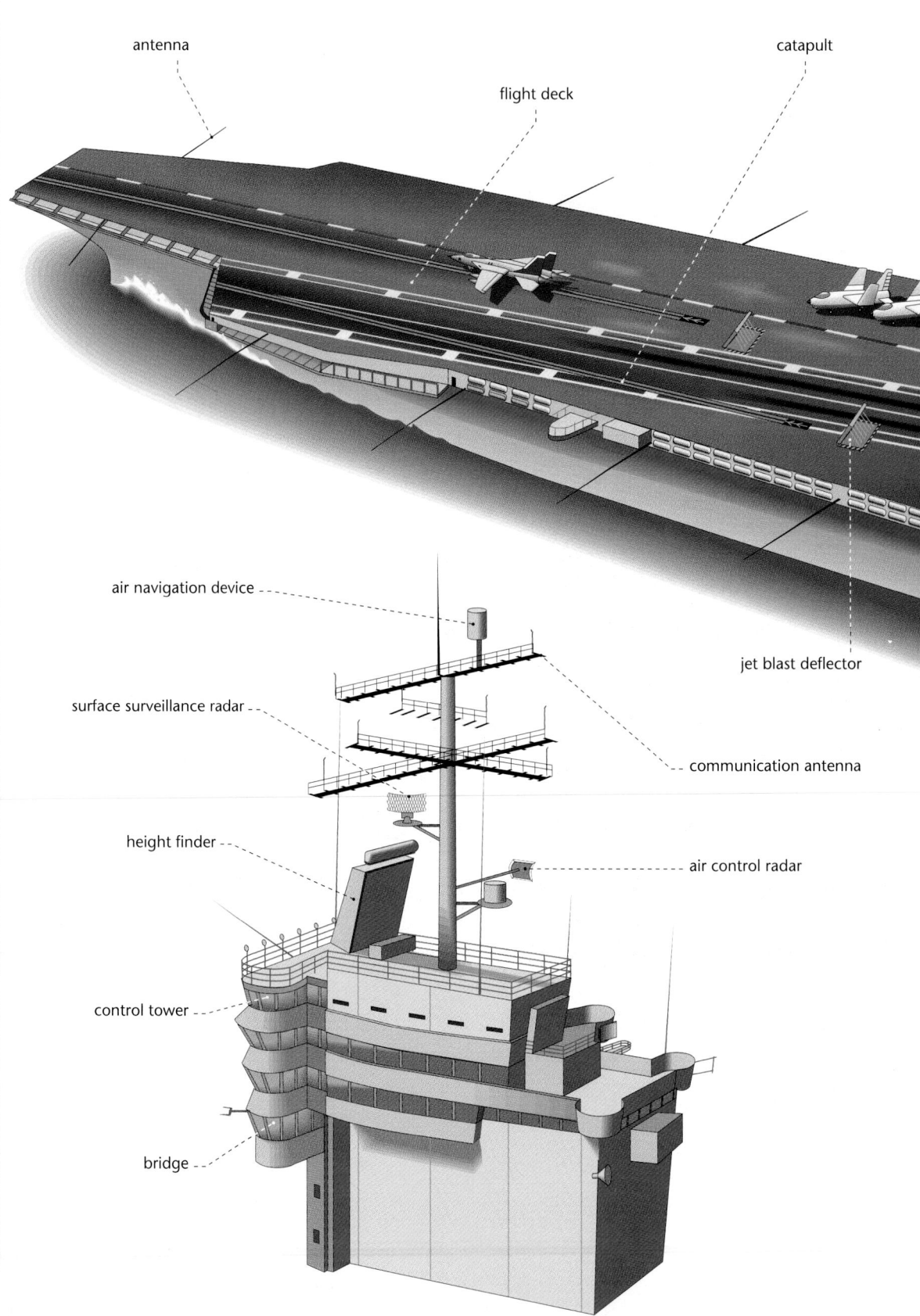

antenna

flight deck

catapult

air navigation device

surface surveillance radar

height finder

control tower

bridge

jet blast deflector

communication antenna

air control radar

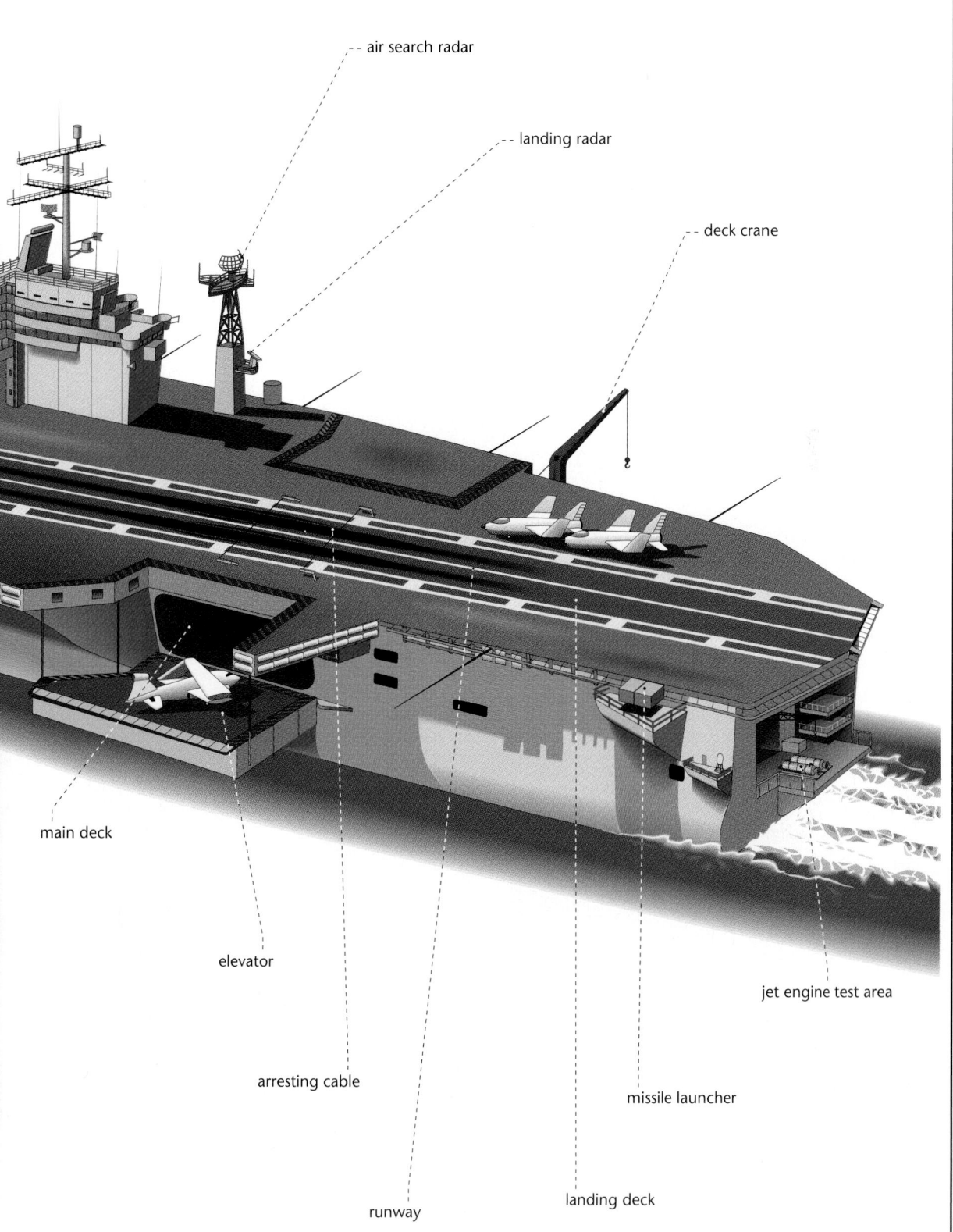

air search radar

landing radar

deck crane

main deck

elevator

jet engine test area

arresting cable

missile launcher

runway

landing deck

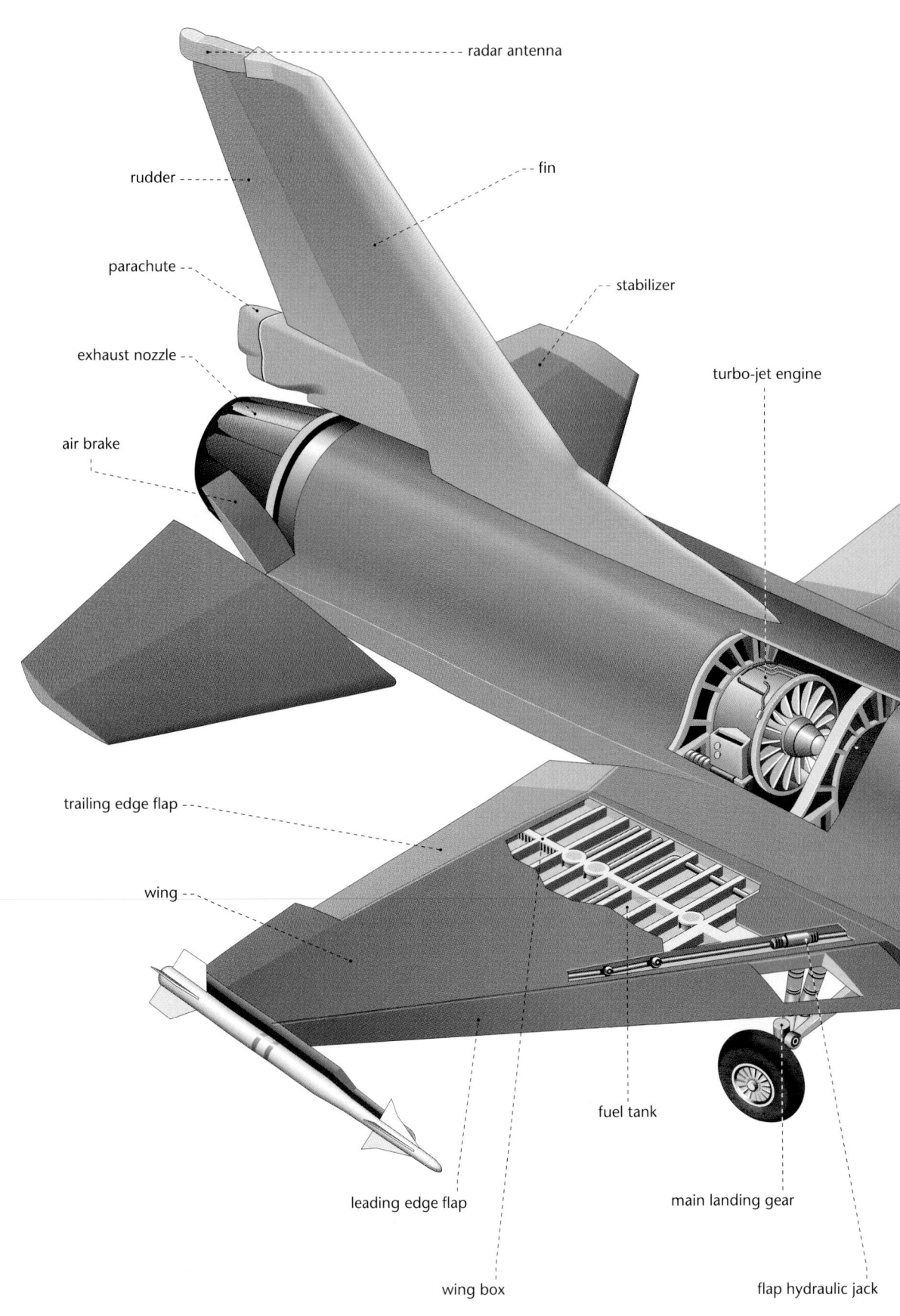

radar antenna

fin

rudder

parachute

stabilizer

exhaust nozzle

turbo-jet engine

air brake

trailing edge flap

wing

fuel tank

leading edge flap

main landing gear

wing box

flap hydraulic jack

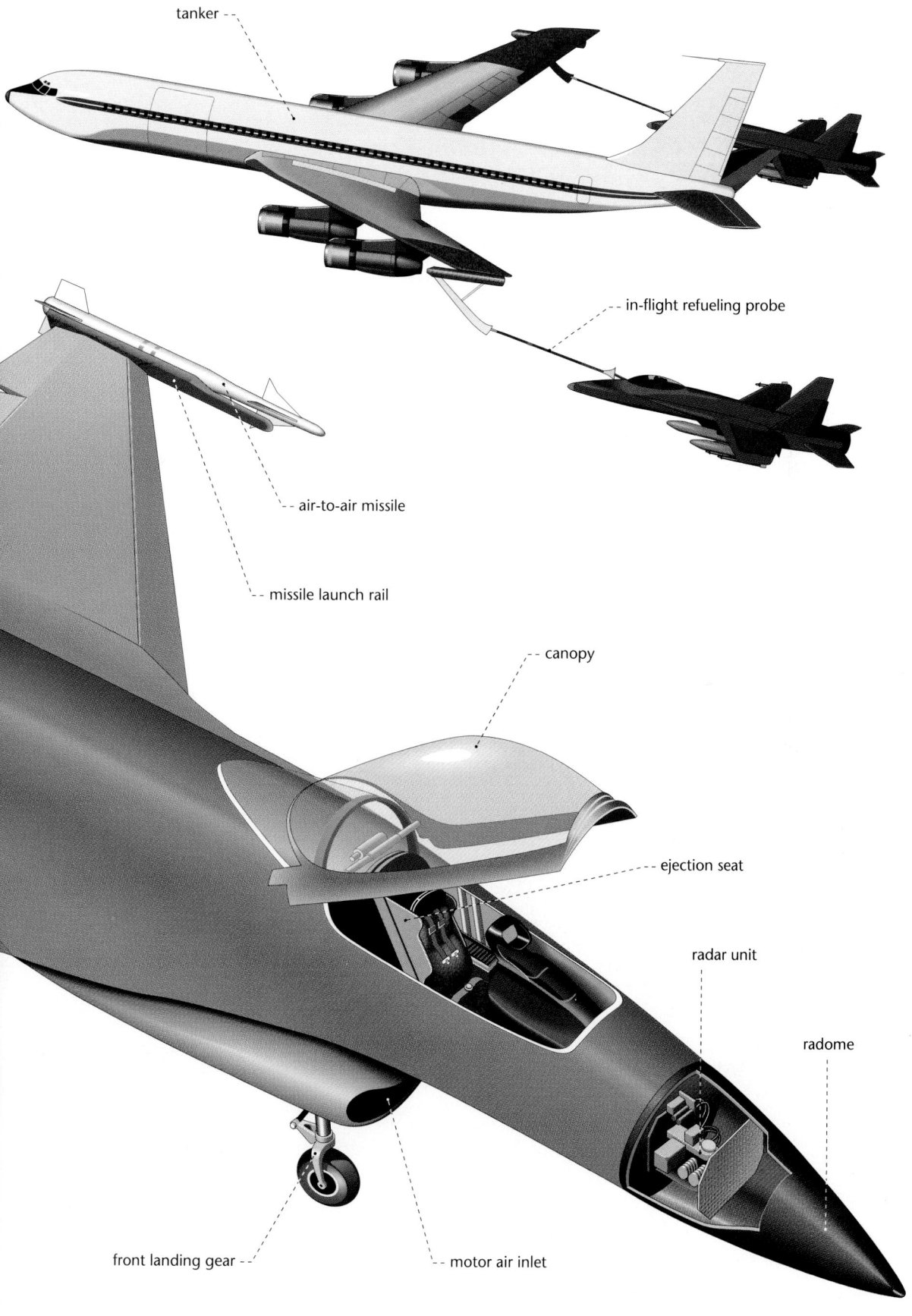

tanker

in-flight refueling probe

air-to-air missile

missile launch rail

canopy

ejection seat

radar unit

radome

front landing gear

motor air inlet

MISSILES

STRUCTURE OF A MISSILE

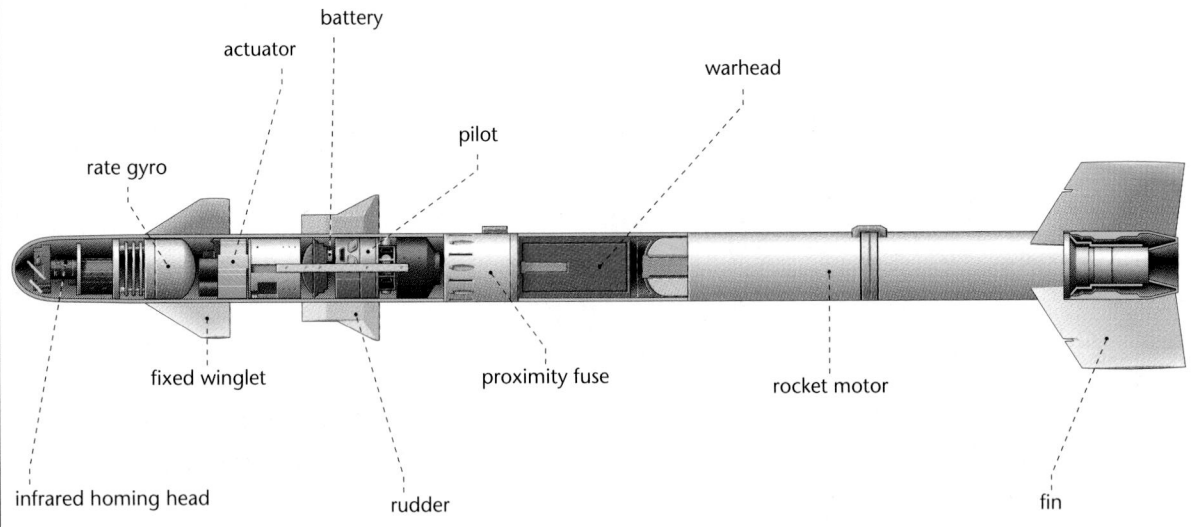

battery

actuator

warhead

pilot

rate gyro

infrared homing head

fixed winglet

proximity fuse

rocket motor

rudder

fin

MAJOR TYPES OF MISSILES

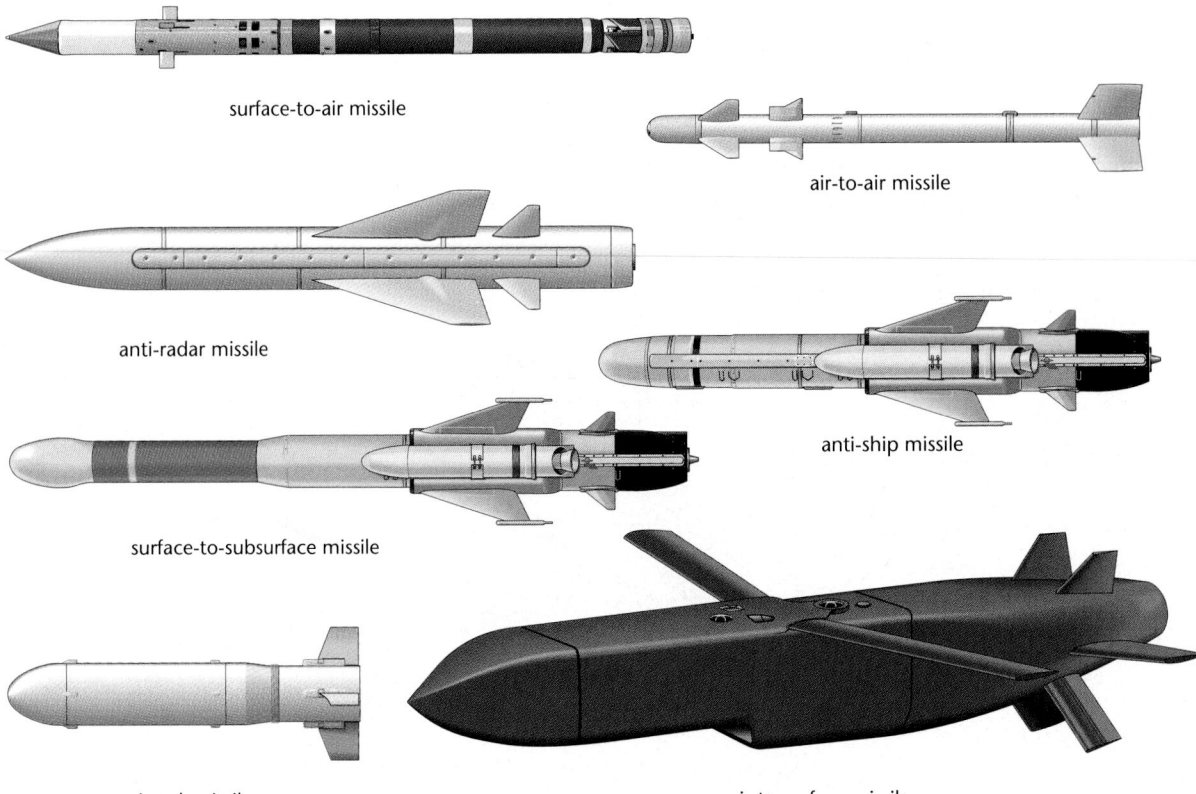

surface-to-air missile

air-to-air missile

anti-radar missile

anti-ship missile

surface-to-subsurface missile

anti-tank missile

air-to-surface missile

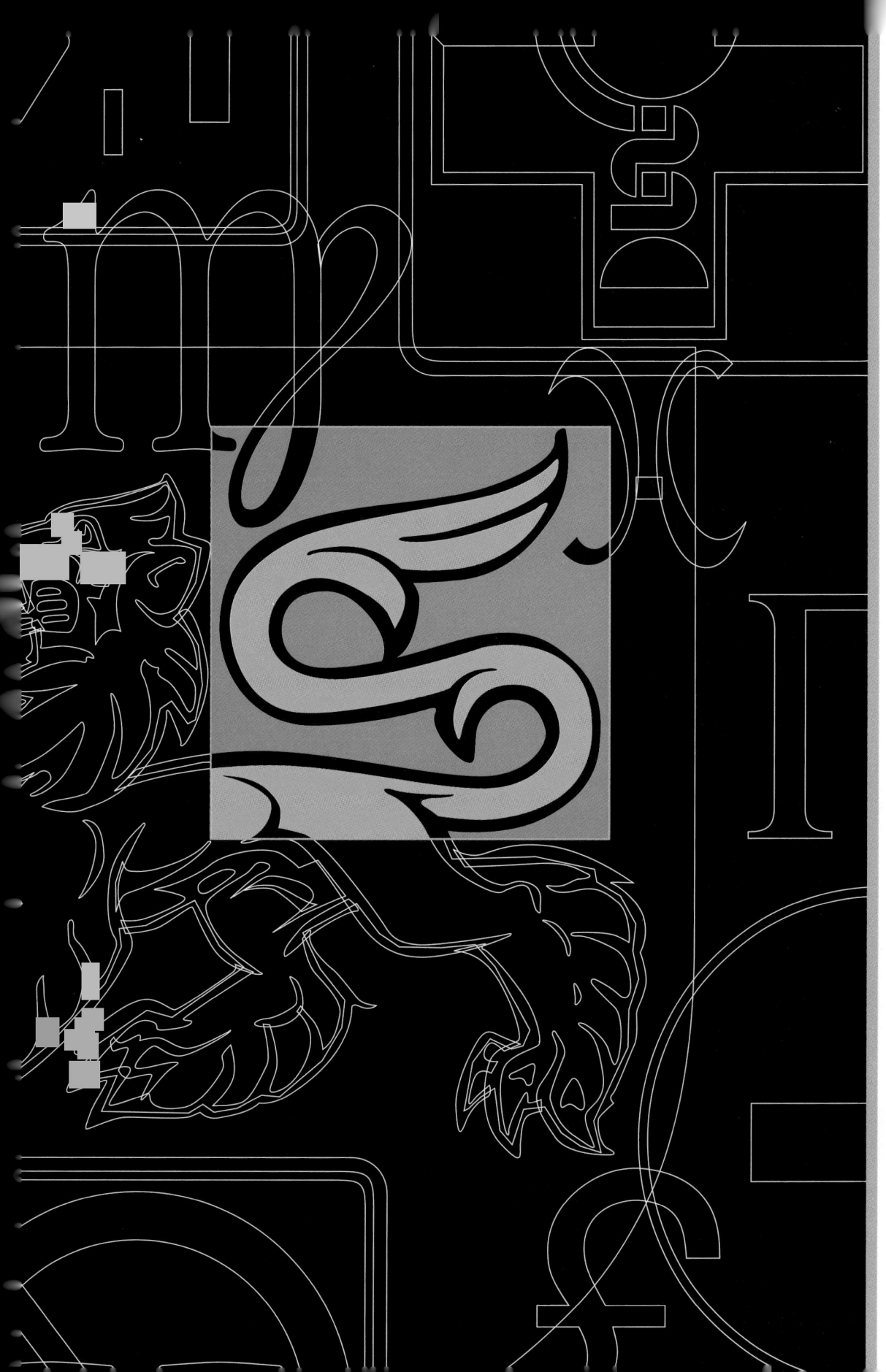

CONTENTS

HERALDRY 817

SIGNS OF THE ZODIAC 820

SAFETY SYMBOLS 821

COMMON SYMBOLS 822

ROAD SIGNS 824

FABRIC CARE 829

COMMON SCIENTIFIC SYMBOLS 830

DIACRITIC SYMBOLS 832

PUNCTUATION MARKS 832

EXAMPLES OF CURRENCY ABBREVIATIONS 832

SYMBOLS

HERALDRY

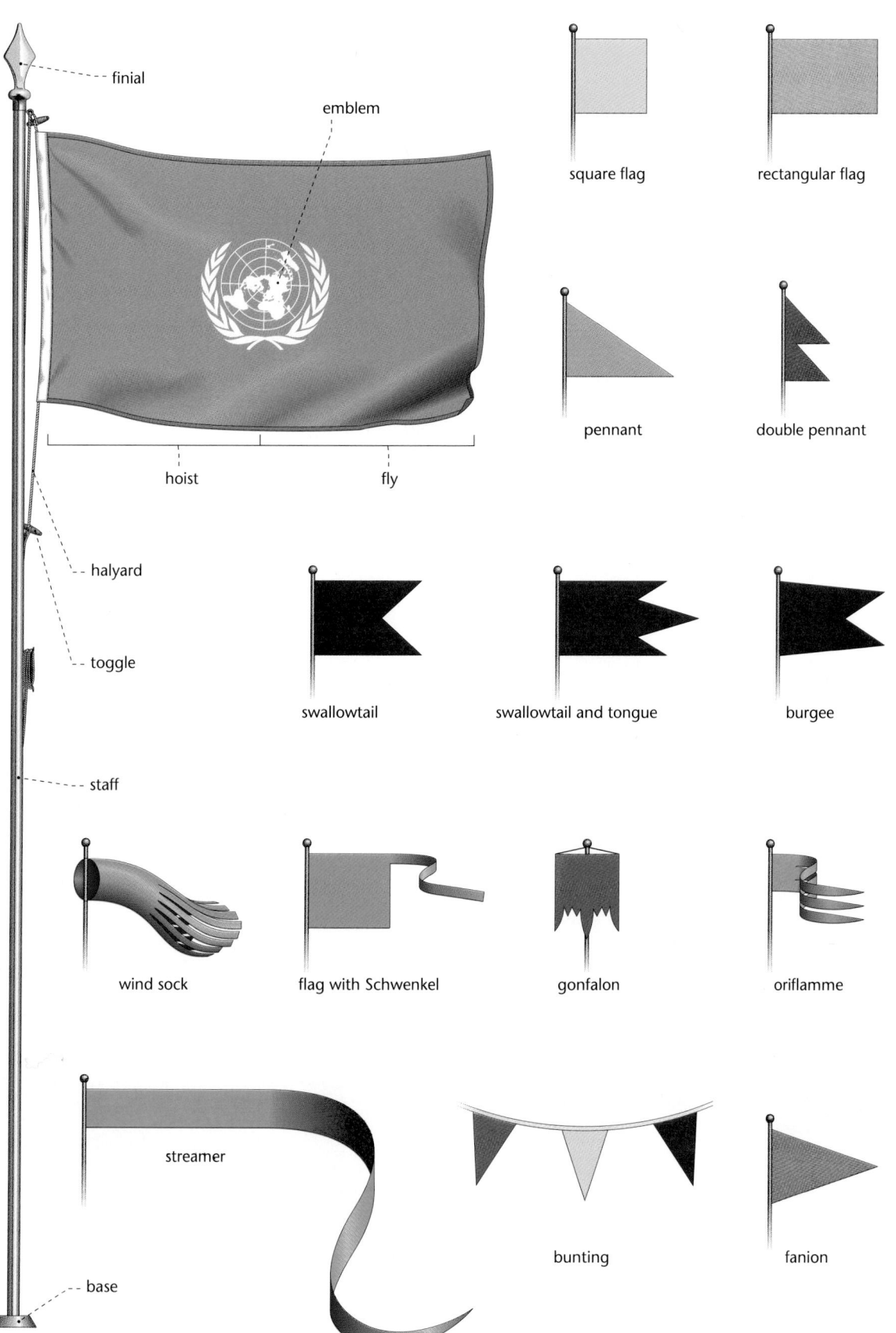

PARTS OF A FLAG

finial

emblem

hoist

fly

halyard

toggle

staff

base

FLAG SHAPES

square flag

rectangular flag

pennant

double pennant

swallowtail

swallowtail and tongue

burgee

wind sock

flag with Schwenkel

gonfalon

oriflamme

streamer

bunting

fanion

817

HERALDRY

SHIELD DIVISIONS

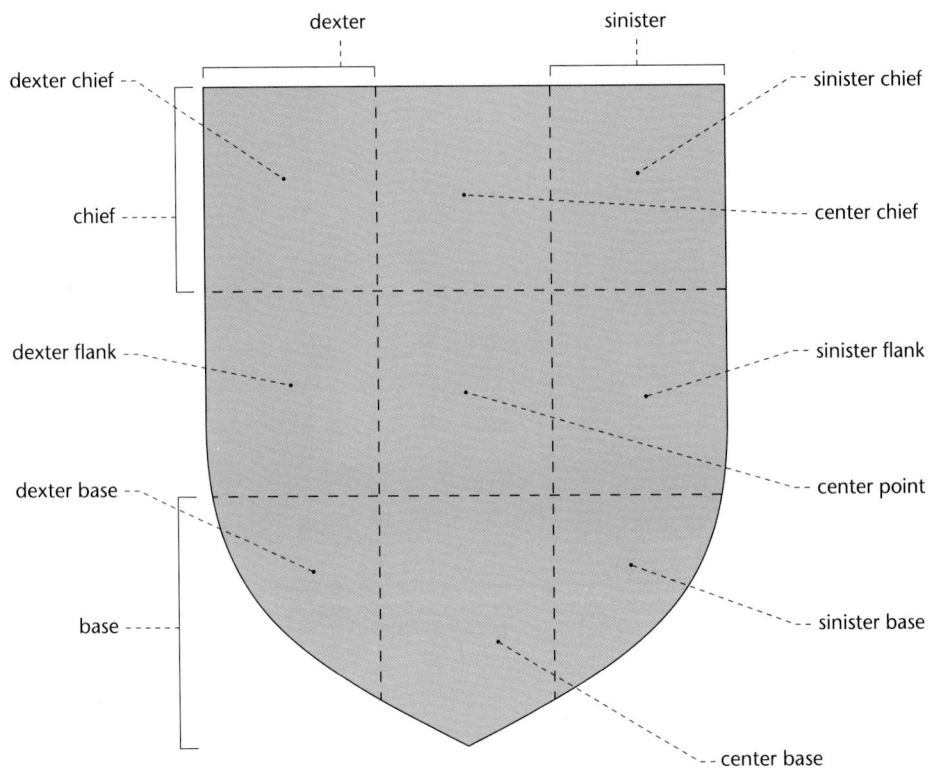

dexter

sinister

dexter chief

sinister chief

chief

center chief

dexter flank

sinister flank

center point

dexter base

sinister base

base

center base

EXAMPLES OF PARTITIONS

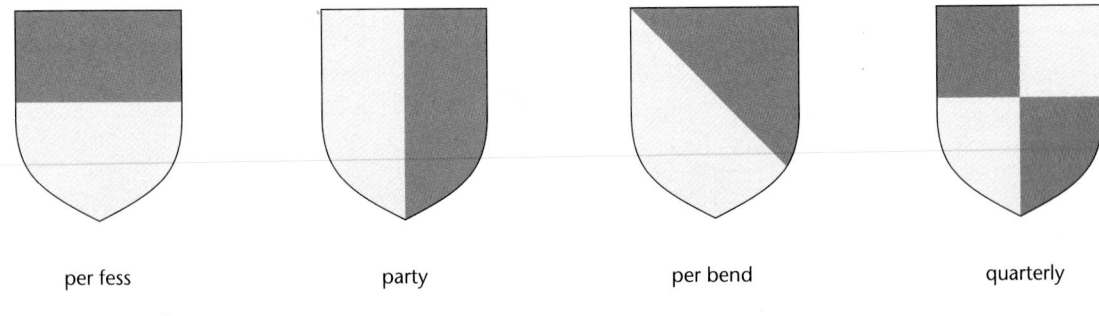

per fess

party

per bend

quarterly

EXAMPLES OF ORDINARIES

chief

chevron

pale

cross

fleur-de-lis

crescent

lion passant

eagle

mulet

EXAMPLES OF METALS

argent

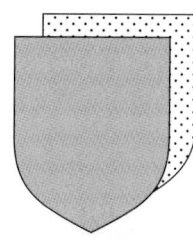

or

EXAMPLES OF FURS

ermine

vair

EXAMPLES OF COLORS

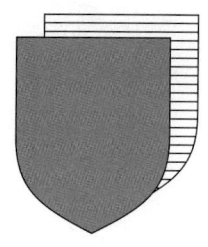

azure

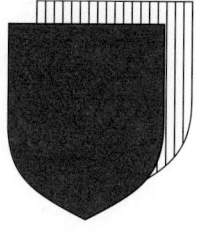

gules

vert

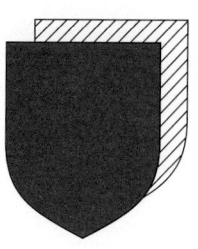

purpure

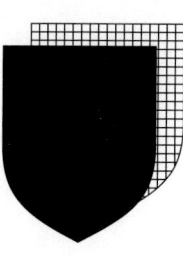

sable

SYMBOLS

SIGNS OF THE ZODIAC

FIRE SIGNS

Aries the Ram (March 21)

Leo the Lion (July 23)

Sagittarius the Archer (November 22)

EARTH SIGNS

Taurus the Bull (April 20)

Virgo the Virgin (August 23)

Capricorn the Goat (December 22)

AIR SIGNS

Libra the Balance (September 23)

Aquarius the Water Bearer (January 20)

Gemini the Twins (May 21)

WATER SIGNS

Cancer the Crab (June 22)

Scorpio the Scorpion (October 24)

Pisces the Fishes (February 19)

SAFETY SYMBOLS

corrosive

electrical hazard

explosive

flammable

radioactive

poison

eye protection

ear protection

head protection

hand protection

feet protection

respiratory system protection

SYMBOLS

coffee shop

telephone

restaurant

men's rest room

women's rest room

access for physically handicapped

pharmacy

no access for wheelchairs

first aid

hospital

police

taxi transportation

camping (tent)

camping prohibited

camping (trailer)

camping (trailer and tent)

picnics prohibited

picnic area

service station

information

information

currency exchange

lost and found articles

fire extinguisher

MAJOR NORTH AMERICAN ROAD SIGNS

stop at intersection

no entry

yield

one-way traffic

direction to be followed

direction to be followed

direction to be followed

direction to be followed

no U-turn

passing prohibited

two-way traffic

merging traffic

stop at intersection

no entry

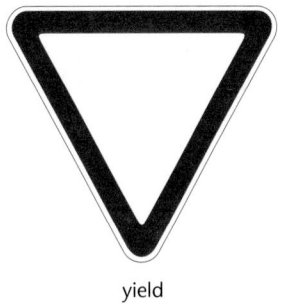

yield

one-way traffic

direction to be followed

direction to be followed

direction to be followed

direction to be followed

no U-turn

passing prohibited

two-way traffic

priority intersection

SYMBOLS

MAJOR NORTH AMERICAN ROAD SIGNS

right bend

double bend

roadway narrows

slippery road

bumps

steep hill

falling rocks

overhead clearance

signal ahead

school zone

pedestrian crossing

road work ahead

right bend

double bend

roadway narrows

slippery road

bumps

steep hill

falling rocks

overhead clearance

signal ahead

school zone

pedestrian crossing

road work ahead

SYMBOLS

MAJOR NORTH AMERICAN ROAD SIGNS

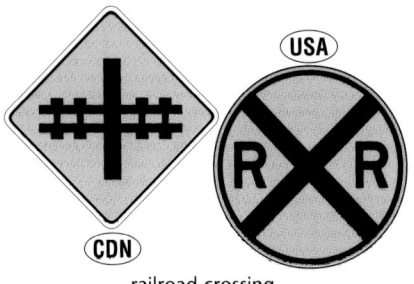

railroad crossing

deer crossing

closed to pedestrians

closed to bicycles

closed to motorcycles

closed to trucks

MAJOR INTERNATIONAL ROAD SIGNS

railroad crossing

deer crossing

closed to pedestrians

closed to bicycles

closed to motorcycles

closed to trucks

FABRIC CARE

do not wash

hand wash in lukewarm water

machine wash in lukewarm water at a gentle setting/reduced agitation

machine wash in warm water at a gentle setting/reduced agitation

machine wash in warm water at a normal setting

machine wash in hot water at a normal setting

do not use chlorine bleach

use chlorine bleach as directed

DRYING

hang to dry

dry flat

tumble dry at medium to high temperature

tumble dry at low temperature

drip dry

IRONING

do not iron

iron at low setting

iron at medium setting

iron at high setting

SYMBOLS

829

COMMON SCIENTIFIC SYMBOLS

MATHEMATICS

— subtraction	**+** addition	**X** multiplication	**÷** division
= is equal to	**≠** is not equal to	is approximately equal to	is equivalent to
≡ is identical with	**≢** is not identical with	**±** plus or minus	**Ø** empty set
> is greater than	**≥** is equal to or greater than	**<** is less than	**≤** is equal to or less than
∪ union	**∩** intersection	**⊂** is contained in	**%** percent
∈ belongs to	**∉** does not belong to	**√** square root of	**Σ** sum
	∞ infinity	**∫** integral	**!** factorial

GEOMETRY

○ degree	**′** minute	**″** second	**π** pi	**⊥** perpendicular
∠ acute angle	**∟** right angle	obtuse angle	**‖** is parallel to	**∦** is not parallel to

male

female

birth

blood factor positive

Rh-
blood factor negative

death

CHEMISTRY

negative charge

positive charge

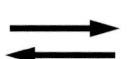
reversible reaction

reaction direction

MISCELLANEOUS

recycled

recyclable

ampersand

registered trademark

copyright

prescription

pause/still

stop

rewind

play

fast forward

DIACRITIC SYMBOLS

acute accent

umlaut

grave accent

circumflex accent

cedilla

tilde

PUNCTUATION MARKS

; semicolon

. period

, comma

. . . ellipses

: colon

* asterisk

« » quotation marks (French)

' ' single quotation marks

" " quotation marks

— dash

( ) parentheses

/ virgule

! exclamation point

? question mark

[ ] square brackets

EXAMPLES OF CURRENCY ABBREVIATIONS

$ dollar

¢ cent

£ pound

¥ yen

F franc

DM deutsche mark

Dr drachma

L lira

Kr krone

IS shekel

ECU European Community Currency

Esc escudo

Pta peseta

Fl florin

a, 537
abacus, 166, 167
abdomen, 78, 79, 81, 91, 108, 116, 118
abdominal aorta, 126, 132
abdominal cavity, 127, 128
abdominal rectus, 120
abdominal segment, 78
ablutions fountain, 172, 173
aboveground pipeline, 740
abruptly pinnate, 56
absorbent cotton, 725
absorbing plate, 768
absorbing surface, 772
abutment, 176, 454, 455, 456
abyssal hill, 29
abyssal plain, 29
abyssal plain, 29
acanthus leaf, 167, 220
acceleration lane, 452
accelerator cable, 271
accelerator control, 272
accent mark, 539
accept machine, 764
access for physically handicapped, 822
access gallery, 747
access panel, 207
access road, 502
access shaft, 752
access window, 529
accessory box, 568
accessory gear box, 501
accessory pocket, 429
accessory pouch, 684
accessory shoe, 391, 409
accidentals, 538
accordion, 536
accordion bag, 380
accordion pleat, 335
account book, 518
Ace, 695
acetylene cylinder, 306
acetylene valve, 306
achene, 62, 66
acid precipitation, 32, 33, 35
acorn nut, 279
acoustic ceiling, 189
acoustic guitar, 546
acoustic meatus, 138, 139
acromion, 123
acroterion, 167, 168
action lever, 541
action of wind, 35
active tracking, 402
actual temperature, 213, 705
actuator, 814
actuator arm, 529
actuator arm motor, 529
acute accent, 832
acute angle, 830
Adam's apple, 116
adaptor, 399
add in memory, 523
add key, 523
addition, 830
additional production personnel, 412
adductor muscle, 92
adhesive bandage, 725
adhesive disk, 85
adhesive tape, 725
adipose tissue, 129, 136
adjustable antenna, 722
adjustable channel, 278
adjustable clamp, 234
adjustable frame, 277
adjustable lamp, 234
adjustable platen, 521
adjustable seat, 460
adjustable spud wrench, 299
adjustable strap, 350
adjustable waist tab, 322
adjuster, 728
adjusting band, 406
adjusting buckle, 645
adjusting catch, 641
adjusting lever, 539
adjusting screw, 278, 282, 306
adjusting tube, 659, 661
adjustment band, 406
adjustment for horizontal-circle image, 713
adjustment for vertical-circle image, 713
adjustment knob, 428
adjustment pedal, 591
adjustment slide, 323
adjustment wheel, 311

administrative building, 752
advertising panel, 474
advertising sign, 477
adze, 587
adze, 681
aerator, 294, 295
aerial ladder truck, 780
aerodynamic brake, 774
Africa, 21
Afro pick, 368
aft shroud, 16
afterbay, 746, 747, 749, 750
afterfeather, 110
aftermast, 478
agitator, 258
aileron, 498, 638
air, 437
air bladder, 89
air brake, 638, 812
air brake handle, 639
air bulb shutter release, 393
air cap, 304
air chamber, 298
air communications, 417
air compression unit, 458
air compressor, 469
air concentrator, 370
air conditioner, 449
air conditioner compressor, 435
air conditioning, 214
air conditioning unit, 415
air control radar, 810
air data computer, 500
air fan, 161
air filter, 210, 272, 469
air flow, 590
air gap, 772
air hole, 385, 389
air horn, 440
air hose, 590, 627, 734
air hose connection, 304
air inlet, 443, 501, 508
air inlet control, 204
air intake, 14, 493
air leg, 734
air lock, 806
air mattress, 687
air navigation device, 810
air pressure, measure, 41
air pump, 453
air purifier, 210
air relief valve, 743
air scoop, 445
air sealing gland, 543
air search radar, 809, 811
air signs, 820
air space, 14, 109
air start unit, 506
air temperature, 38
air tube, 209
air unit, 352
air valve, 304, 590
air vent, 257
air-cleaner filter, 783
air-inlet grille, 370
air-outlet grille, 370
air-pressure pump, 710
air-supply tube, 777
air-to-air missile, 813, 814
air-to-surface missile, 814
air/fuel mixture, 436
airbrush, 590
airbrush, cross section, 590
aircraft carrier, 810
aircraft maintenance truck, 506
airframe, 637
airlock, 14
airplane, 722
airport, 502, 504, 506
airport, 52
airspeed indicator, 639
aisle, 177
ala, 141
alarm threshold display button, 485
alarm threshold setting, 485
albumen, 109
alcohol bulb, 705
alcohol column, 705
alidade, 41, 713
alidade level, 713
alighting board, 82
alley, 614, 618
almond, 63, 66
alphanumeric keyboard, 422, 530
alpine skier, 640
alpine skiing, 640
Alsace glass, 237
Altar, 13
altazimuth mounting, 15

alteration line, 565
alternator, 434, 468
alternator warning light, 431
altimeter, 635, 639
altitude clamp, 720, 721
altitude fine adjustment, 720, 721
altitude scale, 19
altocumulus, 44
altostratus, 44
alula, 110
aluminum layer, 405
alveolar bone, 144
AM antenna, 400
ambulatory, 177
American betting layout, 700
American corn bread, 153
American football, playing field, 604
american plug, 309
American roulette wheel, 700
American white bread, 153
amethyst, 362
ammunition stowage, 805
ampersand, 831
amphibians, 84
amplification of seismic waves, 714
amplifier, 402
amplifier, 714
amplifier's back, 400
ampulla of fallopian tube, 129
anal fin, 87
anal proleg, 78
analog watch, 706
analytical balance, 709
anchor, 483
anchor, 656
anchor pin, 432
anchor wires, 738
anchor-windlass room, 495, 497
anchorage block, 456
anchors, types, 483
ancient costume, elements, 315, 316, 318
anconeus, 121
andirons, 205
Andromeda, 11
anemometer, 41
Anik-E, 418
animal cell, 115
ankle, 116, 118
ankle boot, 357
ankle length, 325
ankle/wrist weight, 665
anklet, 344
announcer turret, 407
annual ring, 59
annular combustion chamber, 501
annular eclipse, 8
annulet, 167
anode rod, 297
anorak, 353
ant, 77
Antarctic Circle, 3
Antarctica, 20
antefix, 169
antenna, 16, 43, 78, 79, 80, 81, 91, 408, 427, 498, 508, 613, 805, 810
antennae cleaner, 80
antennule, 90
anterior chamber, 140
anterior end, 95
anterior notch, 139
anterior root, 135
anterior tibial, 120
anterior tibial artery, 126
anther, 60
anti-aircraft missile, 808
anti-friction pad, 641
anti-radar missile, 814
anti-ship missile, 814
anti-skating device, 404
anti-slip shoe, 302, 661
anti-tank missile, 814
anti-tank rocket, 804
anti-torque tail rotor, 508
anti-vibration handle, 272
anticline, 737
anticollision light, 498
antihelix, 139
antimissile self-defense, 808
antireflection coating, 768
antiseptic, 725
antitragus, 139
anus, 89, 92, 127, 128, 131
anvil, 711
aorta, 125, 130
aortic valve, 125
aperture, 94

aperture changer, 717
aperture diaphragm, 717
aperture door, 16
aperture scale, 396
aperture/exposure value display, 396
apex, 83, 94, 143, 144
apical foramen, 144
apocrine sweat gland, 136
apogee motor firing, 419
apogee passage, 419
apple, 64
apple, 64
appoggiatura, 538
appointment book, 518
approach, 654, 655, 657, 683
approach ramp, 456
approach wall, 492
apricot, 63
apron, 219, 220, 223, 502, 669
apse, 177
apsidiole, 177
Apus, 13
aquamarine, 362
Aquarius, 13
Aquarius the Water Bearer (January 20), 820
aquastat, 209
aquatic bird, 111
aquatic bird, 111
aqueous humor, 140
Aquila, 11
Ara, 13
arbor, 263
arc welding, 305
arc welding machine, 305
arcade, 176
arch, 174
arch, 14, 455
arch bridge, 455
arch bridges, types, 455
arch dam, 750
arch dam, cross section, 750
arch of aorta, 125, 126
arch of foot artery, 126
arch of the aorta, 124
archboard, 518
archer, 684
Archer, 13
archery, 684
arches, types, 174, 455
archipelago, 51
architectural styles, 166
architrave, 166, 168
Arctic, 20
Arctic Circle, 3, 47
arctic continental, 38
arctic maritime, 38
Arctic Ocean, 21
area of ice, 620
arena, 654
Arenberg parquet, 200
areola, 129
argent, 819
Aries, 11
Aries the Ram (March 21), 820
arm, 100, 117, 119, 157, 220, 234, 264, 483, 535, 561, 568, 718, 727, 782, 785
arm cylinder, 782, 785
arm elevator, 404
arm guard, 602
arm lock, 668
arm nut, 568
arm pad, 609
arm position, 625
arm rest, 404
arm slit, 331
arm stump, 220
armchair, 220
armchairs, principal types, 220
armet, 792
armet, 792
armguard, 684
armhole, 325
armoire, 225
armor, 792
armor, 805
armored cord, 422
armored plate, 805
armpit, 116, 118
armrest, 428, 429, 727
armstand, 624
armstand dive, 625
arpeggio, 539
arresting cable, 811
arris, 167
arrow, 684
Arrow, 11, 793
arrow rest, 684

The terms in **bold type** indicate the title of an illustration.

arteries, 126
artichoke, 69
articulated mannequin, 592
articulated road train, 440
articulation, 431
artificial fly, 670
artificial satellite, 19
ascending aorta, 124
ascending colon, 131
ascot tie, 324
ash, 386
ash layer, 25
ashtray, 386
Asia, 21
asparagus, 72
asphalt, 745
asphalt shingle, 286
asphalt still, 745
aspirin, 725
assist grip, 429
assistant timer, 626
asterisk, 832
asteroid belt, 4
asthenosphere, 22
astragal, 167, 800
astronomical observatory, 14
asymmetrical bars, 659
athletic shirt, 325
Atlantic Ocean, 20
atlas, 102, 123
atmosphere, 22, 31
atoll, 28
atrium, 170
attaché case, 378
attached curtain, 228
attack line, 613
attack on human being, 35
attack on nature, 35
attack periscope, 807
attack zone, 613
attacking zone, 608
audio console, 407, 412, 415
audio control room, 412, 415
audio monitor, 407, 412, 413, 415
audio monitoring selector, 413
audio system, 430
audio technician, 412, 415
audio volume unit meters, 413
audio/video preview unit, 413
auditorium, 16
auditory ossicles, 138
auditory ossicles, 139
auger bit, 281
auger bit, 270
auricle, 81, 138
auricle, ear, 139
auriculars, 109
Auriga, 11
Australia, 21
auto answer indicator, 420
auto reverse, 408
auto/manual range, 310
autofocus on/off switch, 397
automatic dialer index, 420
automatic drip coffee maker, 247
automatic rifle, 796
automatic sorting trays, 532
automatic tank gauge, 741
automatically-controlled door, 504
automobile, 425, 426, 428, 430, 432, 434, 438
automobile car, 473
autopilot controls, 500
autumn, 8
autumn squash, 69
autumnal equinox, 8
auxiliary facilities room, 412
auxiliary handle, 280
auxiliary heating, 211
auxiliary tank, 441
auxiliary projector, 16
auxiliary video switcher, 413
avenue, 52
average key, 396
avocado, 68
awl, 688
awning channel, 449
axial compressor blade, 501
axial rib, 94
axillary artery, 126
axillary bud, 57
axillary nerve, 133
axillary vein, 126
axis, 123
axle, 468, 645
axon, 135
axon hillock, 135
azimuth clamp, 720, 721
azimuth fine adjustment, 720, 721
azure, 819

B

b, 537
baby doll, 348
back, 322
back, 101, 106, 108, 117, 119, 223, 239, 240, 241, 242, 277, 288, 727, 793
back beam, 573
back belt, 330
back binding, 633
back board, 577
back boundary line, 618
back check, 541
back crossbar, 645
back judge, 603, 605
back line, 611
back pad, 609, 653
back pocket, 323
back score line, 620
back strap, 653
back wall, 616, 617
back zone, 613
back-hoe, 782
back-hoe controls, 782
backboard, 610
backcourt, 614, 617
backdrop, 188
backgammon, 697
backguard, 255, 258, 259
backing, 579
backing board, 579
backing hammer, 579
backing plate, 432
backing press, 579
backrest, 428, 445
backstay, 479, 644
backstep, 778
backstretch, 651
backstroke, 623
backstroke start, 623
backstroke turn indicator, 621
backup light, 429
backward, 624
backward bucket, 782
backward bucket cylinder, 782
backward dive, 625
badminton, 618
badminton racket, 618
badminton, court, 618
badminton, net, 618
baffle, 216, 742
bag well, 679
baggage cart, 463
baggage check-in counter, 504
baggage claim area, 504
baggage compartment, 458, 508
baggage conveyor, 507
baggage lockers, 463
baggage racks, 492
baggage room, 462
baggage trailer, 507
bagpipes, 536
baguette cut, 363
bail, 599
bail arm, 671
bail arm opening mechanism, 671
bailey, 180
Bailey bridge, 457
baize, 675
bakelite body, 804
baking utensils, 245
balaclava, 329
balalaika, 535
balance beam, 659
balance control, 402
balance rail, 541
balcony, 189
balk area, 674
balk line, 674
balk line spot, 674
ball, 598, 795
ball, 530, 566, 575, 683
ball assembly, 294
ball bearing, 389
ball boy, 614
ball of clay, 584
ball peen, 275
ball return, 683
ball stand, 683
ball winder, 575
ball-cock supply valve, 293
ball-peen hammer, 275
ball-type faucet, 294
ballast, 466
ballerina, 356
balloon, 634
balloon, 634
balloon curtain, 229

ballooning, 634
ballpoint pen, 389, 515
ballroom, 497
balustrade, 194
banana, 68
band, 404
band ring, 364
band selector, 402
bandage, 669
banding wheel, 584
bangle, 364
banister, 201
banjo, 535
bank, 451, 752
bank of heliostats, 770, 771
banquette, 222
bar, 104, 376, 554, 663, 665, 697
bar frame, 235
bar line, 537
bar nose, 272
bar shot, 801
bar stool, 222
barb, 38, 110, 671
barbell, 663
barber comb, 368
barbican, 180
baren, 582
bargraph type peak meter, 407
bark, 59
barley, 152
barn, 148
barograph, 41
barometer scales, 710
barometer/thermometer, 710
barometric pressure, 38
barometric tendency, 38
barrack buildings, 179
barred spiral galaxy, 9
barrel, 800
barrel, 370, 389, 698, 795, 796, 797, 798, 799, 802, 804
barrel jacket, 796
barrette, 369
barrier, 186
bartizan, 178, 181
basaltic layer, 22
base, 166, 204, 232, 233, 236, 252, 283, 368, 404, 410, 450, 466, 471, 579, 656, 661, 708, 712, 718, 774, 799, 817, 818
base course, 451
base line, 719
base of splat, 220
base plate, 40, 284, 404, 641, 713, 719
base plug, 804
base ring, 800
base width, 756
baseball, 595, 596
baseball, cross section, 596
baseball, field, 597
baseboard, 199, 201, 399
baseboard register, 207
baseline, 614
basement, 190
basement, 197
basement window, 197
baseplate, 803
basic building materials, 286
basic components, 528, 530
basic source of food, 31
basic weaves, 576
basil, 74
basilic vein, 126
basin, 752
basin side, 752
basin wrench, 299
basket, 610, 635
basket, 247, 252, 258, 610, 634, 641, 642
basket handle, 174
basket handle, 635
basket stitch, 567
basket suspension cables, 634
basket weave pattern, 200
basketball, 610
basketball, court, 610
bass bridge, 540
bass clarinet, 556
bass drum, 552, 557
bass keyboard, 536
bass pickup, 547
bass register, 536
bass tone control, 402
bass trap, 412
bassoon, 548
bassoons, 557
baster, 246
bastion, 179
bat, 112, 596, 598

bat, 160, 595, 598
bateau neck, 343
bath, 215
bathing wrap, 349
bathrobe, 348
bathroom, 292
bathroom, 194, 195
bathroom scale, 709
bathtub, 194, 292
batsman, 599
batten, 188, 231, 628, 631, 637
batten pocket, 628, 631
batter, 595
batter, 597
batter head, 552, 553
batter's helmet, 595
battery, 393, 439
battery, 409, 468, 528, 769, 777, 814
battery box, 441
battery case, 439
battery cover, 439
battery eject switch, 409
battery modules, 43
battery radiator, 49
batting glove, 595
battlement, 179, 181
batwing sleeve, 339
bay, 7, 51
bay antler, 105
bay window, 197
bayonet base, 232
bayonet mount, 392
bazooka, 804
beach, 23, 30
bead, 433
bead wire, 433
beam, 105, 156, 659, 708
beam balance, 708
beam bridge, 454
beam bridges, types, 454
beam diameter reduction, 717
beam gantry, 756
beam reach, 629
bean bag chair, 222
bean sprouts, 72
bearer, 543
bearing pad, 765
beater, 156, 250, 572
beater ejector, 250
beater handtree, 572
beater sley, 572
beaters, 250
beaver, 98
beaver, 792
bed, 224, 687
bed, 450, 578, 659
bed chamber, 170
bed lamp, 234
bedrock, 714
bedroom, 194, 195, 685
beer mug, 237
beet, 71
beginner's course, 646
belfry, 175, 176
bell, 549, 551
bell bottoms, 336
bell brace, 549
bell roof, 183
bell tower, 175
bellow, 543
bellows, 399, 536
bellows strap, 536
belly, 101
belly scale, 97
belongs to, 830
belt, 323
belt, 319, 433, 668
belt drive, 492
belt highway, 52
belt loader, 733
belt loop, 319, 323, 688
bench, 222
bench, 475, 663, 733
bench height, 733
bench seat, 428
bend, 376, 671
bent blade, 587
Berenice's Hair, 11
beret, 329
bergère, 220
bergschrund, 26
Bering Sea, 21
berm, 748
Bermuda sail, 482
Bermuda shorts, 336
berries, major types, 62
berry fruits, 62
berry, section, 62
berth, 460
bertha collar, 342

bevel, 726
bevel square, 713
bezel, 364
bezel facet (8), 363
bias, 566
bias-ply tire, 433
bib, 349
bib, 350, 351, 667
bib necklace, 361
biceps of arm, 120
biceps of thigh, 121
biconcave lens, 722
biconvex lens, 722
bicorne, 318
bicycle, 446, 448
bicycle bag, 448
bicycle, accessories, 448
bidet, 292
bifocal lens, 376
bikini, 347
bikini briefs, 325
bill, 108, 483
bill compartment, 379
bill-file, 516
billfold, 379
billhook, 269
billiard spot, 675
billiards, 673
billiards cue, 675
bills, principal types, 111
bimetallic helix, 705
bimetallic thermometer, 705
binder, 159
binding, 328, 633, 642
binocular microscope, 718
biology, 831
biomedical monitoring sensor, 512
biosphere, structure, 31
biparous cyme, 60
bipod, 796, 803
bird, 108, 110
Bird of Paradise, 13
bird of prey, 111
bird of prey, 111
bird, morphology, 108
birth, 831
Bishop, 696
bishop sleeve, 340
bit, 385, 648, 734, 737
bits, types, 650
bitt, 743
bitter taste, 143
bivalve shell, 95
Black, 696, 700, 701
black ball, 673
black currant, 62
black rye bread, 153
black salsify, 71
Black Sea, 21
black square, 696
black stone, 697
blade, 783
blade, 57, 214, 239, 242, 251, 256,
  268, 271, 276, 277, 284, 285, 291,
  304, 309, 369, 374, 562, 564, 607,
  609, 619, 627, 632, 644, 666, 672,
  681, 754, 774, 783, 784
blade close stop, 369
blade guard, 285
blade height adjustment, 285
blade injector, 374
blade lever, 578
blade lift cylinder, 783
blade lift fan, 492
blade lifting mechanism, 784
blade locking bolt, 284
blade rotation mechanism, 784
blade tilting lock, 284
blade tilting mechanism, 284, 285
blade with two beveled edges, 587
blades, major types, 587
blank, 695
blanket, 224
blanket insulation, 287
blanket sleepers, 350
blast valve, 635
blastodisc, 109
blazer, 338
bleeder valve, 208
blender, 250
blending attachment, 250
blinker, 653
block, 542, 656, 787
block bracket, 230
block cutter, 581, 587
blockboard, 288
blood circulation, 124, 126
blood circulation, schema, 124
blood factor negative, 831
blood factor positive, 831

blood vessel, 136
blood vessels, 112
blouses, types, 337
blow pipe, 536
blower, 207, 213, 543, 760
blower motor, 207, 214
blucher oxford, 355
blue ball, 673
blue beam, 410
blue cap, 626
blue flag, 626
blue line, 608
blue mussel, 93
blueberry, 62
blueprint reading, 193, 195
blusher brush, 366
board, 288
board, 288, 631
board cutter, 578
board insulation, 287
boarding room, 505
boarding step, 508
boarding walkway, 503
boards, 608
boater, 328
bobber, 672
bobbin, 570
bobbin, 561, 562, 570, 573
bobbin case, 562
bobbin lace, 570
bobbin winder, 575
bobbin winder, 561
bobby pin, 369
bobeche, 236
bobsled, 643
bobstay, 479
bodies, types, 425
body, 426
body, 143, 252, 281, 294, 295, 445,
  449, 453, 542, 546, 549, 645, 658,
  670, 707, 719
body flap, 511
body guard molding, 449
body of fornix, 134
body of nail, 137
body pad, 609
body shirt, 337
body side molding, 427
body suit, 345
body temperature control unit, 512
body tube, 718
body whorl, 94
body wire, 666
boiler, 209
boiler, 208, 771
boiling-water reactor, 763
bole, 59
bolero, 338
boletus, 55
bolster, 224, 239, 242
bolt, 279
bolt, 278, 282, 290, 793
bolt assist mechanism, 796
bonding jumper, 312
bone folder, 577
boning knife, 242
bonnet, 294, 295
book ends, 517
bookbinding leather, 579
booking hall, 462
boom, 628, 782, 785
boom cylinder, 782, 785
boom truck, 506
boom vang, 628
booster intermediate station, 740
booster parachute, 510
boot, 356
boot, 542, 627, 635, 644, 645, 648
boot jack, 358
bootee, 354
Bootes, 11
borage, 74
bordeaux glass, 237
border, 188, 189
bore, 801
bottle cart, 306
bottle opener, 244, 688
bottom, 633, 640
bottom bracket axle, 448
bottom cylinder, 581
bottom deck, 741
bottom deckboard, 787
bottom line, 621
bottom of the pool, 626
bottom pocket, 675
bottom rail, 202, 225, 231
bottom ring, 753
bottom road, 736
bottom side rail, 470
bottom-end transverse member, 470

bottom-fold portfolio, 378
bottomboard, 543
boulevard, 52, 184
bound book, 577
bow, 544, 793
bow, 328, 497, 628, 631, 793
bow collar, 342
bow door, 493
bow loading door, 494
bow saw, 690
bow thruster, 497
bow tie, 324
bow window, 197
bowl, 682
bowl, 241, 251, 385, 484, 784
bowl with serving spout, 251
bowler, 599
bowline, 691
bowline on a bight, 691
bowling, 683
bowling ball, 683
bowling crease, 599
bowling lane, 683
bowls and petanque, 682
bows, 793
bowsprit, 479
bowstring, 684, 793
box, 156, 189, 204, 209
box bag, 381
box car, 470, 472
box end wrench, 279
box pallet, 787
box pleat, 228
box spring, 224
boxer, 669
boxer shorts, 325
boxer shorts, 353
boxing, 669
boxing gloves, 669
bra, 346
brace, 281
brace, 198, 302, 757
bracelets, 364
brachial, 120
brachial artery, 126
brachial plexus, 133
brachioradialis, 120, 121
bracket, 231
bracket base, 225
bract, 66
braided rope, 692
brail, 480
brain, 88
brake, 664, 727
brake cable, 447
brake caliper, 442
brake handle, 445
brake lever, 447
brake line, 432
brake lining, 432
brake loop, 636
brake pad, 432
brake pedal, 430
brake shoe, 432
brakelight, 429
brakeman, 643
branch, 58
branch, 59, 61, 72, 104, 215, 649, 726
branch clip, 726
branch duct, 206
branch return pipe, 208
branch supply pipe, 208
branches, 59
branching, plumbing, 298
brandy snifter, 237
brass family, 550
brassiere cup, 346
brattice, 181
brayer, 581
Brazil nut, 66
bread, 153
bread and butter plate, 238
bread guide, 252
bread knife, 242
break line, 341
breaker, 30
breast, 129
breast, 108, 116, 118
breast beam, 572
breast collar, 653
breast dart, 320
breast pocket, 320, 324
breast welt pocket, 322
breastplate, 792
breaststroke, 622
breaststroke kick, 622
breaststroke turn, 622
breather valve, 741
breathing in, 622
breathing out, 622

breech, 549
breech guard, 549
breechblock, 798, 799, 802
breechblock operating lever assembly,
  802
breeches, 315
breeches, 317, 667, 791
brick, 286
brick wall, 199
bricklayer's hammer, 291
bridge, 674
bridge, 52, 230, 376, 491, 544, 546,
  719, 810
bridge assembly, 547
bridging, 198
bridle, 649
bridle, 653
bridle assembly, 486
bridle tape, 541
briefcase, 378
briefs, 325, 346
brig, 482
brigantine, 482
brightness control, 529
brilliant cut facets, 363
brilliant full cut, 362
brim, 328, 329
briolette cut, 363
bristle, 373, 374
bristles, 304
broad beans, 72
broad ligament of uterus, 129
broad reach, 629
broad welt side pocket, 339
broad welt side pocket, 319, 330
broad-leaved endive, 73
**broadcast satellite
  communication**, 416
broadest of back, 121
broadsword, 794
broccoli, 69
brooch, 364
brood chamber, 82
brook, 676
broom, 205
brow brush and lash comb, 367
brow reinforce, 792
brow tine, 105
browband, 649
brown ball, 673
Brunn's membrane, 142
brush, 304, 582, 589
brush, 152, 373
brush and rails, 647
brush and rails, 646
Brussels sprouts, 73
bubble, 443
bucket, 754, 782
bucket cylinder, 782, 785
bucket hinge pin, 782
bucket lever, 782
bucket ring, 754
bucket seat, 428
bucket tooth, 782
bucket wheel excavator, 733
buckle, 566
buckle, 323, 380, 428, 641
buckwheat, 152
bud, 70
buffer tank, 740
buffet, 227
bugle, 550
building materials, 286, 288
building server, 216
building sewer, 215
built-in microphone, 409
bulb, 72, 104, 232, 233, 310, 743
bulb dibble, 268
bulb unit, 752
bulb vegetables, 70
bulbil, 70
bulbocavernous muscle, 127
bulk terminal, 490
bulkhead, 441
bulkhead flat car, 473
Bull, 11
bull's-eye, 698
bulldozer, 783
bulldozer, 733
bullet, 798
bullion stitch, 571
bulls-eye, 684
bulwark, 478
bumper, 260, 426, 440, 441, 464
bumper guard, 617
bumps, 826, 827
bunch, 384
bunch of grapes, 61
bund wall, 741
bundle, 72, 756

837

The terms in **bold type** indicate the title of an illustration.

bunker, 676
bunker oil, 745
bunker silo, 149
bunting, 817
bunting bag, 349
buoyage regions, 488
buoyancy compensator, 627
burgee, 817
burgundy glass, 237
burned gases, 436
burner, 209, 248, 634, 635, 689
burner frame, 689
burner gas tube, 297
burner ring, 248
burnisher, 582
burr, 105
bursting charge, 804
bus, 190
bus module, 49
bus shelter, 186
bus stop, 186
busbar, 747
bush, 263
bushing, 746, 747, 757
bustle, 316
butane tank, 386
butt, 386, 568, 579, 615, 670, 675, 796, 797
butt cap, 670
butt end, 609
butt grip, 671
butt guide, 671
butt plate, 795, 798, 799
butt section, 670
butt welding, 307
butt-strap, 376
butte, 46
butter compartment, 254
butter curler, 242
butter dish, 238
butter knife, 239
butterfly, 78, 79
butterfly kick, 623
butterfly stroke, 623
butterfly turn, 623
butterfly, hind leg, 78
buttock, 117, 119, 127, 128
button, 232, 324, 326, 530, 536, 666, 800
button loop, 323
button strap, 351
buttondown collar, 324
buttoned placket, 324, 326
buttonhole, 319
buttress, 176, 750
buttress dam, 750
buttress dam, cross section, 750
by-pass taxiway, 502
bypass duct, 501
bypass feeder, 532

C

c, 537
c clef, 537
C degrees, 705
C-clamp, 282
cab, 147, 160, 445, 782, 783, 784, 785
cabbage lettuce, 73
cabin, 496, 508
cabinet, 258, 259, 410
cable, 692
cable, 280, 406, 408, 660, 663, 684, 692
cable distributor, 416
cable drum compartment, 415
cable guard, 684
cable ripper, 311
cable shutter release, 393
cable sleeve, 280
cable stay anchorage, 456
cable stitch, 567
cable-stayed bridges, 456
cables, 414
cabochon cut, 363
caboose, 473
cabriole leg, 220
cabriolet, 220
Caelum, 13
café curtain, 228
cake mascara, 367
cake pan, 245
cakes, 588
calamus, 110
calandria, 759
calcaneus, 103, 123
calcar, 112
calculator, 523
calculator, 379

calculator dial, 396
calendar pad, 518
calf, 151
calf, 117, 119
caliper, 583
caliper, 432
call director telephone, 422
Callisto, 4
calls indicator, 420
calm, 38
calyx, 60, 62, 67, 132
cam ring, 281
cambium, 59
Camelopardus, 11
camera, 414
camera, 16, 412, 414
camera back, 390
camera body, 391
camera control area, 415
camera control technician, 412, 415
camera control unit, 412, 415
camera pedestal, 414
camera platform, 393
camera platform lock, 393
camera screw, 393
camera viewfinder, 414
camisole, 345
camping, 685, 686, 690
camping (tent), 823
camping (trailer and tent), 823
camping (trailer), 823
camping equipment, 688, 690
camping prohibited, 823
camping tools, 690
camping, accessories, 689
camshaft, 434
can opener, 256
can opener, 244, 688
Canadian football, playing field, 604
canal bed, 492
canal lock, 492
canal lock, 490
Cancer, 11
Cancer the Crab (June 22), 820
candlepin, 683
cane pen, 389
canes, 728
Canes Venatici, 11
canine, 98, 144
Canis Major, 13
Canis Minor, 11
canister vacuum cleaner, 260
canned failed fuel, 764
cannon, 101, 805
canopy, 636
canopy, 375, 636, 685, 785, 813
canopy release knob, 639
cantaloupe, 69
canteen, 690
cantilever, 750
cantilever bridge, 454
cantilever span, 454
cantle, 649
canvas, 589
canvas, 669
canvas divider, 685
cap, 301, 328
cap, 55, 201, 250, 309, 389, 398, 590, 773
cap iron, 277
cap sleeve, 339
cape, 331
cape, 51
capillary blood vessel, 137
capillary bore, 705
capital, 51, 166
capitulum, 60
caponiere, 179
capped column, 37
capped tee, 205
Capricorn the Goat (December 22), 820
Capricornus, 13
capstan button, 541
capsule, 725
capsule, section, 67
captain, 643
captain's quarters, 497
captain's seat, 500
capture, 697
car, 470
car, 630
car cleaning yard, 465
car coat, 330
car deck, 494
car repair shop, 465
car wash, 453
carabiner, 681
carabiner, 680

caraco jacket, 316
carafe, 247
carapace, 91, 96
caravan, 449
caraway seeded rye bread, 153
carbon dioxide gas coolant, 760
carbon dioxide reactor, 760
carburetor, 442
card case, 379
card case, 379
card games, 695
card games, symbols, 695
card reader, 422
card support, 40
cardboard, 589
cardigan, 326
cardinal marks, 488
cardoon, 72
Caribbean Sea, 20
caribou, 105
Carina, 13
carnassial, 98
carnivore's jaw, 98
carnivores, 31, 33
carom billiards, 673
carpal pad, 106
carpenter's hammer, 275
carpentry: tools, 275
carpentry: tools, 276
carpentry: tools, 278
carpentry: tools, 280
carpentry: tools, 282
carpentry: tools, 284
carpus, 102, 122
carriage, 800
carriage, 787, 802
carriage control dial, 569
carriage handle, 568
carriage return, 525
carriages, 568
carrier, 230, 446
carrier bag, 381
carrot, 71
carry-on bag, 382
carrying handle, 796
cart path, 676
cartography, 47, 50, 52
carton, 384
cartridge, 797
cartridge, 291, 295, 389, 404, 527, 730
cartridge (rifle), 798
cartridge (shotgun), 799
cartridge drive, 527
cartridge faucet, 295
cartridge film, 395
cartridge fuse, 312
cartridge stem, 295
cartridge tape recorder, 407
cartwheel hat, 329
carver's bench screw, 586
carving, 586
carving fork, 242
carving knife, 242
case, 358, 365, 539, 540, 705, 706, 710, 711, 798
casement, 203
casement window, 203
cash readout, 453
cashew, 66
casing, 211, 214, 271, 702
casing first string, 740
Caspian Sea, 21
cassette, 403
cassette, 408, 526
cassette compartment, 409, 411
cassette deck, 407
cassette drive, 526
cassette eject switch, 409, 411
cassette film, 395
cassette holder, 403
cassette player, 408
cassette player controls, 408
cassette tape deck, 403
cassette tape deck, 400
Cassiopeia, 11
cast-on stitches, 567
castanets, 554
castanets, 556
caster, 260, 553
castle, 180
castle, 180
casual shoe, 356
cat, 107
cat's head, 107
catalytic converter, 439
catalytic reforming plant, 744
catapult, 810
catch glove, 609
catcher, 595

catcher, 541, 597
catcher's glove, 595
catenary, 459
catering vehicle, 507
caterpillar, 78
cathedral, 176
cathedral, 184
cathedral, plan, 177
catwalk, 188
caudal fin, 87
caudal vertebrae, 103
cauliflower, 69
caulking gun, 291
cave, 24
cave, 30
cavernous body, 127
CD/ROM player, 526
cecum, 131
cedilla, 832
ceiling, 205, 616, 617
ceiling bracket, 230
ceiling collar, 205
ceiling fan, 214
ceiling fitting, 236
ceiling joist, 198
ceiling projector, 41
ceiling register, 207
celeriac, 71
celery, 72
celestial coordinate system, 3
celestial equator, 3
celestial meridian, 3
celestial sphere, 3
celiac trunk, 124, 132
cell, 79, 82
cell body, 135
cell membrane, 115
cell wall, 115
cello, 545
cellos, 557
cellular telephone, 417
Celsius scale, 705
cement screed, 200
cementum, 144
cemetery, 52
cent, 832
Centaur, 13
Centaurus, 13
center, 603, 605, 608, 610, 611, 697
center aisle, 460
center back, 601, 612, 613
center back vent, 322
center base, 818
center chief, 818
center circle, 601, 610
center console, 430
center court, 617
center divider strip, 186
center electrode, 439
center face-off circle, 608
center field, 597
center fielder, 597
center flag, 601
center forward, 601, 607, 612, 613
center half, 607
center hole, 404
center keelson, 743
center line, 607, 608, 610, 612, 618, 619, 620, 666, 682
center mark, 614
center pocket, 674
center point, 818
center post, 225, 427
center service line, 614
center span, 456
center spot, 601, 674
center strap, 614
center third, 611
center wheel, 706, 707
centerboard, 628
centering, 524
centering control, 529
Central America, 20
central circle, 611
central column, 774
central focusing wheel, 719
central incisor, 144
central nave, 173
central nervous system, 134
central pumping station, 740
central screw, 579
centrifugal compressor, 501
centriole, 115
cephalic vein, 126
cephalothorax, 90
Cepheus, 11
cereals, major types, 152
cerebellum, 134
cerebrum, 134
cervical vertebra (7), 123

INDEX

The terms in **bold type** indicate the title of an illustration.

cervical vertebrae, 102
Cetus, 11, 13
chain, 448, 661, 707
chain brake, 272
chain drive, 156, 158
chain guide, 448
chain mail, 792
chain of dunes, 46
chain of neurons, 135
chain pipe wrench, 299
chain stay, 446
chain stitch, 571
chain wheel A, 448
chain wheel B, 448
chainsaw, 272
chainsaw chain, 272
chairs, types, 223
chaise longue, 223
chalaza, 109
chalk, 675
Chamaeleon, 13
Chameleon, 13
chamois leather, 358
champagne flute, 237
chandelier, 236
change sign key, 523
channel scan buttons, 411
channel selector control, 411
chanter, 536
chanterelle, 55
Chantilly parquet, 200
chapel, 181
character correction, 525
charcoal, 588
charge, 799
charge indicator, 374
charges, examples, 819
charging handle, 796
charging light, 374
charging plug, 374
Charioteer, 11
Charleston cymbal, 552
charm bracelet, 364
charms, 364
Charon, 5
chart room, 494
chase, 800
check nut, 40
check valve, 216, 306
check-rail, 467
checkbook, 379
checkbook, 379
checkbook/secretary clutch, 379
cheek, 100, 106, 118, 275, 670, 800
cheek ring, 650
cheek strap, 649
cheese knife, 239
chemical treatment, 745
chemise, 181
chemistry, 831
cherimoya, 68
cherry, 63
chervil, 74
chess, 696
chess notation, 696
chessboard, 696
chess, men, 696
chess, movements, 696
chest, 100, 116, 118
chest expander, 665
chest protector, 595, 602, 684
chesterfield, 221
chestnut, 66, 100
chevet, 177
chevron, 818
chevron stitch, 571
chick, 150
chick peas, 72
chicory, 73
chief, 818
chief, 818
chief timekeeper, 621
chiffonier, 226
children's clothing, 349, 350
chimney, 205
chimney, 197, 209
chimney connection, 204
chimney pot, 197
chimney stack, 197
chin, 108, 118
chin guard, 777
chin protector, 443
chin rest, 544
chin strap, 602, 777
China Sea, 21
Chinese cabbage, 73
chisel, 581
Chisel, 13
chive, 70
chloroplast, 115

chock, 681
chock, 680
choir, 177
choir organ manual, 542
choker, 361
chord, 539
choroid, 140
Christmas tree, 740
Christmas tree, 738, 740
chromatin, 115
chromosphere, 6
chrysalis, 78
chrysalis, 82
chuck, 276, 280, 281, 283, 735
chuck key, 281
chukka, 354
church, 185
chute, 736
cicada, 77
cigar, 384
cigar band, 384
cigarette, 384
cigarette holder, 384
cigarette pack, 384
cigarette papers, 384
ciliary body, 140
ciliate, 56
cine scale, 396
circuit breaker, 212, 747
circuit vent, 215
circular body, 535
circular needle, 567
circular route, 52
circular saw, 284
circular saw blade, 284
circulating pump, 208, 772
circulation pump, 763
circumflex accent, 832
cirque, 7
cirrocumulus, 44
cirrostratus, 44
cirrus, 44
citrus fruits, 65
citrus fruits, major types, 65
citrus fruit, section, 65
citrus juicer, 243, 251
city, 51
city houses, 187
city limit, 52
clam, 93
clam cleat, 630
clam cleat, 630
clamp, 309, 370, 575, 578, 642
clamp binder, 519
clamp lever, 370
clamp spotlight, 235
clarinet, 548
clarinets, 556
clasp, 378, 380
class ring, 364
classic blouse, 337
classification yard, 465
clavicle, 122
claw, 78, 80, 90, 91, 97, 106, 107, 108, 112, 275, 364, 579
claw hammer, 275
claw, extended, 107
claw, retracted, 107
clay core, 748
cleaning brush, 374
cleaning tools, 260
cleanout, 296
clear key, 523
clear sky, 39
clear space, 613
clear-entry key, 523
cleat, 630
cleat, 628
cleated shoe, 602
cleaver, 242
clefs, 537
clew, 631
clew line, 481
click, 706, 707
cliff, 7, 23, 27, 30
climate control, 430
climates of the world, 45
climber, 664
climbing harness, 680
climbing iron, 358
climbing plant, 263
clinical thermometer, 705
clip, 515
clip, 230, 389, 711
clip earrings, 361
clipboard, 519
clippers, 369
clitoris, 128
cloche, 329
clock, 407, 413, 415, 430, 714

clock operator, 610
clock timer, 253, 255
clog, 357
close hauled, 629
close reach, 629
close-up lens, 392
closed stringer, 201
closed to bicycles, 828
closed to motorcycles, 828
closed to pedestrians, 828
closed to trucks, 828
closeness setting, 374
closet, 194, 226
closure rail, 467
cloth roller, 572
clothing guard, 727
cloud, 36
cloud ceiling, measure, 41
cloud of volcanic ash, 25
clouds, 44
clouds of vertical development, 44
clouds symbols, 44
cloudy sky, 39
clove hitch, 691
cloverleaf, 452
cloverleaf, 450
club, 695
club chair, 221
clubhouse, 651, 676
clubhouse turn, 651
clubs, golf, 678
clutch bag, 381
clutch housing, 444
clutch lever, 272, 442, 444
clutch pedal, 430
coach car, 460
coach's box, 597
coal mine, 733, 734, 736
coarse adjustment knob, 718
coastal features, 30
coat dress, 332
coat hook, 522
coat rack, 522
coat tree, 522
coats, types, 330
cob, 72
coccyx, 122
cochlea, 139
cochlear nerve, 139
cock, 795
cocking lever, 804
cockle, 93
cockleshell, 220
cockpit, 639
cockpit, 628
cockpit canopy, 638
cockpit ventilation, 639
cocktail cabinet, 227
cocktail glass, 237
coconut, 66
code, 524
coffee makers, 247
coffee mill, 256
coffee mug, 238
coffee pot, 688
coffee shop, 822
coffee spoon, 241
coil, 714
coil spring, 231
coiling, 584
coin chute, 702
coin purse, 379
coin reject slot, 702
coin return bucket, 422
coin slot, 422, 702
colander, 243
cold air, 501, 772
cold air inlet, 438
cold coolant, 771
cold heavy water, 761
cold shed, 491
cold-water circuit, 215
cold-water line, 293, 297
cold-water riser, 215
cold-water supply line, 296, 298
collar, 341
collar, 57, 319, 322, 324, 352, 374, 663
collar bar, 364
collar point, 324, 341
collar stay, 324
collaret, 318, 341
collars, types, 341, 342
collateral, 135
collecting funnel, 40
collecting vessel, 40
collector, 753
collet, 283, 393
colon, 832

color chart, 592
color control, 532
color display, 569
color filter, 392
color selection filter, 410
color spray, 190
color television camera, 512
colored pencils, 588
colors, examples, 819
colter, 156, 158
colter's shaft, 156
Columba, 13
columella, 94
columella fold, 94
column, 24, 36, 166, 168, 169, 208, 236, 283, 393, 399, 455, 561, 621, 700, 701
column crank, 393
column lock, 393
column of mercury, 705
column radiator, 208
coma, 9
Coma Berenices, 11
comb, 574
comb, 792
combat aircraft, 812
combination box and open end wrench, 279
combination lock, 378
combine harvester, 160
combine harvester, 155
combs, 368
combustion, 436, 437, 501
combustion chamber, 434, 438
comet, 9
comforter, 224
comma, 832
command control dial, 391
command key, 530
command module, 509
commander's seat, 805
commando knife, 794
commercial area, 190
commissure of lips of mouth, 142
common carotid artery, 126
common extensor of fingers, 121
common iliac artery, 126, 132
common iliac vein, 132
common periwinkle, 83
common peroneal nerve, 133
common scientific symbols, 830
common symbols, 822
common whipping, 691
communicating ramus, 135
communication antenna, 810
communication devices, 526
communication module, 418
communication panels, 500
communication set, 477
communication tunnel, 510
communications volume controls, 512
commuter train, 464
compact, 366
compact disk, 405
compact disk, 408
compact disk player, 405
compact disk player, 400, 407, 408
compact disk player controls, 408
compact disk unit, 527
compartment, 701
compass, 639
compass bridge, 494, 495, 497
compass card, 484, 719
compass meridian line, 719
competition ring, 646
competitive course, 621
completion, 692
complex dune, 46
complexus, 121
compluvium, 170, 171
compound bow, 684
compound eye, 79, 80, 81
compound leaves, 52
compressed air reservoir, 469
compressed-air cylinder, 627, 777
compression, 436, 437, 501
compression coupling, 296
compression fitting, 300
compression link, 147
compression/admission, 436
compressor, 212, 517
compressor turbine, 438, 501
computer communication, 417
computer room, 807
computer screen intensity controls, 512
computer table, 521
concave, 160
concave lens, 722
concha, 139
Concorde, 19

The terms in **bold type** indicate the title of an illustration.

concrete base, 714
concrete block, 286
concrete drain, 741
concrete shielding, 760, 761, 762, 763
concrete wall, 772
condensation, 35
condensation of steam into water, 767
condensation pool, 763
condenser, 717, 718, 758, 771
condenser adjustment knob, 718
condenser backwash inlet, 759
condenser backwash outlet, 759
condenser coil, 214
condenser cooling water inlet, 759
condenser cooling water outlet, 759
condenser fan, 214
condenser height adjustment, 718
condominiums, 187
conductor's podium, 556
cone, 24, 58
**configuration of an office
    automation system**, 526
conic projection, 50
conical broach roof, 183
conical buoy, 487
conical buoy, 489
conical washer, 293
conifer, 58
conjunctiva, 140
connecting cable, 400, 406, 585
connecting module, 528
connecting rod, 434, 436
connecting terminal, 561
connection, 697
connection box, 412
connection cable, 530
connection point, 757
connective tissue, 137
connector, 300, 312, 406
conning tower, 807
**constellations of the Northern
    Hemisphere**, 10
**constellations of the Southern
    Hemisphere**, 12
constriction, 705
consumer, 417
consumer number, 712
contact, 697
contact, 233
contact lever, 235
contact printer, 398
container, 470
container, 40, 250, 304, 495
container car, 473
container hold, 495
container ship, 494
container ship, 490
container terminal, 491
container-loading bridge, 490
container/pallet loader, 507
containment building, 765, 766
contents identification cardboard, 743
contest area, 668
contestant, 668
continent, 29
continental climates, 45
continental margin, 29
continental rise, 29
continental shelf, 22, 29
continental slope, 22, 29
continents, configuration, 20
continuity tester, 310
continuous beam, 454
continuous drizzle, 39
continuous rain, 39
continuous snow, 39
contour feather, 110
contrabassoons, 556
contrast control, 529, 532
control bar, 637
control box, 297
control cable, 270, 448
control column, 500
control console, 16, 500
control deck, 493, 699
control key, 530
control keys, 421
control knob, 255, 257, 258, 259
control knobs, 531
control lever, 735
control pad, 699
control panel, 257, 532
control panel, 210, 214, 253, 255,
    258, 259, 391, 532, 717, 779
control rod, 760, 761, 762, 763
control room, 14, 15, 16, 189, 407,
    746, 759
control rooms, television, 412
control room, radio, 407
control stand, 468

control stick, 508, 639
control tower, 502, 810
control tower cab, 502
control valve, 689
control visual display, 717
control wheel, 500, 778
convection zone, 6
convector, 211
convenience outlet, 310
convention center, 184
converging lenses, 722
convertible, 425
convex lens, 722
conveyor, 733, 735
conveyor belt, 504
cook's knife, 242
cookie cutters, 245
cookie sheet, 245
cooking set, 688
cooking surface, 253
cooking utensils, 248
cooktop, 255
cooktop edge, 255
cool tip, 370
coolant, 766
coolant, 771
coolant inlet, 768
coolant outlet, 768
coolant transfers the heat to the steam
    generator, 766
coolant: boiling water, 763
coolant: carbon dioxide, 760
coolant: pressurized heavy water,
    761
coolant: pressurized water, 762
cooler, 690
cooling, 744
cooling fan, 434, 438
cooling/heating coils, 213
copper plate, 582
copper to plastic, 301
copper to steel, 301
coprocessor, 528
copy output mode, 532
copy quantity, 532
copyright, 831
corbel, 180, 181
corbel piece, 204
cord, 231, 256, 260, 268, 271, 310,
    578
cord grip, 658
cord sleeve, 283, 305
cord tieback, 229
cordate, 56
cordless telephone, 422
core, 6, 64, 677, 692, 798
coriander, 74
corinthian order, 167
cork ball, 596
cork tip, 618
corkscrew, 688
corn, 72, 152
corn salad, 73
cornea, 140
corner, 577, 669
corner arc, 601
corner cap, 470
corner cupboard, 227
corner fitting, 470
corner flag, 601, 607
corner pad, 669
corner pin, 682
corner stool, 669
corner structure, 470
corner stud, 198
corner tower, 180
cornerpiece, 383
cornet, 550, 556
cornice, 166, 168, 196, 202, 225, 229
corolla, 60
corona, 6
Corona Australis, 13
Corona Borealis, 11
corona radiata, 128
coronet, 101
corpus callosum, 134
correction fluid, 515
correction key, 569
correction paper, 515
corridor connection, 461
corrosive, 821
corselette, 347
corset, 346
cortex, 132
Corvus, 13
corymb, 60
cosmetic tray, 382
costal shield, 97
cot, 726
cotehardie, 316

cottage, 187
cottage curtain, 228
cotter pin, 290
cotton applicators, 725
couched stitches, 571
counter, 352
counter reset button, 403
counterguard, 179
counterjib, 786
counterjib ballast, 786
counterscarp, 178
countersink, 281
counterweight, 15, 147, 404, 457,
    471, 721, 784, 785, 786
country, 51
coupler head, 471
coupler head, 147, 156, 157, 158,
    159, 162, 469
coupler knuckle, 471
coupler knuckle pin, 471
coupler-tilt tablet, 542
coupling bolt, 754
coupling guide device, 459
course, golf, 676
court referee, 612
courtyard, 172, 173
couscous kettle, 249
couter, 792
cover, 375
cover, 213, 251, 309, 386, 532, 596,
    677, 705, 712, 719, 796, 804
covered parapet walk, 180
covered way, 178
covering, 579
covering, 619
covering disk, 158
covering grille, 208
covering materials, 286
cow, 151
cow hitch, 691
cowl, 426
cowl neck, 342
Cowper's gland, 127
cowshed, 149
coxa, 78, 80
coxed four, 632
coxed pair, 632
coxless four, 632
coxless pair, 632
Crab, 11, 90
cradle, 399, 720, 721, 802
crak rye bread, 153
crakow, 318
crampon strap, 680
cranberry, 62
Crane, 13, 14, 738
crane runway, 786
cranial nerves, 133
crank, 281, 448, 671, 793
crank handle, 583
crankcase, 436
crankshaft, 434, 436
crash helmet, 643
crater, 7, 13, 25, 733
crawl kick, 622
crawler tractor, 783
crayfish, 90
creamer, 238
crease, 323
credenza, 520
creel, 672
cremaster, 78
crenate, 56
crenel, 181
crenulate margin, 95
crepidoma, 166, 168, 169
crescendo pedal, 542
crescent, 819
crescent wrench, 279
crescentic dune, 46
crest, 27, 30, 596, 790
crest of spillway, 746
crevasse, 26
crevice tool, 260
crew neck, 350
crew neck sweater, 326
crew quarters, 494
crew's locker, 461
cribriform plate of ethmoid, 141
cricket, 598
cricket ball, 598
cricket player, 598
cricket shoe, 598
cricquet, field, 599
crimping, 799
crisper, 254
crisscross curtains, 229
crochet hook, 567
croissant, 153
crook, 548

crook key, 548
crop elevator, 160
cross, 818
cross brace, 727
cross cut, 736
cross handle, 701
cross head, 276
cross rail, 223
**cross section of an electron
    microscope**, 717
cross stitches, 571
cross-country ski, 642
cross-country ski, 642
cross-country skier, 642
cross-country skiing, 642
cross-headed tip, 276
cross-tip screwdriver, 688
crossarm, 756, 757
crossbar, 446, 535, 574, 578, 626,
    637, 657
crossbeam, 572
crossbow, 793, 793
crossbuck sign, 471
crosshead, 787
crossing, 176, 177
crossing gate mechanism, 471
crossover back straps overalls,
    351
crossover cargo deck line, 743
crosspiece, 219, 572, 728
crosstree, 628
crosswise grain, 566
crotch, 325
crotch piece, 337
croup, 101, 661
Crow, 13
crown, 59, 109, 144, 328, 329, 363,
    483, 545, 553, 590, 706
crown block, 737
crown tine, 105
crownpiece, 649
crude oil, 744
crude-oil pipeline, 740
crus of helix, 139
crushing roll, 158
crustacean, 90
Crux, 13
crystal button, 236
crystal drop, 236
cucumber, 69
cue ball, 673
cuff, 315
cuff, 323, 324, 354, 609
cuff link, 339
cuirass, 791
cuisse, 792
culet, 363
culottes, 334
cultivated mushroom, 55
cultivating soil, steps, 154
cultivator, 157
cultivator, 154
cumulonimbus, 44
cumulus, 44
cup, 238, 688
Cup, 13, 798
cup gasket, 730
cupola, 486
cupule, 66
curb, 186
curb bit, 650
curb bit, 649
curb chain, 649, 650
curb hook, 650
curb rein, 649
curled endive, 73
curled kale, 73
curler, 620
curling, 620
curling brooms, 620
curling brush, 370
curling iron, 370
curling stone, 620
curling, rink, 620
currant, 62
**currency abbreviations,
    examples**, 832
currency exchange, 823
current coil, 712
cursor movement keys, 530
curtain, 229
curtain, 178, 383, 414
curtain pole, 230
curtain track, 230
curtain wall, 180
curtains, types, 228
curved jaw, 278
customer's service entrance, 757
customs control, 505
customs house, 491

cut for gemstones, 363
cut-off trench, 748, 749
cuticle nippers, 365
cuticle pusher, 365
cuticle scissors, 365
cuticle trimmer, 365
cutlery basket, 257
cutlery set, 688
cutter, 311
cutter bar, 158, 160
cutter link, 272
cutting blade, 250, 256, 578
cutting cylinder, 271
cutting edge, 239, 242, 369, 783, 784
cutting guide, 578
cutting line, 565
cutting oxygen handle, 306
cutting tip, 306
cutting torch, 306
cutting wire, 584
cyclorama, 414
Cygnus, 11
cylinder, 290, 295, 436, 784, 797
cylinder case, 290
cylinder head cover, 435
cylinder pressure gauge, 306
cylindrical buoy, 486
cylindrical projection, 50
cymbal, 552
cymbals, 554
cymbals, 557
cypress scalelike leaves, 58
cytoplasm, 115, 128

D

d, 537
«D», 674
dabber, 581
dagger, 794
daggerboard, 631
daggerboard well, 631
dairy, 149
dairy compartment, 254
dairy products, 33
dam, 746
damper, 206, 541, 585
damper lever, 541
damper pedal, 540, 555
damper rail, 541
dandelion, 73
danger, 488
danger area, 668
Danish rye bread, 153
darkness, 489
dart, 698
dart, 565
dartboard, 698
dart, playing area, 698
dash, 832
dashboard, 430, 430
dashboard, 442
data bus, 528, 531
data display, 396, 409, 411, 421
data display illumination button, 396
data hold, 310
data record system, 717
data storage devices, 526
date, 63
dater, 516
dating nail, 466
davit, 478, 742
daymark, 486, 487
daymarks (region B), 489
dead ball line, 606
dead bolt, 289, 290
dead bowl area, 682
deadly poisonous mushroom, 55
death, 831
decanter, 237
deceleration lane, 452
decimal key, 523
decimal tab, 524
deck, 441, 454, 455, 456, 736
deck arch bridge, 455
deck crane, 811
declination, 3
declination axis, 14
declination setting scale, 720, 721
décolleté bra, 346
decorative braid, 349
decoy launcher, 809
deep fryer, 252
deep peroneal nerve, 133
deep-sea floor, 22
deer antlers, 105
deer crossing, 828
deer family, 105
deer, kinds, 105
defending zone, 608

defense, 603, 605
defense third, 611
deferent duct, 127
deflector, 210, 264, 271
degree, 830
Deimos, 4
delete key, 530
delicious lactarius, 55
delivery, 682
delivery entrance, 190
delivery ramp, 184
Delphinus, 11
delta wing, 499
deltoid, 120
deluge gun, 778
demilune, 179
demitasse, 238
dendrite, 135
dental alveolus, 144
dental care, 373
dental floss, 373
dentate, 56
dentil, 166, 167
dentin, 144
departure time indicator, 463
deployment mechanism, 49
depressed-center flat car, 473
depth adjustment, 283
depth gauge, 627
depth of focus, 23
depth scale, 485
depth stop, 283
depth-adjustment mechanism, 277
depth-of-field preview button, 391
depth-of-field scale, 392
derby, 328
dermis, 137
derrick, 737, 738, 740, 743
derrick mast, 743
descender, 681
descending aorta, 124
descending colon, 131
desert, 46
desert, 45
designed orbit, 48
desk lamp, 234
desk mat, 520
desk tray, 517
desktop video unit, 527
despun section, 42
dessert fork, 240
dessert knife, 239
dessert spoon, 241
destination, 463
destroying angel, 55
detachable control, 253
detection of seismic waves, 714
detergent dispenser, 257
detonator, 804
deuterium oxide upgrading, 759
developer bath, 399
developing baths, 399
developing tank, 398
dew, 37
dew pad, 106
dew shield, 721
dewclaw, 106
dexter, 818
dexter base, 818
dexter chief, 818
dexter flank, 818
diacritic symbols, 832
diagonal, 756
diagonal buttress, 177
diagonal movement, 696
diagram of weaving, diagram of principle, 576
dial, 705, 706, 707, 708, 712
dial-type display, 485
diamond, 362, 695
diamond interchange, 451
diamond mesh metal lath, 286
diamond point, 225
diaper, 349
diaphragm, 130, 390, 400, 406
diastema, 98
dibble, 268
dice, 699
dice cup, 697
die, 697
diesel engine, 437
diesel engine, 469, 495, 782, 785
diesel engine ventilator, 468
diesel engines, 809
diesel lift engine, 493
diesel motor, 783
diesel oil, 745
diesel propulsion engine, 492

diesel shop, 464
diesel-electric locomotive, 468
diffuser, 396
diffuser pin, 264
digestive gland, 92
digestive system, 131
digit, 84
digital audio tape recorder, 407
digital display, 310, 709, 710
digital frequency display, 402
digital nerve, 133
digital pad, 106, 107
digital pulp, 137
digital video effects monitor, 413
digital video special effects, 413
digital watch, 706
digitizing pad, 526
dike, 25
dill, 74
dimmer room, 412
dimmer switch, 309
dimple, 677
dining car, 460
dining room, 171, 195, 496, 807
dining section, 460
dinner fork, 240
dinner knife, 239
dinner plate, 238
dinnerware, 238
diode, 769
dioptric ring, 486
dioxide, 33
dip switch, 444
dipper, 592
dipper bucket, 785
direct home reception, 416
direct-reading rain gauge, 40
direction of Mecca, 173
direction of points, 488
direction to be followed, 824, 825
directional sign, 475
director's chair, 220
disc faucet, 295
discharge bay, 764
discharge line, 216
discharge liner, 753
discharge pipe, 742
discus, 658
discus and hammer throw, 654
disgorger, 672
dishwasher, 257, 298
dishwasher, 298
disk, 157, 432, 433, 529, 583, 663, 712
disk brake, 432
disk brake, 442
disk camera, 395
disk compartment, 405
disk compartment control, 405
disk drive, 555
disk drive port, 528
disk motor, 529
disk spacing lever, 158
diskette, 526
diskette drive, 526
disks, 251
display, 420, 422, 523, 709
display cabinet, 227, 522
display setting, 420
disposable camera, 394
disposable fuel cylinder, 299, 307
disposable razor, 374
distal phalanx, 107, 122, 123, 137
distal sesamoid, 102
distance, 376
distance scale, 392
distance travelled, 711
distribution board, 757
distribution box, 216
distribution by cable network, 416
distributor cap, 435
distributor service loop, 757
district, 52
district limit, 52
ditch, 451, 682
diverging lenses, 722
diversion canal, 746
divide key, 523
divider, 160, 378
dividers, 519
dividing breeching, 779
diving, 624
diving glove, 627
diving installations, 624
diving tower, 624
diving, entries, 624
diving, flights, 624
diving, starting positions, 624
division, 830
do not iron, 829

do not use chlorine bleach, 829
do not wash, 829
dock, 490
document folder, 519
document handler, 532
document receiving, 421
document-to-be-sent position, 421
does not belong to, 830
dog, 106
dog ear collar, 341
dog's forepaw, 106
dog, morphology, 106
dollar, 832
Dolphin, 11
dome roof, 183
dome shutter, 14
dome tent, 686
domestic appliances, 250, 252, 254, 256, 257, 258, 260
dominoes, 695
door, 202, 429
door, 173, 225, 253, 259, 427, 449, 498, 617, 685, 686
door access, 709
door handle, 427
door lock, 427
door open warning light, 431
door panel, 225
door shelf, 254
door stop, 254, 471
door switch, 259
doorknob, 202, 289
doors, types, 202
Dorado, 13
doric order, 167
dormant volcano, 24
dorsalis pedis artery, 126
dorsum of nose, 141
dot matrix printer, 531
dot matrix printer, 527
double, 646
double bass, 545
double basses, 557
double bend, 826, 827
double boiler, 249
double curtain rod, 230
double flat, 538
double glazing, 772
double handles, 633
double kitchen sink, 215
double oxer, 647
double oxer, 646
double pennant, 817
double plate, 198
double pole breaker, 312
double reed, 549
double ring, 698
double scull, 632
double seat, 477
double sharp, 538
double sheet bend, 691
double zero, 700
double zero key, 523
double-blank, 695
double-breasted buttoning, 319
double-breasted jacket, 322
double-decked pallet, 787
double-edge blade, 374
double-edge razor, 374
double-leaf bascule bridge, 457
double-six, 695
double-twist auger bit, 281
doubles pole, 614
doubles service court, 618
doubles sideline, 614, 618
doublet, 316
doublet, 695
doubling die, 697
doubly dentate, 56
dough hook, 250
dousing water tank, 759, 766
dousing water valve, 759
Dove, 13
dovetail, 718
down tube, 447
down wind, 629
downspout, 197
downstream face, 749
downstream shoulder, 748
downstream toe, 748
downtown, 184
dozen (1 to 12), 700, 701
dozen (13 to 24), 700, 701
dozen (25 to 36), 700, 701
drachma, 832
Draco, 11
draft arm, 784
draft hole, 209
draft tube, 747, 753, 784
drafting machine, 591

drafting table, 591
drag, 670
Dragon, 11
dragonfly, 77
drain, 215
drain hose, 257, 258, 298
drain tile, 199
drain valve, 297, 741
drainage blanket, 748
drainage layer, 748
draining circuit, 215
draining spoon, 244
draped neck, 343
draped neckline, 343
draped swag, 229
draw drapery, 229
draw hoe, 266
draw tube, 718
drawbar, 803
drawbar lock, 803
drawbridge, 180
drawer, 219, 226, 255
drawers, 325
drawing, 586, 588, 590, 592
drawing, accessories, 591, 592
drawing, equipment, 589
drawstring, 320, 381
drawstring bag, 381
drawstring hood, 351
dredger, 246
dress with bustle, 316
dress with crinoline, 318
dress with panniers, 317
dresser, 226
dresses, types, 332
dressing room, 189
dressmaker's model, 564
drift, 736
drill, 280
drill collar, 737
drill pipe, 737
drill press, 283
drill rod, 734
drill ship, 739
drilling drawworks, 737
drilling rig, 737
drip bowl, 255
drip dry, 829
drip molding, 427
drive belt, 258
drive chain, 446
drive shaft, 492, 508
drive wheel, 256, 280
drive wheels, 784
driver, 652, 678
driver's cab, 459, 468
driver's seat, 805
driveway, 193, 196
driving glove, 327
driving turbine, 438
driving wheel, 147, 575
drone, 81
drone pipe, 536
drop earrings, 361
drop light, 310
drop waist dress, 332
drop-leaf, 219
drum, 167, 231, 259, 432, 484, 707, 714
drum brake, 432
drums, 552
drupelet, 62
dry continental - arid, 45
dry continental - semiarid, 45
dry dock, 490
dry flat, 829
dry fruits, 66
dry gallery, 24
dry point, 582
dry subtropical, 45
dry well, 763
drying, 829
drypoint, 583
dual seat, 443
dual swivel mirror, 368
duck, 150
duckpin, 683
duffel bag, 380, 381
duffle coat, 320
dugout, 597
dumbbell, 665
dump, 733, 734
dump body, 785
dump truck, 785
dune, 30
duo, 558
duodenum, 131
dura mater, 134, 135
dust, 34, 35
dust cover, 404

dust receiver, 260
dust tail, 9
dusting brush, 260
Dutch oven, 249
duty-free shop, 505
dynamic brake, 468
dynamic microphone, 406
dynamics propeller, 492

E

e, 537
eagle, 819
Eagle, 11
ear, 107, 112, 116, 223
ear cushion, 406
ear drum, 139
ear flap, 328
ear loaf, 153
ear plugs, 729
ear protection, 729
ear protection, 821
earphone, 406
earpiece, 376, 726
earrings, 361
Earth, 4, 8
Earth coordinate system, 3
earth foundation, 450
earth radiation scanner, 43
earth radiation sensor, 43
earth sensor, 42, 43, 49
earth signs, 820
Earth's atmosphere, profile, 19
Earth's crust, 22, 23
Earth's crust, section, 22
earthquake, 23
Earth, structure, 22
ear, auricle, 139
ear, parts, 138
easel, 398, 591
East, 488
East cardinal mark, 489
East reflector deployment, 419
Eastern hemisphere, 47
Eastern meridian, 47
eccrine sweat gland, 136
echinus, 167
echo, 722
echo sounder, 485
echo sounder probe, 485
eclipse crossing, 419
eclipse preparation, 419
eclipses, types, 8
ecliptic, 3
ecology, 31, 32, 34
edge, 288, 564, 640, 643, 644, 719
edger, 271
edging, 263
edible crustaceans, 90
edible gastropods, 83
edible mollusks, 93
edible mushrooms, 55
edit/search buttons, 409
effluent, 216
egg, 109, 128
egg, 82
egg beater, 245
egg butt snaffle bit, 650
egg poacher, 249
egg slicer, 246
egg timer, 244
egg tray, 254
eggplant, 69
eggs, 84, 89
Egyptian reed pen, 389
eight, 632
eight cut, 362
eighth note, 538
eighth rest, 538
ejaculatory duct, 127
eject button, 403
ejection port, 796
ejection seat, 813
ejector, 784
elastic, 224
elastic ligament, 92, 107
elastic strainer, 685, 686
elastic support bandage, 725
elastic waistband, 321
elastic webbing, 323
elasticized leg opening, 325
elbow, 301
elbow, 100, 106, 112, 117, 119, 206
elbow pad, 602, 609
elbow, 45°, 301
electric baseboard radiator, 210
electric circuit, 233
electric connection, 207, 213
electric drill, 280
electric dryer, 259

electric foil, 666
electric furnace, 207
electric golf cart, 679
electric guitar, 547
electric kiln, 585
electric motor, 209, 268, 271, 438
electric range, 255
electric razor, 374
electric variometer, 639
electrical box, 309
electrical connection, 441
electrical connection panel, 415
electrical hazard, 821
electrical inlet, 585
electrical payout linkage, 702
electrical power unit, 506
electrical scoring apparatus, 666
electrician's tools, 311
electricity, 309, 310, 312, 746, 748, 750, 752, 754, 756
electricity cable, 186
electricity meter, 757
electricity production, 767
electricity production room, 806
electricity transmission, 757
electricity transmission, 767
electricity transmission network, 771
electricity, tools, 310, 311
electrode, 232, 305
electrode assembly, 209
electrode holder, 305
electrode lead, 305
electron beam, 410, 717
electron beam positioning, 717
electron gun, 410
electron gun, 410, 717
electron microscope, 717
electron microscope elements, 717
electronic ballast, 233
electronic flash, 393
electronic instruments, 555
electronic piano, 555
electronic scales, 709
electronic typewriter, 524
electronic viewfinder, 409
elevating arc, 802
elevating cylinder, 780, 786
elevating handle, 803
elevation, 193
elevation adjustment, 718
elevator, 15, 190, 499, 639, 736, 764, 811
elevon, 511
ellipses, 832
elliptical galaxy, 9
embankment, 450
embankment dam, 748
embankment dam, cross section, 748
emblem, 817
embrasure, 179
embroidered fabric, 571
embroidery, 571
emerald, 362
emerald cut, 362
emergency brake, 477
emergency electric motor, 806
emergency regulator, 627
emergency support vessel, 739
emergency switch, 444
emery boards, 365
emery pack, 563
emission antenna, 418
emission/reception antenna, 418
empty set, 830
emptying hose, 258
en prison, 700, 701
enamel, 144
enclosure, 149
end bracket, 230
end button, 230
end button, 544
end cap, 230, 765
end door, 470
end grain, 288
end joist, 198, 199
end ladder, 470
end line, 604, 610, 613, 619
end piece, 127
end plate, 765
end stop, 230, 630
end wall, 621
end zone, 604
end-piece, 674
endocarp, 63, 64
endoplasmic reticulum, 115
endpaper, 577
endpiece, 376
energy saving bulb, 233
engagement ring, 364

engine, 147, 442, 737, 784, 787, 805
engine and crew alarm display, 500
engine block, 435
engine control room, 742
engine fuel valves, 500
engine housing, 272
engine mounting pylon, 499
engine room, 496, 806
engines, 510
engines, types, 436
English billiards, 673
English billiards and snooker, 674
English cane, 728
English horn, 548
English horns, 557
English loaf, 153
enlarger, 399
enlarger timer, 399
enlarging lens, 399
ensiling, 155, 162
ensiling tube, 162
entablature, 166, 168, 202
enter key, 530
entire, 56
entrance, 82, 452
entrance slide, 82
entrance turnstile, 474
entries, 624
entry, 625, 787
envelope, 634
epaulet, 319
epaulet sleeve, 340
épée, 666
épéeist, 667
epicalyx, 62
epicenter, 23
epicondyle, 123
epidermis, 137
epiglottis, 130, 142, 143
epitrochlea, 123
equal key, 523
equalizing buckle, 231
equator, 3, 47
equilateral, 174
equilibrator, 802
equipment compartment, 458
equipment lock, 764
equipment rack, 412, 415
equipment section, 16
Equuleus, 11
erase button, 420
eraser, 515
eraser holder, 515
erecting lenses, 718
Eridanus, 13
ermine, 819
escalator, 189, 190, 474
escape wheel, 706, 707
escapement mechanism, 539
escudo, 832
escutcheon, 95, 289, 295, 296
esophagus, 88, 92, 97, 130, 131, 142
espadrille, 357
espresso coffee maker, 247
etching press, 581
Eurasia, 21
Europa, 4
Europe, 21
European Community Currency, 832
European plug, 309
Eustachian tube, 139, 141
Eutelsat II, 418
euthynteria, 166, 168
evaporation, 34, 35
evaporator blower, 214
evaporator coils, 214
even, 700, 701
evening glove, 327
examples of instrumental groups, 558
exclamation point, 832
excretory opening, 83
executive desk, 520
executive length, 325
exercise wear, 353
exhalation valve, 730
exhaust, 436, 437, 501
exhaust duct, 501
exhaust gas admission, 438
exhaust guide vanes, 501
exhaust manifold, 435, 437, 438, 439
exhaust nozzle, 812
exhaust pipe, 438, 439, 443, 444, 508, 735
exhaust port, 436, 735
exhaust stack, 147, 440, 784
exhaust system, 439
exhaust tube, 232
exhaust valve, 435, 436, 438

INDEX

The terms in **bold type** indicate the title of an illustration.

exit, 452
exit cone, 82
exit taxiway, 505
exit turnstile, 474
exocarp, 62, 63, 64
exosphere, 19
expandable file pouch, 378
expanding file, 517
expansion bolt, 276
expansion chamber, 485, 705
expansion connector, 528
expansion diaphragm, 485
expansion space, 466
expansion tank, 208, 772
expert drivers course, 646
explosion, 436
explosive, 821
export pipeline, 738
exposure adjustment knob, 391
exposure meter, 396
exposure mode, 391
exposure value, 396
exposure-time scale, 396
extended character, 530
extended claw, 107
extension, 219
extension ladder, 302
extension pipe, 260
extension table, 219
exterior dome shell, 14
exterior door, 202
exterior gauge, 578
exterior of a house, 196
exterior pocket, 378, 382
exterior sign, 474
external ear, 138
external gills, 84
external jugular vein, 126
external oblique, 120, 121
external tank, 510
external tooth lock washer, 278
extrados, 174
eye, 140
eye, 83, 90, 96, 97, 107, 118, 275,
    562, 563, 573, 649, 671, 681
eye guard, 777
eye makeup, 367
eye protection, 729
eye protection, 821
eye ring, 109
eyeball, 140
eyeball, 84
eyebrow, 140
eyebrow pencil, 367
eyebrow stripe, 109
eyebrow tweezers, 365
eyeglasses, 376
eyeglasses case, 379
eyeglasses parts, 376
eyeglasses, major types, 377
eyelash, 140
eyelash curler, 367
eyelashes, 107
eyelet, 230, 353, 354, 381, 569, 644
eyelet tab, 354
eyelid, 97
eyepiece, 390, 396, 409, 718, 719,
    720, 721
eyepiece holder, 721
eyeshadow, 367
eyestalk, 83

F

f, 537
f clef, 537
F degrees, 705
F-1 engine, 509
fabric care, 829
fabric guide, 256
fabric structure, 566
façade, 175
face, 116, 179, 275, 277, 579, 619,
    677, 733, 736
face mask, 602, 609, 643
face shield, 308
face side, 288
face-off circle, 608
face-off spot, 608
facepiece, 730
faceplate, 289, 290
facial makeup, 366
facial nerve, 139
facsimile machine, 421
facsimile machine, 417
factorial, 830
faculae, 6
Fahrenheit scale, 705
failed fuel bay, 764
failed fuel canning, 764

fairing, 442
fairlead, 630
fairway, 676
fall, 341
fall front, 226
falling rocks, 826, 827
fallopian tube, 128
fallopian tubes, 128
fallout, 35
fallow, 148
false rib (3), 123
false tuck, 349
family tent, 685
fan, 162, 209, 212, 259, 501, 528
fan belt, 434
fan brush, 366, 589
fan cable stays, 456
fan control, 214
fan heater, 211
fan housing, 370
fan motor, 214
fan thermostat, 438
fan trellis, 263
fan's tube, 162
fang, 96
fanion, 817
fantail, 773
far turn, 651
farm animals, 150
farm pollution, 32
farmhouse, 148
farmhouse bread, 153
farmstead, 148
farmyard, 148
fascia, 166
fast data entry control, 555
fast forward, 831
fast forward, 411
fast forward button, 411
fast operation, 405
fast-forward button, 403, 408, 420
fastener binder, 519
fasteners, 566
fastening device, 230
fastening system, 661
faucet, 292
fault, 23
feather crown, 618
feather stitch, 571
feathering, 684
feed dog, 562
feed lever, 283
feed pin, 531
feed table, 162
feed tube, 251
feeder header, 759
feeder output tray, 532
feeding tube, 160
feedwater, 760, 761, 762, 763
feet, 579
feet protection, 730
feet protection, 821
feet-first entry, 586
feet, principal types, 111
felt, 581
felt hat, 328, 329
felt tip pen, 588
female, 831
female cone, 58
female ferrule, 670
female genital organs, 128, 129
femoral artery, 126
femoral nerve, 133
femoral vein, 126
femur, 78, 80, 103, 122
fence, 148
fencer, 667
fencing, 666
fencing shoe, 667
fencing weapons, 666
fencing, parts of the weapon, 666
fencing, piste, 666
fencing, positions, 667
fencing, target areas, 667
fender, 426, 440, 446
fennel, 72
ferrule, 304, 369, 375, 675, 678
ferry, 494
ferryboat, 491
fertilizers, 32
fertilizing soil, 154, 156
fetlock, 101
fetlock joint, 101
fettling knife, 585
fiber, 692
fibula, 102, 122, 315
field hockey, 607
field judge, 605
field lens, 718
field lens adjustment, 718

fielder's glove, 596
fielders, 599
15 yards line, 606
fifth, 537
5th metacarpal, 112
fifth wheel, 440
fifty-yard line, 604
figure skate, 644
figure ski, 633
figure skiing handle, 633
figure-eight knot, 691
filament, 6, 60, 232
filament support, 233
file, 277
file, 688
file guides, 518
filing box, 517
fill opening, 256
filler, 384
filler cap, 271, 438, 440
filler rod, 307
filler tube, 293
fillet, 166, 167
filleting knife, 242
filling hole, 804
filling inlet, 741
film, 390
film advance mode, 391
film cartidge chamber, 390
film disk, 395
film drying cabinet, 398
film guide rail, 390
film guide roller, 390
film leader, 395
film leader indicator, 390
film pack, 395
film recorder, 527
film rewind knob, 391
film rewind system, 390
film speed, 391, 396
film sprocket, 390
films, 395
filter, 207, 252, 255, 385, 772
filter cover, 730
filter tip, 384
fin, 210, 499, 508, 627, 633, 812, 814
fin-mounted tail unit, 498
finderscope, 720, 721
fine adjustment knob, 718
fine bookbinding, 577, 578
fine data entry control, 555
fine guidance system, 16
finely threaded screw, 711
finger, 137
finger, 596
finger board, 535, 544, 547
finger button, 550
finger flange, 726
fingernail, 137
finial, 817
finish, 646
finish line, 654
finishing, 586
finishing line, 651
finishing post, 654
fir needles, 58
fire engine, 778, 780
fire extinguisher, 823
fire hose, 778
fire hydrant, 186
fire hydrant wrench, 779
fire irons, 205
fire pot, 204, 209
fire prevention, 777
fire signs, 820
firebrick, 204
firebrick back, 204
fireman, 777
fireman's hatchet, 781
fireplace, 204
fireplace, 195
fireproof and waterproof garment, 777
firestopping, 198
firing, 585
firing accessories, 801
firing chamber, 585
firing lanyard, 802
firing mechanism, 804
firing shaft, 802
firing tube, 807
firmer chisel, 587
first aid, 822
first aid equipment, 726
first aid kit, 725
first aid manual, 725
first base, 597
first baseman, 597
first classification track, 465
first dorsal fin, 86

first floor, 194
first floor, 197
first focal room, 15
first molar, 144
first officer's seat, 500
first premolar, 144
first quarter, 6
first reinforce, 800
first space, 610
first stage, 509
first valve slide, 550
first violins, 556
first-class cabin, 498
fish, 86, 88
fish fork, 240
fish knife, 239
fish platter, 238
fish poacher, 248
fish scaler, 688
fish wire, 311
fishbone stitch, 571
fisherman's knot, 691
Fishes, 11
fisheye lens, 392
fishhook, 671
fishhook, 670
fishing, 670, 672
fishing garment, 672
fishing vest, 672
fishplate, 466
fishplate bolt, 466
fish, anatomy, 88
fish, morphology, 86
fission of uranium fuel, 766
fitness equipment, 663, 664
fitted sheet, 224
fitting, 778
fittings, 301
fittings, 383
5 m platform, 624
5 yards line, 606
five-number bet, 700
fivepin, 683
fixative, 592
fixed arch, 455
fixed base, 282
fixed blade, 578
fixed bridges, 454, 456
fixed distance marking, 505
fixed jaw, 279, 282
fixed platform, 739
fixed weight, 539
fixed winglet, 814
fixed-roof tank, 741
fixing bath, 399
fixture drain, 215
flag, 606
flag shapes, 817
flag with Schwenkel, 817
flagstone, 263
flag, parts, 817
flail mower, 158
flail mower, 154
flame adjustment wheel, 386
flame spreader tip, 307
flammable, 821
flank, 101, 108, 179, 579
flank forward, 606
flanker, 605
flanking tower, 180
flap, 322, 380, 649
flap hydraulic jack, 812
flap lever, 500
flap pocket, 339
flap pocket, 320, 322
flare, 6, 738
flare joint, 300
flare nut wrench, 279
flash hider, 796
flash lamp, 393
flashcube, 393
flashing, 205
flashing light, 471
flashtube, 393
flat, 538
flat brush, 589
flat car, 473
flat end pin, 231
flat head, 276
flat mirror, 14, 720
flat part, 567
flat roof, 182
flat sheet, 224
flat shuttle, 573
flat stitches, 571
flat tip, 276
flat washer, 278
flat-back brush, 368
flat-bed, 561
flat-plate solar collector, 768

The terms in **bold type** indicate the title of an illustration.

flatbed, 441
flatbed pushcart, 788
flesh, 62, 63, 64
fleshy fruits, 62, 65
fleshy leaf, 70
fleur-de-lis, 819
flews, 106
flexible hose, 260, 735
flexible hose connection, 735
flexible rubber hose, 298
flexible skirt, 493
flexible tube, 726
flies, 188
flight, 625, 698
flight bag, 637
flight deck, 500
flight deck, 498, 508, 510, 810
flight information board, 505
flight instruments, 635
flight management computer, 500
flight of stairs, 201
flights, 624
flint, 307, 795
flint arrowhead, 791
flint knife, 791
flintlock, 795
flip turn, 622, 623
float, 216, 485, 803
float ball, 293
float clamp, 216
floater, 626
floating bridge, 457
floating crane, 490
floating head, 374
floating rib, 122
floating roof, 741
floating sleeve, 316
floating-roof tank, 741
floodlight, 414
floodlight on pantograph, 414
floor, 205, 616, 617, 773
floor board, 200
floor brush, 260
floor drain, 215
floor joist, 198, 199
floor lamp, 236
floor tile, 286
floorboard, 200
floppy disk, 529
floppy disk drive, 528
florin, 832
flotation section, 486
flow, 493
flow bean, 740
flow tube, 768
flower, 57
flower bed, 263
flower bud, 57
flowering, 61
flower, inflorescences, 60
flower, structure, 60
flue, 297, 542
flue hat, 297
flue pipe, 542
fluid adjustment screw, 304
fluid cup, 590
fluke, 483
fluorescent tube, 232
fluorescent tube, 233
flush, 695
flush bushing, 301
flush handle, 293
flute, 166, 167, 281, 548
fluted land, 281
fluted pole, 230
fluted shaft, 431
fluteroni, 587
flutes, 556
Fly, 13, 77, 323, 325, 350, 817
fly agaric, 55
fly front closing, 330, 351
fly line, 670
fly reel, 670
fly rod, 670
flying buttress, 175, 176
Flying Fish, 13
flying jib, 481
flyleaf, 577
flywheel, 435, 581, 584, 664
FM antenna, 400
foam, 30
foam cushion, 729
foam insulation, 287
foam monitor, 743
foam pad, 687
foam-rubber insulation, 287
focal plane shutter, 390
focus, 23
focus mode selector, 391

focus setting ring, 392
focusing knob, 720, 721
focusing lenses, 717
focusing magnifier, 399
focusing ring, 719
focusing screen, 390
fodder corn, 149
fog, 37, 39
fog light, 429, 440
foible, 666
foil, 666
foil warning line, 666
foilist, 667
fold, 315
fold line, 565
foldaway ladder, 303
folder, 518
folding chair, 223
folding cot, 687
folding door, 202
folding door, 194, 292
folding grill, 690
folding nail file, 365
folding ramp, 494
folding shovel, 690
foliage, 59
follicle, 67
follicle, section, 67
follow-through, 682
fondue fork, 240
fondue pot, 248
fondue set, 248
food chain, 31
food pollution, 32
food processor, 251
foot, 83, 112, 116, 117, 118, 119,
    225, 350, 542, 545, 553, 631, 670,
    671
foot control, 561
foot cushion, 675
foot fault judge, 614
foot hole, 542
foot pocket, 627
foot score line, 620
foot strap, 631
foot support, 664
football, 602, 604
football player, 602
footboard, 224, 445
footbridge, 180, 464, 475
footing, 198, 199
footless tights, 353
footlights, 188
footrest, 584, 727
footrope, 478
footstool, 222
footstrap, 336, 664
forage blower, 162
forage blower, 155
forage harvester, 162
forage harvester, 155
foramen cecum, 143
forced hot-water system, 208
forced warm-air system, 206
fore edge, 577
fore royal sail, 481
forearm, 106, 117, 119, 798
forearm crutch, 728
forearm support, 728
forecastle, 495, 497
forecourt, 614
forehead, 109, 116
foreleg, 79, 80
foreleg, honeybee, 80
forelimb, 84
forelock, 100
foremast, 479, 743
foresail, 481
forest, 27
forestay, 628
forewing, 79, 81
fork, 240
fork, 105, 447, 688, 707, 721, 787
fork pocket, 470
forked tongue, 96
forklift truck, 787
forks, 787, 788
forks, major types, 240
formeret, 177
forming, 692
Fornax, 13
forte, 666
fortified wall, 172
forward, 624
forward dive, 625
forward slide change, 397
forward swing, 682
forward/reverse, 272
foul line, 597, 683

foundation, 198, 199, 750
foundation blockage, 750
foundation of dam, 748
foundation of tower, 456
foundation slip, 345
foundations, 199
fountain pen, 389, 515
four blade beater, 250
four-door sedan, 425
four-four time, 537
four-masted bark, 478, 480
4 m line, 626
four-of-a-kind, 695
four-stroke-cycle engine, 436
four-toed hoof, 99
fourchette, 327
fourth, 537
4th metacarpal, 112
fourth wheel, 706
fovea, 140
foyer, 189
fractionating tower, 744
fraise, 318
frame, 198, 572
frame, 82, 156, 157, 159, 204, 225,
    272, 282, 302, 319, 323, 378, 382,
    383, 443, 484, 536, 554, 583, 595,
    615, 645, 659, 660, 685, 711, 726,
    768, 769, 773, 785, 787, 788
frame push, 783
frame stile, 225
frames, 376
frame, embroidery, 571
framing square, 275
franc, 832
Francis turbine, 754
free margin, 137
free throw lane, 610
free throw line, 610, 612
free-rolling seat, 664
freeway, 184, 452
freewheel, 448
freezer bucket, 251
freezer compartment, 254
freezer door, 254
freezing rain, 39
freight car, 464
freight cars, types, 472
freight expedition, 505
freight hold, 499
freight reception, 505
freight station, 464
French betting layout, 701
French bread, 153
French cuff, 339
French cut, 363
French horn, 551
French horns, 551
French knot stitch, 571
French loaf, 153
French roulette wheel, 701
French window, 203
fresco, 170
fret, 546, 547, 701
friction strip, 307, 386
frieze, 166, 168, 225
frigate, 808
fringe, 318
fringe trimming, 229
frock coat, 317
frog, 84
frog, 104, 156, 320, 467, 544
frog-adjustment screw, 277
frog, life cycle, 84
front, 322, 324
front apron, 324
front axle, 784
front beam, 708
front binding, 633
front board, 577
front brake, 447
front brake lever, 444
front crawl stroke, 622
front crossbar, 645
front derailleur, 446, 448
front fender, 442
front flap, 386
front foil, 495
front footrest, 443, 444
front grip, 804
front knob, 277, 281
front landing gear, 813
front leg, 223
front lights, 189
front pocket, 381
front point, 680
front runner, 643
front sight, 795, 797, 798, 799, 804
front sight housing, 796

front tip, 256
front top pocket, 323
front view, 147
front wall, 616, 617
front wheel, 147, 727, 784
front-end loader, 782
frontal, 120
frontal bone, 122
frontal sinus, 141
frontcourt, 617
fronts, 39
frontwall, 441
frost, 37
fruit branch, 61
fruit tree, 149
fruit vegetables, 69
fruit-picking ladder, 303
fruition, 61
frying pan, 249, 688
fuel, 766
fuel, 761
fuel bundle, 765
fuel bundle, 765
fuel control, 501
fuel handling sequence, 764
fuel indicator, 431
fuel injector, 437
fuel lines, 635
fuel oil, 744
fuel pellet, 765
fuel tank, 272, 440, 442, 468, 508,
    805, 812
fuel transfer pipe, 509
fuel: enriched uranium, 762
fuel: enriched uranium, 763
fuel: natural uranium, 760
fuel: natural uranium, 761
fueling machine, 759, 760, 761, 764
fulcrum, 624
full and by, 629
full back, 606
full cheek snaffle, 650
full cheek snaffle bit, 650
full deployment, 419
full face mask, 777
full house, 695
full moon, 7
full-load adjustment screw, 712
fullback, 603, 605
fumarole, 24
fume extractor, 805
function button, 699
function display, 555
function key, 530
function keys, 421, 422, 709
function selector, 214, 402
function selectors, 420
funiculus, 62, 67
funnel, 243
funnel, 410, 496
fur, 107
furlong chute, 651
Furnace, 13, 206, 770
furs, examples, 819
fuse, 757, 769
fuse body, 804
fuse box, 312
fuse cutout, 757
fuse holder, 757
fuse puller, 311
fuselage, 499, 639
fuselage mounted tail unit, 498
fuses, 312

G

g, 537
g clef, 537
gable, 175, 197
gable roof, 182
gable stud, 198
gable vent, 197
gaff, 478
gaff sail, 482
gaff sail boom, 478
gaff topsail, 480
gain control, 485
gaits, horse, 101
galaxy, 9
galaxy, classification, 9
gall bladder, 97
gallbladder, 131
gallery, 175, 189, 486, 773
galley, 498
Gallic warrior, 791
gallop, 101
game cartridge, 699
game of darts, 698
gangway, 742

The terms in **bold type** indicate the title of an illustration.

gantry crane, 786
gantry crane, 746, 747
Ganymede, 4
gap, 671
garage, 196
garbage disposal sink, 296
garbage disposal unit, 296
garden, 171
garden hose, 265
garden line, 268
garden sorrel, 73
gardening equipment, 264, 266, 268, 270, 272
gardening tools, 264, 266, 268, 270, 272
garlic, 70
garlic press, 243
garment bag, 382
garment fabric, 565
garment strap, 383
garment, fishing, 672
garnet, 362
garrison cap, 328
garter, 347
garter belt, 347
garter stitch, 567
gas, 34, 35, 232, 737, 744
gas burner, 297
gas cock, 297
gas cylinder, 796
gas lift module, 738
gas lighter, 386
gas main, 186
gas pedal, 430
gas tail, 9
gas tank cap, 444
gas tank door, 427
gas water-heater tank, 297
gasket, 257, 300
gaskin, 101
gasoline, 744, 745
gasoline engine, 434
gasoline pump, 453
gasoline pump, 453
gasoline pump hose, 453
gastrocnemius, 120, 121
gastropod, 83
gate, 647
gate, 462, 490, 646, 681, 747, 752
gate arm, 471
gate arm lamp, 471
gate arm support, 471
gate operating ring, 753
gate-leg, 219
gate-leg table, 219
gather, 337
gather skirt, 335
gathering, 577
gauge, 578
gauntlet, 308, 327
gauntlet, 327, 662
gauze bandage, 662
gauze roller bandage, 725
gear, 575
gear housing, 671
gear shift, 444
gearbox, 495, 583
gearshift lever, 430, 443
gelatin capsule, 725
Gemini, 11
Gemini the Twins (May 21), 820
generator, 753
generator, 446, 758
generator unit, 753
generator unit, 747
genital opening, 83
geometry, 830
geostationary satellite, 42
geostationary orbit, 43
germ, 152
German rye bread, 153
geyser, 25
gill, 55
gill filament, 87
gill raker, 87
gills, 87
gills, 88, 92
gimbal ring, 485
Giraffe, 11
girder, 14, 198
girdle, 346
girdle, 363
girth, 649, 651
girth strap, 649
glacial cirque, 26
glacier, 26
glacier tongue, 26
glacis, 178
gladius, 791

glans penis, 127
glass, 768, 769
glass case, 709
glass cover, 254
glass curtain, 228
glass dome, 484
glass lens, 376
glass slide, 718
glass sphere, 40
glass-fronted display cabinet, 227
glass-lined tank, 297
glassed roof, 190, 195, 462
glassware, 237
glider, 638
gliding, 638
globe, 689
glottis, 96, 142
glove, 512, 598, 609, 635, 642, 643, 667
glove compartment, 430
glove finger, 327
gloves, 327
glue, 200
glue stick, 515
gluteal nerve, 133
gnomon, 706
go, 697
goal, 601, 604, 606, 607, 608, 612, 626
goal area, 601, 612
goal area line, 612
goal attack, 611
goal circle, 611
goal crease, 608
goal defense, 611
goal judge, 608, 626
goal line, 601, 604, 606, 607, 608, 612, 626
goal line referee, 612
goal post, 604, 611
goal shooter, 611
goal third, 611
goalkeeper, 609
goalkeeper, 601, 607, 608, 611, 612, 626
goalkeeper's pad, 609
goalkeeper's stick, 609
goat, 150
Goat, 13
gob hat, 329
goggles, 308
goggles, 635
golf, 676, 678
golf bag, 679
golf ball, 677
golf ball, cross-section, 677
golf cart, 679
golf clubs, 678
golf clubs, types, 677
golf course, 676
golf glove, 679
golf shoe, 679
golf, iron, 678
golf, wood, 678
Golgi apparatus, 115
gondola car, 473
gonfalon, 817
gong, 554
gong, 557
goose, 150
goose-neck, 201
gooseberry, 62
gooseneck, 784
gored skirt, 334
gorge, 24
gorget, 792
gothic cathedral, 175, 176
gouge, 587
gour, 24
go, board, 697
grab handle, 440, 449, 461, 779
grade slope, 193
grader, 784
graduated arc, 484
graduated dial, 719
graduated scale, 708, 709, 710
grafting knife, 269
grain, 288
grain auger, 161
grain elevator, 161
grain of wheat, section, 152
grain pan, 161
grain tank, 160
grain terminal, 490
grain tube, 158
grandfather clock, 707
grandstand, 651
granitic layer, 22
granivorous bird, 111

granny knot, 691
granulation, 6
grape, 61, 62
grape, 61, 62
grape leaf, 61
grape leaf, 73
grapefruit, 65
grapefruit knife, 242
grapeshot, 801
graphic equalizer, 400
grapnel, 483
grassbox, 271
grasshopper, 77
grater, 243
grating, utensils for, 243
grave accent, 832
gravel, 199, 216
gravity band, 483
gravity dam, 749
gravity dam, cross section, 749
gravy boat, 238
gray matter, 135
grease well, 253
greases, 745
great adductor, 121
Great Bear, 11
Great Dog, 13
great organ manual, 542
great saphenous vein, 126
great scallop, 93
greater alar cartilage, 141
greater covert, 110
greater pectoral, 120
greater trochanter, 123
greatest gluteal, 121
greave, 792
Greek bread, 153
Greek temple, 168
Greek temple, plan, 169
green, 682
green ball, 673
green beam, 410
green bean, 69
green cabbage, 73
green peas, 72
green russula, 55
green walnut, 66
greenhouse, 149
Greenland Sea, 20
grid, 188, 410
grid system, 47
griddle, 253
grille, 168, 214, 426, 438, 536
grinding, utensils for, 243
grip, 632, 665, 677, 684
grip handle, 277
grips, tennis table, 619
grips, types, 619
groin, 116, 118
groove, 578
groove, 562, 598, 641, 678, 793
ground, 312, 741
ground air conditioner, 506
ground airport equipment, 506
ground bond, 312
ground clamp, 305
ground connection, 312, 400
ground electrode, 439
ground fault circuit interrupter, 312
ground moraine, 26
ground sill, 178
ground surface, 733
ground wire, 312, 757
ground-wire peak, 756
ground/neutral bus bar, 312
grounded receptacle, 216
grounding prong, 309
grow sleepers, 350
growth line, 83, 95
Grus, 13
guard, 201, 242, 310, 666
guard rail, 254
guardhouse, 178, 180
guava, 68
guide, 670
guide bar, 272
guide handle, 283
guide mark, 612
guide roller, 403
guiding and current bar, 476
guiding tower, 457
guillotine trimmer, 398
gules, 819
gulf, 51
gum, 142, 144
gun, 291
gun body, 304
gun flap, 319
gunner's sight, 805

gusset, 378, 380
gusset pocket, 339
gusset pocket, 338
Gutenberg discontinuity, 22
gutta, 167
gutter, 105, 197, 683
guy cable, 660
guy line, 685
guy wire, 774
guyot, 28
gymnasium, 496
gymnastics, 659, 660
gypsum tile, 286

H

H, 38
hack, 620
hackle, 670
hacksaw, 277, 299
hail, 37
hail shower, 39
hair, 117, 119, 136, 544
hair bulb, 136
hair clip, 369
hair dryer, 370
hair follicle, 136
hair roller, 369
hair roller pin, 369
hair shaft, 136
hairbrushes, 368
haircutting scissors, 369
hairdressing, 368, 370
hairpin, 369
hairspring, 706
hairstyling implements, 369
half barb, 38
half cell, 636
half court line, 616
half handle, 242
half indexing, 525
half note, 538
half rest, 538
half-distance line, 626
half-glasses, 377
half-mask respirator, 730
half-side, 787
half-slip, 345
half-through arch bridge, 455
halfback, 605
hall, 189
hall, 194, 496
hallah, 153
hallway, 194
halyard, 480, 817
ham knife, 242
hammer, 311, 658
hammer, 540, 541, 797, 798, 799
hammer ax, 681
hammer ax, 680
hammer butt, 541
hammer drill, 734
hammer felt, 541
hammer head, 681
hammer rail, 540, 541
hammer shank, 541
hand, 137
hand, 117, 119
hand blender, 250
hand brake gear housing, 470
hand brake wheel, 470
hand brake winding lever, 470
hand drill, 280
hand fork, 268
hand grenade, 804
hand grip, 670
hand lamp, 777
hand mixer, 250
hand mower, 271
hand protection, 821
hand protector, 268
hand shield, 308
hand truck, 788
hand vacuum cleaner, 260
hand vice, 582
hand warmer pocket, 330
hand warmer pouch, 339
hand wash in lukewarm water, 829
hand wheel, 561
hand-warmer pocket, 321
hand-wheel, 579
handbags, 380
handball, 612
handball, court, 612
handgrip, 442, 728
handgrips, 665
handguard, 796
handhold, 652

The terms in **bold type** indicate the title of an illustration.

handicap spot, 697
handle, 633
handle, 204, 224, 239, 240, 241, 250,
  251, 252, 253, 254, 255, 256, 260,
  265, 270, 271, 272, 275, 276, 277,
  278, 279, 281, 282, 284, 291, 294,
  295, 304, 306, 310, 370, 373, 374,
  375, 378, 380, 382, 383, 408, 544,
  563, 564, 570, 573, 579, 596, 598,
  607, 615, 619, 620, 640, 643, 658,
  666, 670, 671, 679, 688, 727, 735,
  793
handlebar, 272, 664
handlebars, 445, 447
handrail, 201, 477
handsaw, 277
handset, 420, 422
handset cord, 420
hang glider, 637
hang gliding, 637
hang point, 637
hang to dry, 829
hang-up ring, 370
hanger, 397
hanger bracket, 727
hanger loop, 326
hanging basket, 263
hanging file, 518
hanging glacier, 26
hanging pendant, 236
hanging sleeve, 316
hanging stile, 202, 203, 225
hank, 630
harbor, 490
hard disk bus, 528
hard disk drive, 529
hard disk drive, 526, 528
hard palate, 141, 142
hard shell clam, 93
hard top gondola, 472
hardboard, 289
hardwood base, 635
Hare, 13
harmonica, 536
harness, 573, 627, 635, 636, 637, 645
harness racing, 652
harnesses, 572
harp, 545
harp cable stays, 456
harps, 556
harquebus, 795
harvesting, 155, 159, 160, 162
hasp, 383
hastate, 56
hatband, 328
hatch, 510, 805
hatchback, 425
hatchet, 690
hatching, 576
haulage road, 733
hawk, 291
hay baler, 159
hay baler, 155
hayloft, 148
hazelnut, 66
hazelnut, section, 66
head, 112
head, 9, 72, 78, 79, 80, 83, 117, 119,
  124, 127, 275, 276, 279, 283, 373,
  374, 384, 386, 466, 544, 546, 547,
  554, 561, 567, 570, 579, 615, 658,
  670, 677, 681
head cover, 679
head cushion, 674
head harness, 730
head linesman, 603
head number, 653
head of femur, 123
head of frame, 203
head of humerus, 123
head pole, 653
head protection, 729
head protection, 821
head roller, 572
head tube, 306, 447
head-first entry, 624
headband, 406, 408, 577, 615, 642,
  729, 730
headbay, 746
headboard, 224
headcap, 577
header, 161
header, 198, 202
headframe, 736
headgear, 328
headings, types, 229
headlamp, 447
headland, 30
headlight, 147, 426, 440, 442, 444,
  445, 459, 469, 805

headlight/turn signal, 430
headlights, 429
headphone, 406
headphone, 408
headphone jack, 402, 408, 555
headphone plug, 408
headpin, 683
headrail, 231
headrest, 428
headwind, 629
head, bat, 112
head, bird, 109
hearing, 138
heart, 125, 695
heart, 88, 92, 97, 130
heartwood, 59
heat control, 209
heat deflecting disc, 232
heat exchanger, 209, 760, 772
heat production, 766
heat pump, 212
heat ready indicator, 370
heat selector switch, 370
heat shield, 510
heat transport pump, 759
heater, 689
heating, 204, 206, 208, 210, 212
heating coil, 635
heating duct, 259
heating element, 207, 209, 257, 259,
  305, 585
heating grille, 477
heating oil, 745
heating/air conditioning equipment,
  494
**heating, forced hot-water
  system**, 208
heating, forced warm-air system,
  206
heating, registers, 207
heaving line knot, 691
heavy drifting snow low, 39
heavy duty boot, 355
heavy gasoline, 744
heavy machinery, 785
heavy thunderstorm, 39
heavy vehicles, 782, 784
heavy-water reactor, 761
heddle rod, 574
heddles, 573
heddles, 572, 574
hedge, 263
hedge shears, 269
hedge trimmer, 268
heel, 104, 117, 119, 156, 242, 277,
  325, 352, 354, 544, 546, 596, 609,
  644, 678
heel flange, 641
heel grip, 354
heel loop, 727
heel piece, 633, 640
heel rest, 250, 256
heel stop, 645
heel-piece, 641
heeled shoe, 318
heelplate, 642, 643
height adjustment, 157, 159, 659,
  661, 664
height adjustment scale, 284
height adjustment screw, 641
height control, 399
height finder, 810
height of the dive, 625
height scale, 399
helicopter, 508
helicopter, 808
helicopter flight deck, 808
helicopter hangar, 808
helipad, 738
helium sphere, 509
helix, 139
helm roof, 183
helmet, 777
helmet, 512, 602, 609, 635, 636, 680,
  777, 791
helmet lamp, 680
helmet ring, 512
hem, 231
hemispheres, 47
hemlath, 773
hemline, 565
hen, 150
hen house, 148
hennin, 318
hepad, 42
hepatic vein, 124
heraldry, 817, 818
herbivore's jaw, 98
herbivores, 31, 33
herbs, 74

Hercules, 11
Herdsman, 11
herringbone parquet, 200
herringbone pattern, 200
herringbone stitch, 571
Hertzian wave transmission, 416
hex nut, 439
hexagon bushing, 301
hidden pocket, 379
high (19 to 36), 700, 701
high beam, 429
high beam indicator light, 431
high beam warning indicator, 445
high card, 695
high clouds, 44
high focal plane buoy, 487
high jump, 657
high jump, 654
high pressure center, 38
high warp loom, 574
high-back overalls, 350
high-pressure steam inlet, 758
high-rise apartment, 187
high-rise apartment, 185
high-speed exit taxiway, 502
high-speed train, 458
high-voltage tester, 310
highball glass, 237
highland climates, 45
highland climates, 45
highlight key, 396
highlighter pen, 515
highway, 52, 452
highway crossing, 471
highway crossing bell, 471
highway number, 52
hill, 27, 770
hilted bayonet, 794
hind leg, 79, 81
hind leg, butterfly, 78
hind leg, honeybee, 81
hind limb, 84, 85
hind toe, 108, 111
hind wing, 79, 81
hinge, 202, 203, 225, 253, 257, 378,
  382, 404, 429, 585, 641, 719
hinge pin, 785
hinge tooth, 95
hinged door, 195
hinged presser foot, 561, 562
hip, 117, 119
hip pad, 602
hip roof, 182
hip-and-valley roof, 183
hitch pin, 540
hitting area, 596
hive, 82
hive, 149
hive body, 82
hobble, 652
hobble hanger, 652
hobo bag, 380
hock, 101, 106
hockey ball, 607
hockey skate, 644
hockey, playing field, 607
hoe, 267
hoe-fork, 266
hog score line, 620
hoist, 188, 817
hoist room, 735
hoisting block, 786
hoisting ring, 483
hoisting rope, 302, 786
hoisting system, 786
holdback, 229
holding, 668
holding area marking, 504
holding timekeeper, 668
holds, judo, 668
hole, 583, 676
hollow barrel, 726
hollow shot, 801
home plate, 597
home-plate umpire, 597
homestretch, 651
honey cell, 82
honeybee, 80, 82
honeybee, foreleg, 80
honeybee, hind leg, 81
honeybee, middle leg, 80
honeycomb, 82
honeycomb section, 82
hood, 204, 260, 320, 349, 426, 440,
  627, 680
hooded sweat shirt, 352
hoof, 104
hoof, 101
hoofs, types, 99
hoof, plantar surface, 104

hook, 267
hook, 203, 230, 310, 562, 566, 567,
  568, 644, 674, 709, 711, 726, 786
hook and eyes, 566
hook ladder, 303
hook ladder, 781
hooker, 606
hoop, 571
hoop earrings, 361
hopper, 158, 162
hopper car, 472
hopper ore car, 472
horizon mirror, 484
horizon shade, 484
horizontal bar, 660
horizontal clamp, 713
horizontal control, 529
horizontal end handhold, 470
horizontal member, 756
horizontal motion lock, 393
horizontal movement, 696
horizontal pivoting window, 203
horizontal seismograph, 714
horizontal stabilizer, 499, 508, 639
horizontal-axis wind turbine, 774
horn, 364
horn, 430, 444, 468, 779
horns, 83
horns of giraffe, 99
horns of mouflon, 99
horns of rhinoceros, 99
horns, major types, 99
horny beak, 97
hors d'oeuvre dish, 238
horse, 98, 100, 102, 104
horse, 661
horse racing, 651
horseradish, 71
horseshoe, 104, 174, 364
horseshoe, 104
horseshoe mount, 14
horse, gaits, 101
horse, morphology, 100
horse, skeleton, 102
hose, 344
hose, 306, 347, 780
hose connector, 264
hose nozzle, 265
hose trolley, 265
hospital, 822
hot air, 501
hot bus bar, 312
hot coolant, 771
hot line connector, 757
hot pepper, 69
hot-air outflow, 207
hot-air outlet, 204
hot-air register, 206
hot-shoe contact, 391
hot-water circuit, 215
hot-water heater, 215
hot-water outlet, 208, 297
hot-water riser, 297
hot-water supply, 298
hot-water supply line, 296, 298
hotel, 185
hotel reservation desk, 504
houppelande, 317
hour angle gear, 14
hour hand, 707
house, 193, 620
house drain, 298
house dress, 333
house, exterior, 196
house, foundations, 199
house, frame, 198
house, structure, 198
housing, 233, 280, 305, 310, 374,
  403, 406, 422, 485, 486
hovercraft, 492
hub, 447, 727, 754, 774
hub cover, 754
Hubble space telescope, 16
Hubble's classification, 9
huckleberry, 62
hull, 67, 628
hull column, 738
hull sonar, 809
human body, 116, 118
human denture, 144
humerus, 102, 122
humid - long summer, 45
humid - short summer, 45
humid subtropical, 45
humidifier, 210
humidity, 210
humidity, measure, 41
hump, 465
hump lead, 465
hump office, 465

The terms in **bold type** indicate the title of an illustration.

Hunter, 11, 13
hunting cap, 328
Hunting Dogs, 11
hunting weapons, 798
hurdle, 656
hurricane, 39
hurricane lamp, 690
husk, 66
husk, 72
hut, 165
Hydra, 11, 13
hydrant intake, 778, 779
hydraulic coupler, 147
hydraulic cylinder, 147, 788
hydraulic hose, 156, 157, 158
hydraulic jack, 449
hydraulic pallet truck, 788
hydraulic resistance, 664
hydraulic shovel, 785
hydraulic system, 787
hydroelectric complex, 746
hydroelectric power station, cross section, 747
hydrofoil boat, 495
hydrologic cycle, 34
hydrometer, 439
hydrosphere, 31
hydrostatic pad, 14
Hydrus, 13
hygrograph, 41
hygrometer, 210
hypha, 55
hyssop, 74

I

ice, 34
ice ax, 681
ice ax, 680
ice cream freezer, 251
ice cream scoop, 246
ice cube tray, 254
ice dispenser, 453
ice hockey, 608
ice hockey player, 609
ice hockey, rink, 608
ice piton, 680
ice screw, 680
icing syringe, 245
identification bracelet, 364
identification tag, 383
idler wheel, 445
igloo, 165
igneous rocks, 23
ignition box, 501
ignition key, 271
ignition switch, 430, 444, 445
ignition transformer, 209
ileum, 131
iliohypogastric nerve, 133
ilioinguinal nerve, 133
ilium, 122
illumination mirror, 713
imagesetter, 527
imperial roof, 183
impervious rock, 737
impluvium, 170, 171
impost, 174
impulse sprinkler, 264
in goal, 606
in-flight refueling, 813
in-flight refueling probe, 813
inactive dyke, 752
inbound line, 604
incandescent lamp, 232
incandescent lamp, 486, 769
incised figure, 580
incisor, 98
incisors, 144
incoming message cassette, 420
incus, 138
indent, 524
index arm, 484
index card cabinet, 517
index card drawer, 517
index cards, 517
index finger, 137
index hole, 529
index mirror, 484
index shade, 484
Indian, 13
Indian chapati bread, 153
Indian fig, 68
Indian naan bread, 153
Indian Ocean, 21
indicator, 710
indicator board, 462, 654
indicator lights, 531
indicator needle, 396
indicators, 405, 410

indoor shutters, 231
indoor unit, 213
Indus, 13
industrial communications, 417
industrial pollution, 32, 33
inert gas, 232, 233
inferior cymbal, 552
inferior dental arch, 142
inferior mesenteric artery, 132
inferior nasal concha, 141
inferior umbilicus, 110
inferior vena cava, 124, 125, 126, 132
infield, 597
infiltration, 34
infinity, 830
inflated carrying tire, 476, 477
inflated guiding tire, 476, 477
inflator, 687
inflator, 627
inflator valve, 627
inflator-deflator, 687
inflorescences, types, 60
inflorescent vegetables, 69
information, 823
information console, 627
information counter, 504
information processing, 722
infrared homing head, 814
infrared sounder, 43
infraspinous, 121
infundibulum of fallopian tube, 129
inhalation valve, 730
injection/explosion, 437
injector, 434
ink, 581, 588
ink, 389, 581
inked surface, 580
inking slab, 581
inlaid parquet, 200
inlet hose, 399
inlet valve, 434, 436
inner boot, 641, 645
inner circle, 620
inner core, 22
inner door shell, 429
inner edge, 104
inner hearth, 204
inner jib, 481
inner lining, 433
inner lip, 94
inner stators, 501
inner table, 697
inner tent, 685, 686
inner toe, 108
input devices, 526
input monitors, 413
input selector, 402
input terminal, 310
insectivores, 31
insectivorous bird, 111
insects, 77
inset pocket, 339
inside, 601
inside knob, 290
inside left, 601
inside linebacker, 603
inside right, 601
inside-leg snap-fastening, 350
insole, 358
inspection plug, 216
instep, 325
instrument pallet, 511
instrument panel, 431
instrument panel, 430
instrument platform, 43
instrument shelter, 41
instrument unit, 509
insulated blade, 310
insulated handle, 310, 311
insulating materials, 287
insulating sheet, 528
insulating sleeve, 309
insulation, 209, 297, 768
insulation layers, 512
insulator, 439, 757
intaglio printing, 580
intaglio printing process, 582
intaglio printing process, equipment, 582
intake, 436, 437
intake manifold, 434, 437
intake port, 436
integral, 830
integral bayonet, 794
Intelsat VII, 418
interchangeable end assembly, 14
interchangeable studs, 600
interchanges, major types, 450
intercom microphone, 413

intercom station, 413
intercooler, 438
intercostal nerve, 133
interfacing, 565
interfemoral membrane, 112
interior dome shell, 14
interior door handle, 429
interior door lock button, 429
interior pocket, 383
interlining, 565
interlock, 576
intermittent drizzle, 39
intermittent rain, 39
intermittent snow, 39
internal boundary, 51
internal ear, 138
internal filum terminale, 134
internal iliac artery, 124, 126, 132
internal iliac vein, 124
internal jugular vein, 126
internal tooth lock washer, 278
international boundary, 51
international road signs, 825, 827, 828
international weather symbols, 39
internode, 57
interrupted projection, 50
intersection, 830
intertragic notch, 139
interval, 489
intervals, 537
intestine, 88, 92, 97, 124
intrados, 174
intrusive rocks, 23
invert, 476
inverted pleat, 228, 335
inward dive, 625
Io, 4
ionic order, 166
iris, 140
Irish bread, 153
iron, 677
iron at high setting, 829
iron at low setting, 829
iron at medium setting, 829
iron curtain, 188
ironing, 829
iron, golf, 678
irregular crystal, 37
irregular galaxy, 9
is approximately equal to, 830
is contained in, 830
is equal to, 830
is equal to or greater than, 830
is equal to or less than, 830
is equivalent to, 830
is greater than, 830
is identical with, 830
is less than, 830
is not equal to, 830
is not identical with, 830
is not parallel to, 830
is parallel to, 830
isba, 165
ischium, 123
island, 51, 452
isobar, 38
isolated danger mark, 489
isoseismal line, 23
isthmus, 51
isthmus of fallopian tube, 129
isthmus of fauces, 142
ivory ball, 701

J

J-2 engine, 509
jabot, 342
jack, 682, 695
jack, 400, 541, 682
jack field, 407
jack spring, 541
jack-up platform, 739
jacket, 321, 331
jacket, 331, 529, 667, 668, 798
jackets, 338
jackleg drill, 734
jackpot box, 702
jackpot feed, 702
jalousie, 203
jamb, 202, 203, 204
Japan plum, 64
Japanese persimmon, 68
javelin, 791
javelin throw, 654
javelins, 658
jaw, 276, 280, 281, 311, 365
jaws, types, 98
jaw, carnivore's, 98
jaw, herbivore's, 98

jaw, rodent's, 98
jazz band, 558
jeans, 336
jejunum, 131
jersey, 602
Jerusalem artichoke, 71
jet blast deflector, 810
jet engine test area, 811
jet fuel, 745
jet refueler, 506
jet tip, 373
Jew's harp, 536
jewel, 706
jewel cap, 485
jewelry, 361, 362, 364
Jewish hallah, 153
jib, 628, 786
jib tie, 786
jibsheet, 628
jigger topgallant staysail, 480
jigger topmast staysail, 480
jingle, 554
jockey, 651
jockey rollers, 448
jodhpur, 648
joint, 389, 577, 670, 675
joint filler, 291
jointed mouth, 650
jointed mouth bit, 650
joist, 200
Joker, 695
journal box, 468
joystick, 526
judge, 666, 668, 669
judge's stand, 651
judo, 668
judo suit, 668
juice sac, 65
juicer, 251
jump rope, 665
jump ski, 633
jumper, 333
jumpsuit, 336, 349, 351
junction box, 471
Jupiter, 4
justaucorps, 315

K

K-frame, 756
Kaplan turbine, 754
keel, 637
keep, 181
keeper ring, 670
kelly, 737
kernel, 72
kerosene, 744, 745
kerosene tank, 509
ketch, 482
kettle, 252
kettledrum, 553
key, 290, 536, 539, 540, 541, 543, 549
key case, 379
key finger button, 549
key guard, 549
key lever, 549
key lock, 378
key signature, 538
keybed, 540
keyboard, 530
keyboard, 422, 526, 527, 540, 555, 683
keyboard instruments, 540
keyboard port, 528
keystone, 174, 177
keyway, 290
kick pleat, 335
kickstand, 443
kidney, 89, 97, 124
kilt, 335
kimono, 348
kimono sleeve, 340
King, 695
King, 11, 696
king post, 199, 637
King's side, 696
kingpin, 441
kiosk, 453, 475
kitchen, 171, 195, 460, 807
kitchen knife, 242
kitchen knives, types, 242
kitchen scale, 244
kitchen timer, 244
kitchen utensils, 242, 244, 246
kitchenette, 195
kiwi, 68
knapsack, 680
knee, 100, 106, 116, 118
knee boot, 653
knee boot suspender, 653

The terms in **bold type** indicate the title of an illustration.

knee pad, 595, 602, 609
knee roll, 649
knee sock, 642
knee-high sock, 344
knickers, 336
knife, 239, 581, 587, 690
knife, 688
knife pleat, 335
knife pleat, 323
knife-blade cartridge fuse, 312
Knight, 696
knit cap, 329
knit shirt, 326
knitting, 567
knitting machine, 568
knitting measure, 567
knitting needles, 567
knives, major types, 239
knob, 219, 596
knob handle, 284
knockout, 312
knot, 576
knot stitches, 571
knots, 691, 692
knurled bolt, 304
kohlrabi, 71
krone, 832
kumquat, 65

L

L, 38
label, 404
label holder, 517
label maker, 516
labial palp, 79, 81, 92
labium majus, 128, 129
labium minus, 128, 129
laboratory, 15
laccolith, 25
lace, 596, 644, 669
lace carriage, 568
Lacerta, 11
lacing, 645
lacrimal duct, 140
lactiferous duct, 129
ladder, 449, 487, 493, 741, 773, 785
ladder and hose strap, 777
ladder pipe nozzle, 781
ladder scaffold, 303
ladders, 302
ladle, 801
ladle, 244
Lady chapel, 177
Lady in the chair, 11
ladybug, 77
lagging, 741
lagoon, 30
lake, 7, 27, 51
lam, 572
lamb, 150
laminboard, 288
lamp, 718
lamp base, 486
lamp socket, 309
lamphouse elevation control, 399
lamphouse head, 399
lanceolate, 56
lancet, 174
land, 281
landing, 194, 201, 736
landing area, 655, 657
landing deck, 811
landing gear lever, 500
landing light, 508
landing net, 672
landing radar, 811
landing window, 508
lane, 683
lane, 621, 655
lane line, 656
lane number, 621
lane rope, 621
lane timekeeper, 621
language display button, 422
languid, 542
lantern, 689
lantern, 263, 486
lantern pane, 486
lapel, 322, 341
lapiaz, 24
lapis lazuli, 362
larch, 58
large blade, 688
large intestine, 131
large wheel, 727
larger round, 121
larva, 82
larynx, 130, 142
laser beam, 405

laser printer, 527
last quarter, 7
latch, 253, 257, 383, 568, 681
latch bolt, 289, 290
latch lever, 562
latch needle, 568
latch needle, 569
lateen sail, 482
lateral bar, 663
lateral condyle of femur, 123
lateral cutaneous nerve of thigh, 133
lateral filing cabinet, 520
lateral great, 120, 121
lateral groove, 104
lateral incisor, 144
lateral line, 87, 620
lateral mark, 489
lateral moraine, 27
lateral rectus muscle, 140
lateral semicircular canal, 139
lateral-adjustment lever, 277
lath, 231
lath tilt device, 231
latitude, 3
latitude scale, 40
latrines, 171
launch escape system, 509
launcher/satellite separation, 419
launching into orbit, 419
launching orbit, 48
laundry room, 194
lava flow, 25
lava layer, 25
lavatory, 195
lavatory truck, 506
lawn, 193, 263
lawn aerator, 266
lawn edger, 266
lawn rake, 267
leach field, 216
lead, 620
lead ball, 804
lead pencil, 389
lead screw, 281
lead-in wire, 232
leader, 672
leading edge, 341, 499, 636, 638
leading edge flap, 812
leading edge tube, 637
leaf, 56
leaf, 57, 72
leaf axil, 56
leaf margin, 56
leaf node, 57
leaf vegetables, 73
leakproof cap, 689
lean-to roof, 182
leash rod, 574
leather end, 323
leather goods, 378
leather sheath, 690
leather sheath, 632
leather skin, 598
leaves, types, 56
leaves, types of, 58
ledger, 198
ledger line, 537
leech, 631
leek, 70
left atrium, 124, 125
left back, 601, 607, 612, 613
left center, 606
left channel, 401
left cornerback, 603, 605
left defense, 608
left defensive end, 603, 605
left defensive tackle, 603, 605
left field, 597
left fielder, 597
left forward, 610, 613
left guard, 603, 605, 610
left half, 601, 607
left halfback, 603
left inner, 607
left kidney, 132
left lung, 124, 130
left outside linebacker, 605
left pulmonary vein, 125
left safety, 603
left safety back, 605
left service court, 614, 616
left tackle, 603, 605
left valve, shell, 95
left ventricle, 124, 125
left wing, 606, 607, 608
left winger, 612
leg, 97, 117, 119, 156, 219, 224, 270, 325, 553, 619, 659, 671
leg curl bar, 663
leg extension bar, 663

leg position, 625
leg-of-mutton sleeve, 340
leg-warmer, 353
legging, 680
legume, section, 67
lemon, 65
length post, 651
lengthwise bulkhead, 742
lengthwise grain, 565, 566
lens, 140, 390, 392
lens accessories, 392
lens aperture scale, 392
lens cap, 392
lens hood, 392, 409, 484
lens mount, 390
lens release button, 391
lens system, 719
lenses, 392, 722
lenticular galaxy, 9
lentils, 72
Leo, 11
Leo Minor, 11
Leo the Lion (July 23), 820
leotard, 353
Lepus, 13
lesser covert, 110
letter opener, 515
letter scale, 516
leucoplast, 115
level, 736
level crossing, 464
leveling foot, 257, 258, 259
leveling head, 713
leveling head level, 713
leveling head locking knob, 713
leveling screw, 40, 709, 713
leveling-adjustment foot, 397
lever, 252, 278, 295, 296, 365, 453, 583, 702, 798
lever corkscrew, 244
lever cover, 295
levigator, 583
Libra, 13
Libra the Balance (September 23), 820
license plate light, 429
lid, 247, 248, 251, 252, 253, 256, 258, 398, 585
lid brace, 585
lierne, 177
life buoy, 495
life raft, 492
life support system, 512
life support system controls, 512
lifeboat, 478, 494, 496, 738
lift, 478
lift arm, 782
lift bridge, 457
lift chain, 293
lift cord, 231
lift cord lock, 231
lift span, 457
lift-arm cylinder, 782
lift-fan air inlet, 493
lifting chain, 787
lifting handle, 803
lifting hook, 737
lifting lever, 147
lifting link, 147
ligament, 95
ligature, 548
light, 477, 486, 487, 489, 720, 721
light bar, 779
light machine gun, 796
light sensor, 390
light shield, 16
light signal, 539
light-load adjustment screw, 712
light-reading scale, 396
lightbox, 398
lighted mirror, 368
lighthouse, 486
lighthouse, 491
lighthouse lantern, 486
lighting, 368, 500
lighting board, 412
lighting board operator, 412
lighting cable, 449
lighting grid, 414
lighting grid access, 412
lighting technician, 412
lighting/camera control area, 412
lightning, 36
lightning arrester, 747, 757
lightning rod, 197
lights, 232, 234, 236, 429
limb, 59, 684
limb top, 718
limousine, 425
limpet, 83

line, 537, 700, 701
line guide, 671
line hook, 492
line judge, 603, 605
line map, 474
line of scrimmage, 603, 605
linear, 56
lineman's pliers, 311
linen, 224
linen, 460
linen chest, 226
lines of latitude, 47
lines of longitude, 47
linesman, 601, 605, 606, 608, 613, 614, 618
lingual papillae, 143
lingual tonsil, 143
lining, 322, 324, 352, 354, 378, 565, 644
linseed oil, 592
linstock, 801
lint filter, 258
lint trap, 259
lintel, 175, 204
lion, 98
Lion, 11
lion passant, 819
lip, 100, 107
lip makeup, 366
lip strap ring, 650
lipbrush, 366
lipid droplet, 115
lipliner, 366
lipstick, 366
liqueur glass, 237
liquid compass, 484
liquid compass, cross section, 485
liquid cooling and ventilation garment, 512
liquid eyeliner, 367
liquid foundation, 366
liquid hydrogen tank, 509
liquid mascara, 367
liquid nitrogen tank, 717
liquid oxygen tank, 509
liquid oxygen tank baffle, 509
liquid-crystal display, 706
liquid/gas separator, 439
lira, 832
listen button, 420
lists, 181
litchi, 68
litho crayon, 583
litho pencil, 583
lithographic press, 583
lithographic printing, 580
lithographic stone, 583
lithographic tusche, 583
lithography, 583
lithography, equipment, 583
lithosphere, 31
Little Bear, 11
Little Dog, 11
little finger, 137
little finger hook, 551
Little Horse, 11
Little Lion, 11
liver, 88, 97, 124, 131
liverpool bit, 650
livestock car, 472
living room, 195, 685
Lizard, 11
load support, 635
loading area, 764
loading bunker, 734
loading dock, 190
loading door, 204
loafer, 355
lobate, 56
lobate toe, 111
lobby, 190, 504
lobe, 111
lobster, 90
lobule, 139
local station, 416
location of the statue, 169
lock, 289, 290
lock, 202, 225, 289, 380, 383, 429, 448, 752
lock dial, 530
lock emptying system, 492
lock filling and emptying opening, 493
lock filling and emptying system, 492
lock filling intake, 493
lock filling opening, 493
lock forward, 606
lock nut, 40, 711
lock rail, 202
lock ring, 397
lock switch, 396

848

INDEX

lock washer, 278
lock-chamber, 493
locked groove, 404
locker, 522
locket, 361
locking button, 260
locking device, 260, 302
locking lever, 471
locking pliers, 278
locking ring, 276, 802
locknut, 296
locomotive track, 465
loculus, 64
log, 288
log carrier, 205
log chute, 746
log tongs, 205
log, section, 288
loin, 101, 117, 119
long adductor, 120
long and short stitch, 571
long extensor of toes, 120
long jump take-off board, 655
long palmar, 120
long peroneal, 120
long radial extensor of wrist, 121
long residue, 744
long service line, 618
long-range jet, 498
longitude, 3
longitudinal dunes, 46
loop, 324, 452
loop stitches, 571
loophole, 181
loose curtain, 228
loose fill insulation, 287
loose powder, 366
loose powder brush, 366
lopping shears, 269
lore, 109
lorgnette, 377
lost and found articles, 823
loudspeaker, 779
loudspeakers, 400
lounge, 496
louver, 214
louver-board, 175
louvered window, 203
lovage, 74
love seat, 221
low (1 to 18), 700, 701
low bar, 659
low beam, 429
low clouds, 44
low fuel warning light, 431
low pressure center, 38
low warp loom, 572
low-pressure steam, 758
low-tension distribution line, 757
lower blade guard, 284
lower bowl, 247
lower cheek, 650
lower chord, 455
lower eyelid, 84, 107, 140
lower fore topgallant sail, 481
lower fore topsail, 481
lower gate, 492
lower gill arch, 87
lower girdle facet (16), 363
lower guard retracting lever, 284
lower lateral lobe, 61
lower lateral sinus, 61
lower level, 493
lower limb, 793
lower lip, 142, 542
lower lobe, 130
lower mandible, 109
lower mantle, 22
lower mast, 478
lower shell, 641
lower sphere clamp, 40
lower support screw, 40
lubber's line, 485
lubricants plant, 744
lubricating oils, 745
lubricating system, 469
lubricator, 735
Luer-Lock tip, 726
luff, 631
lug, 432, 553
luge, 643
luggage, 382
luggage carrier, 382
luggage elastic, 382
luggage rack, 445, 449, 461
lumbar pad, 602
lumbar plexus, 133
lumbar vertebra, 135
lumbar vertebra (5), 123
lumbar vertebrae, 103

lunar eclipse, 8
lunar features, 7
lunar module, 509
lung, 97
lunula, 137
lunule, 95
Lynx, 11
Lyra, 11
lyre, 535
Lyre, 11
lysosome, 115

M

macaroni, 587
machete, 794
machicolation, 181
machicolation, 180
machine gun, 805
machine hall, 746, 747
machine wash in hot water at a
    normal setting, 829
machine wash in lukewarm water
    at a gentle setting/reduced
    agitation, 829
machine wash in warm water at a
    gentle setting/reduced
    agitation, 829
machine wash in warm water at a
    normal setting, 829
machinery shed, 148
macro set button, 409
magazine, 795, 796, 797
magazine base, 797
magazine catch, 795, 797
magma, 25, 28
magma chamber, 25
magnet, 563
magnet, 406, 485, 714
magnetic compass, 719
magnetic damping system, 708
magnetic field, 410
magnetic gasket, 254
magnetic lid holder, 256
magnetic needle, 719
magnetic suspension, 712
magnetometer, 42
magnifier, 688
main breaker, 312
main carriage, 568
main circuit vent, 215
main cleanout, 215
main deck, 743, 811
main duct, 206
main electric motor, 806
main engines, 511
main entrance, 190, 194
main fan, 734
main handle, 280
main inlet, 741
main landing gear, 499, 812
main lanes, 452
main leg, 756
main lever, 590
main line, 464
main lower topgallant sail, 481
main lower topsail, 481
main mirror, 720
main parachute, 635
main power cable, 312
main preview monitor, 413
main reflex mirror, 390
main return pipe, 208
main royal sail, 481
main sail, 481
main scope tube, 718
main section, 700, 701
main sewer, 186
main stalk, 61
main stand, 443
main steam header, 759
main steam pipes, 759
main supply pipe, 208
main switch, 757
main transformer, 458
main tube, 720, 721
main upper topgallant sail, 481
main upper topsail, 481
main vent, 25
main wheel, 707
mainmast, 479
mainsail, 628
mainsheet, 628
maintenance, 453
maintenance area, 415
maintenance hangar, 503
maintenance shop, 734
major amphibians, 85
major inner reaping throw, 668
major outer reaping throw, 668

makeup, 366
malar region, 109
male, 831
male cone, 58
male ferrule, 670
male genital organs, 127
male urethra, 127
mallet, 275, 581, 586
mallet, 552
mallets, 553
malleus, 138
mammary gland, 129
mandarin, 65
mandarin collar, 342
mandible, 78, 80, 81, 86, 102, 122
mandolin, 535
mane, 100
maneuvering bar, 162
maneuvering engine, 511
maneuvering lever, 787, 788
mango, 63
manhole, 186, 741, 742
manicure, 365
manicure set, 365
manicuring implements, 365
manifold, 738
manned maneuvering unit, 512
manometer, 741
manrope, 457
mansard roof, 183
mantel, 204
mantel shelf, 204
mantle edge, 92
manual, 543
manual focusing knob, 397
manual release, 641
manual/automatic mode, 585
manually-operated switch, 467
manuals, 542
manure spreader, 156
manure spreader, 154
manway, 736
map projections, 50
Marconi cutter, 482
margin, 57
margin control, 525
margin release, 524
marginal shield, 96
marine, 45
marine diesel, 745
maritime buoyage system, 488
maritime communications, 417
maritime signals, 486
maritime transport, 735
marker, 389, 515
marker, 683
marker light, 440, 441
marker pen, 588
marking dot, 565
marks by night, rhythm, 489
Mars, 4
mars light, 781
martingale, 666
mascara brush, 367
mask, 595, 627, 667
mason's trowel, 291
masonry, 291
mass, 714
masseter, 120
mast, 464, 471, 508, 628, 631, 787,
    788
mast foot, 631
mast sleeve, 631
master bedroom, 194
master carrier, 230
master cord, 645
master gate valve, 740
masthead, 479, 631
masthead light, 495
masting, 478
mat, 668
mat, 682
matchbook, 386
matchbox, 386
matchstick, 386
material handling, 786, 788
mathematics, 830
matinee-length necklace, 361
mattress, 687
mattress, 224, 726
mattress cover, 224
maulstick, 591
maxilla, 81, 86, 90, 122, 141
maxillary bone, 144
maxillipeds, 90
maximum thermometer, 41
meadow, 149
measure of air pressure, 41
measure of angles, 713
measure of cloud ceiling, 41

measure of distance, 711
measure of humidity, 41
measure of length, 711
measure of pressure, 710
measure of rainfall, 40
measure of seismic waves, 714
measure of snowfall, 41
measure of sunshine, 40
measure of temperature, 41, 705
measure of thickness, 711
measure of time, 706
measure of weight, 708
measure of wind direction, 41
measure of wind strength, 41
measuring button, 396
measuring cups, 244
measuring spoons, 244
measuring tube, 40
measuring, utensils, 244
meat, 33
meat grinder, 243
meat keeper, 254
meat thermometer, 244
mechanical connectors, 300
mechanical pencil, 389, 515
mechanical shovel, 733
mechanical stage, 718
mechanical stage control, 718
mechanical variometer, 639
mechanical watch, 706
mechanics, 453
medial condyle of femur, 123
medial great, 120
medial moraine, 26
medial rectus muscle, 140
median, 452
median groove, 104
median lingual sulcus, 143
median nerve, 133
median strip, 184
Mediterranean Sea, 21
Mediterranean subtropical, 45
medium, 666
medium format SLR (6 x 6), 395
medium tension distribution line, 757
medulla, 132
medulla oblongata, 134
Meissner's corpuscle, 136
melody strings, 535
meltwater, 27
memo pad, 518
memory button, 402, 420
memory cancel, 396, 523
memory key, 396, 405
memory recall, 523
memory recall key, 396
men, 697
men's bag, 380
men's clothing, 319, 320, 322, 324
men's rest room, 822
Mercury, 4, 232
mercury barometer, 41
mercury bulb, 705
merging traffic, 824
méridienne, 221
merlon, 181
mesa, 46
mesh, 619
mesocarp, 62, 63, 64, 65
mesosphere, 19
mesothorax, 78
message display, 532
metacarpus, 102, 107, 122
metal A, 307
metal arm, 264
metal B, 307
metal counterhoop, 553
metal frame, 540
metal head, 658
metal rail, 517
metal rod, 554
metal structure, 463
metallic contact grid, 768
metallic plastron, 667
metals, 33
metals, examples, 819
metamorphic rocks, 23
metatarsus, 80, 103, 122
metathorax, 78
meteorology, 38
meteorology, measuring
    instruments, 41
meteorology, station model, 38
meteors, 39
metope, 167
metronome, 539
mezzanine, 195, 474
mezzanine floor, 194
mezzanine stairs, 195
Michigan snowshoe, 645

The terms in **bold type** indicate the title of an illustration.

micrometer caliper, 711
micrometer screw, 484, 713
microphone, 407, 414, 420, 639
microphone boom, 412, 414
microphone boom tripod, 414
microprocessor, 528
microwave dish, 415
microwave oven, 253
microwave scanner, 43
microwave transmitter, 415
mid-calf length, 325
mid-ocean ridge, 28
middle clouds, 44
middle covert, 110
middle ear, 138
middle finger, 137
middle jib, 481
middle leg, 79, 80
middle leg, honeybee, 80
middle linebacker, 603, 605
middle lobe, 130
middle nasal concha, 141
middle panel, 202
middle phalanx, 107, 122, 123, 137
middle piece, 127
middle primary covert, 110
middle sole, 352
middle toe, 108
middle torus, 167
middy, 337
midfield, 606
midfield line, 601
midrange, 16, 400
midrange pickup, 547
midrib, 56, 67
midriff band, 346
Mihrab, 173
Mihrab dome, 173
military communications, 417
milk bread, 153
Milky Way, 11
millet, 152
minaret, 172, 173
Minbar, 173
miners' changing-room, 735
mini shirtdress, 337
mini-floppy disk, 529
minimum thermometer, 41
minivan, 425
mint, 74
minute, 830
minute hand, 706, 707
mirror, 292, 382, 442, 444
missile launch rail, 813
missile launcher, 811
missile stowage, 808
missiles, 814
missiles, major types, 814
missile, structure, 814
mist, 37, 39
miter gate recess, 493
miter gauge, 285
miter gauge slot, 285
mitochondrion, 115
mitral valve, 125
mitt, 327
mitten, 308, 327
mitten, 680
mixing bowl, 250
mixing bowls, 245
mixing chamber, 306
mizzen royal brace, 480
mizzen royal staysail, 480
mizzen sail, 480
mizzen topgallant staysail, 480
mizzen topmast staysail, 480
mizzenmast, 478
moat, 178, 181
mobile drawer unit, 521
mobile filing unit, 521
mobile passenger stairs, 507
mobile unit, 415
mobile unit, 416
moccasin, 355
mock pocket, 330
mode, 525
mode selector, 402
mode selectors, 408
modem, 526
modem port, 528
moderator, 766
moderator tank, 761
moderator: graphite, 760
moderator: heavy water, 761
moderator: natural water, 762
moderator: natural water, 763
modern bow, 793
modern howitzer, 802
modern mortar, 803
modesty panel, 521

modillion, 167
modulation wheel, 555
Mohorovicic discontinuity, 22
moist surface, 580
moistener, 516
moisture in the air, 34
molar, 98
molars, 144
molar, cross section, 144
moldboard, 156
molded insulation, 287
molding, 199
mollusk, 92
monitor roof, 182
monitor wall, 412, 413, 415
monocle, 377
mons pubis, 128
monster, 605
monument, 52
Moon, 7
Moon, 4, 8
Moon dial, 707
Moon's orbit, 8
moons, 4
Moon, phases, 6
mooring chain, 486
mooring winch, 743
moose, 105
mordent, 538
morel, 55
mortar, 243, 803
mortise, 385
mortise lock, 290
mosaic, 171
mosque, 172
mosque, plan, 173
moss stitch, 567
motor, 161, 214, 257, 258, 259, 270,
   271, 272, 283, 284
motor air inlet, 813
motor car, 476, 477
motor end plate, 134
motor home, 449
motor neuron, 135
motor root, 135
motor truck, 459
motor unit, 250, 251, 256, 260, 373,
   458
motorcycle, 442, 444
motorcycle dashboard, 445
motorcycle, dashboard, 445
motorized earth auger, 270
mount frame binder, 397
mountain, 27
mountain mass, 51
mountain range, 7, 23, 51
mountain slope, 27
mountain torrent, 27
mountaineer, 680
mountaineering, 680
mountaineering boot, 680
mountaineering shovel, 680
mountaineering, equipment, 681
mounting, 666
mounting bracket, 684
mounting foot, 393
mounting plate, 233
mounting point, 501
mouse, 530
mouse, 526, 527
mouth, 142
mouth, 83, 84, 92, 118, 542, 650
mouthparts, 81
mouthpiece, 548, 550, 627, 669
mouthpiece receiver, 550
mouthpipe, 550
movable bridges, 457
movable jaw, 279, 282
movable maxillary, 96
movie theater, 496
moving coil, 406
mowing, 154, 158
Mt Everest, 19
mud flap, 427, 440, 441
mud injection hose, 737
mud pit, 737
mud pump, 737
mudguard, 147
muff, 381
muffin pan, 245
muffler, 439
muffler felt, 540
muffler pedal, 540
mule, 355
mullet, 819
multi-ply plywood, 288
multi-purpose ladder, 303
multimeter, 310
multiple exposure mode, 391
multiple use key, 523

multiple-span beam bridge, 454
multiplication, 830
multiply key, 523
multipurpose antenna, 807
multipurpose tool, 311
multipurpose vehicle, 425
mummy, 687
muntin, 202, 203
Musca, 13
muscle arrector pili, 136
muscle fiber, 134
muscle scar, 95
muscle segment, 89
muscles, 120
museum, 185
mushroom, 55
mushroom anchor, 483
mushroom, structure, 55
music rest, 539
music stand, 539
music stand, 542, 555
musical accessories, 539
musical advisers, 412
musical notation, 537, 538
muskmelon, 69
mustard, 67
mute, 551
mutule, 167
muzzle, 100, 106, 107, 797, 798, 799,
   800, 803
muzzle loading, 800
muzzle loading, cross section, 801
mycelium, 55
myelin sheath, 135

N

nacelle, 774
nacreous cloud, 19
nail, 275
nail, 104
nail bed, 137
nail cleaner, 365
nail clippers, 365
nail file, 365
nail hole, 104
nail matrix, 137
nail nick, 688
nail scissors, 365
nail shaper, 365
nail whitener pencil, 365
naked strangle, 668
name plate, 280, 712
nameplate, 364
naos, 169
nape, 108, 117, 119
naris, 141
nasal bone, 141
nasal cavity, 130
nasal fossae, 141
nasopharynx, 141
national broadcasting network, 416
national park, 52
natural, 538
natural arch, 30
natural sponge, 367
nave, 177
navel, 116, 118
navette cut, 363
navigation devices, 484
navigation display, 500
navigation light, 493, 499
navigation periscope, 807
Neapolitan coffee maker, 247
neck, 97, 100, 117, 118, 119, 127,
   144, 240, 241, 410, 544, 545, 546,
   547, 579, 661, 678
neck end, 324
neck guard, 777
neck of femur, 123
neck of uterus, 128
neck strap, 729
neckhole, 325
necklaces, 361
necklines, 343
neckroll, 224
necks, 343
neckstrap eyelet, 390
necktie, 324
nectarine, 63
needle, 562, 632
needle, 36, 561, 562, 563, 590, 726
needle assembly, 590
needle bar, 562
needle bed, 568
needle bed, 568
needle bed groove, 568
needle clamp, 562
needle clamp screw, 562
needle hub, 726

needle plate, 561
needle position selector, 561
needle threader, 563
needle tool, 585
needle-nose pliers, 311
negative, 399
negative carrier, 399
negative carrier, 399
negative charge, 831
negative contact, 768, 769
negative meniscus, 722
negative plate, 439
negative plate strap, 439
negative region, 768
negative terminal, 439
negligee, 348
neon lamp, 310
neon tester, 310
Neptune, 5
nerve, 136
nerve fiber, 136
nerve termination, 136
nervous system, 133, 134
nest of tables, 219
net, 613, 614, 618
Net, 13, 610, 612, 613, 614, 618,
   619, 626
net band, 614
net judge, 614
net stocking, 344
net support, 619
netball, 611
netball, court, 611
network communication, 527
network port, 528
neural spine, 89
neurons, 135
neutral conductor, 757
neutral indicator, 445
neutral service wire, 312
neutral wire, 312
neutral zone, 603, 605, 608
new crescent, 6
new fuel storage room, 764
new moon, 6
newel post, 201
next call, 422
nib, 389
nictitating membrane, 107
nightgown, 348
nightwear, 348
nimbostratus, 44
nipple, 301
nipple, 116, 118, 129
no access for wheelchairs, 822
no entry, 824, 825
no U-turn, 824, 825
no. 8 forward, 606
no. 8 iron, 678
no. 5 iron, 678
no. 5 wood, 678
no. 4 iron, 678
no. 9 iron, 678
no. 7 iron, 678
no. 6 iron, 678
no. 3 iron, 678
no. 3 wood, 678
nock, 684, 793
nocking point, 684
noctilucent cloud, 19
node, 756
node of Ranvier, 135
non-add/subtotal, 523
North, 488
North America, 20
North American road signs, 824,
   826, 828
North celestial pole, 3
North Pole, 3
North Sea, 21
North Star, 11
Northeast, 488
Northern Crown, 11
Northern hemisphere, 3, 47
Northwest, 488
nose, 141
nose, 100, 118, 498, 637, 638, 792,
   798
nose cone, 501
nose landing gear, 498
nose leaf, 112
nose leather, 107
nose of the quarter, 352, 354
nose pad, 376
noseband, 649
nosing, 201
nostril, 84, 86, 96, 100, 109
notch, 322, 341, 565, 656, 674, 708
**notched double-edged thinning
   scissors**, 369

The terms in **bold type** indicate the title of an illustration.

notched edge, 369
notched lapel, 319, 320
notched single-edged thinning scissors, 369
note symbols, 538
nozzle, 209, 264, 291, 304, 509, 510, 590, 778
nuchal shield, 97
nuclear boiler room, 806
nuclear energy, 758, 760, 762, 764, 766
nuclear envelope, 115
nuclear fuel handling sequence, 764
nuclear generating station, 758
nuclear reactor, 765
nuclear whorl, 94
nucleolus, 115, 128
nucleus, 9, 115, 128, 135
number, 656, 701
number key, 421, 523
number of decimals, 523
number of tracks sign, 471
number three, 620
number two, 620
numbering machine, 516
numeric keyboard, 422, 709
numeric keypad, 530
nut, 279
nut, 278, 279, 290, 300, 466, 544, 546, 547, 793
nutcracker, 243
nuts, 66
nuts, major types, 66
nylon rumba tights, 349
nylon yarn, 271

O

o-ring, 294, 295
oar, 664
oarlock, 632
oars, types, 632
oasis, 46
oats, 152
object balls, 673
objective, 718
objective lens, 391, 392, 396, 397, 405, 718, 719, 721
oboe, 548
oboes, 557
obscured sky, 39
observation deck, 505
observation window, 510
observatory, 14
obstacles, 647
obturator nerve, 133
obtuse angle, 830
occipital, 121
occipital bone, 123
occluded front, 39
ocean, 7, 35, 51
ocean floor, 28
Oceania, 21
ocean, topography, 28
oche, 698
octave, 537, 667
octave mechanism, 548
odd, 700, 701
odd pinnate, 56
odometer, 431
offense, 603, 605
office, 453, 462
office building, 190
office building, 185, 491
office furniture, 520, 522
office tower, 184, 190
officers' quarters, 807, 808
officials' bench, 608
offset, 301
offshore drilling, 739
offshore well, 740
ogee, 174
ogee roof, 182
oil, 737, 738, 740, 742, 744
oil, 737
oil burner, 209
oil drain plug, 434
oil paint, 588
oil pan, 272, 434
oil pan gasket, 434
oil pastel, 588
oil pressure warning indicator, 445
oil processing area, 738
oil pump, 209
oil supply inlet, 209
oil supply line, 209
oil terminal, 491
oil warning light, 431
oil-filled heater, 211

oil/gas separator, 738
oiler, 734
oilstone, 582
okra, 69
old crescent, 7
old-fashioned glass, 237
olecranon, 102, 123
olfactory bulb, 88, 142
olfactory membrane, 142
olfactory nerve, 88, 142
olive, 63
on guard line, 666
on the wind, 629
on-air warning light, 407
on-deck circle, 597
on-off button, 256
on-off indicator, 370
on-off switch, 234, 247, 260, 305, 368, 370, 373, 374, 485
on/off, 408
on/off light, 420
on/off switch, 391, 397, 406
on/off/volume, 408
on/play button, 420
1 m springboard, 624
one pair, 695
one way head, 276
one-arm shoulder throw, 668
one-bar shoe, 356
one-person tent, 686
one-piece coverall, 635
one-piece suit, 643
1/10th second hand, 706
120-volt circuit, 312
one-toe hoof, 99
one-way traffic, 824, 825
opal, 362
open end wrench, 279
open stringer, 201
open strings, 535
open-air terrace, 497
open-face spinning reel, 671
open-pit mine, 733
opening, 327
opening, utensils, 244
opera glasses, 377
opera-length necklace, 361
operating cord, 230
operating dam, 752
operating floor, 752
operating rod, 796
operation control room, 807
operation keys, 422
operator's cab, 786
operculum, 84, 86
Ophiuchus, 11, 13
opisthodomos, 169
opposite prompt side, 189
optic chiasm, 134
optic nerve, 140
optical disk, 527
optical disk drive, 527
optical scanner, 526
optical sight, 713
or, 819
oral cavity, 130, 131
oral hygiene center, 373
oral irrigator, 373
orange, 65
orange, 65
orbicular of eye, 120
orbiculate, 56
orbit of the satellites, 43
orbits of the planets, 4
orchard, 149
orchestra pit, 188
orchestra seats, 188
order, 175
ordinaries, examples, 818
ordinary die, 699
ore, 733
ore pass, 736
oregano, 74
organ, 542
organ console, 542
organ, mechanism, 543
organ, production of sound, 543
Oriental couching stitch, 571
oriflamme, 817
original overlay, 532
Orion, 11, 13
ornamental tree, 148, 263
ornaments, 538
ortho-cane, 728
oscillating sprinkler, 264
otolith, 88
ottoman, 222
outbound track, 465
outdoor condensing unit, 212
outdoor light, 196

outdoor unit, 212
outer boundary line, 616
outer circle, 620
outer core, 22
outer edge, 104
outer jacket, 297
outer jib, 481
outer lip, 94
outer shell, 309
outer stators, 501
outer table, 697
outer toe, 108
outfield, 597
outgoing announcement cassette, 420
outlet, 309
outlet, 449
outlet grille, 211
outlet hose, 399
output devices, 527
output jack, 547
output monitor, 413, 415
outrigger, 632, 780, 785, 786
outside counter, 354
outside knob, 290
outside left, 601
outside linebacker, 603
outside mirror, 426
outside mirror control, 429
outside right, 601
outside ticket pocket, 322
outsole, 353, 355
outwash plain, 27
oval cut, 363
oval head, 276
ovary, 60, 128, 129
ovate, 56
oven, 255
oven control knob, 255
over-blouse, 337
overalls, 335
overburden, 733
overcast sky, 39
overcheck, 653
overcoat, 320, 331
overdrapery, 229
overflow, 215, 292
overflow pipe, 297
overflow protection switch, 257
overflow tube, 293, 399
overhand knot, 691
overhead clearance, 826, 827
overhead connection, 757
overhead frame, 784
overhead ground wire, 756
overhead guard, 787
overhead switch panel, 500
overlap carrier, 230
overlay flooring, 200
overpass, 452, 454
ovule, 60
ox, 151
oxer, 646
oxford shoe, 354
oxyacetylene welding, 306
oxygen cylinder, 306
oxygen feeding control, 639
oxygen feeding knob, 639
oxygen pressure actuator, 512
oxygen valve, 306
oyster, 92
oyster, 93
oyster fork, 240
oyster knife, 242
oyster mushroom, 55
ozone, 19

P

pace, 101
Pacific Ocean, 20
Pacinian corpuscle, 136
packing, 294
packing nut, 294
packing retainer ring, 294
pad, 598
pad arm, 376
pad plate, 376
padding, 635
paddock, 651
pagoda sleeve, 340
paint roller, 304
painted line, 452
Painter's Easel, 13
painting, 588, 590, 592
painting knife, 589
painting upkeep, 304
painting, accessories, 591, 592
painting, equipment, 589
pajamas, 348
palatine tonsil, 143

palatoglossal arch, 142
pale, 818
palette with dipper, 592
palette with hollows, 592
paling fence, 263
pallet, 543, 707, 787
pallet spring, 543
pallet truck, 788
pallial line, 95
pallial sinus, 95
palm, 105, 137, 327, 483, 596
palm grove, 46
palmar pad, 106
palmate, 56
palmette, 220
pan, 708, 709, 795
pan cover, 795
pan hook, 708
panama, 328
pancake pan, 249
pancreas, 131
pane, 203
panel, 589
panel, 202, 229, 323, 346, 634, 649, 736, 756
panoramic head, 393
panoramic window, 190, 460
panpipe, 536
pantograph, 458
pantry, 195
pants, 323
pants, 353, 595, 602, 609, 680
pants, types, 336
panty corselette, 347
panty girdle, 346
panty hose, 344
papaya, 68
paper, 589
paper, 384, 580
paper advance setting, 531
paper bail, 524, 531
paper bail release lever, 525
paper bail roller, 531
paper catcher, 521
paper clamp, 531
paper clips, 515
paper fasteners, 515
paper feed channel, 521
paper feed key, 523
paper guide, 421, 531
paper in reserve, 532
paper punch, 516
paper release lever, 525
paper support, 525
paper tray, 521
paper trays, 532
papilla, 136, 140
papillary muscle, 125
parabolic antenna, 415
parabolic dune, 46
parabolic mirror, 770
parabolic reflector, 15
parachute, 812
parachute valve, 634
parade ground, 178
paraffins, 745
paragliding, 636
paragliding pilot, 636
parallel, 47
parallel bars, 661
parapet, 454
parapet walk, 181
parcels office, 462
parentheses, 832
parietal bone, 123
parietal pleura, 130
paring knife, 242
park, 52, 184
parka, 321
parka, 680
parking, 190, 193, 464
parking area, 503
parking brake lever, 430
parking lot, 185, 491, 504
parsley, 74
parsnip, 71
parterre, 189
partial eclipse, 8
particle board, 289
partition, 520
partition, 66
partitions, examples, 818
partlow chart, 441
party, 818
pass, 27
passenger cabin, 493, 494, 495, 499
passenger car, 477
passenger car, 458, 476
passenger liner, 496
passenger platform, 462

INDEX

The terms in **bold type** indicate the title of an illustration.

passenger station, 462
passenger station, 184, 464
passenger terminal, 504
passenger terminal, 491, 503
passenger train, 462
passenger transfer vehicle, 507
passenger transfer vehicle, 505
passing lane, 452
passing prohibited, 824, 825
passport case, 379
passport control, 505
pasta maker, 243
pastern, 101
pastry bag and nozzles, 245
pastry brush, 245
pastry cutting wheel, 245
patch pocket, 339
patch pocket, 320, 322, 350
patella, 103, 122
patera, 220
path, 263
patio, 193, 263
patio door, 195
pattern, 565, 586
pattern, 570
pattern start key, 569
pauldron, 792
pause, 539
pause button, 403
pause/still, 411, 831
pavilion, 363
pavilion facet (8), 363
pavilion roof, 183
Pavo, 13
pawl, 281
Pawn, 696
pay phone, 422
payload, 509
payload bay, 510
payload bay door, 510
payload module, 49
payout tray, 702
payout trigger, 702
pea, 67
pea, 67
pea jacket, 330
peach, 63
peach, 63
Peacock, 13
peak, 27, 328, 329, 729
peak level meter, 403
peaked lapel, 322
peanut, 66
pear, 64
pear-shaped body, 535
pear-shaped cut, 363
pearl, 105
pearls, 105
pecan nut, 66
pecten, 81
pectoral deck, 663
pectoral fin, 86
pectoral limb, 124
pedal, 446, 448, 545, 552, 553, 656, 664
pedal key, 542
pedal keyboard, 542
pedal pushers, 336
pedal rod, 540
pedestal, 453, 545
pedestal-type sump pump, 216
pedestrian crossing, 826, 827
pedestrian crossing, 186
pedicel, 60, 61, 62, 63, 64
pedicle, 105
pediment, 166, 168, 707
pedometer, 711
peeled veneer, 288
peeler, 242
peep hole, 471
peg, 225, 385, 544, 546, 571, 575
peg box, 544
Pegasus, 11
pelerine, 330
pelerine, 330
pellets, 799
peltate, 56
Pelton turbine, 754
pelvic fin, 86
pelvic limb, 124
pelvis, 103, 132
pen, 714
pen blade, 688
pen holder, 379
pen holder, 378
penalty arc, 601
penalty area, 601
penalty bench, 608
penalty line, 612

penalty spot, 601
pencil, 389, 515
pencil, 765
pencil pleat heading, 229
pencil point tip, 299, 307
pencil sharpener, 515, 516
pendant, 361
pendulum, 707
pendulum bar, 539
pendulum rod, 707
penholder grip, 619
peninsula, 51
penis, 116, 127
pennant, 817
pennant, 38
penstock, 746, 747, 752
pentaprism, 390
peplos, 315
pepper shaker, 238
per bend, 818
per fess, 818
percent, 830
percent key, 523
perching bird, 111
percolator, 247
percussion bar, 780
percussion instruments, 552, 554
perforated hardboard, 289
perforated pipe, 216
perforated toe cap, 355
perforation, 327, 395
pergola, 263
pericardium, 130
pericarp, 65, 66
period, 832
period, 489
periodontal ligament, 144
periople, 104
peripheral device port, 528
peripheral joint, 750
peripheral nervous system, 133
periscopic sight, 805
peristyle, 168, 169, 171
peritoneum, 127, 128
permanent pasture, 148
peroxide, 725
perpendicular, 830
perpetual snows, 27
perron, 196
Perseus, 11
personal AM-FM cassette player, 408
personal communications, 417
personal computer, 526
personal computer (view from above), 528
peseta, 832
pesticides, 32
pestle, 243
petal, 60
petanque bowl, 682
Peter Pan collar, 341
petiolar sinus, 61
petiole, 56
petrochemical industry, 744
petrochemicals, 745
phalanx prima, 103
phalanx secunda, 103
phalanx tertia, 103
pharmacy, 822
pharynx, 130, 131
phase conductor, 757
phases of the Moon, 6
philtrum, 141
phloem, 59
Phobos, 4
Phoenix, 13
phosphorescent coating, 232
photocopier, 532
photocopy control, 532
photoelectric cell, 393
photographic accessories, 393
photographic chamber, 717
photographic picture, 397
photography, 390, 392, 394, 396, 398
photosphere, 6
photovoltaic panel, 486, 487
physical map, 51
physician, 669
pi, 830
piano, 556
piccolo, 548, 557
pick, 267
pick, 385, 681
pickguard, 547
pickling onion, 70
pickup cylinder, 159, 162

pickup reel, 158, 160
pickup selector, 547
pickup truck, 425
picnic area, 823
picnics prohibited, 823
Pictor, 13
picture tube, 410
pie pan, 245
piedmont glacier, 27
pier, 739
pier, 174, 175, 454, 455
pierce lever, 256
pierced earrings, 361
pig, 151
piggyback car, 473
pigsty, 149
pike pole, 780
pike position, 624
pile dwelling, 165
pillar, 176, 545, 714, 736
pillar buoy, 487
pillar buoy, 489
pillbox hat, 329
pillion footrest, 443, 444
pillow, 570
pillow, 224, 570
pillow protector, 224
pillowcase, 224
pilot, 459, 469, 637, 814
pilot gas tube, 297
pin, 232, 233, 563, 683, 780
pin base, 232
pin block, 540
pin cushion, 563
pince-nez, 377
pinch, 232
pinch pleat, 228
pine needles, 58
pine nut, 66
pine seed, 58
pineal body, 134
pineapple, 68
pinion, 280, 707
pink ball, 673
pinking shears, 564
pinnacle, 176, 181
pinnatifid, 56
pinocytotic vesicle, 115
pins, 364
pins, types, 683
pip, 62, 64, 65, 695
pipe, 385
pipe, 260, 543
pipe A, 300
pipe B, 300
pipe cleaners, 385
pipe coupling, 301
pipe diffusers, 501
pipe rack, 385
pipe section, 205
pipe threader, 299
pipe tools, 385
pipe wrench, 299
pipe-wrapping insulation, 287
pipeline, 740
pipework, 543
pipe, cross section, 385
Pisces, 11
Pisces the Fishes (February 19), 820
Piscis Austrinus, 13
pistachio nut, 66
piste, 666
pistil, 60
pistol, 797
pistol grip, 795, 796, 798, 799
pistol grip handle, 280, 305
pistol nozzle, 264
piston, 432, 435, 436, 438
piston lever, 291
piston release, 291
piston skirt, 434
pit, 96, 405, 683
pita bread, 153
pitch, 599
pitch, 599
pitch scale, 524
pitch wheel, 555
pitched roof, 182
pitcher, 597
pitcher's mound, 597
pitcher's plate, 597
pitchfork comb, 368
pitching, 748
pitching wedge, 678
pith, 59
pithead, 734
pithead, 736
piton, 681

piton-carrier, 680
pituitary gland, 134
pivot, 311, 369, 374, 484, 485, 539, 564, 590, 719
pivot cab, 785
placard board, 471
placing judge, 621
plain, 51
plain gypsum lath, 286
plain pole, 230
plain weave, 576
plan reading, elevation, 193
plane, 277
plane figure, 580
plane projection, 50
planetarium, 16
planetarium, 184
planetarium projector, 16
planets, 4
planets, orbits, 4
plano-concave lens, 722
plano-convex lens, 722
plant cell, 115
plantar, 121
plantar interosseous, 120
plantar pad, 107
plantar surface of the hoof, 104
planting, 154, 158
planting box, 657
plant, structure, 57
plasmodesma, 115
plaster bat, 584
plastic case, 799
plastic insulator, 312
plastic pants, 349
plastic-laminated particle board, 289
plastron, 96
plate, 688
plate, 253, 393
plate crystal, 36
plate grid, 439
plateau, 27, 51
platen, 524, 531, 579
platen knob, 531
platform, 302, 457, 475, 504, 621, 709
platform edge, 462, 475
platform entrance, 463
platform ladder, 302
platform number, 462
platform pallet truck, 788
platform shelter, 464
platter, 238
platter, 404
play, 831
play, 411
play button, 403, 408, 411
play/pause, 405
player, 626
player's number, 602
player's stick, 609
players' bench, 604, 608, 610, 612, 613
playing area, 496
playing surface, 619
playing window, 403
pleasure garden, 263
pleasure garden, 193
pleated heading, 229
pleats, types, 228, 335
plectrum, 535
plenum, 206, 207
pleural cavity, 130
plexus of nerves, 144
plinth, 707
plotter, 527
plow anchor, 483
plowing soil, 154, 156
plug, 280, 400, 406, 485
plug adapter, 374
plug bayonet, 794
plug fuse, 312
plum, 63
plumber's snake, 299
plumbing, 292, 294, 296, 298, 299, 300
plumbing system, 215
plumbing tools, 299
plunger, 247, 299
plunger, 726
plungerhead, 159
plunging neckline, 343
plus or minus, 830
plus/equals key, 523
Pluto, 5
ply, 288
pneumatic armlet, 710
pneumatic hammer, 735

pocket, 378, 673, 679, 683
pocket calculator, 523
pocket camera, 395
pocket handkerchief, 322
pockets, types, 339
podium, 190
podium, 190
point, 240, 242, 389, 544, 562, 567, 644, 671, 684, 697, 698
point of interest, 52
point wire, 467
pointed tab end, 324, 339
pointer, 213, 705, 708, 709, 710
poison, 821
poisonous mushroom, 55
poker, 205
poker die, 699
poker, standard hands, 695
polar axis, 14
polar climates, 45
polar ice cap, 45
polar lights, 19
polar maritime, 38
polar orbit, 43
polar tundra, 45
polar-orbiting satellite, 43
Polaris, 11
polarizing filter, 392
Polaroid® Land camera, 394
pole, 657
pole, 230, 479
pole grip, 642
pole shaft, 642
pole tip, 643
pole vault, 657
pole vault, 655
poleyn, 792
police, 822
polished stone hand axe, 791
political map, 51
pollen basket, 81
pollen brush, 80, 81
pollen cell, 82
pollen packer, 81
pollution, atmospheric, 34
pollution, food, 32
polo collar, 342
polo dress, 333
polo shirt, 337
polo shirt, 615
polojama, 351
pome fleshy fruits, 64
pome fruits, major types, 64
pome fruit, section, 64
pomegranate, 68
pommel, 649, 661, 666
pommel horse, 661
poncho, 331
pond, 263
poniard, 794
pons Varolii, 134
pontoon, 457, 738
pool, 673
pool, 772
poop, 478
pop-up tent, 686
popping crease, 599
poppy, 67
porch, 172, 177
porch dome, 172, 173
pore, 67, 115, 136
Porro prism, 719
port, 650, 764
port glass, 237
port hand, 488, 489, 497
port sail plane, 807
portable AM-FM cassette recorder, 408
portable cellular telephone, 422
portable fire extinguisher, 780
portable shower head, 292
portable sound systems, 408
portal, 175
portal bridge, 455
portal frame, 455
portal vein, 124, 126
porthole, 496
position light, 459, 508
position marker, 546, 547
position of the ligament, 95
positive charge, 831
positive contact, 768, 769
positive meniscus, 722
positive plate, 439
positive plate strap, 439
positive region, 768
positive terminal, 439
positive/negative junction, 768
post, 572, 613, 618, 626, 773

post and plank, 647
post and plank, 646
post and rail, 647
post binder, 519
post lantern, 235
post mill, 773
posterior chamber, 140
posterior cutaneous nerve of thigh, 133
posterior end, 95
posterior root, 135
posterior rugae, 117, 119
posterior semicircular canal, 139
postern, 179, 181
potable water truck, 506
potato, 71
potato masher, 244
potential coil, 712
pothole, 24
pottery, 584
pottery, tools, 584, 585
pouch, 380
pouch of Douglas, 128
poulaine, 792
poultry shears, 246
pound, 832
powder blusher, 366
powder chamber, 801
powder flask, 795
powder puff, 366
power button, 402, 405, 410, 411
power car, 459
power cord, 374
power indicator, 529
power mower, 271
power plant, cross section, 752
power plug, 408
power station, 752
power supply cord, 370, 401
power switch, 529, 555
power switch machine, 467
power takeoff, 147
power train, 448
power turbines, 501
power zoom button, 409
power-off/slide-select bar, 397
power-on button, 420
power-on light, 420
power-takeoff shaft, 156, 159, 162
power/light switch, 561
powerhouse, 746
practice green, 676
prairie, 51
prayer hall, 172, 173
precious stones, 362
precipitation, 34, 35
precipitation area, 38
precipitations, 36
preferred channel, 489
premaxilla, 86
premolar, 98
premolars, 144
prepuce, 127
prescription, 831
present state of weather, 38
preset buttons, 411
preset tuning button, 402
president, 666
press bar, 663
press bed, 581, 583
press chamber, 159
press wheel, 158
pressed area, 405
pressed powder, 366
presser bar, 562
presser foot, 562
pressing, 579
pressing board, 579
pressure bar, 540
pressure change, 38
pressure control, 373
pressure control valve, 710
pressure cooker, 248
pressure demand regulator, 777
pressure dial, 561
pressure gauge, 627, 710, 740
pressure plate, 390
pressure regulator, 306
pressure regulator, 248, 306, 689
pressure relief valve, 209
pressure screw, 581, 583
pressure tube, 765
pressure vessel, 762
pressure-relief valve, 297
pressurized heavy water, 761
pressurized-water reactor, 762
pressurizer, 761
prestressed concrete, 286
preview monitor, 415
preview monitors, 413

price per gallon/litre, 453
pricker, 570
primaries, 110
primary consumers, 31
primary covert, 110
primary flight display, 500
primary mirror, 14, 16
primary root, 57
prime, 667
prime focus, 14
prime focus observing capsule, 14
prime meridian, 47
primer, 798, 799, 804
princess dress, 332
princess seaming, 345
principal rafter, 199
print drying rack, 399
print head, 531
print head drive, 531
print washer, 399
printed circuit, 528
printed image, 580
printer, 421
printer, 523
printer port, 528
printer table, 521
printing, 580
printing calculator, 523
printing of messages, 421
printing unit, 524
printout, 709
priority intersection, 825
prism binoculars, 719
private broadcasting network, 416
probe, 310
probe receptacle, 253
proboscis, 79
procedure checklist, 512
producer, 412, 415
producer turret, 407
product code, 709
production adviser, 412
production control room, 413
production control room, 412, 415
production desk, 413
production of electricity from nuclear energy, 766
production of electricity from solar energy, 771
production of electricity, steps, 755
production platform, 738
production platform, 740
production video switcher, 413
production/export riser system, 738
program selector, 555
progressive wave, 30
projectiles, 801
projection dome, 16
projection screen, 397
proleg, 78
promenade deck, 496
prominence, 6
prompt box, 188
prompt side, 189
pronaos, 168, 169
prop forward, 606
propane gas cylinder, 449
propellant, 798
propellant level gauge, 512
propeller, 160, 495, 496, 742, 806
propeller duct, 492
propeller shaft, 495
propellers, 808
property line, 193
propulsion machinery control room, 806
propulsion module, 418
proscenium, 188
prostate, 127
protect tab, 529
protection layer, 512
protective cup, 602, 609
protective equipment, 602
protective girdle, 609
protective helmet, 443
protective helmet, 448
protective surround, 698
protective window, 410
prothorax, 78
protoneuron, 135
protractor, 713
province, 51
proximal phalanx, 107, 122, 123
proximal sesamoid, 102
proximity fuse, 814
pruning knife, 269
pruning saw, 269
pruning shears, 269

psychrometer, 41
pubis, 116, 118
public building, 52
public garden, 190
puck, 608
puff sleeve, 340
pull bail, 397
pull rod, 467
pull strap, 383
pulley, 230, 302, 434, 793
pulley block, 793
pulley safety guard, 283
pulling ring, 726
pullman case, 383
pulmonary artery, 126, 130
pulmonary opening, 83
pulmonary trunk, 125
pulmonary valve, 125
pulmonary vein, 126
pulp, 65, 144
pulp canal, 144
pulp chamber, 144
pulverizing soil, 154, 157
pulvino, 750
pumice correcting pencil, 583
pump, 356
pump, 257, 258, 689, 761, 762, 771
pump island, 453
pump motor, 216
pump nozzle, 453
pump room, 742
pump suction head, 216
pumper, 778
pumpernickel bread, 153
pumping station, 740
pumpkin, 69
punch, 586
punch hole, 323, 353, 355
punctuation marks, 832
pup tent, 686
pupil, 107, 140
Puppis, 13
purfling, 544, 546
purge valve, 627
purple border, 315
purpure, 819
purse, 379
push button, 250, 257, 375
push buttons, 420, 422
push rim, 727
push-button, 290, 389, 397
push-button telephone, 422
push-up bra, 347
push-up stand, 664
pusher, 251
putter, 677
putter, 678
putting green, 676
pygal shield, 96
pyloric cecum, 88
pyramid spot, 663
pyrometric cone, 585
Pyxis, 13

Q

Qibla wall, 173
quad cane, 728
quarte, 667
quarter, 104, 352, 354
quarter note, 538
quarter rest, 538
quarter window, 427
quarter-deck, 496
quarterback, 603, 605
quarterly, 818
quartet, 558
quartz metronome, 539
quay, 490
quay ramp, 490
quayside crane, 490
quayside railway, 491
Queen, 695
Queen, 696
queen cell, 82
queen excluder, 82
Queen's side, 696
queen, honeybee, 81
question mark, 832
quiche plate, 245
quick release system, 393
quill, 389
quill, 281, 283
quill brush, 368
quince, 64
quinte, 667
quintet, 558
quiver, 684
quotation marks, 832
quotation marks (French), 832

R

raceme, 60
rachis, 110
rack, 674
rack, 248, 252, 255, 257, 656
rackboard, 543
rackboard support, 543
racquetball, 617
racquetball racket, 617
racquetball, court, 617
radar, 722
radar, 493, 494, 495, 497
radar antenna, 48, 807, 812
radar mast, 742
radar reflector, 487
radar unit, 813
Radarsat satellite, 49
radial nerve, 133
radial passenger loading area, 503
radial ply, 433
radial thruster, 42
radial tire, 433
radiant heater, 211
radiation zone, 6
radiator, 438
radiator, 16, 208, 469
radiator grille, 440
radiator hose, 438
radiator panel, 510
radicle, 57, 59
radio, 639
radio antenna, 494, 495, 497, 742, 807
radio mast, 738
radio telescope, 15
radio wave, 15
radioactive, 821
radiometer, 42, 43
radish, 71
radius, 102, 112, 122
radome, 813
rafter, 198
raglan, 330
raglan sleeve, 340
raglan sleeve, 319, 330, 350
rail, 225, 466, 568, 627, 675
rail joint, 466
rail section, 466
rail track, 735
railroad, 184
railroad crossing, 828
railroad line, 52
railroad station, 464
railroad station, 52
railroad track, 466
railway shuttle service, 504
rain, 36
rain cap, 205
rain gauge recorder, 40
rain shower, 39
rainbow, 36
raincoat, 319
raindrop, 36
rainfall, measure, 40
rainfly, 685, 686
raining, utensils for, 243
raised band, 577
raised figure, 580
rake, 159, 267
rake, 155
rake bar, 159
rake comb, 368
Ram, 11
ramekin, 238
rammer, 801
ramp, 168, 452, 733
rampart, 178, 180
ramrod, 795
random access memory (RAM) module, 528
range hood, 255
rangefinder, 394
rapier, 794
rasp, 587
raspberry, section, 62
ratchet, 276, 281, 573, 670
ratchet box end wrench, 279
ratchet knob, 711
ratchet wheel, 573, 706, 707
rate gyro, 814
rattle, 97
rattlesnake, 97
razor clam, 93
razors, 374
reaction direction, 831
reaction engine assembly, 43
reactor, 759, 764, 766, 806
reactor building, 759, 765

reactor building airlock, 758
reactor core, 760, 762, 763
reactor tank, 763
reactor vessel, 765
read-only memory (ROM) module, 528
read/write head, 529
reading, 376
reading mirror, 512
reading start, 405
reamer, 251
rear apron, 324
rear beam, 708
rear brake, 446
rear brake pedal, 444
rear bumper, 445
rear derailleur, 446, 448
rear foil, 495
rear leg, 223
rear light, 446
rear limit line, 666
rear runner, 643
rear seat, 428
rear shock absorber, 443
rear sight, 795, 796, 797, 798, 804
rear view, 147
rearview mirror, 430
récamier, 221
receiver, 15, 420, 614, 616, 618, 795, 796
receiver volume control, 420
receiving line, 617
receiving station, 722
receiving yard, 465
receptacle, 60, 62
receptacle analyzer, 310
reception bay, 764
reception hall, 172, 173
recharging base, 260
reclining back, 726
recoil sleigh, 802
recoilless rifle, 804
record, 404
record, 411
record announcement button, 420
record button, 403, 411
record control, 402
record muting button, 403
recorder, 621
recording level control, 403
recording tape, 403
recording unit, 40
rectangular, 687
rectangular flag, 817
rectum, 127, 128, 131
recuperator cylinder, 802
recuperator cylinder front head, 802
recyclable, 831
recycled, 831
Red, 697, 700, 701
red ball, 673
red balls, 673
red beam, 410
red flag, 626, 668
red ocher pencil, 583
red safelight filter, 399
Red Sea, 21
reduce/enlarge, 532
reducing coupling, 301
redundant bracing, 756
reed, 548, 572
reed hooks, 573
reed pipe, 542
reeds, 549
reef band, 480
reef point, 480
reel, 398, 666, 702
reel plate, 702
reel seat, 670, 671
referee, 601, 603, 605, 606, 608, 610, 613, 621, 626, 668, 669
refill, 389
refill tube, 293
refinery, 740
refinery products, 744
reflecting surface, 770
reflecting telescope, 720
reflecting telescope, cross section, 720
reflective stripe, 730, 777
reflector, 310, 441, 445, 446
reflex camera, cross section, 390
refracting telescope, 721
refracting telescope, cross section, 721
refractory brick, 585
refrigerant tank, 212
refrigerant tubing, 213
refrigeration unit, 441
refrigerator, 254

refrigerator car, 472
refrigerator compartment, 254
register, 712
registered trademark, 831
registers, types, 207
regulating button, 541
regulating valve, 208
regulator first stage, 627
regulator second stage, 627
rehearsing room, 188
reheater, 758
rein, 651
rein ring, 650
reinforced concrete, 286
reinforced toe, 730
release lever, 278
release setting screw, 641
release treadle, 573
relief printing, 580
relief printing process, 581
relief printing process, equipment, 581
relocation, 525
remote command antenna, 49
remote control, 411
remote control, 397
remote control sensor, 405, 410
remote control terminal, 391
remote detection satellite, 48
remote-control arm, 510
remote-controlled switch, 467
removable-bottomed pan, 245
renal artery, 126, 132
renal hilus, 132
renal papilla, 132
renal vein, 126, 132
reniform, 56
repeat keys, 405
repeat mark, 537
reptile, 96
rerebrace, 792
reserve parachute, 635
reservoir, 247, 543, 746, 747, 748, 749, 750
reservoir-nib pen, 589
reset, 532
reset button, 297, 411, 706, 711
reset key, 421
resine surface, 405
resistance adjustment, 664
resonator, 406, 542, 554
respirator, 730
respiratory system, 130
respiratory system protection, 730
respiratory system protection, 821
rest area, 52
rest symbols, 538
restaurant, 822
restaurant, 185, 190, 494
restricted area, 610
restricting circle, 610
retainer, 735
retaining ring, 295
retarding magnet, 712
reticle, 718
Reticulum, 13
retina, 140
retractable handle, 378
retractable step, 449
retracted claw, 107
retrenchment, 178
retriever, 613
return, 521
return air, 206, 207
return crease, 599
return key, 530
return spring, 432
reverse dive, 625
reverse slide change, 397
reverse stitch button, 561
reversible reaction, 831
reversing device, 212
revolver, 797
revolving cylinder, 570
revolving nosepiece, 718
revolving sprinkler, 264
rewind, 831
rewind, 411
rewind button, 403, 408, 411, 420
rhubarb, 72
rhythm selector, 555
rib, 72, 97, 102, 129, 375, 544, 546, 729, 785
rib joint pliers, 278
rib pad, 602
rib stitch, 567
ribbing, 326, 350, 670
ribbing plow, 156
ribbing plow, 154

ribbon cartridge, 531
ribosome, 115
ribs, 584
ribs, 122
rice, 152
rider, 648
ridge, 27
ridge beam, 199
riding, 646, 648
riding cap, 648, 651
riding crop, 648, 651
riding glove, 648
riding jacket, 648
riffler, 587
rifle (rifled bore), 798
rift, 28
rigging, 478
rigging wire, 637
right angle, 830
right ascension, 3
right ascension setting scale, 720, 721
right atrium, 124, 125
right back, 601, 607, 612
right bend, 826, 827
right bronchus, 130
right center, 606
right channel, 401
right cornerback, 603, 605
right defense, 608
right defensive end, 603, 605
right defensive tackle, 603, 605
right elevating handwheel, 802
right field, 597
right fielder, 597
right forward, 610, 613
right guard, 603, 605, 610
right half, 601, 607
right halfback, 603
right inner, 607
right kidney, 132
right lung, 124, 130
right outside linebacker, 605
right pulmonary vein, 125
right safety, 603
right safety back, 605
right service court, 614, 616
right tackle, 603, 605
right trail, 803
right ventricle, 124, 125
right wing, 606, 607, 608
right winger, 612
rigs, types, 482
rim, 147, 376, 433, 442, 447, 610, 658
rim flange, 433
rim soup bowl, 238
rinceau, 220
rind, 65
ring, 669
ring, 55, 230, 290, 375, 434, 483, 551, 566, 660, 681, 706, 709, 754
ring binder, 519
ring gate, 753
ring nut, 300
ring post, 669
ring step, 669
ringing volume control, 420
rings, 364, 660
ringside, 669
rink, 608, 620
rink, 620, 682
rink corner, 608
rinse-aid dispenser, 257
rip fence, 284, 285
rip fence guide, 285
rip fence lock, 285
rip fence rule, 285
rip fence slot, 285
ripeness, 61
ripening, 61
ripper, 783
ripper cylinder, 783
ripper tip, 783
ripper tooth, 783
rise, 201
riser, 201, 636
river, 51, 52
River Eridanus, 13
river estuary, 30, 51
rivet, 242, 278
road, 52
road communications, 417
road map, 52
road number, 52
road signs, 824, 826, 828
road system, 450, 452
road transport, 491
road work ahead, 826, 827
roadway, 186, 450
roadway narrows, 826, 827

The terms in **bold type** indicate the title of an illustration.

road, cross section, 450
roasting pans, 248
Roberval's balance, 708
rock, 30
rock basin, 26
rock garden, 263
rock step, 26
rocker arm, 435
rocket, 509
rocket motor, 814
rocking chair, 221, 223
rocking tool, 582
rocky desert, 46
rod, 214, 539, 573
rodent's jaw, 98
roll, 341
roll film, 395
roll-up blind, 231
roller, 270
roller, 230, 231, 369, 530, 583, 788
roller board and arms, 543
roller cover, 304
roller frame, 304
roller shade, 231
roller skate, 645
rolling ladder, 303
rolling pin, 245
romaine lettuce, 73
Roman house, 170
Roman legionary, 791
Roman metal pen, 389
roman shade, 231
Romanian couching stitch, 571
rompers, 351
roof, 82, 171, 197, 205, 427, 470, 733
roof pole, 686
roof truss, 199
roof vent, 196, 215, 449
roofs, 182
Rook, 696
room, 736
room air conditioner, 214
room thermostat, 213, 705
rooster, 150
root, 70, 143, 144, 240
root cap, 57
root hairs, 57
root of nail, 137
root of nose, 141
root rib, 498
root system, 57, 61
root vegetables, 71
root-hair zone, 59
rope, 361
rope, 669, 680, 692
rope ladder, 303
rose, 265, 289, 290, 546
rose cut, 363
rose window, 175
rosemary, 74
rosette, 167
rostrum, 90
rotary engine, 437
rotary file, 516
rotary hoe, 157
rotary system, 737
rotary table, 737
rotating auger, 160, 162
rotating dome, 14
rotating dome truck, 14
rotating drum, 714
rotating track, 15
rotating wheel, 701
rotor, 161, 290, 437, 753, 773, 774
rotor blade, 508
rotor head, 508
rotor hub, 508
rotunda, 190
rotunda roof, 183
rough, 676
roughing out, 586
roulette, 582
roulette table, 700
round brush, 368
round end pin, 231
round eye, 566
round head, 276
round ligament of uterus, 129
round neck, 343
round pronator, 120
router, 283
routing cardboard, 471, 743
row, 373
row counter, 568
row number display, 569
rower, 664
rowing (one oar), 632
rowing and sculling, 632
rowing boats, 632
royal agaric, 55

royal antler, 105
royal flush, 695
royal mast, 479
rub rail, 441
rubber, 355
rubber boot, 777
rubber bulb, 726
rubber gasket, 296
rubber mat, 404
rubber snaffle bit, 650
rubber stamp, 516
rubber thread, 677
rubber tip, 302, 728
rubber wall, 433
rubbing alcohol, 725
rubbing strip, 433
ruby, 362
ruching, 349
rudder, 492, 496, 499, 511, 628, 639, 742, 812, 814
rudder pedal, 639
Ruffini's corpuscle, 136
ruffle, 228, 317
ruffled rumba pants, 349
ruffled skirt, 334
rug and floor brush, 260
rugby, 606
rugby ball, 606
rugby, field, 606
ruler, 578, 591, 688
rump, 109
run, 201, 599
rung, 302
runner, 643, 697, 753
runner blade, 752, 753, 754
running, 654
running bowline, 691
running rail, 476
running shoe, 352
running surface, 466
running track, 786
runway, 504
runway, 476, 811
runway center line markings, 504
runway designation marking, 504
runway side stripe markings, 504
runway threshold markings, 505
runway touchdown zone marking, 505
Russian pumpernickel, 153
rutabaga, 71
rye, 152

S

S-band antenna, 43
S-band high gain antenna, 42
S-band omnidirectional antenna, 42
sabaton, 792
saber, 794
saber, 666
saber and épée warning line, 666
sable, 819
sabreur, 667
sacral plexus, 133
sacral vertebrae, 103
sacrum, 122, 123
saddle, 649
saddle, 386, 397, 636, 648, 651, 661
saddle pad, 648
saddlecloth, 648, 651
safari jacket, 338
safe water mark, 489
safelight, 398
safest water, 488
safety, 796
safety area, 668
safety binding, 641
safety boot, 730
safety cage, 654
safety cap, 729
safety cap, 804
safety chain, 449
safety earmuff, 729
safety glasses, 729
safety goggles, 729
safety handle, 271
safety line, 475
safety match, 386
safety pad, 659
safety pin, 566
safety rail, 302, 468
safety scissors, 365
safety suit connection, 512
safety symbols, 821
safety tank, 761
safety tether, 512
safety thermostat, 259
safety thong, 617
safety valve, 248, 766
safety vest, 730

sage, 74
Sagitta, 11
Sagittarius, 13
Sagittarius the Archer (November 22), 820
sail, 631, 637, 773
sail cloth, 773
sail panel, 628
sailbar, 773
sailboard, 631
sailboat, 628
sailing, 628, 629, 630
sailing, points, 629
sailor collar, 342
sails, 480
sails, types, 482
salad bowl, 238
salad fork, 240
salad plate, 238
salad spinner, 243
salamander, 85
salient angle, 178
saline lake, 46
salivary glands, 131
salsify, 71
salt marsh, 30
salt shaker, 238
salt taste, 143
sample, 567
sand, 748
sand bar, 30
sand island, 30
sand shoe, 441
sand wedge, 678
sandal, 356, 357
sandal, 791
sandbox, 469
sandstorm or dust storm, 39
sandy desert, 46
saphenous nerve, 133
sapphire, 362
sapwood, 59
sarong, 334
sartorius, 120
sash frame, 203
sash window, 203
satchel bag, 380
satellite, 416
satin weave, 576
Saturn, 5
sauce pan, 688
saucepan, 249
sauté pan, 249
savory, 74
sawing-in, 578
sawtooth roof, 182
saxhorn, 551
saxophone, 548
saxophone, 548
scale, 537
scale, 87, 96, 97, 111, 705, 711, 719, 726
scale leaf, 70
Scales, 13
scallion, 70
scallop, 93
scalper, 653
scampi, 91
Scandinavian crak bread, 153
scapula, 102, 122, 123
scapular, 110
scarp, 178
scatter cushion, 224
scattered sky, 39
scenery lift, 188
scenery storage, 188
scenic route, 52
schedules, 463
school zone, 826, 827
schooner, 482
sciatic nerve, 133
scientific air lock, 511
scientific instruments, 16, 511
scissors, 564
scissors, 688, 725
scissors crossing, 464
scissors cut, 362
scissors-glasses, 377
sclera, 140
scoop, 385
score-console, 683
scoreboard, 698
scorer, 610, 613, 666, 668
scoring light, 666
Scorpio the Scorpion (October 24), 820
Scorpion, 13
Scorpius, 13
scotia, 166, 167
scraper, 304, 582, 784

scraper, 583
scraper bar holder, 583
screen, 161, 374, 397, 410, 747
screen case, 397
screen print, 350
screen window, 685
screw, 276
screw, 544
screw base, 232
screw earrings, 361
screw locking nut, 670, 671
screwdriver, 276
screwdriver, 688
screwsleeve, 681
scrimmage, 603
scrimmage in Canadian football, 605
script assistant, 412
scroll, 544
scroll case, 747
scroll foot, 220
scrotum, 116, 127
scrum half, 606
scuba diver, 627
scuba diving, 627
scuffle hoe, 266
sculling (two oars), 632
sculling boats, 632
scythe, 267
sea, 7, 51, 752
sea anchor, 483
sea bag, 381
sea level, 22, 28
sea side, 752
sea-level pressure, 38
Sea-Serpent, 13
sea-to-sea missile, 809
seal, 295
sealed cell, 82
sealing ring, 741
seam, 327, 384, 598
seam allowance, 565
seam gauge, 563
seam line, 565
seam pocket, 339
seam pocket, 330
seaming, 322
seamount, 29
search-and-rescue antennas, 43
seasons of the year, 8
seat, 220, 223, 292, 293, 428, 445, 446, 584, 639, 649, 652, 664, 727
seat belt, 428
seat cover, 293
seat post, 446
seat stay, 446
seat tube, 446
seat-belt warning light, 431
seats, 222
sebaceous gland, 136
second, 830
second, 537, 669
second base, 597
second baseman, 597
second classification track, 465
second dorsal fin, 86
second floor, 194
second floor, 196
second focal room, 15
second hand, 706
2nd metacarpal, 112
second molar, 144
second premolar, 144
second reinforce, 800
second space, 610
second stage, 509
second valve slide, 550
second violins, 556
secondaries, 110
secondary channel, 489
secondary consumers, 31
secondary inlet, 741
secondary mirror, 16, 390
secondary reflector, 15
secondary road, 52
secondary root, 57
seconde, 667
secretarial desk, 521
secretary, 226
secretary, 612, 626
section of a bulb, 70
security casing, 271
security check, 504
security trigger, 272
sedimentary rocks, 23
seed, 62, 63, 64, 65, 66, 67
seed coat, 63, 152
seed drill, 158
seed drill, 154
seed leaf, 57

seed vegetables, 72
seeder, 268
segment, 65
segment score number, 698
seismic wave, 23
seismogram, 714
selector switch, 310
self-adhesive labels, 518
self-contained breathing apparatus, 777
self-inflating mattress, 687
self-timer indicator, 391
selvage, 566
semaphore, 464
semi-circle, 610
semi-detached cottage, 187
semi-fisheye lens, 392
semi-mummy, 687
semi-submersible platform, 739
semicircular arch, 174
semicolon, 832
semimembranous, 121
seminal vesicle, 127
semiprecious stones, 362
semitendinous, 121
semitrailer, 441
semitrailer, 440, 742
sense organs, 136, 138, 140, 141
sense receptor, 134
senses of smell, 142
senses of taste, 142
sensor probe, 253
sensory impulse, 135
sensory neuron, 134
sensory root, 135
sent document recovery, 421
sepal, 60, 62, 64
separator, 439, 742, 758
separator steam release, 758
septal cartilage of nose, 141
septic tank, 216
septime, 667
septum, 67, 141
septum pellucidum, 134
sequencer control, 555
serac, 26
Serpens, 11, 13
Serpent, 11, 13
Serpent Bearer, 11, 13
server, 613, 614, 616, 618
service area, 52, 503, 613
service box, 616, 617, 757
service box line, 617
service building, 764
service judge, 614, 618
service line, 614, 616, 617
service main, 186
service module, 418, 509
service road, 502
service room, 172, 173
service station, 453, 823
service zone, 617
serving bowl, 238
serving cart, 219
sesame seeded pita, 153
set, 525
set of utensils, 244
set-in sleeve, 324, 326
setting, 364
setting indicator, 641
setup, 683
setup, 683
7.5 m platform, 624
seventeenth-century cannon, 800
seventeenth-century mortar, 803
seventh, 537
sew-through buttons, 566
sewer, 186
sewing, 561, 562, 564, 566, 578
sewing frame, 578
sewing machine, 561
sewing, accessories, 563, 564
sewn-in floor, 685, 686
Sextans, 13
sextant, 484
Sextant, 13
sextet, 558
shackle, 630
shade, 234, 236
shade cloth, 231
shadow, 706
shadow key, 396
shadow roll, 651
shady arcades, 172, 173
shaft, 38, 166, 575, 584, 609, 615, 632, 652, 658, 674, 675, 677, 681, 684, 698, 705, 753, 808
shaft head, 734
shaft holder, 653
shake-hands grip, 619

shallot, 70, 542
shallow root, 59
sham, 224
shank, 275, 276, 281, 369, 375, 385, 483, 562, 563, 564, 567, 568, 671
shank button, 566
shank protector, 783
shapka, 328
share, 156
sharp, 538
sharpening steel, 242
shaving brush, 374
shaving mug, 374
shawl collar, 341
sheath, 690
sheath, 56, 101, 106, 688, 692
sheath dress, 332
sheath of Schwann, 135
sheath skirt, 334
sheathing, 198, 199
shed, 193, 263
shed stick, 574
sheep, 150
sheep shelter, 149
sheepshank, 691
sheepskin jacket, 321
sheer curtain, 229
sheet, 480, 577
sheet bend, 691
sheet film, 395
sheet lead, 630
sheet of paper, 714
shekel, 832
shelf, 226, 254, 302
shelf channel, 254
shell, 96
shell, 66, 83, 92, 109, 256, 383, 553, 643, 741
shell membrane, 109
shell, valve, 95
shield, 426, 791
shield divisions, 818
shift key, 524, 530
shift lock key, 524, 530
shifter, 447, 448
shin boot, 648, 652
shin guard, 595, 600
shin pad, 609
shingle, 286
ship's anchor, 483
Ship's Compass, 13
Ship's Keel, 13
ship's motor boat, 809
Ship's Sails, 13
Ship's Stern, 13
shirred heading, 229
shirt, 324, 349
shirt, 656
shirt collar, 341
shirt sleeve, 340
shirttail, 324, 337
shirtwaist dress, 333
shock absorber, 445
shoe, 397
shoe polish, 358
shoe polisher, 358
shoe rack, 358
shoebrush, 358
shoehorn, 358
shoelace, 358
shoelace, 352
shoes, 354, 356, 358
shoeshine kit, 358
shoes, accessories, 358
shoes, major types, 354, 355, 356
shoetree, 358
shoe, parts, 354
shoot, 57, 59
shooting adjustment keys, 409
shooting star, 19
shop, 170
shopping bag, 381
shore, 30
short extensor of toes, 120
short glove, 327
short line, 616, 617
short palmar, 121
short peroneal, 121
short radial extensor of wrist, 121
short service line, 618
short sleeve, 318
short sock, 344
short splice, 692
shorts, 336
shorts, 351, 600, 656
shortstop, 597
shot, 658
shot, 801
shot put, 655
shotgun (smooth-bore), 799

shoulder, 100, 106, 116, 118, 279, 451, 545, 615, 670
shoulder bag, 380
shoulder belt, 428
shoulder blade, 117, 119
shoulder bolt, 279
shoulder pad, 602, 609, 804
shoulder rest, 804
shoulder strap, 346, 375, 380, 382, 679
shovel, 205, 266
shovel, 640, 642
shower, 194
shower and tub fixture, 215
shower head, 292
shower stall, 292
shrimp, 90
shroud, 479, 628
shutoff switch, 216
shutoff valve, 215, 293, 296, 298
shutter, 203, 529, 772
shutter release button, 391
shutter speed setting, 396
shutting stile, 202
shuttle, 573
shuttle, 510
shuttlecock, 618
sickle, 269
side, 239, 479, 787
side back vent, 322
side chair, 223
side chapel, 176
side door, 477
side footboard, 469
side handle, 280
side handrail, 477
side judge, 605
side ladder, 470
side lane, 452
side line, 619
side mirror, 368
side panel, 319
side post, 199
side rail, 302, 441
side span, 456
side vent, 25, 449
side wall, 104, 470, 492, 616, 617, 621
side wall line, 616
side-marker light, 429
side-tilt lock, 393
sideline, 604, 607, 610, 611, 612, 613
sidewalk, 186
sidewall, 441
sieve, 161
sifter, 245
sight, 140
sight, 684, 719, 803
sighting line, 719
sighting mirror, 719
sigmoid colon, 131
signal ahead, 826, 827
signal background plate, 471
signal gantry, 464
signal lamp, 247, 252, 255, 256, 257, 585
signature, 577
signet ring, 364
signs of the zodiac, 820
silencer, 735
silique, section, 67
silk, 72
sill, 24, 199
sill of frame, 203
sill plate, 198, 199
sill step, 470
silos, 490
silverware, 239, 240
sima, 166
simple eye, 78, 80, 81
simple leaves, 56
simple-span beam bridge, 454
single curtain rod, 230
single pole breaker, 312
single quotation marks, 832
single reed, 549
single scull, 632
single seat, 477
single twist, 281
single zero, 700, 701
single-breasted jacket, 322
single-burner camp stove, 689
single-decked pallet, 787
single-family home, 187
single-handle kitchen faucet, 296
single-leaf bascule bridge, 457
single-lens reflex (SLR) camera, 391
single-lens reflex camera, 394
singles pole, 614

singles service court, 618
singles sideline, 614, 618
sinister, 818
sinister base, 818
sinister chief, 818
sinister flank, 818
sink, 215, 292, 296
sinker, 486, 672
sinkhole, 24
sinus, 315
siphon, 24
siphonal canal, 94
site plan, 193
sitting room, 195
sixte, 667
sixteenth note, 538
sixteenth rest, 538
sixth, 537
sixty-fourth note, 538
sixty-fourth rest, 538
skate, 609
skate guard, 644
skating, 644
skeg, 631
skeleton, 122
skeleton, horse, 102
ski, 445, 641
ski boot, 641
ski boot, 640
ski glove, 640
ski goggles, 640
ski hat, 640, 642
ski pants, 336
ski pole, 640, 642
ski stop, 640, 641
ski suit, 640, 642
ski tip, 642
skid, 508
skimmer, 244
skin, 136
skin, 62, 63, 64, 84, 134
skin surface, 137
skip, 620, 736
skirt, 331, 615, 649, 792
skirt finger, 493
skirt marker, 564
skirts, types, 334
skull, 88, 102, 116, 134, 792
skullcap, 328
sky coverage, 39
sky diver, 635
sky diving, 635
skylight, 194, 197
skyscraper, 185
slab, 288
slab building, 584
slalom ski, 633
slat, 571
sled, 264, 643
sleeper-cab, 440
sleepers, 350
sleeping bags, 687
sleeping car, 460
sleeping compartment, 460
sleet, 37, 39
sleeve, 318, 322, 662, 663, 667
sleeve strap, 319
sleeve strap loop, 319
sleeveless jersey, 662
sleeves, types, 339, 340
slender, 121
slide, 257, 397, 566, 797
slide chair, 467
slide plate, 561, 562
slide projector, 397
slide tray, 397
slide-bar, 568
slider, 543
sliding block, 476
sliding breech, 802
sliding channel, 470
sliding cheek bit, 650
sliding cover, 484
sliding door, 202
sliding folding door, 202
sliding folding window, 203
sliding lever, 428
sliding rail, 428, 630
sliding sunroof, 427
sliding weight, 539, 708
sliding window, 203
slight drifting snow low, 39
slightly covered sky, 39
sling back shoe, 356
slip, 345
slip joint, 278
slip joint pliers, 278
slip-stitched seam, 324
slippery road, 826, 827
slit, 576

INDEX

856

The terms in **bold type** indicate the title of an illustration.

slope, 451
sloped turret, 183
sloping cornice, 168
slot, 188, 240, 252, 276, 379, 578
slot machine, 702
slotback, 605
slow-burning stove, 204
slow-motion, 411
slower traffic, 452
sludge, 216
small decanter, 237
small hand cultivator, 268
small intestine, 131
smaller round, 121
smell, 141
smock, 337
smoke, 39
smoke baffle, 204
smoke bomb discharger, 805
smoking accessories, 384, 386
smoking candle, 582
smoking-apparatus, 582
snaffle bit, 650
snaffle bit, 649
snaffle rein, 649
snaffle strap, 649
snail, 83
snail dish, 246
snail tongs, 246
snap, 566
snap, 672
snap fastener, 321, 327
snap shackle, 630
snap-fastening front, 350
snap-fastening tab, 321
snap-fastening waist, 350
snare, 553
snare drum, 553
snare drum, 552, 557
snare head, 553
snare strainer, 553
snelled fishhook, 672
snooker, 673
snorkel, 627
snout, 84
snow, 34
snow crystals, classification, 36
snow gauge, 41
snow guard, 445
snow pellet, 37
snow shower, 39
snowfall, measure, 41
snowmobile, 445
snowshoe, 645
snowsuit, 351
soap dish, 292
soccer, 600
soccer ball, 600
soccer player, 600
soccer shoe, 600
soccer, playing field, 601
sock, 344
sock, 602, 615
socket, 309, 401, 566
socket bayonet, 794
socket head, 276
socks, 325
sofa, 221
soft palate, 141, 142
soft pastel, 588
soft pedal, 540, 555
soft ray, 87
soft shell clam, 93
soft-drink dispenser, 453
soil, 750
solar array, 42, 48, 418
solar array deployment, 419
solar array drive, 42
solar cell, 768
solar cell, 523, 769
solar cell panel, 769
solar cells, 42
solar collector, 772
solar eclipse, 8
solar energy, 768, 770, 772
solar furnace, 770
solar house, 772
solar panel, 16
solar radiation, 768, 769, 770, 771, 772
solar ray reflected, 770, 771
solar reflectors, 418
solar shield, 512
solar system, 4
solar-cell system, 769
solder, 307
soldering, 305, 306, 308
soldering gun, 305
soldering iron, 305
soldering torch, 299, 307

sole, 104, 325, 641, 644, 678
soleplate, 256
soleus, 120
solid body, 547
solid rubber tire, 788
solid shot, 801
solid-rocket booster, 510
solitaire ring, 364
solvent extraction unit, 744
sorghum, 152
sound alarm, 485
sound digitizing processor, 528
sound hole, 544
sound receiver, 726
sound reproducing system, 400, 402, 404
sound reproducing system, components, 400
sound signal, 539
soundboard, 535, 540, 544, 545, 546
soundbox, 545
soup bowl, 238
soup spoon, 241
soup tureen, 238
sour taste, 143
South, 488
South America, 20
South cardinal mark, 489
South celestial pole, 3
South Pole, 3
Southeast, 488
Southern Cross, 13
Southern Crown, 13
Southern Fish, 13
Southern hemisphere, 3, 47
Southern Triangle, 13
Southwest, 488
southwester, 329
sow, 151
soybeans, 72
space, 537
space bar, 525, 530
space probe, 19
space shuttle, 510
space shuttle at takeoff, 510
space shuttle in orbit, 510
spacelab, 511
spacer, 727, 765
spacesuit, 512
spade, 266, 632, 695
spade, 803
spading fork, 266
spadix, 60
spaghetti tongs, 246
spandrel, 174
spanker, 480
spar, 498
spar buoy, 489
spark, 436
spark plug, 439
spark plug, 271, 435, 437
spark plug body, 439
spark plug cable, 435
spark plug gap, 439
spark plug gasket, 439
spark plug terminal, 439
sparkling wine glass, 237
spatial dendrite, 36
spatula, 589
spatula, 244, 581
spatulate, 56
speaker, 408, 420, 500
speaker cover, 400
speaker selector, 402
spear, 72, 791
speargun, 627
special mark, 489
specimen chamber, 717
specimen positioning control, 717
spectrometer, 717
speed control, 250, 271
speed controller, 561
speed course, 646
speed selector, 251, 404
speed selector switch, 370
speed skate, 644
speedbrake lever, 500
speedometer, 431, 445, 664
spelling corrector, 524
spencer, 338
spent fuel discharge bay, 758
spent fuel port, 764
spent fuel storage bay, 758, 764, 765
spermatic cord, 127
spermatozoon, 127
sphenoidal sinus, 141
sphere support, 40
sphincter muscle of anus, 131
spicules, 6

spider, 77
spider, 77
spike, 60, 466, 656, 680, 681
spiked shoe, 595
spillway, 746
spillway chute, 746
spillway gate, 746
spinach, 73
spinal cord, 89, 134, 135
spinal ganglion, 135
spinal nerve, 135
spindle, 223, 251, 290, 294, 404, 707, 711, 712
spine, 577
spine of scapula, 123
spine of the book, 579
spinner, 672
spinning rod, 671
spinous process, 135
spiny lobster, 91
spiny ray, 86
spiracle, 78, 79
spiral, 276, 404
spiral arm, 9
spiral beater, 250
spiral binder, 519
spiral case, 753
spiral galaxy, 9
spiral rib, 94
spiral screwdriver, 276
spiral staircase, 741
spiral-in groove, 404
spire, 94, 175
spirit level, 291
spit, 30
splash plate, 741
splat, 220
splay, 175
spleen, 88, 124
splenius muscle of head, 121
spline, 439
splints, 725
split bet, 700, 701
split end, 603, 605
split link, 672
spoiler, 442, 498
spoke, 447
spoked wheel, 652
sponge, 801
sponge-tipped applicator, 367
sponges, 367
spool, 570, 670, 671
spool pin, 561
spool rack, 575
spoon, 241
spoon, 688
spoon blade, 587
spoons, major types, 241
spores, 55
sports car, 425
sportswear, 352
spot, 235
spot white ball, 673
spotlight, 414, 777, 778, 780
spotmeter, 396
spout, 162, 247, 252, 294, 295
spout assembly, 296
spray, 256
spray arm, 257
spray button, 256
spray control, 256
spray head, 296
spray hose, 292, 296
spray nozzle, 264
spray nozzle, 741
spray paint gun, 304
sprayer, 264
spread collar, 324
spreader, 270
spreader, 375
spreader adjustment valve, 304
spring, 8, 234, 258, 278, 290, 294, 389, 469, 659, 804
spring balance, 709
spring binder, 519
spring housing, 230
spring linkage, 702
spring wing, 276
spring-metal insulation, 287
springboard, 659
springer, 174
sprinkler hose, 265
sprinklers, 766
sprocket, 445
sprocket wheel, 783, 805
spur, 27, 80, 281, 552, 648
squall, 39
square, 184, 577
square bet, 700, 701
square brackets, 832

square flag, 817
square head plug, 301
square knot, 691
square movement, 696
square neck, 343
square root key, 523
square root of, 830
square sail, 482
square trowel, 291
square-headed tip, 276
squash, 616
squash ball, 616
squash racket, 616
squash, court, 616
stabilizer, 636, 684, 812
stabilizer fin, 496
stabilizing fin, 509
stabilizing shaft, 788
stable, 651
stack, 30, 494
stacking chairs, 223
stadium, 185
staff, 537
staff, 817
stage, 189
stage, 188, 717, 718
stage clip, 718
stage curtain, 188, 189
stained glass, 175
stairs, 201
stairs, 194, 474, 741
stairwell, 194
stake, 263, 685, 686
stake loop, 685, 686
stake pocket, 441
stalactite, 24
stalagmite, 24
stalk, 62, 63, 64, 72
stalk vegetables, 72
stamen, 60, 64
stamp, 384
stamp pad, 516
stamp rack, 516
stanchion, 644
stand, 651
stand, 236, 248, 250, 341, 370, 382, 552, 586, 714
stand-off half, 606
stand-up collar, 342
standard A, 539
standard lens, 392
standardbred pacer, 652
standby airspeed indicator, 500
standby altimeter, 500
standby attitude indicator, 500
standing press, 579
standpipe, 298
staples, 138
staple remover, 515
stapler, 515
staples, 515
star anise, 67
star diagonal, 721
star facet (8), 363
star tracker, 16
starboard diving plane, 806
starboard hand, 488, 489, 497
starch, 152
starch granule, 115
start, 532
start and finish, 646
start button, 706
start key, 421
start line, 655, 656
start switch, 259
start wall, 621
start-up key, 530
starter, 271, 272, 621
starter handle, 272
starting bar (backstroke), 621
starting block, 621, 656
starting block, 621
starting cable, 270
starting dive, 622
starting position, 625
starting step, 201
state, 51
station circle, 38
station entrance, 474
station name, 474
station platform, 464
station wagon, 425
stationary bicycle, 664
stationary bowl, 701
stationary front, 39
stationery, 515, 516, 518
stationery cabinet, 522
stator, 290, 753
stay, 479
stay ring, 753

The terms in **bold type** indicate the title of an illustration.

stay vane blade, 753
stays, 456
staysail-stay, 479
steak knife, 239
steam generator, 759, 761, 762, 771, 806
steam generator room cooler, 759
steam iron, 256
steam outlet, 760, 761, 762, 763
steam pressure drives turbine, 767
steam release pipes, 759
steel, 286
steel, 346, 795
steel bar, 660
steel belted radial tire, 433
steel pen, 389
steel safety wheel, 476
steel spring, 795
steel to plastic, 301
steelyard, 708
steep hill, 826, 827
steeple hurdle, 656
steeplechase, 655
steering axle, 788
steering cylinder, 784
steering lever, 788
steering wheel, 147, 430
stellar crystal, 36
stem, 55, 57, 70, 232, 247, 385, 447, 479, 705
stem bulb, 497
stem faucet, 294
stem holder, 294
stem washer, 294
step, 147, 302, 440
step chair, 222
step cut, 363
step groove, 201
step setting, 711
step stool, 302
stepladder, 302
stepladders, 302
steppe, 45
stereo camera, 395
stereo control, 408
stereo phase monitor, 413
sterile pad, 725
stern, 496, 631
stern post, 742
sternocleidomastoid, 120
sternum, 102, 122
stethoscope, 726
steward's desk, 461
stick, 375, 607
stick, 544
stick eraser, 515
stick umbrella, 375
stickpin, 364
sticks, 553
stifle, 101
stigma, 60, 66
stile, 223
stile groove of sash, 203
stile tongue of sash, 203
stiletto, 794
still cameras, 394, 395
still video camera, 395
still video film disk, 395
still water level, 30
stilt, 585
stilted, 174
stimulator tip, 373
stinger, 81
stipule, 56
stirrup, 793
stirrup iron, 648
stirrup leather, 649
stirrup sock, 595
stitch, 352, 355
stitch control buttons, 569
stitch length regulator, 561
stitch pattern memory, 569
stitch patterns, 567
stitch selector, 561
stitch width selector, 561
stitches, 596
stitches, embroidery, 571
stitching, 327
stock, 483, 536, 773, 798, 799
stock pot, 249
stockade, 181
stocked anchor, 483
stocking, 667
stocking cap, 329
stocking stitch, 567
stockless anchor, 483
stomach, 88, 92, 97, 124, 131
stomach throw, 668
stomacker, 317

stone, 286
stone, 63, 364
Stone Age arms, 791
stone fleshy fruits, 63
stone fruits, major types, 63
stone fruit, section, 63
stoner, 246
stop, 831
stop, 106, 411, 532, 566, 570, 632
stop at intersection, 824, 825
stop bath, 399
stop button, 272, 403, 411, 420, 706
stop knob, 542, 543
stop rod, 543
stop watch, 407
stop/clear key, 405
stopwatch, 706
storage compartment, 397, 440, 449, 778, 780
storage door, 254
storage furniture, 225, 226
storage space, 461
storage tank, 744, 772
storage tray, 591, 764
storm collar, 205
storm sewer, 186
stormy sky, 36
stove oil, 745
straight, 695
straight bet, 700, 701
straight blade, 587
straight eye, 566
straight flush, 695
straight jaw, 278
straight ladder, 303
straight muscle of thigh, 120
straight position, 624
straight razor, 374
straight skirt, 334
straight wing, 499
straight-up ribbed top, 325
straight: post and rail, 646
strainer, 243
strainer, 251, 685
strainer body, 296
strainer coupling, 296
straining, utensils for, 243
strait, 51
strand, 692
strap, 365, 596, 660, 662, 706, 777
strap wrench, 299
strapless brassiere, 346
stratocumulus, 44
stratosphere, 19
stratum basale, 136
stratum corneum, 136
stratum granulosum, 136
stratum lucidum, 136
stratum spinosum, 136
stratus, 44
straw spreader, 161
strawberry, section, 62
streamer, 817
street, 52, 184, 190
street bet, 700, 701
street light, 185, 186
street, cross section, 186
stretcher, 219, 726
strike plate, 290
striker, 307
striker, 804
striker wheel, 386
striking circle, 607
string, 541, 544, 545
stringed instruments, 544, 546
stringer, 787
stringing, 615
strings, 540
strip flooring with alternate joints, 200
strip light, 235
strip mine, 733
stroke judge, 621
strokes, types, 622
strongbox, 702
structure of the Sun, 6
strut, 199, 495, 553, 774
stud, 198, 353
studio, 407
studio floor, 412
studio, radio, 407
studio, television, 412, 414
studs, 598
stummel, 385
stump, 59
stump, 598, 599
style, 60, 62, 63, 64, 67
styling brush, 370
stylobate, 166, 168

stylus, 389
stylus cartridge, 404
sub-base, 40
subarctic climates, 45
subarctic climates, 45
subbase, 451
subclavian artery, 126
subclavian vein, 126
subcutaneous tissue, 137
subfloor, 198, 199, 200
subgrade, 451
sublimation, 34
submachine gun, 795
submarine, 806
submarine canyon, 29
submarine pipeline, 740
subsidiary track, 464
substation, 752
substitute corridor, 612
substructure, 737
subterranean stream, 24
subtract from memory, 523
subtract key, 523
subtraction, 830
subtropical climates, 45
suburban commuter railroad, 464
suburbs, 52
subway, 474, 476
subway, 190
subway map, 475, 477
subway station, 474
subway train, 476
subway train, 474
sucker, 61
suction hose, 778
sudoriferous duct, 136
sugar bowl, 238
suit, 331
sulcus terminalis, 143
sulky, 652
sum, 830
sumie, 589
summer, 8
summer solstice, 8
summer squash, 69
summit, 27
sump, 216, 736
Sun, 6
Sun, 4, 8
Sun mode position, 419
sun sensor, 42, 43, 49
sun visor, 430, 449
sundae spoon, 241
sundeck, 497
sundial, 706
sundress, 332
sunglasses, 377
sunshade, 42
sunshine recorder, 40
sunshine, measure, 40
sunspot, 6
Sun, structure, 6
super, 82
superficial peroneal nerve, 133
superior cymbal, 552
superior dental arch, 142
superior mesenteric artery, 126, 132
superior mesenteric vein, 126
superior nasal concha, 141
superior semicircular canal, 139
superior umbilicus, 110
superior vena cava, 124, 125, 126, 130
superstructure, 486
supply duct, 213
supply line, 215
supply point, 757
supply tube, 296
support, 40, 223, 230, 232, 574, 720
support leg, 156, 441, 449
support leg crank, 441
support structure, 15, 48
supports, 589
suprarenal gland, 132
sural nerve, 133
surcingle, 653
surface cold front, 39
surface course, 450
surface element, 255
surface insulation, 510
surface of the water, 624
surface runoff, 32, 34
surface scum, 216
surface surveillance radar, 809, 810
surface warm front, 39
surface-piercing foils, 495
surface-to-air missile, 814
surface-to-subsurface missile, 809, 814
surroyal antler, 105

suspended span, 454
suspender, 456
suspender clip, 323
suspenders, 323
suspension, 477
suspension arm, 258
suspension band, 729
suspension bridge, 456
suspension cable, 456
suspension insulator string, 756
suspension lines, 636
suspension spring, 707
suspension truck, 458
suspensory ligament, 140
suture, 67, 94
swagger stick, 375
swallow hole, 24
swallowtail, 817
swallowtail and tongue, 817
Swan, 11
sweat pants, 352
sweat shirt, 352
sweater, 326
sweaters, 326, 338
sweeping hip throw, 668
sweeping score line, 620
sweet bay, 74
sweet peas, 72
sweet pepper, 69
sweet potato, 71
sweet taste, 143
sweetheart neckline, 343
swell organ manual, 542
swell pedals, 542
swept-back wing, 499
swift, 575
swimmerets, 91
swimming, 621, 622
swimming pool, 496, 621, 626
swimming trunks, 353
swimsuit, 353
swing bridge, 457
swinging door, 202
Swiss army knife, 688
Swiss chard, 72
switch, 309
switch, 254, 280, 283, 285, 464
switch lock, 280
switch plate, 309
switch point, 467
switch rod, 467
switch signal, 467
switch stand, 467
switch tower, 464
swivel, 658, 672, 737
swivel base, 282
swivel cord, 370
swivel head, 282
swivel lock, 282
swivel wall lamp, 234
swivel-tilter armchair, 520
Swordfish, 13
symbol, 702
symbols, dangerous materials, 821
symbols, protection, 821
sympathetic ganglion, 135
symphony orchestra, 556
symphysis pubis, 127, 128
synapse, 135
synthesizer, 555
synthetic sponge, 367
syringe, 726
syringe for irrigation, 726
system buttons, 555
systems display, 500

T

T-shirt dress, 351
T-strap shoe, 356
T-tail unit, 498
tab, 518
tab, 319, 375, 378, 379, 566, 649
tab key, 530
tab setting, 525
table, 219, 674
table, 283, 285, 363, 578
table cut, 363
table extension, 285
table lamp, 236
table mixer, 250
table saw, 285
table tennis, 619
table tennis ball, 619
table tennis paddle, 619
table-locking clamp, 283
tablespoon, 241
tables, major types, 219

INDEX

The terms in **bold type** indicate the title of an illustration.

tablet, 725
table, tennis, 619
tablinum, 170
tabulator, 524
tachometer, 431, 445
tack, 631
tackle box, 672
tadpole, 84
tag, 352, 354
tail, 91, 96, 97, 101, 106, 107, 112,
    127, 499, 579, 633, 638, 641, 642,
    643, 645, 670
tail assembly, 499
tail boom, 508
tail comb, 368
tail edge, 577
tail feather, 109
tail of helix, 139
tail pipe, 439
tail pipe extension, 439
tail pole, 773
tail shapes, types, 498
tail skid, 508
tail-out groove, 404
tailing auger, 161
taillight, 147, 429, 441, 443, 444
taillights, 429
tailored collar, 341
tailored collar, 330
tailored sleeve, 340
tailpiece, 296, 544
tailrace, 747
take-up handle, 572
take-up reel, 403
take-up spool, 390
talon, 111
talus, 123
tambourine, 554
tamper, 385
tandem disk harrow, 157
tandem disk harrow, 154
tang, 239, 242, 291
tank, 805
tank, 216, 398, 399, 689, 742, 743,
    780
tank ball, 293
tank car, 472, 743
tank farm, 740
tank gauge float, 741
tank hatch, 743
tank lid, 293
tank sprayer, 265
tank top, 351, 353
tank trailer, 742
tank wall, 742
tanker, 742
tanker, 491, 813
tanks, 511
tap connector, 265
tape, 566, 571, 607, 613, 711, 804
tape counter, 403
tape dispenser, 516
tape lock, 711
tape measure, 563, 711
tape selector, 403
tape-guide, 403
tapered wing, 499
tapestry bobbin, 574
tapestry bobbin, 574
taproot, 59
tar paper, 286
target, 684
target area, 770
target areas, 667
target detection radar, 809
tarlatan, 582
tarragon, 74
tarsus, 78, 80, 103, 108, 122
tassel, 229, 231
tasset, 792
taste sensations, 143
Taurus, 11
Taurus the Bull (April 20), 820
taxi transportation, 822
taxiway, 502
taxiway line, 503
tea ball, 246
team bench, 626
team shirt, 595, 600
teapot, 238
tear tape, 384
tear-off calendar, 518
teaser comb, 368
teaspoon, 241
technical equipment compartment,
    415
technical identification band, 405
technical producer, 412, 415
technical producer monitor, 413

technical specifications, 433
tedding, 155, 159
teddy, 345
tee, 301
tee, 298, 620, 677
teeing ground, 676
teeth, 144
teeth, 566
tele-converter, 392
telecommunication antenna, 494, 497,
    809
telecommunication satellites, 418
telecommunication satellites,
    examples, 418
telecommunication terminal, 422
telecommunications by satellite,
    417
telecommunications by telephone
    network, 417
telephone, 822
telephone, 413
telephone answering machine,
    420
telephone cable, 186
telephone index, 516
telephone index, 420
telephone network, 417
telephone set, 420
telephone set, 415, 417
telephones, types, 422
telephone, communication, 420,
    422
telephoto lens, 392
teleport, 417
teleprompter, 414
telescope, 14
telescope, 14, 42, 484, 713
telescope base, 14
telescopic boom, 780, 786
telescopic corridor, 503
telescopic front fork, 442
telescopic leg, 726
telescopic sight, 718
telescopic sight, 798
telescopic umbrella, 375
telescoping leg, 393
telescoping uncoupling rod, 470
television, 410, 412, 414
television set, 410
television set, 401
telex, 421
telex, 417
telltale, 616, 628
telson, 91
temperate climates, 45
temperature, 210
temperature control, 213, 252, 256,
    297
temperature control knob, 585
temperature indicator, 431
temperature of dew point, 38
temperature scale, 19
temperature scales, 710
temperature selector, 253, 258, 259
temperature set point knob, 705
temperature, measure, 41
template, 738
temple, 573
temple, 116, 376, 578
tempo control, 555
tempo scale, 539
temporal bone, 122
10 m platform, 624
10 yards line, 606
tenaille, 179
tendon, 107
tendon guard, 644
tendril, 61
tennis, 614
tennis ball, 615
tennis player, 615
tennis racket, 615
tennis shoe, 355
tennis shoe, 615
tennis, court, 614
tennis, net, 614
tenon saw, 578
tenor drum, 553
tenpin, 683
tensiometer, 710
tension adjustment, 671
tension block, 562, 569
tension block, 561
tension dial, 562, 568, 569
tension disk, 562, 569
tension guide, 569
tension pulley wheel, 230
tension rod, 553
tension screw, 552

tension spring, 431, 562, 569, 665
tensor of fascia lata, 120
tentacle, 83
tents, major types, 686
tepee, 165
terminal, 421
terminal, 255, 309, 312, 740, 757
terminal arborization, 135
terminal box, 769
terminal bronchiole, 130
terminal bud, 57
terminal filament, 134
terminal lobe, 61
terminal moraine, 27
terminal tackles, 672
terreplein, 179
terrestrial sphere, 3
tertial, 110
tertiary consumers, 31
test pattern, 414
testicle, 127
text, 524
text display, 524
theater, 188
theodolite, 713
theodolite, 41
thermal barrier, 42
thermal louver, 43
thermocouple, 297
thermocouple tube, 297
thermometer, 705
thermometer, 627, 635, 741
thermos, 690
thermosphere, 19
thermostat, 210, 214, 252, 297
thermostat control, 254
thigh, 101, 106, 108, 117, 119, 127,
    128
thigh pad, 602
thigh-boot, 357
thigh-high stocking, 344
thimble, 563
thimble, 711
thinning razor, 369
third, 537
third base, 597
third baseman, 597
third finger, 137
3rd metacarpal, 112
third stage, 509
third valve slide, 551
third wheel, 706, 707
35 mm still camera, 512
thirty-second note, 538
thirty-second rest, 538
thong, 357
thoracic legs, 90
thoracic vertebra (12), 123
thoracic vertebrae, 102
thorax, 78, 79, 80, 116, 118
thread, 276, 294
thread guide, 561, 562
thread take-up lever, 561
thread trimmer, 562
threaded cap, 301
threaded rod, 279
three-four time, 537
three-hinged arch, 455
three-of-a-kind, 695
3 m platform, 624
3 m springboard, 624
three-quarter coat, 321
three-quarter sleeve, 339
three-toed hoof, 99
threshing area, 161
threshold, 202
throat, 108, 282, 483, 615, 671
throat latch, 649
throat protector, 595, 609
throttle valve, 735
throttles, 500
through arch bridge, 455
throwing circle, 654, 655
throwings, 658
thrust, 455
thrust bearing, 753
thrust device, 389
thrust tube, 389
thruster, 49, 512
thrusting and cutting weapons,
    794
thumb, 112, 137, 327, 596
thumb hook, 550
thumb piston, 542
thumb rest, 549, 726
thumb tacks, 515
thumbscrew, 279
thunderstorm, 39
thyme, 74

tibia, 78, 80, 103, 112, 122
tibial nerve, 133
ticket collector, 463
ticket collector's booth, 474
ticket control, 463
ticket counter, 504
tidal power plant, 752
tie, 375, 466, 539
tie bar, 364
tie beam, 198
tie closure, 375
tie plate, 466
tie rod, 553
tieback, 228
tiepin, 364
tierce, 667
tierceron, 177
tight end, 603, 605
tightener, 661
tightening band, 40
tilde, 832
tile, 286
tile, 169, 170, 511
tiller, 272
tiller, 628, 793
tilt tube, 231
tilt-back head, 250
timber, 168, 170
time signatures, 537
timed outlet, 255
timekeeper, 610, 612, 626, 666, 668,
    669
timer, 398
timer, 252, 585, 664
timing belt, 434
timpani, 557
tine, 157, 240, 272
tip, 57, 72, 239, 241, 275, 276, 284,
    291, 305, 306, 323, 375, 633, 637,
    640, 645, 658, 670, 675
tip cleaners, 307
tip of nose, 141
tip protector, 726
tip section, 670
tip-ring, 670, 671
tipping lever, 727
tire, 433
tire, 440, 447
tire pump, 446
tire valve, 447
tissue holder, 292
Titan, 5
toad, 85
toaster, 252
tobacco, 384
tobacco hole, 385
tobacco pouch, 385
toe, 104, 106, 111, 116, 118, 277,
    325, 678
toe binding, 642
toe box, 644
toe clip, 104, 446, 448
toe guard, 730
toe guard, 595
toe hole, 645
toe pick, 644
toe piece, 633, 640
toe piston, 542
toe strap, 633
toe-piece, 641
toenail scissors, 365
toeplate, 642
toga, 315
toggle, 817
toggle bolt, 276
toggle fastening, 320
toggles, 650
toilet, 293
toilet, 215, 292, 461
toilet bowl, 293
toilet tank, 292
tom-tom, 552
tomato, 69
tombolo, 30
tone arm, 404
tone control, 547
tone leader generator, 407
tongs, 246
tongue, 81, 88, 131, 142, 323, 352,
    354, 536, 542, 566, 641, 644
tongue sheath, 96
tongue, dorsum, 143
tonsil, 142
tool, 735
tool holder, 283
tool tether, 512
tool tray, 302
tools, carpentry, 275, 276, 278, 280,
    282, 284

The terms in **bold type** indicate the title of an illustration.

tools, electricity, 310, 311
tools, plumbing, 299
tools, wood carving, 587
tooth, 96, 158, 159, 160, 162, 268, 277, 284, 369, 785
toothbrush, 373
toothbrush, 373
toothbrush shaft, 373
toothbrush well, 373
toothed jaw, 278
toothpaste, 373
top, 59, 219, 302, 478
top bar, 659
top central manhole, 743
top coat, 331
top cylinder, 581
top deck, 741
top deckboard, 787
top edge, 577
top hat, 328
top ladder, 781
top lift, 354
top of dam, 746, 748, 749, 752
top plate, 525
top pocket, 675
top rail, 202, 223, 225
top rail of sash, 203
top road, 736
top stitched pleat, 335
top stitching, 323, 350
top-end transverse member, 470
topaz, 362
topgallant mast, 479
topmark, 486, 488
topmast, 479
topping, 670
topping lift, 478
toque, 329
torpedo, 807
torpedo room, 807
torque converter, 258
torus, 166, 167
total, 709
total eclipse, 8
tote bag, 380, 382
tote board, 651
Toucan, 13
touch, 136
touch line, 601, 606
touring boot, 642
tourmaline, 362
tow bar, 506
tow bar, 158, 159, 162, 449, 633
tow line, 633
tow release knob, 639
tow tractor, 506, 507
towel bar, 292
tower, 756
tower, 176, 456, 486, 770, 771, 773, 774, 786
tower body, 756
tower crane, 786
tower foot, 756
tower ladder, 781
tower mast, 786
tower silo, 149
tower top, 756
tower window, 756
towing eye, 803
towing hitch, 147, 449
town houses, 187
tracery, 175, 176
trachea, 130
tracing wheel, 563
track, 476, 651
track, 230, 445, 463, 474, 783
track and field athletics, 654, 656, 658
track idler, 783
track lighting, 235
track link, 805
track number, 405
track roller frame, 783
track search keys, 405
track shoe, 656, 805
trackball, 526
tracker, 543
tractor, 147
tractor, 742
tractor engine, 784
trade building, 185
trade name, 384
traditional houses, 165
traditional musical instruments, 535, 536
traffic circle, 52, 450
traffic island, 184
traffic lane, 452
traffic light, 186

tragus, 112, 139
trailer, 449
trailing edge, 498, 636, 637, 638
trailing edge flap, 498, 812
trainer, 669
training set, 351
training suit, 352
training wall, 746
trampoline, 659
trampoline, 659
transcription of seismic waves, 714
transducer, 485
transept, 177
transept spire, 176
transfer canal, 764
transfer dispensing machine, 475
transfer of heat to water, 766
transfer port, 436
transfer ramp, 452
transfer scale, 396
transform fault, 28
transit shed, 490
transition fittings, 301
translation wave, 30
transmission, 258
transmission cable, 485
transmission of the electrical current, 714
transmission/reception of messages, 421
transmitted pulse, 722
transmitter, 420
transmitting station, 722
transparency slide, 397
transpiration, 35
transporter bridge, 457
transverse bulkhead, 743
transverse colon, 131
transverse dunes, 46
transverse process, 135
trap, 301
trap, 215, 293, 296
trap coupling, 296
trapeze dress, 332
trapezius, 120, 121
traveler, 630
traveler, 628
traveling block, 737
traveling crane, 747
traverse arch, 177
traverse rod, 230
traversing handle, 803
tray, 210, 226, 270, 304, 383
tread, 201, 433, 649
tread bar, 147
tread design, 433
treadle, 572
treadle cord, 572
treatment plant, 735
treble, 646
treble bridge, 540
treble fishhook, 672
treble keyboard, 536
treble pickup, 547
treble register, 536
treble tone control, 402
tree, 59
tree, 649
tree frog, 85
tree pruner, 269
trees, 676
tree, structure, 59
tree, trunk, 59
trefoil, 174
trefoil, 175
trench, 28, 733
trench coat, 319
triangle, 554
Triangle, 11, 556
triangular bandage, 725
triangular body, 535
triangular fossa, 139
Triangulum, 11
Triangulum Australe, 13
triceps bar, 663
triceps of arm, 121
tricorne, 318
tricuspid valve, 125
trifoliolate, 56
trigger, 268, 304, 780, 793, 795, 796, 797, 798, 799, 804
trigger guard, 795, 797, 798, 799
trigger switch, 284
triglyph, 167
trill, 538
trim, 383
trim panel, 429
trim ring, 255

trimmer, 374
trimming, 578
trimming, 379
trimming tool, 585
trio, 558
trip lever, 264, 293
trip odometer, 431
triple bars, 647
triple bars, 646
triple jump take-off board, 654
triple jump take-off line, 654
triple ring, 698
triple tail unit, 498
tripod, 393
tripod, 397, 415, 539, 721
tripod accessories shelf, 721
tripod stand, 552
tripod tail support, 507
Triton, 5
trochanter, 78, 80
trolley, 265, 457, 786
trolley crank, 265
trolley pulley, 786
Trombe wall, 772
Trombe wall, 772
trombone, 550
trombones, 556
tropic of Cancer, 3, 47
tropic of Capricorn, 3, 47
tropical climates, 45
tropical fruits, 68
tropical fruits, major types, 68
tropical maritime, 38
tropical rain forest, 45
tropical savanna, 45
tropical storm, 39
troposphere, 19
trot, 101
trough, 30, 38
trousers, 668
trowel, 268
truck, 476
truck, 468, 645
truck crane, 786
truck frame, 468
truck tractor, 440
truck tractor, 440
truck trailer, 440
trucking, 440
truffle, 55
trumpet, 550
trumpet, 550
trumpet interchange, 451
trumpets, 556
trunk, 383
trunk, 59, 61, 117, 119, 427
trunk hose, 316
trunks, 662
trunk, cross section, 59
trunnion, 800
trussed arch, 455
tub, 257, 258, 263
tub platform, 292
tub rim, 258
tuba, 551, 557
tube, 588
tube, 397, 710, 803, 804
tube cutter, 299
tube end, 300
tube flaring tool, 299
tube retention clip, 233
tuber vegetables, 71
tubing, 740
tubing head, 740
tubing valve, 740
tubular bells, 554
tubular bells, 556
tubular element, 255
tubular heater, 744
tubular ice screw, 681
tubular lock, 290
tubular member, 738
tubular structure, 487
Tucana, 13
tuck, 384
tuck position, 624
Tudor, 174
tumble dry at low temperature, 829
tumble dry at medium to high temperature, 829
tuner, 400, 402
tuner, 408
tungsten filament, 233
tungsten-halogen lamp, 233
tunic, 337
tunic, 791
tunic dress, 333
tuning control, 402, 408

tuning controls, 410
tuning fork, 539
tuning gauge, 553
tuning mode, 402
tuning peg, 545, 547
tuning pin, 540
tuning slide, 551
tuning switch, 408
tuning wire, 542
tunnel, 474
turban, 329
turbine, 753
turbine, 758
turbine building, 758
turbine headcover, 753
turbine runner, 752
turbine shaft turns generator, 767
turbine stop valve, 758
turbine-compressor shaft, 501
turbo-alternator, 771, 806
turbo-compressor engine, 438
turbo-jet engine, 812
turbofan engine, 501
turbojet engine, 499
turkey, 150
turn, 538
turn and slip indicator, 639
turn and slip knob, 639
turn signal, 429, 441, 442, 443, 444
turn signal indicator, 431, 445
turnbuckle, 630
turnbuckle, 669
turner, 244
turning, 584
turning handle, 280
turning judge, 621
turning wall, 621, 622
turning wheel, 584
turnip, 71
turntable, 404
turntable, 250, 400, 407, 457, 784, 785
turntable mounting, 780
turpentine, 592
turquoise, 362
turret, 180, 805, 809
turret cap, 718
turtle, 97
turtle neck, 642
turtleneck, 326, 342
turtleneck, 338
tusks of elephant, 99
tusks of walrus, 99
tusks of wart hog, 99
tusks, major types, 99
TV mode, 411
TV power button, 411
TV/video button, 411
tweeter, 16, 400
tweezers, 725
25 ring, 698
25 yards line, 606, 607
twig, 57, 59
twill weave, 576
twin skis, 633
twin-lens reflex camera, 394
twin-set, 338
Twins, 11
twist bar, 665
twist dive, 625
twist drill, 281
twist grip throttle, 444
twisted rope, 692
two columns split bet, 700
two dozens split bet, 701
240-volt circuit, 312
240-volt feeder cable, 312
2 m line, 626
two pairs, 695
two-burner camp stove, 689
two-door sedan, 425
two-hand clean and jerk, 662
two-hand snatch, 662
two-hinged arch, 455
two-person tent, 685
two-sided copies, 532
two-stroke-cycle engine, 436
two-toed hoof, 99
two-two time, 537
two-way collar, 319
two-way traffic, 824, 825
tympanum, 84, 97, 166, 168, 175
type of fuel, 453
type of high cloud, 38
type of low cloud, 38
type of middle cloud, 38
type of the air mass, 38
types of heads, 276
types of passenger cars, 460
typist's chair, 521

The terms in **bold type** indicate the title of an illustration.

U

U-bend, 301
U-shaped gouge, 581
UHF antenna, 42
ulna, 102, 122
ulnar extensor of wrist, 121
ulnar flexor of wrist, 120, 121
ulnar nerve, 133
ultraviolet spectrometer, 43
umbel, 60
umbo, 95
umbra shadow, 8
umbrella, 375
umbrella pine, 58
umbrella sheath, 679
umbrella stand, 375
umlaut, 832
umpire, 599, 603, 605, 611, 613, 614, 618
under tail covert, 109
underarm crutch, 728
underarm portfolio, 378
underarm rest, 728
underground flow, 32, 35
underground mine, 736
underground passage, 464
underground stem, 70
underlining, 565
underlying fabrics, 565
underpass, 454
undershirt, 595
underwater camera, 394
underwear, 325, 345, 346
underwiring, 347
union, 300, 830
union nut, 300
union suit, 325
uniparous cyme, 60
unison, 537
unit price, 709
univalve shell, 94
universal step, 507
unleavened bread, 153
unloading tube, 161
uphaul, 631
upholstery nozzle, 260
upper, 641
upper blade guard, 284
upper bowl, 247
upper cheek, 650
upper chord, 455
upper cold front, 39
upper cuff, 641
upper deck, 498
upper edge, 619
upper eyelid, 84, 107, 140
upper fore topgallant sail, 481
upper fore topsail, 481
upper gate, 493
upper gill arch, 87
upper girdle facet (16), 363
upper laboratory, 15
upper lateral lobe, 61
upper lateral sinus, 61
upper level, 493
upper limb, 793
upper lip, 81, 142, 542
upper lobe, 130
upper mandible, 109
upper mantle, 22
upper rudder, 806
upper shell, 641, 645
upper sphere clamp, 40
upper strap, 641
upper support screw, 40
upper tail covert, 109
upper warm front, 39
upperboard, 543
upperworks, 630
upright, 573, 574, 578, 579, 657, 659, 660, 661, 728
upright piano, 540
upright piano action, 541
upstage, 188, 189
upstream blanket, 748
upstream face, 749
upstream shoulder, 748
upstream toe, 748
Uranus, 5
urban map, 52
ureter, 132
urethra, 128, 129, 132
urinary bladder, 89, 127, 128, 132
urinary meatus, 127
urinary system, 132
urogenital aperture, 89
uropod, 91
Ursa Major, 11

Ursa Minor, 11
use chlorine bleach as directed, 829
utensils, set, 244
uterovesical pouch, 128
uterus, 128, 129
utility case, 382
utility liquids, 592
uvula, 141, 142

V

V-neck, 322, 326
V-neck cardigan, 326
V-neck cardigan, 338
V-shaped gouge, 581
V-shaped neck, 343
vacuole, 115
vacuum chamber, 710, 717
vacuum coffee maker, 247
vacuum diaphragm, 435
vacuum distillation, 744
vacuum manifold, 717
vacuum system console, 717
vagina, 128, 129
vair, 819
valance, 224, 228
valley, 27
valve, 67, 95, 550
valve casing, 550
valve seat, 294
valve seat shaft, 293
valve seat wrench, 299
valve spring, 434
vambrace, 792
vamp, 353, 355
vane, 110, 259
vanity cabinet, 292
vanity case, 382
vanity mirror, 430
vaporizer, 210
vaporizing grille, 210
variable geometry wing, 499
variable spacer, 525
variation keys, 569
variometer, 635
various dry fruits, 67
varnish, 592
varnish-roller, 582
Vauban fortification, 178
vault, 177
vaulting horse, 659
VCR controls, 411
VCR mode, 411
VCR power button, 411
vector/waveform monitor, 413
vegetable bowl, 238
vegetable brush, 246
vegetable garden, 148, 193
vegetable sponge, 367
vegetable steamer, 249
vegetables, 69, 70, 71, 72, 73
vegetables, 33
veil, 670
vein, 56
veins, 126
Vela, 13
Velcro® closure, 349
velum, 80
velvet-band choker, 361
Venetian blind, 231
venom canal, 96
venom gland, 96
venom-conducting tube, 96
venomous snake's head, 96
vent, 214, 430, 800, 801
vent brush, 368
vent door, 441
vent hole, 304
ventail, 792
ventilated rib, 798
ventilating circuit, 215
ventilating fan, 469
ventilating grille, 260
ventilation, 772
ventilation hood, 486
ventilator, 477
ventral aorta, 88
ventricular septum, 125
venturi, 804
venturi fastening lever, 804
Venus, 4
vermiform appendix, 131
vernal equinox, 3, 8
vernier, 708
vernier scale, 484
Versailles parquet, 200
vert, 819
vertebral body, 135
vertebral column, 89, 122, 134

vertebral shield, 97
vertical control, 529
vertical cord lift, 256
vertical frame, 574
vertical movement, 696
vertical pivoting window, 203
vertical pocket, 316
vertical pupil, 96
vertical shaft, 736
vertical side band, 613
vertical stabilizer, 639
vertical-axis wind turbine, 774
very cloudy sky, 39
vest, 315, 322, 338
vestibular nerve, 139
vestibule, 139, 170, 461
vestibule door, 461
VHF antenna, 808
viaduct, 454
vial, 725
vibrating mudscreen, 737
vibrato arm, 547
video camera, 409
video camera, 526
video cassette recorder, 526
video connection panel, 415
video entertainment system, 699
video monitor, 529
video monitor, 526, 527
video monitoring selector, 413
video port, 528
video switcher technician, 412, 415
videocassette recorder, 411
videocassette recorder, 401
videotape operation controls, 409
Vienna bread, 153
view camera, 394
viewfinder, 390
viewfinder adjustment keys, 409
vine shoot, 61
vine stock, 61
vine, maturing steps, 61
vinyl grip sole, 350
vinyl insulation, 287
viola, 545
violas, 556
violin, 544
violin, 545
violin family, 545
Virgin, 11, 13
Virgo, 11, 13
Virgo the Virgin (August 23), 820
virgule, 832
vise, 282
vision slit, 792
visor, 443, 471, 642, 730, 792
visor hinge, 443
visual display, 699
visual display unit, 421, 422
visual transmission, 717
visualization of seismic waves, 714
vitelline membrane, 109
vitreous body, 140
vocal cord, 130
voice edit buttons, 555
voice selector, 555
Volans, 13
volcanic bombs, 25
volcanic island, 28
volcano, 25
volcano, 23
volcano during eruption, 25
volleyball, 613
volleyball, court, 613
volleyball, net, 613
voltage increase, 767
voltage tester, 310
volume control, 402, 408, 411, 420, 422, 547, 555
volume readout, 453
volume unit meters, 407
volute, 166, 167, 220
volva, 55
voussoir, 174
vulva, 118, 128

W

wad, 799, 801
waders, 672
wading bird, 111
waferboard, 288
waffle iron, 253
wagon, 162
wagon tent, 686
waist, 117, 119, 354, 544, 756
waistband, 320, 323, 325
waistband extension, 323
waistcoat, 317
walk, 101

walk-in, 195
walker, 728
walking aids, 728
walking leg, 78
walking stick, 375
walking stick, 728
wall, 647
wall, 7, 65, 104, 646, 685
wall and rails, 647
wall and rails, 646
wall bracket, 230
wall fitting, 234
wall lantern, 235
wall register, 207
wall side, 743
wall stack section, 206
wall stud, 199
wall tent, 686
wallet, 379
wallet, 523
walnut, 66
walnut, section, 66
waning gibbous, 7
wapiti, 105
wardrobe, 226
wardrobe, 195
warhead, 814
warm air, 772
warm air outlet, 438
warm-air baffle, 204
warming plate, 247
warning device, 777
warning lights, 431
warning plate, 280
warning track, 597
warp, 573, 574
warp roller, 573
warp thread, 576
warping frame, 575
warty skin, 85
wash tower, 257
washer, 258, 298
washer, 215, 294, 298
washer nozzle, 426
washers, 278
washing, 829
wasp-waisted corset, 347
Wassily chair, 221
waste pipe, 293
waste stack, 215
waste tee, 298
Water Bearer, 13
water bottle, 447
water bottle clip, 447
water carrier, 690
water cools the used steam, 767
water goblet, 237
water hazard, 676
water hose, 257, 734
water inlet, 295
water intake, 747
water is pumped back into the steam generator, 767
water jump, 647
water jump, 646
water key, 551
water level, 210, 247
water main, 772
water meter, 215
water pitcher, 238
water polo, 626
water polo ball, 626
water polo, goal, 626
water polo, playing area, 626
water pressure gauge, 778
water separator, 734
water service pipe, 215
water signs, 820
water skiing, 633
water skiing handles, types, 633
water skiing skis, types, 633
Water Snake, 11, 13
water table, 24
water tank, 210, 373, 469
water tower, 465
water turns into steam, 766
water-heater tank, 772
water-level selector, 258
water-level tube, 256
water/alcohol, 485
watercolor and gouache, 588
watercress, 73
waterfall, 27
watering can, 265
waterline, 487
watermelon, 69
waterproof pants, 349
watt-hour meter, 712
watt-hour meter, mechanism, 712
wave, 30

The terms in **bold type** indicate the title of an illustration.

wave base, 30
wave clip, 369
wave guide, 415
wave height, 30
wave length, 30
wave wall, 748
wax seal, 293
waxing gibbous, 6
weapons in the age of the Romans, 791
weather map, 38
weather radar, 498
weather satellite, 42
weatherboard, 202, 203
weaving, 572, 574, 576
weaving pattern brush, 568
weaving pattern lever, 568
weaving, accessories, 573, 575
web, 84, 111, 466, 596
web frame, 743
webbed foot, 84
webbed toe, 111
webbing, 428, 571, 634
wedding ring, 364
wedge, 542, 800
wedge iron, 277
wedge lever, 277
weeder, 268
weeding hoe, 266
weekender, 383
weft, 573, 574
weft thread, 576
weighing platform, 709
weight, 658, 665, 707, 708, 709
weight belt, 627
weight stack exercise unit, 663
weight-driven clock mechanism, 707
weightlifter, 662
weightlifting, 662
weightlifting belt, 662
weightlifting shoe, 662
weights, 663
weld bead, 307
welding, 305, 306, 308
welding curtain, 308
welding torch, 306
welding torch, 306, 307
well flow line, 738
welt, 322, 355
welt pocket, 339
welt pocket, 322, 326
West, 488
West cardinal mark, 489
West Coast mirror, 440
Western hemisphere, 47
Western meridian, 47
wet suit, 627
wet well, 763
Whale, 11, 13
whale boat, 482
wheat, 152
wheat, grain, 152
wheel, 433
wheel, 270, 383, 427, 440, 563, 583, 645, 684, 800, 805
wheel chock, 506
wheel cover, 427
wheel cylinder, 432
wheel head, 584
wheel loader, 782
wheel tractor, 782

wheelbarrow, 270
wheelchair, 727
wheelchair, 461
whelk, 83
whipping, 678
whisk, 245
whiskers, 107
whistle, 252
White, 696, 697
white balance sensor, 409
white cabbage, 73
white cap, 626
white cue ball, 673
white flag, 626
white light, 488
white line, 104
white matter, 135
white spot ball, 673
white square, 696
white stone, 697
white tape, 618, 619
white wine glass, 237
white-tailed deer, 105
whole note, 538
whole rest, 538
whole wheat bread, 153
wholemeal bread, 153
whorl, 83, 94
wicker basket, 635
wicket, 599
wicket, 599
wicket gate, 753
wicketkeeper, 599
wide-angle lens, 392
wigwam, 165
willow, 598
winch, 630
wind, 38
wind, 629
wind abeam, 629
wind arrow, 38
wind chest, 543
wind chest table, 543
wind deflector, 440
wind direction, 38
wind direction and speed, 38
wind direction, measure, 41
wind duct, 543
wind energy, 773, 774
wind guard, 634
wind indicator, 628
wind instruments, 548, 550
wind sock, 817
wind speed, 38
wind strength, measure, 41
wind supply, 543
wind trunk, 543
wind vane, 41
windbag, 536
windbreaker, 320
winder, 706
winding adjustment, 718
winding mechanism, 231, 707
winding shaft, 736
winding tower, 735
windmill, 773
window, 203
window, 194, 195, 253, 255, 379, 399, 427, 429, 477, 498, 631
window accessories, 228, 230
window canopy, 685
window regulator handle, 429

window sill, 198
window tab, 518
windows, 379
windows, types, 203
windscreen, 14, 406
windshaft, 773
windshield, 426, 440, 442, 445, 498, 500
windshield wiper, 431
windshield wiper, 426
windshield wiper blade, 431
wine waiter corkscrew, 244
wing, 316
wing, 78, 108, 499, 511, 637, 638, 670, 812
wing attack, 611
wing box, 812
wing covert, 108
wing defense, 611
wing membrane, 112
wing nut, 279
wing pallet, 787
wing rib, 498
wing shapes, types, 499
wing slat, 499
wing tip, 638
wing vein, 79
Winged Horse, 11
winglet, 499
wings, 112, 189
wings, bat, 112
wing, bird, 110
winning line, 702
winter, 8
winter solstice, 8
winze, 736
wiper, 431
wiper arm, 431
wiper switch, 430
wire, 641, 658, 714
wire beater, 250
wire brush, 553
wire cutter, 311
wire sling, 681
wire stripper, 311
wire stripper, 311
wire support, 689
wisdom tooth, 144
wishbone boom, 631
withers, 100, 106
wok, 248
wok set, 248
women's clothing, 330, 332, 334, 336, 338, 340, 342, 344, 346, 348
women's rest room, 822
wood, 288, 677
wood carving, 586
wood chip car, 472
wood chisel, 275
wood engraving, 581
wood flooring, 200
wood flooring, 199
wood flooring arrangements, 200
wood flooring on cement screed, 200
wood flooring on wooden structure, 200
wood ray, 59
wood-based materials, 288, 289
woodbox, 204
woodcut, 581
wooden bar, 661

wooden modeling tools, 585
woods, 52
woodwind family, 548
wood, golf, 678
woofer, 16, 400
word correction, 525
work lead, 305
worker, honeybee, 80
worker, honeybee, 81
working area, 16
working pressure gauge, 306
worm, 801
worm, 575
wraparound dress, 333
wraparound skirt, 334
wrapover top, 337
wrapper, 384
wrist, 106, 112, 117, 119, 137
wrist pad, 602
wrist sling, 681
wrist strap, 640, 642
wrist-length glove, 327
wristband, 615
write protect notch, 529
writing brush, 389
writing case, 378
writing instruments, 389

X

X-band antenna, 49
xylophone, 554
xylophone, 556

Y

Y-branch, 301
Y-tube, 726
yard, 465
yard, 478
yard line, 604
yarn, 692
yarn ball, 596
yarn clip, 569
yarn feeder, 569
yarn rod, 569
yarn tension unit, 569
yellow ball, 673
yellow onion, 70
yen, 832
yield, 824, 825
yoke, 230, 320, 324, 337
yoke skirt, 334
yolk, 109
yurt, 165

Z

zenith, 16
zenith S-band antenna, 49
zest, 65
zester, 242
zipper, 566
zipper, 321, 350, 365, 382, 685
zipper line, 565
zither, 535
zona pellucida, 128
zoom lens, 392
zoom lens, 409, 414
zucchini, 69
zygomatic bone, 122

The terms in **bold type** indicate the title of an illustration.